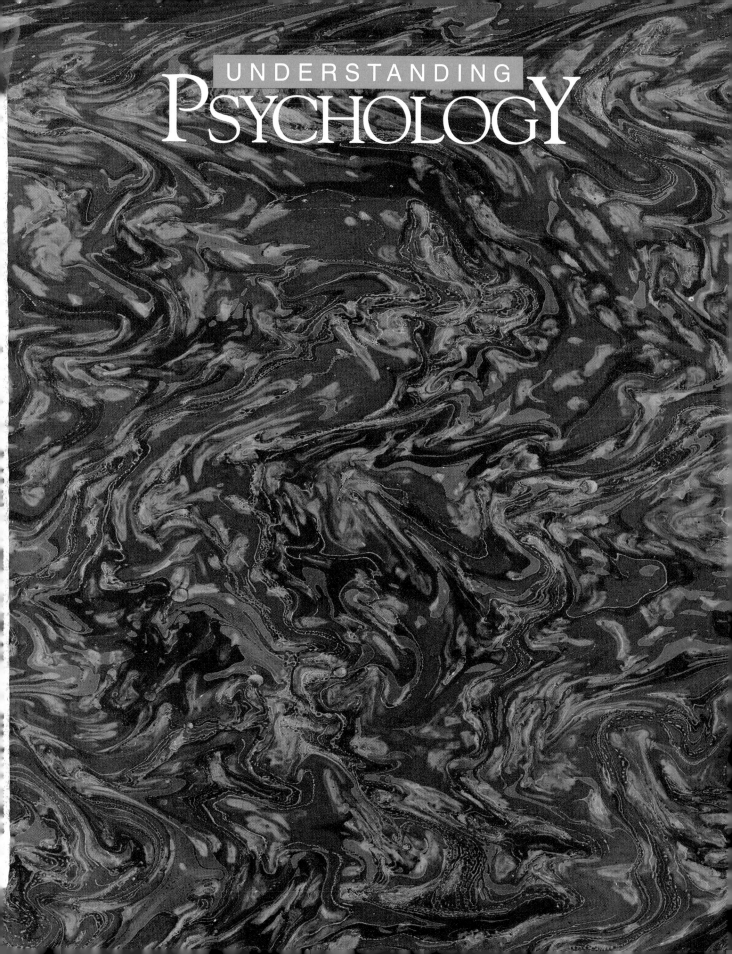

UNDERSTANDING
PSYCHOLOGY

ROBERT S. FELDMAN

University of Massachusetts–Amherst

UNDERSTANDING
PSYCHOLOGY

SECOND EDITION

McGRAW-HILL PUBLISHING COMPANY

New York | St. Louis | San Francisco | Auckland | Bogotá | Caracas | Hamburg
Lisbon | London | Madrid | Mexico | Milan | Montreal | New Delhi | Oklahoma City
Paris | San Juan | São Paulo | Singapore | Sydney | Tokyo | Toronto

UNDERSTANDING PSYCHOLOGY

1 2 3 4 5 6 7 8 9 0   VNH   VNH   8 9 4 3 2 1 0 9

ISBN 0-07-020531-0

This book was set in Garamond by Waldman Graphics, Inc.
The editors were Elisa Adams, James D. Anker, and David Dunham;
the designer was Nicholas Krenitsky;
the production supervisor was Leroy A. Young.
Cover photograph by Bohdan Hrynewych, *Stock, Boston*.
New drawings were done by J & R Services, Inc.
Von Hoffmann Press, Inc., was printer and binder.

Library of Congress Cataloging-in-Publication Data

Feldman, Robert S. (Robert Stephen), (date).
    Understanding psychology / Robert S. Feldman.—2nd ed.
        p.   cm.
    Bibliography: p.
    Includes indexes.
    ISBN 0-07-020531-0
    1. Psychology.   I. Title.
BF121.F35   1990   89-12210
150—dc20

ABOUT THE AUTHOR

Robert S. Feldman is Professor of Psychology at the University of Massachusetts at Amherst. A graduate of Wesleyan University and the University of Wisconsin-Madison, he is a former Fulbright Senior Research Scholar and Lecturer. He is a Fellow of the American Psychological Association and the American Psychological Society and author of more than eighty scientific articles, book chapters, and papers. His research interests include nonverbal behavior and the social psychology of education. He has written or edited six books, including *Social Psychology: Theories, Research, and Applications* (McGraw-Hill), and *The Social Psychology of Education* (Cambridge University Press). His spare time is most often devoted to serious cooking and earnest, but still inelegant, piano playing. He lives with his wife, also a psychologist, and three children overlooking the Holyoke mountain range in Amherst, Massachusetts.

TO

Jonathan, Joshua, and Sarah,
and, of course, Kathy

REVIEWERS

I am grateful to the following people, who reviewed all or part of the manuscripts of the first or second edition of *Understanding Psychology*.

Robert S. Feldman

Phillip Ackerman
University of Minnesota
Louis Banderet
Northeastern University
Gordon Barr
Hunter College
Brenda Bennett
Vincennes University
David Berg
Community College of Philadelphia
Allen E. Bergin
Brigham Young University
Jeanine Bloyd
Spoon River College
Allen R. Branum
South Dakota State University
David M. Brodzinsky
Rutgers University
Peter Burzynski
Vincennes University
Jay Caldwell
California State University
Bernardo Carducci
Indiana University Southeast
Steve Coccia
Orange County Community College
Larry Cology
Owens College
Helen Joan Crawford
University of Wyoming
James Dailey
Vincennes University
Joyce Dennis
Southern Union State University
William Dwyer
Memphis State University
Marsha Epstein
Middlesex Community College

Walter Essman
Queens College
Richard Ettinger
Eastern Oregon State College
William Ford
Bucks County Community College
Judith Gentry
Columbus State Community College
Marvin W. Goldstein
Rider College
David A. Griesé
S.U.N.Y. at Farmingdale
Gloria Griffith
Tennessee Tech University
David Harnison
Virginia Polytechnic Institute
Earl Harper
Bunker Hill Community College
Lynn Hasher
Temple University
Donna Hummel
Trinity College
Janet Hyde
University of Wisconsin
Carroll Izard
University of Delaware
Don Kaesser
Des Moines Area Community College
Lynne Kiorpes
New York University
Michael Knight
Central State University
Angela La Sala
Suffolk Community College
Ken Le Sure
Cuyahoga Community College
Harold Mansfield
North Dakota State University

CONTENTS IN BRIEF

CONTENTS

xiv

CHAPTER 4

PERCEPTION   125

PART THREE

LEARNING AND THINKING   152

CHAPTER 5

LEARNING   155

MEMORY   197

PART FOUR

FEELING AND EXPERIENCING THE WORLD 288

CHAPTER 9

MOTIVATION AND EMOTION 291

PART FIVE

INDIVIDUAL DEVELOPMENT AND DIFFERENTIATION   408

CHAPTER 12

CHAPTER 13

CHAPTER 14

PERSONALITY   479

PART SIX

PHYSICAL AND MENTAL HEALTH   512

CHAPTER 17

PART EIGHT

THE PSYCHOLOGICAL CONTEXT OF THE WORLD AROUND US   682

CHAPTER 20

ORGANIZATIONS AND THE WORKPLACE   685

CHAPTER 21

TECHNOLOGY AND CONTEMPORARY SOCIETY   709

APPENDIX

PREFACE

When I wrote the preface to the first edition of *Understanding Psychology*, I began it in this way:

> As I look out the window, the form of Mount Norwottock, an ancient glacial mountain, rises above the landscape. I can see a farmer in the valley below Norwottock methodically plowing his fields, as, closer to home, a mother walks her child to school. A crew of carpenters is building a new house on land nearby, working together and following complicated architectural plans.
>
> At the same time as I look out on this peaceful scene, the morning newspaper lying across my desk reports another terrorist attack, a Mideast treaty broken, and a murder in a small town nearby. It tells of a march of members of a Nazi-like organization who want to expel minorities from the United States, and of the upcoming release from a mental hospital of a killer judged innocent by reason of insanity.

For better or worse, little has changed over the past few years. More homes are being built in the valley below Norwottock, but the scene is still primarily one of open fields. And my newspaper reports the same variety of behavior and thinking that defies easy explanation. We still see selfishness and self-sacrifice; thoughtfulness and irrationality; cooperation and violent competition among the peoples of the world.

What has changed, though, is the discipline of psychology. It has come closer to its goal of explaining the behavior and thought that we find around us and of meeting the challenge of understanding human behavior. This second edition of *Understanding Psychology* reflects these advances in the field, as well as presenting the fundamentals on which the discipline is built.

INTRODUCING THE SECOND EDITION OF *UNDERSTANDING PSYCHOLOGY*

As with the first edition, the second edition of *Understanding Psychology* has three major goals. First, it is intended to provide effective and broad coverage of the field of psychology, introducing readers to the theories, research, and applications that constitute the science. Second, it is meant to provide an impetus for students to begin to think as psychologists, even after the recall of specific content has waned, and to foster an appreciation for the scientific basis of psychology. Finally, this book is designed to be engaging and interesting, arousing students' intellectual curiosity and building an appreciation of how psychology can increase their understanding of the world around them.

These goals, of course, are interdependent. In fact, I would argue that if the text is successful in accurately communicating the nature of psychology, an understanding of and interest in the field will follow naturally. To that end, the writing style of this book has received considerable attention. The style is intended to provide as close a facsimile to two people sitting down and discussing psychology as can be conveyed by the written word.

Furthermore, this text has special features that are designed to highlight seminal investigations and findings fundamental to the field (Research Classics boxes), challenge students (Cutting Edge boxes with the latest findings), demonstrate the everyday relevance of psychology (Psychology at Work boxes), and improve the quality of readers' own lives (Informed Consumer of Psychology sections). It is also a book that has been carefully designed to promote learning. Material is presented in rational, manageable chunks, each of which is followed by a succinct summary (called a "Recap") and a set of questions on the material (a "Review"). A reader who answers these questions—and then checks the answers, which are provided on a following page—will be able to assess the degree of initial mastery of the material, as well as having a head start on long-term recall and understanding of the information.

In sum, *Understanding Psychology* is, as I reiterate in the first chapter, designed to be user-friendly. It is a book that is meant not to merely expose students to the content—and promise—of psychology, but to do so in a way that will bring alive the excitement of the field, and to keep that excitement alive long after readers have completed their introduction to the discipline.

WHAT'S NEW IN THE SECOND EDITION?

Much thought has gone into the changes incorporated into this edition of *Understanding Psychology.* Because the basic structure and features of the first edition met with such a positive response from both students and professors, the fundamental attributes of the book remain intact. At the same time, additions were made to reflect important advances that have occurred in the field of psychology.

To begin with, several of the chapters have been completely rewritten or substantially expanded. Specifically, a major section on gender differences has been added to the material on human sexuality in Chapter 10. The use of technological innovations, ranging from everyday objects to computers, is discussed in a new final chapter of the book. This chapter also covers disasters and crises, including terrorism, reactions to nuclear war, and psychology's contributions to the promotion of peace.

Several new themes also emerge in this edition. Greater emphasis has been placed on gender differences and the psychology of women, not only in terms of the major addition to Chapter 10 but throughout the book. For example, gender differences in moral development, social clocks, depression, *DSM-III-R* categorization, and persuasibility are discussed. In addition, more work on stereotyping and ethnic concerns is found throughout this edition. The psychological issues associated with the use of computers are discussed in several contexts: learning, artificial intelligence, neural networks, therapy, and technology. Finally, reflecting the burgeoning interest in forensic psychology, legal issues are considered throughout the book, ranging from discussions of signal detection theory to legal definitions of insanity and abnormal behavior.

Overall, a wealth of contemporary research is cited in this edition. Reflecting what is current in psychology, literally hundreds of new citations have been added. Furthermore, scores of new topics not considered in the first edition have been added, and new information has been added to substantially expand others. A sampling of just some of the subjects new or substantially expanded in this edition gives a flavor of the advances that are included: neurometrics, feature detection, parvo, blob, and magno visual system processing, perceptual training, biochemistry of memory, alternate memory models, memory schemas, life-cycle memories, memory disorders, neural networks, teaching critical thinking, natural concepts and prototypes, genetic bases of obesity, bulimia and anorexia nervosa, sex differences in need for power, training need for achievement, AIDS, safe sex, touching and bonding in infants, sex differences in household activities, genetic determinants of personality, the hardy personality, social support, politics of mental disorder, reverse discrimination, the value of illusion, technology, computers, terrorism, nuclear war, and the psychology of peace.

AN OVERVIEW OF *UNDERSTANDING PSYCHOLOGY*

Understanding Psychology includes extensive coverage of the traditional topical areas of psychology, including the biological foundations of behavior, sensation and perception, learning, memory, cognition, human development, personality, abnormal behavior, and social psychological foundations of behavior. Notably, however, it also includes several distinctive chapters that focus primarily on applications of psychological theory and research in non-laboratory, field settings. For example, there are separate chapters on health psychology, organizations and the workplace, and technology, crises, and war and peace—burgeoning areas that represent the most important applied topics currently undergoing investigation.

The flexibility of this text's organizational structure is considerable. Each chapter is divided into three or four manageable, self-contained units, allowing instructors to choose and omit sections in accordance with their syllabus. Furthermore, because chapters are self-contained, it is possible to use this book in either biologically oriented or socially oriented introductory psychology courses by choosing only those chapters that are relevant. In addition, because the applications material is well-integrated throughout, even in the chapters that cover the most traditional, theoretical topics, those courses that omit the more applied topical chapters will still be successful in conveying the relevance of psychology to readers.

Overall, then, the book reflects a combination of traditional core topics and contemporary applied subjects, providing a broad, eclectic—and current—view of the field of psychology. It should be apparent that the volume is *not* an applied psychology text; nor is it a theories-oriented volume. Instead, it draws from theoretical and applied approaches, and integrates the two along with objective presentations of research that illustrate the way in which the science of psychology has evolved and grown. Indeed, the book exemplifies the view that a theory-application dichotomy is a false one. Applications are not presented as devoid of theory, but rather are placed in a theoretical context, grounded in research findings. Likewise, when theoretical material is presented, practical implications are drawn from it.

Some examples can illustrate this approach. If you turn to Chapter 3, you will find that it includes the traditional material on hearing in the ear.

But the text moves beyond a mere recitation of the various parts of the ear and explanations of hearing and balance; it also explores current work involving an electronic ear implant in the cochlea to help the deaf. Similarly, Chapter 12 includes a presentation of the theory behind the nature-nurture issue and developmental research strategies. These are tied to a presentation of classic longitudinal studies which then lead to exciting new findings on the importance for newborns of being touched and stroked, as well as contemporary issues on the effects of day-care. Finally, the chapter on abnormal behavior not only explores the development of models of abnormality and the *DSM-III-R* classification system, but also discusses the politics behind the deletion of several disorders just prior to publication of the *DSM-III-R*. Furthermore, the issues of identification of abnormality is exemplified by real-life cases such as that of Joyce Brown, a homeless women who fights—and ultimately defeats—a court order to be placed in a shelter. In each of these instances, the text demonstrates how applications grow out of the theoretical and research base of the field.

LEARNING AIDS AND FEATURES OF *UNDERSTANDING PSYCHOLOGY*

Understanding Psychology has been designed with its ultimate consumer—the student—in mind. As you can see from the following full list of elements that are common to every chapter, the book incorporates educational features, based on learning and cognitive instructional design theory and research, that are meant to make the book an effective learning device and, at the same time, enticing and engaging:

▶ *Chapter Outline.* Each chapter opens with an outline of the chapter structure. Not only does the outline provide a means of understanding the interrelationships of the material within the chapter, but it serves as a chapter organizer, helping to bridge the gap between what a reader already knows and the subsequent chapter content.

▶ *Prologue.* Each chapter starts with an account of a real-life situation that involves major aspects of the topics of the chapter. These scenarios demonstrate the relevance of basic principles and concepts of psychology to actual issues and problems. For example, the chapter on the biology underlying behavior begins with a description of a patient undergoing a controversial operation in which adrenal tissue is implanted in his brain; the chapter on cognition discusses how the mystery of the Challenger space shuttle explosion is solved; and one of the chapters on social psychology begins with an account of the defense mounted in the trial of an admitted killer, who attributes the blame for his crime to his victim.

▶ *Looking Ahead.* Following the prologue, a chapter overview is presented. It articulates the key themes and issues and lists a set of questions that are answered in the chapter.

▶ *Research Classics.* Research Classics boxes present important, pivotal, or frequently cited seminal studies, enabling readers to develop a sense of both the research process and the historical influences on the field. For instance, Chapter 2 considers Sperry's Nobel Prize-winning work on split-brain patients, the Fels longitudinal study is covered in the development chapter, and the Hawthorne studies are discussed in the chapter on organizations and the workplace.

▶ *Psychology at Work.* The Psychology at Work boxes illustrate an application of psychological theory and research findings to a real-world problem. For example, Chapter 4 discusses how psychologists' theoretical findings on perception have led to new developments in areas as diverse as sexing chicks to distinguishing tanks; the memory chapter includes a discussion of eyewitness identification in judicial settings; and the chapter on technology and the psychological environment discusses the use of computers for therapy.

▶ *The Cutting Edge.* These boxed inserts describe a contemporary research program that is in the forefront of the discipline—suggesting where the field of psychology is heading. This feature helps provide a sense of the growing and developing status of the science of psychology. For instance, the perception chapter discusses current work on the parvo, blob, and magno visual systems in the brain, the memory chapter presents work on the biochemical basis of memory, the motivation chapter considers the genetic determinants of obesity, the states of consciousness chapter discusses development of a pill to produce sobriety after alcohol consumption, and the chapter on organizations and the workplace discusses the psychology behind Japanese management systems.

▶ *The Informed Consumer of Psychology.* Every chapter includes information designed to make readers more informed consumers of psychological information and knowledge by giving them the ability of critically evaluate what the field of psychology offers. For example, this feature covers treatment for dyslexia (perception chapter), dealing with drugs and alcohol (states-of-consciousness chapter), evaluating computer-assisted instructional programs (learning chapter), personality and vocational testing (personality chapter), choosing a physician (health and stress chapter), and evaluating psychological therapy (treatment chapter).

▶ *Recap and Review.* Research clearly indicates the importance of careful organization of textual material, learning material in relatively small chunks, and actively reviewing material. Consequently, each chapter is divided into three or four sections, each of which concludes with a Recap and Review. The Recaps summarize the key points of the previous section, and the Reviews present a variety of types of questions for students to answer—including multiple choice, fill-in, short answer, and matching questions—in order to test both recall and higher-level understanding of the material.

▶ *Running Glossary.* Key terms are highlighted in boldface type where they are introduced, and they are defined in the margin of the text, with pronunciation guides for difficult words. There is also an end-of-book glossary.

▶ *Looking Back.* To facilitate the review of the material covered in each chapter and to aid in the synthesis of the information covered, a numbered summary is included at the end of every chapter. The summary emphasizes the key points of the chapter.

▶ *Key Terms and Concepts.* A list of key terms and concepts, including the page numbers where they were first introduced, is also provided at the end of each chapter.

► *For Further Research and Application.* An annotated bibliography is at the end of each chapter. This bibliography contains two types of selections— books and articles which deal with theory and others that are more oriented towards applications.

► *A full-color graphic design.* To support the instructional design features of the text, a team of graphic designers has developed a design structure to enhance the pedagogy of the text. The beautiful design and photos make the text inviting and a book from which it is easy to learn.

ANCILLARY MATERIALS

Understanding Psychology is accompanied by an extensive ancillary package that enhances the value of the text as a teaching and learning tool. The *Study Guide,* by Valerie J. Sasserath, includes an introductory section on how to study and how to use the Guide effectively with the text. Following this material are chapters (corresponding to each text chapter) which include chapter outlines and overviews, learning objectives, more than one thousand questions in a variety of formats, and application exercises. *Micro Study Guide,* a computerized version, is also available for use with the Apple and IBM PC computers. The Study Guide also will be available in an English-as-a-Second Language (ESL) version to facilitate the use of the text by non-native English speakers.

The Test File in this package offers more than 4,800 multiple-choice and true-false questions that test both factual recall and higher order understanding. This Test File was prepared by Louis Banderet of Northeastern University, Lynne Kiorpes of New York University, Charles Noble of North Georgia College, and Edward Pflaumer of Loma Linda University. Dennis Clare of the College of San Mateo was consultant for quality and construction. The Test File is available in a computerized format for use with mainframe and microcomputers.

The *Instructor's Manual* offers chapter overviews, lecture objectives and topics, key terms, discussion topics, "Take a Stand" sections (which outline issues for debate), demonstrations and projects, essay questions with answers, and an annotated bibliography of audiovisual resources.

A *Guide to Critical Thinking* also will be available to users of *Understanding Psychology.* This guide, written by the text author, discusses using critical thinking to evaluate psychological research and theory, and applications of critical thinking to studying and test-taking.

In addition to the print supplements described above, the ancillary package includes a set of fifty overhead transparencies of illustrations in the text. These transparencies can be used in conjunction with the 110 generic overheads in the *McGraw-Hill Introductory Psychology Overhead Transparency Set.* The *McGraw-Hill Introductory Psychology Slide Set,* consisting of 110 slides which duplicate the generic overheads, McGraw-Hill/CRM Films, and a series of videotapes covering the major areas of psychology are also available to adopters.

Psychworld by John C. Hay of the University of Wisconsin in Milwaukee is an acclaimed generic software package that contains fourteen simulations of classic psychology experiments. Professors can use it in the classroom and students can use it in the lab. In addition, *MacLaboratory for Psychology* by Douglas L. Chute of Drexel University and Robert S. Daniel of the University of Missouri is available for use on Apple Macintosh computers. This software consists of thirteen projects that convert the computer into various pieces of laboratory equipment. You local McGraw-Hill sales representative can explain the details of *Psychworld* and *MacLaboratory for Psychology*.

A newsletter prepared by the text author will be issued on a twice yearly basis to adopters of the text. Although intended primarily for instructors, it may be photocopied or reproduced for students. It will discuss Cutting Edge research findings in psychology, and all material will be keyed to text pages, thus assisting professors in integrating the newsletter contents into lecture and class discussions.

ACKNOWLEDGMENTS

As the long list of reviewers on pages viii-ix attests, this book involved the efforts of many psychologists. They lent their expertise to evaluate all or part of the manuscript, providing an unusual degree of quality control. Their careful work and thoughtful suggestions have improved the manuscript many times over from its first-draft incarnations. I am grateful to them all for their comments.

My thinking has been shaped by many teachers along the way. I was introduced to psychology at Wesleyan University, where several committed and inspiring teachers—and in particular Karl Scheibe—made the excitement and relevance of the field clear to me, and by the time I left Wesleyan I could envision no other career but that of psychologist. Although the nature of the University of Wisconsin, where I did my graduate work, could not have been more different from the much smaller Wesleyan, the excitement and inspiration were similar. Once again, a cadre of excellent teachers—led, in particular, by the late Vernon Allen—molded my thinking and taught me the beauty and science of the discipline of psychology.

My colleagues and students at the University of Massachusetts at Amherst provide an ongoing intellectual stimulation, and I thank them for making the University a very fine place to work. Several people also provided extraordinary research and editorial help; they include Carolyn Dash, Richard Fleming, Wendy Copes, Frances Ramos, Lisa Beck, and Kate Cleary. I also thank James M. Royer, who provided a draft of the material in the statistics appendix.

I am very grateful to Elisa Adams, who was developmental editor for this edition of *Understanding Psychology.* Her skillful editing and insightful comments improved the book immeasurably. And all readers of this book owe a debt to Rhona Robbin, the developmental editor of the first edition, whose relentless pursuit of excellence shaped the underlying quality of this book. I've been lucky enough to have two of the best editors in the publishing field work on this book with me.

Jim Anker, sponsoring editor, was instrumental in ensuring the production of the high-quality volume you see here, and I value his unceasing strong contributions and support. Other people at McGraw-Hill were central to the design and production process; these include David Dunham—whose attention to detail continues to astound me and touch deep chords of gratitude that there are people in the world like him—Elsa Peterson, and Nick Krenitsky. I am proud to be a part of this first-class team.

Finally, I am, as always, indebted to my family. The love and support of my parents, Leah Brochstein and the late Saul D. Feldman, remain a foundation of my life. Other family members also play a central role in my life;

these people include, more or less in order of age, my nieces and nephews, my brother, various brothers- and sisters-in-law, Ethel Radler, and Harry Brochstein. My late mother-in-law, Mary Evans Vorwerk, had an important influence on this book, and I remain grateful to her.

Ultimately, my children, Jonathan, Joshua, and Sarah, and my wife, Katherine, remain the focal point of my life. I thank them, with great love.

Robert S. Feldman

USING

UNDERSTANDING

PSYCHOLOGY

STRATEGIES FOR EFFECTIVE STUDY AND CRITICAL THINKING

Understanding Psychology has been written with the reader in mind, and it therefore includes a number of unique features that will help you to maximize your learning of the concepts, theories, facts, and other kinds of information that make up the field of psychology. To take advantage of these features, there are several steps that you should take when reading and studying this book. By following these steps, you will not only get the most out of this book, but you will also develop habits that will help you to study other texts more effectively and to think critically about material you are learning. Among the most important steps to follow:

▶ Familiarize yourself with the logic of the book's structure. Begin by reading the Table of Contents. It provides an overview of the topics that will be covered and gives a sense of the way the various topics are interrelated. Next, review the Preface, which describes the book's major features. Note how each chapter is divided into three or four self-contained units; these provide logical starting and stopping points for reading and studying. Also note the major highlights of each chapter: a chapter-opening outline, a Prologue, a Looking Ahead section that includes chapter objectives, Recaps and Reviews of key information following each of the major units, and—at the end of every chapter—a Looking Back section, Key Terms and Concepts, and a Further Study and Application section. Because every chapter is structured in the same way, you are provided with a set of familiar landmarks as you chart your way through new material, allowing you to organize the chapter's content more readily.

▶ Use a study strategy. Although we are expected to study and ultimately learn a wide array of material throughout our schooling, we are rarely taught any systematic strategies that permit us to study more effectively. Yet, just as we wouldn't expect a physician to learn human anatomy by trial and error, it is the unusual student who is able to stumble upon a truly effective studying strategy.

Psychologists, however, have devised several excellent (and proven) techniques for improving study skills, two of which are described here. By employing one of these procedures—known by the initials "SQ3R" and "MURDER"—you can increase your ability to learn and retain information and to think critically, not just in psychology classes but in all academic subjects.

The SQ3R method includes a series of five steps, having the initials S-Q-R-R-R. The first step is to *survey* the material by reading the chapter outlines, chapter headings, figure captions, recaps, and Looking Ahead and Looking Back sections, providing yourself with an overview of the major points of the chapter. The next step—the "Q" in SQ3R—is to *question*. Formulate questions—either aloud or in writing—prior to actually reading a section of the material. For instance, if you had first surveyed this section of the book, you might jot down in the margin, "what do "SQ3R" and "MURDER" stand for?" The reviews that end each section of the chapter are also a good source of questions. But it is important not to rely on them entirely; making up your own questions is critical. *Understanding Psychology* has wide margins in which you can write out your own questions. Such questioning helps you to focus in on the key points of the chapter, while putting you in an inquisitive frame of mind as well.

It is now time for the next, and most crucial, step: to *read* the material. Read carefully and, even more important, actively and critically. For instance, while you are reading, answer the questions you have asked yourself. You may find yourself coming up with new questions as you read along; that's fine, since it shows you are reading inquisitively and paying attention to the material. Critically evaluate material by considering the implications of what you are reading, thinking about possible exceptions and contradictions, and examining the assumptions that lie behind the assertions made by the author.

The next step—the second "R"—is the most unusual. This "R" stands for *recite*, in which you look up from the book and describe and explain to yourself, or to a friend, the material you have just read and answer the questions you have posed earlier. Do it aloud; this is one time when talking to yourself is nothing to be embarrassed about. The recitation process helps you to clearly identify your degree of understanding of the material you have just read. Moreover, psychological research has shown that communicating material to others (even imaginary others, if you are reciting aloud to yourself and not a friend) aids you in learning it in a different—and deeper—way than material which you do not intend to communicate. Hence, your recitation of the material is a crucial link in the studying process.

The final "R" refers to *review*. As we will discuss in Chapter 6, reviewing is a prerequisite to fully learning and remembering material you have studied. Look over the information; reread the Recaps and Looking Back summaries; answer in-text review questions; and use any ancillary materials you may have available. (There is both a traditional and a computerized student study guide available to accompany *Understanding Psychology*.) Reviewing should be an active process, in which you consider how different pieces of information fit together and develop a sense of the overall picture.

An alternative approach to studying—although not altogether dissimilar to SQ3R—is provided by the MURDER system of Dansereau (1978). Despite the unpleasant connotations of its title, the MURDER system is a useful study strategy.

In MURDER, the first step is to establish an appropriate mood for studying by setting goals for a study session and choosing a time and place in which you will not be distracted. Next comes reading for understanding, in which careful attention is paid to the meaning of the material being studied. Recall is an immediate attempt to recall the material from memory, without referring to the text. Digesting the material comes next; you should correct any recall errors, and attempt to organize and store newly learned material in memory.

You should work next on expanding (analyzing and evaluating) new material, and try to apply it to situations that go beyond the applications discussed in the text. By incorporating what you have learned into a larger information network in memory, you will be able to recall it more easily in the future. Finally, the last step is review. Just as with the SQ3R system, MURDER suggests that systematic review of material is a necessary condition for successful studying.

Both the SQ3R and MURDER systems provide a proven means of increasing your study effectiveness. It is not necessary, though, to feel tied to a particular strategy; you might want to combine other elements into your own study system. For example, learning tips and strategies for critical thinking will be presented throughout *Understanding Psychology*, such as in Chapter 6 when the use of mnemonics (memory techniques for organizing material to help its recall) are discussed. If these tactics help you to successfully master new material, stick with them.

▶ The last aspect of studying that warrants mention is that *when* and *where* you study are in some ways as important as *how* you study. One of the truisms of the psychological literature is that we learn things better, and are able to recall them longer, when we study material in small chunks over several study sessions, rather than massing our study into one lengthy period. This implies that all-night studying just prior to a test is going to be less effective—and a lot more tiring—then employing a series of steady, regular study sessions. If you have always had trouble with deadlines and have difficulty scheduling regular study sessions, you should also investigate formal time management techniques, discussed in Chapter 5.

In addition to carefully timing your studying, you should seek out a special location to study. It doesn't really matter where it is, as long as it has minimal distractions and is a place that you use *only* for studying. Identifying a special "territory" allows you get in the right mood for study as soon as you begin.

A final comment

By using the proven study strategies presented above, as well as by making use of the pedagogical tools integrated in the text, you will maximize your understanding of the material in this book and you will master techniques that will help you learn and think critically in all your academic endeavors. More importantly, you will optimize your understanding of the field of psychology. It is worth the effort: the excitement, challenge, and promise that psychology holds for you is immense.

UNDERSTANDING
PSYCHOLOGY

PART ONE

THE SCIENCE OF PSYCHOLOGY

In this introductory part of the book, we encounter an Olympic athlete who overcomes a progression of hardships to attain personal triumph. We discover a group of people who hear the screams of terror of a woman being attacked—and do not even bother to call the police. And we consider how the science of psychology plays a role in everyone's lives.

This part of the book provides an introduction to psychology. We learn what psychology is and the diverse topics that psychologists study. After looking at the places in which psychologists are employed, we consider how psychologists solve scientific—and practical—problems by carrying out research. Finally, we find out how we can be informed consumers of psychology.

In Chapter 1, then, the focus is on the science of psychology, encompassing its past, present, and future.

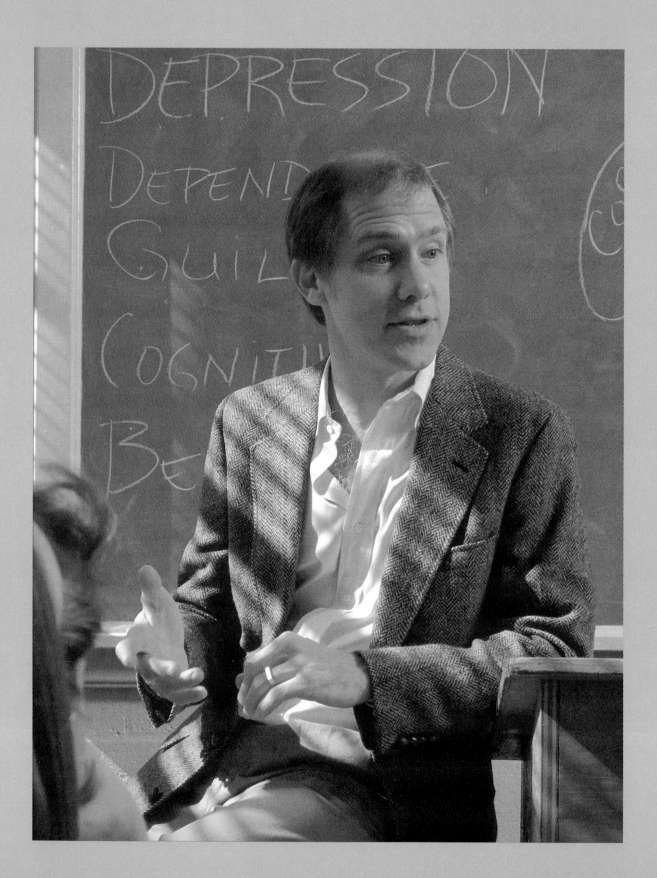

CHAPTER

1

INTRODUCTION TO PSYCHOLOGY

Greg Louganis. (Reuters/Bettmann News-photos)

PROLOGUE:
GREG LOUGANIS

Springing off the diving board almost 3 feet toward the sky, the diver tucked, spun, and somersaulted through the air, until he slipped, at 40 miles per hour, into a tiny spot in the blue water below. There was a moment of awed silence, and then the crowd broke into exuberant cheers.

For Greg Louganis, the precision performance was hardly unusual. This dive, though, was anything but routine, for it was his final dive in the Olympics. As the scores were posted, the perfect ratings of the judges were enough to bring him his fourth gold medal. Through his performance, he became the only person in the world to sweep the platform and springboard gold medals in two world Olympics.

The apparent ease of the dive stood in sharp contrast to the hurdles that Louganis had been forced to overcome throughout his 29 years. Put up for adoption at the age of 9 months by his teenage parents, he grew up suffering from dyslexia, a reading disorder, and he stuttered. He was teased by classmates for his academic problems; but the racial taunts and slurs, brought about by the dark skin inherited from his Samoan father, were even worse. Beatings from neighborhood bullies were an everyday occurrence.

Later, when his talent as a diver became apparent, new difficulties arose: problems with alcohol, injuries, and the constant, gnawing apprehension that comes to every diver—the fear of "losing the water," becoming disoriented and hitting the water so badly that life-threatening injuries result.

Yet Louganis persevered, relentlessly motivated to practice and compete. And success ultimately came: Louganis is without peer in the realm of diving. He is, simply put, the best diver in the world.

LOOKING AHEAD ▶

Despite its storybook qualities, Louganis's life clearly has not been one of easy, unceasing success. As with most of us, his life's highs have been offset by down periods.

To psychologists seeking to understand both the successes and the difficulties faced by Louganis, there is no simple explanation. In fact, different psychologists would take considerably disparate approaches to the question:

▶ Psychologists who specialize in studying the biology underlying behavior would consider the ways in which Louganis's body reacts to the stress of competition and the means by which his body can be trained to react with such precision during dives.

▶ Psychologists who study the senses would investigate Louganis's dyslexia—a reading disorder that involves the distortion of printed material—to understand its impact on his life.

▶ Psychologists who focus on the changes that occur with age might examine Louganis's childhood, considering how his adoption at an early age, and his childhood problems of stuttering and dyslexia, affected his development.

▶ Psychologists specializing in learning would reflect on how Louganis learned his diving skills.

▶ Psychologists interested in explaining motivation would focus on Louganis's almost overpowering need to hone and improve his skills.

▶ Health psychologists and clinical (or abnormal) psychologists would consider the periods of depression and the smoking and alcohol problems experienced by Louganis.

▶ Social psychologists, interested in our interactions with others, would see Louganis's concern for his friends and coaches as an indication of how the social world shapes his behavior.

THE COMMON LINK AMONG PSYCHOLOGISTS:
The Study of Behavior and Mental Processes

Although the approaches taken by different psychologists in considering Greg Louganis are very diverse, the common link among them is that each represents a specialty area within the general area of study called psychology. **Psychology** is the scientific study of behavior and mental processes.

This definition, although clear-cut and accurate, is also deceptively simple. In order to encompass the breadth of the field, "behavior and mental processes" must be understood to mean many things: It includes not just what people do but also their thoughts, their feelings, their perceptions, their reasoning processes, their memories, and even, in one sense, the biological activities that keep their bodies functioning.

When psychologists speak of "studying" behavior and mental processes, their interests are equally broad. To psychologists, it is not enough simply to describe behavior. As with any science—and psychologists clearly consider their discipline a science—psychology attempts to explain, predict, modify, and ultimately improve the lives of people and the world in which they live.

Psychology: The scientific study of behavior and mental processes

Can the sign language Roger Fouts uses to communicate with the chimp Lucy be similar in sophistication to the language used when human beings converse? As discussed in Chapter 7, the answer is controversial. (Paul Fusco/Magnum)

Psychologists seek to achieve these goals through scientific methods. They do not consider it sufficient to rely on intuition, insight, and logic to study behavior; too often, people are simply wrong in their guesses about human behavior (Kohn, 1988). For instance, how many of the following statements do you think are correct?

1. The primary reason babies love their mothers is that their mothers provide food and satisfy other basic biological needs.

2. People who are geniuses generally have poor social adjustment.

3. The best way to make sure that a desired behavior will continue after training is completed is to reward that behavior every single time it occurs during training, rather than reward it only periodically.

4. A schizophrenic is someone with at least two distinct personalities.

5. If you are having trouble sleeping, the best way to get to sleep is to take a sleeping pill.

6. Children's IQ scores have very little to do with how well they do in school.

7. Frequent masturbation can lead to mental illness.

8. Once people reach old age, their leisure activities change radically.

9. Most people would refuse to give painful electric shocks to others.

10. One of the least important factors affecting how much we like another person is that person's physical attractiveness.

You may be surprised to know that *all* these statements have been proved false by psychological research employing well-controlled, methodical, scientific techniques. If you guessed wrong, don't be too concerned; the statements represent opinions that students who enter introductory psychology classes are most likely to hold (Lamal, 1979).

By using scientific procedures, psychologists are able to find answers to questions about the nature of human behavior that are far more valid than what mere intuition and guesses provide. And what a variety and range of questions psychologists pose. Consider these examples: How do we see colors? What is intelligence? Can abnormal behavior be cured? Is a hypnotic trance the same as sleep? Can aging be delayed? How does stress affect us? What is the best way to study? What is normal sexual behavior?

These questions—whose answers you will know by the time you finish reading this book—provide just a hint of the range of topics that will be presented as we explore the field of psychology. Our discussions will take us across the spectrum of what is known about behavior and mental processes. At times, we will leave the realm of humans and explore animal behavior, since many psychologists study nonhumans in order to determine general laws of behavior that pertain to *all* organisms, and since animal behavior can provide important clues to answering questions about human behavior. But we will always return to the usefulness of psychology in helping to solve the everyday problems that confront all human beings.

In this introductory chapter, we cover a number of topics that are central to an understanding of psychology. We begin by introducing the different

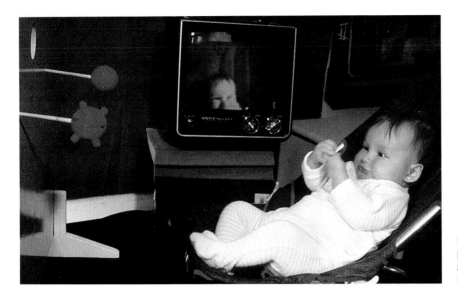

Developmental psychologists conduct sophisticated experiments to study infants and their abilities. (Philippe Plailly/Science Photo Library/Photo Researchers)

types of psychologists and the roles they play. Next, we discuss the major approaches and models that are used to guide the work psychologists do. Finally, we describe the research methods psychologists employ in their search for the answers to questions that will help them to better understand behavior.

In covering this introductory material, we also introduce the text itself. This book is intended to provide as close a facsimile to two people sitting down and discussing psychology as one can convey with the written word; when I write "we," I am talking about the two of us—reader and writer. To borrow a phrase from the folks who spend most of their time with computers, the book is meant to be "user-friendly."

You will find, then, material to demonstrate the ways in which psychologists apply what they have learned to everyday life (Psychology at Work boxes), discussion of how psychologists carry out research and collect data (Research Classics boxes), and material to show you what the future of psychology holds (Cutting Edge boxes). There are also sections in each chapter that are intended to make you a more knowledgeable consumer of psychological information by enhancing your ability to critically evaluate the contributions psychologists offer society. These sections, called The Informed Consumer of Psychology, include concrete recommendations for incorporating psychology into your life.

The book itself is designed to make it easier for you to learn the material we discuss. Based on the principles that psychologists who specialize in learning and memory have developed, information is presented in relatively small chunks, with each chapter including three or four major sections. Each of these sections is followed by a Recap and Review that lists the key points that have been covered and asks you a series of questions. (Answers to the questions are provided on the page following the review.) This kind of quick review will help you in learning, and later recalling, the material.

In sum, after reading this chapter, you will be able to answer the following questions:

▶ What is psychology and why is it a science?

▶ What are the different kinds of psychologists?

▶ What assumptions do psychologists make about the world?

▶ How do psychologists use theory and research to answer questions of interest?

▶ What are the different forms of research employed by psychologists?

PSYCHOLOGISTS AT WORK

Wanted: Industrial/Organizational Psychologist. Ph.D. required. Psychologist will work with other psychologists who are responsible for generating accurate job descriptions, developing and administering training programs, designing performance evaluation systems, and developing and implementing a program for the early identification of managerial talent within the company.

▲ ▲ ▲

Wanted: Counseling Psychologist. Ph.D. required, including internship and experience relevant to understanding both college student development and higher education environments. Responsibilities include counseling/therapy with individuals and groups, and consultation with campus units. Innovation in devising new counseling methods and developing new programs is encouraged.

▲ ▲ ▲

Wanted: Psychology Instructor, Community College. Master's degree required. Instructor will teach one to three sections of introductory psychology and two to four classes from interest areas including family relations, child and adult development, educational psychology, personality, social psychology, and experimental psychology. Additional duties will include advising entering and first-year students (American Psychological Association, 1980).

Many people mistakenly believe that almost all psychologists analyze and treat abnormal behavior. However, as the actual job descriptions reprinted above indicate, the range and scope of the field of psychology are much broader than this common misconception would suggest. We can examine the major branches and specialty areas of psychology by describing them in the general order in which they are discussed in this book. Figure 1-1 displays the percentage of psychologists who are engaged in each of the major specialty areas. It also shows the proportion of published articles relevant to each area, indicating which of the specialties currently are the heaviest contributors to the psychological research literature.

THE BIOLOGICAL FOUNDATIONS OF PSYCHOLOGY: Biopsychologists

In the most fundamental sense, people are biological entities, and some psychologists emphasize how the physiological functions and structures of our body work together with our mind to influence our behavior. **Biopsychology** is the branch of psychology that specializes in the biological bases of behavior. Biopsychologists study a broad range of topics with a focus on the operation of the brain and nervous system. For example, they may in-

Biopsychology: The branch of psychology that studies the biological basis of behavior

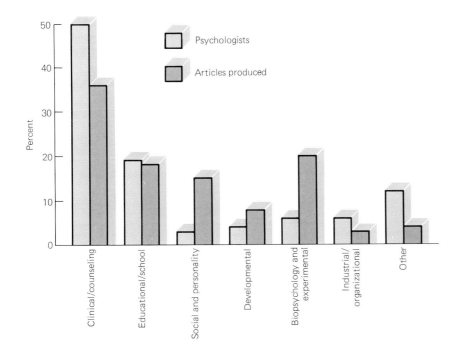

FIGURE 1-1

The major specialties within the field, represented by the percentage of psychologists falling into each category and the number of publications produced in each category between 1967 and 1986. (Sources: Stapp, Tucker, & VandenBos, 1985 (table 2), p. 1324; *PsychINFO Training Manual,* 1987.)

vestigate the ways in which specific sites in the brain are related to a disorder such as Parkinson's disease (see Chapter 2), or they may attempt to determine how bodily sensations are related to emotion (see Chapter 9).

SENSING, PERCEIVING, LEARNING, AND THINKING: Experimental Psychologists

If you have ever wondered how acute your vision is, how you experience pain, or how you can most effectively study, you have raised a question that is most appropriately answered by an experimental psychologist. **Experimental psychology** is the branch of psychology that studies the processes of sensing, perceiving, learning, and thinking about the world.

The work of experimental psychologists overlaps that done by biopsychologists, as well as that done in other branches of psychology. Actually, the term "experimental psychologist" is somewhat misleading, since psychologists in every branch use experimental techniques, and experimental psychologists do not limit themselves to only experimental methods.

Several subspecialties have grown out of experimental psychology and have become central parts of the field in their own right. For example, **cognitive psychology** is the branch of psychology that specializes in the study of higher mental processes, including thinking, language, memory, problem solving, knowing, reasoning, judging, and decision making. Covering a wide swath of human behavior, cognitive psychologists have, for instance, identified more efficient ways of remembering and better strategies for solving problems involving logic.

Experimental psychology: The branch of psychology that studies the processes of sensing, perceiving, learning, and thinking about the world

Cognitive psychology: The branch of psychology that considers higher mental processes including thinking, language, memory, problem solving, knowing, reasoning, judging, and decision making

UNDERSTANDING CHANGE AND INDIVIDUAL DIFFERENCES: Developmental and Personality Psychologists

A baby producing its first smile . . . taking its first step . . . saying its first word.

These events, which can be characterized as universal milestones in development, are also singularly special and unique for each person. Developmental psychologists, whose work is discussed in Chapters 12 and 13, trace the changes in behavior and in people's underlying capabilities throughout their lives.

Developmental psychology is the branch of psychology that studies how people grow and change throughout the course of their lives. Another branch, **personality psychology**, attempts to explain both consistency and change in a person's behavior over time, as well as the individual traits that differentiate the behavior of one person from another when each confronts the same situation. The major issues relating to the study of personality will be considered in Chapter 14.

Developmental psychology: The branch of psychology that studies how people grow and change throughout their lives

Personality psychology: The branch of psychology that studies consistency and change in people's behavior and the characteristics that differentiate people

PHYSICAL AND MENTAL HEALTH: Health, Clinical, and Counseling Psychologists

If you have difficulty getting along with others, continual unhappiness in your life, or a fear that prevents you from carrying out your normal activities, you might consult one of the psychologists who devote their energies to the study of physical or mental health: health psychologists, clinical psychologists, and counseling psychologists.

Health psychology explores the relationship between psychological factors and physical ailments or disease. For instance, health psychologists are interested in how long-term stress (a psychological factor) can affect physical health. They are also concerned with identifying ways of promoting behavior related to good health (such as increased exercise) or discouraging unhealthy behavior such as smoking, as we will discuss in Chapter 15.

Health psychology: The branch of psychology that explores the relationship of physical and psychological factors

For clinical psychologists, the focus of activity is on the treatment and prevention of psychological disturbance. **Clinical psychology** is the branch of psychology that deals with the study, diagnosis, and treatment of abnormal behavior. Clinical psychologists are trained to diagnose and treat problems ranging from the everyday crises of life—such as grief due to the death of a loved one—to more extreme conditions, such as loss of touch with reality. Some clinical psychologists also conduct research, investigating issues that range from identifying the early signs of psychological disturbance to studying the relationship between how family members communicate with one another and psychological disorder.

Clinical psychology: The branch of psychology that studies diagnosis and treatment of abnormal behavior

As we will see when we discuss abnormal behavior and its treatment in Chapters 16 and 17, the kinds of activities carried out by clinical psychologists are varied indeed. It is the clinical psychologist who administers and scores psychological tests and who provides psychological services in community mental-health centers. Even sexual problems, as we will see when we consider human sexuality in Chapter 10, are often treated by the clinical psychologist.

Counseling psychology is the branch of psychology that focuses on educational, social, and career adjustment problems. Almost every college has a counseling center staffed with counseling psychologists, where students can get advice on the kinds of jobs they might be most suited for, on methods of studying effectively, and on strategies for resolving everyday difficulties, from problems with roommates to concerns about a specific professor's grading practices.

Counseling psychology: The branch of psychology that focuses on educational, social, and career adjustment issues

Two close relatives of counseling psychology are educational psychology and school psychology. **Educational psychology** considers how the educational process affects students; it is, for instance, concerned with ways of understanding intelligence, developing better teaching techniques, and understanding teacher-student interaction. **School psychology**, in contrast, is the speciality devoted to assessing children in elementary and secondary schools who have academic or emotional problems and to developing solutions to such problems.

Educational psychology: The branch of psychology that considers how the educational process affects students

School psychology: The branch of psychology that considers the academic and emotional problems of elementary and secondary school students

UNDERSTANDING THE SOCIAL WORLD: Social, Industrial-Organizational, and Environmental Psychologists

None of us lives in isolation; rather, we are all part of a complex network of interrelationships. These networks with other people and with society as a whole are the focus of study for many different kinds of psychologists.

Social psychology, as we will see in Chapters 18 and 19, is the study of how people's thoughts, feelings, and actions are affected by others. Social psychologists focus on such diverse topics as understanding human aggression, learning why people form relationships with one another, and determining how we are influenced by advertisements.

Social psychology: The branch of psychology that studies how people's thoughts, feelings, and actions are affected by others

Industrial-organizational psychology is concerned with the psychology of the workplace. Such questions as "How do you increase productivity and worker accuracy?" "How can you select the right person for a job?" and "Can an employee's job satisfaction be increased?" are asked by industrial and organizational psychologists, as will be discussed in Chapter 20.

Industrial-organizational psychology: The branch of psychology that studies the psychology of the workplace, considering productivity, job satisfaction, and related issues

If you were interested in designing an inner-city apartment building that wouldn't be prone to vandalism, you might turn to an environmental psychologist. **Environmental psychology** considers the relationship between people and the physical environment. As you will read in Chapter 21, environmental psychologists (along with psychologists studying the impact of modern technological advances) have made important progress in understanding how our physical environment affects, for example, the way we behave toward others, our emotions, and how much stress we experience in a particular setting.

Environmental psychology: The branch of psychology that considers the relationship between people and their physical environment

Many veterans faced psychological difficulties after returning from the war in Vietnam. Clinical and counseling psychologists often used a treatment technique with them that consisted of discussion groups, like this one in Walla Walla, Washington. (Eric Kroll/Taurus Photos)

Forensic psychology: The branch of psychology that studies insanity and other legal issues

Consumer psychology: The branch of psychology that considers our buying habits and the effects of advertising on buyer behavior

Program evaluation: The assessment of large-scale programs to determine their effectiveness in meeting their goals

EMERGING AREAS OF STUDY

As the field of psychology matures, the number of specialty areas continues to grow (Matarazzo, 1987). For example, **forensic psychology** focuses on legal issues, such as deciding what criteria indicate that a person is legally insane and whether larger or smaller juries make fairer decisions (Weiner & Hess, 1987; Monahan & Walker, 1988). **Consumer psychology** considers the factors underlying consumers' buying habits and the ways in which people respond to advertisements. Psychologists interested in **program evaluation** also constitute a growing body; they focus on assessing large-scale programs, usually run by the government, to determine whether they are effective in meeting their goals. For example, psychologists specializing in evaluation have examined the effectiveness of such governmental social services as the Head Start day-care program and Medicaid (Woodhead, 1988).

HERE, THERE, EVERYWHERE: Where Do Psychologists Work?

Given the diversity of roles that psychologists play, it is not surprising that they are employed in a variety of settings. As you can see in Figure 1-2, the primary employers are institutions of higher learning: universities, two- and four-year colleges, and medical schools. The next-most-frequent employment settings are hospitals, clinics, community mental-health centers, and counseling centers. A substantial number of psychologists are also employed in private practice. Other settings include human-services organizations, research and consulting firms, and business and industry (Oskamp, 1988).

Why are so many psychologists found in academic settings? The primary reason is that the three major roles played by psychologists in society— teacher, scientist, and professional—are easily carried out in such an environment. Very often professors of psychology are also actively involved in

FIGURE 1-2

Where psychologists work: The major settings in which psychologists are employed. (Adapted from Stapp, Tucker, & VandenBos, 1985 (table 4), pp. 1326–1327.)

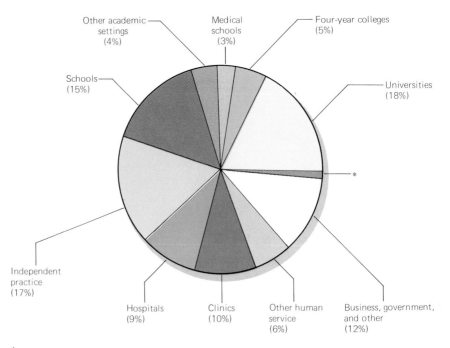

Other academic settings (4%)
Medical schools (3%)
Four-year colleges (5%)
Schools (15%)
Universities (18%)
Independent practice (17%)
Hospitals (9%)
Clinics (10%)
Other human service (6%)
Business, government, and other (12%)
*

*Unspecified (1%)

research or in serving clients. Whatever their particular job setting, however, psychologists share a commitment to better both individual lives and society in general (DeLeon, 1988), and the topics they explore range from a person's inner life to far reaches of outer space (see the Cutting Edge box).

THE CUTTING EDGE

As the rocket headed into space after takeoff, the astronauts unstrapped themselves from their seats to begin the mission tasks. Their first order of business: meeting with the crew psychologist, whose job it was to ensure the psychological adjustment of the crew and to keep its performance at a high level.

Although there has yet to be a psychologist on a space mission, the scenario described above may well become a reality in the future. This prediction is based on the arguments of a growing number of experts, who suggest that psychological problems among astronauts are likely to increase as space exploration becomes more common and voyages last longer.

There are several reasons to expect that psychology will play a critical role in space exploration (Helmreich, 1986; Conners, Harrison, & Akins, 1986). Among them:

● As space flight becomes an everyday occurrence, rocket travel will have little more significance than flying in an airplane. Parades and White House visits for astronauts will be a thing of the past. As these kinds of rewards for space flight diminish, the costs—in terms of danger, isola-

PUSHING THE LIMITS: PSYCHOLOGY IN OUTER SPACE

tion, and crowding—will take on greater significance to space voyagers. It is likely, then, that psychological problems will become more common.

● Because crews on early space flights were relatively homogeneous in background and experience, there was a comparatively low chance of friction among crew members. But as the crews grow in diversity, the possibility of conflict will increase. In fact, it may become necessary to carry out even more rigorous psychological screening of crew members than the National Aeronautics and Space Administration (NASA) currently does.

● As the length of space missions increases, good social relations may become more and more difficult to maintain, and stress levels may rise and never abate. Astronauts on long flights report feeling that they are "never off duty," in a state of "constant alertness" (Douglas, 1984; Bluth, 1984). Whether astronauts can ever completely adapt to the

perception that they are always "on call"—and can ever fully relax—may have an important effect on the amount of stress they experience.

● Isolated groups are subject to poor decision making, a phenomenon called "groupthink" that we discuss in Chapter 20 (Janis & Mann, 1976). Consequently, the decisions made by astronauts in flight must be carefully monitored to ensure their soundness.

● The lack of leisure activities on longer missions will likely become a stumbling block of greater importance. Work carried out by psychologists in other settings—such as underseas laboratories—suggests that crews can work most effectively only when their leisure and recreational needs are met (Nowlis, 1972). Privacy needs and the possibility of sexual tensions in mixed-sex crews must also be taken into account.

The realization that psychological issues will play an important role in space flight suggests, then, that psychologists may come to play an increasingly important part in the space exploration program. Indeed, psychology texts of the future might include "space psychology" among the branches of the field.

RECAP AND REVIEW I

Recap

◀ Psychology is the scientific study of behavior and mental processes.

◀ Among the major kinds of psychologists are biopsychologists; experimental psychologists; cognitive psychologists; developmental and personality psychologists; health, clinical, and counseling psychologists; educa-

tional and school psychologists; and environmental psychologists. Other emerging areas include forensic psychology, consumer psychology, and the psychology of program evaluation.

◀ Most psychologists are employed by institutions of higher learning; the balance are employed by hospitals, clinics, and community health centers or are engaged in private practice.

Review

1. Most of present-day psychology has its foundation in
   a. Intuition
   b. Observation and experimentation
   c. Trial and error
   d. Metaphysics

2. Match each branch of psychology with the issues or questions posed below.
   a. _____ Biopsychology
   b. _____ Experimental psychology
   c. _____ Cognitive psychology
   d. _____ Developmental psychology
   e. _____ Personality psychology
   f. _____ Health psychology
   g. _____ Clinical psychology
   h. _____ Counseling psychology
   i. _____ Educational psychology
   j. _____ School psychology
   k. _____ Social psychology
   l. _____ Industrial psychology
   m. _____ Consumer psychology

   1. Joan, a college freshman, is panicking. She needs to learn better organizational skills and study habits to cope with the demands of college.
   2. At what age do children generally begin to acquire an emotional attachment to their fathers?
   3. It is thought that pornographic films that depict violence against women may prompt aggressive behavior in some men.
   4. What chemicals are released in the human body as a result of a stressful event? What are their effects on behavior?
   5. John is fairly unique in his manner of responding to crisis situations, with an even temperament and a positive outlook.
   6. The general public is more apt to buy products that are promoted by attractive and successful actors.
   7. Eight-year-old Jack's teachers are concerned that he has recently begun to withdraw socially and to show little interest in school work.
   8. Janet's job is demanding and stressful. She wonders if this lifestyle is leaving her more prone to certain illnesses such as cancer and heart disease.
   9. A psychologist is intrigued by the fact that some people are much more sensitive to painful stimuli than others.
   10. A strong fear of crowds leads a young woman to seek treatment for her problem.
   11. What mental strategies are involved in solving complex word problems?
   12. What teaching approaches most effectively motivate elementary school students to successfully accomplish academic tasks?
   13. Jessica is asked to develop a management strategy that will encourage safer work practices in an assembly plant.

3. A large proportion of psychologists are employed in academic institutions because that type of environment makes it easier for them to carry out the roles of
   _____, _____, and _____.

(Answers to review questions are on page 18.)

A SCIENCE EVOLVES: THE PAST AND THE FUTURE

Some half-million years ago, primitive peoples assumed that psychological problems were caused by the presence of evil spirits. To allow these spirits to escape, an operation called trephining was performed. Trephining consisted of chipping away at the skull with crude stone instruments until a hole was cut through the bone. Because archeologists have found skulls with signs of healing around the opening, we can assume that patients sometimes survived the cure.

▲ ▲ ▲

The famous Greek physician Hippocrates thought that personality was made up of four temperaments: sanguine (cheerful and active), melancholic (sad), choleric (angry and aggressive), and phlegmatic (calm and passive). These temperaments were influenced by the presence of "humors," or fluids, in the body. For instance, a sanguine person was thought to have more blood than other people.

▲ ▲ ▲

Franz Josef Gall, an eighteenth-century scientist, argued that a trained observer could discern intelligence, moral character, and other basic personality traits from the shape and number of bumps on a person's skull. His theory gave rise to the "science" of phrenology, employed by hundreds of practitioners.

▲ ▲ ▲

According to the philosopher Descartes, nerves were hollow tubes through which "animal spirits" conducted impulses in the same way that water is transmitted through a tube. When people put a finger too close to a fire, then, the heat was transmitted via the spirits through the tube, directly into the brain.

While these "scientific" explanations sound farfetched to us, at one time they represented the most advanced thinking regarding what might be called the psychology of the era. Even without knowing much about modern-day psychology, you can surmise that our understanding of behavior has advanced tremendously since these earlier views were formulated. Yet most of the advances have occurred relatively recently, for, as sciences go, psychology is one of the newcomers on the block.

Although its roots can be traced back to the ancient Greeks and Romans, and though philosophers have argued for several hundred years about some of the same sorts of questions that psychologists grapple with today, the formal beginning of psychology is generally set at 1879. In that year, the first laboratory devoted to the experimental study of psychological phenomena was established in Germany by Wilhelm Wundt; at about the same time, the American William James set up his laboratory in Cambridge, Massachusetts.

Throughout its some 11 decades of formal existence, psychology has led an active life, developing gradually into a true science. As part of this evolution, it has produced a number of conceptual **models**—systems of interrelated ideas and concepts used to explain phenomena—that have guided the work being carried out. Some of these models have been discarded—

Models: Systems of interrelated ideas and concepts used to explain phenomena

In the 1800s, it was widely believed that phrenology (the study of the contours of an individual's head) could reveal important information about a person. (Culver Pictures)

Names of the Organs.

1. Amativeness.
2. Philoprogenitiveness
3. Adhesiveness.
4. Inhabitiveness.
5. Continuity.
6. Combativeness.
7. Destructiveness.
8. Alimentiveness.
9. Acquisitiveness.
10. Secretiveness.
11. Cautiousness.
12. Approbativeness.
13. Self-Esteem.
14. Firmness.
15. Conscientiousness.
16. Hope.
17. Marvelousness.
18. Veneration.
19. Benevolence
20. Constructiveness.

Names of the Organs.

21. Ideality.
B. Sublimity.
22. Imitation
23. Mirthfulness.
24. Individuality.
25. Form.
26. Size.
27. Weight.
28. Color.
29. Order.
30. Calculation.
31. Locality.
32. Eventuality.
33. Time.
34. Tune.
35. Language.
36. Causality.
37. Comparison.
C. Human Nature.
D. Agreeableness.

"I look upon Phrenology as the guide to Philosophy and the handmaid to Christianity. Whoever disseminates true Phrenology is a public benefactor."
—Hon. Horace Mann.

just as have the views of Hippocrates and Descartes—but others have been developed and elaborated on and provide a set of maps for psychologists to follow.

Each of the models provides a distinct perspective, emphasizing different factors. Just as we may employ not one but many maps to find our way around a particular geographical area—one map to show the roads, one the major landmarks, and one the topography of the hills and valleys—psychologists also find that more than one approach may be useful in understanding behavior. Given the range and complexity of behavior, no single model will invariably provide an optimal explanation—but together, the models provide us with a means to explain the extraordinary breadth of behavior.

THE ROOTS OF PSYCHOLOGY: Historical Perspectives

When Wilhelm Wundt set up the first psychology laboratory in Leipzig, Germany, in 1879, he was interested in studying the building blocks of the mind. Formally defining psychology as the study of conscious experience, he developed a model that came to be known as structuralism. **Structuralism** focused on the fundamental elements that form the foundation of thinking, consciousness, emotions, and other kinds of mental states and activities.

To come to an understanding of how basic sensations combined into our awareness of the world, Wundt and other structuralists used a procedure called introspection to study the structure of the mind. In **introspection,** people were presented with a stimulus—such as a bright green object or a sentence printed on a card—and asked to describe, in their own words and in as much detail as they could manage, what they were experiencing as they were exposed to it. Wundt argued that psychologists could come to understand the structure of the mind through the reports that people made of their reactions.

Wundt's structuralism did not stand the test of time, however, for psychologists became increasingly dissatisfied with the assumption that introspection could unlock the fundamental elements of the mind. For one thing, people had difficulty describing some kinds of inner experiences, such as emotional responses. (For example, the next time you experience anger, try to analyze and explain the primary elements of what you are feeling.) Moreover, breaking down objects into their most basic mental units sometimes seemed to be a most peculiar undertaking. A book, for instance, could not be described by a structuralist as merely a book, but instead had to be broken down into its various components, such as the material on the cover, the colors, the shapes of the letters, and so on. Finally, introspection was not a truly scientific technique; there was little way that an outside observer could verify the accuracy of the introspections that people did make. Such drawbacks led to the evolution of new models, which largely supplanted structuralism.

Interestingly, however, important remnants of structuralism still exist. As we shall see in Chapter 7, the past twenty years have seen a resurgence of interest in people's descriptions of their inner experience. Cognitive psychologists, whose interests center on higher mental processes such as think-

Structuralism: An early approach to psychology which focused on the fundamental elements underlying thoughts and ideas

Introspection: A method in which subjects are asked to describe in detail their thoughts and feelings

---

ANSWERS (REVIEW I):
1. b   **2.** a-4,   b-9,   c-11,   d-2,   e-5,   f-8,   g-10,   h-1,   i-12,   j-7,   k-3,   l-13,   m-6
3. Teacher, scientist, and professional

Wilhelm Wundt, in the center of this photo, established the first laboratory to study psychological phenomena in 1879. (Archives of the History of American Psychology)

ing, memory, and problem solving, have developed innovative techniques for understanding people's conscious experience that overcome many of the difficulties inherent in introspection.

The model that largely replaced structuralism in the evolution of psychology was known as functionalism. Rather than focusing on the mind's components, **functionalism** concentrated on what the mind *does*—the functions of mental activity. Functionalists, whose model rose to prominence in the early 1900s, asked what roles behavior played in allowing people to better adapt to their environments. Led by the American psychologist William James, the functionalists, rather than raising the more abstract questions about the processes of mental behavior, examined the ways in which behavior allows people to satisfy their needs. The famous American educator John Dewey took a functionalist approach and from it developed the field of school psychology, theorizing about how students' needs could best be met through the educational system.

Another reaction to structuralism was the development of Gestalt psychology in the early 1900s. **Gestalt psychology** is a model of psychology focusing on the study of how perception is organized. Instead of considering the individual parts that make up thinking, Gestalt psychologists took the opposite tack, concentrating on how people consider individual elements as units or wholes. Their credo was "The whole is greater than the sum of its parts," meaning that, when considered together, the basic elements that comprise our perception of objects produce something greater and more meaningful than those individual elements alone. As we shall see when we examine perception in Chapter 4, the contributions of Gestalt psychologists to the understanding of perception are substantial.

Today, several major models have evolved from the roots of structuralism, functionalism, and gestalt psychology, each of them emphasizing different aspects of behavior. These include the biological, psychodynamic, cognitive, behavioral, and humanistic models.

Each of these models varies in a number of critical dimensions, as summarized in Table 1-1. One model may have a basically positive and optimistic view of human nature, focusing on the potential for good in people's behavior, while another may be oriented more toward the negative aspects of human behavior, such as selfishness and aggression. The models may also differ in the degree of emphasis they place on mental processes, with some

Functionalism: An early approach to psychology that considered the role of mental activity in adapting to one's environment

Gestalt (geh SHTALLT) **psychology:** An approach to psychology that focuses on the organization of perception and thinking in a "whole" sense, rather than on the individual elements of perception

William James, one of the first American psychologists, rejected structuralism and promoted the model of functionalism. (Culver Pictures)

TABLE 1-1

TABLE 1-1

Comparison of the Major Models of Psychology

Model	Conceptual Focus	View of Human Nature	Importance of Mental Processes	Emphasis: Environment or Person
Biological	Biological functions as basis of behavior	Neutral	Moderate	Person
Psychodynamic	Unconscious determinants of behavior	Negative	Maximum (for unconscious)	Person
Cognitive	Nature of thought processes and understanding of world	Neutral	Maximum	Both
Behavioral	Observable behavior	Neutral	Minimum	Environment
Humanistic	Human desire to reach potential	Positive	Maximum	Person

essentially ignoring thought processes and focusing on observable behavior and others placing primary emphasis on thinking. Finally, some theories consider environmental causes of behavior as predominant, while others base their explanations for behavior more on the nature of the individual.

As we discuss each of the models, keep in mind how they differ in these major dimensions.

BLOOD, SWEAT, AND FEARS: Biological Approaches

Biological model: The psychological model that views behavior in terms of biological functioning

When we get down to the basics, behavior is carried out by living creatures made of skin and guts. According to the **biological model**, the behavior of both people and animals should be considered from the perspective of their biological functioning: how the individual nerve cells are joined together, how the inheritance of certain characteristics from parents and other ancestors influences behavior, how the functioning of the body affects hopes and fears, what behaviors are due to instincts, and so forth. Even more complex kinds of behaviors—emotional responses such as fear, for example—are viewed as having critical biological components by psychologists using the biological model.

Because every behavior can at some level be broken down into its biological components, the biological model has broad appeal. Psychologists who subscribe to this model have contributed important advances in the understanding and betterment of human life, advances that range from suggesting cures for deafness to identifying drugs that help people with severe mental disorders.

UNDERSTANDING THE INNER PERSON: Psychodynamic Approaches

Psychodynamic model: The psychological model based on the belief that behavior is brought about by unconscious inner forces over which an individual has little control

To many people who have never taken a psychology course, psychology begins and ends with the **psychodynamic model**. Proponents of the psychodynamic perspective believe that behavior is brought about by inner forces over which the individual has little control. Dreams and slips of the tongue are viewed as indications of what a person is truly feeling within a seething caldron of subconscious psychic activity.

The psychodynamic view is intimately linked with one individual: Sig-

Sigmund Freud, a Viennese physician, developed the psychodynamic model in which people's behavior was considered to be determined by unconscious processes. (Bettmann Archive)

mund Freud. Freud was a Viennese physician in the early 1900s whose ideas about unconscious determinants of behavior had a revolutionary effect on twentieth-century thinking, not just in psychology but in related fields as well. Although many of the basic principles of psychodynamic thinking have been roundly criticized, the model that has grown out of Freud's work has provided a means not only for treating mental disorders but for understanding everyday phenomena such as prejudice and aggression.

UNDERSTANDING UNDERSTANDING: Cognitive Approaches

The route to understanding behavior leads some psychologists straight into the mind. Evolving in part from structuralism, which, as we noted earlier, was concerned with identifying the various parts of the mind, the **cognitive model** focuses on how people know, understand, and think about the world. The emphasis, though, has shifted away from learning about the structure of the mind itself to learning how people understand and represent the outside world within themselves (Rouse & Morris, 1986).

Cognitive model: The psychological model that focuses on how people know, understand, and think about the world

Psychologists relying on this model ask questions ranging from whether a person can watch television and study a book at the same time (the answer is "probably not") to how people figure out the causes of human behavior. The common element that links cognitive approaches is the emphasis on how people understand the world.

UNDERSTANDING THE OUTER PERSON: Behavioral Approaches

While the biological, psychodynamic, and cognitive approaches look inside the organism to determine the causes of its behavior, the behavioral model takes a very different approach. The **behavioral model** grew out of a rejection of psychology's early emphasis on the inner workings of the mind, suggesting instead that observable behavior should be the focus of the field.

Behavioral model: The psychological model that suggests that observable behavior should be the focus of study

John B. Watson, the first major American psychologist who championed a behavioral approach, was firm in his view that a full understanding of

Rejecting psychology's initial emphasis on the inner workings of the mind, John B. Watson proposed a behavioral approach which focused on observable behaviors. (Culver Pictures)

Humanistic model: The psychological model that suggests that people are in control of their lives

Free will: The human ability to make decisions about one's own life

behavior could be obtained by studying and modifying the environment in which people operated. In fact, he believed rather optimistically that by properly controlling a person's environment, any desired sort of behavior could be obtained, as his own words make clear: "Give me a dozen healthy infants, well-formed, and my own specified world to bring them up in and I'll guarantee to take any one at random and train him to become any type of specialist I might select—doctor, lawyer, artist, merchant-chief, and yes, even beggar-man and thief, regardless of his talents, penchants, tendencies, abilities, vocations and race of his ancestors" (Watson, 1925).

As we will see, the behavioral model crops up along every byway of psychology. Along with the influence it has had in the area of learning processes—much of our understanding of how people learn new behaviors is based on the behavioral model—can also be found in such diverse areas as the treatment of mental disorders, the curbing of aggression, the solution of sexual problems, and even halting drug addiction.

THE SPECIAL QUALITIES OF *HOMO SAPIENS:* Humanistic Approaches

Although it emerged in the 1950s and 1960s, the **humanistic model** is still considered the newest of the major approaches. Rejecting the views that behavior is largely determined by automatic, biological forces or unconscious processes, it suggests instead that people are in control of their lives. Humanistic psychologists maintain that people are naturally inclined to develop toward higher levels of maturity and fulfillment and that, if given the opportunity, they will strive to reach their full potential. The emphasis, then, is on **free will**, the human ability to make decisions about one's life.

More than any other approach, the humanistic model stresses the role of psychology in enriching people's lives and helping them to achieve self-fulfillment. While not as all-encompassing as some of the other general models, the humanistic perspective has had an important influence on the thinking of psychologists, reminding them of their commitment to the individual person and society.

A FINAL WORD ABOUT MODELS

You may be wondering about how the five major models of psychology we have just discussed relate to the different branches of psychology that were presented earlier. The models and branches of psychology actually present two separate and independent ways of approaching the science. Thus a psychologist from any given branch might choose to employ any one, or more, of the major models. (See Table 1-2.) For example, a developmental psychologist might subscribe to a psychodynamic model *or* a behavioral model *or* any of the other models. Although some kinds of psychologists are more or less likely to adhere to a particular model, as the table indicates, in theory at least each of the models is available to any psychologist who chooses to employ it. And don't let the abstract qualities of the models fool you: They each have very practical implications, implications that will concern us throughout this book. (See, for instance, the accompanying Psychology at Work box.)

TABLE 1-2

Major Models of Psychology as Used by Different Kinds of Psychologists.
(Models That Are Used Most Frequently by a Particular Type of Psychologist Are Shaded.)

Type of Psychologist	Model				
	Biological	Psychodynamic	Cognitive	Behavioral	Humanistic
Biopsychologist					
Experimental					
Cognitive					
Developmental					
Personality					
Health					
Clinical					
Counseling					
Educational					
School					
Social					
Industrial-organization					
Environmental					

PSYCHOLOGY AT WORK

BREAKING THE CYCLE OF ADDICTION

At the age of 14, Andrea Schiros had it all. A popular honor student and a cheerleader, she had what seemed to be an ideal life. But when she was suspended from the cheerleading squad for a petty offense, she sought solace in the school's drug culture, and once she began to take drugs, her life went into a tailspin. "I was strung out on coke, acid—everything I could put into my body." Eventually, she ran away from home, and her descent into drugs probably would have been total had it not been for a friend who told her desperate parents where to find her. Two police officers found her in a seedy apartment and brought her to Charter Brook Hospital, a drug rehabilitation center for youths. Although she was hysterical and trying to escape when brought in, Andrea eventually became determined to give up drugs. After seven months of being locked up in the inpatient center, she was allowed to leave the hospital. But her care continues, and she still attends a drug prevention program nightly (Johnson, 1986).

Schiros is one of the lucky ones; she remains free of drugs. Yet thousands of others find it impossible to break the bonds of drug addiction. Even when they are no longer taking drugs, former users are constantly at risk: Everyday sights, smells, and sounds—such as the similarity in appearance between white flour and cocaine—can be enough to bring on a strong craving for drugs.

One obstacle to ending drug abuse is that even after people stop taking an addictive drug, they may experience debilitating physical after-effects as a result of the sudden withdrawal of that drug from their body, as psychologists using the biological model have found. Furthermore, even though medicine administered by health-care providers can control physical withdrawal symptoms, users must still move through several distinct psychological stages before they can be considered free of drugs (Gawin & Ellinwood, 1988).

In one new treatment approach, researchers have developed training that is currently being evaluated (O'Brien et al., 1988). Using principles of learning based on the behavioral model, the training process teaches addicts behavior that disrupts behavioral patterns associated with drug use. For instance, former addicts see videos of people using drugs or handling drug paraphernalia. They are shown that users display increased heart rate, reduced skin temperature, and other signals of increased arousal—something about which they are often unaware.

Through training, they learn to decrease their physical arousal at the sight of drug stimuli—thereby learning to be less responsive to drugs in future encounters.

But such training does not work by itself. The best results occur in people who receive psychological therapy—typically based on psychodynamic, cognitive, or humanistic models—along with the training. It seems, then, that the optimum combination of therapies includes those based on several of the major models of the field.

Although even a complex mix of different therapies is not sufficient to ensure that cocaine addiction is cured, the strategy is a promising one. Furthermore, as the encouraging results of this approach reveal, psychology *is* at work—and *does* work. As we will see throughout this book in other Psychology at Work boxes, the basic principles of the science of psychology are providing both the potential for and the realization of meaningful and significant improvement in the quality of people's lives.

THE FUTURE OF PSYCHOLOGY

Where is psychology heading? Although crystal balls looking into the future of scientific disciplines are notoriously cloudy, a few trends can be safely foretold.

▶ Psychologists will become increasingly specialized. In a field in which practitioners must be experts on such diverse topics as the intricacies of the transmission of electrochemical impulses across nerve endings and the communication patterns of employees in large organizations, no one person can be expected to master the field. It is likely, then, that specialization will increase as psychologists delve into new areas (Altman, 1987; Spence, 1987).

▶ New models will emerge. As a growing, evolving science, psychology will produce new models to supplant the ones it now has. Moreover, older models may be merged to form new ones. We can be certain, then, that as psychologists accumulate more knowledge they will become increasingly sophisticated in their understanding of behavior and mental processes (Marx & Hillix, 1987).

▶ Psychological treatment will become more readily available. The number of health-service providers—such as clinical, counseling, and school psychologists—is increasing at a rapid pace; in fact, it is growing more rapidly than any other segment of the field (Howard et al., 1986). As the number of practitioners grows, the services they provide will become more accessible to the general public.

▶ There will be increasing emphasis on applications of psychological knowledge (Matarazzo, 1987; DeLeon, 1988). The research reported throughout this book is a testament to the fact that the knowledge acquired by psychologists can be applied to the betterment of the human condition.

RECAP AND REVIEW II

Recap

◀ The foundation of today's major models rests on the earlier models of structuralism, functionalism, and gestalt psychology.

◀ The dominant contemporary conceptual models of psychology encompass biological, psychodynamic, cognitive, behavioral, and humanistic approaches.

◀ In the future, psychologists are likely to become more specialized, new models will emerge, psychological treatment will be more available, and there will be increasing emphasis on applications of psychological knowledge.

Review

1. An experimental psychology lab was established in Germany in 1879 by
   a. Descartes b. Freud c. James d. Wundt
2. Match each of the three early models in psychology with its appropriate description.

   a. ____ Structuralism   1. Focuses on studying how perception is organized

   b. ____ Functionalism   2. Focuses on the fundamental elements that underlie thinking and other significant mental activities

   c. ____ Gestalt psychology   3. Focuses on what the mind does
3. Early psychologists studied the mind by asking people to describe what they were experiencing when exposed to various stimuli. This procedure was known as _____ .
4. Jeanne's therapist asks her to recount a violent dream she recently experienced in order to gain insight into the unconscious forces affecting her behavior. Jeanne's therapist is working from a _____ model.
5. "It is behavior that can be observed which should be studied, not the suspected inner workings of the mind." This statement was most likely made by someone following the perspective of a
   a. Cognitive model   c. Humanistic model
   b. Biological model   d. Behavioral model
6. Recent studies of schizophrenia have identified peculiar arrangements of nerve cells, possibly inherited, as a suspected cause of that mental illness. Research such as this is typical of a _____ model.
7. "My therapist is wonderful! She always points out my positive traits. She dwells on my uniqueness and strength as an individual. I feel much more confident about myself—as if I'm really growing and reaching my potential." The therapist referred to above probably practices from a _____ model.
8. In the future, psychologists will probably be trained to be generalists. True or false? _____

(Answers to review questions are on page 26.)

PSYCHOLOGICAL RESEARCH

It took her killer some thirty minutes to finish the job. When Kitty Genovese was first attacked, she managed to free herself and run toward a police call box into which she screamed, "Oh, my God, he stabbed me. Please help me!" In the stillness of the night, her screams were heard by no fewer than thirty-eight neighbors. Windows opened and lights went on. One couple pulled chairs up to the window and turned off the lights so they could see better. Someone yelled, "Let that girl alone." But shouts were not enough to scare off the killer. He chased Kitty, stabbing her eight more times and sexually molesting her before leaving her to die.

And how many of the thirty-eight witnesses came to her aid? Not one.

The Kitty Genovese case remains one of the most horrifying and dismaying examples of "bad Samaritanism." Both the general public and psychologists found it difficult to explain how so many people could stand by without coming to the aid of an innocent victim whose life might well have been saved had there been any active intervention on the part of even one bystander.

Social psychologists in particular puzzled over the problem for many years, and they finally reached a strange conclusion: Kitty Genovese might well have been better off had there been far fewer than thirty-eight people who heard her cries. In fact, had there been just one bystander present, the chances of that person intervening might have been fairly high. For it turns out that the *fewer* witnesses present in a situation such as this one, the better the victim's chances of getting help.

But how could anyone come to such a conclusion? After all, logic and

As Kitty Genovese got out of her car in the parking lot (1), she noticed a man standing nearby. She headed for a police call box (2). At that point, the man caught up with her and stabbed her. She tried to run away, but he caught her and attacked her again at locations 3 and 4. (AP/Wide World Photos.)

common sense would clearly suggest that more bystanders would mean a greater likelihood that someone would help a person in need. This seeming contradiction—and the way psychologists resolved it—illustrates the crux of a problem central to the field of psychology: the challenge of asking and answering questions of interest.

ASKING THE RIGHT QUESTIONS: Theories and Hypotheses

This challenge has been met through reliance on the joint use of theory and research to guide psychologists in searching for answers to questions that concern them. **Theories** are broad explanations and predictions of phenomena of interest. Because they grow out of the diverse models of psychology that we discussed earlier, theories vary both in their breadth and in terms of the particular levels of explanation that they employ. For example, one theory might seek to explain and predict such a narrow topic as how people communicate the emotion of happiness after receiving good news, whereas a broader theory might purport to explain emotional experience in general.

Although all of us carry around our own theories of human behavior—

Theories: Broad explanations and predictions concerning phenomena of interest such as "People are basically good" and "People's behavior is usually motivated by self-interest"—psychologists develop more formal and focused ones (Sternberg, 1985). For example, social psychologists Bibb Latané and John Darley responded to the Kitty Genovese case by developing a theory based on a phenomenon they called *diffusion of responsibility* (Latané & Darley, 1970). According to their theory, the greater the number of bystanders or witnesses to an event that requires helping, the more the responsibility for helping is felt to be shared by all the bystanders. Because of this sense of shared responsibility, then, the more people present in an emergency situation, the less personally responsible each person feels—and the less likely it is that any single person will come forward to help.

Developing Hypotheses

While such a theory makes sense, these psychologists could not stop there. Their next step was to devise a way of testing whether their reasoning was correct. To do this, they needed to derive a hypothesis. **Hypotheses** are predictions stated in a way that allows them to be tested. Just as we have our own broad theories about the world, so do we develop hypotheses about events and behavior (ranging from trivialities, such as why our English professor is such an eccentric, to what is the best way for people to study). Although we rarely test them systematically, we do try to determine whether they are right or not. Perhaps we might try cramming for one exam but studying over a longer period of time for another. By assessing the results, we have created a way to compare the two methods.

> **Hypothesis** (hy POTH eh sis): A prediction that can be tested experimentally

Latané and Darley's hypothesis was a straightforward derivation from their more general theory: The more people who witness an emergency situation, the less likely it is that help will be given to a victim. They could, of course, have chosen another hypothesis (for instance, that people with greater skills related to emergency situations will not be affected by the presence of others), but their initial derivative seemed to offer the most direct test of the theory.

There are several reasons why psychologists use theories and hypotheses. For one thing, these postulations allow sense to be made of individual observations, by placing them together within a framework that organizes and summarizes them. In addition, they offer psychologists the opportunity to move beyond facts that are already known about the world and to make deductions about phenomena that have not yet been explained. In this way, theories and hypotheses provide a reasonable guide to the direction that future investigation ought to take.

In sum, then, theories and hypotheses help psychologists ask the right questions. But how do they answer such questions? The answers come from psychological **research**, systematic inquiry aimed at the discovery of new knowledge.

> **Research**: Systematic inquiry aimed at discovering knowledge

FINDING ANSWERS: Psychological Research

Just as we can derive several theories and hypotheses to explain particular phenomenon, so we can use a considerable number of alternate ways to carry out research. The way that is chosen to test the hypothesis is known as operationalization. **Operationalization** refers to the process of taking a hypothesis and translating it into the particular procedures that are used in the experiment. There is no single way to go about this; it depends on logic, the equipment and facilities available, and the ingenuity of the researcher.

> **Operationalization**: The process of translating a hypothesis into experimental procedures

THE SCIENCE OF PSYCHOLOGY

We will consider several of the major weapons in the psychologist's research arsenal.

Studying One Person to Learn About Many: The Case Study

When Kitty Genovese's killer was identified, many people found themselves asking what it was in his background that might have led to his behavior. In order to answer this question, a psychologist might conduct a **case study**, an in-depth interview of a single individual. In a case study, psychologists might well include psychological testing, in which a carefully designed set of questions is used to gain some insight into the personality of the person being studied. In using case studies as a research technique, the goal is often not only to learn about the individual, but to use the insights gained to better understand people in general.

Case study: An in-depth interview of an individual in order to better understand that individual and to make inferences about people in general

Studying the Records: Archival Research

If you were interested in finding out more about emergency situations in which bystanders did not provide help, you might start by examining historical records. In **archival research**, existing records are examined to confirm a hypothesis. By using newspaper accounts, for example, we might find support for the notion that a decrease in helping behavior accompanies an increase in the number of bystanders.

Archival research: The examination of written records for the purpose of understanding behavior

Studying What is There: Naturalistic Observation

Although archival research allows us to test a hypothesis for which data already exist, researchers typically aren't lucky enough to find sufficient appropriate data intact. They often turn instead to naturalistic observation to carry out their research.

In **naturalistic observation**, the investigator simply observes some naturally occurring behavior and does not intervene in the situation. For example, a researcher investigating helping behavior might turn to a high-crime area of a city and observe there the kind of help that is given to victims of crime. The important point about naturalistic observation is that the researcher is passive and simply meticulously records what occurs.

Naturalistic observation: Observation without intervention, in which the researcher records information about a naturally occurring situation in a way that does not influence the situation

While the advantage of naturalistic observation is obvious—we get a sample of what people do in their "natural habitat"—it also has an important drawback: the inability to control any of the factors of interest. For example, we might find so few naturally occurring instances of helping behavior that we would be unable to draw any conclusions. Because naturalistic observation prevents researchers from making changes in a situation, they must wait until appropriate conditions occur. Similarly, if people know that they are being watched, they may react in such a way that the behavior observed is not truly representative of the group in question.

Asking For Answers: Survey Research

There is no more straightforward way of finding out what people think, feel, and do than by asking them directly. For this reason, surveys represent an important research method. In **survey research**, people chosen to represent some larger population are asked a series of questions about their behavior, thoughts, or attitudes (Fink & Kosecoff, 1985). Survey methods have become so sophisticated that even using a very small sample is sufficient to infer with great accuracy how a larger group would respond. For instance, sampling just a few thousand voters is sufficient to predict within one or two per-

Survey research: Sampling a group of people by assessing their behavior, thoughts, or attitudes, then generalizing the findings to a larger population

"Next question: I believe that life is a constant striving for balance, requiring frequent tradeoffs between morality and necessity, within a cyclic pattern of joy and sadness, forging a trail of bittersweet memories until one slips, inevitably, into the jaws of death. Agree or disagree?"

As suggested here, the wording of survey questions affects how people respond. (Drawing by A. B. Price; © 1989 The New Yorker Magazine, Inc.)

centage points who will win a presidential election—if the sample is chosen with care.

Researchers interested in helping behavior might conduct a survey asking people their reasons for not wanting to come forward to help. Similarly, researchers concerned with sexual behaviors have carried out surveys to learn which sexual practices are common and which are not, and to chart the changes in sexual morality that have occurred as time has passed (as we discuss in Chapter 10).

Although asking people directly about their behavior in some ways seems like the most straightforward approach to understanding what people do, survey research has several potential drawbacks. For one thing, people may give inaccurate information because of lapses of memory or because they don't want to let the researcher know what they really feel. Moreover, people sometimes make responses they think the researcher wants to hear—or, in just the opposite instance, responses they think the researcher *doesn't* want to hear.

CORRELATIONAL RESEARCH   One of the possibilities available to researchers using the survey method as well as the other forms of research we have discussed is to determine the relationship between two behaviors, or between responses to two questions. For instance, we might want to find if people who report that they attend religious services also report that they are more helpful to strangers in emergency situations. If we did find such a relationship, we could say that there was a correlation between attendance at religious services and being helpful in emergencies.

Correlational research: Research to determine whether there is a relationship between certain behaviors and responses

In research that is **correlational**, the relationship between two sets of factors is examined to determine whether they are associated, or "correlated." The strength of a relationship is represented by a mathematical score ranging from +1.0 (a perfect positive relationship, where perfect means that if you know the value of one variable, you can predict the value of the other variable with certainty) to −1.0 (a perfect negative relationship). Although actual correlations are rarely perfect, the closer the correlation is to +1.0 or −1.0, the stronger the relationship. (You can read more about the concept of correlation, and how statistics in general are used by psychologists, in the appendix at the end of the book.)

Although correlational techniques cannot tell us whether one factor *causes* changes in another, they can indicate whether knowing the value of one factor allows us to predict the value of another variable. We may not be able to tell, then, if attending religious services *causes* people to be helpful in emergencies, but correlational procedures will tell us whether knowing that specific people attend religious services will help us to predict how they will behave in an emergency situation.

Another example illustrates the critical point that correlations tell us nothing about cause and effect but only provide a measure of the strength of a relationship between two factors. For instance, we might find that children who watch a lot of television programs having aggressive content are apt to demonstrate a relatively high degree of aggressive behavior, while those who watch few television shows that portray aggression are apt to exhibit a relatively low degree of such behavior (see Figure 1-3). We cannot say that the aggression is *caused* by the TV viewing, since it is just as likely to be caused by some other factor. For example, we may learn that children of low socioeconomic status watch more programs having aggressive content *and* are more aggressive. Factors relating to a family's socioeconomic status, then, may be the true cause of the children's higher incidence of aggression. In fact, there may be several factors that underlie both the aggressive behav-

FIGURE 1-3

If we find that frequent viewing of television programs having aggressive content is associated with high levels of aggressive behavior, we might cite several plausible causes, as suggested in this figure. Correlational findings, then, do not permit us to determine causality.

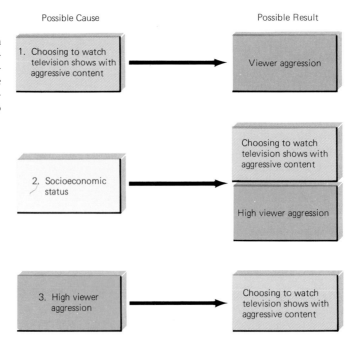

Possible Cause

Possible Result

1. Choosing to watch television shows with aggressive content → Viewer aggression

2. Socioeconomic status → Choosing to watch television shows with aggressive content / High viewer aggression

3. High viewer aggression → Choosing to watch television shows with aggressive content

ior and the television viewing. It is even possible that people who show high aggressiveness choose to watch shows with high aggressive content *because* they are aggressive. It is clear, then, that any number of causal sequences are possible—none of which can be ruled out by correlational research.

The inability of correlational research to answer questions of a cause-and-effect nature is a crucial drawback. There is, though, an alternative technique that establishes causality: the experiment.

DETERMINING CAUSE-AND-EFFECT RELATIONSHIPS:
Experimental Research

The *only* way that psychologists can establish cause-and-effect relationships through research is by carrying out an experiment. In a formal **experiment**, the relationship between two (or more) factors is investigated by deliberately producing a change in one factor and observing the effect that change has upon other factors. The change deliberately produced is called the **experimental manipulation**. Experimental manipulations are used to detect relationships between **variables**, behaviors, events, or other characteristics that can change, or vary, in some way.

There are several steps in carrying out an experiment, but the process typically begins with the development of one or more hypotheses for the experiment to test. Recall, for example, the hypothesis derived by Latané and Darley to test their theory of helping behavior: The more people who witness an emergency situation, the less likely it is that help will be given to a victim. We can trace the way they developed an experiment to test this hypothesis.

The first step was to operationalize the hypothesis by translating it into actual procedures that could be used in an experiment. Operationalizing their hypothesis required that Latané and Darley take into account the fundamental principle of experimental research that we mentioned earlier. There must be a manipulation of at least one variable in order to observe what effects the manipulation has on another variable. But this manipulation cannot be viewed in isolation; if a cause-and-effect relationship is to be established, the effects of the manipulation must be compared with the effects of no manipulation or a different manipulation.

Experimental research requires, then, that at least two groups be compared with each other. One group will receive some special **treatment**—the manipulation implemented by the experimenter—while another group receives either no treatment or a different treatment. The group receiving the treatment is called the **treatment group**, while the other group is called the **control group**. (In some experiments, however, there are multiple treatment and control groups, each of which is compared with another.)

By employing both a treatment and a control group in an experiment, researchers are able to rule out the effects of factors not associated with the experimental manipulation as a source of any changes seen in the experiment. If we didn't have a control group, we couldn't be sure that some other factor—such as the temperature at the time we were running the experiment or the mere passage of time—wasn't causing the changes observed. Through the use of control groups, then, researchers can be sure that the causes of effects are isolated—and cause-and-effect inferences can be drawn.

To Latané and Darley, a means of operationalizing their hypothesis, based on the requirement of having more than one treatment group, was readily available. They decided they would create a bogus emergency situ-

Experiment: A study carried out to investigate the relationship between two or more factors in order to establish causality

Experimental manipulation: The intentional alteration of factors in an experiment to affect responses or behaviors

Variable: A behavior or event that can be changed

Treatment: The manipulation implemented by the experimenter to influence results in a segment of the experimental population

Treatment group: The experimental group receiving the treatment, or manipulation

Control group: The experimental group receiving no treatment

THE SCIENCE OF PSYCHOLOGY

Independent variable: The variable that is manipulated in an experiment

Dependent variable: The variable that is measured and is expected to change as a result of experimenter manipulation

Subject: A participant in research

Random assignment to condition: The assignment of subjects to given groups on a chance basis alone

ation which would require the aid of a bystander. As their experimental manipulation, they decided to vary the number of bystanders present. They could have just had an experimental group with, for instance, two people present, and a control group for comparison purposes with just one person present. Instead, they settled on a more complex procedure in which there were three groups that could be compared with one another, consisting of two, three, and six people.

Latané and Darley now had identified what is called the experimenter's **independent variable**, the variable that is manipulated. In this case, it was the number of people present. The next step was to decide how they were going to determine what effect varying the number of bystanders had on participants' behavior. Crucial to every experiment is the **dependent variable**, which is the variable that is measured and is expected to change as a result of changes caused by the experimenter's manipulation. Experiments have, then, both an independent and a dependent variable. (To remember the difference, you might recall that a hypothesis predicts how a dependent variable *depends* on the manipulation of the independent variable.)

How, then, should the dependent measure be operationalized for Latané and Darley's experiment? One way might have been to use a simple "yes"-or-"no" measure of whether a **subject**—as a participant in research is known—helped or didn't help. But the two investigators decided they also wanted a measure that provided a finer-grained analysis of helping behavior, so they assessed the amount of time it took for a subject to provide help.

Latané and Darley now had all the components of an experiment. The independent variable, manipulated by them, was the number of bystanders present in an emergency situation. The dependent variable was whether the bystanders in each of the groups provided help and the amount of time it took for them to do so. *All* true experiments in psychology fit this straight-forward model.

The Final Step: Random Assignment of Subjects to Treatments

To make the experiment a valid test of the hypothesis, the researchers needed to add a final step to the design: properly assigning subjects to a specific treatment group. Why should this step be so important?

The reason becomes clear when we examine various alternative procedures. For example, the experimenters might have considered the possibility of assigning just males to the group with two bystanders, just females to the group with three bystanders, and both males and females to the group with six bystanders. Had they done so, however, it would have become clear that any differences they found in responsive behavior could not be attributed to the group size alone, but might just as well be due to the composition of the group. A more reasonable procedure would be to ensure that each group had the same composition in terms of sex; then they would be able to make comparisons across groups with considerably more accuracy.

Subjects in each of the treatment groups ought to be comparable, and it is easy enough to create similar groups in terms of sex. The problem becomes a bit more tricky, though, when we consider other subject characteristics. How can we ensure that subjects in each treatment group will be equally intelligent, extroverted, cooperative, and so forth, when the list of characteristics—any one of which may be important—is potentially endless?

The solution to the problem is a simple but elegant procedure called **random assignment to condition**. In random assignment, subjects are as-

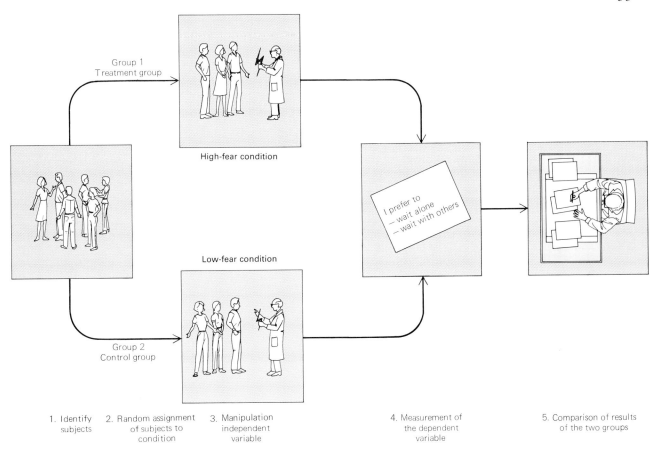

Group 1
Treatment group

High-fear condition

I prefer to
— wait alone
— wait with others

Low-fear condition

Group 2
Control group

1. Identify
subjects

2. Random assignment
of subjects to
condition

3. Manipulation
independent
variable

4. Measurement of
the dependent
variable

5. Comparison of results
of the two groups

signed to different experimental groups or "conditions," on the basis of chance and chance alone. The experimenter might, for instance, put the names of all potential subjects into a hat and draw names to make assignments to specific groups. The advantage of this technique is that subject characteristics have an equal chance of being distributed across the various groups. By using random assignment, the experimenter can be confident that each of the groups will have approximately the same proportion of intelligent people, cooperative people, extroverted people, males and females, and so on. (For an example of another experiment, see Figure 1-4.)

Who Should Participate?: Choosing the Appropriate Subjects

Latané and Darley, both college professors, turned to the people who were most readily accessible to them when they were looking for participants in their experiment: college students. In fact, this group is used so frequently in experiments that psychology has sometimes been called the "science of the behavior of the college sophomore" (Rubenstein, 1982).

The use of college students as subjects has both advantages and drawbacks. The big benefit is their availability: Since most research occurs in university settings, college students are readily available. Typically, they participate for either extra course credit or a relatively small monetary payment, making the cost to the researcher minimal.

The problem with relying on college students for subjects is that they may not adequately represent the general population. College students tend

FIGURE 1-4

This depiction of a classic study, on the effects of fear on affiliation with others, includes the essential elements of an experiment (Schachter, 1959). A group of people—the subjects of the experiment—were randomly assigned to one of two groups. Subjects randomly assigned to group 1 were exposed to a treatment, designed to produce high fear, in which they were told that they would be receiving painful shocks as part of the experiment. In comparison, subjects randomly assigned to group 2, the control group, were in the low-fear condition; they were told that the shocks they were to receive would be mild, resembling a slight tingle. The production of high or low fear was the independent variable. To determine the effects of fear on affiliation, subjects were asked whether they wished to wait for the start of the experiment either alone or in a room with several other people. The choice that subjects made was the dependent variable. (The results? As the experimenter had hypothesized, subjects in the high-fear condition were considerably more likely to choose to wait with others than those in the low-fear condition.)

to be disproportionately white and middle class, more intelligent, and certainly younger and better educated than the rest of the population of the United States. Moreover, their attitudes are likely to be less well formed, and they are apt to be more susceptible to social pressures from authority figures and peers than older adults (Sears, 1986). Given these characteristics, the degree to which we may generalize beyond college students is open to question, and many researchers strive to use subjects who are more representative of the general population.

The issue of subject representativeness becomes even more pronounced when we consider research conducted by psychologists on animals other than humans. If we are concerned that college students are not representative of the population at large, isn't representativeness even more of a problem with research that uses rats, monkeys, gerbils, or pigeons as subjects?

The answer is that the 7 or 8 percent of psychological research that does employ animals has a different focus and is designed to answer different questions from research that uses humans. For example, the shorter life span of animals (rats live an average of two years) allows us to learn about the effects of aging in a much more rapid time frame than if we studied aging directly on humans, with their much longer life. Moreover, the very complexity of human beings may obscure information about fundamental phenomena that can be more plainly identified in animals. Finally, some studies require large numbers of subjects who share similar backgrounds or who have been exposed to particular environments—conditions that could not be met with human beings.

Research using animals as subjects has provided psychologists with information that has profound benefits for humans (King et al., 1988). For instance, animal research has furnished us with the keys to learning how to detect eye disorders in children early enough to prevent permanent damage, how to communicate more effectively with severely retarded children, and how to reduce chronic pain in people, to name just a few results (American Psychological Association, 1988). In the end, of course, animals are not people, and in any experiment it is important to be aware of the limitations in generalizing beyond the subject group used in a study.

Threats to Experiments: Experimenter and Subject Expectations

You may be thinking that, having chosen college students as subjects, Latané and Darley by this point should have been ready to run their experiment. But they had to take into account a few further considerations to avoid **experimental bias**—factors that could distort their understanding of how the independent variable affected the dependent variable.

One problem they needed to avoid was **experimenter expectations**, whereby an experimenter unintentionally transmits cues to subjects about the way they are expected to behave in a given experimental condition. The danger is that these expectations will bring about an "appropriate" behavior—one that may not have otherwise occurred. For example, if Latané and Darley had behaved toward subjects in the two-bystander condition as if they expected them to help, but let on that they had low expectations for helping in the six-person bystander condition, such variations in experimenter behavior—no matter how unintentional—might have affected the results.

A related problem is **subject expectations** about what is appropriate behavior. If you have ever been a subject in an experiment, you know that

Experimental bias: Factors that could lead an experimenter to an erroneous conclusion about the effect of the independent variable on the dependent variable

Experimenter expectations: An experimenter's unintentional message to a subject about results expected from the experiment

Subject expectations: A subject's interpretation of what behaviors or responses are expected in an experiment you quickly develop ideas about what is expected of you, and it is typical for people to develop their own hypothesis about what the experimenter hopes to learn from the study. If these expectations influence a subject's behavior, it becomes a cause for concern, since it is no longer the experimental manipulation producing an effect, but rather the subject's expectations.

To guard against the problem of subject expectations biasing the results of an experiment, the experimenter may disguise the true purpose of the experiment. Subjects who are unaware that helping behavior is being studied, for example, are more likely to act in an unbiased manner than if they are told the purpose of the experiment is to study their helping behavior. Latané and Darley decided to tell their subjects, then, that the actual purpose of the experiment was to hold a discussion among college students about their personal problems. In doing so, they expected that their subjects would not suspect the true purpose of the experiment.

In some experiments, it is impossible to hide the actual purpose of the research. In cases such as these, other techniques are available. For example, suppose you were interested in testing the ability of a new drug to alleviate the symptoms of severe depression. If you simply gave the drug to half your subjects and not to the other half, subjects given the drug might report feeling less depressed merely because they knew they were getting a drug. Similarly, the subjects who got nothing might report feeling no better because they knew that they were in a no-treatment control group.

To solve this problem, psychologists typically use a procedure in which subjects in the control group do receive treatment, sometimes in the form of a pill called a placebo. A **placebo** is a "sugar pill," without any significant chemical properties. Because members of both groups are kept in the dark as to whether they are getting a real or a bogus pill, any differences that are found can be attributed to the quality of the drug and not to the possible psychological effects of being administered a pill.

Placebo (pla SEE bo): A biologically ineffective pill used in an experiment to keep subjects, and sometimes experimenters, from knowing whether or not the subjects have received a behavior-altering drug

But there is still one more thing that a careful researcher must do in an experiment such as this. In order to overcome the possibility that experimenter expectations will affect the subject, the person who administers the drug shouldn't know whether it is actually the true drug or the placebo. By keeping both the subject and the experimenter who interacts with the subject "blind" as to the nature of the drug that is being administered—a method known as the **double-blind procedure**—researchers can more accurately assess the effects of the drug.

Double-blind procedure: The technique by which both the experimenter and the subject are kept from knowing which subjects received a drug, making any observed behavior variations more reliable

Were Latané and Darley Right?: The Data Answer

By now, you must be wondering whether Latané and Darley were right when they hypothesized that increasing the number of bystanders present in an emergency situation would lower the degree of helping.

According to the results of the experiment they carried out, their hypothesis was right on target. In their test of the hypothesis, they used a laboratory setting in which subjects were told that the purpose of the experiment was to hold a discussion about personal problems associated with college. The discussion was to be held over an intercom in order to avoid the embarrassment of face-to-face contact. This was not, of course, the true purpose of the experiment, but one used to keep subjects' expectations from biasing their behavior. (Consider how they would have been affected if they had been told that their helping behavior in emergencies was being tested.

The experimenters could never have gotten an accurate assessment of what the subjects would actually do in an emergency; by definition, emergencies are rarely announced in advance.)

The sizes of the discussion groups were two, three, and six people, which constituted the manipulation of the independent variable of group size. Subjects were randomly assigned to one of these groups upon their arrival at the laboratory.

As the subjects in each group were holding their discussion, they suddenly heard one of the other participants (in reality a trained **confederate** of the experimenters) lapse into what sounded like an epileptic seizure:

> I-er-um-I think I-I need-er-if-if- could-er-er-somebody er-er-er-er-er-er-er give me a little-er give me a little help here because-er-I-er-I'm-er-er-h-h-having a-a-a real problem-er-right now and I-er-if somebody could help me out it would-it-would-er-er s-s-sure be-sure be good . . . because-er-there-er-er-a cause I-er-I-uh-I've got a-a one of the-er-sei---er-er-things coming on and-and-and I could really-er-use some help so if somebody would-er-give me a little h-help-uh-er-er-er-er-er c-could somebody-er-er-help-er-us-us-us [choking sounds]. . . .I'm gonna die-er-er-I'm . . . gonna die-er-help-er-er-seizure-er-[choking sounds, then silence] (Latané and Darley, 1970, p. 379).

The subjects' behavior was now what counted. The dependent variable was the time that elapsed from the start of the "seizure" to the time a subject began trying to help the "victim." If six minutes went by without a subject's offering help, the experiment was ended.

As predicted by the hypothesis, the size of the group had a large effect on whether a subject provided help (Latané & Darley, 1970). In the two-person group (in which subjects thought they were alone with the victim), the average elapsed time was 52 seconds; in the three-person group (the subject, the victim, and one other person), the average elapsed time was 93 seconds; and in the six-person group (the subject, the victim, and four others), the average time was 166 seconds. Considering a simple "yes"-or-"no" measure of whether help was given corroborates the elapsed-time pattern. When the group size was two, 85 percent helped; when it was three, 62 percent helped; and when it was six, 31 percent responded (see Figure 1-5).

Because these results are so straightforward, it seems clear that the original hypothesis was confirmed. However, Latané and Darley could not be sure

Confederate: A participant in an experiment who has been instructed to behave in ways that will affect the responses of other subjects

FIGURE 1-5

The results of the Latané and Darley experiment showed that as the size of the group witnessing an emergency increased, helping behavior decreased. (Based on Latané & Darley, 1968.)

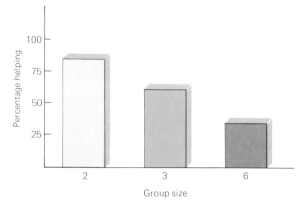

that the results were truly meaningful until they examined their data using formal statistical procedures. As discussed in this book's appendix, statistical procedures—which entail several kinds of mathematical calculations—allow a researcher to determine precisely the likelihood that results are meaningful and not merely the outcome of chance.

The Latané and Darley study contains all the elements of an experiment: an independent variable, a dependent variable, random assignment to conditions, and multiple treatment groups. Because it does, we can say with some confidence that group size *caused* changes in the degree of helping behavior.

Of course, one experiment alone does not resolve forever the question of bystander intervention in emergencies. Psychologists require that findings be **replicated**, or repeated, using other procedures in other settings, with other groups of subjects, before full confidence can be placed in the validity of any single experiment. [In this case, the experiment has stood the test of time: In a review of some fifty studies that were carried out in the ten years following their experiment, the finding that an increase in bystanders leads to decreased helping has been replicated in numerous other studies [Latané & Nida, 1981).]

In addition to replicating experimental results, psychologists also need to test the limitations of their theories and hypotheses in order to determine under what specific circumstances they hold and under what conditions they do not apply. It seems unlikely, for instance, that increasing numbers of bystanders *always* results in less helping, and it is therefore critical to understand the conditions in which exceptions to this general rule occur. For example, we might speculate that under conditions of shared outcomes, in which onlookers experience a sense that a victim's difficulties may later affect them in some way, help would be more readily forthcoming (Aronson, 1988). To test this hypothesis—for which, in fact, there is some support—it is necessary to carry out still further experimentation. Like any science, then, psychology increases our understanding in small, incremental steps, with each step building upon previous work.

Replication: The repetition of an experiment in order to verify the results of the original experiment

KNOWING WHAT'S RIGHT: The Ethics of Research

If you were to put yourself in the place of one of the subjects in the Latané and Darley experiment, how would you feel when you learned that the person who you thought was having a seizure was in reality a confederate of the experimenter?

Although at first you might experience relief that there was no real emergency, you might also feel some resentment that you were deceived by the experimenter. And you might also experience concern that you were placed in an unusual situation in which, depending on how you behaved, you may have had a blow to your self-esteem.

Most psychologists argue that the use of deception is sometimes necessary in order to avoid having subjects influenced by what they think is the study's true purpose. (If you knew the Latané and Darley study was actually concerned with your helping behavior, wouldn't you be tempted to intervene in the emergency?) In order to avoid such behavior, researchers sometimes must use deception.

Because research has the potential to violate the rights of participants, psychologists adhere to a strict set of ethical guidelines aimed at protecting subjects (American Psychological Association, 1981). These guidelines advocate the protection of subjects from physical and mental harm, the right of subjects to privacy regarding their behavior, the assurance that participation in research is completely voluntary, and the necessity of informing the subjects about the nature of procedures prior to participation in the experiment. Although the guidelines do allow the use of deception, the experiment must be reviewed by an independent panel prior to its use—as must all research that uses human beings as subjects (Ceci, Peters, & Plotkin, 1985; Keith-Spiegel & Koocher, 1985; Christensen, 1988).

One of the key ethical principals followed by psychologists is that of **informed consent**. Prior to participating in an experiment, subjects must sign a document affirming that they have been told the basic outlines of the study and are aware of what their participation will involve, what risks the experiment may hold, and the fact that their participation is purely voluntary and may be terminated at any time. The only time informed consent can be dispensed with is in experiments in which the risks are minimal, as in a purely observational study on a street corner or other public location.

It is not just psychologists working with humans who operate under strict ethical constraints; researchers who use animals as subjects have their own set of exacting guidelines to ensure that animals do not suffer. Specifically, they must make every effort to minimize discomfort, illness, and pain, and procedures subjecting animals to distress are used only when an alternative procedure is unavailable and when the goal of research is justified by its prospective value. Moreover, there are federal regulations specifying how animals are to be housed, fed, and maintained.

Because some research with important implications for alleviating human suffering—such as devising techniques for saving mentally disturbed patients who would otherwise starve themselves to death or finding new drugs and procedures to alleviate human pain and depression—cannot be ethically carried out on humans, guidelines permit the use of animals in such cases where the potential benefits clearly outweigh the costs (Gallup & Suarez, 1985; Miller, 1985b). Still, there are stringent regulations that prohibit researchers from inflicting unnecessary pain.

Despite these ethical guidelines, the use of animals for psychological research remains controversial (Goodall, 1987; Holden, 1988; Novak & Suomi, 1988), with some people calling for a complete ban on the practice. However, most psychologists feel that existing ethical guidelines are sufficiently stringent to provide protection for animals while still allowing valuable animal research to continue.

Informed consent: A document signed by subjects prior to an experiment in which the study and conditions and risks of participation are explained

THE INFORMED CONSUMER OF PSYCHOLOGY:
Distinguishing Good Psychology from Bad Psychology

 Penetrate the Minds of Others—with Mind Prober! Psychologists agree that most of us conceal our fears, hopes, and inner desires from our closest friends, and even from ourselves! Now you can use the power of your personal computer to unlock those hidden truths about anyone in your life. With Mind Prober software, you'll gain useful, accurate insight into anyone you choose as a subject. There is no limit to the number of people you may analyze. If you'd like to reveal hidden truths about people you know (or think you know), order Mind Prober today!

▲ ▲ ▲

"Hello, this is Dr. Joy Browne on WITS," says the agreeable voice on the Boston radio station. "Today we're having an open-line program. You can call in with any problem on any topic." The first call comes from Steve, who opens with "Hi, Dr. Joy," and tells about his fainthearted attempts to reestablish contact with an old flame, now married. Dr. Joy analyzes Steve's problem as "a classic case of approach-avoidance," advises him to stop being "so tentative" and to go ahead and "play it by ear." She asks him to call back to "let me know what happens" (Rice, 1981, p. 39).

▲ ▲ ▲

More than any book ever written, *Self-Creation* shows you who you are and reveals the secret to controlling your own life. . . . With it you will discover how to conquer bad habits, solve sexual problems, overcome depression and shyness, deal with infuriating people, be decisive, enhance your career, increase creativity. . . . You created you. Now you can start to reap the boundless benefits of self-confidence, self-reliance, self-determination with *Self-Creation* (excerpted from the back cover; Weinberg, 1979).

From advertisements to talk shows, we are bombarded daily with information about psychology. We are told how to become smarter, happier, and better adjusted, and how to improve our lives by learning psychology's secrets.

Yet the promises are usually empty ones. If things were this easy, we would live in a nation of happy-go-lucky, fully satisfied, and completely fulfilled individuals. Obviously the world is not quite so simple, and the quality of advice supposedly based on psychological truths, provided by self-styled experts—and even by some less-than-reputable psychologists—varies widely. For this reason, there are several points to keep in mind when you evaluate information of a psychological nature.

▶ There's no free ride. If you could, in fact, buy a computer program that

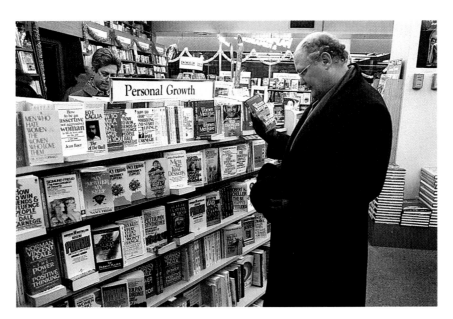

From advertisements to talk shows, we are bombarded daily with psychology. It is important to distinguish between pop psychology and psychological information that is based on reliable research. (Innervisions)

would really "unlock the hidden truths" about others, wouldn't you have heard about it already? If your problems could be assessed, analyzed, and resolved in five minutes of radio air time, don't you think people would be clogging the phone lines with their calls, rather than spending hundreds of hours in treatment for their problems? The point is that difficult problems require complex solutions, and you should be wary of simple, glib responses on how to resolve major difficulties.

▶ If advice that is dispensed by psychologists is accepted by a consumer, the consequences of following that advice should be critically monitored, evaluated, and—if necessary—modified to ensure that it is producing desirable effects. In the case of talk-show psychology, this almost never occurs; it is rare that we discover how well the advice that was dispensed in a given case worked. Both the people with the problems *and* the other listeners and viewers may be getting bad advice—but they never have any way of knowing without follow-up.

▶ No single psychologist or psychological method can solve all problems. The range of difficulties bound up with the human condition is so broad that no person can be an expert in all areas, and any individual or any method that purports to resolve all problems is making an inappropriate claim.

Despite these cautions, the field of psychology has produced a wealth of important information that can be drawn upon for suggestions about every phase of people's lives. As explained earlier in this chapter, one of the major goals of this book is to make you a more informed consumer of psychological knowledge by enhancing your ability to evaluate what psychologists have to offer. Ultimately, this book should provide you with the tools you need to critically evaluate the theories, research, and applications that psychologists have developed. In doing so, you will be able to appreciate the contributions that the field of psychology has made in improving the quality of human life.

RECAP AND REVIEW III

Recap

◀ Psychologists use theories and hypotheses to guide their research.

◀ In correlational research, the relationship between two variables is examined to determine whether they are associated, although cause-and-effect associations cannot be established.

◀ In a formal experiment—which is the only means of determining cause-and-effect associations—the relationship between factors is investigated by deliberately producing a change in one factor and observing the change in the other.

◀ Threats to experiments include experimenter expectations and subject expectations.

Review

1. According to the diffusion-of-responsibility theory, people in a group are more apt to help individually if they have the support of a large group. True or false?

_____

2. Many types of research are often conducted in psychology. Match each example at the right with the type of research it describes.

a. ____ Archival research

b. ____ Survey research

c. ____ Naturalistic observation

d. ____ Case study

1. Distributing a questionnaire to a group representing a larger population to assess attitudes on abortion

2. Interviewing a mass murderer and conducting psychological tests to determine the causes of such behavior

3. Reviewing existing records to confirm a hypothesis about the behavior of terrorists

4. Watching the interactions of young children in various nursery school settings to determine differences in social behavior

3. If we wanted to test our hunch that students who underline chapters as they read retain the information better than those who do not, we would first have to state this prediction in testable terms, that is, develop
   a. An experiment
   b. A theory
   c. A hypothesis
   d. A hunch

4. In the experiment on retention described in question 3, we might want to deliberately produce a change in students' study habits to see if the change does have an effect on how long they remember facts. This process is known as the _____ .

5. We decide to perform our experiment on a large scale, with two groups. We arrange for one group to change its study habits; this group is called the _____ group. We arrange for another group to study as usual; this group is called the _____ group.

6. The variable being measured in our experiment—retention of factual information—is called the _____ variable.

7. What if the students we assign to one group happen to be more intelligent or more motivated than those of the other group? That would certainly cloud our comparison. What procedure should we use to avoid such a problem?

8. Suppose that a group of researchers conducted an experiment with college students as subjects and claimed that the results would hold for factory workers. We could criticize their claim on the grounds of
   a. Experimental design flaws
   b. Representativeness of subjects
   c. Gender differences
   d. Validity of the dependent variable

9. We are concerned that some of the researchers we employ in our study might give subtle cues to subjects about how they should respond. This type of experimental bias is known as
   a. Experimenter expectations
   b. Subject expectations
   c. Demand characteristics
   d. The placebo effect

10. An experimenter knowingly administers a sugar pill to subjects in a control group so that both groups think they are being treated. This is called a double-blind procedure. True or false? _____

11. Statistical procedures usually allow experimenters to determine whether their apparent results are truly meaningful or merely the outcome of chance. True or false? _____

12. Ethical research begins with the concept of informed consent. Before signing up to participate in an experiment, subjects should be informed of
   a. The procedure of the study, stated generally
   b. The risks that may be involved
   c. Their right to withdraw at any time
   d. All of the above

(Answers to review questions are on page 42.)

◀ **LOOKING BACK**

1. Although the definition of psychology—the scientific study of behavior and mental processes—is clear-cut, it is also deceivingly simple, since "behavior" encompasses not just what people do, but their thoughts, feelings, perceptions, reasoning, memory, and biological activities.

2. Psychology has a number of major areas in which psychologists specialize. Biopsychologists focus on the biological basis of behavior, while experimental psychologists study the processes of sensing, perceiving, learning, and thinking about the world. Cognitive psychology, an outgrowth of experimental psychology, considers the study of higher mental processes, including thinking, language, memory, problem solving, knowing, reasoning, judging, and decision making.

3. The branches of psychology that study change and individual differences are developmental and personality psychology. Developmental psychologists study how people grow and change throughout their life span. Personality psychologists consider the consistency and change in an individual's behavior as he or she moves through different situations, as well as the individual differences that distinguish one person's behavior from another's when each is placed in the same situation.

4. Health, clinical, and counseling psychologists are primarily concerned with promoting physical and mental health. Health psychologists study psychological factors that affect physical disease, while clinical psychologists consider the study, diagnosis, and treatment of abnormal behavior. Counseling psychologists focus on educational, social, and career adjustment problems.

5. Educational psychologists investigate how the educational process affects students, while school psychologists specialize in assessing and treating children in elementary and secondary schools who have academic or emotional problems.

6. Social psychology is the study of how people's thoughts, feelings, and actions are affected by others. Industrial-organizational psychologists focus on how psychology can be applied to the workplace, while environmental psychologists explore the relationship between people and their physical environment.

7. Psychologists are employed in a variety of settings. Although the primary employment sites are universities and colleges, many psychologists are found in hospitals, clinics, community mental-health centers, and counseling centers. Many also have practices in which they treat patients privately.

8. The foundations of psychology were established by Wilhelm Wundt in Germany in 1879. Early conceptual models that guided the work of psychologists were structuralism, functionalism, and gestalt theory. Structuralism focused on identifying the fundamental elements of the mind, largely by using introspection. Functionalism concentrated on the functions played by mental activities. Gestalt psychology focused on the study of how perception is organized into meaningful units. Modern-day psychologists rely primarily on five models: the biological, psychodynamic, cognitive, behavioral, and humanistic models.

9. The biological model focuses on the biological functioning of people and animals, reducing behavior to its most basic components. The psychodynamic model takes a very different approach; it suggests that there are powerful, unconscious inner forces about which people have little or no awareness and which are primary determinants of behavior.

10. Cognitive approaches to behavior consider how people know, understand, and think about the world. Growing out of early work on introspection and later work by the gestaltists and functionalists, cognitive models study how people understand and represent the world within themselves.

11. Behavioral models deemphasize internal processes and concentrate instead on observable behavior. They suggest that an understanding and control of a person's environment is sufficient to fully explain and modify behavior.

12. Humanistic models are the newest of the major models of psychology. They emphasize that humans are uniquely inclined toward psychological growth and higher levels of functioning and that human beings will strive to reach their full potential.

13. Three major trends seem to be emerging in terms of the future of psychology. Psychology will become increasingly specialized, new models will emerge, and there will be increasing emphasis on applications of psychological knowledge.

14. Research in psychology is guided by theories (broad explanations and predictions of phenomena of interest) and hypotheses (derivations of theories that are predictions stated in a way that allows them to be tested).

15. The case study represents an in-depth interview and examination of one person, while archival research uses existing records such as old newspapers or other documents to confirm a hypothesis. In naturalistic observation, the investigator mainly acts as an observer, making no change in a naturally occurring situation. In survey research, people are asked a series of questions about their behavior, thoughts, or attitudes. These techniques rely on correlational studies, which describe associations between various factors but cannot determine cause-and-effect relationships.

16. In a formal experiment, the relationship between factors is investigated by deliberately producing a change—called the experimental manipulation—in one of them and observing the change in the other. The factors that are changed are called variables, behaviors or events that are capable of change and can take on two or more levels. In order to test a hypothesis, it must be operationalized: The abstract concepts of the hypothesis are translated into the actual procedures used in the study.

17. In an experiment, at least two groups must be compared with each other in order to assess cause-and-effect relationships. The group receiving the treatment (the special procedure devised by the experimenter) is the treatment group, while the second group (which receives no treatment) is the control group. There also may be multiple treatment groups, each of which is subjected to a different procedure and can then be compared with the others. The variable that is manipulated is the independent variable; the variable that is measured and expected to change as a result of manipulation of the independent variable is called the dependent variable.

18. In a formal experiment, subjects must be assigned to treatment conditions randomly so that subject characteristics are evenly distributed across the different conditions.

19. The frequent use of college students as subjects has the advantage of easy availability. However, there are drawbacks: Students do not represent the general population well. The use of animals as subjects also has costs in terms of generalizability, although the benefits of using animals in research have been profound.

20. Experiments are subject to a number of threats, or biases. Experimenter bias occurs when an experimenter unintentionally transmits cues to subjects about his or her expectations regarding their behavior in a given experimental condition. Subject expectations can also bias an experiment. To help eliminate bias, researchers use placebos and double-blind procedures.

21. One of the key ethical principals followed by psychol-

ANSWERS (REVIEW III):
1. False; the more people in the group, the less responsibility is shared by each individual **2.** a-3, b-1, c-4, d-2 **3.** c **4.** Experimental manipulation **5.** Treatment, control **6.** Dependent **7.** Random assignment to condition **8.** b **9.** a **10.** False; in a double-blind procedure, the experimenter who administers the "drug" shouldn't know whether it is a placebo or the real drug **11.** True **12.** d

ogists is informed consent. Subjects must be told, prior to participation, what the basic outline of an experiment is and the risks and potential benefits of their participation. Researchers working with animals must also follow a rigid set of ethical guidelines for the protection of the animals.

22. Informed use of psychology requires that consumers be aware that answers to psychological problems are complex, that advice offered by psychologists should be monitored and evaluated, and that no single method is a cure for every difficulty.

KEY TERMS AND CONCEPTS ▶

psychology (p. 7)
biopsychology (10)
experimental psychology (11)
cognitive psychology (11)
developmental psychology (12)
personality psychology (12)
health psychology (12)
clinical psychology (12)
counseling psychology (12)
educational psychology (13)
school psychology (13)
social psychology (13)
industrial-organizational
     psychology (13)
environmental psychology (13)
forensic psychology (14)
consumer psychology (14)
program evaluation (14)
models (18)

structuralism (18)
introspection (18)
functionalism (19)
gestalt psychology (19)
biological models (20)
psychodynamic models (20)
cognitive models (21)
behavioral models (21)
humanistic models (22)
free will (22)
theories (26)
hypotheses (27)
research (27)
operationalization (27)
case study (28)
archival research (28)
naturalistic observation (28)
survey research (28)
correlational research (30)

experiment (31)
experimental manipulation (31)
variable (31)
treatment (31)
treatment group (31)
control group (31)
independent variable (32)
dependent variable (32)
subject (32)
random assignment to condition (32)
experimental bias (34)
experimenter expectations (34)
subject expectations (34)
placebo (35)
double-blind procedure (35)
confederate (36)
replication (37)
informed consent (38)

FOR FURTHER STUDY AND APPLICATION ▶

American Psychological Association (1987). *Careers in psychology.* Washington, DC: American Psychological Association.

This booklet, which can be obtained free of charge by writing to the American Psychological Association at 1200 17th Street, N.W., Washington, DC 20036, provides a clear overview of the many roles that psychologists play. It also discusses some of the possibilities for students who are interested in pursuing a career in psychology.

Martin, D. W. (1985). *Doing psychology experiments* (2nd ed.). Monterey, CA: Brooks/Cole.

This is a fine introduction to the ins and outs of doing research in psychology. After reading this book, you should be in a position to carry out simple psychological experiments on your own.

Gregory, W. L., & Burroughs, W. I. (Eds.) (1989) *Introduction to applied psychology.* Glenview, Ill.: Scott, Foresman.

This volume is devoted to taking the theories and research of psychology and applying them to everyday life. By looking through this book you can get a feel for the many contributions that psychology has made.

Leahey, T. (1987). *History of psychology: main currents in psychological thought* (2nd ed.). Englewood Cliffs, NJ: Prentice-Hall.

Marx, M. H., & Hillix, W. A. (1987). *Systems and theory in psychology* (4th ed.). New York: McGraw-Hill.

These two books provide well-written, comprehensive, and scholarly views of the background of modern psychology.

Woods, P. J. (Ed.) (1987). *Is psychology the major for you?* Washington, D.C.: American Psychological Association.

An excellent resource for students who are considering psychology as a major. It includes information on the value of a psychology degree and on careers in psychology.

PART TWO

THE BIOLOGICAL FOUNDATIONS OF PSYCHOLOGY

This part of the book takes us into many worlds. We encounter a man whose body is racked from tremors until, as the last resort, he turns to a controversial treatment that implants tissue from another part of his body into his brain. We meet a woman racked with excruciating pain and a boy who is incapable of experiencing any pain at all. And we see how a series of perceptual errors leads to the death of 269 passengers as an airplane is shot down—by mistake.

In the next three chapters, we examine how psychologists have explored the ways that the biological structures and functions of the body affect behavior. We see how the brain and nervous system work together to affect every aspect of our psychological lives. We also consider how the body takes in information through its sense organs and how the information is understood and interpreted.

In Chapter 2, the focus is on the relationship between behavior and the brain, nervous system, and other biological structures.

In Chapter 3, we learn how the body is able to incorporate and use outside stimuli and information.

In Chapter 4, we turn to the way in which we perceive and organize the world—and some of the common mistakes we make as we interpret what our senses experience.

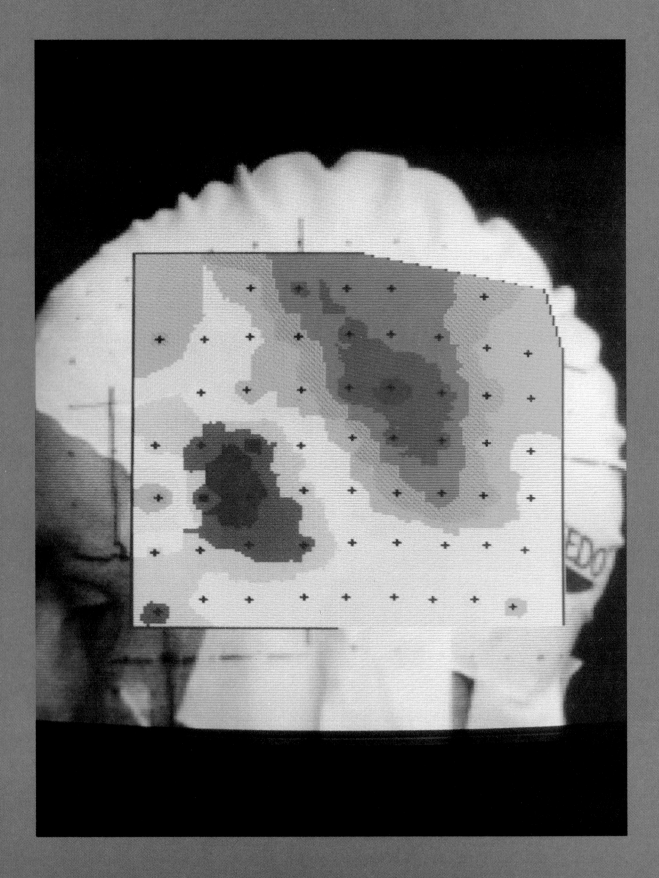

CHAPTER 2

THE BIOLOGY UNDERLYING BEHAVIOR

Nelson Martinez holds his wife's hand sixteen hours after undergoing controversial surgery to treat his symptoms of Parkinson's disease. (Sergio Dorates/The New York Times)

PROLOGUE:
NELSON MARTINEZ

For fourteen years, Nelson Martinez's life had become increasingly nightmarish. Suffering from Parkinson's disease, he was racked with tremors, could not speak properly, and endured frequent nausea and stiffness—all classic characteristics of the disease. He reached the stage at which he was no longer able to work, drink from a cup, or feed himself, and felt as if he were doomed to spend the rest of his life as an invalid.

After exhausting all standard treatments for Parkinson's disease, Martinez was desperate to stop the progression of the illness. In a last-ditch effort, he turned to an experimental treatment and became the first American to undergo a controversial procedure. During a six-hour operation, researchers implanted eight chunks of tissue from Martinez's left adrenal gland (located near his kidneys) into his brain.

The rationale for the procedure was based on an understanding of the cause of Parkinson's disease, which occurs when there is a deterioration of nerve cells in a region of the brain that produces the chemical dopamine. Because the adrenal gland also produces dopamine, researchers hypothesized that the implantation would provide the brain with sufficient amounts of the chemical to end the symptoms.

The operation was painstaking. Peering through a high-powered microscope, a surgeon used tiny stainless steel clips to fasten eight microscopic chunks of tissue, together weighing just over 1 gram, to the surface of the area of the brain that controls body movement. Had the surgeon made a false move, Martinez could have been left completely paralyzed on one side of his body.

The outcome of this high-stakes operation was a success, with the immediate results both dramatic and promising. Just after surgery, Martinez's tremors stopped almost completely, and he lost the stiffness in his body. If his recovery were to follow the predicted course, there would be some setbacks, but ultimately his improvement would be almost total, as his transplanted adrenal gland began to produce a steady output of dopamine. Although his recovery was far from assured—the long-term benefits of the operation are still unproven—his spirits were high: In the words of his wife, "After all these years of suffering, we feel like we've just been reborn" (Rohter, 1987; Lewin, 1988).

LOOKING AHEAD ▶

The results of the operation performed on Nelson Martinez are no less than miraculous. But the greater miracle rests on the object of the surgical procedure: the brain itself. As we shall see in this chapter, the brain, an organ roughly half the size of a loaf of bread, controls our behavior through every waking and sleeping moment. The brain and its pathways extending throughout the body compose the human **nervous system**. Our movements, thoughts, hopes, aspirations, dreams—the very awareness that we are human—are all intimately related to this system.

Nervous system: The brain and its pathways extending throughout the body

Because of the importance of the nervous system in controlling behavior, and because human beings at their most basic level are biological entities, psychologists and researchers from other fields as diverse as computer science, zoology, medicine, and physics—experts collectively called **neuro-scientists**—have paid special attention to the biological underpinnings of behavior (Davis et al., 1988).

Psychologists who specialize in considering the ways in which biological structures and functions of the body affect behavior are known as **biopsy-chologists**. These specialists seek to answer questions such as these: What are the bases for voluntary and involuntary operation of the body? How are messages communicated from one part of the body to another? What is the physical structure of the brain, and how does this structure affect behavior? Can the causes of psychological disorders be traced to biological factors, and how can such disorders be treated?

These questions and others are addressed in this chapter, which focuses on those biological structures of the body that are most closely related to the interests of biopsychologists. Initially, we discuss nerve cells, called neurons, and the nervous system, which allow messages to travel from one part of the body to another. We will see that through their growing knowledge of neurons and the nervous system, psychologists are increasing their understanding of human behavior and are uncovering important clues in their efforts to cure certain kinds of diseases. The structure and main divisions of the nervous system are then presented, with explanations of how they work to control voluntary and involuntary behaviors and the way the various parts of the nervous system operate together in emergency situations to produce life-saving responses to danger.

Next, we consider the brain itself, examining its major structures and the ways in which these affect behavior. We see how the brain controls movement, the five senses, and our thought processes. We also consider the fascinating notion that the two halves of the brain may operate independently of each other.

As we discuss the biological characteristics that are of interest to biopsychologists, it is important to keep in mind the basic rationale for doing so: Our understanding of human behavior cannot be complete without knowledge of the fundamentals of the brain and the rest of the nervous system. As we shall see, much of our behavior—our moods, motivations, goals, and desires—has a good deal to do with our biological makeup.

In sum, after reading this chapter, you will be able to answer these questions:

▶ What are the basic elements of the nervous system?

▶ How does the nervous system communicate electrical and chemical messages from one part to another?

▶ How can an understanding of the nervous system help us to relieve disease and pain?

▶ In what way are the structures of the nervous system tied together?

▶ What are the major parts of the brain, and what are the behaviors for which the parts are responsible?

▶ In what ways do the two halves of the brain operate independently of each other?

Neuroscientists: People from diverse fields who study the nervous system

Biopsychologists: Psychologists who study the ways biological structures and body functions affect behavior

THE BASICS OF BEHAVIOR: NEURONS
AND THE NERVOUS SYSTEM

If you have ever watched the precision with which a well-trained athlete or dancer executes a performance, you may have marveled at the complexity—and wondrous abilities—of the human body. But even the most everyday tasks—picking up a pencil, writing, speaking—require a sophisticated sequence of activities that is impressive. For instance, the difference between saying the words "dime" and "time" rests primarily on whether the vocal cords are relaxed or tense during a period lasting no more than one-hundredth of a second. Yet it is a distinction that almost everyone can make with ease.

The nervous system provides the pathways that permit us to carry out such precise activities. To understand how the nervous system is able to provide such exacting control over our bodies, we must begin by examining the most basic parts of the nervous system and considering the way in which nerve impulses are transmitted throughout the human body.

BEGINNING WITH THE BASICS: The Neuron

The ability to play the piano, drive a car, or hit a tennis ball depends, at one level, merely on muscle coordination. But if we consider *how* the muscles involved in such activities are activated, we see that there are other, more

FIGURE 2-1

The primary components of the specialized cell called the neuron, the basic element of the nervous system.

Dendrites

Nucleus

Cell body

Movement of electrical impulse

Myelin sheath

Axon

Incoming messages

Outgoing messages

Terminal buttons

FIGURE 2-2

fundamental processes involved. It is necessary for the body to provide messages to the muscles and to coordinate those messages in order to produce the complex movements that characterize successful physical activity.

Such messages are passed through specialized cells called **neurons**, the basic elements of the nervous system. Their quantity is staggering; it is estimated that there are between 100 billion and 200 billion neurons in the brain alone. Although there are several types of neurons, each has a similar basic structure, as illustrated in Figures 2-1 and 2-2 (Levy, Anderson & Lehmkuhle, 1984).

Unique among all the body's cells, neurons have a distinctive feature: the ability to communicate with other cells. As you can see in Figure 2-1, neurons have a cluster of fibers called **dendrites** at one end; it is from these fibers, which look like the twisted branches of a tree, that they receive messages from other neurons. At the opposite end, neurons have a long, slim, tubelike extension called an **axon**, which carries messages destined for other cells through the neuron. The axon is considerably longer than the rest of the neuron; most axons are 1 to 2 inches long, though some may reach 3 feet in length. In contrast, the remainder of the neuron is only a fraction of the size of the axon. (The scale drawing of the neuron in Figure 2-3 illustrates the relative proportions of the various parts.) Finally, at the end of the axon are small branches called **terminal buttons** through which messages are relayed to other cells.

The messages that travel through the neuron are purely electrical in nature. They generally move across neurons as if they were traveling on a one-way street, following a route that begins with the dendrites, continues into the cell body, and leads ultimately down the tubelike extension, the axon. Dendrites, then, detect messages from other neurons; axons carry signals away from the cell body.

In order to prevent messages from short-circuiting one another, it is necessary for the axons to be insulated in some fashion (analogous to the

These two photographs, made with an electron microscope, show a single neuron (*a*) and a group of interconnected neurons in the cerebral cortex, a part of the brain (*b*). (*Source: Manfred Kage/Peter Arnold, Inc.*)

Neurons: The basic elements of the nervous system that carry messages

Dendrites: Fibers at one end of a neuron that receive messages from other neurons

Axon: A long extension from the end of a neuron that carries messages

Terminal buttons: Small branches at the end of an axon that relay messages to other cells

Cell body

Dendrites

Axon

FIGURE 2-3

This representation of a neuron, enlarged 250 times, shows the proportions of its various parts drawn to scale. As you can see, the axon, which is folded so that it can fit within the diagram, is considerably longer than the other parts of the neuron. (*Stevens, 1979, p. 56.*)

Myelin sheath: An axon's protective coating, made of fat and protein

way electric wires must be insulated). In most axons, this is done with a protective coating known as the **myelin sheath**, made up of a series of specialized cells of fat and protein that wrap themselves around the axon.

The myelin sheath also serves to increase the velocity with which the electric impulses travel through the neurons, with those neurons that carry the most important and urgently required information having the greatest concentrations of myelin. If you touch a hot stove, for example, the information is passed through neurons that contain a relatively large quantity of myelin, speeding the message of pain. In certain diseases, such as multiple sclerosis, the myelin sheath surrounding the axon deteriorates, exposing parts of the axon that are normally covered. The result is a kind of short circuit, producing a disturbance in messages between the brain and muscles and resulting in symptoms such as the inability to walk, vision difficulties, and general muscle impairment.

Although the electric impulse always moves across the neuron in a dendrite-to-cell-body-to-axon sequence, research shows that some substances travel within parts of the neuron in the opposite direction (Schmeck, 1984). For instance, axons allow a reverse flow toward the cell body, whereby chemical substances needed for the nourishment of the cell are brought into the cell nucleus. Certain diseases, such as amyotrophic lateral sclerosis (ALS), or Lou Gehrig's disease (named for its most famous victim), may be caused by the inability of the neuron to transport vital materials in this reverse direction, eventually causing the neuron to figuratively die from starvation. Similarly, rabies is caused by the transmission of the rabies poison by reverse flow along the axon from the terminal buttons.

The movement of material along the dendrite may also be multidirectional: Rather than consistently transmitting information from other neurons to the cell body, a dendrite may occasionally "leak" information intended for its cell body, thereby inadvertently sending messages to other neurons. In fact, some scientists now suspect that such leaks may cause epilepsy, the disorder in which a person suffers from periodic seizures and convulsions. When electric discharges are leaked from dendrites, communicating unintended messages in an uncontrolled manner, furious electric storms are produced in the brain.

GUN CONTROL: Firing the Neuron

Like a gun, a neuron either fires or doesn't fire; there is nothing in between. Pulling harder on the trigger is not going to make the bullet travel faster or more surely. Similarly, neurons follow an **all-or-none law**: They are either on or off; once triggered beyond a certain point, they will fire. When they are off—that is, in a **resting state**—there is a negative electric charge of about − 70 millivolts within the neuron (a millivolt is one-thousandth of a volt). This charge is caused by the presence of more negatively charged ions (a type of molecule) within the neuron than outside it. You might think of the neuron as one of the poles of a miniature battery, with the inside of the neuron representing the negative pole and the outside of the neuron the positive pole.

However, when a message arrives from another neuron, the cell walls allow the entry of positively charged ions, which in turn permits the charge within that part of the cell to change momentarily from negative to positive. When the charge reaches a critical level, the "trigger" is pulled, and an electric nerve impulse, known as an **action potential**, then travels down the neuron (see Figure 2-4).

The action potential moves from one end of the neuron to the other like a flame moves across a fuse toward an explosive. As the impulse moves toward the end of the neuron, the movement of ions causes a sequential change in charge from negative to positive along the cell (see Figure 2-5). After the passage of the impulse, positive ions are pumped out of the neuron, and the neuron charge returns to negative.

Just after an action potential has passed, the neuron cannot be fired again—it is in its **absolute refractory period**. It is as if the gun has to be reloaded after each shot. Following the absolute refractory period, there is also a **relative refractory period**, in which it is more difficult than usual to fire the neuron. During this period, although an impulse can pass through the neuron, it takes a stronger stimulus to set it off than if the neuron had been given sufficient time to reach its normal resting potential. Eventually,

All-or-none law: The principle governing the state of neurons, which are either on (firing) or off (resting)

Resting state: The nonfiring state of a neuron when the charge equals about − 70 millivolts

Action potential: An electric nerve impulse that travels through a neuron when it is set off by a "trigger," changing the cell's charge from negative to positive

Absolute refractory period: The period following the triggering of a neuron in which the neuron recovers and prepares for another impulse

Relative refractory period: The period during which a neuron, not yet having returned to its resting state, requires more than the normal stimulus to be set off

54

FIGURE 2-4

Changes in the electrical charge of a neuron during the passage of an action potential. In its normal resting state, a neuron has a negative charge of around −70 millivolts. When an action potential is triggered, however, the cell charge becomes positive, increasing to about +40 millivolts. Following the passage of the action potential, the charge becomes even more negative than it is in its typical state. It is not until the charge returns to its resting potential that the neuron will be fully ready to be triggered once again.

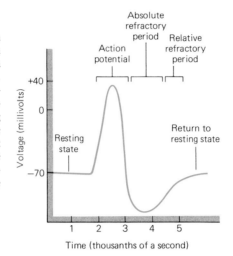

FIGURE 2-5

Movement of an action potential across a neuron can be seen in this series of three drawings. Just prior to time 1, positively charged ions enter the cell walls, changing the charge within that part of the cell from negative to positive. The action potential is thus triggered, traveling down the neuron, as illustrated in the changes occurring from time 1 to time 3 (from top to bottom in this drawing). Following the passage of the action potential, positive ions are pumped out of the neuron, restoring its charge to negative. The change in voltage illustrated at the top of the neuron can be seen in greater detail in Figure 2-4.

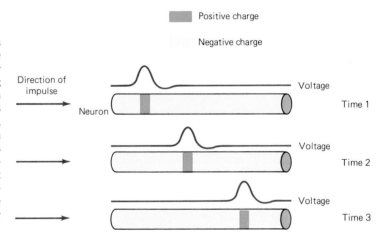

though, the neuron returns to its resting state and is ready to be fired once again.

These complex events occur at speeds that are a function of the size of the axon and the thickness of the myelin sheath. Neurons with small diameters carry impulses at about 2 miles per hour; longer and thicker ones can average speeds of more than 225 miles per hour.

In addition to varying according to how quickly an impulse moves across them, neurons differ in their potential rate of firing. Some neurons have the potential to fire as many as 1000 times per second; others have a maximum potential rate that is much lower. The intensity of a stimulus that provokes a neuron determines how much of this potential rate is reached: A strong stimulus, such as a bright light or loud sound, leads to a higher rate of firing than does a less intense stimulus. Thus, while there are no differences in the strength or speed at which an impulse moves across a given neuron—as the all-or-none law suggests—there is variation in the frequency of impulses, providing a mechanism by which we can distinguish the tickle of a feather from the weight of someone standing on our toe.

The structure, operation, and functions of the neuron illustrate how fundamental biological aspects of the body underlie several primary psychological processes. Our understanding of the way we sense, perceive, and learn about the world would be greatly restricted without the information about the neuron that biopsychologists have acquired.

RECAP AND REVIEW I

Recap

◀ Neurons are the basic elements of the nervous system; they allow the transmission of messages that coordinate the complex activities of the human body.

◀ All neurons have a similar basic structure: They receive messages through the dendrites and transmit them through the axon to other neurons.

◀ Neurons fire according to an all-or-none law; they are either firing or resting.

Review

1. Psychologists concerned with the ways in which biological factors influence behavior are called
   a. Neurologists
   b. Biopsychologists
   c. Chemists
   d. Clinical psychologists

2. The specialized cells that function as the basic elements of the nervous system are called _____ .

3. Clusters of fibers transmitting messages to the neuron are called _____ .

4. Just as electric wires have an outer coating, so axons are insulated by a coating called the _____
   _____ .

5. Do neurons that carry the most important information have the greatest or least concentration of myelin? _____

6. The sensory movement disabilities suffered by individuals with multiple sclerosis are due to a loss of cells in the
   a. Axon
   b. Dendrite
   c. Myelin sheath
   d. Terminal buttons

7. Substances always travel through the neuron in a dendrite-to-cell-body-to-axon sequence. True or false? _____

8. The electric nerve impulse which travels down a neuron is called a(n) _____
   _____ .

9. A stronger stimulus than usual is needed to set off an electric impulse in the neuron during the
   a. Relative refractory period
   b. Action potential period
   c. Absolute refractory period
   d. Resting state

(Answers to review questions are on page 56.)

BRIDGING THE GAP: Where Neuron Meets Neuron

Have you ever put together a radio kit? If you have, you probably remember that the manufacturer supplied you with wires that had to be painstakingly connected to one another or to some other component of the radio; every piece had to be physically connected to something else.

The human body is considerably more sophisticated than a radio, or any other manufactured apparatus, for that matter. It has evolved a neural transmission system that in some parts has no need for a structural connection between its components. Instead, a chemical connection known as a **synapse** bridges the gap between two neurons (see Figure 2-6*a*). When a nerve impulse comes to the end of the axon and reaches a terminal button, the terminal button releases a chemical called a **neurotransmitter**. Neurotransmitters carry specific chemical messages across the synapse to the dendrite (and sometimes the cell body) of a receiver neuron. Although messages travel in electrical form *within* neurons, then, they move *between* neurons through a chemical transmission system.

There are several types of neurotransmitters, and not all receiver neu-

Synapse: The gap between neurons through which chemical messages are communicated

Neurotransmitter: A chemical, secreted when a nerve impulse comes to the end of an axon, that carries messages between neurons

56

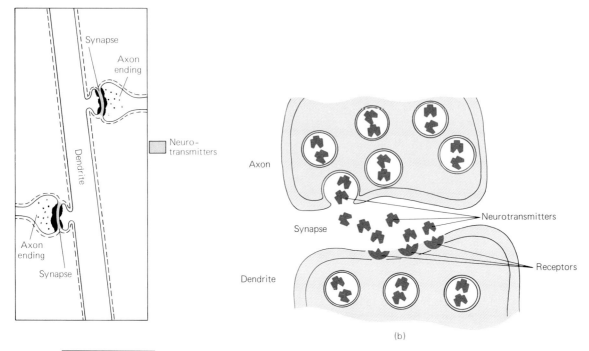

Synapse
Axon ending
Dendrite
Neuro-transmitters
Axon ending
Synapse

Axon
Neurotransmitters
Synapse
Receptors
Dendrite

(b)

FIGURE 2-6

(*a*) A synapse is the junction between an axon and a dendrite. The gap between the axon and the dendrite is bridged by chemicals called neurotransmitters. (*b*) Just as the pieces of a jigsaw puzzle can fit in only one specific location in a puzzle, each kind of neurotransmitter has a distinctive configuration that allows it to fit into a specific type of receptor cell.

Excitatory message: A chemical secretion that "tells" a receiving neuron to fire

Inhibitory message: A chemical secretion that prevents a receiving neuron from firing

Reuptake: The reabsorption of neurotransmitters by a terminal button

rons are capable of receiving the chemical message carried by every neurotransmitter. In the same way that a jigsaw puzzle piece can fit in only one specific location in a puzzle, so each kind of neurotransmitter has a distinctive configuration that allows it to fit into a specific type of receptor cell on the receiving neuron (see Figure 2-6*b*). It is only when a neurotransmitter fits precisely into a receptor cell that successful chemical communication is possible.

If a neurotransmitter does fit into a receiving neuron, the chemical message that arrives with it is basically one of two types: excitatory or inhibitory. **Excitatory** messages make it more likely that a receiving neuron will fire and an action potential will travel down its axons. **Inhibitory** messages, in contrast, do just the opposite; they provide chemical information that prevents or decreases the likelihood that the receiving neuron will fire.

Because the dendrites of a neuron receive many messages simultaneously, some of which are excitatory and some inhibitory, the neuron must integrate the messages in some fashion. It does this through a kind of summation process; if the number of excitatory messages outweighs the number of inhibitory ones, an action potential will occur. On the other hand, if the number of inhibitory messages outweighs the excitatory ones, nothing will happen. The neuron will remain in its resting state.

If neurotransmitters remained at the site of the synapse, effective communication would no longer be possible, since there would be continual stimulation of the receptor cells. Instead, neurotransmitters are either deactivated by enzymes or—more frequently—reabsorbed by the terminal button in an example of chemical thriftiness called **reuptake**. Certain drugs, such as

---

ANSWERS (REVIEW I):
1. b **2.** Neurons **3.** Dendrites **4.** Myelin sheath **5.** Greatest **6.** c **7.** False; axons allow a reverse flow of substances toward the cell body **8.** Action potential **9.** a

cocaine, inhibit the reuptake of some kinds of neurotransmitters, thereby prolonging their effects and producing a "high."

Varieties of Neurotransmitters

So far, some fifty chemicals have been found to act as neurotransmitters, and some experts feel that several hundred may ultimately be identified (Snyder, 1980). Particular neurotransmitters produce the excitation or inhibition of neurons at different rates and in different concentrations. Furthermore, the effects of a given neurotransmitter vary depending on the portion of the nervous system in which it is produced. The same neurotransmitter, then, can cause a neuron to fire when it is secreted in one part of the brain and can inhibit the firing of neurons when it is produced in another part. (The major neurotransmitters are shown in Table 2-1.)

One of the most common neurotransmitters is **acetylcholine** (or **ACh**, its chemical symbol), which produces contractions of skeletal muscles (Blusztajn & Wurtman, 1983; Kasa, 1986). The venom of the deadly black widow spider causes the continuous release of ACh, eventually killing the victim through muscle spasms. ACh is also related to the drug curare, used in the poison arrows of South American Indians. Curare blocks reception of ACh, thereby paralyzing the skeletal muscles and ultimately producing death by suffocation, since the victim is unable to breathe. On the brighter side, the study of ACh has helped provide insights into such medical conditions as myasthenia gravis, a disease in which there is a gradual loss of muscle control. Specifically, treatments have been devised in which drugs can be administered to prevent the destruction of ACh by the body, thereby allowing the normal transmission of impulses across the synapses and restoration of muscle control.

Acetylcholine (a see tul KO leen) **(ACh):** A common neurotransmitter that produces contractions of skeletal muscles

TABLE 2-1

Major Neurotransmitters

Name	Location	Effects
Acetylcholine (ACh)	Brain, spinal cord, peripheral nervous system, especially some organs of the parasympathetic nervous system	Deficiency: paralysis (curare and botulism); Alzheimer's disease Excess: violent muscle contraction (black widow spider venom)
Dopamine (DA)	Brain	Deficiency: muscular rigidity and uncontrollable tremors (Parkinson's disease)
Enkephalins and endorphins	Brain, spinal cord	Pain reduction
Gamma-amino butyric acid (GABA)	Brain	Deficiency: mental deterioration (Huntington's chorea)
Norepinephrine (NE)	Brain, some organs of sympathetic nervous system	Deficiency: depression
Serotonin	Brain	Deficiency: depression

Alzheimer's (ALZ high merz) **disease**: A progressive disorder characterized by a loss of memory

Some psychologists now suggest that **Alzheimer's disease**, a progressively degenerative disorder that ultimately produces loss of memory, confusion, and changes in personality in its victims, is related to the production of ACh. Evidence is growing that ACh is closely related to memory capabilities, and some research now shows that Alzheimer's patients have restricted production of ACh in portions of their brains. If this research is corroborated, it may lead to treatments in which production of ACh can be restored (Wolozin, Pruchnicki, Dickson & Davies, 1986).

Dopamine (DA): A common neurotransmitter that inhibits certain neurons and excites others

Another major neurotransmitter is **dopamine (DA)**, which has an inhibitory effect on some neurons and an excitatory effect on others, such as those of the heart. The discovery that certain drugs can have a marked effect on dopamine release has led to the development of effective treatments for a wide variety of physical and mental ailments. For instance, Parkinson's disease, the severe medical condition of Nelson Martinez (whose case was discussed at the start of the chapter) marked by varying degrees of muscular rigidity and shaking, seems to be caused by a deficiency of dopamine in the brain. Drugs have been developed to stimulate the production of dopamine, and they have proved highly effective in reducing the symptoms of Parkinson's in many patients. In extreme cases, such as that of Martinez, production of dopamine has been stimulated by implantation of cells into the brain from other parts of the body.

Researchers have also hypothesized that schizophrenia and some other mental disturbances are affected or perhaps even caused by the overproduction of dopamine (Wong et al., 1986; Wong et al., 1988). Drugs that inhibit dopamine production have been successful in reducing the appearance of abnormal behavior in people diagnosed as schizophrenic—as we will examine further when we consider abnormal behavior and its treatment in Chapters 16 and 17.

A NATURAL HIGH: Endorphins

Unless he was jogging, David Bartlett was a quiet, unassuming person. Most people who knew him tended to think of him as an introvert. But when he jogged, a noticeable change seemed to come over David. By the time he finished his daily 5- or 6-mile run he was excited, happy—even euphoric at times—and talkative. Anyone who was with David after a run noticed the change. In fact, some of his friends joked about it, saying that he acted as if he were "high" on something he had taken while he was out running.

What happened to David Bartlett when he was jogging? Given our current discussion, you might suspect that his behavior related to a neurotransmitter—an explanation that appears well founded.

Endorphins: Chemicals produced by the body that interact with an opiate receptor to reduce pain

Opiate receptor: A neuron that acts to reduce the experience of pain

The specific neurotransmitter involved is likely to be an endorphin. **Endorphins** are chemicals produced by the body that interact with a particular kind of neuron called an **opiate receptor**. Opiate receptors act to reduce the experience of pain, and in fact many painkilling drugs, such as morphine, are used to activate the opiate receptors. Endorphins are a kind of "natural" morphine produced by the body to reduce pain. For instance, people who are afflicted with diseases that produce long-term, severe pain often develop large concentrations of endorphins in their brains—suggesting an attempt by the body to control the pain (Watkins & Mayer, 1982).

Endorphins like morphine and other opiates may go even further than mere pain reduction: They may also produce the kind of euphoric feelings that jogger David Bartlett experienced after running. It is possible that the amount of exercise and perhaps even the pain involved in a long run stimulate the production of endorphins—ultimately resulting in what has been called a "runner's high" (Hathaway, 1984).

Endorphin release may also explain other phenomena that have long puzzled psychologists, such as the reasons that acupuncture and placebos— pills that contain no actual drugs but that patients *believe* will make them better—are sometimes effective in reducing pain (Bolles & Fanselow, 1982). Specifically, it is possible that acupuncture and placebos both act to release endorphins, thereby bringing about positive results. The study of endorphins may also help biopsychologists to develop new, more effective painkillers based on the natural functions of the body.

STRINGING NEURONS TOGETHER: THE NERVOUS SYSTEM

Given the complexity of individual neurons and the neurotransmission process, it should come as no surprise that the structures formed by the neurons are likewise complicated in their own right. However, there is a certain logic—even an elegance—to the human nervous system.

THE NEAR AND THE FAR: Central and Peripheral Nervous Systems

As you can see from Figure 2-7, the nervous system is divided into two main parts: the central nervous system and the peripheral nervous system. The **central nervous system (CNS)** is composed of the brain and spinal cord. The **spinal cord** is a bundle of nerves, about the thickness of a pencil, that leaves the brain and runs down the length of the back (see Figure 2-8). It is the main means for transmitting messages between the brain and the body.

Some simple kinds of behaviors are organized entirely within the spinal

"Runner's high" may occur from the release of endorphins, or natural painkillers, in the brain. (Jim Anderson/Woodfin Camp & Assoc.)

Central nervous system (CNS): The system that includes the brain and the spinal cord

Spinal cord: A bundle of nerves running along the spine, carrying messages between the brain and the body

FIGURE 2-7

A schematic diagram of the relationship of the parts of the nervous system.

Brain

Spinal cord

FIGURE 2-8

The central nervous system consists of the brain and spinal cord. (Gruppo Editorial Fabbri/Milano.)

Reflexes: Simple movements carried out by the spinal cord without input from the brain

Sensory (afferent) neurons: Neurons that transmit information from the body to the nervous system

Motor (efferent) neurons: Neurons that transmit information from nervous system to muscles and glands

Interneurons: Neurons that transmit information between sensory and motor neurons

cord. A common example is the knee jerk, which occurs when the knee is tapped with a rubber hammer. Such behaviors, called **reflexes**, represent an involuntary response to an incoming stimulus which is "reflected" back out of the body, without the involvement of the brain.

For example, when you touch a hot stove and immediately withdraw your hand, a reflex is at work: Although eventually the brain analyzes the pain, the initial withdrawal is directed only by neurons in the spinal cord. Three sorts of neurons are involved in reflexes: **sensory (afferent) neurons**, which transmit information from the periphery of the body to the central nervous system; **motor (efferent) neurons**, which communicate information from the nervous system to muscles and glands of the body; and **interneurons**, which connect sensory and motor neurons, carrying messages between the two.

The importance of the spinal cord and reflexes is illustrated by the outcome of accidents in which the cord is injured or severed. In one resulting injury, **paraplegia**, a person is unable to voluntarily move any muscles in the lower half of the body. However, even though the cord is severed, the undamaged area of the spinal cord is still able to produce some simple reflex actions, if stimulated appropriately. For instance, if a paraplegic's knee is tapped lightly, the lower leg will jerk slightly forward. Similarly, in some kinds of spinal cord injuries, people will move their legs in an involuntary response to a pinprick, even though they do not experience the sensation of pain.

The spinal cord is related to other basic biological functions as well. For instance, if a male paraplegic's genitals are stimulated, he is capable of having an erection and ultimately ejaculating. However, with a damaged spinal cord, the paraplegic would not experience the sensations that are normally a part of sexual activity and thus would not be able to perceive his arousal.

As suggested by its name, the **peripheral nervous system** branches out from the spinal cord and brain and reaches the peripheries of the body. Made up of long axons and dendrites, the peripheral nervous system encompasses all parts of the nervous system other than the brain and spinal cord. There are two major divisions, the somatic division and the autonomic division, both of which connect the central nervous system with the sense organs, muscles, glands, and other organs. The **somatic division** specializes in the control of voluntary movements—such as the motion of the eyes to read this sentence or of the hand to turn this page—and the communication of information to and from the sense organs. On the other hand, the **autonomic division** is concerned with the parts of the body that keep us alive—the heart, blood vessels, glands, lungs, and other organs that function involuntarily without our awareness. As you are reading along right now, the autonomic division of the peripheral nervous system is pumping the blood through your body, pushing your lungs in and out, overseeing the digestion of the meal you had a few hours ago, and so on—all without a thought or care on your part.

EMERGENCY!: Activating the Autonomic Nervous System

The autonomic division plays a particularly crucial role during emergency situations. Suppose as you are reading you suddenly sense that there is a stranger watching you through the window. As you look up, you see the glint of something that just might be a knife. As confusion races through your mind and fear overcomes your attempts to think rationally, what happens to your body? If you are like most people, you react immediately on a physiological level: Your heart rate increases, you begin to sweat, and you develop goose bumps all over your body.

The physiological changes that occur result from the activation of one part of the autonomic division: the sympathetic division. The **sympathetic division** acts to prepare the body in stressful emergency situations, engaging all the organism's resources to respond to a threat, a response that often takes the form of "fight or flight." In contrast, the **parasympathetic division** acts to calm the body after the emergency situation is resolved. When you find, for instance, that the stranger at the window is actually your roommate who has lost his keys and is climbing in the window to avoid waking you, your parasympathetic division begins to predominate, lowering your heart rate, stopping your sweating, and returning your body to the state it was in prior to your fright. The parasympathetic division also provides a means for

Paraplegia: The inability, as a result of injury to the spinal cord, to move any muscles in the lower half of the body

Peripheral nervous system: All parts of the nervous system *except* the brain and the spinal cord (includes somatic and autonomic divisions)

Somatic division: The part of the nervous system that controls voluntary movements of the skeletal muscles

Autonomic division: The part of the nervous system that controls involuntary movement (the actions of the heart, glands, lungs, and other organs)

Sympathetic division: The part of the autonomic division of the peripheral nervous system that prepares the body to respond in stressful emergency situations

Parasympathetic division: The part of the autonomic division of the peripheral nervous system that calms the body, bringing functions back to normal after an emergency has passed

THE BIOLOGICAL FOUNDATIONS
OF PSYCHOLOGY

Organ	Sympathetic	Parasympathetic
Heart	Accelerates	Slows
Pupil of eye	Widens	Constricts
Sweat glands	Increase	(no effect)
Lungs	Swell	Constrict
Salivary glands	Decrease	Increase
Digestive functions of stomach and intestines	Slow	Increase

FIGURE 2-9

The major functions of the autonomic nervous system. The sympathetic division acts to prepare certain organs of the body for stressful emergency situations, and the parasympathetic division acts to calm the body after the emergency situation is resolved.

the body to maintain storage of energy sources such as nutrients and oxygen. The sympathetic and parasympathetic divisions work together to regulate many functions of the body (see Figure 2-9). For instance, sexual arousal is controlled by the parasympathetic division, while sexual orgasm is a function of the sympathetic division.

Recap

◄ The specific site of transmission from one neuron to another is called the synapse. Messages moving *across* synapses are chemical in nature, although they travel *within* neurons in an electrical form.

◄ Neurotransmitters are the specific chemicals that make the chemical connection at the synapse; these act either to excite other neurons into firing or to inhibit neurons from firing.

◄ The central nervous system (CNS) is made up of the brain and spinal cord, a thick bundle of nerves running from the brain down the length of the back. The spinal cord provides the major route for transmission of messages between the brain and the rest of the body.

◄ The peripheral nervous system includes all parts of the nervous system other than the brain and spinal cord. It has two major parts: the somatic division (for voluntary movements) and the autonomic division (for involuntary movements).

◄ The autonomic division, which has two parts (sympathetic and parasympathetic divisions), plays a major role during emergency situations.

Review

1. The gap between neurons, across which messages are communicated, is called the _____ ; the chemical which bridges the gap is called a(n) _____ .

2. Do messages *within* neurons travel in electrical or chemical form? _____

3. Receiver neurons are typically capable of receiving many different types of neurotransmitters. True or false? _____

4. It is more likely that the action potential will travel down the axons of a neuron when it has received a(n) _____ message.

5. Acetylcholine is now thought to play a role in
   a. Alzheimer's disease
   b. Lou Gehrig's disease
   c. Muscular dystrophy
   d. Multiple sclerosis

6. Match the description in the right-hand column with the neurotransmitter whose release most likely explains the effect given.

   a. _____ Dopamine

   b. _____ Endorphins

   c. _____ Acetylcholine

   1. The poison had the effect of paralyzing the victim's muscles, thereby causing death by suffocation.
   2. Medications have helped sufferers of mental illness by regulating the production of a neurotransmitter.
   3. Sharon finished her longest run yet, pushing herself well beyond the discomfort stage. As a result, she felt a "runner's high."

7. Opiate receptors are activated by painkilling drugs such as morphine. True or false? _____

8. The brain and spinal cord compose the _____ nervous system, whereas the _____ nervous system branches out from the brain and spinal cord.

9. Barbara saw a young boy run into the street and get hit by a car. When she got to the fallen child, she was in a state of panic. She was sweating and her heart was racing. Her physiological state resulted from the activation of what division of the autonomic nervous system?
   a. Parasympathetic
   b. Somatic
   c. Peripheral
   d. Sympathetic

(Answers to review questions are on page 64.)

TYING THE NERVOUS SYSTEM TOGETHER: THE BRAIN

When you come right down to it, it is not a very pretty sight. Soft, spongy, mottled, and pinkish-gray in color, one could hardly say that it possesses much in the way of physical beauty. Despite its physical appearance, however, it ranks as the greatest natural marvel that we know and possesses a beauty and sophistication all its own.

The object to which this description applies is, as you might guess, the brain. The brain is responsible for our loftiest thoughts—and our most primitive urges. It is the overseer of the intricate workings of the human body.

THE BIOLOGICAL FOUNDATIONS
OF PSYCHOLOGY

The soft, spongy gray matter of the brain has capabilities far more spectacular than its appearance would lead one to suspect. (A. Glauberman/Photo Researchers)

If one were to attempt to design a computer to mimic the capabilities of the brain, the task would be nearly impossible; in fact, it has proved difficult to even come close (Hellerstein, 1988). Just the sheer quantity of nerve cells in the brain is enough to daunt even the most ambitious computer engineer. Many billions of nerve cells make up a structure weighing just 3 pounds in the average adult. However, it is not the number of cells that is the most astounding thing about the brain but its ability to allow human intellect to flourish as it guides our behavior and thoughts.

EXPLORING AND MAPPING THE UNKNOWN: Studying the Brain

The brain has always posed a challenge to those wishing to study it. For most of history, it could be examined only after an individual was dead—for only then was it possible to open up the skull and cut into the brain without the risk of causing serious injury. While informative, such a limited procedure could hardly tell us much about the functioning of the healthy brain.

Today, however, the story is different. Probably the most important advances that have been made in the study of the brain use the **brain scan**, a technique by which a picture of the internal workings of the brain can be taken without having to surgically cut into a patient's skull (Turkington, 1985). The main kinds of scanning techniques are described below and illustrated in Figure 2-10.

Brain scan: A method of "photographing" the brain without opening the skull

ANSWERS (REVIEW II):
1. Synapse, neurotransmitter **2.** Electrical **3.** False; distinctive neurotransmitters have to fit precisely into the specific receptor cell of the neuron **4.** Excitatory **5.** a **6.** a-2; b-3; c-1 **7.** True **8.** Central, peripheral **9.** d

(a)

(b)

(c)

(d)

FIGURE 2-10

Brain scans produced by different techniques. (*a*) A computer-produced EEG image. (*b*) The CAT scan shows the structures of the brain. (*c*) The NMR scan uses a magnetic field to detail the parts of the brain. (*d*) PET scans display the functioning of the brain at a given moment in time and are sensitive to the person's activities. [(a) *Dr. Richard Coppola/NIMH,* (b) *Dan McCoy/ Rainbow,* (c) *Courtesy of J. C. Mazziotta and M. E. Phelps, UCLA School of Medicine.*]

▶ The **electroencephalogram (EEG)**, records the electrical signals being transmitted inside the brain through electrodes placed on the outside of the skull. Although traditionally the EEG could produce only a graph of electrical wave patterns, new techniques now are able to transform the brain's electrical activity into a pictorial representation of the brain that allows the diagnosis of such problems as epilepsy and learning disabilities (see the Psychology at Work box).

Electroencephalogram (ee LEK tro en SEF uh lo gram) (**EEG**): A technique that records the brain's electrical activity

▶ The **computerized axial tomography (CAT)** scan uses a computer to construct an image of the brain by combining thousands of separate x-rays taken at slightly different angles. It is extremely useful for showing abnor-

Computerized axial tomography (CAT) scan: A scanning procedure that shows the structures within the brain

USING THE BRAIN AS A DIAGNOSTIC DEVICE: NEUROMETRICS

A new field of science is promising to revolutionize the diagnosis of the most subtle kinds of brain dysfunction. Called **neurometrics,** it measures and analyzes electrical activity in the brain of an individual and compares it with a norm. Early indications are that specific kinds of deviations from average patterns can be used not only to infer that an individual is suffering from some kind of psychological or medical problem but to determine the particular nature of the problem as well (John, Prichep, Fridman & Easton, 1988).

Major advances in neurometrics have come from the development of an innovative technique for measuring electrical activity in the brain. Using a procedure called **brain electrical activity mapping (BEAM),** scientists have been able to produce a computerized snapshot of electrical activity within the brain at a given moment, supplementing data from electroencephalograms. By comparing BEAM scans of normal people with those of patients suffering from particular kinds of psychological and medical problems, researchers have been able to detect specific patterns of brain activity. Figure 2-11 shows average BEAM scans for a group of individuals suffering from several kinds of problems.

The diagnostic possibilities implicit in neurometrics are extraordinary. For example, in cases in which two patients display identical symptoms, neurometrics may enable scientists to determine that the underlying problems causing the symptoms are actually quite different. This, in turn, may lead to more precise and individualized treatments.

Even more interesting is the possibility of identifying psychological difficulties before any overt symptoms have emerged. In this way, psychological problems can be prevented from disrupting people's lives *before* they occur—a true advance for the field of psychology.

Neurometrics: The study of brain electrical activity, allowing for the comparison of brain functioning in normal and disordered individuals

Brain electrical activity mapping (BEAM): A computerized scan technique that indicates electrical activity within the brain

---

Nuclear magnetic resonance (NMR) scan: A scan produced by a magnetic field which shows brain structures in great detail

Positron emission tomography (PET) scan: A scan technique which indicates how the brain is functioning at a given moment

Central core: The "old brain," which controls such basic functions as eating and sleeping and is common to all vertebrates

malities in the structure of the brain, such as swelling and enlargement of certain parts, but does not provide information about brain activity.

▶ The **nuclear magnetic resonance (NMR)** scan produces a powerful magnetic field to provide a detailed, computer-generated image of brain activity. Although still considered experimental, it is becoming the scan of choice because of the wealth of detail that can be constructed.

▶ The **positron emission tomography (PET)** scan indicates how the brain is functioning at a given moment in time. After radioactive sugar is injected into a patient, a computer that measures radiation in the brain displays whether the brain is functioning normally.

Each of these techniques provides exciting possibilities not only for the diagnosis and treatment of brain disease and injuries but also for an increased understanding of the normal functioning of the brain.

UNCOVERING THE "OLD BRAIN": The Central Core

While the capabilities of the human brain far exceed those of the brain of any other species, it is not surprising that the basic functions—such as breathing, eating, and sleeping—that we share with more primitive animals are directed by a relatively primitive part of the brain. A portion of the brain known as the **central core** (see Figure 2-12) is quite similar to that found in all vertebrates (species with backbones). The central core is often referred

	Delta	Theta	Alpha	Beta

Normal

Unipolar depression

Bipolar depression

Alcoholism

Schizophrenia

Mild cognitive impairment

Dementia

FIGURE 2-11

This series of brain scans shows average BEAM scans for groups of people who are normal (top) and for patients diagnosed with the psychological disorders of unipolar depression, bipolar depression, alcoholism, schizophrenia, mild cognitive impairment, and dementia. Each of the four columns focuses on a different type of electrical wave pattern. (*Courtesy of E. Roy John and Leslie Prichep, NYU School of Medicine/ by permission of* Science.)

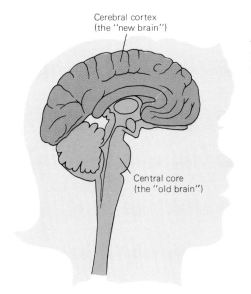

Cerebral cortex
(the "new brain")

Central core
(the "old brain")

FIGURE 2-12

The major divisions of the brain: the "new" brain (the cerebral cortex) and the "old" brain (the central core or subcortex).

68

(a)

FIGURE 2-13

(*a*) A three-dimensional view of the structures within the brain. (Nauta & Feirtag, 1979.) (*b*) In this view, we can see the inside of a brain that has been cut in half; we are viewing the inner surface of the right side. (From Thompson, 1967).

Medulla: The part of the central core of the brain that controls many important body functions such as breathing and heartbeat

Pons: The part of the brain that joins the halves of the cerebellum, transmitting motor information to coordinate muscles and integrate movement between the right and left sides of the body

Cerebellum (ser rah BELL um): The part of the brain that controls bodily balance

Reticular formation: A group of nerve cells in the brain that arouses the body to prepare it for appropriate action and screens out background stimuli

(b)

to as the "old brain" because it is thought to have evolved relatively early in the development of the human species.

If we were to move up the spinal cord from the base of the skull to locate the structures of the central core of the brain, the first part we would come to would be the medulla (see Figure 2-13). The **medulla** controls a number of important body functions, the most important of which are breathing and maintenance of heartbeat. The pons comes next, joining the two halves of the cerebellum, which lies just adjacent to it. Containing large bundles of nerves, the **pons** acts as a transmitter of motor information, permitting the coordination of muscles and the integration of movement between the right and left halves of the body.

The **cerebellum** is found just above the medulla and behind the pons. Without the help of the cerebellum we would be unable to walk a straight line without staggering and lurching forward, for it is the job of the cerebellum to control bodily balance. It constantly monitors feedback from the muscles to coordinate their placement, movement, and tension. In fact, drinking too much alcohol seems to depress the activity of the cerebellum, leading to the unsteady gait and movement characteristic of drunkenness.

So far our description of the parts of the brain has suggested that it is made up of a series of individual, well-defined separate structures. However, its parts do not simply follow one another in a sequential order; they are found both within and between other structures. An example of this is the **reticular formation**, which extends from the medulla through the pons. The reticular formation is made up of a group of nerve cells that serves as a kind of guard that immediately activates other parts of the brain to cause a general arousal of the body. If, for example, you are startled by a loud noise, your reticular formation is likely to engage your body in immediate vigilance, prompting a heightened state of awareness to determine whether a response is necessary. In addition, it serves a different function when you are sleeping, seeming to screen out background stimuli to allow you to sleep undisturbed.

The final structures that are part of the "old brain" are the thalamus and the hypothalamus. The **thalamus**, located centrally within the "old brain," acts primarily as a relay station, mostly for messages concerning sensory information (Casey & Morrow, 1983). Messages from the eyes, ears, and skin travel to the thalamus to be communicated upward to higher parts of the brain. The thalamus also integrates information from higher parts of the brain, sorting it out so that it can be sent to the cerebellum and medulla.

The **hypothalamus** is located just below the thalamus. Although tiny—about the size of the tip of a finger—the hypothalamus plays an inordinately important role in the functioning of the body. One of its major functions is to maintain **homeostasis**, a steady internal environment for the body; as we will discuss further in Chapter 9, the hypothalamus helps provide a constant body temperature and monitors the amount of nutrients stored in the cells. A second major function is equally important: It produces and regulates behavior that is important to the basic survival of the species—eating, drinking, sexual behavior, fighting, and nurturance of offspring.

Thalamus: The part of the brain's central core that transmits messages from the sense organs to the cerebral cortex and from the cerebral cortex to the cerebellum and medulla

Hypothalamus: Located below the thalamus of the brain, its major function is to maintain homeostasis

Homeostasis: The process by which an organism tries to maintain an internal biological balance or steady state

OF CHEMICALS AND GLANDS: The Endocrine System

As we move upward through the brain, we need to pause a moment to consider the **endocrine system**, a chemical communication network that sends messages throughout the nervous system via the bloodstream. Although not a structure of the brain itself, the endocrine system is intimately tied to the hypothalamus. The job of the endocrine system is to secrete **hormones**, chemicals that circulate through the blood and affect the functioning or growth of other parts of the body (Crapo, 1985; Kravitz, 1988).

Like neurons, endocrines transmit messages throughout the body, although the speed and mode of transmission are quite different. Whereas neural messages are measured in thousandths of a second, hormonal communications may take minutes to reach their destination. Furthermore, neural messages move across neurons in specific lines (as with wires strung along telephone poles), whereas hormones travel throughout the entire body, similar to the way radio waves transmit across the entire landscape. Just as radio waves evoke a response only when a radio is tuned to the correct station, so hormones flowing through the bloodstream activate only those cells that are receptive and "tuned" to the appropriate hormonal message.

The major component of the endocrine system is the **pituitary gland**, found near—and regulated by—the hypothalamus. The pituitary gland is sometimes called the "master gland," because it controls the functioning of the rest of the endocrine system. But the pituitary gland is more than just the taskmaster of other glands; it has important functions in its own right. For instance, hormones secreted by the pituitary gland control growth. Extremely short people—dwarfs—and unusually tall ones—giants—usually have pituitary gland deficiencies. Other endocrine glands, shown in Figure 2-14, affect emotional reactions, sexual urges, and energy levels.

Endocrine system: A chemical communication network that sends messages throughout the nervous system and secretes hormones that affect body growth and functioning

Hormones: Chemicals that circulate throughout the blood and affect the functioning and growth of parts of the body

Pituitary gland: The "master gland," the major component of the endocrine system, which secretes hormones that control growth

THE BIOLOGICAL FOUNDATIONS
OF PSYCHOLOGY

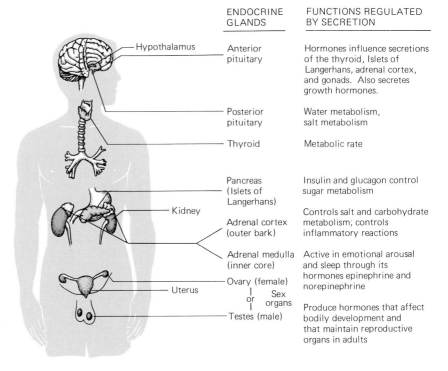

ENDOCRINE GLANDS	FUNCTIONS REGULATED BY SECRETION
Anterior pituitary	Hormones influence secretions of the thyroid, Islets of Langerhans, adrenal cortex, and gonads. Also secretes growth hormones.
Posterior pituitary	Water metabolism, salt metabolism
Thyroid	Metabolic rate
Pancreas (Islets of Langerhans)	Insulin and glucagon control sugar metabolism
Adrenal cortex (outer bark)	Controls salt and carbohydrate metabolism; controls inflammatory reactions
Adrenal medulla (inner core)	Active in emotional arousal and sleep through its hormones epinephrine and norepinephrine
Ovary (female)	or Sex organs
Testes (male)	Produce hormones that affect bodily development and that maintain reproductive organs in adults

Other labels in figure: Hypothalamus, Kidney, Uterus

FIGURE 2-14

Location and function of the major endocrine glands. (Source: Rosenzwig & Leiman, 1982.)

The uncoordinated behavior characteristic of a person who has been drinking occurs because the ingestion of alcohol causes a reduction in the activity of the cerebellum. (Dan Chidester/The Image Works)

Limbic system: The part of the brain located outside the "new brain" that controls eating and reproduction

Despite its label as the "master gland," the pituitary is actually a servant of the brain, which is ultimately responsible for the endocrine system's functioning. The brain regulates the internal balance of the body, ensuring that homeostasis is maintained through the hypothalamus. Moreover, the road from brain to endocrine system is not strictly a one-way street: Hormones may permanently modify the way in which brain cells are organized. For example, adult sexual behavior is thought to be affected by the production of hormones that modify cells in the hypothalamus.

PASSING BEYOND THE CENTRAL CORE: The Limbic System

In a bizarre view of the future, some science fiction writers have suggested that people will someday routinely have electrodes implanted in their brains, allowing them to receive tiny shocks that produce the sensation of pleasure by stimulating certain centers of the brain. When they feel upset, people will simply activate their electrodes to achieve an immediate high.

Although farfetched—and ultimately probably unachievable—such a futuristic fantasy is based on fact: The brain does have pleasure centers in an area known as the **limbic system.** Consisting of a series of interrelated structures, the limbic system borders the top of the central core and connects with it and with the cerebral cortex (located in Figure 2-12 roughly at the boundaries between the two colors).

The structures of the limbic system jointly control a variety of basic functions relating to self-preservation—such as eating, aggression, and reproduction—and injury to the limbic system can produce striking changes in behavior. It can turn animals that are usually docile and tame into belligerent savages. Conversely, those that are usually wild and uncontrollable may become meek and obedient (Fanelli, Burright & Donovick, 1983).

Probably the most thought-provoking finding to emerge from the study of the limbic system comes from research that has examined the effects of mild electric shocks to certain parts of the system (Olds & Milner, 1954). In one experiment, rats with an electrode implanted in their limbic systems were given the opportunity to pass an electric current through the electrode by pressing a bar. Even starving rats on their way to food would stop to press the bar as many times as they could. In fact, if allowed to do so, the rats would stimulate their limbic systems literally thousands of times an hour—until they collapsed with fatigue (Routtenberg & Lindy, 1965).

The extraordinarily pleasurable quality of certain kinds of limbic-system stimulation has also been found in humans, who have—usually as part of some treatment of brain dysfunction—received electrical stimulation to certain areas of the limbic system. Although they are at a loss to describe just what it feels like, these people report the experience to be intensely pleasurable—similar in some respects to sexual orgasm.

The limbic system also plays an important role in learning and memory, a finding demonstrated in patients with epilepsy who, in an attempt to stop their seizures, have had portions of the limbic system removed. Such individuals sometimes have difficulty learning and remembering new information. In one case (discussed again when we focus on memory in Chapter 6) a patient who had undergone surgery was unable to remember where he lived, although he had resided at the same address for eight years. Further, even though the patient was able to carry on animated conversations, he was unable, a few minutes later, to recall what had been discussed (Milner, 1966).

The limbic system, then, is involved in several important functions, including self-preservation, learning, memory, and the experience of pleasure. These functions are hardly unique to humans; in fact, the limbic system is sometimes referred to as the "animal brain" because its structures and functions are so similar to those of other mammals. To find that which is uniquely human, we need to turn to another part of the brain—the cerebral cortex.

RECAP AND REVIEW III

Recap

◀ The central core of the human brain—sometimes referred to as the "old brain"—is similar to that found in all vertebrates.

◀ If we trace the CNS from the top of the spinal cord up into the brain, the first structure we find is the medulla, which controls such functions as breathing and heartbeat. Next is the pons, which acts to transmit motor information. The cerebellum is involved in the control of motion.

◀ The reticular formation, extending from the medulla through the pons, arouses and activates the body but also censors outside stimulation during sleep.

◀ The thalamus acts primarily as a sensory-information relay center, whereas the hypothalamus maintains homeostasis, a steady internal environment for the body.

◀ The endocrine system, a chemical communication network that sends messages throughout the nervous system, secretes hormones, chemicals that affect the growth and function of the body.

◀ Eating and reproductive behavior are controlled to a large extent by the limbic system, which also produces an extraordinarily pleasurable experience when stimulated electrically.

Review

1. _____ is an emerging field of science that may revolutionize the detection and diagnosis of even subtle types of brain dysfunction.

2. BEAM stands for _____ _____ _____ _____ .

3. Breathing and heartbeat are controlled by that part of the central core of the brain known as the _____ .

4. "I was staggering drunk!" Jeff exclaimed. "Let me state it more technically," his roommate offered snidely. "You consumed an excess of liquor, which served to depress the activity of your _____ , which in turn caused your instability."

5. The structure of the brain which maintains the body's homeostasis is called the
   a. Reticular formation
   b. Hypothalamus
   c. Thalamus
   d. Pons

6. The _____ _____ activates the body into a state of arousal when it is startled.

7. Hormones which control growth are secreted by the _____ gland.

8. Experimental evidence has demonstrated that stimulating the limbic system produces extremely unpleasant feelings. True or false? _____

(Answers to review questions are on page 74.)

UP THE EVOLUTIONARY LADDER: THE CEREBRAL CORTEX

As we have moved up the spinal cord and into the brain, our discussion has centered on the areas of the brain that control functions similar to those found in less sophisticated organisms. But where, you may be asking, are the parts of the brain that enable humans to do the things they do best, things that distinguish humankind from all other animals? Those unique features of the human brain—indeed the very capabilities that allow you to come up with such a question in the first place—are embodied in the ability to think and remember. And the central location of these abilities, along with many others, is the **cerebral cortex**.

The cerebral cortex—sometimes called the "new brain" because of its relatively recent evolution—is a mass of deeply folded, rippled, convoluted tissue. Although it is only about one-twelfth of an inch thick, if flattened out it would cover a 2½-foot-square area. This physical configuration allows the surface area of the cortex to be considerably greater than if it were more loosely and smoothly packed into the skull. It also allows the neurons within the cortex to be intricately connected to one another, permitting the highest level of integration of neural communication within the brain, and therefore the most sophisticated processing of information.

Cerebral cortex: The "new brain," responsible for the most sophisticated information processing in the brain; contains the lobes

The lobes of the brain. (A. Glaubermann/ Photo Researchers, Inc.)

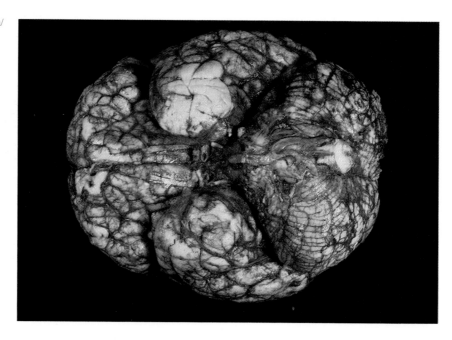

The cortex has four major sections, called **lobes**. If we take a side view of the brain, the **frontal lobes** lie at the front center of the cortex, and the **parietal lobes** lie behind them. The **temporal lobes** are found in the lower center of the brain, with the **occipital lobes** lying behind them. These four sets of lobes are physically separated by deep grooves called sulci. Figure 2-15*a* shows the four areas.

Another way of describing the brain is by considering the functions associated with a given area. Figure 2-15*b* shows the specialized regions within the lobes related to specific functions and areas of the body. Three major areas have been discovered: the motor area, the sensory and somatosensory area, and the association area. Although we will discuss them as though they were separate and independent entities, this is something of an

Lobes: Major structures of the brain

Frontal lobes: The brain structure located at the front center of the cortex containing major motor and speech and reasoning centers

Parietal lobes: The brain structure to the rear of the frontal lobes; the center for bodily sensations

Temporal lobes: The portion of the brain located beneath the frontal and parietal lobes

Occipital lobes: The structures of the brain lying behind the temporal lobes

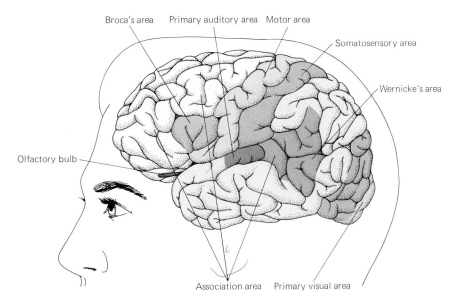

FIGURE 2-15

The cerebral cortex of the brain. (*a*) The major physical *structures* of the cerebral cortex are called lobes. (*b*) This figure illustrates the *functions* associated with particular areas of the cerebral cortex.

Frontal lobe

Parietal lobe

Occipital lobe

Temporal lobe

(a)

Broca's area   Primary auditory area   Motor area

Somatosensory area

Wernicke's area

Olfactory bulb

Association area   Primary visual area

(b)

THE BIOLOGICAL FOUNDATIONS
OF PSYCHOLOGY

oversimplification: In most instances, behavior is influenced simultaneously by several structures and areas within the brain, operating interdependently.

THE MOTOR AREA OF THE BRAIN

Motor area: One of the major areas of the brain, responsible for voluntary movement of particular parts of the body

If you look at the frontal lobe in Figure 2-15*b*, you will see a shaded portion labeled the **motor area**. This part of the brain is largely responsible for voluntary movement of particular parts of the body. In fact, every portion of the motor area corresponds to a specific locale within the body. If we were to insert an electrode into a particular part of the motor area of the brain and apply mild electrical stimulation, there would be involuntary movement in the corresponding part of the body (Kertesz, 1983). If we moved to another part of the motor area and stimulated it, a different part of the body would move.

The motor area has been so well mapped that it is possible to devise the kind of schematic representation shown in Figure 2-16. This weird-looking model illustrates the amount and relative location of cortical tissue that is used to produce movement in specific parts of the human body. As you can see, the control of body movements that are relatively large-scale and require little precision—such as movement of a knee or a hip—is centered in a very small space in the motor area. On the other hand, movements that must be precise and delicate—such as facial expressions and the use of the fingers—are controlled by a considerably larger portion of the motor area. In sum, the brain's motor area provides a clear guide to the degree of complexity and the importance of the motor capabilities of specific parts of the body.

THE SENSORY AREA OF THE BRAIN

Given the one-to-one correspondence between motor area and body location, it is not surprising to find a similar relationship between specific por-

FIGURE 2-16

The correspondence between the amount and location of tissue in the brain's motor area and the specific body parts where movement is controlled by that tissue. (Penfield & Rasmussen, 1950.)

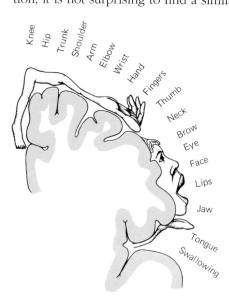

tions of the brain and the senses. The **sensory area** of the cortex includes three regions: one that corresponds primarily to touch, one relating to sight, and a third relating to sound. The **somatosensory area** encompasses specific locations associated with the ability to perceive touch in a specific area of the body. As with the motor area, the amount of brain tissue related to a specific body part determines the degree of sensitivity of that part: The greater the space within the brain, the more sensitive the part. As you can see from Figure 2-17, parts such as the fingers are related to proportionally more space in the sensory area and are the most sensitive.

The senses of sound and sight also are represented in specific areas of the cerebral cortex. An auditory area located in the temporal lobe is responsible for the sense of hearing. If the auditory area is stimulated electrically, a person will hear sounds such as clicks or hums. It also appears that particular locations within the auditory area respond to specific pitches.

The visual center in the brain operates analogously to the other sensory areas; stimulation by electrodes produces the experience of flashes of light or colors, suggesting that the raw sensory input of images from the eyes is received in this area of the brain and transformed into meaningful stimuli. The visual area also provides another example of how areas of the brain are intimately related to specific areas of the body: Particular areas of the eye are related to a particular part of the brain—with, as you might guess, more space in the brain given to the most sensitive portions of the eye.

THE ASSOCIATION AREA OF THE BRAIN

Twenty-five-year-old Phineas Gage, a railroad employee, was blasting rock one day in 1848 when an accidental explosion punched a 3½-foot-long spike, about an inch in diameter, completely through his skull. The spike entered just under his left cheek, came out the top of his head, and flew into the air. He immediately suffered a series of convulsions,

Sensory area: The site in the brain of the tissue that corresponds to each of the senses, with the degree of sensitivity relating to the amount of tissue

Somatosensory area: The area within the cortex corresponding to the sense of touch

FIGURE 2-17

If the parts of our bodies reflected proportionally the space that the brain gives to the body parts' sensations, we might look like this strange creature. (British Museum of Natural History.)

THE BIOLOGICAL FOUNDATIONS
OF PSYCHOLOGY

yet a few minutes later was talking with rescuers. In fact, he was able to walk up a long flight of stairs before receiving any medical attention. Amazingly, after a few weeks his wound healed, and he was physically close to his old self again. Mentally, however, there was a difference: Once a careful and hard-working person, Phineas now became enamored with wild schemes and was flighty and often irresponsible. As one of his physicians put it, "Previous to his injury, though untrained in the schools, he possessed a well-balanced mind, and was looked upon by those who knew him as a shrewd, smart businessman, very energetic and persistent in executing all his plans of operation. In this regard his mind was radically changed, so decidedly that his friends and acquaintances said he was 'no longer Gage' " (Harlow, 1869, p. 14).

What had happened to the old Gage? Although there is no way of knowing for sure—science being what it was in the 1800s—we might speculate that the accident may have injured the association area of Gage's cerebral hemisphere.

If you return one last time to our diagram of the cerebral cortex (Figure 2-15b), you will find that the motor and sensory areas take up a relatively small portion of the cortex; the remainder contains the association area. The **association area** is generally considered to be the site of higher mental processes such as thinking, language, memory, and speech. Most of our understanding of the association area comes from patients who have suffered some brain injury—from natural causes such as a tumor or a stroke, either of which would block certain blood vessels within the cerebral cortex, or, as in the case of Phineas Gage, from accidental causes. Damage to this area can result in unusual behavioral changes, indicating the importance of the association area to normal functioning.

Consider, for instance, the condition known as **apraxia**. Apraxia occurs when a person is unable to integrate activities in a rational or logical manner. For example, a patient asked to get a soda from the refrigerator might go to the refrigerator and open and close the door repeatedly, or might take bottle after bottle of soda out of the refrigerator, dropping each to the floor. Similarly, a person with apraxia who is asked to open a lock with a key may be unable to do so in response to the request—but, if simply left alone in a locked room, wishing to leave, will unlock the door (Lechtenberg, 1982).

Apraxia is clearly not a muscular problem, since the person is capable of carrying out the individual components of the overall behavior. Moreover, if asked to perform the individual components of a larger behavioral pattern one at a time, a patient is often quite successful. It is only when asked to carry out a sequence of behaviors requiring a degree of planning and foresight that the patient shows deficits. It appears, then, that the association area may act as a kind of "master planner," that is, the organizer of actions.

Other difficulties that arise because of injury to the association area of the brain relate to the use of language. Problems with verbal expression, known as **aphasia**, can take many forms. In **Broca's aphasia** (caused by damage to the part of the brain first identified by a French physician, Paul Broca), speech becomes halting and laborious. The speaker is unable to find the right words—in a kind of tip-of-the-tongue phenomenon that we all experience from time to time—except that in the case of the person with aphasia, it happens almost constantly. Patients with aphasia also speak in "verbal

Association area: One of the major areas of the brain, the site of the higher mental processes such as thought, language, memory, and speech

Apraxia: The inability to perform activities in a logical way

Aphasia: A disorder resulting in problems with verbal expression due to brain injury

Broca's aphasia: A syndrome in which speech production is disturbed

THE BRAIN TRANSPLANT: SOLVING OLD PROBLEMS—AND CREATING NEW ONES?

The successful operation carried out on Nelson Martinez (described at the beginning of this chapter), in which he received relief from the symptoms of Parkinson's disease by having cells from his adrenal glands transplanted into his brain, raises the possibility of a far more radical procedure in the future: the brain transplant. Although it sounds like something out of a science fiction movie, scientists are taking some tentative first steps toward making such an eerie prospect come true.

In 1976, scientists successfully performed the essential first step in the brain transplant process (White, 1976). They removed the brain of a chimpanzee and kept it alive for more than twenty-four hours by supplying it with oxygen and other essential nutrients. More recent research with Parkinson's patients like Martinez has provided further evidence of the possibilities inherent in brain transplants (Snyder, 1987; Lewin, 1987).

Such work is promising, raising the possibility that damaged areas of the brain may someday be routinely repaired by the introduction of compatible, healthy cells. Similar procedures may prove useful in providing therapy for a variety of problems of the nervous system, including strokes, spinal cord injuries, and brain tumors (Rosenberg et al., 1988). However, the possibility of an actual brain transplant raises a set of psychological and ethical issues that transplants of other organs do not. One issue concerns the distinction between the mind and the body, an ancient philosophical question that we discuss in Chapter 11. If we assume that the mind is separate from the body, whose mind will regulate the recipient's body—the do-

nor's or the recipient's? If we reject the separation of body and mind—as most psychologists do—we have a hard-to-imagine situation: a new mind taking control of the recipient's body.

Brain transplants hold out even more complexities. Because others frequently react to us on the basis of our physical appearance (as we shall see in Chapter 18), a brain inhabiting someone else's body would have to adjust to a whole new set of reactions from others. Who would this new brain-in-a-body be?

While these issues may not be of immediate concern, they must be considered carefully because of their implications. And they may need to be addressed sooner than we think: In the words of neurologist Abraham Lieberman, "Five years ago, when you talked about brain transplantation, you were talking about Boris Karloff and Frankenstein. Today it's no longer science fiction" (Jaroff, 1987, p. 57).

telegrams." A phrase like "I put the book on the table" comes out as "I . . . put . . . book . . . table" (Lechtenberg, 1982).

In **Wernicke's aphasia**, named for its discoverer, Carl Wernicke, there are difficulties in understanding the language of others. Found in patients with damage to a particular area of brain first identified by Wernicke, the disorder produces speech that appears to be fluent—but makes no sense. For instance, one Wernicke's patient, Philip Gorgan, was asked what brought him to the hospital. He replied, "Boy, I'm sweating, I'm awful nervous, you know, once in a while I get caught up, I can't mention the tarripoi, a month ago, quite a little, I've done a lot well, I impose a lot, while, on the other hand, you know what I mean, I have to run around, look it over, trebbin and all that sort of stuff" (Gardner, 1975, p. 68).

Wernicke's aphasia: A syndrome involving problems with understanding language, resulting in fluent but nonsensical speech

TWO BRAINS OR ONE?: THE SPECIALIZATION OF THE HEMISPHERES

The most recent development—at least in evolutionary terms—in the organization and operation of our brain probably occurred in the last million

THE BIOLOGICAL FOUNDATIONS
OF PSYCHOLOGY

Hemispheres: Symmetrical left and right halves of the brain

Lateralization: The dominance of one hemisphere of the brain in specific functions

years: a specialization of the functions controlled by the two sides of the brain, which has symmetrical left and right halves.

Specifically, the brain structure can be divided into two roughly similar mirror-image halves—just as we have two arms, two legs, and two lungs. Because of the way nerves are connected from the brain to the rest of the body, these two symmetrical left and right halves, called **hemispheres,** control the side of body opposite to their location. The left hemisphere of the brain, then, generally controls the right side of the body, and the right hemisphere controls the left side of the body. Thus damage to the right side of the brain is typically indicated by functional difficulties in the left side of the body.

Yet the structural similarity between the two hemispheres of the brain is not reflected in all aspects of its functioning; it appears that certain activities are more likely to occur in one hemisphere than in the other. Early evidence for the functional differences between halves of the brain came from studies of people with aphasia; researchers found that people with the speech difficulties characteristic of aphasia tended to have physical damage to the left hemisphere of the brain. In contrast, physical abnormalities in the right hemisphere of the brain tended to produce far fewer problems with language (Corballis & Beales, 1983). The conclusion? For most people, language is **lateralized,** or located more in one hemisphere than the other—in this case, in the left side of the brain.

It now seems clear that the two hemispheres of the brain specialize in different functions. The left hemisphere concentrates on tasks that require verbal strength, such as speaking, reading, thinking, and reasoning. The right hemisphere has its own strengths, particularly in nonverbal areas such as spatial understanding, recognition of patterns and drawings, music, and emotional expression (see Figure 2-18).

In addition, the way in which information is processed seems somewhat different in each hemisphere: The left hemisphere considers information sequentially, one bit at a time, while the right hemisphere tends to process information globally, considering it as a whole (Gazzaniga, 1983; Levy, 1983; Springer & Deutsch, 1985.) Moreover, there is even evidence suggesting that

FIGURE 2-18

This series of PET scans shows the activity of the left and right hemispheres while the person is performing various activities. (Courtesy of J. C. Mazziotta and M. E. Phelps, UCLA School of Medicine.)

the two hemispheres develop at slightly different rates during the course of people's lives (Thatcher, Walker & Giudice, 1987, Hahn, 1987).

There is also great variation in the degree and nature of lateralization from one person to another. If, like most people, you are right-handed, the portion of your brain that controls language is probably concentrated on the left side of your brain. By contrast, if you are among the 10 percent of people who are left-handed or are ambidextrous (you use both hands interchangeably), it is much more likely that the language centers of your brain are located in the right hemisphere or are divided equally between left and right hemispheres (Geschwind & Galaburda, 1985; Gazzaniga, 1985; Beaton, 1986).

It also turns out that males and females show some intriguing sex differences in brain lateralization. Most males tend to show greater lateralization of language in the left hemisphere: For them, language is clearly relegated largely to the left side of the brain. In contrast, women display less lateralization, with language abilities apt to be more evenly divided between the two hemispheres (Gur et al., 1982). Such differences in brain lateralization may account, in part, for the superiority of females often found on some measures of verbal skills, such as the onset and fluency of speech.

You can readily demonstrate which half of someone's brain is processing information by looking at the direction in which the eyes move when the person is thinking of the answer to a question. To try this, ask someone to perform the following tasks and watch to see in what direction his or her eyes move. If the person's eyes move to the right, it suggests that the subject is using the left half of the brain; if they move to the left, it suggests that the individual is using the right half. (This will work only if your subject is right-handed; left-handed people show great variability.)

1. Think of what your mother looked like the last time she got angry with you.

2. Use a sentence with the words "brain" and "behavior."

3. Describe the last sunset you saw.

4. Define the word "lateralization."

Because items 1 and 3 call upon primarily spatial and emotional abilities, most people use right-hemisphere processing and therefore should look toward the left. In contrast, items 2 and 4 call for verbal skills, resulting in left-hemisphere processing; people usually look to the right when responding (Schwartz, Davidson & Maer, 1975).

Is the functioning of one hemisphere more important than that of the other? The fact that language and formal reasoning capabilities are two of the primary functions that distinguish humans from other species might seem to suggest that the left hemisphere is of greater importance. The issue, however, is really a matter of values. In our computerized western culture, a brain that operates in a logical, sequential fashion might be preferred. But there are many cultures in which thinking proceeds in a less direct and less logical fashion and is organized pictorially rather than mathematically and verbally. In cultures such as these, a strong right hemisphere might be preferable (Annett, 1985).

Luckily, none of us has to choose between the two hemispheres of our brains; unless there is brain damage, both halves will be intact and will function together and interdependently (Best, 1985; Kosslyn, 1988). Moreover, people (especially young children) who suffer brain damage to the left side of their brain and lose linguistic capabilities often recover the ability to speak—because the right side of the brain pitches in and takes over some of the functioning of the left side (Weiderhold, 1982). The brain, then, is remarkably adaptable and can modify its functioning—to some extent at least—in respect to adverse circumstances (McConnell, 1985; Beaton, 1986; Kucharski & Hall, 1987).

The differences in hemispheric functioning at least suggest the possibility that there may be individual differences in the strengths of each hemisphere. For example, we might speculate that a talented writer has a brain in which the left side is particularly dominant, while an artist or architect might have more strength in the right hemisphere. What we do best in life, then, may be a function of which side of our brain has the greater strengths. (For a view of the way the two hemispheres work together and separately, see the Research Classics box.)

RESEARCH CLASSICS

When the seizures first started, Cindy Gluccles thought her physician would be able to give her a drug that would prevent their recurrence. Her physician and her neurologist were both optimistic, maintaining that in most cases seizures could be controlled with the proper drugs. But the seizures got worse and more frequent, and no drug treatment seemed to help. Further examination revealed that the seizures were caused by remarkably large bursts of electrical activity that were starting in one hemisphere and moving to the other. Finally, her doctors prescribed a last-ditch measure: surgically cutting the bundle of nerves that connected the two hemispheres to each other. Almost magically, the seizures stopped. The operation was clearly a success—but was Cindy the same person she had been before the operation?

That issue has evoked a great deal of interest on the part of brain researchers and, in fact, has earned a Nobel Prize for Roger Sperry. Sperry, with a group of colleagues, explored the behavior of patients who had had the links between the two hemispheres of the brain surgically cut. The research team found that, in most ways, there were no

UNDERSTANDING THE TWO HEMISPHERES: SPLIT-BRAIN PATIENTS

major changes in either personality or intelligence.

On the other hand, patients like Cindy Gluccles, called **split-brain patients,** did occasionally display some unusual behavior. For instance, one patient reported pulling his pants down with one hand and simultaneously pulling them up with the other. In addition, he mentioned grabbing his wife with his left hand and shaking her violently, while his right hand tried to help his wife by bringing his left hand under control (Gazzaniga, 1970).

Interest in this occasional curious behavior, however, was peripheral to the rare opportunity that split-brain patients provided for research in the independent functioning of the two hemispheres of the brain, and Sperry developed a number of ingenious techniques for studying how each hemisphere operated (Sperry, 1982). In one experimental procedure, blindfolded subjects were allowed to touch an object with their right hand and were asked to name it. Because the right side of the body

is connected to the left side of the brain—the hemisphere that is most responsible for language—the split-brain patient was able to name it. But if the blindfolded subject touched the object with his or her left hand, naming it aloud was not possible. However, the information had registered: When the blindfold was taken off, the subject could choose the object that he or she had touched. Information can be learned and remembered, then, using only the right side of the brain. (By the way, this experiment won't work with you—unless you have had a split-brain operation—since the nerves connecting the two halves of a normal brain immediately transfer the information from one half of the brain to the other.)

In another demonstration of the relative independence and specialization of the two hemispheres, Sperry and his colleague Michael Gazzaniga asked a split-brain patient to match a relatively simple pattern shown in a picture using a four-block puzzle which, when put together, could produce the figure in the picture (Springer & Deutsch, 1985). When using his left hand—which is controlled by the right side of the brain, the "specialist" in visual patterns—the patient had little trouble arranging the puzzle to match the drawing. But when asked to use his right hand, which is controlled by the less spatially oriented left hemisphere, the patient had grave difficulties. In fact, at one point, the patient's left hand reached toward the blocks, in an apparent effort to help the less adept right hand.

It is clear from experiments such as these that the right and left hemispheres of the brain specialize in handling different sorts of information. At the same time, it is important to realize that they are both capable of understanding, knowing, and being aware of the world—although in somewhat different ways. The two hemispheres, then, should be seen as different in terms of the efficiency with which they process certain kinds of information, rather than viewed as two entirely separate brains. Moreover, in people with normal, nonsplit brains, the hemispheres work interdependently to allow the full range and richness of thought of which humans are capable.

Split-brain patient: A person who suffers from independent functioning of the two halves of the brain, as a result of which the sides of the body work in disharmony

---

THE INFORMED CONSUMER OF PSYCHOLOGY: Learning to Control Your Heart—and Brain—through Biofeedback

When her blood pressure rose to unacceptably high levels, Carla Lewitt was first given the option of undergoing a standard treatment with drugs. When she asked whether there was any alternative, her physician suggested an approach that would entail her learning to control her blood pressure voluntarily. Although Carla didn't think she was capable of controlling something she wasn't even aware of, she agreed to give it a try. Within three weeks, her blood pressure had come down to normal levels.

▲ ▲ ▲

Bill Jackson had experienced excruciatingly painful headaches all his life. No drug seemed to stop them, and they were often accompanied by a loss of appetite and vomiting. When a friend suggested he try a new procedure designed to enable him to voluntarily control the headaches by learning to control the constriction of muscles in his head, he laughed. "I've been trying to learn to stop these headaches all my life," he said, "and it's never worked." Convinced by his friend that it was worth a try, though, he went to a psychologist specializing in biofeedback—and in four weeks had put an end to his headaches.

We typically think of our heart, respiration rate, blood pressure, and other bodily functions as being under the control of parts of the brain over which we have no influence. But, as the cases above illustrate, psychologists are finding that what were once thought of as entirely involuntary biological responses are proving to be susceptible to voluntary control—and, in the process, they are learning about important treatment techniques for a variety of ailments.

The technique that both lowered Carla Lewitt's blood pressure and stopped Bill Jackson's headaches was the same: biofeedback. **Biofeedback** is a procedure in which a person learns to control internal physiological processes such as blood pressure, heart rate, respiration speed, skin temperature, sweating, and constriction of certain muscles (Yates, 1980).

How can people learn to control such responses, which are typically considered "involuntary"? They do so through training with electronic de-

Biofeedback: A technique for learning to control internal physiological processes through conscious thought

Psychologist Weinstock uses biofeedback to help patients. (Dan McCoy/Rainbow)

vices that provide continuous feedback on the physiological response in question. For instance, a person interested in controlling her blood pressure might be hooked up to an apparatus that constantly monitors and displays her blood pressure. As she consciously thinks about altering the pressure, she receives immediate feedback as to the measure of her success. In this way she can eventually learn to bring her pressure under control. Similarly, if an individual wanted to control headaches through biofeedback, he might have electronic sensors placed on certain muscles in his head and thereby learn to control the constriction and relaxation of those muscles. Then, when he felt a headache coming on, he could relax the relevant muscles and abort the pain.

While the control of physiological processes through the use of biofeedback is not easy to learn, it has been employed with success in a variety of ailments, including emotional problems (such as anxiety, depression, phobias, tension headaches, insomnia, and hyperactivity); medical problems with a psychological component (such as asthma, high blood pressure, ulcers, muscle spasms, and migraine headaches); and physical problems (such as nerve-muscle injuries due to stroke, cerebral palsy, and—as we see in Figure 2-19—curvature of the spine).

Given that biofeedback is still experimental, we cannot assume that treatment is going to be successful in every case (Roberts, 1985). What is certain, however, is that learning through biofeedback has opened up a number of exciting possibilities for treating people with physical and psychological problems. Moreover, some psychologists speculate that the use of biofeedback may become a part of everyday life one day in the future.

For instance, one researcher has suggested that students whose minds wander during studying might be hooked up to apparatus that gives them feedback as to whether they are paying attention to the information they are studying (Ornstein, 1977). If they stop paying attention, the computer will alert them—putting them back on the right track.

FIGURE 2-19

The traditional treatment for curvature of the spine employs an unsightly, cumbersome brace. In contrast, biofeedback treatment employs an unobtrusive set of straps attached to a small electronic device that produces tonal feedback when the patient is not standing straight. The person learns to maintain a position that gradually decreases the curvature of the spine until the device is no longer needed. [*Miller, 1985(a).*]

Recap

◀ The cerebral cortex contains three major areas: the motor, sensory, and association areas. These areas control voluntary movement, the senses, and higher mental processes (including thought, language, memory, and speech), respectively.

◀ The two halves, or hemispheres, of the brain are structurally similar, but they seem to specialize in different functions. The left side of the brain is most closely related to language and verbal skills; the right side, to nonverbal skills such as mathematical and musical ability, emotional expression, pattern recognition, and the processing of visual information.

◀ Biofeedback is a procedure in which a person learns to control certain internal physiological processes, thereby bringing relief to a variety of specific ailments.

Review

1. The _____ lobes lie behind the frontal lobes, and the _____ lobes lie behind the temporal lobes.
2. The motor, sensory, and associative areas each influence behavior independently of the others. True or false? _____
3. Fine motor movements are controlled by a larger portion of the motor area of the cerebral cortex than are gross motor movements. True or false? _____
4. Touch, sight, and hearing are associated with what area within the cerebral cortex? _____
5. As a result of an injury to the association area of the brain, the patient was subsequently unable to understand what was said to her. This condition is labeled
   a. Broca's aphasia
   b. Wernicke's aphasia
   c. Apraxia
   d. Broca's apraxia
6. Men and women show equally great lateralization of language in the left hemisphere. True or false? _____
7. When Sam is asked a series of questions, his eyes shift reliably to the right as he thinks about each answer. This demonstrates that he is using the _____ half of his brain.
8. Biofeedback can be used in the treatment of
   a. Migraine headaches
   b. Muscle spasms
   c. Emotional problems
   d. All of the above

(Answers to review questions are on page 84.)

◀ LOOKING BACK

1. In this chapter we have seen that understanding human behavior requires knowledge of the biological influences underlying that behavior. This chapter reviews what biopsychologists (psychologists who specialize in studying the effects of biological structures and functions on behavior) have learned about the human nervous system.
2. Neurons, the most basic elements of the nervous system, allow nerve impulses to pass from one part of the body to another. Information generally enters a neuron through its dendrite, is passed on to other cells via its axon, and finally exits through its terminal buttons.
3. Most neurons are protected by a coating called the myelin sheath. When a neuron receives a message to fire, it releases an action potential, an electric charge that travels through the cell. Neurons operate according to an all-or-none law: They are either at rest or an action potential is moving through them. There is no in-between state.
4. Once a neuron fires, nerve impulses are carried to other neurons through the production of chemical substances, neurotransmitters, which actually bridge the gaps—known as synapses—between neurons. Neurotransmitters may be either excitatory, telling other neurons to fire, or inhibitory, preventing or decreasing the likelihood of other neurons firing. Among the major neurotransmitters are acetylcholine (ACh), which produces contractions of skeletal muscles, and dopamine, which has been linked to Parkinson's disease and certain mental disorders such as schizophrenia and Alzheimer's disease.
5. Endorphins, another type of neurotransmitter, are related to the reduction of pain. By interacting with opiate receptors—specialized neurons that reduce the experience of pain—they seem to produce a natural kind of morphine and are probably responsible for creating the kind of euphoria that joggers sometimes experience after running.
6. The nervous system is made up of the central nervous system (the brain and spinal cord) and the peripheral nervous system (the remainder of the nervous system). The peripheral nervous system is made up of the somatic division, which controls voluntary movements and the communication of information to and from the sense

organs, and the autonomic division, which controls involuntary functions such as those of the heart, blood vessels, and lungs.

7. The autonomic division of the peripheral nervous system is further subdivided into the sympathetic and parasympathetic divisions. The sympathetic division prepares the body in emergency situations, and the parasympathetic division helps the body return to its typical resting state.

8. The central core of the brain is made up of the medulla (which controls such functions as breathing and the heartbeat), the pons (which coordinates the muscles and the two sides of the body), the cerebellum (which controls balance), the reticular formation (which acts to heighten awareness in emergencies), the thalamus (which communicates messages to and from the brain), and the hypothalamus (which maintains homeostasis, or body equilibrium, and regulates basic survival behaviors). The functions of the central core structures are similar to those found in other vertebrates; this part of the brain is sometimes referred to as the "old brain."

9. The endocrine system secretes hormones, allowing the brain to send messages throughout the body. Its major component is the pituitary gland, which affects growth. The limbic system, found on the border of the "old" and "new" brains, is associated with eating, reproduction, and the experiences of pleasure and pain.

10. The cerebral cortex—the "new brain"—has areas that control voluntary movement (the motor area); the senses (the sensory area); and thinking, reasoning, speech, and memory (the association area). It is divided into two halves, or hemispheres, each of which generally controls the opposite side of the body from that in which it is located. However, each hemisphere can be thought of as specialized in the functions it carries out: The left is best at verbal tasks, such as logical reasoning, speaking, and reading; the right is best at nonverbal tasks, such as spatial understanding, pattern recognition, and emotional expression.

11. Biofeedback is a procedure in which a person learns to control internal physiological processes. By controlling what were previously considered involuntary responses, people are able to relieve anxiety, tension, migraine headaches, and a wide range of other psychological and physical problems.

KEY TERMS AND CONCEPTS ▶

nervous system (p. 48)
neuroscientist (49)
biopsychologist (49)
neuron (51)
dendrite (51)
axon (51)
terminal button (51)
myelin sheath (52)
all-or-none law (53)
resting state (53)
action potential (53)
absolute refractory period (53)
relative refractory period (53)
synapse (55)
neurotransmitter (55)
excitatory message (56)
inhibitory message (56)
reuptake (56)
acetylcholine (57)
Alzheimer's disease (58)
dopamine (58)
endorphin (58)
opiate receptor (58)
central nervous system (59)
spinal cord (59)

reflexes (60)
sensory (afferent) neurons (60)
motor (efferent) neurons (60)
interneurons (60)
paraplegia (61)
peripheral nervous system (61)
somatic division (61)
autonomic division (61)
sympathetic division (61)
parasympathetic division (61)
brain scan (64)
electroencephalogram (EEG) (65)
computerized axial tomography (CAT)
    scan (65)
neurometrics (66)
brain electrical activity mapping
    (BEAM) (66)
nuclear magnetic resonance (NMR)
    scan (66)
positron emission tomograph (PET)
    scan (66)
central core (66)
medulla (68)
pons (68)
cerebellum (68)

reticular formation (68)
thalamus (69)
hypothalamus (69)
homeostasis (69)
endocrine system (69)
hormones (69)
pituitary gland (69)
limbic system (70)
cerebral cortex (70)
frontal lobes (70)
parietal lobes (70)
temporal lobes (70)
occipital lobes (70)
motor area of the brain (74)
sensory area of the brain (74)
somatosensory area of the brain (74)
association areas of the brain (76)
apraxia (76)
aphasia (76)
Broca's aphasia (76)
Wernicke's aphasia (77)
hemisphere (78)
lateralization (78)
split-brain patient (81)
biofeedback (81)

ANSWERS (REVIEW IV):
1. Parietal, occipital **2.** False; separating the three areas helps us discuss different functions but is in actuality an oversimplification **3.** True **4.** Sensory area **5.** b **6.** False; women's language abilities tend to be more evenly divided between the two hemispheres **7.** Left **8.** d

<h2>FOR FURTHER STUDY AND APPLICATION ▶</h2>

Carlson, N. R. (1988). *Foundations of physiological psychology.* Boston: Allyn & Bacon.

This text provides a comprehensive view of the physiological underpinnings of human behavior while remaining readable and straightforward.

Netter, F. H. (1953). *The Ciba collection of medical illustrations (Vol. 1: Nervous system).* Summit, NJ: Ciba Pharmaceutical Co.

Although some aspects of these illustrations are dated, they are for the most part the best drawings we have of the human nervous system. The drawings convey a sense of the intricacies and marvels underlying the operation of our bodies.

Wiederhold, W. C. (Ed.). (1982). *Neurology for non-neurologists.* New York: Academic Press.

This volume provides a series of chapters, written by experts but designed for the nonexpert, on various disorders of the nervous system and on methods of treatment.

Gardner, H. (1974). *The shattered mind: The person after brain damage.* New York: Random House.

This fascinating book discusses a number of case histories of individuals who have suffered brain damage in light of what their difficulties might suggest about normal brain function.

Baskin, Y. (1983, August). Interview with Roger Sperry. *OMNI,* pp. 68–73, 98–100.

An insightful interview with one of the pioneers and leading experts on the brain, this article summarizes his accomplishments and discusses where work on the brain is heading.

Penfield, W. (1975). *The mystery of the mind.* Princeton, NJ: Princeton University Press.

Written by an expert on the brain, this book provides fascinating glimpses into the operation and mysteries of the mind.

Bloom, F. E., & Lazerson, A. (1988). *Brain, mind, and behavior* (2nd ed.). New York: W. H. Freeman.

This book provides an up-to-date discussion of the brain, with some beautiful illustrations.

Springer, S. P., & Deutsch, G. (1985). *Left brain, right brain.* New York: W. H. Freeman.

This text gives an excellent overview of the differences in strengths between the brain's left and right hemispheres.

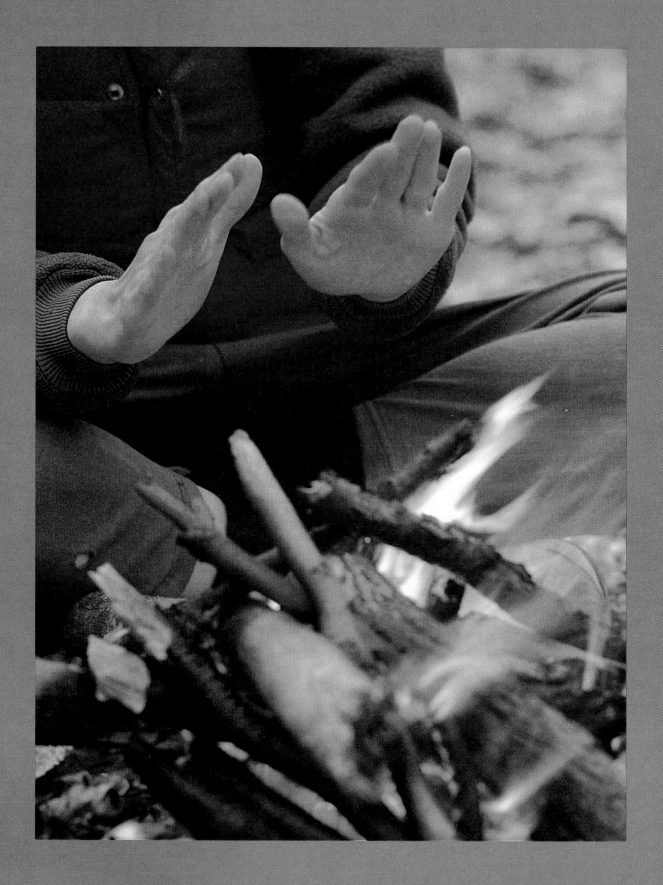

CHAPTER 3

SENSATION

PROLOGUE:
GALE SCHOENLEBER

Gale Schoenleber and her daughter. (*Brad Bower/Picture Group*)

The pain of childbirth was nothing compared with the headaches Gale Schoenleber experienced for years. A 36-year-old Pennsylvania mother, Schoenleber had her first severe headache when she was 12, and the attacks grew worse over the years. They became so intense that she would go to the hospital for shots of morphine, and during one recent year she spent two months in bed. She lost weight—and she lost self-esteem, unable as she was to live a normal existence.

Schoenleber suffered from migraine headaches, a severe form of headache so painful that sufferers are almost at a loss for words to describe it. Some call migraines "throbbing," "hammerlike," or "burning." Author Joan Didion says they start like a "pounding terror," and the fact "that no one dies of migraine seems, to someone deep into an attack, an ambiguous blessing."

For Schoenleber, however, all this changed when she was referred to Seymour Solomon, director of the headache unit at Montefiore Medical Center in New York. Solomon immediately prescribed a change in medicine, placing Shoenleber on a mild tranquilizer and increasing the dosage of a beta blocker, a kind of drug that reduces arousal in certain parts of the nervous system. The result of the new treatment: Schoenleber hasn't had a headache since.

Unfortunately, Schoenleber still has to deal with headaches—those of her 8-year-old daughter, Michele. Migraine headaches run in families, and Michele seems to be developing severe headaches similar to those suffered by her mother for so many years. At least now, however, Schoenleber's freedom from pain allows her to care for her daughter, something she was unable to do before her own successful treatment (Monmaney, 1987).

LOOKING AHEAD ▶

Fortunately, most of us do not suffer the debilitating pain of migraine headaches. Yet the presence of this kind of misery among our fellow human beings clearly illustrates the profound effect our bodily sensations have on our day-to-day behavior.

Pain, of course, is just one of the sensations to which we are sensitive; we respond also to light, sound, tastes, smells, and a variety of other stimulation that comes from the world around us. In this chapter we focus on the area of psychology concerned with the nature of information our body takes in through its senses. Our senses provide us with a tie to the reality of the outside world and permit us to develop our own understanding of what is happening to us. To a psychologist who is interested in the causes of behavior, then, sensation represents an elemental topic, since so much of our behavior is based on our reactions to the stimulation we receive from the world around us.

In this chapter, we will be concerned with how physical stimulation (energy that produces a response in a sense organ) is translated into our own personal sensory experience. We will consider issues ranging from such basics as identifying the fundamentals of vision and hearing to understanding how we know whether ice or fire is colder, how we can tell whether sugar or lemon is sweeter, and how we distinguish a backfiring car from the barking of a dog.

After reading this chapter, then, you will be able to answer questions such as the following:

▶ How keen are the senses?

▶ What is the relationship between the nature of a physical stimulus and the kinds of sensory responses that result from it?

▶ What are the major senses, and what are the basic mechanisms that underlie their operation?

As we explore these questions, we will see how the senses work together to provide us with an integrated view and understanding of the world.

SENSING THE WORLD AROUND US

To someone lying on the quiet shore of a lake, the environment may seem serene and tranquil—a silent refuge from the sights and sounds of a clamorous world. Yet to members of nonhuman species, more acute in their natural abilities, the same lake may provide a challenge in sorting out the many stimuli that are actually present—stimuli that people, because of the limitations of the human body, cannot detect through their senses.

To a dog wandering by, for instance, the lake may unleash an enticing set of smells, a symphony of random sounds, and a bustling scene of swarming insects and other tiny organisms. Furthermore, the area abounds with other forms of physical energy, of which no person or animal, nor any other living organism, has an awareness: radio waves, ultraviolet light, and tones that are extremely high or low in pitch.

To understand how a psychologist might consider such a scene, we first need a basic working vocabulary. In formal terms, if any passing source of physical energy activates a sense organ, the energy is known as a **stimulus.** A stimulus, then, is energy that produces a response in a sense organ. The

Stimulus: A source of physical energy that activates a sense organ

This tranquil scene is actually teeming with stimuli, most of which are not perceived by the human sensory system. (*James H. Simon/The Picture Cube.*)

Sensation: The process by which an organism responds to a stimulus

Magnitude: The strength of a stimulus

Psychophysics: The study of the relationship between the physical nature of stimuli and a person's sensory responses to them

Absolute threshold: The smallest amount of physical intensity by which a stimulus can be detected

term **sensation** is used to describe the process by which an organism responds to the stimulus.

Stimuli vary in both kind and strength. Different kinds of stimuli activate different sense organs. For instance, we can differentiate light stimuli, which activate our sense of sight and allow us to see the colors of a tree in autumn, from sound stimuli, which permit us to hear the sounds of an orchestra through our sense of hearing.

Each sort of stimulus that is capable of activating a sense organ can also be considered in terms of its strength, or **magnitude**. For instance, such questions as how bright a light stimulus needs to be before it is capable of being detected or how much perfume a person must wear before it is noticed by others relate to stimulus magnitude.

The issue of how the magnitude of a stimulus is related to sensory responses falls into a branch of psychology known as psychophysics. **Psychophysics** is the study of the relationship between the physical nature of stimuli and a person's sensory responses to them. Psychophysics played a central role in the development of the field of psychology; many of the first psychologists studied issues related to psychophysics. It is easy to see why: Psychophysics bridges the physical world outside and the psychological world within.

LET THERE BE LIGHT: Absolute Thresholds

It is obvious that people are not capable of detecting all the physical stimuli that are present in the environment, as noted earlier in our example of the seemingly quiet lake. Just when does a stimulus become strong enough to be detected by our sense organs? The answer to this question requires an understanding of the concept of absolute thresholds. An **absolute threshold**

FIGURE 3-1

These examples of absolute thresholds illustrate the extraordinary sensitivity of our senses.

Sight
Candle flame seen from a distance of 30 miles

Hearing
Ticking of a watch 20 feet away

Taste
One teaspoon sugar dissolved in 2 gallons of water

Smell
One drop of perfume in a three-room house

Touch
The wing of a bee falling on your cheek from a distance of 1 centimeter

is the smallest amount of physical intensity of a stimulus that must be present for it to be detected. Although we previously compared the sensory capabilities of humans unfavorably with those of dogs, in fact, absolute thresholds in human sensory organs are quite extraordinary. Consider, for instance, these examples of absolute thresholds for the various senses (see Figure 3-1):

▶ Sight: A candle flame can be seen 30 miles away on a dark, clear night.

▶ Hearing: The ticking of a watch can be heard 20 feet away under quiet conditions.

▶ Taste: Sugar can be discerned when 1 teaspoon is dissolved in 2 gallons of water.

▶ Smell: Perfume can be detected when one drop is present in a three-room apartment.

▶ Touch: A bee's wing falling from a distance of 1 centimeter can be felt on a cheek (Galanter, 1962).

Such thresholds permit a wide range of sensory stimulation to be detected by the human sensory apparatus. In fact, the capabilities of our senses are so fine-tuned that we might have problems if they were any more sensitive. For instance, if our ears were just slightly more sensitive, we would be able to hear the sound of air molecules in our ears knocking into each other—something that would surely prove distracting and might even prevent us from hearing sounds outside our bodies as well.

Of course, the absolute thresholds we have been discussing are measured under ideal conditions; normally our senses cannot detect stimulation quite so well because of the presence of noise. **Noise**, as defined by psychophysicists, is background stimulation that interferes with the perception of other stimuli. Hence noise refers not just to auditory stimuli, the most obvious example, but also to those stimuli that affect the other senses. Picture a talkative group of people crammed into a small, crowded, smoke-filled

Noise: Background stimulation that interferes with the perception of other stimuli

The noise in P. J. Clarke's, Chicago, is not just auditory; the crowded conditions produce noise that affects the senses of vision, smell, taste, and touch as well. (*Michael L. Abramson/Woodfin Camp & Assoc.*)

THE BIOLOGICAL FOUNDATIONS
OF PSYCHOLOGY

room at a party. The din of the crowd makes it hard to hear individual voices, and the smoke makes it difficult to see—and even to taste the food. In this case, the smoke and crowded conditions would be considered "noise," since they are preventing sensation at more discriminating and sensitive levels.

Signal Detection Theory

Noise is not the only factor that influences our sensitivity to stimulation; our expectations about whether any stimulus is present, our knowledge about the nature of the stimulus, and our motivation all affect our detection capabilities. For example, a baseball player's ability to visually track a pitch—and ultimately to hit the ball—will be better if the player knows that the pitcher has thrown a curve ball than if the player does not know what kind of pitch to expect. Similarly, the high motivation of a physician to identify abnormalities when listening through a stethoscope is apt to increase the likelihood of detecting stimuli that suggest a problem.

Signal detection theory: The theory that addresses the questions of whether a person can detect a stimulus and whether a stimulus is actually present at all

Hence our ability to detect faint stimuli is not just a function of properties of the stimulus; it is also affected by our psychological state. **Signal detection theory** is an outgrowth of psychophysics that seeks to explain the role of psychological factors in producing variations in our ability to identify stimuli (Swets & Pickett, 1982; Gescheider, 1985).

The theory acknowledges that observers may err in one of two ways: in reporting that a stimulus is present when it is not or in reporting that a stimulus is not present when it actually is. By applying statistical procedures, psychologists using signal detection theory are able to obtain an understanding of how different kinds of decisions—which may involve such factors as observer expectations and motivation—relate to judgments about sensory stimuli in different situations. Statistical methods also allow them to increase the reliability of predictions about what conditions will cause observers to be most accurate in their judgments.

Such findings have immense practical importance, not only in the case of radar operators who are charged with identifying and distinguishing incoming enemy missiles from the radar images of passing birds, but in other areas as well. One arena in which signal detection theory has practical implications is the judicial system. Witnesses who are asked to view a lineup find themselves in a classic signal detection situation, in which misidentification can have grave consequences for an individual (if an innocent person is incorrectly identified as a perpetrator) and for society (if an actual perpetrator is not detected). However, many witnesses have biases stemming from prior expectations about the socioeconomic status and race of criminals, attitudes toward the police and criminal justice system, and other biases that impede accurate judgment.

Unlike this cook, who has habituated to the smells and heat, a person walking into the kitchen of this swank Los Angeles restaurant might find the situation less than tolerable. (*Margot Granitsas/The Image Works*)

Using signal detection theory, psychologists have been able to make suggestions to increase the accuracy of witness identification (Ellson & Buckhout, 1981). For example, it is helpful to tell witnesses viewing a lineup that the prime suspect just might not be in the lineup at all. Moreover, justice is better served when the people in the lineup appear equally dissimilar from one another, which seems to reduce the chances of witnesses guessing.

COMPARING APPLES WITH APPLES: Just Noticeable Differences

Suppose a shopkeeper said you could choose six lemons from a barrel, and you wanted to compare them in a number of aspects to see which half dozen were best—which were bigger, which were yellower, which tasted more tart. One approach to this problem would be to systematically compare one lemon with another until you were left with a few so similar that you could not tell the difference between them (see Figure 3-2).

Psychologists have discussed this comparison problem in terms of the **difference threshold**, the smallest detectable difference between two stimuli—also known as a **just noticeable difference**. They have found that the stimulus value that constitutes a just noticeable difference depends on the initial intensity of the stimulus. For instance, you may have noticed that the light change which comes in a three-way bulb when you switch from 75 to 100 watts appears greater than when you switch from 100 to 125 watts, even though the wattage increase is the same in both cases. Similarly, when the moon is visible during the late afternoon, it appears relatively dim—yet against a dark night sky, it seems quite bright.

The relationship between changes in the original value of a stimulus and the degree to which the change will be noticed forms one of the basic laws of psychophysics: Weber's law. **Weber's law** states that a just noticeable difference is a constant proportion of the magnitude of an initial stimulus. Therefore, if a 10-pound increase in a 100-pound weight produces a just noticeable difference, it would take a 1000-pound increase to produce a noticeable difference if the initial weight were 10,000 pounds. In both cases, the same proportional increase is necessary to produce a just noticeable difference—1:10 (10:100 = 1000:10,000). (Actually, Weber found the true proportional increase in weight that produces a just noticeable difference to be between 2 and 3 percent.) Similarly, the just noticeable difference distinguishing changes in loudness between sounds is larger for sounds that are initially loud than for sounds that are initially soft—as exemplified by the fact that a person in a quiet room is more apt to be startled by the ringing of a telephone than a person in a room that is already noisy. In order to produce the same amount of reaction in a noisy room, a telephone ring might have to approximate the loudness of cathedral bells.

Weber's law seems to hold for all sensory stimuli, although its predictions are less accurate at extremely high or extremely low levels of stimu-

Difference threshold: The smallest detectable difference between two stimuli

Just noticeable difference: (See difference threshold)

Weber's law: The principle that states that the just noticeable difference is a constant proportion of the magnitude of an initial stimulus

FIGURE 3-2

One way of choosing six lemons from a bin would be to compare one lemon with another systematically in pairs. (*Mark Antman/The Image Works.*)

Adaptation: An adjustment in sensory capacity following prolonged exposure to stimuli

lation. Moreover, the law helps explain psychological phenomena that lie beyond the realm of the senses. For example, imagine that you own a house you would like to sell for $150,000. You might be satisfied if you received an offer of $145,000 from a potential buyer, even though it was $5000 less than the asking price. On the other hand, if you were selling your car and asking $10,000 for it, an offer of $5000 less than your asking price would probably not make you happy. Although the absolute amount is the same in both cases, the psychological value of the $5000 is very different.

BECOMING ACCUSTOMED TO STIMULATION: Sensory Adaptation

As the circus strongman carries a group of five acrobats across the circus tent, someone asks him if they aren't awfully heavy. He replies, "Not if you've just been carrying an elephant."

This story illustrates the phenomenon of **adaptation**, an adjustment in sensory capacity following prolonged exposure to stimuli. Adaptation occurs as people get used to a stimulus and change their frame of reference. Consequently, they do not respond to the stimulus in the way they did earlier.

One example of adaptation is the decrease in sensitivity that occurs after frequent exposure to a stimulus. If, for example, you were to repeatedly hear a loud tone, it would begin to sound softer after a while. This apparent decline in sensitivity to sensory stimuli is due to the inability of the sensory nerve receptors to constantly fire off messages to the brain. Because these receptor cells are most responsive to *changes* in stimulation, constant stimulation is not effective in producing a reaction. In fact, most receptor cells are incapable of constant firing, and their reaction to unvarying stimulation is a steady decline in the rate at which impulses are communicated.

Adaptation occurs with all the senses. For example, if you were able to stare unblinkingly at the exact same spot on this page for a long period of time—something that is impossible to do because of minute, involuntary movements of the eye—the spot would eventually disappear as the visual neurons lost their ability to fire.

Judgments of sensory stimuli are also affected by the context in which the judgments are made. Carrying five trapeze artists seems like nothing to the strongman who has just carted an elephant around the tent. The reason is that judgments are made, not in isolation from other stimuli, but in terms of preceding sensory experience.

You can demonstrate this for yourself by trying a simple experiment. Take two envelopes, one large and one small, and put fifteen nickels in each. Now lift the large envelope, put it down, and lift the small one (see Figure 3-3). Which seems to weigh more?

Most people report that the small one is heavier—although, as you know, the weights are identical. The reason for this misconception is that the physical context of the envelope interferes with the sensory experience of weight; adaptation to the context of one stimulus (the size of the envelope) alters responses to another stimulus (the weight of the envelope) (Coren, Porac & Ward, 1984).

Sensory-adaptation phenomena provide another illustration that a person's reaction to sensory stimuli is not always an accurate representation of the physical stimuli that brought it about. This point will become even more

To determine the effects of context on judgments of sensory stimuli, try this simple experiment in which you place 15 nickels into each of two envelopes of different sizes. If you then compare the weight of the two envelopes, it will seem that the nickels in the smaller envelope weigh more—demonstrating that the context of one stimulus (the envelope size) modifies responses to another stimulus (the envelope weight).

apparent as we move from consideration of sensation—which is the direct response of an organism to physical stimuli—and begin to discuss the specific senses of the human body.

RECAP AND REVIEW I

Rooap

◀ Sensation occurs when an organism responds to a stimulus, which is any form of energy that activates a sense organ. Psychophysics studies the relationship between the physical nature of stimuli and sensory responses that are made.

◀ An absolute threshold is the smallest amount of physical intensity by which a stimulus can be detected. The level of the absolute threshold is affected by noise—background interference from other stimuli—and by a person's expectations and motivation.

◀ Signal detection theory is used to predict the accuracy of sensory judgments; an observer may err in one of two ways. By reporting the presence of a stimulus when there is none or by reporting the absence of a stimulus when there actually is one.

◀ Difference threshold, or just noticeable difference, refers to the smallest detectable difference between two stimuli. According to Weber's law, a just noticeable difference is a constant proportion of the intensity of an initial stimulus.

◀ Sensory adaptation occurs when people are exposed to a stimulus for so long that they become used to it and therefore no longer respond to it.

Review

1. Our initial contact with and response to a stimulus is known as
   a. Psychophysics
   b. Sensation
   c. Perception
   d. Orientation

2. A researcher is investigating the effects of noise levels on human sensory responses. The area of psychology she is working in is known as _____ .

3. Match the descriptive statements in the right column with the appropriate label in the left column.

   a. ____ Noise
   1. The minimum amount of magnitude of a stimulus needed for it to be detected

   b. ____ Absolute threshold
   2. Background stimuli which interfere with and impede sensory discrimination

   c. ____ Adaptation
   3. The smallest detectable difference between two stimuli

   d. ____ Just noticeable difference
   4. Adjustment of our sensory capacity following extended exposure to a stimulus

4. Signal detection theory extends beyond the ability of a person to detect a stimulus when it is present; it also addresses the phenomenon of detecting a stimulus when it is *not* present. True or false? _____

5. _____ states that the difference threshold is a constant proportion of the magnitude of the initial stimulus.
   a. Psychophysics

b. Sensory adaptation
   c. Weber's law
   d. Signal detection theory

6. After completing a very difficult rock climb in the morning, Rick found the afternoon climb unexpectedly easy. This case illustrates the phenomenon of _____.

(Answers to review questions are on page 98.)

THE FIVE + SENSES

As she sat down to Thanksgiving dinner, Rhona reflected on how happy she was to leave dormitory food behind—at least for the long holiday weekend. She was just plain tired of seeing and smelling the same monotonous cafeteria food. Even chewing the stuff was distasteful—it all felt like mush. "In fact," she thought to herself, "if I have to eat toast covered with chipped beef one more time, I may never eat again." But this thought was soon interrupted when she saw her father carry in the turkey on a tray and place it squarely in the center of the table. The noise level, already high from the talking and laughter of the family members, grew still louder. As she picked up her fork, the smell of the turkey reached her and she felt her stomach growl hungrily. With the sight and sound of her family around the table—not to speak of the smell and taste of all that food—she felt more relaxed than she had since she had left for college in the fall. "Ah, home, sweet home," she thought.

Put yourself in this scene and consider how different it might be if any one of your senses were not functioning. What if you were blind and unable to see the faces of your family—or the welcome shape of the succulent turkey? What if you had no sense of hearing and could not listen to the family's talk, or were unable to feel your stomach growl, or smell the dinner, or taste the food? Clearly, an important dimension of the situation would be lacking, and no doubt the dinner would evoke a very different experience for you than it would for someone whose sensory apparatus was intact.

Moreover, the sensations mentioned above barely scratch the surface of sensory experience. Although most of us have been taught at one time or another that there are just five senses—sight, sound, taste, smell, and touch—this enumeration is far too modest, since human sensory capabilities go well beyond the basic five senses. It is well established, for example, that we are sensitive not merely to touch, but to a considerably wider set of stimuli—pain, pressure, temperature, vibration, and more. In addition, the ear is responsive to information that allows us not only to hear but to keep our balance as well. In fact, psychologists now believe that there are at least a dozen distinct senses—all of which are interrelated.

Although all the senses, alone and in combination, play a critical role in determining how we experience the world, most psychological research has focused on vision and hearing—the two sensory modes that are most conspicuous in allowing us to successfully interact with our environment.

THE EYES HAVE IT: Vision

To understand how our sense of vision allows us to view the world, we must first begin outside the body and consider the nature of the stimulus that produces vision—**light**. Although we are all familiar with light, having all our lives basked in the sun or an artificial equivalent, its underlying physical qualities are less apparent.

Light: The stimulus that produces vision

The stimuli that register as light in our eyes are actually electromagnetic radiation waves to which our bodies' visual apparatus happens to be sensitive and capable of responding. As you can see in Figure 3-4, electromagnetic radiation is measured in wavelengths, with the size of the wavelength corresponding to different sorts of energy. The range of wavelengths that humans are sensitive to—called the **visual spectrum**—is actually relatively small, but the differences among wavelengths within that spectrum are sufficient to allow us to see a range of all the colors, running from violet at the low end of the visual spectrum to red at the top. Colors, then, are associated with a particular wavelength within the visual spectrum.

Visual spectrum: The range of wavelengths to which humans are sensitive

Light waves coming from some object outside the body (imagine the light reflected off the face of the Mona Lisa, as in Figure 3-5) first encounter the only organ that is capable of responding to the visual spectrum: the eye. Strangely enough, most of the eye is concerned not with reacting directly to light but with shaping the entering image into something that can be used by the neurons that will serve as messengers. The neurons themselves take up a relatively small percentage of the total eye. In other words, most of the eye is a mechanical device, analogous in many respects to a camera without film, as you can see in Figure 3-5. (It is important to realize, though, the limitations of this analogy: Vision involves processes that are far more complex and sophisticated than any camera is capable of mimicking.)

Illuminating the Structure of the Eye

The ray of light we are following as it is reflected off the Mona Lisa first travels through the **cornea**, a transparent, protective window that is constantly being washed by tears, keeping it moist and clean. After moving through the cornea, the light traverses the pupil. The **pupil** is a dark hole found in the center of the **iris**, the colored part of the eye, which ranges in humans from a light blue to a dark brown. The size of the pupil opening depends on the amount of light in the environment: The dimmer the surroundings, the more the pupil opens in order to allow more light to enter.

Cornea: A transparent, protective window into the eyeball

Pupil: A dark hole in the center of the eye's iris which changes size as the amount of incoming light changes

Iris: The colored part of the eye

Why shouldn't the pupil be opened all the way all the time, thereby allowing the greatest amount of light into the eye? The answer has to do

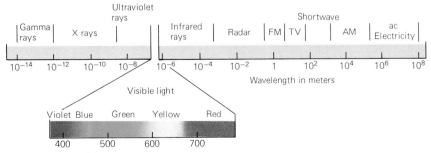

Violet Blue   Green   Yellow   Red

Visible light

FIGURE 3-4

The visual spectrum—the range of wavelengths to which people are sensitive—represents only a small part of the kinds of wavelengths present in our environment.

FIGURE 3-5

Although human vision is far more complicated than the most sophisticated camera, in some ways basic visual processes are analogous to those used in photography.

Lens: The part of the eye located behind the pupil that bends rays of light to focus them on the retina

Accommodation: The ability of the lens to vary its shape in order to focus incoming images on the retina

with the basic physics of light. A small pupil greatly increases the range of distances at which objects are in focus; with a wide-open pupil, the range is relatively small, and details are harder to discern. (Camera buffs know this in terms of the aperture or f-stop setting that they must adjust on their cameras.) The eye takes advantage of bright light by decreasing the size of the pupil and thereby becoming more discerning; in dim light the pupil expands in order to enable us to view the situation better—but at the expense of visual detail. Perhaps one reason that candlelight dinners are often thought of as romantic is that the dimness of the light prevents one from seeing the details of a lover's flaws.

Once light passes through the pupil, it enters the **lens,** which is located directly behind the pupil. The lens acts to bend the rays of light coming from the Mona Lisa so that they are properly focused on the rear of the eye. The lens focuses the light by changing its own thickness, a process called **accommodation.** The kind of accommodation that occurs depends on the location of the object in relation to the body. Distant objects require a relatively flat lens; in this case, the muscles controlling the lens relax, allowing the fluid within the eye to flatten the lens. In contrast, close objects are viewed best through a rounded lens. Here, then, the muscles contract, taking tension off the lens—and making it rounder.

ANSWERS (REVIEW I):
1. b **2.** Psychophysics **3.** a-2, b-1, c-4, d-3 **4.** True **5.** c **6.** Adaptation

Having traveled through the pupil and lens, our image of the Mona Lisa is finally able to reach its ultimate destination in the eye—the **retina**—where the electromagnetic energy of light is converted into messages that the brain can use. It is important to note that—again because of the physics of light—the image has reversed itself as it traveled through the lens, and it reaches the retina upside down (relative to its original position). Although you might think this would cause major difficulties in understanding and moving about the world, it turns out not to be a problem, because the brain rearranges the image back to its proper position. In fact, if we were ever to put on mirrored glasses that righted the image before it reached the brain, we would have a hard time, because everything would look upside down to us—although eventually we would adjust to the new orientation.

Retina: The part of the eye that converts the electromagnetic energy of light into useful information for the brain

The retina is actually a thin layer of nerve cells at the back of the eyeball (see Figure 3-6). There are two kinds of light-sensitive receptor cells found in the retina, and the names they have been given describe their shapes: **rods**, which are long and cylindrical, and **cones**, which are short, thick, and tapered. The rods and cones are distributed unevenly throughout the retina, with the greatest concentration of cones on the part of the retina called the **fovea** (refer back to Figure 3-5). The fovea is a particularly sensitive region of the retina; if you want to focus in on something of particular interest, you will probably center the image from the lens onto the area of the fovea.

Rods: Long, cylindrical, light-sensitive receptors in the retina that perform well in poor light but are largely insensitive to color and small details

Cones: Cone-shaped, light-sensitive receptor cells in the retina that are responsible for sharp focus and color perception, particularly in bright light

The farther away from the fovea, the fewer the number of cones there are on the retina. Conversely, there are no rods in the fovea—but the number increases rapidly toward the edges of the eye. Because the fovea covers only a small portion of the eye, there are fewer cones (about 7 million) than there are rods (about 125 million).

Fovea: A very sensitive region of the retina that aids in focusing

The rods and cones are not only structurally dissimilar, but they play distinctly different roles in vision (Cohen & Lasley, 1986). Cones are primarily responsible for the sharply focused perception of color, particularly in brightly lit situations, while rods are related to vision in dimly lit situations and are largely insensitive to color and to details as sharp as those the cones

This microscopic photo of the rods and cones of the eye clearly reveals their distinctive shapes. (*Lennart Nilsson*/Behold Man/*Little, Brown & Company*)

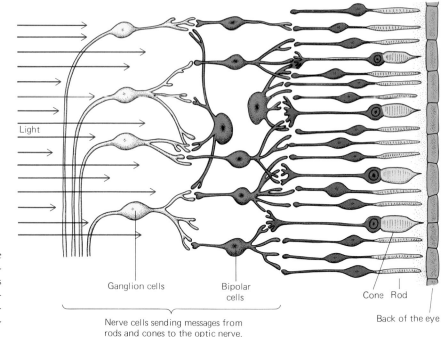

Light

Ganglion cells

Bipolar
cells

Cone Rod

Back of the eye

Nerve cells sending messages from
rods and cones to the optic nerve.

FIGURE 3-6

The basic cells of the eye. Light entering the eye travels through the ganglion and bipolar cells and strikes the light-sensitive rods and cones. The rods and cones then transmit nerve impulses to the brain via the bipolar and ganglion cells. (*Coren, Porac, & Ward, 1979.*)

Peripheral vision: The ability to see objects behind the eyes' main center of focus

are capable of recognizing. The rods are used for **peripheral vision**—seeing objects that are outside the main center of focus—and for night vision. In both cases, the level of detail that can be discerned is far lower when the rods come into play than when the cones are activated—as you know from groping your way across a dark room at night. Although you may just dimly see the outlines of furniture, it is almost impossible to distinguish color and the other details of obstacles in your path. You may also have noticed that you can improve your view of an object at night by looking slightly away from it. The reason? If you shift your gaze off-center, the image from the lens falls not on the relatively night-blind foveal cones but on the more light-sensitive rods.

The distinctive abilities of rods and cones make the eye analogous to a camera that is loaded with two kinds of film. One type is a highly sensitive black-and-white film (the rods); the other type is a somewhat less sensitive color film (the cones).

Shedding Light on Vision: Sending the Message from the Eye to the Brain
When light energy strikes the rods and cones, it starts the first in a chain of events that transforms light into neural impulses that can be communicated to the brain. In fact, even before the neural message reaches the brain, some initial alteration of the visual information takes place.

When light energy first strikes the retina, what happens is partially dependent on whether it strikes a rod or a cone. Rods contain **rhodopsin,** a complex, reddish-purple substance whose composition changes chemically when energized by light and thereby sets off a reaction. The substance found in cone receptors is different, but the principles are similar: Stimulation of the nerve cells in the eye triggers a neural response that is transmitted to other nerve cells, called bipolar cells and ganglion cells, leading to the brain.

Bipolar cells receive information directly from the rods and cones, and

Rhodopsin (ro DOP sin): A complex reddish-purple substance that changes when energized by light, causing a chemical reaction

Bipolar cells: Nerve cells leading to the brain that are triggered by nerve cells in the eye

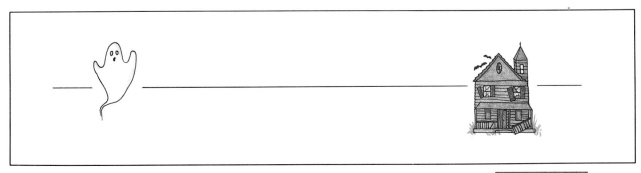

FIGURE 3-7

this information is then communicated to the ganglion cells. **Ganglion cells** collect and summarize visual information, which is gathered and moved out of the back of the eyeball through a bundle of ganglion axons called the **optic nerve.**

Because the opening for the optic nerve pushes through the retina, there are no rods or cones in the area, which creates a blind spot. Normally, however, this absence of nerve cells does not interfere with vision, because you automatically compensate for the missing part of your field of vision. (To find your blind spot, see Figure 3-7.)

Once beyond the eye itself, the neural signals relating to the image of the Mona Lisa we have been following move through the optic nerve. As the optic nerve leaves the eyeball, its path does not take the most direct route to the part of the brain right behind the eye. Instead, the optic nerves from each eye meet at a point roughly between the two eyes—called the **optic chiasma**—where each optic nerve then splits.

When the optic nerve splits, the nerve impulses coming from the right half of each retina are sent to the right side of the brain, and the impulses arriving from the left half of each retina are sent to the left side of the brain. Because the image on the retina is reversed and upside down, however, those images coming from the right half of the retina are actually included in the field of vision to the left of the person, and images coming from the left half of the retina represent the field of vision to the right of the individual (see Figure 3-8). In this way, our nervous system ultimately produces the phenomenon we discussed first in Chapter 2, in which each half of the brain is associated with the functioning of the opposite side of the body.

One of the most frequent causes of blindness is a restriction of the impulses across the optic nerve. **Glaucoma**, which strikes between 1 and 2 percent of those over age 40, occurs when pressure in the fluid of the eye begins to build up, either because it cannot be properly drained or because it is overproduced. When this first begins to happen, the nerve cells that communicate information about peripheral vision are constricted, leading to a decline in the ability to see anything outside a narrow circle directly ahead. This problem is called **tunnel vision**. Eventually, the pressure can become so great that all the nerve cells are contracted, leading to total blindness. However, if detected early enough, glaucoma is highly treatable, either through medication that reduces the pressure in the eye or through surgery.

From Light to Sight: Processing the Visual Message

By the time a visual message reaches the brain, it has passed through several stages of processing. One of the initial sites is the ganglion cells. Each ganglion cell gathers information from a group of rods and cones in a particular

To find your blind spot, close your right eye and look at the haunted house with your left eye. You will see the ghost on the periphery of your vision. Now, while staring at the house, move the page toward you. When the book is about a foot from your eye, the ghost will disappear. At this moment, the image of the ghost is falling on your blind spot.

But also notice how, when the page is at that distance, not only does the ghost seem to disappear, but the line seems to run continuously through the area where the ghost used to be. This shows how we automatically compensate for missing information by using nearby material to complete what is unseen. That's the reason you never notice the blind spot: What is missing is replaced by what is seen next to the blind spot.

Ganglion cells: Nerve cells that collect and summarize information from rods and carry it to the brain

Optic nerve: A bundle of ganglion axons in the back of the eyeball that carry visual information to the brain

Optic chiasma (ky AZ muh): A point between and behind the eyes at which nerve impulses from the optic nerves are reversed and "righted" in the brain

Glaucoma (glaw KO muh): A dysfunction of the eye in which fluid pressure builds up and causes a decline in visual acuity

Tunnel vision: An advanced stage of glaucoma in which vision is reduced to the narrow circle directly in front of the eye

THE BIOLOGICAL FOUNDATIONS
OF PSYCHOLOGY

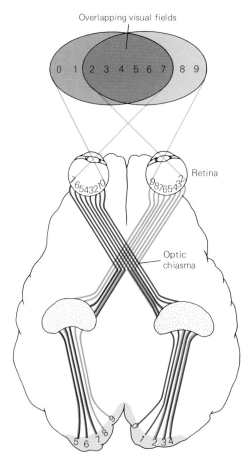

FIGURE 3-8

Because the optic nerve coming from each eye splits at the optic chiasma, the image to a person's right is sent to the left side of the brain, and the image to the person's left is transmitted to the right side of the brain. (*Based on Lindsay & Norman, 1977.*)

Feature detection: The activation of neurons in the cortex by visual stimuli of specific shapes or patterns

area of the eye, and compares the amount of light entering the center of that area with the amount of light in the area around it. In some cases, ganglion cells are activated by light in the center (and darkness in the surrounding area). In other cases, the opposite is true: Some ganglion cells are activated when there is darkness in the center and light in the surrounding areas. The ultimate effect of this process is to maximize the detection of variations in light and darkness. The neural image that is passed on to the brain, then, is an enhanced version of the actual visual stimulus outside the body.

The ultimate processing of visual images takes place in the visual cortex of the brain, of course, and it is here that the most complex kinds of processing occur (Hurlbert & Poggio, 1988). Nobel-prize winning psychologists David Hubel and Torsten Wiesel have found that many neurons in the cortex are extraordinarily specialized, being activated only by visual stimuli of a particular shape or pattern—a process known as **feature detection**. For example, some cells are activated only by lines of a particular width, shape, or orientation. Other cells are activated only by moving, as opposed to stationary, stimuli (Hubel & Wiesel, 1979). The specialization of these cells is extraordinary (see the Research Classics box).

THE MONKEY'S PAW: NEURONS THAT RECOGNIZE SPECIFIC PATTERNS

A monkey's paw—celebrated for providing good luck in a well-known short story—also represents an important breakthrough in the study of the responsivity of neurons of the brain to specific stimuli.

The story began in the early 1970s, when psychologist Charles Gross and colleagues were studying the response of single cells related to vision in a portion of the cortex of the brain of macaque monkeys (Gross, Rocha-Miranda & Bender, 1972). As part of an ongoing study, one day they found a cell that seemed at first to be completely unresponsive to any kind of light stimulus. As they were about to give up, however, one of the scientists waved a hand in front of the screen on which stimuli were presented—and the cell produced an energetic response.

The next twelve hours were spent testing various kinds of paper cutouts to determine what specific feature had produced the response. The researchers were successful in identifying only one particular physical feature that made the cell fire: the similarity of the stimulus to a monkey's paw. The closer in shape to the shadow of a paw, the greater the likelihood that the cell would fire!

Ongoing work by Gross has shown that there are several kinds of specific stimuli to which individual cells respond. For example, recent experiments have found that some cells respond selectively to the faces of monkeys. And some of these cells are so selective that they respond only to faces that are held in particular orientations (see Figure 3-9).

While it is clear that monkeys possess specialized cells, our understanding of the reasons behind their operation is not complete (Bruce, Desimone & Gross, 1986).

We do not know whether such specialized recognition is a result of experience with objects that are important to the everyday existence of an organism, nor how much of the operation of such cells is due to inborn genetic factors. It is also possible that some underlying physical dimension—such as size or configuration—that is unrelated to the nature of particular objects themselves is responsible for the firing of the cells.

Currently, there is no evidence that cells are selective to specific objects other than hands and faces. Gross speculates that using other stimuli that are important to monkeys—such as tropical fruits, tree branches, or monkey rumps (important in sexual activities)—may permit the identification of other selective cells. On the other hand, it may be that paws and faces are so critically important to the survival of monkeys that they are the only two classes of objects to which specialized reactions are produced (Gross, Desimone, Albright & Schwartz, 1985).

Researchers have also found that the cells of the visual cortex are organized spatially in a way that represents a visual scene being viewed. In other words, cells that correspond to neighboring areas of the visual field on the retina are located next to each other on the cortex. However, the representation is distorted, with more space on the cortex being devoted to the areas with the most rods and cones. In addition, the brain simultaneously

FIGURE 3-9

The upper row shows the electrical responses of certain neurons in a monkey's brain to the stimuli below it. As you can see, these neurons were stimulated most by intact monkey faces held at particular angles. (*Source: Gross, 1985, Fig. 3.*)

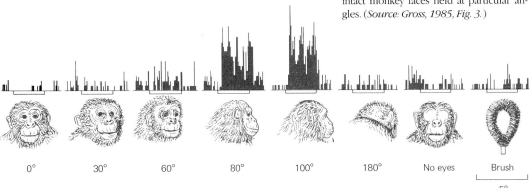

| 0° | 30° | 60° | 80° | 100° | 180° | No eyes | Brush |

5°

contains not one but several spatial representations of information coming from the visual field. In fact, there appear to be at least ten separate complete representations of the visual world, all of which are integrated by the brain (Merzenich & Kaas, 1980).

From Light to Dark: Adaptation

Have you ever walked into a movie theater on a bright, sunny day and stumbled into your seat, barely being able to see at all? Do you also recall later getting up to buy some popcorn and having no trouble navigating your way up the aisle?

Light adaptation: The eye's temporary insensitivity to light dimmer than that to which it has become accustomed

Your initial trouble seeing in the dimly lit theater was due to **light adaptation**, a phenomenon in which the eye grows insensitive to light that is dimmer than the level to which it has been most recently exposed. In contrast, the fact that you were later able to see relatively well is due to **dark adaptation**, a heightened sensitivity to light that results from being in relative dimness.

Dark adaptation: A heightened sensitivity to light resulting from being in low-level light

The speed at which both dark and light adaptation occur is a function of the rate at which changes occur in the chemical composition of the rods and cones. As you can see in Figure 3-10, the changes occur at different speeds for the two kinds of cells, with the cones reaching their greatest level of adaptation in just a few minutes, but the rods taking close to thirty minutes to reach the maximum level. On the other hand, the cones never reach the level of sensitivity to light that the rods attain. When rods and cones are considered jointly, though, dark adaptation is complete in a darkened room in about half an hour.

The 7-Million-Color Rainbow: Color Vision and Color Blindness

Although the range of wavelengths to which humans are sensitive is relatively narrow, at least in comparison to the entire electromagnetic spectrum, the portion to which we are capable of responding still allows us great flexibility in sensing the world. Nowhere is this clearer than in terms of the colors we can discern: A person with normal color vision is capable of distinguishing no less than 7 million different colors (Bruce & Green, 1984).

Although the variety of colors that people are generally able to distin-

FIGURE 3-10

Dark adaptation—the heightened sensitivity to light that occurs after moving to a dimmer environment—occurs at different rates for rods and cones. As this graph shows, the visual threshold (the lowest amount of light needed to be detected) is lower for rods than cones after about 30 minutes in a dimly lit environment. (*Adapted from Cornsweet, 1970.*)

(a) (b) (c) (d)

FIGURE 3-11

(*a*) Six-year-old Paula Vergara playing on a teeter-totter looks like this to someone with normal vision. (*b*) A person with red-green color blindness would see the scene like this, in hues of blue and yellow. (*c*) A person who is blue-yellow blind, conversely, would see it in hues of red and green. (*d*) A monochromat, or person with total color blindness, would see the scene like this. (*Elsa Peterson.*)

guish is vast, there are certain individuals whose ability to perceive color is quite limited—the color-blind. Interestingly, the condition of these individuals has provided some of the most important clues for understanding how color vision operates (Nathans et al., 1986).

Look, for a moment, at the photos shown in Figure 3-11. If you cannot see any difference in the series of photos, you probably are one of the 2 percent of men or 2 out of 10,000 women who are color-blind.

For most people who are color-blind, the world looks quite dull: Red fire engines look yellow, green grass looks yellow, and the three colors of a traffic light all look yellow. In fact, in the most common form of color blindness, all red and green objects are seen as yellow. There are other forms of color blindness as well, but they are quite rare. In yellow-blue blindness, people are unable to tell the difference between yellow and blue, and in the most extreme case an individual perceives no color at all: The world to such a person looks something like the picture on a black-and-white television set.

To understand why some of us are color-blind, it is necessary to consider the basics of color vision. There appear to be two processes involved. The first process is based on what has been labeled the **trichromatic theory**. It suggests that there are three kinds of cones in the retina, each of which responds primarily to a specific range of wavelengths. One is most responsive to blue-violet colors, one to green, and the other to yellow-red (Brown & Wald, 1964). According to trichromatic theory, perception of color is influenced by the relative strength with which each of the three kinds of cones is activated. If, for instance, we see a blue sky, the blue-violet cones are primarily triggered, while the others show less activity. The trichromatic theory provides a straightforward explanation of color blindness: It suggests that one of the three cone systems malfunctions, and colors covered by that range are perceived improperly.

However, there are phenomena that the trichromatic theory is less successful at explaining. For instance, it cannot explain why pairs of colors can combine to form gray, and it does not explain what happens after you stare at something like the flag shown in Figure 3-12 for about a minute. Try this yourself, and then move your eyes to the white space below. You will see an image of the traditional red, white, and blue American flag. Where there

Trichromatic theory of color vision: The theory that suggests that the retina has three kinds of cones, each responding to a specific range of wavelengths, perception of color being influenced by the relative strength with which each is activated

THE BIOLOGICAL FOUNDATIONS
OF PSYCHOLOGY

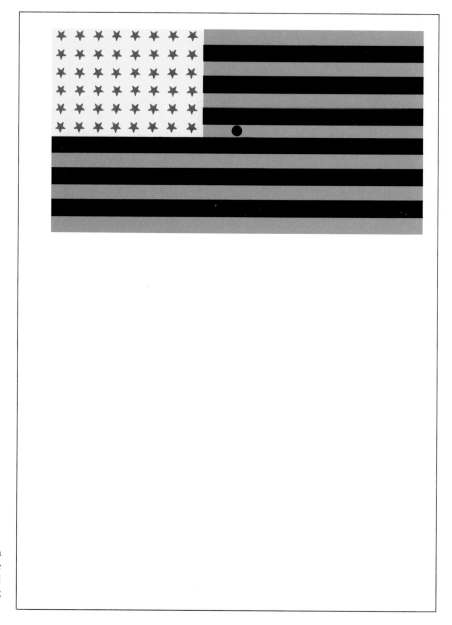

If you stare at the dot in this flag for about a minute and then look at a piece of white paper, the afterimage phenomenon will make a traditional red, white, and blue flag appear.

Afterimage: The image appearing when the eyes shift from a particular image to a blank area

Opponent-process theory of color vision: The theory that suggests that members of pairs of different receptor cells are linked together to work in opposition to each other

was yellow, you'll see blue, and where there were green and black, you'll see red and white.

The phenomenon you have just experienced is called an **afterimage**, and it occurs because activity in the retina continues even when you are no longer staring at the original picture. However, it also demonstrates that the trichromatic theory does not explain color vision completely. Why should the colors in the afterimage be different from those in the original?

Because trichromatic processes do not provide a full explanation of color vision, an alternative, the **opponent-process theory**, has been proposed. According to the theory, receptor cells are linked in pairs, working in opposition to each other. Specifically, there is a blue-yellow pairing, a red-green pairing, and a black-white pairing. If an object reflects light that contains more blue than yellow, it will stimulate the firing of the blue receptors, simultaneously discouraging or inhibiting the firing of yellow receptors—and the object will appear blue. If, on the other hand, a light contains more yellow than blue, the yellow receptors will be stimulated to fire while the blue ones are inhibited, and the object will appear yellow.

The opponent-process theory allows us to explain afterimages very directly. When we stare at the yellow in the figure, for instance, our receptor cells for the yellow component of the yellow-blue pairing begin to get fatigued and will be less able to respond to yellow stimuli. On the other hand, the blue part of the pair is not tired, since it is not being stimulated. When we look at a white surface, the light reflected off it would normally stimulate both the yellow and the blue receptors equally. But the fatigue of the yellow receptors prevents this; they temporarily do not respond to the yellow, which makes the white light appear to be blue. Since the other colors in the figure do the same thing relative to their specific opponents, the afterimage produces the opponent colors—for a while, at least. Of course, the afterimage lasts only a short time, since the fatigue of the yellow receptors is soon overcome, and the white light begins to be perceived more accurately.

Most psychologists assume that both opponent processes and trichromatic mechanisms are at work in allowing us to see colors, although they operate in different parts of the visual sensing system. It seems most likely that trichromatic processes work within the retina itself, while opponent processes operate at a later state of neuronal connections and processing (Beck, Hope & Rosenfeld, 1983). The ultimate explanation for our color-sensing capabilities still eludes us. We are nevertheless getting an increasingly clear picture that promises to provide psychologists with new applications in such areas as remedying color blindness and devising traffic signals that are effective in reducing accidents (Botstein, 1986; Boynton, 1988).

RECAP AND REVIEW II

Recap

◄ Although people have traditionally thought in terms of five senses, psychologists studying sensation have found that the number is actually far greater.

◄ The eyes are sensitive to electromagnetic radiation waves of certain wavelengths; these waves register as light.

◄ As light enters the eye, it passes through the cornea, pupil, iris, and lens and ultimately reaches the retina, where the electromagnetic energy of light is converted into nerve impulses usable by the brain. These impulses leave the eye via the optic nerve.

◄ The retina is composed of nerve cells called rods and cones, which play differing roles in vision and are responsible for dark and light adaptation.

◄ Humans are able to distinguish around 7 million colors. Color vision is believed to involve two processes: trichromatic mechanisms and an opponent-processing system.

Review

1. The visual spectrum can best be described as
   a. The existing wavelengths of the universe
   b. The stimulation of the retina by a variety of wavelengths
   c. The wavelengths not visible to the naked eye
   d. The range of wavelengths to which human beings are sensitive

2. Perception of the myriad colors visible at the beach on a sunny day is the responsibility of the receptor cells of the eye known as _____ . On the other hand, discriminating features in a dimly lit restaurant is the job of the _____ .

3. The area on the retina containing the greatest concentration of cones is the
   a. Fovea
   b. Optic chiasma
   c. Rhodospin
   d. Optic nerve

108

4. Match each definition in the right column with the correct word in the left column. All words relate to the structure or function of the eye.

a. ____ Lens
b. ____ Accommodation
c. ____ Iris
d. ____ Retina
e. ____ Cornea
f. ____ Pupil

1. Kept moist by tears, this part of the eye could be considered a protective window.
2. This action performed by the lens serves to focus the light passing through it.
3. The colored part of the eye, it ranges from light blue to dark brown in humans.
4. This dark hole is centered in the colored part of the eye.
5. This feature of the eye bends rays of light so they are focused on the rear of the eye.
6. At this site, the visual image is transformed into messages that the brain can use.

5. _____ is the chemical substance contained in the rods.

6. Ganglion cells receive information directly from the rods and cones and communicate it to the bipolar cells. True or false? _____

7. _____ is a disease in which pressure in the fluid of the eye begins to build up, resulting in a decline in peripheral vision known as _____.

8. Many neurons in the visual cortex are specialized, being activated only by visual stimuli of a particular shape or pattern. This phenomenon is known as _____.

9. John was to meet his girlfriend in the movie theater. As was typical, he was late and the movie had begun. He stumbled down the aisle, barely able to see because of _____ adaptation. Unfortunately, the woman he sat down beside and attempted to put his arm around was not his girlfriend. He sorely wished he had given his eyes a chance and waited for _____ adaptation to occur.

10. The _____ theory suggests that there are three kinds of cones in the retina, each of which responds primarily to a specific range of wavelengths.
    a. Opponent-process
    b. Afterimage
    c. Trichromatic
    d. Color-blindness

(Answers to review questions are on page 110.)

HEARING AND MOVING ABOUT THE WORLD:
The Sense of Sound and Balance

The blast-off was easy compared with what the astronaut was experiencing now: space sickness. The constant nausea and vomiting were enough to make him consider calling Mission Control and asking to return to base. Even though he had been warned that there was a 50 percent chance that his first experience in space would cause such sickness, he wasn't prepared for how terribly sick he really felt. How could he live and work on the space station for the next three months feeling like this?

Whether or not our mythical astronaut turns his rocket around and heads back to earth, his experience—which is a major problem for space travelers—is related to a basic sensory process that is centered in the ear and its adjacent structure: the sense of motion and balance, which allows people to navigate their bodies through the world and maintain an upright position without falling. Along with hearing, the process by which sound waves are translated into understandable and meaningful forms, the sensing of motion and balance represent the major functions of the ear.

The Site of Sound: The Ear
While many of us think primarily of the **outer ear** when we consider hearing, this part is little more than a reverse megaphone, designed to collect and

Outer ear: The visible part of the ear that acts as a sound collector

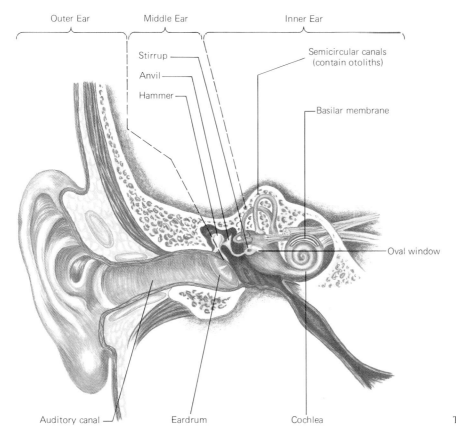

Outer Ear   Middle Ear   Inner Ear

Stirrup

Anvil

Hammer

Semicircular canals
(contain otoliths)

Basilar membrane

Oval window

Auditory canal   Eardrum   Cochlea

FIGURE 3-13

The ear.

bring sounds into the internal portions of the ear, illustrated in Figure 3-13. **Sound** is the movement of air molecules brought about by the vibration of an object. Sounds travel through the air in wave patterns similar in shape to those made by a stone thrown into a still pond.

Once sounds, which arrive in the form of wave vibrations, have been funneled into the **auditory canal**, a tubelike passage, they reach the **eardrum**. The eardrum is aptly named because it operates like a miniature drum, vibrating when sound waves hit it. The louder the sound, the more it vibrates. These vibrations are then transmitted into the **middle ear**, a tiny chamber containing just three bones called, because of their shapes, the **hammer**, the **anvil**, and the **stirrup**. These bones have one function: to transmit vibrations to the **oval window**, a thin membrane leading to the inner ear. Because of their shape, the hammer, anvil, and stirrup do a particularly effective job not only transmitting vibrations but actually increasing their strength, since they act as a set of levers. Moreover, since the opening into the middle ear is considerably larger than the opening out of it, the force of sound waves on the smaller area becomes amplified. The middle ear, then, acts as a tiny mechanical amplifier, making us aware of sounds that would otherwise go unnoticed.

The **inner ear** is the portion of the ear that actually changes the sound vibrations into a form that allows them to be transmitted to the brain. It also contains the organs that allow us to locate our position and determine how we are moving through space. When sound enters the inner ear through the oval window, it moves into the **cochlea**, a coiled tube filled with fluid that

Sound: The movement of air molecules brought about by the vibration of an object

Auditory canal: A tubelike passage in the ear through which sound moves to the eardrum

Eardrum: The part of the ear that vibrates when sound waves hit it

Middle ear: A tiny chamber containing three bones—the hammer, the anvil, and the stirrup—which transmit vibrations to the oval window

Hammer: A tiny bone in the middle ear that transfers vibrations to the anvil

Anvil: A tiny bone in the middle ear that transfers vibrations to the stirrup

Stirrup: A tiny bone in the middle ear that transfers vibrations to the oval window

Oval window: A thin membrane between the middle ear and the inner ear that transmits vibrations while increasing their strength

Inner ear: The interior structure that changes sound vibrations into a form that can be transmitted to the brain

Cochlea (KOKE lee uh): A coiled tube filled with fluid that receives sound via the oval window or through bone conduction

Basilar membrane: A structure dividing the cochlea into an upper and a lower chamber

Hair cells: Tiny cells covering the basilar membrane that, when bent by vibrations entering the cochlea, transmit neural messages to the brain

looks something like a snail. Inside the cochlea is the **basilar membrane**, a structure that runs through the center of the cochlea, dividing it into an upper and a lower chamber (see Figure 3-13). The basilar membrane is covered with **hair cells**. When these hair cells are bent by the vibrations entering the cochlea, a neural message is transmitted to the brain (Scharf & Baas, 1986).

Although sound typically enters the cochlea via the oval window, there is an additional method of entry: bone conduction. Because the ear rests on a maze of bones within the skull, the cochlea is able to pick up subtle vibrations that travel across the bones from other parts of the head. For instance, one of the ways you hear your own voice is through bone conduction, which explains why you sound different to yourself than to other people who hear your voice. (Listen to yourself on a tape recorder sometime to hear what you *really* sound like!) The sound of your voice reaches you both through the air and via bone conduction and therefore sounds richer to you than to everyone else.

The Physical Aspects of Sound

As we mentioned earlier, what we refer to as sound is actually the physical movement of air molecules in regular, wavelike patterns caused by the vibration of an object (see Figure 3-14). Sometimes it is even possible to view these vibrations, as in the case of a stereo speaker that has no enclosure. If you have ever seen one, you know that, at least when the lowest notes are

FIGURE 3-14

The waves produced by different stimuli are transmitted—usually through the air—in different patterns, with lower frequencies indicated by fewer peaks and valleys per second.

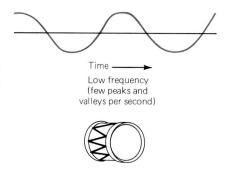

Time ⟶
Low frequency
(few peaks and
valleys per second)

Time ⟶
High frequency
(numerous peaks and
valleys per second)

ANSWERS (REVIEW II):
1. d   **2.** Cones, rods   **3.** a   **4.** a-5, b-2, c-3, d-6, e-1, f-4   **5.** Rhodopsin
6. False; bipolar cells communicate the information to the ganglion cells   **7.** Glaucoma, tunnel vision   **8.** Feature detection   **9.** Light, dark   **10.** c

playing, you can see the speaker moving in and out. What is less obvious is what happens next: The speaker pushes air molecules into waves with the same pattern as its movement. These wave patterns soon reach your ear, although their strength has been weakened considerably during their travels. All other stimuli that produce sound work in essentially the same fashion, setting off wave patterns that move through the air to the ear. Air—or some other medium, such as water—is necessary to make the vibrations of objects reach us; there can be no sound in a vacuum.

We are able to see the speaker moving when low notes are played because of a primary characteristic of sound called frequency. **Frequency** is the number of wave crests that occur in a second. With very low frequencies there are relatively few, and therefore slower, up-and-down wave cycles per second—which are visible to the naked eye as vibrations in the speaker. Low frequencies are translated into a sound that is very low in pitch. (**Pitch** is the characteristic that makes sound "high" or "low.") For example, the lowest frequency that humans are capable of hearing is 20 cycles per second. Higher frequencies translate into higher pitch; at this end of the sound spectrum, people can detect sounds with frequencies as high as 20,000 cycles per second.

While sound frequency allows us to enjoy the sounds of the high notes of a piccolo and the bass notes of a tuba, **intensity** is a feature of wave patterns that allows us to distinguish between loud and soft sounds. Intensity refers to the size of the difference between the peaks and valleys of air pressure in a sound wave as it travels through the air. Waves with small peaks and valleys produce soft sounds, while those that are relatively large produce loud sounds.

We are sensitive to a broad range of sound intensity: The loudest sounds we are capable of hearing are about 10 million times as intense as the very weakest sound we can hear. This range is measured in **decibels**, which can be used to place everyday sounds along a continuum (see Figure 3-15). When sounds get higher than 120 decibels, they become painful to the human ear, and long-term exposure to such high levels eventually leads to a permanent hearing loss—a phenomenon all too familiar to many rock musicians (and some of their fans).

How are our brains able to sort out wavelengths of different frequencies and intensities? One clue comes from studies of the basilar membrane, the area within the cochlea that translates physical vibrations into neural impulses. It turns out that sounds affect different areas of the basilar membrane, depending on the frequency of the wave. The part of the basilar membrane nearest the oval window is most sensitive to high-frequency sounds, while the part nearest the cochlea's inner edge is most sensitive to low-frequency sounds. This finding has led to the **place theory of hearing**, which says that different areas of the basilar membrane respond to different frequencies.

On the other hand, other mechanisms are also involved. The **frequency theory of hearing** suggests that the entire basilar membrane acts like a microphone, vibrating as a whole in response to a sound. According to the theory, the nerve receptors send out signals that are tied directly to the frequency (the number of wave crests per second) of the sounds to which we are exposed, with the number of nerve impulses being a direct function of the sound's frequency. Thus, the higher the pitch of a sound (and therefore the greater the frequency of its wave crests), the greater the number of nerve impulses that are transmitted up the auditory nerve to the brain.

Most research points to the conclusion that both the place theory and

Frequency: The number of wave crests occurring each second in any particular sound

Pitch: The "highs" and "lows" in sound

Intensity: A feature of wave patterns that allow us to distinguish between loud and soft sounds

Decibel: A measure of sound loudness or intensity

Place theory of hearing: The theory that states that different frequencies are responded to by different areas of the basilar membrane

Frequency theory of hearing: The theory that suggests that the entire basilar membrane acts like a microphone, vibrating in response to sound

112

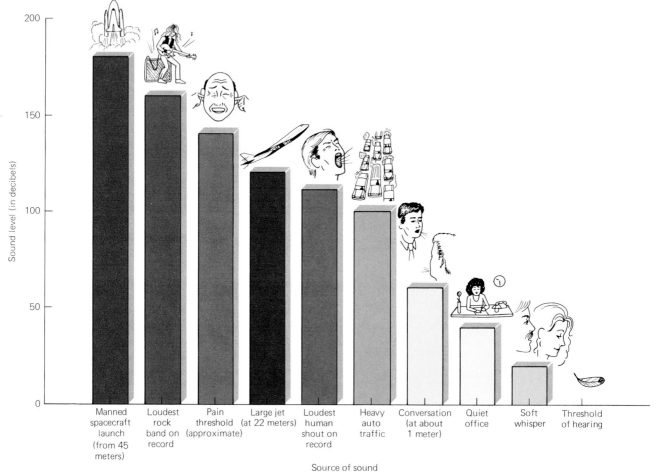

FIGURE 3-15

Illustrations of decibel levels (measures of sound intensity).

the frequency theory provide accurate descriptions of the processes that underlie hearing, although not at every frequency. Specifically, the place theory seems a better explanation of the sensing of high-frequency sounds, whereas the frequency theory explains what happens when low-frequency sounds are encountered. Sounds with pitch in between seem to incorporate both processes.

After an auditory message leaves the ear, it is transmitted to the auditory cortex of the brain through a complex series of neural interconnections. As the message is transmitted, it is communicated through neurons that respond to specific types of sounds. Within the auditory cortex itself, there are neurons that respond selectively to very specific sorts of sound features, such as clicks or whistles. Moreover, some neurons respond only to a specific pattern of sounds, such as a steady tone but not an intermittent one.

If we were to analyze the configuration of the cells in the auditory cortex, we would find that neighboring cells are responsive to similar frequencies. The auditory cortex, then, provides us with a "map" of sound frequencies, just as the visual cortex furnishes a representation of the visual field. (To learn about the latest attempts at helping people with hearing problems, see the Psychology at Work box.)

SENSE ORGAN REPLACEMENTS: ELECTRONIC EARS FOR THE DEAF AND EYES FOR THE BLIND

What appeared to be science fiction just a few years ago is considerably closer to becoming a reality: the replacement of malfunctioning human sense organs with artificial ones.

The greatest step forward has come in the realm of hearing. Because of technological advances, some 60,000 to 200,000 partially deaf people in the United States are now able to hear sounds such as automobile horns and doorbells for the first time. Making this advance possible is an electronic ear implant connected directly to the cochlea.

The device works in some cases of deafness in which the hair cells in the cochlea are damaged and unable to convert vibrations into the electrical impulses that the brain is able to use. A tiny microphone outside the ear is used to pick up sounds, which are then sent to a speech processor worn on a shoulder strap or belt that allows a user to squelch background noise with a button. The electronic signal is then sent from the processor to a transmitter behind the ear and broadcasts a radio wave to a receiver implanted inside the skull. The implanted receiver is directly connected to the cochlea by twenty-two thin wires (see Figure 3-16) and

emits electrical signals that stimulate the cochlea, sending a message to the brain that sound is being heard (Molotsky, 1984; Clark, 1987).

Although the device does not allow people to pick up words distinctly—users report that the quality of speech is like that of Donald Duck—about half the users of state-of-the-art implants are able to understand familiar voices and speak on the phone. Implants also enable users to detect changes in tone of voice and volume. Moreover, as the technology continues to improve, it is likely that sounds will be made more distinct, perhaps one day approaching the sensitivity of the ear itself.

New technological advances have brought hope to the blind, as well. For example, Bach-Y-Rita (1982) and his colleagues at the Smith-Kettlewell Institute of Visual Science in San Francisco have employed a miniature television camera, which is mounted on spectacle frames worn by a blind person. The picture from the camera is analyzed by a small computer, which translates the picture into 400 dots, varying in darkness. Next, the degree of darkness of each of the spots is transformed into vibrations of varying intensity that are relayed to the blind person's abdomen, with darker spots being represented by more rapid vibrations. With just a small amount of training, blind people are able to "see" and recognize common objects, and eventually they are able to open doors, negotiate their way through halls, and pick up small objects.

The technology is still not as advanced as that employed in ear transplants, since the sensation of sight must be "translated" first into sensations of touch. And neither ear nor eye substitutes have reached the ultimate level of sophistication, in which signals can be fed directly into the brain and perceived as sound or sight. Still, the innovations described here offer real hope to thousands of deaf and blind people now, and the possibility of future improvements is high.

Balancing the Ups and Downs of Life

The ear has several other structures that are related more to our sense of balance than to our hearing. The **semicircular canals** of the inner ear consist of three tubes containing fluid that sloshes through them when the head moves, signaling rotational or angular movement to the brain. The pull on our bodies caused by the acceleration of forward, backward, or up-and-down motion, as well as the constant pull of gravity, is sensed by the **otoliths**, tiny, motion-sensitive crystals within the semicircular canals. When we move, these crystals shift like sands on a windy beach. The brain's inexperience in interpreting messages from the weightless otoliths is the cause of the space sickness experienced by the astronaut in our earlier example—a problem that is actually quite common among space travelers.

Semicircular canals: Part of the inner ear containing fluid that moves when the body moves to control balance

Otoliths: Crystals in the semicircular canals that sense body acceleration

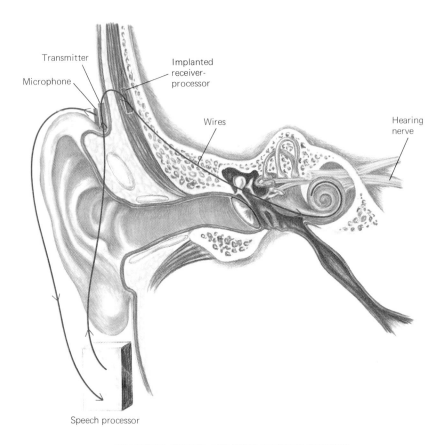

FIGURE 3-16

A cochlear implant. (Newsweek, *1987.*)

MAKING SENSE OF THE OTHER SENSES:
Smell, Taste, and the Skin Senses

When Audrey Warner returned home after a day's work, she knew that something was wrong the minute she opened her apartment door. The smell of gas—a strong, sickening smell that immediately made her feel weak—permeated the apartment. She left her apartment, ran to the pay phone across the street, and called the gas company. As she was explaining what she smelled, Audrey heard a muffled explosion and then saw flames begin to shoot out of her apartment window. Her life had been saved by her ability to smell the gas.

Although there are few instances in which the sense of smell provides such drama, it is clear that our lives would be considerably less interesting if we could not smell freshly mowed hay, sniff a bouquet of flowers, or enjoy the odor of an apple pie baking. Like our senses of vision and hearing, each of the remaining senses that we now consider—smell, taste, and the skin senses—plays an important role in our lives.

Smell and Taste
Although many animals have keener abilities to detect odors than we do—a point reflected by the fact that a greater proportion of their brains is related to the sense of smell than ours is—we are still able to detect a wide range of smells. People can be trained to make sophisticated, complex judgments of smells; there are even professions in which the major task is to continually assess the quality of the odor of a manufactured product. For instance, the

beer industry has developed the odor wheel (see Figure 3-17), which is used during the production of beer as part of quality-control checks.

Results of "sniff tests" have shown that women generally have a better sense of smell than do men and that a nonsmoker's sense of smell is better than a smoker's. In addition, the sense of smell changes with age: Sensitivity to smells is greatest between the ages of 30 and 60, declining from age 60 on. Moreover, a small number of people cannot smell at all. Such a condition may result from a head injury, nasal growths, or sometimes just a bad case of the flu (Doty, 1986; Gilbert & Wysocki, 1987).

For some animals, smells represent an important mode of communication. By releasing **pheromones**, chemicals that produce a reaction in other members of the species, they are able to send such messages as sexual availability. For instance, certain substances in the vaginal secretions of female monkeys contain a chemical that stimulates sexual interest in male monkeys.

Pheromones: Chemicals that produce a reaction in other members of a species

Although it seems reasonable that humans might also communicate through the release of pheromones, the evidence is still scanty. Women's vaginal secretions contain chemicals similar to those found in monkeys, but the smells do not seem to be related to sexual activity in humans. On the other hand, the presence of these substances might explain why women who live together for long periods tend to show similarity in the timing of their menstrual cycles (Engen, 1982; 1987). In addition, women are able to identify their babies solely on the basis of smell just a few hours after birth (Porter et al., 1983).

Some researchers suggest that it was the sense of smell that led to the

FIGURE 3-17

The beer industry has devised the set of descriptive terms in this flavor wheel to help in the production and quality control of beer. Both odors and tastes are included in the wheel. (*American Society of Brewing Chemists.*)

evolution and development of the cerebral cortex of the brain (Bloom & Lazerson, 1988). They base this notion on evidence from the existence of a now-extinct group of shrewlike mammals that roamed the earth at the time of the dinosaurs, some 100 million years ago. The long noses and small eyes of these animals suggest that they used smell as their primary tool of survival. According to this hypothesis, any animal that relied on smell had to develop such higher-order mental capabilities as remembering, planning, and tracking—in contrast to animals that relied solely on visual cues. The hypothesis suggests that animals developed this capability through growth in the part of the brain that was the forerunner of the cerebral cortex.

We know considerably less about the mechanisms underlying smell than we do about those concerning sight and sound. It is clear that the sense of smell comes into play when molecules of a substance enter the nasal passages and meet **olfactory cells**, the receptor cells of the nose. Each of these cells has hairlike structures that stick out into the air and are capable of transforming the passing molecules into nerve impulses that can be used by the brain.

Olfactory cells: The receptor cells of the nose

More is understood about the sense of taste, which is intimately related to smell. There are only four fundamental sensations responsible for the myriad tastes that we experience: sweet, sour, salty, and bitter. Every other taste is simply a combination of these four basic qualities.

The receptor cells for taste are located in **taste buds**, which are distributed across the tongue. However, the distribution is uneven, and certain areas of the tongue are more sensitive to certain of the fundamental tastes than are others (Bartoshuk, 1971). As we can see in Figure 3-18, the tip of the tongue is most sensitive to sweetness; in fact, a granule of sugar placed on the rear of the tongue will hardly seem sweet at all. Similarly, only the sides of the tongue are very sensitive to sour tastes, and the rear specializes in bitter tastes.

Taste buds: The location of the receptor cells of the tongue

The different taste areas on the tongue correspond to different locations in the brain. Neurons responding to sour and bitter tastes are located on one end of the area of the cortex corresponding to taste, whereas sweet tastes stimulate neurons on the opposite end of the cortex. In contrast, salty tastes stimulate neurons that are distributed across the entire taste area of the brain (Yamamoto et al., 1981).

Of course, the sense of taste does not operate simply through the tongue, as anyone with a stuffy nose can confirm. The smell, temperature, texture, and even appearance of food all affect our sense of taste. Furthermore, some people are more sensitive to certain tastes than are others, and the ability to taste certain substances runs in some families. Our own behavior and habits also play a role in our tasting capabilities; smoking, for example, dulls the taste of food.

Senses of the Skin: Touch, Pressure, Temperature, and Pain

For the Gale Schoenlebers of the world, who suffer from debilitating migraine headaches (described at the beginning of this chapter), pain is the central aspect of life. Yet an inability to experience pain can be just as tragic. Consider the following description of a boy born with an extremely rare inherited defect that made him insensitive to pain:

His arms and legs are deformed and bent, as though he had suffered from rickets. Several fingers are missing. A large open wound covers

FIGURE 3-18

Particular portions of the tongue are sensitive to tastes that are bitter, sour, sweet, or salty.

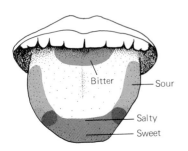

Bitter
Sour
Salty
Sweet

one knee, and the smiling lips are bitten raw. He looks, to all the world, like a battered child.... His fingers were either crushed or burned because he did not pull his hands away from things that were hot or dangerous. His bones and joints were misshapen because he pounded them too hard when he walked or ran. His knee had ulcerated from crawling over sharp objects that he could not feel. Should he break a bone or dislocate a hip, he would not feel enough to cry out for help (Wallis, 1984, p. 58, p. 60).

Clearly, the consequences of a painfree existence can be devastating. If, for example, you did not experience pain, instead of recoiling when your arm brushed against a hot teapot, you might lean against it, not noticing that you were being severely burned. Similarly, without the warning sign of stomach pain that typically accompanies an inflamed appendix, your appendix might go on to rupture, spreading a fatal infection through your body. Such examples underscore the vital importance of our sense of pain.

In fact, all our **skin senses**—touch, pressure, temperature, and pain—play a critical role in survival, making us aware of potential danger to our bodies. Most of these senses operate through nerve receptor cells located at various depths throughout the skin, although they are not evenly distributed. When we consider receptors sensitive to pressure, for example, some areas—such as the fingertips—have many more cells and are therefore more sensitive to pressure than others—such as the middle of the back (see Figure 3-19).

Probably the most extensively researched skin sense is pain, and with good reason: People consult physicians and take medication for pain more

Skin senses: The senses that include touch, pressure, temperature, and pain

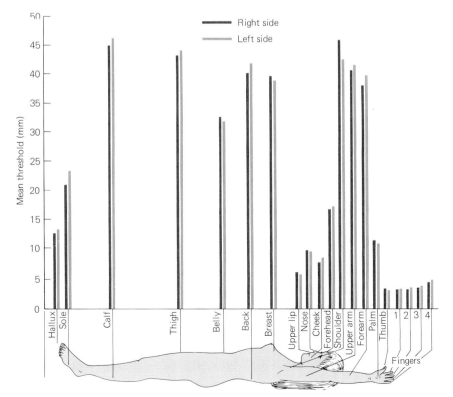

FIGURE 3-19

Skin sensitivity of various parts of the body. The shorter a line, the more sensitive the body part is. The fingers and thumb, lips, nose, cheeks, and big toe are the most sensitive. (*Weinstein, 1968.*)

THE BIOLOGICAL FOUNDATIONS
OF PSYCHOLOGY

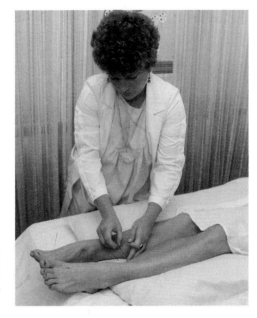

The gate-control theory of pain may explain the effectiveness of acupuncture, in which sharp needles inserted into the skin produce pain relief. (*Ellis Herwig/The Picture Cube*)

Gate-control theory of pain: The theory that suggests that particular nerve receptors lead to specific areas of the brain related to pain; when these receptors are activated by an injury or bodily malfunction, a "gate" to the brain is opened and pain is sensed

than for any other symptom or condition. Nearly one-third of the population of the United States has problems with persistent or recurrent pain—and many of these individuals are disabled to the point of being unable to function normally in society.

Until fairly recently, little was understood about the biology and psychology of pain—and even less about how to treat it (Fordyce, 1988). Today, however, the major theory relating to the experience of pain, called the gate-control theory, is providing us with new clues for understanding how we can control pain. The **gate-control theory** suggests that particular nerve receptors lead to specific areas of the brain related to pain (Melzack & Wall, 1965). When these receptors are activated because of some injury or problem with a part of the body, a "gate" to the brain is opened, allowing the sensation of pain to be experienced.

However, another set of neural receptors is able, when stimulated, to close the "gate" to the brain, thereby reducing the experience of pain. The gate may be shut for two different reasons. First, other impulses can overwhelm the nerve pathways to the brain that the pain would otherwise use. In this case, nonpainful stimuli compete with and sometimes displace the neuronal message of pain, thereby shutting off the painful stimulus. This explains why rubbing the skin around an injury helps reduce pain: The competing stimuli from the rubbing may alleviate the painful ones. Similarly, scratching is able to relieve itching (which is technically classified as a kind of pain stimulus).

A second way in which a gate may be activated is through the brain itself. The brain is able to close a gate by sending a message down the spinal cord to an injured area, producing a reduction in or relief from pain. Thus a soldier who is injured in battle may experience no pain (the surprising situation in more than half of all combat injuries), because he experiences such relief at still being alive that his brain sends a signal to the injury site to shut down the pain gate (Sternbach, 1987).

The gate-control theory may explain the effectiveness of **acupuncture**, an ancient Chinese technique in which sharp needles are inserted into var-

Acupuncture: A Chinese technique of relieving pain through the placement of needles in specific areas of the body

FIGURE 3-20

Acupuncture has existed for centuries. This Ming dynasty chart from around the fourteenth century illustrates locations where needles are to be inserted. (*British Museum.*)

ious parts of the body (see Figure 3-20). The sensation from the needles may close the gateway to the brain, reducing the experience of pain. It is also possible that the body's own painkillers, the endorphins (discussed in Chapter 2), as well as positive and negative emotions, may play a role in opening and closing the gate (Wall & Melzack, 1984; Warga, 1987).

THE INFORMED CONSUMER OF PSYCHOLOGY:
How Do You Spell Relief—from Pain?

You've been hurting for months, perhaps even years. You have tried every home remedy, and your family physician is unable to determine the cause of your pain. As the pain lingers, it begins to affect every aspect of your daily life. Where do you go next?

One place to consider is a comprehensive pain clinic. Numbering about 150 worldwide, pain clinics are designed for people who suffer from lingering, chronic pain that has resisted previous treatment. They offer a multidisciplinary approach to the relief of pain (Holzman & Turk, 1985; Budiansky, 1987). In the typical clinic, the patient is first evaluated thoroughly by a team of health practitioners, including physicians, psychologists, and various medical specialists, and then a treatment is prescribed. The major antipain weapons in the arsenal of the pain clinic include:

Transcutaneous electrical nerve stimulation: A method of providing relief from pain by passing a low-voltage electric current through parts of the body.

▶ Drugs: Drugs remain the most popular treatment in fighting pain. Drugs range from those that treat the source of the pain—such as reducing swelling in painful joints—to those that work on the symptom of the pain.

▶ Hypnosis: Some 15 to 20 percent of the people who can be hypnotized can achieve a major degree of pain relief.

▶ Biofeedback: As we discussed in the previous chapter, biofeedback is a process in which people learn to control such "involuntary" functions as heartbeat and respiration. If the pain involves muscles, such as in tension headaches or back pain, biofeedback can be helpful (Dolce & Raczynski, 1985).

▶ Nerve and brain stimulation: Low-voltage electric current passed through painful parts of the body in a process called **transcutaneous electrical nerve stimulation (TENS)** can sometimes bring pain relief. In extreme cases, electrodes can be surgically implanted into the brain, and a handheld battery pack can stimulate nerve cells to provide direct relief.

▶ Relaxation techniques: People can be trained to systematically relax their bodies, thereby decreasing the pain caused by tension.

▶ Surgery: One of the most extreme methods, surgery can be used to cut certain nerve fibers carrying pain messages to the brain. Still, because there is a danger that other functions of the body will be affected, surgery is a treatment of last resort.

▶ Psychological counseling: In cases where pain cannot be successfully treated (it is important to keep in mind that there are no "miracle cures"), psychological counseling is employed to help a patient cope more effectively with the experience of pain.

RECAP AND REVIEW III

Recap

◀ The senses of hearing, motion, and balance are centered in the ear.

◀ The major parts of the ear are the outer ear (which includes the auditory canal and eardrum), the middle ear (with the hammer, anvil, and stirrup), and the oval window leading to the inner ear. The inner ear contains the cochlea, basilar membrane, and hair cells.

◀ The sense of balance is centered in the ear's semicircular canals and otoliths.

◀ The physical aspects of sound include frequency and intensity. Both place and frequency processes are believed to operate in the transformation of sound waves into the experience of sound.

◀ Less is known about the senses of smell and taste and the skin senses (touch, pressure, temperature, and pain) than about vision and hearing. One major research focus has been on understanding the causes of pain and devising ways to alleviate it, often by using drugs, hypnosis, biofeedback, nerve and brain stimulation, relaxation techniques, surgery, and psychotherapy.

Review

1. Trace the path of sound through an ear by ordering, from the outside in, the following structures: eardrum, auditory canal, outer ear, middle ear, inner ear, oval window.

2. The hammer, anvil, and stirrup are tiny bones contained in the
   a. Outer ear
   b. Middle ear
   c. Inner ear
   d. Oval window

3. The process by which the cochlea picks up subtle vibrations moving across the skull is known as bone conduction. True or false? _____

4. The structure of the ear that senses the constant pull of gravity is the
   a. Basilar membrane
   b. Semicircular canal
   c. Otolith
   d. Eardrum

5. High- and low-pitched sounds are characterized by

waves of different _____ , whereas loud and soft sounds are characterized by waves of different _____ .

6. The _____ theory appears to offer an explanation of how we sense high-frequency sounds, whereas the _____ theory seems to explain how we sense low-frequency sounds.

7. The _____ cortex provides us with a map of sound frequencies.

8. Chemical messages, such as those signaling sexual availability, are sent by some animals through the release of _____ .

9. Our sense of smell is activated through contact with the _____ _____ .

10. The sour taste of a lemon is most distinct when exposed to what part of the tongue?
a. Tip b. Underside c. Sides d. Rear

11. Which *two* descriptions explain how the "gate" to the brain might be closed to pain according to the gate-control theory?
a. The brain sends a message down the spinal cord to the injured site.
b. The brain opens up more nerve pathways to disperse the pain.
c. Messages are sent from the injured site up the spinal cord to the brain.
d. Nonpainful stimuli compete with and displace the neural message of pain.

(Answers to review questions are on page 122.)

◀ **LOOKING BACK**

1. This chapter has examined the way our senses respond to the world around us. Sensation is our initial contact with stimuli (forms of energy that activate a sense organ). Sensation has traditionally been investigated by the branch of psychology called psychophysics, which studies the relationship between the physical nature of stimuli and a person's sensory responses to them.

2. One major area of psychophysics is the study of the absolute threshold, the smallest amount of physical intensity by which a stimulus can be detected. Although under ideal conditions absolute thresholds are extraordinarily sensitive, the presence of noise (background stimuli that interfere with the other stimuli) reduces detection capabilities. Moreover, factors such as an individual's expectations and motivations affect success in detecting stimuli. Signal detection theory is now used to predict the accuracy of judgments by systematically taking into account two kinds of errors made by observers—reporting the presence of a stimulus when there is none and reporting the absence of a stimulus when one is actually present.

3. Difference thresholds relate to the smallest detectable difference between two stimuli, known as a just noticeable difference. According to Weber's law, a just noticeable difference is a constant proportion of the magnitude of an initial stimulus.

4. Sensory adaptation occurs when we become accustomed to a constant stimulus and change our evaluation of it. Repeated exposure to a stimulus results in an apparent decline in sensitivity to it.

5. Human sensory experience goes well beyond the traditional five senses, although most is known about just two: vision and hearing. Vision depends on sensitivity to light, electromagnetic waves that are reflected off objects outside the body. The eye shapes the light into an image that is transformed into nerve impulses and interpreted by the brain.

6. When light first enters the eye, it travels through the cornea and then traverses the pupil, a dark hole in the center of the iris. The size of the pupil opening adjusts according to the amount of light entering the eye. Light then enters the lens, which, by a process called accommodation, acts to focus light rays onto the rear of the eye. On the rear of the eye is the retina, which is composed of light-sensitive nerve cells called rods and cones. The rods and cones are unevenly spaced over the retina, with the greatest concentration of cones occurring in an area called the fovea.

7. The visual information gathered by the rods and cones is transferred via bipolar and ganglion cells through the optic nerve, which leads to the optic chiasma—the point where the optic nerve splits. Because the image on the retina is reversed and upside down, images from the right half of the retina are actually from the field of vision to the left of the person, and vice versa. Moreover, because of the phenomenon of adaptation, it takes time to adjust to situations that are either measurably lighter or measurably darker than the previous environment.

8. Color vision seems to be based on two processes described by the trichromatic theory and the opponent-process theory. The trichromatic theory suggests that there are three kinds of cones in the retina, each of which is responsive to a certain range of colors. The opponent-process theory presumes pairs of different types of cells in the eye. These cells work in opposition to each other.

9. Sound, motion, and balance are centered in the ear. Sounds, in the form of vibrating air waves, enter through the outer ear and travel through the canal until they reach the eardrum. The vibrations of the eardrum are

transmitted into the middle ear, which consists of three bones: the hammer, the anvil, and the stirrup. These bones transmit vibrations to the oval window, a thin membrane leading to the inner ear. In the inner ear, vibrations move into the cochlea, which encloses the basilar membrane. Hair cells on the basilar membrane change the mechanical energy of sound waves into nerve impulses which are transmitted to the brain. In addition to processing sound, the ear serves as the site of the organs that sense balance and motion through the semicircular canals and otoliths.

10. Sound has a number of important characteristics. One is frequency, the number of wave crests that occur in a second. Differences in the frequency of sound waves create different pitches. Another aspect of sound is intensity, the variations in pressure produced by a wave as it travels through the air. Intensity is measured in decibels. The place theory of hearing and the frequency theory of hearing explain the processes by which we distinguish sounds of varying frequency and intensity.

11. Considerably less is known about smell, taste, and the skin senses than about vision and hearing. Still, it is clear that smell employs olfactory cells (the receptor cells of the nose) and that taste is centered in the tongue's taste buds, which are capable of sensing combinations of sweet, sour, salty, and bitter flavors.

12. The skin senses are responsible for the experiences of touch, pressure, temperature, and pain. We know the most about pain, which can be explained by the gate-control theory. The theory suggests that particular nerve receptors lead to specific areas of the brain related to pain. When these receptors are activated, a "gate" to the brain is opened, allowing the sensation of pain to be experienced. In addition, there is another set of receptors which, when stimulated, close the gate, thereby reducing the experience of pain. Endorphins, internal painkillers, may also affect the operation of the gate.

13. In cases of severe, long-term pain, pain clinics can sometimes offer relief. Among the current techniques used to alleviate pain are administration of drugs, hypnosis, biofeedback, nerve and brain stimulation, relaxation techniques, surgery, and psychotherapy.

KEY TERMS AND CONCEPTS ▶

stimulus (p. 89)
sensation (90)
magnitude (90)
psychophysics (90)
absolute threshold (90)
noise (91)
signal detection theory (92)
difference threshold (93)
just noticeable difference (93)
Weber's law (93)
adaptation (94)
light (97)
visual spectrum (97)
cornea (97)
pupil (97)
iris (97)
lens (98)
accommodation (98)
retina (99)
rods (99)
cones (99)
fovea (99)

peripheral vision (100)
rhodopsin (100)
bipolar cells (100)
ganglion cells (101)
optic nerve (101)
optic chiasma (101)
glaucoma (101)
tunnel vision (101)
feature detection (102)
light adaptation (104)
dark adaptation (104)
trichromatic theory (104)
afterimage (106)
opponent-process theory (106)
outer ear (108)
sound (109)
auditory canal (109)
eardrum (109)
middle ear (109)
hammer (109)
anvil (109)
stirrup (109)

oval window (109)
inner ear (109)
cochlea (109)
basilar membrane (110)
hair cells (110)
frequency (111)
pitch (111)
intensity (111)
decibel (111)
place theory of hearing (111)
frequency theory of hearing (111)
semicircular canals (113)
otoliths (113)
pheromones (115)
olfactory cells (116)
taste buds (116)
skin senses (117)
gate-control theory of pain (118)
acupuncture (118)
transcutaneous electrical nerve
    stimulation (TENS) (120)

ANSWERS (REVIEW III):
1. Outer ear, auditory canal, eardrum, middle ear, oval window, inner ear   **2.** b   **3.** True   **4.** c   **5.** Frequency, intensity
6. Place, frequency   **7.** Auditory   **8.** Pheromones   **9.** Olfactory cells   **10.** c   **11.** a, d

FOR FURTHER STUDY AND APPLICATION ▶

Coren, S., & Ward, L. M. (1989). *Sensation and perception* (3rd ed.). New York: Harcourt Brace Jovanovich.

Goldstein, E. B. (1989). *Sensation and perception* (3rd ed.). Belmont, CA: Wadsworth.
These are fine general overviews of sensation and the senses, including a broad and balanced treatment of theories, principles, and findings.

Gregory, R. L. (1978). *The psychology of seeing* (3rd ed.). New York: McGraw-Hill.
This volume focuses on the operation of the eye and on the nature of human sight.

Sternbach, R. A. (Ed.) (1987). *The psychology of pain*. New York: Raven Press.

Hendler, N. H., Long, D. M., & Wise, T. N. (1982). *Diagnosis and treatment of chronic pain*. Boston: J. Wright.
These books provide an overview of treatments and strategies for pain reduction.

CHAPTER 4

PERCEPTION

PROLOGUE:
KAL FLIGHT 007

The disaster was one that could have been avoided. But because of an apparent series of perceptual errors, one compounding another, 269 people were killed when a Soviet fighter shot down Korean Air Lines Flight 007 as it strayed off course and passed over the eastern coast of the Soviet Union.

The first mistake appears to have been made by the pilot and other crew members of the Boeing 747, who may have erroneously programmed the plane's navigational computer and brought the plane over a sensitive Soviet military installation, some 500 kilometers to the west of where it should have been. Compounding the initial mistake, the crew members failed to perceive the error, ignoring information from instruments that could have told them that they were in the wrong place.

The fatal perceptual error, which ultimately led to the destruction of the plane, seems to have occurred on the part of a Soviet military pilot, who mistook the Boeing 747 for an RC-135, a sophisticated American plane used for spying. Although the RC-135 is smaller, the shape of its frame is similar to that of the 747, and a Soviet pilot flying below and behind the 747 could have easily misperceived it as an RC-135 (see Figure 4-1). Convinced he was confronting a spy plane, the Russian pilot radioed for instructions to his commanders—and was ordered to fire the missile that sent the 747 plunging into the sea.

LOOKING AHEAD ▶

Although the complete story of the downing of Korean Air Lines Flight 007 may never be known, it is apparent that perceptual errors played a central role in the tragedy. Despite the sophistication of our sensory system, our ultimate understanding of the world is based, not on a complete and perfectly

FIGURE 4-1

Soviet officials argued that their pilot mistook a Korean Air Lines jumbo jet for a U.S. Air Force spy plane. Although the profiles of the planes are quite different, from beneath they look similar.

accurate reproduction of the information that our senses provide us with, but on our *interpretation* of that information.

At the same time, our knowledge of the world's myriad and varied stimuli is surprisingly accurate much of the time. For example, we can recognize the face of an old friend whom we have not seen in twenty years, even though he or she may have aged considerably, and we can perceive the tiny shapes on this page as letters and turn them into meaningful words and sentences.

The processes underlying our ability to give meaning to stimuli have been explored by psychologists who study perception. **Perception** is the sorting out, interpretation, analysis, and integration of stimuli from our sensory organs. The study of perception is directed at finding out how we take stimuli and form conscious representations of the environment.

Perception is clearly an outgrowth of sensation, and it is sometimes difficult to distinguish the two. (Indeed, psychologists—and philosophers, as well—have argued for years over the distinction.) The primary difference is that sensation can be thought of as an organism's first encounter with a raw sensory stimulus, while perception is the process by which it is interpreted, analyzed, and integrated with other sensory information. For instance, if we were considering sensation, we might ask how bright a stimulus appears; if we were considering perception, we might ask whether someone recognizes the stimulus and what it means to that person.

To understand the importance of perception, we might consider for a moment what the world would be like if we responded only to the raw, sensory stimuli presented to us. Because of the vast number of stimuli to which we are constantly exposed, the world would be filled with an overwhelming array of sights, sounds, and other sensations, and we would be unable to respond coherently to them. Perception, however, enables us to take those different stimuli and place them in a context that provides us with meaning and understanding.

After reading this chapter, you will be able to answer the following questions relating to perception:

▶ What principles underlie our organization of the stimuli to which our sense organs are exposed, allowing us to make sense of our environment?

▶ How are we able to perceive the world in three dimensions when our retinas are capable of sensing only two-dimensional images?

▶ How do we sort out auditory stimuli, paying attention to particular stimuli and ignoring others?

▶ What clues do visual illusions give us about our understanding of general perceptual mechanisms?

Perception: The sorting out, interpretation, analysis, and integration of stimuli from our sensory organs

VIEWING THE WORLD: PERCEPTUAL ORGANIZATION

Look, for a moment, at the shapes in Figure 4-2. Most of us would report that we saw a figure on a horse in Figure 4-2*a*, a set of brackets in Figure 4-2*b*, rows of circles and squares in Figure 4-2*c*, and an oval and a square intersecting in Figure 4-2*d*. But are these the only interpretations that could

(a)

(b)

FIGURE 4-2

Perceptual organization at work. Although the figure in (*a*) can be seen as a series of unrelated splotches, (*b*) as lines with protrusions at top and bottom, (*c*) as columns of alternating circles and squares, and (*d*) as three separate shapes, most of us see in (*a*) a horse and rider, in (*b*) a series of brackets, in (*c*) rows of circles and squares, and in (*d*) an overlapping oval and square. [(a) *Mednick, Higgins, & Kirschbaum, 1975).*]

(c)

(d)

be given? A reasonable person could argue that there are a series of unrelated blotches in Figure 4-2*a*, ten lines with two protrusions coming off each line in Figure 4-2*b*, seven columns of alternating circles and squares in Figure 4-2*c*, and three distinct enclosed areas in Figure 4-2*d*.

The fact that most of us are apt to interpret the shapes as meaningful wholes illustrates some of the basic processes of perception at work: We try to simplify the complex stimuli presented to us by the environment. If we did not reduce the complex into something understandable, the world would present too much of a challenge for us to function, and—unless we lived as hermits in drab, colorless, silent caves—we would spend all our time just sorting through its myriad stimuli. Ironically, psychologists have found that the process of simplifying the world requires an impressive amount of perceptual effort.

WHOLES FROM PARTS: The Gestalt Laws of Organization

The basic perceptual processes operate according to a series of principles that describe how we organize bits and pieces of information into meaningful wholes. These are known as **gestalt laws of organization**, set forth in the early 1900s by a group of German psychologists who studied patterns—or **gestalts** (Wertheimer, 1923). They discovered a number of important principles which are valid for visual and auditory stimuli:

▶ **Closure**—Groupings are usually made in terms of enclosed or complete figures rather than open ones. We tend to ignore the breaks, then, in Figure 4-2*a* and *b* and concentrate on the overall forms.

▶ **Proximity**—Elements that are closer together are grouped together. Because of this, we tend to see pairs of dots rather than a row of single dots in the following:

      . . . .

Gestalt (geh SHTALLT) **laws of organization**: A series of principles that describe how we organize pieces of information into meaningful wholes; they include closure, proximity, similarity, and simplicity

Gestalts: Patterns studied by the gestalt psychologists

Closure: The tendency to group according to enclosed or complete figures rather than open or incomplete ones

Proximity: The tendency to group together those elements that are close together

T.M.

▶ **Similarity**—Elements that are similar in appearance are grouped together. We see, then, horizontal rows of circles and squares in Figure 4-2c instead of vertical mixed columns.

Similarity: The tendency to group together those elements that are similar in appearance

▶ **Simplicity**—In a general sense, the overriding gestalt principle is one of simplicity: When we observe a pattern, we perceive it in the most basic, straight-forward manner that we can (Hochberg, 1978). For example, Figure 4-2d is seen as an interlocking of the simpler two figures, rather than as two separate forms. If we have a choice in interpretations, we generally opt for the simpler one.

Simplicity: The tendency to perceive a pattern in the most basic, straightfor-ward, organized manner possible—the overriding gestalt principle

HALF FULL OR HALF EMPTY?: Figure and Ground

Look at the logo from the movie *Batman* in Figure 4-3. It was designed to be ambiguous, so that sometimes people see a figure of a bat and at other times they see teeth in a gaping mouth.

Chances are that you first saw one but very soon after perceived the other. Most people, in fact, shift back and forth between these two interpretations. The difficulty we face is that because the figure is two-dimensional, the usual means we employ for distinguishing the **figure** (the object being perceived) from the **ground** (the background or spaces within the object) do not work.

Figure/ground: Figure refers to the object being perceived, whereas ground refers to the background of or spaces within the object

The fact that we can look at the same figure in either of two ways illustrates an important point first emphasized by the gestalt psychologists: We do not just passively respond to visual stimuli that happen to fall on our retinas. Instead, we actively try to organize and make sense of what we see (see Figure 4-4). Perception, then, is typically a constructive process by which we go beyond the stimuli that are presented to us and attempt to construct a meaningful situation (Haber, 1983; Kienker et al., 1986).

WHERE 1 + 1 EQUALS MORE THAN 2: The Whole Is Greater Than Its Parts

If someone were to try to convince you that 1 plus 1 equals more than 2, you would think that person needed to brush up on some basic arithmetic. Yet the idea that two objects considered together form a whole that is greater than the simple combination of the objects was a fundamental principle of

130

FIGURE 4-4

What does this message say? You probably read it as "My phone number is area code 604, 876-1569. Please call!" If you did, however, you were being affected by the context of the message. Go back and look more carefully at it, and you will notice the word "is" and the number "15" are written identically. You'll also note that the "h" in the word "phone" and "b" in the word "number" are the same, as well as the "d" in the word "code" and the "l" in the word "please." You probably had no trouble in sorting these similarities out, though, because of your prior experience and because of the context that the message provided. (*Coren, Porac, & Ward, 1979.*)

> My phone number is area
> code 604, 876-1569. Please call!

Perceptual constancy: The phenomenon by which physical objects are perceived as unvarying despite changes in their appearance or the surrounding environment

the gestalt psychologists. They argued—quite convincingly, in fact—that perception of stimuli in our environment goes well beyond the individual elements that we sense and represents an active, constructive process carried out within the brain, where bits and pieces of sensations are put together to make something greater—and more meaningful—than the individual elements separately.

Consider, for instance, Figure 4-5. As you examine the black patches, it is likely that you will perceive the form of a dog. The dog represents a gestalt, or perceptual whole. Although you can see the individual parts that make up the figure, putting each of them together forms something greater than these individual parts. The whole, then, is greater than the sum of the individual elements.

One outgrowth of this active perceptual processing is **perceptual constancy**, a phenomenon in which physical objects are perceived as unvarying and consistent, despite changes in their appearance or in the physical environment. For instance, consider what happens as you finish a conversation with a friend and she begins to walk away from you. As you watch her walk down the street, the image on your retina becomes smaller and smaller. Yet you do not think she is shrinking, despite this change in sensory experience. Instead, because you factor into your thinking the knowledge that she is also getting farther away, the phenomenon of perceptual constancy compensates for the change in retinal image, and you ultimately perceive her as the same size no matter how far away she moves.

FIGURE 4-5

Although at first it is difficult to distinguish anything in this drawing, you probably will eventually be able to discern the figure of a dog. (*Ronald C. James, from Carraher, R. G., and Thurston, J. B. (1966). Optical Illusions in the Visual Arts. New York: Von Nostrand Reinhold.*)

One of the most dramatic examples of perceptual constancy occurs with the rising moon. When the moon first appears at night, close to the horizon, it seems to be huge—considerably larger than when it is high in the sky later in the evening. You may have thought that the size difference was caused by the moon's being physically closer to the earth when it first appears, but in fact this is not the case at all (Reed, 1984). Instead, the moon appears to be larger when it is close to the horizon because of a breakdown in perceptual constancy. Intervening terrain and objects such as trees convey a greater sense of distance when the moon is on the horizon; when the moon is higher in the sky, we see it by itself. To prove this, try looking at the moon when it is low through a paper-towel tube; the moon will suddenly appear to "shrink" back to normal size.

Perceptual constancy occurs not just with size but with shape and color as well. The image on your retina varies as a plane approaches, flies overhead, and disappears, yet you do not perceive the plane as changing shape. Instead, you perceive it as unchanging, despite the physical variations that occur. Similarly, the soft lighting in a dimly lit restaurant might allow you to notice for the first time that a companion's eyes are an entrancing shade of blue. Yet you probably would not complain the next day when the bright sunlight produced a somewhat different color of blue. In fact, you probably wouldn't even notice the difference: Because of color constancy, you would perceive the blue as the same shade.

Although perceptual constancy aids us in simplifying the world, not all its outcomes are positive ones. For instance, the higher accident rate experienced by drivers of small cars may be due in part to other drivers' underestimating the closeness of smaller cars, since at a particular distance a small car produces a smaller retinal image than a larger one (Eberts & MacMillan, 1985).

The exact process by which we experience perceptual constancy is not completely understood and has given rise to two competing theories. One explanation—**unconscious inference theory**—suggests that we use our prior experience about the size of an object to make unconscious inferences about its location (Lindsay & Norman, 1977; Rock, 1983). Because we have learned the size of particular stimuli from earlier experience, we compensate for changes in its size on the retina by inferring its location.

In contrast, **ecological theory** suggests that the relationships among different objects in a scene give us clues about their sizes (Gibson, 1979). According to this theory, when a friend walks away from us into the distance, not only is she farther away, but so are the objects she is close to. Therefore, all objects near her are going to produce an image that is proportionally smaller on our retina. Ecological theory suggests that we consider the scene as a whole and that perceptual constancy is brought about by direct perception of all the stimuli in the scene.

While we cannot say whether unconscious inference theory or ecological theory provides a more complete account of perception, it is clear that perceptual abilities develop early in life (Treisman & Gormican, 1988; Gibson, 1988). Indeed, perception is quite sophisticated even at birth (see Chapter 12), although learning and experience clearly play a critical role in its development.

Various theories have tried to explain the breakdown in perceptual constancy that occurs in the "moon illusion"—the phenomenon of the moon close to the horizon looking so much larger than it looks when higher in the sky. (*Mark Antman/The Image Works*)

Unconscious inference theory: A process whereby unconscious inferences about an object's location are made on the basis of prior experience of the object's size

Ecological theory: A theory suggesting that the relationship between objects in a scene gives clues about the objects' sizes

Recap

◄ Perception refers to the process by which sensory stimuli are interpreted, analyzed, and integrated.

◄ Among the gestalt laws of organization are closure, proximity, and similarity. The overriding principle, however, is simplicity.

◄ People do not respond passively to visual stimuli; rather, they try to separate a given figure from the background.

◄ Two competing theories seek to explain perceptual constancy: unconscious inference theory and ecological theory.

Review

1. An organism's initial encounter with a stimulus is referred to as _____ ; the subsequent interpretation, analysis, and integration of the stimulus is known as _____ .

2. The principles that describe how we sort separate pieces of information into organized wholes are known as the _____ .

3. Match the perceptual experiences described in the right-hand column with the principles of gestalt laws of organization in the left-hand column.

    a. ____ Proximity

    1. Jill identified the horse and rider by disregarding the breaks in the picture and concentrating on the whole.

    b. ____ Similarity

    2. Cary described the pattern in terms of the most basic design she perceived.

    c. ____ Simplicity

    3. Jim found that by grouping together the elements of the figure closest to one another, he could perceive a meaningful whole.

    d. ____ Closure

    4. In another picture, Jim found that by grouping together like elements, he was able to perceive order in its design.

4. Even though an oncoming car appears to grow in size as it approaches, the phenomenon of _____ _____ explains why we perceive the automobile as consistent in size.

5. The phenomenon referred to in question 4 occurs with shape and color as well as size. True or false? _____

6. The theory that explains perceptual constancy in terms of the relationships between stimuli in the environment being viewed is known as the _____ theory. The theory that credits prior learning for providing us with the ability to perceive accurately is known as the _____ theory.

(Answers to review questions are on page 134.)

TRANSLATING 2-D TO 3-D: Depth Perception

As sophisticated as the retina is, the images that are projected onto it are flat and two-dimensional. Yet the world around us is three-dimensional, and we perceive it that way. How do we make the transformation from 2-D to 3-D?

The ability to view the world in three dimensions and to perceive distance—an ability known as **depth perception**—is due largely to the fact that we have two eyes. Because there is some distance between the eyes, a slightly different image reaches each retina, and the brain integrates them into one composite view. But it does not ignore the difference in images, which is known as **binocular disparity**; the disparity allows the brain to estimate the distance of an object from us.

Generally speaking, the farther away a stimulus is, the less the retinal disparity; and the closer the object, the greater the disparity between the two images. You can see this for yourself. Hold a pencil at arm's length and look at it first with one eye and then with the other. There is little difference between the two views relative to the background. Now bring the pencil just 6 inches away from your face, and try the same thing. This time you will perceive a greater difference between the two views. The fact that the discrepancy between the two eyes varies according to object distance provides you with a means of determining distance: Greater discrepancies are inter-

Depth perception: The ability to view the world in three dimensions and to perceive distance

Biocular disparity: The difference between the images that reach the retina of each eye; this disparity allows the brain to estimate distance

Moviegoers in the 1950s, such as these people watching *Bwana Devil,* could enjoy a sense of three-dimensionality by wearing specially designed glasses. (*Culver Pictures*)

preted to mean that an object is closer, while smaller discrepancies are interpreted to mean that an object is farther away.

Filmmakers, whose medium compels them to project images in just two dimensions, have tried to create the illusion of depth perception by using two cameras, spaced slightly apart, to produce slightly different images, each destined for a different eye. In a 3-D movie, the two images are projected simultaneously. This produces a double image, unless special glasses are worn to allow each image to be viewed by the eye for which it is intended. The special glasses—familiar to moviegoers since the first 3-D movie, *Bwana Devil,* appeared in 1952—provide a genuine sense of depth. Similar processes are being developed to show 3-D movies on television (Rogers, 1988).

Processes analogous to binocular disparity in the eye give the ear a sense of sound localization—of where a sound is coming from. Because the ears are several inches apart, wave patterns in the air enter each ear at a slightly different time, permitting the brain to use the discrepancy to locate the place from which the sound is originating.

However, it is important to realize that depth or location can be perceived by even a single sense organ. For example, it is not always necessary to use two eyes to perceive depth; certain cues permit us to obtain a sense of depth and distance with just one eye (Burnham, 1983). These cues are known as **monocular cues.** One monocular cue—**motion parallax**—is the change in position of an object on the retina as the head moves from side to side. The brain is able to calculate the distance of the object by the amount of change in the retinal image. Similarly, experience has taught us that if two objects are the same size, the one that makes a smaller image on the retina is farther away than the one that provides a larger image—an example of the monocular cue of **relative size.**

Finally, anyone who has ever seen railroad tracks that seem to join together in the distance knows that distant objects appear to be closer together than nearer ones, a phenomenon called **linear perspective** (see Figures 4-6, 4-7, and 4-8). People use linear perspective as a monocular cue in estimating distance, allowing the two-dimensional retinal image to register the three-dimensional world (Bruce & Green, 1984).

Monocular cues: Signals that allow us to perceive distance and depth with just one eye

Motion parallax: The movement of the image of objects on the retina as the head moves, providing a monocular cue to distance

Relative size: The phenomenon by which, if two objects are the same size, the one that makes a smaller image on the retina is perceived to be farther away

Linear perspective: The phenomenon by which distant objects appear to be closer together than nearer objects

FIGURE 4-6

It appears that the edges of this road come closer together as they move away from the driver, illustrating the depth cue of linear perspective. (*Joel Gordon.*)

FIGURE 4-7

Artists are trained to use linear perspective to promote the feeling of distance in their work, as this Van Gogh painting illustrates. (*Source: Van Gogh,* Hospital Corridor at Saint Remy. *1889. Collection, The Museum of Modern Art, New York. Abby Aldrich Rockefeller Bequest.*)

ANSWERS (REVIEW I):
1. Sensation, perception   **2.** Gestalt laws of organization   **3.** a-3,   b-4,   c-2,   d-1
4. Perceptual constancy   **5.** True   **6.** Ecological, unconscious inference

FIGURE 4-8

A clever use of linear perspective cues in this M. C Escher painting creates an impossible scene, as monks walk along a staircase that never ends. (*Source: M. C. Escher, Ascending and Descending. 1960. Haags Gemeentemuseum, by permission of M. C. Escher Heirs, Cordon Art, Baarn, The Netherlands.*)

AS THE WORLD TURNS: Motion Perception

When a batter tries to hit a pitch, the most important factor is the motion of the ball. How is a batter able to judge the speed and location of a target that is moving at some 90 miles per hour?

The answer rests, in part, on several cues that provide us with relevant information about the perception of motion. For one thing, the perceived movement of an object across the retina is typically made relative to some stable, nonmoving background. Moreover, if the stimulus is heading toward us, the image on the retina may expand in size, filling more and more of the visual field. In such cases, we assume that the stimulus is approaching—and not that it is an expanding stimulus viewed at a constant distance.

It is not, however, just the movement of images across the retina that brings about the perception of motion. If it were, we would perceive the world as moving every time we moved our heads. Instead, one of the critical things we learn about perception is to factor information about head and eye movements along with information about changes in the retinal image.

In some cases, movement is so fast that we are unable to follow it. In those instances, we may be able to anticipate where an object will end up on the basis of our prior experience. For example, computer tracking of baseball pitches has shown that most fast balls thrown in major-league games travel too fast for the eye to follow. Indeed, if a batter tried to follow a fast ball from the moment it left a pitcher's hand, he would lose sight of it by the time it got about five feet from the plate (Bahill, 1984). Research suggests that good hitters take their eyes off the ball during the middle of its trip and shift their vision closer to home plate, waiting for the ball's arrival and (hoped-for) impact with the bat. Thus, instead of relying on the raw sensory input from the traveling ball—the process of sensation—they employ perceptual processes, using what they have learned to expect about the way balls travel.

THE DIRECTION OF PERCEPTION: Top-down and Bottom-up Processing

Ca- yo- re-d t-is -en-en-e, w-ic- ha- ev-ry -hi-d l-tt-r mis-in-? After a bit of thought, you'll probably be able to figure out that it says, "Can you read this sentence, which has every third letter missing?"

The fact that you are able to recognize such an imprecise stimulus illustrates that perception proceeds along two different avenues, called top-down processing and bottom-up processing. In **top-down processing**, perception is guided by higher-level knowledge, experience, expectations, and motivations. You were able to figure out the meaning of the sentence with the missing letters because of your prior reading experience, and because of the fact that written English contains redundancies: Not every letter of each word is necessary to decode its meaning. Moreover, your expectations played a role in your being able to read the sentence; you were probably expecting a statement that had *something* to do with psychology, and not the lyrics to a U2 song.

Top-down processing: Perception guided by knowledge, experience, expectations, and motivations

Even though top-down processing allows you to fill in the gaps, you would be unable to perceive the meaning of the sentence without **bottom-up processing**, which consists of recognizing and processing information about the individual components of the stimuli. You would make no headway in your recognition of the sentence without being able to perceive the individual shapes that make up the letters. Some perception, then, occurs at the level of the patterns and features of each of the separate letters.

Bottom-up processing: Recognition and processing of individual components of a stimulus

It should be apparent that both top-down and bottom-up processing occur simultaneously, and interact with each other, in our perception of the world around us. It is bottom-up processing that allows us to process the fundamental characteristics of stimuli, whereas top-down processing allows us to bring our experience to bear on perception. And as we learn more about the complex processes involved in perception, we are developing a better understanding of how our brain continually interprets information from our senses and permits us to make responses appropriate to the environment. (For another view of the importance of perception, see the Cutting Edge box.)

The fields of psychology, art, and brain science are beginning to meet in ways that may help to unravel puzzles in each of the three fields, according to psychologist Margaret Livingstone. She and her colleague David Hubel are investigating the manner in which the brain processes visual information in order to explain how both visual illusions and works of art are perceived.

Livingstone and Hubel suggest that the brain processes and ultimately perceives visual information coming from the eye using three separate systems of structures and neural pathways (Livingstone, 1988; Livingstone & Hubel, 1988). The systems differ in their ability to perceive color, their sensitivity to contrast, their acuity, and the speed at which they process information, although all three systems are eventually integrated into the perception of an object.

The first system, the "parvo," considers high-resolution information about borders of figures that are formed by contrasting colors. The neurons in this system that first receive the information from the eye are responsive to particular colors; later neural processing does not carry information about specific colors. This system is particularly important in allowing us to perceive stationary objects in great detail.

WHERE PSYCHOLOGY, ART, AND THE BRAIN MEET: THE PROCESSING AND PERCEPTION OF VISUAL INFORMATION

The second system, which Livingstone and Hubel refer to as the "blob" (after the configuration of the brain cells involved), processes information about color and shades of gray but is not concerned with information regarding movement, shape, and depth. Although it sees in color, it does not carry as much detail as the first system does.

The third system, the "magno," carries information about movement and depth. This system is particularly sensitive to motion and therefore is good at perceiving moving objects but not stationary ones. Moreover, it is insensitive to color.

The presence of the three systems helps to explain many kinds of reactions to visual stimuli that previously have not been well understood (Reinhardt-Rutland, 1988). For example, some of the unusual effects of modern art probably occur because particular color combinations strongly activate the parvo system while simultaneously being relatively weak activators of the magno system. Because the parvo system is

able to indicate an object's shape while the magno system is unable to respond to its borders (and hence is not able to indicate either movement or position of the stimulus), a stimulus may appear to move around or vibrate on a canvas (see Figure 4-9).

Similarly, advertisements sometimes contain key phrases in colors that are equal in brightness to the background. Even though it is harder to read the text when there is no variation in brightness, advertisers have found that words printed in this fashion have an unusual, jumpy appearance that draws the reader's attention.

Livingstone and Hubel's work holds several implications for the future. For one thing, their research may be useful in practical ways, such as in the construction of more effective surveillance systems. It may also enable people to more accurately judge blurry, fuzzy images, such as x-rays, by encouraging processing in particular systems in the brain (for example, using movement to engage the magno system). Even more important, their work is providing a more complete and accurate description of the way in which visual stimuli are processed and perceived by the brain.

SORTING OUT THE WORLD: Selective Attention

The scene: a crowded, noisy party. As the woman next to you drones on about her new car, you suddenly hear snatches of conversation from behind you about your friend Terry, who seems to have left the party with another guest. Straining to hear what is being said by the person behind you, you lose track of what the woman is saying about her car—until suddenly you realize she has asked a question that requires a response. Brightly you say, "Pardon me—I didn't hear what you said, with all the noise."

Anyone who has been stuck listening to a bore go on and on about something trivial is probably familiar with situations similar to the one de-

THE BIOLOGICAL FOUNDATIONS
OF PSYCHOLOGY

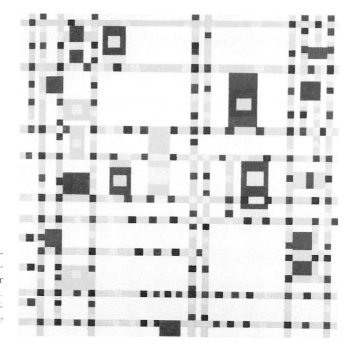

FIGURE 4-9

This op art painting by Piet Mondrian produces an illusion of movement and vibration through the activation of particular visual systems in the brain. (*Piet Mondrian. Broadway Boogie-Woogie. 1942-43. Collection, the Museum of Modern Art, New York. Given anonymously.*)

Selective attention: The perceptual process of choosing a stimulus to attend to

Stroop task: An exercise requiring the division of our attention between two competing stimuli—the meaning of words and the colors in which they are written

Dichotic (dy KOT ik) **listening:** A procedure in which an individual wears earphones through which different messages are sent to each ear at the same time

scribed above. Psychologists interested in perception are also familiar with circumstances such as this one, in which there are many stimuli to pay attention to simultaneously. The psychologist's interest lies primarily in the question of how we are able to sort out and make sense of multiple stimuli.

Selective attention is the perceptual process of choosing which stimulus to pay attention to. We are particularly attentive to stimuli that appear exceptionally bright, large, loud, novel, or high in contrast. We also pay greater attention to stimuli that are particularly meaningful or relevant to our own motivations (Whalen & Liberman, 1987; Posner & Presti, 1987). For example, if we feel hungry, we are more apt to be sensitive to food and food-related stimuli.

Advertisers are well aware of the phenomenon of selective attention. For instance, advertisements often include bright contrasts, and television and radio commercials are typically broadcast at higher volumes than the shows they sponsor. Furthermore, television and radio ads are often run at times of the day when people are particularly sensitive to their content (as when food advertisements are shown at the dinner hour).

In some cases, out attention must be divided between two stimuli. For instance, try the task shown in Figure 4-10, in which you are asked to say aloud the color of the ink used in each of the words—not the color the word spells out. Known as the **Stroop task**, the exercise is a frustratingly difficult one because it encompasses the perception of two powerful stimuli, and you are forced to divide your attention between the color and the meaning of the words (Stroop, 1935). Because both are potent stimuli and because, like most people, you are more experienced with reading than with naming colors, your attention is apt to be drawn away from the color of the ink toward the meaning of the words.

In order to study selective attention in the auditory realm, psychologists have developed a procedure called **dichotic listening**, whereby a person wears earphones through which a different message is sent to each ear at

BLUE   GREEN

GREEN   ORANGE

PURPLE   ORANGE

GREEN   BLUE

RED   RED

GRAY   GRAY

RED   BLUE

BLUE   PURPLE

FIGURE 4-10

To try the Stroop task, name the colors in which each of these words are printed as quickly as you can, ignoring the word that is spelled out. For most people, the task is frustratingly difficult.

the same time. The individual is asked to repeat one of the messages aloud as it comes into one ear—a process known as **shadowing**, since the listener's voice acts as a verbal "shadow" of the message being received.

The question of interest is not so much whether the person is able to shadow the message adequately (most people can do so fairly easily); instead, it revolves around the effects of the message coming into the other ear. It turns out that although the content of the second message typically cannot be recalled, certain characteristics of the message can be remembered (Cherry, 1953). For instance, listeners accurately report whether the speaker was a man or a woman and whether the sex of the speaker changed during the course of the message. About one-third of the time, they can also report hearing whether their names were spoken.

One factor that seems particularly important is the meaningfulness of the message being shadowed. If a message that is being shadowed from one ear suddenly switches to the other, subjects generally "follow" the message to the second ear and begin to shadow from the second ear, even though they have been specifically instructed to shadow only what is being heard in the first ear (see Figure 4-11). Moreover, they are usually not even aware that they have made the switch (Treisman, 1960).

Experiments such as these suggest that although people may fully concentrate on only one message at a time, they still pay attention on some level to other information. This, then, explains our ability to eavesdrop on one conversation at a party but to know when it is time to make a response to someone to whom we are supposedly listening at the same time.

The phenomena involved in selective attention are of particular importance to people whose jobs require the constant monitoring of gauges or dials: pilots, air traffic controllers, nuclear power plant operators, and so on. Ironically, however, research has shown that as the importance of accurately attending to deviations from normal readings increases, people are less successfully able to carry out the task (Wickens, 1984). For example, in the late 1970s the nuclear power plant at Three Mile Island suffered a loss of cooling fluid that ultimately led to the leak of clouds of radioactive steam. At the time, information was available that could have rectified the crisis at an early stage. However, the operators on duty attended only to certain portions of the information, which turned out to be erroneous. Had they been attentive to information that was indicated on other instruments, they would have

Shadowing: A technique used during dichotic listening in which a subject is asked to repeat one of the messages aloud as it comes into one ear

Jet pilots face a dizzying array of information, making selective attention a critical process. (*Copyright © 1989 Roger Ressmeyer—Starlight*)

FIGURE 4-11

A shadowing experiment. Subjects are told to shadow—or repeat—only the message being heard in their right ear, as the two messages shown in the captions are heard simultaneously. Although subjects are unaware that they are doing it, if the message switches to the opposite ear, they will typically begin to shadow that message, despite the experimenter's instructions.

been able to stop the leakage before serious damage had been done. Similarly, had the pilot of the Korean Air Lines jet (discussed at the beginning of the chapter) heeded the information available to him about the plane's flight path, he could have avoided straying off course.

In order to increase the accuracy with which people are able to scan and selectively attend to many stimuli simultaneously, psychologists have developed several principles for designing instruments that provide important information (Sanders & McCormick, 1987). Among the major ones are minimizing the number of sources of information, simplifying the display of information, and keeping sources of information physically close to one another. These guidelines have helped to improve the accuracy of perception as well as to reduce stress levels among those workers monitoring the instruments (Wiener & Nagel, 1988).

RECAP AND REVIEW II

Recap

◀ Depth perception occurs because of binocular disparity, motion parallax, and relative size of images on the retina.

◀ The movement of images across the retina, combined with information about head and eye movements, brings about the perception of motion.

◀ Perception occurs with top-down and bottom-up processing.

◀ Selective attention is the perceptual process of choosing which stimulus to pay attention to.

REVIEW

1. The images that are projected onto our retinas are three-dimensional. True or false? _____

2. Match each term with its descriptor by placing the appropriate number in each blank.

   a. _____ Depth perception

   b. _____ Binocular disparity

   c. _____ Monocular cues

   1. The differences in images received by our retinas

   2. A monocular cue relating near and far objects

   3. The phenomenon by which two parallel lines appear to converge in the distance

d. _____ Motion parallax

e. _____ Relative size

f. _____ Linear perspective

4. The means by which we can obtain a sense of depth with just one eye

5. The relative movement of objects as our head moves from side to side.

6. Our ability to view the world in three dimensions and to discriminate distance

3. Good hitters in baseball are those who keep their eyes on the ball right up until the time it reaches the plate. True or false? _____

4. Cory was able to look at and figure out the problem by relying on expectations based on past experience, a phenomenon known as _____ - _____ processing, as well as by dis-

criminating specific components, a phenomenon known as _____ - _____ processing.

5. By broadcasting an advertisement at a higher volume, advertisers are capitalizing on the process of _____ _____ .

6. As a research subject, you are asked to repeat a message as it is delivered into your left ear, while simultaneously receiving a different message in your right ear. This research procedure is referred to as _____.

7. An interesting finding of experiments such as the one described above is that individuals can rarely recall any features of the message they are not asked to repeat. True or false? _____

8. As the importance of selectively attending to many stimuli at once increases, people appear to be less able to do so accurately. True or false? _____

(Answers to review questions are on page 142.)

PERCEPTION IN EVERYDAY LIFE

For sight follows gracious contours, and unless we flatter its pleasure by proportionate alternations of these parts (so that by adjustment we offset the amount to which it suffers illusions), an uncouth and ungracious aspect will be presented to the spectators.

The phenomenon to which Vitruvius, a Greek architect who lived around 30 B.C., refers so elegantly in this quote is that people do not always view the world accurately, and that it is important to consider how people's eyes and brains perceive buildings when designing architectural works.

Consider the Parthenon, one of the most famous buildings of ancient Greece. Although it looks true and straight to the eye, it was actually built with a bulge on one side. This protrusion fools viewers into thinking it is straight. If it didn't have that bulge—and quite a few other "tricks" like it, such as columns that incline inward—it would look as if it were crooked and about to fall down.

The fact that the Parthenon appears to be completely upright, with its lines straight and right angles at every corner, is the result of a series of **visual illusions**, physical stimuli that consistently produce errors in perception (Coren & Ward, 1989). As you can see in Figure 4-12a, if the building were completely square it would seem to be sagging, since there is a common visual illusion that makes angles placed above a line give the line the appearance of being bent (as in Figure 4-12b). If this had not been compensated for, the Parthenon would have looked as it does in Figure 4-12c. Therefore, the Parthenon was built with a slight upward curvature (as in Figure 4-12d).

Such perceptual insights did not stop with the Greeks; modern-day architects and designers also take visual distortions into account in their planning (see Figure 4-15). For example, the New Orleans Superdome makes use of several visual tricks: Its seats vary in color throughout the stadium in order to give the appearance, from a distance, that there is always a full

Visual illusion: A physical stimulus that consistently produces errors in perception (often called an optical illusion)

PART 2

THE BIOLOGICAL FOUNDATIONS
OF PSYCHOLOGY

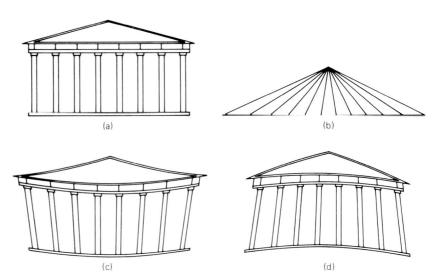

FIGURE 4-12

In building the Parthenon, the Greeks constructed an architectural wonder that looks perfectly straight, with right angles at every corner, as in (*a*). However, the visual illusion illustrated in (*b*) would have made it look as it appears in (*c*) if it actually had been built with true right angles. To compensate for this illusion, the Parthenon was designed to have a slight upward curvature, as shown in (*d*). (*Coren, Porac, & Ward, 1979, p. 6.*)

(a)

(b)

(c)

(d)

PSYCHOLOGY AT WORK

SEXING CHICKS: GETTING PERCEPTION RIGHT

How do you sex a chick?

To chicken farmers, this is hardly an idle question. One of their greatest challenges is identifying the sex of newborn chicks, whose sex organs are, to say the least, obscure (see Figure 4-13). It takes years to learn to differentiate male and female day-old chicks accurately—although expert sexors can eventually classify them at a rate of about 1000 per hour, with 98 percent accuracy (Lunn, 1948).

To psychologists Irving Biederman and Margaret Shiffrar, the chick-sexing problem has implications well beyond the barnyard. For example, it has much in common with the difficulty of learning to perceive subtle differences in a wide variety of stimuli. Thus the Soviet fighter pilot who apparently had difficulty perceiving the difference between the Korean Air Lines 747 passenger jet and a military attack plane was clearly unable to make a critical

perceptual differentiation. Radar operators must be able to make subtle differentiations among a myriad of tiny blips on a radar screen.

To better understand the problems involved in learning to make critical perceptual distinctions, Biederman and Shiffrar (1987) considered the question using an "expert systems analysis." By observing an expert chick sexor and ascertaining the criteria employed by the expert, they were able to find that there was one basic, critical difference between the contours of the genitals of male and female chicks: In males, the genital eminence—the size of a pin head—is convex; in females; it is flat or concave. Biederman and Shif-

frar were then able to devise a simple training sequence, shown in Figure 4-14, which provided instructions for chick sexing. Their training was successful: Following exposure to the training materials, subjects improved dramatically in their sexing ability, getting some 84 percent of their choices correct, compared with a rate of 54 percent correct among sexors in an untrained group.

Because perceptual distinctions are so often of critical importance, the procedure developed by Biederman and Shiffrar has wide applicability, ranging from the military arena (distinguishing enemy tanks from friendly ones) to the judicial (identifying suspects in a lineup). Their work, and that of their colleagues, demonstrates the importance of perception in the world around us and provides a means of improving our perceptual abilities.

ANSWERS (REVIEW II):
1. False; they are two-dimensional **2.** a-6, b-1, c-4, d-5, e-2, f-3 **3.** False; when movement is too fast to follow, we rely on past learning to anticipate the path of an object, such as occurs with good hitters who take their eyes off the ball **4.** Top-down, bottom-up **5.** Selective attention **6.** Shadowing **7.** False; people usually still direct some attention to the other message. **8.** True

FIGURE 4-13

Chick sexors are highly trained in perceiving the tiny differences between the genitals of male and female baby chicks. (*Amchick, Lansdale, PA*)

house. The carpeting in some of the sloping halls has perpendicular stripes that make people slow their pace by producing the perception that they are moving faster than they actually are. The same illusion is used at toll booths on superhighways: Stripes painted on the pavement in front of the toll booths make drivers feel that they are moving more rapidly than they actually are and cause them to decelerate quickly. (For other practical applications of psychological research on perception, see the Psychology at Work box.)

Now you will be asked to sex-type another set of chickens. You should use the following rules to discriminate between the male and female genitals. The first part of your task should be to locate the informative region. In order to find this point, you should look for the two large cylindrical side lobes near the bottom of each picture. The genitals are located either between the ends of these two lobes (1) or slightly above the ends (2).

After you have found this area, you should study the swellings present there. It is at this point that males may be differentiated from females. Male chicken genitals tend to look round and fullish like a ball or watermelon. Here are two examples:

Female chicken genitals can take on two different appearances. They can look pointed, like an upside down pine tree, or flattish. Here are two examples:

FIGURE 4-14

These experimental instructions, excerpted here, were successful in teaching the differences between the genitals of male and female chicks. (*Biederman & Shiffrar, 1987.*)

FIGURE 4-15

In order to make it appear that the yard of this house in Houston was longer, architects designed a small pool that was being installed to have a tapered shape. The wider end of the pool is closest to the house. (*Timothy Hursley.*)

MISPERCEPTIONS OF THE EYE: Visual Illusions

The implications of visual illusions go beyond the attractiveness of buildings. For instance, suppose you were an air traffic controller watching a radar screen like the one shown in Figure 4-16*a*. You might be tempted to sit back and relax as the two planes, whose flight paths are indicated in the figure, drew closer and closer together. If you did, however, you might end up with an air disaster: Although it looks as if the two planes will miss each other, they are headed for a collision. In fact, investigation has suggested that some 16 percent of all airplane accidents are caused by misperceptions of one sort or another (Kraft & Elworth, 1969; Hurst, 1984; Wiener & Nagel, 1988).

The flight-path illustration provides an example of a well-known visual illusion called the **Poggendorf illusion**. As you can see in Figure 4-16*b*, the Poggendorf illusion, when stripped down to its basics, gives the impression

Poggendorf illusion: An illusion involving a line that passes diagonally through two parallel lines

FIGURE 4-16A

Put yourself in the shoes of a flight controller and look at the flight paths of the two planes on this radar screen. A first glance suggests that they are headed on different courses and will not hit each other. But now take a ruler and lay it along the two paths. Your career as a flight controller might well be over if you were guiding the two planes and you allowed them to continue without a change in course. (*Coren, Porac, & Ward, p. 7.*)

Flight path

Flight path

FIGURE 4-16B

The Poggendorf illusion, in which the two diagonal lines appear (incorrectly) as if they would not meet if extended toward each other.

145

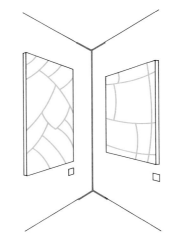

FIGURE 4-17A

The Müller-Lyer illusion, in which the upper horizontal line appears longer than the lower one.

FIGURE 4-17B

An explanation for the Müller-Lyer illusion suggests that the line with arrow points directed out is interpreted as the relatively close end of a rectangular object extended out toward us (as in the building corner), and the line with arrow points directed inward are viewed as the inside corner of a rectangle extending away from us (as in the room corner). Our previous experience with distance cues leads us to assume that the outside corner is closer than the inside corner and that the inside corner must therefore be longer.

that line X would pass *under* line Y if it were extended through the pipelike figure, instead of heading directly toward line Y as it actually does.

The Poggendorf illusion is just one of many that consistently fool the eye (Perkins, 1983; Greist-Bousquet & Schiffman, 1986). Another is the one illustrated in Figure 4-17 called the **Müller-Lyer illusion**. Although the two lines are the same length, the one with the arrow tips pointing inward (Figure 4-17*a*, top) appears to be longer than the one with the arrow tips pointing outward (Figure 4-17*a*, bottom).

Although all kinds of explanations for visual illusions have been suggested, most concentrate either on the eye's visual sensory apparatus itself or—as in Figure 4-18—on the interpretation that is given a figure by the brain (Schiffman, 1982). Visual explanations for the Müller-Lyer illusion suggest, for example, that eye movements are greater when the arrow tips point inward, making us perceive the line as longer than when the arrow tips face outward.

Other evidence suggests that the cause of the illusion rests on the brain's interpretive errors. For instance, one hypothesis assumes that the Müller-

Müller-Lyer illusion: An illusion in which two lines of the same length appear to be of different lengths because of the direction of the arrows at the ends of each line; the line with arrows pointing out appears shorter than the line with arrows pointing in

FIGURE 4-18

The right-side-up, upside-down cake. It seems clear that the cake is missing one slice. But now hold the picture upside down; you're looking at just one slice of cake, but one that is right-side up. The reason for this illusion is that you have no experience in viewing cake attached to the underside of a plate. When you see it for the first time with the plate on top, your brain reinterprets the situation in a way that seems more reasonable to you. Therefore, no matter how many times you rotate the picture back and forth, it will always appear as if the hands are holding the dish upright.

FIGURE 4-19

The "devil's tuning fork" has three prongs
. . . or does it have just two?

Lyer illusion is a result of the meaning we give to each of the lines (Gregory, 1978). When we see the top line in Figure 4-17*a*, we tend to perceive it as if it were the inside corner of a room extending away from us, as illustrated on the right in Figure 4-17*b*. On the other hand, when we view the bottom line in Figure 4-17*a*, we perceive it as the relatively close outside corner of a rectangular object such as the building on the left in Figure 4-17*b*. Because previous experience leads us to assume that the outside corner is closer than the inside corner, we make the further assumption that the inside corner must therefore be larger.

Given all the underlying assumptions, it may seem unlikely that this explanation is correct, but in fact there is a good degree of convincing evidence for it. One of the most telling pieces of support comes from cross-cultural studies that show that people raised in areas where there are few right angles—such as the Zulu in Africa—are much less susceptible to the illusion than people who grow up where most things are built using right angles and rectangles (Segall, Campbell & Herskovits, 1966).

Several kinds of cultural factors affect the ways in which we perceive the world. Consider, for example, the drawing in Figure 4-19. Sometimes called the "devil's tuning fork," it is likely to produce a mind-boggling effect, as the center tine of the fork alternates between appearing and disappearing.

Now try to reproduce the drawing on a piece of paper. Chances are that the task is nearly impossible for you—unless you are a member of an African tribe with little experience with western cultures. For such individuals, the task is simple; they have no trouble in reproducing the figure. The reason seems to be that western people automatically interpret the drawing as some-

FIGURE 4-20

Is the man about to spear the elephant or the antelope? Westerners assume that the differences in size between the two animals indicate that the elephant is further away, and therefore the man is aiming for the antelope. On the other hand, members of some African tribes, not used to depth cues in two-dimensional drawings, assume that the man is aiming for the elephant. The same lack of depth cues can be seen in the art of various cultures, such as this manuscript illumination from India. [*(drawing) Based on Deregowski, 1973; (illumination) Indian (Mughal) manuscript 07.271*. Rama and Lakshman Battle the Demon Rakshasas. *Late 16th century. Courtesy of the Freer Gallery of Art, Smithsonian Institution, Washington, D.C.*]

(a)

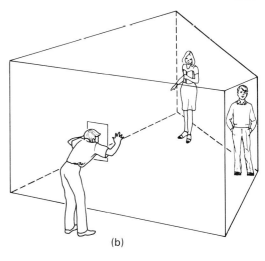
(b)

thing that cannot exist in three dimensions, and they are therefore inhibited from reproducing it. The African tribal members, on the other hand, do not make the assumption that the figure is "impossible" and instead view it in two dimensions, which enables them to copy the figure with ease (Deregowski, 1973).

Cultural differences are also reflected in depth perception. A western viewer of Figure 4-20 would interpret the drawing as one in which the hunter is trying to spear the antelope in the foreground while an elephant stands under the tree in the background. A member of an isolated African tribe, however, interprets the scene very differently by assuming that the hunter is aiming at the elephant. Westerners use the difference in sizes between the two animals as a cue that the elephant is farther away than the antelope (Hudson, 1960).

The misinterpretations created by visual illusions are ultimately due, then, to errors in both fundamental visual processing and in the way the brain interprets the information it receives (Coren & Porac, 1983; see also Figure 4-21). But visual illusions also illustrate something fundamental about perception that makes them more than mere psychological curiosities: There is a basic connection between our prior knowledge, needs, motivations, and expectations about how the world is put together and the way we perceive it. Our view of the world is very much a function, then, of fundamental psychological factors. Furthermore, each of us perceives the environment in a way that is unique and special—a fact that allows each of us to make our own special contribution to the world.

FIGURE 4-21

Despite the fact that the two people in (a) look like a giant and dwarf, the woman is actually considerably taller than the child. The reason for their perceived differences in size is that we assume that the room is rectangular, with the back walls at right angles to the side walls. Actually, the room forms a trapezoid, as the floorplan (b) shows, and the woman seen in (a) is standing considerably further back than the child. Because the images that reach our retina differ—the image of the woman is considerably smaller than that of the child—we make the only logical assumption: there is a size discrepancy. In fact, even when we know the truth about the room, the illusion is compelling and it is hard to dispel the notion of size discrepancy. (© *Baron Wolman/Woodfin Camp & Assoc.*)

THE INFORMED CONSUMER OF PSYCHOLOGY:
Discovering and Treating Dyslexia

At first glance, Chris King is the model American teenager. The 18-year-old student is president of the senior class at Staples High School in Westport, Connecticut, and this weekend he is playing the lead role in the drama club's production of *Mr. Roberts.* Next fall he hopes to move on to Boston University.

The youth, though, is the first to concede that he is by no means an ideal model. "I reverse letters when I read and have trouble taking my

Dyslexia (dis LEX ee uh): A disability with a perceptual basis that can result in the reversal of letters during reading and writing, confusion between left and right, and difficulties in spelling

thoughts and organizing them on paper," he explained recently. "If I'm rushed, I'll mix words up and come out with something like 'attack-a-heart.' I've learned that I can do just about anything I set out to do, but I have to work a lot harder than other people to do it" [Fiske, 1984, 12(1)].

Chris King suffers from dyslexia. So do perhaps as many as 10 percent of all Americans, including Greg Louganis, whose case is discussed at the beginning of this book. **Dyslexia** is a reading disability with a perceptual basis. To a dyslexic, every letter that is underlined in this sentence might appear to be reversed. Dyslexics often have handwriting that is difficult to read, confuse right and left, make unusual and very obvious spelling errors, and appear clumsy in comparison with their peers (Pavlidis & Fisher, 1986).

The causes of dyslexia are far from apparent, although they do seem to be related to abnormal development of the brain prior to birth. The brains of dyslexics tend to show overdevelopment of the right hemisphere, suggesting that there may be some kind of tension between the left hemisphere (normally the dominant hemisphere for language) and the right hemisphere for control of language processes (Galaburda, 1988).

Although the reason for such abnormal brain development is not known, some researchers speculate that it may be related to the presence before birth of abnormally high levels of the male hormone testosterone in the mother (Bannatyne, 1971) or to small strokes, stress, or a virus during pregnancy. Whatever the cause, dyslexia is not related to low intelligence. Many exceptional individuals, including inventor Thomas Edison, sculptor Auguste Rodin, and President Woodrow Wilson, were dyslexic.

What should be done if a child is suspected of having dyslexia? Most important, a psychologist who specializes in learning disabilities should be consulted. The psychologist will conduct a series of tests designed to measure the level of perceptual skills that the child has and will also analyze the specific nature of the child's perceptual errors. Most children, at one time or another, make the kinds of mistakes that dyslexics make, and so it is

People with dyslexia have difficulty copying even simple words printed on a black-board. (Richard S. Orton)

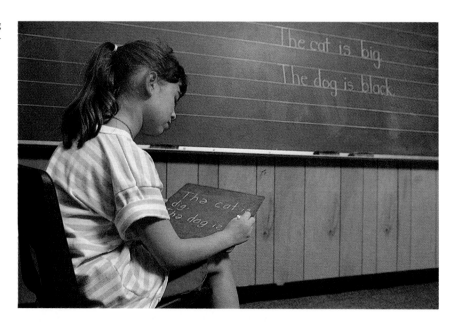

important that a specialist and not just the child's parents or a classroom teacher make the diagnosis.

Over the past few years, many new treatment techniques have been devised. Practice with sounding out words is usually assumed to be the key to successful intervention. Children practice viewing a letter, hearing its sound, pronouncing it, and writing it over and over again. Once they master the basics, they try to create words from the letters and sounds. Building the self-esteem of children with dyslexia is also an important component of any successful treatment program, since such children often experience scholastic failure. To build self-confidence, one should try to emphasize a dyslexic's strengths in other areas, which are often considerable. In addition, older students with dyslexia should make their disability known to their instructors and should try to arrange for alternate test-taking procedures—such as oral tests. (Even standardized tests, such as the SATs, can be taken in an untimed version if prior arrangements are made.)

In the past, many cases of dyslexia were overlooked or misdiagnosed, and so it is possible that an adult suffering from reading problems might be mildly dyslexic. If you hold that suspicion—about yourself, a relative, or a friend—the best course of action is to arrange for an examination by a psychologist. Dyslexia is no longer the mystery it once was, and the reading difficulties experienced by dyslexics can be overcome with appropriate training.

RECAP AND REVIEW III

Recap

◀ Visual illusions are physical stimuli that consistently produce errors in perception. Among the most common are the Poggendorf illusion and the Müller-Lyer illusion.

◀ Illusions occur both in visual processing and in the way the brain interprets this information.

◀ Dyslexia is a reading disability that is caused by perceptual difficulties. People with dyslexia reverse letters, confuse right and left, and make unusual and obvious spelling errors.

Review

1. The illusion of flight paths which, when viewed on a screen, appear as though they won't cross, is known as the _____ illusion.

2. Which of the following has *not* been proposed as an explanation of why we perceive visual illusions?
   a. Variations in the eye's visual sensory apparatus
   b. Small distance between eyeballs
   c. Interpretive errors made by the brain
   d. Previous learning experience

3. Jessica frequently perceives letters to be reversed when reading. Her teacher also notes that she makes unusual and very obvious spelling errors. It is likely that Jessica suffers from _____ .

4. Jessica's disability is often associated with low intelligence or mild mental retardation. True or false? _____

(Answers to review questions are on page 150.)

◀ LOOKING BACK

1. Perception is the process by which we sort out, interpret, analyze, and integrate stimuli to which our senses are exposed. Perception follows the gestalt laws of organization. These laws provide a series of principles by which we organize bits and pieces of information into meaningful wholes, known as gestalts. Among the most important laws are those of closure, proximity, similarity, and simplicity.

2. Work on figure-ground distinctions shows that perception is a constructive process in which people go beyond the stimuli that are physically present and try to construct a meaningful situation. Moreover, the gestalt psychologists demonstrated convincingly that perception follows the general rule: "The whole is greater than the sum of its parts."

3. Perceptual constancy permits us to perceive stimuli as

150

unvarying and consistent, despite changes in the environment or the appearance of the objects being perceived. Two competing theories seek to explain constancy effects: unconscious inference theory, which suggests that we use our prior experience about size to make unconscious inferences about location, and ecological theory, which suggests that the relationship between different environmental cues in a scene gives us information about their size.

4. Depth perception is the ability to perceive distance and to view the world in three dimensions, even though the images projected on our retinas are two dimensional. We are able to judge depth and distance as a result of binocular disparity (the difference in images as seen by each of the eyes) and monocular cues, such as motion parallax (the apparent movement of objects as one's head moves from side to side), the relative size of images on the retina, and linear perspective.

5. Motion perception depends on several cues. They include the perceived movement of an object across our retina and information about how the head and eye are moving.

6. Processing of perceptual stimuli occurs in both a top-down and a bottom-up fashion. In top-down processing, perception is guided by higher-level knowledge, experience, expectations, and motivations. In bottom-up processing, perception involves recognition and processing of information about the individual components of stimuli.

7. Selective attention is the perceptual process of choosing which stimulus to pay attention to. Psychologists study attention using a dichotic-listening procedure, in which a message is presented in each ear and the person is asked to repeat, or shadow, one of the messages.

8. Visual illusions are physical stimuli that consistently produce errors in perception, causing judgments that do not accurately reflect the physical reality of the stimulus. Among the best-known illusions are the Poggendorf illusion and the Müller-Lyer illusion. Most evidence suggests that visual illusions are a result of errors in the brain's interpretation of visual stimuli.

9. Dyslexia is a reading disability that has a perceptual basis. Sufferers of dyslexia often reverse letters, have poor handwriting, make unusual and obvious spelling errors, and may appear clumsy. If dyslexia is properly diagnosed, treatment can be successful.

KEY TERMS AND CONCEPTS ▶

perception (p. 127)
gestalt laws of organization (128)
gestalts (128)
closure (128)
proximity (128)
similarity (129)
simplicity (129)
figure-ground (129)
perceptual constancy (130)

unconscious inference theory (131)
ecological theory (131)
depth perception (132)
binocular disparity (132)
monocular cues (133)
motion parallax (133)
relative size (133)
linear perspective (133)
top-down processing (136)

bottom-up processing (136)
selective attention (138)
stroop task (138)
dichotic listening (138)
shadowing (139)
visual illusion (141)
Poggendorf illusion (145)
Müller-Lyer illusion (146)
dyslexia (148)

FOR FURTHER STUDY AND APPLICATION ▶

Coren, S., & Girgus, J. S. (1978). *Seeing is deceiving: The psychology of visual illusions.* Hillsdale, NJ: Erlbaum.

This book provides a fascinating glimpse at and clear understanding of illusions.

Matlin, M. M. (1988). *Sensation and perception.* (2nd ed.). Boston: Allyn & Bacon.

Schiff, W. (1980). *Perception: An applied approach.* Boston: Houghton Mifflin.

These volumes cover the fundamentals of perception and relate them to a variety of real-world applications.

Foundation for Children with Learning Disabilities. (1984). *Their world.* New York: Foundation for Children with Learning Disabilities.

This book, written for the layperson, describes current approaches to dyslexia and other learning disabilities, with sound advice for those with problems. The foundation will be happy to send you a copy if you write to them at 99 Park Avenue, New York, NY 10016.

ANSWERS (REVIEW III)
1. Poggendorf **2.** b **3.** dyslexia **4.** False; while the cause is not known, many exceptional individuals have been dyslexic.

PART THREE

LEARNING AND THINKING

PART
THREE

LEARNING
AND
THINKING

We now move from the basic biological foundations of human behavior to consider the ways in which we learn and think about the world. In this next part of the book, we encounter a person whose profound physical disabilities are overcome with the aid of an unlikely non-human helper. We meet a movie star who is affected with a debilitating memory disorder—as well as someone who can remember almost everything to which he is exposed. We learn how creative problem solving uncovered the mystery of the cause of the Challenger space shuttle disaster and how a profoundly retarded person has, despite limited intellectual capabilities, produced critically acclaimed paintings.

These diverse topics are related by the fundamental principles of learning and thinking that have been identified by psychologists. We examine how basic research on learning has been used to account for mastery of the most complex material. We consider how we are able to remember obscure details from our past but may still forget the name of a person whom we have just met. We examine our basic thinking and reasoning processes and explore the ways in which language provides a vehicle for communication and thought. Finally, we discuss differences in intellectual capabilities and the effects such capabilities have on behavior.

In Chapter 5, the focus is on learning, ranging from the most simple to the most complex.

In Chapter 6, the discussion turns to memory and how it is structured and operates.

In Chapter 7, we consider the processes that underlie our capabilities to think and reason about the world and how we use language.

In Chapter 8, we examine intelligence and the abilities of which it is composed.

CHAPTER 5

LEARNING

155

FIGURE 5-1

Capuchin monkey Jo helps quadriplegic Gary Finkle perform many everyday tasks.

PROLOGUE:
GARY FINKLE (AND JO)

Try this: Take the most comfortable chair you own into the pleasantest room in your house, arrange it in a convenient location, and sit down. Don't move. Wait fifteen or twenty minutes for your muscles to loosen up. Relax. Look around; take stock of your surroundings. If any visitors walk in, you can turn your head to greet them but you can't stand or shake hands. You can admire the view out your window, but you can't crack it open for a breath of fresh air if the room becomes stuffy or warm. Wait another hour. Are you bored yet? Hungry? Thirsty? Sorry, but you'll just have to wait until somebody happens by. Don't worry, it shouldn't be too long—probably no more than a couple of hours (MacFadyen, 1987, p. 125).

Welcome to Gary Finkle's world—and that of some 90,000 other Americans who have suffered spinal cord injuries that have left them without feeling or movement below their shoulders. Finkle, though, has an advantage over most of those who have suffered similar accidents: Jo, a female capuchin monkey.

Finkle is one of the first participants in a program called Helping Hands: Simian Aides for the Disabled. The organization trains capuchins to reduce the dependence of the disabled on family and friends and to increase their self-reliance.

Through careful and systematic training, Jo has become Finkle's arms and legs. By using his mouth to control a laser attached to his wheelchair, Finkle is able to direct Jo to turn the pages of a book, take a sandwich out of the refrigerator, turn lights on and off, comb his hair, put a tape into a cassette player, and even wipe up a spill.

Jo's miraculous capabilities did not just happen, of course. They are the result of meticulous training procedures based on basic principles of learning. For example, in one training procedure, Jo was taught to fetch any article to which a laser beam was pointed. She began by learning the subcomponents of the task: first learning to merely look at the beam, then learning to go to the place where the beam was pointed, then touching the object, and so forth, until she mastered the entire task. Whenever she successfully completed an assignment, she was immediately given a reward—typically a sip of sticky, strawberry-flavored Nutrament. And if she failed at a task, she received nothing. Through this simple procedure, the inventory of tasks Jo could accomplish was gradually expanded and refined (Blumenthal, 1987; MacFadyen, 1987).

To Gary Finkle, the process by which Jo was able to learn so much is less important than the changes that have occurred in his own life. Her presence has given him the opportunity to maintain a considerable degree of independence, one of the most precious commodities for a disabled person. "I definitely cannot imagine living without her," he says.

LOOKING AHEAD ▶

The same processes that allowed trainers to harness and shape Jo's capabilities to benefit Gary Finkle are at work in each of our lives, as we read a book, drive a car, play poker, study for a test, or perform any of a myriad of other activities central to us. Like Jo, each of us must acquire and then hone our skills and abilities through learning.

A fundamental topic for psychologists, learning underlies many of the diverse areas discussed throughout this book. For example, a psychologist studying perception might ask, "How do we learn that people who look small from a distance are just far away and not simply tiny?" A developmental psychologist might inquire, "How do babies learn to distinguish their mothers from other people?" A clinical psychologist might wonder, "Why do some people learn to be afraid when they see a spider?" A social psychologist might ask, "How do we learn to feel that we are in love?" Each of these questions, although drawn from very different fields of psychology, can be answered only with reference to learning processes. In fact, learning plays a central role in almost every topic of interest to psychologists.

What do we mean by learning? Although psychologists have identified a number of different types of learning, a general definition encompasses them all: **Learning** is a relatively permanent change in behavior brought about by experience. What is particularly important about this definition is that it permits us to distinguish between performance changes due to **maturation** (the unfolding of biologically predetermined patterns of behavior due simply to getting older) and those changes brought about by experience. For instance, children become better tennis players as they grow older partially because their strength increases with their size—a maturational phenomenon. Such maturational changes need to be distinguished from improvements due to learning, which are a consequence of practice.

Similarly, we must distinguish between short-term changes in behavior that are due to factors other than learning, such as declines in performance resulting from fatigue or lack of effort, and performance changes that are due to actual learning. For example, if Chris Evert Lloyd performs poorly in a tennis game because of tension or fatigue, this does not mean that she has not learned to play correctly or has forgotten how to play well.

The distinction between learning and performance is critical, and not always easy to make. Learning is an *inferred* process; we cannot see it happening directly, and we can assume that learning has occurred only by observing changes in performance. This fact makes the learning psychologist's task a difficult one, since there is not always a one-to-one correspondence between learning and performance—as those of us who have done poorly on an exam because we were tired and made careless mistakes can well understand. Poor performance, then, does not necessarily indicate an absence of learning.

In this chapter, we examine basic learning processes in order to answer a number of fundamental questions:

▶ What are the different forms of learning, and how can we differentiate among them?

▶ What is the role of reward and punishment in learning?

▶ What is the role of thinking in learning?

▶ How can we formally analyze behavior, and how does this lead to techniques for modifying and controlling it?

▶ What are some practical methods for bringing about behavior change, both in others and in ourselves?

Learning: A relatively permanent change in behavior brought about by experience

Maturation: The unfolding of biologically predetermined patterns of behavior due to aging

PAVLOV'S DOGS AND THE GOLDEN ARCHES: CLASSICAL CONDITIONING

What do you think of when you catch a glimpse of the golden arches in front of McDonald's? If the mere sight of them makes your stomach rumble a bit and your thoughts turn to hamburgers and french fries, you are displaying a rudimentary form of learning called classical conditioning.

The processes that underlie classical conditioning explain such diverse phenomena as crying at the sight of a bride walking down the aisle at a wedding, fearing the dark, and falling in love with the boy or girl next door. To understand classical conditioning, however, it is necessary to move back in time and place to the early part of the century in Russia.

CANINE CONDITIONING

Ivan Pavlov, a Russian physiologist, never intended to do psychological research. In 1904 he won the Nobel Prize for his work on digestion, testimony to his contribution to that field. Yet Pavlov is remembered not for his physiological research, but for his experiments on basic learning processes—work that he began quite accidentally.

Pavlov had been studying the secretion of stomach acids and salivation in dogs in response to the ingestion of varying amounts and kinds of food. While doing so, he observed a curious phenomenon: Sometimes stomach secretions and salivation would begin when no food had actually been eaten; the mere sight of a food bowl, the individual who normally brought the food, or even the sound of the footsteps of that individual was enough to produce a physiological response in the dogs. Pavlov's genius was his ability to recognize the implications of this rather basic discovery. He saw that the dogs were responding not only on the basis of a biological need (hunger), but also as a result of learning—or, as it came to be called, classical conditioning. In **classical conditioning**, an organism learns a response to a neutral stimulus that normally does not bring about that response.

To demonstrate and analyze classical conditioning, Pavlov ran a series of experiments (Pavlov, 1927). In one, he attached a tube to the salivary gland of a dog, allowing him to measure precisely the amount of salivation that

Classical conditioning: A kind of learning in which a previously neutral stimulus comes to elicit a response through its association with a stimulus that naturally brings about the response

Ivan Pavlov (center, with white beard), a Russian physiologist, was the first to recognize the importance of the learning processes represented in classical conditioning. (Culver Pictures, Inc.)

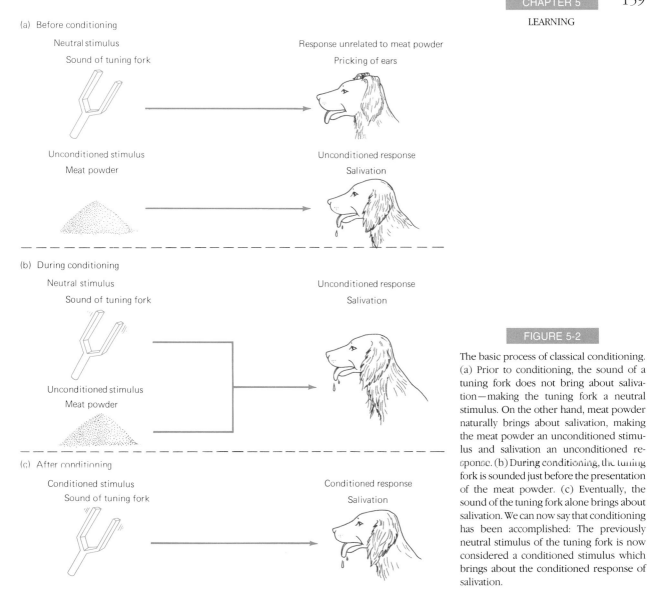

(a) Before conditioning

Neutral stimulus
Sound of tuning fork

Response unrelated to meat powder
Pricking of ears

Unconditioned stimulus
Meat powder

Unconditioned response
Salivation

(b) During conditioning

Neutral stimulus
Sound of tuning fork

Unconditioned response
Salivation

Unconditioned stimulus
Meat powder

(c) After conditioning

Conditioned stimulus
Sound of tuning fork

Conditioned response
Salivation

FIGURE 5-2

The basic process of classical conditioning. (a) Prior to conditioning, the sound of a tuning fork does not bring about salivation—making the tuning fork a neutral stimulus. On the other hand, meat powder naturally brings about salivation, making the meat powder an unconditioned stimulus and salivation an unconditioned response. (b) During conditioning, the tuning fork is sounded just before the presentation of the meat powder. (c) Eventually, the sound of the tuning fork alone brings about salivation. We can now say that conditioning has been accomplished: The previously neutral stimulus of the tuning fork is now considered a conditioned stimulus which brings about the conditioned response of salivation.

occurred. He then sounded a tuning fork and, just a few seconds later, presented the dog with meat powder. This pairing, carefully planned so that exactly the same amount of time elapsed between the presentation of the sound and the meat, occurred repeatedly. At first the dog would salivate only when the meat powder itself was presented, but soon it began to salivate at the sound of the tuning fork. In fact, even when Pavlov stopped presenting the meat powder, the dog still salivated after hearing the sound. The dog had been classically conditioned to salivate to the tone.

As you can see in Figure 5-2, the basic processes of classical conditioning underlying Pavlov's discovery are straightforward, although the terminology he chose has a technical ring. Consider first the diagram in Figure 5-2*a*. Prior to conditioning, we have two unrelated stimuli: the sound of a tuning fork and meat powder. We know that the sound of a tuning fork leads not to salivation but to some irrelevant response such as perking of the ears or, perhaps, a startle reaction. The sound in this case therefore is called the

Neutral stimulus: A stimulus that, before conditioning, has no effect on the desired response

Unconditioned stimulus (UCS): A stimulus that brings about a response without having been learned

Unconditioned response (UCR): A response that is natural and needs no training (e.g., salivation at the smell of food)

Conditioned stimulus (CS): A once-neutral stimulus that has been paired with an unconditioned stimulus to bring about a response formerly caused only by the unconditioned stimulus

Conditioned response (CR): A response that, after conditioning, follows a previously neutral stimulus (e.g., salivation at the sound of a tuning fork)

neutral stimulus because it has no effect on the response of interest. We also have meat powder, which, because of the biological makeup of the dog, naturally leads to salivation, the particular response that we are interested in conditioning. The meat powder is considered an **unconditioned stimulus**, or **UCS**, because food placed near a dog's mouth automatically causes salivation to occur. The response that the meat powder produces is called an **unconditioned response**, or **UCR**—a response that is not associated with previous learning. Unconditioned responses are natural and innate responses that need no training, and they are always brought about by unconditioned stimuli.

Figure 5-2*b* illustrates what happens during conditioning. The tuning fork is repeatedly sounded just before presentation of the meat powder. The goal of conditioning is for the tuning fork to develop into a substitute for the unconditioned stimulus (meat powder) and therefore to bring about the same sort of response as the unconditioned stimulus. During this period, salivation gradually increases each time the tuning fork is sounded until the tuning fork alone causes the dog to salivate.

When conditioning is complete, the tuning fork has evolved from a neutral stimulus to what is now called a **conditioned stimulus**, or **CS**. At this time, salivation that occurs as a response to the conditioned stimulus (tuning fork) is considered a **conditioned response**, or **CR**. This situation is depicted in Figure 5-2*c*. The conditioned stimulus evokes the conditioned response.

The sequence and timing of the presentation of the unconditioned stimulus and the conditioned stimulus is particularly important (Rescorla, 1988). Like a signal light at a railroad crossing that does not operate until after a train has passed by, a neutral stimulus that follows an unconditioned stimulus has little chance of becoming a conditioned stimulus. On the other hand, just as a warning light works best if it goes on right before a train is about to go by, a neutral stimulus that is presented just before the unconditioned stimulus is most apt to result in successful conditioning. Research has shown, in fact, that conditioning is most effective if the conditioned stimulus precedes the unconditioned stimulus by between a half second and several seconds, depending on what kind of response is being conditioned.

Although the terminology employed by Pavlov to describe classical conditioning may at first seem confusing, the following rules of thumb can help to make the relationships between stimuli and responses easier to understand and remember:

▶ *Un*conditioned stimuli lead to *un*conditioned responses, and *un*conditioned stimulus–*un*conditioned response pairings are *un*learned and *un*trained.

▶ Conditioned stimuli lead to conditioned responses, and conditioned stimulus–conditioned response pairings are a consequence of learning and training.

▶ Unconditioned responses and conditioned responses are similar (such as salivation in the example described above), but the conditioned response is learned, whereas the unconditioned response occurs naturally.

APPLYING CONDITIONING PRINCIPLES TO HUMAN BEHAVIOR

Although the initial classical conditioning experiments were carried out with animals, the principles that underlie the early work were soon found to explain many aspects of everyday human behavior. Consider someone whose stomach begins to rumble and whose mouth waters at the sight of McDonald's golden arches. The cause of this reaction is classical conditioning: The previously neutral arches have come to be associated with the food inside the restaurant (the unconditioned stimulus), causing the arches to become a conditioned stimulus that brings about the conditioned response of salivation.

Emotional responses are particularly apt to be learned through classical conditioning processes. For instance, how do some of us develop fears of mice, spiders, and other creatures that—if we thought about it much—do not seem intrinsically more ferocious or potentially harmful than a pet dog or cat? In a now-famous experiment designed to show that classical conditioning was at the root of such fears, an 11-month-old infant named Albert, who initially showed no fear of rats, was exposed to a loud noise at the same time that a rat was presented to him (Watson & Rayner, 1920). The noise (the UCS) evoked fear (the UCR); after just a few pairings, Albert began to show fear of the rat by itself. The rat, then, had become a CS that brought about the CR, fear. Similarly, it is likely that the pairing of the appearance of certain species with the fearful comments of an adult causes children to develop the same fears their parents have.

In adulthood, learning via classical conditioning occurs a bit more subtly. You may come to know that a professor's mood is particularly menacing when her tone of voice changes; in the past you may have seen that the professor uses that tone only when she is about to criticize someone's work. Likewise, you may not go to a dentist as often as you should because of prior associations with dentists and pain. Or you may have a particular fondness for the color blue because that was the color of your childhood bedroom. Classical conditioning, then, explains many of the reactions we have to stimuli in the world around us (Gomezano, Prokasy & Thompson, 1987).

UNLEARNING WHAT YOU HAVE LEARNED: Extinction

As long as you can remember, you have hated broccoli. The very sight of it makes you queasy. Yet your new girlfriend's parents seem to love it, serving it every time you come to visit. Being polite, you feel you must eat a little of it. The first few times it is torture; you feel as if you are about to embarrass yourself by getting sick at the table, but you steel yourself to keep the broccoli down. After a few weeks it becomes easier. In fact, after a couple of months, you are surprised to realize that you no longer feel sick at the thought of eating broccoli.

Your behavior can be explained by one of the basic phenomena of learning: extinction. **Extinction** occurs when a previously conditioned response becomes weaker and eventually disappears. To produce extinction, one needs to end the association between conditioned and unconditioned stimuli. If we had trained a dog to salivate at the sound of a bell, we could bring about extinction by ceasing to provide meat after the bell was sounded. At first the dog would continue to salivate when it heard the bell, but after a few such instances, the amount of salivation would probably decline, and the dog would eventually stop responding to the bell altogether. At that point, we could say that the response had been extinguished. In sum, extinction occurs when the conditioned stimulus is repeatedly presented without the unconditioned stimulus.

As we will describe more fully in Chapter 17, psychologists have treated

Extinction: The weakening and eventual disappearance of a conditioned response

Systematic desensitization: A form of therapy in which fears are minimized through different degrees of exposure, with the patient eventually learning to feel comfortable in the presence of the object of his or her former fears

people with irrational fears or phobias using a form of therapy called **systematic desensitization**, in which the goal is to bring about the extinction of the phobia. For instance, a person who has an intense fear of heights and has been undergoing systematic desensitization therapy might be told to climb to the first floor of a building and look out the window. When he is on the first floor, he uses relaxation procedures he has been taught by the therapist until he feels comfortable at that height. To feel truly relaxed, he may have to repeat this process several times. Next he is told to climb to a somewhat higher floor and do the same thing. By increasing the height to which he climbs each time—and discovering that there are no negative consequences—he may eventually be able to overcome his fear of high places.

The basic goal of systematic desensitization is to bring about the extinction of the phobia in question. When the treatment begins, the patient demonstrates a conditioned response to the feared object; in our example, for instance, a high place acts as a conditioned stimulus that produces the conditioned response of fear. Each time the person is exposed to the conditioned stimulus (being in a high place) without experiencing the unconditioned stimulus (negative consequences), the likelihood that the conditioned stimulus will evoke the undesirable response is weakened. Eventually, then, the conditioned response is extinguished.

THE RETURN OF THE CONDITIONED RESPONSE: Spontaneous Recovery

Once a conditioned response has been extinguished, is it lost forever? Not necessarily. As Pavlov discovered, if he returned to his previously conditioned dog the day after the conditioned behavior had been extinguished and rang a bell, the dog would once again salivate. Similarly a person once "cured" of a phobia may find that the phobia returns after a long period of absence from the feared object.

Spontaneous recovery: The reappearance of a previously extinguished response after a period of time during which the conditioned stimulus has been absent

This phenomenon is called **spontaneous recovery**—the reappearance of a previously extinguished response after time has elapsed without exposure to the conditioned stimulus. Usually, however, responses that return through spontaneous recovery are weaker than they were initially and can be extinguished more readily than before.

A ROSE IS A ROSE: Generalization and Discrimination

Despite differences in color and shape, to most of us a rose is a rose is a rose: The pleasure we experience at the beauty, smell, and grace of the flower is similar for different roses. Pavlov noticed an analogous phenomenon: His dogs often salivated not only at the sound of the tuning fork that was used during their original conditioning but at the sound of a bell or a buzzer as well.

Stimulus generalization: Response to a stimulus that is similar to but different from a conditioned stimulus; the more similar the two stimuli, the more likely generalization is to occur

Such behavior is the result of stimulus generalization. **Stimulus generalization** takes place when a conditioned response follows a stimulus that is similar to the original conditioned stimulus. The greater the similarity of the two stimuli, the greater the likelihood of stimulus generalization. Baby Albert, who, as we mentioned earlier, was conditioned to be fearful of rats, was later found to be afraid of other furry white things; he was fearful of white rabbits, white fur coats, and even a white Santa Claus mask. On the other hand, according to the principle of stimulus generalization, it is unlikely that he

In Watson's work with Little Albert, the boy's conditioned fear of white rats was generalized to include many furry white objects, including the Santa Claus mask worn by Watson in this photo. (Courtesy of Dr. Benjamin Harris, University of Wisconsin-Kenosha)

would be afraid of a black dog, since its color would differentiate it sufficiently from the original fear-evoking stimulus.

The conditioned response that is evoked by the new stimulus is usually not as intense as the original conditioned response, although the more similar the new stimulus is to the old one, the more similar the new response will be. It is unlikely, then, that Albert's fear of the Santa Claus mask was as great as his learned fear of a rat. Still, stimulus generalization permits us to know that we ought to brake at all red lights, even if there are minor variations in size, shape, and shade.

If stimuli are sufficiently distinct from one another so that the presence of one evokes a conditioned response but the other does not, we can say that stimulus discrimination has occurred. In **stimulus discrimination**, an organism learns to differentiate among different stimuli and restricts its responding to one stimulus rather than to others. Without the ability to discriminate between a red and a green traffic light, we would be mowed down by oncoming traffic; and if we could not discriminate a cat from a mountain lion, we might find ourselves in uncomfortable straits on a camping trip.

Stimulus discrimination: The process by which an organism learns to differentiate among stimuli, restricting its response to one in particular

WHEN A CS BECOMES A UCS: Higher-order Conditioning

If you are knocked over a few times by your neighbor's vicious Doberman, Rover, it would not be surprising that merely hearing the dog's name called would produce an unpleasant emotional reaction. This represents an example of higher-order conditioning. **Higher-order conditioning** occurs when a conditioned stimulus that has been established during earlier conditioning is then paired with a neutral stimulus, and the neutral stimulus comes to evoke a conditioned response similar to the original conditioned stimulus. The original conditioned stimulus, in effect, acts as an unconditioned stimulus.

Higher-order conditioning: A form of conditioning that occurs when an already-conditioned stimulus is paired with a neutral stimulus until the neutral stimulus evokes the same response as the conditioned stimulus

Our example of Rover can illustrate higher-order conditioning. You have learned to associate the sight of vicious Rover, who originally was a neutral stimulus, with rough behavior. The mere sight of Rover, then, has become a conditioned stimulus, which evokes the conditioned response of fear.

Later, however, you realize that every time you see Rover, its owner is calling the dog's name, saying, "Here, Rover." Because of this continual pairing of the name of Rover (which was originally a neutral stimulus) with the sight of Rover (now a conditioned stimulus), you become conditioned to experience a reaction of fear and loathing whenever you hear the name Rover, even though you may be safely inside your house. The name "Rover," then, has become a conditioned stimulus because of its earlier pairing with the conditioned stimulus of the sight of Rover. Higher-order conditioning has occurred: The sound of Rover's name has become a conditioned stimulus evoking a conditioned response.

Theoretically, it ought to be possible to keep producing unlimited higher-order response chains, associating one conditioned stimulus with another, and in fact Pavlov hypothesized that all learning is nothing more than long strings of conditioned responses. However, this notion has not been supported by subsequent research, and it turns out that classical conditioning provides us with only a partial explanation of how people and animals learn.

For instance, there are many cases in which learning does not build upon natural, innate responses such as salivation when exposed to food or avoidance of unpleasant stimuli (Catania, 1984). Furthermore, there have been challenges to some of the basic notions of classical conditioning. For example, work done by John Garcia, a leading researcher in learning processes, has disputed the supposition that optimum learning occurs only when the conditioned stimulus immediately follows the unconditioned stimulus.

Like Pavlov, Garcia made his major contribution while studying something unrelated to learning; he was initially concerned with the effects of exposure to nuclear radiation on laboratory animals. In the course of his experiments, he realized that rats in a radiation chamber drank almost no water, while in their home cage they drank eagerly. The most obvious explanation, that it had something to do with the radiation, was soon ruled out: Garcia found that even when the radiation was not turned on, the rats still drank little or nothing in the radiation chamber.

Initially puzzled by the rats' behavior, Garcia was eventually able to put the pieces together and understand what was happening. He noticed that the drinking cups in the radiation chamber were made of plastic, thereby giving the water an unusual, plasticlike taste, whereas those in the home cage were made of glass and left no abnormal taste.

After a series of experiments to rule out several alternative explanations, only one possibility remained: Apparently, the plastic-tasting water had become repeatedly paired with illness brought on by exposure to radiation, and had led the rats to form a classically conditioned association. The process began with the radiation acting as an unconditioned stimulus evoking the unconditioned response of sickness; with repeated pairings, the plastic-tasting water had become a conditioned stimulus that evoked the conditioned response of sickness (Garcia, Hankins & Rusiniak, 1974).

The problem with this finding was that it violated some of the basic rules of classical conditioning—that an unconditioned stimulus should *immediately* follow the conditioned stimulus for optimal conditioning to occur. Instead, Garcia's findings showed that conditioning could occur when there was an interval of as long as eight hours between exposure to the conditioned stimulus and the response of sickness. Furthermore, the conditioning persisted over very long periods and sometimes occurred after just one exposure to water that resulted in illness.

These findings have had important practical implications. In order to prevent coyotes from killing their sheep, some ranchers now routinely lace a sheep carcass with a drug and leave the carcass in a place where coyotes will find it. The drug temporarily makes the coyotes quite ill, but it does not permanently harm them. After just one exposure to a drug-laden sheep carcass, coyotes tend to avoid sheep, which are normally one of their primary natural victims. The sheep, then, have become a conditioned stimulus to the coyotes. This procedure is a far more humane one than shooting, the traditional response of ranchers to predators (Gustavson, Garcia, Hankins & Rusiniak, 1974).

Recent research in classical conditioning has identified another area that may have significant implications for people who suffer from allergic reactions and diseases such as asthma which are triggered by unknown factors. In the research, rats were exposed to a situation in which a flashing light and humming fan were repeatedly paired with the presentation of egg albumin—a substance that naturally produces a response of the rat's immune system (its natural defenses against disease). After repeated pairings, the light and noise alone were capable of producing a similar response—indicating that they had become a conditioned stimulus. The research suggests that allergic or asthmatic reactions may be caused by the process of classical conditioning, in which the reaction is actually the response to some previously unsuspected conditioned stimulus (MacQueen et al., 1989).

RECAP AND REVIEW I

Recap

◄ Learning is a relatively permanent change in behavior brought about by experience.

◄ Classical conditioning is a kind of learning in which an initially neutral stimulus, which does not evoke a relevant response, is paired repeatedly with an unconditioned stimulus until the previously neutral stimulus evokes a response similar to that brought about by the unconditioned stimulus.

◄ Classical conditioning underlies many sorts of everyday learning, such as the acquisition of emotional responses.

◄ Among the basic phenomena of classical conditioning are extinction, systematic desensitization, spontaneous recovery, stimulus generalization and discrimination, and higher-order conditioning.

Review

1. Learning involves changes brought about by experience, whereas _____ describes changes due to biological development.

Refer to the passage below to answer questions 2 through 5.
The last three times Theresa visited Dr. Noble for checkups, he administered a painful preventive immunization shot that left her in tears. When her mother takes her for another checkup, Theresa begins to sob as soon as she comes face to face with Dr. Noble, even before he has had a chance to say hello.

2. The painful shot that Theresa received during each visit was a(an) _____ _____ , which elicited the _____ _____ , her tears.

3. Dr. Noble is upset because his presence has become a _____ _____ for Theresa's crying.

4. When elicited by Dr. Noble's presence alone, Theresa's crying is referred to as a(an) _____ _____ .

5. Fortunately, Dr. Noble gave Theresa no more shots for quite some time. Over that time she gradually stopped crying and even came to like him. _____ had occurred.

6. Systematic desensitization is based on the process of extinction. True or false? _____

7. Responses made during a spontaneous recovery are generally stronger than those made before extinction. True or false? _____

8. Responding to one relevant stimulus and not to others is known as
   a. stimulus generalization.
   b. stimulus discrimination.
   c. an unconditioned response.
   d. inferred learning.

9. Classical conditioning theory is challenged by Garcia's finding that in spite of a relatively long delay between the onset of the neutral stimulus and the onset of the unconditioned response, conditioning may still take place. True or false? _____

(Answers to review questions are on page 166.)

THE REWARDS OF REINFORCEMENT:
OPERANT CONDITIONING

Very good ... What a clever idea ... Far out ... I agree ... Thank you ... Excellent ... This is the best paper you've ever written; you get an A ... You are really getting the hang of it ... I'm impressed ... Let me give you a hug ... You're getting a raise ... Have a cookie ... You look great ... I love you ...

Few of us would mind having any of the above comments directed at us. But what is particularly noteworthy about them is that each of these simple statements can be used to bring about powerful changes in behavior and to teach the most complex tasks through a process known as operant conditioning. Operant conditioning forms the basis for much of the most important kinds of human, and animal, learning (Davey & Cullen, 1988).

Operant conditioning: Learning that occurs as a result of certain positive or negative consequences; the organism operates on its environment in order to produce a particular result

Operant conditioning describes learning in which people make responses as a result of positive or negative consequences that are contingent (or dependent) on their responses. Unlike classical conditioning, in which the original responses are the natural, biological outgrowth of the presence of some stimulus such as food, water, or pain, operant conditioning applies to voluntary responses, which an organism performs willfully—in order to produce a desirable outcome. The term "operant" emphasizes this point: The organism *operates* on its environment in order to produce some desirable result. For example, operant conditioning is at work when we learn that working diligently can bring about a raise, or that cleaning our room produces words of praise from our parents, or that studying hard results in good grades.

Like the roots of classical conditioning, the foundations for understanding operant conditioning were laid by work with animals. We turn now to some of that early research, which began with a simple inquiry into the behavior of cats.

As these students at New York City's High School for Music and Art may be finding out, operant conditioning plays a part in every day conversations: the more the other person agrees with your opinions, the more likely you will be to express additional opinions. (Margot Granitsas/The Image Works)

ANSWERS (REVIEW I):

1. Maturation   **2.** Unconditioned stimulus, unconditioned response   **3.** Conditioned stimulus   **4.** Conditioned response   **5.** Extinction   **6.** True; a previously conditioned response such as fear may be weakened through extinction   **7.** False; responses are typically weaker   **8.** b   **9.** True

FIGURE 5-3

Edward L. Thorndike devised this puzzle box to study the process by which a cat learns to press a paddle to escape the box and receive food. (Thorndike, 1932; Sepp Seitz/Woodfin Camp. & Assoc.)

CAT-IN-A-BOX: Thorndike's Law of Effect

If you placed a hungry cat in a cage and then put a small piece of food outside, chances are the cat would eagerly search for a way out of the cage. The cat might first claw at the sides or push against an opening. Suppose, though, that you had rigged things so that the cat could escape by stepping on a small paddle that released the latch to the door of the cage (see Figure 5-3). Eventually, as it moved around the cage, the cat would happen to step on the paddle, the door would open, and the cat would eat the food.

What would happen if you then returned the cat to the box? The next time, it would probably take a little less time for the cat to step on the paddle and escape. After a few trials, the cat would deliberately step on the paddle as soon as it was placed in the cage. What would have occurred, according to Edward L. Thorndike (1932), who studied this situation extensively, was that the cat would have learned that pressing the paddle was associated with the desirable consequence of getting food. Thorndike summarized that relationship by formulating the **law of effect**, which states that responses that are satisfying are more likely to be repeated, and those that are not satisfying are less likely to be repeated.

Thorndike felt that the law of effect operated as automatically as leaves falling off a tree in autumn. It was not necessary for an organism to understand that there was a link between a response and reward. Instead, he thought that over time and through experience, the organism would form a direct connection between the stimulus and the response without any awareness that the connection existed.

Law of effect: Thorndike's theory that responses that satisfy are more likely to be repeated, whereas those that don't satisfy will be discontinued

FROM CAT-IN-THE-BOX TO SKINNER BOX: The Basics of Operant Conditioning

Thorndike's early research formed the foundation for the work of the most famous contemporary psychologist, B. F. Skinner. You may have heard of the Skinner box (shown in one form in Figure 5-4), a chamber with a highly controlled environment used to study operant conditioning processes with laboratory animals. Whereas Thorndike's goal was to get his cats to learn to obtain food by leaving the box, animals in a Skinner box learn to obtain food by operating on their environment within the box. Skinner became interested in specifying how behavior varied as a result of alterations in the environment.

Skinner, whose work goes far beyond perfecting Thorndike's earlier

FIGURE 5-4

A Skinner box, used to study operant conditioning. Laboratory animals learn to press the lever in order to obtain food, which is delivered in the tray. (Sepp Seitz/Woodfin Camp. & Assoc.)

apparatus, is considered the father of a whole generation of psychologists studying operant conditioning. To illustrate Skinner's contribution, let's consider what happens to a pigeon in the typical Skinner box.

Suppose you want to teach a hungry pigeon to peck a key that is located in its box. At first the pigeon will wander around the box, exploring the environment in a relatively random fashion. At some point, however, it will probably peck the key by chance, and when it does, it will receive a food pellet. The first time this happens, the pigeon will not learn the connection between pecking and receiving food and will continue to explore the box. Sooner or later the pigeon will again peck the key and receive a pellet, and in time the frequency of the pecking response will increase. Eventually, the pigeon will peck the key continually until it satisfies its hunger, thereby demonstrating that it has learned that the receipt of food is contingent on the pecking behavior.

Reinforcing Desired Behavior

Reinforcer: Any stimulus that increases the probability that a preceding behavior will be repeated

In a situation such as this one, the food is called a reinforcer. A **reinforcer** is any stimulus that increases the probability that a preceding behavior will occur again. Here, food is a reinforcer because it increases the probability that the behavior of pecking the key (formally referred to as the "response" of pecking) will take place. Bonuses, toys, and good grades could also serve as reinforcers, since they strengthen a response that comes before the introduction of the reinforcer. In each case, it is critical that the organism learn that the delivery of the reinforcer is contingent on the response occurring.

Of course, we are not born knowing that 50 cents can buy us a candy bar. Rather, through experience we learn that money is a valuable commodity because of its association with stimuli, such as food, drink, and shelter, that are naturally reinforcing. This fact suggests a distinction that can be drawn regarding whether something is a primary reinforcer or a secondary reinforcer. A **primary reinforcer** satisfies some biological need and works naturally, regardless of a person's prior experience; food for the hungry person, warmth for the cold person, and cessation of pain for a person who is hurting would all be classified as primary reinforcers. A **secondary reinforcer**, in contrast, is a stimulus that becomes reinforcing because of its association with a primary reinforcer. For instance, we know that money is valuable

Primary reinforcer: A reward that satisfies a biological need (e.g., hunger or thirst) and works naturally

Secondary reinforcer: A stimulus that becomes reinforcing by its association with a primary reinforcer (e.g., money, which allows us to obtain food, a primary reinforcer)

because it allows us to obtain other desirable objects, including primary reinforcers such as food and shelter; money thus becomes a secondary reinforcer.

What makes something a reinforcer is very individualistic. While a Hershey bar may act as a reinforcer for one person, an individual who hates chocolate might find 50 cents much more desirable. The only way we can know if a stimulus is a reinforcer for a given organism is to observe whether the rate of response of a previously occurring behavior increases after the presentation of the stimulus.

Positive Reinforcers, Negative Reinforcers, and Punishment

In many respects, reinforcers can be thought of in terms of rewards; both a reinforcer and a reward increase the probability that a preceding response will occur again. But the term "reward" is limited to *positive* occurrences, and this is where it differs from a reinforcer—for it turns out that reinforcers can be positive or negative.

A **positive reinforcer** is a stimulus added to the environment that brings about an increase in a preceding response. If food, water, money, or praise is provided following a response, it is more likely that that response will occur again in the future. The paycheck I get at the end of the month, for example, increases the likelihood that I will work the following month.

In contrast, a **negative reinforcer** refers to a stimulus whose *removal* is reinforcing, leading to an increase in the probability that a preceding response will occur in the future. For example, if you have cold symptoms that are relieved when you take medicine, you are more likely to take the medicine when you experience such symptoms again. Similarly, if the radio is too loud and hurts your ears, you are likely to find that turning it down relieves the situation; lowering the volume is negatively reinforcing and you are more apt to repeat the action in the future. Negative reinforcement, then, teaches the individual that taking an action removes a negative condition that exists in the environment.

It is important to note that negative reinforcement is not the same as punishment. **Punishment** refers to unpleasant or painful stimuli—termed **aversive stimuli**—that are *added* to the environment if a certain behavior occurs; the result is a *decrease* in the probability that that behavior will occur again. In contrast, negative reinforcement is associated with the *removal* of an unpleasant or painful stimulus, which produces an *increase* in the behavior that brought an end to the unpleasant stimulus. If we receive a shock for behaving in a particular fashion, then, we are receiving punishment; but if we are already receiving a shock and do something to stop that shock, the behavior that stops the shock is considered to be negatively reinforced. In the first case, a specific behavior is apt to decrease because of the punishment; in the second, we are likely to increase the behavior because of the negative reinforcement (Azrin & Holt, 1966).

While punishment is typically considered in terms of applying some aversive stimulus—the back of the hand for being disobedient or ten years in jail for committing a crime—it may also consist of the removal of something positive. For instance, when a teenager is told she will no longer be able to use the family car because of her poor grades, or when an employee is told that he has been demoted with a cut in pay because of poor job evaluations, punishment in the form of the removal of a positive reinforcer is being administered.

Positive reinforcer: A stimulus added to the environment that brings about an increase in the response that preceded it

Negative reinforcer: A stimulus whose removal is reinforcing, leading to a greater probability that the response bringing about this removal will occur again

Punishment: An unpleasant or painful stimulus that is added to the environment after a certain behavior occurs, decreasing the likelihood that the behavior will occur again

Aversive stimuli: Unpleasant or painful stimuli

TABLE 5-1

Types of Reinforcement and Punishment

Nature of Stimulus	Application	Removal or Termination
Positive	*Positive reinforcement* Example: Giving a raise for good performance Result: Increase in frequency of response (good performance)	*Punishment by removal* Example: Removal of favorite toy after misbehavior Result: Decrease in frequency of response (misbehavior)
Negative	*Punishment by application* Example: Giving a spanking following misbehavior Result: Decrease in frequency of response (misbehavior)	*Negative reinforcement* Example: Terminating a headache by taking aspirin Result: Increase in frequency of response (taking aspirin)

The distinctions between the types of punishment, as well as positive and negative reinforcement, may appear confusing at first glance, but the following rules of thumb (and the summary in Table 5-1) can help you to distinguish these concepts from one another:

▶ Reinforcement is meant to *increase* the behavior preceding it; punishment is meant to *decrease* the behavior preceding it.

▶ The *application* of a *positive* stimulus is intended to bring about an increase in behavior and is referred to as positive reinforcement; the *removal* of a *positive* stimulus is meant to decrease behavior and is called punishment by removal.

▶ The *application* of a *negative* stimulus is intended to reduce behavior and is called punishment by application; the *removal* of a *negative* stimulus that results in an increase in behavior is termed negative reinforcement.

Why Reinforcement Beats Punishment: The Pros and Cons of Punishment
Is punishment an effective means of modifying behavior? Punishment often presents the quickest route to changing behavior that, if allowed to continue, might be dangerous to an individual. For instance, we may not have a second chance to warn a child not to run into a busy street, so punishing the first incidence of this behavior might prove to be wise. Moreover, the use of punishment to suppress behavior, even temporarily, provides the opportunity to reinforce a person for behaving in a more desirable way.

There are some instances in which punishment may be the most humane approach to certain deep-seated psychological problems. For example, some children suffer from autism, a rare psychological disorder in which they may abuse themselves, tearing at their skin or banging their heads against the wall, injuring themselves severely in the process. In such cases, punishment in the form of a quick but intense electric shock—sometimes with remarkable results—has been used to prevent self-injurious behavior when all other treatments have failed (Lovaas & Koegel, 1973). Such punishment, however, is used only as a treatment of last resort, keeping the child safe and buying time until positive reinforcement procedures can be initiated.

Autistic children must sometimes wear physical restraints to prevent them from injuring themselves when they engage in self-destructive behavior. (Joel Gordon)

Several disadvantages make the routine use of punishment questionable. For one thing, it is frequently ineffective, particularly if the punishment is not delivered shortly after the behavior being suppressed or if the individual is able to withdraw from the setting in which the punishment is being given. An employee who is reprimanded by the boss may quit; a teenager who loses the use of the family car may run away from home. In such instances, then, the initial behavior that is being punished may be replaced by one that is even less desirable.

Even worse, physical punishment may convey to the recipient the idea that physical aggression is permissible and perhaps even desirable. A father who yells and hits his son teaches the son that aggression is an appropriate, adult response, and the son may soon copy his father's behavior and act aggressively toward others. In addition, physical punishment is often administered by people who are themselves angry or enraged. It is unlikely that individuals in such an emotional state will be able to think through what they are doing or to carefully control the degree of punishment they are inflicting.

The use of physical punishment produces the risk that the people administering the punishment will grow to be feared. Furthermore, unless people who are being punished can be made to understand the reasons—that the punishment is meant to change behavior and that it is independent of the punishers' view of them as individuals—punishment may lead to lowered self-esteem.

Finally, punishment does not convey any information about what an alternative, more appropriate behavior might be. In order to be useful in bringing about more desirable behavior in the future, punishment must be paired with specific information about what is being punished, along with information about a more desirable behavior. To punish a child for staring out the window in school may lead her to stare at the floor instead. Unless we teach her the appropriate way to respond, we have just substituted one undesirable behavior for another. If punishment is not combined with reinforcement for alternative behavior that is more appropriate, little will be accomplished. In sum, reinforcing desired behavior is a more appropriate technique for modifying behavior than is using punishment. In the scientific arena, then, reinforcement usually beats punishment.

RECAP AND REVIEW II

Recap

◁ Operant conditioning is a form of learning in which a response is made because of the positive or negative consequences that follow the response or because of the negative conditions that are ended or avoided by the response.

◁ A reinforcer is any stimulus that increases the probability that a preceding response will occur.

◁ Primary reinforcers are those that satisfy a biological need and therefore are effective without prior experience; secondary reinforcers are stimuli that, because of their previous association with primary reinforcers, begin to elicit the same responses as primary reinforcers.

◁ A positive reinforcer is a stimulus that is added to the environment to increase the likelihood of a response. A negative reinforcer is a stimulus whose removal leads to an increase in the probability that a preceding response will occur in the future.

◁ Punishment is the administration of an unpleasant stimulus, following a response, which is meant to decrease or suppress behavior; it may also consist of the removal of a positive reinforcer.

◁ The distinction between punishment and negative reinforcement is critical: In punishment, the goal is to decrease or suppress undesired behavior by administering a stimulus; in negative reinforcement, the goal is to increase a desired behavior by removing a stimulus.

1. _____ _____ focuses on responses that are learned as a result of the positive or negative consequences contingent upon the response.

2. A warm campfire would be a _____ reinforcer to a cold hiker, whereas an award for hiking a large number of miles would be a _____ reinforcer.

3. Sandy had had a rough day, and his son's noisemaking was not helping him relax. Not wanting to resort to scolding, Sandy lowered his tone of voice and told his son in a serious manner the he was very tired and would like the boy to play quietly for an hour. This approach worked. For Sandy, the change in his son's behavior was
   a. positively reinforcing.
   b. secondarily reinforcing.
   c. punishing.
   d. negatively reinforcing.

4. Sandy was pleased. He had not been happy with himself a week earlier, when he yelled loudly at his son. On that occasion he had halted his son's excessive noise through
   a. removal of a reinforcer.
   b. punishment.
   c. negative reinforcement.
   d. extinction.

5. Fortunately, there is little danger that a child who is punished by a parent will learn that punishment is an acceptable behavior. True or false? _____

6. Reinforcing desired behavior to take the place of undesired behavior is usually a more effective approach than using punishment. True or false? _____

(Answers to review questions are on page 174.)

TIMING LIFE'S REWARDS: Schedules of Reinforcement

The world would be a different place if a cardplayer stopped playing as soon as he was dealt a losing hand, a fisherman stopped fishing as soon as he missed a catch, or a door-to-door salesperson stopped selling at the first house at which she was turned away. The fact that such unreinforced behaviors continue, often with great frequency, illustrates that reinforcement need not be received continually in order for behavior to be learned and maintained. In fact, behavior that is reinforced only occasionally may ultimately be learned better than behavior that is always reinforced.

When we refer to the frequency and timing of reinforcement following desired behavior we are talking about **schedules of reinforcement**. Behavior that is reinforced every time it occurs is said to be on a **continuous reinforcement schedule**; if it is reinforced some but not all of the time, it is on a **partial reinforcement schedule**. Although learning occurs more rapidly under a continuous reinforcement schedule, learned behavior lasts longer after reinforcement stops when it is learned under a partial reinforcement schedule.

Why should partial reinforcement schedules result in stronger, longer-lasting learning than continuous reinforcement schedules? We can answer the question by examining how we might behave when using a soda vending machine compared with a Las Vegas slot machine. When we use a vending machine, prior experience has taught us that the schedule of reinforcement is continuous—every time we put in 75 cents, the reinforcement, a soda, ought to be delivered. In comparison, a slot machine offers a partial reinforcement schedule: We have learned that after putting in 75 cents, most of the time we will not receive anything in return. At the same time, though, we know that we will occasionally win something.

Now suppose that, unbeknownst to us, both the soda vending machine and the slot machine are broken, and neither one is able to dispense anything. It will not be very long before we stop depositing coins into the broken soda machine; probably at most we would try only two or three times before leaving the machine in disgust. But the story would be quite different with

Schedules of reinforcement: The frequency and timing of reinforcement following desired behavior

Continuous reinforcement: The reinforcing of a behavior every time it occurs

Partial reinforcement: The reinforcing of a behavior some, but not all of the time

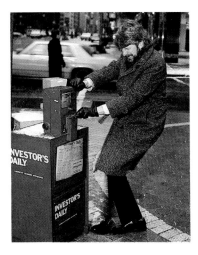

Because we expect continuous reinforcement from vending machines—e.g., every time we insert the required coins, we get a newspaper—we become frustrated very quickly when the reinforcement is not forthcoming. (Innervisions)

the broken slot machine. Here, we would throw in money for a considerably longer time, even though no response would be forthcoming.

In formal terms, we can see the difference between the two reinforcement schedules: Partial reinforcement schedules (such as those provided by slot machines) maintain performance longer than do continuous reinforcement schedules (such as those established in soda vending machines) before extinction occurs.

Using a **cumulative recorder**, a device that automatically records and graphs the pattern of responses made in reaction to a particular schedule (see Figure 5-5), learning psychologists have found that certain kinds of partial reinforcement schedules produce stronger and lengthier responding before extinction than do others. Although many different partial reinforcement schedules have been examined, they can be most readily classified into two categories: schedules that consider the *number of responses* made before reinforcement is given—called fixed-ratio and variable-ratio schedules—and those that consider the *amount of time* that elapses before reinforcement is provided—called fixed-interval and variable-interval schedules.

Cumulative recorder: A device that automatically records and graphs the pattern of responses made in reaction to a particular reinforcement schedule

Counting Responses: Fixed- and Variable-Ratio Schedules

In a **fixed-ratio schedule**, reinforcement is given only after a certain number of responses are made. For instance, a pigeon might receive a food pellet every tenth time it pecked a key; here, the ratio would be 1:10. Similarly,

Fixed-ratio schedule: A schedule whereby reinforcement is given only after a certain number of responses is made

FIGURE 5-5

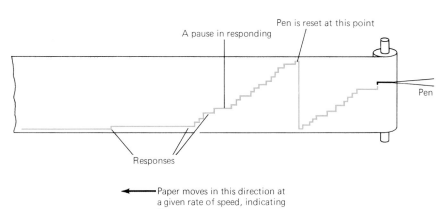

Pen is reset at this point

A pause in responding

Pen

Responses

Paper moves in this direction at a given rate of speed, indicating time

A cumulative recorder. As the paper slowly unrolls, the pen indicates when a response has been made by moving a notch upward. Pauses in responding are indicated by a lack of upward movement of the line. As is the case in this example, it is typical for the time between initial responses to decrease as the organism learns to make the response.

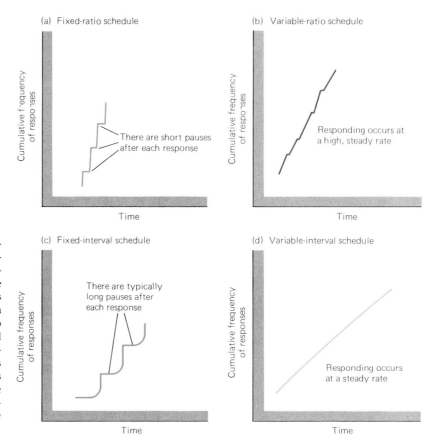

(a) Fixed-ratio schedule

Cumulative frequency of responses

There are short pauses after each response

Time

(b) Variable-ratio schedule

Cumulative frequency of responses

Responding occurs at a high, steady rate

Time

(c) Fixed-interval schedule

Cumulative frequency of responses

There are typically long pauses after each response

Time

(d) Variable-interval schedule

Cumulative frequency of responses

Responding occurs at a steady rate

Time

FIGURE 5-6

Typical outcomes of different reinforcement schedules. (a) In a fixed-ratio schedule, short pauses occur following each response. Because the more responses, the more reinforcement, fixed-ratio schedules produce a high rate of responding. (b) In a variable-ratio schedule, responding also occurs at a high rate. (c) A fixed interval schedule produces lower rates of responding, especially just after reinforcement has been presented, since the organism learns that a specified time period must elapse between reinforcement. (d) A variable-interval schedule produces a fairly steady stream of responses.

garment workers are generally paid on fixed-ratio schedules: They receive *x* dollars for every ten blouses they sew. Because a greater rate of production means more reinforcement, people on fixed-ratio schedules are apt to work as quickly as possible. Even when rewards are no longer offered, responding comes in bursts—although pauses between bursts become longer and longer until the response peters out entirely (see Figure 5-6).

In a **variable-ratio schedule**, reinforcement occurs after a varying number of responses rather than after a fixed number. Although the specific number of responses necessary to receive reinforcement varies, the number of responses usually hovers around a specific average. Probably the best example of a variable-ratio schedule is that encountered by a door-to-door salesperson. She may make a sale at the third, eighth, ninth, and twentieth houses she visits without being successful at any of the houses in between. Although the number of responses that must be made before making a sale varies, it averages out to a 20 percent success rate. Under these circumstances, you might expect that the salesperson would try to make as many calls as possible in as short a time as possible. This is the case with all variable-ratio schedules; they promote a high rate of response and a high resistance to extinction.

Variable-ratio schedule: A schedule whereby reinforcement occurs after a varying number of responses rather than after a fixed number

Passing Time: Fixed- and Variable-Interval Schedules

In contrast to fixed- and variable-ratio schedules—in which the crucial factor is the number of responses—fixed- and variable-*interval* schedules focus on the amount of *time* that has elapsed since a person or animal was rewarded. One example of a fixed-interval schedule is a weekly paycheck. For people who receive regular, weekly paychecks, it makes little difference how much they produce in a given week—as long as they show up and do *some* work.

Because a **fixed-interval schedule** provides a reinforcement for a response only if a fixed time period has elapsed, overall rates of response are relatively low. This is especially true in the period just after reinforcement when the time before another reinforcement is relatively great. Students' study habits often exemplify this reality: If the periods between exams are relatively long (meaning that the opportunity for reinforcement for good performance is fairly infrequent), students often study minimally or not at all until the day of the exam draws near. Just before the exam, however, students begin to cram for it, signaling a rapid increase in the rate of their studying response (Mawhinney et al., 1971). As you might expect, just after the exam there is a rapid decline in the rate of responding, with few people opening a book the day after a test.

One way to decrease the delay in responding that occurs just after reinforcement, and to maintain the desired behavior more consistently throughout an interval, is to use a variable-interval schedule. In a **variable-interval schedule**, the time between reinforcements varies around some average rather than being fixed. For example, a professor who gives surprise quizzes that vary from one every three days to one every three weeks, averaging one every two weeks, is using a variable-interval schedule. Students' study habits would most likely be very different as a result of such an unpredictable schedule than those we observed with a fixed-interval schedule: Students would be apt to study more regularly since they would never know when the next surprise quiz would be coming. Variable-interval schedules, in general, are more likely to produce relatively steady rates of responding than are fixed-interval schedules, with responses that take longer to extinguish after reinforcement ends.

Fixed-interval schedule: A schedule whereby a reinforcer is given at established time intervals

Variable-interval schedule: A schedule whereby reinforcement is given at various times, usually causing a behavior to be maintained more consistently

DISTINGUISHING THE RIGHT STIMULUS FROM THE WRONG: Discrimination and Generalization in Operant Conditioning

It does not take a child long to learn that a red light at an intersection means stop, while a green light indicates that it is permissible to continue. Just as in classical conditioning, then, operant learning involves the phenomena of discrimination and generalization.

The process by which people learn to discriminate stimuli is known as stimulus control training. In **stimulus control training**, an organism is reinforced in the presence of a specific stimulus, but not in its absence. For example, one of the most difficult discriminations many people face is determining when someone's friendliness is not mere friendliness, but a signal of romantic interest. People learn to make the discrimination by observing the presence of certain subtle nonverbal cues—such as increased eye contact and touching—that indicate romantic interest; when such cues are absent, they learn that no romantic interest is indicated. In this case, the nonverbal cue acts as a **discriminative stimulus**, one to which an organism learns to respond during stimulus control training. A discriminative stimulus signals the likelihood that reinforcement will follow a response. For example, if you wait until your roommate is in a good mood before asking her to lend you her favorite record, your behavior can be said to be under stimulus control.

Stimulus control training: Training in which an organism is reinforced in the presence of a certain specific stimulus, but not in its absence

Discriminative stimulus: A stimulus to which an organism learns to respond as part of stimulus control training

Just as in classical conditioning, the phenomenon of stimulus generalization, in which an organism learns a response to one stimulus and then applies it to other stimuli, is also found in operant conditioning. If you have learned that being polite produces the reinforcement of getting your way in a certain situation, you are likely to generalize your response to other situations. Sometimes, though, generalization can have unfortunate consequences, such as when people behave negatively toward all members of a racial group because they have had an unpleasant experience with one member of the racial group.

SUPERSTITIOUS BEHAVIOR

Whenever Phil Esposito, a hockey star for eighteen years, drove to a game, he always wore a black tie and always passed through the same tollbooth he had driven through on the way to his last winning game. When he arrived at the site of the game, he would put on the black turtleneck he wore when he became the team's high scorer. He then arranged his wardrobe in a particular order (underwear, pants, skates, and laces), and was sure to include a pack of gum plus one additional stick of gum. Next, he arranged his skating paraphernalia with black tape on the bottom, then white tape, and then his gloves, which he carefully aligned and placed palms up on each side of his hockey stick. As the game was about to start he would say a Hail Mary and the Lord's Prayer and would pray that his team played well and that the game would be free of injuries. *Then* he was ready to play hockey.

While it is easy to scoff at Phil Esposito's elaborate pregame ritual of **superstitious behavior**, such behavior is relatively common among athletes (Zimmer, 1984). In fact, many of us have some superstitions of our own; wearing a special shirt when we take a test or go•for a job interview, telling ourselves that if we make all the traffic lights on a certain road we'll have good luck for the rest of the day, or—an old favorite—avoiding a black cat in our path.

Where do such superstitions come from? To learning psychologists, there is a simple answer, having to do with the principles of reinforcement. As we have discussed, behavior that is followed by a reinforcer tends to be strengthened. Occasionally, however, the behavior that occurs prior to the reinforcement is entirely coincidental. Imagine, for instance, that a baseball player hits his bat against the ground three times in a row and then gets a home run. The hit is, of course, coincidental to the batter's hitting the ground, but to the player it may be seen as somehow related. Because the association is made in the player's mind, he may hit the ground three times every time he is at bat in the future. And because he will be at least partially reinforced for this behavior—batters usually get a hit 25 percent of the time—his ground-hitting behavior will probably be maintained.

Do superstitions actually affect subsequent behavior? In fact, they do. According to some psychologists, superstitious behavior allows people to cope with anxiety by providing routines or rituals that can give them a sense of control over a situation (Zimmer, 1984). In this way, wearing a "lucky" shirt helps to calm a person—which, in fact, may lead to better performance when taking a test or during a stressful interview. As you can see, then, your superstitions may shape your subsequent behavior.

Superstitious behavior: The mistaken belief that particular ideas, objects, or behavior will cause certain events to occur, as a result of learning based on the coincidental association between the idea, object, or behavior and subsequent reinforcement

Superstitious behavior is learned through the coincidental association between an idea, object, or behavior and subsequent reinforcement. Because the number 13 has come to be associated with bad luck, many buildings do not include a thirteenth floor. (Innervisions)

WHAT IS REINFORCING FOR YOU MAY BE PUNISHMENT TO ME:
The Premack Principle

It is clear that food is a reinforcer to someone who is hungry and water is a reinforcer to someone who is thirsty. It is considerably less clear, however, whether two tickets to a concert will be reinforcers, nor is it clear whether the concert tickets would be better reinforcers than two tickets to a basketball game. It is only by examining the prior history of a given individual that we would be able to ascertain which tickets would be of greater value—or whether they would be of any value at all.

To account for differences in reinforcers, psychologist David Premack developed what has come to be known as the Premack principle. The Premack principle states that organisms have different preferences for performing various behaviors, and that the preferences can be rank-ordered. Furthermore, an organism will perform behaviors that are low in rank in order to obtain the opportunity to perform a more preferred behavior (Premack, 1965).

The principle suggests, then, that to determine what is reinforcing to an organism we must first develop a ranking for various activities. Suppose, for instance, we find that a person prefers attending basketball games to concerts. We can then use the higher-ranked activity—in this case, basketball game attendance—as a reinforcer in training other behaviors. Moreover, if we were interested in teaching the person to attend concerts, we could reinforce concert going (the lower-ranked activity) by providing the opportunity to attend basketball games (the higher-ranked one).

The Premack principle reminds us that reinforcers are individualistic, and that we need to consider an organism's prior history when designing ways of modifying behavior. Although there are some exceptions to the principle, the notion of preference rankings for activities is a critical one.

REINFORCING WHAT DOESN'T COME NATURALLY: Shaping

Consider the difficulty of using operant conditioning to teach people to repair an automobile transmission. If you had to wait until they fixed it perfectly before you provided them with reinforcement, the Model T might be back in style long before they ever mastered the repair.

There are many complex behaviors, ranging from auto repair to zebra hunting, which we would not expect to occur naturally as part of anyone's spontaneous behavior. In cases such as these, in which there otherwise might be no opportunity to provide reinforcement for the particular behavior (since it never occurs in the first place), a procedure known as shaping is used. **Shaping** is the process of teaching a complex behavior by rewarding closer and closer approximations of the desired behavior. In shaping, any behavior that is at all similar to the behavior you want the person to learn is reinforced at first. Later, you reinforce only responses that are closer to the behavior you ultimately want to teach. Finally, you reinforce only the desired response. Each step in shaping, then, moves only slightly beyond the previously learned behavior, permitting the person to link the new step to the behavior learned earlier.

Shaping: The process of teaching a complex behavior by rewarding closer and closer approximations of the desired behavior

Shaping even allows lower animals to learn complex responses that naturally would never occur, ranging from porpoises trained to jump through hoops and walk on the water with their tails, to pigeons trained to rescue people lost at sea (see the Psychology at Work box later in the chapter).

Shaping also underlies the learning of many complex human skills. For instance, the organization of most textbooks is based on the principles of shaping. Typically, material is presented so that new material builds on previously learned concepts or skills. Thus the concept of shaping could not be presented in this chapter until we had discussed the more basic principles of operant learning.

WHERE PROFESSORS ARE PROGRAMS: Using Programmed Instruction in College Classes

Chemistry students can mix chemicals to their hearts' delight without risk of explosion. Medical students can perform simulated operations without endangering a patient's life. Physics students can see the path electrons travel in response to different forces (Pollack, 1987, p. D6).

The opportunity to carry out each of these activities comes not from a resourceful and clever classroom teacher but from an inanimate replacement: a computer. According to proponents of the use of computers to teach college students, the increasingly widespread availability of computers and an increase in computer literacy on many college campuses will lead to a revolution in instruction. In this view, computers may be routinely used to supplement human instruction, or to teach courses entirely, in the not-too-distant future.

The use of computers in classrooms is based on a procedure first developed some sixty years ago (Benjamin, 1988). Called programmed instruction or computer-assisted instruction, it represents one of the most common applications of shaping (Cherry, 1983; Skinner, 1984). **Programmed instruction** explicitly uses the principles of learning in the design of instructional material. A student using such material is first asked to type into the computer very simple responses that are printed on the screen; then the student moves on to increasingly complex problems. Correct responses are immediately reinforced, while mistakes evoke a review of previous material. The reinforcement for correct responses may be explicit, in the form of encouragement printed on the screen ("Good," "Great job, Wendy," "Keep it up," and the like), or the user may simply be allowed to move on to the next part of the lesson, which in itself can act as a powerful reinforcer. Each correct response shapes the student's behavior to bring him or her closer to the final desired behavior—mastery of a relatively complex body of material.

The advantages of using programmed instruction are many (Hassett & Dukes, 1986). Computers never become fatigued, and they are available whenever the student is. Sophisticated programs can critically analyze students' patterns of errors and present material in a manner that is specifically suited to the learning capabilities of the student. In addition, the computer is capable of providing sophisticated simulations that permit students to experience situations that would otherwise be physically impossible or excessively expensive. State-of-the-art computers use optical discs—newer versions of the compact discs used for music—to deliver stereo sound, photos, and moving pictures, along with enough written text to fill a small library (Rogers, 1988).

For instance, using one computer program, students can learn physiology by determining how the power exerted by a muscle varies with the muscle's length and the weight of the load it must lift. They can also "par-

Programmed instruction: The development of learning by building gradually on basic knowledge, with review and reinforcement when appropriate

FIGURE 5-7

This example of computerized programmed instruction—drawn from *Psych-World,* a set of programs that accompany *Understanding Psychology*—shows the operation of parts of the brain. (John Hay, Psychworld, McGraw-Hill, 1989.)

ticipate" in a bicycle race on the video screen, experimenting with the effects of shifting gears to modify the output of certain muscles (Pollack, 1987). Similarly, programmed instruction designed by John Hay shows the effects of inserting electrodes in particular parts of the brain (see Figure 5-7).

Programmed instruction is not without its critics, however. Some people feel that the excessive use of simulations will not provide students with an understanding of what actually happens in the real world, such as when laboratory experiments go awry. Others feel that the inability of students to ask questions beyond those that have been programmed is too restrictive.

Still, most data suggest that carefully designed programmed instruction can be an effective teaching technique (Wilkinson, 1983; Mandl & Lesgold, 1988). Computers are also helping to illuminate basic learning processes, as you can see in the accompanying Cutting Edge box.

THE CUTTING EDGE

COMPUTERS LEARN TO LEARN

A computer is teaching itself to read out loud. Initially, its attempts sound like gibberish, since it has not been given any rules about what the sounds of particular letters are. However, after electronically receiving corrective feedback following each mistake it makes, it soon begins to produce babylike babbling sounds as it learns to distinguish between vowels and consonants. After an evening of computing, it reads with only minor errors (Pollack, 1987).

A new breed of computer programs, such as this one developed by Terrence Sejnowski of Johns Hopkins University, are demonstrating that they can learn how to learn—and, in the process, are illuminating the manner in which human beings themselves learn. These new programs employ a technology called "neural networks" and hold the promise of a generation of computers that in essence program themselves, without requiring a person to produce a set of rules and procedures for the computer to follow (Ballard, Hinton & Sejnowski, 1983; Roberts, 1989).

Computers using neural networks operate in a manner analogous to the way neurons in the brain operate during learning. Many of the computer's processing units (called "nodes") operate simultaneously on a problem, as do the billions of neurons in the brain. Each of these nodes is connected to many others, again analogous to the way in which the brain's neurons are connected via synapses to other neurons, with the strength of the connections varying.

Each node has a particular activation level that determines whether or not it will "fire," thereby sending information to another node. Furthermore, not only does the activation level vary, but the magnitude of the connection between two nodes may differ. Either of these variables can be set by the computer programmer in advance, or the computer itself can, through trial and error, set its own levels, according to the nature of the problem on which it is working (Ackley, Hinton & Sejnowski, 1985).

When faced with a problem, the computer network processes information simultaneously on many levels. Unlike traditional computers, in which the rules must be completely specified in advance (for example, the letter "t" is pronounced differently when it is followed by an "h" than when it is followed by a vowel), neural network computers can develop their own rules based on the feedback they receive (see Figure 5-8 on the next page).

What is particularly interesting is how the computer's use of the electronic feedback it is provided mimics the shaping procedures that underlie the learning of complex information that has been discovered by psychologists. Moreover, neural network computers are helping to unravel the question of how much learning is due to the mere application of rules, and under what conditions classical conditioning and operant conditioning theories are most pertinent.

Still, computers have yet to approach the learning capabilities of human beings. Given the fact there are literally billions of neurons in the human brain, the likelihood that any computer will soon reach the level of human learning is low. However, the day may come when a computer can be made to learn effectively—helping us to better understand how humans learn in the process.

FIGURE 5-8

A neural network mimics human processes in learning to recognize the letter *A*. Initially, the system makes random guesses. (a) When the system makes a wrong choice, a weakening occurs in the circuits involved. (b) When the system makes an appropriate selection, the accountable circuits are strengthened. (c) Finally, after making numerous choices with differing forms of the letter in which particular circuits are either strengthened or weakened, the system learns to identify the letter with a high degree of accuracy (Lertola, 1988).

DISCRIMINATING BETWEEN CLASSICAL AND OPERANT CONDITIONING

Up to this point, we have been discussing classical and operant conditioning as though they were two entirely distinct approaches. However, these two types of conditioning share several features.

For example, generalization and discrimination processes are found in operant conditioning, just as they are in classical conditioning. A pigeon that has learned to peck a red key to receive food will probably do the same thing to a blue key, illustrating that generalization has occurred. Similarly, discrimination processes are also present in operant conditioning. When a child learns from the reinforcers his parent provides that he ought to stay away from strangers but be polite and friendly to acquaintances, we can see an example of discrimination.

The fact that generalization and discrimination are present in both classical and operant conditioning suggests that the distinction between these two types of learning is not always clear-cut. Consider, for instance, what happens when you are called into the house for dinner. As you hear the call for dinner, you begin to salivate, and the smells of the food get stronger as you walk toward the kitchen. You quickly reach the table and receive your reward for coming: a big helping of roast beef, potatoes, and salad.

Is your behavior the result of classical conditioning or operant conditioning? Actually, it is both. Your salivation reflects classical conditioning; you have learned to associate being called in to dinner with the food that follows it. But the footsteps taking you to the table, which actually allow you to receive the reinforcement of food, reflect a behavioral pattern learned through operant conditioning; you have purposefully responded in a way that gets you a reward.

As you see, the distinction between classical and operant conditioning is not always clear when we consider specific instances of behavior, since both processes are often at work in terms of a particular sequence of behavior. Moreover, even some of the most basic differences between operant and classical conditioning have been called into question. For example, as we discussed in Chapter 2, people are able to learn to control "involuntary" responses, such as blood pressure and heart rate, through biofeedback. What would typically be thought of as a response involving classical conditioning, then, can be viewed in terms of operant conditioning.

To complicate matters, even the essential nature of classical conditioning is open to question. Robert Rescorla (1988) has suggested that rather than being viewed in terms of learning based on the close pairing of stimuli, classical conditioning should be seen as the learning of relations among events, in which the organism is able to predict an unconditioned stimulus by the conditioned stimulus. In this manner, a person or animal is able to represent the structure of its environment through classical conditioning.

Still, although there are many unresolved questions regarding classical and operant conditioning, the two processes are distinct in most of the cases of behavior that psychologists analyze: In classical conditioning, the unconditioned stimulus precedes the response; the response is elicited by the unconditioned stimulus. In operant conditioning, in contrast, the response is made prior to the reinforcement and is therefore performed intentionally—that is, the response is made to obtain the reward. In classical conditioning, then, the response is basically involuntary, whereas in operant conditioning the response is voluntary.

YOU CAN'T TEACH AN OLD DOG DIFFICULT TRICKS: Biological Constraints on Learning

Keller and Marian Breland were pleased with their idea. As professional animal trainers for the circus, they came up with the notion of having a pig place a wooden disk into a piggy bank. With their experience in training animals through operant conditioning, they thought the task would be easy to teach, given that it was certainly well within the range of the pig's physical capabilities. Yet every time they tried out the procedure, it failed: Upon viewing the disk, the pigs were willing to do nothing but root the wooden disk along the ground. Apparently, the pigs were biologically programmed to push stimuli in the shape of disks along the ground.

Their lack of success with porkers led the Brelands to substitute a raccoon. Although the procedure worked fine with one disk, when two disks were used, the raccoon refused to deposit either of them and instead rubbed the two together, as if it were washing them. Once again, it appeared that the disks evoked biologically innate behaviors that were impossible to supplant with even the most exhaustive training (Breland & Breland, 1961).

The Brelands' difficulties illustrate an important point: Not all behaviors can be trained in all species equally well. Instead, there are **biological constraints**, built-in limitations, in the ability of animals to learn particular be-

Biological constraints: Built-in limitations in an organism's ability to learn particular behaviors

haviors. In some cases, an organism will have a special bent that will aid in its learning a behavior (such as behaviors which involve pecking in pigeons); in other cases, biological constraints will act to prevent or inhibit an organism from learning a behavior. In either instance, it is clear that animals have specialized learning mechanisms which influence how readily both classical and operant conditioning function, and each species is biologically primed to develop particular kinds of associations and to face obstacles in learning others (Hollis, 1984).

At the same time, the range of behaviors that can be taught is remarkable. As noted in the Psychology at Work box, operant procedures have been employed to teach an extraordinary variety of behaviors.

A PIGEON POSSE: SAVING LIVES WITH OPERANT CONDITIONING

Your sailboat has capsized in the Pacific and you have been drifting for three days. Your mouth is dry, your stomach hungers for food, and you don't know how much longer you can hang on to the side of the boat. Suddenly, you see a speck in the sky off in the distance. It gets closer and closer until it is flying directly above, and you can see on it the markings of a Coast Guard rescue helicopter. As it hovers above, you wonder how you will ever be able to repay the pilots of the helicopter who have saved your life.

Actually, if you did thank the pilots for rescuing you, you might well be thanking the wrong people—or more accurately, the wrong species. For in reality you might owe your life to three pigeons caged in the belly of the helicopter.

These pigeons, trained in Sea Hunt, a Navy program currently under development, represent a dramatic example of the use of operant conditioning principles. The director of the Sea Hunt project, James Simmons, has taken ordinary pigeons and, using operant conditioning,

trained them to peck a series of keys at the sight of an orange speck in the ocean—such as a downed sailor wearing a life jacket (Cusack, 1984).

The training uses basic shaping procedures: Pigeons are first taught in a Skinner box to peck a key to receive food, and then to peck it only when an orange light is present. Next, the size of the light is decreased so the pigeons learn to peck only when an orange speck of light is present. (Lasers are used to control with exact precision the size of the light beam.) Finally the pigeons are taken out to sea and taught to peck at the key only when they see an orange stimulus in the ocean. The entire training process takes from six to ten months (Simmons, 1984).

In operation, the Sea Hunt system is simplicity itself. When the pigeons, which are strapped in the belly of a search helicopter (see Fig-

ure 5-9), peck a key to indicate the sighting of an orange stimulus, a signal is sent to the pilot. With three trained birds being used simultaneously, each in a separate chamber with a different viewing area, the pilot knows in what direction to orient the search. Because their visual acuity is far superior to that of humans, pigeons can spot a target 90 percent of the time the first time they are over an area—considerably better than the 40 percent success rates of human searchers. Moreover, they are less apt to be affected by sun glare and the problems of concentration and boredom that pilots experience during long searches.

Because the Sea Hunt system is effective, easy to use, reliable, and economical, the Navy is giving serious consideration to routinely using pigeons trained through operant conditioning as part of rescue operations. If you are ever stranded at sea, then, you should not be too surprised if you are saved not by a human search party but by a feathered one.

FIGURE 5-9

In the Sea Hunt system, pigeons trained by operant conditioning to identify downed sailors wearing orange life jackets are strapped into the belly of a search helicopter. When a pigeon spots an appropriate stimulus, it pecks a key, which alerts the helicopter pilot. (Based on Simmons, 1984.)

RECAP AND REVIEW III

Recap

◀ Reinforcement need not be constant in order for behavior to be learned and maintained; partial schedules of reinforcement, in fact, lead to greater resistance to extinction than continuous schedules of reinforcement.

◀ In fixed-ratio schedules, reinforcement is given only after a set number of responses is made. In variable-ratio schedules, reinforcement is given after a varying number of responses.

◀ In fixed-interval schedules, reinforcement is given after a desired response only if a specified period of time has elapsed since the last reinforcement. In contrast, in variable-interval schedules, the time between delivery of reinforcement varies around some average period of time.

◀ Generalization, discrimination, and shaping are among the basic phenomenon of operant conditioning.

◀ There are biological constraints on learning which aid, prevent, or inhibit learning.

Review

1. Carl decides to reward himself for studying by listening to music for a period of time following each hour of studying. What kind of reinforcement schedule has he arranged?
   a. Fixed-ratio
   b. Variable-interval
   c. Fixed-interval
   d. Variable-ratio

184

2. It just isn't working! Carl finds himself staring at one or two pages for an hour. He comes up with a great idea. He will listen to music only after reading fifteen pages. His reinforcement schedule would now be termed
   a. fixed-ratio.
   b. variable-interval.
   c. fixed interval.
   d. variable-ratio.

3. Feeling inquisitive, Carl decides to have his roommate, Jim, provide him access to music contingent upon differing numbers of pages read. Carl instructs Jim to provide access to music at times after eight pages or so, but at other times after perhaps thirty pages, with Jim choosing the number randomly but keeping the average around fifteen pages. This new schedule would be called
   a. fixed-ratio.
   b. variable-interval.
   c. fixed-interval.
   d. variable-ratio.

4. One day Cathy decided to alter her path to work and crossed the street to look at storefront displays. As she passed a flower cart, the vendor reached out and gave her a free rose. Cathy thereafter established a new route

to work, even though the vendor was rarely stationed across the street. This could be termed an example of _____ _____ .

5. A shop owner found that when he allowed his employees to choose a desirable task following completion of a less desirable one, the employees came to enjoy the less desirable task more. This is an example of the _____ _____ .

6. At first, Julie had all she could do to balance on her bicycle. However, after lots of encouragement from her parents for achieving small successes, she now rides beautifully. Julie's parents used _____ to teach her.

7. Computer simulations designed to gradually shape a student's ability to perform a specific task represent an application of _____ _____ .

8. Name two distinctions between operant and classical conditioning.

9. Classical and operant conditioning procedures work consistently well with all species of animals, despite built-in biological differences between them. True or false? _____

(Answers to review questions are on page 186.)

THINKING ABOUT LEARNING THEORY: COGNITIVE APPROACHES TO LEARNING

The criminal in the television movie hits a police officer's head against a brick wall. By knocking the officer out, the criminal manages to escape. He smiles triumphantly and coolly steps on the body as he runs away.

▲ ▲ ▲

An 8-year-old boy, who has seen the movie the previous evening, gets into a fight with his brother. Although in the past the fights have never involved physical violence, this time the boy knocks his brother into a wall and tries to step on him.

The impetus for the boy's new behavior is clear: It is the television movie. But the underlying process that accounts for his conduct cannot easily be explained by either classical or operant conditioning. Knocking people into a wall would not seem to be either an unconditioned or conditioned response, nor, given the fact that the boy had never had fights of this sort in the past, would he have had the opportunity to be reinforced for such behavior. Instances such as these suggest that some kinds of learning involve higher-order thinking processes in which people's thoughts and memories and the way they process information account for their responses.

Some psychologists have concentrated on the thought processes that underlie learning—an approach known as **cognitive learning theory**. Although psychologists using cognitive learning theory do not deny the importance of classical and operant conditioning, they have developed approaches that focus on the unseen mental processes that occur during the

Cognitive learning theory: The study of the thought processes that underlie learning

learning process, rather than concentrating solely on external stimuli, responses, and reinforcements.

In its most basic formulation, cognitive learning theory suggests that it is not enough to say that people make responses because there is a hypothetical link between a stimulus and a response due to a past history of reinforcement for the response. Instead, according to this point of view, people—and even animals—develop an *expectation* that they will receive a reinforcer upon making a response.

Evidence for this point of view comes from a famous series of experiments that revealed a type of cognitive learning called **latent learning**. In latent learning, a new behavior is learned but is not demonstrated until reinforcement is provided for displaying it (Tolman & Honzik, 1930). In the studies, the behavior of rats in a maze such as that shown in Figure 5-10*a* was examined. In one representative experiment, a group of rats was allowed to wander around the maze once a day for seventeen days without ever receiving any reward; understandably, these rats made many errors and spent a relatively long time reaching the end of the maze. A second group, however, was always given food at the end of the maze, and these rats learned to run quickly and directly to the food box, making few errors.

A third group of rats started out in the same situation as the unrewarded rats, but only for the first ten days. On the eleventh day, a critical experimental manipulation was instituted: From that point on, the rats in this group were given food for completing the maze. The results of this manipulation were dramatic, as you can see from the graph in Figure 5-10*b*. The previously unrewarded rats, who had earlier seemed to wander about aimlessly, showed reductions in running time and declines in error rates that almost immediately matched those of the group that had received rewards from the start.

To cognitive theorists, it seemed clear that the unrewarded rats had learned the layout of the maze early in their explorations; they just never displayed their latent learning until the reinforcement was offered. Instead, the rats seemed to develop a **cognitive map** of the maze—a mental representation of spatial locations and directions.

People, too, develop cognitive maps of their surroundings, based primarily on particular landmarks. When they first encounter a new environment, their maps tend to rely on specific paths—such as the directions we

Latent learning: Learning in which a new behavior is acquired but not readily demonstrated until reinforcement is provided

Cognitive map: A mental "picture" of locations and directions

FIGURE 5-10

(a) In an attempt to demonstrate latent learning, rats were allowed to roam through a maze of this sort once a day for seventeen days. (b) Those rats that were never rewarded (the nonrewarded control condition) consistently made the most errors, whereas those that received food at the finish every day (the rewarded control condition) made far fewer errors. But the results also showed latent learning: Rats that were initially unrewarded but began to be rewarded only after the tenth day (the experimental group) showed an immediate reduction in errors and soon matched the error rate of the rats that had been consistently rewarded. According to cognitive learning theorists, the reduction in errors indicates that the rats had developed a cognitive map—a mental representation—of the maze. (Tolman & Honzik, 1930.)

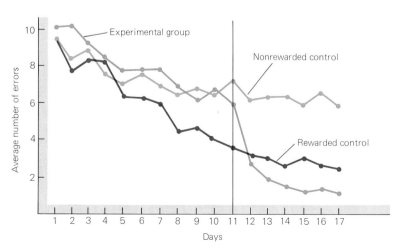

(a)   (b)

might give someone unfamiliar with an area: "Turn right at the stop sign, make a left at the bridge, and then go up the hill." However, as people become more familiar with an area, they develop an overall conception of it and an abstract cognitive map of the area. Using such a map, they are eventually able to take shortcuts as they develop a broad understanding of the area.

Unfortunately, though, our cognitive maps tend to be riddled with errors, representing simplifications of the actual terrain. We tend to develop maps that ignore curving roads and instead conceive of areas in terms of straight grids of intersecting roadways (Tversky, 1981). Our cognitive maps, then, are imperfect versions of actual maps.

Despite their inadequacies, the possibility that we develop our cognitive maps through latent learning presents something of a problem for strict reinforcement theorists. If we consider the results of Tolman's maze experiment, for instance, it is unclear what the specific reinforcement was that allowed the rats that received no reward to initially learn about the layout of the maze, since there was no obvious reinforcer present. Although we might speculate on the presence of internal reinforcers—such as the fulfillment of the organism's curiosity—such talk leaves behavioral psychologists uneasy. Given their focus on external and environmental reinforcement, psychologists who rely on operant conditioning explanations of learning are left with a theoretical question that has yet to be resolved satisfactorily.

LEARNING BY COPYING: Observational Learning

Although latent learning suggests how a behavior may be learned but not demonstrated, it does not explain the case of the boy who imitates a response that he has earlier observed in a television movie. In order to account for how a person who has no direct experience in carrying out a particular behavior learns and carries out the behavior, psychologists have proposed another form of cognitive learning: observational learning.

According to psychologist Albert Bandura and colleagues, a major part of human learning consists of **observational learning**, which they define as learning through observing the behavior of another person, a **model** (Bandura, 1977). Bandura and his colleagues demonstrated rather dramatically the ability of models to stimulate learning. In what is now considered a classic experiment, young children saw a movie of an adult wildly hitting a 5-foot-tall inflatable punching toy called a Bobo doll (Bandura, Ross & Ross, 1963). Later the children were given the opportunity to play with the Bobo doll themselves and, sure enough, they displayed the same kind of behavior, in some cases mimicking the aggressive behavior almost identically.

It is not only negative behaviors that are acquired through observational learning. In one experiment, for example, children who were afraid of dogs were exposed to a model—dubbed the Fearless Peer—playing with a dog (Bandura, Grusec & Menlove, 1967). Following exposure, observers were considerably more likely to approach a strange dog than were children who had not viewed the Fearless Peer.

Observational learning: Learning through observations of others (models)

Model: A person serving as an example to an observer; if a model's behavior is rewarded, the observer may imitate that behavior

ANSWERS (REVIEW III):
1. c **2.** a **3.** d **4.** Superstitious behavior **5.** Premack principle **6.** Shaping **7.** Programmed instruction **8.** Classical: Unconditioned stimulus occurs before the response; response is involuntary. Operant: Response is made before reinforcement; response is voluntary **9.** False; biological constraints on learning differ across species

Observational learning has taken place when a child imitates a behavior which she or he has seen someone else display. (Michal Heron/Woodfin Camp & Assoc.)

According to Bandura, observational learning takes place in four steps: (1) paying attention and perceiving the most critical features of another person's behavior; (2) remembering the behavior; (3) reproducing the action; and (4) being motivated to learn and carry out the behavior. Instead of learning occurring through trial and error, then, with successes being reinforced and failures punished, many important skills are learned through observational processes.

Observational learning is particularly important in acquiring skills in which shaping is inappropriate. Piloting an airplane and performing brain surgery, for example, would hardly be behaviors that could be learned using trial-and-error methods without grave cost—literally—to those involved in the learning.

Not all behavior that we witness is learned or carried out, of course. One crucial factor that determines whether we later imitate a model depends on the consequences of the model's behavior. If we observe a friend being rewarded for putting more time into her studies by receiving higher grades, we are more likely to model her behavior than if her behavior results in no increase in grades but rather greater fatigue and less social life. Models who are rewarded for behaving in a particular way are more apt to be mimicked than models who receive punishment. Interestingly, though, observing the punishment of a model does not necessarily stop observers from learning the behavior. Observers can still recount the model's behavior—they are just less apt to perform it (Bandura, 1977).

ACCEPTING THE UNACCEPTABLE: Learned Helplessness

Have you ever heard someone say, "You can't fight city hall"; "No matter how hard I study I'll never pass this course"; or "I'll never learn to play tennis, regardless of how much I practice"? According to psychologist Martin Seligman, each of these statements may represent an example of **learned helplessness**, the learned belief of a person or animal that no control can be exerted over the environment (Seligman, 1975).

Learned helplessness: An organism's learned belief that it has no control of the environment

Learned helplessness was first demonstrated in experiments in which dogs were exposed to a series of moderately painful but not physically damaging shocks that they could not avoid. Although at first the dogs tried desperately to escape, they eventually accepted the shocks. But the next phase of the experiment was the most revealing: The dogs were placed in a box with two compartments, separated by a low barrier that they could easily jump over. By jumping the barrier, they could avoid any shock administered in the first compartment. In comparison with dogs who had not received

shocks previously and who quickly learned to jump into the next compartment, the dogs who had received the inescapable shocks earlier tended to
give up rapidly, lie down, and wait for the shock to be over. The conclusion
drawn by Seligman was that the dogs had learned to be helpless. They expected that nothing they did would be useful in preventing the shocks and
therefore simply accepted them.

People, too, can learn to be helpless (Mineka & Hendersen, 1985). For
example, in one experiment, groups of college students were exposed to a
loud tone from which they could not escape. When later they were asked to
complete a task and were given the opportunity to escape a loud noise, they
made fewer attempts to escape and performed more poorly than a control
group of subjects completing the task who had earlier been exposed to a
tone from which they could escape. The students had seemingly learned to
be helpless in the face of something that, if they had only tried, they could
have escaped (Hiroto & Seligman, 1975).

The concept of learned helplessness provides an explanation for several
puzzling phenomena. For instance, battered children sometimes do not seek
relief even when given the oppportunity and may come to accept their beatings. One explanation is that they have learned helplessness in the face of
what they perceive to be inescapable punishment. Similarly, as we will discuss in Chapter 16, learned helplessness may underlie cases of severe human
depression in which people come to feel that they are victims of events
beyond their control and are helpless in their environment.

THE UNRESOLVED CONTROVERSY OF COGNITIVE LEARNING THEORY

The degree to which learning is based on unseen internal factors rather than
on external factors remains one of the major issues dividing learning theorists today. Both classical conditioning and operant conditioning consider
learning in terms of external stimuli and responses—a kind of "black box"
analysis in which all that matters are the observable features of the environment, not what goes on inside a person's head. To the cognitive learning
theorists, such an analysis misses the mark; what is crucial is the mental
activity—in the form of thoughts and expectations—that takes place.

Some psychologists feel that neither approach, by itself, is sufficient to
explain all learning. Rather than viewing behavioral and cognitive approaches
as contradictory, they see them as addressing learning through differing but
complementary approaches. Such a theoretical outlook has allowed psychologists to make important advances in such areas as the treatment of
certain kinds of abnormal behavior, as we will see in Chapter 16.

Still, while the controversy surrounding different approaches to learning
rages on as a major issue of psychology, tremendous advances are taking
place in the practical application of principles derived from the various theories, as we shall see in the remainder of this chapter.

BEHAVIOR ANALYSIS AND BEHAVIOR MODIFICATION

A couple who had been married for three years began to fight more and
more frequently. The issues ranged from the seemingly petty, such as who
was going to do the dishes, to the more profound, such as the quality of
their love life and whether they found each other interesting. Disturbed
about this increasingly unpleasant pattern of interaction, they went to a be-

havior analyst, a psychologist who specialized in behavior-modification techniques. After interviewing each of them alone and then speaking to them together, he asked them to keep a detailed written record of their interactions over the next two weeks—focusing, in particular, on the events that preceded their arguments.

When they returned two weeks later, he carefully went over the records with them. In doing so, he noticed a pattern that the couple themselves had observed after they had started keeping their records: Each of their arguments had occurred just after one or the other had left some household chore undone. For instance, the wife would go into a fury when she came home from work and found that her husband, a student, had left his dirty lunch dishes on the table and had not even started dinner preparations. The husband would get angry when he found his wife's clothes draped on the only chair in the bedroom; he insisted it was her responsibility to pick up after herself.

Using the data that had been collected, the behavior analyst devised a system for the couple to try out. He asked them to list all of the chores that could possibly arise and assign each one a point value depending on how long it took to complete. Then he had them divide the chores equally and agree in a written contract to fulfill the ones assigned to them. If either failed to carry out one of the assigned chores, he or she would have to place $1 per point in a fund for the other to spend. They also agreed to a program of verbal praise, promising to verbally reward each other for completing a chore.

Although skeptical about the value of such a program, the couple agreed to try it for a month and to keep careful records of the number of arguments they had during this period. To their surprise, the number declined rapidly, and even the more basic issues in their marriage seemed on the way to being resolved.

The case described above provides an illustration of **behavior modification**, a formalized technique for promoting the frequency of desirable behaviors and decreasing the incidence of unwanted ones. Using the basic principles of learning theory, behavior-modification techniques have proved to be helpful in a variety of situations (Wielkiewicz, 1985). Severely retarded people have learned the rudiments of language and, for the first time in their lives, have started dressing and feeding themselves. Behavior modification has also helped people to lose weight, give up smoking, and behave more safely (Cooper, Heron & Heward, 1987).

The variety of techniques used by behavior analysts is as varied as the list of processes that modify behavior—including the use of reinforcement scheduling, shaping, generalization training, discrimination training, and extinction. Behavioral approaches do, however, typically follow a series of similar basic steps in a behavior-change program (Royer & Feldman, 1984). These steps include:

▶ Identifying goals and target behaviors. The first step is to define "desired behavior." Is it an increase in time spent studying? A decrease in weight? An increase in the use of language? A reduction in the amount of aggression displayed by a child? The goals must be stated in observable terms and lead to specific targets. For instance, a goal might be "to increase study time," while the target behavior would be "to study at least two hours per day on weekdays and an hour on Saturdays."

Behavior modification: A formalized technique for promoting the frequency of desirable behaviors and decreasing the incidence of unwanted ones

▶ Designing a data-recording system and recording preliminary data. In order to determine whether behavior has changed, it is necessary to collect data before any changes are made in the situation. This provides a baseline against which future changes can be measured.

▶ Selecting a behavior-change strategy. The most crucial step is to select an appropriate strategy. Since all the principles of learning can be employed to bring about behavior change, a "package" of treatments is normally used. This might include the systematic use of positive reinforcement for desired behavior (verbal praise or something more tangible, such as food), as well as a program of extinction for undesirable behavior (ignoring a child who throws a tantrum). Selecting the right reinforcers is critical; you may have to experiment a bit to find out what is important to a given individual. Avoid threats, since they are merely punishing and are not very effective in bringing about long-term changes in behavior.

▶ Implementing the program. The next step is to institute the program. Probably the most important aspect of program implementation is consistency; if the program is not consistently applied, the chances for success are greatly reduced. It is also important to make sure that you are reinforcing the behavior you want to reinforce. For example, suppose you want a child to spend more time on her homework, but as soon as she sits down to study, she asks for a snack. If you get one for her, you are likely reinforcing her delaying tactic, not her studying. Instead, you might tell her that you will provide her with a snack after a certain time interval has gone by during which she has studied—thereby using the snack as a reinforcement for studying.

▶ Keeping careful records after the program is implemented. Another crucial task is record keeping; if the target behaviors are not monitored, there is no way of knowing whether the program has actually been successful. Don't rely on your memory, because it is all too easy for memory lapses to occur.

▶ Evaluating and altering the ongoing program. Finally, the results of the program should be compared with preimplementation data to determine its effectiveness. If successful, the procedures employed can be gradually phased out. For instance, if the program called for reinforcing every instance of picking up one's clothes from the bedroom floor, the reinforcement schedule could be modified to a fixed-ratio schedule in which every third instance was reinforced. On the other hand, if the program had not been successful in bringing about the desired behavior change, consideration of other approaches might be advisable.

Behavior-change techniques based on these general principles have had wide success and have proved to be one of the most powerful means of modifying behavior. We turn now to an area of particular applicability to most of our lives: better management of time.

THE INFORMED CONSUMER OF PSYCHOLOGY:
Using Behavior-Modification Techniques to Manage Your Time

Do you ever feel that you don't have enough time for everything you want to accomplish? Most of us, at one time or another, have such feelings, especially during our college years when numerous courses make separate and equally important demands on us—not to mention our extracurricular activities, social lives, and a host of other tasks that we want to accomplish. And such demands do not cease once one leaves college; life is filled with competing demands on our time. How can one meet these demands successfully?

Psychologists specializing in learning have devised a technique—called **time management**—that can teach us to use our time most effectively. Although the specifics vary, it is generally agreed that tasks must be broken down into their most basic components and that these components must be scheduled on a day-by-day basis. One system, designed specifically for use by college students in scheduling their study time, includes the following steps (Chase & Schulze, 1984):

Time management: A method of planning our time to make the most efficient use of it

▶ Buy two calendars that have spaces to write in activities and events for each day. One calendar should be reserved for long-term events; a calendar that displays the semester on one page might be appropriate here. The second should permit you to pencil in daily events. Having two calendars allows you to hold both a long-term focus, giving you an idea of when you should begin more ambitious projects, such as papers and studying for major exams, and a short-term focus for the day-to-day details. Put the calendars where you can see them every time you come into your room—don't hide them behind a door or in a desk drawer. The object is to see them often enough so that they act as a stimulus for an appropriate response.

▶ Collect every schedule, syllabus, and school calendar that will affect you over the semester, and use them to record on your calendars all pertinent deadlines, tests, papers due, social activities, athletic events, and the like. Also list your regular classes, job commitments, meetings, and so forth.

▶ A very general rule of thumb—which varies widely, but at least gives you a start—is to allow yourself *at least* two hours of study time for each hour you spend in the classroom. For instance, if your introductory psychology class is a three-credit course that meets three hours per week, it is wise to leave at least six hours per week for studying. Include additional study time for special projects, such as a term paper due at the end of the semester. If after scheduling your other classes and activities you find you do not have sufficient study time available to meet this goal, it is probably wise to cut back on some nonacademic activity or perhaps to enroll in one less course.

▶ Mark your study time on your calendar, considering what time of day you work best. The time you schedule for yourself to study should be as important—and free from interruption—as the events that others schedule for you. Guard it, and don't be tempted to fill it up with activities that come up on the spur of the moment.

▶ As any good learning theorist would say, be sure to build some rewards into your schedule. Give yourself breaks during your study time, perhaps saving a candy bar or soda until after you have studied for a certain period. It is also important to reinforce yourself by scheduling some "time off" every once in a while, particularly after very busy periods of the semester. And don't overschedule yourself—leave time for the unexpected.

▶ Finally, review your schedule each day and revise it according to the demands of the school term. Reviewing will enable you to make out a daily list of tasks you intend to accomplish—and, most rewarding of all, check off the accomplishments of the previous day.

As you can see from the preceding suggestions, the key to time management is specifying your goals and structuring the situation so that you are most apt to meet those goals—and are reinforced for reaching them. Because time management is so rewarding, it is a behavior that is likely to be maintained and generalized beyond the college years, giving you continuing control over one of life's most precious commodities—time.

RECAP AND REVIEW IV

Recap

◀ Cognitive learning theory focuses on the unseen, internal mental processes that are occurring within a person.

◀ Modeling consists of learning from the observation of others' behavior. The rewards that a model receives contribute to the imitation of the model.

◀ Learned helplessness is the learned belief of a person or animal that no control can be exerted over the environment.

◀ Behavior modification, a formal technique for promoting desirable behaviors and reducing undesirable ones, has been used successfully in changing both one's own and others' behavior.

Review

1. Six-year-old Judy unexpectedly performed a break-dancing maneuver similar to one she had observed at a show the previous week. Her parents found it charming and complimented Judy through their laughter and hugs. Now Judy performs the move frequently. Cognitive learning theorists might refer to Judy's behavior as an example of
   a. operant conditioning.
   b. expectation.
   c. latent learning.
   d. classical conditioning.

2. Judy had perhaps formulated a _____ _____ of the dance movement prior to receiving reinforcement from her parents.

3. Cognitive maps are typically extremely precise and accurate. True or false? _____

4. Remembering the television show she had seen on cabinetmaking and being motivated to construct her own cabinets, Jenny was able to reproduce many of the skills she had seen and eventually complete the project. The process by which Jenny came to acquire her skills is known as _____ _____.

5. Jeremy had consistently been unsuccessful in trying to overcome bouts of mild depression. According to the theory of _____ _____, it should not be too surprising if he discontinued trying new coping techniques and instead came to accept his depression.

6. Fill in the key steps missing in the behavior-analysis model:
   a. identifying goals and target behaviors.
   b. _____
   c. selecting a behavior-change strategy.
   d. implementing the program.
   e. keeping careful records.
   f. _____

(Answers to review questions are on page 194.)

◀ LOOKING BACK

1. Learning, a relatively permanent change in behavior due to experience, is a basic topic of psychology, although it is a process that must be assessed indirectly (we can only assume that learning has occurred by observing performance, which is susceptible to such factors as fatigue and lack of effort).

2. One major form of learning is known as classical conditioning. First studied by Ivan Pavlov, classical conditioning occurs when a neutral stimulus—one that brings about no relevant response—is repeatedly paired with a stimulus (called an unconditioned stimulus) that brings about a natural, untrained response. For instance, a neutral stimulus might be a buzzer; an unconditioned stimulus might be a dish of ice cream. The response ice cream might bring about in a hungry person—salivation—is called an unconditioned response; it occurs naturally, owing to the physical makeup of the individual being trained.

3. The actual conditioning occurs when the neutral stimulus is repeatedly presented just before the unconditioned stimulus. After repeated pairings, the neutral stimulus begins to bring about the same response as the unconditioned stimulus. When this occurs, we can say that the neutral stimulus is now a conditioned stimulus, and the response made to it is the conditioned response. For example, after a person has learned to salivate to the sound of the buzzer, we say the buzzer is a conditioned stimulus, and the salivation is a conditioned response.

4. Learning is not always permanent, however. Extinction occurs when a previously learned response weakens and eventually disappears. Extinction provides the basis for systematic desensitization, a treatment designed to decrease people's strong, irrational fears.

5. Stimulus generalization occurs when a conditioned response follows a stimulus that is similar to the original conditioned stimulus. The greater the similarity between the two stimuli, the greater the likelihood of stimulus generalization; the closer the new stimulus to the old one, the more similar the new response. The converse phenomenon, stimulus discrimination, occurs when an organism learns to respond to one stimulus but not to another.

6. Higher-order conditioning occurs when an established conditioned stimulus is paired with a neutral stimulus, and the new neutral stimulus comes to evoke the same conditioned response as the original conditioned stimulus. The neutral stimulus changes, then, into another conditioned stimulus.

7. A second major form of learning is operant conditioning. Moving beyond Edward Thorndike's original work on the law of effect, which states that responses producing satisfying results are more likely to be repeated than those that do not, B. F. Skinner carried out pioneering work on operant learning.

8. According to Skinner, the major factor underlying learning is the reinforcer—any stimulus that increases the probability that the preceding response will occur again. We can determine whether a stimulus is a reinforcer only by observing its effects upon behavior. If behavior increases, the stimulus is, by definition, a reinforcer. Primary reinforcers involve rewards that are naturally effective without prior exposure because they satisfy a biological need. Secondary reinforcers, in contrast, begin to act as if they were primary reinforcers through frequent pairings with a primary reinforcer.

9. Positive reinforcers are stimuli that are added to the environment and lead to an increase in a preceding response. Negative reinforcers are stimuli whose removal from the environment leads to an increase in the preceding response.

10. Punishment is the administration of an unpleasant stimulus following a response in order to produce a decrease in the incidence of that response. Punishment is also characterized by the removal of a positive reinforcer. In contrast to reinforcement, in which the goal is to increase the incidence of behavior, punishment is meant to decrease or suppress behavior. Although there are a number of advantages to the use of punishment, its disadvantages usually outweigh its positive effects.

11. Schedules and patterns of reinforcement affect the strength and duration of learning. Generally, partial reinforcement schedules—in which reinforcers are not delivered on every trial—produce stronger and longer-lasting learning than do continuous reinforcement schedules.

12. Among the major categories of reinforcement schedules are fixed- and variable-ratio schedules, which are based on the number of responses made, and fixed- and variable-interval schedules, which are based on the time interval that elapses before reinforcement is provided when a desired response occurs. Fixed-ratio schedules provide reinforcement only after a certain number of responses are made; variable-ratio schedules provide reinforcement after a varying number of responses are made—although the specific number typically settles around some average. In contrast, fixed-interval schedules provide reinforcement after a fixed amount of time has elapsed since the last reinforcement; variable-interval schedules provide reinforcement over varying amounts of time, although the times form a specific average.

13. Generalization and discrimination are phenomena that operate in operant conditioning as well as classical conditioning. Generalization occurs when an organism makes the same or a similar response to a new stimulus that it has learned to make in the past to a similar stimulus. Discrimination occurs when the organism responds to one stimulus, but does not respond to a similar (but different) stimulus.

14. Among the phenomena associated with operant conditioning are superstitious behavior and the Premack principle. Superstitious behavior is the mistaken belief that particular ideas, objects, or behavior will cause certain events to occur, as a result of learning that is based on the coincidental association between a stimulus and subsequent reinforcement. The Premack principle states that because organisms have different preferences for performing behaviors, less-preferred behaviors will be performed to obtain the opportunity to engage in more-preferred ones.

15. Shaping is a process for teaching complex behaviors by rewarding closer and closer approximations of the desired final behavior. Shaping forms the basis for learning and teaching many everyday skills and is central to presenting complicated information in textbooks and in computerized programmed instruction.

16. There are biological constraints, or built-in limitations, on the ability of an organism to learn. Because of these constraints, certain behaviors will be relatively easy to learn, whereas other behaviors will be either difficult or impossible to learn.

17. Cognitive learning seeks to explain phenomena such as latent learning—in which a new behavior is learned but not performed until reinforcement is provided for its performance—and the apparent development of cognitive maps. Learning also occurs through the observation of the behavior of others, known as models. The major factor that determines whether a behavior will actually be performed is the nature of reinforcement or punishment a model receives. Learned helplessness, the learned belief of a person or animal that it cannot exert control over the environment, also suggests the impor-

tance of cognitive processes in learning.

18. Behavior modification is a method for formally using the principles of learning theory to promote the frequency of desired behaviors and to decrease or eliminate unwanted ones. The typical steps in a behavior-change program are identifying goals and target behaviors, designing a data-recording system, recording preliminary data, selecting a behavior-change strategy, implementing the strategy, and evaluating and altering the ongoing program.

KEY TERMS AND CONCEPTS ▶

learning (p. 157)
maturation (157)
classical conditioning (158)
neutral stimulus (160)
unconditioned stimulus (UCS) (160)
unconditioned response (UCR) (160)
conditioned stimulus (CS) (160)
conditioned response (CR) (160)
extinction (161)
systematic desensitization (162)
spontaneous recovery (162)
stimulus generalization (162)
stimulus discrimination (163)
higher-order conditioning (163)
operant conditioning (166)

law of effect (167)
reinforcer (168)
primary reinforcer (168)
secondary reinforcer (168)
positive reinforcer (169)
negative reinforcer (169)
aversive stimulus (169)
punishment (169)
schedules of reinforcement (172)
continuous reinforcement (172)
partial reinforcement (172)
cumulative recorder (173)
fixed-ratio schedule (173)
variable-ratio schedule (174)
fixed-interval schedule (175)

variable-interval schedule (175)
stimulus control training (175)
discriminative stimulus (175)
superstitious behavior (176)
shaping (177)
programmed instruction (178)
biological constraints (181)
cognitive learning theory (184)
latent learning (185)
cognitive map (185)
observational learning (186)
model (186)
learned helplessness (187)
behavior modification (189)
time management (191)

FOR FURTHER STUDY AND APPLICATION ▶

Klein, S. B. (1987). *Learning: Principles and applications.* New York: McGraw-Hill.

This is a basic, well-written, understandable introduction to learning theory and its application.

Hill, W. F. (1981). *Principles of learning: A handbook of applications.* Sherman Oaks, CA: Alfred Publishing.

This book provides a practical overview of learning theories and how they may be applied to everyday problems involving the mastery of new material.

Sulzer-Azaroff, B., & Mayer, R. (1986). *Achieving educational excellence using behavioral strategies.* New York: Holt.

This interesting book is filled with insights into the use of operant conditioning to improve scholastic performance.

Epstein, R. (Ed.). (1982). *Skinner for the classroom: Selected papers.* Champaign, IL: Research Press.

This is an excellent collection of B. F. Skinner's papers, with commentary that provides a context for the work and explains its importance in the study of operant conditioning.

Pavlov, I. P. (1927). *Conditioned reflexes.* New York: Oxford University Press.

Surprisingly readable, this volume describes Pavlov's original work—which may leave you salivating to learn more about classical conditioning.

Skinner, B. F. (1948). *Walden two.* New York: Macmillan.

A number of communities are actually trying to follow the approach laid out by Skinner in this fascinating book, which details his utopian vision, based on the principles of operant conditioning.

Ferner, J. D. (1980). *Successful time management.* New York: Wiley.

This practical volume is devoted to procedures for using time better through operant conditioning. The methods described are comprehensive—and the rewards of gaining more time for oneself are well worth the effort.

ANSWERS (REVIEW IV):

1. c **2.** Cognitive map **3.** False; they tend to be oversimplified **4.** Observational learning **5.** Learned helplessness **6.** b—designing a recording system and recording preliminary data; f—evaluating and altering the ongoing program

CHAPTER 6

MEMORY

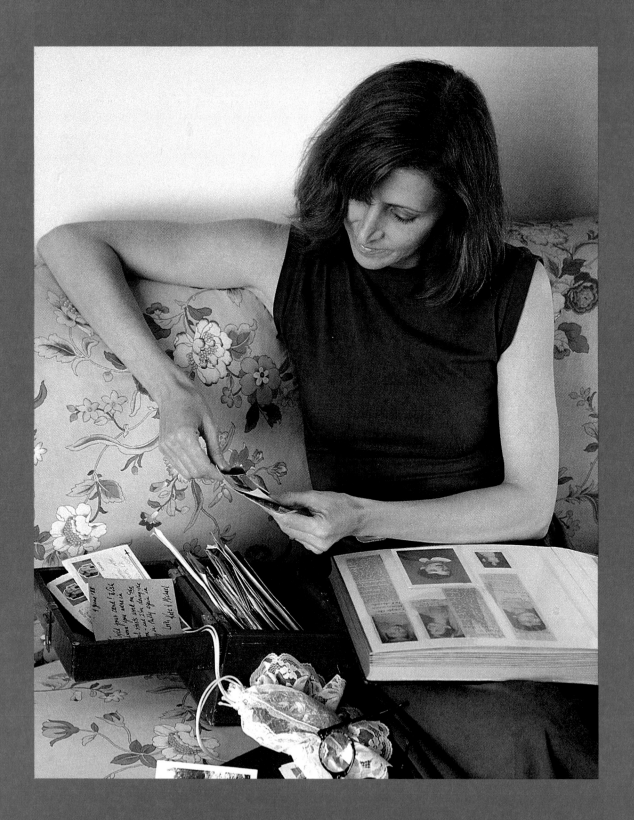

CHAPTER 6

MEMORY

One of the most famous victims of Alzheimer's disease, Rita Hayworth was widely admired as an actress and dancer. (UPI/ Bettmann Newsphotos)

PROLOGUE: RITA HAYWORTH

Glamorous, beautiful, and romantic were the words routinely used to describe Rita Hayworth, and appropriately. Leading a most public existence, she made sixty-one films and became one of the most recognizable and revered movie stars of her time.

In the end, though, the glamour took a sad turn. By the time she was 60, Hayworth's behavior became increasingly erratic. She would get off an elevator and become confused, forgetting where she was headed. At times, when her daughter recounted a story about close friends, Hayworth would be unable to comprehend the story and would look at her daughter as if she were a stranger. Her memory showed increasingly frightening lapses; she would forget appointments and eventually could not remember the names of old acquaintances.

After a round of doctors had been consulted, a diagnosis for the strange symptoms was eventually found: Alzheimer's disease. Alzheimer's disease produces degeneration first of memory and eventually of the entire body; people with the disease ultimately remember no one and cannot take care of their most basic needs. This was the death that Hayworth suffered—remembering nothing of her fabled past.

LOOKING AHEAD ▶

Complete memory failures, such as those brought on by Alzheimer's disease, are the most dramatic illustrations of how drastically our lives would be altered without the ability to recall information from our past. But most of us do not need to be reminded of the importance of memory—and of the fluctuations in our abilities that occur daily. For instance, we are able to retrieve a vast array of information to which we have been exposed, such as the name of a friend we haven't seen or been in touch with for ten years or a picture that hung in our bedroom as a child. At the same time, it is not uncommon to forget where we left the keys to the car or to be unable to answer an exam question about material that we studied just a few hours before.

In this chapter, we address a number of issues about memory that psychologists are investigating. We examine the ways in which information is stored and retrieved. We discuss evidence showing that there are actually three separate types of memory, and we explain how each type operates in a somewhat different fashion to allow us to remember material to which we have been exposed. The problems of retrieving information from memory and the reasons information is sometimes forgotten are examined, and we consider the biological foundations of memory. Finally, we discuss some practical means of increasing memory capacity.

After reading this chapter, then, you will be able to answer the following questions:

▶ What is memory and how does it operate?

▶ Are there different kinds of memory?

▶ How are we able to recall material from long ago, yet forget information to which we have been exposed very recently?

▶ Can we improve our memory?

MEMORY'S THREE R'S: RECORDING, RETAINING, AND RETRIEVING INFORMATION

What is memory, and why do we remember certain events and activities and forget others? Psychologists define **memory** as the capacity to record, retain, and retrieve information—the three R's of remembering (see Figure 6-1). Without memory, learning would be impossible; people could not build on past experiences or adapt their knowledge to new situations.

Memory: The capacity to record, retain, and retrieve information

Each of the three parts of the definition of memory—recording, retention, and retrieval—represents a different process in remembering and allows us to systematically consider the point at which memory may fail. For example, suppose, in the middle of a game of Trivial Pursuit, you are asked to name the crime Al Capone was finally imprisoned for in 1931. If you can't, the source of your failure may reside in the initial recording stage; you may never, for instance, have been exposed to the information. In this case, your failure relates to **encoding**, the process by which information is recorded in a form usable by memory.

Encoding: The process by which information is initially recorded in a form usable to memory

Even if you were exposed to the information and originally knew of the crime, you may still be unable to recall it because of a failure in the retention process. Memory specialists speak of placing information in **storage**, the location in the memory system in which material is saved. If the material is not stored adequately in the first place, it cannot later be recalled.

Storage: The location in the memory system in which material is saved.

Memory depends on one last process: retrieval. In **retrieval**, material in memory storage is located, brought into awareness, and used. Your ineptitude in recalling Capone's conviction, then, may rest on your inability to retrieve the information that you learned earlier. (In case your own memory has failed, Capone was convicted of income tax evasion.)

Retrieval: The process by which material in memory storage is located, brought into awareness, and used

THE SHORT AND LONG OF IT: The Three Stages of Memory

Although the processes of recording, retaining, and retrieving information are necessary for memory to operate successfully, they do not describe the specific manner in which material is entered into our storehouse of memories. Many psychologists studying memory suggest that there are different stages through which information must travel if it is to be remembered.

According to one influential theory, there are three kinds of memory, which vary in terms of their function and the length of time information is retained (Atkinson & Shiffrin, 1968). As shown in Figure 6-2, **sensory memory** refers to the initial, momentary storage of information, lasting only an instant; it is recorded by the person's sensory system as a raw, nonmeaningful stimulus. **Short-term memory** holds information for fifteen to twenty-five seconds; in this phase, the information is stored in terms of its meaning rather than mere sensory stimulation. The third type of memory is **long-term memory**. Here, information is relatively permanent, although it may be difficult to retrieve.

Sensory memory: The initial, short-lived storage of information recorded as a meaningless stimulus

Short-term memory: The storage of information for fifteen to twenty-five seconds

Long-term memory: The storage of information on a relatively permanent basis, although retrieval may be difficult

FIGURE 6-1

Memory is built on three basic processes.

200

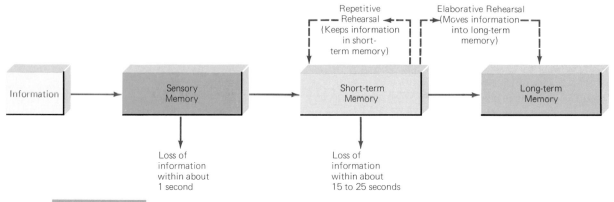

FIGURE 6-2

In this three-stage model of memory, information initially recorded by the person's sensory system enters sensory memory, which momentarily holds the information. It then moves to short-term memory, which stores the information for fifteen to twenty-five seconds. Finally, the information can move into long-term memory, which is relatively permanent. Whether the information moves from short-term to long-term memory depends on the kind and amount of rehearsal of the material that is carried out. (After Atkinson & Shiffrin, 1968.)

Iconic (i KON ik) **memory:** The storage of visual information
Echoic (eh KO ik) **memory:** The storage of information obtained from the sense of hearing

THE INITIAL ENCOUNTER: Sensory Memory

A momentary flash of lightening, the sound of a twig snapping, and the sting of a pinprick all represent stimulation of exceedingly brief duration, but they may nonetheless provide important information that can require some response. Such stimuli are initially—and briefly—stored in sensory memory, the first repository of the information that the world presents to us. Actually, the term "sensory memory" encompasses several types of sensory memories, each related to a different source of sensory information. There is an **iconic memory**, which reflects information from our visual system, an **echoic memory**, which stores information coming from the ears, as well as corresponding memories for each of the other senses.

Regardless of the individual subtypes, sensory memory in general is able to store information for only a very short time, and if material does not pass to another form of memory, that information is lost for good. For instance, iconic memory seems to last less than a second, although, if the initial stimulus is very bright, the image may last a little longer (Long & Beaton, 1982). Echoic memory fades within three or four seconds (Darwin, Turvey & Crowder, 1972). However, despite the brief duration of sensory memory, its precision is high: It is able to store an almost exact replica of each stimulus to which it is exposed.

If the storage capabilities of sensory memory are so limited and information stored within sensory memory so fleeting, it would seem almost impossible to find evidence for its existence; new information would be constantly replacing older information, even before a person could report its presence. Not until psychologist George Sperling (1960) conducted a series of clever and now-classic studies was sensory memory well understood. Sperling briefly exposed people to a series of twelve letters arranged in the following pattern:

F T Y C
K D N L
Y W B M

When exposed to this pattern for just one-twentieth of a second, most people could accurately recall only four or five of the letters. Although they knew that they had seen more, the memory had faded by the time they reported the first few letters. It was possible, then, that the information had initially been accurately stored in sensory memory, but during the time it took to verbalize the first four or five letters the memory of the other letters faded.

To test that possibility, Sperling had a high, medium, or low tone sounded just after a person had been exposed to the full pattern of letters. People were told to report the letters in the highest line if a high tone were sounded, the middle line if the medium tone occurred, or the lowest line at the sound of the low tone. Because the tone occurred after the exposure, people had to rely on their memory to report the correct row.

The results of the study showed very clearly that people had been storing the complete pattern in memory: They were quite accurate in their recollection of the letters in the line that had been indicated by the tone, regardless of whether it was the top, middle, or bottom line. Obviously, *all* the lines they had seen had been stored in sensory memory. Despite its rapid loss, then, the information in sensory memory was an accurate representation of what the people had seen.

By gradually lengthening the time between the presentation of the visual pattern and the tone, Sperling was able to determine with some accuracy the length of time that information existed in sensory memory. The ability to recall a particular row of the pattern when a tone was sounded declined progressively as the period between visual exposure and tone lengthened but leveled off when it reached about one second in duration. The conclusion: The entire visual image was stored in sensory memory for less than a second.

In sum, sensory memory operates as a kind of snapshot that stores information—which may be of a visual, auditory, or other sensory nature—for a brief moment in time. But it is as if each snapshot, immediately after being taken, is destroyed and replaced with a new one. Unless the information in the snapshot is transferred to some other type of memory, it is lost.

(Drawing by Richter; © 1982 The New Yorker Magazine, Inc.)

"Well, here I sit, surrounded by my memorabilia, and I can't remember having done a damn thing."

Because the information that is stored briefly in our sensory memories consists of representations of raw sensory stimuli, it is not necessarily meaningful to us. In order for us to make sense of it and to allow for the possibility of long-term retention, the information must be transferred to the next stage of memory, short term memory. Short-term memory, sometimes referred to as working memory, is the memory in which material initially has meaning, although the maximum length of retention is relatively short.

The specific process by which sensory memories are transformed into short-term memories is not yet clear. Some theorists suggest that the information is first translated into graphical representations or images, and others hypothesize that the transfer occurs when the sensory stimuli are changed to words (Baddeley, 1985). What is clear, however, is that unlike sensory memory, which holds a relatively full and detailed—if shortlived—representation of the world, short-term memory has incomplete representational capabilities.

In fact, the specific amount of information that can be held in short-term memory has been identified: seven items, or "chunks," of information, with variations up to plus or minus two chunks. A **chunk** is a meaningful grouping of stimuli that can be stored as a unit in short-term memory. According to George Miller (1956), it could be individual letters, as in the following list:

Chunk: A meaningful grouping of stimuli that can be stored as a unit in short-term memory

C T N Q M W N

Each letter here qualifies as a separate chunk, and—as there are seven of them—they are easily held in short-term memory.

But a chunk might also consist of larger categories, such as words or other meaningful units. For example, consider the following list of letters:

TWACIAABCCBSMTVUSAAAA

Clearly, because the list exceeds seven chunks, it is difficult to recall the letters after one exposure. But suppose they were presented to you as follows:

TWA CIA ABC CBS MTV USA AAA

In this case, even though there are still twenty-one letters, it would be possible to store them in memory, since they represent only seven chunks.

You can see how chunking works in your own memory process by trying to memorize the shapes in Figure 6-3 after looking at them for just a few moments. Although it may at first seem to be an impossible task, just one hint will guarantee that you can easily memorize all the shapes: Each figure represents part of the letters in the word "PSYCHOLOGY."

FIGURE 6-3

Try looking at the shapes in this figure for a few moments, and memorize them in the exact sequence in which they appear.

If you consider this an impossible task, here's a hint that will guarantee that you can easily memorize all of them: They are the shapes of each part of the letters in the word "PSYCHOLOGY." The reason the task suddenly becomes so simple is that the shapes can be grouped together into one chunk—a word that we all recognize. Rather than being considered as nineteen separate shapes, the symbols are recoded in the memory as just one chunk.

The reason the task suddenly became so simple was that the shapes could be grouped together into one chunk—a word that we all recognize. Rather than being nineteen separate symbols with no meaning, they are recoded as just one chunk.

Chunks can vary in size from single letters or numbers to categories that are far more complicated, and the specific nature of what constitutes a chunk varies according to one's past experience. You can see this for yourself by trying an experiment that was first carried out comparing expert and inexperienced chess players (deGroot, 1966).

Examine the chessboard on the top of Figure 6-4 for about five seconds, and then, after covering up the board, try to reproduce the position of the pieces on the blank chessboard on the bottom. Unless you are an experienced chess player, you will likely have great difficulty carrying out such a task. Yet chess masters—the kind who win tournaments—do quite well: Ninety percent are able to correctly reproduce it. In comparison, inexperienced chess players typically are able to reproduce only 40 percent of the board properly.

The chess masters do not have superior memories in other respects; they generally test normally on other measures of memory. What they can do better than others is to chunk the board into meaningful units and reproduce the chess pieces by using these units. An analogous skill is found among electronics technicians, who are able to glance at a complicated circuit drawing and recall it without difficulty because of their ability to chunk it into meaningful configurations, as you can see in Figure 6-5 (Egan & Schwartz, 1979).

Although it is possible to remember seven or so relatively complicated sets of information entering short-term memory, the information cannot be held there very long. Just how short term is short-term memory? Anyone who has looked up a telephone number at a pay phone, struggled to find coins, and forgotten the number at the sound of the dial tone knows that information in short-term memory does not remain there terribly long. Most psychologists believe that information in short-term memory is lost after fifteen to twenty-five seconds—unless it is transferred to long-term memory.

Rehearsal

The transfer of material from short- to long-term memory proceeds largely

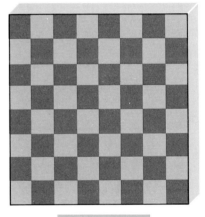

FIGURE 6-4

Look at the top chessboard for about five seconds, and then cover it with your hand. Now try to recreate the chess pieces on the blank board below it. Unless you are an experienced chess player, you will probably have a good deal of difficulty recalling the configuration and types of chess pieces. On the other hand, expert chess players have little difficulty recreating the board on the left. (deGroot, 1966.)

FIGURE 6-5

Although most of us would have difficulty memorizing this circuit schematic, experienced electronics technicians recall it with ease because they are able to view it as a meaningful unit or chunk. (Egan & Schwartz, 1979.)

Feedback network

Amplifier 1

Rectifier

Filter

Load

Ground

Amplifier 2

This California student may be confronted with the limitations of short-term memory when he looks up a phone number, only to forget it as soon as he closes the directory. (Lawrence Migdale/Photo Researchers)

Rehearsal: The transfer of material from short- to long-term memory via repetition

on the basis of **rehearsal**, the repetition of information that has entered short-term memory. Rehearsal accomplishes two things. First, as long as the information is repeated, it is kept alive in short-term memory. More important, however, rehearsal allows the material to be transferred into long-term memory.

Whether the transfer is made from short- to long-term memory seems to depend largely on the kind of rehearsal that is carried out. If the material is simply repeated over and over again—as we might do with a telephone number while we rush from the phone book to the telephone—it is kept current in short-term memory but it will not necessarily be placed in long-term memory. Instead, as soon as we stop dialing, the number is likely to be replaced by other information and will be completely forgotten.

On the other hand, if the information in short-term memory is rehearsed using a process called elaborative rehearsal, it is much more likely to be transferred into long-term memory (Craik & Lockhart, 1972). **Elaborative rehearsal** occurs when the material is considered and organized in some fashion. The organization might include expanding the information to make it fit into a logical framework, linking it to another memory, turning it into an image, or transforming it in some other way. For example, a list of vegetables to be purchased at a store could be woven together in memory as items being used to prepare an elaborate salad; they could be linked to the items bought on an earlier shopping trip; or they could be thought of in terms of the image of a farm with rows of each item.

Elaborative rehearsal: Organizing information into a logical framework to assist in recalling it

By using organizational strategies called mnemonics, we can vastly improve our retention of information (Higbee & Kunihira, 1985). **Mnemonics** are formal techniques for organizing material in a way that makes it more likely to be remembered. For instance, when a beginning musician learns that the spaces on the music staff spell the word "FACE" or when we learn the rhyme "Thirty days hath September, April, June, and November; all the rest have . . . ," we are using mnemonics.

Mnemonics (neh MON ix): Formal techniques for organizing material to increase the likelihood of its being remembered

THE FINAL REPOSITORY: Long-term Memory

Material that makes its way from short-term memory to long-term memory enters a repository of almost unlimited capacity. Like a new book delivered to a library, the information in long-term memory is filed and cataloged so that it can be retrieved when we need it.

Evidence of the existence of long-term memory, as distinct from short-term memory, comes from a number of sources. For example, people with certain kinds of brain injury have no long-term recall of new information following the injury, although people and events in memory prior to the injury remain (Milner, 1966). Because short-term memory following the injury appears to be operative—new material can be recalled for a very brief period—and because information from before the injury is intact, we might infer that there are two distinct memories, one for short-term and one for long-term storage.

Evidence from laboratory experiments is also consistent with the notion of separate short- and long-term memories. For example, in one set of studies people were asked to recall a relatively small amount of information (such as a set of three letters)—but then, to prevent practice of the initial information, were required to recite some extraneous material aloud, such as counting backward by three (Brown, 1958; Peterson & Peterson, 1959). By varying the amount of time between which the initial material was first presented and its recall was required, investigators found that recall was quite good when the interval was near zero, but it declined rapidly thereafter. In fact, after fifteen seconds had gone by, recall hovered at around 10 percent of the material initially presented.

Apparently, counting backward prevented almost all the initial material from reaching long-term memory. Initial recall was good because it was coming from short-term memory, but these memories were lost at a rapid rate. Eventually, all that could be recalled was the small amount of material that had made its way into long-term storage despite the distractions of counting backward.

Episodic and Semantic Memories

There are actually two kinds of memories held in long-term memory: episodic and semantic (Tulving, 1983). **Episodic memories** relate to our individual lives, recalling what we have done and the kinds of experiences we have had. When you recall your first date, the time you fell off your bicycle, or what you felt like when you graduated from high school, you are recalling episodic memories. The information in episodic memory is connected with specific times and places. In contrast, **semantic memories** consist of organized knowledge and facts about the world; because of semantic memory, we know that $2 \times 2 = 4$, the earth is round, and "memoree" is misspelled.

Episodic memories: Stored information relating to personal experiences

Semantic memories: Stored, organized facts about the world (e.g., mathematical and historical data)

Looking at photos taken years ago can trigger episodic memories, sharp recollections of past events. (Willie Hill, Jr./The Image Works)

Like this Bowdoin College student, we store facts that we have learned or read in semantic memory. (Seth Resnick/Stock Boston)

Episodic memories can be surprisingly detailed. Consider, for instance, what your response would be if you were asked to identify what you were doing on a specific day two years ago. An impossible task? You might think otherwise as you read the following exchange between a researcher and a subject who was asked, in a memory experiment, what he was doing "on Monday afternoon in the third week of September two years ago."

Subject: Come on. How should I know?

Experimenter: Just try it anyhow.

Subject: OK. Let's see: Two years ago ... I would be in high school in Pittsburgh.... That would be my senior year. Third week in September—that's just after summer—that would be the fall term.... Let me see. I think I had chemistry lab on Mondays. I don't know. I was probably in chemistry lab. Wait a minute—that would be the second week of school. I remember he started off with the atomic table—a big fancy chart. I thought he was crazy trying to make us memorize that thing. You know, I think I can remember sitting.... (Lindsay & Norman, 1977).

Episodic memory, then, can provide information from events that happened long in the past (Reynolds & Takooshian, 1987). But semantic memory is no less impressive: By calling upon it, all of us are able to dredge up thousands of facts ranging from the date of our birthday to the knowledge that $1 is less than $5. Both individual pieces of information and the rules of logic for deducing other facts are stored in semantic memory.

Storage in Long-Term Memory

There are several ways in which both episodic and semantic information is stored in long-term memory. One of the primary ways is through the **linguistic code**, which relies on language. The linguistic code allows us to store information abstractly without having to rely on a specific image. For instance, we may be able to recall that someone talking about a sloth is discussing an animal, even while we are unable to conjure up a specific image of what it looks like.

An **imaginal code**, in contrast, is memory storage that is based on visual images. If someone asked you to describe the path you take on the way from your psychology class to your home or dormitory, you would likely recall the images you have seen when taking the route in the past.

The third type of coding in long-term memory is the **motor code**, storage that is based on memories of physical activities. Your ability to ride a bicycle is based on motor memories; you probably would be hard-pressed to recall in verbal terms how you are able to do it. Motor codes are particularly well remembered. Even after years of never riding a bicycle, you would probably have little trouble remembering how to do it.

LEVELS OF PROCESSING

As an alternative to the notion that the processing of information proceeds along three sequential stages, some psychologists, in an increasingly influential view, suggest that a single process accounts for how well information is remembered: the way in which material is first perceived and considered.

The **levels-of-processing** approach emphasizes the degree to which new material is mentally analyzed (Craik & Lockhart, 1972). In contrast to the

Linguistic code: Memory storage relying on language

Imaginal code: Memory storage based on visual images

Motor code: Memory storage based on physical activities

Levels-of-processing theory: The theory which suggests that the way information is initially perceived and learned determines recall view that there are sensory, short-term, and long-term memories, levels-of-processing theory suggests that the amount of information processing that occurs when material is initially encountered is central in determining how much of the information is ultimately remembered. According to this approach, the depth of processing during exposure to material—meaning the degree to which it is analyzed and considered—is critical; the greater the intensity of its initial processing, the more likely we are to remember it.

Because we do not pay close attention to much of the information to which we are exposed, only scant mental processing takes place, and we forget it almost immediately. However, information to which we pay more attention is processed more thoroughly. Therefore, it enters memory at a deeper level—and is less apt to be forgotten than information processed at more shallow levels.

The theory goes on to suggest that there are considerable differences in the way information is processed at various levels of memory. At shallow levels, information is processed merely in terms of its physical and sensory aspects; for example, we may pay attention only to the shapes that make up the letters in the word "dog." At an intermediate level of processing, the shapes are translated into meaningful units—in this case, letters of the alphabet. These letters are considered in the context of words, and a specific sound of the word may be attached to the letters.

At the deepest level of processing, information is analyzed in terms of its meaning. It may be seen in a wider context, and associations between the meaning of the information and broader networks of knowledge may be drawn. For instance, we may think of dogs not merely as animals with four legs and a tail, but in terms of their relation to cats and other mammals. We may form an image of our own dog, relating it to our own lives.

According to the levels-of-processing approach, the deeper the initial level of processing of specific information, the longer the information will be retained. The approach suggests, then, that the best way to remember new information is to consider it thoroughly when you are first exposed to it—reflecting on how it relates to information that you currently have.

The levels-of-processing theory considers memory as involving more active mental processes than does the three-stage approach to memory. However, neither model has been able to account for all phenomena relating to memory. Because of this, other models of memory have been proposed. For example, psychologist Nelson Cowan (1988) has suggested that the most accurate representation of memory comes from a model in which short-term storage is considered a part of long-term storage, rather than representing a separate stage. Still, it is too early to tell—let alone remember—which model represents the most accurate representation of memory.

RECAP AND REVIEW I

Recap

◀ Memory is the capacity to record, retain, and retrieve information.

◀ Sensory memory contains a brief but accurate representation of physical stimuli to which a person is exposed. Each representation is constantly being replaced with a new one, however.

◀ Short-term memory has a capacity of seven (plus or minus two) chunks of information. Memories remain in short-term storage for fifteen to twenty-five seconds and are then either transferred to long-term memory or lost through interference or decay.

◀ Long-term memories are either episodic or semantic, and they enter long-term storage through rehearsal.

An alternative to the three-stage model of memory, the levels-of-processing approach suggests that information is analyzed at different levels, with material processed at deeper levels being retained the longest.

Review

1. At one time, Frances was able to rattle off the phone numbers of her five best college friends. Now she can't remember one. Her failure to remember has to do with the process of
   a. encoding.
   b. retrieval.
   c. recording.
   d. storage.
2. As your friend Beth rushes off, she looks back and shouts her new phone number, 747-0190. Unless you make some effort to organize these numbers, they will probably remain only briefly (fifteen to twenty-five seconds) in your
   a. sensory memory.
   b. short-term memory.
   c. long-term memory.
   d. semantic memory.
3. Suppose that in the above encounter you paused and thought, "Okay, 19 is my age. The last part of Beth's number is my age surrounded by zeros. And 747 is a type of jet." You think this through once more, before going about your business. This strategy of organization is referred to as _____ .
4. Your strategy above would probably result in the phone number entering your _____ _____ memory.
5. Craig awoke to the crashing sound of a large branch falling outside. This event immediately entered Craig's
   a. iconic memory.
   b. short-term memory.
   c. echoic memory.
   d. long-term memory.
6. Unless stored in another form of memory, the event Craig experienced will last for only
   a. less than one second.
   b. three to four seconds.
   c. four to five seconds.
   d. ten to fifteen seconds.
7. The average capacity for short-term memory is seven chunks. True or false? _____
8. _____ are formal techniques that facilitate memory through the organization of material.
9. Recalling the first time you drove a car on your own is an example of
   a. semantic memory.
   b. echoic memory.
   c. iconic memory.
   d. episodic memory.
10. If asked to describe the mountain ranges you saw during your last vacation, you would rely on a(n) _____ code to do so.
11. The levels-of-processing theory discounts the importance of paying careful attention to something as a means of bettering your memory of it. True or false? _____

(Answers to review questions are on page 210.)

MISPLACED OR LOST FOR GOOD?: RECALLING LONG-TERM MEMORIES

An hour after his job interview, Rich was sitting in a coffee shop, telling his friend Laura about his apparent success, when the woman who had interviewed him walked in. "Well, hello, Rich. How are you doing?" Trying to make a good impression, Rich began to introduce Laura, but then realized he could not remember the name of the interviewer. Stammering, he desperately searched his memory for her name but couldn't remember. "I *know* her name," he thought to himself, "but here I am, looking like a jerk. I can kiss this job goodbye."

Tip-of-the-tongue phenomenon: The inability to recall information that one realizes one knows—a result of the difficulty of retrieving information from long-term memory

Have you ever tried to remember someone's name, absolutely certain that you knew it, but unable to recall it no matter how hard you tried? This not infrequent occurrence—known as the **tip-of-the-tongue phenomenon**—

Memory retrieval cues include drawings and photographs, such as these being viewed by Sgt. Mark Tracy of Santa Cruz, California. (Rick Browne/Stock Boston)

exemplifies the difficulties that can occur in retrieving information stored in long-term memory (Harris & Morris, 1984).

One reason recall is not perfect is the sheer quantity of recollections that are stored in long-term memory. Although the issue is far from settled, many psychologists have suggested that the material that makes its way there is relatively permanent (Tulving & Psotka, 1971). If they are correct, this suggests that the capacity of long-term memory is vast, given the variety of people's experiences and learning. For instance, if you are like the average college student, your vocabulary includes some 50,000 words, you know hundreds of mathematical "facts," and you are able to conjure up images—such as the way your childhood home looked—with no trouble at all. In fact, simply cataloging all your memories would probably take years of work.

How do we sort through this vast array of material and retrieve specific information at the appropriate time? One of the major ways is through the use of retrieval cues. A **retrieval cue** is a stimulus that allows us to more easily recall information that is located in long-term memory (Tulving & Thompson, 1973). It may be a word, an emotion, a sound; whatever the specific cue, a memory will suddenly come to mind when the retrieval cue is present. For example, the smell of roasting turkey may evoke memories of Thanksgiving or family gatherings.

Retrieval cues guide people through the vast array of information stored in long-term memory in much the same way as the cards in a card catalog guide people through a library. They are particularly important when *recalling* information, as opposed to being asked to *recognize* material stored in memory. In **recall**, a specific piece of information must be retrieved—such as that needed to fill in the blanks or write an essay on a test. In contrast, **recognition** occurs when people are presented with a stimulus and asked whether they have been exposed to it previously, or are asked to identify it from a list of alternatives.

As you might guess, recognition is generally much easier than recall.

Retrieval cue: A stimulus such as a word, smell, or sound that allows one to more easily recall information located in long-term memory

Recall: Drawing from memory a specific piece of information for a specific purpose

Recognition: Acknowledging prior exposure to a given stimulus, rather than recalling the information from memory

Suppose, for instance, you witnessed a robbery and were asked to describe the thief—a recall task. Clearly, this would be harder than being shown a police "mug book" and asked to pick out the robber—a recognition problem. The reason that recall is more difficult is that it consists of a series of processes: a search through memory, retrieval of potentially relevant information, and then a decision regarding whether or not the information you have found is accurate. If it appears correct, the search is over, but if it does not, the search must continue. On the other hand, recognition is simpler since it involves fewer steps (Anderson & Bower, 1972). (For more on memory retrieval, see the Research Classics box.)

RESEARCH CLASSICS

Suppose you wanted to find the word "mnemonics" in the dictionary, and you couldn't remember how to spell it. There are several approaches you could use. One way—probably the most inefficient—is to start at the beginning of the dictionary, working your way through every word until you came to the "m's" and finally reached "mnemonics"—a **serial search,** in which information is examined one piece at a time. A more reasonable approach, however, would be one in which you scan the entire dictionary simultaneously, examining many words at once. Searching for information all at once is an example of **parallel search,** and it is clearly a more efficient process.

To investigate whether people use serial or parallel searches in retrieving information from short-term memory, psychologist Saul Sternberg (1966, 1969) carried out a classic series of studies. He presented subjects with a list of one to six digits (such as 5-3-4), which they saw for a little over one second. They were then presented with a target number

RETRIEVING INFORMATION: WHAT SEARCH STRATEGY DO WE USE?

and asked to determine whether the target number had been part of the original list.

Sternberg reasoned that if the time subjects took in responding was related to the number of digits they had been originally presented, a serial search would be taking place: Subjects would be systematically examining each number in turn, leading to higher response times with recall of more original numbers. On the other hand, if people were using a parallel-search process, there should be no difference in response time according to the number of digits originally presented. In this case, they would be examining all the digits simultaneously.

When Sternberg measured how long it took subjects to respond, he found the pattern displayed in Figure 6-6. The more numbers there were on the original list, the longer it took

subjects to respond. On this basis, he concluded that people were using a serial-search strategy: They were examining each of the numbers in short-term memory to see if it matched the target number.

Subsequent research confirmed not only that serial-search strategies were used to retrieve information from short-term memory but that people used an "exhaustive serial-search strategy." Rather than stopping their search as soon as they matched the target digit, subjects continued through the entire list. It is as if, in our earlier example, once we had found the word "mnemonics" in the dictionary, we continued looking until we had reached the end of the "z's." Sternberg's research, then, is clear in suggesting that the retrieval of information from short-term memory, while exhaustive, is not the most efficient strategy.

Serial search: A method of retrieving information from memory one piece at a time
Parallel search: Searching memory for stored information all at once

---

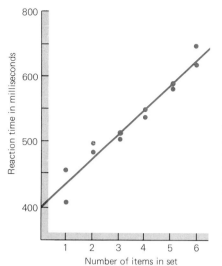

FIGURE 6-6

This pattern of responses clearly suggests that subjects in Sternberg's experiment were using a serial search strategy, sequentially examining each of the numbers that they were presented, since the more numbers that had been on the original list, the longer it took them to respond. It seems, then, as if they were examining each of the numbers in short-term memory to see if it matched the target number. (Sternberg, 1966.)

FLASHBULB MEMORIES

Ask anyone over the age of 40 what he or she was doing on first hearing that President John F. Kennedy was assassinated, and that person is likely to be able to provide you with a thorough description of his or her activities some thirty years ago.

Similarly, it may be easy for you to recall events that took place last New Year's Eve. What makes this possible is a phenomenon known as flashbulb memories. **Flashbulb memories** are memories centered around a specific, important event that are so clear it is as if they represented a snapshot of the event. For example, common flashbulb memories among college students are involvement in a car accident, meeting one's roommate for the first time, and the night of high school graduation (Rubin, 1985). (See Figure 6-7.)

Of course, not every detail of an original scene is recalled in a flashbulb memory (McCloskey et al., 1988). Even though I may remember that I was sitting in Mr. Sharp's tenth-grade geometry class when I heard that President Kennedy was shot, and I remember where my seat was located and what my classmates did, I may not recall what I was wearing or what I had for lunch that day.

Still, flashbulb memories are extraordinary because of the details they do include. An analysis of people's recollections of the Kennedy assassination found that their memories tended to have a number of features in common (Brown & Kulik, 1977). Most contained information regarding where the person heard the news, who told him or her about it, what event was interrupted by the news, the emotions of the informant, the person's own emotions, and some personal details of the event (such as seeing a robin fly by while the information was being given).

Flashbulb memories illustrate a more general phenomenon about memory: Memories that are distinctive are more easily retrieved than those relating to events that are commonplace. We are more likely, for example, to recall a particular number if it appears in a group of twenty words than if it appears in a group of twenty other numbers. The more distinctive a stimulus, then, the more likely we are to recall it later—the **von Restorff effect**, a phenomenon named after its discoverer (von Restorff, 1933).

Flashbulb memories: Memories of a specific event that are so clear they seem like "snapshots" of the event

von Restorff effect: The phenomenon by which distinctive stimuli are recalled more readily than less distinctive ones

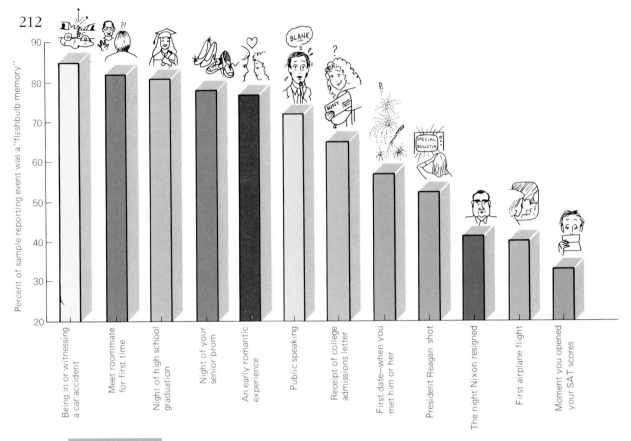

FIGURE 6-7

The most common flashbulb memories of a sample of college students are shown here. (Rubin, 1985.)

Constructive processes: Processes in which memories are influenced by the interpretation and meaning we give to events

Schemas: General themes in terms of which we remember a situation

The von Restorff effect operates in our own lives: We are far better at remembering unusual, atypical events that happen to us than the mundane, routine occurrences that take up most of our time. For instance, in one study, a group of college students were equipped with beepers that went off at random intervals, at which time they wrote down what they were doing. Most of what the students had done was soon forgotten; what was recalled best were distinctive, unusual events, such as a student's first date (Brewer & Dupree, 1983).

BUILDING MEMORIES: Constructive Processes in Memory

Although it is clear that we can have detailed recollections of significant and distinctive events, it is difficult to gauge the accuracy of such memories. In fact, it is apparent that our memories reflect, at least in part, **constructive processes**, processes in which memories are influenced by the meaning that we give to events. When we retrieve information, then, the memory that is produced is affected not just by the direct prior experience we have had with the stimulus, but by our guesses and inferences about its meaning as well.

The notion that memory is based on constructive processes was first put forward by Sir Frederic Bartlett, a British psychologist, who suggested that people tend to remember information in terms of **schemas**, general themes that contain relatively little specific detail (Bartlett, 1932). He argued that such schemas were based on the information provided not just by a stimulus but by our understanding of the situation, our expectations about the situation, and our awareness of the motivation underlying people's behavior.

In a demonstration of the operation of schemas, researchers have employed a process known as **serial reproduction**, in which information from memory is passed sequentially from one person to another. For an example of serial reproduction, briefly look at the cartoon in Figure 6-8, and then try to describe it to someone else without looking back at it. Then ask that person to describe it to another, and repeat the process with still one more person.

If you listen to the last person's report of the contents of the cartoon, you are sure to find that it differs in important respects from the cartoon itself. Many people recall the cartoon as showing a razor in the hand of the black person—obviously an incorrect recollection, given that the razor is held by the white person (Allport & Postman, 1958).

This example, which is drawn from a classic experiment, illustrates the role of expectations in memory. The migration of the razor from the white person's hand to the black person's hand in memory clearly indicates that expectations about the world—reflecting, in this case, the prejudice that blacks may be more violent than whites and thus more apt to be holding a razor—have an impact upon how events are recalled.

Bartlett thought that schemas affected recall at the time of retrieval of information, and that the information had been entered into memory accurately. However, subsequent work has shown that our expectations and prior knowledge affect the way information is initially entered into memory. For example, read and try to remember the following passage:

> The procedure is actually quite simple. First you arrange items into different groups. Of course, one pile may be sufficient, depending on how much there is to do. If you have to go somewhere else due to lack of facilities, that is the next step; otherwise, you are pretty well set. It is important not to overdo things. That is, it is better to do too few things at once than too many. In the short run this may not seem important but complications can easily arise. A mistake can be expensive as well. At first, the whole procedure will seem complicated. Soon, however, it will become just another facet of life. It is difficult to foresee any end to the necessity for this task in the immediate future, but then one can

Serial reproduction: The passage of interpretive information from person to person, often resulting in inaccuracy through personal bias and misinterpretation

FIGURE 6-8

When one person views this cartoon and then describes it from memory to a second person, who in turn describes it to a third, and so on—in a process known as serial reproduction—the last person to repeat the contents of the cartoon typically gives a description that differs in important respects from the original. (Allport & Postman, 1958.)

never tell. After the procedure is completed, one arranges the materials into different groups again. Then they can be put into their appropriate places. Eventually, they will be used once more and the whole cycle will then have to be repeated. However, this is a part of life. (Bransford & Johnson, 1972, p. 722).

As the results of a study that used this passage revealed, your ability to recall it—as well as understand it initially—would have been far superior if you had known prior to reading it that it referred to washing laundry (Bransford & Johnson, 1972). Our prior understanding of information, then, can facilitate our ability to remember it.

The Soap Opera Effect: Motivations and Memory

Just as our expectations and prior knowledge have an impact on what we recall, so our understanding of a person's motivations leads to constructive processes in recall. In what has been called the **soap opera effect**, knowledge about what motivates an individual can lead to elaborations in memory of a prior event involving that person.

The soap opera effect gets its name from soap opera characters making seemingly innocent statements that are fraught with significance for viewers who are aware of the character's real motives. To demonstrate that such awareness of the characters' actual motivations affects memory, in one experiment subjects read a series of scenarios about a college student who was going about her everyday, routine activities (Owens, Bower & Black, 1979). For some of the subjects, information provided an understanding of what the student's motivations were. For example, in one of the scenarios the student was described as visiting a physician, who smiled at her and said, "Well, it seems my expectations have been confirmed." Those subjects who received the additional information were first told, "Nancy woke up feeling sick again and wondered if she were really pregnant. How would she tell the college professor she had been seeing? And the money was another problem." The other subjects did not receive this information.

In a test of recall that took place one day later, subjects who had been provided with information about the student's motivation for the visit correctly recalled more facts about the situation than those who had not. More interestingly, those subjects who had been given the additional information also recalled more *incorrect* facts. For example, subjects tended to think that the physician had said, "Your fears have been confirmed"—a statement that would be congruent with knowing that the student worried that she was pregnant.

It is clear that our understanding of the motivations behind a person's behavior, as well as our expectations about the world, affects the reliability of our memories. As discussed in the Psychology at Work box, the imperfections of our recollections can have important consequences.

Soap opera effect: The phenomena by which memory of a prior event involving a person is more reliable when we understand that person's motivations

It is a scene immortalized in scores of old television shows and movies: A lineup is called and a beautiful, nervous heroine picks out one of five suspects, saying with confidence, "He's the one. I'm certain of it."

Ongoing research on eyewitness memory for details of crimes suggests that most eyewitnesses should be considerably less confident than they often are in their ability to recall either the identity of a suspect or any other details of a crime. Work on eyewitness identification has shown that witnesses are apt to make substantial errors when they try to recall details of criminal activity (Bishop, 1988; Kassin, 1985).

Consider the three faces shown below. As you can see, the men share certain characteristics; they are all wearing glasses and have mustaches and similar hairstyles. Their similarity led to near-tragic consequences when one of them was arrested for several rapes and another for a robbery, all crimes that the third person had actually committed. The bases of their arrests were the mistaken impressions of eyewitnesses who—before the actual criminal had been found—felt sure that they had identified the right person as the perpetrator.

This case of mistaken identification is not an isolated event, according to research on the topic; eyewitnesses are prone to frequent errors

MEMORY ON TRIAL: WITNESS FALLIBILITY

in memory (Wells & Loftus, 1984; Cutler & Penrod, 1988). For instance, viewers of a twelve-second film of a mugging that was shown on a New York City television news program were later given the opportunity to pick out the assailant from a six-person lineup. Of some 2000 viewers who called the station after the program, only 15 percent were able to pick out the right person—a figure just slightly higher than if they had guessed randomly (Buckhout, 1975).

Other research suggests that the mistakes witnesses make show wide variability. For example, one study found that witnesses of staged crimes disagreed by as much as 2 feet in their estimates of the height of a perpetrator and averaged a difference of 8 inches from his true height. There was a discrepancy from the true age averaging eight years, hair color was recalled incorrectly 83 percent of the time, and about a quarter of all witnesses left out more than half of the details they had actually seen (Gardner, 1933).

Even the specific wording of a question posed to a witness can affect the way in which something is recalled, as a number of experiments illustrate. For example, in one

experiment subjects were shown a film of two cars crashing into each other. Some were then asked the question, "About how fast were the cars going when they *smashed* into each other?" They estimated the speed to be an average of 40.8 miles per hour. In contrast, when another group of subjects was asked, "About how fast were the cars going when they *contacted* each other?" the average estimated speed was only 31.8 miles per hour (Loftus & Palmer, 1974).

In sum, the memories of eyewitnesses are far from infallible. Furthermore, it is not just the memory processes of witnesses that determine how fairly justice is meted out, but the memories of jurors as well. In complex cases, jurors must sort through a vast array of information, typically using only their memory of what was presented to them in the courtroom (Hastie, Penrod & Pennington, 1983). In addition, they sometimes are directed to *forget* information to which they have been exposed, when told by a judge to disregard information that may not be legally considered during their deliberations. As you might guess, it is almost impossible for jurors to disregard information that they are directed to forget, especially if they consider the information to be important or relevant to their deliberations (Allen, 1988).

In a case of mistaken identification, the men in the photos on the left and right were arrested for crimes actually committed by the man in the center. Both of the innocent men had been identified as guilty in separate lineups by victims of the real criminal. (After Buckhout, 1975/The New York Times)

Where Past Meets Present: Memories of Our Own Lives

Your memory of your own past might well be a fiction—or at least a distortion of what actually occurred. The reason for this is that the same constructive processes that act to make us inaccurately recall the behavior of others also depress the accuracy with which we recall facts about our own lives (Bradburn, Rips & Shevell, 1987).

For example, people tend to forget information about their past that is incongruent with the way in which they currently see themselves. One study found that adults who were well adjusted but who had been treated for emotional problems during the early years of their lives tended to forget important but troubling childhood events. For instance, they forget such details as their family's receipt of welfare when they were children, being in foster care, and living in a home for delinquents (Robbins, 1988). Similarly, people who are depressed remember sad events from their past more easily than do happy people, and people who report being happy in adulthood remember more happy events than depressing ones (Bower & Cohen, 1982).

It is not just certain kinds of events that are distorted; particular periods of life are remembered more easily than others (Rubin, 1985). Furthermore, there are remarkable commonalities among people in what periods are remembered best. As you can see in Figure 6-9, 70-year-olds tend to recall details of their lives from their twenties and thirties best, whereas 50-year-olds tend to have more memories of their teenage years and their twenties. In both cases, it is the recollection of details of the more recent decades of people's lives, in comparison with earlier years, that suffers most.

FIGURE 6-9

We selectively recall certain periods of our lives. At age 70, people remember more of their twenties than their forties and fifties, while people age 50 remember more of their teenage years. (Rubin, 1986).

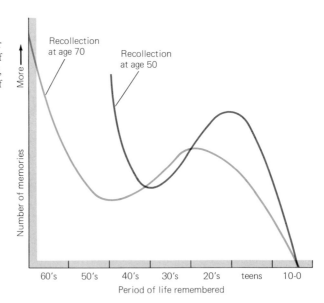

RECAP AND REVIEW II

Recap

◀ The tip-of-the-tongue phenomenon refers to the inability to recall something that a person is sure he or she knows.

◀ Retrieval cues are particularly important when recalling information—as opposed to recognizing it.

◀ Flashbulb memories are memories that are centered around a specific, important event and are so clear it is as if they represent a snapshot of the event.

◀ Memories reflect, at least in part, constructive processes, in which they are influenced by the meaning that we give to events. Our recollections of our own lives, for instance, are distorted.

Review

1. A classmate asks whether you can remember that important word about memory discussed in your last psychology class. You just can't think of it, but when you glance at the glossary terms in your book, you immediately discover the word. It was "recall." You remembered the word through the process of
   a. retention.
   b. recall.
   c. recognition.
   d. forgetting.

2. Hearing an old song again brought back a number of associated memories. The song served as a _____ _____ for those memories.

3. You can easily remember the details of the moment you received your diploma during your high school graduation. This is an example of
   a. flashbulb memory.
   b. the von Restorff effect.
   c. figural representation.
   d. sensory memory.

4. It is easier to remember the letter "B" on the car license plate 617 B36 than on the plate C12 HBL because of the phenomenon known as
   a. flashbulb memory.
   b. recognition.
   c. the von Restorff effect.
   d. serial reproduction.

5. "I think I remember the argument so well because I was surprised at how aggressively Bill acted in such a volatile situation." This statement demonstrates memory of a situation through a _____ .

6. Constructive processes refer to the way in which memories vary as a function of the number of times we are exposed to an event. True or false? _____

7. "You may not remember so clearly what he said, but I do because I know from experience that he is always thinking about making a sale." The speaker recalls the event so well as a result of the _____ _____ effect.

8. "The more you go back in years, the fuzzier the memories." Is this statement apt to be true or false for a 70-year-old? _____

(Answers to review questions are on page 218.)

WHEN MEMORY FAILS: FORGETTING WHAT YOU HAVE REMEMBERED

He could remember, quite literally, nothing — nothing, that is, that had happened since the loss of his temporal lobes and hippocampus during experimental surgery to reduce epileptic seizures. Until that time, his memory had been quite normal. But after the operation he was unable to recall anything for more than a few minutes, and then the memory was seemingly lost forever. He did not remember his address, or the name of the person to whom he was talking. He would read the same magazine over and over again. According to his own description, his life was like waking from a dream and being unable to know where he was or how he got there (Milner, 1966).

The difficulties faced by a person without a normal memory are legion, as exemplified in the case described above of a patient immortalized in the annals of memory research as "H. M." All of us who have experienced even routine instances of forgetting—such as not remembering an acquaintance's name or a fact on a test—understand the serious consequences of memory failure.

The first attempts to study forgetting were made by German psychologist Hermann Ebbinghaus about a hundred years ago. Using himself as his only subject, he memorized lists of three-letter nonsense syllables—meaningless sets of two consonants with a vowel in between, such as FIW and BOZ. By measuring how easy it was to relearn a given list of words after varying periods of time from initial learning had passed, he found that forgetting occurred systematically, as shown in Figure 6-10. As the figure indicates, the most rapid forgetting occurs in the first nine hours, and particularly in the

218

In his classic work, Ebbinghaus found that the most rapid forgetting occurs in the first nine hours after exposure to new material. However, the rate of forgetting then slows down and declines very little even after many days have passed. (Ebbinghaus, 1885.)

Decay: The loss of information through nonuse

Memory trace: A physical change in the brain corresponding to the memory of material

Interference: The phenomenon by which recall is hindered because of other information in memory

first hour. After nine hours, the rate of forgetting slows and declines little, even after the passage of many days.

Despite his primitive methods, Ebbinghaus's research had an important influence on subsequent research, and his basic conclusions have been upheld. There is almost always a strong initial decline in memory, followed by a more gradual drop over time. Furthermore, relearning of previously mastered material is almost always faster than starting from scratch, whether the material is academic information or a motor skill such as riding a bike.

Efforts at understanding *why* we forget have produced two major explanations. One theory explains forgetting in terms of a process called **decay**, or the loss of information through its nonuse. The theory assumes that when new material is learned, a **memory trace** or engram—an actual physical change in the brain—occurs. In decay, the trace simply fades away with nothing left behind, because of the mere passage of time.

Although there is some evidence that decay does occur, it does not seem to be the complete solution to the puzzle of forgetting. The difficulty with relying on decay as an explanation is that there is often no relationship between how long ago a person was exposed to information and how well it is recalled. If decay explained all forgetting, we would expect that the longer the time between the initial learning of information and our attempt to recall it, the harder it would be to remember it, since there would be more time for the memory trace to decay. Yet people who take several sequential tests on the same material often recall more of the initial information when taking later tests than they did on earlier tests. If decay were operating, we would expect the opposite to occur (Payne, 1986).

Because decay is not able to fully account for forgetting, memory specialists have proposed an additional mechanism: interference. In **interference**, information in memory displaces or blocks out other information, preventing its recall.

To distinguish between decay and interference, think of the two processes in terms of a row of books on a library shelf. In decay, the old books are constantly crumbling and rotting away, leaving room for new arrivals. Interference processes suggest that new books knock the old ones off the shelf, where they become inaccessible.

Most research suggests that interference is the key process in forgetting (Glass & Holyoak, 1985). We mainly forget things not because the memory trace has decayed, but because new memories interfere with the retrieval of old ones.

THE BEFORE AND AFTER OF FORGETTING:
Proactive and Retroactive Interference

There are actually two sorts of interference that influence forgetting: proactive and retroactive. In **proactive interference**, information learned earlier interferes with recall of newer material. Suppose, as a student of foreign languages, you first learned French in tenth grade, and then in eleventh grade you took Spanish. When it comes time to take a college achievement test in the twelfth grade in Spanish you may find you have difficulty recalling the Spanish translation of a word because all you can think of is its French equivalent. On the other hand, **retroactive interference** refers to difficulty in recall of information because of later exposure to different material. If, for example, you have difficulty on a French achievement test because of your more recent exposure to Spanish, retroactive interference is the culprit (see Figure 6-11). One way of remembering the difference between proactive and retroactive interference is to keep in mind that *pro*active interference

Proactive interference: The phenomenon by which information stored in memory interferes with recall of material learned later

Retroactive interference: The phenomenon by which new information interferes with the recall of information learned earlier

Study French in tenth grade

Time 1

Study Spanish in eleventh grade

Time 2

Take college achievement tests in twelfth grade

Proactive interference:

Spanish Test:
Translate "hello" into Spanish.

I remember that the French word for "hello" is "bonjour," but I can't remember what the Spanish word is . . .

Time 3

Retroactive interference:

French test:
Translate "hello" into French.

I remember that the Spanish word for "hello" is "hola," but I can't remember what the French word is . . .

FIGURE 6-11

Proactive interference occurs when material learned earlier interferes with recall of newer material. In this example, exposure to French prior to learning Spanish interferes with performance on a Spanish test. In contrast, retroactive interference exists when material learned after initial exposure to other material interferes with the recall of the first material. In this case, retroactive interference occurs when recall of French is impaired because of later exposure to Spanish.

moves forward in time—the past interferes with the present—whereas *retro-*active interference retrogresses in time, working backward as the present interferes with the past.

Although the concepts of proactive and retroactive interference suggest why material may be forgotten, they do not explain whether forgetting is caused by the actual loss of information or by problems in retrieval of information. Most research suggests that material that has apparently been lost because of interference can eventually be recalled if appropriate stimuli are presented (Tulving & Psotka, 1971), but the question has not been fully answered. In an effort to resolve the issue, some psychologists have begun to study the biological bases of memory in order to better understand what is remembered and what is forgotten—an increasingly important avenue of investigation discussed in the accompanying Cutting Edge box.

THE CUTTING EDGE

THE BIOLOGICAL BASES OF MEMORY: THE SEARCH FOR THE ENGRAM

Just where is the engram—the physical, neural trace that represents a memory in the brain—located?

This question has proved to be a major puzzle to psychologists interested in memory and has become the focus of a good deal of ongoing work. The search began in the 1920s, when psychologist Karl Lashley ran a series of experiments in which he removed portions of the cortex of rats. He found that rats who were made to relearn a problem involving running a maze showed learning deficits in proportion to the extent of the damage to their cortex; when more material was removed from the cortex, greater learning difficulties took place.

More intriguing, however, was the finding that the time it took to relearn the problem was unrelated to the specific *location* of the injury. Regardless of the particular portion of the brain that had been removed, the degree of learning deficit was comparatively similar, suggesting that memory traces are somewhat evenly distributed across the brain. Results of Lashley's work—summarized in a famous paper titled "In Search of the Engram"—led to the view held for several decades that stored memories are widely and fairly equally distributed across the brain (Lashley, 1950).

Contemporary research, however, seems to be coming to a differ-

ent conclusion. Such research starts from findings on the physiology of learning that show that separate, distinct areas of the cortex simultaneously process information about particular dimensions of the world, including visual, auditory, and all the other sensory stimuli that the world presents. Because different areas of the cortex are simultaneously involved in processing information about particular aspects of a stimulus, it seems reasonable that information storage might be linked to the specific neural systems that are used during learning and localized to those particular areas.

If these assumptions are correct, the location of an engram is dependent on the nature of the material that is being learned and the specific neural system that processed the information (Squire, 1986; 1987). For example, a portion of the cortex known as the inferotemporal area is the final part of the brain involved in the visual processing of patterns that begins in a different area of the cortex (the striate cortex) and has passed through several stages. Consequently, it may be that the inferotemporal cortex not only pro-

vides the location of this visual processing but is the site of the visual memories as well. Traces of a specific memory may be located in the area of the brain associated with how that memory was learned initially (Alkon, 1987).

How can we reconcile the growing contemporary view that memory is related to specific neural processing employed during learning when we consider Lashley's findings that memory deficits were unrelated to the location of injury to the cortex? One answer is that the contradiction between the two findings is more apparent than real. It is likely, for example, that Lashley's procedure of having rats run through a maze actually involves several kinds of information and learning—including visual information, spatial configuration, smells, and perhaps even sounds. Assuming this to be the case, learning and processing of information must have been occurring in several modalities simultaneously, although presumably in different locations in the brain. If each of these processing modalities resulted in a separate memory trace, then removing any particular portion of the cortex would still leave the other memory traces intact—and produce the same apparent deficit in performance, independent of which area of the cortex was removed.

In sum, it appears that memory is

localized to specific areas in that a particular memory trace is related to a particular information processing system in the brain. But in a larger sense, memory traces are distributed, given that several brain processing systems are involved in any learning situation—leading to the distribution of the traces throughout various areas of the brain (Weinberger, McGaugh & Lynch, 1985; Squire, 1987; Bear, Cooper & Ebner, 1987).

Other investigators are following different paths to learn about the biological basis of memory. For instance, recent work suggests that the brain's hippocampus and amygdala are particularly crucial in the formation of new memories (Hostetler, 1988; Squire, 1988). The hippocampus, in particular, appears to play a central role in the conversion of new sensory information into a form that allows it to be stored in other parts of the brain.

Furthermore, some work has found that administration of particular kinds of drugs in animals can lead to impairment or facilitation of memory (Flood, Smith & Morley, 1987; Gibbs & Ng, 1977). In one study, chicks were trained to avoid pecking a bitter solution. Some then received a drug that inhibited protein synthesis, and they showed significantly poorer performance on a measure of recall than those not receiving the drug. In addition, the administration of the drug arecholine in one experiment improved verbal learning in humans—but only for those who had relatively low scores without the drug. The drug was useful, then, in leading people to show recall at their optimal level—but the results suggest that it may not be possible to improve memory if people are already operating at their maximum level of performance.

According to Mark Rosenzweig, a leading researcher in memory at the University of California at Berkeley, the recent advances in our understanding of memory suggest a number of possible applications. In particular, it may be possible to help people who suffer from deficiencies of memory (such as Rita Hayworth, who suffered from Alzheimer's disease) and people with certain forms of mental retardation. According to Rosenzweig, "It may even be possible to aid those with 'normal' memory to perform better or at least to perform at their best level most of the time" (Rosenzweig, 1984, p. 373). Sometime in the future, all our memories may benefit from research on the biological bases of memory.

AFFLICTIONS OF FORGETTING: Memory Dysfunctions

To a casual observer, Harold appears to be a brilliant golfer. He seems to have learned the game perfectly; his shots are almost flawless.

Yet anyone accompanying him on the course is bound to notice some startling incongruities. Although he is immediately able to size up a situation and hit the ball exactly where it should go, he cannot remember where the ball has just landed. At the end of each hole, he forgets the score (Blakeslee, 1985, p. C1).

Harold's problem: he suffers from **Alzheimer's disease**, the illness that counts severe memory problems among its symptoms. Alzheimer's, discussed first at the beginning of the chapter, strikes about 7 percent of people over the age of 65.

In its initial stages, Alzheimer's appears as simple forgetfulness of things like appointments and birthdays. As the disease progresses, memory loss becomes more profound, and even the simplest tasks—such as how to dial a telephone—are forgotten. Ultimately, victims can forget their own names or family members' faces. In addition, physical deterioration sets in, and language abilities may be lost entirely.

Although the causes of Alzheimer's disease are not fully understood, recent evidence points to deterioration in the nerve cell pathways between the hippocampus and the cerebral cortex of the brain. In some cases, such deterioration is so profound that it can be seen without a microscope (Van Hoesen, 1988). The cause of this deterioration remains to be determined. One clue is that Alzheimer's patients have an unusually low level of the neurotransmitter acetylcholine (see Chapter 2).

Alzheimer's disease: An illness associated with aging that includes severe memory loss, physical deterioration, and loss of language abilities

LEARNING AND THINKING

Amnesia: Memory loss unaccompanied by other mental difficulties

Retrograde amnesia: Memory loss of occurrences prior to some event

Anterograde amnesia: Memory loss of events following an injury

Korsakoff's syndrome: A disease among long-term alcoholics involving memory impairment

Alzheimer's disease is just one of several memory dysfunctions that plague their victims. Another is **amnesia**, memory loss that occurs without other mental difficulties. The classic case—immortalized in many a drama—is a victim who receives a blow to the head and is unable to remember anything from his or her past. In reality, amnesia of this type, known as retrograde amnesia, is quite rare. In **retrograde amnesia**, memory is lost for occurrences prior to a certain event. There is usually a gradual reappearance of lost memory, although it may take as long as several years for a full restoration to occur. In certain cases, some memories are lost forever (Baddeley, 1982).

A second type of amnesia is exemplified by the case of "H. M.," the man we discussed earlier who could remember nothing of his current activities. In **anterograde amnesia**, loss of memory occurs for events following an injury. Information cannot be transferred from short-term to long-term memory, resulting in the inability to remember anything other than what was in long-term storage prior to the accident.

Amnesia is also displayed by people who suffer from **Korsakoff's syndrome**, a disease that afflicts long-term alcoholics who have also had an impaired diet, resulting in a thiamine deficiency. Although many of their intellectual abilities may be intact, they display a strange array of symptoms, including hallucinations; repeating questions, even after being told the answer; and repeating the same story over and over again.

Fortunately, most of us have memories that are intact, and the occasional failures that we do suffer may in fact be preferable to having a perfect memory. Consider, for instance, the case of a man who had total recall. After reading passages of the *Divine Comedy* in Italian—a language he did not speak—he was able to repeat it back from memory even some fifteen years later. He could memorize lists of fifty unrelated words and recall them at will more than a decade later. He could even repeat the same list of words backward, if asked (Luria, 1987).

Such a skill might at first seem to have few drawbacks, but it actually presented quite a problem. The man's memory became a jumble of lists of words, numbers, and names, and when he tried to relax, his mind was filled

When memory becomes a burden: A woman with total recall would remember every word and every scene of every movie she saw, whether or not she liked the film! (E. L. Miller/Stock Boston)

with images. Even reading was difficult, since every word evoked a flood of thoughts from the past that interfered with his ability to understand the meaning of what he was reading. Partially as a consequence of the man's unusual memory, psychologist A. R. Luria, who studied his case, found him to be a "disorganized and rather dull-witted person" (Luria, 1968, p. 65).

We may be grateful, then, that being somewhat forgetful plays at least some useful role in our lives.

THE INFORMED CONSUMER OF PSYCHOLOGY:
Improving Your Memory

Apart from the advantages of forgetting, say, the details of a gruesome science fiction movie, most of us still would like to find ways of improving our memories. Given our understanding of memory, is it possible to find practical ways of increasing our recall of information? Most definitely. A good deal of research has revealed a number of strategies that can be used to help us develop better memories. Among the best:

▶ The keyword technique. Suppose you are taking a class in a foreign language and need to learn long lists of vocabulary words. One way of easing this process is to use the **keyword technique**, in which a foreign word is paired with a common English word that has a similar *sound*. This English word is known as the keyword. For example, to learn the Spanish word duck (*pato,* pronounced *pot-o*), the keyword might be "pot"; for the Spanish word for horse (*caballo,* pronounced *cob-eye-yo*), the keyword might be "eye."

Keyword technique: The pairing of a foreign word with a common, similar-sounding English word to aid in remembering the new word

Once you have thought of a keyword, you form a mental image of it graphically "interacting" with the English translation of the word. For instance, you might envision a duck taking a bath in a pot to remember the word *pato,* or a horse with a large, bulging eye in the center of its head to recall *caballo.* This technique has produced considerably superior results in learning foreign language vocabulary than have more traditional techniques involving memorization of the words themselves (Pressley & Levin, 1983; Pressley, 1987).

▶ Method of loci. If you have ever had to give a talk in class, you know the difficulty of keeping in mind all the things you want to say. One technique that works quite effectively was developed by the ancient Greeks: When Greek orators sought to memorize long speeches, they used the **method of loci** (*loci* is the Latin word for places) to organize their recollections of what they wanted to say. With this technique, each part of a speech is imagined as "residing" in a different location of a building.

Method of loci (LO sy): Assigning words or ideas to places, thereby improving recall of the words by envisioning those places

For instance, you might think of the preface of a talk as being in your house's entryway, the first major point being in the living room, the next major point residing in the dining room, and so forth, until the end of the speech is reached at the back bedroom of the house. This technique can easily be adapted to learning lists of words; each word on the list is imagined as being located in a series of sequential locations. The method works best by using the most outlandish images possible: If you wanted to remember a list of groceries consisting of bananas, ketchup, and milk, for instance, you might think of a banana intertwined in the leaves of your living-room begonia, the ketchup spilled over the end table, and the milk spraying from the top of a table lamp. When you got to the supermarket, you could mentally "walk" through your living room, recalling the items easily.

Context-dependent memory: The phenomenon by which memory of information is enhanced when recalled under the same conditions as when it was learned

▶ Context-dependent memory. Some research suggests that we remember information best in the same environment in which we learned it—a phenomenon known as **context-dependent memory**. You will probably do better on a test, then, if you study in the same classroom in which the test is going to be given (Saufley, Otaka & Bavaresco, 1985). Similarly, you will remember more about lectures you have attended if you study and are tested in the room in which the lectures were held.

▶ Organization of text material. Most of life's more important recall tasks involve not lists of words but rather texts that have been read. How can you facilitate recall of such material? One proven technique for improving recall of written material consists of organizing the material in memory as it is being read for the first time. To do this, you should first identify any advance information about the structure and content of the material—scanning by using the table of contents, chapter outline, headings, and even the end-of-chapter summary—before reading the chapter itself. By understanding the structure of the material, you will recall it better.

Another technique is to ask yourself questions that integrate the material you have read, and then answer them. By asking questions, you will be able to form networks between the various specific facts and promote the processing of the material at a deeper level—which, as the levels-of-processing approach to memory that we discussed earlier suggests, will aid later recall (Royer & Feldman, 1984). For example, you might at this moment ask yourself, "What are the major techniques for remembering material in textbooks?" and then try to answer the question.

▶ Organization of lecture notes. "Less is more" is perhaps the best advice for taking lecture notes that aid in recall. Rather than trying to take down every detail of a lecture, it is better to listen and think about the material, taking down the main points after you have considered them in a broader context. In effective note taking, thinking about the material initially is more important than writing it down. This is one reason that borrowing someone else's notes is a bad proposition, since you will have no framework in memory to use in understanding them (Peper & Mayer, 1978).

These orchestra players at C. W. Post College are taking advantage of the fact that rehearsal aids performance. (Sepp Seitz/ Woodfin Camp & Assoc.)

▶ Practice and rehearsal. Although practice does not necessarily make perfect, it does help. By studying and rehearsing material past the point of initial mastery—a process called **overlearning**—people are able to show better long-term recall than if they stop practicing after they have learned the material initially.

Overlearning: Rehearsing material beyond the point of mastery to improve long-term recall

Eventually, of course, practice has little or no effect; you probably already know your address so well that no amount of additional practice will make you recall it any better than you already do. But it is safe to say that, given the volume of material covered in most courses, academic material is rarely so securely retained, and you would generally be wise to review material a few times even after you feel you have learned it, in order to reach a true level of overlearning.

Research on the outcomes of elaborative rehearsal, discussed earlier in the chapter, also suggests that it is important that the practice of asking and rehearsing the answers to questions be as active as possible. In this way, the connections between the parts of the material are likely to become explicit, aiding in its later recall by providing ample retrieval cues.

Finally, people who cram for tests should note that the best retention comes from practice that is distributed over many sessions, rather than left for one long session. Research clearly demonstrates that fatigue and other factors prevent long practice sessions from being as effective as distributed practice.

RECAP AND REVIEW III

Recap

◀ Decay and interference are the primary explanations for forgetting.

◀ There are two kinds of interference: proactive interference (when information learned earlier interferes with recall of newer information) and retroactive interference (when new information interferes with recall of information learned earlier).

◀ The major memory dysfunctions include Alzheimer's disease, retrograde amnesia, anterograde amnesia, and Korsakoff's syndrome.

◀ Specific techniques for increasing the recall of information include the keyword technique, the method of loci, the use of context-dependent memory, the organization of information in textbooks, good note taking, and practice and rehearsal.

Review

1. It appears that decay is the major cause of loss in long-term memory. True or false? _____
2. Yesterday, Sue mentioned the name of the new movie starring your favorite actress. But today, all you can recall are the names of the actress's earlier films. The culprit interfering with your memory is
   a. memory trace.
   b. decay.
   c. proactive interference.
   d. retroactive interference.
3. The onset of Alzheimer's disease is marked by an almost immediate profound loss of memory. True or false? _____
4. Loss of memory for events subsequent to an injury is known as _____ amnesia.
5. Alcoholics with inadequate diets may experience amnesia as a result of _____ syndrome.
6. In order to help himself remember who was at the business meeting, Jim imagined each of the attendees standing in a different room in his house. His technique is known as
   a. rehearsal.
   b. the method of loci.
   c. overlearning.
   d. the keyword technique.
7. Based on the phenomenon of context-dependent memory, would you be apt to perform better on a test if it were given in your lecture room or in a novel location?
8. Research clearly shows that the best way to study before a test is to overlearn the material in one long session just before the exam. True or false? _____

(Answers to review questions are on page 226.)

226

1. Memory is defined by the three R's of remembering; it consists of the capacity to record, retain, and retrieve information. There are three basic kinds of memory storage: sensory memory, short-term memory, and long-term memory.

2. Sensory memory (made up of memories corresponding to each of the sensory systems) is the first place where information about the world is saved, although the memories are very brief. For instance, iconic memory (made up of visual sensations) lasts less than a second, and echoic memory (corresponding to auditory sensations) lasts less than four seconds. Despite their brevity, sensory memories are very precise, storing almost an exact replica of each stimulus to which a person is exposed. Unless they are transferred to other types of memory, however, sensory memories appear to be lost.

3. Roughly seven (plus or minus two) chunks of information are capable of being transferred and held in short-term memory. A chunk is a meaningful bit of information, ranging in size from a letter or a single digit to more complicated categorizations. Information in short-term memory is held from fifteen to twenty-five seconds and, if not transferred to long-term memory, is lost primarily through interference, as well as through decay. Interference is the loss of material through the displacement of older material by newer information, whereas decay is the loss of information through its nonuse.

4. Memories are transferred into long-term storage through rehearsal. The most effective type is elaborative rehearsal, in which the material to be remembered is organized and expanded. Formal techniques for organizing material are called mnemonics.

5. If memories are transferred into long-term memory, they become relatively permanent. Long-term memories are of two types: episodic and semantic. Episodic memories relate to our individual lives (such as recalling what a grade-school teacher looked like); semantic memories consist of organized knowledge and facts about the world (for example, $4 \times 5 = 20$).

6. The levels-of-processing approach to memory suggests that the way in which information is initially perceived and analyzed determines the success with which the information is recalled. The deeper the initial processing, the greater the recall of the material.

7. The tip-of-the-tongue phenomenon refers to the experience of trying in vain to remember information that one is certain one knows. A major way of successfully recalling information is to use retrieval cues, stimuli that permit a search through long-term memory.

8. Flashbulb memories are memories centered around a specific, important event. The memories are so clear that they appear to represent a "snapshot" of the event. Flashbulb memories illustrate the broader point that the more distinctive a memory, the more easily it can be retrieved—a phenomenon called the von Restorff effect.

9. Memory is a constructive process in which we relate memories to the meaning, guesses, and expectations that we give to the events the memory recalls. Specific information is recalled in terms of schemas, or general themes that contain relatively little detail.

10. Even with the use of retrieval cues, some information appears irretrievable, owing to decay or interference. Interference seems to be the major cause of forgetting. There are two sorts of interference: proactive interference (when information learned earlier interferes with recall of material to which one is exposed later) and retroactive interference (when new information interferes with recall of information to which one has been exposed earlier).

11. Current research on the biology underlying memory is concerned with the site of the engram, or memory trace. Other work has found changes in brain chemistry following training of animals. Furthermore, certain drugs impair or aid memory in animals, suggesting that drugs may be used to improve the memory of people in the future.

12. There are several memory dysfunctions. Among them are Alzheimer's disease, which leads to a progressive loss of memory, and amnesia, a memory loss that occurs without other mental difficulties and that can take two forms. In retrograde amnesia, there is loss of memory for occurrences prior to some event; in anterograde amnesia, there is loss of memory for events following an injury. Korsakoff's syndrome is a disease that afflicts long-term alcoholics, resulting in memory impairment.

13. Psychologists have developed a number of specific techniques to improve memory. These include using the keyword technique to memorize foreign vocabulary, applying the method of loci to learn lists, using context-dependent memory, organizing text material, and practicing enough so that overlearning—studying and rehearsing past the point of initial mastery—occurs.

ANSWERS (REVIEW III):
1. False; decay does not offer a full explanation of forgetting **2.** c **3.** False; memory loss is gradual **4.** Anterograde **5.** Korsakoff's **6.** b **7.** In the lecture room where prior learning took place **8.** False; practice is best distributed over several sessions

FOR FURTHER STUDY AND APPLICATION ▷

Stern, L. (1985). *The structures and strategies of human memory.* Homewood, IL: Dorsey.

Norman, D. A. (1982). *Learning and memory.* San Francisco: W. H. Freeman.

These two useful and readable accounts of memory are written by experts in the field.

Neisser, U. (1982). *Memory observed: Remembering in natural context.* San Francisco: W. H. Freeman

An excellent, comprehensive guide to remembering, this volume reports on fascinating phenomena that you will not easily forget.

Wells, G. L., & Loftus, E. A. (Eds.) (1984). *Eyewitness testimony.* New York: Cambridge University Press.

This work provides a number of interesting, although technical, perspectives on the accuracy and processes involving eyewitness testimony. It also gives concrete suggestions for changing courtroom procedures to ensure the fairness of trials.

Luria, A. R. (1987). *The mind of a mnemonist.* Cambridge, MA: Harvard University Press.

The author recounts the fascinating story of a man with an extraordinary memory. As the book makes clear, remembering so much is a mixed blessing.

Reason, J., & Mycielska, K. (1982). *Absentminded? The psychology of mental lapses and everyday errors.* Englewood Cliffs, NJ: Prentice-Hall.

The title speaks for itself. The book contains a deft combination of laboratory and everyday examples of absentmindedness.

Solomon, P. R., Goethals, G. R., Kelley, C. M., & Stephens, B. R. (Eds.) (1988). *Memory: Interdisciplinary approaches.* New York: Springer-Verlag.

This volume provides a broad overview of memory, taken from the perspectives of biopsychology, cognitive psychology, developmental psychology, and social psychology.

CHAPTER

7

COGNITION AND LANGUAGE

Physicist Richard Feyman shows how the material which the solid rocket booster O-rings are made of fails in cold weather. (UPI/Bettmann Newsphotos)

PROLOGUE:
RICHARD FEYNMAN

When the *Challenger* space shuttle blew up, killing all the astronauts aboard, it represented more than a human tragedy. To NASA engineers, and the members of a presidential commission appointed to determine the cause of the accident, it also represented a scientific puzzle of the most important kind: Without a clear understanding of the reason for the accident, space travel by the United States could not proceed.

To one member of the commission, Nobel-prize winning physicist Richard Feynman, at least part of the answer to the problem was apparent early in the investigation. In a briefing he received soon after being appointed to the commission, Feynman was apprised of a problem with the O-ring seals, which later were judged to be the actual cause of the accident. But Feynman was frustrated in his attempts to pursue the issue. When he tried to obtain information from the NASA bureaucracy about the resiliency of the O-ring rubber at low temperatures, he received only a stack of papers with the answer to a question he didn't ask.

Feynman was ultimately able to obtain the answer to his question in a novel and eye-opening way. In his words, "Later I'm feeling lousy and I'm eating dinner; I look at the table, and there's a glass of ice water. I think, 'Damn it, *I* can find out about the rubber *without* sending notes to NASA and getting back a stack of papers; all I've got to do is get a sample of the rubber, stick it in ice water and see how it responds when I squeeze it!' " (Feynman, 1988, p. 30).

After obtaining a piece of rubber from NASA—not an easy task (NASA is very careful with its supplies, and every piece of material is checked and counted and controlled)—Feynman went to a hardware store to purchase screwdrivers, pliers, clamps, and other supplies needed to carry out a small experiment.

The experiment itself was a simple demonstration. To lower the temperature of the rubber, Feynman thrust it into a pitcher of ice water and left it there for a few minutes. When he took it out, it was brittle and broke apart. To observers, his point had been made: At lowered temperatures, the rubber in the O-rings was rendered inadequate for the job of sealing the rocket joints. The cause of the shuttle accident had been demonstrated in a way the world could understand (Feynman, 1988).

LOOKING AHEAD ▶

Feynman's simple demonstration produced an understanding of the causes of the shuttle accident in a simple and elegant manner. In addition, it raised a number of issues of interest to psychologists: How do people use and retrieve information to devise innovative solutions to problems? How is such knowledge transformed, elaborated upon, and utilized? More basically, how do people think about, understand, and, using language, describe the world?

These questions and others are being addressed by **cognitive psychologists**, who specialize in the study of cognition. **Cognition** encompasses the higher mental processes of humans, including how people know and understand the world, process information, make judgments and decisions, and describe their knowledge and understanding to others. The realm of cognitive psychology is broad, then, and includes the research on memory ex-

Cognitive psychology: The branch of psychology that specializes in the study of cognition
Cognition: The higher mental processes by which we understand the world, process information, make judgments and decisions, and communicate knowledge to others

230

amined in the previous chapter and much of the work on intelligence that we discuss in the next chapter.

In this chapter, we concentrate on two issues that are central to the field of cognitive psychology: problem solving and language. We examine various ways to approach problems, means of generating solutions, and ways of making judgments about the usefulness and accuracy of solutions. In our focus on language, we consider how language is developed and acquired, its basic characteristics, and whether language is a uniquely human skill. Finally, we explore the relationship between thinking and language.

After reading this chapter, then, you will be able to answer a number of basic questions:

▶ How do people approach and solve problems?

▶ What are the major obstacles to problem solving?

▶ How do people use language, and how does it develop?

COGNITIVE PROCESSES IN PROBLEM SOLVING

According to legend, a group of monks in Vietnam devote a considerable amount of their time attempting to solve a problem called the Tower of Hanoi puzzle. If they are successful in finding a solution, the monks expect that it will bring an end to the world as we know it (Raphael, 1976). (Happily, there is no need for immediate concern; according to one estimate, the monks' puzzle is so complex that it will take about a trillion years to reach a solution.)

In a simpler version of the puzzle, illustrated in Figure 7-1, there are three posts on which three disks are to be placed in the order shown. The goal of the puzzle is to move all three disks to the third post in the same order, using as few moves as possible. But there are two restrictions: Only one disk can be moved at a time, and no disk can ever cover a smaller one during a move.

Start

Finish

FIGURE 7-1

The goal of the Tower of Hanoi puzzle is to move all three disks from the first post to the last and still preserve the original order of the disks, using the least number of moves possible while following the rules that only one disk at a time can be moved and no disk can cover a smaller one during a move. Try it yourself before you look at the solution, which is listed according to the sequence of moves. (Solution: Move C to 3, B to 2, C to 2, A to 3, C to 1, B to 3, and C to 3.)

Why are cognitive psychologists interested in the Tower of Hanoi problem? The answer is that the way people go about solving this puzzle and simpler ones like it helps illuminate the processes by which people solve more complex problems that they encounter in school and at work. For example, psychologists have found that problem solving typically follows three major steps: preparation for the creation of solutions, production of solutions, and evaluation of solutions that have been generated.

PREPARATION: Understanding and Diagnosing the Problem

When presented with a problem such as the Tower of Hanoi, most people begin by trying to ensure that they thoroughly understand the problem. If the problem is novel, they will likely pay particular attention to any restrictions placed on coming to a solution and the initial status of the components of the problem. If the problem is familiar, they are apt to spend considerably less time in this stage than if it is completely new to them.

Problems vary from well defined to ill defined (Reitman, 1965). For a well-defined problem—such as a mathematical equation or the solution to a jigsaw puzzle in which no pieces have been lost—both the nature of the problem itself and the information needed to solve the problem are available and clear. Thus, straightforward judgments can be made about whether a potential solution is appropriate. With an ill-defined problem, such as how to increase morale on an assembly line, not only may the specific nature of the problem be unclear, but the information required to solve the problem may be even less obvious.

The clarity of a problem has important effects on the ultimate success of the problem solver. Consider a physician encountering a patient who complains, rather vaguely, that he feels tired. The way in which the physician defines and frames this initial complaint is likely to have an important impact on the physician's ultimate success in solving the problem.

Kinds of Problems

Problems typically fall into one of the three categories exemplified in Figure 7-2: arrangement, inducing structure, and transformation (Greeno, 1978). Each requires somewhat different kinds of psychological skills and knowledge to solve.

Arrangement problems require that a group of elements be rearranged or recombined in a way that will satisfy a certain criterion. There are usually several different possible arrangements that can be made, but only one or a few of the arrangements produce a solution. Anagram problems and jigsaw puzzles represent arrangement problems.

In problems of **inducing structure**, a person must identify the relations that exist among the elements presented and construct a new relationship among them. In such a problem, it is necessary to determine not only the relationships among the elements but the structure and size of the elements involved. In the example shown in Figure 7-2, a person must first determine that the solution requires the numbers to be considered in pairs (14-24-34-44-54-64). It is only after that part of the problem is identified that the solution rule (the first number of each pair increases by one, while the second number remains the same) can be determined.

The Tower of Hanoi puzzle represents a third kind of problem. **Transformation problems** consist of an initial state, a goal state, and a series of methods for changing the initial state into the goal state. In the Tower of

---

Arrangement problems: Problems whose solution requires the rearrangement of a group of elements in order to satisfy a certain criterion

Inducing structure problems: Problems whose solution requires the identification of existing relationships among elements presented so as to construct a new relationship among them

Transformation problems: Problems to be solved using a series of methods to change an initial state into a goal state

A. ARRANGEMENT PROBLEMS

ANAGRAMS: Rearrange the letters in each set to make an English word:

EFCTA
IAENV
BODUT
LIVAN
IKCTH

B. PROBLEMS OF INDUCING STRUCTURE

1. What number comes next in this series?

142434445464

2. Complete the analogy:
baseball is to bat as tennis is to

a. kick
b. court
c. racket

C. TRANSFORMATION PROBLEMS

1. HOBBITS AND ORCS:

Three hobbits and three orcs stand on one side of a river. On their side of the river is a boat which will hold up to two creatures. The problem is to transport all six creatures to the other side of the river. However, if orcs ever outnumber hobbits, orcs will eat the hobbits. How should they get across?

2. WATER JARS

A person has three jars having the capacities listed. How can the person measure exactly 11 ounces of water?
Jar A—28 ounces
Jar B— 7 ounces
Jar C— 5 ounces

(Solutions are on page 234.)

FIGURE 7-2

The major categories of problems: (a) arrangement, (b) inducing structure, and (c) transformation. (Bourne et al., 1986.)

Hanoi problem, the initial state is the original configuration; the goal state consists of the three disks on the third peg; and the method consists of the rules for moving the disks.

Whether the problem is one of arrangement, inducing structure, or transformation, the initial stage of understanding and diagnosing is critical in problem solving because it allows us to develop our own cognitive representation of the problem and to place it within a personal framework. The problem may be divided into subparts, or some information may be ignored, as we try to simplify the task. Winnowing out the inessential information is often a critical step in problem solving.

Representing and Organizing the Problem

A crucial aspect of the initial encounter with a problem is the way in which we represent it to ourselves and organize the information presented to us. Consider the following problem:

A man climbs a mountain on Saturday, leaving at daybreak and arriving at the top near sundown. He spends the night at the top. The next day, Sunday, he leaves at daybreak and heads down the mountain, following the same path that he climbed the day before. The question is this: Will there be any time during the second day when he will be at exactly the same point on the mountain as he was at that time on the first day?

If you try to solve this problem by using algebraic or verbal representations, you will have a good deal of trouble. However, if you represent the problem with the kind of simple diagram illustrated in Figure 7-3, the solution becomes apparent.

Successful problem solving, then, requires that a person form an appropriate representation and organization of the problem. However, there is no one optimal way of representing and organizing material, since that is dependent on the nature of the problem. Sometimes simply restructuring a problem, from a verbal form to a pictorial or mathematical form for instance, can help point out a direct solution (Mayer, 1982).

PRODUCTION: Generating Solutions

If a problem is relatively simple, a direct solution may already be stored in long-term memory, and all that is necessary is to retrieve the appropriate information. If the solution cannot be retrieved, or is not known, a process by which possible solutions are generated and compared with information in long- and short-term memory is instigated.

At the most primitive level, solutions to problems can be obtained through trial and error. Thomas Edison was able to invent the light bulb only because he tried thousands of different kinds of material for a filament before he found one that worked (carbon). The difficulty with trial and error is, of course, that some problems are so complicated it would take close to forever to try out every possibility. For example, according to one estimate, there are some 10^{120} possible sequences of chess moves.

In place of trial and error, more complex problem solving requires the use of algorithms and heuristics. An **algorithm** is a set of rules which, if followed, guarantee a solution, even if the reason it works is not understood. For example, you may know that the length of the third side of a right triangle can be found by using the formula $a^2 + b^2 = c^2$. You may not have the foggiest notion why it works, but this algorithm is always accurate and provides you with a solution to a particular problem.

Heuristics, in contrast, are rules of thumb or mental shortcuts that may lead to a solution but are not guaranteed to do so (Groner, Groner & Bischof, 1983). For example, a heuristic that chess players often follow is to gain control of the center of the board. The tactic doesn't guarantee that they will

Algorithm: A set of rules that, if followed, guarantee a solution, though the reason they work may not be understood by the person using them

Heuristic (hyur ISS tik): A rule of thumb that may bring about a solution to a problem but is not guaranteed to do so

FIGURE 7-3

Using a graph, it is easy to solve the problem posed in the text. Remember, the goal is not to determine the time, but just to indicate whether an exact time exists. (Anderson, 1980.)

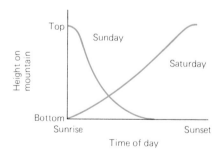

Answers to problems posed in Figure 7-2

A. facet, naive, doubt, anvil, thick

B. 1. 7
   2. c

C. 1. Hobbits and Orcs. (Using h = hobbit, o = Orc, F = forward boat move, B = backward boat move; for example, F/2o means move the boat forward with two orcs): F/2o (or F/1h, 1o), B/1o (or B/1h), F/2o, B/1o, F/2h, B/1h, 1o, F/2h, B/1o, F/2o, B/1h (or B/1o), F/1h, 1o (or F/2o).

   2. Fill jar A, empty into jar B once and into jar C twice. What remains in jar A is 11 oz.

win, but it does increase their chances. Similarly, students may follow the heuristic of preparing for a test by ignoring the assigned textbook reading and studying only their lecture notes—a strategy that may or may not pay off.

Several general heuristics tend to be employed in solving problems that require making judgments or decisions. **Representativeness** is the heuristic in which people determine whether a given example is a member of a particular category by evaluating how representative it is of that category. Suppose, for instance, you are the owner of a fast-food store and you have been robbed many times by people who come into your store looking nervous and shifty. The next time someone who fits this description enters your store, it is likely that—if you employ the representativeness heuristic— you will assume that danger lurks, since your prior experience suggests that the person is likely to be a member of a class of people you have come to know as "thief."

The **availability** heuristic involves judging the probability of an event by how easily the event can be recalled from memory (Tversky & Kahneman, 1973). According to this heuristic, we assume that events we recall easily are likely to have occurred more frequently in the past, and we further assume that the same sort of event is more likely to occur in the future. The availability heuristic explains why, after we hear about an airplane crash, we estimate a greater likelihood of being in a crash ourselves.

Probably the most frequently applied heuristic is a means-ends analysis. In a **means-ends analysis**, a person repeatedly tests for differences between the desired outcome and what currently exists, trying each time to reduce the difference between the possible solution and desired outcome. For example, people using a means-ends analysis to search for the correct sequence of roads to get to a city that they can see in the distance would analyze their solutions in terms of how much closer each individual choice of roadways brings them to the ultimate goal of arriving at the city. Such a strategy is effective, though, only if there is a direct solution to the problem. If the problem is such that indirect steps have to be taken that appear to *increase* the discrepancy between the current state and the solution, means-ends analyses can be counterproductive. In our example, if roadways are laid out in such a way that a person must temporarily move *away* from the city in order to reach it eventually, a means-ends analysis will keep the person from reaching the goal.

In fact, for some problems the converse of a means-ends approach is the most effective: working backward by beginning with the goal and moving toward the starting state. Instead of altering the elements of a problem in a series of steps that move closer and closer to the solution, people can work in the opposite direction, moving away from the goal and aiming to reach the beginning point (Bourne et al., 1986; Malin, 1979).

Subgoals

Another commonly used heuristic is to divide a problem into intermediate steps, or subgoals, and to solve each of those steps. For instance, if you return to the Tower of Hanoi problem, there are several obvious subgoals that could be chosen, such as moving the largest disk to the third post.

If solving a subgoal is part of the ultimate solution to a problem, then identifying subgoals is an appropriate strategy. There are cases, however, in which the formation of subgoals is not all that helpful and may actually take

Representativeness heuristic: A rule in which people and things are judged by the degree to which they represent a certain category

Availability heuristic: A rule for judging the probability that an event will occur by the ease with which it can be recalled from memory

Means-ends analysis: Repeated testing to determine and reduce the distance between real and desired outcomes in problem solving the problem solver longer to find a solution (Reed, 1988; Hayes, 1966). For example, some problems cannot be subdivided. Others are so difficult to subdivide that it takes longer to identify the appropriate subdivisions than to solve the problem by other means. Finally, even when a problem is divided into subgoals, it may be unclear what to do when the subgoal has been reached.

Insight

Some approaches to problem solving focus less on step-by-step processes than on the sudden bursts of comprehension that may come when solving a problem. Just after World War I, German psychologist Wolfgang Kohler examined the learning and problem-solving processes in chimps (Kohler, 1927). In his studies, Kohler exposed chimps to challenging situations in which the elements of the solution were all present; what was necessary was for the chimps to put them together.

For example, in one series of studies, chimps were kept in a cage in which boxes and sticks were strewn about, with a bunch of tantalizing bananas hanging high in the cage out of their reach. Initially, the chimps engaged in a variety of trial-and-error attempts at getting to the bananas: They would throw the stick at the bananas, jump from one of the boxes, or leap wildly from the ground. Frequently, they would seem to give up in frustration, leaving the bananas dangling temptingly overhead. But then, in what seemed like a sudden revelation, they would leave whatever activity they were involved in and stand on a box in order to be able to reach the bananas

In a remarkable display of problem solving, Kohler's chimp Sultan sees a bunch of bananas out of his reach (a). He then retrieves several crates sitting in the room (b), and stacks them up so that he can reach the bananas (c). (The Photo Source)

(a) (b) (c)

with a stick. Kohler called the cognitive processes underlying the chimps' behavior **insight**, a sudden awareness of the relationships among various elements that had previously appeared to be independent of one another.

Although Kohler emphasized the apparent suddenness with which solutions were revealed, subsequent research has shown that prior experience and initial trial-and-error practice in problem solving are prerequisites for producing the appearance of insight (Metcalfe, 1986). One study demonstrated that only chimps who had experience in playing with sticks could successfully solve the problem; inexperienced chimps never made the connection between standing on the box and reaching the bananas (Birch, 1945). Some researchers have suggested that the behavior of the monkeys represented little more than the chaining together of previously learned responses, no different from the way a pigeon learns, by trial and error, to peck a key (Epstein, 1987; Epstein et al., 1984). It is clear that insight depends on previous experience with the elements involved in a problem.

JUDGMENT: Evaluating the Solutions

The final step in problem solving consists of judging the adequacy of a solution. Often, this is a simple matter: If there is a clear solution—as in the Tower of Hanoi problem—we will know immediately whether we have been successful. On the other hand, if the solution is less concrete, or if there is no single correct solution, evaluating solutions becomes more difficult.

If there is more than one solution to a problem, or if the solution criteria are vague, we must decide which solution alternative is best. Unfortunately, we are sometimes quite inaccurate in estimating the quality of our own ideas: there is often little relationship between our own judgments of the quality of our ideas and more objective criteria (Johnson, Parrott & Stratton, 1968).

Theoretically, if the heuristics and information we rely on to make decisions are appropriate and valid, we can make accurate choices among problem solutions. However, as we see next, there are several kinds of obstacles and biases in problem solving that affect the quality of the decisions we make.

RECAP AND REVIEW I

Recap

◀ Cognitive psychologists specialize in the study of the higher mental processes of humans, including problem solving, knowing, reasoning, judging, and decision making.

◀ One major goal of cognitive psychologists is to identify the thinking processes that underlie problem solving. Typically, people pass through a series of three steps in problem solving: preparation, production, and judgment.

◀ Problem solvers frequently use algorithms (sets of rules that, if followed, guarantee a solution will be reached) and heuristics (rules of thumb that may lead to a solution).

◀ Insight is the sudden awareness of the relationships among various elements that had earlier seemed independent of one another.

Review

1. Match the statement in the right column with the problem-solving state it represents in the left column.

   a. _____ Preparation

   b. _____ Production of solutions

   c. _____ Evaluation of solutions

   1. Bryan pulled out a piece of paper and listed a dozen ways that might help him crack the problem.

   2. Jill is carefully assessing the peer relationships in her class to try to figure out why the students are so disruptive.

   3. "Well, I can think of several ways of solving this, but I wonder which one is the best."

2. Four patterned blocks were laid out in front of Ben. He was asked to arrange them in a specific configuration to match a model. Ben is faced with
   a. a transformation problem.
   b. a problem of inducing structure.
   c. an anagram problem.
   d. an arrangement problem.
3. _____ are rules which, if followed, may in fact lead to a solution, whereas _____ are sets of rules which, if followed, guarantee a solution.
4. Two-year-old Sam, accustomed to playing with balls, decided that the tomato was just another ball and threw it across the room. In doing so, Sam used the _____ heuristic.
5. On a recent rock climb, Phil tried to overcome a difficult section by trying to find the straightest path to a large ledge visible above. His attempt to solve the problem employed
   a. subgoals.
   b. insight.
   c. an availability heuristic.
   d. means-ends analysis.
6. _____ refers to the sudden discovery of solutions which don't appear (at least on the surface) to be the result of any step-by-step process.
7. Research suggests that we should feel confident in our ability to estimate the quality of our own ideas accurately when we attempt to choose among solutions to a vague problem. True or false? _____

(Answers to review questions are on page 240.)

OVERCOMING OBSTACLES TO PROBLEM SOLVING

Consider the following problem-solving test (Duncker, 1945): You are presented with a set of tacks, candles, and matches in small boxes, and told your goal is to place three candles at eye level on a nearby door, so that wax will not drip on the floor as the candles burn (see Figure 7-4). How would you approach this challenge?

If you have difficulty solving the problem, you are not alone: Most people are unable to solve it when it is presented in the manner illustrated in the figure, in which the objects are located *inside* the boxes. On the other hand, if the objects were presented *beside* the boxes, just resting on the table, chances are you would solve the problem much more readily—which, in case you are wondering, requires tacking up the boxes and then placing the candles on top of them (see Figure 7-5).

The difficulty you probably had in solving the problem stems from its presentation and relates to the fact that you were misled at the initial preparation stage. In fact, significant obstacles to problem solving exist at each of the three major stages. Although cognitive approaches to problem solving suggest that thinking proceeds along fairly rational, logical lines as a person confronts a problem and considers various solutions, there are actually a number of factors acting to hinder the development of creative, appropriate, and accurate solutions.

FIGURE 7-4

The problem here is to place three candles at eye level on a nearby door so that the wax will not drip on the floor as the candles burn—using only materials in the figure (tacks, candles, and matches in boxes). For a solution, turn to page 240, Figure 7-5.

Given jars with these capacities (in quarts)			Obtain
1.	21	127	3	100
2.	14	163	25	99
3.	18	43	10	5
4.	9	42	6	21
5.	20	59	4	31
6.	28	76	3	25

Try this classic demonstration, which illustrates the importance of mental set in problem solving. The object is to use the jars in each row to measure out the designated amount of liquid. After you figure out the solution for the first five rows, you'll probably have trouble with the sixth row—even though the solution is actually easier. In fact, if you had tried to solve the problem in the sixth row first, you probably would have had no difficulty at all.

PREPARATION HINDRANCES: Jumping to Conclusions

The reason that most people experience difficulty with the candle problem rests on a phenomenon known as **functional fixedness**, the tendency to think of an object only in terms of its typical use. Functional fixedness occurs because the objects are first presented inside the boxes which are then seen simply as containers for the objects they hold rather than as a potential part of the solution.

Functional fixedness is an example of a broader phenomenon known as **mental set**, the tendency for old patterns of problem solving to persist. This phenomenon was demonstrated in a classic experiment carried out by Abraham Luchins (1946). As you can see in Figure 7-6, the object of the task is to use the jars in each row to measure out the designated amount of liquid. (Try it yourself to get a sense of the importance of mental set before moving on.)

If you have tried the problem, you know that the first five parts are all solved in the same way: Fill the largest jar (B) and from it fill the middle-size jar (A) once and the smallest jar (C) two times. What is left in B is the designated amount. (Stated as a formula, it is B − A − 2C.) The demonstration of mental set comes with the sixth part of the problem, a point at which you probably encountered some difficulty. If you are like most people, you tried the formula and were perplexed when it failed. Chances are, in fact, that you missed the simple (but different) solution to the problem, which simply involves subtracting C from A. Interestingly, those people who were given problem six *first* had no difficulty with it at all.

Mental set can be perceptual in nature: It can prevent you from seeing your way beyond the apparent constraints of a problem. For example, in the following grid, try to draw four straight lines so that they pass through all nine dots—without lifting your pencil from the page.

Functional fixedness: The tendency to think of an object in terms of its most typical use

Mental set: The tendency for old patterns of problem solving to persist

. . .

. . .

. . .

240

FIGURE 7-5

A solution to the problem posed in Figure 7-4 involves tacking the boxes to the wall and placing the candles on the boxes.

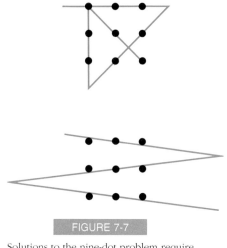

FIGURE 7-7

Solutions to the nine-dot problem require the use of lines drawn beyond the boundaries of the figure—something that our mental set may prevent us from easily seeing.

If you had difficulty with the problem, it was probably because you felt compelled to keep your lines within the grid. If you had gone outside the boundaries, however, you would have succeeded with solutions such as those shown in Figure 7-7.

PRODUCTION HINDRANCES: Biases in Algorithms and Heuristics

Suppose you encounter a person named Tom who is highly intelligent, neat, and orderly but lacks true creativity. His writing is rather dull, although it is occasionally enlivened by corny puns and flashes of sci-fi imagination. Being rather self-centered, he does not have much feeling and is not sympathetic to others, but he does have a strong moral sense.

If you were asked whether he is a computer science major or a humanities major, what would you guess? To answer such a question, the first thing you would probably do is to employ the heuristic of representativeness and determine how well the person fits your mental image of "computer science major" or "humanities major." If you are like most people, you'll probably opt for computer science major.

However, what if you were to learn that Tom is a member of a class of 100 students, of whom 80 are humanities majors and 20 are computer science majors? Has your guess changed on the basis of this new information?

Your answer is most likely "no." But if you were to follow the laws of logic and probability more precisely, your answer *should* have changed, despite the representativeness heuristic: chances are that any one person from the class would most likely belong to the group of 80 who are humanities majors, regardless of any personality characteristics that that person may display (Kahneman & Tversky, 1973).

ANSWERS (REVIEW I):
1. a-2, b-1, c-3 **2.** a **3.** Heuristics, algorithms **4.** Representativeness **5.** d **6.** Insight **7.** False; when the solution criteria are vague, our ideas are sometimes inaccurate

Although algorithms and heuristics most frequently help us to solve problems, their use may sometimes backfire. In one of the major obstacles to problem solving, we may apply algorithms and heuristics to situations in which they are not relevant, thereby coming up with incorrect solutions or applying them erroneously. Consider the following information:

> There are two programs in a high school. Boys are a majority (65 percent) in program A and a minority (45 percent) in program B. There are an equal number of classes in each of the two programs. You enter a class at random and observe that 55 percent of the students are boys. What is your best guess: Does the class belong to program A or to program B? (Kahneman & Tversky, 1972, p. 433).

Most people rely on the heuristic of representativeness to come up with the answer that the class belongs to program A—a solution that is incorrect. They assume that just because there are more boys in the class, and there are more boys than girls in program A, this particular class is more likely to represent program A.

However, there are several considerations that lead to a different—and more accurate—conclusion. First, recall that there are equal numbers of classes in the two programs, and therefore any class that one enters is equally likely to be in either program. Moreover, the specific percentage of boys found in the class (55 percent) is halfway between the percentage of boys in program A (65 percent) and the percentage of boys in program B (45 percent). In fact, the most reasonable answer is that it is no more likely for the class to be in either program A or B. In this case, the representativeness heuristic leads people astray.

The availability heuristic, in which judgments of the probability of an event are based on how easily the event can be recalled, is also a potential source of error in problem solving. Suppose you were asked to pick up a dictionary and randomly choose a word with at least three letters. After you have chosen a word, would you think it more likely that the first letter or the third letter of the word would be an "r"?

Most people conclude that the first letter would more likely be an "r," which is erroneous. (The letter "r" actually occurs more frequently as the third letter than the first in the English language.) The reason for the mistaken judgment? It is considerably easier to retrieve words from memory that start with a given letter (run, rats, root) than it is to retrieve words on the basis of their third letter (bar, tart, purse).

As you see, the same heuristics that assist in problem solving can also be misapplied and act as hindrances in finding the correct solution to problems. But it is not only at the production stage that heuristics can hinder problem solving; even during the final evaluation stage, the misuse of heuristics can lead to confusion.

JUDGMENT HINDRANCES:
Obstacles to Accurate Evaluation of Solutions

When the nuclear power plant at Three Mile Island in Pennsylvania suffered its initial malfunction in 1979—a disaster that almost led to a nuclear meltdown—the plant operators were faced immediately with solving a problem of the most serious kind. Several monitors indicated contradictory informa-

Confirmation bias: A bias in problem solving favoring an initial hypothesis and disregarding contradictory information suggesting alternative solutions

Creativity: The combining of responses or ideas in novel ways

tion about the source of the problem: One suggested that the pressure was too high, leading to the danger of an explosion; others indicated that the pressure was too low, which could lead to a meltdown. Although the pressure was in fact too low, the supervisors on duty relied on the one monitor—which was faulty—that suggested the pressure was too high. Once they had made their decision and acted upon it, they ignored the contradictory evidence from the other monitors (Wickens, 1984).

One reason for the operators' mistake is the **confirmation bias**, in which initial hypotheses are favored and contradictory information supporting alternative hypotheses or solutions is ignored. Even when we find evidence that contradicts a solution we have chosen, then, we are apt to stick with our original hypothesis.

There are several reasons for the confirmation bias. One is that it takes cognitive effort to rethink a problem that appears to be already solved, so we are apt to stick with our first solution. Another is that evidence contradicting an initial solution may present something of a threat to our self-esteem, leading us to hold to the solutions that we have come up with first (Rasmussen, 1981; Fischoff, 1977).

CREATIVITY

Despite obstacles to problem solving, people are very adept at coming up with creative solutions to problems. In fact, one of the enduring questions that cognitive psychologists have tried to answer is what factors underlie **creativity**, which is usually defined as the combining of responses or ideas in novel ways (Mumford & Gustafson, 1988).

Although being able to identify the stages of problem solving helps us to understand how people approach and solve problems, it does little to explain why some people come up with better solutions than others. Solutions to even the simplest of problems often show wide discrepancies. Consider, for example, how you might respond to the question "How many uses can you think of for a newspaper?" Compare your own solution with this one proposed by a 10-year-old boy:

> You can read it, write on it, lay it down and paint a picture on it. . . . You could put it in your door for decoration, put it in the garbage can, put it on a chair if the chair is messy. If you have a puppy, you put newspaper in its box or put it in your backyard for the dog to play with. When you build something and you don't want anyone to see it, put newspaper around it. Put newspaper on the floor if you have no mattress, use it to pick up something hot, use it to stop bleeding, or to catch the drips from drying clothes. You can use a newspaper for curtains, put it in your shoe to cover what is hurting your foot, make a kite out of it, shade a light that is too bright. You can wrap fish in it, wipe windows, or wrap money in it. . . . You put washed shoes in newspaper, wipe eyeglasses with it, put it under a dripping sink, put a plant on it, make a paper bowl out of it, use it for a hat if it is raining, tie it on your feet for slippers. You can put it on the sand if you had no towel, use it for bases in baseball, make paper airplanes with it, use it as a dustpan when you sweep, ball it up for the cat to play with, wrap your hands in it if it is cold (Ward, Kogan & Pankove, 1972).

It is obvious that this list shows extraordinary creativity. Unfortunately, it has proved to be considerably easier to identify *examples* of creativity than to identify its causes. There are several factors, however, that seem to be associated with creativity (Richards et al., 1988).

One factor closely related to creativity is divergent thinking. **Divergent thinking** refers to the ability to generate unusual, but still appropriate, responses to problems or questions. This type of thinking contrasts with **convergent thinking**, which produces responses that are based primarily on knowledge and logic. For instance, convergent thinking answers "You read it" to the query "What do you do with a newspaper?" In contrast, "You use it as a dustpan" is a more divergent—and creative—response.

Another ingredient of creativity is **cognitive complexity**, the use of and preference for elaborate, intricate, and complex stimuli and thinking patterns. Similarly, creative people often have a wider range of interests and are more independent and more interested in philosophical or abstract problems than are less creative individuals (Barron, 1969).

Certain transitory factors also seem to be able to enhance creativity, at least temporarily. Humor, for instance, is useful. In a recent experiment, psychologist Alice Isen and colleagues found that people who had just watched a humorous film of television "bloopers" were more likely to come to a creative (and appropriate) solution to the candle problem discussed earlier (Figures 7-4 and 7-5) than were people who had not viewed the film. Also, people who watched the comedy sequence seemed to think more generally, perceiving relationships among different sorts of information. Being in a good mood, then, may help us to be more creative and to think more broadly (Isen, Daubman, & Nowicki, 1987).

One factor that is *not* closely related to creativity is intelligence. In fact, because most tests of intelligence focus on convergent thinking skills—their problems are well defined and have only one acceptable answer—creative people who are divergent thinkers may find themselves at a disadvantage. This may explain why researchers consistently find that creativity is only slightly related to intelligence or school grades, particularly when intelligence is measured using typical intelligence tests (Barron & Harrington, 1981; Sternberg, 1986). For more on creativity, see the Cutting Edge box.

Divergent thinking: The ability to generate unusual, but appropriate, responses to problems or questions

Convergent thinking: A type of thinking which produces responses based on knowledge and logic

Cognitive complexity: The use of and preference for elaborate, intricate, and complex stimuli and thinking patterns

---

THE CUTTING EDGE

CREATING AN INDEX OF CREATIVITY

The most obvious kinds of creativity—writing a poem, drawing a picture—are easy enough to identify. But isn't there potentially an equal degree of creativity to be found in the work of a grade-school teacher tutoring a difficult student, or in the efforts of a business executive to put together a complex deal?

To understand the role of creativity in people's everyday lives, psychologists Ruth Richards, Dennis Kinney, and colleagues (1988) developed a measurement system that evaluates two aspects of creativity. One index assesses peak creativity,

the most innovative behavior that is shown in a person's life and that is considered to reflect an individual's innate creative capacity. The second index looks at creativity over time, assessing how much motivation or inclination a person displays toward creativity.

The results—based on comprehensive, structured interviews of 461

men and women—show that people can be placed in one of six categories, ranging from "exceptional creativity" to "no significant creativity" (see Table 7-1). The "exceptionally creative" person values creativity so much that he or she may make important sacrifices in other aspects of life—such as spending so much time on perfecting inventions that personal relationships suffer. At the other end of the spectrum, the person with "no significant creativity" leads a routine, passive existence, watching television or cleaning the house.

244

People who fall in the middle of the creativity scale may display creativity on occasion, such as an amateur chef who comes up with a new recipe every once in a while, or a person whose otherwise mundane life is shaken up by a decision to take a risky trip to an exotic part of the world.

According to the research of Richards and Kinney, less than 1 percent of all men and women show "exceptional" creativity, and only about 10 percent fall into the "high creativity" category. Most people—60 percent—are considered as having either "moderate" or "some" creativity.

Other ongoing research is examining the link between creativity and mental disorders. For example, the rapid mood swings associated with one specific disorder, manic depression (which we discuss in Chapter 16), seem to facilitate creativity (Richards et al., 1988; Andreasen, 1987).

It is still too early to know how people are able to reach their optimal level of creativity. It is clear, though, that there are many paths to a creative life.

TABLE 7-1

The Creative Life: A Scale

Level of Involvement in Creativity	Example
1. **Exceptional involvement**: a pervasive preoccupation with innovative activity, often to the exclusion of other aspects of life	An amateur botanist who strictly limits hours at his regular job and often spends "twenty-hour days" to complete botanical experiments
2. **High involvement**: a marked emphasis on creative efforts	A used-equipment dealer who collects and restores unusual gadgets and invents tools
3. **Moderate involvement**: making innovations in a common activity	A chef who devised menus for the restaurants he worked at and later managed his own restaurant
4. **Some involvement**: occasional innovation, not highly unusual	A sports enthusiast who took a journalism course and writes on sporting events for a community newspaper
5. **Minor involvement**: routine living broken by rare innovation	A secretary who sometimes edited books on the side
6. **No significant involvement**: a life given over to prescribed routines	A bricklayer for twenty years who inherited a trust fund and retired, spending most of his time watching television

Source: Adapted from Richards et al. (1988).

LEARNING TO THINK CRITICALLY:
Teaching People Problem-solving Skills

Can people be taught to be better problem solvers? A growing body of evidence supports the notion that people can in fact learn to perform better in problem-solving situations, including school-related tasks (Adams, 1989).

In one program, for example, researchers have developed a technique called Pair Problem Solving, in which two students work together on specially designed problems (Lochhead, 1985). The partners alternate in taking one of two roles: One partner reads a description of the problem and tries to reach a solution by thinking it through out loud, while the other listens. The listener is not passive, however; he or she continually checks for the partner's accuracy and constantly urges the problem solver to think aloud. Thinking aloud is a critical part of the program, because it allows the listener to examine any erroneous assumptions and check the accuracy of the speaker; it also makes speakers themselves aware of fuzziness in their logic.

To facilitate the Pair Problem Solving process, students are sometimes given samples of problems, with illustrations of how experienced problem solvers attack and solve them (see Figure 7-8). By demonstrating how problems must be broken down into small steps, as well as how important initial assumptions are, the sample problems play an important role in the development of the participants' thinking processes.

Does the program work? Accumulating evidence seems to indicate that it does (Konnold, 1985; Perkins, Lochhead & Bishop, 1987; Clement, in press). Moreover, research from other training programs supports the view

FIGURE 7-8

A problem used in teaching thinking skills, with an illustration of the way in which experienced problem-solvers work it out. (Lochhead, 1985.)

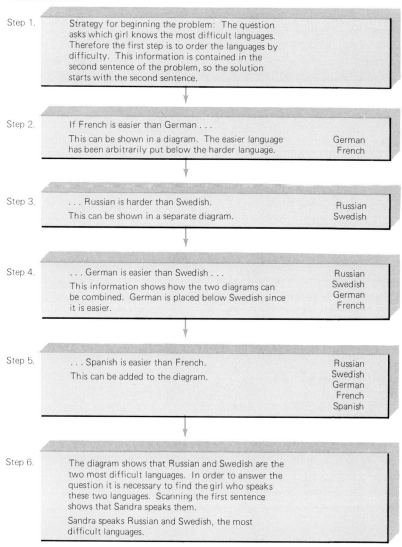

Original Problem

Cathy knows French and German, Sandra knows Swedish and Russian, Cindy knows Spanish and French, Paula knows German and Swedish. If French is easier than German, Russian is harder than Swedish, German is easier than Swedish, and Spanish is easier than French, which girl knows the most difficult languages?

Problem Solution

Step 1. Strategy for beginning the problem: The question asks which girl knows the most difficult languages. Therefore the first step is to order the languages by difficulty. This information is contained in the second sentence of the problem, so the solution starts with the second sentence.

Step 2. If French is easier than German . . .
This can be shown in a diagram. The easier language has been arbitrarily put below the harder language.

German
French

Step 3. . . . Russian is harder than Swedish.
This can be shown in a separate diagram.

Russian
Swedish

Step 4. . . . German is easier than Swedish . . .
This information shows how the two diagrams can be combined. German is placed below Swedish since it is easier.

Russian
Swedish
German
French

Step 5. . . . Spanish is easier than French.
This can be added to the diagram.

Russian
Swedish
German
French
Spanish

Step 6. The diagram shows that Russian and Swedish are the two most difficult languages. In order to answer the question it is necessary to find the girl who speaks these two languages. Scanning the first sentence shows that Sandra speaks them.

Sandra speaks Russian and Swedish, the most difficult languages.

that abstract rules of logic and reasoning may be taught, and that such training improves the way in which people are able to reason about the underlying causes of everyday life events (Nisbett et al., 1987). Ultimately, cognitive psychologists may routinely teach students not only to increase the skill with which they are able to solve problems, but to think more critically as well.

TEACHING COMPUTERS TO THINK: Artificial Intelligence

Therapist: What seems to be your problem?

Patient: My mother drinks too much.

Therapist: Who else in your family drinks too much?

A reasonable exchange between therapist and patient? Actually, the therapist is a computer program named "Eliza," responding to a "patient" who has typed his problem into the computer (Weizenbaum, 1966). This interchange represents one of the first efforts in a new area of interest to cognitive psychologists: **artificial intelligence** demonstrated by computers and other sophisticated machines.

The central question being asked by investigators of artificial intelligence is whether a computer is capable of simulating the thinking and problem-solving capabilities of human beings. Will we one day be able to go up to our home computer and ask it what kind of new auto insurance policy to buy? Or get it to tell us what courses we should register for? Or ask it for advice on what type of washing machine to buy or where we might find our house keys?

Such questions are not as farfetched as they sound. Roger Schank and his colleagues at Yale University are working on computers that are capable of understanding, and ultimately thinking in and responding to, the English language—which is proving to be no easy task (Schank, 1985). Consider the following sentence:

> John sold Mary a book for two dollars.

Although seemingly simple, to a computer it represents some serious problems. The computer has to know that other sentences presented to it mean the same thing, such as: "John gave Mary a book and she gave him two dollars," "Mary paid John two dollars and received a book," "The book that Mary bought from John cost two dollars." Moreover, the computer needs to know the implications of the act: Mary now has the book; she didn't have it before; John has two dollars more than when he began the transaction. Although these are not necessarily logical implications, most human listeners would assume them to be true—so the computer must make the assumptions as well (Kendig, 1983).

The complexities of artificial intelligence are such that truly intelligent machines have not yet been developed, although computers are becoming increasingly sophisticated in mimicking human thinking processes (Dehn & Schank, 1982). Moreover, by developing computers that are fashioned after human thinking processes, scientists are moving closer to the day when machines can respond to queries—and even more important—learn new information, thereby growing "smarter" (Epp, Kalin & Miller, 1988; Waldrop, 1988).

Artificial intelligence: Intelligence demonstrated by computers and other sophisticated machines

Perhaps the reality is that someday a computer *will* be able to tell you where to look for your missing house keys. For now, though, it is humbling to consider what happened when one computer, programmed to translate from English to Russian and then back to English, worked on the biblical phrase "The spirit is willing, but the flesh is weak." After a series of translations, the final version read, "The wine was agreeable, but the meat was spoiled."

THE INFORMED CONSUMER OF PSYCHOLOGY: Thinking Critically and Creatively

On the basis of the research we have discussed on problem solving, thinking, and creativity, there are several strategies that can help you think more critically and evaluate problems more creatively—whether they be the challenges of everyday life or more academically oriented problems such as finding the correct solution to a question on a test (Reese et al., 1976; Baron & Sternberg, 1987). Suggestions for increasing critical thinking and creativity include:

▶ Redefine problems. The boundaries and assumptions you hold can be modified; the problem can be rephrased at a more abstract or more concrete level, depending on how it is initially presented; or it can be divided into separate parts (Rice, 1984).

▶ Adopt a critical perspective. Rather than passively accepting assumptions or arguments, critically evaluate material by considering its implications and thinking about possible exceptions and contradictions.

▶ Use analogies. Analogies not only help us uncover new understanding, they provide alternative frameworks for interpreting facts. One particularly effective means of coming up with analogies is to look for them in the animal kingdom when the problem concerns people, and in physics or chemistry when the problem concerns inanimate objects.

▶ Think divergently. Instead of thinking in terms of the most logical or most common use for an object, think of how it might be of help if you were forbidden to use it in its usual way.

▶ Take the perspective of another person, either one who is involved in the situation or who is a disinterested bystander. In doing so, you may get a fresh view on the situation.

▶ Use heuristics. As mentioned earlier, heuristics are rules of thumb that can help bring about a solution to a problem. If the nature of the problem is such that it has a single, correct answer, and a heuristic is available—or can be constructed—using the heuristic frequently helps to develop a solution more rapidly and effectively.

▶ Experiment with different solutions. Don't be afraid to use different routes to solutions to problems (verbal, mathematical, graphic, even acting out a situation). Try coming up with every conceivable idea you can, no matter how wild or bizarre it may seem at first. After you have come up with a list of solutions, you can go back over each and try to think of ways of making what at first appeared impractical seem more feasible.

Recap

◀ Among the obstacles to successful problem solving are mental set and functional fixedness, the faulty application of algorithms and heuristics, and the confirmation bias.

◀ Creativity is related to divergent thinking and cognitive complexity.

◀ Critical thinking skills can be taught.

◀ Artificial intelligence is becoming increasingly sophisticated.

◀ Some methods of enhancing critical thinking and solving problems creatively include redefining a problem, using analogies, using divergent thinking, taking another perspective, using heuristics, and experimenting with different solutions.

Review

1. Using a drinking glass to form the towers of a sand castle is an example of overcoming _____ _____ .

2. While often useful, algorithms and heuristics can lead us to biased and incorrect solutions. True or false? _____

3. "Charlie seems to rely almost solely on his past experience and logic to solve problems. Our psychology professor labeled that _____ thinking, as opposed to more creative thinking, which she called _____ thinking."

4. Intelligence tests are good measures of creative thinking ability. True or false? _____

5. One student thinks aloud while another listens and provides feedback as part of a technique called _____ _____ _____ which has been used to teach better problem solving skills.

6. Computers are easily programmed to make common assumptions that human beings make routinely. True or false? _____

7. People who have been trained to think creatively in a specific area have been found to transfer that ability to other areas. True or false? _____

(Answers to review questions are on page 250.)

COMMUNICATING WITH OTHERS: LANGUAGE

'Twas brillig, and the slithy toves
    Did gyre and gimble in the wabe:
All mimsy were the borogoves,
    And the mome raths outgrabe.

Although few of us have ever come face to face with a tove, we have little difficulty in discerning that in Lewis Carroll's (1872) poem "Jabberwocky," the expression "slithy toves" contains an adjective, "slithy," and the noun it modifies, "toves."

Our ability to make sense out of nonsense, if the nonsense follows typical rules of language, illustrates both the sophistication of human language capabilities and the complexity of the processes that underlie the development and use of language. The way in which people are able to use **language**—the systematic, meaningful arrangement of symbols—clearly represents an important ability, one that is indispensable for communicating with others. But language is not only central to communication, it is closely tied to the very way in which we think about and understand the world, for there is a crucial link between cognition and language. It is not surprising, then, that psychologists have devoted considerable attention to studying the topic of language.

Language: The systematic, meaningful arrangement of symbols

THE LANGUAGE OF LANGUAGE: Grammar

In order to understand how language develops, and its relationship to cognition, we first need to discuss some of the formal elements that constitute language. The basic structure of language rests on grammar. **Grammar** is the framework of rules that determine how our thoughts can be expressed.

Grammar deals with three major components of language: phonology, syntax, and semantics. **Phonology** refers to the smallest unit of sounds, called **phonemes**, that affect the meaning of speech and to the way we use those sounds to produce meaning by placing them into the form of words. For instance, the "a" in "fat" and the "a" in "rake" represent two different phonemes in English.

Although English-speakers use just forty-two basic phonemes to produce words, the basic phonemes of other languages range from as few as fifteen to as many as eighty-five (Akmajian, Demers & Harnish, 1984). The differences in phonemes underlies one reason why people have difficulty in learning other languages: for example, to the Japanese-speaker, whose native language does not have an "r" phoneme, English words such as "roar" present some difficulty.

Syntax refers to the rules that indicate how words and phrases can be combined to form sentences. Every language has intricate rules that guide the order in which words may be strung together to communicate meaning. English-speakers have no difficulty in knowing that "Radio down the turn" is not an appropriate sequence, while "Turn down the radio" is. The importance of appropriate syntax is demonstrated by the changes in meaning that come from the differing order of words in the following three sequences: "John kidnapped the boy," "John, the kidnapped boy," and, "The boy kidnapped John."

The third major component of language is semantics. **Semantics** refers to the rules governing the meaning of words and sentences. Semantic rules allow us to use words to convey the most subtle of nuances. For instance, we are able to make the distinction between "The truck hit Laura" (which we would be likely to say if we had just seen the vehicle hitting Laura) and "Laura was hit by a truck" (which we would probably say if asked why Laura was missing class while she recuperated).

Despite the complexities of language, most of us acquire the basics of grammar without even being aware that we have learned its rules (Rice, 1989). Moreover, even though we might have difficulty explicitly stating the rules of grammar that we employ, our linguistic abilities are so sophisticated that they enable us to utter an infinite number of different statements. We turn now to how such sophisticated abilities are acquired.

DEVELOPING A WAY WITH WORDS: Language Development

To parents, the sounds of their infant babbling and cooing are music to the ears (except, perhaps, at three o'clock in the morning). These sounds also serve an important function: They mark the first step on the road to the development of language.

Children **babble**—making speechlike but meaningless sounds—from around 3 months to a year. While babbling, they may produce, at one time or another, any of the sounds found in all languages, not just the one to which they are exposed. However, babbling increasingly begins to reflect the specific language that is being spoken in the environment, initially in terms of pitch and tone, and eventually in terms of specific sounds (Reich, 1986).

Grammar: The framework of rules that determine how our thoughts can be expressed

Phonology: The study of the sounds we make when we speak and of how we use those sounds to produce meaning by forming them into words
Phonemes (FONE eems): The smallest units of sound used to form words

Syntax: The rules that indicate how words are joined to form sentences

Semantics: The rules governing the meaning of words and sentences

Babble: Speechlike but meaningless sounds

By the time the child is around a year old, sounds that are not in the language disappear. It is then a short step to the production of actual words. In English, these are typically short words that start with a consonant such as "b," "d," "m," "p," or "t"—helping to explain why "mama" and "dada" are so often among the first words to be said. Of course, even before they produce their first words, children are capable of understanding a fair amount of the language they hear. Language comprehension, then, precedes language production.

After the age of 1 year, children begin to learn more complicated forms of language. They produce two-word combinations, which become the building blocks of sentences, and there is an acceleration in the number of different words they are capable of using. For example, by the age of 2 years, the average child has a vocabulary of more than fifty words. Just six months later, the vocabulary has grown to several hundred. At that time, children can produce short sentences, although they use **telegraphic speech**—sentences that literally sound as if they were part of a telegram, in which words not critical to the message are dropped. Rather than saying, "I showed you the book," a child using telegraphic speech might say, "I show book," and "I am drawing a dog" might become "Drawing dog." As the child gets older, of course, the use of telegraphic speech declines and sentences become increasingly complex (see Table 7-2).

By the time children are 3 years old, they learn to make plurals by adding "s" to nouns, and they are able to form the past tense by adding "ed" to verbs. This ability also leads to errors, since children tend to apply rules

Telegraphic speech: Sentences containing only the most essential words

TABLE 7-2

Children's Imitation of Sentences, Showing Decline of Telegraphic Speech

	Eve, 25½ Months	Adam, 28½ Months	Helen, 30 Months	Ian, 31½ Months	Jimmy, 32 Months	June, 35½ Months
I showed you the book.	I show book.	(I show) book.	C	I show you the book.	C	Show you the book.
I am very tall.	(My) tall.	I (very) tall.	I very tall.	I'm very tall.	Very tall.	I very tall.
It goes in a big box.	Big box.	Big box.	In big box.	It goes in the box.	C	C
I am drawing a dog.	Drawing dog.	I draw dog.	I drawing dog.	Dog.	C	C
I will read the book.	Read book.	I will read book.	I read the book.	I read the book.	C	C
I can see a cow.	See cow.	I want see cow.	C	Cow.	C	C
I will not do that again.	Do—again.	I will that again.	I do that.	I again.	C	C

C = correct imitation
Source: Brown & Fraser, 1963.

indiscriminately. This phenomenon is known as **overregularization**, whereby children apply rules even when the application results in an error. Thus, although it is correct to say "he walked" for the past tense of "walk," the "ed" rule doesn't work quite so well when children say "he runned" for the past tense of "run."

Toddlers' acquisition of language is assisted by the nature of language that their parents use with them. When speaking with children, adults use a form of language that is atypical of their everyday speech but promotes language development: They speak more slowly, use a more primitive vocabulary, substitute nouns for pronouns, and in general simplify sentence structure (deVilliers & deVilliers, 1978). Furthermore, parents who speak *with* their children, not *at* them, encourage language development. Listening to children and providing opportunities for them to respond to questions, then, is a better strategy than merely talking to them a lot (Brody, 1987).

Much of children's acquisition of the basic rules of language is complete by the time they are 5. However, a full vocabulary and the ability to comprehend and use subtle grammatical rules are not attained until later. For example, if you showed a 5-year-old boy a blindfolded doll and asked, "Is the doll easy or hard to see?" he would have great difficulty answering the question. In fact, if he were asked to make the doll easier to see, he would probably try to take off the doll's blindfold. On the other hand, 9-year-olds have little difficulty understanding the question, realizing that the doll's blindfold has nothing to do with an observer's ability to see the doll (Chomsky, 1969).

Overregularization: Applying rules of speech in instances in which they are inappropriate

THE ROOTS OF LANGUAGE: Understanding Language Acquisition

While anyone who is around children will notice the enormous strides that are made in language development throughout childhood, the reasons for

As children develop, their language becomes more and more sophisticated. (a) During the earliest period, children babble and begin to make the sounds appropriate to their particular language. (b) Later, they learn to produce specific, meaningful words. (c) By the age of 5, they are able to communicate in a surprisingly sophisticated fashion, even adjusting the complexity of their speech to match the comprehension level of the listener. [(a) Richard Pasley/Stock Boston, (b) Frank Siteman/The Picture Cube, (c) Bob Daemmrich/Stock Boston]

(a)

(b)

(c)

this rapid growth are less obvious. Two major explanations have been put forward: one based on learning theory and the other on innate processes.

The learning-theory approach suggests that language acquisition follows the principles of reinforcement and conditioning we discussed in Chapter 5. For example, a child who utters the word "mama" is hugged and praised by her mother, thereby reinforcing the behavior and making its repetition more likely. This view suggests that children first learn to speak by being rewarded for making sounds that approximate speech. Ultimately, through a process of shaping, language becomes more and more like adult speech (Skinner, 1957).

The learning-theory approach is less successful when it comes to explaining the acquisition of language rules. Children are reinforced not only when they use proper language, but also when they respond incorrectly. For example, parents answer "Why the dog won't eat?" as eagerly as they do the correct "Why won't the dog eat?"; both sentences are understood equally well. Learning-theory views do not seem to provide the full story of language acquisition.

Universal grammar: An underlying structure shared by all languages, the basis of Chomsky's theory that certain language characteristics are based in the brain's structure and are, therefore, common to all people

Language-acquisition device: A neural system of the brain hypothesized to permit understanding of language

An alternative model is provided by Noam Chomsky (1968, 1978), who argues that innate mechanisms play an important role in learning a language. He suggests that humans are born with an innate linguistic capability that emerges primarily as a function of maturation. According to his analysis, all the world's languages share a similar underlying structure—what he calls a **universal grammar**—which is based on the structure and functions of the human brain. The brain has a neural system, the **language-acquisition device**, which not only permits the understanding of the structure of a language but also provides people with strategies and techniques for learning the unique characteristics of a native language. According to this view, then, language is a uniquely human phenomenon brought about by the presence of the language-acquisition device.

Chomsky's view, as you might suspect, is not without its critics, particularly among learning theorists, who contend that the fact that animals can seemingly be taught the fundamentals of human language (see the Psychology at Work box) argues against the innate view. The issue of how humans acquire language thus remains hotly contested (Rice, 1989).

PSYCHOLOGY AT WORK

EXPLORING HUMAN LANGUAGE—BY COMMUNICATING WITH ANIMALS

Deaf, mute, and retarded since birth, 23-year-old Sandra was written off by her doctors as a hopeless case. But in the past two years the once hostile, violent young woman has been transformed. Today, she can request her favorite foods and communicate with her teachers—thanks to a computer-based language that was originally developed for the study of chimpanzees. "Sandra's learned to express herself," says Steve Watson, director of the Developmental Learning Center at Atlanta's Georgia Regional Hospital, where she lives.

"That's a way of being set free" (Keerdoja, 1985, p. 66).

The language that liberated Sandra is **Yerkish,** initially developed at the Yerkes Primate Center in Atlanta to study the communicative abilities of chimpanzees. It consists of some 225 geometric symbols, each representing a common English word, that can be pressed on a computer keyboard to make sentences (Savage-Rumbaugh, Rumbaugh & Boysen, 1980).

Yerkish was developed to investigate an enduring issue that has long puzzled psychologists: whether language is uniquely human or whether lower animals are able to acquire it as well. It is clear that many animals communicate with one another in some rudimentary forms, such as fiddler crabs that wave their claws to signal, bees whose dance indicates the direction in which food will be found, or certain birds that say "zick, zick" during courtship and "kia" when they are about to fly away. But researchers have yet to demonstrate conclusively that these animals use true language, which is characterized in part by the ability to produce and communicate new and unique meanings following a formal grammar.

Psychologists have, however, been able to teach chimps to communicate at surprisingly high levels. For instance, Kanzi, a 4-year-old pygmy chimpanzee, has Yerkish linguistic skills that are close to those of a 1- or 2-year-old human being (Keerdoja, 1985). Koko, a lowland gorilla, developed a large vocabulary of sign language (Patterson, 1978); another chimp, Washoe, was taught American Sign Language (originally developed for the deaf) and has been able to join signs together to form new meanings. For example, after learning the sign "more" in reference to tickling (which she loved), she used the sign later to request more food and more brushing (Klima & Bellugi, 1973). Chimps can combine the signs into "sentences," use them to express humor or be deceptive, and even form new words by combining different signs (Ristau & Robbins, 1982). David Premack, who taught a chimp named Sarah to manipulate plastic symbols that represented words and relations, contends that there are several fundamental similarities between children's and chimps' language acquisition, in terms of both grammar and the function of particular words (Premack, 1985).

Despite the skills displayed by primates, the language that they use still lacks a grammar and other sufficiently complex and novel constructions to approach human capabilities (Terrace, 1985). In fact, critics contend that the chimps are displaying a skill no different from that of a dog which learns to lie down on command in order to get a reward.

Most evidence supports the contention that humans are better equipped than animals to produce and organize language in the form of meaningful sentences. But the question of whether animals are capable of being taught to communicate in a way that more closely resembles human language remains a controversial one (Terrace, Pettitto, Sanders & Bever, 1981; Herman & Forestell, 1985). In the meantime, ongoing research promises to produce even more sophisticated techniques for improving the communication abilities of people such as Sandra.

Yerkish: A language system, taught to chimpanzees, that consists of about 225 geometric symbols representing English words

FIGURE 7-9

Kanzi's ability to communicate in Yerkish has implications for the treatment of humans with language disabilities. (Elizabeth Rubert/Yerkes Primate Research Center.)

DOES LANGUAGE DETERMINE THOUGHT— OR DOES THOUGHT DETERMINE LANGUAGE?

When an Eskimo woman peers outside her igloo and sees that it is snowing, she doesn't simply announce, "It's snowing." For Eskimos have at their disposal more than twenty individual words to describe different sorts of snow. This linguistic prowess suggests an important question: Do Eskimos *think* about snow differently than do English-speakers?

LEARNING AND THINKING

Linguistic-relativity hypothesis: The theory claiming that language shapes and may even determine the way people perceive and understand the world

The answer to that question is controversial. According to the **linguistic-relativity hypothesis**, language shapes and, in fact, may determine the way people of a particular culture perceive and understand the world (Whorf, 1956). According to this view, Eskimos think about snow in a way that is qualitatively different from the way English-speakers think about it, since the range of linguistic categories provided by the Eskimo language permits finer discriminations than the more limited English language.

Let us consider another possibility, however. Suppose that, instead of language being the *cause* of certain ways of thinking about the world, language is a *result* of thinking about and experiencing relevant stimuli in the environment. In this view, thought *produces* language. The only reason Eskimos have more words for "snow" than we do is that snow is considerably more relevant to them than it is to people in most other cultures. According to this point of view, if we were to move to the Arctic Circle (or become ski bums), we would be perfectly capable of differentiating various types of snow. Our language usage might not be particularly eloquent (we might say "deep, crunchy, hard-packing snow that is going to be on the ground all winter"), but we would have no trouble perceiving and thinking about the differences in snow.

To try to tease out which of the two descriptions (language produces thought versus thought produces language) provides the more accurate account, investigators have carried out a significant amount of research. In one study, Eleanor Rosch (1972) compared perception of colors in Americans and in members of the Dani tribe of New Guinea. The Dani have only two names for color: one for cold, dark colors and one for warm, lighter colors. In English, of course, there are hundreds of color names, but eleven of them represent major color categories (red, yellow, green, blue, black, gray, white, purple, orange, pink, and brown). Rosch argued that if the linguistic relativity hypothesis were accurate, English speakers should be more efficient at recognizing and distinguishing colors that represent the major categories than colors that were not members of major categories. In contrast, she reasoned that the Dani tribe members should show no difference in recognition between colors that were members of major or nonmajor categories, since there were no words in their vocabulary to describe any of them.

However, the results were not supportive of this hypothesis. There was no difference in the way that either English-speakers or Dani perceived the colors; both perceived colors in the major categories more efficiently than colors in the nonmajor categories. According to these results, then, language differences do not produce effects on perception.

Subsequent research is congruent with Rosch's study and by and large has been unsupportive of the linguistic relativity hypothesis (Brown, 1986). It seems most appropriate to conclude that, in general, cognition influences language and not the other way around. On the other hand, language *does* affect thinking and cognition in some ways. For instance, the manner in which information is stored in memory—and how well such information can subsequently be retrieved—is related to language (Cairns & Cairns, 1976). Likewise, the linguistic categories available in a given language affect the way that concepts (which we consider next) are formed. Finally, our impressions and memory of others' personality and behavior are affected by the linguistic categories provided us by the language we speak (Hoffman, Lau & Johnson, 1986). Although language does not determine thought, then, it certainly influences it.

If someone asked you what was in your kitchen cabinet, you might answer with a detailed list of every item ("a jar of Skippy peanut butter," "three chipped dinner plates," and so forth). More likely, though, you would respond with some broader categories, such as "food" and "dishes."

The categorization that you use reflects the operation of concepts. **Concepts** are categorizations of objects, events, or people that share common properties. Through the use of concepts, we are able to distill the complexities of the world into more simplified—and therefore more easily usable—cognitive categories.

When cognitive psychologists first studied concepts, they focused on "artificial concepts"—ones that are clearly defined by a set of properties or features which nonexamples of the category do not have. For example, an equilateral triangle is a shape that has three sides of equal length. If an object has these characteristics, it is an equilateral triangle; and if it does not have these characteristics, it is not an equilateral triangle.

Other concepts—the ones that have the most relevance to our everyday lives—are much fuzzier and more difficult to define. For example, how would you formally define "table" or "bird"? Both are examples of **natural concepts**—ones that represent familiar objects, are simple, and share a set of characteristic features. Unlike "artificial concepts," natural concepts do not have unvarying, universal defining features. Instead, they are defined by a set of general, relatively loose characteristic features and are exemplified by prototypes. **Prototypes** are typical, highly representative examples of a concept. For instance, a prototype of the concept "bird" is a robin; a prototype of "table" is a coffee table. Relatively high agreement exists among people as to which examples of a natural concept are prototypes and which examples fit less well with the concept. Cars and trucks, for instance, are viewed by most people as good examples of vehicles, whereas elevators and wheelbarrows are not, thereby making cars and trucks prototypes of the natural concept of vehicle.

Prototypes lead to faster and easier learning of the underlying concept than do examples that are less central to the concept (Rosch, 1973). Natural concepts also allow us to classify newly encountered objects into a form that is understandable in terms of our past experience. For example, we are able to tell that a small, four-legged creature with a wagging tail is probably a dog—even if we have never encountered that specific animal before. Ultimately, concepts influence behavior; we would assume, for instance, that it would be appropriate to pet the animal, given its canine categorization.

The importance of concepts lies in their ability to allow us to think about and deal with a complex, intricate world in a more manageable and capable manner (Markham & Callahan, 1984). For example, the judgments we make about the causes behind others' actions are based on the way we classify their behavior. Similarly, the way in which a physician categorizes our medical symptoms or a psychologist classifies a mental disorder into a diagnosis is based in part on the conceptual framework that is brought to bear on the problem. Understanding how people classify their knowledge of the world thus represents an important undertaking for cognitive psychologists.

Concept: A categorization of objects, events, or people that share common properties

Natural concepts: Simple concepts that represent familiar objects and share a set of characteristic features

Prototypes: Typical, highly representative examples of a concept

Recap

◀ Language is characterized by grammar, a framework of rules that determine how our thoughts can be expressed.

◀ Language acquisition proceeds rapidly from birth and is largely complete by the age of 5, although there are subsequent increases in vocabulary and sophistication.

◀ The learning-theory view suggests that language is learned through the principles of reinforcement and conditioning. In contrast, Chomsky's view suggests that language capabilities are innate, a result of the existence of a language-acquisition device in the brain.

◀ The question of whether language determines thought (the linguistic-relativity hypothesis) or thought determines language remains controversial.

◀ Concepts are categorizations of objects, events, or people that share common properties. Natural concepts, consisting of prototypes, represent familiar objects, are simple, and share a set of characteristic features.

Review

1. A change in the statement "Throw down the stairs the keys" to "Throw the keys down the stairs" exemplifies increasing sophistication in

   a. phonology.
   b. semantics.
   c. linguistic meaning.
   d. syntax.

2. Babbling plays no functional role in language acquisition. True or false? _____

3. The child who wants to play with a toy might say "I get toy," which is an example of _____ _____ .

4. "I getted toy" is an example of _____ .

5. Chomsky suggests that acquisition of language is guided by an innate _____ - _____ device in the brain.

6. Learning theorists emphasize the role of the social environment in language acquisition, whereas linguists such as Chomsky accentuate the role of innate structures. True or false? _____

7. Rosch's research supports the view that
   a. color words represent an inappropriate research variable.
   b. language and thought are not causally related.
   c. language produces thought.
   d. thought produces language.

8. An apple is a _____ of the _____ _____ of fruit.

(Answers to review questions are on page 258.)

◀ LOOKING BACK

1. Cognitive psychologists study cognition, which encompasses the higher mental processes. These processes include the way people know and understand the world, process information, make judgments and decisions, and describe their knowledge and understanding to others.

2. Problem solving typically follows three major steps: preparation, production of solutions, and evaluation of solutions that have been generated. Preparation begins when people try to understand the problem. Some problems are well defined, with clear solution requirements; other problems are ill defined, with ambiguities in both the information required for a solution and the solution itself.

3. In arrangement problems, a group of elements must be rearranged or recombined in a way that will satisfy a certain criterion. In problems of inducing structure, a person must identify the relationships among the elements presented and construct a new relationship among them. Finally, transformation problems consist of an initial state, a goal state, and a series of methods for changing the initial state into the goal state.

4. A crucial aspect of the preparation stage is the representation and organization of the problem. Sometimes restructuring a problem from a verbal form to a pictorial or mathematical form can help point the way to the solution.

5. In the production stage, people try to generate solutions. The solutions to some problems may already be in long-term memory and can be directly retrieved. In addition, some problems may be solved through simple trial-and-error. More complex problems, however, require the use of algorithms (rules which, if followed, guarantee a solution) and heuristics (rules of thumb that may lead to a solution but are not guaranteed to do so).

6. There are several kinds of heuristics. In the representativeness heuristic, people decide whether a given example is a member of a particular category by evaluating how representative of that category the example is. The availability heuristic consists of judging the probability of an event by how easily the event can be recalled from memory. In a means-ends analysis, a person will repeatedly test for differences between the desired outcome and what currently exists, trying each time to come closer to the goal. Another heuristic is to divide a problem into intermediate steps or subgoals and solve each of those steps.

7. One approach to problem solving is exemplified by

Kohler's research with chimps, in which the elements of the situation had to be manipulated in a novel fashion in order for the chimps to solve the problem. Kohler called the cognitive processes underlying the chimps' behavior insight, a sudden awareness of the relationships among elements that had previously seemed independent.

8. Several factors hinder effective problem solving. Functional fixedness (the tendency to think of an object only in terms of its most typical use), is an example of a broader phenomenon known as mental set. Mental set is the tendency for old patterns of problem solving to persist. The inappropriate use of algorithms and heuristics can also act as an obstacle to the production of solutions to problems. Finally, the confirmation bias, in which initial hypotheses are favored, can hinder the accurate evaluation of solutions to problems.

9. Creativity is the combining of responses or ideas in novel ways. Divergent thinking is the ability to respond with unusual, but still appropriate, responses to problems or questions and is associated with creativity. Cognitive complexity, the use of and preference for elaborate, intricate, and complex stimuli and thinking patterns, is also related to creativity.

10. A growing body of evidence supports the idea that people can learn to perform better in problem-solving situations. By learning abstract rules of logic and reasoning, people are able to think critically about the underlying causes of everyday events.

11. Artificial intelligence is intelligence demonstrated by computers and other machines. By devising computer programs fashioned after human thinking processes, scientists are moving closer to developing machines that respond to queries and that learn new information.

12. Suggestions for solving problems creatively include redefining the problem, using analogies, thinking divergently, taking the perspective of another person, using heuristics, and experimenting with different solutions.

13. Language is the systematic, meaningful arrangement of symbols. All languages have a grammar—a framework of rules that determine how our thoughts can be expressed—which encompasses the three major components of language: phonology, syntax, and semantics. Phonology refers to the sounds (called phonemes) we make when we speak and the use of those sounds to produce meaning; syntax refers to the rules that indicate how words are joined together to form sentences; and semantics refers to the rules governing the meaning of words and sentences of language.

14. Language production, preceded by language comprehension, develops out of babbling (speechlike but meaningless sounds), which leads to the production of actual words. After a year, children use two-word combinations and their vocabulary increases. They first use telegraphic speech, in which words not critical to the message are dropped. By the age of 5, acquisition of language rules is relatively complete.

15. There are two major theories of language acquisition. Learning theorists suggest that language is acquired simply through reinforcement and conditioning. In contrast, Chomsky suggests that there is an innate language-acquisition device which guides the development of language. The degree to which language is a uniquely human skill remains controversial.

16. The linguistic-relativity hypothesis suggests that language shapes and may determine the way people think about the world. Most evidence suggests that although language does not determine thought, it does affect the way information is stored in memory and how well it can be retrieved.

17. Concepts are categorizations of objects, events, or people that share common properties. Natural concepts (which are concepts that represent familiar objects, are simple, and share a set of characteristic features) consist of prototypes, representative examples of the concept.

KEY TERMS AND CONCEPTS ▶

cognitive psychology (p. 230)
cognition (230)
arrangement problems (232)
inducing structure (232)
transformation problems (232)
algorithm (234)
heuristic (234)
representativeness heuristic (235)
availability heuristic (235)
means-ends analysis (235)
insight (237)
functional fixedness (239)

mental set (239)
confirmation bias (242)
creativity (242)
divergent thinking (243)
convergent thinking (243)
cognitive complexity (243)
artificial intelligence (246)
language (248)
grammar (249)
phonology (249)
phonemes (249)
syntax (249)

semantics (249)
babble (249)
telegraphic speech (250)
overregularization (250)
universal grammar (252)
language-acquisition device (252)
Yerkish (253)
linguistic-relativity hypothesis (254)
concept (255)
natural concepts (255)
prototypes (255)

258

FOR FURTHER STUDY AND APPLICATION ▶

Reed, S. K. (1988). *Cognition: Theory and applications* (2nd ed.). Monterey, CA: Brooks/Cole.

Bourne, L. E., **Dominowski**, R. L., **Loftus**, E. F., & **Healy**, A. F. (1986). *Cognitive processes* (2nd ed.). Englewood Cliffs, NJ: Prentice-Hall.

Two fine overviews of cognitive psychology. Both use interesting case reports to carefully explain phenomena related to memory, cognition, and concepts.

Mayer, R. E. (1983). *Thinking, problem solving, and cognition.* NY: Freeman.

This work summarizes research on the ways in which people are able to solve problems.

Nickerson, R. S., **Perkins**, D. N., & **Smith**, E. E. (1985). *The teaching of thinking.* Hillsdale, NJ: Erlbaum.

This volume addresses the question of whether thinking and problem solving can be taught and comes up with an affirmative answer. It provides a theoretical and practical overview of the area of cognitive psychology that seeks to improve human cognitive capabilities.

Clark, H. H., & **Clark**, E. V. (1977). *Psychology and language: An introduction to psycholinguistics.* New York: Harcourt Brace Jovanovich.

Reich, P. A. (1986). *Language development.* Englewood Cliffs, NJ: Prentice-Hall.

The first volume remains one of the best introductions to language. Well-written and comprehensive, it shows in detail how psychologists approach the area. The second book provides a good overview of the development of language.

Feynman, R. P. (1988, February). An outsider's inside view of the *Challenger* inquiry. *Physics Today,* pp. 26–37.

This insightful account of the inquiry into the *Challenger* space shuttle investigation illustrates problem solving in action.

ANSWERS (REVIEW III):

1. d   **2.** False; babbling children produce sounds which will eventually develop into language   **3.** Telegraphic speech   **4.** Overregularization   **5.** Language-acquisition   **6.** True   **7.** d   **8.** Prototype, natural concept

CHAPTER 8
INTELLIGENCE

CHAPTER 8
INTELLIGENCE

Artist Richard Wawro, shown with his father, has produced hundreds of paintings, such as the one below called "Washday in Pakistan." Critics have called him an artistic genius, and his paintings have won many awards. What makes his accomplishments particularly extraordinary, however, is that Wawro is mentally retarded, having the mental capabilities of a young child. [(a) Stanley Farrar/American Statesman, (b) Courtesy of Dr. Laurence Becker]

PROLOGUE: RICHARD WAWRO

The paintings are varied. Some are landscapes, others are portraits, while still others depict the early-morning light casting its shadows on a wintry scene. All are drawn, according to one critic, with "the precision of a mechanic and the vision of a poet." They have appeared in galleries all over the world, and more than 1000 pictures have sold, ranging in price from $100 to $2000. Some observers have labeled the pictures as works of an artistic genius.

The artist is 35-year-old Richard Wawro. But he is no ordinary artist. What makes him unique is that he is mentally retarded, with the mental capabilities of a young child. Furthermore, he is legally blind, suffering from severe visual deficiencies; he has diabetes; he did not produce an understandable word until he was 11 years old, and even now he can hold only the simplest of conversations. Yet despite his multiple handicaps—and the fact that by most standards he lacks so much—his contributions to the artistic world are extraordinary, far beyond the capabilities of most people with "normal" intelligence.

Wawro's condition, called the "savant syndrome," is a very rare one in which an individual, despite being mentally retarded, demonstrates spectacular talent in a specific area. In one case, for example, a severely retarded savant who could not do the simplest arithmetic problem could, for each year during the 1900s, name the months in which the eighteenth day fell on a Saturday. Another could compute square roots in his head, and still another could play a tune on the piano perfectly after hearing it only once.

If you asked Wawro how he is able to draw such sensitive, sophisticated pictures, he would be unable to explain it to you. What he does say in response to praise is this: "Being happy is a good idea. I am happy when my pictures make people feel good. I can see feeling good" (Blank, 1983).

Page 263

LOOKING AHEAD

Although the capabilities of Richard Wawro and other savants have yet to be explained satisfactorily, one thing is clear: Intelligence is an unusually complex phenomenon. It is also a major focal point for psychologists intent on understanding how people are able to adapt their behavior to the world in which they live and how individuals differ from one another in their capacity to learn about and understand the world.

In this chapter, we consider the challenges involved in defining and measuring intelligence. If you are like most people, you have probably wondered how smart you are; psychologists too have pondered the nature of intelligence. We will examine some of the answers they have found, including the development and use of standardized intelligence tests, and the way results of these tests are used to provide the measure of intelligence. We will also consider the two groups displaying extremes of individual differences in intelligence: the mentally retarded and the gifted. The special challenges of each population will be discussed along with special programs that have been developed to help individuals from both groups reach their full potential. Finally, we will discuss what are probably the two most controversial issues surrounding intelligence: the degree to which intelligence is influenced by heredity and the environment, and whether traditional tests of intelligence are biased toward the dominant cultural groups in society.

After reading this chapter, then, you will be able to answer the following questions:

▶ How is intelligence conceived of and defined by psychologists?

▶ What are the major approaches to measuring intelligence?

▶ How can the extremes of intelligence be differentiated, and what are some of the special programs designed to help people maximize their full potential?

▶ To what degree is intelligence influenced by the environment and by heredity?

▶ Are traditional IQ tests culturally biased?

DEFINING INTELLIGENT BEHAVIOR

It is typical for members of the Trukese tribe, a small Micronesian society, to sail a hundred miles in open ocean waters. Although their destination may be just a small dot of land less than a mile across, the Trukese are able to sail unerringly toward it—without the aid of compass, chronometer, sextant, or any of the other sailing tools that are at the heart of modern western navigation. They are able to sail accurately even when prevailing winds do not allow a direct approach to the island and they must take a zigzag course (Gladwin, 1964).

How are the Trukese able to navigate so effectively? If you ask them, they could not explain it. They might tell you that they use a process that takes

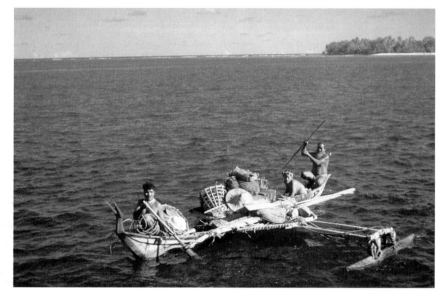

The flawless Trukese navigational techniques, although primitive by western standards, are indicative of intelligence that is not easily measured on traditional intelligence tests. (Eugenia Clark/American Museum of Natural History)

into account the rising and setting of the stars and the appearance, sound, and feeling of the waves against the side of the boat. But at any given moment as they are sailing along, they could not identify their position or say why they are doing what they are doing. Nor could they explain the navigational theory underlying their sailing technique.

Some might say the inability of the Trukese to explain how their sailing technique works is a sign of primitive and even unintelligent behavior. In fact, if we made Trukese sailors take a standardized western test of navigational knowledge and theory, or for that matter a traditional test of intelligence, they might very well do poorly on it. Yet, as a practical matter, it is hard to accuse the Trukese of being unintelligent: Despite their inability to explain how they do so, they are able to navigate successfully through the open ocean waters.

The way in which the Trukese navigate points out the difficulty in coming to grips with what is meant by intelligence. To a westerner, traveling in a straight line along the most direct and quickest route using a sextant and other navigational tools would likely represent the most "intelligent" kind of behavior; a zigzag course, based on the "feel" of the waves, would not seem very reasonable. To the Trukese, however, who are used to their own system of navigation, the use of complicated navigational tools might well seem so overly complex and unnecessary that they might think of western navigators as lacking in intelligence.

It is clear that the term "intelligence" can take on many different meanings. If, for instance, you lived in a remote African village, the way you differentiate between more intelligent and less intelligent people might be unlike the way someone living in the middle of New York City would distinguish individual differences. To the African, high intelligence might be represented by extraordinary hunting or other survival skills; to the New Yorker, it might be exemplified by dealing effectively with a mass-transit system, by achieving success as a member of a high-salaried, prestigious profession, or by getting good grades at a rigorous private school.

In fact, each of these conceptions of intelligence is reasonable, for each represents an instance in which more intelligent people are better able to use the resources of their environment than are less intelligent people, a distinction that we would assume to be basic to any definition of intelligence. Yet it is also clear that these conceptions represent very different views of intelligence.

That two such different sets of behavior can exemplify the same psychological concept has proved to be a problem to psychologists. They have long grappled with the issue of devising a general definition of intelligence that would remain independent of a person's specific culture and other environmental factors. Interestingly, untrained laypersons have fairly clear conceptions of intelligence (Sternberg, 1985). For example, in one survey that asked a group of people to define what they meant by intelligence, three major components of intelligence emerged (Sternberg, Conway, Ketron & Bernstein, 1981). First, there was problem-solving ability: People who reason logically and identify more solutions to problems were seen as intelligent. Second, verbal abilities were thought to exemplify intelligence. Finally, intelligence was assumed to be indicated by social competence: the ability to show interest in others and interact effectively with them.

The definition of intelligence that psychologists employ is more focused, although it contains many of the same elements contained in the layperson's conception. To psychologists, **intelligence** is the capacity to understand the world, think with rationality, and use resources effectively when faced with challenges (Wechsler, 1975).

Unfortunately, neither the layperson's nor the psychologist's conception of intelligence is much help when it comes to distinguishing, with any degree of precision, more intelligent people from less intelligent ones. To overcome this problem, psychologists interested in intelligence have focused much of their attention on the development of batteries of tests, known, quite appropriately, as **intelligence tests**, and have relied on such tests to identify a person's level of intelligence. These tests have proved to be of great benefit in identifying students in need of special attention in school, in diagnosing cognitive difficulties, and in helping people make optimal educational and vocational choices. At the same time, their use has proved quite controversial.

Intelligence: The capacity to understand the world, think rationally, and use resources effectively when faced with challenges

Intelligence tests: A battery of measures to determine a person's level of intelligence

The French psychologist Alfred Binet developed the first intelligence test. (Bettman Archive)

SEPARATING THE INTELLIGENT FROM THE UNINTELLIGENT: Measuring Intelligence

The first intelligence tests followed a simple premise: If performance on certain tasks or test items improved with age, then performance could be used to distinguish more intelligent people from less intelligent ones within a particular age group. Using this principle, Alfred Binet, a French psychologist, devised the first formal intelligence test, which was designed to identify the "dullest" students in the Paris school system in order to provide them with remedial aid.

Binet began by presenting tasks to same-age students who had been labeled "bright" or "dull" by their teachers. If a task could be completed by the bright students but not by the dull ones, he retained the task as a proper test item; otherwise it was discarded. In the end he came up with a test that distinguished between the bright and dull groups, and—with further work— one that distinguished among children in different age groups (Binet & Simon, 1916).

On the basis of the Binet test, children were assigned a score that cor-

Mental age: The typical intelligence level found for people at a given chronological age

Chronological age: A person's physical age

Intelligence quotient (IQ) score: A measure of intelligence that takes into account an individual's mental and chronological ages

Deviation IQ score: A calculation of an IQ score that allows one person's performance to be measured in relation to others'

Stanford-Binet test: A test of intelligence that includes a series of items varying in nature according to the age of the person being tested

responded to their **mental age**, the average age of children taking the test who achieved the same score. For example, if a 10-year-old boy received a score of 45 on the test and this was the average score received by 8-year-olds, his mental age would be considered to be 8 years. Similarly, a 14-year-old girl who scored an 88 on the test—matching the mean score for 16-year-olds—would be assigned a mental age of 16 years.

Although assigning a mental age to students provided an indication of whether they were performing at the same level as their peers, it did not allow for adequate comparisons among people of different **chronological**, or physical, **ages**. By using mental age alone, for instance, we would assume that an 18-year-old responding at a 16-year-old's level would be as bright as a 5-year-old answering at a 3-year-old's level, when actually the 5-year-old would be displaying a much greater *relative* degree of slowness.

A solution to the problem came in the form of the **intelligence quotient**, or **IQ score**, a measure of intelligence that takes into account an individual's mental *and* chronological ages. To calculate an IQ score, the following formula is used, in which MA stands for mental age and CA for chronological age:

$$\text{IQ score} = \frac{\text{MA}}{\text{CA}} \times 100$$

Using this formula, we can return to the earlier example of an 18-year-old performing at a mental age of 16 and calculate an IQ score of $(16 \div 18) \times 100 = 88.9$. In contrast, the 5-year-old performing at a mental age of 3 comes out with a considerably lower IQ score: $(3 \div 5) \times 100 = 60$.

As a bit of trial and error with the formula will show you, anyone who has a mental age equal to his or her chronological age will have an IQ equal to 100. Moreover, people with a mental age that is greater than their chronological age will have IQs that exceed 100.

Although the basic principles behind the calculation of an IQ score still hold, IQ scores are figured in a somewhat different manner today and are known as **deviation IQ scores**. First, the average test score for everyone of the same age who takes the test is determined, and this average score is assigned an IQ of 100. Then, with the aid of mathematically sophisticated techniques, IQ values are assigned to other test scores for the age group on the basis of how much the test score deviates from the average for that group.

As you can see in Figure 8-1, approximately two-thirds of all individuals fall within 15 IQ points of the average score of 100. As scores increase or fall beyond that range, the percentage of people in a category falls considerably.

MEASURING IQ: Stanford-Binet, Wechsler, et al.

Just what is an IQ test like? It is probable that sometime during your academic career you have taken one; almost all of us are given IQ tests at one time or another.

The original test is still with us, although it has been revised many times and in its modern incarnation bears little resemblance to the original version. Now called the **Stanford-Binet test**, it was last revised in 1985 (Hagen, Sattler & Thorndike, 1985; Thorndike, Hagan & Sattler, 1986). The test consists of a series of items which vary in nature according to the age of the person

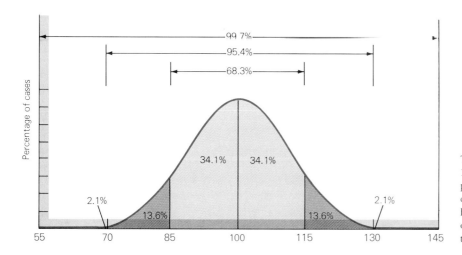

FIGURE 8-1

The average and most frequent IQ score is 100, and approximately 68 percent of all people are within a 30-point range centered on 100. Some 95 percent of the population have scores that are within 30 points above or below 100, and 99.7 percent have scores that are between 55 and 145.

being tested. For example, young children are asked to copy figures or answer questions about everyday activities. Older people are asked to solve analogies, explain proverbs, and describe similarities that underlie sets of words.

The test is administered orally. An examiner begins by finding a mental age level at which the person is able to answer all questions correctly and then moves on to successively difficult problems. When a mental age level is reached at which no items can be answered, the test is over. By examining the pattern of correct and incorrect responses, the examiner is able to compute an IQ score for the person being tested.

The other IQ test frequently used in America was devised by psychologist David Wechsler and is known as the **Wechsler Adult Intelligence Scale—Revised**, or, more commonly, the **WAIS-R**. There is also a children's version, the **Wechsler Intelligence Scale for Children—Revised**, or **WISC-R**. Both the WAIS-R and the WISC-R have two major parts: a verbal scale and a performance—or nonverbal—scale. As you can see from the sample questions in Figure 8-2, the two scales include questions of very different types. Whereas verbal tasks consist of more traditional kinds of problems, including vocabulary definition and comprehension of various concepts, the nonverbal part consists of assembling small objects and arranging pictures in a logical order. Although an individual's scores on the verbal and performance sections of the test are generally close to each other, the scores of a person with a language deficiency or from a background of severe environmental deprivation may show a relatively large discrepancy. By providing separate scores, the WAIS-R and WISC-R give a more precise picture of a person's specific abilities.

Because the Stanford-Binet, WAIS-R, and WISC-R all require individualized administration, it is relatively difficult and time-consuming to administer and score them on a wide-scale basis. Consequently, there are now a number of IQ tests that allow for group administration (Carroll, 1982). Rather than having one examiner ask one person at a time to respond to individual items, group IQ tests are strictly paper-and-pencil measures, in which those taking the tests read the questions and provide their answers in writing. The primary advantage of group tests is their ease of administration.

There are, however, sacrifices made in group testing which, in some cases, may outweigh the benefits. For instance, group tests generally sample

Wechsler Adult-Intelligence Scale—Revised (WAIS-R). A test of intelligence consisting of verbal and nonverbal performance sections, providing a relatively precise picture of a person's specific abilities

Wechsler Intelligence Scale for Children—Revised (WISC-R): An intelligence test for children; see Wechsler Adult Intelligence Scale—Revised

Verbal scale

Information	Where does milk come from? Who invented the telephone?
Comprehension	Why do we put food in the refrigerator? What should you do if you see a person leave his or her groceries on a bus?
Arithmetic	Stacey had two crayons and the teacher gave her two more. How many did she have all together? How long will it take a train traveling at 80 miles an hour to reach the station 320 miles away?
Similarities	In what way are cows and horses alike? In what way are rivers and roads the same?
Digit span	Repeat the following numbers: 5, 8, 2 Repeat the following numbers in reverse order: 3, 2, 9, 7, 4, 1, 4.
Vocabulary	What is a candle? What does administer mean?

Performance scale

Digit symbol
(Match symbols to numbers using the key.)

Picture completion
(Identify what is missing.)

(Pieces of a table)

Object assembly
(Put jigsaw puzzle together.)

Picture arrangement
(Arrange pictures to tell a logical story.)

FIGURE 8-2

Typical kinds of items found on the verbal and performance scales of the Wechsler Intelligence Scales for Children (WISC-R).

a narrower range of behaviors than tests administered individually. Furthermore, people may be more motivated to perform at their highest ability level when working on a one-to-one basis with a test administrator. Finally, in some cases, it is simply impossible to employ group tests, particularly with young children or people with unusually low IQs.

Achievement and Aptitude Tests

IQ tests are not the only kind of tests that you have taken during the course of your schooling. Two other kinds of tests related to intelligence but designed to measure somewhat different phenomena are achievement tests and aptitude tests. An **achievement test** is a test meant to ascertain the level of knowledge in a given subject area; rather than measuring general ability as an intelligence test does, an achievement test concentrates on the specifics of what a person has learned.

Achievement test: A test intended to determine a person's level of knowledge in a given subject

An **aptitude test** is designed to predict a person's ability in a particular area or line of work. You may have already taken the most famous aptitude test of them all: the Scholastic Aptitude Test, or SAT. The SAT is meant to predict how well people will do in college and has proved over the years to correlate very strongly with college grades.

Although in theory the distinction between intelligence, aptitude, and achievement tests can be precisely drawn, as a practical matter there is a good deal of overlap between them. For example, the SAT has been roundly criticized for being less of a predictive aptitude test than one that actually measures achievement. It is difficult, then, to devise tests that predict future performance but do not rely on past achievement.

Aptitude test: A test designed to predict ability in a particular line of work

IQ TESTS DON'T TELL ALL: Alternative Formulations of Intelligence

Although Binet's procedure for measuring intelligence, exemplified by the modern Stanford-Binet and WAIS-R intelligence tests, remains one of the most frequently employed, some theorists argue that it lacks an underlying conception of what intelligence is. To Binet and his followers, intelligence was generally conceived of as what his test measured. That was, and remains, an eminently practical approach, but it depends not on an understanding of the nature of intelligence but primarily on comparing one person's performance with that of others. For that reason, the intelligence test of Binet and his successors does little to increase our understanding of what intelligence is all about; it merely measures behavior that is assumed to exemplify intelligence.

This does not mean, however, that researchers and theoreticians have ignored the question of what intelligence really is. One important issue is whether intelligence is a single, unitary factor, or whether it is made up of particular subcomponents (Weinberg, 1989). The earliest psychologists interested in intelligence made the assumption that there was a general factor for mental ability, called **g**, or the **g-factor** (Spearman, 1927). This factor was thought to underlie performance on every aspect of intelligence, and it was the g factor that was presumably being measured on tests of intelligence.

G or g-factor: A single general factor accounting for mental ability

Later psychologists, however, disputed the view that intelligence is unidimensional. For instance, L. L. Thurstone (1938) suggested that there are several primary mental abilities underlying general intelligence. By using innovative statistical techniques, he identified a variety of subcomponents of intelligence, including numerical ability, reasoning, verbal fluency, memory, and verbal comprehension.

More contemporary theoreticians have suggested that there are really two different kinds of intelligence: fluid intelligence and crystallized intelligence (Cattell, 1967, 1987). **Fluid intelligence** is the ability to deal with new problems and encounters. If you were asked to group a series of letters according to some criterion or to remember a set of numbers, you would be using fluid intelligence. **Crystallized intelligence** is the store of information, skills, and strategies that people have acquired through their use of fluid intelligence. You would likely rely on crystallized intelligence, for instance, if you were asked to solve a puzzle or deduce the solution to a mystery, drawing upon your past unique experience. The differences between fluid and crystallized intelligence become particularly evident in the elderly, who—as we will discuss further in Chapter 13—show declines in fluid, but not crystallized, intelligence.

Fluid intelligence: The ability to deal with new problems and encounters

Crystallized intelligence: The store of specific information, skills, and strategies that people have acquired through experience

Other theoreticians divide intelligence into even more detailed subdivisions. For instance, by examining the talents of people who display unusual talent in certain areas (such as Richard Wawro, discussed at the start of the chapter) psychologist Howard Gardner (1983; 1985) has suggested that we have not one but seven multiple intelligences, each relatively independent of the others. Specifically, he considers our spheres of intelligence to include the seven areas illustrated in Table 8-1.

Although Gardner illustrates the individual intelligences with descriptions of well-known people, it is important to remember that each of us theoretically harbors the same kinds of intelligence. Moreover, although the seven are presented individually, Gardner suggests that these separate intelligences do not operate in isolation. Normally, any activity encompasses several kinds of intelligence, working together.

Going a step further, J. P. Guilford (1968, 1982) suggested that an even finer-grained analysis of intelligence was in order. In his **structure-of-intellect** model, illustrated in Figure 8-3, Guilford provided the most detailed representation of human intelligence to date. On the basis of observations of people's performance on a wide variety of tasks, he proposed that there are 150 separate mental abilities underlying intelligence. These abilities could be sorted along three major dimensions: the content of a task (made up of five subdivisions), the requirements—called "operations"—involved in carrying out the task (made up of five subdivisions), and the product of the task (made up of six subdivisions).

Although such minute distinctions between different components of intelligence present difficulties in terms of reliable measurement, Guilford's model, as well as those of other theorists who propose that intelligence is multifaceted, has led to a number of advances in our understanding of the nature of intelligence. For example, one outgrowth of the models is the development of test items in which more than one answer can be correct, providing the opportunity for the demonstration of creative thinking. Ac-

Structure-of-intellect model: A model of intelligence based on performance along three different dimensions: task content, task requirements, and product

FIGURE 8-3

According to Guilford's structure of intellect model, there are 150 separate mental abilities that fall along the three major dimensions (task content, operations involved in carrying out a task, and task product) represented in this cube. (Guilford, 1982.)

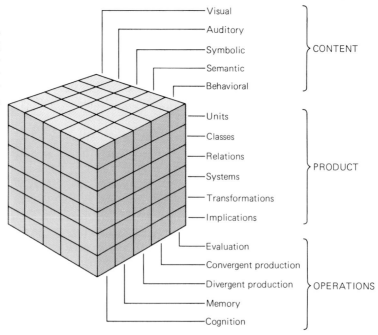

TABLE 8-1

Gardner's Seven Intelligences

1. Musical intelligence (skills in tasks involving music). Case example:

   When he was three years old, Yehudi Menuhin was smuggled into the San Francisco Orchestra concerts by his parents. The sound of Louis Persinger's violin so entranced the youngster that he insisted on a violin for his birthday and Louis Persinger as his teacher. He got both. By the time he was 10 years old, Menuhin was an international performer.

2. Bodily-kinesthetic intelligence (skills in using the whole body or various portions of it in the solution of problems or in the construction of products or displays, exemplified by dancers, athletes, actors, and surgeons). Case example:

   Fifteen-year-old Babe Ruth played third base. During one game, his team's pitcher was doing very poorly and Babe loudly criticized him from third base. Brother Mathias, the coach, called out, "Ruth, if you know so much about it, *you* pitch!" Babe was surprised and embarrassed because he had never pitched before, but Brother Mathias insisted. Ruth said later that at the very moment he took the pitcher's mound, he *knew* he was supposed to be a pitcher.

3. Logical-mathematical intelligence (skills in problem-solving and scientific thinking). Case example:

   Barbara McClintock won the Nobel Prize in medicine for her work in microbiology. She describes one of her breakthroughs, which came after thinking about a problem for half an hour in her office: "Suddenly I jumped and ran back to the [corn] field. At the top of the field (the others were still at the bottom) I shouted, "Eureka, I have it!" . . .

4. Linguistic intelligence (skills involved in the production and use of language). Case example:

   At the age of ten, T. S. Eliot created a magazine called *Fireside,* to which he was the sole contributor. In a three-day period during his winter vacation, he created the eight complete issues.

5. Spatial intelligence (skills involving spatial configurations, such as those used by artists and architects). Case example:

   Navigation around the Caroline Islands . . . is accomplished without instruments. . . . During the actual trip, the navigator must envision mentally a reference island as it passes under a particular star and from that he computes the number of segments completed, the proportion of the trip remaining, and any corrections in heading that are required.

6. Interpersonal intelligence (skills in interacting with others, such as sensitivity to the moods, temperaments, motivations, and intentions of others). Case example:

   When Anne Sullivan began instructing the deaf and blind Helen Keller, her task was one that had eluded others for years. Yet, just two weeks after beginning her work with Keller, Sullivan achieved a great success. In her words, "My heart is singing with joy this morning. A miracle has happened! The wild little creature of two weeks ago has been transformed into a gentle child."

7. Intrapersonal intelligence (knowledge of the internal aspects of oneself; access to one's own feelings and emotions). Case example:

   In her essay "A Sketch of the Past," Virginia Woolf displays deep insight into her own inner life through these lines, describing her reaction to several specific memories from her childhood that still, in adulthood, shock her: "Though I still have the peculiarity that I receive these sudden shocks, they are now always welcome; after the first surprise, I always feel instantly that they are particularly valuable. And so I go on to suppose that the shock-receiving capacity is what makes me a writer."

Source: Adapted from Walters & Gardner (1986).

cording to these approaches, then, different kinds of intelligence may produce contradictory—but equally valid—responses to the same question.

IS INFORMATION PROCESSING INTELLIGENCE?:
Contemporary Approaches

The most recent contribution to understanding intelligence comes from the work of cognitive psychologists. Drawing on the research and theory that we discussed in Chapter 7, cognitive psychologists use an information-processing approach, which assumes that the way people store material in memory and use the material to solve intellectual tasks provides the most accurate conception of intelligence (Sternberg, 1981). Rather than focusing on the structure of intelligence in the form of its subcomponents, cognitive approaches have examined the *processes* underlying intelligent behavior.

By breaking tasks and problems into their component parts and identifying the nature and speed of problem-solving processes, researchers have noted distinct differences between those who score high on traditional IQ tests and those who score lower. Take, for example, a college student who is asked to solve the following analogy problem (Sternberg, 1982):

lawyer is to *client* as *doctor* is to:

(a) *patient* or (b) *medicine*

A student presented with this analogy tends to move through a series of stages in attempting to reach a solution (see Figure 8-4). First she will *encode* the initial information, which means providing each item with identifying cues that help retrieve relevant information buried in long-term memory. For instance, she may think of lawyer in terms of law school, the Supreme Court, an ambulance chaser, Perry Mason, and a courtroom. Each of the other terms will be similarly encoded. Next, she will *infer* any possible relationship between lawyer and client. She may infer that the relevant relationship is that a client employs a lawyer, or alternatively, that a lawyer gives services to a client.

Once she has inferred the relationship, she must *map* the higher-order relationship between the first half of the analogy and the second half—both deal with people who provide professional services for a fee. The crucial stage that follows is one of *application*, in which she tries out each answer option with the relationship she has inferred. She will presumably decide that a doctor provides professional services to a patient, not to medicine. Finally, the last component of solving the problem is responding.

By breaking problems into component parts in this manner, it is possible to identify systematic differences in both quantitative and qualitative aspects of problem solving, and to demonstrate that people with higher intelligence levels differ not only in the number of correct solutions they come up with, but in their method of solving problems. For instance, high scorers are apt to spend more time on the initial encoding stages of a problem, identifying the parts of the problem and retrieving relevant information from long-term memory. This initial emphasis on recalling relevant information pays off in the end; those who spend relatively less time on the initial stages tend to be less able to find a solution. People's use of such information-processing abilities, therefore, may underlie the differences in intelligence.

Applying this cognitive approach to intelligence, psychologist Robert

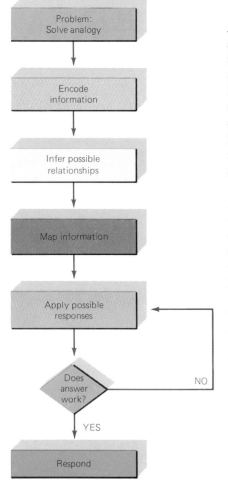

FIGURE 8-4

Information-processing stages in solving analogies (Sternberg, 1982.)

Sternberg (1985) developed what he calls a triarchic theory of intelligence. The **triarchic theory of intelligence** suggests that there are three major aspects to intelligence: componential, experiential, and contextual. The componential aspect focuses on the mental components involved in analyzing information to solve problems, particularly those processes operating when a person displays intelligent behavior. In contrast, the experiential aspect focuses on how a person's prior experiences are related to intelligence and how those experiences are brought to bear on problem-solving situations. Finally, the contextual aspect of intelligence takes into account the success people experience in facing the demands of their everyday environment.

Triarchic theory of intelligence: A theory suggesting three major aspects of intelligence: componential, experiential, and contextual

Recent approaches to intelligence have focused most heavily on Sternberg's third aspect of intelligence (Sternberg & Detterman, 1986). Several new theories emphasize **practical intelligence**—intelligence related to overall success in living, rather than to intellectual and academic performance. For a discussion of the ongoing work on practical intelligence, see the Psychology at Work box.

Practical intelligence: A person's style of thought and approach to problem solving, which may differ from traditional measures of intelligence

PSYCHOLOGY AT WORK

Your year on the job has been generally favorable. Performance ratings for your department are at least as good as they were before you took over, and perhaps even a little better. You have two assistants. One is quite capable. The other just seems to go through the motions and is of little real help. Even though you are well liked, you believe that there is little that would distinguish you in the eyes of your superiors from the nine other managers at a comparable level in the company. Your goal is rapid promotion to the top of the company. The following is a list of things you are considering doing. Rank the importance of each.

1. Find a way to get rid of the "deadwood"—namely, the less helpful assistant and three or four other employees in your department.

2. Participate in a series of panel discussions to be shown on the local public television station.

3. Find ways to make sure your superiors are aware of your important accomplishment.

4. Accept a friend's invitation to join the exclusive country club that many higher-level executives belong to.

IS PRACTICAL INTELLIGENCE DIFFERENT FROM SCHOOL INTELLIGENCE?

5. When making decisions, give a great deal of weight to the way your superiors like things done. (Based on Wagner & Sternberg, 1985, p. 447.)

The way in which you would answer this question may have a lot to do with your future success in a business career, at least according to its author, psychologist Robert J. Sternberg. (The optimal order of choices is given below.) In fact, the question is one of a series designed to help give an indication of your intelligence. It is not traditional intelligence that the question is designed to tap, but rather intelligence of a particular kind: practical intelligence for business (Sternberg & Wagner, 1986).

The test that Sternberg has devised is one of several new intelligence measures now taking form. Each is designed to overcome one of the most glaring limitations of traditional IQ tests: Although literally hundreds of studies have shown that

students with high IQs tend to get high grades and those with low IQs tend to be less successful in school, the fact remains that IQ does not relate to *career* success. For example, while it is clear that successful business executives usually score at least moderately well on IQ tests, the rate at which they advance and their ultimate business achievement are only minimally associated with their specific IQ scores.

A more significant influence, according to psychologist Siegfried Streufert (1984), is the way in which people approach problems and their style of thinking. This kind of intelligence is manifested in successful business leaders through a kind of cognitive complexity in decision making. Instead of being locked into a simple pattern of thinking, successful managers are able to acquire and integrate complex sets of information and to see with clarity the interrelationships among events. Rather than viewing problems in terms of a single goal or factor—such as profit making—leaders with high practical intelligence are able to coordinate differing goals simultaneously when devising solutions to problems.

Business is hardly the only sphere in which this kind of practical intelligence is crucial, and some psychologists are working to develop tests that identify it in various domains of everyday life. For example, Seymour Epstein has developed a test of what he terms "constructive thinking," in which life success can be predicted. Here are some of the kinds of items found on the test (Epstein & Meier, 1989):

1. I am the kind of person who takes action rather than just thinks or complains about a situation. Agree or disagree?

2. I don't let little things bother me. Agree or disagee?

3. I tend to take things personally. Agree or disagree?

4. I get so distressed when I notice that I am doing poorly in something that it makes me do worse. Agree or disagree?

According to Epstein, the skills his test assesses include happiness with social relationships, job success, and even physical and emotional health. His data indicate that the test is far more predictive of actual success in life than are traditional IQ tests.

In sum, it is clear that there are many ways to demonstrate—and

measure—intelligence. A high IQ does not guarantee success in life, especially if it accompanies low practical intelligence.

(By the way, the optimum order of choices for Sternberg's test of practical intelligence for business is 5, 1, 3, 2, 4. In Epstein's test of constructive thinking, the ideal choices are (1) agree, (2) agree, (3) disagree, and (4) disagree. Keep in mind that because these items represent such a small sample of Sternberg's and Epstein's measures, it is impossible to infer how you might score on the complete tests.)

THE INFORMED CONSUMER OF PSYCHOLOGY:
Can You Do Better On Standardized Tests?

 Even though psychologists disagree about the nature of intelligence, standardized intelligence tests—as well as many other kinds of tests—are still widely used in a variety of situations. At one point or another, almost all of us have had to cope with formal testing, be it in school or on the job. And most of us can probably understand the concern expressed by students taking college entrance exams, such as the Scholastic Aptitude Test (SAT), who feel that the success of their future life hangs on the results of one morning's test results.

One outcome of the prevalence of tests in our society is the development of numerous coaching services that purport to train people to raise their scores by reviewing basic skills and teaching test-taking strategies. But do they work?

Although the Educational Testing Service (ETS) at one time suggested that coaching for the SAT was useless, today it takes a more positive approach toward the practice. While still suggesting that the SAT measures underlying competencies so fundamental that a course of a few weeks' duration will provide little advantage, ETS concedes that practice in test taking provided during the course may have a slightly beneficial effect. But ETS goes on to point out that the coaching required to bring about average score increases of more than 20 to 30 points is so extensive that it would be the equivalent of going to school full time (Messick & Jungeblut, 1981).

Most research carried out by psychologists verifies that coaching for the SAT exams produces small effects—usually in the range of 15-point increases in verbal and math scores (Kulik, Bangert-Drowns & Kulik, 1984). On the other hand, research also shows that coaching on other sorts of aptitude and intelligence tests can result in more substantial increases in test scores.

Since some kinds of coaching do help raise the scores people receive on tests, one crucial concern is to determine what kind of coaching is most likely to be effective. Among the points to consider when deciding whether coaching will be an effective and useful strategy for raising your score on an upcoming test are whether the instruction addresses the basic areas covered by the test, particularly those in which you are rusty and may need drill and practice; whether the course is geared to the specific test; whether the instructor has recent public versions of the test that can be used for practice with the mechanics of the test itself; and whether there are data to show that this particular coaching service has previously produced significant gains in the scores of students. Finally, you must ask yourself whether it is worth the cost in time and money to end up with only a small gain on the test— particularly in view of the fact that most people have higher test scores the second time they take a test whether they are coached or not.

Only careful research can answer these questions, and it is wise to be skeptical of the claims of coaches. At the same time, there are certain steps you can take, without the benefit of coaching, to maximize your opportunity to score well on standardized tests. For example, these four points provide good advice for anyone taking a standardized test (Crocetti, 1983):

▶ Preview each section. Not only will it give you a chance to take a deep breath and prevent you from frantically rushing through the section; it will also alert you to any unexpected changes in the test format. Previewing will give you a sense of what to expect as you work through each problem.

▶ Time yourself carefully. The computer that scores your test will not care how deeply you have thought out and considered each answer; all it notes is whether or not you have answered a problem correctly. Therefore, it is important not to spend too much time on initial problems at the expense of later ones. If you are unsure of an answer, try to narrow down the options, then guess and go on to the next problem. Perfection is not your goal; maximizing the number of correct responses is

▶ Check the test-scoring policy to determine whether guessing is appropriate. On the Scholastic Aptitude Test, wrong answers are subtracted from your score, making blind guessing a bad strategy. In comparison, the Graduate Record Exam and many other tests do not penalize you for wrong answers. On tests with penalties for wrong answers, guess only if you can narrow the choices down to two or three. On the other hand, for tests in which wrong answers do not lower your score, it pays to guess, even if you have no idea of the correct response.

▶ Complete answer sheets accurately. Obviously, it makes sense to check your answer sheet when you have finished the test. It is also a good idea to write your answers in the test booklet itself, so that when you go back to review your answers you won't have to refer to the answer sheet.

These tips won't ensure a high score on the next test you take, but they will help to maximize your opportunity for better performance.

Recap

◄ Intelligence is the capacity to understand the world, think with rationality, and use resources effectively when faced with challenges.

◄ The measure of intelligence used in tests is the intelligence quotient, or IQ.

◄ There are a number of alternative formulations of intelligence, including models which look at the subcomponents of intelligence and models which suggest that information-processing strategies provide the most useful understanding of intelligence.

◄ Coaching seems to have some impact on improving test scores, although there is wide variability in its effectiveness.

Review

1. Intelligence is thought to be an innate ability that exists independent of cultural influence. True or false? _____

2. Ten-year-old Sharon is given an intelligence test. She achieves a mental age score of 11. Using the formula for determining intelligence quotient, calculate Sharon's IQ score.

3. Cindy is asked to arrange blocks in a specific pattern as part of the _____ scale of the WAIS-R.

4. _____ tests, such as the SAT, are designed to predict future performance in a given area.

5. Mandy has had a wide range of experiences in dealing with novel situations. Consequently, she has developed a broad set of related skills and strategies. Her storehouse of information and strategies is referred to as
   a. structure of intellect.
   b. crystallized intelligence.
   c. fluid intelligence.
   d. a cognitive map.

6. Roberta's skills as a psychotherapist include the uncanny ability to perceive the feelings and intentions of her clients. Gardner would refer to this as an example of
   a. intrapersonal intelligence.
   b. linguistic intelligence.
   c. spatial intelligence.
   d. interpersonal intelligence.

7. Name the model of J. P. Guilford that divides intelligence into 150 separate mental abilities. _____

8. Cognitive psychologists use an information-processing approach to understanding intelligence. Accordingly, they suggest that when breaking information into components, people with high IQ scores tend to focus on
   a. encoding and inferring.
   b. encoding and applying.
   c. mapping and applying.
   d. applying and responding.

9. Componential, experiential, and contextual aspects highlight the _____ theory of intelligence.

10. According to Sternberg, our view of intelligence should stress _____ intelligence, the ability to be successful at tasks in everyday life, rather than academic abilities.

(Answers to review questions are on page 278.)

ABOVE AND BELOW THE NORM: VARIATIONS IN INTELLECTUAL ABILITY

Bill never liked school all that much. For the first few years he managed to get by, although his parents had to push hard to get him to do a minimally acceptable level of first- and second-grade work. He always seemed slower at learning things that the other kids had no trouble with, and—while he wasn't exactly a poorly behaved child—his attention span was short and he had trouble following what was going on in class. He also seemed tired much of the time, but a physical examination ruled out any medical problems. His teachers began to suspect he was simply lazy and unmotivated, though he did, on occasion, show great interest in lessons that involved working with his hands. Finally, out of desperation, his teachers and parents arranged for him to be evaluated by a psychologist. To their surprise, they found out he had an IQ of 63—so far below average that his fell into the range of IQ scores classified as mentally retarded.

Bill is one of more than 6.5 million people in the United States who have been identified as having intelligence far enough below average to regard it as a serious deficit. Both those people with low IQs, known as the mentally retarded, and those with unusually high IQs, referred to as the intellectually gifted, make up classes of individuals who require special attention to reach their full potential.

FALLING BELOW THE NORM: Mental Retardation

Although sometimes thought of as a rare phenomenon, mental retardation occurs in 1 to 3 percent of the population. There is wide variation among those labeled as mentally retarded—in large part because of the inclusiveness of the definition developed by the American Association on Mental Deficiency. The association suggests that **mental retardation** exists when there is "significantly subaverage general intellectual functioning existing concurrently with deficits in adaptive behavior and manifested during the developmental period" (Grossman, 1983). What this means is that people classified as mentally retarded can range from individuals whose performance differs little in a qualitative sense from those with higher IQs, to those who virtually cannot be trained and who must receive institutional treatment throughout their lives (Reynolds & Mann, 1987).

> **Mental retardation:** A significantly subaverage level of intellectual functioning accompanying deficits in adaptive behavior

Most mentally retarded people have relatively minor deficits and are classified as **mildly retarded**. These individuals have IQ scores ranging from 55 to 69, and they constitute some 90 percent of all retarded individuals. Although their development is typically slower than that of their peers, they can function quite independently by adulthood and are able to hold jobs and have families of their own.

> **Mild retardation:** Mental retardation characterized by an IQ between 55 and 69 and the ability to function independently

At greater levels of retardation—**moderate retardation** (IQs of 40 to 54), **severe retardation** (IQs of 25 to 39), and **profound retardation** (IQs below 25)—the difficulties are more pronounced. With the moderately retarded, deficits are obvious early, with language and motor skills lagging behind those of peers. Although these people can hold simple jobs, they need to have a moderate degree of supervision throughout their lives. The severely and profoundly retarded are generally unable to function independently. Often they have no language ability, poor motor control, and even an inability to be toilet-trained. These people are typically institutionalized for their entire lives.

> **Moderate retardation:** Mental retardation characterized by an IQ between 40 and 54
>
> **Severe retardation:** Mental retardation characterized by an IQ between 25 and 39 and difficulty in functioning independently
>
> **Profound retardation:** Mental retardation characterized by an IQ below 25 and an inability to function independently

Mentally retarded people can lead productive lives as adults; pictured here is the first retarded person to be hired as a page in the U.S. Senate. (Joe Connor/Stock Boston)

Down's syndrome: A common cause of mental retardation, brought about by the presence of an extra chromosome

Familial retardation: Mental retardation in which there is a history of retardation in a family but no evidence of biological causes

Least-restrictive environment: The official phrase from PL94-142 that guarantees the right of full education for retarded people in an environment that is most similar to the educational environment of typical children

Mainstreaming: The integration of retarded people into regular classroom situations

In mainstreaming, the mentally retarded are educated and trained in the least restrictive environment, often being integrated into regular classrooms. (Richard Hutchings/Science Source/Photo Researchers)

What are the causes of mental retardation? In nearly one-third of the cases there is a known biological cause, the most common being Down's syndrome. **Down's syndrome**, which was once referred to as mongolism because the facial configuration of those with the disorder had an oriental appearance, is caused by the presence of an extra chromosome. Birth complications, such as a temporary lack of oxygen, may also cause retardation.

The majority of cases of mental retardation are classified as familial retardation. In **familial retardation** there is no known biological defect but a history of retardation within the person's family. Whether that history is caused by environmental factors—such as extreme, continuous poverty leading to malnutrition—or by some underlying genetic factor inherited from one's parents is usually impossible to determine for certain. What is characteristic of familial retardation is the presence of more than one retarded person in the immediate family.

Regardless of the cause of mental retardation, important advances in the care and treatment of the mentally retarded have been made in the last fifteen years (Turkington, 1987; Garber, 1988; Landesman & Ramey, 1989). Much of this change was instigated by the Education for All Handicapped Children Act of 1975 (Public Law 94-142). In this federal law, Congress ruled that the mentally retarded are entitled to a full education and that they must be educated and trained in the **least-restrictive environment**. The law increased the educational opportunities for the retarded, facilitating their integration into regular classrooms as much as possible—a process known as **mainstreaming**.

The philosophy behind mainstreaming suggests that the interaction of retarded and nonretarded students in regular classrooms will improve the educational opportunities for the mentally retarded, increase their social acceptance, and facilitate their integration into society as a whole. The philosophy was once to segregate the retarded into special-education classes

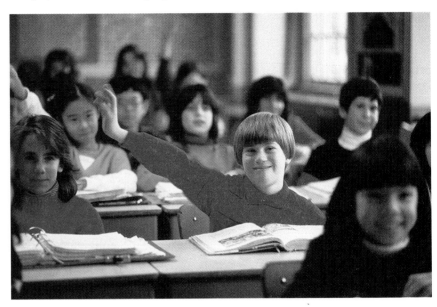

where they could learn at their own pace along with other handicapped students. Mainstreaming attempts to prevent the isolation inherent in special-education classes and to reduce the social stigma of retardation by allowing the handicapped to interact with their age peers as much as possible (Mastropieri & Scruggs, 1987).

Of course, there are still special-education classes; some retarded individuals function at too low a level to benefit from placement in regular classrooms. Moreover, retarded children mainstreamed into regular classes typically attend special classes for at least part of the day. Still, mainstreaming holds the promise of increasing the integration of the mentally retarded into society and allowing them to make their own contributions to the world at large.

THE OTHER END OF THE SPECTRUM: The Intellectually Gifted

While the uniqueness of the mentally retarded is readily apparent, members of another group differ equally from the norm. Instead of having low intelligence, the **intellectually gifted** have higher-than-average intelligence.

Comprising 2 to 4 percent of the population, the intellectually gifted have IQ scores greater than 130. The stereotype associated with the gifted suggests that they are awkward, shy, social misfits unable to get along well with peers, but most research suggests just the opposite: The intellectually gifted are outgoing, well-adjusted, popular people who are able to do most things better than the average person (Stanley, 1980; Horowitz & O'Brien, 1987).

For example, in a long-term study by Lewis Terman that started in the early 1920s and is still going on, 1500 children who had IQ scores above 140 were followed and examined periodically through the next 60 years (Sears, 1977; Terman & Oden, 1947). From the very start, members of this group were physically, academically, and socially more able than their non-gifted peers. They were generally healthier, taller, heavier, and stronger than average. Not surprisingly, they did better in school as well. They also showed better social adjustment than average. And all these advantages paid off in terms of career success: As a group, the gifted received more awards and distinctions and higher incomes and made more contributions in art and

Intellectually gifted: Individuals characterized by higher-than-average intelligence, with IQ scores above 130

Intellectually gifted youngsters, like these students at a high school in Milwaukee, tend to excel socially and athletically as well as academically. (Jeff Lowenthal/Woodfin Camp & Assoc.)

literature. For example, by the time the members of the group were 40 years old they had written over 90 books, 375 plays and short stories, and 2000 articles and had registered more than 200 patents. Perhaps most important, they reported greater satisfaction in life than the nongifted.

On the other hand, the picture of these intellectually gifted people was not unvaryingly positive. Not every member of the group Terman studied was successful, and in fact there were some notable failures. Moreover, other research suggests that high intelligence is not a homogeneous quality; a person with a high overall IQ is not necessarily gifted in every academic subject but may excel in just one or two (Stanley, 1980; Sternberg & Davidson, 1986). A high IQ, then, does not guarantee success in everything.

Although special programs attempting to overcome the deficits of the mentally retarded abound, only recently have ways of encouraging the talents of the intellectually gifted been developed. This lack of special attention has been due in part to the persistent view that the gifted ought to be able to "make it on their own"; if they can't, then they really aren't gifted in the first place (Maeroff, 1977; Berger, 1988). More enlightened approaches, however, have acknowledged that without some form of special attention, the gifted may become bored and frustrated with the pace of their schooling and may never reach their full potential (Reis, 1989; Borland, 1989).

One particularly successful program for the intellectually gifted is a project called the Study of the Mathematically Precocious Youth (SMPY). In the program, seventh graders who have shown unusual mathematical success are enrolled in summer classes in which they are rapidly taught complex mathematical skills, culminating in college-level calculus (Stanley, 1980). In addition, they receive instruction in a variety of other subjects, including the sciences and languages. The ultimate goal of the program, and others like it, is to provide sufficient enrichment and acceleration to the gifted to allow their talents to flourish and to increase the likelihood that they will reach their maximum potential. Although it is too early to tell whether enrichment programs such as SMPY are effective—since the graduates of these programs have yet to reach adulthood—such special programs have been highly rated by participants. (For another facet of intelligence, see the Cutting Edge box.)

THE CUTTING EDGE

ESTABLISHING INTELLIGENCE: THE EARLIEST SIGNS OF IQ

How soon can we determine a child's intelligence?

Until recently, most psychologists would have answered that it is not until a child is 3 or 4 years of age that accurate predictions can be made. However, a growing number of psychologists now feel that relatively accurate estimates of adult intelligence can be made in children as young as 6 months (Bornstein & Sigman, 1986).

For example, certain tests that indicate how babies process information in the first six months of their lives are associated with their per-

formance on IQ tests when they reach school age. According to Marc Bornstein of New York University and Susan Rose of Albert Einstein College of Medicine of New York, tests of visual attentiveness administered during the first six months are correlated with IQ scores at ages 4 and 6. Furthermore, the relationship holds regardless of children's socioeconomic status or the

educational level of their parents (Kolata, 1987).

In Bornstein and Rose's work, a group of 6-month-old children was shown photographs of faces or abstract patterns and geometric shapes. After viewing the first picture, each infant was shown a new one, and the experimenters measured how long the infant spent looking at the new, as opposed to the old, picture. Overall, infants spent an average of 60 percent of their time looking at new pictures, but there were large differences among children. These differences were related statistically to intelli gence test scores at ages 4 and 6.

The reason such a test seems sensitive to the infants' intelligence is that the processes being meas ured seem to go beyond mere per ceptual memory and instead relate to the way in which the infants ac tively process information. It ap pears that the babies not only re member the first photo but also are able to discriminate the novelty of the second one, comparing it with the first.

It is too early to judge the practi cal implications of these findings. For one thing, there are ample pos sibilities for the influence of environ mental factors, since the strength of the association between the results of the six-month visual attentiveness measure and school-age intelli gence is only moderate. Further more, as mentioned earlier in the chapter, IQ scores are not particu larly adequate predictors of ultimate success in life.

Still, these new findings suggest the possibility that interventions can be made in the earliest years of life to help raise the IQs of children who are at risk for poor school per formance (the measure which is most closely associated with IQ scores). The task for psychologists now is not only to hone their measures more finely but to identify the sorts of interventions that would be most successful in raising chil dren's intelligence levels.

Recap

◀ Mental retardation is defined by significantly subaverage general intellectual functioning along with deficits in adaptive behavior.

◀ The levels of retardation include mildly retarded (IQ of 55 to 69), moderately retarded (IQ of 40 to 54), severely retarded (IQ of 25 to 39), and profoundly retarded (IQ below 25).

◀ The most frequent causes of mental retardation are Down's syndrome and familial influences.

◀ The intellectually gifted have IQs above 130 and com prise 2 to 4 percent of the population.

Review

1. Russell displays some deficits in adaptive functioning and scores 59 on a standard IQ test. By definition, he would be classified as
   a. mildly retarded.
   b. moderately retarded.
   c. severely retarded.
   d. profoundly retarded.

2. In general, someone like Russell will probably never be capable of living independently. True or false? _____

3. Russell's younger brother is also mentally retarded. No known biological cause for either boy's retardation has been identified. Such cases of retardation are classified as
   a. Down's syndrome.
   b. genetic retardation.
   c. Mongolism.
   d. familial retardation.

4. Integrating mentally retarded children into regular class rooms is known as _____.

5. Research generally reveals that most intellectually gifted people are poorly adjusted socially. True or false? _____

6. Accurate estimates of intelligence can now be made in children as young as
   a. 1 year.
   b. 3 months.
   c. 6 months.
   d. 3 years.

7. Intelligence can be assessed at such a young age because of the ability to measure
   a. processing of information.
   b. visual acuity.
   c. perceptual memory.
   d. the effects of environmental influence.

(Answers to review questions are on page 282.)

INDIVIDUAL DIFFERENCES IN INTELLIGENCE: HEREDITY, ENVIRONMENT—OR BOTH?

Kwang is often washed with a pleck tied to a _____ .

   (*a*) rundel   (*c*) pove

   (*b*) flink   (*d*) quirj

If you found this kind of item on an intelligence test, you would probably complain that the test was totally absurd and had nothing to do with your intelligence or anyone else's. How could anyone be expected to respond to items presented in a language that was completely unfamiliar?

But suppose you found the following item, which at first glance might look equally foreign:

Which word is most out of place here?

   (*a*) splib   (*d*) spook

   (*b*) blood   (*e*) black

   (*c*) gray

Just as absurd, you say? On the contrary, there is considerably more reason to use this second item on an intelligence test than the first example, which was made up of nonsense syllables. Although this second item may appear meaningless to the white population of the United States, to urban blacks the question might be a reasonable test of their knowledge.

The item is drawn from a test created by sociologist Adrian Dove, who tried to illustrate a problem that has plagued the developers of IQ tests from the beginning. By using terminology that would be familiar to urban blacks with inner-city backgrounds, but typically unfamiliar to whites (and to blacks raised within the dominant white culture), he dramatized the fact that cultural experience could play a critical role in determining intelligence test scores. (The answer to the item presented above, by the way, is *c*. To try your hand at other items drawn from Dove's test, see Table 8-2.)

The importance of devising fair intelligence tests that measure knowledge unrelated to cultural and family background and experience would be minor if it were not for one important and persistent finding: Members of certain racial and cultural groups consistently score lower than members of other groups (MacKenzie, 1984). For example, as a group, blacks tend to average 15 IQ points lower than whites. Does this reflect a true difference in intelligence, or are the questions biased in the kinds of knowledge they test? Clearly, if whites perform better because of their greater familiarity with the kind of information that is being tested, their higher IQ scores are not necessarily an indication that they are more intelligent than members of other groups.

In fact, there is good reason to believe that some standardized IQ tests contain elements that discriminate against minority-group members whose

ANSWERS (REVIEW II):
1. a   **2.** False; mildly mentally retarded individuals are usually capable of independent living   **3.** d   **4.** Mainstreaming   **5.** False; most gifted people are found to be well adjusted   **6.** c   **7.** a

TABLE 8-2

A Culture-*Un*fair Intelligence Test

If you have been raised within the dominant white culture, particularly in a suburban or rural environment, you may have difficulty in answering the following questions, which are designed to illustrate the importance of devising culture-fair intelligence tests.

1. Bird, or Yardbird, was the jacket jazz lovers from coast to coast hung on
(a) Lester Young
(b) Peggy Lee
(c) Benny Goodman
(d) Charlie Parker
(e) Birdman of Alcatraz

2. The opposite of square is
(a) Round
(b) Up
(c) Down
(d) Hip
(e) Lame

3. If you throw the dice and 7 is showing on the top, what is facing down?

(a) 7
(b) Snake eyes
(c) Boxcars
(d) Little Joes
(e) 11

4. Jazz pianist Ahmad Jamal took an Arabic name after becoming really famous. Previously he had what he called his "slave name." What was his previous name?
(a) Willie Lee Jackson
(b) LeRoi Jones
(c) Wilbur McDougal
(d) Fritz Jones
(e) Andy Johnson

5. In C. C. Rider, what does "C. C." stand for?
(a) Civil Service
(b) Church Council
(c) County Circuit Preacher
(d) Country Club
(e) Cheating Charley (the "Boxcar Gunsel")

6. Cheap chitlings (not the kind you purchase at the frozen-food

counter) will taste rubbery unless they are cooked long enough. How soon can you quit cooking them to eat and enjoy them?
(a) Fifteen minutes
(b) Two hours
(c) Twenty-four hours
(d) One week (on a low flame)
(e) One hour

7. A "handkerchief head" is
(a) A cool cat
(b) A porter
(c) An "Uncle Tom"
(d) A hoddi
(e) A "preacher"

Answers It is obvious how this test illustrates, in an exaggerated reverse fashion, the difficulties that a black from an inner-city background might have in responding to items on the typical intelligence test, which mirrors the dominant middle- and upper-class white culture. The correct answers are **1.** *d;* **2.** *d;* **3.** *a;* **4.** *d;* **5.** *c;* **6.** *c;* **7.** *c.*

experiences differ from those of the white majority. Consider the question "What would you do if another child grabbed your hat and ran with it?" Most white middle-class children answer that they would tell an adult, and this response is scored as "correct." On the other hand, a reasonable response might be to chase the person and fight to get the hat back, the answer that is chosen by many urban black children—but one that is scored as incorrect (Albee, 1978; Miller-Jones, 1989).

The possibility of bias and discrimination against minority-group members in traditional IQ tests has led some jurisdictions to ban their use. For example, the state of California does not permit public schools to give black students IQ tests to decide whether they should be placed in special-education classes—regardless of the students' academic background or socioeconomic status, or even following parental request—unless express permission is obtained from the courts (Baker, 1987). (Ironically, because the ban pertains only to black students, and not to whites, Hispanics, and other racial and ethnic groups, some people have argued that the ban itself is discriminatory.)

THE BASIC CONTROVERSY: Heredity versus Environment

In an attempt to produce what has come to be called a **culture-fair IQ test**, one that does not discriminate against members of any minority cultural group, psychologists have tried to devise test items which assess experiences common to all cultures or which emphasize questions that do not require language usage. However, test makers have found this difficult to do, and some culture-fair tests have produced even larger discrepancies between

Culture-fair IQ test: A test that does not discriminate against members of any minority culture group majority and minority groups than traditional tests which rely more heavily on verbal skills (Anastasi, 1988).

The efforts of psychologists to produce culture-fair measures of intelligence relate to a lingering controversy over differences in intelligence between members of minority and majority groups. In attempting to identify whether there are differences between such groups, psychologists have been faced with the broader issue of determining the relative contribution to intelligence of genetic factors (heredity) and experience (environment).

Arthur Jensen, an educational psychologist, fueled the fires of the debate with a 1969 article. He argued that an analysis of IQ differences between whites and blacks demonstrated that, although environmental factors played a role, there were also basic genetic differences between the two races. Jensen based his argument on a number of findings. For instance, on average, whites score 15 points higher than blacks on traditional IQ tests even when socioeconomic class is taken into account. According to Jensen, middle- and upper-class blacks score lower than middle- and upper-class whites, just as lower-class blacks score lower on average than do lower-class whites. Intelligence differences between blacks and whites, Jensen concluded, could not be attributed to environmental differences alone.

Heritability: A measure of the degree to which a characteristic is related to genetic, inherited factors, as opposed to environmental factors

Moreover, intelligence in general shows a high degree of **heritability**, a measure of the degree to which a characteristic is related to genetic, inherited factors. As can be seen in Figure 8-5, the closer the genetic link between two people, the greater the correspondence of IQ scores. Using data such as these, Jensen argued that fully 75 to 80 percent of the variability in IQ scores could be attributed solely to genetic factors. If we rule out environmental causes of differences between races in IQ scores, then, we are left with the conclusion—claimed by Jensen—that these differences in IQs are caused by genetically-based differences in intelligence.

FIGURE 8-5

Summary findings on IQ and closeness of genetic relationship. The length of the line indicates the range of correlations found in different studies, and the arrows show the average correlation. Note, for example, that the average correlation for unrelated people reared apart is quite low, while the correlation for identical twins, reared together, is substantially higher. The more similar the genetic and environmental background of two people, the greater the correlation. (Jencks et al., 1972; Kamin, 1979; Walker & Emory, 1985; Scarr & Carter-Saltzmann, 1985.)

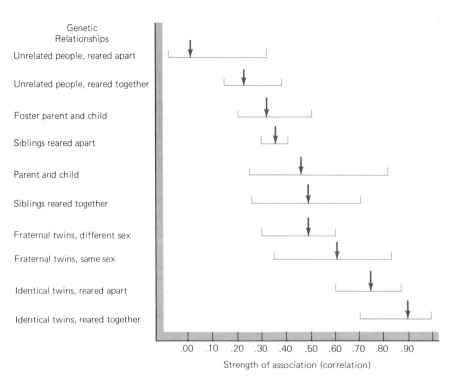

The psychology community reacted quickly to Jensen's contentions and convincingly refuted many of his claims. For one thing, even when socio-economic conditions are supposedly held constant, there remain wide variations among individual households, and no one can convincingly assert that living conditions of blacks and whites are identical even when their socio-economic status is similar. Second, as we discussed earlier, there is reason to believe that traditional IQ tests may discriminate against lower-class urban blacks, asking for information on experiences to which they are unlikely to have been exposed.

Moreover, there is direct evidence that blacks who are raised in enriched environments do not tend, as a group, to have lower IQ scores than whites in similar environments. For example, a study by Sandra Scarr and Richard Weinberg examined black children who were adopted at an early age by white middle-class families of above-average intelligence (Scarr & Weinberg, 1976). The IQ scores of the children averaged 106—about 15 points above the average IQ scores of unadopted black children reared in their own homes, and above the average in scores of the general population. In addition, the younger a child was when adopted, the higher his or her IQ score tended to be. The evidence that genetic factors play the major role in determining racial differences in IQ, then, is not compelling—although the question still evokes controversy (MacKenzie, 1984).

Ultimately, it is crucial to remember that IQ scores and intelligence have greatest relevance in terms of individuals, not groups, and that by far the greatest discrepancies in IQ occur not among mean *group* IQ scores but among the IQ scores of *individuals.* There are blacks who score high on IQ tests and whites who score low, just as there are whites who score high and blacks who score low. For the concept of intelligence to aid in the betterment of society, we must examine how *individuals* perform, not the groups to which they belong, as well as the degree to which intelligence can be improved in a given person (Angoff, 1988).

Other issues make the heredity-versus-environment debate somewhat irrelevant to practical concerns. For example, as we discussed earlier, there are many kinds of intelligence, and traditional IQ scores do not tap many of them. Indeed, some psychologists argue that IQ scores are only weakly linked to intelligence (Flynn, 1987). Furthermore, IQ scores are often inadequate predictors of ultimate work and academic success (as noted earlier in the Psychology at Work box); and actual school achievement differences between whites and blacks appear to be narrowing (Jones, 1984). In sum, questions concerning differences in white and black intelligence levels may prove to be less pertinent than those relating to understanding individual differences in IQ, without regard to race.

NEITHER HEREDITY NOR ENVIRONMENT:
Putting the Question in Perspective

There is no absolute resolution to the question of the degree to which intelligence is influenced by heredity and by environment. The reason is that we are dealing with an issue for which true experiments to unequivocally determine causality cannot be devised. (A moment's thought about how we might experimentally assign infants to enriched or deprived environments will reveal the impossibility of devising ethically reasonable experiments!)

The more critical question to ask, then, is not so much whether it is primarily heredity or environment that underlies intelligence but whether there is anything we can do to maximize the intellectual development of each individual (Scarr & Carter-Saltzman, 1982; Angoff, 1988). We then will be able to make changes in the environment—which may take the form of more enriched homes and schools—that can lead each person to reach his or her highest potential.

RECAP AND REVIEW III

Recap

◄ The issue of whether IQ tests are biased in favor of dominant groups in society arises because blacks tend to average 15 IQ points lower than whites on standardized tests.

◄ Culture-fair IQ tests have been developed in an attempt to avoid discriminating against minority groups.

◄ Probably the most important issue concerning IQ is not the degree to which it is caused by heredity or environment, but what we can do to nurture and maximize the development of intelligence in all individuals.

Review

1. IQ tests have been criticized because of
   a. length.
   b. scoring devices.
   c. the testing environment.
   d. cultural bias.

2. _____ refers to a measure of the degree to which a trait is related to genetic factors.

3. Most evidence now points to genetic differences in intelligence between blacks and whites. True or false? _____

4. Evidence has shown that the average IQ of adopted black children who are reared in white middle-class homes, with parents of above-average intelligence, is higher than the average IQ of unadopted blacks reared in their own homes. True or false? _____

5. The most constructive use of IQ test scores is probably in the assessment of the performance of
   a. groups.
   b. blacks.
   c. individuals.
   d. whites.

(Answers to review questions are on page 287.)

◄ LOOKING BACK

1. Because intelligence can take many forms, defining it presents a challenge to psychologists. One commonly accepted view is that intelligence is the capacity to understand the world, think rationally, and use resources effectively when faced with challenges.

2. Intelligence tests are used to measure intelligence. They provide a mental age which, when divided by a person's chronological age and then multiplied by 100, gives an IQ, or intelligence quotient, score. Specific tests of intelligence include the Stanford-Binet test, the Wechsler Adult Intelligence Scale—Revised (WAIS-R), and the Wechsler Intelligence Scale for Children—Revised (WISC-R). In addition to intelligence tests, other standardized tests take the form of achievement tests (which measure level of knowledge in a given area) and aptitude tests (which predict ability in a given area).

3. Although intelligence tests are able to identify individual differences in intelligence, they do not provide us with an understanding of the underlying nature of intelligence. One of the major issues here is whether there is a single, unitary factor underlying intelligence or whether intelligence is made up of particular subcomponents.

4. The earliest psychologists interested in intelligence made the assumption that there was a general factor for mental ability called g. However, later psychologists disputed the view that intelligence was unidimensional.

5. Some researchers suggest that there are two kinds of intelligence: fluid intelligence and crystallized intelligence. Gardner's theory of multiple intelligences proposes that there are seven spheres of intelligence: musical, bodily-kinesthetic, logical-mathematical, linguistic, spatial, interpersonal, and intrapersonal. At the furthest extreme, Guilford's structure-of-intellect model theorizes that there are 150 separate mental abilities.

6. Information-processing approaches suggest that intelligence should be conceptualized as the way in which people represent and use material cognitively. Rather than focusing on the structure of intelligence, they examine the processes underlying intelligent behavior. One example of an information-processing approach is Sternberg's triarchic theory of intelligence, which sug-

gests three major aspects to intelligence: componential, experiential, and contextual.

7. At the two extremes of intelligence are the mentally retarded and the intellectually gifted. The levels of mental retardation include mild retardation (IQ of 55 to 69), moderate retardation (IQ of 40 to 54), severe retardation (IQ of 25 to 39), and profound retardation (IQ below 25). About one-third of the cases of retardation have a known biological cause, with Down's syndrome being the most common. Most cases, however, are classified as ones of familial retardation, in which there is no known biological cause.

8. There have been a number of recent advances in the treatment of both the mentally retarded and the intellectually gifted, particularly after federal law mandated that the mentally retarded be educated in the least-restrictive environment. In mainstreaming, the mentally retarded are integrated into regular education classrooms as much as possible.

9. Traditional intelligence tests have frequently been criticized for being biased in favor of the white middle-class population majority. That controversy has led to attempts to devise culture-fair tests, IQ measures which avoid questions that depend on a particular cultural background.

10. Two major controversies have grown out of research on intelligence: whether there are racial differences in intelligence and the degree to which intelligence is influenced by heredity and by the environment. Because individual IQ scores vary far more than group IQ scores, it is most critical to ask what we can do to maximize the intellectual development of each individual.

KEY TERMS AND CONCEPTS ▶

intelligence (p. 265)
intelligence test (265)
mental age (266)
chronological age (266)
intelligence quotient (IQ) score (266)
deviation IQ score (266)
Stanford-Binet test (266)
Wechsler Adult Intelligence Scale—
    Revised (WAIS-R) (267)
Wechsler Intelligence Scale for
    Children—Revised (WISC-R) (267)

achievement test (268)
aptitude test (269)
g or g-factor (269)
fluid intelligence (269)
crystallized intelligence (269)
structure-of-intellect model (270)
triarchic theory of intelligence (273)
practical intelligence (273)
mental retardation (277)
mild retardation (277)

moderate retardation (277)
severe retardation (277)
profound retardation (277)
Down's syndrome (278)
familial retardation (278)
least-restrictive environment (278)
mainstreaming (278)
intellectually gifted (279)
culture-fair IQ test (283)
heritability (284)

FOR FURTHER STUDY AND APPLICATION ▶

Wigdor, A. K., & Garner, W. R. (Eds.) (1982). *Ability testing: Uses, consequences, and controversies.* Washington, D.C.: National Academy Press.

This is a comprehensive look at intelligence, ranging from the history of testing to such contemporary issues as the use of IQ scores by schoolteachers.

Sternberg, R. J. (Ed.). (1985). *Handbook of human intelligence.* New York: Cambridge University Press.

Written by the leading experts in the field, this book provides a state-of-the-art view of intelligence. Although technical, it is probably the best single source on intelligence available today.

Eysenck, H. J., & Kamin, L. (1981). *The intelligence controversy.* New York: Wiley.

This intriguing book presents widely divergent views of the nature of intelligence and covers many of the major issues raised by psychologists.

Sternberg, R. J. (1986). *Intelligence applied: Understanding and increasing your intellectual skills.* San Diego: Harcourt Brace Jovanovich.

A leading theoretician takes a practical look at ways of improving your intellectual abilities.

Gould, S. J. (1981). *Mismeasure of man.* New York: Norton.

This careful analysis of the political uses that have been made of intelligence testing traces some of the major controversies and abuses surrounding the measurement of mental abilities.

Gardner, H. (1983). *Frames of mind: The theory of multiple intelligence.* New York: Basic Books.

This interesting and well-written guide describes the different sorts of intelligence that people have.

ANSWERS (REVIEW III):
1. d **2.** Heritability **3.** False; environmental differences in upbringing and cultural bias in IQ tests better account for differences found **4.** True **5.** c

PART FOUR

FEELING AND EXPERIENCING THE WORLD

We move now from the realm of thought to that of motivation and inner experience. We meet a woman whose feelings about food lead to uncontrollable eating binges. We discover a man trapped for forty days in a canyon and see how the motivation to live results in an amazing story of survival. We encounter a woman who masquerades as a man for decades, unbeknownst even to her children. Finally, we meet a man whose sleep disorder leads him to violently act out his dreams as he sleeps.

In this part of the book, we consider how various kinds of motivation affect our choice of behaviors. We examine how emotions influence behavior and how they affect our functioning in everyday life. We consider how gender and human sexuality represent a complex interaction between biology, motivation, and social factors. Finally, we look at consciousness, considering how we experience it and how our usual state of consciousness can be altered.

In Chapter 9, we examine the movitation behind behavior and how our emotions are related to our behavior.

In Chapter 10, the focus is on gender and human sexuality, ranging from basic biological functions to sexual interaction with others.

In Chapter 11, we turn to states of consciousness, including sleep, hypnosis, and drugs.

CHAPTER

9

MOTIVATION AND EMOTION

PROLOGUE:
CHRISTINE BERGEL

She could be the girl next door. Bright, hard-working, successful and good-looking, 20-year-old Christine Bergel was a standard against whom others might compare themselves.

The trouble was that Christine never saw herself in the way others did. She hated how she looked and grew preoccupied with her appearance and weight. To cope with her feelings, Christine secretly began repeated cycles of binging on huge quantities of food, and then eliminating the food by vomiting. During her worst times, she would stuff herself and then force herself to throw up three times a day. Obsessed by the thought that she was too fat, she exercised three hours daily. Her constant binging-and-purging cycles were accompanied by deep feelings of guilt and depression over what she recognized as self-destructive behavior.

Christine's problem is called bulimia, and it is shared by some 10 percent of college-age women. It is one of a number of eating disorders that afflict mainly women of college age, although it can be found in others as well. The habitual binging-and-purging cycles of bulimia can lead to digestive-tract problems, rotted teeth, and even heart failure. Other eating disorders may lead people to literally starve themselves to death.

Christine's story, however, has a happy ending. Realizing the seriousness of her problem, Christine checked herself into the Renfrew Center, the first residential treatment facility in the United States designed exclusively for people with eating disorders. After six weeks of treatment, which included individual and group therapy, Christine came to put her eating behavior, and her obsession with her appearance, in perspective. As she says, "Somebody could look at my picture and say, 'Oh, she's pretty. Bulimia didn't do anything to her.' But that's all I was, my looks. It was such a shallow world" (Kohn, 1987).

Prior to being photographed, Christine Bergel said she was afraid she would appear too fat. Having her body outline traced gave her an opportunity to view her own silhouette more objectively. (Sarah Leen.)

LOOKING AHEAD ▶

Fortunately, few of us have eating behavior problems as severe as those that beset Christine Bergel. In fact, the major question that psychologists face when considering eating is just how we manage to regulate our food intake so effectively. Most of us show only minor variation in weight from one day to another, even though the kind of food we eat and the amount may vary significantly.

Eating behavior is just one aspect of the two central topics of psychology to which we turn our attention in this chapter: motivation and emotion. Motivation looks at the factors that direct and energize the behavior of humans and other organisms. Psychologists who study motivation seek to discover the **motives**, or desired goals, that underlie behavior. Such motives may be as fundamental as eating to satisfy the motive of hunger or as inconsequential as taking a walk to obtain exercise. To the psychologist specializing in the study of motivation, the common factor in both behaviors is that underlying motives are assumed to steer the choice of both activities.

Motives: Desired goals that prompt behavior

The study of **motivation**, then, consists of identifying why people do the things they do. Psychologists studying motivation ask questions such as these: "Why do people choose particular goals for which to strive?" "What specific motives direct behavior?" "What are the individual differences in motivation that account for the variability in people's behavior?"

Motivation: The factors that direct and energize behavior

Whereas motivation is concerned with the forces that direct future behavior, a second, and related, major area of psychology—emotion—deals with the feelings we experience throughout the course of our lives. The study of emotions focuses on our internal experiences at any given moment. Most of us have felt a variety of emotions: happiness at getting an A on a difficult exam, sadness brought about by the death of a loved one, anger at being unfairly treated. Because emotions not only can motivate our behavior but also can reflect our underlying motivation, they play a broad role in our lives, and the study of emotions has been a critical area for psychologists.

In this chapter, we consider motivation and emotion. We begin by focusing on the major conceptions of motivation, discussing how the different motives and needs people experience jointly affect behavior. We consider both primary motives, those that are biologically based and universal such as hunger, as well as motives that are unique to humans: the need for achievement, the need for affiliation, and the need for power. We then turn to the nature of emotional experience on both a physiological and a cognitive level. We consider the roles and functions that emotions play in people's lives, discussing a number of theories meant to explain how people understand what emotion they are experiencing at a given moment. Finally, the chapter ends with a discussion of how emotions are communicated to others through nonverbal behavior.

After you finish this chapter, then, you will be able to answer questions such as these:

▶ What are the biological and social factors that underlie eating behavior, and what are the best strategies for dieting?

▶ How are needs such as the need for achievement, affiliation, and power exhibited?

▶ What factors lead to the experience of an emotion?

▶ What are the major emotions and their functions?

▶ How does nonverbal behavior relate to the expression of emotions?

CONCEPTIONS OF MOTIVATION

Consider the case of 22-year-old Marine Lance Cpl. Karl Bell, who spent forty days in a steep canyon after falling in a freak hiking accident. Avoiding starvation by eating anything he could find, even ants, Bell finally found a way out. He had lost seventy-five pounds, his ankle was fractured, his body was covered with hundreds of cuts, and his clothing was torn to shreds. But he had managed to stay alive, after fighting every day and night to save himself.

What was it that drove Bell on, even in the face of overwhelming odds against survival? Like most questions revolving around motivation, this one has several answers. Clearly, biological aspects of motivation were at work: The need for food, water, and warmth affected Bell's attempts to extricate himself from the canyon. But cognitive factors were also apparent in his belief that he was too young to die. Finally, social factors—his desire to see family and friends—helped keep his will to survive intact.

The complexity of motivation has led to the development of a variety of conceptual approaches to it. Although they vary in the degree to which they encompass biological, cognitive, and social factors, all seek to explain the energy that guides people's behavior in particular directions.

BORN TO BE MOTIVATED: Instincts

Instinct: An inborn pattern of behavior that is biologically determined

Psychologists first sought to explain motivation in terms of **instincts**, inborn patterns of behavior that are biologically determined. According to instinctive theories of motivation, people and animals are born with preprogrammed sets of behaviors essential to their survival. These instincts provide the energy that channels behavior in appropriate directions. Hence, sex might be explained as a response to an instinct for reproduction, and exploratory behavior might be viewed as motivated by an instinct to examine one's territory.

There are several difficulties with such a conception, however. For one thing, psychologists have been unable to agree on what the primary instincts are. One early psychologist, William McDougall (1908), suggested that there were eighteen, including pugnacity and gregariousness. Others found even more—with one sociologist claiming that there were exactly 5,759. Clearly, such an extensive enumeration provides little more than labels for behavior.

No explanation based on the concept of instincts goes very far in explaining *why* a specific pattern of behavior, and not some other, has appeared in a given individual. Furthermore, the variety and complexity of human behavior, much of which is clearly learned, are difficult to explain if instincts are the primary motivational force. Therefore, conceptions of motivation based on instincts have largely been supplanted by newer theories, although instinctual approaches still play a role in contemporary psychology. For example, in later chapters we will discuss Freud's theories, which suggest that such instinctual drives as sex and aggression largely motivate behavior. Moreover, many animal behaviors clearly have an instinctual basis.

In rejecting instinct theory, psychologists first proposed simple **drive-reduction** theories of motivation in its place (Hull, 1943). Drive-reduction theories suggest that when people lack some basic biological requirement such as water, a drive to obtain that requirement (in this case, the thirst drive) is produced.

To understand the approach, we need to begin with the concept of drive. A **drive** is motivational tension, or arousal, that energizes behavior in order to fulfill some need. Many basic kinds of drives, such as hunger, thirst, sleepiness, and sex, are related to biological requirements of the body or of the species as a whole. These are called **primary drives**. Primary drives contrast with **secondary drives**, in which no obvious biological need is being fulfilled. In secondary drives, needs are brought about by prior experience and learning. As we will discuss later, some people have strong needs to achieve academically and in their careers; we can say that their achievement need is a secondary drive motivating their behavior.

We usually try to resolve a primary drive by reducing the need underlying it: After exercising, we may become thirsty and seek out the nearest water fountain. We become hungry after not eating for a few hours and may raid the refrigerator if our next scheduled meal is too far away. If the weather turns cold, we put on extra clothing or raise the setting on the thermostat in order to keep warm.

The reason for such behavior is homeostasis, a basic motivational phenomenon underlying primary drives. **Homeostasis** is the process by which a person or animal tries to maintain some optimal level of internal biological functioning by compensating for deviations from its usual, balanced, internal state. Although not all basic biological behaviors related to motivation fit a homeostatic model—sexual behavior is one example, as we will see in the next chapter—most of the fundamental needs of life, including hunger, thirst, and the need for sleep, can be explained reasonably well by such an approach.

Unfortunately, although drive-reduction theories provide a good explanation of how primary drives motivate behavior, they are inadequate when it comes to explaining behaviors in which the goal is not to reduce a drive, but rather to maintain or even to increase a particular level of excitement or arousal. For example, many of us go out of our way to seek thrills through such activities as riding a roller coaster and steering a raft down the rapids of a river.

Other behaviors seem to be motivated by nothing more than curiosity. Anyone who has rushed to pick up newly delivered mail, or who avidly follows gossip columns in the newspaper, or who yearns to travel to exotic places, knows the importance of curiosity in directing behavior. And it is not just human beings who display behavior indicative of curiosity: Even monkeys will learn to press a bar just to be able to peer into another room, especially if something interesting (such as a toy train moving along a track) can be glimpsed (Butler, 1954). Monkeys will also expend considerable energy solving simple mechanical puzzles, even though their behavior produces no obvious reward (Harlow, Harlow & Meyer, 1950; Mineka & Hendersen, 1985).

Thrill seeking and curiosity are just two kinds of behavior that shed doubt on drive-reduction theories of motivation. In both cases, rather than

Drive-reduction theory: The theory which claims that drives are produced to obtain our basic biological requirements

Drive: A motivational tension or arousal that energizes behavior in order to fulfill a need

Primary drives: Biological needs such as hunger, thirst, fatigue, and sex

Secondary drives: Drives in which no biological need is fulfilled (e.g., need for achievement)

Homeostasis: the process by which an organism tries to maintain an internal biological balance, or "steady state"

seeking to reduce an underlying drive, people and animals appear to be motivated to increase their overall level of stimulation and activity. In order to explain this phenomenon, psychologists have suggested several alternatives to drive reduction.

THE SEARCH FOR STIMULATION: Arousal Theory

Arousal theories seek to explain behavior in which the goal is the maintenance of or an increase in excitement (Berlyne, 1967; Brehm & Self, 1989). According to **arousal theory**, each of us tries to maintain a certain level of stimulation and activity. As with the drive-reduction model, if our stimulation and activity levels become too high, we try to reduce them. But the arousal model also suggests something quite different from the drive-reduction model: If the levels of stimulation and activity are too low, we will try to *increase* them by seeking stimulation.

Arousal theory provides an explanation for one of the oldest principles of psychology, devised by two psychologists in 1908: the **Yerkes-Dodson law**. According to this law and its later revisions, a particular level of motivational arousal produces optimal performance on a task; more specifically, performance on simple tasks usually benefits from higher levels of arousal than does performance on more complex tasks (Hebb, 1955). It seems as if high arousal gets in the way of successful responses to complex tasks, while promoting better performance on simpler tasks (see Figure 9-1).

On the other hand, both complex and simple tasks suffer when the level of arousal is *too* high. In this case, the arousal is distracting and anxiety-producing, decreasing performance regardless of the difficulty of the task (Covington & Omelich, 1987). In sum, consistent with arousal theory, there is an optimal level of arousal for task performance; arousal that is either too high or too low will result in poorer performance.

People vary widely in the optimal level of arousal that they seek out (Mineka & Henderson, 1985). Individuals as diverse as comic John Belushi, DNA researcher Sir Francis Crick, daredevil Evel Knievel, and bank robbers Bonnie and Clyde appear to share a cluster of characteristics that make up what psychologist Frank Farley calls the Type T or thrill-seeking personality (Farley, 1986). Such people seek excitement and stimulation not only in physical domains, through such exploits as mountain climbing and skydiving, but in mental domains, through unusually high levels of creativity and risk-taking behavior. In many cases, the characteristics associated with a thrill-

Arousal theory: The belief that we try to maintain certain levels of stimulation and activity, increasing or reducing them as necessary

Yerkes-Dodson law: The theory that a particular level of motivational arousal produces optimal performance of a task

FIGURE 9-1

The Yerkes-Dodson law claims that the optimal performance on a task will come from different levels of arousal, depending on whether the task is simple as seen in (*a*) or complex as seen in (*b*).

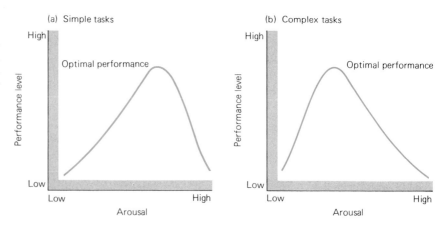

seeking personality lead to positive outcomes, as seen in unusually creative scientific innovations (the case with Sir Francis Crick, the codiscoverer of DNA's structure). But thrill seeking can also lead to destructive results, as seen in criminal behavior (the case with Bonnie and Clyde) or political manipulation.

Few people are pure Type T's, and many of us characteristically seek out relatively low levels of stimulation (for example, people who get excitement from such sedentary exploits as playing chess or Trivial Pursuit). For a sense of your own characteristic level of stimulation, try the questionnaire in Table 9-1.

Arousal theory has significant applications to a variety of fields. For example, students who are highly anxious while taking tests on complex material may perform well below their ability because of their high level of arousal. In a completely different realm—the baseball field—research has shown that batting performance, which represents a complex task, suffers under conditions of high arousal but is enhanced under conditions of low arousal (Jackson, Buglione & Glenwick, 1988).

High sensation seekers may enjoy the physical risk of sky diving. (Craig Aurness/ Woodfin Camp.)

TABLE 9-1

Do You Seek Out Sensation?

How much stimulation do you crave in your everyday life? You will have an idea after you complete the following questionnaire, which lists some items from a scale designed to assess your sensation-seeking tendencies. Circle either A or B in each pair of statements.

1. A I would like a job that requires a lot of traveling.
B I would prefer a job in one location.
2. A I am invigorated by a brisk, cold day.
B I can't wait to get indoors on a cold day.
3. A I get bored seeing the same old faces.
B I like the comfortable familiarity of everyday friends.
4. A I would prefer living in an ideal society in which everyone was safe, secure, and happy.
B I would have preferred living in the unsettled days of our history.
5. A I sometimes like to do things that are a little frightening.
B A sensible person avoids activities that are dangerous.
6. A I would not like to be hypnotized.

B I would like to have the experience of being hypnotized.
7. A The most important goal of life is to live it to the fullest and to experience as much as possible.
B The most important goal of life is to find peace and happiness.
8. A I would like to try parachute jumping.
B I would never want to try jumping out of a plane, with or without a parachute.
9. A I enter cold water gradually, giving myself time to get used to it.
B I like to dive or jump right into the ocean or a cold pool.
10. A When I go on a vacation, I prefer the comfort of a good room and bed.
B When I go on a vacation, I prefer the change of camping out.
11. A I prefer people who are emotionally expressive, even if they are a bit unstable.
B I prefer people who are calm and even-tempered.
12. A A good painting should shock or jolt the senses.
B A good painting should give one a feeling of peace and security.
13. A People who ride motorcycles must have some kind of uncon-

scious need to hurt themselves.
B I would like to drive or ride a motorcycle.

Scoring Give yourself one point for each of the following responses: 1A, 2A, 3A, 4B, 5A, 6B, 7A, 8A, 9B, 10B, 11A, 12A, 13B. Find your total score by adding up the number of points and then use the following scoring key:
0–3 very low sensation seeking
4–5 low
6–9 average
10–11 high
12–13 very high

Keep in mind, of course, that this short questionnaire, for which the scoring is based on the results of college students who have taken it, provides only a rough estimate of your sensation-seeking tendencies. Moreover, as people get older, their sensation-seeking scores tend to decrease. Still, the questionnaire will give you at least an indication of where you stand when it comes to filling your life with sensation. Source: Zuckerman, 1978.

Incentive: An external stimulus anticipated as a reward which directs and energizes behavior

Incentive theory: The theory explaining motivation in terms of external stimuli

Opponent-process theory: The theory that suggests that increases in arousal produce a calming reaction in the nervous system, and vice versa

PULLING BEHAVIOR: Incentive Theory

When a luscious dessert is brought to the table after a filling meal, the attraction we feel has little or nothing to do with internal drives or with the maintenance of arousal. Rather, if we choose to eat the dessert, such behavior is motivated by the external stimulus of the dessert itself, which acts as an anticipated reward. This reward, in motivational terms, is an **incentive**.

Incentive theory attempts to explain why behavior is not always motivated by an internal need such as the desire to reduce drives or to maintain an optimum level of arousal. Instead of focusing on internal factors, incentive theory explains motivation in terms of the nature of the external stimuli—the incentives that direct and energize behavior. In this view, properties of external stimuli largely account for a person's motivation.

Although the theory explains why we may succumb to an incentive (such as an attractive dessert) even though internal cues (such as hunger) are lacking, it seems insufficient to provide a complete explanation of motivation, since organisms seek to fulfill needs even when incentives are not apparent. Because of this, many psychologists feel that the internal drives proposed by drive-reduction theory work in tandem with the external incentives of incentive theory to "push" and "pull" behavior, respectively. Rather than contradicting each other, then, drives *and* incentives may work together in motivating behavior (Hoyenga & Hoyenga, 1984).

THE YIN AND YANG OF MOTIVATION: Opponent-process Theory

When Chinese philosophers suggested long ago that there were two opposing forces in the universe—the Yin and the Yang—which influenced human behavior, they were foreshadowing the development of one further model of motivation called opponent-process theory (Solomon & Corbit, 1974). **Opponent-process theory** helps explain the motivation behind such phenomena as drug addiction and the physiological and emotional reactions that occur as a result of extremes of physical danger, as in skydiving.

According to opponent-process theory, stimuli that first produce increases in arousal later produce an opposite, calming reaction in the nervous system, whereas stimuli that first produce decreases in arousal later produce an increase in arousal. Moreover, with each exposure to a stimulus, the original response to the stimulus remains fairly stable or perhaps even declines, while the opponent process—the reaction to the original response—tends to grow in strength.

Let's look at some concrete examples. Suppose a man takes a drug that produces feelings of unusual happiness. According to the theory, after these initial positive feelings subside, an opponent process will follow, swinging the man toward an opposite of happiness, or depression. In addition, the theory suggests that the opponent process (depression) tends to strengthen each time the drug is taken, whereas the initial process (happiness) tends to weaken. Consequently, the negative reaction will increase after each drug use, whereas the pleasure derived from the drug will decline. Ultimately, the man's motivation to increase the positive process (and avoid the eventual unpleasant opponent process) will lead him to take a larger quantity of the drug—likely resulting in a pattern of addiction.

Opponent processes work in the reverse way when the initial experience is negative. Consider a woman about to make her first skydiving jump from an airplane. Her initial reaction is likely to be one of terror. But there will also be an opponent process at work: a feeling of euphoria after the jump is over. Opponent-process theory suggests that each time she jumps, the original process resulting in terror will grow no stronger and in fact may even weaken, whereas the opponent process resulting in euphoria is likely to increase. Ultimately, then, skydiving may become almost addictive to a skydiver.

In sum, opponent-process theory helps explain why people hold strong motivation for behavior that on the surface has few benefits. It is frequently the opponent process, not the initial reaction, that maintains the motivation to carry out such behavior.

THINKING ABOUT MOTIVES: Cognitive Theory

One contemporary approach to motivation focuses on the role of our thoughts, expectations, and understanding of the world. As we will discuss in detail in Chapter 19, we develop sophisticated explanations for the causes behind other people's behavior, and these explanations have an important impact on our own subsequent behavior. In short, each of us develops our own, personal motivational theories, based on our understanding of the world, in an effort to explain the reasons for others' behavior.

One central distinction psychologists make is intrinsic versus extrinsic motivation. **Intrinsic motivation** causes us to participate in an activity for our own enjoyment, not for any tangible reward that it will bring us. In contrast, **extrinsic motivation** causes us to do something for a tangible reward. According to research on the two types of motivation, we are more apt to persist, work harder, and produce work of higher quality when motivation for a task is intrinsic rather than extrinsic (Lepper, 1984; Deci & Ryan, 1985).

Ongoing work on intrinsic and extrinsic motivation is well illustrated by a recent experiment by Teresa Amabile (1985). She asked a group of volunteers who were experienced in creative writing to compose a short poem. After completing the task, some of the participants were given a list of "extrinsic" reasons for writing poetry (such as making money, impressing others, and becoming well known); another group was given a list of "intrinsic" reasons for writing (such as enjoyment in using words and satisfaction in expressing oneself with precision). In addition, a control group was given no list of reasons.

Next, subjects in all three groups were asked to write a second poem. A group of established poets then judged the overall creativity of each of the two poems written by the participants. There was no difference between the two groups in judged creativity of their first poems. However, the second set of poems revealed a difference. The poems of the writers who were given extrinsic reasons showed a marked decline in creativity from their first attempt—while the poems of those given intrinsic reasons and those in the control group showed no change in creativity between their first and second efforts (see Figure 9-2). Concentrating on extrinsic reasons for writing, then, resulted in a decrease in creativity.

Such research suggests the importance of promoting intrinsic motivation and indicates that providing extrinsic rewards (or, as in this case, simply calling attention to them) may actually undermine the effort and quality of performance. Teachers might think twice, then, about offering their students an A for a good composition. Instead, the work on intrinsic motivation sug-

Intrinsic motivation: Motivation by which people participate in an activity for their own enjoyment, not for the reward it will get them

Extrinsic motivation: Motivation by which people participate in an activity for a tangible reward

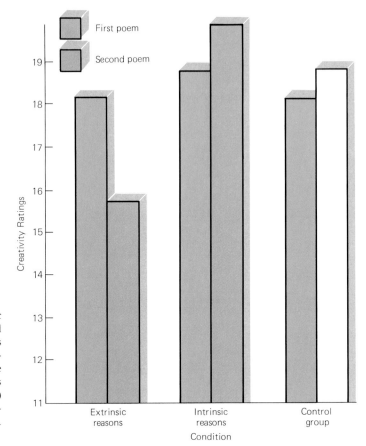

FIGURE 9-2

Subjects who were presented with extrinsic reasons for writing poetry (such as financial gain or fame) subsequently wrote poems that were judged less creative than an earlier poem. In contrast, subjects who were presented with intrinsic reasons (such as writing for the enjoyment of using words) or no reasons showed essentially no difference between their first and second efforts. (Amabile, 1985.)

gests that better results would come from reminding students about the intrinsic reasons—such as the joys of producing a carefully crafted paper—for good performance.

ORDERING MOTIVATIONAL NEEDS: Maslow's Hierarchy

What do Eleanor Roosevelt, Abraham Lincoln, and Albert Einstein have in common? Quite a bit, according to a model of motivation devised by psychologist Abraham Maslow: Each of them reached and fulfilled the highest levels of motivational needs underlying human behavior.

Maslow's model considers different motivational needs to be ordered in a hierarchy, and it suggests that before more sophisticated, higher-order needs can be met, certain primary needs must be satisfied (Maslow, 1970; 1987). The model can be thought of as a pyramid (see Figure 9-3) in which the more basic needs are at the bottom and the higher-level needs are at the top. In order for a particular need to be activated and thereby guide a person's behavior, the more basic needs in the hierarchy must be met first.

The most basic needs are those described earlier as primary drives: needs for water, food, sleep, sex, and the like. In order to move up the hierarchy, a person must have these basic physiological needs met. Safety needs come next in the hierarchy; Maslow suggests that people need a safe, secure environment in order to function effectively. Physiological and safety needs compose the lower-order needs.

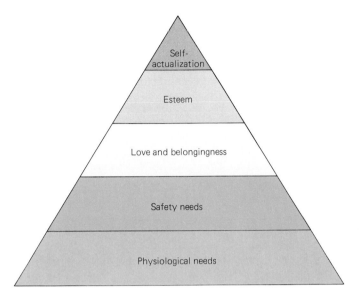

FIGURE 9-3

Maslow's hierarchy shows how our motivation progresses up the pyramid from a basis in the broadest, most fundamental biological needs to higher-order ones. (After Maslow, 1970.)

Only when the basic lower-order needs are met can a person consider fulfilling higher-order needs, consisting of love and belongingness, esteem, and self-actualization. Love and belongingness needs include the need to obtain and give affection and to be a contributing member of some group or society. After these needs are fulfilled, the person strives for esteem. In Maslow's thinking, esteem relates to the need to develop a sense of self-worth by knowing that others are aware of one's competence and value.

Once these four sets of needs are fulfilled—no easy task—the person is ready to strive for the highest-level need, self-actualization. **Self-actualization** is a state of self-fulfillment in which people realize their highest potential. When Maslow first discussed the concept, he used it to describe just a few well-known individuals such as Eleanor Roosevelt, Lincoln, and Einstein. But self-actualization is not limited to the famous. A parent with excellent nurturing skills who raises a family, a teacher who year after year creates an

Self-actualization: In Maslow's theory, a state of self-fulfillment in which people realize their highest potential

Self-actualization is the attainment of one's highest potential for achievement and self-satisfaction. (Michael Grecco/Stock Boston)

environment that maximizes students' success, and an artist who realizes her creative potential might all be self-actualized. The important thing is that people feel at ease with themselves and satisfied that they are using their talents to the fullest. In a sense, reaching self-actualization produces a decline in the striving and yearning for greater fulfillment that marks most people's lives and instead provides a sense of satisfaction with the current state of affairs.

Although there is very little research to validate the exact ordering of the stages of Maslow's theory (Haymes, Green, & Quinto, 1984), the model is important in two ways: It highlights the complexity of human needs, and it emphasizes the fact that until more basic biological needs are met, people are going to be relatively unconcerned with higher-order needs. If people are hungry, their first interest will be in obtaining food; they will not be concerned with such things as love and self-esteem. The model helps explain why victims of such disasters as famine and war may suffer the breakdown of normal family ties and be unconcerned with the welfare of anyone other than themselves.

A Final Word about the Theories of Motivation

Now that we have examined several different theoretical approaches to motivation, it is natural to wonder which provides the fullest account of motivational phenomena. In fact, many of the conceptual approaches are complementary—rather than contradictory—and it is often useful to employ several theories simultaneously in order to understand a particular motivational system. Thus, as we next consider specific motives, such as the needs for food, water, achievement, affiliation, and power, we will draw upon several of the theories in order to gain a full understanding of motivation.

RECAP AND REVIEW I

Recap

◀ The study of motivation looks at the factors that energize and direct people's behavior.

◀ A drive is a motivational tension that energizes behavior to fulfill some need. Primary drives typically operate according to the principle of homeostasis, in which an organism strives to restore any deviations from a balanced, preferred internal state.

◀ Drive-reduction theory proposes that behavior is motivated by drives to reduce biological needs. However, it does not explain why people sometimes seek out stimulation.

◀ Arousal theory suggests that we try to maintain a certain level of stimulation and activity. Arousal theory is consistent with the Yerkes-Dodson law, which demonstrates that too much or too little arousal will result in inferior performance.

◀ Opponent-process theory suggests that changes in arousal level in one direction lead to a reaction in the nervous system in the opposite direction.

◀ According to Maslow's motivational model, motivational needs progress in a hierarchy from most basic to higher-order needs. The specific categories include physiological, safety, love and belongingness, esteem, and self-actualization needs.

Review

1. Much of human behavior is too varied and complex to be explained solely in terms of instincts. True or false? _____

2. Hunger and thirst are related to _____ drives, whereas _____ drives have no biological basis.

3. After running five miles in hot weather, Judie craved fluids and salty foods. Her desires can be explained by the process of _____ .

4. Sarah took up hang gliding to satisfy a need for stimulation she felt. This type of motivation might be explained by _____ theory.

5. According to the Yerkes-Dodson law, very high levels of arousal negatively affect performance on both simple and complex tasks. True or false? _____

6. Salespeople who work especially hard for commissions are evidence for the _____ theory of motivation.

7. Adam was almost sick with fear before his first rock-climbing experience. However, the feelings of fear gradually diminished over time and were replaced by stronger and stronger feelings of euphoria. This seemingly ironic phenomenon is best explained by
   a. incentive theory.
   b. drive reduction theory.
   c. the Yerkes-Dodson law.
   d. opponent-process theory.

8. Based on findings on intrinsic versus extrinsic motivation, which of the following would be the best advice you could give a teacher who wanted to encourage students to work and learn?
   a. Have children earn recess time by completing their schoolwork.

   b. Encourage achievement of good grades.
   c. Praise hard-working children in front of their classmates.
   d. Comment on the positive feelings associated with good academic performance.

9. Which one of the following is true of Maslow's hierarchy of needs?
   a. Basic needs must be met before higher-order needs can be met.
   b. Self-actualization is eventually achieved by nearly everyone.
   c. Love and marriage go together like a horse and carriage.
   d. Love, belongingness, and esteem are lower-order needs.

(Answers to review questions are on page 304.)

EAT, DRINK, AND BE DARING: HUMAN NEEDS AND MOTIVATION

To Bob, doing well in college meant that he would get into a good law school, which he saw as a stepping-stone to a successful future. Consequently, he never let up academically and always tried his best to do well in his courses. But his constant academic striving went well beyond the desire to get into law school; he tried not only to get good grades, but to get *better* grades than his classmates.

In fact, Bob was always trying to be the best at everything he did. He could turn the simplest activity into a competition. Bob couldn't even play poker without acting as if his success at the game were essential. There were, however, some areas in which he didn't compete. He was interested only if he thought he had a fighting chance to succeed; he ignored challenges that were too difficult as well as those that were too easy for him.

What is the motivation behind Bob's consistent striving to achieve? To answer that question, we must begin to consider some of the specific kinds of needs that underlie behavior.

We will examine several of the most important human needs. Because human beings are in a fundamental sense biological creatures, we first consider the primary drive that has received the most attention among psychologists: hunger. But because much of human behavior has no clear biological basis, we will also examine the secondary drives—those uniquely human strivings, based on learned needs and past experience, that help explain behavior such as Bob's.

EATING YOUR NEEDS AWAY: Hunger

With about a quarter of the United States population suffering from **obesity** (defined as being more than 20 percent above the average weight for a

Obesity: The state of being more than 20 percent above the average weight for a person of a particular height person of a given height), losing unwanted weight has become an American obsession. Many people spend untold time, energy, and money attempting to regulate the amount and type of food they eat in order to decrease their weight. Others, with a problem many of us would envy, are concerned with trying to *gain* weight. Yet, in most cases, people who are not monitoring their weight show only minor weight fluctuations in spite of substantial variations in how much they eat and exercise over time. Clearly, then, eating is subject to some form of homeostasis.

Psychologists began their search for an understanding of eating motivation with animals, which are relatively free of the problems of obesity that beset human beings. Most nonhumans, when left in an environment in which food is readily available, do a good job regulating their intake—as anyone knows who makes sure that a dish of food is always available for a pet. Cats, for instance, will eat only until their immediate hunger is satisfied; they leave the remainder, returning to it only when internal cues tell them to eat.

Furthermore, there appear to be internal mechanisms that regulate not only the quantity of food intake, but the kind of food that an animal desires. Hungry rats that have been deprived of particular foods tend to seek out alternatives that contain the specific nutrients their diet is lacking, and laboratory experiments show that animals given the choice of a wide variety of foods in cafeteria-like settings choose a fairly well-balanced diet (Rozin, 1977; del Rio & Stevens, 1989).

The mechanisms by which organisms know whether they require food or should stop eating are complex ones (Keesey & Powley, 1986). It is not just a matter of an empty stomach causing hunger pangs and a full one alleviating hunger, since people who have had their stomachs removed still experience the sensation of hunger (Inglefinger, 1944). Similarly, laboratory animals tend to eat larger quantities when their food is low in nutrients; in contrast, when given a high-nutrient diet, they lower their food intake—despite the degree to which their stomach is empty or full or the amount of time it takes to eat the food (Harte, Travers & Savich, 1948).

It appears, then, that animals, as well as people, are sensitive to both the amount and the nutritional value of the foods they eat (Barker, Best & Domjan, 1977). One mechanism that helps to regulate food intake is a change in the chemical composition of the blood. For instance, experiments show that when glucose, a kind of sugar, is injected into the blood, hunger decreases, and animals will refuse to eat. On the other hand, when insulin, a hormone that is involved in the conversion of glucose into stored fat, is introduced into the bloodstream, hunger increases (Rodin, 1985).

But what part of the body monitors changes in the blood chemistry relating to eating behavior? One particular structure of the brain, the **hypothalamus** (see Figure 9-4), appears to be primarily responsible for food intake. Injury to the hypothalamus has been shown to cause radical changes in eating behavior, depending upon the site of the injury. For example, rats whose **lateral hypothalamus** is damaged may literally starve to death; they refuse food when offered, and unless they are force-fed they eventually die. Rats with an injury to the **ventromedial hypothalamus** display the opposite problem: extreme overeating. Rats with this injury can increase in weight by

Hypothalamus: The structure in the brain that is primarily responsible for regulating food intake

Lateral hypothalamus: The part of the brain which, when damaged, results in an organism's starving to death

Ventromedial hypothalamus: The part of the brain which, when injured, results in extreme overeating

---

ANSWERS (REVIEW I):
1. True **2.** Primary, secondary **3.** Homeostasis **4.** Arousal **5.** True **6.** Incentive **7.** d **8.** d **9.** a

Corpus callosum

Cerebral cortex

Thalamus

Hypothalamus

Pons

Medulla

Cerebellum

Plane of section

FIGURE 9-4

The hypothalamus acts as the brain's "feeding center," being primarily responsible for food intake.

as much as 400 percent (see Figure 9-5). Similar phenomena occur in humans who have tumors of the hypothalamus.

Although it is clear that the hypothalamus plays an important role in regulating food intake, the exact mechanism by which it operates is uncertain. Some researchers think it affects an organism's sense or perception of hunger; others hypothesize that it directly regulates the neural connections that control the muscles involved in eating behavior (Stricker & Zigmond, 1976).

FIGURE 9-5

Following an operation in which its ventromedial hypothalamus was cut, this obviously pudgy rat tipped the scales at something on the order of four times its normal weight. (Courtesy of Neal E. Miller.)

Weight set point: The particular level of weight the body strives to maintain

One theory suggests that injury to the hypothalamus affects the weight set point by which food intake is regulated (Nisbett, 1972). The **weight set point** is the particular level of weight that the body strives to maintain. Acting as a kind of internal weight thermostat, the hypothalamus calls for either greater or less food intake. According to this explanation, injury to the hypothalamus drastically raises or lowers the set point, and the organism strives to meet its internal goal by increasing or decreasing its food consumption.

Social Factors in Eating

You have just finished a full meal and are completely stuffed. Suddenly, your host announces with great fanfare that he will be serving his "house specialty" dessert, flaming bananas, and that he has spent the better part of the afternoon preparing it. Even though you are full and don't even like bananas, you accept a serving of his dessert and eat it completely.

Clearly, internal biological factors are not the full story when it comes to explaining our eating behavior. External social factors, based on societal rules and conventions, and on what we have learned about appropriate eating behavior from our prior experience, also play an important role.

Take, for example, the simple fact that people customarily eat breakfast, lunch, and dinner at approximately the same times every day. Because we are accustomed to eating on schedule every day, we tend to feel hungry as the usual hour approaches—sometimes quite independently of what our internal cues are telling us. Similarly, we tend to take roughly the same amount of food on our plates every day—even though the amount of exercise we may have had, and consequently our need for energy replenishment, varies from day to day. We also tend to prefer particular foods over others; grasshoppers may be a delicacy in certain cultures, but few people in western cultures find them greatly appealing—despite their potentially high nutritional value. In sum, cultural influences and our own individual habits play an important role in determining when, what, and how much we eat (Polivy & Herman, 1985; Boaks, Popplewell, & Burton, 1987).

An oversensitivity to external eating cues based on social convention, and a parallel insensitivity to internal hunger cues, is related to obesity in some individuals. Research has shown, for example, that obese people who are placed in a room next to an inviting bowl of crackers are apt to eat considerably more than nonobese people—even though they may have just finished a filling sandwich (Schachter, Goldman & Gordon, 1968). In addition, obese individuals are more apt to scorn and avoid unpleasant-tasting food—even if they have been deprived of food for a period of time—than nonobese individuals, who tend to be less concerned with the taste of the food, suggesting that the obese respond less to internal hunger cues than the nonobese. Finally, the obese are less apt to eat if doing so involves any sort of work: In one experiment obese subjects were less likely to eat nuts that had to be shelled, but ate copious amounts of nuts that already had their shells removed. Nonobese people, in contrast, ate the same amount of nuts, regardless of whether it was necessary to remove the shells (Schachter, 1971).

At the same time that obese people are overly sensitive to external cues, they may be relatively insensitive to internal hunger cues. In fact, there is essentially no correspondence between reports of hunger in obese individuals and the amount of time they have been deprived of food, in contrast to a significant correlation for people of normal weight (Nisbett, 1968). It thus appears that many obese people give undue attention to external cues and

The appearance of these fat cells, magnified many times, illustrates the outcome of over-eating. (From *Tissues and Organs: A Text-Atlas of Scanning Electron Microscopy* by Richard G. Kessel and Randy H. Kardon, W. H. Freeman and Company. Copyright © 1979)

are less aware of the internal cues that help nonobese people regulate their eating behavior.

On the other hand, many individuals who are highly reliant on external cues never become obese, and there are quite a few obese people who are relatively unresponsive to external cues (Rodin, 1981). Other factors, then, are clearly at work in determining why some people become obese.

The Weight Set Point, Metabolism, and Obesity

One suspect that appears to be a plausible cause of obesity is the weight set point. Specifically, it is possible that overweight people have higher set points than people of normal weight. Because their set points are unusually high, their attempts to lose weight by eating less may make them especially sensitive to external, food-related cues and therefore more apt to eat, perpetuating their obesity.

But why may some people's weight set points be higher than others? One factor may be the size and number of fat cells in the body, which rise as a function of weight increase. Because the set-point level may reflect the number of fat cells a person has, any increase in weight, which raises the number of fat cells, may raise the set point. Moreover, any loss of weight after the age of 2 does not decrease the number of fat cells in the body, although it may cause them to shrink in size (Knittle, 1975). Hence, although fat babies are sometimes considered cute, obese children may have acquired so many fat cells that their weight set point is too high—long after they have reached the age at which being chubby or fat is still appealing.

In sum, according to weight-set-point theory, the presence of too many fat cells may result in the set point becoming "stuck" at a higher level than is desirable. Under such circumstances, losing weight becomes a difficult proposition, since one is constantly at odds with one's own internal set point.

Other factors also work against people's efforts to lose weight. For example, there are large differences in people's **metabolism**, the rate at which energy is produced and expanded by the body. Some people, with a high metabolism rate, seem to be able to eat as much as they want without gaining weight, while others, with low metabolism, may eat only half as much and yet gain weight readily. Actually, those who gain weight easily are biologically

Metabolism: The rate at which energy is produced and expended by the body more efficient: They have the advantage (?) of easily converting food into body tissue. In contrast, those who are able to eat large quantities without gaining weight are inefficient in using the foods they eat; much gets wasted—and they stay thin. (For more on the role of metabolism in obesity, see the Cutting Edge box.)

Still other factors may lead to obesity. Children who are given food after becoming upset may learn, through the basic mechanisms of classical and operant conditioning, that eating is associated with consolation, so they may eat whenever they experience difficulties as adults. When parents provide food as the "treatment" for their child's stress, anxiety, and depression, eating may become a learned response to any emotional difficulty, leading to eating behavior that has little or nothing to do with internal hunger cues (Davis, 1986; Herman & Polivy, 1975).

In the most extreme cases, eating behavior can be so disordered that it becomes life threatening, as described in the case of Christine Bergel at the beginning of the chapter. In one major disorder, **anorexia nervosa**, people may refuse to eat, while denying that their behavior and appearance—which can become skeleton-like—are unusual. Some 15 to 20 percent of anorexics literally starve to death.

Anorexia nervosa afflicts mainly females between the ages of 12 and the early twenties, although both men and women of other ages may develop

Anorexia nervosa: An eating disorder usually striking young women in which symptoms include self-starvation or near self-starvation in an attempt to avoid obesity

---

THE CUTTING EDGE

BORN TO BE FAT? REMOVING THE BLAME FROM THE OBESE

Are some people genetically born to be fat?

Growing evidence suggests the answer may be yes. Several studies indicate that people who are prone to obesity may gain weight mainly because they inherit low rates of metabolism—and not because they overeat. In one experiment, for example, the metabolism rates of members of an Arizona Indian tribe which is prone to obesity—some 80 percent of the tribe members are obese by their early twenties—were carefully studied (Ravussin et al., 1988). As part of the study, metabolism rates were measured over several twenty-four-hour periods, during which the subjects stayed virtually immobile. Over the two years of the study, the subjects who gained the most weight were the ones who initially had the slowest metabolism. Although we cannot rule out the possibility that Indians who gained the most weight were also eating more, the data are clear in suggesting that

most of the weight gain was due to slower metabolism.

Corroborating evidence comes from a study of babies born to a group of obese and thin mothers (Roberts et al., 1988). When the babies were 3 months old, researchers measured their metabolism over a one-week period. Half the babies born to obese mothers had significantly slower metabolism than the other children, and those babies who had the slowest metabolism were overweight by the time they were 1 year old. In contrast, those with a faster metabolism at 3 months of age were of normal weight at 1 year.

Other research is supportive of the view that obesity is inherited. For instance, studies of adults who were adopted as children show them to be considerably more similar in

weight to their biological parents than to their adoptive parents. Also, the closer the biological relationship between two individuals, the more similar they are in weight (Stunkard et al., 1986; Stunkard, Foch & Hrubec, 1986).

Perhaps the most ironic fact to emerge from the current research is that when obese people (who may have a slow rate of metabolism to begin with) diet successfully, their bodies may react by slowing their metabolism still further. Thus, it is necessary for them to eat even less in order to avoid gaining weight—certainly a disheartening thought for the obese.

Ultimately, though, this research brings with it the promise of relief for the obese. The next step on the researchers' agenda is to identify the reason that some people have unusually slow metabolism and ultimately to attempt to modify metabolism rates through treatment (Hirsch & Leibel, 1988).

it. People with the disorder tend to come from stable homes, and they typically are successful, attractive, and relatively affluent. Their lives revolve around food: although they eat little themselves, they may cook for others, go shopping for food frequently, or collect cookbooks (Brunch, 1973; Brumberg, 1988).

Christine Bergel suffered from a related problem, **bulimia**, a disorder in which a person binges on incredibly large quantities of food. An entire gallon of ice cream and a whole pie may easily be consumed in a single sitting. Following such a binge, sufferers feel guilt and depression and typically induce vomiting or take laxatives to rid themselves of the food—behavior known as purging (Hinz & Williamson, 1987). Constant binging-and-purging cycles, and the use of drugs to induce vomiting or diarrhea, may create a chemical imbalance that can lead to heart failure. Typically, though, the weight of a person suffering from bulimia remains normal.

What causes anorexia nervosa or bulimia? Some researchers suspect there is a physiological cause such as a chemical imbalance in the hypothalamus or pituitary gland (Gold et al., 1986). Other psychologists feel that the cause is rooted in societal expectations about the value of slenderness, in social definitions of appropriate eating behavior, or in strained family interactions (Polivy & Herman, 1985). For instance, some evidence suggests that there are clear standards on certain college campuses about "appropriate" binging behavior, and the amount of binging is associated with a woman's popularity (Crandall, 1988). It would not be surprising if anorexia nervosa and bulimia were found to stem from both physiological and social causes, just as eating behavior in general is influenced by a variety of factors.

Bulimia: An eating disorder characterized by vast intake of food that may be followed by self-induced vomiting

THE INFORMED CONSUMER OF PSYCHOLOGY:
Dieting and Losing Weight Successfully

For many people, dieting represents a losing battle: Most people who diet eventually regain the weight they have lost, so they try again and get caught in a seemingly endless cycle of weight loss and gain. Given what we know about the causes of obesity this is not entirely surprising, since there appear to be so many factors that affect eating behavior and weight.

According to Jules Hirsch, an obesity specialist, there are several things to keep in mind when trying to lose weight (Kolata, 1988):

▶ There is no easy route to weight control; you will have to make permanent changes in your life in order to lose weight. The most obvious step, cutting down on the amount of food you eat, is just the beginning of a lifetime commitment to changing your eating habits. You must begin to consider the energy value of the food as well as the overall quantity and the balance in different kinds of nutrients.

▶ Exercise. When you exercise, you burn fat stored in your body, which is used as fuel for the muscles that are working. As this fat is used, you will probably lose weight. Weight-set-point theory suggests another advantage to moderate exercise: It may lower your set point. Although there is some dispute about just how much exercise is sufficient to actually lower weight (Pi-Sunyer, 1987), most experts recommend at least thirty consecutive minutes of moderate exercise at least three times a week. (If nothing else, the release of endorphins following exercise—discussed in Chapter 2—will make you feel better, even if you don't lose weight.)

▶ Decrease the influence of external, social stimuli on your eating behavior. There are a number of things you can do to lower your susceptibility to external food cues. For example, you can give yourself smaller portions of food, or you can leave the table before you see what is available for dessert. Don't even buy snack foods such as peanuts or potato chips; if they're not readily available in the kitchen cupboard, you're not apt to eat them. Wrap foods in the refrigerator in aluminum foil so you cannot see the contents. That way, you won't be tantalized by the sight of food every time you open the refrigerator.

▶ Avoid fad diets. No matter how popular they are at a given time, over the long term extreme diets usually don't work (Charlier, 1988).

▶ When you reach your desired weight, you're not finished. You must maintain the habits you built up while dieting in order to avoid gaining back the weight you have lost. Consider the role that food and eating play in your life, as well as your general values (Schwartz & Inbar-Saban, 1988).

Above all, don't feel guilty if you don't succeed in losing weight. Given the evidence that obesity may be genetically determined, the inability to lose weight should not be seen as a major failure in life. Indeed, you are in good company, for some 90 percent of dieters put back the weight they have lost (Bennett & Gurin, 1982). And even a relatively small weight loss is better than none: just a 10 percent drop in body weight may lower the major health risks that are associated with obesity (Brody, 1987).

YOU ARE WHAT YOU DRINK: Thirst

More than 75 percent of our weight is accounted for by water, and maintenance and regulation of that amount of liquid is no easy task for our bodies. Furthermore, given that we lose a significant amount of water through sweating and urination, drinking represents an important motivational drive. The importance of drinking is underlined by the fact that although we could live for more than a month without food, we would die within several days if deprived of water.

The stimuli that motivate us to drink are mainly internal; the dry mouth that accompanies thirst is a symptom of the need for water rather than the cause. Actually, two primary internal mechanisms produce thirst. First, the salt concentration of the cells of the body vary as a function of the amount of internal fluid, and when the concentration reaches a certain level, it triggers the hypothalamus to act, thereby resulting in the experience of thirst. The second major mechanism that induces thirst is a decrease in the total volume of fluid in the circulatory system (Fitzsimons, 1961). For instance, a person who loses a significant amount of blood through an injury subsequently experiences a powerful sense of thirst.

An increase in body temperature or a significant energy expenditure also produces thirst. This increase is probably due to a rise in the salt concentration in the body, which occurs as a consequence of increased sweating.

STRIVING FOR SUCCESS: The Need for Achievement

While hunger and thirst may represent two of the most potent drives in our day-to-day lives, we are also motivated by powerful secondary drives that have no clear biological basis (McClelland, 1985; Geen, 1984). Among the most prominent of these is the need for achievement.

The **need for achievement** is a stable, learned characteristic in which satisfaction is obtained by striving for and attaining a level of excellence (McClelland, Atkinson, Clark & Lowell, 1953). People with a high need for achievement seek out situations in which they can compete against some standard—be it grades, money, or winning at a game—and prove themselves successful. But they are not indiscriminate when it comes to picking their challenges: They tend to avoid situations in which success will come too easily (which would be unchallenging) or those in which success is unlikely. Instead, people high in achievement motivation are apt to choose tasks that are of intermediate difficulty.

In contrast, people with low achievement motivation tend mainly to be motivated by a desire to avoid failure. As a result, they seek out easy tasks, being sure to avoid failure, or they seek out very difficult tasks for which failure has no negative implications, since almost anyone would fail at them. People with a high fear of failure will stay away from tasks of intermediate difficulty, since they may fail where others have been successful (Atkinson & Feather, 1966).

The outcomes of a high need for achievement are generally positive, at least in a success-oriented society such as our own (Heckhausen, Schmalt & Schneider, 1985; Spence, 1985). For instance, people motivated by a high need for achievement are more likely to attend college than their low-achievement counterparts, and once in college they tend to receive higher grades in classes that are related to their future careers (Atkinson & Raynor, 1974). Furthermore, high achievement motivation is associated with future economic and occupational success (McClelland, 1985).

Measuring Achievement Motivation

How can we measure a person's need for achievement? The technique used most frequently is to administer a **Thematic Apperception Test**, or **TAT**. In the TAT, people are shown a series of ambiguous pictures, such as that in Figure 9-6. They are told to write a story that describes what is happening, who the people are, what led to the situation, what the people are thinking or wanting, and what will happen next. A standard scoring system is then used to determine the amount of achievement imagery in people's stories. For example, someone who writes a story in which the main character is striving to beat an opponent, studying in order to do well at some task, or working hard in order to get a promotion shows clear signs of achievement imagery. It is assumed that the inclusion of such achievement-related imagery indicates an unusually high degree of concern with—and therefore a relatively strong need for—achievement.

Other techniques have been developed for assessing achievement motivation on a societal level (Reuman, Alwin & Veroff, 1984). For example, a good indication of the overall level of achievement motivation in a particular society can be found by assessing achievement imagery in children's stories or folk tales. Researchers who have examined children's reading books for achievement imagery over long periods have found correlations between the amount of imagery in the books and the economic activity in the society over the next few decades (DeCharms & Moeller, 1962). Whether stories incorporating achievement imagery actually influence children or simply reflect growing economic trends cannot be determined, of course. It is clear,

Need for achievement: A stable, learned characteristic in which satisfaction comes from striving for and achieving a level of excellence

Thematic Apperception Test (TAT): A test consisting of a series of ambiguous pictures about which a person is asked to write a story. The story is taken to be a reflection of the writer's personality

FIGURE 9-6

This ambiguous picture is similar to those used in the Thematic Apperception Test to determine people's underlying motivation. (© 1943 by the President and Fellows of Harvard College; © 1971 by Henry A. Murray.)

Fear of success: A fear that being successful will have a negative influence on the way one is perceived

though, that children might be learning more from their books than how to read—they may be acquiring the level of achievement motivation that society expects from them.

There has been one major drawback to the work on achievement motivation: The findings have been considerably more consistent for men than for women, and TAT measures of the need for achievement do not correlate with actual achievement for females as strongly as they do for males. One explanation for the discrepancy is that some women view achievement and success with a certain ambivalence (Horner, 1972). According to this explanation, women who have been raised according to the traditional standards of society—in which competition and independence are deemed inappropriate for females—might find success in a field typically dominated by males as anxiety-provoking. Some women, then, may actually experience a **fear of success**: They are afraid that being successful will have a negative influence on the way others view them and on their definition of themselves as female.

Although the evidence in support of the fear-of-success explanation is far from consistent, it does seem as if women who have a high fear of success do not strive to achieve in areas that are seen as competitive, male-dominated, or challenging. However, we would expect that as society's view of appropriate female behavior becomes less constrained, fear of success ought to be on the decline (Veroff, 1982; Fleming, 1982; Jenkins, 1987).

The work on fear of success provides an illustration of how complex our motivational structures may be (Gama, 1985). Any particular behavior may be motivated simultaneously by several underlying needs, and it is possible that for some of us the need for achievement and the fear of success operate jointly to direct our behavior.

"Well, you can stop lecturing me about my will to fail. I've failed."

Some theories of achievement motivation suggest that certain people may have a fear of success. (Drawing by Ed Arno; © 1978 The New Yorker Magazine, Inc.)

Learning to Achieve: The Development of Achievement Motivation

How do people come to be high in the need for achievement? Several factors seem to be at work, beginning at a very early age. For instance, parents whose children turn out to be high in achievement motivation tend to be relatively strict in their feeding schedules—from birth onward—and in their toilet-training practices (McClelland, 1985). Furthermore, parents who set high standards—even when it comes to everyday tasks such as dressing—who are relatively demanding, and who strongly encourage independence produce children high in need for achievement.

Although parental directiveness may make parents seem rather unpleasant, this is not the case: Such parents are also quick to praise their children's success, and they warmly encourage their children in all areas of endeavor. Even if their child fails, these parents do not complain; instead, they urge their children to find areas in which they will be able to succeed.

Training Achievement Motivation in Adults

Can we teach people to have higher achievement motivation? Such a question is hardly academic, since we know that a high need for achievement is associated with greater economic success.

To answer the question, psychologists David McClelland and David Winter (1969) went to India, a less technologically developed country in which economic needs are profound, and implemented a training program consisting of several components. First, they taught participants—who were all owners of small businesses—such things as the importance of setting moderate goals and taking personal responsibility for meeting them. After reviewing the lives of successful entrepreneurs, participants were told to imagine themselves being successful. They were asked to make concrete, step-by-step plans, and to keep track of their progress toward their goals.

The results of the program were impressive. Compared with a control group made up of business owners who did not receive training, participants increased their level of business activity significantly. They created new jobs, and they expanded their businesses. Even more important was the fact that the gains lasted: The economic achievements of the participants were significantly greater ten years after the program than were those in the control group (McClelland & Winter, 1971; McClelland, 1978). It is never too late, then, to learn higher achievement motivation; even adults can increase their achievement strivings—and consequent success.

STRIVING FOR FRIENDSHIP: The Need for Affiliation

Few of us choose to lead our lives as hermits. Why?

One reason is that most people have a **need for affiliation**, a concern with establishing and maintaining relationships with other people. Individuals with a high need for affiliation write TAT stories that emphasize the desire to maintain or reinstate friendships and show concern over being rejected by friends.

People who are higher in affiliation needs are particularly sensitive to relationships with others. They like to work with their friends and may be more likely to pay attention to the social relationships within work settings than to getting the job done. For example, United States presidents whose inaugural addresses were high in affiliation imagery tend to be rated by historians as relatively inactive and ineffective (Winter, 1976). On the other hand, such presidents also seem to avoid war and to sign weapons-control agreements.

Need for affiliation: A need to establish and maintain relationships with other people

STRIVING FOR IMPACT ON OTHERS: The Need for Power

If your fantasies include being elected President of the United States, running General Motors, or receiving the Nobel Prize, they may be reflecting a high need for power. The **need for power**, a tendency to seek impact, control, or influence over others, and to be seen as a powerful individual, represents an additional type of motivation (Winter, 1973).

As you might expect, people with a strong need for power are more apt to belong to organizations and seek office than those low in the need for power. They also are apt to be in professions in which their power needs may be fulfilled (such as business management and—you may or may not be surprised—teaching). In addition, they try to show the trappings of power: even in college, they are more apt to collect prestigious possessions, such as stereos and sports cars.

There are some significant sex differences in the display of need for power. Men who are high in power needs tend to show unusually high levels of aggression, be heavy drinkers, be sexually exploitative, and participate more frequently in competitive sports—behaviors that collectively represent somewhat extravagant, flamboyant behavior (Winter, 1973). In contrast, women display their power needs in a more restrained manner, congruent with traditional societal restraints on women's behavior: Women high in a need for power are more apt than men to channel their power needs in a

Need for power: A tendency to want to make an impression or have an impact on others in order to be seen as a powerful individual socially responsible manner (such as by showing concern for others or through highly nurturant behavior) (Winter, 1988).

Clearly, needs for power can be fulfilled in several sorts of ways. As with all motives, the way in which a need will be manifested is a combination of people's skills, values, and the specific situation in which they find themselves.

RECAP AND REVIEW II

Recap

◀ Hunger, a primary drive, is affected by internal cues that regulate the amount and kind of food eaten. The hypothalamus plays a particularly important role in determining food intake.

◀ People's weight set point, their sensitivity to external social cues, the number of fat cells they have, their metabolism, and genetic factors all affect eating patterns.

◀ Among the major secondary drives are needs for achievement, affiliation, and power.

Review

1. Research on the activity of the hypothalamus, metabolism, and weight set point has clearly demonstrated that social factors do not play a significant role in people's desire to eat. True or false? _____

2. Obese people seem to be much more sensitive to external cues than people of normal weight. True or false? _____

3. Obese children may find it difficult to lose weight later in life because their weight set point is too high. True or false? _____

4. "Oh, come on! Marcia doesn't have an eating problem!" argued Karen. "Her weight is about normal, and we all have occasional late-night binges."

   "But Karen, she makes herself vomit after those binges. I think something is wrong."

   Marcia may very well be suffering from
   a. a hypothalamus disorder.
   b. bulimia.

c. anorexia nervosa.
d. an intestinal disorder.

5. What are two primary internal mechanisms that produce thirst?

6. Weight lost through the application of the guidelines presented in this chapter will usually stay off, even after one stops following the guidelines. True or false? _____

7. Jim is considered to be a person with a high need for achievement. His boss would probably be correct in assuming that Jim would readily accept the challenge of completing a risky task, where success is doubtful. True or false? _____

8. Children high in achievement motivation tend to have parents who
   a. discourage independence.
   b. punish failure to meet standards.
   c. set high standards.
   d. accept their children's behavior unconditionally.

9. Research shows that achievement motivation of adults can be increased through training in goal-setting, imaginal techniques, systematic planning, and tracking of progress. True or false? _____

10. Shelley's Thematic Apperception Test (TAT) story depicts a young girl who had been rejected by one of her peers and sought to regain her friendship. What major type of motivation is Shelley displaying in her story?
    a. Need for achievement
    b. Need for motivation
    c. Need for affiliation
    d. Need for power

(Answers to this question are on page 316.)

UNDERSTANDING EMOTIONAL EXPERIENCE

Karl Andrews held in his hands the envelope he had been waiting for. It could be his ticket to his future: An offer of admission to his first-choice college. But what was it going to say? He knew it could go either way; his grades were pretty good, and he had been involved in some activities; but his SAT scores had been, to put it bluntly, lousy. He felt so nervous—scared really—that his hands shook as he opened the thin envelope (not a good sign, he thought). Here it comes. "Dear Mr. Andrews," it read. "The President and Trustees of the University are pleased to admit you . . . ." That was all he needed. With a whoop of excitement, Karl found himself gleefully jumping up and down. A rush of emotion overcame him as it sank in that he had, in fact, been accepted. He was on his way.

At one time or another, all of us have felt the strong feelings that accompany both very pleasant and very negative experiences. Perhaps it was the thrill of being accepted into college, the joy of being in love, the sorrow over someone's death, or the anguish of inadvertently hurting someone. Moreover, we experience such reactions on a less intense level throughout our daily lives: the pleasure of a friendship, the enjoyment of a movie, or the embarrassment of forgetting to return a borrowed item.

Despite the varied nature of these feelings, there is a common link between them: They all represent emotions. As we discussed earlier, such emotions are an important component in motivating our behavior, and the behavior that results from motivational needs in turn influences our emotions.

While we all know what it is like to experience an emotion, finding a definition acceptable to psychologists has proven to be an elusive task. One reason is that different theories of emotion—which we will discuss later—emphasize different aspects of emotions, and therefore each theory ultimately produces its own definition. Despite these difficulties, though, we can use a general definition: **Emotions** are feelings that generally have both physiological and cognitive elements and that influence behavior.

Emotions: Feelings (such as happiness, despair, and sorrow) that generally have both physiological and cognitive elements and that influence behavior

Consider, for example, how it feels to be happy. First, you obviously experience a feeling that you can differentiate from other emotions. It is likely you also experience some identifiable physical changes in your body: Perhaps your heart rate increases, or—as in our example earlier—you find yourself "jumping for joy." Finally, the emotion probably encompasses cognitive elements; your understanding and evaluation of the meaning of what is happening in your environment prompts your feelings of happiness.

It is also possible, however, to experience an emotion without the presence of cognitive elements. For instance, we may react with fear to an unusual or novel situation (such as coming into contact with a disturbed, unpredictable individual), or we may experience pleasure over sexual excitation without having cognitive awareness or understanding of what it is about the situation that is exciting.

In fact, some psychologists argue that there are entirely separate systems that govern cognitive responses and emotional responses. One current controversy is whether the emotional response takes predominance over the cognitive response or vice versa. Some theorists suggest that we first respond to a situation with an emotional reaction, and later try to understand it (Zajonc, 1985). For example, we may enjoy a complex modern symphony without understanding it or knowing why we like it.

ANSWERS (REVIEW II):
1. False; eating is also influenced by social factors   **2.** True   **3.** True   **4.** b
5. Fluctuation of salt concentrations in the cells, fluid decreases in the circulatory system
6. False; changes in eating habits must be maintained   **7.** False; people with high achievement needs tend to seek out challenging but attainable tasks   **8.** c   **9.** True
10. c

In contrast, other theorists suggest that people first develop cognitions about a situation and then react emotionally (Lazarus, 1984). This school of thought suggests that it is necessary for us to first think about and understand a stimulus or situation, relating it to what we already know, before we can react on an emotional level.

Both sides of this debate are supported by research, and the question is far from being resolved (Scheff, 1985; Frijda, 1985, 1988). It is possible that the sequence varies from situation to situation, with emotions predominating in some instances and cognitive processes occurring first in others. Whatever the ultimate sequence, however, it is clear that our emotions play a major role in affecting our behavior.

WHAT EMOTIONS DO FOR US:
Understanding the Functions of Emotions

Imagine what it would be like if you had no emotions—no depths of despair, no depression, no feeling apologetic, but at the same time, no happiness, joy, or love. Obviously life would be much less interesting, even dull, without the experience of emotion.

But do emotions serve any purpose beyond making life interesting? Psychologists have identified a number of important functions that emotions play in our daily lives (Scherer, 1984). Among the most important of those functions are the following:

▶ Preparing us for action. Emotions act as a link between events in the external environment and behavioral responses that an individual makes. For example, if we saw an angry dog charging toward us, the emotional reaction (fear) would be associated with physiological arousal of the sympathetic division of the autonomic nervous system, which we discussed in Chapter 2. The role of the sympathetic division is to prepare us for emergency action, which presumably would get us moving out of the dog's way—quickly. Emotions, then, are stimuli that aid in the development of effective responses to various situations.

▶ Shaping our future behavior. Emotions serve to promote learning of information that will assist us in making appropriate responses in the future. For example, the emotional response that occurs when a person experiences something unpleasant—such as the threatening dog—teaches that person to avoid similar circumstances in the future. Similarly, pleasant emotions act as reinforcement for prior behavior and therefore are apt to lead an individual to seek out similar situations in the future. Thus, the feeling of satisfaction that follows giving to a charity is likely to reinforce charitable behavior and make it more likely to occur in the future.

▶ Helping us to regulate social interaction. As we shall discuss in detail later, the emotions we experience are frequently obvious to observers, as they are communicated through our verbal and nonverbal behaviors. These behaviors can act as a signal to observers, allowing them to better understand what we are experiencing and predict our future behavior. In turn, this promotes more effective and appropriate social interaction. For instance, a mother who sees the terror on her 2-year-old son's face when he sees a frightening picture in a book is able to comfort and reassure him, thereby helping him to deal with his environment more effectively in the future.

The emotion of joy is characterized by positive feelings and thoughts. (Charles Gupton/Stock Boston)

If we were to try to list the words in the English language that have been used to describe emotions, we would end up with at least 500 different examples (Averill, 1975). The list would range from such obvious emotions as "happiness" and "fear" to less common ones, such as "adventurousness" and "pensiveness."

One challenge for psychologists has been to try to sort through this list in order to identify the most important, fundamental emotions in our everyday lives, as well as trying to determine how our emotions are related to one another (Shaver et al., 1987; Storm & Storm, 1987). One of the most comprehensive efforts has been carried out by Robert Plutchik (1984), who asked people to rate each of a large set of emotions along thirty-four different rating scales. Then, by mathematically combining the ratings, he was able to determine the relationship among the various emotions, as well as which emotions were most fundamental.

The results were clear: Eight different fundamental emotions (joy, acceptance, fear, surprise, sadness, disgust, anger, and anticipation) emerged, and they formed the pattern within the wheel shown in Figure 9-7. Furthermore, these primary emotions could be consolidated into the two-emotion combinations shown on the outside of the wheel. Emotions nearer one another in the circle are more closely related, while those opposite each other are conceptual opposites. For instance, sadness is opposite joy, and anticipation is opposite surprise.

While Plutchik's configuration of the basic emotions is reasonable, it is not the only plausible one. Other psychologists have come up with somewhat different lists—as we shall see when we discuss the communication of emotion and nonverbal behavior later in this chapter. Still, while we may have trouble coming up with a definitive list of the primary emotions, each of us has little difficulty identifying what we are experiencing at any given moment. The process by which we come to this understanding forms the basis of a number of theories of emotion, which we will discuss next.

KNOWING HOW WE FEEL: UNDERSTANDING OUR OWN EMOTIONS

I've never been so angry before; I feel my heart pounding, and I'm trembling all over . . . I don't know how I'll get through the performance. I feel like my stomach is filled with butterflies . . . That was quite a mistake I made! My face must be incredibly red . . . When I heard the footsteps in the night I was so frightened that I couldn't catch my breath.

If you examine our language, you will find that there are literally dozens of ways to describe how we feel when we are experiencing an emotion, and that the language we use to describe emotions is, for the most part, based on the physical symptoms that are associated with a particular emotional experience (Koveces, 1987).

Consider, for instance, the experience of fear. Pretend that it is late one New Year's Eve. You are walking down a dark road, and you hear a stranger approaching behind you. It is clear that he is not trying to hurry by but is coming directly toward you. You think of what you will do should the stranger attempt to rob you—or worse, hurt you in some way.

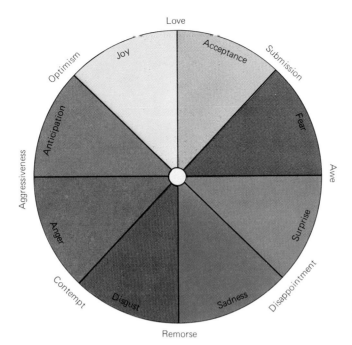

FIGURE 9-7

Plutchik's emotion wheel demonstrates how eight primary emotions are related to one another. (Plutchik, 1980.)

While these thoughts are running through your head, it is almost certain that something rather dramatic will be happening to your body. Among the most likely physiological reactions that may occur, which are associated with activation of the autonomic nervous system (see Chapter 2), are those listed here:

▶ The rate and depth of your breathing will increase.

▶ Your heart will speed up, pumping more blood through your circulatory system.

▶ The pupils of your eyes will open wider, allowing more light to enter and thereby increasing your visual sensitivity.

▶ Your mouth will become dry as your salivary glands, and in fact your entire digestive system, stop functioning. At the same time, though, your sweat glands may increase their activity, since increased sweating will help you rid yourself of excess heat developed by any emergency activity in which you engage.

▶ As the muscles just below the surface of your skin contract, your hair may literally stand on end.

Of course, all these physiological changes are likely to occur without your awareness. At the same time, though, the emotional experience accompanying them will be obvious to you: You would most surely report being fearful.

Although it is a relatively straightforward matter to describe the general physical reactions that accompany emotions, the specific role that these physiological responses play in the experience of emotions has proved to be a major puzzle for psychologists. As we shall see, some theorists suggest that there are specific bodily reactions that *cause* us to experience a particular emotion—we experience fear, for instance, *because* our heart is pounding and we are breathing deeply. In contrast, other theorists suggest that the physiological reaction is the *result* of the experience of an emotion. In this view, we experience fear, and this emotional experience causes our heart to pound and our breathing to deepen.

DO GUT REACTIONS EQUAL EMOTIONS?: The James-Lange Theory

To William James and Carl Lange, who were among the first researchers to explore the nature of emotions, emotional experience is, very simply, a reaction to instinctive bodily events that occurred as a response to some situation or event in the environment. This view is summarized in James's statement, ". . . we feel sorry because we cry, angry because we strike, afraid because we tremble" (James, 1890).

James and Lange took the view that the instinctive response of crying at a loss leads us to feel sorrow; that striking out at someone who frustrates us results in our feeling anger; that trembling at a menacing threat causes us to feel afraid. They suggested that every major emotion has a particular physiological "gut" reaction of internal organs—called a **visceral experience**—attached to it, and it is this specific pattern of visceral response that leads us to label the emotional experience.

In sum, James and Lange proposed that we experience emotions as a result of physiological changes that produce specific sensations. In turn, these sensations are interpreted by the brain as particular kinds of emotional experiences (see Figure 9-8). This view has come to be called the **James-Lange theory of emotion**.

The James-Lange theory has some serious drawbacks, however. In order for the theory to be correct, visceral changes would have to occur at a relatively rapid pace, since we experience some emotions—such as fear upon hearing a stranger rapidly approaching on a dark night—almost instanta-

Visceral (VIS er al) **experience**: The "gut" reaction experienced internally, triggering an emotion (see James-Lange theory)

James-Lange theory of emotion: The belief that emotional experience is a reaction to bodily events occurring as a result of an external situation ("I feel sad because I am crying")

FIGURE 9-8

A comparison of three models of emotion.

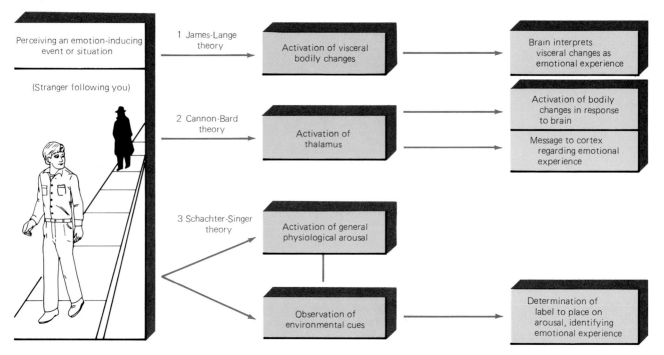

neously. Yet, emotional experiences frequently happen even before many physiological changes have time to be set into motion. Because of the slowness with which some visceral changes take place, it is hard to see how they could be the source of immediate emotional experience.

The James-Lange theory poses another difficulty: Physiological arousal does not invariably produce emotional experience. For example, a person who is jogging has an increased heartbeat and respiration rate, as well as many of the other physiological changes associated with certain emotions. Yet joggers do not typically think of such changes in terms of emotions. There cannot be a one-to-one correspondence, then, between visceral changes and emotional experience, and visceral changes—by themselves— may not be sufficient to produce emotion.

Finally, our internal organs produce relatively limited sensations. It is difficult to imagine how the range of emotions that people are capable of experiencing could be the result of unique visceral changes. Many emotions are actually correlated with relatively similar sorts of visceral changes, a fact that contradicts the James-Lange theory.

PHYSIOLOGICAL REACTIONS AS THE RESULT OF EMOTIONS: The Cannon-Bard Theory

In response to the difficulties inherent in the James-Lange theory, Walter Cannon—and later Philip Bard—suggested an alternative view. In what has come to be known as the **Cannon-Bard theory of emotion**, they proposed the model illustrated in the second part of Figure 9-8 (Cannon, 1929). The major thrust of the theory is to reject the view that physiological arousal alone leads to the perception of emotion. Instead, the theory assumes that both physiological arousal *and* the emotional experience are produced simultaneously by the same nerve impulse, which Cannon and Bard suggested emanates from the brain's thalamus.

According to the theory, after an emotion-inducing stimulus is perceived, the thalamus is the initial site of the emotional response. In turn, the thalamus sends a signal to the viscera, which are then activated, and at the same time communicates a message to the cerebral cortex regarding the nature of the emotion being experienced. Hence, it is not necessary for different emotions to have unique physiological patterns associated with them—as long as the message sent to the cerebral cortex differs according to the specific emotion.

The Cannon-Bard theory seems to have been accurate in its rejection of the view that physiological arousal alone accounts for emotions. However, recent research has provided some important modifications to the theory. As you may recall from Chapter 2, it is now understood that the hypothalamus and the limbic system—not the thalamus—play a major role in emotional experience. In addition, the simultaneity of the physiological and emotional responses—a fundamental assumption of the theory—has yet to be conclusively demonstrated (Pribram, 1984). This ambiguity has allowed room for yet another theory of emotions: the Schachter-Singer theory.

Cannon-Bard theory of emotion: The belief that both physiological and emotional arousal are produced simultaneously by the same nerve impulse

EMOTIONS AS LABELS: The Schachter-Singer Theory

Suppose, as you were being followed down the dark street on New Year's Eve, you noticed a man being followed by a shady figure on the other side of the street. Now assume that instead of reacting with fear, the man begins

FEELING AND EXPERIENCING
THE WORLD

Schachter-Singer theory of emotion: The belief that emotions are determined jointly by a nonspecific kind of physiological arousal and its interpretation, based on environmental cues

to laugh and act gleeful. Might the reactions of this other individual be sufficient to lay your fears to rest? Might you, in fact, decide there is nothing to fear, and get into the spirit of the evening by beginning to feel happiness and glee yourself?

According to an explanation that focuses on the role of cognition, the **Schachter-Singer theory of emotion**, this might very well happen. This final approach to explaining emotions emphasizes that we identify the emotion we are experiencing by observing our environment and comparing ourselves with others (Schachter & Singer, 1962).

A classic experiment found evidence for this hypothesis. In the study, subjects were told that they would receive a vitamin injection of a drug called Suproxin. In reality, they were given epinephrine, a drug that causes an increase in physiological arousal, including higher heart and respiration rates and a reddening of the face—responses that typically occur as part of strong emotional responses. Although one group of subjects was informed of the actual effects of the drug, another was kept in the dark.

Subjects in both groups were then individually placed in a situation where a confederate of the experimenter acted in one of two ways. In one condition, he acted angry and hostile, complaining that he would refuse to answer the personal questions on a questionnaire that the experimenter had asked him to complete. In the other condition, his behavior was quite the opposite: He behaved euphorically, flying paper airplanes and tossing wads of paper, in general acting quite happy with the situation.

The key purpose of the experiment was to determine how the subjects would react emotionally to the confederate's behavior. When they were asked to describe their own emotional state at the end of the experiment, subjects who had been told of the effects of the drug were relatively unaffected by the behavior of the confederate: Being informed of the effects of the epinephrine earlier, they thought their physiological arousal was due to the drug and therefore were not faced with the need to find a reason for their arousal. Hence, they reported experiencing relatively little emotion.

On the other hand, subjects who had not been told of the drug's real effects were influenced by the confederate's behavior. Those subjects exposed to the angry confederate reported that they felt angry, while those exposed to the euphoric confederate reported feeling happy. In sum, the results suggest that uninformed subjects turned to the environment and the behavior of others for an explanation of the physiological arousal they were experiencing.

The results of the Schachter-Singer experiment, then, support a cognitive view of emotions, in which emotions are determined jointly by a relatively nonspecific kind of physiological arousal *and* the labeling of the arousal based on cues from the environment (refer back to the third part of Figure 9-8).

The Schachter-Singer theory has led to some interesting experiments coming from many areas of the field of psychology. For example, psychologists interested in the determinants of interpersonal attraction have drawn applications from the theory. In one intriguing and imaginative experiment, an attractive, college-aged woman stood at the end of a swaying 450-foot suspension bridge that spanned a deep canyon. The woman was ostensibly conducting a survey, and she asked men who made it across the bridge a series of questions. She then gave them her telephone number, telling them that if they were interested in the results of the experiment they could contact her in the upcoming week.

In comparison to members of a control group who had completed the questionnaire after strolling across a stable bridge spanning a shallow stream ten feet below, the men who had come across the dangerous bridge showed significant differences in their questionnaire results: sexual imagery was considerably higher. Furthermore, those crossing the dangerous span were significantly more likely to actually call the woman in the upcoming week, suggesting that their attraction to her was higher. The men whose arousal was increased by the dangerous bridge seemed to have searched for a reason for their physiological arousal—and ended up attributing the cause to the attractive woman (Dutton & Aron, 1974). Consistent with the Schachter-Singer theory, then, the men's emotional response was based on a labeling of their arousal.

Unfortunately, evidence gathered to confirm the Schachter-Singer theory has not always been supportive (Reisenzein, 1983; Leventhal & Tomarken, 1986). Even the original experiment has been criticized on methodological grounds and for certain ambiguities in the results. Furthermore, there is evidence that in some cases physiological arousal is not essential for emotional experience to occur and that physiological factors *alone* can account for one's emotional state without any labeling process occurring (Marshall & Zimbardo, 1979; Chwalisz, Diener, & Gallagher, 1988). For example, some drugs invariably produce depression as a side effect no matter what the nature of the situation or the environmental cues present.

On the whole, however, the Schachter-Singer theory of emotions is important because it suggests that, at least under some circumstances, emotional experiences are a joint function of physiological arousal and the labeling of that arousal. When the source of physiological arousal is unclear to us, we may look to our environment to determine just what it is we are experiencing.

SUMMING UP THE THEORIES OF EMOTION

At this point, you have good reason to ask why there are so many theories of emotion and, perhaps even more important, which is most accurate. Actually, we have only scratched the surface; there are even more explanatory theories of emotion (Scherer & Ekman, 1984; Foz & Kozak, 1986; Frijda, 1987; Izard, 1988).

The explanation as to why there are so many theories and which is the most accurate is actually the same: Emotions are such complex phenomena that no single theory has been able to explain all facets of emotional experience completely satisfactorily. For each of the three major theories there is contradictory evidence of one sort or another, and therefore no theory has proven invariably accurate in its predictions. On the other hand, this is not a cause for despair—or unhappiness, fear, or any other negative emotion. It simply reflects the fact that psychology is an evolving, developing science. Presumably, as more evidence is gathered, the specific answers to questions about the nature of emotions will become more clear. Moreover, the lack of definitive knowledge about the nature of emotions has not stopped people from applying what we now know about emotional responses to some practical problems—as we discuss in the Psychology at Work box.

324

When President Bush took office, many of his new appointees had to take lie-detector tests in order to obtain top-secret clearances.

When an accused rapist wanted to prove his innocence, he asked for, and received, a lie-detector test.

In order to get a job working for a major defense contractor, Jim Tane was told he needed to get a security clearance. The major part of the investigation into his past consisted of a lie-detector test, in which he was asked questions about his allegiance to his country, his past friends and associates, and any possible criminal activity, ranging from occasional drug use to major crimes.

The common element in each of these actual situations is the use of the lie detector, or **polygraph**, an electronic device that is designed to expose people who are telling lies. The basic assumption behind the apparatus is straightforward: The sympathetic nervous system of a person who is not being truthful becomes aroused as his or her emotionality increases, and the physiological changes that are indicative of this arousal can be detected by the polygraph.

Actually a number of separate physiological changes are measured simultaneously by a lie detector, including an irregularity in breathing pattern, an increase in heart rate and blood pressure, and an increase in sweating. In theory, the polygraph operator asks a series

THE TRUTH ABOUT LIES: USING EMOTIONAL RESPONSES TO SEPARATE THE HONEST FROM THE DISHONEST

of questions, some of which he knows will elicit verifiable, truthful responses—such as what a person's name and address are. Then, when more critical questions are answered, the operator can observe the nature of the physiological changes that occur. Answers whose accompanying physiological responses deviate significantly from those accompanying truthful responses are assumed to be false.

Unfortunately, there is no foolproof technique for assessing the extent of the physiological changes that may indicate a lie. Even truthful responses may elicit physiological arousal—if the question is emotion-laden (Waid & Orne, 1982). How many innocent people accused of a murder, for instance, would *not* respond emotionally when asked whether they committed the crime, since they know that their future may hang in the balance?

One further drawback of lie detector tests is that people are occasionally capable of fooling the polygraph (Barland & Raskin, 1973; Honts, 1987). For instance, biofeedback techniques (see Chapter 2) can be employed to produce emotional responses to accompany even truthful statements, meaning that the polygraph operator will be unable to differentiate between honest and

dishonest responses. Even biting one's tongue or hiding a tack in a shoe and pressing on it as each question is answered may be sufficient to produce physiological arousal during each response, making truthful and deceptive responses indistinguishable (Honts, Hodes, & Raskin, 1985).

Because of these sources of error, users of lie detectors often make mistakes when trying to judge another person's honesty (Saxe, Dougherty & Cross, 1985), and the American Psychological Association has adopted a resolution stating that the evidence for the effectiveness of polygraphs "is still unsatisfactory" (APA *Monitor*, 1986). Even the major proponent of the use of polygraphs—the American Polygraph Association—admits an error rate between 4 and 13 percent, and critics suggest that research has shown that the actual rate is closer to 30 percent (Meyer, 1982). Using such evidence, the U.S. Congress has passed a bill that would bar employers from using polygraphs as screening devices for job applicants (Bales, 1988).

Despite the prevalence of lie detector tests in many different areas of society, then, there is good reason to doubt that such tests can determine whether someone is lying. Clearly, you would not want to bet your future on the results of a lie detector test.

Polygraph: An electronic device that measures bodily changes which may signal that a person is lying; often called a lie detector

---

RECAP AND REVIEW III

Recap

◄ Emotions are feelings that generally have both a physiological component and a cognitive component.

◄ Emotions have a number of functions, including preparing us for action, shaping our future behavior, and regulating social interaction.

◄ A number of physiological changes accompany strong emotion, including rapid breathing and increased heart rate, opening of the pupils, dryness in the mouth, increase in sweating, and the sensation of hair "standing on end."

◄ The major theories of emotion are the James-Lange, Cannon-Bard, and Schachter-Singer theories.

Review

1. Evidence has clearly proved that emotional responses occur only after the cognitive process takes place. True or false? _____

2. a. You label as "disgust" the emotion you feel regarding sexist behavior of a person at a party you're attending. Using Plutchik's "emotion wheel," what emotion would you identify as the opposite of what you're experiencing? _____

   b. If you also felt anger in combination with disgust, how would you then label your emotional state according to the emotion wheel? _____

3. _____ _____ is the technical term for "gut reaction."

4. The _____ - _____ theory states that the hypothalamus triggers physiological and emotional reactions simultaneously. In contrast, the _____ - _____ theory suggests that emotions follow physical arousal.

5. The Schachter-Singer theory states that emotions are determined in part by one's interpretation of the environment. True or false? _____

6. Drugs that invariably produce depression, regardless of the environmental cues present, are a challenge to the Schachter-Singer theory. True or false? _____

7. The failure of any one of the theories discussed to completely explain emotions is best interpreted in which of the following ways?

   a. Psychology is an evolving science; in time more questions will be answered.

   b. The study of emotions is beyond the scope of psychology.

   c. Current theories should be discarded and replaced with new ones.

   d. Emotions should be studied strictly from a physiological perspective.

(Answers to review questions are on page 326.)

EXPRESSING EMOTIONS: THE ROLE OF NONVERBAL BEHAVIOR

Ancient Sanskrit writings speak of someone who, on making an evasive answer, "rubs the great toe along the ground, and shivers." Shakespeare writes of Macbeth's face as "a place where men may read strange matters." Old torch songs claim "your eyes are the eyes of a woman in love." Such examples demonstrate how nonverbal behavior has long had the reputation of revealing people's emotions. Only recently, though, have psychologists demonstrated the validity of such speculation, finding that nonverbal behavior does represent a major means by which we communicate our emotions.

We now know that nonverbal behavior communicates messages simultaneously across several **channels**, paths along which communications flow. For example, facial expressions, eye contact, body movements, and even less obvious behaviors such as the positioning of the eyebrows can each be conceptualized as separate nonverbal channels of communication. Furthermore, each separate channel is capable of carrying a particular message—which may or may not be related to the message being carried by the other channels. Because facial expressions represent the primary means of communicating emotional stages, we will concentrate on them, considering their role in the experience of emotions.

Channels: Paths along which verbal and nonverbal behavioral messages are communicated (e.g., facial expressions, eye contact, body movements)

UNIVERSALITY IN EMOTIONAL EXPRESSIVITY

Consider, for a moment, the six photos displayed in Figure 9-9. Can you identify the emotions being expressed by the person in each of the photos?

If you are a good judge of facial expressions, you will conclude that six of the basic emotions are displayed: happiness, anger, sadness, surprise,

FIGURE 9-9

These photos demonstrate six of the primary emotions: happiness, anger, sadness, surprise, disgust, and fear. (Courtesy of Paul Ekman.)

disgust, and fear. These categories are the emotions that emerge in literally hundreds of studies of nonverbal behavior as being consistently distinct and identifiable, even by untrained observers (Wagner, MacDonald & Manstead, 1986).

What is particularly interesting about these six categories is that they are not limited to members of western cultures; they appear to represent the basic emotions expressed universally by members of the human race, regardless of where they have been raised and what learning experiences they have had. This point was demonstrated convincingly by psychologist Paul Ekman, who traveled to New Guinea to study members of an isolated jungle tribe having had almost no contact with westerners (Ekman, Friesen & Ellsworth, 1982). The people of the tribe did not speak or understand English, they had never seen a movie, and they had had very limited experience with Caucasians before Ekman's arrival.

To learn about how the New Guineans used nonverbal behavior in emotional expression, Ekman told them a story involving an emotion and then showed them a set of three faces of westerners, one of which was displaying an emotion appropriate for the story. The task was to choose the face showing the most reasonable expression. The results showed that the New Guineans' responses were quite similar to those of western subjects and New Guinean children showed even greater skill in identifying the appropriate emotion

ANSWERS (REVIEW III):
1. False   **2.** a—acceptance; b—contempt   **3.** Visceral experience   **4.** Cannon-Bard; James-Lange   **5.** True   **6.** True   **7.** a

than did the New Guinean adults. Interestingly, the only difference occurred in identifying fearful faces, which were often confused with surprise by the tribespeople.

In addition to learning whether the New Guinean natives interpreted emotional expression in the same way as westerners did, it was important to find out whether both groups showed similar nonverbal responses. To do this, other natives were told the stories that Ekman had used earlier and were asked to provide a facial expression appropriate to the subject of the story. These expressions were videotaped, and a group of subjects in the United States were asked to look at the faces and identify the emotion being expressed. The results were clear: The western viewers—who had never before seen any New Guineans—were surprisingly accurate in their judgments, with the exception of expressions of fear and surprise.

In sum, convincing evidence exists for universality across cultures in the way basic emotions are displayed and interpreted (Ekman et al., 1987; Aronoff, Barclay & Stevenson, 1988). Because the New Guineans were so isolated, they could not have learned from westerners to recognize or produce similar facial expressions. Instead, their similar abilities and manner of responding emotionally appear to have been present innately. Of course, it is possible to argue that similar experiences in both cultures led to learning of similar types of nonverbal behavior, but this appears unlikely, since the two cultures are so very different. The expression of basic emotions, then, seems to be universal (Zivin, 1985).

What is the mechanism that produces similarity in the expression of basic emotions across cultures? One explanation is based on a hypothesis known as the facial-affect program (Ekman, 1982). The **facial-affect program**—which is assumed to be universally present at birth—is analogous to a computer program that is turned on when a particular emotion is experienced. When set in motion, the "program" activates a set of nerve impulses that make the face display an appropriate expression. Each primary emotion produces a unique set of muscular movements, forming the kind of expressions seen in Figure 9-9. For example, the emotion of happiness is universally displayed by movement of the zygomatic major, a muscle that raises the corners of the mouth—forming what we would call a smile. (For more on the relationship between facial expressions and emotions, see the Research Classics box.)

Facial-affect program: The activation of a set of nerve impulses that make the face display the appropriate expression

SMILE, THOUGH YOU'RE FEELING BLUE: THE FACIAL-FEEDBACK HYPOTHESIS

If you want to feel happy, try smiling.

That is the implication of an intriguing notion known as the **facial-feedback hypothesis.** According to this hypothesis, facial expressions not only *reflect* emotional experience, they also help *determine* how people experience and label emotions (Izard, 1977). The basic idea is that "wearing" an emotional expression provides muscular feedback to the brain which helps produce an emotion congruent with the expression. For instance, the muscles activated when we smile may send a message to the brain indicating the experience of happiness—even if there is nothing in the environment that would produce that particular emotion. Some theoreticians have gone even further, suggesting that facial expressions are *necessary* for an emotion to be experienced (Rinn, 1984). According to this view, if there is no facial expression present, the emotion cannot be felt.

Support for the facial feedback hypothesis comes from what has become a classic experiment carried out by psychologist Paul Ekman and colleagues (Ekman, Levenson & Friesen, 1983). In the study, professional actors were asked to follow

328

very explicit instructions regarding movements of muscles in their faces (see Figure 9-10). You might try this example yourself:

Raise your brows and pull them together; raise your upper eyelids; now stretch your lips horizontally back toward your ears.

After carrying out these directions—which, as you may have guessed, are meant to produce an expression of fear—the actors showed a rise in heart rate and a decline in body temperature, physiological reactions that are characteristic of fear. Overall, facial expressions representative of the primary emotions produced physiological effects similar to those accompanying the emotions in other circumstances.

Although support for the facial-feedback hypothesis is not firm (Matsumoto, 1987), there is sufficient evidence in its favor to suggest that the old lyric "Smile, though you're feeling blue" may not be far from the mark in its suggestion that you will feel better by putting a smile on your face (McCanne & Anderson, 1987; Adelmann & Zajonc, 1989).

Facial-feedback hypothesis: The notion that facial expressions are involved in determining the experience of emotions and in labeling them

FIGURE 9-10

The instructions given this actor were to (*a*) "raise your brows and pull them together," (*b*) "now raise your upper eyelids," and (*c*) "now also stretch your lips horizontally, back toward your ears." If you follow these directions yourself, it may well result in your experiencing fear. (Ekman, Levenson, & Friesen, 1983.)

WHY DON'T WE SMILE WHEN WE ARE SAD?

Although there is ample evidence to suggest a close link between a particular facial expression and an emotional state, neither the facial-affect program nor the facial-feedback hypothesis explains *why* a particular expression is linked to a particular emotion. For instance, although we are used to people smiling when they are happy and frowning when they are sad, there is seemingly no logical reason why this has to be the case. Why don't we smile when we are sad or frown when we are happy?

In the early part of this century, an obscure French physician, Israel Waynbaum (1907), put forward a theory that sought to explain why, in fact, smiling is not associated with sadness. According to him, and to more recent theorizing done by psychologist Robert Zajonc (1985), the configuration of the face affects the flow of blood to particular regions of the brain. When we concentrate, for instance, our brows become furrowed, certain muscles on our face contract, and our jawbone may stick out. All this activity acts as a tourniquet on certain blood vessels in the face, which ultimately leads to more blood being shunted to the cerebral cortex. In turn, the rich concentration of blood allows for more efficient thinking. Using similar reasoning, Zajonc argues that smiling temporarily diverts blood away from the cerebrum of the brain that ultimately produces a surge of positive emotion when the diversion is terminated and the blood is redirected to the cerebrum.

The intriguing hypothesis that links blood flow to the brain and the experience of particular emotions remains just that: an intriguing hypothesis. For instance, it is not clear that changes in brain blood flow are directly associated with specific emotional experiences. Nevertheless, evidence is mounting that the link between specific facial configurations and emotion is an important one (Cacioppo et al., 1988; Adelmann & Zajonc, 1989) and that it is unlikely that a truly sad person will do much in the way of smiling.

THE INFORMED CONSUMER OF PSYCHOLOGY:
Can You "Read" Others' Nonverbal Behavior?

You Can Read a Person Like a Book ... Body Talk ... Body Language. A glance through a bookstore will reveal many titles such as these, all aimed at helping you to understand other people's nonverbal behavior. But do they work?

For a number of reasons, psychologists who study emotional expressivity would urge extreme caution in accepting advice from these books. First, cultural **display rules**—learned rules that inform us about the appropriateness of showing emotion nonverbally—operate to mask and modify emotional displays. Therefore, the facial expressions we see in social situations may be brought about by adherence to a display rule, rather than by an actual emotion.

Display rules: Learned rules that inform us about the appropriateness of showing emotions nonverbally

Moreover, there is not always a one-to-one relationship between a particular emotion and nonverbal behavior. Just as with word homonyms such as "bear" and "bare," which sound the same but have very different meanings, the same nonverbal behavior may sometimes mean one thing and, at other times, quite another. Take, for instance, a smile. A smile may, and probably most frequently does, indicate happiness. On the other hand, people who are highly fearful and preparing to defend themselves aggressively may bare their teeth, presenting an expression which at first glance is surprisingly similar to a smile. The meaning behind the expression, however, is quite different.

Finally, there is no evidence that what has been called "body language" actually has any of the characteristics of a language. There is no evidence for a syntax and grammar of emotional expressions and, except in sign language, people do not put various nonverbal signs and signals together to form a nonverbal equivalent of sentences. The term "body language," then, is misleading.

Despite these cautions, facial expressions often are a true indication of emotions, and it is possible to increase the accuracy with which you understand others' nonverbal behavior. Among the principles you can use are the following:

▶ Look at what is occurring in the environment. When nonverbal behavior represents an emotional response, it reflects what is happening to a person in a given situation. You can use these clues to understand the meaning of a person's nonverbal behavior.

▶ Consider discrepancies between facial expressions and verbal ones. When a facial expression does not match what a speaker is saying, this is a signal for closer observation. Sometimes the facial expression may provide a more accurate indicator of what people are actually experiencing than the words they use.

FIGURE 9-11

(*a*) An example of a true happy smile, genuinely experienced. (*b*) In this photo, the
same woman pretends to be happy when
she actually feels disgusted. (Paul Ekman)

(a)

(b)

▶ Watch for subtleties in facial expression. For example, the differences
between a real smile and one that is feigned while lying—shown in Figure
9-11—rest on variations in just a few muscle groups in the face. Before you
jump to conclusions about the meaning of nonverbal behavior, then, remember how difficult it is to decode nonverbal cues reliably (Ekman, Friesen &
O'Sullivan, 1988).

Perhaps the overriding advice to be drawn from these suggestions is
"proceed with caution." Although emotional expressions do provide insight
into what people are experiencing, it is probably not possible to read others
"like a book."

RECAP AND REVIEW IV

Recap

◀ Six primary emotions are displayed through facial
expressions and understood similarly across different
cultures.

◀ The facial-feedback hypothesis maintains that facial
expressions not only reflect emotional experience, they
may also determine how people experience and label
emotions. Furthermore, one theory suggests that there is
an association between specific facial configuration and
blood flow to the brain, leading to emotional experience.

◀ Although facial expressions can reveal emotions, they do
not always provide an accurate representation of the
emotion being experienced.

Review

1. What are the six primary emotions that can be identified
from facial expressions?

2. Viewed as similar to a computer program, the
_____ _____ program provides a possible
explanation for the universality in the expression of emotions.

3. "I'm smiling on purpose to get myself into a good
mood." What hypothesis would support this reasoning?
_____-_____ hy-
pothesis.

4. According to Zajonc, blood concentration in certain areas
of the brain might trigger specific facial expressions. True
or false? _____

5. Cathy smiled because she felt it was appropriate in the
social situation. Inside, however, she felt angry and had
smiled only out of adherence to a _____
_____ .

6. List three ways by which an astute observer might have
been able to determine Cathy's true feelings.

(Answers to review questions are on page 332.)

1. The topic of motivation considers the factors that direct and energize behavior, whereas the study of emotions focuses on internal experiences. Drive is the motivational tension that energizes behavior in order to fulfill a need. Primary drives relate to basic biological needs; secondary drives are those in which no obvious biological need is fulfilled. Motivational drives often operate under the principle of homeostasis, by which an organism tries to maintain an optimal level of internal biological functioning by making up for any deviations from its usual state.

2. A number of broad theories of motivation move beyond explanations that rely on instincts. Drive-reduction theories, though useful for primary drives, are inadequate for explaining behavior in which the goal is not to reduce a drive but to maintain or even increase excitement or arousal. Arousal theory suggests that we try to maintain a particular level of stimulation and activity. The Yerkes-Dodson law, dealing with the relationship between task difficulty and the optimal level of motivation, is consistent with arousal theory. Finally, opponent-process theory suggests that opponent forces in the nervous system arise when initial arousal results from some stimulus. If the initial arousal is positive, the opponent forces are negative, and vice versa.

3. Maslow's hierarchy of needs suggests that there are five needs (physiological, safety, love and belongingness, esteem, and self-actualization). Only after the more basic needs are fulfilled is a person able to move toward higher-order needs.

4. Eating behavior is subject to homeostasis, since most people's weight stays within a relatively stable range. Organisms tend to be sensitive to the nutritional value of food they eat, with the hypothalamus being closely related to food intake. In addition to the biological factors that affect eating behavior, social factors also play a role. For instance, mealtimes, cultural food preferences, the attractiveness of food, and other learned habits determine when and how much one eats. An oversensitivity to social cues and an insensitivity to internal cues also may be related to obesity. In addition, obesity may be caused by an unusually high weight set point—the weight at which the body attempts to maintain homeostasis—or by the rate of metabolism.

5. The stimuli that motivate drinking are mainly internal. Salt concentration of the body's cells vary as a function of the amount of internal fluid. Furthermore, a decrease in the total volume of fluid in the circulatory system can cause thirst.

6. Need for achievement refers to the stable, learned characteristic in which a person strives to attain a level of excellence. People high in need for achievement tend to seek out tasks that are of moderate difficulty, while those low in need for achievement seek out only very easy and very difficult tasks. However, inconsistent findings regarding females' need for achievement has led some researchers to suggest that women have a fear of success related to achievement motivation. Need for achievement is usually measured through the Thematic Apperception Test (TAT), a series of pictures about which a person writes a story.

7. The need for affiliation is a concern with establishing and maintaining relationships with others, whereas the need for power is a tendency to seek impact on others.

8. One definition of emotion that seems appropriate across differing theoretical perspectives views emotions as feelings that may affect behavior and generally have both a physiological and a cognitive component. What this definition does not do is address the issue of whether there are separate systems that govern cognitive and emotional responses, and whether one has primacy over the other.

9. Among the functions of emotions are to prepare us for action, shape future behavior through learning, and help to regulate social interaction. Although the range of emotions is wide, according to one category system there are only eight primary emotions: joy, acceptance, fear, surprise, sadness, disgust, anger, and anticipation.

10. Among the general physiological responses to strong emotion are opening of the pupils, dryness of the mouth, and increases in sweating, rate of breathing, heart rate, and blood pressure. Because these physiological changes are not the full explanation of emotional experience, a number of distinct theories of emotion have been developed.

11. The James-Lange theory suggests that emotional experience is a reaction to bodily, or visceral, changes that occur as a response to an environmental event. These visceral experiences are interpreted as an emotional response. In contrast to the James-Lange theory, the Cannon-Bard theory contends that visceral movements are too slow to explain rapid shifts of emotion and the fact that visceral changes do not always produce emotion. Instead, the Cannon-Bard theory suggests that both physiological arousal *and* an emotional experience are produced simultaneously by the same nerve impulse. Therefore, the visceral experience itself does not necessarily differ among differing emotions.

12. The third explanation, the Schachter-Singer theory, rejects the view that the physiological and emotional responses are simultaneous. Instead, it suggests that emotions are determined jointly by a relatively nonspecific physiological arousal and the subsequent labeling of that arousal. This labeling process uses cues from the environment to determine how others are behaving in the same situation.

13. Emotions can be revealed through a person's facial expression. In fact, there is universality in emotional expressivity, at least for the basic emotions, across members of different cultures. In addition, there are similar-

ities in the way members of different cultures understand the emotional expressions of others. One explanation for this similarity rests on the existence of an innate facial-affect program which activates a set of muscle movements representing the emotion being experienced.

14. The facial-feedback hypothesis suggests that facial expressions not only are a reflection of emotions but can help determine and produce emotional experience. There is also a theory—still without wide support—that suggests a link between a particular facial configuration and the flow of blood to the brain, which in turn results in the experience of a specific emotion.

KEY TERMS AND CONCEPTS ▶

motives (p. 293)
motivation (293)
instinct (294)
drive-reduction theory (295)
drive (295)
primary drives (295)
secondary drives (295)
homeostasis (295)
arousal theory (296)
Yerkes-Dodson law (296)
incentive (298)
incentive theory (298)
opponent-process theory (298)
intrinsic motivation (299)

extrinsic motivation (299)
self-actualization (301)
obesity (302)
hypothalamus (304)
lateral hypothalamus (304)
ventromedial hypothalamus (304)
weight set point (306)
metabolism (307)
anorexia nervosa (308)
bulimia (309)
need for achievement (311)
Thematic Apperception Test
   (TAT) (311)
fear of success (312)

need for affiliation (314)
need for power (314)
emotions (316)
visceral experience (320)
James-Lange theory of emotion (320)
Cannon-Bard theory of emotion (321)
Schachter-Singer theory of
   emotion (321)
polygraph (324)
channels (325)
facial-affect program (327)
facial-feedback hypothesis (328)
display rules (329)

FOR FURTHER STUDY AND APPLICATION ▶

Buck, R. (1988). *Human motivation and emotion* (2nd ed.). New York: Wiley.

McClelland, D. C. (1985). *Human motivation*. Chicago: Scott Foresman.
   These two volumes provide good, general guides to motivation. Not only do they include the classic issues, but they provide information on a number of applications.

McClelland, D. C., & Winter, D. G. (1969). *Motivating economic achievement*. New York: Free Press.
   This book provides details of the program developed by McClelland and Winter to teach achievement motivation in India. It includes a wealth of other data on the need for achievement.

Polivy, J., & Herman, C. P. (1983). *Breaking the diet habit*. New York: Basic Books.
   This is one of the few popular diet books that can be recommended. Based not on fad diets but on the kinds of principles we discuss in this chapter, the book contains numerous hints for losing weight sensibly.

Buck, R. (1986). *The communication of emotions*. New York: Guilford.

Feldman, R. S., & Rimé, B. (Eds.). (1990). *Fundamentals of nonverbal behavior*. Cambridge, England: Cambridge University Press.
   These are two well-illustrated guides to human emotions and nonverbal behavior.

Darwin, C. (1872). *The expression of emotions in man and animals*. Chicago: University of Chicago Press (1965 reprint).
   This classic on emotions remains surprisingly readable and fascinating, more than 100 years after it was written.

Ekman, P. (1985). *Telling lies*. New York: Norton.
   This guide to deception describes what psychologists know about lying, ways of detecting lies, and how lies are used in society.

ANSWERS (REVIEW IV):
1. Surprise, sadness, happiness, anger, disgust, and fear **2.** Facial affect **3.** The facial-feedback hypothesis **4.** False; Zajonc hypothesized that facial expressions could affect blood flow in the brain, not the other way around **5.** Display rule **6.** a—look for environmental cues; b—consider discrepancies between verbal and facial expressions; c—watch for subtleties in facial expression

CHAPTER

10

SEXUALITY AND GENDER

CHAPTER 10

SEXUALITY AND GENDER

Billy Tipton. (Wide World Photos.)

Gender: The sense of being male or female

PROLOGUE: BILLY TIPTON

When jazz musician Billy Tipton died at the age of 74, his three adopted sons found out something about him they had never once suspected: their father was actually a woman.

Tipton's startling secret was kept since the 1950s, when Tipton first began to appear publicly as a man in order to be more successful in her musical career. According to the woman Tipton said she had married in 1960, the opportunities for a successful career for a woman in the jazz field were limited. "He gave up everything. There were certain rules and regulations in those days if you were going to be a musician."

Although Tipton had a baby face and a high singing voice, even those who worked with her for decades did not know Tipton's true sex. Tipton's adopted sons also had no inkling of the secret, and its revelation left them bewildered. According to one son, who learned the truth four days after Tipton's death, "I'm just lost. He'll always be Dad. But I think that he should have left something behind for us, something that would have explained the truth." (*New York Times,* 1989, p. A18.)

LOOKING AHEAD ▶

The details of Tipton's life will probably remain a mystery, but even the few facts that are known raise many profound psychological issues about her sexuality and her sense of sexual identity. For example, what was the nature of Tipton's sexual behavior (and that of the woman she identified as her wife)? Did she perceive of herself sexually as a female or a male? What stress did she experience in adopting a sex role that was not congruent with her physical sexuality? And what are we to make of Tipton's assumption—which probably was accurate—that success as a jazz musician would come more readily if she posed as a man?

These questions—and the curiosity Tipton's situation arouses—indicate our fascination with a topic which affects all of us. It also illustrates the complexity of the field of human sexuality. Representing an interplay between human biology and psychology, sexual behavior provides a rich area of study for psychologists in a variety of specialty areas. For example, psychologists interested in motivation view sexuality in terms of sexual needs, drives, and gratification; biopsychologists consider it from the perspective of the functioning of the sexual organs and their underlying physiology; and social psychologists focus on society's rules of sexual conduct and the role that sexual behavior plays in interpersonal behavior. In this chapter, we consider sex from several of these vantage points.

We first consider **gender,** the sense of being male or female. We examine the ways in which expectations about how a man and woman should behave differ, and the impact that those expectations have on our lives. Next we turn to sexual behavior, describing the biological aspects of sexual excitement and arousal, and then examining the variations in sexual activities in which people engage. We conclude the chapter with a discussion of nonconsenting sex, sexually transmitted diseases, and the psychological aspects of sexual difficulties.

After reading this chapter, you will be able to answer questions such as these:

▶ What are the major differences between male and female gender roles?

▶ Why, and under what circumstances, do we become sexually aroused?

▶ What is "normal" sexual behavior, and how do most people behave sexually?

▶ Why is rape not a crime of sex, and how prevalent is it and other forms of nonconsenting sex?

▶ What are the major sexual difficulties that people encounter?

GENDER AND SEX

"It's a boy." "It's a girl."

The first words uttered upon the birth of the child are almost always these. The way in which we think about others, and even the way in which we think about ourselves, is based to a large extent on whether we are a male or a female. But the effects of gender go well beyond the mere biological fact of a body which harbors male or female sex organs. Our conclusions about what is or is not "appropriate" behavior for others and ourselves are based on **gender roles**—the set of expectations, defined by society, that indicate what is appropriate behavior for men and women.

Were the expectations associated with men and women's gender roles to be equivalent, they would have only minor impact upon our lives. However, not only do the expectations differ, but in many cases they result in favoritism toward one sex or the other, leading to stereotyping. **Stereotyping** refers to beliefs and expectations about members of a group based on their membership in that group. Stereotypes about gender roles produce **sexism**, negative attitudes and behavior toward a person based on that individual's sex.

Our society holds particularly well-defined stereotypes about men and women, and they prevail regardless of age, economic status, and social and educational background. For example, in an examination of traditional stereotypes about men and women, one study carried out in the early 1970s asked a group of college students (seventy-four men and eighty women) to examine a list of traits and specify which of them were more characteristic of men than women and which were more characteristic of women than men.

Table 10-1 shows the traits seen as applicable to one sex more than the other by at least 75 percent of the subjects (Broverman et al., 1972). From the way in which the traits cluster, you can see that men were more apt to be viewed as having traits involving competence; women, on the other hand, were seen as having traits involving warmth and expressiveness. Because our society traditionally holds competence in higher esteem than warmth and expressiveness, the perceived differences between men and women are biased in favor of men.

Of course, given that Broverman's study was carried out almost two decades ago, one could argue that times—and stereotypes—have changed. Unfortunately, this does not seem to be the case; males are still viewed as holding more competence-related traits, whereas women continue to be seen in terms of warmth and expressiveness (Ruble, 1983; Deaux & Lewis,

Gender roles: Societal expectations about appropriate behavior for women and men

Stereotyping: Beliefs and expectations about members of a group based on their membership in that group

Sexism: Negative attitudes toward a person based on that person's sex

TABLE 10-1

Common Stereotypes about Men and Women

Traits perceived as characteristic of men	Traits perceived as characteristic of women
Aggressive	Talkative
Independent	Tactful
Unemotional	Gentle
Self-confident	Religious
Very objective	Aware of feelings of others
Likes math and science	Interested in own appearance
Ambitious	Neat
Active	Quiet
Competitive	Strong need for security
Logical	Enjoys art and literature
Worldly	Easily expresses tender feelings
Direct	Does not use harsh language
Adventurous	Dependent

College students rated the "typical man" and the "typical female" on a list of adjectives. Some of the traits that most strongly differentiated ratings of men and women are indicated above. As you can see, men are seen as having traits involving competence, while women are viewed as holding traits involving warmth and expressiveness.

Source: Adapted from Broverman et al., 1972.

in press; Martin, 1987). Because society still tends to hold competence in higher esteem than warmth and expressiveness, this perceived difference—and keep in mind we are talking about people's perceptions, and not necessarily factual differences—may have sexist implications (O'Leary & Smith, 1988).

Furthermore, important differences remain in which occupations are seen as appropriate for men and for women, with members of each sex expecting greater success when they enter a profession viewed as appropriate for their sex (Eccles, 1987; Bridges, 1988). Although more women are entering the work force, they continue to be seen as suited to traditionally female jobs: secretaries, nurses, bookkeepers, cashiers, and other female-dominated professions that feature low pay and low status (Glick, Zion & Nelson, 1988). In addition, women hold significantly lower expectations than men about their entering and peak salaries (Major & Konar, 1984; Martin, 1989).

In sum, gender stereotypes seem more positive for men than women. Of course, such stereotypes reflect people's perceptions and not the reality of the world. But because people often act upon their expectations, gender stereotypes can lead to the unfortunate consequence of more favorable behavior to men than to women.

Although the prevalence and clarity of gender stereotypes might lead us to expect that actual differences between men's and women's behavior are large, the reality is quite different. In fact, in considering the differences between men and women that have been well documented, it is important to remember that in most respects men and women are more similar to one another than they are different. Moreover, when differences have been found, their magnitude is usually small. When we compare men and women, then, keep in mind that there is more overlap in behavior and psychological characteristics than there is discrepancy between the sexes. The differences that have been found reflect average male and female group differences and tell us nothing about any given male or female. Even if we find that males, on the whole, tend to be more aggressive than females (as they are), there are going to be many men who are less aggressive than most women, just as there will be many women who act more aggressively than most men.

Personality Differences

As already mentioned, one of the most pronounced differences between men and women is their degree of aggression. By the time they are 2 years old, boys tend to show more aggression than girls, and this higher level of aggression persists throughout the lifespan (Hyde, 1984; Maccoby & Jacklin, 1974). Although the difference is greatest in terms of physical aggression, there are also differences in terms of aggression that produce psychological harm to others. Furthermore, women feel greater anxiety and guilt about their aggressiveness and are more concerned about its effects on their victims than are men (Eagly & Steffen, 1986).

Men and women also differ in average levels of self-esteem (Block, 1983). Women, on the average, have lower self-esteem than men. Furthermore, not

"We're a great team, Sash—you with your small and large motor skills, me with my spatial awareness and hand-eye coördination."

(Drawing by Koren; © 1988 The New Yorker Magazine, Inc.)

only do women tend to downgrade themselves relative to men; their self-denigration translates into lower confidence in their estimates of how well they will succeed on future tasks. Of course, such a state of affairs is not particularly surprising, given the message of incompetence that society's stereotypes are communicating. In fact, when considered in light of their lower aggressiveness, women's lower self-esteem may help explain their reluctance to enter high-prestige professions dominated by men, in which aggression and self-confidence may be a prerequisite for success.

Men and women also differ in both their verbal and nonverbal communication styles. For starters, there is a difference in the amount of talking—but not what stereotypes would have us believe: Men tend to talk more than women (McMillan et al., 1977). The content of men's and women's speech also differs, with women's speech being more precise. At the same time, women's speech patterns lead others to view them as more tentative and less assertive; they more often raise their pitch at the end of sentences, and they more often add "tags" at the end of an opinion, rather than stating the opinion outright: Instead of saying "It's awfully warm today," a female speaker might say instead "It's awfully warm today, *isn't it?*," thereby appearing less certain of her opinion (Matlin, 1987).

In nonverbal areas, women and men also differ in several significant respects. In mixed-sex conversations, women look at a partner significantly more while listening than while speaking, whereas men display more equivalent levels of looking while speaking and looking while listening. The effect of the male's pattern is to communicate power and dominance, while the women's pattern is associated with lower levels of power. Men also are more likely to touch others, while women are more likely to be touched, and women are better than men at decoding the facial expressions of others (Hall, 1978; Dovidio & Ellyson, 1985; Dovidio et al., 1988).

Cognitive Abilities

Although there are no differences between men and women in overall IQ scores, learning, memory, problem solving, and concept-formation tasks, a few disparities in more specific cognitive areas have been identified. However, the true nature of these differences—and even their existence—has been called into question by recent research.

When Eleanor Maccoby and Carol Jacklin carried out a pioneering review of sex differences in 1974, they concluded that girls outperformed boys in verbal abilities, and that there was a gender difference favoring boys over girls in quantitative and spatial abilities. This conclusion was widely accepted as one of the truisms of the psychological literature.

However, recent and more sophisticated analyses have questioned the specific nature and magnitude of these differences. For instance, Alan Feingold (1988) analyzed scores on the Differential Aptitude Tests, a series of tests administered to close to 200,000 students over a thirty-three-year period. Some consistent differences emerged: Girls scored higher than boys on scales of grammar, spelling, and perceptual speed, while boys had higher means on measures of spatial visualization, high school mathematics, and mechanical aptitude. Perhaps most interestingly, gender differences declined in magnitude over the thirty-three-year period, except in one area—the higher performance by boys in high school mathematics has remained unchanged. Similarly, a study of 74,000 children in twenty nations found that in half the countries, boys had an edge in geometry and measurement, but the differences were not large (Hanna, 1988). In many countries the differences were nonexistent, and, in fact, in Belgium, Thailand, Finland, and Hungary, girls outperformed boys in algebra.

Futhermore, a comprehensive analysis of 165 studies of gender differences in verbal ability, representing the testing of close to 1.5 million subjects, led psychologists Janet Hyde and Marcia Linn to an even stronger conclusion. In their words, "We are prepared to assert that there are no gender differences in verbal ability, at least at this time, in American culture, in the standard ways that verbal ability has been measured" (Hyde & Linn, 1988, p. 62).

Current evidence suggests, then, that little is certain about gender differences in cognitive skills. As we amass more sophisticated research, some of the differences that have been traditionally thought to exist may prove to be illusory (Jacklin, 1989).

SOURCES OF GENDER AND SEX DIFFERENCES

If the identification of gender differences has posed a thorny and complex problem for researchers, the search for their causes has proved to be even more elusive and controversial. Given the indisputable fact that sex is a biological variable, it would seem reasonable to look at factors involving biological differences between men and women. But environmental factors can hardly be ruled out, given the obvious importance of growing up in a world in which people are treated differently on the basis of their sex from the time they are born.

Before considering both the biological and environmental factors that help explain sex and gender differences, we should note that it is unlikely that either biological or environmental factors alone are capable of providing a full explanation. Rather, it is probable that some combination of the two, interacting with each other, will ultimately provide us with an understanding of the causes of sex and gender differences.

Biological Causes

Does a difference between male and female brains underlie sex and gender differences? This intriguing suggestion has been put forward in recent years by psychologists studying brain structure and functioning. For example, Julian Stanley and Camilla Benbow (1987) found that groups of children with exceptional talent in mathematics were characterized by an unusual assortment of physical attributes, such as an overrepresentation of left-handedness and a high incidence of allergies and shortsightedness. Such seemingly unrelated characteristics, it turns out, may be associated with the degree of prenatal exposure to **androgens**, male sex hormones, which may slow the growth of the left hemisphere of the brain. According to one theory, the right hemisphere of the brain—which specializes in mathematical problems—then compensates for the deficiencies of the left hemisphere by becoming strengthened, thereby leading to the increased abilities of males in mathematical spheres (Gerschwind, 1985). Similarly, evidence from at least one study suggests that women perform better on tasks involving verbal skill and muscular coordination during periods when their production of the female sex hormone, **estrogen**, is relatively high than when it is low. In contrast, they perform better on tasks involving spatial relationships when their estrogen level is relatively low (Kimura & Sampson, 1988).

We don't yet know the extent to which biological causes may underlie

Androgens: Male sex hormones

Estrogen: The female sex hormone

sex differences, but the evidence is growing that such factors may explain, at least in part, behavioral differences between men and women (Kimura & Sampson, 1988; Witelson, 1989; Gur et al., 1982). However, it is also clear that environmental factors have a critical effect in producing sex and gender differences. Moreover, because environmental factors can be changed, such influences offer us the opportunity to decrease the detrimental effects of sex stereotyping.

Environmental Causes

Starting from the moment of birth, with blue blankets for boys and pink ones for girls, most parents and other adults provide environments that differ in important respects. The kinds of toys that are given to boys and girls differ, and fathers play more roughly with their infant sons than with their daughters (Huston, 1983). Middle-class mothers tend to talk more to their daughters than to their sons (Maccoby & Jacklin, 1974).

Socialization: The process by which individuals learn what society deems appropriate behavior, including gender roles

Such differences in behavior, and there are many more, produce different socialization experiences for men and women. **Socialization** is the process by which an individual learns the rules and norms of appropriate behavior. In this case, it refers to learning what society calls appropriate behavior for men and women. According, then, to the processes of social-learning theory, which we discussed in Chapter 5, boys and girls are taught (and rewarded for performing) behaviors that are thought, by society, to be appropriate for men and women, respectively.

It is not just parents, of course, who provide socialization for children. Society as a whole communicates clear messages to children as they are growing up. Television, for instance, is a particularly potent source of socialization. Despite programs such as *L.A. Law, Designing Women,* and *Rose-anne,* which show women in key roles, men still outnumber women on television and women often are cast in such stereotypic roles as housewife, secretary, and mother. The potency of television as a socialization force is indicated by the fact that some data suggest that the more television children watch, the more sexist they become (Morgan, 1982; Jennings, Geis, & Brown, 1980; McNeil, 1975; Liebert & Sprafkin, 1988).

Our educational system also provides differential treatment of boys and girls. For example, boys are five times as likely to receive more attention from classroom teachers. Boys receive significantly more praise, criticism, and remedial help than do girls. Even in college classes, male students receive more eye contact from their professors than female students; men are called upon more in class, and they are apt to receive extra help from their professors (Epperson, 1988).

Gender schema: A cognitive framework that organizes and guides a child's understanding of gender

According to Sandra Bem (1987), socialization produces a **gender schema**, a cognitive framework that organizes and guides a child's understanding of information relevant to gender. On the basis of what their schemas are regarding what is or is not appropriate for being a male or female, children begin to behave in ways that reflect society's gender roles. Hence, a child who goes to summer camp and is offered the opportunity to sew a potholder may evaluate the activity, not in terms of the intrinsic components of potholder making (such as the mechanics of using a needle and thread), but in terms of whether the activity is compatible with his or her gender schema.

Androgynous: A state in which gender roles encompass characteristics thought typical of both sexes

According to Bem, one way in which gender schemas can be circumvented is by encouraging children to be **androgynous,** a state in which gender roles encompass characteristics thought typical of both sexes. Specifically, an androgynous male may not only be aggressive and forceful (typically viewed by society as masculine characteristics) but simultaneously be compassionate and gentle (typically thought of as feminine characteristics). Conversely, an androgynous female may be affectionate and soft-spoken, while at the same time being assertive and self-reliant.

The concept of androgyny does not suggest that there should be no differences between men and women. Instead, it proposes that differences should be based on choices, freely made, of the best *human* characteristics, and not on an artificially restricted inventory of characteristics deemed by society to be appropriate only for men or only for women.

RECAP AND REVIEW I

Recap

◀ Gender roles, society's expectations about what is appropriate behavior for men and women, lead to sex stereotyping and sexism.

◀ Although there are both personality and cognitive gender differences, the magnitude of the differences tends to be small, and the specific differences can change over time.

◀ Sex and gender differences are caused by the interaction of biological and environmental factors.

REVIEW

1. Gender roles are determined by our biological makeup. True or false? _____

2. The statement "He must be arrogant and lazy if he belongs to that group!" is an example of _____

3. Recent views of the role of women in the labor force contradict earlier stereotypes predicting that women would enter traditionally female jobs of low pay and low status. True or false? _____

4. Which of the following statements is true about male/female differences in aggressiveness?
   a. Males are only more aggressive physically than females during childhood.
   b. Male/female differences in aggressiveness first become evident during adolescence.

   c. Males are more aggressive than females throughout the lifespan.
   d. Females and males feel equally anxious about their aggressive acts.

5. Which statement is *not* true about male/female differences in communication style?
   a. Men tend to talk more than women.
   b. Women tend to look at a partner more while speaking than while listening.
   c. Men look at a partner about equally as much while listening as they do while speaking.
   d. Men are more likely to touch others while communicating.

6. Girls apparently demonstrate poorer math-related skills than boys as a result of lower motivation and lower social expectations. True or false? _____

7. Stanley and Benbow found that talent for mathematics was associated with a variety of physical characteristics which may be a result of prenatal exposure to the male sex hormone _____ .

8. Although Lindall generally acts in a gentle and compassionate manner, she can also be very assertive and independent when the situation warrants it. In terms of gender roles, Lindall might be considered to be _____ .

(Answers to review questions are on page 344.)

THE FACTS OF LIFE: UNDERSTANDING HUMAN SEXUAL RESPONSE

When I started "tuning out," teachers thought I was sick; they kept sending me to the school nurse to have my temperature taken—physically sick. If I'd told them I was carrying on with Cheryl Tiegs in their classes, while supposedly learning my Caesar and my Latin vocabulary, they'd have thought I was—well, delirious. I *was!* I'd even think of Cheryl while jogging; I'd have to stop sometimes because it'd hurt down there! You can't run and have sex—or can you? (Coles & Stokes, 1985, pp. 18–19).

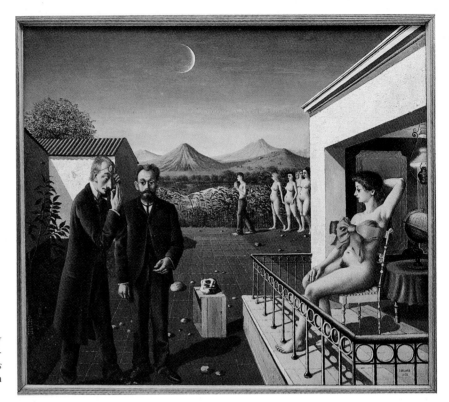

People's sexual fantasies can take many forms, as suggested by this painting by surrealist Paul Delvaux. (Paul Delvaux. *Phases of the Moon*. 1939. Collection, The Museum of Modern Art, New York. Purchase.)

Not everyone's sexual fantasies are as consuming as those reported by this teenage boy. Yet sex is an important consideration in most people's lives, for although the physical aspects of human sex are not all that different from those of other species, the meaning, values, and feelings that humans place on sexual behavior elevate it to a special place. To fully appreciate this difference, however, it is first necessary to understand the basic biology underlying sexual responses.

BASIC BIOLOGY: The Underlying Sex Drive

Anyone who has seen two dogs mating knows that sexual behavior has a biological basis; their sexual behavior appears to occur spontaneously, without much prompting on the part of others. In fact, a number of genetically controlled factors influence the sexual behavior of animals. For instance, animal behavior is affected by the presence of certain hormones in the blood. Moreover, females are receptive to sexual advances only at certain, relatively limited periods of time during the year.

Human sexual behavior, by comparison, is more complicated, although the underlying biology is not all that different from related species. In males, for example, the **testes** secrete androgen, the male sex hormone, beginning

Testes: The male reproductive organs responsible for secreting androgens

---

FIGURE 10-1

Cutaway side views of the female and male sex organs.

at puberty (see Figure 10-1 for the basic anatomy of the male and female **genitals**, or sex organs). Not only does androgen produce secondary sex characteristics, such as the development of body hair and a deepening of the voice; it also increases the sex drive. Although there are long-term changes in the amount of androgen that is produced—with the greatest production occurring just after sexual maturity—its short-term production is fairly constant. Men, therefore, are capable of (and interested in) sexual activities without any regard to biological cycles. Given the proper stimuli leading to arousal, male sexual behavior can occur.

Women show a different, and more complex, pattern. When they reach maturity at puberty, the two **ovaries**, the female reproductive organs, begin to produce estrogen—the female sex hormone. Estrogen, however, is not produced consistently; instead, its production follows a cyclical pattern. The

Genitals: The male and female sex organs

Ovaries: The female reproductive organs

Ovulation: The monthly release of an egg from an ovary

greatest production occurs during **ovulation**, when an egg is released from the ovaries, making the chances of fertilization by a male sperm cell highest. Although in lower animals the period around ovulation is the only time that the female is receptive to sex, human beings are different: Although there are variations in reported sex drive, women are receptive to sex throughout their cycles, depending on the external stimuli they encounter in their environment (Hoon, Bruce & Kinchloe, 1982).

Though biological factors "prime" people for sex, it takes more than hormones to motivate and produce sexual behavior. In animals it is the presence of a partner who provides arousing stimuli that leads to sexual activity. Humans are considerably more versatile; not only other people, but nearly any object, sight, smell, sound, or other stimulus can lead to sexual excitement. Because of prior associations, then, people may be turned on sexually by the smell of Chanel No. 5 or Brut, the sight of a bikini brief, or the sound of a favorite song, hummed softly in their ear. The reaction to a specific, potentially arousing stimulus, as we shall see, is a very individual one—what turns one person on may do just the opposite for another.

WHAT TURNS PEOPLE ON?
The Psychological Aspects of Sexual Excitement

If you were to argue that the major sex organ is the brain, in a sense you would be right. Much of what is considered sexually arousing in our society has little or nothing to do with our genitals but instead is related to external stimuli which, through a process of learning, have come to be labeled as **erotic**, or sexually stimulating.

Erotic: Sexually stimulating

Erogenous (eh RAH jun us) **zones:** Areas of the body that are particularly sensitive because of an unusually rich array of nerve receptors

For example, there are no areas of the body that when touched automatically produce sexual arousal. What are called **erogenous zones**—areas

The obesity of this woman, Princess Ruth Keelikolani, represented the height of sexual attractiveness in Hawaii in the late nineteenth century. (American Museum of Natural History)

of the body that are particularly sensitive because of the presence of an unusually rich array of nerve receptors—are sensitive not just to sexual touch, but to any kind of touch. When a physician touches a breast or a penis, the information sent to the brain by the nerve cells is essentially the same as that sent when a lover touches the same area. What differs is the interpretation given to the touch. Only when a certain part of the body is touched in what people define as a sexual manner is sexual arousal likely to follow (Gagnon, 1977).

Although people can learn to respond sexually to almost any stimulus, there is a good deal of agreement within a society or culture as to what usually represents an erotic stimulus. While in western society, large, full breasts represent a standard against which many males measure female appeal, in many other cultures breast size is irrelevant. For instance, in the last century, Hawaiian males saw female obesity as very arousing, and in some cultures today the female thigh is viewed as very erotic—if sporting a tattoo.

In our own culture, most women prefer men with small buttocks and a moderately large chest. They also see the chest as most sexually stimulating—more so than buttocks, legs, or the penis (Wildman, Wildman, Brown & Trice, 1976). These preferences have led to the development of entire industries that promise consumers enhanced sexual desirability (See Figure 10-2).

Sexual fantasies also play an important role in producing sexual arousal. Not only do people have fantasies of a sexual nature during their everyday activities, but about 60 percent of all people have fantasies during sexual intercourse. Interestingly, such fantasies often include having sex with someone other than one's partner of the moment.

Men's and women's fantasies differ little from each other in terms of content, as you can see in Figure 10-3. For both sexes, thoughts of being sexually irresistible and of engaging in oral-genital sex are most common (Sue, 1979; McCauley & Swann, 1980). It is important to note that fantasies are just that—fantasies—and do not represent a desire to fulfill them in the real world. We should not assume from such data that females want to be sexually overpowered, nor should we assume that in every male lurks a potential rapist desirous of forcing sexual overtures on a submissive victim.

FIGURE 10-2

Society's opinions of what is attractive changes over time, leading to a reliance on fashion magazines for advice on what is currently stylish. (Barbara Alper/Stock, Boston)

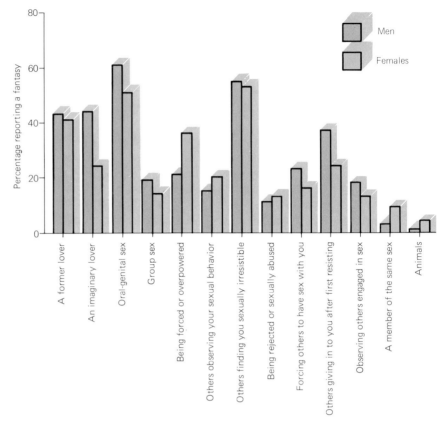

FIGURE 10-3

The kinds of fantasies that men and women have during sexual intercourse are relatively similar. (Sue, 1979.)

THE PHASES OF SEXUAL RESPONSE

Although the kinds of stimuli that produce sexual arousal are to some degree unique to each of us, there are some basic aspects of sexual responsiveness that we all share. According to pioneering work done by William Masters and Virginia Johnson (1966), who studied sexual behavior in carefully controlled, laboratory settings, sexual responses follow a regular pattern consisting of four phases: excitement, plateau, orgasm, and resolution. Although other researchers argue that sexual responses follow a somewhat different form (e.g., Kaplan, 1974; Zilbergeld & Ellison, 1980), Masters and Johnson's research is the most accepted account of what happens when people become sexually excited.

In the **excitement phase**, which can last from just a few minutes to over an hour, an arousing stimulus begins a sequence that prepares the genitals for sexual intercourse. In the male, the **penis** becomes erect when blood flows into it; for females, the **clitoris** swells because of an increase in the blood supply to the area, and the **vagina** becomes lubricated. Women may also experience a "sex flush," a measlelike coloration that typically spreads over the chest and throat.

Next comes the **plateau phase**, the body's preparation for orgasm. During this stage, the maximum level of sexual arousal is attained as the penis and clitoris swell with blood. The size of women's breasts and vagina increases. Heartbeat and blood pressure rise, and the breathing rate increases. Muscle tension becomes greater as the body prepares itself for the next stage, **orgasm**.

Although it is difficult to explain the sensation of orgasm beyond saying

Excitement phase: A period during which the body prepares for sexual intercourse

Penis: The primary male sex organ

Clitoris: The small and very sensitive organ in the female's external genitals

Vagina: The female canal into which the penis enters during sexual intercourse

Plateau phase: A period in which the maximum level of arousal is attained, the penis and clitoris swell with blood, and the body prepares for orgasm

Orgasm: The peak of sexual excitement during which time rhythmic muscular contractions occur in the genitals that it is an intense, highly pleasurable experience, the biological events that accompany the feeling are fairly straightforward. When the orgasm stage is reached, rhythmic muscular contractions occur in the genitals every eight-tenths of a second. In the male, the contractions expel **semen**, a fluid containing sperm, from the penis—a process known as **ejaculation**. Breathing and heart rates reach their maximum.

Although we can't be sure, the subjective experience of orgasm seems identical for males and females, despite the differences in the organs that are involved. In one experiment, a group of men and women wrote down their descriptions of how an orgasm felt to them. These descriptions were given to a group of experts, who were asked to identify the sex of the writer. The results showed that the experts were correct at no better than chance levels, suggesting that there were little means to distinguish the descriptions of orgasms on the basis of gender (Vance & Wagner, 1976). To get a sense of how people describe orgasms, see Table 10-2.

Semen: A fluid containing sperm that is ejaculated through the penis during orgasm

Ejaculation: The expulsion of semen through the penis

TABLE 10-2

Orgasm, Male and Female

What does it feel like to have an orgasm? The following ten descriptions were written by men and women in an introductory psychology class. As you read through them, see if you can tell which were written by men and which by women.

1. Your heart pounds more than 100 miles per hour, your body tenses up, you feel an overwhelming sensation of pleasure and joy.

2. An orgasm feels like blood pulsating through my body, rushing essentially to the genital area, a surge of contraction-like waves paired with a rapidly beating heart and strong pulse; my heart feels like someone is squeezing it, painful, and I have trouble breathing deeply.

3. Feels like being plugged into an electrical socket, but pleasurable rather than painful. Nearly indescribable!

4. It's as if every muscle in your body is being charged with intense electricity; your mind is incapable of thinking about anything, and you become totally incoherent. All the nerves in your body tremble, and you have trouble breathing, and get the urge to scream, or yell, or do something wild.

5. An orgasm to me is like the sensations of hot and cold coming together in one throbbing, thrusting, prolonged moment. It is the ultimate excitement of my passion.

6. Like exquisite torture. The sudden release of all the primal urges in the body. The gladness and yet the sadness that the fun is over.

7. An orgasm is that point when you don't care if anyone hears you screaming out your pleasures of ecstasy.

8. It's like all the cells in my brain popping at once and whirling around, while all the muscles in my body heave upward till I reach ultimate sensory bliss.

9. Tingling, throbbing, pleasurable feeling. Breathing is very fast and not rhythmic. Tend to hold my breath at peak. Possible shaking afterward and tightening/contraction of muscles.

10. An orgasm is a heavenly experience. It can be compared to nothing.

If you thought that men and women experience orgasm differently, you may be surprised at how hard it is to tell the difference from these descriptions. The correct answers:

1. M, 2. F, 3. M, 4. F, 5. F, 6. M, 7. F, 8. M, 9. F, 10. M

(a)

(b)

FIGURE 10-4

A four-stage model of the sexual response cycle for males and females based on the findings of Masters and Johnson (1966). Note how the male pattern (on the left) includes a refractory period. The figure on the right shows three possible female patterns. In (*a*), the pattern is closest to the male cycle, except that the woman has two orgasms in a row. In (*b*), there is no orgasm, whereas in (*c*) orgasm is reached quickly and the woman rapidly returns to an unaroused state. (After Masters & Johnson, 1966.)

Resolution stage: The final stage of sexual arousal during which the body returns to its normal state

Refractory period: Entered by a male after the resolution stage, a temporary period during which he cannot be sexually aroused again

Following orgasm, people move into the last stage of sexual arousal, the **resolution stage**. The body returns to its normal state, reversing the changes brought about by arousal. The genitals resume their normal size and shape, and blood pressure, breathing, and heart rate return to normal.

Male and female responses differ significantly during the resolution stage; these divergences are depicted in Figure 10-4. Women are able to cycle back to the orgasm phase and experience repeated orgasms. Ultimately, of course, females enter the final resolution stage, and they return to their prestimulation state. In contrast, it is generally thought that men enter a **refractory period** during the resolution stage. During the refractory period, males are not able to be aroused and therefore are unable to have another orgasm and ejaculate. The refractory period may last from a few minutes to several hours, although in the elderly it may continue for several days.

Interestingly, some current evidence suggests that the traditional view that males are unable to have multiple orgasms without an intervening refractory period may be in error. In one study, for example, 12 percent of a group of 282 males reported experiencing multiple orgasms before they ejaculated (Hartman & Fithian, 1984; Robbins & Jensen, 1978). Moreover, measures of physiological responses that accompany orgasm confirmed the validity of the subjects' reports. From such research, and from the fact that orgasm and ejaculation are controlled by separate parts of the nervous system, it appears that orgasm and ejaculation may occur independently—a fact that is typically hidden, since they almost always happen together. Although further research is needed, what we now know suggests that it is possible that all men have the ability to have repeated orgasms without ejaculating; it is just that most have not learned the proper technique.

RECAP AND REVIEW II

Recap

◄ Although biological factors prime people for sex, other stimuli are necessary for sexual excitement to occur.

◄ Erogenous zones are areas of the body that are particularly sensitive to touch because of the presence of a rich array of nerve receptors. However, what makes a touch sexual is the context and interpretation given it.

◄ Fantasies, thoughts, and images in people's minds play an important role in producing sexual arousal.

◄ Although there are differences in detail, both men's and women's sexual response follows a regular pattern consisting of four phases: excitement, plateau, orgasm, and resolution.

Review

1. The ovaries produce the female sex hormone _____ , whereas the testes produce the male sex hormone _____ .

2. Whereas men are interested in sexual activity regardless of their biological cycles, women are truly receptive to sex only during ovulation, when the production of their sex hormones is greatest. True or false? _____

3. Areas of the body that are particularly sensitive because of the rich array of nerve receptors are called _____ _____ .

4. Fantasies typically do not occur once a person engages in sexual intercourse. True or false? _____

5. A woman engaged in sexual activity experiences an increased pulse rate and swelling of her vagina and breasts. What phase does this describe?

a. Resolution
b. Excitement
c. Plateau
d. Orgasm

6. The male process of expelling semen during orgasm is called _____ .

7. Marie becomes stimulated again very soon after she and Alex have both experienced orgasm. Alex, however, finds himself unaroused. He has entered the
a. resolution phase.
b. refractory period.
c. plateau period.
d. postorgasm phase.

8. Many males have learned to experience multiple ejaculations. True or false? _____

(Answers to review questions are on page 352.)

DIFFERENT STROKES FOR DIFFERENT FOLKS: THE VARIETIES OF SEXUAL BEHAVIOR

In order to discourage sexual arousal during the Victorian era, people avoided offering a woman a leg of chicken. Piano legs were covered with lace, and books by male and female authors were separated from one another on bookshelves—unless the authors were married to each other (Sussman, 1976; Taylor, 1954).

▲ ▲ ▲

A Chinese sex manual tells how couples will know that they have engaged in too much sex: "If, on the morning after sex, a couple feels worn out, heavy-headed, pain in the thighs or short of breath, or if they detect a loss of appetite, they are having too much sex and should take corrective measures" (Masters, Johnson & Kolodny, 1982, p. 491).

▲ ▲ ▲

"A boy will not feel so vigorous and springy; he will be more easily tired. . . . He will probably look pale and pasty, and he is lucky if he escapes indigestion and getting his bowels confined, both of which will probably give him spots and pimples on his face. . . .

"The results on the mind are the more severe. . . . A boy who practices this habit can never be the best that Nature intended him to be. His wits are not so sharp. His memory is not so good. His power of fixing his attention on whatever he is doing is lessened. . . . A boy like this is a poor thing to look at. . . . [He is] untrustworthy, unreliable, untruthful, and probably even dishonest" (Schofield & Vaughan-Jackson, 1913, pp. 30–42). The source of this condition: masturbation—at least according to the authors of this early twentieth-century sex manual, *What Every Boy Should Know.*

Though each of these views may seem bizarre and farfetched to you—a notion with which experts on human sexual behavior would certainly agree— they were at one time considered perfectly sound and accurate by people

This device allowed Victorian women to expose their legs and have shoes fitted without undue embarrassment. (Mary Evans Picture Library/Photo Researchers)

who were otherwise quite reasonable. Indeed, trivia buffs might be interested to learn that one nineteenth-century physician, J. W. Kellogg, felt that because some foods produced sexual excitation, an alternative of "unstimulating" grains was needed, thereby leading to the first bowl of corn flakes.

Clearly, sex and sex-related behavior are influenced by expectations, attitudes, beliefs, and the state of medical and biological knowledge of a given period. Today we know that sexual behavior may take a variety of forms, and what was once seen as "unnatural" and "lewd" is readily accepted in contemporary society. In fact, as we shall see, distinctions between normal and abnormal sexual behavior are not easily drawn.

WHAT IS NORMAL?: Approaches to Sexual Normality

If we were to develop a scale for "sexual normality," it would not be hard to define the end points. Most people would agree, for instance, that male-female sexual intercourse involving consenting members of a married couple would fit comfortably at one end of the scale, while a person who becomes sexually aroused only while spiders are crawling over his or her body might reasonably be placed at the other end. It is when we consider behaviors that fall in between that defining normality poses difficulties.

One approach—which we will discuss further in the context of defining abnormal behavior (see Chapter 16)—is to define abnormal sexual behavior in terms of deviation from the average, or typical, behavior. In order to determine abnormality, we simply observe what behaviors are rare and infrequent in a society and label these deviations from the norm as abnormal. The difficulty with such an approach, however, is that some behaviors that are statistically unusual hardly seem worthy of concern. Even though most people have sexual intercourse in the bedroom, does the fact that someone prefers sex in the dining room imply abnormality? If some people prefer fat sexual partners, are they abnormal in a society that holds slimness in high esteem? Clearly, the answer to both these questions is "no," and so the deviation-from-the-average definition is inappropriate for determining sexual abnormality.

An alternative approach would be to compare sexual behavior against some standard or ideal. But there is a problem here: What standard should be used? Some might suggest the Bible, some might turn to philosophy, and some might consider psychology the ultimate determinant. The trouble is that none of these potential sources of standards is universally acceptable, and since standards change radically with shifts in societal attitudes and new knowledge, such an approach is undesirable. For instance, until 1973 the American Psychiatric Association listed homosexuality as a mental illness, but then voted to change its official mind and said that homosexuality was no longer a signal of mental disorder. Obviously the behavior had not changed—only the label placed on it by the psychiatric profession had.

Given the difficulties with other approaches, it seems that the most reasonable definition of sexual normality is one that considers the psychological

---

ANSWERS (REVIEW II):
1. Estrogen, androgen **2.** False; women are receptive throughout their cycles depending on the kinds of external stimuli they encounter **3.** Erogenous zones **4.** False; about 60 percent of people have sexual fantasies *during* intercourse **5.** c **6.** Ejaculation **7.** b **8.** False; although some males may be capable of experiencing multiple *orgasms*, they are restricted to one ejaculation without a pause in sexual activities

consequences of the behavior. In this approach, sexual behavior is considered abnormal if it produces a sense of distress, anxiety, or guilt—or if it is harmful to some other person. According to this view, then, sexual behaviors can be viewed as abnormal only when they have a negative impact on a person's sense of well-being or on others.

It is important to recognize that what is seen as normal and what is seen as abnormal in sexual behavior are very much matters of value, resting largely in the eye of the beholder, and that there have been dramatic shifts from one generation to another in definitions of what constitutes appropriate sexual behavior. While people can, and should, make their own personal value judgments about what is appropriate in their own sex lives, there are few universal rights and wrongs when it comes to sexual behavior in general.

The vast variety of sexual behavior in which people engage was largely a mystery shrouded in ignorance until the late 1930s, when Albert Kinsey, a biologist by training, began a series of surveys on the sexual behavior of Americans that was to span eighteen years. The result was the first comprehensive look at sexual practices, and a spate of publicity as well. (See the Research Classics box.)

RESEARCH CLASSICS

KINSEY'S SEX SURVEYS

When Alfred C. Kinsey was tapped to teach a course in marriage at Indiana University in 1938, he was appalled at the level of ignorance that surrounded sexual practices. In an attempt to remedy the situation, he began what turned out to be a lifelong effort to collect data, highlighted by the publication of his landmark volumes, *Sexual Behavior in the Human Male* (1948) and *Sexual Behavior in the Human Female* (1953).

Prior to Kinsey's efforts, there was little systematic attempt at learning about human sexual behavior. What knowledge that existed was based on unsystematic case histories, and no large-scale surveys had ever been attempted. In contrast, Kinsey adopted the goal of collecting 100,000 sexual histories, and although he never reached that ambitious total, he and his colleagues did manage to interview tens of thousands of individuals.

To gather information about sexual practices, Kinsey used in-depth interviews, often lasting several hours. He and his colleagues were masterful at eliciting information that their subjects might otherwise have felt too embarrassed to admit. By treating all responses in a matter-of-fact manner, he encouraged people to report every sexual experience. Questions were worded in a way that was most likely to produce a response. For example, rather than saying, "Have you ever masturbated?" he would ask, "When was the first time you masturbated?" In this way, interviewees were forced to deny a particular sexual practice, rather than being asked to admit to the practice. Similarly, questions were asked in dissimilar ways at different points in the interview regarding the same sexual behavior in order to identify any discrepancies in subjects' reports.

Although Kinsey's interview techniques are still regarded as exemplary, his sampling techniques are open to criticism. By and large, Kinsey's interviews overrepresented college students, young people, well-educated individuals, urban dwellers, and people living in Indiana and the northeast; his interviews underrepresented manual laborers, people of low education, Roman Catholics and Jews, members of racial minorities, and people who lived in rural areas (Kirby, 1977).

Furthermore, as with all surveys of sexual practices, his sample was made up of volunteers, and it is unclear how representative his data are of people who refused to be interviewed. Similarly, because no survey observes behavior directly, it is not simple to assess how accurately people's descriptions of what they do in private match their actual sexual practices. People may be ashamed to admit to certain behaviors, or they may feel embarrassed that they have *not* engaged in practices that they think everyone else has engaged in, such as a virgin who is concerned about "lagging behind" his or her peer group.

Despite these drawbacks, Kinsey's work has remained influential. He showed that sexual behavior could be studied in an objective manner, and his research provided a foundation for much of the work on human sexuality that followed.

Kinsey's work set the stage for later surveys, although it is surprising how few comprehensive national surveys have been carried out since Kinsey did his initial work some forty years ago (Booth, 1988, 1989; McDonald, 1988). However, by examining the common results gleaned from different samples of subjects, we now have a reasonably complete picture of contemporary sexual practices—to which we turn next.

SOLITARY SEX: Masturbation

Masturbation: Sexual self-stimulation

If you were to listen to physicians even fifty years ago, you would have been told that **masturbation**, sexual self-stimulation, often using the hand to rub the genitals, would lead to a wide variety of physical and mental disorders, ranging from hairy palms to insanity. Had they been correct, however, most of us would be wearing gloves to hide the sight of our hair-covered palms— for masturbation is one of the most frequently practiced sexual activities. Some 94 percent of all males and 63 percent of all females have masturbated at least once, and among college students, the frequency ranges from "never" to "several times a day" (Houston, 1981; Hunt, 1974).

The age at which males and females begin to masturbate differs, as you can see in Figure 10-5. Furthermore, males masturbate more often than women, although there are differences in frequency according to age. For instance, male masturbation is most frequent in the early teens and then declines, whereas females both begin and reach a maximum frequency later.

Although masturbation is often considered an activity to engage in only if no other sexual outlets are available, this view bears little relationship to reality. Close to three-quarters of married men surveyed (age 20 to 40) report masturbating an average of twenty-four times a year, and 68 percent of the married women in the same age group masturbate an average of ten times each year (Hunt, 1974).

FIGURE 10-5

The age at which a sample of college students first masturbated. The percentages are based on only those people who have masturbation experience. (Arafat & Cotton, 1974.)

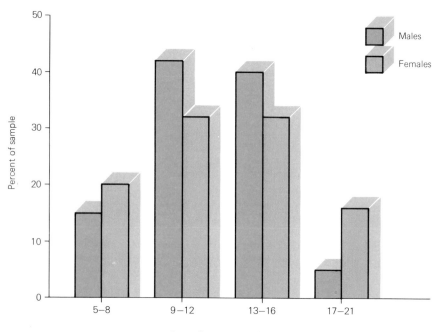

Age at first masturbation

Despite the high incidence of masturbation, attitudes toward it still reflect some of the negative views of yesteryear. For instance, one survey found that around 10 percent of the people who masturbated experienced feelings of guilt, and 5 percent of the males and 1 percent of the females considered their behavior perverted (Arafat & Cotton, 1974). Despite these negative attitudes, however, most experts on sex view masturbation not only as a healthy, legitimate—and harmless—sexual activity, but also as a means of learning about one's own sexuality.

INTERPERSONAL SEX: Heterosexuality

Despite the frequency of masturbation, there is another sexual activity that is probably even more common: **heterosexuality**, or sexual behavior between a man and a woman. People often believe that the first time they have sexual intercourse represents one of life's major milestones. Although heterosexuality goes well beyond sexual intercourse between men and women (it encompasses kissing, petting, caressing, massaging, and other forms of sex play), the focus of sex researchers has been on the act of intercourse, particularly in term of its first occurrence and its frequency.

Premarital Sex

Until fairly recently, premarital sex, at least for women, was considered one of the major taboos of our society. Traditionally, women have been warned by society that "nice girls don't do it"; men have been told that although premarital sex is OK for them, they should make sure they marry virgins. This view, that premarital sex is permissible for males but not for females, is called the **double standard**.

Although as recently as the mid-1960s about 80 percent of adult Americans believed that premarital sex was always wrong, by the 1970s a dramatic

While researchers of heterosexual behavior have focused on intercourse, a heterosexual relationship actually consists of a wide variety of other activities. (Susan Lapides/Design Conceptions)

Heterosexuality: Sexual behavior between a man and a woman

Double standard: The view that premarital sex is permissible for males but not for females

(Drawing by Modell; © 1972, The New Yorker Magazine, Inc.)

"Your friend is more than welcome, dear, but we just want you to know that your father and I didn't do anything funny till after we were married."

shift had occurred: Only about one-third felt this way (Reiss, 1980). Even higher rates of approval for premarital sex are found within certain age groups; for example, 80 percent of the males and 68 percent of the females in one poll of college students agreed that sexual intercourse prior to marriage was permissible (Arena, 1984).

Changes in approval of premarital sex were matched by changes in actual rates of premarital sexual activity in the 1970s and early 1980s. In one survey, for example, close to 80 percent of women under the age of 25 said they had experienced premarital intercourse, while just over 20 percent of those over 55 years of age reported having had premarital sexual intercourse (Horn & Bachrach, 1985), and some figures put the proportion of college-age women who had had premarital sexual intercourse at 59 percent (Arena, 1984). (See Figure 10-6.) Although some statistics suggest that there was a drop in women's sexual activity in the mid-1980s (Gerrard, 1988), overall the general trend over the last two decades has been toward more women engaging in premarital sexual activity.

Males, too, have shown an increase in the rate of premarital sexual intercourse, although the increase has not been as dramatic as it has for females—probably because the rates for males were higher to begin with. For instance, the first surveys carried out in the 1940s showed a rate of 84 percent; recent figures put the figure at closer to 95 percent. Moreover, the average age of males' first sexual experience has also been declining steadily, and some 76 percent of college-age males have already had intercourse (Arena, 1984).

What may be most interesting about these patterns is that they show a convergence of male and female attitudes and behavior in regard to premarital sex. But is the change sufficient to signal an end to the double standard?

The answer appears to be "no." Although in one survey of students, 95 percent of men and women were in favor of identical sexual standards for men and women involved in "love" relationships, the figure slipped to 82 percent when the man and woman were "casual acquaintances." Moreover, where differing standards remained, the attitudes were almost always more

FIGURE 10-6

In this figure, the rate of premarital sex is presented according to age and sex. As you can see, the figures have changed considerably more for women than for men.

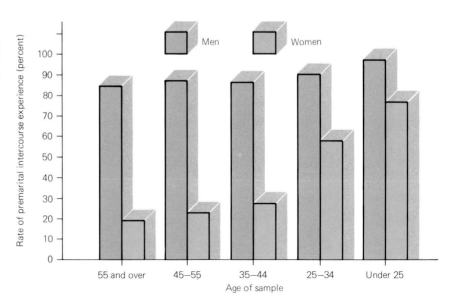

lenient toward the male than the female (Peplau, Rubin & Hill, 1977; Sullivan, 1985). It appears that the double standard, although declining, has yet to disappear. (For a discussion of another contemporary phenomenon relating to sexual behavior—teenage pregnancy—see the Cutting Edge box.)

THE CUTTING EDGE

CHILDREN WITH CHILDREN: THE EPIDEMIC OF TEENAGE PREGNANCIES

By the time they reach the age of 20, one in ten American women will have been pregnant at least once. Furthermore, there are 1.1 million unwanted teen pregnancies each year (Harris, 1987).

These startling statistics, found in a study of nineteen industrialized nations, is even more surprising when one considers that the severity of the problem is unique to the United States. As illustrated in Figure 10-7, teenagers in this country become pregnant and have abortions at significantly higher rates than do teenagers in any other industrialized country (Alan Guttmacher Institute, 1988).

Although the most obvious explanation is the decline of the double standard, leading American teenagers to have sexual intercourse earlier, the problem in fact is more complex. According to statistics, there is little difference among the countries in the age by which most girls have had sexual intercourse—just under 18. Moreover, there is no support for the explanation that teen-age girls become pregnant in order to collect welfare, for welfare payments in other countries are higher than those in the United States.

What does seem different is the use of birth control: It appears that American teenagers are less likely to use contraception than teenagers in other countries. Even when they do use birth control, American teenagers are less likely to use the most effective method, birth-control pills. In contrast, in the other countries studied, birth control is either very inexpensive or free, and its availability is widespread. In France, for instance, family-planning clinics reserve every Wednesday as a special day just for teenagers—a day when the schools are closed. Birth control has been free through these clinics since 1974.

But even the ready availability of birth control in other countries does not provide the full explanation. At the root of the problem, according to some experts, is not so much a looseness in American values about sex but just the opposite: even as the actual rate is increasing, Americans are still basically intolerant of premarital sex and so are unwilling to provide the kind of sex education that would prevent teenage pregnancies (Adler, 1985). In Sweden, for example, sex education is mandatory and taught in every grade, and the society as a whole is more tolerant of sexual activity. As the data in Figure 10-7 indicate, the teenage pregnancy rate in Sweden is considerably lower than it is in the United States.

Whatever the reasons, the teenage pregnancy rate has reached epidemic proportions in the United States. Perhaps what is most surprising about this fact is that the country which is one of the acknowledged leaders in basic human sexuality research has been so unsuccessful in applying that information.

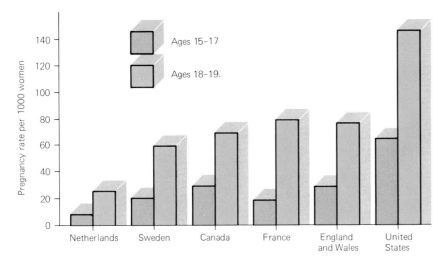

FIGURE 10-7

The degree to which the teenage pregnancy rate in the United States exceeds that of other industrialized countries is shown in this figure. (Alan Guttmacher Institute, 1985.)

The overall level of satisfaction in marriage is related to sexual satisfaction. (Earl Bronsteen/Taurus Photos)

Marital Sex

To judge by the number of articles about sex in marriage, one would think that sexual behavior was the number-one standard by which marital bliss is measured. Married couples are often concerned that they are having too little sex, too much sex, or the wrong kind of sex.

Although there are many different dimensions against which sex in marriage is measured, one is certainly the frequency of sexual intercourse. What is typical? As with most other types of sexual activities, there is no easy answer to the question, since there are such wide variations in patterns between individuals. We do know that the average frequency for married couples is approximately eight times per month (Westoff, 1974; Blumstein & Schwartz, 1983). In addition, there are differences according to the age of the couple; younger couples tend to have sexual intercourse more frequently than older ones (see Figure 10-8).

It also appears that the frequency of marital sexual intercourse is higher

FIGURE 10-8

The average monthly frequency of sexual intercourse between married couples, according to the wife's age. (Westoff, 1974.)

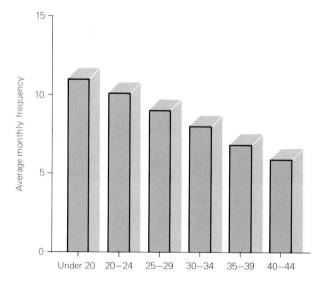

at this point in time than in other recent historical periods. A number of factors account for this increase. Increased availability of birth-control methods (including birth-control pills) and abortion have led couples to be less concerned about unwanted pregnancies. Moreover, several social changes have likely had an impact. As sex becomes more openly discussed in magazines, books, and even television shows, many married couples have come to feel that the frequency of sex is a critical index of the success of their marriage. Furthermore, as women's roles have changed, and the popular media have reinforced the notion that female sexuality is OK, the likelihood that a wife may initiate sex, rather than waiting for her husband's overture as in the more traditional scenario, has increased (Westoff, 1974).

The consequences of the increase in marital intercourse are difficult to assess. It is clear that the degree of sexual satisfaction is related to overall satisfaction with a marriage (Tavris & Sadd, 1977). Yet the *frequency* of sexual intercourse does not appear to be associated with happiness in marriage (Goleman, 1985). The rise in frequency of sexual intercourse does not suggest, then, that there will be an accompanying increase in marital satisfaction.

The increase in the frequency of sexual intercourse in marriage has been accompanied by an increase in the frequency of **extramarital sex**, sexual activity that occurs between a married person and someone who is not his or her spouse. In the 1940s, some 50 percent of all married men and 25 percent of all married women admitted to having had sex at least once with a partner other than their husband or wife. More recent surveys have shown a slight increase for men, but a more significant rise for women. What has not changed at all are people's attitudes toward extramarital sex: There is a high, consistent rate of disapproval, with more than three-quarters of those surveyed saying the practice is wrong (Hunt, 1974). (You'll note that if the statistics are correct, they suggest that some of the people who feel it is wrong must be the same ones who are having extramarital sex!)

Extramarital sex: Sexual activity between a married person and someone who is not his or her spouse

INTERPERSONAL SEX: Homosexuality and Bisexuality

Just as there seems to be no genetic or biological reason for heterosexual women to find men's buttocks particularly erotic, humans are not born with an innate attraction to the special characteristics of the opposite sex. We should not find it surprising, then, that some people, **homosexuals**, are sexually attracted to members of their own sex, while others, **bisexuals**, are sexually attracted to people of the same *and* the opposite sex. In fact, the number of people who choose same-sex sexual partners at one time or another is considerable. Estimates suggest that about 20 to 25 percent of males and about 15 percent of females have had at least one homosexual experience during adulthood, and between 5 and 10 percent of both men and women are estimated to be exclusively homosexual during extended periods of their lives (Hunt, 1974; Kinsey, Pomeroy, & Martin, 1948; Fay et al., 1989).

Homosexuality: A sexual attraction to a member of one's own sex

Bisexuality: A sexual attraction to members of both sexes

Although people often view homosexuality and heterosexuality as two completely distinct sexual orientations, the issue is not that simple. Pioneering sex researcher Alfred Kinsey acknowledged this when he considered sexual orientation along a scale, with exclusively homosexual at one end and exclusively heterosexual at the other. According to this view, bisexuals belong somewhere in the middle of the scale, with the precise location determined by the person's specific sexual experiences (see Figure 10-9).

	Bisexual behavior					
0	1	2	3	4	5	6
Exclusively heterosexual behavior	Incidental homosexual behavior	More than incidental homosexual behavior	Equal amount of heterosexual and homosexual behavior	More than incidental heterosexual behavior	Incidental heterosexual behavior	Exclusively homosexual behavior

FIGURE 10-9

This is the Kinsey scale designed to define the degree to which sexual orientation is heterosexual, homosexual, or bisexual. Although Kinsey saw people as falling along a continuum, most people saw themselves as belonging to a specific category. (After Kinsey, Pomeroy, & Martin, 1948.)

Why are people homosexual? Although there are a number of theories, none has proved completely satisfactory. Some approaches are biological in nature, suggesting that there may be a genetic or hormonal reason for the development of homosexuality (Gladue, 1984; Hutchinson, 1978). There is little conclusive evidence for such an approach, however, although it is still possible that there may be some genetic or biological factor that predisposes a person toward homosexuality, if certain environmental conditions are met (Gartell, 1982).

Other theories of homosexuality have focused on the childhood and family background of homosexuals. For instance, Freud felt that homosexuality occurred as a result of inappropriate identification with the opposite-sex parent during development (Freud, 1922/1959). Similarly, other psychoanalysts suggest that the nature of the parent-child relationship can lead to homosexuality, and that homosexuals frequently have overprotective, dominant mothers and passive, ineffective fathers (Bieber, 1962).

The problem with such theories is that there are probably as many homosexuals who were not subjected to the influence of such family dynamics as who were. The evidence does not support explanations which rely on child-bearing practices or on the nature of the family structure (Bell & Weinberg, 1978).

Another explanation for homosexuality rests on learning theory (Masters & Johnson, 1979). According to this view, sexual orientation is learned through rewards and punishments in much the same way that we might learn to prefer swimming over tennis. For example, a young adolescent who had a heterosexual experience whose outcome was unpleasant might learn to link unpleasant associations with the opposite sex. If that same person had a rewarding, pleasant homosexual experience, homosexuality might be incorporated into his or her sexual fantasies. If such fantasies are then used during later sexual activities—such as masturbation—they may be positively reinforced through orgasm, and the association of homosexual behavior and sexual pleasure might eventually cause homosexuality to become the preferred form of sexual behavior.

Although the learning theory explanation is plausible, there are several difficulties which prevent it from being seen as a complete explanation for homosexuality. Because our society tends to hold homosexuality in low esteem, one ought to expect that the punishments involved in homosexual behavior would outweigh the rewards attached to it (Whitam, 1977). Fur-

Despite the stereotype of the "disturbed" homosexual, studies show that lesbians, gay men, and bisexual individuals enjoy the same overall degree of mental health as heterosexuals. (Joel Gordon)

thermore, children growing up with a homosexual parent statistically are unlikely to become homosexual, thus contradicting the notion that homosexual behavior might be learned from others (Green, 1978).

In yet another approach to explaining homosexuality, some researchers have examined childhood behavioral patterns. For example, some evidence suggests that early behavioral patterns counter to typical gender stereotypes are associated with male homosexuality in adults. Richard Green (1987) found that a group of males who were labeled when children as "sissies" by their peers showed a relatively high incidence of adult homosexuality. The problem with using such a finding as an explanation for homosexuality, however, is that many of the children labeled as sissies were *not* homosexual as adults, and most adult homosexuals do not display behavior outside typical gender stereotypes. Furthermore, it does not explain why children display behavior that runs counter to stereotypes in the first place.

Given the difficulty in finding a consistent explanation, the majority of researchers reject the notion that any single factor orients a person toward homosexuality, and most suspect that a combination of biological and environmental factors is the cause (Money, 1987). Although we don't know at this point exactly why people become homosexual, one thing is clear: There is no relationship between psychological adjustment and sexual preference (Reiss, 1980). Bisexuals and homosexuals enjoy the same overall degree of mental and physical health as do heterosexuals, and they hold equivalent ranges and types of attitudes about themselves, independent of sexual orientation.

RECAP AND REVIEW III

Recap

◀ Definitions of what is sexually normal behavior are influenced by the expectations, attitudes, beliefs, and state of medical knowledge of a given period.

◀ Masturbation (sexual self-stimulation) is common among both men and women, although it is still viewed negatively by many people.

◀ Attitudes regarding premarital heterosexuality still show a double standard, although both a tolerance for and actual acts of premarital sex have increased greatly over the last decades.

◀ Homosexuals are attracted to members of their own sex, and bisexuals are attracted to people of the same and of the opposite sex. Although no theory fully explains why people are homosexual, it is clear that homosexuals and bisexuals are as well adjusted psychologically as heterosexuals.

Review

1. The most reasonable approach to defining sexual normality is one that
   a. considers the psychological and physical consequences of the sexual behavior.
   b. measures deviation of the behavior from the average.
   c. compares the sexual behavior against some standard or ideal.
   d. derives from the study of psychology.

2. Although masturbation among young adults is high, once men and women become involved in intimate relationships, they typically cease masturbating. True or false?

   _____

3. "It's understandable that young men would 'sow their wild oats' before getting married, but respectable young women are those who save their virginity until they are married." This statement represents a _____

   _____ .

4. The increase in premarital sex in recent years has been greater for women than for men. True or false?

   _____

5. Which of the following is true about the frequency of sexual intercourse among married couples?
   a. It has remained relatively stable in recent years.
   b. It does not appear to be related to satisfaction with a marriage.
   c. It has served to decrease extramarital sex.
   d. Attitudes toward extramarital sex have become more liberal as a result of increased frequency.

(Answers to review questions are on page 364.)

WHEN SEX GOES WRONG:
SEXUAL DIFFICULTIES AND TREATMENT

When Joan left the party with her friends one night in March, she had no idea one of her male friends would try to rape her later.

"I knew we'd probably end up kissing each other. In fact, I anticipated it. And we were holding hands and stuff, and that was fine."

After dropping off a couple of people, he drove Joan to the parking lot near her dorm. They turned off the lights and began kissing, which, she says, "seemed OK."

But, upon driving to a more quiet place near Orchard Hill, he began to "touch my chest and worked his way down." That wasn't OK.

"It was like I wasn't me anymore; it was like I was just a thing. He kept trying to take my clothes off. . . ."

Joan protested and told him to stop several times, but all he could say was, 'Maybe we should try another position. Maybe you'd like that better.'. . . The only thing that mattered to him . . . was that he'd be satisfied. It didn't matter who I was or what my name was.

"He couldn't understand why I was crying; he couldn't understand why I was angry.

"He'd laugh at me a little. He made me feel like it was my fault" (Pereira, 1987, p. 1).

The only reason this rape did not occur was that the woman was strong enough to force the man off her, after a forty-five minute physical struggle. But she was left a changed person, filled with anger, distrust, and pain.

When sex—an activity that should be pleasurable, joyful, and intimate—is forced on someone, it becomes one of the ultimate acts of aggression and brutality that people are capable of inflicting on one another. Two sorts of sexual behavior that represent nonconsenting sex—and which unfortunately occur with surprising frequency—are rape and childhood sexual abuse.

NONCONSENTING SEX: Rape

When one person forces another to submit to sexual activity such as inter-course or oral-genital sex, **rape** has occurred. Although it usually applies to a male forcing a female, rape can be said to occur when members of either sex are forced into sexual activities against their will.

Most people think of rape as a rare crime and one committed by strangers. In fact, it occurs far more frequently than is commonly thought, and rapists are typically acquaintances of their victims (Mahoney, 1983; Koss, in press). For instance, a national survey conducted at thirty-five universities revealed the startling finding that one out of eight women reported having been raped, and of that group, about half said the rapists were first dates, casual dates, or romantic acquaintances—a phenomenon called **date rape** (Sweet, 1985). Statistically, then, a woman is more likely to be raped on a date than by a stranger jumping out of the bushes. But whether on a date or alone, a woman's chances of being raped are shockingly high: According to one researcher, there is a 26 percent chance that a woman will be the victim of a rape during her lifetime (Russell & Howell, 1983).

Although on the surface it might appear that rape is primarily a crime of sex, there is evidence that most often other motivations underlie the behavior (Groth, 1979; Lisak & Roth, 1988). In some cases, the rapist uses sex as a means of demonstrating power and control over the victim. As such, there is little that is sexually satisfying about rape to the rapist; instead, the pleasure comes in forcing someone else to be submissive.

In other cases of rape, the primary motivation is anger. Sexual behavior is used to show the male rapist's rage and anger at women in general, usually because of some perceived rejection or hurt that has been suffered in the past. Such rapes are likely to include physical violence and degrading acts against the victim.

Finally, some rapes *are* based on a desire for sexual gratification. Because some men hold the attitude that it is appropriate and desirable for them to actively seek out sex, that sexual encounters represent a form of "war" be-tween the sexes—with winners and losers—and that, in fact, violence is sometimes an appropriate way to obtain that which is desired, they reason that using force to obtain sexual gratification is permissible (Mosher & An-derson, 1986). In addition, there is a common but unsupported societal belief that many women offer token resistance to sex, saying "no" to sex when they mean "yes," and that their protests need not be taken seriously (Muehlenhard & Hollabaugh, 1988).

Although you might expect that only a tiny minority of the population view forced sex as acceptable, this is not the case: Alarmingly enough, there are conditions under which both the typical male and the typical female report approval of rape. For instance, in one study, high school students were given a list of situations and asked whether it was acceptable in those situations for a man to hold a woman down and force sexual intercourse. Just 44 percent of the females and 24 percent of the males thought no situ-ation warranted forced sex; the rest felt that under some conditions rape was acceptable, as you can see in Figure 10-10 (Mahoney, 1983).

Moreover, when college males were asked whether they ever might commit rape, fully 35 percent responded that, under certain circumstances, they might (Malamuth, 1981). This percentage was even higher when the men had just been exposed to pornographic materials, including sequences

Rape: The act whereby one person forces another to submit to sexual activity

Date rape: Rape in which rapist is either a date or an acquaintance

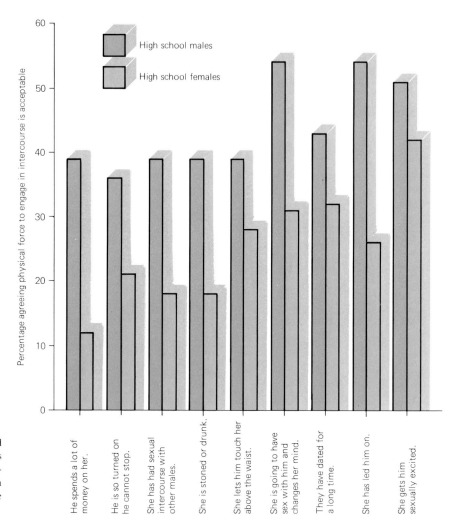

FIGURE 10-10

A sample of high school students indicated the conditions under which they felt it was permissible to force a woman to have sexual intercourse. Only a minority of both men and women felt that the use of force was never permissible. (Mahoney, 1983.)

of aggression toward women. Such figures illustrate the pervasiveness of societal beliefs that degrade women and condone violence toward them, and they suggest that such irrational views will be replaced only with great effort. (We discuss the relationship between pornography and violence toward women more fully in Chapter 19.)

Although the causes of rape are complex, reflecting the rapist's background and attitudes, the drastic effects of rape on the victim are clear. Immediately after being raped, victims report shock, disbelief, fear, extreme anxiety, and suspiciousness, and the psychological reactions are no different whether it was date rape or rape by a stranger (Kilpatrick, Resick & Veronen, 1981; Koss & Burkhart, 1989). These feelings may continue for several months and sometimes years, even though the victim outwardly appears to have "recovered." Eventually, most rape victims enter a reorganization phase, when they try to put their lives back together. Even in this phase, they experience episodes of extreme emotion as a result of the attack: nightmares,

---

ANSWERS (REVIEW III):
1. a **2.** False; men and women alike tend to continue to masturbate even when they have a sexual outlet with a partner. **3.** Double standard **4.** True **5.** b

fear of places similar to those where they were raped, and disruption of sexual behavior are typical.

NONCONSENTING SEX: Childhood Sexual Abuse

One form of sexual behavior that is surprisingly common, yet about which the least is known, is the sexual abuse of children. Although reported cases are low in number and firm data are hard to come by, the frequency of child sexual abuse—instances in which an older person engages in sexual activity with a child—is thought to be relatively high. The reason, of course, is that only the most extreme cases are apt to be reported to authorities; child abuse is a secret crime, where participants are often motivated—although for different reasons—to keep their activities from being discovered. One nationwide survey, however, found that a startling 22 percent of adult Americans who were polled reported having been the victims of some form of child sexual abuse (Timnick, 1985). Sexual intercourse was involved in 55 percent of the molestations, while 36 percent involved fondling.

Who commits child sexual abuse? In most cases it is a relative (23 percent) or acquaintance (42 percent); in only about one-quarter of the cases was the abuse carried out by a stranger. The most vulnerable age for being molested is around 10 years old, and the abusers tend to be about twenty years older than their victims.

Both the short- and long-term consequences of childhood sexual abuse are most typically negative. In terms of initial effects, victims report increased fear, anxiety, depression, anger, hostility, and aggression, and their sexual behavior frequently shows signs of disorder. Long-term effects may include depression and self-destructive behavior, anxiety, feelings of isolation and stigma, poor self-esteem, difficulty in trusting others, substance abuse, and sexual maladjustment. The exact consequences of childhood sexual abuse are related to the specific nature of the abuse. For example, it is known that experiences involving fathers, genital contact, and force are the most damaging (Browne & Finkelhor, 1986; Finkelhor, 1979).

SEXUALLY TRANSMITTED DISEASES (STDS): The Case of AIDS

No factor has had a greater effect on sexual behavior in the last decade than **acquired immune deficiency syndrome**, or **AIDS**. Transmitted only through sexual contact or by exposure to infected blood, AIDS has no cure and is ultimately fatal to those afflicted with it. Because it is primarily spread sexually, AIDS is classified as an **STD** or **sexually transmitted disease**.

Although AIDS began in the United States largely as a disease affecting homosexuals, it has spread to other populations, and in some parts of the world, such as Africa, it primarily affects heterosexuals. In America, it is thought that there are between 945,000 and 1.4 million people presently infected with the AIDS virus, all of whom will die unless a cure is found (Booth, 1988). The worldwide figures are even more daunting: Millions more are thought to carry the AIDS virus, leading to an epidemic of epic proportions.

Although some researchers argue the odds of contracting AIDS from any one sexual encounter are not high (Hearst & Hulley, 1988), others dispute this contention (Masters, Johnson & Kolodny, 1988). However, the outcome of getting the ultimately fatal disease is of such magnitude that AIDS has led

Acquired immune deficiency syndrome (AIDS): A fatal, sexually transmitted disease that is caused by a virus that destroys the body's immune system and has no known cure

Sexually transmitted disease (STD): A disease spread primarily through sexual contact

The spread of AIDS has led to many forms of educational outreach, such as this discussion group led by Ronald Austin of the New Jersey Department of Health. (Robert McElroy/Woodfin Camp & Assoc.)

to several large-scale changes in sexual behavior. People are less likely to engage in "casual" sex with new acquaintances, and the use of condoms during sexual intercourse has increased (Adler, 1985; McKusick, Horstman & Coates, 1985; Bauman & Siegel, 1987).

The only foolproof method of avoiding AIDS is celibacy—a drastic step that most people find an unrealistic alternative. However, as you can see in Table 10-3, there are ways of reducing the risk of contracting AIDS through what have come to be called "safe sex" practices.

AIDS presents several profound psychological issues (Backer et al., 1988; Namir et al., 1987). First, there is the question of how to treat the psychological distress of victims of the disease, who must face the knowledge that their disease is incurable and invariably fatal—and that society is fearful that

---

TABLE 10-3

"Safe Sex": Sexual Practices That Help Prevent the Transmission of AIDS

Despite the specter of AIDS and other sexually transmitted diseases, most people will not choose to become celibate. In the face of this reality, experts have suggested several practices to minimize the risks of contracting AIDS and other sexually transmitted diseases:

▶ *Know your sexual partner—well.* Sexual activities are risky with someone whose sexual history is unfamiliar to you. Before entering into a sexual relationship with someone, be aware of his or her background.

▶ *Avoid the exchange of bodily fluids, particularly semen.* In particular, most experts recommend the avoidance of anal intercourse. The AIDS virus can spread through small tears in the rectum, making anal intercourse without using condoms particularly dangerous.

▶ *Use condoms.* For those in sexual relationships, condoms are the most reliable means of preventing transmission of the AIDS virus.

▶ *Consider the benefits of monogamy.* People in long-term, monogamous relationships with partners who have been faithful are at a lower risk of contracting AIDS.

they will spread the disease. Second, because a blood test can detect whether a person who does not have the disease yet is a carrier of the virus (and therefore at risk to actually contract AIDS in the future), there is an issue of how to deal with the concerns of people who stand a probability of eventually coming down with the disease (Tross & Hirsch, 1988). Finally, psychologists need to devise methods of reducing the anxiety of people whose fears of catching AIDS lead them to demand that extreme measures be taken against the victims of the disease (going so far, for instance, as calling for a quarantine for those with AIDS). Until a cure is found for the disease, AIDS will continue to present difficult problems that are likely to have a profound impact on sexual behavior (Fineberg, 1988).

Other STDs

Although AIDS is the best-known STD, others are considerably more prevalent (see Figure 10-11). For instance, the most widespread is **chlamydia**, an STD which initially produces no symptoms in women but when untreated can lead to pelvic inflammation and even sterility. In men, there is burning on urination and discharge from the penis. Chlamydia affects some 4.5 million women and men and is treated with antibiotics. **Genital herpes** is a virus related to the cold sores that sometimes appear around the mouth. Herpes first appears as small blisters or sores around the genitals which later break open, causing severe pain. These sores heal after a few weeks, but the disease can and often does reappear after an indeterminate interval, and the cycle repeats itself. There is no cure for genital herpes, and during the active phases of the disease it can be transmitted to sexual partners.

Gonorrhea and **syphilis** are the two STDs that have been recognized the longest. Gonorrhea can lead to fertility problems and infection; syphilis, if untreated, may affect the brain, heart, and a developing fetus, and can even be fatal. Syphilis reveals itself first through a small sore at the point of sexual contact. In its secondary stage, it may include a rash. Both gonorrhea and syphilis can be treated successfully with antibiotics if diagnosed early enough.

Chlamydia: (kla MID ee ah) An STD which initially produces no symptoms in women but which can lead to pelvic inflammation and sterility, and produces in men painful urination and discharge from the penis

Genital herpes: A noncurable virus producing small blisters or sores around the genitals; symptoms disappear but often recur

Gonorrhea: An STD which leads to infertility and infection

Syphilis: An STD which, if untreated, may affect brain, heart, and developing fetus, and can be fatal

FIGURE 10-11

Estimates of the number of new cases annually of sexually transmitted diseases. (Center for Disease Control, 1988.)

AIDS 39,000
Syphilis 87,000
Genital herpes 500,000
Gonorrhea 781,000
Venereal warts 1,000,000
Chlamydia 4,000,000
Estimated cases

SECRETS OF THE BEDROOM: Sexual Problems

While few of us would feel embarrassed by a case of appendicitis or a broken leg, most of us would have to admit that sexual difficulties are a cause for major concern, given the importance that society places on "appropriate" sexual conduct. In fact, interest in their own sexuality leads many people to consider and reconsider its every nuance.

While for most people, sexual behavior proceeds relatively smoothly, there are times in almost everyone's life when sexual problems arise. Among the most common are some of the disorders we discuss below.

Erectile failure: A male's inability to achieve or maintain an erection

Primary erectile failure: A long-term inability to achieve or maintain an erection

Secondary erectile failure: A male's temporary inability to achieve or maintain an erection

Erectile failure is the inability of a male to achieve or maintain an erection (Segraves & Schoenberg, 1985). In one rare manifestation, **primary erectile failure**, the male has never been able to have an erection. But in the more common case, **secondary erectile failure**, the male, though now unable to have an erection, has at least once in the past successfully had one.

Erectile failure is not an uncommon problem, and it is the rare man who has never experienced it at least once during his lifetime. This is hardly surprising, since the ability to achieve and hold an erection is sensitive to alcohol, drugs, performance fears, anxiety, and a host of other factors. It becomes a more serious problem when it occurs more than occasionally.

Premature ejaculation: A male's inability to delay ejaculation

In **premature ejaculation**, a male is unable to delay orgasm as long as he wishes. Because "as long as he wishes" is dependent on a man's—and his partner's—attitudes and opinions about how long is appropriate, this is a difficult disorder to define, and sometimes the problem can be resolved simply by having a male redefine how long he wants to delay ejaculation.

Premature ejaculation is most often a psychological problem, since there are rarely physical reasons for it. One cause may be early sexual learning: Because sexual experiences during adolescence are often accompanied by a fear of being caught, some men learn early in their lives to reach orgasm as quickly as possible.

Inhibited ejaculation: A male's inability to ejaculate when he wants to, if at all

Inhibited ejaculation is the opposite problem. In this case, the male is unable to ejaculate when he wants to, if at all. Sometimes learning general relaxation techniques is sufficient to allow men to overcome the difficulty.

Anorgasmia (an or GAZ mee uh): A female's lack of orgasm

Primary orgasmic dysfunction: A female's long-term inability to achieve orgasm

Secondary orgasmic dysfunction: A female's temporary inability to achieve orgasm or her ability to achieve orgasm only under certain conditions (such as masturbation)

Some women experience **anorgasmia**, or a lack of orgasm. In **primary orgasmic dysfunction**, women have never experienced orgasm, while in **secondary orgasmic dysfunction**, a woman is capable of experiencing orgasm only under certain conditions—such as during masturbation but not during sexual intercourse. Because the inability to have orgasm during sexual intercourse is so common, with some one-third of all women reporting they do not receive sufficient stimulation to have orgasm during sexual intercourse, some sex researchers suggest that secondary orgasmic dysfunction is not dysfunctional at all, but merely a normal variation of female sexuality (Kaplan, 1974).

It is important to note that many of the problems we have discussed are common at one time or another during sexual encounters. It is only when these problems persist, cause undue anxiety, and turn sex from play into work that they are cause for concern. Moreover, new techniques that are being developed today for treating sexual disorders have provided solutions to many problems that in the past would have gone unresolved, as we discuss in the Psychology at Work box.

IMPROVING YOUR SEX LIFE WITH THERAPY

St. Louis, Missouri, seems an unlikely place to be thought of as the sex capital of the world. Yet, within the confines of the St. Louis clinic housing the husband-and-wife team of William H. Masters and Virginia E. Johnson, some of the most effective forms of treatment for people with sexual problems are being carried out. As pioneering sex researchers, Masters and Johnson were among the first to describe the phases of sexual excitation of men and women. Their clinic has become the mecca for those with stubborn sexual problems that escape self-remedy.

In the program, couples are treated together by a male-and-female therapist team over a two-week period (Masters & Johnson, 1970). After a thorough physical examination, the couple undergo therapy that consists of education and training using the basic principles of learning theory, with the aim being a change in sexual behavior, technique, and—often most important—a reduction in anxiety.

During the first few days, couples are explicitly told to avoid sexual intercourse or any other sexual act that has been causing them a problem. This reduces anxiety about "performing" properly. A life history is taken, and significant events from the individuals' pasts are brought out into the open, with one important goal being open and shared communication between the partners. The couple also openly discuss their sexual beliefs and values.

The next step in therapy is specific instruction in sexual techniques. The basics of sex-organ biology are reviewed, and the couple is told to use a process called **sensate focus,** in which attention is directed away from intercourse and toward other behaviors that feel pleasurable to the partner, such as caressing the neck or massaging the back. Because sexual intercourse has been forbidden by the therapist, these sensate focus exercises take on importance, allowing the couple to experience their sexuality in a relaxed, non-performance-oriented manner.

Gradually more and more involved sexual activities are allowed by the therapists, who eventually tell the couple it is permissible to have intercourse. Typically the couple is successful. For instance, improvement rates for erectile-failure difficulties are around 74 percent for secondary erectile failure and 60 percent for primary erectile failure.

While other therapeutic techniques have been developed to treat sexual problems, the Masters and Johnson procedure remains one of the most widely imitated. Of course, practical considerations prevent many people from using their method, since not everyone can devote two full weeks to treatment. Other treatments, less costly (in terms of time and money), have been developed—following more traditional schedules such as weekly one-hour sessions for three or four months—and many of these programs are quite successful. Therapy for sexual problems, then, can work quite effectively, and problems that were once left in the secrecy of the bedroom can be brought out into the open and alleviated.

Sensate focus: A method of sexual therapy in which attention is directed away from intercourse and toward other pleasurable behaviors

THE INFORMED CONSUMER OF PSYCHOLOGY:
Recognizing the Promises and Pitfalls of Sex Therapy

Given the importance of sex, both in terms of our society and for each of us as individuals, it is not surprising that problems and concerns with sexuality have become a big business. Clinics for treating sexual problems have sprung up all over the country, and therapists concentrating on the treatment of sexual problems have become more and more common.

Unfortunately, not all sexual problems respond to treatment equally well. Moreover, sex therapy does not operate in the same way that medical treatment for a disease would: A person cannot take a pill or receive an injection and suddenly become "cured." Sexual problems are complex, involving as they do both physical and psychological components.

There are certain factors that informed consumers of sex therapy ought to consider when seeking help for sexual problems. Among those are the following:

▶ The sex therapist should have credentials indicating that he or she has been specially trained in sex therapy. For instance, the American Association of Sex Educators, Counselors, and Therapists (AASECT) has an active certification program.

▶ Sex therapy should *never* involve sexual activity with the therapist. This does not mean that a physical examination is not a typical part of sex therapy, since some sexual problems have physical causes. But it does mean that therapists who suggest that sexual interaction with them is necessary are guilty of incompetent and highly unethical behavior.

▶ Remember that not all sexual "problems" are problems. Holding up your sexual behavior to some standard—such as frequency of sexual intercourse—is not necessarily appropriate. You and your partner are individuals, and if your sex life works for you, don't worry about how it compares to other peoples' sex lives.

▶ A good sex life won't cure a bad relationship. Improving sexual functioning is not a cure-all for helping a relationship; even if a couple's sex life gets better, their relationship may still be in trouble.

▶ Sexual problems do not lie in the genitals alone but reflect the whole person and his or her interactions with others. As we have seen, sexual arousal and satisfaction are complex phenomena, involving physical, cognitive, emotional, social, and societal factors. All must be taken into account when sexual problems are being treated.

RECAP AND REVIEW IV

Recap

◀ Rape occurs when one person forces another to submit to sexual activity. It is most often motivated by power or anger, rather than by desire for sexual gratification.

◀ Child sexual abuse is a surprisingly frequent phenomenon.

◀ The major sexually transmitted diseases (STDs) include AIDS, chlamydia, genital herpes, gonorrhea, and syphilis.

◀ Among the major sexual problems are erectile failure, premature ejaculation, and anorgasmia.

Review

1. A college woman is more apt to be raped by an acquaintance than by a stranger. True or false? _____

2. Which of the following is unlikely to be a motivation for the act of rape?

a. Need for power
b. Desire for sexual intimacy
c. Desire for sexual gratification
d. Anger against women in general

3. Which of the following is *not* a fact of child sexual abuse?
a. Most child sexual abuse is carried out by a relative or acquaintance.
b. Usually only extreme cases are reported.
c. Twenty-two percent of American adults have reported that they have been victims of some form of child sexual abuse.
d. Rarely are any long-term psychological effects experienced by the victim.

4. Which of the following is *not* true about changes in sexual behavior as a result of the AIDS epidemic?
a. The use of condoms has increased.
b. People are less likely to engage in casual sex.

c. Many people have found celibacy to be a realistic alternative.

d. The risk of contracting AIDS may be reduced by engaging in safe-sex practices.

5. Which of the following STDs is the most widespread?
   a. Genital herpes
   b. Gonorrhea
   c. Chlamydia
   d. Syphilis

6. "Some men worry about ejaculating too quickly. I have to worry about whether I will ejaculate at all—sometimes I can and other times I just can't." This man is describing the problem of
   a. inhibited ejaculation.
   b. premature ejaculation.
   c. primary erectile failure.
   d. secondary erectile failure.

7. _____ orgasmic dysfunction refers to a woman's capability of having an orgasm only under certain conditions.

(Answers to review questions are on page 372.)

 ◀ **LOOKING BACK**

1. Our sense of the way in which we think about ourselves is partly determined by gender, the sense of being male or female. Gender roles are the expectations, defined by society, that indicate what is appropriate behavior for men and women. When gender roles show favoritism toward one particular sex, they lead to stereotyping and produce sexism, negative attitudes and behavior based on an individual's sex.

2. The gender-role stereotype for men suggests that they are endowed with competence-related traits, whereas women are seen in terms of warmth and expressiveness. Actual sex differences are much less clear, and of smaller magnitude, than the stereotypes would suggest. There are differences in aggression, self-esteem, communication styles, and perhaps cognitive abilities, but the magnitude of the differences is not great. The differences that do exist are produced by a combination of biological and environmental factors.

3. Biological causes of sex difference are reflected by evidence suggesting a possible difference in brain structure and functioning between men and women and may be associated with differential exposure to hormones prior to birth. In terms of environmental causes, socialization experiences produce gender schema, cognitive frameworks that organize and guide a child's understanding of information relevant to gender.

4. Although biological factors, such as the presence of androgens (the male sex hormone) and estrogens (the female sex hormone) prime people for sex, almost any kind of stimulus can produce sexual arousal, depending on a person's prior experience. Erogenous zones are areas of the body that are particularly sensitive to touch and have become associated with sexual arousal. Fantasies, thoughts, and images are also important in producing arousal.

5. People's sexual responses follow a regular pattern consisting of four phases: excitement, plateau, orgasm, and resolution. Women can experience multiple orgasms, whereas men may enter a refractory period, during which more sex is impossible until a sufficient amount of time has passed. Recent evidence, though, suggests that men may actually be capable of multiple orgasms but not multiple ejaculations.

6. There are a number of approaches to determining normality: deviation from the average, comparison of sexual behavior with some standard or ideal, or—in the approach used most often—consideration of the psychological and physical consequences of the behavior to the person and whether it is harmful to others.

7. Masturbation is sexual self-stimulation. The frequency of masturbation is high, particularly for males. Although attitudes toward masturbation have become more liberal, they are still somewhat negative—even though no negative consequences have been detected.

8. Heterosexuality, or sex between a man and a woman, is the most common sexual orientation. In terms of premarital sex, there is still a double standard: Sex is thought to be more permissible for men than for women. However, approval for premarital sex for women has risen considerably in the last few decades, as has the incidence of the behavior.

9. The frequency of marital sex varies widely. However, younger couples tend to have sexual intercourse more frequently than older ones. In addition, extramarital sex, of which most people disapprove, occurs with about half of all married men and one-quarter of married women.

10. Homosexuals are sexually attracted to members of their own sex; bisexuals are sexually attracted to people of the same and the opposite sex. About one-quarter of males and 15 percent of females have had at least one homosexual experience, and around 5 to 10 percent of all men and women are exclusively homosexual during extended periods of their lives. No explanation for why people become homosexual has been confirmed; among the possibilities are genetic or biological factors, childhood and family influences, and prior learning experiences and conditioning. What is clear is that there is no relationship between psychological adjustment and sexual preference.

11. Rape occurs when one person forces another to submit to sexual activity. Rape does not occur only between strangers; often the victim is acquainted with the rapist.

The motivation for rape is only sometimes sexual gratification; more frequently, though, it is power, aggression, or anger. A surprisingly large percentage of college-age males—some 35 percent—report that they might rape a woman under certain circumstances.

12. Childhood sexual abuse is widespread; some 22 percent of all Americans report some form of sexual abuse as children. Most often the perpetrator is an acquaintance or a family member. Lingering negative effects, even into adulthood, can be experienced by victims of sexual abuse.

13. Acquired immune deficiency syndrome, or AIDS, represents a health problem that is having profound effects on sexual behavior. First limited largely to homosexuals, AIDS now is found in the heterosexual population and is bringing about changes in casual sex and in people's sexual practices. The disease raises a number of psychological issues that are difficult to resolve. Other sexually transmitted diseases include chlamydia, genital herpes, gonorrhea, and syphilis.

14. Among the major sexual problems reported by males are erectile failure (primary, for males who have never had an erection, or secondary, for males who have had erections in the past); premature ejaculation, in which orgasm cannot be delayed; and inhibited ejaculation, in which the male cannot ejaculate during sexual intercourse. For females, the major problem is anorgasmia, or a lack of orgasm. Here, too, the problem may be primary (in women having never experienced an orgasm) or secondary (in women capable of experiencing orgasm, but doing so only under certain conditions).

15. Because of the prevalence of sexual therapists and different forms of treatment, it is important to keep several considerations in mind when seeking therapy. Among them are the credentials of the sex therapist, the fact that there should be no sexual contact between therapist and client, the realization that not all sexual problems may really be problems, that bad relationships won't be resolved by good sex, and that sexual problems affect the whole person.

KEY TERMS AND CONCEPTS ▶

gender (p. 336)
gender roles (337)
stereotyping (337)
sexism (337)
androgens (341)
estrogens (341)
socialization (342)
gender schema (342)
androgynous (342)
testes (344)
genitals (345)
ovaries (345)
ovulation (346)
erotic (346)
erogenous zones (346)
excitement phase (348)

penis (348)
clitoris (348)
vagina (348)
plateau phase (348)
orgasm (348)
semen (349)
ejaculation (349)
resolution stage (351)
refractory period (351)
masturbation (354)
heterosexuality (355)
double standard (355)
extramarital sex (359)
homosexuality (359)
bisexuality (359)
rape (363)
date rape (363)

acquired immune deficiency syndrome (AIDS) (365)
sexually transmitted disease (STD) (365)
chlamydia (367)
genital herpes (367)
gonorrhea (367)
syphilis (367)
erectile failure (368)
primary erectile failure (368)
secondary erectile failure (368)
premature ejaculation (368)
inhibited ejaculation (368)
anorgasmia (368)
primary orgasmic dysfunction (368)
secondary orgasmic dysfunction (368)
sensate focus (369)

FOR FURTHER STUDY AND APPLICATION ▶

Hyde, J. (1990). *Understanding human sexuality* (4th ed.). New York: McGraw-Hill.

Masters, W. H., Johnson, V. E., & Kolodny, R. C. (1985). *Human sexuality.* Boston: Little, Brown.

Here are two fine textbooks that provide a good overview of gender and human sexuality. The latter has a particularly strong emphasis on the scientific methods pioneered by Masters and Johnson. Each indicates specific techniques for overcoming sexual difficulties.

ANSWERS (REVIEW IV):
1. True **2.** b **3.** d **4.** c **5.** c **6.** a **7.** Secondary

Walsh, M. R. (Ed.) (1987). *The psychology of women: Ongoing debates.* New Haven: Yale University Press.

This fine, informative series of "pro" and "con" articles examines basic issues related to gender.

Kinsey, A. C., Pomeroy, W. B., & Martin, C. E. (1948). *Sexual behavior in the human male.* Philadelphia: Saunders.

The publication of this book marked the start of renewed scientific interest in human sexuality and had a large impact on ideas about sex in the United States in the decades that followed.·

Masters, W. H., & Johnson, V. E. (1966). *Human sexual response.* Boston: Little, Brown.

This book, which reports scientific observations of the biological changes during sexual arousal, also had an important impact on the field of human sexuality.

Killman, P., & Mills, K. (1983). *All about sex therapy.* New York: Plenum.

This text provides a comprehensive description and assessment of various types of sex therapies.

Pritchard, C. (1985). *Avoiding rape on and off campus.* Wenonah, NJ: State College Publishing Company.

Designed for college students concerned with rape, this book includes a safety checklist pertaining to the risks associated with rape.

Holden, C. (1988, May). Doctor of sexology. *Psychology Today,* pp. 45–48.

A fascinating interview with John Money, probably the most important researcher on sex and sexual identity. The article contains a wealth of information on his life as well as his views on human sexuality.

Turner, C. F., Miller, H. G., & Moses, L. E. (Eds.). (1989). *AIDS: Sexual behavior and intravenous drug use.* Washington, D.C.: National Academy Press.

This report presents a broad overview of the complex issues involved in the AIDS epidemic.

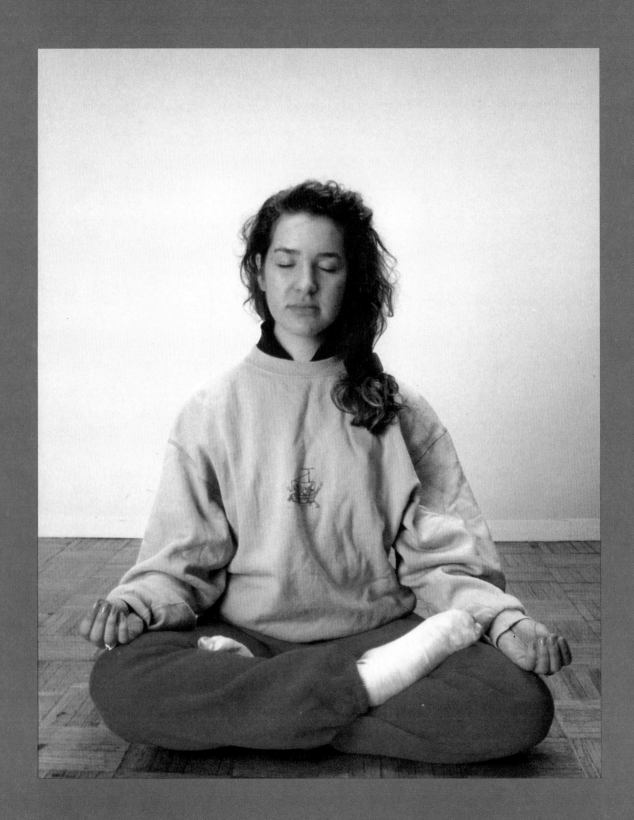

CHAPTER
11
STATES OF CONSCIOUSNESS

Donald J. Dorff, whose sleeping disorder was cured. (Courtesy of Donald J. Dorff)

PROLOGUE: DONALD DORFF

The crowd roared as running back Donald Dorff, age 67, took the pitch from his quarterback and accelerated smoothly across the artificial turf. As Dorff braked and pivoted to cut back over tackle, a huge defensive lineman loomed in his path. One hundred twenty pounds of pluck, Dorff did not hesitate. But let the retired grocery merchandiser from Golden Valley, Minnesota, tell it:

"There was a 280-pound tackle waiting for me, so I decided to give him my shoulder. When I came to, I was on the floor in my bedroom. I had smashed into the dresser and knocked everything off it and broke the mirror and just made one heck of a mess. It was 1:30 A.M." (Long, 1987, p. 787).

Dorff, it turned out, was suffering from a rare malady found in some older men in which the mechanism that usually shuts down bodily movement during dreams does not function properly. People afflicted with the problem have been known to hit others, smash windows, punch holes in walls—all the while being fast asleep.

LOOKING AHEAD ▶

Donald Dorff's problem had a happy ending: With the help of clonazepam, a drug that suppresses movement during dreams, his malady vanished, and he now sleeps through the night in welcome repose. The success of the treatment illustrates just one of the recent advances that has occurred in our understanding of sleep. In fact, our knowledge about all forms of consciousness, including sleep, has been expanding rapidly, as psychologists explore the nature of human consciousness.

Consciousness refers to a person's awareness of the sensations, thoughts, and feelings being experienced at a given moment. It is our subjective understanding of both the environment around us and our private internal world, unobservable to outsiders.

The nature of consciousness at any given moment spans several dimensions (Gazzaniga, 1988). Consciousness can range from being wide awake to being in the deepest state of sleep, with wide variation in how aware we are of outside stimuli. Furthermore, even while we are awake, consciousness can vary from an active state to a passive state (Hilgard, 1980). In more active states, we systematically carry out mental activity, thinking and considering the world around us. In passive waking states, thoughts and images come to us more spontaneously; we daydream or drift from one thought to another. Finally, consciousness can vary in terms of whether it occurs naturally, as when we drift from wakefulness into sleep, or whether it is artificially induced, as in a drug "high."

Because consciousness is so personal a phenomenon—who can say that your consciousness is the same as or, for that matter, different from anyone else's?—psychologists have sometimes been less than eager to study it. In fact, some early psychological theoreticians suggested that the study of consciousness was out of bounds for the psychologist, since it could be understood only by relying on the "unscientific" introspections of subjects about what they were experiencing at a given moment. Proponents of this view argued that the study of consciousness was better left to philosophers, who

Consciousness: A person's awareness of the sensations, thoughts, and feelings that he or she is experiencing at a given moment could speculate at their leisure on such knotty issues as whether consciousness is separate from the physical body, how people know they exist, how the body and mind are related to each other, and how we identify what state of consciousness we are in at a given moment in time.

Most contemporary psychologists reject the view that the study of consciousness is improper for psychology, arguing instead that there are several approaches that allow the scientific study of consciousness. For example, recent insights into the biology of the brain allow measurement of brain-wave patterns under conditions of consciousness ranging from sleep to waking to hypnotic trances. Moreover, new understandings of the effects on behavior of drugs such as marijuana and alcohol have provided insights into the way they produce their positive—and negative—effects. Finally, psychologists have come to understand that there are actually several kinds of consciousness that may be studied separately. By concentrating on particular **altered states of consciousness**—those that differ from a normal, waking consciousness—they have been able to study the phenomenon of consciousness scientifically, even if the more difficult questions, such as whether our consciousness exists separately from our physical bodies, remain unanswered.

Altered states of consciousness: Experiences of sensation or thought that differ from one's normal experience

Although various kinds of altered states of consciousness produce widely disparate effects, all share some characteristics (Ludwig, 1969; Martindale, 1981). One is an alteration in our thinking, which may become shallow, illogical, or impaired in some way. Our sense of time may become disturbed, and our perceptions of the world and of ourselves may be changed. We may experience a loss of self-control, doing things that we would never otherwise do. Finally, we may have a sense of ineffability—the inability to understand an experience rationally or describe it in words.

This chapter considers several states of consciousness, beginning with two that we have all experienced: sleeping and dreaming. Next, we turn to states of consciousness found under conditions of hypnosis and meditation. Finally, we examine drug-induced altered states of consciousness.

Psychologists agree that we may experience different states of consciousness. (Drawing by Frascino, © 1983, The New Yorker Magazine)

"If you ask me, all three of us are in different states of awareness."

After reading this chapter, you will be able to answer questions such as these:

▶ What are the different states of consciousness?

▶ What happens when we sleep, and what is the meaning and function of dreams?

▶ How much do we daydream?

▶ Are hypnotized people in an altered state of consciousness, and can they be made to do things against their will?

▶ What are the major classifications of drugs, and what are their effects?

LIFE IS BUT A DREAM . . . : SLEEP AND DREAMS

I was sitting at my desk thinking about the movie I was going to see that evening. Suddenly I remembered that this was the day of my chemistry final! I felt awful; I hadn't studied a bit for it. In fact, I couldn't even remember where the class was held, and I had missed every lecture all semester. What could I do? I was in a panic, and began running across campus desperately searching for the classroom so that I could beg the professor to give me another chance. But I had to stop at every classroom building, looking in one room after another, hoping to find the professor and the rest of the class. It was hopeless; I knew I was going to fail and flunk out of college.

If you have ever had a dream like this one, you are not alone: This kind of dream is common among people involved in academic pursuits.

After you have awakened and found to your relief that the scene that moments before had seemed so real was only a dream, you may have asked

FIGURE 11-1

Testing Your Knowledge of Sleep and Dreams

Although sleeping is something we all do for a significant part of our lives, many myths and misconceptions about the topic abound. To test your own knowledge of sleep and dreams, try answering the following questions before reading further.

1. Some people never dream. True or false? _____
2. Most dreams are caused by bodily sensations such as an upset stomach. True or false? _____
3. It has been proved that eight hours of sleep is needed to maintain mental health. True or false? _____

4. When people do not recall their dreams it is probably because they are secretly trying to forget them. True or false? _____
5. Depriving someone of sleep will invariably cause the individual to become mentally unbalanced. True or false? _____
6. If we lose some sleep, we will eventually make up all the lost sleep the next night or another night. True or false? _____
7. No one has been able to go for more than forty-eight hours without sleep. True or false? _____
8. Everyone is able to

sleep and breathe at the same time. True or false? _____
9. Sleep enables the brain to rest since there is little brain activity taking place during sleep. True or false? _____
10. Drugs have been proved to provide a long-term cure for sleeping difficulties. True or false? _____

Scoring: This is an easy set of questions to score, for every item is false. But don't lose any sleep if you missed them; they were chosen to represent the most common myths regarding sleep. (Items were drawn from a questionnaire developed by Palladino & Carducci, 1984.)

yourself what such dreams mean and whether they serve any purpose—questions psychologists have themselves considered in their study of sleep and dreams. We turn now to some of the answers they have arrived at. (Before you read on, you might want to test your knowledge of sleep and dreams by answering the questions in Figure 11-1.)

AWAKENING OUR KNOWLEDGE ABOUT SLEEP: The Stages of Sleep

Most of us consider sleep a time of quiet tranquility, as we peacefully set aside the tensions of the day and spend the night in uneventful slumber. However, a closer look at sleep shows that a good deal of activity occurs throughout the night, and what at first appears to be an undifferentiated state is, in fact, quite diverse.

Most of our knowledge of what happens during sleep comes from the **electroencephalogram** or **EEG**, which, as discussed in Chapter 2, is a measurement of electrical activity within the brain. When an EEG machine is attached to the surface of a sleeping person's scalp and face, it becomes readily apparent that instead of being dormant, the brain is active throughout the night, producing electric discharges that form regular, wavelike patterns

Electroencephalogram (ee LEK tro en SEF uh lo gram) **(EEG)**: measure of the brain's electrical activity

Although we generally view sleep as a period of repose and tranquillity, sleep researchers have found that a considerable amount of physical and mental activity occurs during sleep, as this series of photos taken during the course of one night suggests. (Ted Spagna)

that change in height (or amplitude) and speed (or frequency) in regular sequences. Instruments that measure muscle stimulation and eye movements also reveal a good deal of physical activity.

It turns out that there are four distinct stages of sleep through which a person progresses during a night's rest. These stages come and go, cycling approximately every ninety minutes. Each of these four stages is associated with a unique pattern of brain waves, as shown in Figure 11-2. Moreover, there are specific physiological indicators of dreaming.

When people first go to sleep, they move from a waking state in which they are relaxed with their eyes closed—sometimes called stage 0 sleep— into **stage 1** sleep, which is characterized by relatively rapid, low-voltage brain waves. This is actually a stage of transition between wakefulness and sleep. During stage 1 images sometimes appear; it's as if we were viewing still photos. However, true dreaming does not occur during the initial entry into this stage.

Stage 1 sleep: The state of transition between wakefulness and sleep

As sleep becomes deeper, people enter **stage 2**, which is characterized by a slower, more regular wave pattern. However, there are also momentary interruptions of sharply pointed waves called, because of their configuration, "sleep spindles." It becomes increasingly difficult to awaken a person from stage 2 sleep, which accounts for about half of a college-age person's total sleep.

Stage 2 sleep: A sleep deeper than that of stage 1, characterized by sleep spindles

As people drift into **stage 3**, the next stage of sleep, the brain waves become slower, with an appearance of higher peaks and lower valleys in the

Stage 3 sleep: A sleep characterized by slow brain waves, with greater peaks and valleys in the wave pattern

FIGURE 11-2

Brain-wave patterns (measured by an EEG apparatus) and eye movements in the different stages of sleep. (Cohen, 1979.)

Stage 1
Brain wave
Eye movements

Stage 2
Brain wave
Eye movements

Stage 3
Brain wave
Eye movements

Stage 4
Brain wave
Eye movements

REM sleep
Brain wave
Eye movements

FIGURE 11-3

During the night, the typical sleeper passes through all four stages of sleep and several REM periods. (*Source:* Hartmann, E. (1967). *The biology of dreaming.* Springfield, Ill.: Charles C Thomas.)

wave pattern. By the time sleepers arrive at **stage 4**, the pattern is even slower and more regular, and people are least responsive to outside stimulation.

As you can see in Figure 11-3, stage 4 is most likely to occur during the early part of the night when a person has first gone to sleep. In addition to passing through regular transitions between stages of sleep, then, people tend to sleep less and less deeply over the course of the night (Dement & Wolpert, 1958).

Stage 4 sleep: The deepest stage of sleep, during which we are least responsive to outside stimulation

The Paradox of Sleep: REM Sleep

Several times a night, after sleepers cycle from higher stages back into stage 1 sleep, something curious happens: Their heart rate increases and becomes irregular, their blood pressure rises, their breathing rate increases, and males—even male infants—have erections. Most characteristic of this period is the back-and-forth movement of their eyes, as if they were watching an action-filled movie. This period of sleep is called **REM**, or **rapid eye movement** sleep. REM sleep occupies a little over 20 percent of adults' total sleeping time.

Paradoxically, while all this activity is occurring, the major muscles of the body act as if they are paralyzed—except in rare cases such as Donald Dorff's, described at the beginning of the chapter—and it is hard to awaken the sleeper. In addition, REM sleep is usually accompanied by dreams, which, whether people remember them or not, are experienced by *everyone* during some part of the night.

One possible but still unproven explanation for the occurrence of rapid eye movements is that the eyes follow the action that is occurring in the dream (Dement, 1979). For instance, people who have reported dreaming about watching a tennis match just before they were awakened showed regular right-left-right eye movements, as if they were observing the ball flying back and forth across the net.

There is good reason to believe that REM sleep plays an important role in everyday human functioning. People deprived of REM sleep—by being awakened every time they begin to display the physiological signs of the stage—show a **rebound effect** when allowed to rest undisturbed. With this rebound effect, REM-deprived sleepers spend significantly more time in REM sleep than they normally do. It is as if the body requires a certain amount of REM sleep in order to function properly.

Rapid eye movement (REM) sleep: Sleep occupying around 20 percent of an adult's sleeping time, characterized by increased heart rate, blood pressure, and breathing rate; erections; eye movements; and the experience of dreaming

Rebound effect: An increase in REM sleep after one has been deprived of it

FEELING AND EXPERIENCING
THE WORLD

Sleep, in general, seems necessary for human functioning, although surprisingly enough this fact has not been firmly established. It is reasonable to expect that the body would require a tranquil "rest and relaxation" period in order to revitalize itself (Adam & Oswald, 1977). However, several arguments suggest this is not the full explanation. For instance, most people sleep between seven and eight hours each night, but there is wide variability among individuals, with some people needing as little as three hours. Sleep requirements also vary over the course of a person's lifetime; as people age, they generally need less and less sleep (see Figure 11-4). If sleep played a restorative function for the body, it is hard to see why the elderly would need less sleep than those who are younger.

Furthermore, people who have participated in sleep deprivation experiments, in which they are kept awake for stretches as long as 200 hours, show no lasting effects (Dement, 1976). They do experience weariness, lack of concentration, a decline in creativity, irritability, and a tendency toward hand tremors while they are being kept awake (e.g., Horne, 1988), but after being able to sleep once again they bounce back quickly. Just having twice the amount of sleep they get in a normal night enables them to perform at predeprivation levels.

Those of us who worry that the lack of sleep due to long hours of work or study may be ruining our health should feel encouraged, then: As far as anyone can tell, we should suffer no long-term consequences of such sleep deprivation (Eckholm, 1988).

THE REALITY OF DREAMS:
The Function and Meaning of Dreaming

If you have had a dream similar to the one described earlier about missing a final exam, you know how utterly convincing are the panic and fear that

FIGURE 11-4

As people age, the amount of time they sleep declines. (Adapted from Roffwarg, Muzio, & Dement, 1966.)

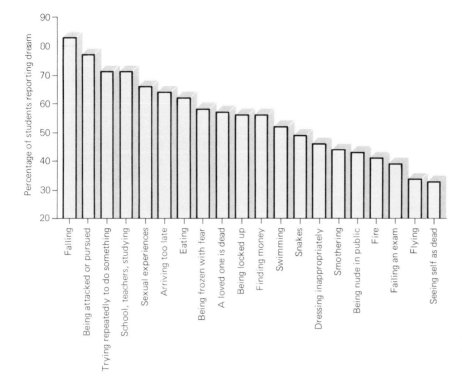

FIGURE 11-5

The twenty most common dreams reported by students. (Griffith, Miyago, & Tago, 1958.)

events in the dream can bring about. Some dreams could not seem more real.

In the case of **nightmares**, dreams are unusually frightening. Sometimes the same nightmare recurs over a period of years. Even worse are **night terrors**, dreams in which a person has a profoundly frightening dream and wakes up, in some cases screaming in horror. Often the terror of the dream is so real that people cannot get back to sleep immediately and need time to regain their emotional composure.

On the other hand, most dreams are much less dramatic, recounting such everyday events as going to the supermarket or preparing a meal. We just seem to remember the more exciting ones more readily (Webb, 1979). The most common dreams are shown in Figure 11-5.

Whether dreams have a specific function is a question that scientists have considered for many years. Sigmund Freud, for instance, used dreams as a guide to the unconscious (Freud, 1900). He thought that dreams represented unconscious wishes that the dreamer wanted to fulfill. However, because these wishes were threatening to the dreamer's conscious awareness, the actual wishes—called the **latent content** of the dream—were disguised. The true subject and meaning of a dream, then, may have little to do with its overt story line, called by Freud the **manifest content**.

To Freud, it was important to pierce the armor of a dream's manifest content to understand its true meaning. To do this, Freud tried to get people to discuss their dreams, associating symbols in the dreams to events in the past. He also suggested that there were certain common symbols with universal meaning that appeared in dreams. For example, to Freud, dreams in which the person was flying symbolized a wish for sexual intercourse. (See Table 11-1 for other common symbols.)

Today many psychologists reject Freud's view that dreams typically rep-

Nightmares: Unusually frightening dreams

Night terrors: Profoundly frightening nightmares which wake up the dreamer

Latent content of dreams: According to Freud, the "disguised" meanings of dreams, hidden by more obvious subjects

Manifest content of dreams: According to Freud, the surface meaning of dreams

This famous painting by Henry Fuseli depicts the phantoms that may inhabit our
dreams. (Henry Fuseli. *The Nightmare*. De-
troit Institute of Arts.)

TABLE 11-1

Dream Symbolism, According to Freud

Symbol	Interpretation
Climbing up a stairway, crossing a bridge, riding an elevator, flying in an airplane, walking down a long hallway, entering a room, train traveling through a tunnel	Sexual intercourse
Apples, peaches, grapefruits	Breasts
Bullets, fire, snakes, sticks, umbrellas, guns, hoses, knives	Male sex organs
Ovens, boxes, tunnels, closets, caves, bottles, ships	Female sex organs

resent unconscious wishes and that particular objects and events in a dream
are symbolic. Instead, the direct, overt action of a dream is considered the
focal point in understanding its meaning. If we dream that we are walking
down a long hallway to take an exam for which we haven't studied, for
instance, it does not relate to unconscious, unacceptable wishes; rather, it
simply means we are concerned about an impending test. Even more complex dreams can usually be interpreted in terms of everyday concerns.

Moreover, we now know that some dreams reflect events occurring in
the dreamer's environment as he or she is sleeping. For example, sleeping
subjects in one experiment were sprayed with water while they were dreaming; these unlucky volunteers reported more dreams involving water than a
comparison group of subjects who were left to sleep undisturbed (Dement

& Wolpert, 1958). Similarly, it is not unusual to wake up to find that the doorbell that was being rung in a dream is actually an alarm clock telling us it is time to get up.

Although the content of dreams clearly can be affected by environmental stimuli, the question of *why* we dream remains unresolved. Some psychologists suggest that dreaming represents an opportunity to resolve our problems and difficulties (Cartwright, 1978). By allowing our emotions to be brought to bear on personal issues in an uninhibited fashion, and by trying out different schemes for resolving our problems, we can safely "rehearse" different solutions during our dreams.

Other psychologists look at dreaming in terms of a more fundamental biological activity (Hobson & McCarley, 1977; Hobson, 1988; Hartmann, 1982). According to an influential theory, the brain produces electrical energy during REM sleep, possibly due to changes in the production of particular neurotransmitters. This electrical energy randomly stimulates different memories lodged in various portions of the brain. The brain then takes these random memories and—because we have a need to make sense of our world, even while asleep—weaves them into a logical story line, filling in the gaps to produce a rational scenario. In this view, then, dreams are closer to a self-generated game of Madlibs than to significant, meaningful psychological phenomena.

Evidence that dreaming represents a response to random brain activity comes from work with people who are injected with drugs similar to the neurotransmitter acetylcholine. Under the influence of the drug, people quickly enter REM sleep and have dreams similar in quality to those occurring in natural sleep (Schmeck, 1987).

Still another theory seeks to explain why we dream: It is possible that dreaming occurs as the by-product of a checking and consolidation process that the brain goes through during REM sleep (Evans, 1984). In a sense, this theory suggests that the dreams represent an attempt of the brain to check out its neural connections during off-peak hours, in the same way that computer operators test their machines during the late evening, when computer demands are at their lowest.

Even if dreams are a by-product of brain activity and do not (as Freud suggested) represent an active attempt to disguise unconscious wishes, this does not mean that they have no psychological significance. It is still possible that the specific content of our dreams is unique to us and represents meaningful patterns and concerns. Dreams may indeed provide clues about the things that on some level of consciousness are most important to us (Cartwright et al., 1984; Hermans, 1987).

DREAMS WITHOUT SLEEP: Daydreams

It is the stuff of magic: Our past mistakes can be wiped out and the future filled with noteworthy accomplishments. Fame, happiness, and wealth can be ours. In the next moment, though, the most horrible of tragedies can occur, leaving us alone, penniless, a figure of pitiful unhappiness.

The source of these scenarios is **daydreams**, fantasies that people construct while awake. Unlike dreaming that occurs while sleeping, daydreams are more under people's control, and therefore their content is often more closely related to immediate events in the environment than is the content of the dreams that occur during sleep. Although they may, as we saw in

Daydreams: Fantasies people construct while awake

Chapter 10, include sexual content, daydreams also pertain to other activities or events that are relevant to a person's life.

Daydreams are a typical part of waking consciousness; but their extent, and the daydreamer's involvement in them, varies from person to person. For example, around 2 to 4 percent of the population spend at least half their free time fantasizing. Although most people daydream much less frequently, almost everyone fantasizes to some degree. Studies that ask people to identify what they are doing at random times during the day have shown that they are daydreaming about 10 percent of the time. As to the content of fantasies, most concern mundane, ordinary events: Paying the telephone bill, picking up the groceries, and solving a romantic problem are typical (Singer, 1975; Lynn & Rhue, 1988; Klinger, 1987).

People who daydream most frequently often report having had lonely childhoods and appear to have developed a pattern of fantasizing to escape a lack of stimulation. On the other hand, this pattern is not universal: Many frequent fantasizers come from rich environments and had parents who encouraged the use of imagination, sometimes to the extent of building joint fantasies about the world (Lynn & Rhue, 1985).

Although frequent daydreaming might seem to suggest psychological difficulties, there actually seems to be little relationship between psychological disturbance and daydreaming (Rhue & Lynn, 1987; Lynn & Rhue, 1988). Except in those rare cases in which a daydreamer is unable to distinguish a fantasy from reality (a mark of serious problems, as we discuss in Chapter 16), daydreaming seems to be a normal part of waking consciousness. Indeed, fantasy may contribute to the psychological well-being of some people by increasing their creativity and by permitting them to use their imagination to understand what other people are experiencing.

SLUMBERING PROBLEMS: Sleep Disturbances

At one time or another, almost all of us have sleeping difficulty—a condition known as **insomnia**. It may be due to a particular situation such as the death of a friend or close relative, or concern about a test score or the loss of a

Insomnia: An inability to get to sleep or stay asleep

The sleeplessness of insomnia affects almost everyone at one time or another. (Innervisions)

job. Some cases of insomnia, however, have no obvious reason or cause. Some people are simply unable to fall asleep easily, or they go to sleep readily but wake up frequently during the night. Insomnia is a problem that afflicts about a quarter of the population of the United States.

Other sleep problems are less common than insomnia. People with **sleep apnea** have difficulty breathing and sleeping simultaneously. The result is disturbed, fitful sleep, as the person is constantly reawakened when the lack of oxygen becomes sufficiently great to trigger a waking response. In some cases, people with apnea wake themselves some 500 times during the course of an evening, resulting in complaints of sleepiness the next day. Sleep apnea may account for **sudden infant death syndrome**, a mysterious killer of seemingly normal infants who die while sleeping.

Narcolepsy is an uncontrollable need to sleep for short periods during the day. No matter what the activity—holding a heated conversation, exercising, or driving—the narcoleptic will suddenly drift into sleep. People with narcolepsy go directly from wakefulness to REM sleep, skipping the other stages. The causes of narcolepsy are not known, although there may be a genetic component, with narcolepsy running in some families.

We know relatively little about sleeptalking and sleepwalking, two fairly harmless sleep disturbances. Both occur during stage 4 sleep and are more frequent in children than in adults. In most cases, sleeptalkers and sleepwalkers have a vague consciousness of the world around them, and a sleepwalker may be able to walk around obstructions in a crowded room in an agile fashion. Unless a sleepwalker wanders into a dangerous environment, sleepwalking typically poses little risk. In fact, the conventional wisdom that one shouldn't awaken sleepwalkers is wrong: No harm will come from waking them, although they will probably be quite confused.

Sleep apnea: A sleep disorder characterized by difficulty in breathing and sleeping simultaneously

Sudden infant death syndrome: A disorder in which seemingly healthy infants die in their sleep

Narcolepsy (NARK o lep see): An uncontrollable need to sleep for short periods during the day

THE INFORMED CONSUMER OF PSYCHOLOGY: Sleeping Better

Fortunately, the most severe sleep disorder from which most of us suffer is insomnia. Yet the fact that things could be worse provides little solace to weary insomniacs, whose difficulty in sleeping can make them feel exhausted every waking moment.

For those of us who spend hours tossing and turning in bed, psychologists studying sleep disturbances have made a number of suggestions for overcoming insomnia. These include:

▶ Exercise during the day; not surprisingly, it helps to be tired before going to sleep! Moreover, learning systematic relaxation techniques and biofeedback (see Chapter 2) can help you unwind from the day's stress and tensions (Woolfolk & McNulty, 1983).

▶ Choose a regular bedtime, and then stick to it. Adhering to a habitual schedule helps your internal timing mechanisms better regulate your body.

▶ Don't use your bed as an all-purpose area; leave studying, reading, eating, watching TV, and other recreational activities to some other area of your room. By following this advice, you can more readily make your bed a conditioned stimulus—leading to the conditioned response of sleeping.

▶ Avoid drinks with caffeine (such as coffee, tea, and some soft drinks) after lunch; their effects can linger for as long as eight to twelve hours after they are consumed.

▶ Drink a glass of warm milk at bedtime. Your grandmother was right, although she probably didn't know the reason why. (Milk contains the chemical tryptophan, which helps people get to sleep.)

▶ Avoid sleeping pills. Although over $100 million a year is spent on sleeping pills in the United States, most of this money is wasted. They can be temporarily effective, but in the long run sleeping pills can cause more harm than good, since they disrupt the normal sleep cycle.

▶ Don't *try* to go to sleep. This advice, which sounds odd at first, actually makes a good deal of sense. Psychologists have found that part of the reason people have difficulty falling asleep is that they are trying so hard. A better strategy is one suggested by Richard P. Bootzin of Northwestern University, who teaches people to recondition their sleeping habits. He tells them to go to bed only when they feel tired. If they don't get to sleep within ten minutes, they should leave the bedroom and do something else, returning to bed only when they do feel tired. This process should be continued, all night if necessary. But in the morning, the patient must get up at his or her usual hour and must not take a nap during the day. After three to four weeks on this regimen, most people become conditioned to associate their beds with sleep—and fall asleep rapidly at night (Youkilis & Bootzin, 1981).

Even if these techniques do not work to your satisfaction and you still feel that insomnia is a problem, there is one consolation: Many people who *think* they have sleeping problems may be mistaken. Observers find that patients who enter sleep laboratories for treatment actually sleep much more than they think they do (Trinder, 1988). For example, researchers have found that some people who report being up all night actually fall asleep in thirty minutes and stay that way all night. Their problem, then, is not insomnia but rather faulty perceptions of their sleeping patterns. In many cases, just becoming aware of how long they really do sleep—and understanding the fact that the older they become the less sleep they need—is enough to "cure" people's perception that they have a sleep disorder.

RECAP AND REVIEW I

Recap

◀ Consciousness refers to a person's awareness of the sensations, thoughts, and feelings being experienced at a given moment.

◀ There are four distinct stages of sleep, as well as REM (rapid eye movement) sleep. These stages recur in cycles during the course of a normal night's sleep.

◀ Dreams may have symbolic meanings, although some psychologists feel that dream content simply reflects the conscious concerns of the dreamer, an attempt to resolve problems, or a reaction to random electrical activity in the brain.

◀ The major sleep disorders include insomnia, narcolepsy, and sleep apnea.

Review

1. Impaired thinking, a disturbed sense of time, and loss of self-control are characteristic of a(n)

   a. passive state of consciousness.
   b. active state of consciousness.
   c. artificial state of consciousness.
   d. altered state of consciousness.

2. Brain activity during sleep can be measured through a(n) _____ .

3. During which stage of sleep do sleep spindles occur?
   a. 1
   b. 2
   c. 3
   d. 4

4. Which of the following does *not* occur during REM sleep?
   a. Breathing rate increases.
   b. Blood pressure rises.
   c. Movement of the major muscles increases.
   d. Heart rate increases and becomes irregular.

5. Many people simply do not dream. True or false? _____

6. People deprived of REM sleep show a _____ _____—a subsequent increase in time spent in REM sleep when they are finally allowed to sleep undisturbed.

7. Which of the following is *not* true of people who have been deprived of sleep?
    a. They are able to catch up fairly quickly.
    b. They cannot expect to be able to catch up on weekends.
    c. They experience weariness and lack of concentration.
    d. They may display hand tremors.

8. According to Freud, the often quizzical themes experienced in dreams actually mask the true wishes of the dreamer. The dream, as experienced, represents the _____ content, whereas the underlying wishes are the _____ content.

9. One theory of why we dream suggests that electrical brain activity stimulates memories, each of which forms a separate dream. True or false? _____

10. Studies have shown that people daydream about _____ percent of the time.
    a. 5
    b. 10
    c. 15
    d. 20

11. Daydreaming is quite often a warning sign of mental disturbance. True or false? _____

12. Gabrielle abruptly fell asleep at the table during a dinner party. Her dinner guests might have considered Gabrielle's behavior a bit rude had her husband not been present to explain that Gabrielle suffered from
    a. sleep apnea.
    b. daydreaming.
    c. insomnia.
    d. narcolepsy.

(Answers to review questions are on page 390.)

ALTERED STATES OF CONSCIOUSNESS: HYPNOSIS AND MEDITATION

You are feeling relaxed and drowsy. You are getting sleepier and sleepier. Your body is becoming limp. Now you are starting to become warm, at ease, more comfortable. Your eyelids are feeling heavier and heavier. Your eyes are closing; you can't keep them open any more. You are totally relaxed.

Now, as you listen to my voice, do exactly as I say. Place your hands above your head. You will find they are getting heavier and heavier—so heavy you can barely keep them up. In fact, although you are straining as hard as you can, you will be unable to hold them up any longer.

An observer watching the above scene would notice a curious phenomenon occurring: Many of the people listening to the voice would, one by one, drop their arms to their sides, as if they were holding heavy lead weights. The reason for this strange behavior is probably no surprise: The people have been hypnotized.

YOU ARE UNDER MY POWER—OR ARE YOU?: Hypnosis

A person under **hypnosis** is in a state of heightened susceptibility to the suggestions of others. In some respects, it appears that a person in a hypnotic trance is asleep (although measures of brain waves show that this is not the case). Yet other aspects of behavior contradict this appearance of sleep, for the person is attentive to the hypnotist's suggestions and carries out suggestions that may be bizarre and silly.

At the same time, people do not lose all will of their own when hypnotized: They will not perform antisocial behaviors, and they will not carry out self-destructive acts. Moreover, people cannot be hypnotized against their will—despite the popular misconceptions.

Hypnosis: A state of heightened susceptibility to the suggestions of others

FIGURE 11-6

If this comic were true to life, Spiderman would have little to fear from the evil Mesmero: Despite common misconceptions to the contrary, people cannot be hypnotized against their will. (Marvel Comics Group, 1981.)

There are wide variations in people's susceptibility to hypnosis (Piccione, Hilgard, & Zimbardo, 1989; Stara & Jaffa, 1987). About 5 to 10 percent of the population cannot be hypnotized at all, while some 15 percent are very easily hypnotized. Most people fall in between. Moreover, the ease with which a person is hypnotized is related to a number of other characteristics. People who are readily hypnotized are also easily absorbed while reading books or listening to music, becoming unaware of what is happening around them, and they often spend an unusual amount of time daydreaming (Hilgard, 1974; Lynn & Rhue, 1985; Lynn & Snodgrass, 1987). In sum, then, they show a high ability to concentrate and to become completely absorbed in what they are doing.

A Different State of Consciousness?

The issue of whether hypnosis represents a state of consciousness that is qualitatively different from normal waking consciousness has long been controversial among psychologists.

Ernest Hilgard (1975) has argued convincingly that hypnosis does represent a state of consciousness that differs significantly from other states. He contends that particular behavioral characteristics clearly differentiate hypnosis from other states, including higher suggestibility; increased ability to recall and construct images, including visual memories from early childhood; a lack of initiative; and the ability to accept uncritically suggestions that clearly contradict reality. Moreover, recent research has found changes in electrical activity in the brain that are associated with hypnosis, supporting the position that hypnotic states represent a state of consciousness different from that of normal waking (Guzelier et al., 1984; Spiegel, 1987).

Still, some theorists reject the notion that hypnosis represents an altered state of consciousness (Spanos, 1986). They argue that altered brain wave patterns are not sufficient to demonstrate that a hypnotic state is qualitatively different from normal waking consciousness, given that there are no other specific physiological changes that occur when a person is in a trance. Fur-

---

ANSWERS (REVIEW I):
1. d **2.** Electroencephalogram **3.** b **4.** c **5.** False; everyone dreams, although some people may not remember their dreams **6.** Rebound effect **7.** b **8.** Manifest, latent **9.** False; the theory suggests that the brain weaves random memories into a dream with a logical story line **10.** b **11.** False, except when the daydreamer fails to distinguish fantasy from reality **12.** d

thermore, some researchers have shown that people merely pretending to by hypnotized show behaviors that are nearly identical to those of truly hypnotized individuals, and that hypnotic susceptibility can be increased through training procedures (Gfeller, Lynn & Pribble, 1987; Spanos et al., 1987). There also is little support for the contention that adults can accurately recall memories of childhood events while hypnotized (Nash, 1987). Such converging evidence suggests that there is nothing qualitatively special about the hypnotic trance (Orne & Evans, 1965; Barber, 1975).

The jury remains out on whether hypnosis represents a state of consciousness that is truly unique. On the other hand, hypnosis has been applied in a number of important areas (see the Psychology at Work box), and as such represents a useful therapeutic tool.

REGULATING YOUR OWN STATE OF CONSCIOUSNESS: Meditation

When traditional practitioners of the ancient eastern religion of Zen Buddhism want to achieve greater spiritual insight, they turn to a technique that has been used for centuries to alter their state of consciousness. This technique is called meditation.

Meditation is a learned technique for refocusing attention that brings about an altered state of consciousness. Although there is an exotic sound to it, some form of meditation is found within every major religion—including Christianity and Judaism. In the United States today, some of the major

Meditation: A learned technique for refocusing attention that brings about an altered state of consciousness

---

PSYCHOLOGY AT WORK

USING HYPNOSIS OUTSIDE THE LABORATORY

Although there is disagreement over the true nature of consciousness associated with hypnotic states, few would dispute the tremendous practical value of hypnosis in a variety of settings. Psychologists working in many disparate areas have found hypnosis to be a reliable, effective tool. Among the range of applications are the following:

● Medical care. Patients suffering from chronic pain may be given the suggestion, while hypnotized, that their pain is eliminated or reduced. Similarly, they may be taught to hypnotize themselves to relieve pain or to gain a sense of control over their symptoms. Hypnosis has proved to be particularly useful during childbirth and dental procedures (Long, 1986).

● Law enforcement uses. Witnesses and victims are sometimes better able to recall details of a crime when hypnotized. In one well-known case, a witness to the kidnapping of a group of California schoolchildren was placed under hypnosis and was able to recall all but one digit of the license number on the kidnapper's vehicle (*Time,* 1976). On the other hand, the evidence regarding the accuracy of recollections obtained under hypnosis is decidedly mixed. In some cases, accurate recall of specific information increases—but so do the number of errors (Dywan & Bowers, 1983). Moreover, there is an increase in a person's confidence about the recollections obtained during hypnosis, even when the memory is in error (Nogrady, Mc-Conkey & Perry, 1985). The hypnotic state may simply make people more willing to report whatever they think they remember. Because of these questions about its usefulness, the legal status of hypnosis has yet to be resolved (Council on Scientific Affairs, 1985).

● Professional sports. Athletes frequently turn to hypnosis to improve their performance. For example, championship fighter Ken Norton used hypnosis prior to a bout to prepare himself for the encounter, and baseball star Rod Carew used hypnotism to increase his concentration when batting (Udolf, 1981).

Hypnosis, then, has many potential applications. Of course, it is not invariably effective: For the significant number of people who cannot be hypnotized, it offers little help. But for people who make good hypnotic subjects, hypnosis has the potential for providing significant benefits.

Meditation has its roots in the ancient oriental religion of Zen Buddhism, but it is practiced today by many westerners in modified techniques that do not use traditional sitting postures. (Jerry Howard/Positive Images)

Mantra: A sound, word, or syllable repeated over and over to take one into a meditative state

---

FIGURE 11-7

An ancient mandala that can be used to focus one's attention while meditating. A mandala is constructed so that attention is drawn to the center of the figure. (Manfred Kage/Peter Arnold, Inc.)

proponents of meditation are followers of Maharishi Mahesh Yogi, who practice a form of meditation called *transcendental meditation,* or *TM,* although several other groups teach various forms of meditation.

The specific meditative technique used in TM involves repeating a **mantra**—a sound, word or syllable—over and over; in other forms of meditation, the focus is on a picture, flame, or specific part of the body (see Figure 11-7). Regardless of the nature of the particular initial stimulus, in most forms of meditation the key to the procedure is concentrating on it so thoroughly that the meditator becomes unaware of any outside stimulation and a different state of consciousness is reached. Following meditation, people report feeling thoroughly relaxed, having sometimes gained new insights into themselves and the problems they are facing.

Studies of the physiological changes that occur during meditation indicate that *something* different is happening in that state, but whether these changes qualify as a true change in consciousness is controversial. For example, oxygen usage decreases, heart rate and blood pressure decline, and brain-wave patterns may change (Wallace & Benson, 1972). On the other hand, similar changes occur during relaxation of any sort, so whether they indicate some special state of consciousness remains an open question (Shapiro & Walsh, 1984; Holmes, 1985).

It *is* clear that you yourself can meditate without exotic trappings by using a few simple procedures developed by Herbert Benson, who has studied meditation extensively (Benson, Kotch, Crassweller & Greenwood, 1977). The basics—which are similar in several respects to those developed as a part of eastern religions but have no spiritual component—include sitting in a quiet room with eyes closed, breathing deeply and rhythmically, and repeating a word or sound over and over. Although the procedure is a bit more complicated than this, most people find themselves in a deeply relaxed state after just twenty minutes. Practiced twice a day, Benson's meditative techniques seem to be just as effective in bringing about relaxation as more mystical methods (Benson & Friedman, 1985).

RECAP AND REVIEW II

Recap

◄ Hypnosis places people in a state of heightened susceptibility to the suggestions of others. People cannot be hypnotized against their will, and they vary in their susceptibility to hypnosis.

◄ One crucial question about hypnosis is whether or not it represents a separate state of consciousness. There is evidence on both sides of the issue.

◄ Meditation is a learned technique for refocusing attention that is meant to bring about an altered state of consciousness.

Review

1. People who are readily hypnotized show
   a. high distractability.
   b. a high degree of gullibility.
   c. a high ability to concentrate.
   d. superior intelligence.

2. Changes in electrical brain activity during hypnosis provide indisputable evidence that the hypnotic state represents an altered state of consciousness. True or false?

3. In which applied area is hypnosis particularly controversial?
   a. Law enforcement
   b. Medical care
   c. Professional sports
   d. Magic

4. Leslie repeats a unique sound, known as a _____, when she engages in transcendental meditation.

5. Meditation can be learned only by following procedures which include some spiritual component. True or false?

(Answers to review questions are on page 394.)

THE HIGHS AND LOWS OF CONSCIOUSNESS: DRUG USE

As the butane torch flame vaporized the cocaine in the bowl of a glass smoking pipe, Amir Vik-Kiv inhaled deeply, held the smoke in his expanded chest, then exhaled in a breathless rush. Suddenly, his eyes bulged and his hands trembled. Beads of sweat broke out on his forehead, and perspiration stains formed under his arms.

The use of cocaine, here being inhaled or "snorted," has damaged the lives of many people. (Jon Feingersh/Stock Boston)

Moments earlier . . . the former television cameraman had "cooked" a gram of refined cocaine in the kitchen of his Northeast Washington apartment. Using a simple recipe of water and baking soda, he had reduced the substance to a potent, insidious form known as "crack."

Within an hour he had "burned" about $100 worth of the drug, but what had happened in his brain just seven seconds after taking the first hit was more like an explosion. Although he had not eaten food in a day or had sex in months, he was no longer hungry for either. . . .

What would happen when the dope ran out was another story. Before long Vik-Kiv would be crawling around the kitchen floor, searching for bits of cocaine that might have spilled. When he found anything white, he would take it—and gag at the taste of what could have been anything from a burning bread crumb to a moldering roach egg. (Milloy, 1986, p. 1.)

Although few of us reach the extremes of this person—who eventually enrolled in a rehabilitation program—almost all of us are experienced drug users. From infancy on, most people take vitamins, aspirin, cold-relief med-

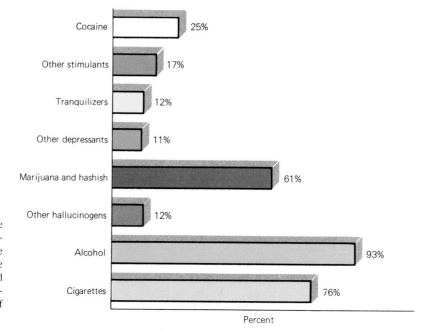

FIGURE 11-8

How many people use drugs? Results of the most recent comprehensive survey of people 18 to 25 years old, carried out by the National Institute of Drug Abuse, show the percentage of respondents who have used various substances for nonmedical purposes at least once. (National Institute of Drug Abuse, 1986.)

Psychoactive drugs: Drugs that influence a person's emotions, perceptions, and behavior

Addictive drugs: Drugs that produce a physical or psychological dependence in the user

icine, and the like. These drugs have little effect on our consciousness, operating primarily on our biological functions. When we speak of drugs that affect consciousness, we are referring instead to **psychoactive drugs**, drugs that influence a person's emotions, perceptions, and behavior. Even these drugs are common in most people's lives; if you have ever had a cup of coffee or sipped a beer, you have had a psychoactive drug. In fact, a large number of people have used more potent—and dangerous—psychoactive drugs than coffee and beer (see Figure 11-8).

Obviously, drugs vary in the nature of the effects they have on users. The most dangerous are those that are addictive. **Addictive drugs** produce a biological or psychological dependence in the user, and their withdrawal leads to a craving for the drug that, in some cases, may be nearly irresistible. Addictions may be biologically based, in which case the body becomes so accustomed to functioning in the presence of a drug that it cannot function in its absence. Or addictions may be psychological, in which case people believe that they need the drug in order to respond to the stresses of daily living. Although we generally associate addiction with drugs such as heroin, everyday sorts of drugs like caffeine (found in coffee) and nicotine (found in cigarettes) have their addictive aspects as well.

We know relatively little about the reasons underlying addiction. One of the problems in identifying the causes is that different drugs (such as alcohol and cocaine) affect the brain in very different ways—and yet may be equally addicting. Furthermore, it takes longer to become addicted to some drugs than to others, even though the ultimate consequences of addiction may be equally grave (Barnes, 1988).

ANSWERS (REVIEW II):
1. c   **2.** False; altered brain-wave patterns are considered by some not to be sufficient evidence   **3.** a   **4.** Mantra   **5.** False; some meditative techniques have no spiritual component

Why do people take drugs in the first place? There are many reasons, ranging from the perceived pleasure of the experience itself, to the escape a drug-induced high affords from the everyday pressures of life, to an attempt to achieve a religious or spiritual state. But other factors, ones that have little to do with the nature of the experience itself, also lead people to try drugs. For instance, the models of prestigious users and the pressures of peers play a role in the decision to use drugs (Stein, Newcomb & Bentler, 1987). In some cases, the motive is simply the thrill of trying something new and perhaps illegal. Regardless of the forces that lead a person to begin to use drugs, drug addiction is among the most difficult of all behaviors to modify, even with extensive treatment (Marlatt et al., 1988).

DRUG HIGHS: Stimulants

It's one o'clock in the morning, and you still haven't finished reading the last chapter of the text on which you are being tested in the morning. Feeling exhausted, you turn to the one thing that may help you keep awake for the next two hours: a cup of strong, black coffee.

If you have ever found yourself in such a position, you have been relying on a major **stimulant**, caffeine, to stay awake. **Caffeine** is one of a number of stimulants that affect the central nervous system by causing a rise in heart rate, blood pressure, and muscular tension. Caffeine is not present in coffee alone; it is an important ingredient in tea, soft drinks, and chocolate as well. The major behavioral effects of caffeine are an increase in attentiveness and a decrease in reaction time. Caffeine can also bring about an improvement in mood, most likely by mimicking the effects of a natural brain chemical, adenosine.

Too much caffeine, however, can result in nervousness and insomnia. People can build up a biological dependence on the drug: If they suddenly stop drinking coffee, they may experience headaches or depression. Many people who drink large amounts of coffee on weekdays have headaches on weekends because of a sudden drop in the amount of caffeine they are consuming (Konner, 1988).

Another common stimulant is **nicotine**, found in cigarettes. The soothing effects of nicotine help explain why cigarette smoking is rewarding for smokers, many of whom continue to smoke despite clear evidence of its long-term health dangers. As we will discuss further in Chapter 15 when we consider health psychology, smoking is addictive; smokers develop a dependence on nicotine, and smokers who suddenly stop develop strong cravings for the drug. According to the U.S. Surgeon General, who changed the designation of smoking from a "habit" to an "addiction" in 1988, the use of nicotine is "driven by strong, often irresistible urges and can persist despite . . . repeated efforts to quit" (Koop, 1988).

"Speed Kills": Amphetamines

The phrase "speed kills" was made popular in the late 1970s when use of **amphetamines**, strong stimulants such as Dexedrine and Benzedrine (popularly known as speed), soared. In small quantities, amphetamines bring about increased confidence, a sense of energy and alertness, and a mood "high." They may also cause a loss of appetite, increased anxiety, and irritability. When taken over long periods of time, amphetamines can cause feelings of being persecuted by others, as well as a general sense of suspicious-

Stimulants: Drugs that affect the central nervous system, causing increased heart rate, blood pressure, and muscle tension

Caffeine: A stimulant found most abundantly in coffee, tea, soda, and chocolate

Nicotine: A stimulant present in cigarettes

Amphetamines: Strong stimulants that cause a temporary feeling of confidence and alertness but may increase anxiety and appetite loss and taken over a period of time, suspiciousness and feelings of persecution

One of the most frequently used stimulants is nicotine, a chief ingredient of cigarettes. (Kindra Clineff/The Picture Cube)

ness. If taken in too large a quantity, amphetamines cause so much stimulation of the central nervous system that convulsions and death can occur—hence the phrase "speed kills." (For a summary of the effects of amphetamines and other illegal drugs, see Table 11-2.)

Cocaine: A stimulant that initially creates feelings of confidence, alertness, and well-being, but eventually causes mental and physical deterioration

Coke Isn't It

One dangerous stimulant that has grown in popularity over the last fifteen years is **cocaine** and its derivative, crack. Cocaine is inhaled or "snorted"

TABLE 11-2

Illegal Drugs and Their Effects

Drug	Street Name	Effects	Withdrawal Symptoms	Adverse/Overdose Reactions
Stimulants Amphetamines Benzedrine Dexedrine Cocaine	Speed Speed Coke, blow, toot, snow, lady, crack	Increased confidence, mood elevation, sense of energy and alertness, decreased appetite, anxiety, irritability, insomnia, transient drowsiness, delayed orgasm	Apathy, general fatigue, prolonged sleep, depression, disorientation, suicidal thoughts, agitated motor activity, irritability, bizarre dreams	Elevated blood pressure, increase in body temperature, face-picking, suspiciousness, bizarre and repetitious behavior, vivid hallucinations, convulsions, possible death
Depressants Barbiturates Nembutal Seconal Phenobarbital Quaalude	Yellowjackets, yellows Reds Ludes, 714s	Impulsiveness, dramatic mood swings, bizarre thoughts, suicidal behavior, slurred speech, disorientation, slowed mental and physical functioning, limited attention span	Weakness, restlessness, nausea and vomiting, headaches, nightmares, irritability, depression, acute anxiety, hallucinations, seizures, possible death	Confusion, decreased response to pain, shallow respiration, dilated pupils, weak and rapid pulse, coma, possible death
Heroin Morphine	H, hombre, junk, smack, dope, horse, crap Drugstore dope, cube, first line, mud	Apathy, difficulty in concentration, slowed speech, decreased physical activity, drooling, itching, euphoria, nausea	Anxiety, vomiting, sneezing, diarrhea, lower back pain, watery eyes, runny nose, yawning, irritability, tremors, panic, chills and sweating, cramps	Depressed levels of consciousness, low blood pressure, rapid heart rate, shallow breathing, convulsions, coma, possible death
Hallucinogens Cannabis Marijuana Hashish Hash oil	Bhang, kif, ganja, dope, grass, pot, smoke, hemp, joint, weed, bone, Mary Jane, herb, tea	Euphoria, relaxed inhibitions, increased appetite, disoriented behavior	Hyperactivity, insomnia, decreased appetite, anxiety	Severe reactions are rare but include panic, paranoia, fatigue, bizarre and dangerous behavior, decreased production of testosterone over long term, immune-system effects

through the nose, whereas crack is smoked. Both are rapidly absorbed into the bloodstream, making their effects apparent almost immediately. Although illegal and expensive, cocaine and crack use are not uncommon: There are some 5 million regular cocaine users, and about 30 percent of all college students will have tried cocaine by their senior year (Washton & Gold, 1987).

When taken in relatively small quantities, cocaine has many of the same effects as amphetamines in general—euphoria, increased confidence, alertness, and a sense of well-being. It also allows people to work for long periods

Drug	Street Name	Effects	Withdrawal Symptoms	Adverse/Overdose Reactions
Hallucinogens (*cont.*) LSD	Electricity, acid, quasey, blotter acid, microdot, white lightning, purple barrels	Fascination with ordinary objects; heightened aesthetic responses to color, texture, spatial arrangements, contours, music; vision and depth distortion; hearing colors, seeing music; slowing of time; heightened sensitivity to faces and gestures; magnified feelings of love, lust, hate, joy, anger, pain, terror, despair; paranoia; panic; euphoria; bliss; impairment of short-term memory; projection of self into dreamlike images	Not reported	Nausea and chills; increased pulse, temperature, and blood pressure; trembling; slow, deep breathing; loss of appetite; insomnia; longer, more intense 'trips"; bizarre, dangerous behavior possibly leading to injury or death
Phencylidine (PCP)	Angel dust, hog, rocket fuel, superweed, peace pill, elephant tranquilizer, dust, bad pizza	Increased blood pressure and heart rate, sweating, nausea, numbness, floating sensation, slowed reflexes, altered body image, altered perception of time and space, impaired immediate and recent memory, decreased concentration, paranoid thoughts and delusions	Not reported	Highly variable and possibly dose-related: disorientation, loss of recent memory, lethargy/stupor, bizarre and violent behavior, rigidity and immobility, mutism, staring, hallucinations and delusions, coma

The crystallized, concentrated form of co-caine called "crack" is highly addictive and poses a major drug problem in many cities. (A. Tannenbaum/Sygma)

of time without feeling tired (although this can be followed by a "crash" in which the user sleeps for long periods of time).

The price paid for these effects is steep. The drug is psychologically addictive, and users may grow obsessed with obtaining it. Their lives become tied to the drug; they deteriorate mentally and physically, losing weight and growing suspicious of others. In extreme cases, cocaine can cause halluci-nations; a common one is that insects are crawling over one's body (Fishman, 1985; Fisher, Rashkin & Uhlenhuth, 1987).

DRUG LOWS: Depressants

Depressants: Drugs that slow down the nervous system

Intoxication: A state of drunkenness

In contrast to the initial effect of stimulants, which is an increase in arousal of the central nervous system, the effect of **depressants** is to impede the nervous system by causing the neurons to fire more slowly. Small doses result in at least temporary feelings of **intoxication**—drunkenness—along with a sense of euphoria and joy. When large amounts are taken, however, speech becomes slurred, muscle control becomes disjointed, causing diffi-culty of motion, and ultimately consciousness may be lost entirely.

The most common depressant is alcohol, although most people would probably claim that it increases their sense of sociability and well-being (Steele & Southwick, 1985). The discrepancy between the actual and the perceived effects of alcohol lies in its initial effects: releasing tension and producing a breakdown in judgment. As the dose of alcohol increases, how-ever, the depressive effects become clearer (Hannon et al., 1985). People may feel emotionally and physically unstable; they become incoherent and may eventually fall into a stupor and pass out (see Table 11-3).

It is only recently that scientists have begun to understand how alcohol brings about its varied effects. According to Ernest Noble, director of the Alcohol Research Center at the University of California at Los Angeles, re-

TABLE 11-3

Effects of Alcohol

Distilled Spirits Consumed in 2 Hours, Ounces	Alcohol in Blood, Percent	Typical Effects, Average-size Adult
3 (2 drinks)	0.05	Judgment, thought, and restraint weakened; tension released, giving carefree sensation
4½ (3 drinks)	0.08	Tensions and inhibitions of everyday life lessened
6 (4 drinks)	0.10	Voluntary motor action affected, making hand and arm movements, walk, and speech clumsy
10 (6.7 drinks)	0.20	Severe impairment—staggering, loud, incoherent, emotionally unstable; 100 times greater traffic risk
14 (9.3 drinks)	0.30	Deeper areas of brain affected, with stimulus response and understanding confused; stuporous
18 (12 drinks)	0.40	Incapable of voluntary action, sleepy, difficult to arouse; equivalent of surgical anesthesia
22 (14.7 drinks)	0.50	Comatose; centers controlling breathing and heartbeat anesthetized; death

Note: A drink refers to a typical 12-ounce glass of beer, a 1.5-ounce shot of hard liquor, or a 5-ounce glass of wine.

searchers have recently learned that alcohol affects the walls or membranes of neurons by decreasing their ability to transmit messages. When most people consume alcohol, the normal pathways of the neurons become less rigid, and messages become garbled and disoriented—resulting in the depressive effects that occur in the central nervous system.

In contrast, alcoholics—people who come to rely on alcohol and drink even though it causes serious problems—develop a tolerance for alcohol; their cell membranes remain rigid even in the presence of alcohol. When alcohol in the blood decreases, alcoholics suffer from withdrawal symptoms, since their cell membranes become unable to process messages in the absence of alcohol (see Figure 11-9).

It is still unclear why certain people become alcoholic and develop a tolerance for alcohol, while others do not (Rivers, 1986; Gallant, 1987). Some evidence suggests a genetic cause; the chances of becoming alcoholic are considerably higher if alcoholics are present in earlier generations, implying that some people are genetically susceptible to alcoholism. On the other hand, not all alcoholics have close relatives who are alcoholics; in these cases, environmental stressors are suspected of playing a larger role (Holden, 1985; Kolata, 1987).

Whatever the specific cause of the increased tolerance to alcohol found in alcoholics, the findings pertaining to the rigidity of the cell membranes suggest some novel approaches to treating alcoholism. Because certain foods affect the density of the neuronal cell membranes, it is possible that changes

FEELING AND EXPERIENCING
THE WORLD

Nonalcoholics
Normal cell
Walls of neuron cells are believed to consist of protein icebergs afloat in seas of fat. Messages controlling emotions and behavior move through channels between these icebergs.

Alcohol-affected
When alcohol is added, the normal fluidity between the icebergs increases. They become disoriented; the channels get disrupted and messages are garbled.

Alcoholics

Alcohol-dependent
After frequent, long-term exposure to alcohol, the walls become more rigid than normal. The brain becomes less sensitive to alcohol.

Alcohol-denied
When alcohol is removed, withdrawal symptoms occur. The channels are unable to recover normal fluidity, causing overactivity in the central nervous system.

FIGURE 11-9

Finding the key to alcoholism. (*Source:* Adapted from Blakeslee, 1984.)

Barbiturates: Depressants used to induce sleep and reduce stress, the abuse of which, especially when combined with alcohol, can be deadly

Morphine: Derived from the poppy flower, a powerful depressant that reduces pain and induces sleep

Heroin: A powerful depressant, usually injected, that gives an initial rush of good feeling but leads eventually to anxiety and depression; extremely addictive

in diet might help people become less susceptible to alcoholism in the same way that dietary changes are recommended to help prevent heart disease. Even more interesting is the possibility of a "sober" pill, which would prevent alcohol from affecting the cell membranes and would thereby prevent the behavioral effects of alcohol from occurring (see the Cutting Edge box).

Barbiturates, which include such drugs as Nembutal, Seconal, and phenobarbital, are another form of depressant. Frequently prescribed by physicians to induce sleep or to reduce stress, barbiturates produce a sense of relaxation. Yet they too are psychologically and physically addictive and, when combined with alcohol, can be deadly, since such a combination relaxes the muscles of the diaphragm to such an extent that the user suffocates. The street drug known as Quaalude is closely related to the barbiturate family and has similar dangers associated with it.

Morphine and Heroin

Two of the most powerful depressants, **morphine** and **heroin**, are derived from the poppy flower. Both reduce pain and cause sleepiness. Although morphine is used medically to control severe pain, heroin is illegal in the United States. This has not prevented its widespread use.

Heroin users usually inject the drug directly into their veins with a hypodermic needle. The immediate effect has been described as a "rush" of positive feeling, similar in some respects to a sexual orgasm—and just as difficult to describe. After the rush, a heroin user experiences a sense of

It has been a rowdy party, and large quantities of liquor have been consumed. As the party draws to a close, however, the host hands each participant a small pill to swallow. In a few minutes, all signs of raucous behavior have disappeared, and the partygoers appear altogether sober.

Such a curious scenario might someday become a reality if scientists are successful in perfecting a recently discovered experimental drug that makes drunk animals appear to be sober. Tentatively called Ro15-4513, the drug not only seems to reverse the effects of alcohol, but it may help to reveal the biochemical basis for alcohol's actions and may hold the future promise of helping alcoholics overcome their problems.

The effect of Ro15-4513 on experimental animals is dramatic (Paul, 1986). In one experiment, rats were given so much alcohol that they became heavily sedated; if they were put on their backs, they did not roll over, and their arms and legs flopped away from their bodies when they lay on their stomachs.

LOOKING FOR A "SOBER" PILL

But two minutes after an injection of Ro15-4513, the animals would get up and walk around, appearing completely sober. Moreover, if the rats received a dose of the drug before they were given alcohol, they never acted intoxicated in the first place.

Some scientists suggest that Ro15-4513 will aid in understanding how alcohol affects behavior—a process that is not now well understood. Moreover, it may prove to be helpful in the treatment of alcoholism, allowing alcoholics to learn to live without alcohol. Recovering alcoholics might take the pill daily in order to prevent intoxication, even if they found themselves in situations in which they felt compelled to take a drink (Kolata, 1986).

The drug holds particular promise because of its lack of side effects. Although other drugs have been found to reverse alcohol's

effects, they have always proved dangerous, producing convulsions and sometimes even death in experimental animals. In contrast, Ro15-4513 is a fairly close relation of such relatively safe drugs as Valium and Librium.

On the other hand, important ethical issues may preclude the widespread use of Ro15-4513 among the general population. For example, although the drug impedes the behavioral effects of alcohol, the amount of alcohol and its metabolism within the body are not affected by Ro15-4513. The harmful side effects of long-term alcohol use, such as the potential of irreversible damage to the liver, would not be remedied by use of the drug.

It thus remains to be seen whether Ro15-4513 will eventually serve as the ultimate nightcap at parties, taken to help people become sober when it is time to drive home after an evening of revelry. Whether or not this use of the drug would represent social progress is an open question.

well-being and peacefulness that lasts three to five hours. When the effects of the drug wear off, however, the user feels extreme anxiety and a desperate desire to repeat the experience. Moreover, larger amounts of heroin are needed each time to produce the same pleasurable effect. This leads to a cycle of biological and psychological addiction: The user is constantly either shooting up or attempting to obtain ever-increasing amounts of the drug. Eventually, the life of the addict becomes centered around heroin.

Because of the powerful positive feelings the drug produces, heroin addiction is particularly difficult to cure. One treatment that has shown some success is the use of methadone. **Methadone** is a chemical that satisfies a heroin user's physiological cravings for the drug without providing the "high" that accompanies heroin. When heroin users are placed on regular doses of methadone they may be able to function relatively normally. The use of methadone has one substantial drawback, however: Although it removes the psychological dependence on heroin, it replaces the biological addiction to heroin with a biological addiction to methadone.

Methadone: A chemical used to detoxify heroin addicts

Heroin, which is typically injected directly into the user's vein, is a powerful drug that produces both biological and psychological addiction. (Joel Gordon)

Hallucinogen (ha LOOS en o jen): A drug that is capable of producing changes in perception, or hallucinations

Marijuana: A common hallucinogen, usually smoked

FLYING HIGH: Hallucinogens

What do mushrooms, jimsonweed, and morning glories have in common? Besides being fairly common plants each can be a source of a powerful **hallucinogen**, a drug that is capable of producing hallucinations, or changes in the perceptual process.

The most common hallucinogen in widespread use today is **marijuana**, whose active ingredient—tetrahydrocannabinol (THC)—is found in a common weed, cannabis. Marijuana is typically smoked in cigarettes, although it can be cooked and eaten. At least one-third of all Americans over the age of 12 have tried it at least once, and among 18- to 25-year-olds, the figure is twice as high (National Institute of Drug Abuse, 1986). Despite its illegality, marijuana use is so prevalent that about 15 percent of those over 15 years old are likely to use it in a given week.

The effects of marijuana vary from person to person, but they typically consist of feelings of euphoria and general well-being. Sensory experiences seem more vivid and intense, and a person's sense of self-importance seems to grow. Memory may be impaired, causing the user to feel pleasantly "spaced out." On the other hand, the effects are not universally positive: Individuals who take marijuana when feeling depressed can end up even more depressed, since the drug tends to magnify both good and bad feelings.

Marijuana has the reputation of being a "safe" drug when used in moderation, and there seems to be no scientific evidence that its use is addictive or that users "graduate" to more dangerous drugs. However, the long-term effects of heavy marijuana usage present some potential hazard. For instance, there is some evidence that heavy use decreases the production of the male sex hormone testosterone, potentially affecting sexual activity and sperm count (Miller, 1975). Similarly, heavy use affects the ability of the immune system to fight off germs and increases stress on the heart, although it is unclear how strong the magnitude of these effects are (Turkington, 1986). One negative consequence of smoking large quantities of marijuana is unquestionable, though: The smoke damages the lungs much the way cigarette smoke does, producing an increased likelihood of developing cancer and other lung diseases (Institute of Medicine, 1982).

In sum, the *short-term* effects of marijuana use appear to be relatively

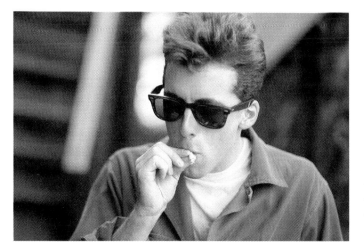

One of the most commonly used illegal drugs is marijuana; studies estimate that about 15 percent of the adult population uses it in any given week. (Richard Hutchings/Photo Researchers)

minor—if users follow obvious cautions, such as avoiding driving or using machinery. However, it is less clear whether the long-term consequences are harmful. The case regarding the use of marijuana is far from closed, and more research is necessary before the question of its safety can be settled.

The Acid Test: LSD and PCP

Two of the strongest hallucinogens are **lysergic acid diethylamide**, or **LSD** (known commonly as acid), and **phencyclidine**, or **PCP** (often referred to as angel dust). Both drugs seem to affect the operation of the neurotransmitter serotonin in the brain, causing an alteration in brain-cell activity and perception (Jacobs, 1987).

LSD produces vivid hallucinations. Perceptions of colors, sounds, and shapes are altered so much that even the most mundane experience—such as looking at the knots in a wooden table—can seem exciting and moving. Time perception is distorted, and objects and people may be viewed in a new way, with some users reporting that LSD increases their understanding of the world. For others, however, the experience brought on by LSD can be terrifying, particularly if users have had emotional difficulties in the past. Furthermore, people can experience flashbacks, in which they hallucinate long after the initial drug usage.

One of the most recent additions to the drug scene, PCP also causes strong hallucinations. However, the potential side effects associated with its use make the drug even more dangerous than LSD. Large doses may cause paranoid and destructive behavior, and in some cases users become violent toward themselves and others.

Lysergic acid diethylamide (LSD): One of the most powerful hallucinogens, affecting the operation of neurotransmitters in the brain and causing brain cell activity to be altered

Phencyclidine (PCP): A powerful hallucinogen that alters brain-cell activity

THE INFORMED CONSUMER OF PSYCHOLOGY:
Identifying Drug and Alcohol Problems

In a society bombarded with commercials for drugs that are guaranteed to do everything from curing the common cold to giving new life to "tired blood," it is no wonder that drug-related problems present a major social issue. Yet many people with drug and alcohol problems deny they have them, and even close friends and family members may fail to realize when occasional social use of drugs or alcohol has turned into abuse.

Certain signs, however, indicate when use becomes abuse (Brody, 1982). Among them:

▶ Always getting high to have a good time

▶ Being high more often than not

▶ Getting high to get oneself going

▶ Going to work or class while high

▶ Missing or being unprepared for class or work because you were high

▶ Feeling bad later about something you said or did while high

▶ Driving a car while high

▶ Coming in conflict with the law because of drugs

▶ Doing something while high that you wouldn't otherwise do

▶ Being high in nonsocial, solitary situations

▶ Being unable to stop getting high

▶ Feeling a need for a drink or a drug to get through the day

▶ Becoming physically unhealthy

▶ Failing at school or on the job

▶ Thinking about liquor or drugs all the time

Any combination of these symptoms is sufficient to alert a person to a serious drug problem. Because drug and alcohol dependence are almost impossible to cure on one's own, people who suspect that they have a problem should seek immediate attention from a psychologist, physician, or counselor.

RECAP AND REVIEW III

Recap

◀ Psychoactive drugs affect a person's emotions, perceptions, and behavior. The most dangerous drugs are those that are addictive—they produce a biological or psychological dependence.

◀ Stimulants produce an increase in the arousal of the central nervous system.

◀ Depressants decrease arousal in the central nervous system; they can produce intoxication.

◀ Hallucinogens produce hallucinations and other modifications of perception.

Review

1. Caffeine produces increases in both attentiveness and reaction time. True or false? _____

2. Smoking has been designated as an addiction. True or false? _____

3. Which of the following is *not* true about cocaine addicts?

   a. They become obsessed with the drug.
   b. They deteriorate physically.
   c. They grow suspicious of others.
   d. They can be assured that their addiction will not produce hallucinations.

4. All of the following are depressants except
   a. alcohol.
   b. morphine.
   c. methadone.
   d. cocaine.

5. It has recently been discovered that when nonalcoholics consume alcohol
   a. the ability of the walls of neurons to transmit messages decreases.
   b. the pathways of the neurons become more rigid, increasing the ability to transmit messages.
   c. messages become more lucid.
   d. the central nervous system is stimulated.

6. When combined with alcohol, barbiturates can relax the

muscles of the diaphragm and cause death by suffocation. True or false? _____

7. Used in the treatment of heroin addiction, methadone
   a. is not addictive.
   b. satisfies the addict's cravings by producing a high similar to heroin.
   c. satisfies the addict's cravings without producing a high.
   d. produces an adverse effect when heroin is taken.

8. Unlike cigarette smoke, marijuana smoke does not damage the lungs or present a cancer risk. True or false? _____

9. A history of emotional difficulties puts an individual at higher risk for having a terrifying experience with LSD. True or false? _____

10. The hallucinogen _____ can produce paranoid and/or destructive behavior.

11. Match each substance with its description.
    a. ____ Marijuana
    b. ____ Cocaine
    c. ____ Alcohol
    d. ____ LSD
    e. ____ Heroin
    f. ____ Caffeine

    1. an addictive stimulant, inhaled for an immediate high
    2. present in many food and drink products
    3. the most commonly used hallucinogen
    4. a depressant that causes an addiction treatable by methadone
    5. a drug that alters brain-cell activity, creating vivid hallucinations
    6. a depressant that at first gives a feeling of well-being

(Answers to review questions are on page 406.)

◀ LOOKING BACK

1. Consciousness refers to a person's awareness of the sensations, thoughts, and feelings being experienced at a given moment. It can vary in terms of how aware of outside stimuli we are, from an active to passive state, and in terms of whether it is artificially induced or occurs naturally.

2. Using the electroencephalogram, or EEG, to study sleep, scientists have found that the brain is active throughout the night, and that sleep proceeds through a series of stages identified by unique patterns of brain waves. In what is sometimes called stage 0, people move out of a waking state, in which they are relaxed with their eyes closed, into stage 1. Stage 1 is characterized by relatively rapid, low-voltage waves, whereas Stage 2 shows more regular, spindle patterns. In stage 3, the brain waves become slower, with higher peaks and lower valleys apparent. Finally, stage 4 sleep includes waves that are even slower and more regular.

3. REM (rapid eye movement) sleep is characterized by an increase in heart rate, a rise in blood pressure, an increase in the rate of breathing and, in males, erections. Most striking is the rapid movement of the eyes, which dart back and forth under closed eyelids. Dreams occur during this stage. REM sleep seems to be critical to human function, although other stages of sleep are less essential.

4. According to Freud, dreams have both a manifest content, their apparent story line, and a latent content, their true meaning. He suggested that the latent content provides a guide to a dreamer's unconscious, showing unfulfilled wishes or desires. Many psychologists disagree with this view; they suggest that the manifest content relates to the actual import of the dream.

5. More recent theories view dreaming in terms of a fundamental biological activity, in which dreams are a result of random electrical energy, possibly due to changes in the production of particular neurotransmitters. This electrical energy randomly stimulates different memories, which are then woven into a coherent story line. Another theory suggests that dreaming occurs as the by-product of a checking and consolidation process that the brain goes through during REM sleep.

6. Daydreaming is a typical part of waking consciousness, although there are wide individual differences in the amount of time devoted to it. There is little relationship between psychological disorders and a high incidence of daydreaming.

7. Insomnia is a sleep disorder characterized by difficulty sleeping. Sleep apnea is reflected in difficulties in sleeping and breathing at the same time; people with narcolepsy have an uncontrollable urge to sleep. Sleepwalking and sleeptalking are relatively harmless.

8. Psychologists and sleep researchers have devised a number of measures to help people overcome insomnia, including increasing exercise during the day, avoiding caffeine and sleeping pills, drinking a glass of warm milk before bedtime, and avoiding *trying* to go to sleep.

9. Hypnosis produces a state of heightened susceptibility to the suggestions of the hypnotist. Although there are no physiological indicators that distinguish hypnosis from normal waking consciousness, significant behavioral characteristics occur, including increased concentration and suggestibility, heightened ability to recall and construct images, lack of initiative, and acceptance of suggestions that clearly contradict reality.

10. Meditation is a learned technique for refocusing attention that brings about an altered state of consciousness. In transcendental meditation, the most popular form

practiced in the United States, a person repeats a mantra (a sound, word, or syllable) over and over, concentrating until he or she becomes unaware of any outside stimulation and reaches a different state of consciousness.

11. Drugs can produce an altered state of consciousness. However, they vary in how dangerous they are and in whether or not they are addictive, producing a physical or psychological dependence. People take drugs for several reasons: to perceive the pleasure of the experience itself, to escape from everyday pressures, to attain religious or spiritual states, to follow the model of prestigious users or peers, or to experience the thrill of trying something new and perhaps illegal. Whatever the cause, drug addiction is one of the most difficult behaviors to modify.

12. Stimulants cause arousal in the central nervous system. Two common stimulants are caffeine (found in coffee, tea, and soft drinks) and nicotine (found in cigarettes). More dangerous are amphetamines, or "speed," and cocaine. Although in small quantities they bring about increased confidence, a sense of energy and alertness, and a "high," in larger quantities they may overload the central nervous system, leading to convulsions and death.

13. Depressants decrease arousal in the central nervous system, causing the neurons to fire more slowly. They may cause intoxication along with feelings of euphoria. The most common depressant is alcohol, which initially relieves tension. Other depressants include barbiturates, morphine, and heroin. Because of their addictive qualities, morphine and heroin are particularly dangerous.

14. Alcohol is the most frequently used depressant. Alcohol affects the walls or membranes of neurons by decreasing their ability to transmit messages. However, alcoholics develop a tolerance for alcohol, and the cell membranes are unable to process messages effectively without the presence of alcohol. Both genetic causes and environmental stressors may lead to alcoholism.

15. Hallucinogens are drugs that produce hallucinations and other changes in perception. The most frequently used hallucinogen is marijuana; its use is common throughout the United States. Although occasional, short-term use of marijuana seems to be of little danger, long-term effects are less clear. The lungs may be damaged; there is the possibility that testosterone levels are lowered in males; and the immune system may be affected. Two other hallucinogens, LSD and PCP, affect the operation of neurotransmitters in the brain, causing an alteration in brain-cell activity and perception.

16. A number of signals indicate when use of drugs becomes abuse. These include frequent usage, getting high in order to get to class or work, driving while high, developing legal problems, and being high alone. A person who suspects that he or she has a drug problem should get professional help; people are almost never capable of solving drug problems on their own.

KEY TERMS AND CONCEPTS ▶

consciousness (p. 376)
altered state of consciousness (377)
electroencephalogram (EEG) (379)
stage 1 sleep (380)
stage 2 sleep (380)
stage 3 sleep (380)
stage 4 sleep (381)
rapid eye movement (REM)
   sleep (381)
rebound effect (381)
nightmares (383)
night terrors (383)
latent content of dreams (383)

manifest content of dreams (383)
daydreams (385)
insomnia (386)
sleep apnea (387)
sudden infant death syndrome (387)
narcolepsy (387)
hypnosis (389)
meditation (391)
mantra (392)
psychoactive drugs (394)
addictive drugs (394)
stimulants (395)
caffeine (395)

nicotine (395)
amphetamines (395)
cocaine (396)
depressants (398)
intoxication (398)
barbiturates (400)
morphine (400)
heroin (400)
methadone (401)
hallucinogen (402)
marijuana (402)
lysergic acid diethylamide (LSD) (403)
phencyclidine (PCP) (403)

ANSWERS (REVIEW III):
1. False; attention increases but reaction time decreases **2.** True **3.** d **4.** d **5.** a
6. True **7.** c **8.** False; the effects on the lungs are similar and there is an increased likelihood of developing cancer and other lung diseases **9.** True **10.** PCP **11.** a. 3, b. 1, c. 6, d. 5, e. 4, f. 2

FOR FURTHER STUDY AND APPLICATION ▶

Wallace, B., & Fisher, L. E. (1987). *Consciousness and behavior* (2nd ed.). Boston: Allyn & Bacon.

This volume provides a thorough introduction to the various states of consciousness.

Hales, D. (1981). *The complete book of sleep.* Reading, MA: Addison-Wesley.

This volume provides a sound, useful guide to those interested in learning more about sleep—or getting a better night's rest each evening.

Dement, W. C. (1974). *Some must watch while some must sleep.* San Francisco: Freeman.

Written by the foremost researcher in sleep and dreams, this book gives a readable account of how research on sleep is carried out and what is known about sleep and dreams.

Udolf, R. (1981). *Handbook of hypnosis for professionals.* New York: Van Nostrand.

Although the title suggests that this book is just for professionals, it provides a clear overview of hypnosis readable by the layperson, and presents a good foundation for the understanding of hypnosis.

Ray, O. (1983). *Drugs, society, and human behavior* (3rd ed.). St. Louis: Mosby, 1983.

This book gives a levelheaded, comprehensive view of the range of consciousness-changing drugs, including their effects on the body's sensations and functioning.

(For help with a drug problem, check your telephone book for a local listing of Narcotics Anonymous, or write to World Service Office, P.O. Box 9999, Van Nuys, CA 91409. For immediate help with a cocaine problem, call a hotline run by the National Institute on Drug Abuse at (800) 662-HELP.)

PART

FIVE

INDIVIDUAL
DEVELOPMENT
AND
DIFFERENTIATION

We come now to the world of the newborn, who begins as a speck of humanity, gradually moving through the years of childhood. We encounter an adolescent's difficult rites of passage, ranging from repeated beatings and mutilations to psychological indignities that must be endured during the transition to adulthood, and we meet an elderly person as she contemplates the final stage of her life. We also meet a man whose notable generosity is a counterpoint to his criminal activities.

In this part of the book, we consider what psychologists have discovered about the universal patterns of growth and change that occur throughout life. We examine what has been learned about the interaction of biologically determined patterns of behavior and the ever-changing environment. We consider the factors that differentiate one person from another and the consistencies in behavior that people display across their own lives.

In Chapter 12, the focus is on the beginning of life, starting at the moment of conception until the onset of adolescence.

In Chapter 13, we look at the remaining stages of development—adolescence, adulthood, old age, and death.

In Chapter 14, we consider personality, both in terms of the characteristics that differentiate one person from another and in the degree of consistency people show as they move from one situation to another.

CHAPTER
12
DEVELOPMENT:
THE BEGINNINGS OF LIFE

PROLOGUE:
GERALD LEVEY AND MARK NEWMAN

Twins Jerry Levey and Mark Newman have many things in common—from their choice of occupation to their favorite brand of beer—despite the fact that they never met until the age of 31. (Peter Byron)

How many bald, 6-foot-6, 250-pound volunteer fire fighters are there in New Jersey who have droopy mustaches and aviator-style eyeglasses and wear a key ring on their belt on the right side?

The answer is: two. Gerald Levey and Mark Newman are twins, separated at birth, who did not even know each other existed until they were reunited—in a fire station—by a fellow fire fighter who knew Newman and was startled to see Levey at a fire fighters' convention.

Their lives, although separate, took remarkably similar paths. Levey went to college, studying forestry; Newman planned to study forestry in college but instead took a job trimming trees. Both had jobs in supermarkets. One has a job installing sprinkler systems; the other installed fire alarms.

Both are unmarried and find the same kind of woman attractive: "tall, slender, long hair." They share similar hobbies, enjoying hunting, fishing, going to the beach, and watching old John Wayne movies and professional wrestling. Both like Chinese food, and they drink the same brand of beer. Their mannerisms are also similar—they both throw their heads back when they laugh. And, of course, there is one more thing: They share a passion for fighting fires (Lang, 1987).

LOOKING AHEAD ▶

Gerald Levey and Mark Newman have been reunited once again, as part of a large-scale, national study of twins being conducted at the Minnesota Center for Twin and Adoption Research, where researchers are finding that the strange degree of similarity between Levey and Newman is mirrored in many other sets of twins. Such coincidences are being studied not as mere curiosities, but because they provide us with important clues about one of the most fundamental questions facing psychologists: how the environment and the natural endowment with which the human being is born interact to produce a unique individual.

This question, and others, falls within the domain of developmental psychology. **Developmental psychology** is the branch of psychology that studies the patterns of growth and change occurring throughout life. In large part, developmental psychologists study the interaction between the unfolding of biologically predetermined patterns of behavior and a constantly changing, dynamic environment. They ask how our genetic background affects our behavior throughout our lives, whether our potential is limited by heredity, and how our built-in biological programming affects our day-to-day development. Similarly, they are committed to understanding the way the environment works with—or against—our genetic capabilities, how the world we live in affects our development, and how we can be encouraged to develop our full potential.

Developmental psychology: The branch of psychology that studies people's growth and change over the life span

More than other psychologists, developmental psychologists consider the day-to-day patterns and changes in behavior that occur across the lifespan. This chapter focuses on the early part of the life cycle, beginning with birth, moving through infancy, and ending with childhood. The following chapter explores aspects of development during the remainder of the life cycle from adolescence to adulthood, and finally to old age and death.

We begin our discussion of development by examining the approaches that have been used to understand and delineate the environmental and genetic factors that direct a person's development. Then we consider the very start of development, beginning with conception and the nine months of life prior to birth. We consider both genetic and environmental influences on the unborn individual, and how these can affect behavior throughout the remainder of the life cycle.

Next, we examine the physical and perceptual developments that occur after birth, witnessing the enormous and rapid growth that occurs during the early stages of life. We also focus on the developing child's social world, indicating what draws the child into relationships with others and membership in society. Finally, we discuss cognitive growth during infancy and childhood, tracing changes in the way children think about the world.

After reading this chapter, you will have the answers to several fundamental questions about development:

▶ How do psychologists study the degree to which development is a joint function of heredity and environmental factors?

▶ What is the nature of development prior to birth, and what factors affect a child during pregnancy?

▶ What are the major milestones of physical, perceptual, and social growth after birth?

▶ How can we best describe cognitive development, and what can parents appropriately do to promote the cognitive development of their children?

NATURE VERSUS NURTURE: A FUNDAMENTAL DEVELOPMENTAL QUESTION

Although the similarities displayed by twins such as Gerald Levey and Mark Newman are startling, they are no less surprising than the dissimilarities that exist among siblings who are raised in almost identical environments. Consider, for instance, the Torres family. Emmanual Torres was convicted of attempting to rape a drama student and then stabbing her to death on a New York City apartment roof; his brother, Alfredo, is a well-respected medical student. Although raised in the same house, with the same parents, the two brothers could not be more different. The differences between them were apparent from childhood; Emmanual continually misbehaved and later had difficulty holding a job, whereas Alfredo showed a fierce ambition from an early age to become a physician (Chambers, 1985).

To the developmental psychologist, one of the central challenges to understanding human development is illustrated by such contrasts, which raise a fundamental question about human development: Can we attribute behavior to causes that are **environmental**—the influence of parents, siblings, family, friends, schooling, nutrition, and all the other experiences to which a child is exposed—or to causes that are **hereditary**—those based on the genetic makeup of an individual that influence growth throughout one's life? A fundamental issue, then, is one we first discussed when we considered the determinants of intelligence in Chapter 8: the **nature-nurture question**, where nature refers to heredity and nurture to environmental influences.

Environment: Influences on behavior that occur in the world around us—in family, friends, school, nutrition, and many other factors

Heredity: Influences on behavior that are transmitted biologically from parents to a child

Nature-nurture question: The issue of the degree to which environment and heredity influence behavior

INDIVIDUAL DEVELOPMENT
AND DIFFERENTIATION

Genetic makeup: Pertaining to the biological factors that transmit hereditary information

Maturation: The unfolding of biologically predetermined behavior patterns

The nature-nurture issue has deep philosophical roots. English philosopher John Locke argued in the 1600s that people were born with the equivalent of a blank slate, a *tabula rasa,* on which the story of their individual experience could be written from scratch. In contrast, the French philosopher Jean Jacques Rousseau suggested a very different conception of development in the 1700s, one in which the environment was seen as corrupting and the "natural" aspects of people (namely, genetic factors) were most influential.

Although the question was first posed as the nature-*versus*-nurture question, today developmental psychologists agree that *both* nature and nurture interact to produce specific developmental patterns. The question has changed from *which* influences behavior to *how* and to what degree environment and heredity produce their effects. No one grows up without being influenced by the environment, nor does anyone develop without being affected by his or her inherited, or **genetic makeup**. However, the debate over the relative influence of the two factors remains an ongoing one, with different approaches and theories of development emphasizing the environment or heredity to a greater or lesser degree.

For example, some developmental theories stress the role of learning in producing changes in behavior in the developing child, relying on the basic principles of learning we discussed in Chapter 5; such theories emphasize the role of environment in accounting for development. In contrast, other approaches, grounded more closely in the biological aspects of the human being we first encountered in Chapter 2, emphasize the physiological makeup and functioning of the individual. Such theories stress the role of heredity and **maturation**—the unfolding of biologically predetermined patterns of behavior—in producing developmental change. Maturation can be seen, for instance, in the development of sex characteristics (such as breasts or body hair) that occur at the start of adolescence.

On some points, however, agreement exists among developmental psychologists of different theoretical persuasions (Plomin, 1989). It seems clear that genetic factors not only provide the potential for particular behaviors or traits to emerge, they also place limitations on the emergence of such behavior or traits. For instance, heredity defines people's general level of intelligence, setting an upper limit which—regardless of the nature of the environment—people cannot exceed. Heredity also provides limits on physical abilities; humans simply cannot run at a speed of 60 miles an hour, nor are they going to grow as tall as ten feet, no matter what the nature of their environment.

Table 12-1 shows some of the characteristics that are most affected by heredity. As you consider the items on the list, it is important to keep in mind that these characteristics are not *entirely* determined by heredity—merely that the best evidence suggests that variations in these factors are due to a relatively large extent to the genetic makeup of an individual.

In most instances, environmental factors play a critical role in enabling people to reach the potential capabilities provided by their genetic background (Case, 1985; Lamb & Bornstein, 1987). Had Albert Einstein received no intellectual stimulation as a child and not been sent to school, it is unlikely that he would have reached his genetic potential. Similarly, a great athlete like baseball star Willie Mays would have been unlikely to display much physical skill had he not been raised in an environment that nurtured his native talent and gave him the opportunity to train and perfect his natural skills.

TABLE 12-1

Characteristics with Strong Genetic Components

Physical Characteristics	Intellectual Characteristics	Emotional Characteristics and Disorders
Height	Memory	Shyness
Weight	Ability as measured on intelligence tests	Extraversion
Obesity		Emotionality
Tone of voice	Age of language acquisition	Neuroticism
Blood pressure	Reading disability	Schizophrenia
Tooth decay	Mental retardation	Anxiety
Athletic ability		Alcoholism
Firmness of handshake		
Age of death		
Activity level		

Source: Papalia & Olds, 1988; Plomin, 1989.

In sum, developmental psychologists take an **interactionist** position on the nature-nurture issue, suggesting that a combination of genetic predisposition and environmental influences produces development. The challenge facing developmental psychologists is to identify the specific kind and relative strength of each of these influences on the individual.

The search for the influence of nature and nurture is not merely academic. Important advances in our understanding of the optimal way to treat children have come from research on heredity and the environment. For instance, the way in which we educate children, how children in institutions such as orphanages are raised, and the kinds of day-care that are considered optimal have all been influenced by our understanding of the interaction of heredity and environment.

Interactionist: One who believes that a combination of genetic predisposition and environmental influences determine the course of development

ADDRESSING THE NATURE-NURTURE QUESTION

Developmental psychologists have confronted the question of determining the relative influence of genetic and environmental factors on behavior in several different ways, although no technique is foolproof. We can, for example, experimentally control the genetic makeup of laboratory animals, carefully breeding them for specific traits. Just as the people who raise Butterball turkeys have learned to produce a breed that grows particularly quickly (so they can be brought to the marketplace less expensively), psychologists are able to breed strains of laboratory animals who share a similar genetic makeup. By observing animals with a similar genetic background in varied environments, they can then ascertain the effects of particular kinds of environmental stimulation. Ultimately, of course, we do have the problem of generalizing the findings of research with animals to a human population, but the animal findings do provide fundamental information that could not be obtained ethically from human subjects.

The study of identical twins raised separately, as were Linda Lackner and April Yamashire, yields valuable insights into the nature-nurture question. (Courtesy Thomas J. Bouchard, Jr., Minnesota Center for Twin and Adoption Research)

Identical twins: Twins with identical genetic makeup

Human twins also provide us with an important source of information about the relative effects of genetic and environmental factors. If **identical twins** (those who are genetically identical) display different patterns of development, we have to attribute such differences to variations in the environment in which they were raised. The most useful data come from identical twins (such as Gerald Levey and Mark Newman) who are adopted at birth by different sets of foster parents and raised apart from each other in different environments. Studies of nontwin siblings who are raised in different environments also shed some light on the issue. Because they share relatively similar genetic backgrounds, siblings who show similarities as adults provide strong evidence for the importance of heredity.

It is also possible to take the opposite tack. Instead of concentrating on people with similar genetic backgrounds who are raised in different environments, we may consider people raised in similar environments who have totally dissimilar genetic backgrounds. If we find, for example, that two adopted children—who have dissimilar genetic backgrounds—raised in the same family develop similarly, we have evidence for the importance of environmental influences on development. Moreover, it is possible to carry out research with animals with dissimilar genetic backgrounds; by experimentally varying the environment in which they are raised, we can determine the influence of environmental factors, independent of heredity, on development.

STUDYING DEVELOPMENT: Research Methods

The specific research methods used by developmental psychologists to consider the nature-nurture issue, as well as other questions of a developmental nature, tend to fall into two categories: cross-sectional and longitudinal. In **cross-sectional research**, people of different ages are compared at the same point in time. Suppose, for instance, you were interested in the development of intellectual ability in adulthood. To carry out a cross-sectional study, you might compare a sample of 25-, 45-, and 65-year olds on an IQ test, seeing how the average scores differ.

Cross-sectional research: A research method in which people of different ages are compared at the same point in time

Cross-sectional research has pitfalls, however. In our example, for instance, it is possible that any differences you found in IQ scores were due not to age differences per se but to the fact that the average educational level attained by the older subjects was lower than that of the younger sample, since far fewer people went to college forty years ago.

One way around the problem is to conduct **longitudinal research**, in which the behavior of one or more subjects is traced as the subjects age. By examining changes over several points in time, we can best understand how individual people develop. (For an example of one of the most famous longitudinal studies ever conducted, see the Research Classics box.)

Unfortunately, there are drawbacks to longitudinal research: It requires an enormous expenditure of time (as the researcher waits for the subjects to get older), and subjects who participate at an earlier stage may drop out, move away, or even die as the research continues. Moreover, subjects who take the same test at several points in time may become "testwise" and perform better each time they take it, just because they are becoming more familiar with the test.

To make up for the drawbacks of cross-sectional research and longitudinal research, investigators have devised an alternative method. Known as **cross-sequential research**, it combines cross-sectional and longitudinal research by taking a number of different age groups and examining them over several points in time. For example, investigators might use a group of 3-, 5-, and 7-year-olds, examining them every six months for a period of several years. This technique allows the developmental psychologist to tease out the effects of age changes themselves from other potentially contaminating factors.

Longitudinal research: A research method which investigates behavior as subjects age

Cross-sequential research: A research method which combines cross-sectional and longitudinal research

THE FELS LONGITUDINAL STUDY

It was fairly easy for parents of newborns to consent to the first request of developmental psychologists working on the Fels Longitudinal Study: Most readily agreed to permit their child to receive a full battery of psychological and physical tests as part of an experimental investigation. The second part of the request, however, proved a bit more difficult to consent to, for parents were asked to allow intensive testing of their child over the next *eighteen* years.

The reason behind these requests was a massive longitudinal study, begun more than five decades ago, that proved to be a milestone in psychological research. The scrutiny given subjects was close. Until children were 12 years old, they and their mothers were observed in their home every six months. To study social interaction with their peers, children from age 3 to 5 were observed in their preschool (the Fels

Institute nursery school) two times a year, and from age 6 to 12, they were observed at a summer day camp. Other data were also collected in school and home settings, providing a massive data pool that investigators could plumb to answer a wide array of questions.

For instance, one set of psychologists studied patterns of independence and dependence among the Fels subjects (Kagan & Moss, 1962). By looking at ratings of the children's behavior at four stages of life (birth to 3 years, 3 to 6 years, 6 to 10 years, and 10 to 14 years), as well as considering the mothers' behavior at each of those ages, the investigators were able to determine how early behavior was reflected in subsequent

behavior. One of the major findings was the high degree of stability in dependent behavior. Although dependent behavior during the first three years fluctuated a great deal and was unrelated to adult behavior, by the time subjects were in preschool, dependent behavior showed a modest relationship with adult behavior. But by the time subjects were 6 to 10 years of age, their behavior bore a strong resemblance to adult behavior.

The Fels Longitudinal Study allowed researchers to answer questions about stability and change in the behavior of individuals in a way that never before had been possible. And, in what is perhaps the longest ongoing psychological study, the Fels Longitudinal Study continues: Each year, a small group of children are enrolled.

INDIVIDUAL DEVELOPMENT
AND DIFFERENTIATION

Conception: The process by which an egg cell is fertilized by a sperm cell

Zygote: The one-celled product of fertilization

Chromosomes: Rod-shaped structures that contain basic hereditary information

Genes: The parts of a chromosome through which genetic information is transmitted

Our understanding of the biology of the start of life—when a male's sperm cell meets a female's egg cell at the moment of **conception**—makes it no less of a miracle. At that single moment, an individual's genetic endowment is established for the rest of his or her life.

When the egg becomes fertilized by the sperm, the result is a one-celled **zygote** that immediately begins to develop. The zygote contains twenty-three pairs of **chromosomes**, rod-shaped structures that contain the basic hereditary information. One member of each pair is from the mother and the other is from the father. Each chromosome contains thousands of **genes**—smaller units through which genetic information is transmitted—that, either individually or in combination, produce particular characteristics in the individual.

While some genes are responsible for the development of systems common to all members of the human species—the heart, circulatory system, brain, lungs, and so forth—others control the characteristics that make each human unique—facial configuration, height, eye color, and the like. The child's sex is also determined by a particular combination of genes. Specifically, a child inherits an X chromosome from its mother, and either an X or Y chromosome from its father. With an XX combination, it is a female; with an XY combination, it develops as a male. Recent findings suggest that male development is triggered by a single gene on the Y chromosome, and without the presence of that specific gene, the individual will develop as a female (Roberts, 1988).

The moment—and miracle—of conception, when a male's sperm cell meets a female's egg cell. (Dr. Landrum B. Shettles)

Rod-shaped chromosomes carry the basic information of heredity. Each chromosome contains thousands of genes. (Howard Sochurek/Woodfin Camp & Assoc.)

The zygote starts out as a microscopic speck, but as it divides through an intricate preprogrammed system of cell division, it grows 10,000 times larger in just four weeks, to about one-fifth of an inch long. At that point it is called an **embryo** and has developed a rudimentary heart (that beats), a brain, an intestinal tract, and a number of other organs. Although all these organs are at a primitive stage of development, they are clearly recognizable. Moreover, by the eighth week, the embryo is about an inch long, and arms, legs, and face can be deciphered (see Figure 12-1).

Embryo: A developed zygote that has a heart, a brain, and other organs

Following the eighth week, the embryo faces what is known as a **critical period**, the first of several stages in development in which specific kinds of growth must occur if the individual is to develop normally. For example, if the eyes and ears do not develop during this stage, they will never form later on, and if they form abnormally, they are permanently damaged. During critical periods, organisms are particularly sensitive to environmental influences such as the presence of certain kinds of drugs, which, as we will see later, can have a devastating effect on subsequent development (Bornstein, 1987; 1989).

Critical period: The first of several stages of development in which specific kinds of growth must occur to enable further normal development

Beginning in the ninth week and continuing until birth, the developing individual is called a **fetus**. At the start of this period, it begins to be responsive to touch; it bends its fingers when touched on the hand. At 16 to 18 weeks, its movements become strong enough for the mother to sense the baby. At the same time, hair may begin to grow on the baby's head, and the facial features become similar to those the child will display at birth. The major organs begin to function, although the fetus could not be kept alive outside the mother. In addition, a lifetime's worth of brain neurons have been produced—although it is unclear whether the brain is capable of thinking in any real sense at this early stage.

Fetus: A developing child, from nine weeks after conception until birth

By the twenty-fourth week, a fetus has many of the characteristics it will display as a newborn. In fact, when an infant is born prematurely at this age, it can open and close its eyes; suck; cry; look up, down, and around; and even grasp things placed in its hands, although it is still unable to survive for long outside the mother.

The fetus continues to develop prior to birth. It begins to grow fatty

FIGURE 12-1

These remarkable photos of live fetuses display the degree of physical development at 4 and 15 weeks. [(*Left*) Lennart Nilsson, *A Child Is Born*/Dell Publishing, Inc., (*Right*) Petit Format/Science Source/Photo Researchers.]

Age of viability: The point at which a fetus can survive if born prematurely

deposits under the skin and it gains weight. The fetus reaches the **age of viability**, the point at which it can survive if born prematurely, at about 28 weeks, although through advances in medical technology, this crucial age is getting earlier. At 28 weeks, the fetus weighs about three pounds and is about 16 inches long. It may be capable of learning: One study found that the infants of mothers who read a certain Dr. Seuss story aloud prior to birth preferred the sound of the Dr. Seuss story over other stories after they were born (Spence & DeCasper, 1982).

In the final weeks of pregnancy, the fetus continues to put on weight and grow, becoming increasingly fit. At the end of the normal 38 weeks of pregnancy the fetus typically weighs around $7\frac{1}{2}$ pounds and is about 20 inches in length.

Genetic Influences on the Fetus

The process of fetal growth that we have been discussing reflects normal development—something that happens in 95 to 98 percent of all pregnancies. Some people are less fortunate, for in the remaining 2 to 5 percent of the cases, children are delivered with major birth defects. One prime cause of such defects is genetic: The information in the chromosomes inherited from one or both of the parents causes a problem. Here are some of the most common genetic difficulties.

Phenylketonuria (FEEN ul kee toe NYUR ee uh) (PKU): The inability to produce an enzyme that resists certain poisons, causing profound mental retardation

▶ *Phenylketonuria (PKU).* A child born with the inherited disease **phenylketonuria** (PKU) cannot produce an enzyme that is required for normal development. This results in accumulation of poisons that eventually cause profound mental retardation. The disease is treatable, however; if it is caught early enough—and most infants today are routinely tested för PKU—children can be placed on a special diet which allows them to develop normally.

Sickle-cell anemia: A disease of the blood that affects about 10 percent of America's black population

▶ *Sickle-cell anemia.* About 10 percent of the American black population has the possibility of passing on **sickle-cell anemia**, a disease that gets its name from the abnormal shape of the red blood cells. Children with the disease may have poor appetites, swollen stomachs, and yellowish eyes; they rarely live beyond childhood.

Tay-Sachs (TAY SAKS) disease: A genetic defect preventing the body from breaking down fat and typically causing death by the age of 3 or 4

▶ *Tay-Sachs disease.* Children born with **Tay-Sachs disease**, a problem found most often in Jews of eastern European ancestry, usually die by the age of 3 or 4 because of the body's inability to break down fat. If both parents carry the genetic defect producing the illness, their child has a 1-in-4 chance of being born with the disease (Navon & Proia, 1989).

Down's syndrome: A disorder caused by the presence of an extra chromosome, resulting in mental retardation

▶ *Down's syndrome.* In Chapter 8, we discussed **Down's syndrome** as a cause of mental retardation. Down's syndrome is brought about not by an inherited trait passed on by the parents, but by a malfunction whereby the zygote receives an extra chromosome at the moment of conception, causing retardation and an unusual physical appearance (which led to an earlier label for the disease: mongolism). Down's syndrome is related to the mother's and father's age; mothers over 35, in particular, stand a higher risk of having a child with the problem.

Prenatal Environmental Influences

Genetic factors are *not* the only causes of difficulties in fetal development; a number of environmental factors also have an effect on the course of development. The major prenatal environmental influences include:

▶ *The mother's nutrition and state of mind.* What a mother eats during her pregnancy can have important implications for the health of her baby. Mothers who are seriously undernourished cannot provide adequate nutrition to the growing baby, and they are likely to give birth to underweight babies or to babies that are more susceptible to disease (Wyden, 1971). Moreover, there is some evidence that the mother's emotional state affects the baby. Mothers who are anxious and tense during the end of their pregnancies are more apt to have infants who are irritable and who sleep and eat poorly (Kagan, Kearsley & Zelazo, 1978). The reason? One hypothesis is that the autonomic nervous system of the fetus becomes especially sensitive as a result of the chemical changes produced by the mother's emotional state.

▶ *Illness of mother.* During 1964 and 1965 an epidemic of **rubella**, or German measles, in the United States resulted in the prenatal death or malformation of close to 50,000 children. Although the disease has relatively minor effects on the mother when contracted during the early part of pregnancy, it is one of a number of illnesses that can have devastating results on the developing fetus. Other maternal diseases that may produce a permanent effect on the fetus include syphilis, diabetes, and high blood pressure.

Rubella: German measles; when contracted by pregnant women, it can cause severe birth defects

AIDS—acquired immune deficiency syndrome—can be passed from mother to child. Sadly, in many cases mothers may not even know they carry the disease and inadvertently transmit it to their children. According to some evidence, the AIDS virus can also be passed on through breast feeding after birth (Heyward & Curran, 1988).

▶ *Mother's drug intake.* Drugs taken by a pregnant woman can have a tragic effect on the unborn child. Probably the most dramatic example was the use of thalidomide, a tranquilizer that was widely prescribed during the 1960s—until it was discovered that it caused such severe birth defects as the absence of arms and legs. The hormone diethylstilbestrol (DES), prescribed until the 1950s to prevent miscarriages, is now known to have placed children of mothers who took it at risk for abnormalities of the cervix and vagina and for developing cancer of the uterus in the case of daughters, and for infertility and reproductive problems in the case of sons.

Alcohol and nicotine are also dangerous to fetal development. For example, **fetal alcohol syndrome**, an ailment resulting in mental and growth

Fetal alcohol syndrome: An ailment producing mental and physical retardation in a baby as a result of the mother's high alcohol intake while pregnant

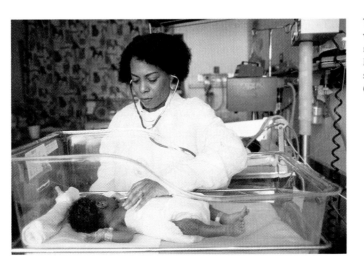

This infant, the child of a cocaine addict, was born addicted. He is undergoing treatment by Dr. Xylina Bean of King Drew Medical Center, Los Angeles for the painful symptoms of withdrawal from the drug. (John Livzey/*Time* Magazine)

retardation, has been found in the children of mothers who consumed high levels of alcohol during pregnancy. Moreover, mothers who take physically addictive drugs run the risk of giving birth to babies similarly addicted, and their newborns suffer painful withdrawal symptoms after birth (Chavez et al., 1979; Miller, 1986).

▶ *Birth complications.* Although most births occur without complication, the process sometimes goes awry, resulting in injury to the infant. For example, the umbilical cord connecting the baby to the mother may become compressed, withholding oxygen from the child. If this occurs for too long, the child may suffer permanent brain damage.

A number of other environmental factors have an impact upon the child prior to and during birth (see Table 12-2). It is important to keep in mind, however, that development represents the interaction of environmental and genetic influences, and that—although we have been discussing the influences of genetics and environment separately—neither factor works alone. Moreover, while we have been flagging some of the points at which development can go awry, the vast majority of births occur without difficulty, and development follows normal patterns—which we discuss next.

TABLE 12-2

Environmental Factors Affecting Prenatal Development

Factor	Possible Effect
Rubella (German measles)	Blindness, deafness, heart abnormalities, stillbirth
Syphilis	Mental retardation, physical deformities, maternal miscarriage
Addictive drugs	Low birth weight, addiction of infant to drug, with possible death, after birth, from withdrawal
Smoking	Premature birth, low birth weight and length
Alcohol	Mental retardation, lower-than-average birth weight, small head, limb deformities
Radiation from x-rays	Physical deformities, mental retardation
Inadequate diet	Reduction in growth of brain, smaller-than-average weight and length at birth
Mother's age—younger than 18 at birth of child	Premature birth, increased incidence of Down's syndrome
Mother's age—older than 35 at birth of child	Increased incidence of Down's syndrome
DES (diethylstilbestrol)	Reproductive difficulties and increased incidence of genital cancer in children of mothers who were given DES during pregnancy to prevent miscarriage

Source: Adapted from Schikendanz, Schikendanz & Forsyth, 1982, p. 95.

Recap

◄ A fundamental issue of developmental psychology is the nature-nurture question, which seeks to determine the relative influence of environmental and genetic factors on development.

◄ During the course of prenatal development, the one-cell zygote evolves into an embryo and subsequently a fetus. Birth typically occurs 38 weeks after conception.

◄ The major difficulties caused by genetic factors are sickle-cell anemia, phenylketonuria (PKU), Tay-Sachs disease, and Down's syndrome. Among the primary environmental influences on prenatal development and newborn health are the mother's nutrition, state of health, and drug intake, and the nature of the baby's delivery.

Review

1. Contemporary developmental psychologists tend to hold a(n) _____ view of the nature-nurture debate.

2. Height, weight, intelligence test scores, and emotionality have been shown to be strongly affected by _____ (genetic/environmental) factors.

3. The age of viability is the stage at which
   a. a fetus can survive if born prematurely.
   b. an embryo is most susceptible to developmental defects.
   c. a newborn is first able to control its own movements.
   d. the chromosomes of the parents first determine a baby's characteristics.

4. Number, from earliest to latest, the following stages of human development.
   ____ Fetus
   ____ Egg/sperm
   ____ Embryo
   ____ Zygote

5. Dr. Jackson described the birth of an infant who lacked the ability to produce an enzyme necessary for human development. Fortunately, early medical testing and intervention saved the infant from a life of profound mental retardation. The genetic disease she described was
   a. Down's syndrome.
   b. phenylketonuria (PKU).
   c. Tay Sachs disease.
   d. sickle-cell anemia.

(Answers to review questions are on page 424.)

HOW WE DEVELOP PHYSICALLY AND SOCIALLY

His head was molded into a long melon shape and came to a point at the back. . . . He was covered with a thick, greasy white material known as "vernix," which made him slippery to hold, and also allowed him to slip easily through the birth canal. In addition to a shock of black hair on his head, his body was covered with dark, fine hair known as "lanugo." His ears, his back, his shoulders, and even his cheeks were furry. . . . His skin was wrinkled and quite loose, ready to scale in creased places such as his feet and hands. The hair, matted with vernix, gave an odd, pasted appearance. . . . His ears were pressed to his head in unusual positions—one ear was matted firmly forward on his cheek. His nose was flattened and pushed to one side by the squeeze as he came through the pelvis (Brazelton, 1969, p. 3).

What kind of creature is this? Although the description hardly fits the Gerber baby in commercials, we are in fact talking about a normal, completely developed child just after the moment of birth. Called a **neonate**, the newborn presents itself to the world in a form that hardly meets the typical standards of beauty against which we normally measure others. Yet ask any parent: No sight is more beautiful or exciting than the first glimpse of their newborn.

Neonate: A newborn child

The neonate's less-than-perfect appearance is brought about by a number of factors. Its travels through its mother's birth canal may have squeezed the incompletely formed bones of the skull together and squashed the nose

424

Vernix: A white lubricant that covers a fetus, protecting it during birth

Lanugo (lan OO go): A soft fuzz covering the body of a newborn

Reflexes: Unlearned, involuntary responses to certain stimuli

Rooting reflex: A neonate's tendency to turn its head toward things that touch its cheek

Sucking reflex: A reflex that prompts an infant to suck at things that touch its lips

Gag reflex: An infant's reflex to clear its throat

Moro (startle) reflex: The reflex action in which an infant, in response to a sudden noise, flings its arms, arches its back, and spreads its fingers

Babinski reflex: The reflex action in which an infant fans out its toes in response to a stroke on the outside of its foot

into the head. It is covered with **vernix**, a white, greasy material which is secreted to protect its skin prior to birth, and it may have **lanugo**, a soft fuzz, over its entire body. Its eyelids may be puffy with an accumulation of fluids because of its upside-down position during birth.

All this changes during the first two weeks of life, as the neonate takes on a more familiar appearance. Even more impressive are the capabilities that the neonate begins to display from the time it is born—capabilities that grow at an astounding rate over the ensuing months and years.

The neonate is born with a number of **reflexes**—unlearned, involuntary responses that occur automatically in the presence of certain stimuli. Many of these reflexes are critical for survival and unfold naturally as a part of an infant's ongoing maturation. The **rooting reflex**, for instance, causes neonates to turn their heads toward things that touch their cheeks—such as a nipple of a mother's breast or a bottle. Similarly, a **sucking reflex** prompts the infant to suck at things that touch its lips. Among the other reflexes are a **gag reflex** (to clear its throat); the **Moro**, or **startle**, **reflex** (a series of movements in which the infant flings out its arms, fans it fingers, and arches its back in response to a sudden noise); and the **Babinski reflex** (the baby's toes fan out when the outer edge of the sole of its foot is stroked).

As these primitive reflexes are lost after the first few months of life, they are replaced by more complex and organized behaviors. Although at birth the neonate is capable of only jerky, limited voluntary movement, during the first year of life the capability to move independently grows enormously. The typical baby is able to roll over by the age of 3 months; at 6 months it can sit without support; it stands alone at about $11\frac{1}{2}$ months; and by the time it is just over a year old, a baby has begun to walk. Not only does the ability to make large-scale movements improve during this time, but fine-muscle movements also become increasingly sophisticated (as illustrated in Figure 12-2).

GROWTH AFTER BIRTH

Perhaps the most obvious sign of development is the physical growth of the child. During the first year of life, children typically triple their birth weight, and their height increases by about half. This rapid growth slows down as the child gets older—think how gigantic adults would be if that rate of growth were constant—and the average rate of growth from age 3 to the beginning of adolescence, around age 13, is a gain of about 5 pounds and 3 inches a year.

The physical changes that occur as children develop are not just a matter of increasing growth; the relationship of the size of the various body parts to one another changes dramatically as children age. As you can see in Figure 12-3, the head of the fetus (and the newborn) is disproportionally large. However, the head soon becomes more in proportion to the rest of the body as growth occurs mainly in the trunk and legs.

TAKING IN THE WORLD: Development of Perception

When proud parents pick up the neonate and peer into its eyes, is the child able to return their gaze? Although it was thought for some time that new-

The grasp reflex is one of the behaviors that is characteristic of newborns. (Elizabeth Crews/The Image Works)

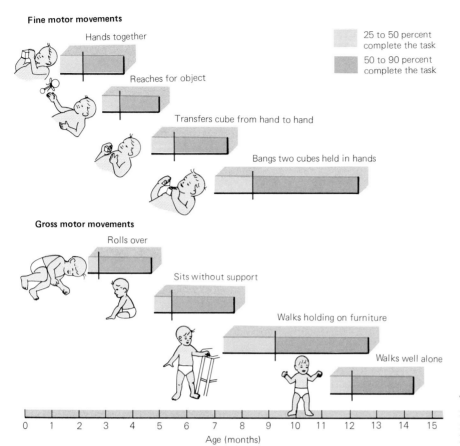

FIGURE 12-2

These landmarks of physical development illustrate the range of ages at which most infants learn various physical tasks. (Frankenburg & Dodds, 1967.)

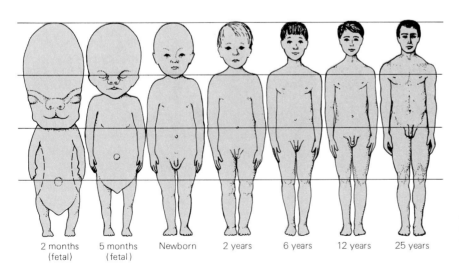

FIGURE 12-3

As development progresses, the relative size of the head—in relation to the rest of the body—decreases until adulthood is reached. (Adopted from Robbins, 1929.)

borns could see only a hazy blur, most current findings indicate that the capabilities of neonates are much more impressive (Aslin & Smith, 1988). Their eyes have limited capacity to modify the shape of the lens, making it difficult to focus on objects that are not within a 7- to 8-inch distance from the face, yet neonates are able to follow objects moving within their field of vision (Bornstein, 1984; Cohen, DeLoache & Strauss, 1979). They also show

Habituation: A decrease in responding to repeated presentations of the same stimulus

By measuring the vigor with which this baby sucks on a nipple, this developmental psychologist is able to determine the baby's interest in the picture being projected on the screen. (Enrico Ferorelli)

the rudiments of depth perception, as they react by raising their hands when an object appears to be moving rapidly toward the face.

You might think that it would be hard to figure out just how well neonates are able to see, since their lack of language ability clearly prevents them from saying what direction the E on a vision chart is facing—even if they were able to read. However, a number of ingenious methods, which rely on physiological responses and innate reflexes of the newborn, have been devised to test their perceptual skills (Hay, 1986).

One important technique relies on changes in an infant's heart rate, for heart rate is closely correlated with the baby's reaction to a stimulus that he or she is looking at—a phenomenon known as habituation. **Habituation** is a decrease in responding to repeated presentations of the same stimulus. Infants who are shown a novel stimulus will pay close attention to it, and their heart rates will show a change in speed. But if the infant is repeatedly shown the same stimulus, his or her attention to it decreases, as indicated by the return to a normal heart rate—showing that habituation has occurred.

However, when a new stimulus is subsequently presented, once again a discernible change in heart rate occurs *if* the child is able to detect that the new stimulus is different from the old one. Using this technique, then, developmental psychologists can tell when a stimulus can be detected and discriminated by a child too young to speak (Bornstein, 1984).

Researchers have developed a number of other methods of measuring neonate and infant perception. In one technique, for instance, babies suck on a nipple attached to a computer; a change in the rate and vigor with which they suck is used to infer that they can perceive variations in stimuli (Milewski, 1976). In other studies, researchers examine babies' eye movements (Hainline & Lemerise, 1982), while still other investigators simply observe which way babies move their heads when presented with a visual stimulus (Kolata, 1987).

Using such research techniques, we now know that infants' visual perception is remarkably sophisticated from the very start of life. At birth, babies show preferences for patterns with contours and edges over less distinct patterns, indicating that they are capable of responding to the configuration of stimuli. In fact, neonates have the skill to discriminate facial expressions—and even to imitate them (Field, 1982). As you can see in Figure 12-4, newborns exposed to an adult with a happy, sad, or surprised facial expression are able to produce a good imitation of the adult's expression. Even newborn children, then, have the capability of responding to the emotions and moods that their care givers' facial expressions reveal.

Other visual abilities grow rapidly after birth. By the end of their first month, babies can distinguish some colors from others, and after 4 months they can readily focus on near or far objects. By 4 or 5 months, they are able to recognize two- and three-dimensional objects, and they can make use of the gestalt patterns that we discussed in relation to adult perception in Chapter 4 (Smith, 1987). Furthermore, there are rapid improvements in perceptual abilities: Sensitivity to visual stimuli, for instance, becomes three to four times greater at 1 year of age than it was at birth (Aslin & Smith, 1988; Norcia & Tyler, 1985).

In addition to vision, newborns' other sensory capabilities are quite impressive. They can distinguish different sounds to the point of being able to recognize their own mothers' voices at the age of three days (DeCasper & Fifer, 1980). They are also capable of making subtle linguistic distinctions

FIGURE 12-4

This newborn infant is clearly imitating the happy, sad, and surprised expressions of the adult model in these amazing photos. (Courtesy of Dr. Tiffany Field.)

that underlie the language abilities we discussed in Chapter 7: At 4 days of age babies can discriminate between such closely related sounds as *ba* and *pa,* and they are soon able to distinguish between their native tongue and foreign languages (Jusczyk & Derrah, 1987; Jusczyk, 1986). By 6 months of age, they are capable of discriminating virtually any difference in sound that is relevant to the production of language (Aslin, 1987). Moreover, they are capable of discriminating different tastes and smells at a very early age (Steiner, 1979). There even seems to be something of a built-in sweet tooth: The neonate prefers liquids that have been sweetened with sugar over their unsweetened counterparts.

As anyone who has seen an infant smiling at the sight of its mother can guess, at the same time infants are growing physically and perceptually, they are also developing socially. In fact, the nature of a child's early social development provides the foundation for social relationships that will last a lifetime.

Attachment: The positive emotional bond that develops between parents and their children

Attachment, the positive emotional bond that develops between a child and a particular individual, is the most important form of social development that occurs during infancy. One of the first investigators to demonstrate the importance and nature of attachment was psychologist Harry Harlow. Harlow found that infant monkeys who were given the choice of a wire "monkey" that provided food or a soft, terrycloth "monkey" that was warm but did not provide food, clearly preferred the cloth one, although they made occasional forays to the wire monkey to nurse (Harlow & Zimmerman, 1959). Clearly, the cloth monkey provided greater comfort to the infants; food alone was insufficient to create attachment (see Figure 12-5).

Building on this initial work, other researchers have suggested that attachment grows through the responsiveness of infants' care givers to the signals the babies provide, such as cries, smiles, reaching, and clinging. The greater the responsiveness of the care giver to the child's signals, the more likely it is that a secure attachment bond will be formed. Full attachment eventually develops as a result of a complex series of interactions between care giver and child known as the Attachment Behavioral System, illustrated in Figure 12-6 (Bell & Ainsworth, 1972). It is important to note that the infant plays as critical and active a role in the formation of an attachment bond as the care giver; infants who respond positively to a care giver promote more positive behavior on the part of the care giver, which in turn elicits even greater attachment from the child.

At what point does attachment begin? According to a hypothesis put forward by Marshall Klaus and John Kennell (1976), a critical period takes

Although the wire "mother" dispensed milk to the hungry infant monkey, the soft, terry-cloth "mother" was preferred. (Harry Harlow Primate Laboratory/University of Wisconsin.)

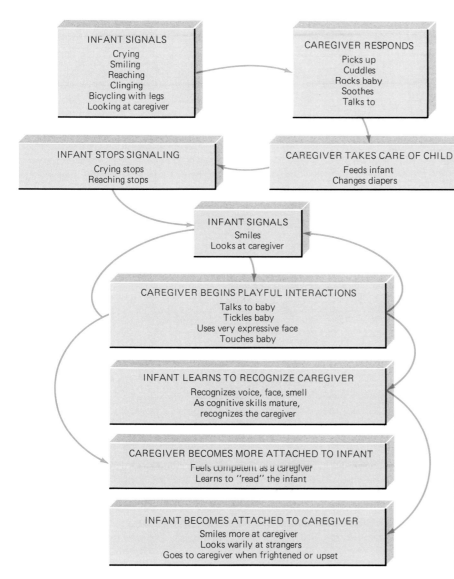

FIGURE 12-6

The Attachment Behavioral System shows the sequence of activities that infants employ to keep their primary caregivers physically close and to bring about attachment. Early in life, crying is the most effective behavior. Later, though, infants are able to keep the caregiver near through other, more socially appropriate behaviors such as smiling, looking, and reaching. After they are able to walk, children are able to play a more active role in staying close to the caregiver. At the same time, the caregiver's behavior interacts with the baby's activities to promote attachment. (Tomlinson, 1985.)

place just after birth. During this juncture, lasting only a few hours, skin-to-skin contact between mother and child was said to lead to emotional bonding. Because the hypothesis received wide publicity, many hospitals changed their procedures to allow immediate contact between newly born children and their parents.

It now appears, however, that there is little support for the hypothesis. Although it does seem that mothers who had early physical contact with their babies were more responsive to them, the effect lasted for only three days. Furthermore, there seems to be no lasting consequences of separation after birth, even when it lasts as long as several days (Goldberg, 1983; Lamb, 1982). For parents who adopt children, or who, because of illness of the child or some other reason, miss out on the opportunity for contact with their child just after its birth, such news is certainly reassuring. (Although skin-to-skin contact does not seem to be crucial for bonding, recent evidence does suggest that physical contact plays a crucial role in the child's development, as we discuss in the Cutting Edge box.)

As her baby fusses and cries, a mother reaches over and gently strokes her newborn infant. The baby stops whimpering and instead begins to coo gently.

Although it is clear that stroking can have a calming influence on newborns, some intriguing new evidence suggests that touch does more than soothe a baby: it may trigger a complex chemical reaction that begins in the baby's brain and allows the baby to grow and thrive.

According to newly discovered evidence, touch has benefits well beyond the communication of affection. Developmental psychologist Tiffany Field (1988) found that premature babies who were massaged for fifteen minutes three times a day gained weight some 50 percent faster than a control group of premature babies who were not massaged and were left in their incubators. The massaged babies also became more active than the control group and more responsive to stimuli such as faces and rattles, suggesting that their nervous systems developed more rapidly. Their greater weight gain seemed attributable to the contact itself: The massaged babies did not eat more than children in the control group but seemed instead to have a more efficient metabolism.

Massage had other effects, as

THE BENEFITS OF TOUCH START IN THE BRAIN

well. The children who were touched were discharged earlier from the hospital, and the medical costs of the massaged infants averaged $3,000 less than those for children in the control group. Furthermore, the effects were long-lasting: Eight months later, the massaged infants performed better on measures of mental and physical abilities than did the unmassaged babies, and they weighed more as well. Touch, apparently, is a potent factor in growth and development.

An explanation for the benefits of touching comes from work with rats carried out by Saul Schanberg, who, in one of the best examples of how research with laboratory animals has led directly to practical applications, studied the behavior of rat pups that were deprived of maternal contact (Schanberg & Field, 1987). Schanberg found that such rats neither gained weight nor developed according to a normal schedule. The reason could be traced to the release of the brain chemical beta-endorphin that occurred during the mother's absence. Apparently, the chemical led to a slowing of metabo-

lism, which subsequently stunted the growth of the organism.

On the other hand, by mimicking a mother's touch, Schanberg was able to reverse the effects of deprivation by inhibiting the release of beta-endorphin. He found that stroking baby rats with a wet paintbrush—the equivalent of a rat mother's wet, rough tongue—kept the beta-endorphin levels under control in deprived rats and led to an increase in the production of proteins and weight gain. Obviously, then, stroking produces important biological effects.

It is not just any touch, however, that yields the beneficial effects of stroking. Field says that a gentle, slow, but firm touch is best. Too light a touch can irritate an infant; too heavy a touch, of course, can hurt a child. Moreover, different kinds of massage produce different effects: to soothe an infant, a light massage on its back and legs or gentle strokes are beneficial. In contrast, a baby will be stimulated by stroking on its face, stomach, or feet (Goleman, 1988).

Clearly, touch plays an important role in the development of infants. As evidence increases on the importance of physical contact in early life (e.g., Meaney et al., 1988), learning to massage a child effectively may become as important as learning what kind of food is best.

Measuring Attachment

Developmental psychologists have devised a quick and direct way of measuring attachment, known as the strange situation. Developed by Mary Ainsworth, the **Ainsworth strange situation** consists of a sequence of events involving a child and (typically) his or her mother. Initially, the mother and baby enter an unfamiliar room, and the mother permits the baby to explore while she sits down. An adult stranger then enters the room, after which the mother leaves. The mother then returns, and the stranger leaves. The mother then once again leaves the baby alone, and the stranger returns. Finally, the stranger leaves, and the mother returns (Ainsworth et al., 1978).

Babies' reactions to the strange situation vary drastically, depending on their degree of attachment to the mother. One-year-old children who are labeled "securely attached" employ the mother as a kind of home base, exploring independently but returning to her occasionally. When she leaves,

The Ainsworth strange situation: A sequence of events involving a child and his or her mother that provide a measurement of attachment they exhibit distress, and they go to her when she returns. Children termed "avoidant" do not cry when the mother leaves, but they seem to avoid her when she returns, appearing to be angry with her. Finally, "ambivalent" children display anxiety before they are separated and are upset when the mother leaves, but they may show ambivalent reactions to her return such as seeking close contact but simultaneously hitting and kicking her.

The nature of attachment between children and their mothers has far-reaching consequences on later development. For example, one study found that boys who were securely attached at age 1 showed fewer psychological difficulties when they were older than did avoidant or ambivalent youngsters (Lewis et al., 1984). Moreover, children who are securely attached to their mothers tend to be more socially and emotionally competent than their less securely attached peers, and they are viewed as more cooperative, capable, and playful (Sroufe, Fox & Pancake, 1983).

The Father's Role

For many years, the father stood in the shadows behind the mother—at least as far as developmental research was concerned. Because traditionally it was thought that the mother-infant bond was the most crucial in a child's life, researchers in earlier decades focused on the mother's relationship with her children. However, the last ten years have seen a host of studies which focus on fathers and their interactions with their children (Lamb, 1987).

Although by and large fathers still spend less time caring for and playing with their children than do mothers—even in households in which both parents are employed full time—fathers can produce attachment bonds as strong as those between mothers and their children. Furthermore, children can be simultaneously attached to both their parents (Lamb, 1982). Yet the nature of attachment is not always identical between mothers and fathers. For instance, infants tend to prefer to be soothed by their mothers, even though fathers are just as adept at comforting and nurturing babies.

The reason for differences in attachment between mothers and fathers may be that mothers spend a greater proportion of their time feeding and directly nurturing their children, whereas fathers spend more time, proportionally, playing with them (Parke, 1981). Moreover, the quality of fathers' play is often different from that of mothers. Fathers engage in more physical, rough-and-tumble sorts of activities, whereas mothers play more verbally oriented games and traditional physical ones such as peekaboo. Such differences in play style are very pronounced, and occur even in the small minority of families in which the mother works to support the family and the father stays at home with the children (Field, 1978; Power & Parke, 1982).

Despite the differences between the behavior of fathers and mothers, each parent is an important attachment figure and plays a major role in the social development of a child. Furthermore, it is becoming increasingly apparent that the amount of time an adult spends with a child is less important than the quality of that time (Hetherington & Parke, 1986).

Social Relationships with Peers

If you have ever seen a preschooler rushing off to play with a neighborhood friend, you know the enjoyment that children derive from being with their peers. In fact, such friendships are crucial to a child's social development. According to development psychologist Willard Hartup, experience is necessary both in "vertical" relationships (those with people of greater knowl-

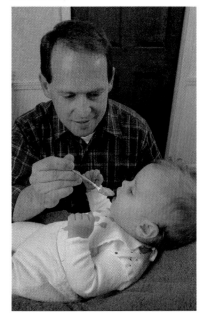

In recent years, fathers have taken a more active role in child care. (David Perdew/ Stock South.)

edge and social power, such as parents) *and* in "horizontal" relationships (those with people who have the same amount of knowledge and social power) in order for effective social competence to develop (Hartup, 1989).

From the age of 2 years, children become less dependent on their parents and more self-reliant, increasingly preferring to play with friends. Initially, play is relatively independent. Two-year-olds pay more attention to toys than to one another when playing. Later, however, children actively interact, modifying one another's behavior and later exchanging roles during play.

As children reach school age, their social interactions become increasingly formalized, as well as more frequent. They may engage in elaborate games, in which they pretend to be superheroes on another planet, and work out elaborate scenarios. Play also becomes more structured, involving teams and games with rigid rules (Mueller & Lucas, 1975).

It is important to realize that children's play serves other purposes than mere enjoyment. It allows them to become increasingly competent in their social interactions with others, learning to take the perspective of other people and to infer others' thoughts and feelings, even when they are not being directly expressed. Furthermore, they learn self-control: They avoid hitting an adversary who bests them, they learn to be polite, and they learn to control their emotional displays and facial expressions, smiling even when receiving a disappointing gift (Selman et al., 1983; Feldman, 1982). Situations that provide children with opportunities for social interaction, then, may enhance their social development—a point illustrated in the Psychology at Work box, which considers the effects of day-care on children.

PSYCHOLOGY AT WORK

WHO IS TAKING CARE OF THE CHILDREN?: DETERMINING THE EFFECTS OF DAY-CARE

A mother and her 3-year-old son head off together at the start of the day. But they are not out for a day's excursion; instead, they head to a day-care center near the mother's office. She says goodbye to her son and leaves for work for the day, knowing that she will not see him again until she picks him up some nine hours later. It is a scene that she and her son repeat five days a week, every week of the year—except during the mother's two weeks of vacation.

One of the biggest societal changes to occur over the last two decades is the upsurge in the number of children enrolled in day-care centers. Roughly a million children, some still in their infancy, are looked after by paid child-care workers, generally in centers outside the home, from a couple of hours a day to all day long. To parents contemplating enrolling their children in such a center, cer-

tain questions are critical: What are the effects of day-care on children? How early can children start? What separates good day-care from bad? Because day-care is a necessity in many families with two working parents or in single-parent families, such questions take on particular urgency.

Fortunately, initial answers to these questions have begun to emerge as a result of research conducted during the last twenty years, and—although the long-term consequences of day-care have yet to be determined definitely—the results are encouraging: Children who attend high-quality day-care centers may not only do as well as children who stay at home with their parents

but in some cases may actually do better (Clarke-Stewart, 1989; Bee, 1985; Scarr, 1986). Among the specific findings that support this suggestion are the following:

● Intellectual development. For children from poor or disadvantaged homes, day-care in specially enriched environments—those with many toys, books, a variety of children and high-quality care providers—may prove to be more intellectually stimulating than the home environment. Such day-care can lead to increased intellectual achievement in terms of higher IQ scores and better language development. For instance, in one study (Ramey, 1981) children from poor families who attended a special day-care center from 2 months until 3 years of age showed higher IQ scores than those who were reared at home (see Figure 12-7). Other researchers have found similar results with children from impoverished backgrounds. The results are less positive with middle- and upper-class families; day-care does *not* seem to improve intellectual performance—nor does it hurt it. The conclusion: Children from middle- and upper-class families—who may already come from intellectually stimulating environments—will not suffer intellectually from day-care, whereas, children from disadvantaged homes can actually benefit intellectually from day-care because of the increased stimulation provided.

● Relationship with parents. Are children less attached to their mothers and fathers when they spend part of the day being cared for by others? This question—raised by many critics of day-care—is a difficult one to answer, and the research on the issue is contradictory. Some evidence suggests that infants who are involved in outside care more than twenty hours a week in their first year show less attachment to their mothers than do those who have not been in day-care (Belsky & Rovine, 1988). On the other hand, most other research finds little or no difference in the strength of parental attachment bonds of infants and toddlers who have been in day-care and those raised solely by their parents, regardless of how long they have been in day-care. Moreover, there is no evidence that children in day-care centers are more attached to the day-care workers than to their parents; in fact, they almost always appear to be more attached to their parents (Rutter, 1982; Ragozin, 1980). In sum, evidence is lacking that children who are in day-care are less attached to their parents than those who are not in day-care.

● Peer relationships. Some difference between children in day-care and those who spend their days at home is revealed in the nature of their peer relationships: Although the data are inconsistent, some studies have found that day-care children are more aggressive and assertive than their peers (e.g., McKinney & Edgerton, 1983). Aside from these findings, no other differences in the quality of peer relationships have emerged from the research on day-care.

In sum, most research has found little difference between children who have been in day-care and those who have not—a comforting state of affairs for parents concerned about the effects of day-care on their children (Deutsch, Jordan, & Deutsch, 1985). Furthermore, long-term follow-up research shows that first-, third-, and fifth-graders whose mothers worked performed better academically, were more socially adjusted, and were more self-reliant than children whose mothers did not work. They were also more involved in school activities and scored higher in IQ tests (Scarr, 1986).

Yet there are many unanswered questions: Is there an age before which day-care should be avoided? How do the effects of good day-care centers differ from the effects of less optimal centers? Does it matter what kind of day-care curriculum is used? What are the critical characteristics to consider when choosing a day-care center? Given the necessity of employment for a significant proportion of the parent population, these questions must be addressed. For many people, then, the significant issue is not whether to choose day-care, but how to make their child's experience as positive as possible (Clarke-Stewart, 1989).

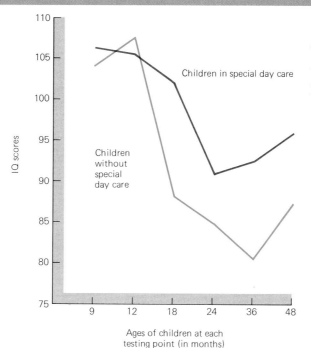

FIGURE 12-7

According to the results of one study, the IQ test scores of children in a day-care center were higher than a comparison group of children raised at home during the day by their mothers. (Ramey, 1981.)

Children in special day care

Children without special day care

IQ scores

Ages of children at each testing point (in months)

INDIVIDUAL DEVELOPMENT
AND DIFFERENTIATION

Authoritarian parents: Parents who are firm and punitive, and who value unquestioning obedience from their children

Permissive parents: Parents who are lax, inconsistent and undemanding, yet warm toward their children

Authoritative parents: Parents who are firm, set clear limits, reason with and explain things to their children

Temperament: Basic, innate disposition

Psychosocial development: Development of individuals' interactions and understanding of each other and of their knowledge and understanding of themselves as members of society

Trust-versus-mistrust stage: According to Erikson, the first stage of psychosocial development, occurring from birth to 18 months of age, during which time infants develop feelings of trust or lack of trust

Although many advances that take place in social development are prompted by peer interaction, parents' child-rearing patterns also shape their children's social competence. Psychologist Diana Baumrind (1971) found that parental styles fall into three main categories. **Authoritarian parents** are firm and punitive and value unquestioning obedience from their children. They have rigid standards and discourage expressions of disagreement. **Permissive parents** give their children lax or inconsistent direction and, although warm, require little of them. Finally, **authoritative parents** are firm, setting limits for their children. As the children get older, these parents try to reason and explain things to them. They also set clear goals and encourage their children's independence.

As you might expect, the three kinds of child-rearing styles were associated with very different kinds of behavior in their children (although there were, of course, many exceptions). Children of authoritarian parents tend to be unsociable, unfriendly, and relatively withdrawn. In contrast, permissive parents' children are immature, moody, and dependent and have low self-control. The children of authoritative parents fare best: Their social skills are high—they are likable, self-reliant, independent, and cooperative.

Before we rush to congratulate authoritative parents and condemn authoritarian and permissive ones, it is important to note that in many cases authoritarian and permissive parents produce children who are perfectly well adjusted. Moreover, children are born with particular **temperaments**—basic, innate dispositions. Some are naturally warm and cuddly, whereas others are irritable and fussy. The kind of temperament a baby is born with may in part elicit particular kinds of parental child-rearing styles. Hence, the upbringing a child receives is a function not just of what child-rearing philosophy a parent holds and employs, but the nature of the child's personality. As is the case with almost all development, then, behavior is a function of a complex interaction of environmental and genetic factors.

ERIKSON'S THEORY OF PSYCHOSOCIAL DEVELOPMENT

In trying to trace the course of social development, some theorists have considered how society and culture present challenges that change as the individual matures. Following this path, psychoanalyst Erik Erikson developed the most comprehensive theory of social development. According to Erikson (1963), the developmental changes occurring throughout our lives can be viewed as a series of eight stages of psychosocial development. **Psychosocial development** encompasses changes in our interactions and understanding of one another as well as in our knowledge and understanding of ourselves as members of society.

Erikson suggests that passage through each of the stages necessitates resolution of a crisis or conflict. Accordingly, each of Erikson's eight stages is represented as a pairing of the most positive and most negative aspects of the crisis of the period. Although each crisis is never resolved entirely—life becomes increasingly complicated as we grow older—it needs to be resolved enough so that we are equipped to deal with demands that the next stage makes.

In the first stage of psychosocial development, **trust versus mistrust** (birth to $1\frac{1}{2}$ years), infants develop feelings of trust if their physical requirements and psychological needs for attachment are consistently met and their interactions with the world are generally positive. On the other hand, inconsistent care and unpleasant interactions with others can lead to the development of mistrust and leave the infant unable to meet the challenges required in the next stage.

In the second stage, **autonomy versus shame and doubt** ($1\frac{1}{2}$ to 3 years), toddlers develop independence and autonomy if exploration and freedom are encouraged, or they experience shame, self-doubt, and unhappiness if they are overly restricted and protected. According to Erikson, the key to the development of autonomy, rather than of shame and doubt, during this period is for the child's care givers to provide the appropriate amount of control. If parents provide too much control, children will be unable to assert themselves and develop their own sense of control over their environment; if parents provide too little control, children themselves become overly demanding and controlling.

Autonomy-versus-shame-and-doubt stage: The period during which, according to Erikson, toddlers (ages 18 months to 3 years) develop independence and autonomy if exploration and freedom are encouraged, or shame and self-doubt if they are restricted and overprotected

The next crisis that children face is that of **initiative versus guilt** (ages 3 to 6). In this stage, the major conflict is between a child's desire to initiate activities independently and the guilt that comes from unwanted and unexpected consequences of such activities. If parents react positively to the child's attempts at independence, they help resolve the initiative-versus-guilt crisis positively.

Initiative-versus-guilt stage: According to Erikson, the period during which children aged 3 to 6 years experience conflict between independence of action and the sometimes negative results of that action

The fourth and last stage of childhood is **industry versus inferiority** (ages 6 to 12). During this period, successful psychosocial development is characterized by increasing competency across all tasks, be they social interactions or academic skills. In contrast, difficulties in this stage lead to feelings of failure and inadequacy.

Industry versus inferiority: According to Erikson, the period during which children aged 6 to 12 years may develop positive social interactions with others or may feel inadequate and become less sociable

Erikson's theory suggests that psychosocial development continues throughout life, and he proposes that there are four more crises to face past childhood (which we discuss in the next chapter). Although his theory has been criticized on several grounds—such as the imprecision of the concepts he employs and an emphasis more on male development than female development—it remains influential and is one of the few that encompasses the entire lifespan.

RECAP AND REVIEW II

Recap

◀ The neonate is born with a number of reflexes, including the rooting, sucking, Moro (or startle), and Babinski reflexes.

◀ Physical growth is initially rapid: During the first year, children typically triple their birth weight, and height increases by 50 percent. Rate of growth declines after age 3, averaging about 5 pounds and 3 inches a year until adolescence.

◀ The perceptual abilities of infants grow rapidly, although they are remarkably sophisticated at birth.

◀ Social development is demonstrated through the growth of attachment, the positive emotional bond that develops between a child and a particular individual. As a child ages, relationships with friends become increasingly important.

◀ Erikson's theory suggests that there are four stages of psychosocial development within childhood, with four other stages spanning the rest of life.

Review

1. The reflex that causes a baby to turn its head toward things that touch its cheeks is called _____ .

2. Which of the following is true about a baby's first simple reflexes?
   a. They disappear within several hours of birth.
   b. They are replaced by more complex, voluntary movements.
   c. They evolve into complex reflexes.
   d. They continue throughout the life cycle.

3. A parent gently shakes a rattle in front of a neonate's eyes. The baby's heart rate increases at first, but with repeated presentations it soon decreases to normal, indicating that _____ has occurred.

4. Harlow demonstrated that infant monkeys preferred a warm, cloth "monkey" over a wire "monkey" that provided food. This is an example of early research on the positive emotional bond known as _____ .

5. Which of the following is *not* true about the effects of day-care centers?

a. They weaken the attachment of a child to his or her parents.

b. They improve the intellectual development of lower-class children.

c. They may make children more aggressive.

d. They do not hurt the intellectual abilities of upper- and middle-class children.

6. Jim's parents make few rules and rarely punish him for disobedience. They could probably be labeled _____ parents on the basis of their child-rearing style.

(Answers to review questions are on page 438.)

OUR MINDS: HOW WE DEVELOP COGNITIVELY

Suppose you had two drinking glasses of different shapes—one short and broad and one tall and skinny. Now imagine that you filled the short, broad one with soda about half way and then poured the liquid from that glass into the tall one. The soda appears to fill about three-quarters of the second glass. If someone asked you whether there was more soda in the second glass than there had been in the first, what would you say?

You might think that such a simple question hardly deserves an answer; of course there is no difference in the amount of soda in the two glasses.

However, most 4-year-olds would be likely to say that there is more soda in the second glass. In fact, if you then poured the soda back into the short glass, they would say there is now less soda than there was in the taller glass.

Why are young children confused by this problem? The reason is not readily apparent. Anyone who has observed preschoolers must be impressed at how far they have progressed from the early stages of development. They speak with ease, know the alphabet, count, play complex games, use a phonograph, tell stories, and communicate quite ably.

Yet, despite this outward sophistication, there are profound gaps in children's understanding of the world. Some theorists have suggested that children are incapable of understanding certain ideas about the world until they reach a particular stage of **cognitive development**—the process by which a child's understanding of the world changes as a function of age and experience. In contrast to theories of physical and social development that were discussed earlier (such as those of Erikson), theories of cognitive development seek to explain the quantitative and qualitative intellectual advances that occur during development.

Cognitive development: The process by which a child's understanding of the world changes as a function of age and experience

STAGES OF UNDERSTANDING:
Piaget's Theory of Cognitive Development

No theory of cognitive development has had more impact than that of Swiss psychologist Jean Piaget. Piaget (1970) suggested that children proceed through a series of four separate stages in a fixed order that is universal across all children. He maintained that these stages differ not only in the *quantity* of information acquired at each, but in the *quality* of knowledge and understanding as well. Taking an interactionist point of view, he suggested that movement from one stage to the next occurred when the child reached an appropriate level of maturation *and* was exposed to relevant types of experiences. Without such experiences, children were assumed to be incapable of reaching their highest level of cognitive growth.

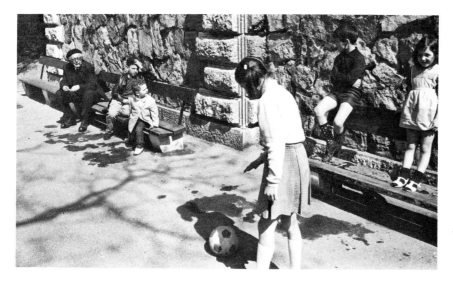

Jean Piaget, a towering figure in developmental psychology, studied children's cognitive development in part by observing them at play. (Yves DeBraine/Black Star)

Piaget's four stages are known as the sensorimotor, preoperational, concrete operational, and formal operational stages (see Table 12-3). Let's examine each of them.

Sensorimotor Stage: Birth to 2 Years

During the initial part of the **sensorimotor stage** the child has relatively little competence in representing the environment using images, language, or other kinds of symbols. Consequently, the infant has no awareness of objects or people who are not immediately present at a given moment, lacking what Piaget calls object permanence. **Object permanence** is the awareness that objects—and people—continue to exist even if they are out of sight.

How can we know that children lack object permanence? Although we cannot ask infants, we can watch their reaction when a toy that they are playing with is hidden under a blanket. Until the age of about 9 months, children will make no attempt to locate the toy. However, soon after this age they will begin to actively search for the object when it is hidden, indicating

Sensorimotor stage: According to Piaget, the stage from birth to 2 years during which a child has little competence in representing the environment using images, language, or other symbols

Object permanence: The awareness that objects do not cease to exist when they are out of sight

TABLE 12-3

A Summary of Piaget's Stages

Approximate Age Range	Stage	Major Characteristics
Birth–2 years	Sensorimotor	Development of object permanence, development of motor skills, little or no capacity for symbolic representation
2–7 years	Preoperational	Development of language and symbolic thinking, egocentric thinking
7–12 years	Concrete operational	Development of conservation, mastery of concept of reversibility
12–adulthood	Formal operational	Development of logical and abstract thinking

Preoperational stage: According to Piaget, the period from 2 to 7 years of age that is characterized by language development

Egocentric thought: Viewing the world entirely from one's own perspective

Principle of conservation: The knowledge that quantity is unrelated to the arrangement and physical appearance of objects

When equal amounts of liquid are poured into containers of different sizes, adults recognize that the level of the liquid is higher in the container with the smaller diameter. A 3-year-old, however, believes that there is actually more liquid in the smaller container because it appears fuller. (Stuart Cohen/Comstock.)

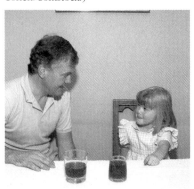

that they have developed a mental representation of the toy. Object permanence, then, is a critical development during the sensorimotor stage.

Preoperational Stage: 2 to 7 Years

The most important development during the **preoperational stage** is in the use of language, described in more detail in Chapter 7. Children develop internal representational systems of the world that allow them to describe people, events, and feelings. They even use symbols in play, pretending, for example, that a book pushed across the floor is a car.

Although children's thinking is more advanced in this stage than in the earlier sensorimotor stage, it still is qualitatively inferior to that of adults. One example of this is in the preoperational child's **egocentric thought**, in which the world is viewed entirely from the child's own perspective. Preoperational children think that everyone shares their own perspective and knowledge. Thus, children's stories and explanations to adults can be maddeningly uninformative, as they are described without any context. For example, a preoperational child may start a story with "He wouldn't let me go," neglecting to mention who "he" is or where the storyteller wanted to go. Egocentric thinking is also seen when children at the preoperational stage play hiding games. For instance, 3-year-olds frequently hide with their faces against a wall, covering their eyes—although they are still in plain view. It seems to them that if *they* cannot see, no one else will be able to see them, since they assume that others share their view.

Another deficiency of the preoperational child is demonstrated by the **principle of conservation**, which is the knowledge that quantity is unrelated to the arrangement and physical appearance of objects. Children who have not mastered this principle do not know that the amount, volume, or length of an object does not change when its shape or configuration is changed. The question about the two glasses—one short and broad, the other tall and thin—with which we began our discussion of cognitive development illustrates this point quite clearly. Children who do not understand the principle of conservation invariably state that the amount of liquid changes as it is poured back and forth; they cannot comprehend that a transformation in appearance does not imply a transformation in amount. Instead, it seems just as reasonable to the child that there is a change in quantity as it does to the adult that there is no change.

There are a number of other ways in which the lack of understanding of the principle of conservation affects children's responses, several of which are illustrated in Figure 12-8. Research on conservation illustrates that principles which are obvious and unquestioned by adults may be completely misunderstood by children during the preoperational period, and it is not until the next stage of cognitive development that children grasp the concept of conservation.

Concrete Operational Stage: Seven to Twelve Years

The beginning of the concrete operation stage is marked by mastery of the principle of conservation. However, there are still some aspects of conservation—such as conservation of weight and volume—that are not fully understood for a number of years.

Type of conservation	Modality	Change in physical appearance	Average age at which invariance is grasped
Number	Number of elements in a collection	Rearranging or dislocating elements	6—7
Substance (mass) (continuous quantity)	Amount of a malleable substance (e.g., clay or liquid)	Altering shape	7—8
Length	Length of a line or object	Altering shape or configuration	7—8
Area	Amount of surface covered by a set of plane figures	Rearranging the figures	8—9
Weight	Weight of an object	Altering shape	9—10
Volume	Volume of an object (in terms of water displacement)	Altering shape	14—15

FIGURE 12-8

These tests are among those used most frequently to assess whether children have learned the principle of conservation across a variety of dimensions. (Schikendanz, Schikendanz, & Forsythe, 1982.)

During the **concrete operational stage**, children develop the ability to think in a more logical manner, and they begin to overcome some of the egocentrism characteristic of the preoperational period. One of the major principles that children learn during this stage is reversibility, the idea that some changes can be undone by reversing an earlier action. For example, children in the concrete operational stage can understand that when a ball of clay is rolled into a long sausage shape, it is possible to recreate the original ball by reversing the action. They can even conceptualize this principle in their heads, without having to see the action performed before them.

Another advance that occurs during the concrete operational stage is the development of a better understanding of time and space. Consider, for instance, the two tracks shown in Figure 12-9. Suppose you were told that the two cars start out at the same time and move along the tracks—which

Concrete operational stage: According to Piaget, the period from 7 to 12 years of age that is characterized by logical thought and a loss of egocentrism

FIGURE 12-9

These two tracks, arranged in this pattern, are used to test children's understanding of space and time.

Track A

Track B

are exactly the same length—at the same speed. Would the cars take the same amount of time to reach the end of the track?

Naturally, you would say. But to children just entering the concrete operational stage, the car traveling along track A would stop first and take less time than the other. In fact, even after being told the contrary, children would claim that the second car started later than the first. The spatial arrangement dominates their judgment.

A little later in the stage, older children might assert that although the two cars start and stop simultaneously, the car moving along track A takes less time. It is not until the end of the concrete operational stage that children understand the problem; at that point their confusion over time and space has cleared up.

Although children make important advances in their logical capabilities during the concrete operational stage, there is still one major limitation to their thinking: They are largely bound to the concrete, physical reality of the world. For the most part, they have difficulty understanding questions of an abstract, hypothetical nature.

Formal Operational Stage: 12 Years to Adulthood

Formal operational stage: According to Piaget, the period from age 12 to adulthood that is characterized by abstract thought

The **formal operational stage** produces a new kind of thinking—that which is abstract, formal, and logical. Thinking is no longer tied to events that are observed in the environment but makes use of logical techniques to resolve problems.

The emergence of formal operational thinking is illustrated by the way in which the "pendulum problem," devised by Piaget, is attacked (Piaget & Inhelder, 1958). The problem solver is asked to figure out what determines how fast a pendulum swings. Is it the length of the string, or the weight of the pendulum, or the force with which the pendulum is pushed? (For the record, the answer is the length of the string.)

Children in the concrete operational stage approach the problem haphazardly, without a logical or rational plan of action. For example, they may simultaneously change the length of the string *and* the weight on the string *and* the force with which they push the pendulum. Since they are varying all factors at once, they are unable to tell which factor is the critical one. In contrast, people in the formal operational stage approach the problem systematically. Acting as if they were scientists conducting an experiment, they examine the effects of changes in just one variable at a time. This ability to rule out competing possibilities is characteristic of formal operational thought.

Although formal operational thought emerges during the teenage years, this type of thinking is, in some cases, used only infrequently (Burbules & Linn, 1988). Moreover, it appears that many individuals never reach this stage at all; most studies show that only 40 to 60 percent of college students and adults fully reach it, with some estimates running as low as 25 percent in the general population (Keating, 1980). In addition, in certain cultures—

particularly those that are less technologically sophisticated than western societies—almost no one reaches the formal operational stage (Chandler, 1976; Super, 1980).

Is Piaget Right?: Stages versus Continuous Development

No other theorist has provided us with as comprehensive a theory of cognitive development as Piaget. Still, some contemporary theorists suggest that a better description of how children develop cognitively can be provided by approaches that do not employ a series of stages (Daehler & Bukato, 1985; Bornstein & Sigman, 1986). Such researchers have found that children are not always consistent in their performance of tasks that—if Piaget's theory were accurate—ought to be performed equally well at a given stage (Tomlinson-Keasey et al., 1979). Furthermore, some developmental psychologists suggest that cognitive development proceeds in a more continuous fashion than Piaget's stage theory implies; they propose that cognitive developmental growth is primarily quantitative, rather than qualitative. They argue that although there are differences in when, how, and to what extent a child is capable of using given cognitive abilities—thereby reflecting quantitative changes—the underlying cognitive processes change relatively little with age (Gelman & Baillargeon, 1983; Sugarman, 1989).

Most developmental psychologists do agree that, although the processes that underlie changes in cognitive abilities may not be those suggested by his theory, Piaget has provided us with an accurate account of age-related changes in cognitive development. Moreover, the influence of the theory has been enormous (Ginsburg & Opper, 1988; Gholson & Rosenthal, 1984). For example, Piaget suggests that increases in cognitive performance cannot be attained unless both cognitive readiness brought about by maturation *and* appropriate environmental stimulation are present. This view has been influential in determining the nature and structure of educational curricula and how children are taught. Piaget's theory and methods have also been used to investigate issues surrounding animal cognition, such as whether primates show object permanence (they seem to; Dore & Dumas, 1987).

ALTERNATIVES TO PIAGET: Information-Processing Approaches

If cognitive development does not proceed in the stagelike fashion suggested by Piaget, what *does* underlie the enormous increases in children's cognitive abilities that are apparent to even the most untutored eye? To many developmental psychologists, the answer can be found in changes in **information processing**, the way in which people take in, use, and store information.

According to this approach, which reflects the cognitive aspects of behavior that we discussed in Chapter 7, quantitative changes occur in children's ability to organize and manipulate information about the world. From this perspective, children are seen as becoming increasingly adept at information processing, analogous to the way a computer program might become more sophisticated as a programmer modifies it on the basis of experience. Information-processing approaches consider the kinds of "mental programs" that children invoke when approaching problems.

Several significant changes occur in children's information processing capabilities. For one thing, speed of processing increases with age as some abilities become more automatic. The speed at which stimuli can be scanned, compared with other stimuli, and recognized increases with age. Attention span also lengthens; with increasing age, children can pay attention to stimuli

Information processing: The way in which people take in, use, and store information longer and are less easily distracted (Manis, Keating & Morrison, 1980; Case, 1985).

Memory also improves dramatically with age. If you recall from Chapter 6, adults are able to keep seven, plus or minus two, chunks of information in short-term memory. In contrast, preschoolers can hold only two or three chunks; 5-year-olds can hold four; and 7-year-olds can hold five. The size of chunks also grows with age, as does the sophistication and organization of knowledge stored in memory (Bjorkland, 1985; Ornstein & Naus, 1988).

Metacognition: An awareness and understanding of one's own cognitive processes

Finally, improvement in information processing is tied to advances in **metacognition**, an awareness and understanding of one's own cognitive processes. Metacognition involves the planning, monitoring, and revising of cognitive strategies. Younger children, who lack knowledge of their cognitive processes, are often unaware of their own incapabilities, causing them to misunderstand others and not even to recognize their errors. It is only later, when metacognitive abilities become more sophisticated, that children are able to know when they *don't* understand (Astington, Harris, & Olson, 1988).

The growth in metacognitive abilities is but one of the many advances we make as part of our continuing development. We have seen in this chapter the enormous strides youngsters make as they move from relatively helpless infants to competent, able children. In the next chapter, we consider the challenges presented by adolescence and adulthood and the ways in which people continue to grow and change throughout their lives.

THE INFORMED CONSUMER OF PSYCHOLOGY:
Maximizing Cognitive Development

Are there ways of maximizing a child's cognitive development? Although our examination of the nature-nurture issue makes clear that genetic background plays a critical role in defining the limits that we can ultimately achieve, it is also apparent that environmental factors can enhance the probability of achieving our potential. In fact, research carried out by developmental psychologists has identified several child-rearing practices that seem to be important in maximizing cognitive development (Meyerhoff & White, 1986; Gottfried, 1984; Bee, 1985; Cataldo, 1987). Among the most crucial:

▶ Provide children with the maximum opportunity to explore and investigate their environments. For instance, if an environment can be made safe, toddlers should not be restricted to playpens.

▶ Be emotionally responsive and involved with children. Parents with high-achieving children are interested in their children's lives and encourage and reinforce their efforts. They are warm and supportive, and act as children's "personal consultants."

▶ Use language that is highly descriptive and accurate when speaking with a child. Avoid "baby talk" and speak with children, not *at* them. Ask questions, listen to babies' responses, and provide further feedback.

▶ Provide *appropriate* play materials. The sheer quantity of toys and other play materials is less important than their appropriateness for the child's age and developmental level.

▶ Give children a chance to make mistakes. Parents of successful children tend to avoid harsh, arbitrary rules and highly restrictive control, and they do not use punishment frequently. Instead, while remaining firmly in control of their children's behavior and without being overly permissive, they are likely to guide their children with a combination of firmness and warmth, providing a rationale for the rules children must follow.

▶ Hold high expectations. Parents should communicate that they expect their children to do well, demonstrating to their children the importance of success and achievement.

▶ Don't push children too hard. Despite the rigors and demands of modern life, childhood should be a time of enjoyment and not viewed as merely a period of preparation for what comes later. Some psychologists feel that we are producing a society of "hurried children," whose lives revolve around rigid schedules and who are so pressed to succeed that their childhood is filled with stress (Elkins, 1981). Remember that—as in the rest of the life-span—it is important to step back and set priorities regarding what is and is not most important.

RECAP AND REVIEW III

Recap

◀ The major theory of cognitive development—the way in which children's understanding of the world changes as a function of age and experience—is Piaget's theory. Piaget proposes four major stages: sensorimotor, preoperational, concrete operational, and formal operational.

◀ Among the hallmarks of cognitive development are the understanding of object permanence, a decline in egocentric thought, and an understanding of the principle of conservation.

◀ Although Piaget's description of what happens within the various stages of cognitive development has largely been upheld, some theorists argue that development is more gradual and continuous and due more to quantitative than to qualitative changes in cognition.

◀ Information-processing approaches to cognitive development focus on the quantitative changes that occur in the way in which people take in, use, and store information. Major changes occur with age in the speed of processing, length of attention span, memory, and metacognitive abilities.

Review

1. The process by which our understanding of the world develops is called
   a. Piaget's theory.
   b. the sensorimotor stage.
   c. developmental psychology.
   d. cognitive development.
2. Match each developmental stage in the left-hand column with the behavior presented at the right.
   ____ Sensorimotor stage
   a. Sandy, who watched her parents unroll their new bathroom rug, returns later to roll it back up into its original form.

____ Preoperational stage

____ Concrete operational stage

____ Formal operational stage

   b. Jenny puts her hands up to her eyes and says to her friend, "You can't see me now."
   c. By systematically testing out his hypothesis, Randy is able to figure out a problem involving a pendulum.
   d. Jonathan does not go searching for his stuffed animal when his father slips it out of sight behind his back. Seemingly, to Jonathan it no longer exists.

3. Now match the examples of behavior in the right-hand column above with the concepts presented below.
   ____ Egocentric thought
   ____ Object permanence
   ____ Logical thought
   ____ Reversibility
4. The understanding that quantity is unrelated to the physical appearance of objects is known as the principle of _____ .
5. The information-processing approach to development is an alternative to Piaget's theory of cognitive development. Which of the following situations does not support the information-processing approach?
   a. Attention span increases.
   b. Memory improves with age.
   c. A child begins to develop knowledge of his or her own cognitive processes.
   d. A child develops mental representations of objects and people.

(Answers to review questions are on page 444.)

1. Developmental psychology is the branch of psychology that studies growth and change throughout life. One fundamental question is how much developmental change is due to nature—heredity and genetic factors—and how much to nurture—environmental factors. Most developmental psychologists feel that heredity defines the upper limits of our growth and change, whereas the environment affects the degree to which the upper limits are reached.

2. Cross-sectional research compares people of different ages with one another at the same point in time. In contrast, longitudinal research traces the behavior of one or more subjects as the subjects become older. Finally, cross-sequential research combines the two methods by taking several different age groups and examining them over several points in time.

3. At the moment of conception, a male's sperm cell and a female's egg cell unite, each contributing to the new individual's genetic makeup. The new cell, a zygote, immediately begins to grow, becoming an embryo measuring about one-fifth of an inch long at four weeks. By the ninth week, the embryo is called a fetus and is responsive to touch and other stimulation. At about twenty-eight weeks it reaches the age of viability: It may survive if born prematurely. A fetus is normally born after thirty-eight weeks of pregnancy, weighing around $7\frac{1}{2}$ pounds and measuring about 20 inches in length.

4. Genetic abnormalities produce birth defects such as phenylketonuria (PKU), sickle-cell anemia, Tay-Sachs disease, and Down's syndrome. Among the prenatal environmental influences on fetal growth are the mother's nutritional status, illnesses, drug intake, and birth complications.

5. The newborn, or neonate, has many capabilities. Among them are the rooting reflex, the Moro (startle) reflex, and the Babinski reflex. After birth, physical development is rapid; children typically triple their birth weights in a year. Perceptual abilities also increase rapidly; infants can distinguish color and depth after just one month. Other sensory capabilities are also impressive at birth; infants can distinguish sounds and discriminate tastes and smells. However, the development of more sophisticated perceptual abilities depends on increased cognitive abilities.

6. Social development in infancy is marked by the phenomenon of attachment—the positive emotional bond between a child and a particular individual. Attachment is measured in the laboratory using the Ainsworth strange situation and is related to later social and emotional adjustment.

7. As children become older, the nature of their social interactions with peers changes. Initially, play occurs relatively independently but becomes increasingly co-operative. Play helps increase social competence and self-control.

8. Different styles of child rearing result in differing outcomes. Authoritarian parents are firm, punitive, and strict; their children tend to be unsociable and withdrawn. Permissive parents provide lax or inconsistent discipline, although they are warm; their children tend to be immature, moody, dependent, and low in self-control. Finally, authoritative parents are firm, setting limits, but using reasoning and explanations. Their children tend to be likable, self-reliant, independent, and high in social skills. Of course, there are many exceptions, depending in part on the temperament of the child.

9. According to Erikson, eight stages of psychosocial development encompass people's changing interactions and understanding of themselves and others. During childhood, there are four stages, each of which relates to a crisis that requires resolution. These stages are labeled trust versus mistrust (birth to 18 months), autonomy versus shame and doubt (18 months to 3 years), initiative versus guilt (3 to 6 years), and industry versus inferiority (6 to 12 years).

10. Piaget's theory suggests that cognitive development proceeds through four stages in which qualitative changes occur in thinking. In the sensorimotor stage (birth to 2 years), children develop object permanence, the awareness that objects and people continue to exist even if they are out of sight. In the preoperational stage (2 to 7 years) children display egocentric thought, and by the end of the stage they begin to understand the principle of conservation—the knowledge that quantity is unrelated to the arrangement and physical appearance of an object. The conservation principle is not fully grasped, however, until the concrete operational stage (7 to 12 years), in which children begin to think more logically, and to understand the concept of reversibility. In the final stage, the formal operational period (12 years to adulthood), thinking becomes abstract, formal, and fully logical.

11. Although Piaget's theory has had an enormous influence, some theorists suggest that the notion of developmental stages is inaccurate. They say that development is more continuous and that the changes occurring within and between stages are reflective of quantitative advances in cognitive development rather than in the quality of thought.

12. Information-processing approaches suggest that quantitative changes occur in children's ability to organize and manipulate information about the world, such as significant increases in speed of processing, attention span, and memory. In addition, there are advances in metacognition, the awareness and understanding of one's own cognitive processes.

ANSWERS (REVIEW III):

1. d **2.** d, b, a, c **3.** b, d, c, a **4.** Conservation **5.** d

13. Because environmental factors play such an important role in cognitive development, child-rearing practices can have an important effect on the degree to which a child realizes his or her genetic potential. Parents can help by giving children the opportunity to explore their environment, being emotionally responsive and involved with their children, being verbally interactive, providing appropriate play materials, giving children a chance to make and learn from mistakes, and holding high expectations.

KEY TERMS AND CONCEPTS ▶

developmental psychology (p. 412)
environment (413)
heredity (413)
nature-nurture question (413)
genetic (414)
maturation (414)
interactionist (415)
identical twins (416)
cross-sectional research (416)
longitudinal research (417)
cross-sequential research (417)
conception (418)
zygote (418)
chromosomes (418)
genes (418)
embryo (419)
critical period (419)
fetus (419)
age of viability (420)

sickle-cell anemia (420)
phenylketonuria (PKU) (420)
Tay-Sachs disease (420)
Down's syndrome (420)
rubella (421)
fetal alcohol syndrome (421)
neonate (423)
vernix (424)
lanugo (424)
reflex (424)
rooting reflex (424)
sucking reflex (424)
gag reflex (424)
Moro (startle) reflex (424)
Babinski reflex (424)
habituation (426)
attachment (428)
Ainsworth strange situation (430)
authoritarian parents (434)

permissive parents (434)
authoritative parents (434)
temperament (434)
psychosocial development (434)
trust-versus-mistrust stage (434)
autonomy-versus-shame-and-doubt stage (435)
initiative-versus-guilt stage (435)
industry-versus-inferiority stage (435)
cognitive development (436)
sensorimotor stage (437)
object permanence (437)
preoperational stage (438)
egocentric thought (438)
principle of conservation (438)
concrete operational stage (439)
formal operational stage (440)
information processing (441)
metacognition (442)

FOR FURTHER STUDY AND APPLICATION ▶

Lamb, M. E., & Bornstein, M. H. (1987). *Development in infancy: An introduction* (2nd ed). New York: Random House.

This book provides an excellent introduction to the world of the infant.

Shaffer, D. R. (1989). *Developmental psychology: Childhood and adolescence* (2nd ed.). Pacific Grove, CA: Brooks/Cole.

Papalia, D., & Olds, S. (1989). *Human development* (4th ed.). New York: McGraw-Hill.

These two fine, broad introductory texts on child development cover the range of childhood changes.

Daehler, M., & Bukato, D. (1985). *Cognitive development.* New York: Random House.

This work offers a good, in-depth introduction to cognitive development.

Bower, T. G. R. (1977). *The perceptual world of the child.* Cambridge, MA: Harvard University Press.

Although perceptual growth can be a dry, complex subject, Bower covers the material in a readable, fascinating manner, clearly stating what we know about the development of perception—and how we know it.

White, B. L. (1975). *The first three years of life.* Englewood Cliffs, NJ: Prentice-Hall.

This book is filled with practical advice on the purchase of toys and games, as well as suggestions on what parents can do to help their children realize their potential during the first few years of life.

Brazelton, T. B. (1969). *Infants and mothers: Differences in development.* New York: Dell.

Brazelton, T. B. (1974). *Toddlers and parents.* New York: Delta.

Written by a physician who has become the new Dr. Spock, these books provide an anecdotal account of three infants' and three toddlers' development in the early stages of life. They give a good understanding of the complexities of child rearing and how development differs across children with unique temperaments.

Scarr, S. (1984). *Mother care/other care.* New York: Basic Books.

This book is filled with practical advice on the choices and outcomes of day-care, written for the layperson by a well-known developmental psychologist.

Bronstein, P., & Cowan, C. P. (Eds.) (1988). *Fatherhood today: Men's changing role in the family.* NY: Wiley.

Written by a distinguished group of social scientists, this volume provides a contemporary view of fathers' effects on their children.

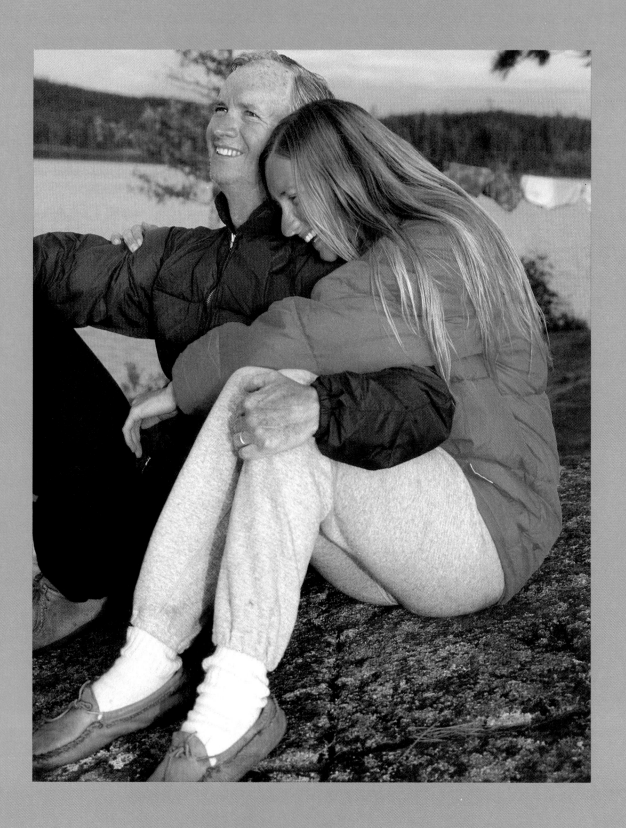

CHAPTER

13

DEVELOPMENT: ADOLESCENCE TO THE END OF LIFE

PROLOGUE:
ADA CUTTING PERRY

Ada Cutting Perry at the age of 100. (Pamela Valois/*Gifts of Age*/Chronicle Books)

Ada Perry lived to be almost 103. Born near Watertown, New York, she led a rigorous life. She had five children, the last of whom was born when Ada was 47. Her husband, a rancher, raised alfalfa and worked as a carpenter. They grew most of their own food, and Ada remembers cooking batches of baked beans and bread to sell to neighbors. She also took the time to help Indians in nearby tribes learn to read and write, as well as schooling her own children.

When she looked back, at age 100, she said the following:

"I realize I am always adapting to the next lesson in life. I have been old now for more than thirty years. I thought I was old at 70 but then thirty more years have just flown away. I've had a lot of adapting to do with each decade. . . .

"I don't feel too different about being 100. After all, it's just a matter of good health and circumstance. I'm glad that I still have the use of my legs, my arms, my hands, my brain. I'm so thankful for common everyday health. I'm hungry, I enjoy food, and I love to eat something that's not good for me.

"I have one more adaptation I must make in life, then I'll be through. It's something I don't talk to a lot of people about because most of them would be bored with it. But I want to adapt to the idea of death. It's important that I shouldn't be afraid of death. There's not as much fear as there was twenty years ago, but I still have work to do. There's a certain laziness that I'm anxious to overcome. I should just go about it calmly and get on better terms with death. I hope I can adapt to it as well as I have to everything else. It might be around the corner" (Painter, 1985, p. 125).

LOOKING AHEAD ▶

Ada Perry is right: Each of our lives is filled with challenges to which we must adapt. Beginning with adolescence, we face a series of critical developmental changes that will continue throughout our lifetimes, ending only with death. Because development is an ongoing process that continues throughout adolescence and adulthood, then, we are not the same person today that we will be when we reach 40, 60, 80, or, if we are lucky, 100 years.

In this chapter, we examine development from adolescence through young adulthood, middle age, and old age. Our discussion of adolescence focuses on some of the major physical, emotional, and cognitive changes that occur during people's entry into adulthood. Next, we consider early and middle adulthood, stages in which people are at the peak of their physical and intellectual abilities; we discuss the developmental changes that people undergo during these periods and their relationship to work, families, and living patterns. Finally, in our discussion of old age, we examine the kinds of physical, intellectual, and social changes that occur as a consequence of the aging process and see that aging may bring about both declines and improvements in various kinds of functioning. We end with a discussion of the ways people prepare themselves for death and mourn for those who have died.

In sum, this chapter provides you with the answers to these fundamental questions about development:

▶ What major physical changes mark the onset of adolescence, and how do our bodies continue to change as we age?

▶ What principal kinds of social and intellectual changes occur in early adulthood, middle adulthood, and old age, and what are their causes?

▶ How does moral development proceed?

▶ What are the stages of psychosocial development in adolescence and adulthood?

▶ How can we adjust to death and mourning?

As each of these questions is addressed, you will see how developmental psychologists have come to understand that adolescence and beyond—the greater part of most people's lives—is a period marked by crucial changes that progress until the very end of life.

BECOMING AN ADULT: ADOLESCENCE

It is not easy to be a male adolescent in the Awa tribe: First come the beatings. Seated around a fire, the boys are hit with sticks and prickly branches, not only for their own past misdeeds but in honor of tribesmen killed in warfare.

But the beatings—which last for two or three days—are just the beginning. In the next phase of the ritual, adults jab sharpened sticks into the boys' nostrils until copious bleeding takes place. Then they force a five-foot length of vine deep into the boys' throats, until they gag and vomit.

Finally, tribesmen make deep cuts in the boys' genitals, and severe bleeding occurs. The boys are then released to bleed into a stream, while adult onlookers laugh, jeer, and poke at the cuts to make them bleed even more.

Although the rites that mark the coming-of-age of boys in the Awa tribe in New Guinea sound horrifying to us, they are comparable to those in other cultures, in which it may be necessary to endure public circumcision and kneeling on hot coals without displaying pain. And it is not just males who must participate in such trials: In some tribes, girls must toss wads of burning cotton from hand to hand and allow themselves to be bitten by hundreds of ants.

Although western society has no rituals as physically and psychologically taxing to represent the entry into adulthood—for which most of us will heave a sigh of relief—the period that follows childhood, adolescence, is still an important time in our lives. For most people, adolescence is marked by profound changes and, sometimes, turmoil. Considerable biological change marks the adolescent's attainment of sexual and physical maturity, rivaled by important social, emotional, and cognitive changes that occur as adolescents strive for independence and move toward adulthood.

Adolescence: The developmental stage between childhood and adulthood during which many physical, cognitive, and social changes take place

Adolescence, which is generally thought of as a developmental stage between childhood and adulthood, represents a critical period in people's development. Given the length of education that precedes starting work in our society, the stage is a fairly lengthy one, starting just before the teenage years and ending just after them. No longer children, but considered by society to be not quite adults, adolescents face a period of rapid physical and social change that affects them for the rest of their lives.

THE CHANGING ADOLESCENT: Physical Development

If you think back to the start of your own adolescence, it is likely that the most dramatic changes you remember are of a physical nature. A spurt in height, the growth of breasts in girls, deepening voices in boys, the development of body hair, and intense sexual feelings are a source of curiosity, interest, and sometimes embarrassment for individuals entering adolescence.

The physical changes that occur at the start of adolescence, which are largely a result of the secretion of various hormones (see Chapter 2), affect virtually every aspect of the adolescent's life; not since infancy has development been so dramatic (see Figure 13-1). Weight and height increase rapidly; a growth spurt begins at around age $10\frac{1}{2}$ for girls and age 12 for boys, and adolescents may grow as much as 5 inches in one year.

Puberty: The period during which maturation of the sexual organs occurs

Puberty, the period at which maturation of the sexual organs occurs, begins at about age 11 or 12 for girls and 13 or 14 for boys. However, there are wide variations, and it is not too rare for a girl to begin to menstruate—the first sign of sexual maturity in females—as early as age 10 or as late as age 16. Furthermore, the average age at which adolescents reach sexual maturity has been steadily decreasing over the last century, most likely a result of better nutrition and medical care (Dreyer, 1982). This change in the onset of puberty provides a good illustration of how changes in the environment interact with heredity to affect development.

The age at which puberty begins has important implications for the way adolescents feel about themselves—as well as how others treat them. Early-maturing boys have a distinct advantage over later-maturing boys; they do better in athletics and they are generally more popular and have higher self-concepts. The picture is less clear for girls. Although early-maturing girls are more sought after as dates and have higher self-concepts than later-maturing girls, initially their early physical maturation is less positive, since the development of such obvious characteristics as breasts sets them apart from their peers and may be a source of ridicule (Atwater, 1983).

FIGURE 13-1

The range of ages during which major sexual changes occur during adolescence is shown by the colored bars. (Based on Tanner, 1978).

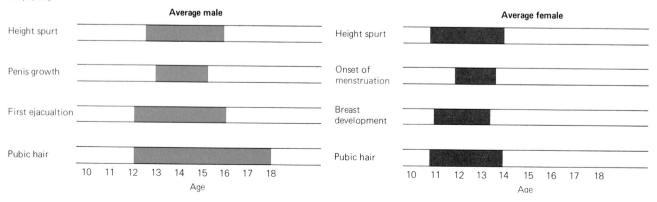

Late maturers, in contrast, may suffer psychological consequences as a result of the delay. Boys who are smaller and less coordinated than their more mature peers tend to be ridiculed and seen as less attractive, and may come to view themselves in the same way. The consequences of late maturation may extend well into a male's thirties (Mussen & Jones, 1957). Similarly, late-maturing girls are at a disadvantage in junior high and high school. They hold a relatively low social status, and they may be overlooked in dating and other male-female activities (Apter et al., 1981; Clarke-Stewart & Friedman, 1987).

Clearly, the rate at which physical changes occur during adolescence can have significant effects on the way people are viewed by others and the way they view themselves. Just as important as physical changes, however, are the psychological and social changes that evolve during adolescence.

DISTINGUISHING RIGHT FROM WRONG:
Moral and Cognitive Development

According to psychologist Lawrence Kohlberg, people pass through a series of stages in the evolution of their sense of justice and in the kind of reasoning they use to make moral judgments (Kohlberg, 1984). Largely because of the various cognitive deficits that Piaget described (see Chapter 12), preadolescent children tend to think either in terms of concrete, unvarying rules ("It is always wrong to steal" or "I'll be punished if I steal") or in terms of the rules of society ("Good people don't steal" or "What if everyone stole?").

Adolescents, however, are capable of reasoning on a higher plane, typically having reached Piaget's formal operational stage of cognitive development. Because they are able to comprehend broad moral principles, they can understand that morality is not always black and white and that conflict can exist between two sets of socially accepted standards.

After extensive research (see the Research Classics box), Kohlberg (1984) suggests that the changes occurring in moral reasoning can be understood best as a three-level sequence, which, in turn, is divided into six stages. These levels and stages are shown in Table 13-1, which also includes samples of subjects' reasoning at each stage. Note that the arguments either in favor of or against stealing the drug can be categorized into the same stage of moral reasoning. It is the nature and sophistication of the argument that determine into what category it falls.

Kohlberg's category system assumes that people move through the six stages in a fixed order, and that they are not capable of reaching the highest stage until about the age of 13—primarily because of deficits in cognitive development that are not overcome until that age. However, many people never reach the highest level of moral reasoning. In fact, Kohlberg suggests that only about 25 percent of all adults rise above stage 4 of his model.

Moral Development in Women

Psychologist Carol Gilligan (1982; 1987) has pointed out an important shortcoming in Kohlberg's original research: It was first carried out using only male subjects and is thus more applicable to them than to women. Furthermore, she convincingly argues that, because of differing socialization experiences, a fundamental difference exists in the manner in which men and women view moral behavior. According to her, men view morality primarily in terms of broad principles such as justice and fairness, whereas women

In Europe, a woman is near death from a special kind of cancer. The one drug that the doctors think might save her is a form of radium that a druggist in the same town has recently discovered. The drug is expensive to make, and the druggist is charging ten times the cost, or $2000, for a small dose. The sick woman's husband, Heinz, goes to everyone he knows to borrow the money, but he can get together only about $1000. He tells the druggist that his wife is dying and asks him to sell the drug cheaper or let him pay later. The druggist says, "No, I discovered the drug and I'm going to make money from it." Heinz is desperate and considers breaking into the man's store to steal the drug for his wife.

What would you tell Heinz he should do?

In the view of Lawrence Kohlberg, the advice you give Heinz is a reflection of your level of moral development. In pioneering research on morality, Kohlberg devised a series of scenarios, such as the one above, that described a moral dilemma. No dilemma had a right or wrong answer; rather, each pitted one set of fundamental principles against another—in this case, prin-

ASSESSING MORAL DEVELOPMENT: KOHLBERG'S STAGES

ciples in favor of protecting human life versus principles against stealing from others.

After constructing the scenarios, Kohlberg asked a large number of subjects of varying ages to read them and describe how they would resolve them. He then categorized the responses according to the kind and sophistication of the argument that each subject made, and found that moral development fell into the six stagelike categories shown in Table 13-1 (Colby & Kohlberg, 1987).

Extensive research has shown that the stages identified by Kohlberg generally provide a valid representation of moral development. Yet the research raises several methodological issues. One major problem is that Kohlberg's procedure measures moral *judgments*, not *behavior*. Although Kohlberg's theory seems to be a generally accurate account of how moral judgments develop, some research finds that such judgments are not always related to

moral behavior (Snarey, 1985; Malinowski & Smith, 1985). On the other hand, other investigators suggest that a relationship between moral judgments and behavior does exist. For example, one study found that students who were most likely to commit acts of civil disobedience were those whose moral judgments were at the highest levels (Candee & Kohlberg, 1987). Still, the evidence is mixed on this question; knowing right from wrong does not mean that we will always act in accordance with our judgments.

Another difficulty with Kohlberg's research is that although it provides a description of the different stages of moral development, it is far less precise in identifying the underlying mechanisms which produce them. Thus we don't know what specific factors lead to more sophisticated morality. Furthermore, Kohlberg's reliance on hypothetical moral dilemmas, which are removed from everyday life, has been criticized.

Despite these theoretical and methodological concerns, Kohlberg's work has provided us with one of the most comprehensive accounts of moral development, and his research remains a classic contribution to our understanding of morality.

see it in terms of responsibility toward individuals and willingness to sacrifice to help a specific individual within the context of a particular relationship. Compassion for individuals is a more salient factor in moral behavior for women than it is for men.

Thus, because Kohlberg's model conceives of moral behavior largely in terms of principles of justice, it is inadequate in describing the moral development of females. This factor accounts for the surprising finding that women typically score at a lower level than men on tests of moral judgment using Kohlberg's stage sequence. In Gilligan's view, women's morality is centered on individual well-being rather than moral abstractions, and the highest levels of morality are represented by compassionate concern for other's welfare.

According to Gilligan's research, women's moral development proceeds in three stages. In the first stage, termed "orientation toward individual survival," a woman concentrates on what is practical and best for her. During

TABLE 13-1

Kohlberg's Sequence of Moral Reasoning

Level	Stage	Sample Moral Reasoning of Subjects	
		In Favor of Stealing	**Against Stealing**
Level 1 Preconventional morality: At this level, the concrete interests of the individual are considered in terms of rewards and punishments.	*Stage 1* Obedience and punishment orientation: At this stage, people stick to rules in order to avoid punishment, and obedience occurs for its own sake.	"If you let your wife die, you will get in trouble. You'll be blamed for not spending the money to save her, and there'll be an investigation of you and the druggist for your wife's death."	"You shouldn't steal the drug because you'll be caught and sent to jail if you do. If you do get away, your conscience will bother you thinking how the police will catch up with you at any minute."
	Stage 2 Reward orientation: At this stage, rules are followed only for a person's own benefit. Obedience occurs because of rewards that are received.	"If you do happen to get caught, you could give the drug back and you wouldn't get much of a sentence. It wouldn't bother you much to serve a little jail term, if you have your wife when you get out."	"You may not get much of a jail term if you steal the drug, but your wife will probably die before you get out, so it won't do much good. If your wife dies, you shouldn't blame yourself; it isn't your fault she has cancer."
Level 2 Conventional morality: At this level, people approach moral problems as members of society. They are interested in pleasing others by acting as good members of society.	*Stage 3* "Good boy" morality: Individuals at this stage show an interest in maintaining the respect of others and doing what is expected of them.	"No one will think you're bad if you steal the drug, but your family will think you're an inhuman husband if you don't. If you let your wife die, you'll never be able to look anybody in the face again."	"It isn't just the druggist who will think you're a criminal; everyone else will too. After you steal the drug, you'll feel bad thinking how you've brought dishonor on your family and yourself; you won't be able to face anyone again."
	Stage 4 Authority and social-order-maintaining morality: People at this stage conform to society's rules and consider that "right" is what society defines as right.	"If you have any sense of honor, you won't let your wife die just because you're afraid to do the only thing that will save her. You'll always feel guilty that you caused her death if you don't do your duty to her."	"You're desperate and you may not know you're doing wrong when you steal the drug. But you'll know you did wrong after you're sent to jail. You'll always feel guilty for your dishonesty and lawbreaking."
Level 3 Postconventional morality: At this level, people use moral principles which are seen as broader than those of any particular society.	*Stage 5* Morality of contract, individual rights, and democratically accepted law: People at this stage do what is right because of a sense of obligation to laws which are agreed upon within society. They perceive that laws can be modified as part of changes in an implicit social contract.	"You'll lose other people's respect, not gain it, if you don't steal. If you let your wife die, it will be out of fear, not out of reasoning. So you'll just lose self-respect and probably the respect of others too."	"You'll lose your standing and respect in the community and violate the law. You'll lose respect for yourself if you're carried away by emotion and forget the long-range point of view."
	Stage 6 Morality of individual principles and conscience: At this final stage, a person follows laws because they are based on universal ethical principles. Laws that violate the principles are disobeyed.	"If you don't steal the drug, and if you let your wife die, you'll always condemn yourself for it afterward. You won't be blamed and you'll have lived up to the outside rule of the law but you won't have lived up to your own standards of conscience."	"If you steal the drug, you won't be blamed by other people, but you'll condemn yourself because you won't have lived up to your own conscience and standards of honesty."

Source: Adapted from Kohlberg, 1969.

this stage, there is a transition from selfishness to responsibility, in which the woman thinks about what would be best for others.

At the second stage of moral development, termed "goodness as self-sacrifice," a woman begins to think that she must sacrifice her own wishes to what other people want. Ultimately, though, she makes the transition from "goodness" to "truth," in which she takes into account her own needs plus those of others.

In the third stage, "morality of nonviolence," a woman comes to see that hurting anyone is immoral—including hurting herself. This realization establishes a moral equality between herself and others and represents, according to Gilligan, the most sophisticated level of moral reasoning.

As you can see, Gilligan's sequence of stages is very different from that presented by Kohlberg, and some psychologists have suggested that her rejection of Kohlberg's work is too sweeping (Colby & Damon, 1987). It is clear, though, that gender plays an important role in determining what is seen as moral, and that men and women have differing conceptions of what constitutes moral behavior (McGraw & Bloomfield, 1987).

SEARCHING FOR IDENTITY: Psychosocial Development

To most adolescents, answering the questions "Who am I?" and "How do I fit into the world?" is one of life's major challenges. Although these questions continue to be posed throughout a person's lifetime, they take on particular significance during the adolescent years.

Erikson's theory of psychosocial development, which we first discussed in Chapter 12, places particular importance on this search for identity during the adolescent years. As noted earlier, psychosocial development encompasses how people's understanding of themselves, one another, and the world around them changes as a part of development (Erikson, 1963).

The fifth stage of Erikson's theory (summarized, with the other stages, in Table 13-2) is labeled the **identity-versus-role-confusion** period and encompasses adolescence. This stage is a time of major testing, as people try to determine what is unique and special about themselves. They attempt to discover who they are, what their skills are, and what kinds of roles they are best suited to play for the rest of their lives—in short, their **identity**. Confusion over the most appropriate role to follow in life can lead to lack of a stable identity, adoption of a socially unacceptable role such as that of a social deviant, or difficulty in maintaining close personal relationships later in life (Kahn et al., 1985).

During the identity-versus-role-confusion period, pressures to identify what one wants to do with one's life are acutely felt. Because these pressures come at a time of major physical changes and important changes in what society expects of them, adolescents can find the period a particularly difficult one. The identity-versus-role-confusion stage has another important characteristic: a decline in reliance on adults for information, with a shift toward using the peer group as a source of social judgments. The peer group becomes increasingly important, enabling adolescents to form close, adultlike relationships and helping them clarify their personal identities.

During the college years, most students enter the **intimacy-versus-isolation** stage (spanning the period of early adulthood, from around age 18 to age 30), in which the focus is on developing close relationships with others. Difficulties during this stage result in feelings of loneliness and a fear of

Identity-versus-role-confusion stage: According to Erikson, a time in adolescence of testing to determine one's own unique qualities

Identity: The distinguishing character of the individual: who each of us is, what our roles are, and what we are capable of

Intimacy-versus-isolation stage: According to Erikson, a period during early adulthood that focuses on developing close relationships

TABLE 13-2

A Summary of Erikson's Stages

Stage	Approximate Age	Positive Outcomes	Negative Outcomes
1. Trust vs. mistrust	Birth–1½ years	Feelings of trust from environmental support	Fear and concern regarding others
2. Autonomy vs. shame and doubt	1½–3 years	Self-sufficiency if exploration is encouraged	Doubts about self, lack of independence
3. Initiative vs. guilt	3–6 years	Discovery of ways to initiate actions	Guilt from actions and thoughts
4. Industry vs. inferiority	6–12 years	Development of sense of competence	Feelings of inferiority, no sense of mastery
5. Identity vs. role confusion	Adolescence	Awareness of uniqueness of self, knowledge of role to be followed	Inability to identify appropriate roles in life
6. Intimacy vs. isolation	Early adulthood	Development of loving, sexual relationships and close friendships	Fear of relationships with others
7. Generativity vs. stagnation	Middle adulthood	Sense of contribution to continuity of life	Trivialization of one's activities
8. Ego-integrity vs. despair	Late adulthood	Sense of unity in life's accomplishments	Regret over lost opportunities of life

relationships with others, while successful resolution of the crises of the stage results in the possibility of forming relationships that are intimate on a physical, intellectual, and emotional level.

Erikson goes on to describe the last stages of adulthood, in which development continues. During middle adulthood, people are in the **generativity-versus-stagnation** stage. Generativity refers to a person's contribution to his or her family, community, work, and society as a whole. Success in this stage results in positive feelings about the continuity of life, while difficulties lead to feelings of triviality regarding one's activities and a sense of

Generativity-versus-stagnation stage: According to Erikson, a period in middle adulthood during which we take stock of our contributions to family and society

Peer relationships are very important during the adolescent years. (James H. Karales/ Peter Arnold, Inc.)

Ego-integrity-versus-despair stage: According to Erikson, a period from late adulthood until death during which we review life's accomplishments and failures

stagnation or of having done nothing for upcoming generations. In fact, if a person has not successfully resolved the identity crisis of adolescence, he or she may still be floundering toward identifying an appropriate career.

Finally, the last stage of psychosocial development, the period of **ego-integrity-versus-despair**, comprises later adulthood and continues until death. Success in resolving the difficulties presented by this stage of life is signified by a sense of accomplishment; difficulties result in regret over what might have been achieved, but was not.

One of the most noteworthy aspects of Erikson's theory is its suggestion that development does not stop at adolescence but continues throughout adulthood. Prior to Erikson, the prevailing view was that psychosocial development was largely complete after adolescence. He helped to establish that considerable development continues throughout our lives.

STORMY ADOLESCENCE: Myth or Reality?

Does puberty invariably foreshadow a stormy, rebellious period of adolescence?

At one time most children entering adolescence were thought to enter a period fraught with stress and unhappiness, but psychologists are now finding that such a characterization is largely a myth. Most young people, it seems, pass through adolescence without appreciable turmoil in their lives (Steinberg, 1985, 1987; Peterson, 1988).

This is not to say that adolescence is completely tranquil (Rowlison & Felner, 1988). There is clearly a rise in the amount of arguing and bickering in most families. Young teenagers, as part of their search for identity, tend to experience a tension between their attempts to become independent from their parents and their actual dependence on them. Happily, though, for the majority of families such tensions tend to stabilize during middle adolescence—around age 15 or 16—and eventually decline around age 18 (Montemayor, 1983).

One of the reasons for the increase in discord in adolescence appears to be the protracted period in which children stay at home with their parents. In prior historical periods—and in some cultures today—children leave home immediately following puberty. Today, however, sexually mature adolescents may spend as much as seven or eight years with their parents (Steinberg, 1985). In addition, adolescence brings with it a variety of stresses outside the home. Typically, adolescents change schools at least twice (from elementary to middle or junior high, then to senior high school), and friendships and peer groups are particularly volatile. Such stressors can lead to unusual tensions at home.

Teenage Suicide

Although the vast majority of teenagers pass through adolescence without major psychological difficulties, some experience unusually severe psychological tension. In some cases, the problems become extreme—such as the case of teenage suicide, which is the third leading cause of death of adolescents in the United States. Current statistics show that a teenager commits suicide every 90 minutes.

Over the last two decades, the occurrence of teenage suicide has tripled (see Figure 13-2). In fact, the reported rate of suicide may actually be low,

FIGURE 13-2

The rate of increase in suicide in 15- to 24-year-olds has been dramatic over the last two decades, as indicated by these figures, displaying the number of suicides per 100,000 white males. (National Center for Health Statistics, 1987.)

since medical personnel are reluctant to report suicide as a cause of death, preferring to label a death as an accident in order to "protect" the survivors.

Adolescent suicide has several causes (Schneidman, 1987). According to some studies, one major factor that underlies suicide is depression, characterized by unhappiness, extreme fatigue, and—something that seems particularly important—a profound sense of hopelessness (Beck, 1985). In other cases, adolescents who commit suicide are perfectionists, inhibited socially and prone to extreme anxiety when faced with any social or academic challenge (Holden, 1986).

Family background and adjustment difficulties are also related to suicide (Jacobs, 1971). There may be a long-standing history of conflicts between the parents and children. These conflicts may lead to adolescent behavior problems, such as delinquency, dropping out of school, and aggressive tendencies. In addition, teenage alcoholics and abusers of other drugs have a relatively high rate of suicide.

Psychologists have developed a set of warning signs that indicate when a teenager's problems may be severe enough to warrant concern about the possibility of a suicide attempt (Hart & Keidel, 1979; Dunne, McIntosh & Dunne-Maxim, 1987). They include:

▶ School problems, such as missing classes, truancy, and a sudden change in grades

▶ Running away from home

▶ Frequent incidents of self-destructive behavior, such as careless accidents

▶ Loss of appetite or excessive eating

▶ Withdrawal from friends and peers

▶ Sleeping problems

▶ Signs of depression, tearfulness, or overt indications of psychological difficulties, such as hallucinations

▶ A preoccupation with death, an afterlife, or what would happen "if I died"

▶ Putting affairs in order, such as giving away prized possessions, making arrangements for the care of a pet, and drawing up a will

▶ An explicit announcement that the person is thinking about suicide

Of course, in some cases of teenage suicide none of these signs appears, and in some teenagers, some of the symptoms are present and suicide is never attempted. Yet if an adolescent shows indications that suicide is a possibility, it is unreasonable to ignore them, and it is wise to urge the person to seek professional help. Because suicidal people feel that they cannot be helped, assertive action may be needed, such as enlisting the assistance of family members or friends. Talk of suicide is a signal for help, not a confidence to be kept. As yet, no sure way of predicting the likelihood of suicide exists, and it is better to be safe than sorry.

RECAP AND REVIEW I

Recap

◀ Adolescence is the developmental stage between childhood and adulthood.

◀ Several critical physical changes occur during puberty. Early maturing is generally socially beneficial, whereas late maturing is usually disadvantageous.

◀ According to Kohlberg, moral development passes through a series of increasingly sophisticated levels. In Gilligan's contrasting view of moral development, women, more than men, focus on principles involving compassion toward the individual rather than on abstract principles of justice or fairness.

◀ During adolescence, people enter the crucial identity-versus-role-confusion stage, which may include an identity crisis.

◀ Although adolescence was once thought of as a stormy, rebellious period, psychologists now feel that such a view reflects more myth than reality.

◀ The rate of teenage suicide has tripled over the last two decades.

Review

1. Physical maturation occurring in adolescence is a result of the secretion of _____ .

2. Early-maturing females and males generally enjoy a higher self-concept. True or false? _____

3. The concept that there are fundamental differences in the ways men and women view moral behavior was proposed by
   a. Erik Erikson.
   b. Lawrence Kohlberg.
   c. Carol Gilligan.
   d. Carolyn Dash.

4. Match the example in the right-hand column with its corresponding stage of Erikson's psychosocial development theory on the left.

   ____ Identify vs. role confusion a. A few years back, Paul felt that his contributions to his family, work, and other commitments were insignificant. He now values his contributions and is optimistic about his future.

   ____ Intimacy vs. isolation b. Joni is having an emotionally trying adolescence. She finds herself grasping at different ways of behaving, trying to get a handle on who she really is.

   ____ Generativity vs. stagnation c. Mark has never felt the desire for such an intimate relationship as he does now with his college classmate Alicia.

5. Trouble in school, changes in appetite, and depression
   a. are normal adolescent behaviors.
   b. are consequences of late maturation in teenagers.
   c. may be warning signs that a teenager is at risk of suicide.
   d. are signs of a low level of moral development.

(Answers to review questions are on page 460.)

THE MIDDLE YEARS OF LIFE:
EARLY AND MIDDLE ADULTHOOD

At some point it just dawned on me: I'm an adult now. I've got a wife, I've got children, a mortgage, I complain about my taxes—I'm not too different from my own father, in fact. Probably the biggest change in my life that made me feel like an adult was having kids. Here were other people who were dependent on me. I couldn't just say to heck with it, walk away, and go on. . . . I had responsibilities. And I couldn't think any longer, "Someday I'll do this, someday I'll do that." Someday was *here*. If I wasn't successful, if I messed up my life, there would be no second chances.

The sentiments expressed by this young adult are common during the years of life known as early and middle adulthood. During this period, people "grow up"; they are considered both legally and socially to be full-fledged adult members of society.

Psychologists generally consider early adulthood to begin at around age 20 and last until about age 40 to 45, and middle adulthood to last from about age 40 to 45 to around age 65. Despite the enormous importance of these periods of life—in terms of both the accomplishments that occur within them and their overall length (together they span some forty years)—they have been studied less than any other stages by developmental psychologists. One reason is that the physical changes during these periods are less apparent and occur more gradually than do those at other times during the life span. In addition, the social changes are so diverse that they prevent simple categorization. Still, there has been a recent upsurge of interest in adulthood among developmental psychologists, with a special focus on the social changes that occur in terms of the family, marriage, divorce, and careers for women.

Young adulthood often brings added responsibilities. (Mark Antman/The Image Works.)

THE PEAK OF HEALTH: Physical Development

For most people, early adulthood marks the peak of physical health. From about 18 to 25 years of age, people's strength is greatest, their reflexes are quickest, and their chances of dying from disease are quite slim. Moreover, reproductive capabilities are at their highest level.

The changes that begin at age 25 are largely of a quantitative rather than a qualitative nature. The body begins to operate slightly less efficiently and becomes somewhat more prone to disease. Overall, however, ill health remains the exception; most people stay remarkably healthy. (Can you think of any machine other than the body that can operate without pause for so long a period?)

The major biological change that does occur pertains to reproductive capabilities during middle adulthood. On average, during their late forties or early fifties, women begin **menopause**, the point at which they stop menstruating and are no longer fertile. Because menopause is accompanied by a reduction in estrogen, a female hormone, women sometimes experience symptoms such as hot flashes, or sudden sensations of heat. Most symptoms of menopause, though, are successfully treated with artificial estrogen.

Menopause: The point at which women stop menstruating, generally at around age 45

Menopause was once blamed for a host of psychological symptoms, including depression, but most research now suggests that such problems, if they do occur, are caused more by women's perceived reactions to reaching an "old" age in a society that values youth so highly than by menopause itself. Society's attitudes, then, more than the physiological changes of menopause, may produce psychological difficulties (Ballinger, 1981).

For men, the aging process during middle adulthood is somewhat more subtle, since there are no physiological signals of increasing age equivalent to the end of menstruation in women. Moreover, men remain fertile and are capable of fathering children until well into old age. However, some gradual physical declines appear: Sperm production decreases and the frequency of orgasm tends to decline. Once again, though, any psychological difficulties that do occur are usually brought about, not so much by physical deterioration, but by the inability of the aging individual to meet the exaggerated standards of youthfulness held in high regard by society.

WORKING AT LIFE: Social Development

Whereas physical changes during adulthood reflect development of a quantitative nature, social developmental transitions are more profound. It is during this period that people typically launch themselves into careers, marriage, and families.

Psychologist Daniel Levinson (1986) has proposed a model of adult development based on a comprehensive study of major events in the lives of a group of forty men. Although his initial sample was small and consisted only of males, the study is important because it provided one of the first comprehensive descriptions of the stages through which people pass following adolescence. According to Levinson, six major stages occur from the entry into early adulthood through the end of middle adulthood (see Figure 13-3).

After a transitional period at around age 20, the stages in early adulthood relate to leaving one's family and entering the adult world. An individual envisions what Levinson calls "The Dream"—an all-encompassing vision

ANSWERS (REVIEW I):
1. Hormones **2.** True **3.** c **4.** b, c, a **5.** c

FIGURE 13-3

Developmental periods over the course of adulthood. (Source: Levinson, 1986.)

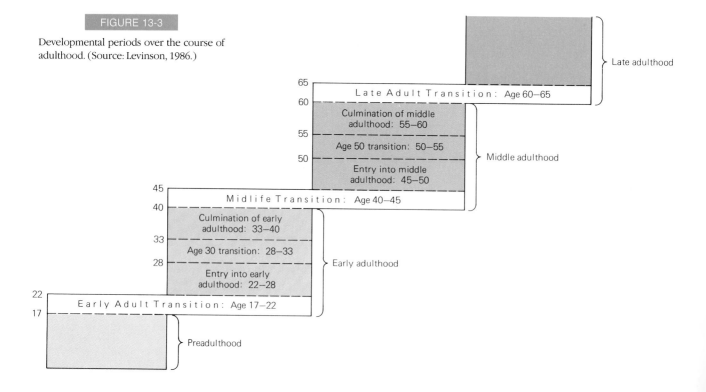

about what goals are desired from life, be it writing the great American novel or becoming a physician. Career choices are made, and perhaps discarded, during early adulthood, until eventually long-term decisions are reached. This leads to a period of settling down in the late thirties, during which people establish themselves in a particular set of roles and begin to evolve and work toward a vision of their own future.

Around the age of 40 or 45, people generally begin to question their lives as they enter a period called the **midlife transition**, and the idea that life is finite becomes paramount in their thinking. Rather than maintaining a future-oriented view of life, people begin to ask questions about their past accomplishments, assessing what they have done and how satisfying it has been to them (Gould, 1978). They realize that not all they had wanted to accomplish will be completed before their life ends.

Midlife transition: Beginning around the age of 40, a period during which we come to the realization that life is finite

In some cases, people's assessments of their lives are negative, and they may enter what has been popularly labeled a **midlife crisis**. As they face signs of physical aging, they become aware that their careers are not going to progress considerably further. Even if they have attained the heights to which they aspired—be it company president or well-respected community leader—they find that the reality of their accomplishments is not all that they had hoped it would be. As they look at their past, they may also be motivated to try to define what went wrong and how they can remedy old dissatisfactions.

Midlife crisis: The negative feelings that accompany the realization that we have not accomplished in life what we had hoped to

In most cases, though, the passage into middle age is relatively calm, and some developmental psychologists even question whether the midlife crisis occurs in most people (Whitbourne, 1986). Most 40-year-olds view their lives and accomplishments sufficiently positively that their midlife transition proceeds relatively smoothly, and the forties and fifties are a particularly rewarding period of life. Rather than looking to the future, people at this stage concentrate on the present, and their involvement with their families, friends, and other social groups takes on new importance. A major developmental thrust of this period of life is learning to accept that the die has been cast, and that one must come to terms with one's circumstances.

Finally, during the last stages of middle adulthood—the fifties—people generally become more accepting of others and their lives and less concerned about issues or problems which once bothered them. Rather than being driven to achieve as they were in their thirties, they come to accept the realization that death is inevitable, and they try to understand their accomplishments in terms of the broader meaning of life (Gould, 1978). Although people may begin, for the first time, to label themselves as "old," many also develop a sense of wisdom and feel freer to enjoy life (Karp, 1989).

Because most work on the phases of social development in adulthood has been based on the study of men's lives, it is important to consider whether women's lives follow the same patterns. We might expect significant gender differences on several grounds (Gilligan, 1982). For one thing, women often play different roles in society than men, either by choice or because of societal expectations. Moreover, women's roles have undergone rapid social change in the last decade, as we shall discuss next, making generalizations about women's development during early and middle adulthood difficult.

Unfortunately, there is as yet no clear answer to the question of how women's social development differs from men's, since a sufficiently large body of data focusing directly on women has only begun to be accumulated. Some recent research suggests, however, that there are both similarities and differences between men and women (see the Cutting Edge box). Levinson (in press), for example, argues that women generally go through the same stages at the same ages as men, although disparities exist in the specific details of some of the stages. For instance, important differences appear during "The Dream," the stage in which people develop a vision of what their future life will encompass. Women often have greater difficulty than men in forming a clear dream, for they may experience conflict between the goals of working and of raising a family. For men, this conflict tends to be much less important, since a man who wishes to marry and have a family usually views working as the means of taking care of his family.

One study of early adulthood suggests that there is a major period of disruption, reassessment, and reorientation around the age of 30 for women (Reinke, Holmes & Harris, 1985). Although it is not clear why this disruption occurs, the age-30 transition appears to have greater impact on women than the age-40 transition. In contrast, for men the midlife transition at age 40 is typically more powerful. Further research must be carried out, of course, before the universality of these findings can be determined.

THE CUTTING EDGE

MARKING TIME: CHARTING THE SOCIAL CLOCKS OF LIFE

Completing school. Finding a job. Getting married. Having a child. Changing jobs. Becoming a grandparent.

Each of these events constitutes a tick on what has been called the **social clock**, the psychic timepiece that indicates the major milestones in adult life (Neugarten, 1979). We all carry a social clock within ourselves, providing a sense of whether we have reached life's milestones on time or whether, in comparison with our peers, we are early or late.

According to psychologist Ravenna Helson and colleagues, who have been carrying out a long-term study of the social clocks of a sample of women who graduated from college in the early 1960s, there are several timepieces from which to choose—and the choice has consequences for social and personality development during adulthood (Helson & Moane, 1987). Helson drew distinctions between women whose social clocks were focused on their families, those who sought their place in society through high-level

careers, and those who had chosen neither of those social clocks and followed a different pattern.

After analyzing the results of several questionnaires and measures of personality administered when the women graduated from college, when they were 27 years old, and again when they were 43, Helson found several significant patterns. For the sample as a whole, there were increases in self-discipline and commitment to duties, in independence and confidence, and in coping skills. Scores on measures of behavior traditionally associated with femininity changed direction over time; they increased from age 21 to 27 but decreased between ages 27 and 43. Helson speculates that the increase was due to a rise in sex-role specialization as women engaged in mothering, whereas the later decrease

was produced by a decline in child-care responsibilities as their offspring aged.

What is perhaps most interesting about the results is that women who chose to pursue either family or career patterns showed the most positive—and similar—social and personality development; those who neither had families nor were greatly invested in their careers showed little, or even negative, change. Thus, it is not so much the particular pattern of choices made by the subjects that resulted in their social and personality development, but rather their engagement in some socially legitimate and acceptable social-clock pattern. It seems as if many of the activities of young adulthood, with their demands for independence, perseverance, and interpersonal skills, spur developmental change.

Social clock: The psychic timepiece that indicates major milestones in adult life

FAMILY TIES: Marriage, Children, and Divorce

In many a fairy tale, the typical ending has a dashing young man and a beautiful woman marrying, having children, and living happily ever after. Unfortunately, such a scenario is just that—a fairy tale. In most cases, it does not match the realities of love and marriage in the 1980s. Today, it is likely that the man and woman would first live together, then get married and have children—but ultimately end up getting divorced.

According to census figures, the percentage of unmarried couples in U.S. households has increased dramatically over the last two decades, and the average age at which marriage takes place is higher than at any time since the turn of the century (U.S. Census Bureau, 1985). When people do marry, anywhere from one in eight marriages (for older couples) to as many as one in two (for couples whose marriages began after 1970) end in divorce, and nearly two-thirds of the marriages that break up are in families with children (Hetherington, 1986). Even though divorce rates have actually declined since a peak in 1981, if current trends continue, a child born in the mid-1980s will have a 40 percent chance of seeing his or her parents divorce and a 20 percent chance of experiencing a second parental divorce (Blakeslee, 1984; *Time*, 1987). Because of these trends, society has witnessed almost a doubling in single-parent households since 1970 (see Figure 13-4).

Divorce and subsequent life in a single-parent household presents the potential for the development of several kinds of psychological difficulties, for both parents and children. Children initially may be exposed to high levels of parental conflict, leading to heightened anxiety and aggressive behavior. Later separation from one or the other parent is a painful experience and may result in obstacles to establishing close relationships throughout life. In many cases, good child-care is hard to find, producing psychological stress and sometimes guilt over the arrangements working parents must, for economic reasons, make. Time is always at a premium in single-parent families. Finally, children in single-parent families may feel deprived at not having a living arrangement that matches the typical one in society.

On the other hand, most evidence suggests that children from single-parent families are as well adjusted as those from two-parent families (Svanum, Bringle & McLaughlin, 1982). Moreover, it is clear that children are more successful growing up in a relatively tranquil single-parent family than in a family in which the parents are engaged in continuous conflict with one another (Hetherington, Cox & Cox, 1978; Hetherington, 1986).

Do current statistics suggest that marriage is as obsolete as the horse and buggy? At first they may seem to, but a closer look reveals that this is

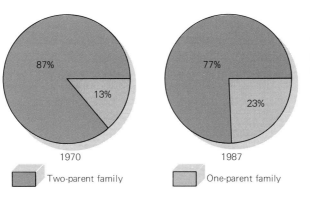

FIGURE 13-4

The proportion of one-parent families has almost doubled over the last two decades. (U.S. Census Bureau, 1988.)

1970   1987

Two-parent family   One-parent family

Working wives, whether they are executives
or waitresses, usually do most of the household chores in addition to their paid jobs.
(John Lei/Stock Boston.)

not the case. For one thing, survey data show that most people want to get
married at some time in their lives, and close to 95 percent eventually do
(Strong, 1978). Even people who divorce are more likely than not to get
remarried, some for three or more times—a phenomenon known as serial
marriage (Brody, Neubaum & Forehand, 1988). Finally, individuals who are
married report being happier than those who are not (Glenn, 1987).

Although marriage thus remains an important institution in our culture,
the roles that men and women play within a marriage are changing. More
women than ever before either want, or are forced by their economic situation, to act simultaneously as wives, mothers, and wage earners—in contrast
to the traditional marriage, in which the husband was the sole wage earner
and the wife took primary responsibility for caring for the home and children
(Gottfried & Gottfried, 1988). In fact, statistics show that 71 percent of all
married women with school-aged children are employed outside the home
and that the number of women in the work force has increased dramatically
(U.S. Bureau of Labor Statistics, 1987). In 1940 only one-quarter of the work
force was female, but by 1980 it had risen to just over one-half.

Although married women are more likely than they once were to be out
of the house working, they are not out of the kitchen, for the distribution of
household tasks between husbands and wives has not changed substantially.
Working wives are still more likely to view themselves as responsible for the
traditional homemaking tasks such as cooking and cleaning, whereas husbands of working wives still view themselves as responsible primarily for
such household tasks as repairing broken appliances, putting up screens in
the summer, and doing yard work (Burros, 1988).

In addition, the way in which time is spent by married men and women
during the average week is quite different. As you can see in Figure 13-5,
although married men average slightly more work hours per week than
married women, they spend considerably less time on household chores and
child-care. Overall, working women spend much more time than working
men on combined job and family demands (Googins & Burden, 1987).

Families in which both parents work still tend to view the mother as
holding primary responsibility for child rearing. Consequently, rather than
careers supplanting what women do at home, they often exist in addition to
the role of homemaker. This factor has led to resentment toward husbands
who spend less time than wives may have expected on child-care and house-

FIGURE 13-5

The number of hours per week devoted to home chores and child care differ considerably for men and women, even though they spend almost the same number of hours on the job. (Googins & Burden, 1987.)

work (Ruble et al., 1988; Williams, 1983). For women, the competing demands of family and work makes social development during early adulthood particularly arduous.

On the other hand, the benefits of work may outweigh the disadvantages of having major responsibilities in multiple roles. For instance, women who work, particularly those in high-prestige occupations, report feeling a greater sense of mastery, pride, and competence than nonworking women (Baruch, Barnett & Rivers, 1983). The value of work, then, goes beyond merely earning a salary and extends to providing self-satisfaction and a sense of contributing to society (Hoffman, 1989).

It is clear that success at work has important psychological consequences for both men and women. People report feeling happier and more in control of their lives, have higher self esteem, and even feel that they have better marriages when they are successful at their jobs. Conversely, work failures—such as being fired—can lead to depression, impotence, and a host of other psychological symptoms (Gruenberg, 1980). In sum, for men and women in the middle years of life, job-related achievement represents an important aspect of continued growth and development.

RECAP AND REVIEW II

Recap

◀ The peak of physical strength occurs from about age 18 to age 25, after which there are declines in strength and general health.

◀ According to a model developed by Levinson, social development during early and middle adulthood proceeds through a series of stages.

◀ Although many marriages end in divorce, marriage is still highly valued by society, with most people saying that they want to get married and ultimately doing so.

◀ The proportion of working women has increased, although the division of household roles between husband and wife has not altered radically.

Review

1. We experience our greatest physical fitness between

   a. ages 12 and 22.
   b. ages 18 and 22.
   c. ages 18 and 25.
   d. ages 22 and 28.

2. Women's reproductive years end with the onset of _____ , at which point there is a decrease in the female hormone _____ .

3. Men undergo a loss of fertility during the middle years. True or false? _____

4. Forty-year-old Martin recently found himself surveying his goals and accomplishments to date. Although he has accomplished a lot, he realizes that many of his goals will not be met in his lifetime. Levinson would term this stage in Martin's life the _____ _____ .

5. Early research points to the probability that men and women both undergo their most powerful life transitions

at about age 40. True or false? _____

6. In Helson's research on social clocks, women's scores on measures of traditional femininity _____ between the ages of 21 and 27, and _____ between the ages of 27 and 43.

7. For both men and women, success at work is usually accompanied by
   a. a decline in the importance of family life.
   b. resentment toward one's spouse.
   c. depression, impotence, and psychological symptoms.
   d. higher self-esteem and greater satisfaction with marriage.

(Answers to review questions are on page 468.)

THE LATER YEARS OF LIFE: GROWING OLD

I can't quite figure out where all the time went. Seventy-six years old. It sounds ancient, even to me.

The funny part is I really don't *feel* any older. Oh, my body has its share of aches and pains, and I don't move around as fast as I used to. And I forget things. But I've been forgetting things all my life.

I guess the most surprising thing is that it doesn't bother me all that much to be old and to know that death can't be too far away. It's quite a contrast to how I felt when I was younger—I used to be so afraid of getting old and of dying. Now, though, things are different. Of course, I'm not ready to die, and I sure don't want to. But it doesn't scare me the way it once did. After all, we all die sometime, don't we?

The fact that death is indeed a universal experience has not stopped it from being a source of fear and concern to many people, just as it once was to the speaker above. And many younger people exhibit similar negative feelings toward the entire period of old age.

However, old age is rapidly being viewed in a more favorable light as **gerontologists**, specialists who study aging, have begun to debunk many misconceptions regarding old age. Focusing on the period that starts at around age 65, gerontologists have made important contributions in clarifying the capabilities of the elderly and demonstrated that significant developmental processes continue even during old age.

Gerontologists: Specialists who study aging

THE OLD BODY: Physical Changes in the Elderly

Napping, eating, walking, conversing. It probably doesn't surprise you that these relatively unvigorous activities represent the typical pastimes of the elderly. But what is striking about this list is that these activities are identical to the most common leisure activities reported in a survey of college students. Although the students cited more active pursuits—such as sailing and playing basketball—as their favorite activities, in actuality they engaged in such sports relatively infrequently, spending most of their free time napping, eating, walking, and conversing (Harper, 1978).

Although the leisure activities in which the elderly engage may not differ all that much from those that younger people pursue, many physical changes are, of course, brought about by the aging process. The most obvious are those of appearance—hair thinning and turning gray, skin wrinkling and folding, and sometimes a slight loss of height as the size of the disks between vertebrae in the spine decreases—but there are also more subtle changes in

The physical changes that come with age can be seen in these four self-portraits by Rembrandt. (Top left, Indianapolis Museum of Art/The Clowes Fund Collection; top right, Gemaldegalerie Alte Meister/Staatliche Kunstammlungen Kassel; bottom right, National Galleries of Scotland/Duke of Sutherland; bottom left, © copyright Scala Art Resource, 1986.)

the body's biological functioning (Munnichs, Mussen, Obrich & Coleman, 1985).

For example, sensory acuity decreases as a result of aging; vision and hearing are less sharp, and smell and taste are not as sensitive. Reaction time slows. There are changes in physical stamina. Because oxygen intake and heart-pumping ability decline, the body is unable to replenish lost nutrients as quickly—and therefore the rebound from physical activity is slower (Shock, 1962). Of course, none of these changes begins suddenly at age 65; gradual declines in some kinds of functioning start earlier. It is in old age, however, that these changes become more apparent.

What are the reasons for these physical declines? There are two major explanations: genetic preprogramming theories and wear-and-tear theories (Bergener, Ermini & Stahelin, 1985; Whitbourne, 1986). **Genetic preprogramming theories** suggest that there is a built-in time limit to the reproduction of human cells, and that after a certain time they are no longer able to divide (Hayflick, 1974). A variant of this idea is that some cells are genetically preprogrammed to become harmful to the body after a certain amount

Genetic preprogramming theories of aging: Theories that suggest a built-in time limit to the reproduction of human cells

INDIVIDUAL DEVELOPMENT
AND DIFFERENTIATION

Wear-and-tear theories of aging: Theories that suggest that the body's mechanical functions cease efficient activity and, in effect, wear out

of time has gone by, causing the internal biology of the body to "self-destruct" (Pereira-Smith, 1988).

The second approach for understanding physical declines due to aging is based on the same factors that force people to buy new cars every so often: mechanical devices wear out. According to **wear-and-tear theories**, the mechanical functions of the body simply stop working efficiently. Moreover, wastes that are by-products of energy production eventually accumulate, and mistakes are made when cells reproduce. Eventually the body, in effect, wears out.

We do not know which of these theories provides a better explanation of the physical aging process; it may be that both contribute. It is important to realize, however, that physical aging is not a disease, but rather a natural biological process (Rowe & Kahn, 1987). Many physical functions do not decline with age. For example, sex remains pleasurable well into old age (although the frequency of sexual activity decreases), and some elderly people even report that the pleasure they derive from sex increases (Lobsenz, 1975).

Furthermore, neither genetic preprogramming theories nor wear-and-tear theories successfully explain a fact that is immediately apparent to anyone studying aging: Women live longer than men. Throughout the industrialized world, women outlive men by a margin of four to ten years (Holden, 1987). The female advantage begins just after conception. Although more males are conceived than females, males have a higher rate of prenatal, infant, and childhood death, and by age 30 there are equal numbers of males and females. By age 65, 84 percent of females and 70 percent of males are still alive.

Happily, though, the gender gap is not increasing—mainly because of positive changes in men's health habits, including decreased smoking and consumption of cholesterol and greater exercise. But health habits do not provide the complete explanation for the gap, and an explanation of why women live longer than men remains to be found. What is clear is that women, more often than men, must make the profound adjustments needed following the death of a spouse. Women's longer lives are something of a mixed blessing: The end of life must frequently be faced without a partner.

THINKING ABOUT—AND DURING—OLD AGE: Cognitive Changes

Three women were talking about the inconveniences of growing old.

"Sometimes," one of them confessed, "when I go to my refrigerator, I can't remember if I'm putting something in or taking something out."

"Oh, that's nothing," said the second woman. "There are times when I find myself at the foot of the stairs wondering if I'm going up or if I've just come down."

"Well, my goodness!" exclaimed the third woman. "I'm certainly glad I don't have any problems like that"—and she knocked on wood. "Oh," she said, starting up out of her chair, "there's someone at the door" (Dent, 1984, p. 38).

ANSWERS (REVIEW II):
1. c **2.** Menopause, estrogen **3.** False; males remain fertile well into old age **4.** Midlife transition **5.** False; research suggests that women undergo their most important transition at around age 30 **6.** Increase, decrease **7.** d

At one time, many gerontologists would have agreed with the view—suggested by the story above—that the elderly are forgetful and confused. Today, however, most research tells us that this is far from an accurate assessment of elderly people's capabilities.

One reason for the change in view is the use of more sophisticated research techniques. For example, if we were to give a group of elderly people an IQ test, we might find that the average score was lower than for a group of younger people. We might conclude that this signifies a decline in intelligence. But if we looked a little closer at the specific test, we might find that such a conclusion was unwarranted. For instance, many IQ tests include portions based on physical performance (such as arranging a group of blocks) or on speed. In such a case, poorer performance on the IQ test may be due to increases in reaction time—a physical decline that accompanies old age—and have little or nothing to do with the intellectual capabilities of the elderly (Schaie, 1988; Cornelius & Caspi, 1987).

Other difficulties hamper research into the cognitive functioning of the elderly. For example, the elderly are more likely than younger people to suffer from physical ill health. Some studies of IQ in the past inadvertently compared a group of physically healthy younger people with a group of elderly people who were generally less healthy, with the finding of significantly lower scores for the elderly group. However, when only *healthy* elderly people are observed, intellectual declines are markedly less evident (Riegel & Riegel, 1972; Avorn, 1985). Furthermore, it is unfair to compare the test results of an elderly group with those of a younger group of subjects when the mean level of education is probably lower in the older group (for historical reasons) than in the younger one.

Similarly, declines in the IQ scores of the elderly may be caused by their having lower motivation to perform well on intelligence tests than younger people. Finally, traditional IQ tests may not be the most appropriate measures of intelligence in the elderly. For example, as we discussed in Chapter 8, some researchers contend that several kinds of intelligence exist, and in fact some researchers have found that the elderly perform better on tests of everyday problems and social competence than do younger individuals (Cornelius & Caspi, 1987).

On the other hand, some declines in the intellectual functioning of the elderly have been found, even when using more sophisticated research methods (Cerella, 1985; Schaie & Willis, 1985). If you recall from Chapter 8, intelligence can be conceptualized in terms of **fluid intelligence**—the ability to deal with new problems and situations—and **crystallized intelligence**—intelligence based on the accumulation of particular kinds of knowledge and experience as well as on strategies that have been acquired through the use of fluid intelligence. Tests show clear, although not substantial, declines in fluid intelligence in old age. It is noteworthy, however, that such changes actually begin to appear in early adulthood, as indicated in Figure 13-6 (Baltes & Schaie, 1974; Schaie, 1985).

Crystallized intelligence, in contrast, does not decline; it actually improves with age, as shown in Figure 13-6. For example, an elderly woman asked to solve a geometry problem (which taps fluid intelligence) might have greater difficulty than she once did, but she might be better at solving verbal problems that require reasoned conclusions.

One possible reason for the developmental differences between fluid and crystallized intelligence during old age is that fluid intelligence may be

Fluid intelligence: The ability to deal with new problems and situations

Crystallized intelligence: Intelligence based on the store of specific information, skills, and strategies that people have acquired through experience

FIGURE 13-6

Although crystallized intelligence remains steady and even seems to increase slightly in the elderly, fluid intelligence does show a decline. (Schaie, 1984.)

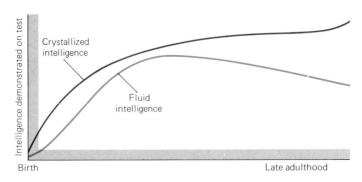

more sensitive to changes in the nervous system than crystallized intelligence (Horn, 1985). Another factor may be the degree to which the two kinds of intelligence are used during a person's lifetime. Whatever the reason, people compensate for the decline. They can still learn what they want to; it just may take more time (Storandt, 1984).

Furthermore, new evidence suggests that cognitive declines might be remedied by increasing the amount of blood in the brains of the elderly. In support of this reasoning, in one experiment the drug Nimodipine—which increases blood flow—was given to a group of elderly rabbits. The rabbits that received the drug learned a classically conditioned response significantly faster than a control group of rabbits that did not receive the drug. In fact, the rabbits that received the drug learned as rapidly as a group of young rabbits (Deyo, Straube, & Disterhoft, 1989). (Other ways of increasing intellectual functioning are explored in the Psychology at Work box.)

Are the Elderly Forgetful? Memory Changes in Old Age
One of the characteristics most frequently attributed to the elderly is forgetfulness. How accurate is this assumption?

Most evidence suggests that memory change is not inevitable in the aging process, although some elderly people show declines. Moreover, when memory deficits do exist, they most typically occur only in long-term memory; the capacity of short-term memory rarely declines, except in cases of illness (Craik, 1977).

Some cases of memory failures are due merely to changes in the lives of the elderly (Ratner, 1987). For instance, it is not surprising that a retired person, who may no longer face the same kind of consistent intellectual challenges encountered on the job, might well be less practiced in using memory or even be less motivated to remember things, leading to an apparent decline in memory. Even in cases in which long-term memory declines, the elderly person can usually profit from compensatory strategies. In fact, when the elderly are provided with the kind of mnemonic procedures that we discussed in Chapter 6, long-term memory not only can be prevented from deteriorating, but actually may improve (Perlmutter & Mitchell, 1986; Brody, 1987).

In the past, elderly people with severe cases of memory decline, accompanied by other cognitive difficulties, were viewed as suffering from senility. **Senility** is a broad, imprecise term typically applied to elderly people who experience progressive deterioration of mental abilities, including memory loss, disorientation to time and place, and general confusion.

Once thought to be an inevitable state that accompanies aging, senility

Senility: A broad, imprecise term used in reference to elderly people who experience progressive deterioration of mental abilities, including memory loss, confusion of time and place, and general disorientation

Winston Churchill becomes British prime minister for the first time. Age: 65.

Grandma Moses, who began to paint only ten years earlier, has her first one-person exhibit. Age: 80.

▲ ▲ ▲

Cellist Pablo Casals gives a concert some eight years before his death. Age: 88.

Although the stereotype of old age suggests that senility and declining awareness of what is happening in the world are inevitable, many elderly people—like the three celebrities mentioned above—clearly rebut this mistaken notion. Still, for some people, the stereotype becomes reality, and a decline in cognitive abilities occurs as they age.

On the other hand, there are large individual differences; some people keep and even increase their intellectual capabilities well into their eighties and nineties. The fact that

OLDER BUT WISER: INCREASING INTELLECTUAL PERFORMANCE IN THE ELDERLY

some elderly perform so well cognitively raises the question of whether intellectual declines are truly inevitable (Rowe & Kahn, 1987). In fact, some gerontologists have argued that, with appropriate environmental stimulation, cognitive deterioration might largely be prevented—and in some cases even reversed.

In clear support of this hypothesis, K. Warner Schaie and Sherry L. Willis of Pennsylvania State University devised a five-hour training program involving the teaching of reasoning and spatial skills to the elderly (Schaie & Willis, 1986). The subjects were 229 men and women whose ages ranged from 64 to 95, with a mean age of 73. Participants in the program were taught general strategies for dealing with problems,

and they also completed practice test items typical of those used to measure cognitive skills.

After completing the training program, subjects were tested on a variety of measures, and the program was demonstrated to be a success. Of those participants who had previously shown declines in reasoning and spatial skills, most began to improve, and the training even enhanced the performance of participants whose abilities had remained relatively stable. Specifically, more than 55 percent of the subjects who had prior declines in intellectual functioning showed significant improvement, and over 39 percent of the stable subjects achieved significant increments following training.

The results argue quite clearly that declines in cognitive functioning in old age should not be considered unavoidable. Intellectual abilities in the elderly remain resilient, and even when reductions have occurred, it seems that they may be reversed through appropriate kinds of training.

is now viewed by most gerontologists as a label that has outlived its usefulness. Rather than senility being the cause of certain symptoms, the symptoms are deemed to be caused by some other factor. In some cases there is an actual disease, such as **Alzheimer's disease**, the progressive brain disorder discussed in Chapter 6 which leads to a gradual and irreversible decline in mental abilities. In other cases, the symptoms of senility are caused by tem-

Alzheimer's disease: A progressive brain disease leading to an irreversible decline in mental and physical abilities

By engaging in activities that provide stimulation, older people can keep their coordination, reaction time, and cognitive skills in shape. (Charles Gupton/Stock Boston.)

INDIVIDUAL DEVELOPMENT
AND DIFFERENTIATION

porary anxiety and depression, which may be successfully treated, or may even be due to overmedication. The danger is that people suffering such symptoms may be labeled senile and left untreated, thereby continuing their decline—even though treatment would have been beneficial.

OLD BUT NOT ALONE: The Social World of the Elderly

Just as the view that senility is an inevitable outcome of old age has proved to be wrong, so has the view that old age inevitably brings loneliness. In fact, the elderly most often see themselves as functioning members of society, with one representative poll showing that just 12 percent of people 65 and over view loneliness as a serious problem (Harris, 1975).

Still, the social patterns and behaviors of the elderly are different in some respects from those of younger individuals. Two major approaches have been suggested to explain patterns of successful aging and the nature of elderly people's social environment: disengagement theory and activity theory.

Disengagement theory of aging: A theory that suggests that aging is a gradual withdrawal from the world on physical, psychological, and social levels

Disengagement theory sees aging as a gradual withdrawal from the world on physical, psychological, and social levels (Cumming & Henry, 1961). Physically, lower energy levels produce less activity; psychologically, the focus shifts from others to the self; and socially, there is less interaction with others and a reduction in the level of participation in society at large. But rather than viewing this disengagement in a negative light, theorists suggest that it should be seen positively, since it provides for increased reflectiveness and decreased emotional investment in others at a time of life when social relationships will inevitably be ended by death.

Disengagement theory has been criticized because of its suggestion that disengagement is an automatic process, marking a sharp departure from earlier behavior patterns. Even more important are data showing that the elderly who report being the happiest are those who remain the most active (Havighurst, 1973).

Grand Master cyclist Fred Knoller, photographed at age 87, illustrates the view that the elderly who age most successfully are those who maintain the activities of their earlier years. (James Kamp/Black Star.)

Such criticisms have led to the development of an alternative approach describing social adjustment to aging. **Activity theory** suggests that the elderly who age most successfully are those who maintain the interests and activities they had during middle age and who resist any decline in the amount and kind of social interaction they have with others (Blau, 1973). According to activity theory, old age should reflect a continuation, as much as possible, of the activities in which people participated during the earlier part of their lives, as well as activities to replace those lost through changes such as retirement.

Activity theory is not without its critics. For instance, activity alone does not guarantee happiness. Rather, the *nature* of activities in which people engage is probably more critical (Gubrium, 1973). Furthermore, not all elderly people need a life filled with activities and social interaction to be happy; as in every stage of life, there are those who are just as satisfied leading a relatively inactive, solitary life as one filled with activity and social relationships.

We cannot say whether disengagement theory or activity theory presents a more accurate view of the elderly, probably because there are vast individual differences in how people cope with becoming old. Clearly, however, the elderly are not just marking time until death. Rather, old age is a time of continued growth and development, as important as any other period of life.

Activity theory of aging: A theory that suggests that the elderly who age most successfully are those who maintain the interests and activities they had during middle age

THE INFORMED CONSUMER OF PSYCHOLOGY: Adjusting to Death

At some time in your life, you will face death—certainly your own, and probably the deaths of friends and loved ones. Although there is nothing more inevitable in life than death, it remains a frightening, emotion-laden topic. In fact, there may be nothing more stressful than the death of a loved one or the contemplation of your own imminent death, and preparing for death will likely represent one of your most crucial developmental tasks.

Not too long ago, talk of death was taboo. The topic was never mentioned to dying people, and gerontologists had little to say about it. That changed, however, with the pioneering work of Elisabeth Kübler-Ross (1969), who brought the subject out into the open with her observation that those facing death move through five stages.

▶ Denial. In this first stage, people resist the idea that they are dying. Even if told that their chances for survival are small, they refuse to admit that they are facing death.

▶ Anger. After moving beyond the denial stage, dying people are angry—angry at people around them who are in good health, angry at medical professionals for being ineffective, angry at God. They ask the question "Why me?" and are unable to answer it without feeling anger.

▶ Bargaining. Anger leads to bargaining, in which the dying try to think of ways to postpone death. They may decide to dedicate their lives to religion if God saves them; they may say, "If only I can live to see my son married, I will accept death then." Such bargains are rarely kept, most often because the dying person's illness keeps progressing and invalidates any "agreements."

▶ Depression. When dying people come to feel that bargaining is of no use, they move to the next stage: depression. They realize that the die is cast, that they are losing their loved ones and their lives really are coming to an end. They are experiencing what Kübler-Ross calls "preparatory grief" for their own death.

▶ Acceptance. In this last stage, people are past mourning for the loss of their own lives, and they accept impending death. Usually, they are unemotional and uncommunicative; it is as if they have made peace with themselves and are expecting death without rancor.

Although not everyone experiences each of these stages in the same way, if at all, Kübler-Ross's theory remains our best description of people's reactions to their approaching death. There are, however, vast individual differences, depending on the specific cause of death as well as the person's sex, age, and personality and the type of support received from family and friends (Kastenbaum, 1975; Goleman, 1988).

Mourning

For the survivors of a loved one's death, there remains a painful period of mourning and coming to terms with death. Most adults pass through four major stages of grief, not altogether unrelated to what the dying person experienced prior to death (Greenblat, 1978; Malinak, Hoyt & Patterson, 1979).

The first stage is one of shock, denial, and disbelief, usually lasting a few days, although sometimes extending over a period of weeks or even months. This phase is followed by a period of depression, of yearning for the dead person, and wishing he or she could somehow return. Crying, anger, fear, sleeplessness, and other symptoms of grief are common during this period, which peaks within five days to two weeks. In some cases, it lasts much longer—up to a year or more—going beyond what is considered normal.

In the second and third stages, the person comes to terms with the death. After a period of mourning, people pick up the pieces of their lives, turning to others and beginning to free themselves from some of the bonds that held them to the loved one. Finally, in the fourth stage they begin to construct a new identity, one that is independent of the lost loved one. They form new relationships and may come to understand themselves better. In fact, around half of all people who reach this stage report that the death helped them grow as human beings, forcing them to be more self-reliant and more appreciative of life.

As with the stages of dying, not everyone moves through the same stages of mourning in the same manner; people will experience grief in their own way, partly dependent on the nature of their relationship with the deceased. Furthermore, some deaths are particularly difficult to deal with, such as a sudden, untimely death or the death of one's child, when grief is so profound that the person is immobilized, when mourning continues for extraordinarily long periods, when physical symptoms develop, or when there are general, long-lasting changes in personality, the mourner may require some professional guidance for dealing with his or her grief (Sanders, 1988; Goleman, 1988; Weiss, 1988).

Few of us enjoy the contemplation of death. Yet awareness of its psychological effects and consequences can make its inevitable coming less anxiety-producing and perhaps more understandable.

Recap

◀ The leisure activities of the elderly do not differ substantially from those of younger people, but a number of physical declines do occur with age. These declines are explained by two classes of theories: genetic preprogramming theories and wear-and-tear theories.

◀ Fluid and crystallized intelligence and memory are affected by aging.

◀ Disengagement theory and activity theory seek to explain changes in social activity during old age.

◀ People approaching death move through a series of stages, as do people mourning another's death.

Review

1. Psychologists who study old age are called _____ .
2. a. The idea that the reproduction of cells is finite in all humans is a common factor in _____ theories.
   b. _____ theories hold that, like machines, the mechanical functions of the body eventually stop working efficiently.
3. Which of the following is false?
   a. Aging is accompanied by a decline in fluid intelligence.
   b. Elderly people generally score higher than young people on most sections of intelligence tests.
   c. As a result of cultural and historical factors, average education levels of different age groups are not the same.
   d. Skills measured by IQ tests include speed and agility, a fact that may cause elderly people to score lower.
4. Memory deficits in the elderly
   a. are a result of neural wear and tear.
   b. are an unavoidable part of aging.
   c. may result from lack of practice.
   d. are more pronounced in men than in women.
5. Lois feels that, in her old age, she has gradually decreased her social contacts and has become more self-oriented. A proponent of _____ theory interprets the situation as a result of Lois's not maintaining her past interests. A supporter of _____ theory views her behavior in a more positive light, suggesting that it is a natural process accompanied by enhanced reflectiveness and declining emotional investment.
6. Name the five stages in Elisabeth Kübler-Ross's theory of preparation for death.

(Answers to review questions are on page 476.)

◀ LOOKING BACK

1. Adolescence, the developmental stage between childhood and adulthood, is marked by the onset of puberty, the point at which sexual maturity occurs. The age at which puberty begins has implications for the way people view themselves and the way they are seen by others.

2. Moral judgments during adolescence increase in sophistication, according to Kohlberg's three-stage, six-level model. Although Kohlberg's stages are an adequate description of males' moral judgments, they seem not to be as applicable in describing females' judgments. Specifically, Gilligan suggests that women view morality in terms of concern for individuals rather than in terms of broad, general principles of justice or fairness; in her view, moral development in women proceeds in three stages.

3. According to Erikson's model of psychosocial development, adolescence may be accompanied by an identity crisis, although this is by no means universal. Adolescence is followed by three stages of psychosocial development which cover the remainder of the life span.

4. Early adulthood marks the peak of physical health. Physical changes occur relatively gradually in men and women during adulthood, although one major change occurs at the end of middle adulthood for women: They begin menopause, after which they are no longer fertile. For men, the aging process is more subtle, since they remain fertile.

5. Levinson's model of adult development suggests that six major stages occur, beginning with entry into early adulthood at around age 20 and ending at around age 60 or 65. One of the most critical transitions—at least for men—occurs during midlife (around age 40 to 45), when people typically experience a midlife transition in which the notion that life is not infinite becomes more important. In some cases this can lead to a midlife crisis; usually, however, the passage into middle age is relatively calm. Although Levinson suggests that women's lives follow the same pattern as men's, several differences have been identified (for instance, in "The Dream" stage), and some research suggests that, for women, the transition around age 30 is of greater importance than the age-40 transition.

6. As aging continues during middle adulthood, people realize in their fifties that their lives and accomplishments are fairly well set, and they try to come to terms with them.

7. Among the most important developmental milestones during adulthood are marriage, family changes, and di-

vorce. Although divorce is more prevalent than ever before, most people still view marriage as important and desirable. Another important determinant of adult development is work. Recently, single and married women have joined the work force in historically high numbers.

8. Old age may bring marked physical declines. Although the activities of the elderly are not all that different from those of younger people, elderly people do experience reaction-time increases, as well as sensory declines and a decrease in physical stamina. These declines might be caused by genetic preprogramming, which sets a time limit on the reproduction of human cells, or they may simply be due to wear and tear on the mechanical parts of the body.

9. Although intellectual declines were once thought to be an inevitable part of aging, most research suggests that this is not necessarily the case. Fluid intelligence does decline with age, and long-term memory abilities are sometimes impaired. In contrast, crystallized intelligence shows slight increases with age, and short-term memory remains at about the same levels. Senility, then, is no longer seen as a universal outcome of old age.

10. Disengagement theory sees successful aging as a process accompanied by gradual withdrawal from the physical, psychological, and social worlds. In contrast, activity theory suggests that the maintenance of interests and activities from earlier years leads to successful aging. Because there are vast individual differences, it is unclear whether either of the two theories is completely accurate.

11. According to Kübler-Ross, dying people move through five stages as they face death: denial, anger, bargaining, depression, and acceptance. Following the death of a loved one, mourners also appear to move through a series of stages in coming to terms with death.

KEY TERMS AND CONCEPTS ▶

adolescence (p. 450)
puberty (450)
identity-versus-role-confusion stage (454)
identity (454)
intimacy-versus-isolation stage (454)
generativity-versus-stagnation stage (455)
ego-integrity-versus-despair stage (456)

menopause (459)
midlife transition (461)
midlife crisis (461)
social clock (462)
gerontologists (466)
genetic preprogramming theories of aging (467)

wear-and-tear theories of aging (468)
fluid intelligence (469)
crystallized intelligence (469)
senility (470)
Alzheimer's disease (471)
disengagement theory of aging (472)
activity theory of aging (473)

FOR FURTHER STUDY AND APPLICATION ▶

Steinberg, L. (1989). *Adolescence* (2nd ed.) New York: Knopf.
Rice, F. P. (1984). *The adolescent: Development, relationships, and culture* (4th ed.). Boston: Allyn & Bacon.

These two books provide a solid overview of the adolescent period of development—probably the best-researched period past childhood.

Whitbourne, S. K. (1986). *Adult development.* New York: Praeger.

This volume presents an excellent summary of postadolescent development.

Cunningham, W. R., & Brookbank, J. W. (1988). *Gerontology: The psychology, biology, and sociology of aging.* New York: Harper & Row.

This text focuses on old age, covering the period from a variety of viewpoints.

Sheehy, G. (1976). *Passages.* New York: Dutton.

Although not sophisticated in a scientific sense, this book describes patterns of development during adulthood, and provides rich insights into the kinds of changes that occur during life.

Kübler-Ross, E. (1981). *Living with death and dying.* New York: Macmillan.

This sensitive look at the end of life was written by one of the foremost experts on the psychological processes associated with death.

ANSWERS (REVIEW III):
1. Gerontologists   **2.** a—genetic preprogramming; b—wear-and-tear   **3.** b   **4.** c
5. Activity, disengagement   **6.** Denial, anger, bargaining, depression, acceptance

CHAPTER 14

PERSONALITY

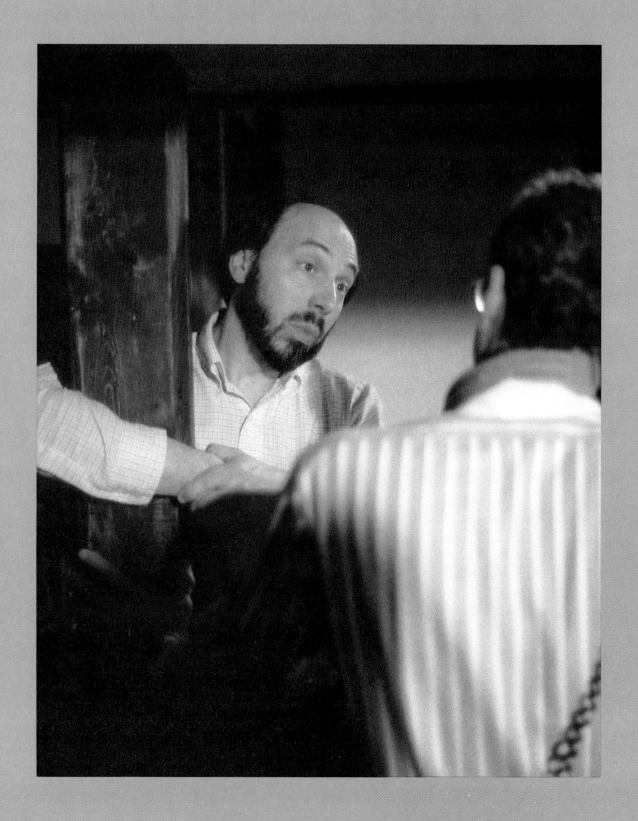

CHAPTER
14
PERSONALITY

Frank Costello testifies before the Senate Crime Investigating Committee in 1951. Despite his criminal activities, he was also known for his charitable contributions.

PROLOGUE: FRANK COSTELLO

His generosity was undeniable. For instance, as vice-chairman of the Salvation Army's fund-raising drive, Frank Costello helped raise $3500 at a $100-a-plate dinner he organized at the Copacabana in New York. To that sum he added $6500 of his own money, a goodly amount in 1949. He was also active in other charities and was a member of the Men's Committee of the Legal Aid Society.

Costello cut a dapper figure. His meticulous attention to his clothing was legendary among his acquaintances—a habit he insisted on even when it might have worked against him. When a lawyer suggested that wearing one of his hand-tailored suits at a trial might hurt his case with the jury, Costello refused to change to off-the-rack clothing, saying he would rather blow the case.

The fact that Frank Costello was involved in a trial at all, however, was related to another side to his personality. Along with generosity and concern over his appearance, Costello had a somewhat more unusual set of attributes: As a member of one of the most prominent organized crime syndicates in the United States, he was a thief, gambler, and murder mastermind.

Costello began his life of crime at age 14, when he robbed the landlady of his parents' apartment. He quickly graduated to assault and robbery and eventually moved through the ranks of organized crime to the very top position, where he routinely arranged for the murder of those he considered his enemies (Sifakis, 1987).

LOOKING AHEAD ▶

Will the real Frank Costello please stand up?

Although you probably don't know many cases as extreme as that of Costello, you may be acquainted with people who behave one way in one situation and display characteristics that are quite the opposite in another. (In fact, you might include yourself in this category.) At the same time, you probably know people whose behavior is so predictable that you can tell, almost without thinking, what they are going to do in a particular situation—people whose behavior is almost entirely consistent from one setting to the next.

To psychologists, understanding the characteristic ways in which people behave makes up the core of the area of psychology known as **personality**. The term itself is used in two different, but related, ways: On the one hand, personality refers to the characteristics that differentiate people—those behaviors that make an individual unique. On the other hand, personality is used as a means of explaining the stability in people's behavior that leads them to act uniformly both in different situations and over extended periods of time.

In this chapter we will consider a number of theories meant to explain personality. We begin with the broadest and most comprehensive approach to personality: Freud's psychoanalytic theory. Next, we turn to more recent theories of personality. We will consider approaches that concentrate on identifying the most fundamental personality traits that differentiate one person from another, on theories that emphasize how personality is a set of

Personality: The sum total of characteristics that differentiate people, or the stability in a person's behavior across different situations learned behaviors, and on approaches, known as humanistic theories, that highlight the uniquely human aspects of personality. The chapter ends with a discussion of the ways in which personality is measured and the ways personality tests can be used.

After reading this chapter, you will have the answers to questions such as these:

▶ How do psychologists define and use the concept of personality?

▶ What is the structure and development of personality according to Freud and his successors?

▶ What are the major aspects of trait, learning, and humanistic theories of personality?

▶ How can we most accurately assess personality, and what are the major types of personality measures?

EXPLAINING THE INNER LIFE: PSYCHOANALYTIC THEORIES OF PERSONALITY

Oscar Madison: sloppy, disheveled, unkempt.

Felix Unger: neat, precise, controlled.

As anyone who has seen the play or the old television series *The Odd Couple* can attest, two people could hardly seem to possess more dissimilar personalities. Yet to one group of personality theorists, **psychoanalysts**, the two might actually be quite similar—at least in terms of the underlying part of personality that motivates their behavior. According to psychoanalysts, our behavior is triggered largely by powerful forces found in a part of personality about which we are not aware. These hidden forces, shaped to a great degree by childhood experiences, play an important role in energizing and directing our everyday behavior.

Psychoanalysts: Physicians or psychologists who specialize in psychoanalysis

The most important of the theorists to hold such a view, and indeed one of the best-known figures in all psychology, is Sigmund Freud. An Austrian physician, Freud was the originator of **psychoanalytic theory** in the early 1900s.

Psychoanalytic theory: Freud's theory that unconscious forces act as determinants of personality

WHAT YOU SEE IS NOT WHAT YOU GET: Freud's Psychoanalytic Theory

The college student was intent on sounding smooth and making a good first impression with an attractive woman he spotted across a crowded room at a party. As he walked toward her, he mulled over a line he had heard in an old movie the night before: "I don't believe we've been properly introduced yet." To his horror, what came out was a bit different. After threading his way through the crowded room, he finally reached the woman and blurted out, "I don't believe we've been properly seduced yet."

Although this may seem to be merely an embarrassing slip of the tongue, according to psychoanalytic theory such a mistake is not an error at all (Motley, 1987). Rather, it is an indication of deeply felt emotions and thoughts that are harbored in the **unconscious**, a part of the personality of which a

Unconscious: A part of the personality of which a person is unaware and which is a potential determinant of behavior

INDIVIDUAL DEVELOPMENT
AND DIFFERENTIATION

Instinctual drives: Infantile wishes, desires, demands, and needs hidden from conscious awareness

person is not aware. Many of life's experiences are painful, and the unconscious provides a "safe" haven for our recollection of such events, a place where they can remain without continually disturbing us. Similarly, the unconscious contains **instinctual drives**: infantile wishes, desires, demands, and needs that are hidden from conscious awareness because of the conflicts and pain they would cause us if they were part of our everyday lives.

To Freud, conscious experience is just the tip of the iceberg; like the unseen mass of a floating iceberg, the material found in the unconscious dwarfs the information about which we are aware. Much of people's everyday behavior is viewed as being motivated by unconscious forces about which they know little. For example, a child's concern over being unable to please his strict and demanding parents may lead him to have low self-esteem as an adult, although he may never understand why his accomplishments—which may be considerable—seem insufficient. Indeed, consciously the child may recall his childhood with great pleasure; it is his unconscious, which holds the painful memories, that provokes the low self-evaluation.

According to Freud, to fully understand personality, it is necessary to illuminate and expose what is in the unconscious. But because the unconscious disguises the meaning of material it holds, it cannot be observed directly. It is therefore necessary to interpret clues to the unconscious—slips of the tongue, fantasies, and dreams—in order to understand the unconscious processes directing behavior. A slip of the tongue, such as the one quoted earlier, might be interpreted as revealing the speaker's underlying unconscious sexual interests.

If the notion of an unconscious does not seem so farfetched to most of us, it is only because Freudian theory has had such a widespread influence, with applications ranging from literature to religion. In Freud's day, however, the idea that the unconscious could harbor painful material from which people were protecting themselves was revolutionary, and the best minds of the time summarily rejected his ideas as being without basis and even laughable. That it is now so easy to accept the existence of a portion of personality about which people are unaware—and one that is responsible for much of our behavior—is a tribute to the influence of Freud's theory.

Structuring Personality: Id, Ego, and Superego

To describe the structure of personality, Freud developed a comprehensive theory which held that personality consisted of three separate but interacting

According to Freudian psychoanalytic theory, the honesty of a customer who returns the excess change she has received from a cashier might be brought about by her superego.

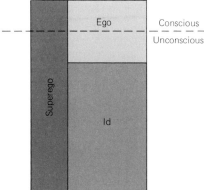

FIGURE 14-1

In Freud's model of personality, there are three major components: the id, the ego, and the superego. As the schematic shows, only a small portion of personality is conscious. This figure should not be thought of as an actual, physical structure, but rather as a model of the interrelationships between the parts of personality.

parts: the id, the ego, and the superego. Although Freud described these parts in very concrete terms, it is important to realize that they are not actual physical structures found in a certain part of the brain; instead, they represent parts of a general *model* of personality that describes the interaction of various processes and forces within one's personality that motivate behavior. Yet Freud suggested that they can be depicted diagrammatically to show how the three components of personality are related to the conscious and the unconscious (see Figure 14-1).

If personality consisted only of primitive, instinctual cravings and longings, it would have but one component: the id. The **id** is the raw, unorganized, inherited part of personality whose sole purpose is to reduce tension created by primitive drives related to hunger, sex, aggression, and irrational impulses. The id operates according to the **pleasure principle**, in which the goal is the immediate reduction of tension and the maximization of satisfaction.

Unfortunately for the id—but luckily for people and society—reality prevents the demands of the pleasure principle from being fulfilled in most cases. Instead, the world produces constraints: We cannot always eat when we are hungry, and we can discharge our sexual drives only when time, place—and partner—are willing. To account for this fact of life, Freud suggested a second part of personality, which he called the ego.

The **ego** provides a buffer between the id and the realities of the objective, outside world. In contrast to the pleasure-seeking nature of the id, the ego operates according to the **reality principle**, in which instinctual energy is restrained in order to maintain the safety of the individual and help integrate the person into society. In a sense, then, the ego is the "executive" of personality: It makes decisions, controls actions, and allows thinking and problem solving of a higher order than the id is capable of. The ego is also the seat of higher cognitive abilities such as intelligence, thoughtfulness, reasoning, and learning.

The **superego**, the final personality structure to develop, represents the rights and wrongs of society as handed down by a person's parents, teachers, and other important figures. It becomes a part of personality when children learn right from wrong and continues to develop as people begin to incorporate into their own standards the broad moral principles of the society in which they live.

The superego actually has two parts, the **conscience** and the **ego-ideal**. The conscience *prevents* us from doing morally bad things, while the ego-ideal *motivates* us to do what is morally proper. The superego helps to

Id: The raw, unorganized, inherited part of personality whose purpose is to reduce tension created by biological drives and irrational impulses

Pleasure principle: The principle by which the id operates, in which the person seeks the immediate reduction of tension and the maximization of satisfaction

Ego: The part of personality that provides a buffer between the id and the outside world

Reality principle: The principle by which the ego operates, in which instinctual energy is restrained in order to maintain an individual's safety and integration into society.

Superego: The part of personality that represents the morality of society as presented by parents, teachers, and others

Conscience: The part of the superego that prevents us from doing what is morally wrong

Ego-ideal: The part of the superego that motivates us to do what is morally proper

484

This baby is going through what Freud described as the oral stage. An adult who has a fixation at this stage might engage in excessive eating, smoking, or chewing gum. (Joel Gordon.)

Oral stage: According to Freud, a stage from birth to 12–18 months, in which an infant's center of pleasure is the mouth

Fixation: Behavior reflecting an earlier stage of development

control impulses coming from the id, making them less selfish and more virtuous.

Although on the surface the superego appears to be the opposite of the id, the two share an important feature: Both are unrealistic in that they do not consider the actualities of society. While this lack of reality within the superego pushes the person toward greater virtue, if left unchecked it would create perfectionists who were unable to make the compromises that life requires. Similarly, an unrestrained id would create a primitive, pleasure-seeking, thoughtless individual, seeking to fulfill every desire without delay. The ego, then, must compromise between the demands of the superego and the id, permitting a person to obtain some of the gratification sought by the id while keeping the moralistic superego from preventing the gratification.

Developing Personality: A Stage Approach

Freud did not stop after describing the components of adult personality; his theory also provides a view of how personality develops throughout a series of stages during childhood.

Particularly important about the sequence, summarized in Table 14-1, is that it suggests how experiences and difficulties during a particular childhood stage may predict specific sorts of idiosyncracies in adult personality. The theory is also unique in focusing each stage on a major biological function, which is assumed to be the focus of pleasure in a given period.

In the first period of development, called the **oral stage**, the baby's mouth is the focal point of pleasure. During the first 12 to 18 months of life, children suck, mouth, and bite anything that will fit into their mouths. To Freud, this behavior suggested that the mouth was the primary site of a kind of sexual pleasure, and if infants were either overly indulged (perhaps by being fed every time they cried) or very frustrated in their search for oral gratification, they might become fixated at this stage. Displaying **fixation** means that an adult shows personality characteristics that are related to an earlier stage of development. For example, fixation at the oral stage might produce an adult who was unusually interested in overtly oral activities—eating, talking, smok-

TABLE 14-1

The Stages of Personality Development According to Freud's Psychoanalytic Theory

Stage	Age	Major Characteristics
Oral	Birth to 12–18 months	Interest in oral gratification from sucking, eating, mouthing, biting
Anal	12–18 months to 3 years	Gratification from expelling and withholding feces; coming to terms with society's controls relating to toilet training
Phallic	3 to 5–6 years	Interest in the genitals; coming to terms with Oedipal/Electra conflict, leading to identification with same-sex parent
Latency	5–6 years to adolescence	Sexual concerns largely unimportant
Genital	Adolescence to adulthood	Reemergence of sexual interests and establishment of mature sexual relationships

ing—or who showed symbolic sorts of oral interests: being "bitingly" sarcastic or being very gullible ("swallowing" anything).

From around 12 to 18 months until 3 years of age—where the emphasis in most cultures is on toilet training—the child enters the **anal stage**. At this point, the major source of pleasure changes from the mouth to the anal region, and children derive considerable pleasure from both retention and expulsion of feces. If the external concerns of society in the form of toilet training are particularly demanding, the result may be fixation. If fixation occurs during the anal stage, Freud suggested that adults might show unusual rigidity, orderliness, punctuality—or extreme disorderliness or sloppiness, as in our earlier examples of Oscar and Felix.

At about age 3, the **phallic stage** begins, at which point there is another major shift in the primary source of pleasure for the child. This time, interest focuses on the genitals and the pleasures derived from fondling them. This is also the stage of one of the most important points of personality development, according to Freudian theory: the **Oedipal conflict**. As children focus their attention on their genitals, the differences between male and female anatomy become more salient. Furthermore, at this time Freud felt that the male begins to develop sexual interests in his mother, starts to see his father as a rival, and harbors a wish to kill his father—as Oedipus did in the ancient Greek tragedy. But because he views his father as too powerful, he develops a fear of retaliation in the form of "castration anxiety." Ultimately, this fear becomes so powerful that the child represses his desires for his mother and instead chooses to **identify** with his father, trying to be as much like him as possible.

For girls, the process—occasionally referred to as a resolution of the "Electra complex"—is a little different. Freud reasoned that girls begin to feel sexual arousal toward their fathers and—in a suggestion that was to later bring serious, and not unreasonable, accusations that he viewed women as inferior to men—that they begin to experience **penis envy**: They wish they had the anatomical part that, at least to Freud, seemed most clearly "missing" in girls. They blame their mothers for their lack of a penis, believing that their mothers are responsible for their "castration." As with males, though, they find that in order to resolve such unacceptable feelings, they must identify with the same-sex parent by behaving like her and adapting her attitudes and values. In this way, a girl's identification with her mother is completed.

At this point, the Oedipal conflict is said to be resolved, and, if things have gone smoothly, Freudian theory assumes that both males and females move on to the next stage of development. If difficulties arise during this period, however, all sorts of problems are thought to occur, including a lack of conscience and improper sex-role behavior.

Following the resolution of the Oedipal conflict, typically at around age 5 or 6, children move into the **latency period**, which lasts until puberty. During this period, not much of interest is occurring, according to Freud; sexual concerns are more or less put to rest, even in the unconscious. Then, during adolescence, sexual feelings reemerge, marking the start of the final period, the **genital stage**, which extends until death. The focus in the genital stage is on mature, adult sexuality, which Freud defined as sexual intercourse.

Dealing with the Dangers from Within: Defense Mechanisms

Freud's efforts to describe and theorize about the underlying dynamics of

Anal stage: According to Freud, a stage, from 12–18 months to 3 years of age, in which a child's pleasure is centered on the anus

Phallic stage: According to Freud, a period beginning around age 3 during which a child's interest focuses on the genitals

Oedipal (ED ih pul) **conflict:** A child's sexual interest in his or her opposite-sex parent, typically resolved through identification with the same-sex parent

Identification: A child's attempt to be similar to his or her same-sex parent

Penis envy: According to Freud, a girl's wish, developing around age 3, that she had a penis

Latency period: According to Freud, the period, between the phallic stage and puberty, during which children's sexual concerns are temporarily put aside

Genital stage: According to Freud, a period from puberty until death, marked by mature sexual behavior (i.e., sexual intercourse)

INDIVIDUAL DEVELOPMENT
AND DIFFERENTIATION

Anxiety: A feeling of apprehension or tension

Neurotic anxiety: Anxiety caused when irrational impulses from the id threaten to become uncontrollable

Defense mechanisms: Unconscious strategies people use to reduce anxiety by concealing its source from themselves and others

Repression: The primary defense mechanism, in which unacceptable or unpleasant id impulses are pushed back into the unconscious

Regression: Behavior reminiscent of an earlier stage of development, carried out in order to have fewer demands put upon oneself

Displacement: The expression of an unwanted feeling or thought, directed toward a weaker person instead of a more powerful one

Rationalization: A defense mechanism whereby people justify a negative situation in a way that protects their self-esteem

Denial: A refusal to accept or acknowledge anxiety-producing information

Projection: A defense mechanism in which people attribute their own inadequacies or faults to someone else

Sublimation: A defense mechanism, considered healthy by Freud, in which a person diverts unwanted impulses into socially acceptable thoughts, feelings, or behaviors

personality and its development were motivated by very practical problems that his patients faced in dealing with **anxiety**, an intense, negative emotional experience. According to Freud, anxiety is a danger signal to the ego. Although anxiety may arise from realistic fears—such as seeing a poisonous snake about to strike—it may also occur in the form of **neurotic anxiety**, in which irrational impulses emanating from the id threaten to burst through and become uncontrollable. Because anxiety, naturally, is unpleasant, Freud believed that people develop a range of defense mechanisms to deal with it. **Defense mechanisms** are unconscious strategies people use to reduce anxiety by concealing the source from themselves and others (Cramer, 1987).

The primary defense mechanism is **repression**, in which unacceptable or unpleasant id impulses are pushed back into the unconscious. Repression is the most direct method of dealing with anxiety; instead of handling an anxiety-producing impulse on a conscious level, one simply ignores it. For example, a college student who feels hatred for her mother might repress these personally and socially unacceptable feelings; they remain lodged within the id, since acknowledging them would be so anxiety-provoking. This does not mean, however, that they would have no effect: True feelings might be revealed through dreams, slips of the tongue, or symbolically in some other fashion. The student might, for instance, have difficulty with authority figures such as teachers and do poorly in school. Alternatively, she might join the military, where she could give harsh orders to others and never have them questioned.

If repression is ineffective in keeping anxiety at bay, other defense mechanisms may be called upon. For example, **regression** might be used, whereby people behave as if they were at an earlier stage of development. By retreating to a younger age—for instance by complaining and throwing tantrums—they might succeed in having fewer demands put upon them.

Anyone who has ever been angered by a professor and then returned to the dorm and yelled at his or her roommate knows what displacement is all about. In **displacement**, the expression of an unwanted feeling or thought is redirected from a more threatening, powerful person to a weaker one. A classic case is yelling at one's secretary after being criticized by the boss.

Rationalization, another defense mechanism, occurs when we distort reality by justifying what happens to us: We develop explanations that allow us to protect our self-esteem. If you've ever heard someone say that he didn't mind being stood up for a date because he really had a lot of work to do that evening, you have probably seen rationalization at work.

In **denial**, a person simply refuses to accept or acknowledge an anxiety-producing piece of information. For example, when told that his wife has died in an automobile crash, a husband may at first deny the tragedy, saying that there must be some mistake, and only gradually come to conscious acceptance that she actually has been killed. In extreme cases, denial may linger; the husband may continue to expect that his wife will return home.

Projection is a means of protecting oneself by attributing unwanted impulses and feelings to someone else. For example, a man who feels sexually inadequate may complain to his wife that *she* is sexually inept.

Finally, one defense mechanism that Freud considered to be particularly healthy and socially acceptable is **sublimation**. In sublimation, people divert unwanted impulses into socially approved thoughts, feelings, or behaviors. For example, a person with strong feelings of aggression may become a butcher—and hack away at meat instead of people. Sublimation allows the

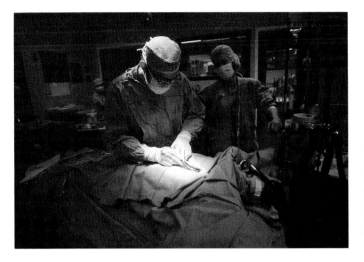

One of the healthier defense mechanisms is sublimation, in which people channel their unwanted impulses into socially approved behavior. For example, Freud might suggest that a surgeon's choice of profession is influenced by unconscious aggressive tendencies. (George Gardner/The Image Works.)

butcher the opportunity not only to release psychic tension but to do so in a way that is socially acceptable.

All of us employ defense mechanisms to some degree, according to Freudian theory. Yet some people use them so much that a large amount of psychic energy must be constantly directed toward hiding and rechanneling unacceptable impulses, making everyday living difficult. In this case, the result is a neurosis, a term referring to mental disorders produced by anxiety that we will discuss in the chapter on abnormal behavior.

Evaluating Freudian Theory

More than almost any other psychological theory we have discussed, Freud's personality theory presents an elaborate and complicated set of propositions—some of which are so removed from everyday explanations of behavior that they may appear difficult to accept. But laypeople are not the only ones to be concerned about the validity of Freud's theory; personality psychologists, too, have been quick to criticize its inadequacies.

Among the most compelling criticisms is the lack of scientific data to support the theory. Although there are a wealth of individual assessments of particular people that *seem* to support the theory, we lack definitive evidence showing that the personality is structured and operates along the lines Freud laid out—due, in part, to the fact that Freud's conception of personality is built on unobservable abstractions. Moreover, while we can readily employ Freudian theory in after-the-fact explanations, it is extremely difficult to predict how certain developmental difficulties will be displayed in the adult. For instance, if a person is fixated at the anal stage, he might, according to Freud, be unusually messy—or he might be unusually neat. Freud's theory offers no guidance for predicting which manifestations of the difficulty will occur. It produces good history, then, but not such good science. Finally, Freud made his observations—albeit insightful ones—and derived his theory from a limited population: primarily upper-class Austrian women living in the strict, puritanical era of the early 1900s. How far one can generalize beyond this population is a matter of considerable question.

Despite these criticisms, which cannot be dismissed, Freud's theory has had an enormous impact on the field of psychology—and indeed on all of western thinking. The ideas of the unconscious, anxiety, defense mechanisms, and the childhood causes of adult psychological difficulties have per-

488

Carl Jung posed for this chalk drawing in 1934. (The Granger Collection.)

Neo-Freudian psychoanalysts (neo-Freudians): Theorists who place greater emphasis than did Freud on the functions of the ego and its influence on our daily activities

Collective unconscious: A concept developed by Jung proposing that we inherit certain personality characteristics from our ancestors and the human race as a whole

Archetypes: According to Jung, universal, symbolic representations of a particular person, object, or experience

meated people's views of the world and their understanding of the causes of their own behavior and that of others.

Furthermore, Freud's emphasis on the unconscious has been partially supported by some of the current research findings of cognitive psychologists. This work has revealed that mental processes about which people are unaware have an important impact on thinking and actions. In addition, new experimental techniques have been developed that allow the unconscious to be studied in a more scientifically sophisticated manner, overcoming the reliance of traditional Freudian approaches on single-subject case studies and unconfirmable theoretical interpretations of dreams and slips of the tongue for support (Kihlstrom, 1987; Kline, 1987).

The importance of psychoanalytic theory is underscored by the fact that it spawned a significant—and enduring—method of treating psychological disturbances, as we will discuss further in Chapter 17. For a variety of reasons, then, Freud's psychoanalytic theory remains a significant contribution to our understanding of personality.

REVISING FREUD: The Neo-Freudian Psychoanalysts

One particularly important outgrowth of Freud's theorizing was the work done by a series of successors who were trained in traditional Freudian theory but who later strayed from some of its major points. These theorists are known as **neo-Freudian psychoanalysts.**

The neo-Freudians placed greater emphasis than did Freud on the functions of the ego, suggesting that it had more control than the id over day-to-day activities. They also paid greater attention to social factors and the effects of society and culture on personality development. Carl Jung (pronounced "yoong"), for example, who initially adhered closely to Freud's thinking, later rejected the notion of the primary importance of unconscious sexual urges—a key notion of Freudian theory—and instead looked at the primitive urges of the unconscious more positively. He suggested that people had a **collective unconscious,** a set of influences we inherit from our own particular ancestors, the whole human race, and even animal ancestors from the distant past. This collective unconscious is shared by everyone and is displayed by behavior that is common across diverse cultures—such as love of mother, belief in a supreme being, and even behavior as specific as fear of snakes.

Jung went on to propose that the collective unconscious contained **archetypes,** universal symbolic representations of a particular person, object, or experience. For instance, a mother archetype, which contains both our own experiences with our mother and reflections of our ancestors' relationships with mother figures, is suggested by the prevalence of mothers in art, religion, literature, and mythology. (Think of the Virgin Mary, Earth Mother, wicked stepmothers of fairy tales, Mother's Day, and so forth!) A more sinister archetype is the shadow, which Jung said contained the more depraved attributes from our prehuman predecessors. The shadow archetype forms the basis for representations of sin and the devil which are found throughout religious history.

To Jung, archetypes play an important role in determining our day-to-day reactions, attitudes, and values. For instance, Jung might explain the popularity of a movie such as *Batman* as being due to its use of broad archetypes of good (Batman), evil (the Joker), and innocence (Vicki Vail).

To Jung, Superman and his enemy General Zod would represent broad archetypes of good and evil. (*Superman II,* A Warner Bros. Release/ © DC Comics Inc./Film Stills Archive, The Museum of Modern Art, New York.)

Alfred Adler, another important neo-Freudian psychoanalyst, considered Freudian theory's emphasis on sexual needs as misplaced. Instead, Adler proposed that the primary human motivation was a striving for superiority, not in terms of superiority over others, but as a quest to achieve self-improvement and perfection. Adler used the term **inferiority complex** to describe situations in which adults have not been able to overcome the feelings of inferiority that they developed as children, when they were small and limited in their knowledge about the world. Early social relationships with parents have an important effect on how well children are able to outgrow feelings of personal inferiority and instead orient themselves toward attaining more socially useful goals such as improving society.

Other neo-Freudians, such as Erik Erikson (whose theory we discussed in Chapters 12 and 13) and Karen Horney (1937), also focused less than Freud on inborn sexual and aggressive motivation and more on the social and cultural factors behind personality. Horney, for example, suggested that personality developed in terms of social relationships and depended particularly on the relationship between parents and child and how well the child's needs were met. She rejected Freud's suggestion that women had penis envy, asserting that what women coveted most in men was not their anatomy but the independence, success, and freedom that women were often denied. Horney was one of the first feminist psychologists.

Inferiority complex: A phenomenon whereby adults have continuing feelings of weakness and insecurity

Karen Horney was one of Freud's top students, although she eventually broke with him over issues related to women's behavior. (Culver Pictures.)

Recap

◀ Freud's psychoanalytic theory proposes that many deeply felt emotions, feelings, and thoughts are found in the unconscious, the part of personality of which a person is unaware. Personality consists of three components: the id, the ego, and the superego.

◀ According to psychoanalytic theory, personality develops during a series of stages in which the focus of pleasure is on a particular part of the body. The stages are the oral, anal, phallic (which leads to the Oedipal conflict), latency, and genital stages.

◀ Defense mechanisms are unconscious strategies that people use to reduce anxiety by concealing its source. Among the most important are repression, regression, displacement, rationalization, projection, and sublimation.

◀ Although Freud's theory may be criticized on a number of grounds—including its inability to be scientifically tested and its failure to permit clear-cut predictions rather than after-the-fact explanations—it has been enormously influential.

◀ Among the neo-Freudian psychoanalysts who built and modified psychoanalytic theory are Jung, who developed the concepts of the collective unconscious and archetypes, Adler, who coined the term "inferiority complex," and Horney, who viewed personality development in terms of social relationships.

Review

1. Which of the following is *not* true?
   a. Freud's theory is responsible for the widespread acceptance of the notion of the unconscious
   b. Psychoanalytic theory has been proven correct by a great deal of scientific evidence
   c. Freud has been criticized for his explanation of female development.
   d. Many theories of personality are based on Freud's psychoanalytic model.
2. Match each of the following with a description on the right.

_____ Id

_____ Ego

_____ Superego

_____ Sublimation

_____ Archetypes

_____ Inferiority complex

_____ Rationalization

_____ Fixation

a. Diverting unwanted impulses into socially accepted behaviors
b. The personality's decision maker
c. The distortion of reality to protect self-esteem
d. Feelings of inadequacy based on one's life position
e. Attachment to some earlier form of gratification
f. Primitive, instinctive drives
g. Universal symbolic representations of people, objects, or experiences
h. The component of personality responsible for moral behavior

3. According to Freud, the Oedipal conflict is resolved by
   a. entering the stage of mature sexuality.
   b. aggression toward the same-sex parent.
   c. identification with the same-sex parent.
   d. the development of defense mechanisms.
4. A woman who is angry with her husband yells at her son and sends him to his room. This might be an example of
   a. repression.
   b. regression.
   c. displacement.
   d. projection.
5. The idea of a collective unconscious was proposed by _____ .
6. Which of the following theorists suggested that our primary motivation is a striving for superiority?
   a. Freud
   b. Horney
   c. Jung
   d. Adler

(Answers to review questions are on page 492.)

IN SEARCH OF PERSONALITY: TRAIT, LEARNING, AND HUMANISTIC APPROACHES

"Tell me about Roger, Sue," said Wendy.

"Oh, he's just terrific. He's the friendliest guy I know—goes out of his way to be nice to everyone. He hardly ever gets mad. He's just so even-tempered, no matter what's happening. And he's really smart, too. About the only thing I don't like is that he's always in such a hurry to get things done; he seems to have boundless energy, much more than I have."

"He sounds great to me, especially in comparison to Richard," replied Wendy. "He is so self-centered and arrogant it drives me crazy. I sometimes wonder why I ever started going out with him."

Friendly. Even-tempered. Smart. Energetic. Self-centered. Arrogant.

If we were to analyze the conversation printed above, the first thing we would notice is that it is made up of a series of trait characterizations of the two people being discussed. In fact, most of our understanding of the reasons behind others' behavior is based on the premise that people possess certain traits that are assumed to be consistent across different situations. A number of formal theories of personality employ variants of this approach. We turn now to a discussion of these and other personality theories, all of which provide alternatives to the psychoanalytic emphasis on unconscious processes in determining behavior.

LABELING PERSONALITY: Trait Theories

If someone were to ask you to characterize another person, it is probable that—like the two people in the conversation just presented—you would come up with a list of that individual's personal qualities, as you see them. But how would you know which of these qualities were most important in determining the person's behavior?

Personality psychologists have asked similar questions themselves. In order to answer them, they have developed a sophisticated model of personality known as **trait theory**. **Traits** are enduring dimensions of personality characteristics along which people differ from one another.

Trait theorists do not assume that some people have a trait and others do not; rather, they propose that all people have certain traits, but that the degree to which the trait applies to a specific person varies and can be quantified. For instance, you might be relatively friendly, whereas I might be relatively unfriendly. But we both have a "friendliness" trait, although you would be quantified with a higher score and I with a lower one. The major challenge for trait theorists taking this approach has been to identify the specific primary traits necessary to describe personality—and, as we shall see, different theorists have come up with surprisingly different sets.

Getting Down to Basics: Allport's Trait Theory

When personality psychologist Gordon Allport carefully leafed through an unabridged dictionary, he came up with some 18,000 separate terms that could be used to describe personality. Although he was able to pare down the list to a mere 4,500 descriptors after eliminating synonyms, he obviously was still left with a problem crucial to all trait theories: Which of these were the most crucial?

Allport answered this question by suggesting that there were three basic categories of traits: cardinal, central, and secondary (Allport, 1961, 1966). A **cardinal trait** is a single characteristic that directs most of a person's activities. For example, a totally selfless woman might direct all her energy toward humanitarian activities; another person might be driven by all-consuming power needs.

Most people, however, do not develop all-encompassing cardinal traits; instead, they possess a handful of central traits that make up the core of

Trait theory: A model that seeks to identify the basic traits necessary to describe personality

Traits: Enduring dimensions of personality characteristics differentiating people from one another

Cardinal trait: A single personality trait that directs most of a person's activities (e.g., greed, lust, kindness)

492

Central traits: A set of major characteristics that make up the core of a person's personality

Secondary traits: Less important personality traits (e.g., preferences for certain clothes or movies) that do not affect behavior as much as central and cardinal traits do

Factor analysis: A statistical technique for combining traits into broader, more general patterns of consistency

Surface traits: According to Cattell, clusters of a person's related behaviors that can be observed in a given situation

Source traits: The sixteen basic dimensions of personality that Cattell identified as the root of all behavior

Introversion-extroversion: According to Eysenck, a dimension of personality traits encompassing the shyest to the most sociable people

Neuroticism-stability: Eysenck's personality spectrum encompassing people from the moodiest to the most even-tempered

personality. **Central traits,** such as honesty and sociability, are the major characteristics of the individual; they usually number from five to ten in any one person. Finally, **secondary traits** are characteristics that affect behavior in fewer situations and are less influential than central or cardinal traits. For instance, a preference for ice cream or a dislike of modern art would be considered a secondary trait.

Factoring out Personality: The Theories of Cattell and Eysenck

More recent attempts at discovering primary traits have centered on a statistical technique known as factor analysis. **Factor analysis** is a method of summarizing the relationships among a large number of variables into fewer, more general patterns. For example, a personality researcher might administer a questionnaire to many subjects, asking them to describe themselves along an extensive list of traits. By statistically combining responses and computing which traits are associated with one another in the same person, a researcher can identify the most fundamental patterns or combinations of traits—called factors—that underlie subjects' responses.

Using factor analysis, personality psychologist Raymond Cattell (1965) suggested that the characteristics that can be observed in a given situation represent 46 **surface traits,** or clusters of related behaviors. For example, you might encounter a friendly, gregarious librarian who goes out of his way to be helpful to you, and from your interactions with him decide that he possesses the trait of sociability—in Cattell's terms, a surface trait.

However, such surface traits are based on people's perceptions and representations of personality; they do not necessarily provide the best description of the underlying personality dimensions that are at the root of all behavior. Carrying out further factor analysis, Cattell found that sixteen **source traits** represented the basic dimensions of personality. Using these source traits, he developed the Sixteen Personality Factor Questionnaire, or 16 PF, a measure that provides scores for each of the source traits. Figure 14-2 shows the pattern of average scores on each of the source traits for three different groups of subjects—airplane pilots, creative artists, and writers.

Another trait theorist, psychologist Hans Eysenck (1975; Eysenck & Eysenck, 1985), also used factor analysis to identify patterns within traits, but he came to a very different conclusion about the nature of personality. He found that personality could best be described in terms of just two major dimensions: **introversion-extroversion** and **neuroticism-stability.** On the one extreme of the introversion-extroversion dimension are people who are quiet, careful, thoughtful, and restrained (the introverts), and on the other are those who are outgoing, sociable, and active (the extroverts). Independent of that, people can be rated as neurotic (moody, touchy, sensitive) versus stable (calm, reliable, even-tempered). By evaluating people along these two dimensions, Eysenck has been able to make accurate predictions of behavior in a number of situations (see Figure 14-3).

Still other theorists, also using factor analysis, have produced trait models that encompass anywhere from three to seven primary dimensions. For example, one study determined that five major factors produce the optimal description of personality: sociability, activity, impulsivity, socialization (au-

---

ANSWERS (REVIEW I):
1. b **2.** f, b, h, a, g, d, c, e **3.** c **4.** c **5.** Carl Jung **6.** d

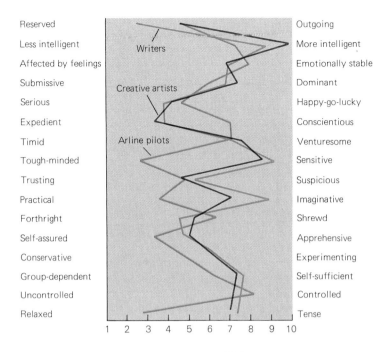

Reserved — Outgoing
Less intelligent — More intelligent
Affected by feelings — Emotionally stable
Submissive — Dominant
Serious — Happy-go-lucky
Expedient — Conscientious
Timid — Venturesome
Tough-minded — Sensitive
Trusting — Suspicious
Practical — Imaginative
Forthright — Shrewd
Self-assured — Apprehensive
Conservative — Experimenting
Group-dependent — Self-sufficient
Uncontrolled — Controlled
Relaxed — Tense

1 2 3 4 5 6 7 8 9 10

Writers
Creative artists
Arline pilots

FIGURE 14-2

Personality profiles for source traits developed by Cattell for three groups of subjects: airline pilots, creative artists, and writers. The average score for the general population is between 4.5 and 6.5 on each scale. (Adapted from Cattell, Ebver, & Tatsuoka, 1970. Copyright © 1970 by the Institute for Personality and Ability Testing. Reproduced by permission.)

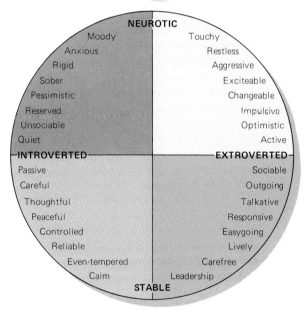

NEUROTIC

Moody   Touchy
Anxious   Restless
Rigid   Aggressive
Sober   Exciteable
Pessimistic   Changeable
Reserved   Impulsive
Unsociable   Optimistic
Quiet   Active

INTROVERTED ——— **EXTROVERTED**

Passive   Sociable
Careful   Outgoing
Thoughtful   Talkative
Peaceful   Responsive
Controlled   Easygoing
Reliable   Lively
Even-tempered Carefree
Calm   Leadership

STABLE

FIGURE 14-3

According to Eysenck, personality can be viewed as lying along two major dimensions: introversion-extroversion and neuroticism-stability. Other personality characteristics can be ordered along the circular figure depicted here. (Eysenck, 1973.)

tonomy versus conformity), and emotionality (Zuckerman, Kuhlman & Camac, 1988). However, the specific number and kinds of traits remain a source of heated debate among trait theorists.

Which Theorist's Traits Are the Right Ones?:
Evaluating Trait Theories of Personality

Trait theories have several virtues. They provide a clear, straightforward explanation of people's behavioral consistencies. Furthermore, traits allow us to readily compare one person with another. Because of these advantages, trait conceptions of personality have had an important practical influence on the development of several personality measures that we discuss later in the chapter.

On the other hand, trait theories have several drawbacks. For example, we have seen that trait theories describing personality come to quite different conclusions about which traits are the most fundamental and descriptive. The difficulty in determining which of the theories is most accurate has led many psychologists to question the validity of trait conceptions of personality in general.

Actually, there is an even more fundamental difficulty with trait approaches. Even if we are able to identify a set of primary traits, we are left

---

THE CUTTING EDGE

The identical twins, separated at birth but reunited in adulthood for a study of twins, looked eerily similar. Each wore a blue double-breasted suit, mustache, and wire-rimmed glasses. Stranger, though, was the fact that they both had quick tempers and an unusual sense of humor, exemplified by their enjoyment of startling others by sneezing in elevators (Holden, 1987).

Although most traditional theories of personality view parents and the family environment as the primary determinants of personality traits, increasing evidence suggests that heredity plays an important role. In fact, a major new study of identical twins reared apart from each other suggests that more than half the variation in people's traits is brought about by heredity, with a minority of the influence being due to the environment.

In an ongoing study, Auke Tellegen and colleagues at the University of Minnesota have been examining the personality traits of some 350 pairs of twins (Tellegen et al., 1988). Forty-four of the pairs were genetically identical but raised apart from each other, providing the opportunity of determining the influence of genetic factors on personality. Each of the twins was given a battery of tests, including one that measured eleven key personality traits. The results of the test, called the Multidimensional Personality Question-

THE ROOTS OF PERSONALITY: THE INHERITANCE OF TRAITS

naire, indicated that in major respects the twins were quite similar to each other in personality. Moreover, certain traits were more influenced by heredity than others. For example, social potency (the degree to which a person takes mastery and leadership roles in social situations) and traditionalism (the following of authority) had particularly strong genetic components, whereas achievement and social closeness had relatively weak genetic components (see Figure 14-4).

Other studies support Tellegen's findings and show that the effects of heredity appear quite early in life and that stability can be seen in a variety of areas. In one major longitudinal study, for example, infants who were exceptionally easy (readily adapting to regular schedules and having a generally good mood) or exceptionally difficult (crying a great deal and generally behaving unpredictably) showed relatively stable temperaments across the first five years of life (Thomas et al., 1963). Similarly, a more recent study showed that most of a group of children who were unusually shy at age 2 were still quiet, cautious, and avoidant of social contact with unfamiliar children at age 7. Conversely, those who were unusually outgoing and spontaneous at

age 2 were talkative and uninhibited at age 7 (Kagan, Reznick & Snidman, 1988).

Other work shows that the expression of both altruism and aggression is affected by heredity (Rushton, Fulker, Neale, Nias & Eysenck, 1986). Even human sexuality and political attitudes—at least in terms of basic conservatism and authoritarianism—are related to genetic factors (Eysenck, 1976; Eaves & Eysenck, 1974).

It seems, then, that heredity plays an important role in determining an individual's personality. Does this mean that parental influence and other environmental factors are of only minor importance? The answer is a clear no, since parents and other figures in the child's environment shape the extent to which traits produced by heredity assert themselves (Loehlin, Willerman & Horn, 1987; Rose et al., 1988). It is possible, for instance, to reduce the degree of self-absorption in children who are high in that trait by exposing them to constructive experiences that involve them with other children. Similarly, highly assertive children might have their assertiveness reduced through experiences that make them more aware of the feelings of others. Still, if the current data are valid, it seems that it might be difficult to have children with a disposition toward timidity become unusually brave.

with little more than a label or description of personality—rather than an explanation of behavior. If we say that someone donates money to charity because he or she has the trait of generosity, we still do not know *why* the person became generous in the first place, or the reasons for displaying generosity in a given situation (see the Cutting Edge box). Traits, then, provide nothing in the way of explanations of behavior; they are merely descriptive labels.

Is Personality a Myth?: Personality versus Situational Factors

Perhaps the biggest problem with trait conceptions is one that is fundamental to the entire area of personality: Is behavior really as consistent over different situations as trait conceptions would imply? How, for instance, would a trait theorist explain Frank Costello's behavior described at the beginning of this chapter? Trying to answer this question has provided personality theory with one of its most vexing and controversial problems.

When personality psychologist Walter Mischel began to review the literature on the strength of the relationship between people's personality traits and their behavior in the late 1960s, he found a curious situation: Broad personality traits could be used to explain only a minor, insignificant portion of behavior. Instead, it seemed to Mischel that most behavior could be ex-

Social potency   61%
A person high in this trait is masterful, a forceful leader who likes to be the center of attention.

Traditionalism   60%
Follows rules and authority, endorses high moral standards and strict discipline.

Stress reaction   55%
Feels vulnerable and sensitive and is given to worries and easily upset.

Absorption   55%
Has a vivid imagination readily captured by rich experience; relinquishes sense of reality.

Alienation   55%
Feels mistreated and used, that "the world is out to get me."

Well-being   54%
Has a cheerful disposition, feels confident and optimistic.

Harm avoidance   51%
Shuns the excitement of risk and danger, prefers the safe route even if it is tedious.

Aggression   48%
Is physically aggressive and vindictive, has taste for violence and is "out to get the world."

Achievement   46%
Works hard, strives for mastery, and puts work and accomplishment ahead of other things.

Control   43%
Is cautious and plodding, rational and sensible, likes carefully planned events.

Social closeness   33%
Prefers emotional intimacy and close ties, turns to others for comfort and help.

FIGURE 14-4

The roots of personality. The percentages indicate the degree to which eleven major personality characteristics reflect the influence of heredity. (Tellegen et al., 1988.)

plained primarily by the nature of the situation in which the people found themselves—not by their personalities (Mischel, 1968).

Mischel's views fanned the flames of a raging controversy that continues to be one of the major issues dividing personality theorists: the degree to which people's behavior is caused by personality versus situational factors. On one side of the controversy are traditional personality theorists who argue that traits, if measured appropriately, provide a valid explanation of behavior across diverse situations. For instance, Seymour Epstein (Epstein & O'Brien, 1985) argued that it is necessary to consider behavior over repeated settings and times to get a true picture of the degree of consistency displayed. When this was done—a group of subjects were repeatedly assessed over a period of months—there were strong indications of consistency, contrary to Mischel's suggestions.

In response, Mischel has argued that even though his critics may have demonstrated consistency over time, they have not shown consistency over situations. For instance, an office supervisor may be verbally aggressive toward her staff day in and day out, thereby showing consistency over time, but may not be verbally aggressive toward her boss—demonstrating *in*consistency over situations. It is this inconsistency across situations that makes personality-trait approaches suspect to Mischel (Mischel & Peake, 1982, 1983).

Although the controversy shows little indication of abating, several important facts have emerged as a result of it (Kenrick & Funder, 1988). Trait ratings are most accurate when they are done by raters who are thoroughly familiar with the person being rated, when multiple ratings and multiple raters are used, and when the observed behavior is directly relevant to the trait in question. On the other hand, lower accuracy is apt to be obtained in situations in which only one sample of behavior is observed or in which powerful forces are pushing an individual toward certain behavior. Thus, when a sergeant orders a private to peel potatoes, the subsequent behavior could hardly be viewed as an indication of a trait relating to the private's culinary interest.

The controversy has also led personality theorists to focus more directly on the nature of person-situation interactions—how the specific characteristics of a situation will influence the behavior of an individual with a specific type of personality (Magnusson & Endler, 1977). By considering such person-situation interactions, personality psychologists are developing a more accurate portrait of the role of personality in the particular situations and environments that are part of people's everyday lives (Kenrick & Funder, 1988). Still, the final chapter in the controversy over the consistency of behavior across situations has yet to be written.

EXPLAINING THE OUTER LIFE, DISREGARDING THE INNER LIFE:
Learning Theories of Personality

Whereas psychoanalytic and trait theories concentrate on the inner person—the stormy fury of an unobservable but powerful id or a hypothetical but critical set of traits—learning theories of personality focus on the outer person. In fact, to a strict learning theorist, personality is simply the sum of learned responses to the external environment. Internal events such as thoughts, feelings, and motivations are ignored; though their existence is not denied, learning theorists say that personality is best understood by looking at features of a person's environment.

According to the most influential of the learning theorists, B. F. Skinner (whom we discussed first in terms of operant conditioning in Chapter 5), personality is a collection of learned behavior patterns (Skinner, 1975). Similarities in responses across different situations are caused by similar patterns of reinforcement that have been received in such situations in the past. If I am sociable both at parties and at meetings, it is because I have been reinforced previously for displaying social behaviors—not because I am fulfilling some unconscious wish based on experiences during my childhood or because I have an internal trait of sociability.

Strict learning theorists such as Skinner are less interested in the consistencies in behavior across situations, however, than in ways of modifying behavior. In fact, their view is that humans are infinitely changeable; if one is able to control and modify the patterns of reinforcers in a situation, behavior that other theorists would view as stable and unyielding can be changed and ultimately improved. Learning theorists are optimistic in their attitudes about the potential for resolving personal and societal problems through treatment strategies based on learning theory—methods we will discuss further in Chapter 17.

Where Freud Meets Skinner: Dollard and Miller's Stimulus-Response Theory

Not all learning theories of personality take such a strict view in rejecting the importance of what is "inside" the person by focusing solely on the "outside." John Dollard and Neal Miller (1950) are two theorists who tried to meld psychoanalytic notions with traditional stimulus-response learning theory in an ambitious and influential explanation of personality.

Dollard and Miller translated Freud's notion of the pleasure principle— trying to maximize one's pleasure and minimize one's pain—into terms more suitable for learning theory by suggesting that both biological *and* learned drives energize an organism. If the consequence of a particular behavior is a reduction in drive, the drive reduction is viewed as reinforcing. This in turn increases the probability of the behavior occurring again in the future.

According to Dollard and Miller, the Freudian notion of repression, in which anxiety-producing thoughts are pushed into the unconscious through innate processes, can be looked at instead as an example of "learned not-thinking." Suppose the thought of sexual intercourse makes you anxious. Freud might propose that you deal with the anxiety by avoiding conscious thought about intercourse and instead relegating the idea to your unconscious—that is, by repressing the thought, where repression is an unlearned phenomenon. In contrast, Dollard and Miller might suggest that "not think-ing" about the topic will become reinforcing to you because you find that doing so leads to a reduction in the unpleasant state of anxiety that thinking about the topic evokes. "Not thinking," then, will become an increasingly likely behavior.

Where the Inner Person Meets the Outer One: Social Learning Theories of Personality

Unlike other learning theories of personality, **social learning theory** emphasizes the influence of a person's thoughts, feelings, expectations, and values in determining personality. According to Albert Bandura, the main proponent of this point of view, people are able to foresee the possible outcomes of certain behaviors in a given setting without actually having to carry them out. This takes place mainly through the mechanism of **observational learning**—

Social learning theory (of personality): The theory that suggests that personality develops through observational learning

Observational learning: Learning that is the result of viewing the actions of others and observing the consequences viewing the actions of others and observing the consequences (Bandura, 1977).

For instance, as we first discussed in Chapter 5, children who view a model behaving in, say, an aggressive manner tend to copy the behavior if the consequences of the model's behavior are seen to be positive. If, on the other hand, the model's aggressive behavior has resulted in no consequences or negative consequences, children are considerably less likely to act aggressively. According to social learning theory, personality thus is developed by repeated observation of others' behavior.

As an example of how observational learning produces personality characteristics, psychologist Joan Grusec and colleagues designed an experiment in which kindergarten children were tempted by desirable toys to abandon a task they had been instructed to carry out (Grusec et al., 1979). Prior to being tempted, they were exposed to a model who either succumbed to temptation or resisted. The results of the study showed that children who were exposed to the resistant model were considerably more apt to resist themselves than those who saw a nonresisting model. Moreover, the effect lingered; two weeks later, those who had seen a model who resisted temptation were still better able to hold themselves back than subjects who had seen a model who had yielded to temptation (see Figure 14-5). The study suggests a mechanism through which the personality characteristic of resistance to temptation might be acquired.

More than other learning theories, social learning theory considers how we can modify our own personalities through the exercise of self-reinforcement. We are constantly judging our own behavior on the basis of our internal expectations and standards and then providing ourselves with cognitive rewards or punishments. For instance, a person who cheats on her income tax may mentally punish herself, feeling guilty and displeased with herself. If, just before mailing her tax return, she corrects her "mistake," the positive feelings she will experience will be rewarding and will serve to reinforce her view of herself as a law-abiding citizen.

FIGURE 14-5

Children's observation of a model who resisted temptation or who yielded to temptation affected the amount of time they themselves later spent playing with a "forbidden" toy—even two weeks after they viewed the model. (Grusec et al., 1979.)

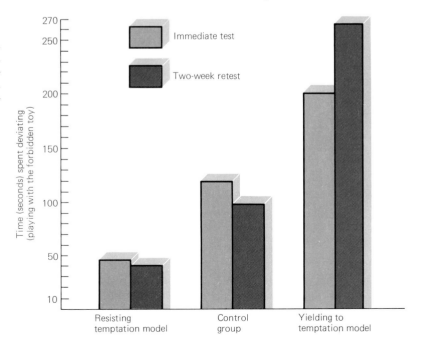

Social learning theories are also distinct in the emphasis they place on the reciprocity between individuals and their environment. Not only is the environment assumed to affect personality, but people's behavior and personalities are assumed to "feed back" and modify the environment—which in turn affects behavior (Bandura, 1981).

Evaluating Learning Theories of Personality

By ignoring the internal processes that are uniquely human, traditional learning theorists such as Skinner have been accused of oversimplifying personality so much that the concept becomes meaningless. In fact, reducing behavior to a series of stimuli and responses, and excluding thoughts and feelings from the realm of personality, leaves behaviorists practicing an unrealistic and inadequate form of science, at least in the eyes of their critics.

Of course, some of these criticisms are blunted by social learning theory, which explicitly considers the role of cognitive processes in personality. Still, all learning theories share a highly **deterministic** view of human behavior, a view maintaining that behavior is shaped primarily by forces outside the control of the individual. In the eyes of some critics, determinism disregards the ability of people to pilot their own course through life.

Determinism: The view suggesting that people's behavior is shaped primarily by factors outside their control

On the other hand, learning approaches have had a major impact in a variety of ways. For one thing, they have helped make the study of personality an objective, scientific venture by focusing on observable features of people and the environments in which they live. Beyond this, learning theories have produced important, successful means of treating personality disorders. The degree of success these treatments have enjoyed provides confidence that learning theory approaches have merit.

UNDERSTANDING THE SELF: Humanistic Theories of Personality

Where, in all these theories of personality, is an explanation for the saintliness of a Mother Teresa, the creativity of a Michelangelo, the brilliance and perseverance of an Einstein? An understanding of such unique individuals—as

Mother Teresa's selflessness can be explained by humanistic theories of personality. (UPI/Bettmann Newsphotos.)

Humanistic theory (of personality): The theory that emphasizes people's basic goodness and their natural tendency to rise to higher levels of functioning

Self-concept: The impression one holds of oneself

Unconditional positive regard: Supportive behavior from another individual, regardless of one's words or actions

Self-actualization: A state of self-fulfillment in which people realize their highest potential

well as more ordinary sorts of people who share some of the same attributes—comes from humanistic theory.

According to humanistic theorists, the theories of personality that we have discussed share a fundamental error in their views of human nature. Instead of seeing people as controlled by unconscious, unseen forces (as does psychoanalytic theory), a set of stable traits (trait theory), or situational reinforcements and punishments (learning theory), **humanistic theory** emphasizes people's basic goodness and their tendency to grow to higher levels of functioning. It is this conscious, self-motivated ability to change and improve, along with people's unique creative impulses, that make up the core of personality.

The major representative of the humanistic point of view is Carl Rogers (1971). Rogers suggests that people have a need for positive regard that reflects a universal requirement to be loved and respected. Because others provide this positive regard, we grow dependent on them. We begin to see and judge ourselves through the eyes of other people, relying on their values.

According to Rogers, one outgrowth of placing import on the values of others is that there is often some degree of mismatch between a person's experiences and his or her **self-concept**, or self-impression. If the discrepancy is minor, so are the consequences. But if it is great, it will lead to psychological disturbances in daily functioning, such as the experience of frequent anxiety.

Rogers suggests that one way of overcoming the discrepancy between experience and self-concept is through the receipt of unconditional positive regard from others—a friend, a spouse, or a therapist. As we will discuss further in Chapter 17, **unconditional positive regard** consists of supportive behavior on the part of an observer, no matter what a person says or does. This support, says Rogers, allows people the opportunity to evolve and grow both cognitively and emotionally as they are able to develop more realistic self-concepts.

To Rogers and other humanistic personality theorists (such as Abraham Maslow, whose theory of motivation we discussed in Chapter 9), an ultimate goal of personality growth is self-actualization. **Self-actualization** is a state of self-fulfillment in which people realize their highest potential: This, Rogers would argue, occurs when their experience with the world and their self-concept are closely matched. People who are self-actualized accept themselves as they are in reality, which enables them to achieve happiness and fulfillment.

Evaluating Humanistic Theories

Although humanistic theories suggest the value of providing unconditional positive regard toward people, unconditional positive regard toward humanistic theories has been less forthcoming from many personality theorists. The criticisms have centered on the difficulty of verifying the basic assumptions of the theory, as well as on the question of whether unconditional positive regard does, in fact, lead to greater personality adjustment.

Humanistic approaches have also been criticized for making the assumption that people are basically "good"—a notion which is unverifiable and, equally important, one in which nonscientific values are used to build supposedly scientific theories. Still, humanistic theories have been important in highlighting the uniqueness of human beings and in guiding the development of a significant form of therapy designed to alleviate psychological difficulties.

By now, you have come across the question of which theory is right a number of times in connection with psychology. The response, once again, is the same: This is not the most appropriate question to be asking. Each theory looks at somewhat different aspects of personality and holds different premises, and in many cases personality is most reasonably viewed from a number of perspectives simultaneously. Of course, the potential exists that someday there will be a unified theory of personality, but the field has not yet reached that point, and the likelihood of its happening in the near future is slim.

In the meantime, it is possible to highlight and compare the major differences between each of the theories. Listed below are the most important dimensions along which the theories differ:

▶ The unconscious versus the conscious. Psychoanalytic theory emphasizes the importance of the unconscious; humanistic theory stresses the conscious; and trait and learning theories largely disregard both.

▶ Nature (genetic factors) versus nurture (environmental factors). Psychoanalytic theory stresses genetic factors; learning theory focuses on the environment; trait theory varies; and humanistic theory stresses the interaction between both in the development of personality.

▶ Freedom versus determinism. Humanistic theories stress the freedom of individuals to make choices in their lives; other theories stress determinism, the view that behavior is directed and caused by factors outside people's willful control. Determinism is particularly evident in psychoanalytic and learning theories, as well as in most trait theories; in such approaches, people's behavior is assumed to be brought about by factors largely outside their control.

▶ Stability versus modifiability of personality characteristics. Psychoanalytic and trait theories emphasize the stability of characteristics across a person's life; learning and humanistic theories stress that personality remains flexible and resilient throughout the life span.

▶ Nomothetic versus idiographic approaches. **Nomothetic** approaches to personality accentuate the broad uniformities across behavior, whereas **idiographic** approaches to personality emphasize what makes one person unique—different from all others. Although each of the theories contains nomothetic and idiographic aspects, psychoanalytic theory, which posits broad developmental stages, and trait theory, which searches for universal characteristics, are more closely allied to nomothetic approaches than the others. Learning theory and humanistic theory are more idiographic, stressing the consequences of a person's particular background and environment on personality.

Nomothetic approaches to personality: A study of personality accentuating the broad uniformities across behavior

Idiographic approaches to personality: A study of personality emphasizing what makes one person different from others and unique

RECAP AND REVIEW II

Recap

◀ Traits are relatively enduring dimensions along which people differ from one another. Trait theorists have tried to identify the major traits that characterize personality.

◀ Allport divided traits into cardinal, central, and secondary traits. Using a statistical technique called factor analysis,

Cattell identified 46 surface traits and sixteen basic source traits, whereas Eysenck found just two major dimensions: introversion-extroversion and neuroticism-stability.

◀ Learning theories of personality concentrate on how environmental factors shape personality. Among the most important approaches are Skinner's reinforcement theory, Dollard and Miller's stimulus-response theory, and social learning theories.

◀ Humanistic theories view the core of personality as the ability to change, improve, and be creative in a uniquely human fashion.

◀ The major characteristics along which personality theories differ include the role of the unconscious versus the conscious, nature (genetic factors) versus nurture (environmental factors), freedom versus determinism, stability versus modifiability of personality characteristics, and nomothetic versus idiographic approaches to personality.

Review

1. a. Carl's determination to succeed is the dominant force in all his activities and relationships. According to Gordon Allport's theory, this is an example of a _____ trait.

   b. In contrast, Cindy's fondness for old Western movies is an example of a _____ trait.

2. a. The notion that an individual's behavior is determined more by the nature of the situation than by stable personality traits was proposed by _____ .

   b. In opposition to this idea, _____ argued that consistency can be demonstrated by measuring behavior over repeated settings and times.

3. Which trait theorist used surface traits and source traits to explain behavior on the basis of sixteen personality dimensions?

   a. Hans Eysenck
   b. Walter Mischel
   c. Gordon Allport
   d. Raymond Cattell

4. What is the major premise of Eysenck's trait theory?

5. Learning theorists Dollard and Miller believed that people are energized by
   a. a desire for pleasure.
   b. the need for a positive self-concept.
   c. the need for love and respect.
   d. biological and learned drives.

6. Observational learning was demonstrated by
   a. B. F. Skinner.
   b. John Dollard and Neal Miller.
   c. Carl Rogers.
   d. Albert Bandura.

7. Fill in each blank with the letter of the appropriate theory.

   ____ Emphasizes role of thoughts, feelings, expectations, and values in determining behavior

   ____ Criticized for its limitations in labeling, but not explaining, personalities

   ____ Focuses on observable traits, responses to environment, and behavior modification

   ____ Begins with the idea that people are basically good

   ____ Suggests personality is determined partially by unconscious forces.

   a. Trait theory
   b. Behaviorism
   c. Humanistic theory
   d. Social learning theory
   e. Psychodynamic theory

(Answers to review questions are on page 504.)

DETERMINING WHAT MAKES YOU SPECIAL: ASSESSING PERSONALITY

You have a need for other people to like and admire you.

You have a tendency to be critical of yourself.

You have a great deal of unused potential that you have not turned to your advantage.

Although you have some personality weaknesses, you are generally able to compensate for them.

Your adjustment to the opposite sex has presented problems to you.

More disciplined and self-controlled outside, you tend to be worrisome and insecure inside.

At times you have serious doubts as to whether you have made the right decision or done the right thing.

You prefer a certain amount of change and variety and become dissatisfied when hemmed in by restrictions and limitations.

You do not accept others' statements without satisfactory proof.

You have found it unwise to be too frank in revealing yourself to others.

If you think these statements provide a surprisingly accurate account of your personality, you are not alone: Most college students think that the statements are tailored just to them. In fact, though, the descriptions are intentionally designed to be so vague as to be applicable to just about anyone (Forer, 1949; Russo, 1981).

The ease with which we can agree with such imprecise statements underscores the difficulty in coming up with accurate and meaningful assessments of people's personalities (Johnson, Cain, Falke, Hayman & Perillo, 1985). Just as trait theorists were faced with the problem of determining the most critical and important traits, psychologists interested in assessing personality must be able to define the most meaningful measures of discriminating between one person's personality and another's. To do this, they use **psychological tests**, standard measures devised to assess behavior objectively. Such tests are used by psychologists to help people make decisions about their lives and understand more about themselves; they are also employed by researchers interested in the causes and consequences of personality.

Psychological tests: Standard measures devised to objectively assess behavior

THE KEYS TO PERSONALITY ASSESSMENT: Reliability and Validity

When we use a ruler, we expect to find that it measures an inch in the same way as the last time we used it. When we weigh ourselves on the bathroom scale, we hope that the variations we see on the scale are due to changes in our weight and are not errors on the part of the scale (unless the change in weight is in an unwanted direction!).

In the same way, we hope that psychological tests have **reliability**—that they measure what they are trying to measure consistently. We need to be sure that each time we administer the test, a person taking the test will get the same results—assuming that nothing about the person has changed relevant to what is being measured.

Reliability: Consistency in the measurements made by a test

Suppose, for instance, that when you first took the College Board exams you scored a 300 on the verbal section of the test. Then, when taking the test again a few months later, you scored a 700. Upon receiving your new score, you might well stop celebrating for a moment to question whether the test is reliable, since it is unlikely that your abilities could have changed enough to raise your score by 400 points.

But suppose your score changed hardly at all, and both times you received a score of about 300. Though you couldn't complain about a lack of reliability, if you knew your verbal skills were above average you might be concerned that the test did not adequately measure what it was supposed to measure. The question has now become one of validity rather than of reliability. A test has **validity** when it actually measures what it is supposed to measure.

Validity: The ability of a test to measure what it is supposed to measure

Knowing that a test is reliable is no guarantee that it is also valid. For instance, we could devise a very reliable means for measuring the circumference of the skull, if we decided that skull size is related to trustworthiness. But there is certainly no guarantee that the test is valid, since one can assume with little danger of being contradicted that skull size has nothing to do with trustworthiness. In this case, then, we have reliability without validity.

On the other hand, if a test is unreliable, it cannot be valid. Assuming that all other factors—a person's motivation, knowledge of the material, health, and so forth—are similar, if someone scores high the first time she takes a specific test and low the second time, the test cannot be measuring what it is supposed to measure, and is therefore both unreliable and not valid.

Test validity and reliability are prerequisites for accurate personality assessment—as well as for any other measurement task carried out by psychologists. Thus the intelligence tests that we discussed in Chapter 8, clinical psychologists' assessment of psychological disorders that we will consider in Chapters 16 and 17, and social psychologists' measures of attitudes must meet the tests of validity and reliability in order for the results to be meaningful. We turn now to some of the specific sorts of measures used by psychologists in their study of personality.

ASKING A LITTLE TO LEARN MUCH: Self-Report Measures of Personality

If someone wanted to assess your personality, one useful method would be to carry out an extensive interview with you in order to determine the most important events of your childhood, your social relationships, and your successes and failures. Obviously, though, such a technique would be extraordinarily costly in terms of time and effort.

It is also unnecessary. Just as physicians do not need to drain your entire blood supply in order to test it, psychologists can utilize **self-report measures** that ask people about a relatively small sample of their behavior. This sampling of self-reports is then used to infer the presence of particular personality characteristics.

One of the best examples of a self-report measure, and the most frequently used personality test, is the **Minnesota Multiphasic Personality Inventory (MMPI)**, developed by a group of researchers in the 1940s and revised several times (Hathaway, Monachesi & Salasin, 1970). Although the original purpose of the measure was to differentiate people with specific sorts of psychological difficulties from those without disturbances, it has been found to predict a variety of other behaviors. For instance, MMPI scores have been shown to be good predictors of whether college students will marry within ten years and whether they will get an advanced degree (Dworkin & Widom, 1977). Police departments use the test to measure whether police officers are prone to use their weapons. The Soviets even administer a modified form of the MMPI to their cosmonauts and Olympic athletes (Holden, 1986).

The test itself consists of a series of 704 true-false items (for adults) and 654 items (in an adolescent version) to which a person responds "true,"

Self-report measures: A method of gathering data about people by asking them questions about a sample of their behavior

Minnesota Multiphasic Personality Inventory (MMPI): A test used to identify people with psychological difficulties

---

"false," or "cannot say." The questions cover a variety of issues, ranging from mood ("I am happy most of the time") to occupational aspirations ("I would like to be a soldier") to physical and psychological health ("I am seldom troubled by constipation" and "Someone has control over my mind"). There are no right or wrong answers, of course. Instead, interpretation of the results rests on the pattern of responses. The test yields scores on ten separate scales (see Figure 14-6) plus three scales meant to measure the validity of the respondent's answers. For example, there is a "lie scale" that indicates (from items such as "I can't remember ever having a bad night's sleep") when people are falsifying their responses in order to present themselves more favorably.

How did the authors of the MMPI know what specific patterns of responses indicate? The procedure they used is typical of personality test construction—a process known as test standardization. To devise the test, groups of psychiatric patients with a specific diagnosis, such as depression or schizophrenia, were asked to complete a large number of items. The test authors then determined which items best differentiated members of these groups from a comparison group of normal subjects, and these specific items were included in the final version of the test. By systematically carrying out this procedure on groups with different diagnoses, the test authors were able to

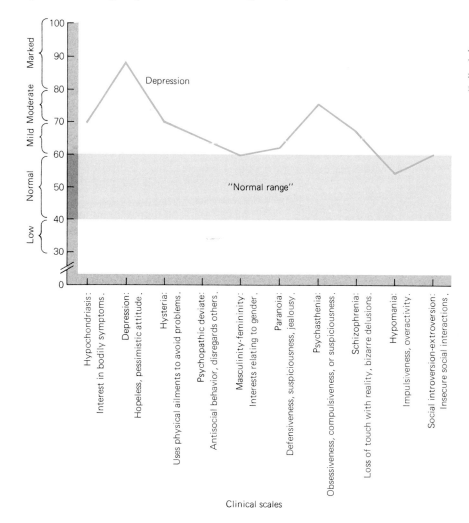

FIGURE 14-6

A sample profile on the MMPI of a person who has been diagnosed as suffering from severe depression. (Adapted from Kleinmuntz, 1967, and Rosen, 1958.)

PART 5

INDIVIDUAL DEVELOPMENT
AND DIFFERENTIATION

Norms: Standards of test performance

devise a number of subscales which identified different forms of abnormal behavior.

As with any test standardization procedure, it was necessary for the MMPI authors to establish **norms**, standards of test performance. To develop a norm, test designers calculate the average score, and also establish the amount and nature of scores that differ from the norm. Test takers are then able to consider the meaning of their raw scores relative to the scores of others who have taken the test, giving them a qualitative sense of their performance.

Over the last decade, the norms of the MMPI were updated, and individual items were revised to eliminate such problems as sexist and antiquated word usage (Holden, 1986; Offord, 1987). According to James N. Butcher, a psychologist at the University of Minnesota, about 15 percent of the items underwent change. For example, an item stating "Sometimes at elections I vote for men about whom I know very little" was typical of several sexist questions which assumed that a target person would be male. Moreover, a number of items asked about men's views of women, while not one asked about how women view men. And an item that asked about playing the game drop-the-handkerchief was typical of those which were puzzling to people under the age of 40.

More important than wording changes, however, were changes in assumptions about abnormality. For instance, a woman who answers affirmatively to questions such as "I like mechanics magazines" and "I would like to be a soldier" no longer is assumed to be unusual.

When the MMPI is used for the purposes for which it was devised—identification of personality disorders—it has proved to do a reasonably good job (Butcher & Owen, 1978). However, like other personality tests, it presents the opportunity for abuse. For instance, employers who use it as a screening tool for job applicants may interpret the results improperly, relying too heavily on the results of individual scales instead of taking into account the overall patterns of results, which require skilled interpretation. Other tests, such as the California Psychological Inventory and the Edwards Personal Preference Schedule are more appropriately used for screening job applicants, as well as for providing people with information about their personalities to help them make informed career choices and to identify their strengths and weaknesses (see the Psychology at Work box).

LOOKING INTO THE UNCONSCIOUS: Projective Methods

If you were shown the kind of inkblot presented in Figure 14-7 and asked what it represented to you, you might not think that your impressions would mean very much. But to a psychoanalytic theoretician, your responses to such an ambiguous figure would provide valuable clues to the state of your unconscious, and ultimately to your general personality characteristics.

The inkblot in the figure is representative of **projective personality tests**, in which a person is shown an ambiguous stimulus and asked to describe it or tell a story about it. The responses are then considered to be "projections" of what the person is like.

The best-known projective test is the **Rorschach test**. Devised by Swiss psychiatrist Hermann Rorschach (1924), the test consists of showing a series of symmetrical stimuli, similar to the one in Figure 14-7, to people who are then asked what the figures represent to them. Their responses are recorded,

Projective personality test: An ambiguous stimulus presented to a person for the purpose of determining personality characteristics

Rorschach (ROAR shock) **test**: A test consisting of inkblots of indefinite shapes, the interpretation of which is used to assess personality characteristics

Wanted: People with "kinetic energy," "emotional maturity" and the ability to "deal with large numbers of people in a fairly chaotic situation."

CAN YOU PASS THE JOB PERSONALITY TEST?

This job description may seem as if it specifies qualities required for a co-host of *Wheel of Fortune*. In actuality, American MultiCinema (AMC), one of the major movie theater chains in America, is searching for candidates who possess such skills to manage its theaters (Dentzer, 1986). To find them, AMC has developed a battery of personality measures for aspiring job applicants to complete. In developing its tests, AMC joined scores of companies, ranging from General Motors to J. C. Penney, which employ personality tests to help determine who gets hired and, once on the job, who gets promoted or even who gets fired.

Companies in the United States now spend about $50 million a year on testing procedures, and the amount is rising annually (Tuller, 1985). One reason for the growth of such tests is computerization. Before the advent of inexpensive micro-

computers, many companies had to send test responses to a central scoring facility, waiting as long as two weeks for results. Today, however, scores can be determined immediately through computerized scoring procedures, aiding in timely decision making.

An even more important factor in the growth of testing has been the development of more sophisticated, valid, and bias-free tests. For instance, a group of power companies has devised a series of tests for a number of job categories. The companies now have specific tests to measure decision-making capability for systems operators, mechanical aptitude for maintenance workers, and language skills for clerical positions. The power companies estimate that they are saving at least $20 million per year because of the

improvement in employee selection procedures (Tuller, 1985).

The use of personality tests for employee selection is not without its potential dangers, however. For one thing, although personality tests may be good at predicting the abilities of large numbers of people, any one individual—particularly someone who has difficulties performing well on standardized tests—may not receive an adequate assessment of his or her abilities. Furthermore, no single test, by itself, gives a complete picture of the range of skills, traits, and abilities a person may have (Angleitner & Wiggins, 1986). Finally, it is difficult to construct a test that is both reliable and valid, and tests designed by nonexperts may be worse than no test at all.

Despite their potential shortcomings, the use of personality tests is on the rise in employment settings (Sweetland & Keyser, 1988). Given their increasing use, you should not be surprised if the first thing you are given when you apply for a new job is not a traditional job interview, but a personality test.

and through a complex set of clinical judgments on the part of the examiner, people are classified into different personality types. For instance, respondents who see a bear in one inkblot are thought to have a strong degree of emotional control, according to the rules developed by Rorschach.

FIGURE 14-7

This inkblot is similar to the type used in the Rorschach personality test. What do *you* see in it?

508

Thematic Apperception Test (TAT): A test consisting of a series of ambiguous pictures about which a person is asked to write a story, which is then taken to be a reflection of the writer's personality

The **Thematic Apperception Test (TAT)** is another well-known projective test. As noted when we discussed achievement motivation in Chapter 9, the TAT consists of a series of pictures about which a person is asked to write a story. The stories are then used to draw inferences about the writer's personality characteristics.

By definition, tests with stimuli as ambiguous as the Rorschach and TAT require particular skill and care in their interpretation. In fact, they are often criticized as requiring too much inference on the part of the examiner. However, they are widely used, particularly in clinical settings, and their proponents suggest that their reliability and validity are high.

BEHAVIORAL ASSESSMENT

If you were a psychologist subscribing to a learning approach to personality, you would likely object to the indirect nature of projective tests. Instead, you would be more apt to use **behavioral assessment**—direct measures of an individual's behavior used to describe characteristics indicative of personality. As with observational research (discussed in Chapter 1), behavioral assessment may be carried out naturalistically by observing people in their own settings: in the workplace, at home, or in school, for instance. In other cases, behavioral assessment occurs in the laboratory, under controlled conditions in which a psychologist sets up a situation and observes an individual's behavior.

Behavioral assessment: Direct measures of an individual's behavior used to describe characteristics indicative of personality

Regardless of the setting in which behavior is observed, an effort is made to ensure that behavioral assessment is carried out objectively, quantifying behavior as much as possible. For instance, an observer might record the number of social contacts a person initiates, the number of questions asked, or the number of aggressive acts. Another method might be to measure duration of events: the length of a temper tantrum in a child, the length of a conversation, the amount of time spent working, or the time spent in cooperative behavior.

Behavioral assessment is particularly appropriate for observing—and eventually remedying—specific behavioral difficulties, such as increasing socialization in shy children. It provides a means of assessing the specific nature and incidence of a problem and subsequently allows psychologists to determine whether intervention techniques have been successful.

Techniques based on behavioral assessment and learning theories of personality also have made important contributions to the treatment of certain kinds of psychological difficulties. Indeed, the knowledge of normal personality provided by the theories we have discussed throughout this chapter has led to significant advances in our understanding and treatment of both physical and psychological disorders, as we will see in the next chapter.

THE INFORMED CONSUMER OF PSYCHOLOGY:
Assessing Personality Assessments

It is not unusual today to be required to take a personality test before being offered a job. Likewise, there are many organizations which—for a hefty fee—will give you a battery of personality tests that purport to steer you toward a career for which your personality is particularly suited.

Before you rely on the results of such testing too heavily—as a potential employee, employer, or consumer of testing services—you should keep the following points in mind:

▶ Understand what the test purports to measure. Standard personality measures are accompanied by information that discusses how the test was developed, to whom it is most applicable, and how the results should be interpreted. If possible, you should read the accompanying literature; it will help you understand the meaning of any results.

▶ Remember that decisions should not be based solely on the results of any one test. Test results should be interpreted in the context of other information—academic records, social interests, and home and community activities. Without these data, individual scores are relatively uninformative at best and may even be harmful.

▶ Tests are not infallible. The results may be in error; the test may be unreliable or invalid; you may have had a "bad day" when you took the test; the person scoring and interpreting the test may have made a mistake. You should not place undue stock in the results of the single administration of any test.

In sum, it is important to keep in mind the complexity of human behavior—particularly your own. No one test can provide an understanding of the intricacies of someone's personality without considering a good deal more information than can be provided in a single testing session.

RECAP AND REVIEW III

Recap

◀ Psychological tests are standard measures used to measure behavior objectively. They must be reliable, measuring with consistency what they are trying to measure, and valid, measuring what is supposed to be measured.

◀ Self-report measures of personality ask people about a sample range of their behaviors. The results are then used to infer personality characteristics.

◀ Projective personality tests present ambiguous stimuli which the person is asked to describe or tell a story about. Responses are used as an indication of information about the individual's personality.

◀ Behavioral assessment employs direct measures of an individual's behavior to describe characteristics indicative of personality.

Review

1. The primary application of personality tests is
   a. determining whether someone is honest.
   b. analyzing someone's qualifications for a particular position.
   c. providing an objective measure of behavior.
   d. determining whether the taker is depressed or schizophrenic.

2. _____ refers to the consistency of multiple scores on a test.

3. _____ refers to what a test measures and how well it does so.

4. The Rorschach Test employs symmetrical inkblots which resemble specific objects. A subject who sees something different from the typical response is likely to have a psychological disturbance, often requiring treatment. True or false? _____

5. The study of personality based on direct measures of behavior is known as
   a. projective testing.
   b. behavioral assessment.
   c. the MMPI.
   d. behaviorism.

6. Which of the following is *not* true?
   a. Personality testing is often the best way to determine whether a job applicant should be hired.
   b. Personality tests should be used only by professionals who are trained to administer the test and interpret the results correctly.
   c. A valid employment test will be good at predicting who will succeed on the job.
   d. The MMPI was designed to aid in the diagnosis of psychiatric disorders.

(Answers to review questions are on page 510.)

1. In this chapter, we have examined characteristics and behaviors that make people different from one another—those behaviors that psychologists consider to be at the root of personality. More formally, personality is thought of in two different, but related, ways: First, it refers to the characteristics that differentiate one person from another. Second, it provides a means of explaining the stability in people's behavior that leads them to act uniformly both in different situations and over extended periods of time.

2. According to psychoanalysts, much of behavior is caused by parts of personality which are found in the unconscious, and of which we are unaware. Freud's theory suggests that personality is composed of the id, the ego, and the superego. The id is the unorganized, inherited part of personality whose purpose is to immediately reduce tensions relating to hunger, sex, aggression, and other primitive impulses. The ego restrains instinctual energy in order to maintain the safety of the individual and to help the person be a member of society. The superego represents the rights and wrongs of society and consists of the conscience and the ego-ideal.

3. Freud's psychoanalytic theory suggests that personality develops through a series of stages, each of which is associated with a major biological function. The oral stage is the first period, occurring during the first year of life. Next comes the anal stage, lasting from approximately age 1 to age 3. The phallic stage follows, with interest focusing on the genitals. At age 5 or 6, near the end of the phallic stage, children experience the Oedipal conflict, a process through which they learn to identify with the same-sex parent by acting as much like that parent as possible. Then follows a latency period lasting until puberty, after which people move into the genital stage, a period of mature sexuality.

4. Defense mechanisms, used for dealing with anxiety relating to impulses from the id, provide people with unconscious strategies to reduce anxiety. The most common defense mechanisms are repression, regression, displacement, rationalization, denial, projection, and sublimation.

5. Freud's psychoanalytic theory has provoked a number of criticisms. These include a lack of supportive scientific data, the theory's inadequacy in making predictions, and its limitations owing to the restricted population on which it is based. Still, the theory remains a pivotal one. For instance, the neo-Freudian psychoanalytic theorists built on Freud's work, although they placed greater emphasis on the role of the ego and paid greater attention to social factors in determining behavior.

6. Trait theories have tried to identify the most basic and relatively enduring dimensions along which people differ from one another—dimensions known as traits. For example, Allport suggested that there were three kinds of traits—cardinal, central, and secondary. Later theorists employed a statistical technique called factor analysis to identify the most crucial traits. Using this method, Cattell identified sixteen basic traits, while Eysenck found two major dimensions: introversion-extroversion and neuroticism-stability.

7. Learning theories of personality concentrate on observable behavior. In fact, to the strict learning theorist, personality is the sum of learned responses to the external environment. In contrast, Dollard and Miller's stimulus-response theory combines psychoanalytic concepts with learning approaches, and social learning theory concentrates on the role of thoughts, feelings, expectations, and values in determining personality. Social learning theory pays particular attention to observational learning.

8. Humanistic theory emphasizes the basic goodness of people and their tendency to grow into higher levels of functioning. It considers as the core of personality a person's unique creative impulses and his or her ability to change and improve. Rogers' concept of the need for positive regard suggests that a universal requirement to be loved and respected underlies personality.

9. The major personality theories differ along a number of important dimensions, including the role of the unconscious versus the conscious, nature versus nurture, freedom versus determinism, stability versus modifiability of personality characteristics, and nomothetic (focusing on the broad uniformities across behavior) versus idiographic (emphasizing the differentiation between people) approaches.

10. Psychological tests are standard assessment tools that objectively measure behavior. They must be reliable, measuring what they are trying to measure consistently, and valid, measuring what they are supposed to measure.

11. Self-report measures ask people about a sample range of their behaviors. These reports are used to infer the presence of particular personality characteristics. The most commonly used self-report measure is the Minnesota Multiphasic Personality Inventory (MMPI), designed to differentiate people with specific sorts of psychological difficulties from normal individuals.

12. Projective personality tests present an ambiguous stimulus; the observer's responses are then used to infer information about the observer. The two most frequently used projective tests are the Rorschach, in which reac-

---

ANSWERS (REVIEW III):
1. c **2.** Reliability **3.** Validity **4.** False; the Rorschach test is designed to provide a trained examiner with clues to the respondent's general personality characteristics **5.** b
6. a

tions to inkblots are employed to classify personality types, and the Thematic Apperception Test (TAT), In which stories about ambiguous pictures are used to draw inferences about the storyteller's personality.

13. Behavioral assessment is based on the principles of learning theory. It employs direct measurement of an individual's behavior to determine characteristics related to personality.

KEY TERMS AND CONCEPTS ▶

personality (p. 480)
psychoanalyst (481)
psychoanalytic theory (481)
unconscious (481)
instinctual drives (483)
id (483)
pleasure principle (483)
ego (483)
reality principle (483)
superego (483)
conscience (483)
ego-ideal (483)
oral stage (484)
fixation (484)
anal stage (485)
phallic stage (485)
Oedipal conflict (485)
identification (485)
penis envy (485)
latency period (485)
genital stage (485)
anxiety (486)
neurotic anxiety (486)

defense mechanisms (486)
repression (486)
regression (486)
displacement (486)
rationalization (486)
denial (486)
projection (486)
sublimation (486)
neo-Freudian psychoanalyst (488)
collective unconscious (488)
archetypes (488)
inferiority complex (489)
trait theory (491)
trait (491)
cardinal trait (491)
central trait (492)
secondary trait (492)
factor analysis (492)
surface trait (492)
source trait (492)
introversion-extroversion (492)
neuroticism-stability (492)
social learning theory (497)

observational learning (497)
determinism (499)
humanistic theory (500)
self-concept (500)
unconditional positive regard (500)
self-actualization (500)
nomothetic approaches to personality (501)
idiographic approaches to personality (501)
psychological tests (503)
reliability (503)
validity (503)
self-report measures (504)
Minnesota Multiphasic Personality Inventory (MMPI) (504)
norms (506)
projective personality test (506)
Rorschach test (506)
Thematic Apperception Test (TAT) (508)
behavioral assessment (508)

FOR FURTHER STUDY AND APPLICATION ▶

Phares, E. J. (1989). *Introduction to personality* (2nd ed.). Glenview, IL: Scott, Foresman.

Hall, C. S., & Lindzey, G. (1978). *Theories of personality* (3rd ed.). New York: Wiley.

Each of these books provides a solid overview of the various theories of personality, with the Hall & Lindzey work being at a somewhat higher level.

Freud, S. (1962). *New introductory lectures on psychoanalysis.* London: Hogarth Press.

This English translation of Freud's original lectures lays out his theory in an understandable fashion, using many examples and case histories.

Anastasi, A. (1989). *Psychological testing* (6th ed.). NY: Macmillan.

This classic textbook describes the key procedures of psychological testing.

Sweetland, R. C., & Keyser, D. J. (1988). *Tests: A comprehensive reference for assessments in psychology, education, and business* (2nd ed.). Kansas City, MO: Test Corporation of America.

This thorough review of the major tests and measures now available—some 3000—provides a capsule description of each one.

American Psychological Association (1974). *Standards for educational and psychological tests.* Washington, D.C.: American Psychological Association.

If you are interested in how psychologists go about creating and using formal tests, this booklet gives you the answers.

PART SIX
PHYSICAL AND MENTAL HEALTH

We now venture into the stress-filled world of an administrative aide, and we enter a physician's examination room, where a patient is describing his symptoms. We encounter a woman working in an office who just a few months earlier had been homeless and shouting obscenities at passers-by. And we eavesdrop on a psychologist's therapy session, in which a patient with psychological difficulties is receiving treatment.

As you'll see in the next three chapters, psychologists have focused their attention on a variety of issues related to physical and psychological health. They have looked at the causes and consequences of stress, health problems such as smoking and heart disease, and physician-patient relationships. They have considered ways of defining and classifying abnormal behavior and have devised means of treating various disorders.

In Chapter 15, we explore the psychological aspects of physical health, including the relationship between stress and health.

In Chapter 16, we turn to psychological health, discussing the distinctions between normal and abnormal behavior, the theories of and explanations for abnormality, and the various types of abnormal behavior.

In Chapter 17, we look at the techniques used in the treatment of psychological disorders and the ways of distinguishing among them.

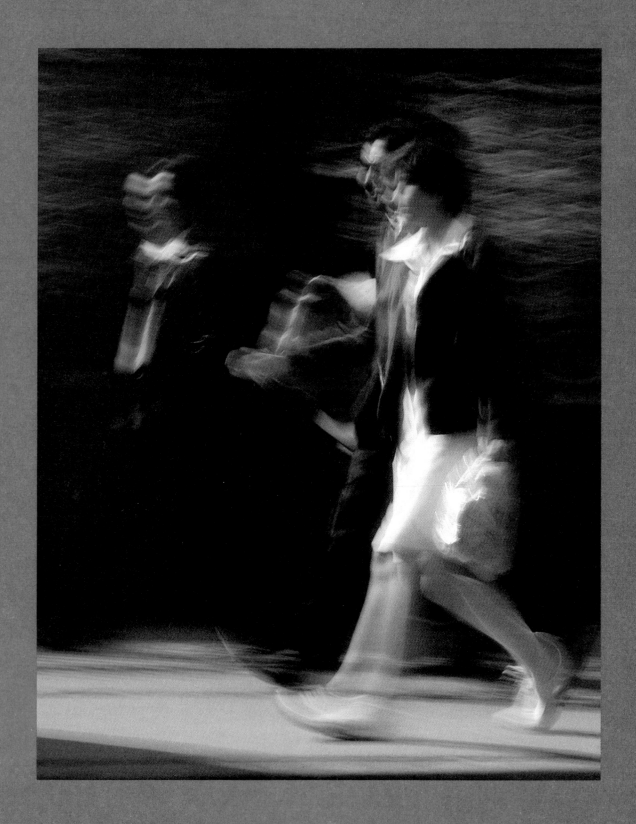

CHAPTER

15

HEALTH PSYCHOLOGY: STRESS, COPING, AND HEALTH

Cathy Collins is being outfitted with the apparatus that measured how much stress she experienced during a normal workday. (*Andy Levin.*)

PROLOGUE:
CATHY COLLINS

It is now 10:26 A.M. Cathy Collins, a Teaneck, New Jersey, mother, wife, and administrative aide in a metropolitan hospital has already been up for five hours, having left breakfast for her children and taken two buses to reach her tiny, windowless office.

She is standing with a phone cradled on her shoulder, contending with:

▶ A patient sitting at her desk, waiting to ask her some questions

▶ A secretary with a question about another patient's chart

▶ Two calls on hold, and her intercom buzzing

▶ Several forms to be completed on her desk, which she attempts to fill out between calls

▶ A stack of paperwork three inches high in her "in" box

▶ A boss who has just walked out of his office and asked for something to be copied

At this moment, a mechanism strapped to Cathy's waist and arm measures her blood pressure and heartbeat, finding that both are elevated 25 and 15 percent, respectively, over earlier readings. As it happened, it was not the biggest increase of the day for Collins (Tierney, 1988).

LOOKING AHEAD ▶

Because Cathy Collins was participating in a hospital study of stress in the workplace, we know for certain about her hidden physiological reactions to the events of the moment. And although no measurements were taken of her emotional reactions, few of us would have difficulty in guessing what she would report experiencing during this same period: stress.

Stress has long been a major topic of study for psychologists as they have attempted to develop an understanding of its causes and devise ways for people to cope with it. In recent years, however, psychologists have begun to consider stress and coping within the broader context of a new field of study known as health psychology. **Health psychology** is the area of psychology applied to the prevention, diagnosis, and treatment of medical problems. It considers questions about the way in which illness is influenced and in some cases caused by psychological factors and how treatments for disease and illness can be based on psychological principles and findings. It also is concerned with issues of prevention: how health problems such as heart disease and stress can be avoided by more healthful behavior.

Health psychologists take a strong stand on the perennial mind-body issue that philosophers, and later psychologists, have argued over since the time of the ancient Greeks (and that we first discussed in Chapter 1). They suggest that, rather than the mind and body being distinct, unrelated systems, the two are clearly linked, and physical health is interwoven with psychological factors. It is now clear, in fact, that good health and the ability to cope with illness when it does occur are affected by psychological factors such as the ability to manage stress and an individual's health habits. Even our attitudes and emotions, working through the **immune system**—the complex

Health psychology: The branch of psychology that explores the relationship between physical and psychological factors

Immune system: The body's natural defenses that fight disease

516

system of organs, glands, and cells that comprise the body's natural defenses in fighting disease—appear to have a direct influence on our health. The mind and the body are thus viewed by health psychologists as two parts of a whole human being that cannot be considered independently.

In this chapter, we discuss ways in which psychological factors affect health, focusing first on the causes and consequences of stress, as well as on the means of coping with it. Next, we explore the psychological aspects of several major health problems, including heart disease, cancer, and smoking. Finally, we examine the ways in which patient-doctor interactions influence our health, and offer suggestions for increasing people's compliance with behavior that will improve their well-being.

In sum, after reading this chapter, you will be able to answer questions such as these:

▶ What is stress, how does it affect us, and how can we best cope with it?

▶ How do psychological factors affect such health-related problems as smoking, coronary heart disease, and cancer?

▶ What are the best ways to encourage behavior that improves health?

▶ Does the nature of our interactions with physicians affect our health?

▶ How can we ensure patient compliance to medical advice?

Despite her gusto in eating these French fries, this woman is probably well aware that the long-term effects on her health from salty, fatty foods are not beneficial. Health psychologists are concerned with devising ways of changing people's habits and lifestyles to help them prevent future disease. (*Renée Lynn/Photo Researchers.*)

STRESS AND COPING

For better or worse, most of us need little introduction to the phenomenon of **stress**, formally defined as the response to events that threaten or challenge a person. Whether it be a paper or exam deadline, a family problem, or even a cumulative series of small events such as those faced by Cathy Collins on the job, life is full of circumstances—known as **stressors**—that produce threats to our well-being. Even pleasant events—such as planning a party or beginning a sought-after job—can produce stress, although negative events result in greater detrimental consequences than positive ones (Sarason, 1978).

All of us face stress in our lives; in fact, some health psychologists believe that daily life involves a series of repeated sequences of perceiving a threat, considering ways of coping with it, and ultimately adapting to the threat, with greater or lesser success (Gatchel & Baum, 1983). Although adaptation is often minor and occurs without our being aware of it, in those cases in which the stress is more severe or longer lasting, adaptation requires major effort and may produce physiological and psychological responses that result in health problems.

Stress: The response to events that are threatening or challenging

Stressors: Circumstances that produce threats to our well-being

THE HIGH COST OF STRESS

Stress can take its toll in many ways, producing physiological and psychological consequences. Often the most immediate reaction to stress is a physiological one, for exposure to stress induces a rise in certain hormones secreted by the adrenal glands, an increase in heart rate and blood pressure, and changes in how well the skin conducts electrical impulses (Mason, 1975;

PHYSICAL AND MENTAL HEALTH

Stress is not necessarily a bad thing, as performers and others who must be "up" to do their jobs know. (*Paul Goode.*)

Selye, 1976). On a short-term basis, these responses may be adaptive because they produce an "emergency reaction"—the response of the sympathetic nervous system discussed in Chapter 2—and may allow more effective coping with the stressful situation.

However, continued exposure to stress results in a decline in the body's overall level of biological functioning because of the continued secretion of the stress-related hormones. Over time, in fact, stressful reactions can promote actual deterioration of body tissues such as the blood vessels and the heart. Ultimately, we become more susceptible to disease as our ability to fight off germs is lowered (Kiecolt-Glaser & Glaser, 1986; Schneiderman, 1983).

In addition to major health difficulties, many of the minor aches and pains that we experience may be caused or worsened by stress. These include headaches, backaches, skin rashes, indigestion, fatigue, and constipation (Brown, 1984). Moreover, a whole class of medical problems, known as **psychosomatic disorders**, often result from stress. These medical problems are caused by an interaction of psychological, emotional, and physical difficulties. Among the most common psychosomatic disorders are ulcers, asthma, high blood pressure, and eczema. In fact, the likelihood of onset of any major illness seems to be related to the number of stressful events a person experiences (see Table 15-1).

On a psychological level, high levels of stress prevent people from coping with life adequately. Their view of the environment can become clouded (a minor criticism made by a professor is blown out of proportion), and—at the greatest levels of stress—emotional responses may be so severe that people are unable to act at all. Moreover, people become less able to deal with new stressors. The ability to contend with future stress, then, declines as a result of past stress (Eckenrode, 1984).

Psychosomatic (sy ko so MAT ik) **disorders:** Medical problems caused by an interaction of psychological, emotional, and physical difficulties

General adaptation syndrome (GAS): A theory developed by Selye that suggests that a person's response to stress consists of three stages: alarm and mobilization, resistance and exhaustion

CHARACTERIZING STRESS: The General Adaptation Syndrome Model

The effects of stress are best illustrated by a model developed by Hans Selye, a major stress theorist (Selye, 1976). This model, the **general adaptation**

TABLE 15-1

TABLE 15-1

Predicting the Illness of the Future from the Stress of the Past

Is there a stress-related illness in your future? Survey research has shown that the number of stressors in a person's life is associated with the experience of a major illness (Rahe & Arthur, 1978).

To find out the degree of stress in your life, take the stressor value given beside each event you have experienced and multiply it by the number of occurrences over the past year (up to a maximum of four), then add up these scores.

50	Entered college
77	Married
38	Had trouble with your boss
43	Held a job while attending school
87	Experienced the death of a spouse
34	Had a major change of sleeping habits
77	Experienced the death of a close family member
30	Had a major change in eating habits
41	Changed your choice of major field of study
45	Revised personal habits
68	Experienced the death of a close friend
22	Were found guilty of minor violations of the law
40	Had an outstanding personal achievement
68	Experienced pregnancy or fathered a pregnancy
56	Experienced a major change in the health or behavior of a family member
58	Had sexual difficulties
42	Had trouble with in-laws

26	Had a major change in the number of family get-togethers
53	Had a major change in financial status
50	Gained a new family member
42	Changed residence or living conditions
50	Had a major conflict or change in values
36	Had a major change in church activities
58	Experienced a marital reconciliation with your mate
62	Were fired from work
76	Were divorced
50	Changed to a different line of work
50	Had a major change in the number of arguments with your spouse
47	Had a major change in responsibilities at work
41	Had your spouse begin or cease work outside the home
42	Had a major change in working hours or conditions
74	Experienced a marital separation from mate
37	Had a major change in type and/or amount of recreation
52	Had a major change in use of drugs
52	Took on a mortgage or loan of less than $10,000
65	Had a major personal injury or illness
46	Experienced a major change in use of alcohol
43	Had a major change in social activities
38	Had a major change in amount of participation in school activities

49	Had a major change in amount of independence and responsibility
33	Took a trip or vacation
54	Became engaged to be married
50	Changed to a new school
41	Changed dating habits
44	Had trouble with school administration
60	Ended a marital engagement or a steady relationship
57	Had a major change in self-concept or self-awareness

Scoring If your total score is above 1435, you are in a high-stress category, which, according to Marx, Garrity & Bowers (1975), puts you at risk for experiencing a stress-related illness in the future. On the other hand, you should not assume that a high score destines you to a future illness. Because the research on stress and illness is correlational, major stressful events cannot be viewed as necessarily causing illness (Dohrenwend, Dodson & Shrout, 1984; Lakey & Heller, 1985). Moreover, some research suggests that future illness is better predicted by the daily, ongoing hassles of life, rather than by the major events depicted in the questionnaire (Lazarous, DeLoungis, Folkman & Green, 1985). Still, a high level of stressful events in one's life is a concern, and it is not unreasonable to take measures to reduce stress (Marx, Garrity & Bowers, 1975, p. 97; Maddi, Bartone & Puccetti, 1987).

syndrome (GAS), suggests that the same set of physiological reactions to stress occurs regardless of the particular cause of stress. As shown in Figure 15-1, the model has three phases. The first stage, the **alarm and mobilization stage**, occurs when people become aware of the presence of a stressor. Suppose, for instance, you learned at the end of the first term of college that you were on academic probation because of your low grades. You likely would respond first with alarm, feeling concerned and upset. Subsequently, though, you would probably begin to mobilize your efforts, making plans and promises to yourself to study harder for the rest of the school year.

In the next stage of the model, the **resistance stage**, you would prepare

Alarm and mobilization stage: In Selye's general adaptation syndrome, a person's initial awareness of the presence of a stressor

Resistance stage: The second stage of Selye's general adaptation syndrome: coping with the stressor

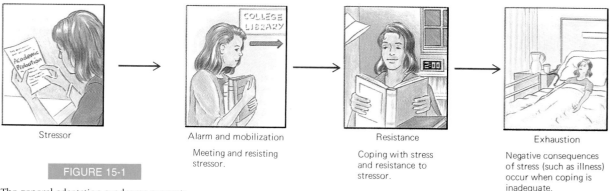

Stressor	Alarm and mobilization	Resistance	Exhaustion
	Meeting and resisting stressor.	Coping with stress and resistance to stressor.	Negative consequences of stress (such as illness) occur when coping is inadequate.

FIGURE 15-1

The general adaptation syndrome suggests that there are three major stages in people's response to stress. (Selye, 1976.)

Exhaustion stage: The third stage of Selye's general adaptation syndrome: failure to adapt to a stressor, leading to physical, psychological, and emotional problems

yourself to fight the stressor. During resistance, a person uses various means to cope with the stressor—sometimes successfully—but at a cost of some degree of physical or psychological general well-being. For instance, your resistance might take the form of devoting long hours to studying. You may ultimately be successful in raising your grades, but it may be at the expense of a loss of sleep and hours of worry.

If resistance is not adequate, the last stage of the model, exhaustion, is reached. During the **exhaustion stage**, a person's ability to adapt to the stressor declines to the point where negative consequences of stress appear: physical illness, psychological symptoms in the form of an inability to concentrate, heightened irritability, or, in severe instances, disorientation and a loss of touch with reality. If you become overwhelmed by pressure to perform well in your courses, for example, you may become sick or find it impossible to study altogether.

The GAS has had a substantial impact on our understanding of stress. For instance, by suggesting that the exhaustion of resources in the third stage of the model produces physiological damage, it has provided a specific model to explain how stress can lead to illness. Furthermore, the model offers a general explanation for stress that cuts across humans and animals. (In fact, as the Research Classics box describes, the model was developed from research on animals.)

On the other hand, some of the specifics of the GAS model have been questioned. Among the most important criticisms is that certain stressors seem to produce distinct physiological reactions, such as the secretion of specific hormones (Mason, 1974). Furthermore, the model's reliance on physiological factors leaves little room for attention to psychological factors, particularly in terms of the way in which stressors are appraised differently by different people (Mikhail, 1981). Still, the model provides a substantial foundation for our understanding of stress.

MY STRESS IS YOUR PLEASURE: The Nature of Stressors

The general adaptation syndrome model is useful in explaining how people respond to stress, but it is not specific about what constitutes a stressor for a given person. Although it is clear that certain kinds of events—such as the death of a loved one or participation in combat during a war—are almost universally stressful, other situations may or may not be stressful to a particular person (Fleming, Baum & Singer, 1984; Lazarus & Cohen, 1977). Consider, for instance, automobile racing. Some of us would find driving cars at

DEVELOPING A MODEL: THE GENERAL ADAPTATION SYNDROME

Hans Selye, who developed the general adaptation syndrome (GAS) model, was initially interested in the effects of sex hormones on the physiological functioning of rats. In the course of this work, it was necessary to expose the rats to a variety of stressful manipulations and observe their responses.

Selye soon noticed a puzzling phenomenon—a phenomenon whose discovery would ultimately bring him far greater notice than his work on sex hormones. Regardless of the specific stressor he introduced into the rats' environment, the rats responded in much the same way. Specifically, the adrenal cortex in the brain became enlarged, the thymus and lymph glands became smaller, and the stomach developed ulcers. After systematically exposing rats to extreme cold, hunger, and fatigue, Selye found that their biological responses were similar.

Ultimately, Selye came to understand the underlying mechanisms at work. He suggested that when an organism confronts a stressor, it becomes mobilized for action by the adrenal glands, which produce activity on the part of the sympathetic nervous system (which we discussed in Chapter 2). Regardless of the cause of the stress, the response of the adrenal glands is the same, leading to similar stress reactions. In time, as the number of stress reactions accumulates, the physiological functioning of several parts of the body is affected, leading to such consequences as the development of stomach ulcers.

Although Selye's model has not been free from criticism, it remains a cornerstone of work on stress. Not only has his research become a classic in health psychology; it illustrates the way in which research with animals has direct relevance to humans.

---

breakneck speeds to be a very stressful event, and the activity would be likely to produce reactions similar to those of other stressful occurrences. However, there are those for whom car racing is a challenging and fun-filled activity; instead of experiencing stress, they look forward to driving around a track at 200 miles per hour. Whether or not car racing is stressful depends in part, then, on individual perceptions of the activity.

For people to consider an event to be stressful, they must perceive it as threatening and must lack the resources to deal with it effectively (Folkman et al., 1986). Consequently, the same event may at times be stressful and at other times evoke no stress at all. For instance, a young man might experience stress when he is turned down for a date—if he attributes the refusal to his unattractiveness or unworthiness. But if he attributes it to some factor unrelated to his self-esteem, such as a previous commitment of the woman he asked, the experience of being refused might create no stress at all.

A number of factors also influence the severity of stress. For example, stress is greater when the importance and number of goals that are threatened are high, when the threat is immediate, or when the anticipation of the threatening event extends over a long period (Paterson & Neufeld, 1987).

Categorizing Stressors

What kinds of events tend to be seen as stressful? There are three general classes of events: cataclysmic stressors, personal stressors, and background stressors (Gatchel & Baum, 1983; Lazarus & Cohen, 1977). **Cataclysmic events** are strong stressors that occur suddenly and affect many people simultaneously. Natural disasters, such as tornadoes and plane crashes, are examples of cataclysmic events that can affect hundreds or thousands of people simultaneously. Curiously, however, cataclysmic events may sometimes be less stressful in the long run than events that are initially less intense. One reason is that such events have a clear resolution: once they are over and done with, people can look forward to the future knowing that the worst

Cataclysmic events: Strong stressors that occur suddenly, affecting many people at once (e.g., natural disasters)

Cataclysmic events, such as the Mexico City earthquake of 1985, can be less stressful than individual disasters, as people often pitch in to help others and thereby help themselves recover from the trauma of the experience. (*Dorantes/Sygma.*)

is behind them. Moreover, the stress induced by cataclysmic events is shared by others who have also experienced the disaster (Cummings, 1987). This permits people to provide one another with social support and a firsthand understanding of the difficulties the others are going through.

Posttraumatic stress syndrome: A phenomenon in which victims of major catastrophes reexperience the original stress event and associated feelings in flashbacks or dreams

On the other hand, some victims of major catastrophes can experience a **posttraumatic stress syndrome**, in which the original events and the feelings associated with them are reexperienced in vivid flashbacks or dreams. Fifteen percent of the veterans of the Vietnam War suffer from posttraumatic stress syndrome, which leads to sleep difficulties, problems in relating to others, and—in some cases—alcohol and drug abuse (Roberts, 1988). The fact that the suicide rate for Vietnam veterans is 86 percent higher than for the general population indicates the difficulties faced by veterans of this war (Blank, 1982).

Personal stressors: Major life events, such as the death of a family member, that have immediate negative consequences which generally fade with time

Personal stressors include major life events such as the death of a parent or spouse, the loss of one's job, a major personal failure, and diagnosis of a life-threatening illness. Typically, personal stressors produce an immediate major reaction that soon tapers off. For example, stress arising from the death of a loved one tends to be greatest just after the time of death, but people begin to feel less stressed and are better able to cope with the loss after the passage of time.

In some cases, though, the effects of stress are lingering. Victims of rape sometimes suffer lasting consequences long after the event, facing major difficulties in adjustment. Similarly, the malfunction of the Three Mile Island nuclear plant in Pennsylvania in the early 1980s, which exposed people to the stressor of a potential nuclear meltdown, produced emotional, behavioral, and physiological consequences that lasted more than a year and a half (Baum, Gatchel & Schaeffer, 1983). (The consequences of such disasters are examined in more detail in Chapter 21.)

Background stressors: Daily hassles, such as being stuck in traffic, that cause minor irritations but have no long-term ill effects, unless they continue or are compounded by other stressful events

Standing in a long line at a bank and getting stuck in a traffic jam are examples of **background stressors** or, more informally, "daily hassles" (Lazarus & Cohen, 1977). These stressors represent the minor irritations of life that we all face time and time again: delays, noisy cars and trucks, broken appliances, other people's irritating behavior, and so on. Background stressors also consist of long-term, chronic problems such as dissatisfaction with school or job, unhappy relationships, or living in crowded quarters without privacy.

By themselves, daily hassles do not require much coping or even re-sponse on the part of the individual, although they certainly do produce unpleasant emotions and moods (Clark & Watson, 1988). Yet daily hassles add up—and ultimately they may produce as great a toll as a single, more stressful incident. In fact, there is an association between the number of daily hassles that people face and the number of psychological symptoms they report (Kanner et al., 1981; Zika & Chamberlain, 1987). Even health problems (such as flu, sore throat, headaches, and backaches) have been linked to daily hassles (DeLongis, Folkman & Lazarus, 1988; Jones, Brantley & Gilchrist, 1988).

Although the nature of daily hassles differs from day to day and from person to person, background stressors do have certain characteristics in common. One critical factor is related to the degree of control people have over aversive, unpleasant stimuli in the environment (Folkman, 1984; Rodin, 1986). When people feel that they can control a situation and determine its outcome, stress reactions are reduced considerably. For instance, people exposed to high levels of noise suffer fewer adverse effects if they know they are able to control the noise than those exposed to the same amount of noise who are unable to control its intensity and duration (Glass & Singer, 1972).

The flip side of hassles are **uplifts**, those minor positive events that make one feel good—even if only temporarily. As indicated in Table 15-2, uplifts range from relating well to a companion to finding one's surroundings pleas-ing. What is especially intriguing about these uplifts is that they are associated with people's psychological health in just the opposite way that hassles are: The greater the number of uplifts experienced, the fewer the psychological symptoms people later report.

Uplifts: Minor positive events that make one feel good

OUT OF CONTROL: Learned Helplessness

You've probably heard someone complaining about an intolerable situation that she couldn't seem to resolve, have heard her say that she was tired of "hitting her head against the wall," and was giving up and accepting things the way they were. This example illustrates one of the possible consequences

Everyday hassles, like having to wait forever for a bus after a snowstorm, are the most common cause of stress overload. (*Joel Gordon.*)

TABLE 15-2

The Ten Most Frequently Reported Hassles and Uplifts

Below are the items that a group of people identified as the hassles and uplifts they experienced most frequently over a nine-month period. The "percentage of times checked" figures represent the mean number of times an item was checked each month, averaged over the nine monthly administrations.

Items	Percentage of Times Checked
Hassles	
1. Concerns about weight	52.4
2. Health of a family member	48.1
3. Rising price of common goods	43.7
4. Home maintenance	42.8
5. Too many things to do	38.6
6. Misplacing or losing things	38.1
7. Yard work or major outside home maintenance	38.1
8. Property investment or taxes	37.6
9. Fears of crime	37.1
10. Physical appearance	35.9
Uplifts	
1. Relating well with spouse or lover	76.3
2. Relating well with friends	74.4
3. Completing a task	73.3
4. Feeling healthy	72.7
5. Getting enough sleep	69.7
6. Eating out	68.4
7. Meeting your responsibilities	68.1
8. Visiting, phoning, or writing someone	67.7
9. Spending time with family	66.7
10. Home (inside) pleasing to you	65.5

Source: Kanner, A. D., Coyne, J. C., Schaefer, C., & Lazarus, R. S. (1981). Comparison of two modes of stress measurement: Daily hassles and uplifts versus major life events. *Journal of Behavioral Medicine,* 4:14, Table 3. Used with permission.

Learned helplessness: A learned belief that one has no control over the environment

of being in an environment in which control over a situation is not possible—a state that produces learned helplessness. According to psychologist Martin Seligman, **learned helplessness**, as discussed first in Chapter 5, occurs when people conclude that unpleasant or aversive stimuli cannot be controlled—a pattern that becomes so ingrained that they do not try to remedy the aversive circumstances, even if they can exert some influence (Seligman, 1975). With learned helplessness, then, people decide that there is no link between the responses they make and the outcomes that occur.

Take, for example, what often happens to elderly people when they are placed in nursing homes or hospitals after living a long life of independence. One of the most striking features of their new environment is that they no longer have control over the most basic activities. They are told what and when to eat, they have their sleeping schedules arranged by someone else, and they are told when they may watch TV or participate in recreational activities. It is not hard to see how this loss of control can have negative effects upon people suddenly placed, often reluctantly, in such a situation.

In fact, the result of the loss of control and the ensuing stress is frequently poorer health—and even a likelihood of earlier death, a fact confirmed dramatically in an experiment conducted in a nursing home where elderly residents in one group were encouraged to make more choices and take greater control of their day-to-day activities (Langer & Janis, 1979). As a result, members of the group were more active and happier than a comparison group of residents who were encouraged to let the nursing home staff care for them. Moreover, an analysis of the residents' medical records showed that six months after the experiment, the group encouraged to be self-sufficient showed significantly greater health improvement than the comparison group. Even more startling was an examination of the death rate: Eighteen months after the experiment began, only 15 percent of the "independent" group had died—compared with 30 percent of the comparison group.

Other research confirms that learned feelings of helplessness have negative consequences, and not just for the elderly. People of all ages report more physical symptoms and depression when they have little or no control than when they feel control over a situation (Pennebaker, Burnam, Schaeffer & Harper, 1977; Peterson & Raps, 1984; Rodin, 1986).

Although the concept of learned helplessness applies to many situations, it does not provide a complete explanation of the circumstances under which stress produces feelings of helplessness. For instance, it does not explain why some individuals experience helplessness in certain situations while others do not.

To help specify the conditions leading to helplessness, Seligman and his colleagues reformulated their original model (Abramson, Garber & Seligman, 1980). Rather than focusing on whether people believe that they lack control in a situation, the revised model addresses people's explanations for their lack of control. Specifically, it suggests that people are most apt to experience helplessness when they perceive the causes of the lack of control to be related to something about their own personal characteristics (as opposed to outside, environmental forces); when they view the causes as stable and enduring (rather than just temporary); and when they see the causes are global and universal (cutting across many situations, rather than in just one sphere of life).

A sense of control over one's daily activities is vital to mental health, for the elderly as well as for younger people. This gentleman spends part of his week volunteering in a local school. (*J. L. BarKan/The Picture Cube.*)

COPING WITH STRESS

Stress is a normal part of living. As Hans Selye has noted, to avoid stress totally, a person would likely have to cease living. Yet, as we have seen, too much stress can take its toll on both physical and psychological health. How do people deal with stress? Is there a way to reduce its negative effects?

The efforts to control, reduce, or learn to tolerate the threats that lead to stress are known as **coping**. We habitually use certain coping responses to help ourselves deal with stress. Most of the time, we're not aware of these responses—just as we may be unaware of the minor stressors of life until they build up to sufficiently aversive levels.

Coping: The efforts to control, reduce, or learn to tolerate the threats that lead to stress

One means of dealing with stress that occurs on an unconscious level is the use of **defense mechanisms**. As we discussed in Chapter 14, defense mechanisms are reactions that maintain a person's sense of control and self-worth by distorting or denying the actual nature of the situation. For example, one study showed that California students who live close to a geological fault in dormitories which are rated as being unlikely to withstand an earthquake

Defense mechanisms: Unconscious strategies people use to reduce anxiety by concealing its source from themselves and others were significantly more likely to deny the seriousness of the situation and to doubt experts' predictions of an impending earthquake than those who lived in safer structures (Lehman & Taylor, 1988).

Another defense mechanism sometimes used to cope with stress is emotional insulation, in which a person stops experiencing any emotions at all, thereby remaining unaffected and unmoved by both positive and negative experiences. The problem with defense mechanisms, of course, is that they do not deal with reality but merely hide the problem.

People use other, more direct and potentially more positive means for coping with stress, as shown in several studies (Aldwin & Revenson, 1987; Compas, 1987; Miller, Brody & Summerton, 1988). For example, in one experiment 100 men and women were asked to record how they coped with a number of different stressors in their lives over a seven-month period. The results showed that people used two major sorts of techniques for dealing with stress: the conscious regulation of emotions, called **emotion-focused coping**, and the management of the stressful problem or stimulus, called **problem-focused coping**. Examples of emotion-focused coping included such strategies as "accepted sympathy and understanding from someone" and "tried to look on the bright side," whereas examples of problem-focused strategies included "got the person responsible to change his or her mind" and "made a plan of action and followed it." In over 98 percent of the stressful incidents reported, *both* emotion-focused and problem-focused strategies were employed. However, more emotion-focused strategies were used in circumstances perceived as being unchangeable, and more problem-focused approaches were used in situations seen as relatively modifiable (Folkman and Lazarus, 1980).

Coping Style: The Hardy Personality

Most of us cope with stress in a characteristic manner, employing a "coping style" that represents our general tendency to deal with stress in a specific way. For example, you may know people who habitually react to even the smallest amount of stress with hysteria, and others who calmly confront even the greatest stress in an unflappable manner. These kinds of people clearly have quite different coping styles (Taylor, 1986).

Among those who cope with stress most successfully are people with a coping style that has come to be called "hardiness." **Hardiness** is a personality characteristic associated with a lower rate of stress-related illness and consisting of three components: commitment, challenge, and control (Kobasa, 1979; 1982).

Commitment is a tendency to throw ourselves into whatever we are doing—a sense that our activities are important and meaningful in all our encounters. Hardy people are also high in a sense of challenge, the second component; they believe that change, rather than stability, is the standard condition of life. To them, the anticipation of change acts as an incentive rather than a threat to their security. Finally, hardiness is marked by a sense of control—the perception that they can influence the events in their lives.

Hardiness seems to act as a buffer against stress-related illness. The hardy individual approaches stress in an optimistic manner and is apt to take direct action to learn about and deal with stressors, thereby changing stressful events into less threatening ones. As a consequence, a person with a hardy personality style is less likely to suffer the negative outcomes of high stress.

Although the concept of hardiness is a useful one, researchers disagree about whether it is a single phenomenon, or if actually just one or two of

Emotion-focused coping: The conscious regulation of emotion as a means of dealing with stress

Problem-focused coping: The management of a stressful stimulus as a way of dealing with stress

Hardiness: A personality characteristic associated with a lower rate of stress-related illness, consisting of three components: commitment, challenge, and control its underlying components account for the positive effects on health that are typically found (Hull, Treuren & Virnelli, 1987). What is clear is that people with hardier personality styles are better able to cope with stress than those with less hardy styles (Allred & Smith, 1989).

Turning to Others: Seeking Social Support

The nature of our relationships with others also provides an important means of coping with stress. Researchers have found that **social support**, the knowledge that we are part of a mutual network of caring, interested others, enables people to experience lower levels of stress and to be better able to cope with the stress they do undergo (Schaefer, Coyne & Lazarus, 1981; Dunkel-Schetter, Folkman & Lazarus, 1987).

Social support: Knowledge of being part of a mutual network of caring, interested others

Other people provide the social and emotional support that helps in dealing with stress in several ways (Lieberman, 1982; Taylor, 1986). For instance, they demonstrate that a person is an important and valued member of a social network. Similarly, other people can provide information and advice about appropriate ways of dealing with stress—as well as being available as a sounding board.

Finally, people who are part of a social support network can provide tangible goods and services. For instance, they can supply a person whose house has burned down with temporary living quarters, or they can help a student who is experiencing stress due to academic performance to study for a test.

THE INFORMED CONSUMER OF PSYCHOLOGY:
Coping Strategies that Work

How does one cope most effectively with stress? Researchers working in the area have made a number of recommendations for dealing with the problem. There is no universal solution for coping with stress, of course, since effective coping depends on the nature of the stressor and the degree to which control is possible. Still, some general guidelines can be followed (Folkman, 1984; Holahan & Moos, 1987):

In an example of turning threat into challenge, Diana Golden, who lost her lower right leg to cancer as a child, continued to ski and in 1988 won the world championship with the U.S. Disabled Ski Team. (*Brooks Dodge/Sharf Marketing Group, Inc.*)

▶ *Turning threat into challenge.* When a stressful situation might be controllable, the best coping approach is to treat the situation as a challenge, focusing on ways to control it. For instance, if you are stressed by poor academic performance, one reasonable approach is to analyze your performance and develop strategies for more effective studying.

▶ *Making a threatening situation less threatening.* When a stressful situation seems to be uncontrollable, a different approach must be taken. It is possible to change one's appraisal of the situation, to view it in a different light, and to modify one's attitudes toward it (Smith & Ellsworth, 1987). The old truism "Look for the silver lining in every cloud" seems to be supported by research findings that show that people who discover something good in negative situations show less distress and better coping ability than those who do not look for the positive side of things (Silver & Wortman, 1980).

▶ *Changing one's goals.* When a person is faced with an uncontrollable situation, another reasonable strategy is to adopt new goals that are practical in view of the particular situation. For example, a dancer who has been in an automobile accident and has lost full use of her legs may no longer aspire to a career in dance—but might modify her goals and try to become a dance

"Stress inoculation" is the technique of preparing oneself for a stressful event before it happens, as this patient about to undergo a spinal tap operation is doing. (*John Griffin/ The Image Works.*)

Inoculation (for stress): Preparation for stress before it is encountered

instructor. Similarly, an executive who has lost his job may change his goal of becoming wealthy to that of obtaining a more modest, but secure, source of income.

▶ *Taking physical action.* Another approach to coping with stress is to bring about changes in one's physiological reactions to it. For example, biofeedback, discussed in Chapter 2, can alter basic physiological processes, allowing people to reduce blood pressure, heart rate, and other consequences of heightened stress. In addition, exercise can be effective in reducing stress in several ways. For one thing, regular exercise reduces heart rate, respiration rate, and blood pressure (although these responses temporarily increase during exercise periods). Furthermore, exercise gives people a sense of control over their bodies, plus a feeling of accomplishment. It even provides a temporary respite from the environment that is causing the stress in the first place, and it helps people sleep better at night

Finally, sometimes a change in diet is helpful in coping with stress. For instance, people who drink large quantities of caffeine are susceptible to feeling jittery and anxious; simply decreasing the amount they consume may be sufficient to reduce the experience of stress. Similarly, being overweight may itself be a stressor, and losing excess weight may be an effective measure for reducing stress—unless dieting is so tension-filled that it becomes stressful.

▶ *Preparing for stress before it happens.* A final strategy for coping with stress is **inoculation**: preparing for stress *before* it is encountered. First developed as a means of preventing postsurgical emotional problems among hospital patients, inoculation methods prepare people for stressful experiences—of either a physical or an emotional nature—by explaining, in as much detail as possible, the difficult events they are likely to encounter. As part of the process, people are asked to imagine how they will feel about the circumstances and to consider various ways of dealing with their reactions—all before the experience has actually occurred. Probably the most crucial element, however, is providing individuals with clear, objective strategies for handling the situation, rather than simply telling them what to expect (Janis, 1984).

When carried out properly, inoculation works. Coping is greater for people who have received inoculation treatments prior to facing a stressful event than for those who have not (MacDonald & Kuiper, 1983; Anderson, 1987).

RECAP AND REVIEW I

Recap

◁ Stress is the process by which events threaten an individual's ability to deal adequately with the situation.

◁ According to Selye's general adaptation model, stress follows three stages: alarm and mobilization, resistance, and exhaustion.

◁ The specific nature of stressors varies from person to person; what is stressful for one person may be invigorating to another. There are, however, three general categories of stressors: cataclysmic events, personal stressors, and background stressors (or daily hassles).

◁ Perceptions of control typically reduce stress. In some instances, though, learned helplessness occurs—people perceive that aversive stimuli cannot be controlled.

◁ Coping devices may take the form of adopting defense mechanisms, turning threat into challenge, reducing the perception of threat, changing goals, and preparing for stress through inoculation.

Review

1. Circumstances that produce threats to our well-being are known as _____ .

2. Medical problems resulting from an interaction of psy-

chological, emotional, and physical difficulties are called
   a. ulcers.
   b. nervous disorders.
   c. psychosomatic disorders.
   d. stress.
3. Name the three stages of response to stress, according to Selye's general adaptation syndrome theory.
4. The concept of learned helplessness was proposed by
   a. Hans Selye.

   b. Ivan Pavlov.
   c. Martin Seligman.
   d. B. F. Skinner.
5. In a visit to Tim's hospital room, Dr. Lewis explains in detail the adverse consequences that could occur as a result of the following day's surgery; she and Tim then discuss possible responses to each situation. As a method of reducing stress, this preparation is called _____ .

(Answers to review questions are on page 530.)

PSYCHOLOGICAL ASPECTS OF MAJOR HEALTH PROBLEMS

The process starts off silently in childhood. There is no symptom, no pain, no warning. A small globule of fat attaches itself to a wall in an artery leading to the heart. Slowly, as the years pass by, other fat cells join the first, building up a lingering deposit that eventually clogs the passageway through which oxygen-rich blood must pass. Then, one day, a blood clot breaks off in the bloodstream. As it reaches the small passageway in the artery that is already obstructed with fat, so much of the blood flow is cut off that a part of the heart dies from lack of oxygen. The result: a heart attack.

Twenty years ago, a recounting of the processes that bring about coronary heart disease—the leading cause of death in the United States—would have been largely complete with the description above, which focuses on the biological aspects of the problem. Today, however, a growing body of research demonstrates the importance of psychological factors in problems that were once seen in purely physiological terms. We focus now on the major health problems of heart disease, cancer, and smoking.

THE A'S AND B'S OF CORONARY HEART DISEASE

Have you ever seethed in impatience at being caught behind a slow-moving vehicle, felt anger and frustration at not finding material you needed at the library, or experienced a sense of competitiveness with almost all your classmates?

Many of us experience these sorts of feelings at one time or another, but for some people they represent a pervasive, characteristic set of personality traits known as the **Type A behavior pattern**. Type A individuals are competitive, show a continual sense of urgency about time, are aggressive, exhibit a driven quality regarding their work, and are hostile—especially when interrupted while trying to complete a task (Matthews, 1982; Friedman & Ulmer, 1984; Yarnold, Grimm & Mueser, 1986). On the other hand, individuals who show what is called the **Type B behavior pattern** display essentially the opposite set of behaviors: They are far less competitive, not especially time-oriented, and not usually aggressive, driven, or hostile. Although people are typically not "pure" Type A's or Type B's, showing instead a combination of both behavior types, they generally do fall into one or the other category.

Type A people lead fast-paced, driven lives. They put in longer hours at

Type A behavior: A pattern of behavior characterized by competitiveness, impatience, tendency toward frustration, and hostility

Type B behavior: A pattern of behavior characterized by noncompetitiveness, nonaggression, and patience in times of potential stress

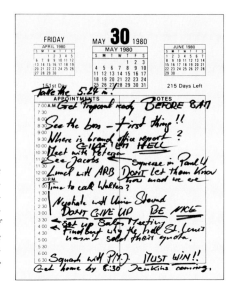

The notations on this calendar indicate quite clearly the characteristics of competitive, aggressive, and driven Type A behavior—behavior that is associated with coronary heart disease. (*From "The Stress of Excellence" by Siegfried Steufert, Across the Board, October 1983. Reprinted with permission of the author and the Conference Board.*)

work than Type B's and are impatient with other people's performance, which they typically perceive as too slow. They also engage in what is known as polyphasic thinking: concentrating on several activities simultaneously. A classic—and true—example is the case of a man who built a desk onto the front of his exercise bike. When seated on the bike, which he positioned in front of the television, he was able to get his daily exercise, sign letters, read, and view television—all at the same time. He noted that his wife could always tell when there had been an exciting football play: He pumped the pedals so quickly that she could hear the bike in the next room.

Type A behaviors would be of little more than passing interest to health psychologists were it not for the fact that the Type A behavior pattern has been repeatedly linked to coronary heart disease. For example, a major eight-year study of some 3000 men who were diagnosed initially as being free of heart disease and as having the Type A pattern developed coronary heart disease twice as often, suffered significantly more fatal heart attacks, and reported five times as many coronary problems as those classified as having the Type B pattern (Roseman, Brand, Sholtz & Friedman, 1976). Moreover, the Type A pattern predicted who was going to develop heart disease as well as—and independently of—any other single factor, including age, blood pressure, smoking habits, and cholesterol levels in the body. The Type A behavior pattern is generally associated, then, with a heightened risk of coronary heart disease.

Why should Type A behavior be linked to coronary heart disease? The most convincing theory is that Type A's tend to become excessively aroused physiologically whenever they are placed in stressful situations; this arousal results in increased production of the hormones epinephrine and norepinephrine, as well as increased heart rate and blood pressure. Such exaggerated physiological responsivity, in turn, seems to be tied to an increased incidence of cardiovascular disease. Ultimately, these reactions to stress may damage the arteries, leading to the increased incidence of coronary heart disease (Matthews, 1982). Because the effects of being a Type A begin in the

ANSWERS (REVIEW I):

1. Stressors **2.** c **3.** Alarm and mobilization, resistance, exhaustion **4.** c
5. Inoculation

first decade of life—there is research, for instance, showing that preschoolers who display Type A behavior (by being competitive, aggressive, and quick to anger) also show more volatile physiological reactions—the consequences associated with Type A behavior may build up throughout an individual's life (Brown & Tanner, 1988; MacEvoy et al., 1988).

Paradoxically, not all research evidence consistently shows a strong, clear link between Type A behavior and coronary heart disease. For example, the results of one study suggest that men who fit the Type A pattern may be more likely to survive a second heart attack than men fitting the Type B pattern—even though the Type A men are more likely to have an initial heart attack (Ragland et al., 1988). In light of such puzzling evidence, a small minority of researchers go so far as to claim that the relationship between Type A behavior and coronary heart disease is illusory (Tierney, 1985; Fischman, 1987).

However, the most recent and definitive summaries of the literature find that there is at least a modest relationship between the two factors, although certain components of Type A behavior seem to be more closely associated with coronary heart disease than others (Booth-Kewley & Friedman, 1987; Wright, 1988). For example, the hard-driving and competitive aspects of Type A people are major factors in coronary heart disease; impatience in completing tasks seems less important.

Overall, the most important concept to emerge from recent research is that people who experience frequent negative emotions—whether aggressive competitiveness, frustration, anger, depression, or some combination—are most prone to coronary heart disease. Because Type A people are more likely than Type B's to experience such negative emotions, then, they may be more apt to experience coronary heart disease.

If you display Type A behaviors, you may be worrying about whether you are destined to have coronary heart disease. The answer is no, particularly if you are female. The great majority of research has been carried out on men, since the rates of coronary heart disease are significantly higher for males than for females. Thus we know much less about Type A behavior in women and its links to heart disease.

In addition, the evidence relating Type A behavior and coronary heart disease is correlational; we cannot say for sure whether Type A behavior *causes* heart disease or whether, instead, some other factor causes both heart disease and Type A behavior. Indeed, some evidence suggests that rather than focusing on Type A behavior as the cause of heart disease, we should concentrate on Type B behavior, which appears to be critical in the *prevention* of heart disease (Krantz, Glass, Schaeffer & Davia, 1982).

More important, even if a causal link between Type A behavior and coronary heart disease exists, there is evidence that people may be able to learn to change from their A behaviors to B behaviors and, as a consequence, decrease their risk of heart disease—as we point out in the Psychology at Work box on page 532.

MIND OVER TUMOR?: Psychological Aspects of Cancer

Hardly any disease is more feared than cancer. Most people think of cancer in terms of lingering pain, and being diagnosed with the disease is typically viewed as receiving a death sentence.

Although a diagnosis of cancer is not as grim as you might at first sus-

TURNING A'S INTO B'S: CHANGING ATTITUDES AND BEHAVIOR TO DECREASE THE RISK OF HEART ATTACK

If you fit the description of Type A but are trained to modify your behavior so that you begin to act more like Type B, will you lessen your chances of developing coronary heart disease?

Given the relationship between Type A behavior and an increased risk of coronary heart disease, it does seem logical. That assumption was the basis of an extensive program carried out in the San Francisco Bay Area where 600 Type A men were trained to act more like Type B's (Friedman et al., 1984). In the study, the subjects—all of whom had previously suffered heart attacks and, therefore, were at a relatively high risk for future heart disease—were taught specific techniques to modify their reactions to stressful situations.

Several training techniques were used (Friedman et al., 1984). One strategy was intended to change the way Type A's interpreted situations that had in the past produced stress. For example, suppose a Type A were in a long, slow-moving line at a bank. This person's characteristic reaction would be to fume, feel anxious, think about where he or she had to go and how much was not being

accomplished because of the delay. Type B's, on the other hand, would tend to take a more leisurely view of the situation, possibly even welcoming the delay as an opportunity to pause and reflect. The training suggested that program participants should consider how a Type B would view the situation, and react similarly—thereby lowering their level of anxiety. To learn to do so, Type A's were told to look for lines and practice patiently standing and waiting.

Other techniques were directed toward the participants' physiological reactions to stress. Participants were trained in muscle relaxation procedures and in moderating their general physical activity level. Finally, they were urged to make changes in their lifestyles, including the renewal of old friendships and the adoption of hobbies unrelated to their careers.

The results of the program were

highly encouraging. Compared with a control group of heart attack victims who received traditional medical treatment and information about heart attacks, those enrolled in the program fared significantly better—with a dramatically lower incidence of repeat heart attacks (Friedman et al., 1984).

We cannot say for sure that a reduction in Type A behavior led directly to a reduced risk of coronary heart disease, since a variety of treatment procedures were used in the program and since it is unclear what specific Type A factor might account for the reduction in heart attacks (Friedman, Hall, & Harris, 1985).

There is something else to consider: Type A behaviors are associated with many of the highly esteemed cultural norms of our society, including achievement, competitiveness, and the importance of the work ethic (Carver & Humphries, 1982). If psychologists are successful in reducing the incidence of Type A behavior, the result may be a physically healthier individual, but not necessarily a more productive one.

pect—several kinds of cancer have a high cure rate if found early enough—cancer remains the second leading cause of death after coronary heart disease. The precise trigger for the disease is not well understood, but the process by which cancer spreads is straightforward. Certain cells in the body become altered and multiply rapidly and in an uncontrolled fashion. As these cells grow, they form tumors, which, if left unchecked, suck nutrients from healthy cells and body tissue, ultimately destroying the body's ability to function properly.

Although the process involved in the spread of cancer is basically physiological in nature, accumulating evidence suggests that the emotional response of cancer patients to their disease may have a critical effect on its course. For example, one experiment found that people who adopt a fighting spirit ("I don't care what the odds are, I'm going to lick this disease") are more likely to recover than those who pessimistically suffer and resign themselves to death ("I'm a goner"). The study analyzed the survival rates of women who had undergone the removal of a breast because of cancer (Pettingale, Morris, Greer & Haybittle, 1985). The results suggested that the survival rates were related to the psychological response of the women three months following surgery (see Figure 15-2). Women who stoically accepted their fate, trying not to complain, and those who felt the situation was hopeless and that nothing could be done, showed the lowest survival rates; most of these women were dead after ten years. On the other hand, the survival rates of women who showed a fighting spirit (predicting that they would overcome the disease and planning to take steps to prevent its recurrence) and the survival rates of women who (erroneously) denied that they had ever had cancer (saying that the breast removal was merely a preventative step) were significantly higher. In sum, according to this study, cancer patients with a positive attitude were more likely to survive than those with a more negative one.

Studies such as these suggest that the emotional response of the patient may have an effect on the course of the disease. Although the exact mechanism by which the process could occur is not well understood, accumulating evidence suggests that a patient's emotional state may affect the immune system, the body's natural defenses that fight disease. In the case of cancer, for instance, it is possible that positive emotional responses to the disease may produce natural "killer" cells that help to control the size and spread of cancerous tumors.

The notion that a positive mental state increases longevity is supported by other studies. Psychologist Sandra Levy and colleagues, for example, found that a factor they labeled "joy"—referring to mental resilience and vigor— was the strongest predictor of survival times for a group of patients with recurrent breast cancer (Levy et al., 1988).

Other research has examined the relationship between social support and the development of cancer. For instance, one fifteen-year-long study found that people who developed cancer reported little closeness in their families (Thomas, Duszynski & Shaffer, 1979). Moreover, researchers have tried to find whether a particular personality type is linked to cancer. Some

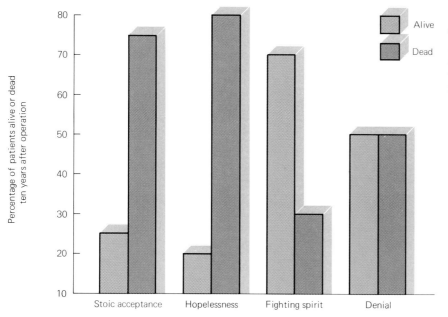

FIGURE 15-2

The relationship between women's psychological response to breast cancer three months after surgery and their survival ten years after the operation. (Pettingale, Morris, Greer, & Haybittle, 1985.)

findings suggest that cancer patients are less emotionally reactive, suppress anger, and lack outlets for emotional release. However, the data are still too tentative and inconsistent to suggest firm conclusions about a link between personality characteristics and cancer (Smith, 1988; Hughes, 1987). Furthermore, it is certainly unreasonable to assume that people who develop cancer would not have done so if their personality had been of a different sort or if their attitudes had been more positive.

It is still too early to draw conclusions about the relationship between personality and cancer, but increasing evidence clearly demonstrates that the immune system is affected by people's attitudes in several other medical realms. For instance, research has shown that patients with genital herpes are more likely to report outbreaks of the disease when they feel depressed than when they are not depressed—and that such outbreaks have a physiological basis associated with a decline in the cells that play an important role in controlling the virus (Kemeny, 1985). Furthermore, it is clear that stress, in general, alters functioning of the immune system and increases susceptibility to disease (Jemmott & Locke, 1984).

If stress and negative attitudes lead to suppression of the immune system, do positive attitudes help it function more effectively? The question is far from answered, but certainly the possibility is a real one. In sum, although this area of research remains controversial—with some investigators entirely dismissing the effects of mental state on the course of disease (Angell, 1985)—most psychologists believe that there are significant links between people's emotional states and their illnesses.

SMOKING

Would you go into a supermarket and purchase an item with a label warning you that its consumption was considered dangerous by the Surgeon General? Although most of us would probably answer no, millions of us make such a purchase every day: a pack of cigarettes. Moreover, we do this despite clear, well-publicized evidence that smoking is linked to cancer, heart attacks, strokes, bronchitis, emphysema, and a host of other serious illnesses. According to government reports and the U.S. Surgeon General, smoking is the greatest preventable cause of death in America.

Why do people smoke, despite all the evidence showing that it is bad for their health? It is not that they are somehow unaware of the association between smoking and disease; surveys show that 71 percent of *smokers* agree with the statement "Cigarette smoking frequently causes disease and death" (U.S. Department of Health and Human Services, 1981). One explanation is that smokers develop the smoking habit in a number of stages, only gradually becoming hooked on the behavior. But once smoking becomes a habit, it is as hard to stop as an addiction to cocaine or heroin (U.S. Surgeon General, 1988).

Psychologists have found that smokers go through four basic stages that culminate in the smoking habit (Hirschman, Leventhal & Glynn, 1984; Leventhal & Cleary, 1980).

▶ Preparation. Old movie buffs ought to recall that many of the movie characters in the 1940s were avid smokers; in fact, female leads often used the skillful manipulation of their cigarettes in suggestive poses, thereby communicating the idea that smoking was sexy. Although movies today are less apt to use this ploy, powerful images are still conveyed by the media and other sources which promote the view that smoking is socially desirable. This view sets the first stage of smoking: a relatively positive attitude about it, generally gleaned from the media, peers, and advertising, and expressed in one of three guises: Smoking is "cool" or sophisticated; smoking is a rebellious act; smoking helps one perform calmly under stressful situations.

▶ Initiation. Smoking a cigarette is often a "rite of passage" for adolescents, tried at the urging of friends and viewed as a sign of growing up. One or two cigarettes do not usually make a lifetime smoker, but if people go on to smoke even ten cigarettes at some early age, they stand an 80 percent chance of becoming regular smokers (Salber, Freeman & Abelin, 1966).

▶ Becoming a smoker. In this crucial stage, smoking becomes a habit. Probably the most important hallmark of this stage is that people begin to consider themselves smokers, and smoking becomes part of their self-concept. Moreover, they become tolerant of, and potentially dependent on, the physiological effects of smoking, since nicotine, a primary ingredient of tobacco, is highly addictive (Jarvick, 1979; Russell, 1979; U.S. Surgeon General, 1988).

▶ Maintaining the smoking habit. In this final stage there is an interaction of both psychological and biological factors that makes smoking a routine behavior. The most important psychological mechanisms include the establishment of a learned habit, positive emotional reactions such as stimulation and relaxation, a decrease in negative emotional reactions such as tension and anxiety, and social factors such as peer-group approval and support from other smokers (Oskamp, 1984). But it is also clear that apart from the purely psychological factors, there are biological reasons for maintenance of smoking. People develop a physiological dependence on the nicotine content of cigarettes. Ultimately, a complex relationship develops between smoking, nicotine levels, and the smoker's emotional state (Leventhal & Cleary, 1980). Specifically, it seems that smoking tends to affect and regulate people's emotions. Because smoking raises the nicotine level in the blood, a certain nicotine level eventually becomes associated with a given emotional state. People smoke, then, in an effort to regulate *both* emotional states and nicotine levels in the blood.

Quitting Smoking

Because smoking has both psychological and biological causes, few habits are as difficult to break (Pomerleau & Pomerleau, 1977; Swann & Denk, 1988). In fact, long-term successful treatment typically occurs in just 15 percent of those trying to "kick the habit." Behavioral strategies, which view smoking as a learned habit and concentrate on changing the smoking response, have been most effective: Initial "cure" rates of 60 percent have been found, and one year after treatment more than half of those who quit have not resumed smoking (Lictenstein, 1982; Pomerleau, Adkins & Pertschuk, 1978).

What may prove to be the most effective means of reducing smoking are the broad changes that are now occurring in societal norms and attitudes about smoking and the kinds of people who smoke. For instance, many cities and towns have made smoking in public places illegal, and other legislation restricting smoking in such places as college classrooms and buildings—based on strong popular sentiment—is being passed with greater and greater frequency.

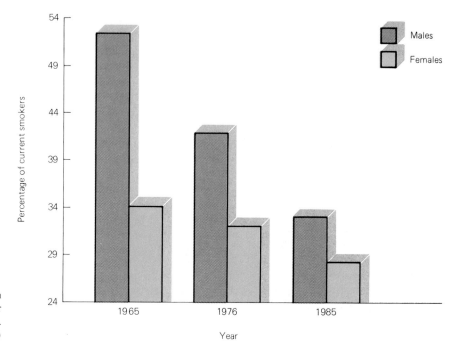

FIGURE 15-3

The percentage of both men and women who smoked declined substantially over the twenty-year period from 1965 to 1985. (National Center for Health Statistics, 1987.)

The long-term effect of the constant barrage of information regarding the negative consequences of smoking on people's health is bound to be substantial. In fact, one estimate suggests that without the antismoking publicity of recent decades, the number of smokers today—approximately 33 percent of men and 28 percent of women—would be 20 to 30 percent higher (Warner, 1977). In sum, although the threat to public health represented by smoking is far from over, the trend is headed in the right direction (see Figure 15-3).

RECAP AND REVIEW II

Recap

◀ Among the major problems studied by health psychologists are coronary heart disease, cancer, and smoking.

◀ The Type A behavior pattern is associated with a higher incidence of coronary heart disease. Type A's are competitive, show a sense of time urgency, appear to be unduly driven, and are relatively aggressive and hostile, especially when they are interrupted. Type B's tend to display the opposite sorts of behaviors.

◀ The success of cancer treatment may be affected by patients' attitudes.

◀ Smokers pass through four basic stages: preparation, initiation, becoming a smoker, and maintaining the smoking habit.

Review

1. Research has shown that Type A behavior
   a. causes heart disease.
   b. prevents heart disease.
   c. is linked with heart disease.
   d. has no relationship to physical health.
2. Evidence is accumulating that a patient's emotional state may affect his or her defenses against disease, or _____ system.
3. Name the four stages associated with developing a smoking habit.
4. The addictive element in cigarettes is _____ .

(Answers to review questions are on page 538.)

GOING TO THE DOCTOR: PSYCHOLOGICAL FACTORS RELATED TO PHYSICAL ILLNESS

When Stuart Grinnel first noticed the small lump in his arm, he assumed that it was just a bruise from the touch-football game he had played last week. But as he thought about it, he envisioned more serious possibilities and decided that he better get it checked out by a physician at the university health service. The visit—like most of his encounters with physicians—was less than satisfactory. A shy and inarticulate person, Stuart felt embarrassed and inept about communicating his medical problems. Then, after answering all the questions he was asked, he couldn't even understand the doctor's list of possible problems. All he heard was medical jargon and gobbledygook. Why couldn't the physician just have carried out a physical examination to find out what was wrong? After all, hadn't the doctor gone to medical school in order to be able to make a diagnosis on the basis of physical symptoms?

Stuart Grinnel's attitudes toward doctors and his view of a physician's role are shared by many of us. Yet not everything of importance *can* be discerned from a physical examination alone; several critical psychological factors, such as the nature of physician-patient communication, influence a health-care practitioner's effectiveness in diagnosing and treating medical problems.

SPEAKING TO THE DOCTOR: Physician-Patient Communication

It may surprise you that many patients are reluctant to describe their symptoms to their physicians. But the situation is a common one: Many individuals believe that physicians are so skilled that they can easily identify a patient's problems through a thorough physical examination, the way a good mechanic can diagnose car problems (Leigh & Reiser, 1980; Mentzer & Snyder, 1982). Moreover, physicians' relatively high social prestige and power may intimidate patients by making them feel that their problems are trivial and unimportant, or making them reluctant to volunteer information that might cast them in a bad light (Taylor, 1982).

Conversely, physicians may have difficulties encouraging their patients to give the proper information (see Table 15-3). In many cases, physicians

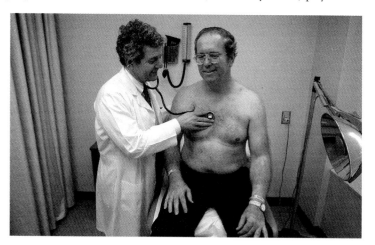

People often do not discuss the full extent of their medical symptoms with their physicians, assuming (erroneously) that the physical examination will identify anything of importance. (*Charles Gupton/Stock Boston.*)

TABLE 15-3

A Patient Talks to Her Physician

The following excerpt from a case study used at the Harvard Medical School is an example of poor interviewing technique on the part of the physician.

Patient: I can hardly drink water.

Doctor: Um hum.

Patient: Remember when it started? . . . It was pains in my head. It must have been then.

Doctor: Um hum.

Patient: I don't know what it is. The doctor looked at it . . . said something about glands.

Doctor: OK. Um hum, aside from this, how have you been feeling?

Patient: Terrible.

Doctor: Yeah.

Patient: Tired . . . there's pains . . . I don't know what it is.

Doctor: OK. . . . Fevers or chills?

Patient: No.

Doctor: OK. . . . Have you been sick to your stomach or anything?

Patient: (Sniffles, crying) I don't know what's going on. I get up in the morning tired. The only time I feel good . . . maybe like around suppertime . . . and everything (crying) and still the same thing.

Doctor: Um hum. You're getting the nausea before you eat or after? (Goleman, 1988, p. B16).

Although the frequent "um hum's" suggest that the physician is listening to the patient, in fact they do not encourage the patient to disclose more pertinent details. Late in the interview, the physician ignores the patient's emotional distress and coldly continues through the list of questions.

dominate an interview with questions of a technical nature, while patients attempt to communicate a personal sense of their illness and the impact it is having on their lives (Goleman, 1988).

The reluctance of patients to reveal medical information fully to health-care providers, and the difficulties that providers experience in eliciting information from patients, may prevent providers from understanding the full nature of the difficulties that led the patients to seek medical care in the first place. Furthermore, the inability to provide patients with an environment in which they can disclose their problems may lead to other problems as well, as we see in the Cutting Edge box.

The view held by many patients that physicians are "all-knowing" results in serious communication problems. For instance, many patients do not understand their treatment yet fail to ask their doctors for clearer explanations of a prescribed course of action. Research has shown that about half of all patients cannot accurately report how long they are to continue taking

ANSWERS (REVIEW II):
1. c   **2.** Immune   **3.** Preparation, initiation, becoming a smoker, maintaining the habit
4. Nicotine

CONFESSION: NOT JUST GOOD FOR THE SOUL

You have probably heard that confession is good for the soul; a new line of research suggests that it may be even better for the body. According to work carried out by health psychologist James W. Pennebaker and colleagues, providing people with an opportunity to air their most personal and disturbing experiences—those which they normally keep to themselves—has real health-related benefits.

Pennebaker has been exploring the consequences of revealing information that is usually kept hidden. In one experiment, for instance, a group of healthy undergraduates was asked to write anonymously about their most traumatic, emotionally upsetting, and stressful life experiences for four consecutive days (Pennebaker & Beall, 1986). One group of subjects was told to write about the facts surrounding the traumatic events, another group was told to write about feelings about the events but not facts, and a third group was asked to describe both feelings and facts concerning the traumatic events. There was also a control group that wrote about trivial assigned topics for the four days.

The results were clear—and compelling. Subjects who wrote about the emotions or about the combined facts and emotions of past traumatic events reported feeling the most upset following the study. Even more important were the results of a questionnaire that all subjects completed six months after being in the study. Subjects who had written about the emotions, or about the combined facts and emotions, reported feeling healthier and experiencing fewer illnesses and fewer days of restricted activity due to illness than subjects in the other groups. Apparently, the disclosure of traumatic information, although initially upsetting, proved to have long-term benefits which improved people's perceptions of health and decreased the number of visits to physicians.

What is the reason for the benefits of confession? Pennebaker suggests that the act of inhibiting or restraining traumatic information requires physiological effort, which ultimately leads to increased stress on the body and heightened rates of illness and symptoms. However, disclosure—even if temporary—provides a respite in the body's efforts to suppress information, thereby reducing stress and enhancing health.

Later research has provided support for this reasoning. In a study that examined the relationship between the disclosure of past traumatic events and the biological reactions of the body, subjects who divulged intensely personal material showed significantly lower levels of skin conductance of electrical charges, heart rate, and blood pressure than subjects who did not disclose such information, indicating lower stress levels (Pennebaker, Hughes & O'Heeron, 1987). On a long-term basis, then, we might expect that the physiological effort associated with secret, unconfessed information could well be damaging to a person's health.

The implications of this ongoing research extend to many realms. Confession and self-disclosure have traditionally been viewed as important components of religion and psychological therapy and are seen as having spiritual and psychological benefits. It now seems as if the advantages of confession reach into the physical realm as well.

---

a medication prescribed for them, and about a quarter do not even know the purpose of the drug (Svarstad, 1976). In fact, some patients are not even sure, as they are about to be rolled into the operating room, why they are having surgery!

One reason for patient-physician communication difficulties is that very frequently the material that needs to be communicated is too difficult or too technical for patients, who may lack fundamental knowledge about the body and basic medical practices (Ley & Spelman, 1967). Moreover, the use of professional jargon can be confusing. Suppose, for instance, you were told that you had "essential hypertension" and that you had to "take hydrochlorathiazide twice a day and reduce sodium intake." These instructions obviously would have been a lot easier to comprehend if you had been told you had high blood pressure, should take a drug that eliminates fluids, and should reduce the amount of salt in your diet (DiMatteo & DiNicola, 1982).

Sometimes medical practitioners take the opposite tack and use baby talk or overly simplistic explanations. A physician who said, "Nurse, would you just pop off her things for me? I want to examine her," elicited the following comments from a patient:

> In the hospital, everything is "popped" on or off, "slipped" in or out. I don't think I met a single doctor who, in dealing with patients, didn't resort to this sort of nursery talk. I once heard one saying to a patient, an elderly man, "We're just going to pop you into the operating theater to have a little peep into your tummy" (Toynbee, 1977).

Obviously, there is a middle ground between the extremes of technical jargon and baby talk. Unfortunately, because they deal with so many patients, health practitioners often have difficulty determining just how much individuals actually do understand about their conditions. As a consequence, practitioners routinely underestimate what patients understand (McKinley, 1975).

Another difficulty in patient-physician communication is that patients typically construct their own theories about their illnesses—theories which may have little basis in reality (Leventhal, Nerenz & Leventhal, 1985). For example, a patient who has been prescribed medication for high blood pressure may think (erroneously) that headaches are a symptom of the high blood pressure. Because of this erroneous assumption, she may think it necessary to take her medicine only when she has a headache—even if she has been told to take it every day. Her mistake is reinforced because she measures her blood pressure only when she has a headache—and then finds that it is high. Of course, if she were to take her blood pressure at other times, she would find it high then, too, and the inaccuracy of her theory would become apparent. But this is unlikely to happen, so the woman will continue to resist appropriate treatment because of her own misunderstanding of her medical problem.

Still, there are ways of combatting physician-patient communication problems. For example, when patients are taught to ask forthright questions, they receive better medical care and ultimately feel better. Similarly, physicians who are taught to follow simple rules of courtesy—such as saying hello, addressing patients by name, explaining the purpose of a procedure while they are treating the patient, and saying goodbye—are perceived as warmer and more supportive than physicians who do not follow such rules (DiMatteo & DiNicola, 1982; Thompson, 1988).

LISTENING TO THE DOCTOR: Complying with Physicians' Orders

One major consequence of patient-physician communication difficulties is a lack of compliance with medical advice. The problem is a serious one: Surveys show that only 40 to 70 percent of patients follow a physician's advice or take their prescribed medicine (Gatchel & Baum, 1983). Such noncompliance can take many forms—for example, failing to show up for scheduled appointments, not following diets or not giving up smoking, discontinuing medication during treatment, and failing to take prescribed medicine at all.

Compliance with medical advice is also linked to the degree of satisfaction patients have with their physicians. Patients who are satisfied with their physicians and view them as friendly and interested in their care are more apt to comply with their advice than patients reporting a lower level of satisfaction with their physician (Korsch & Negrets, 1972).

Although compliance with a physician's advice does not guarantee that the patient's medical problems will go away, it does optimize the possibility that the patient's condition will improve. What, then, can physicians do to produce greater compliance on the part of their patients? One approach is for physicians to demonstrate greater friendliness and interest in their patients. It is likely that patients who are comfortable with their physicians are able to process information more completely than are those under the stress of working with a physician who is perceived as aloof or unpleasant, and therefore they can comply more readily with the physician's advice.

It is also reasonable to assume that patients who view their physicians positively may feel an enhanced sense of control over their own care. Rather than perceiving themselves as merely following the advice of a powerful physician, they perceive that they are part of a partnership, jointly determining their medical care. In fact, feelings of patient control have been directly linked to increased compliance (Rodin & Janis, 1979; Langer, 1983).

Of course, patient compliance is a complex process involving both physician and patient, and powerful psychological forces can operate to prevent both partners from modifying their behavior. For instance, consider the suggestion that physicians communicate with their patients in a warmer and more open manner and offer clear advice and information. Some would argue that in many cases it is better for physicians to maintain emotional distance between themselves and their patients (Parsons, 1975). According to proponents of this view, physicians can thereby diagnose and treat patients in a more objective manner.

Furthermore, evidence suggests that in many cases physicians themselves may be motivated by psychological factors to keep patients in the dark about the true nature of their illnesses, about what to expect in terms of the difficulties and pain involved in treatment, and about the potential for a disease to lead to a patient's death. Surveys show that physicians typically want to avoid telling dying patients that their illnesses are terminal. The experience that produces the greatest amount of anxiety for first-year medical students is discussing a fatal illness with a patient (Feifel, 1963; Saul & Kass, 1969). However, almost every survey reveals that most people say that they want to be informed of the details of their illnesses—even if it means they learn that they are dying (Blumenfield, Levy & Kaplan, 1979; Miller & Mangan, 1983). In fact, the strongest predictor of how satisfied patients are with their doctors is the amount of information the doctor gives about their condition and its treatment (Hall, 1988).

In sum, patients generally prefer to be well informed, and their degree of satisfaction with their medical care is linked to how well and how accurately physicians are able to convey the nature of their medical problems and treatment. The ultimate result of enhanced patient satisfaction is not just increased compliance with a physician's advice but more positive treatment outcomes as well. Patients who like their physicians tend to have greater confidence in the physician's technical expertise, which, in turn, leads to a reduction in patient anxiety (Ben-Sira, 1976). In addition, an increase in patient satisfaction is likely to have a positive influence on the recuperation process of patients who have had surgery, since the level of anxiety patients experience—related in part to their confidence in their physician—is itself related to postoperative recovery (Langer, Janis & Wolfer, 1975).

THE INFORMED CONSUMER OF PSYCHOLOGY:
The Dangers of Being a "Good Patient"

To be a "patient" is a unique status because one thinks it means that one has relinquished the right to ask questions, although one must accept the obligation of answering questions and permitting oneself to be examined. Asking questions seems to be the right of everyone else—especially physicians, strangers, and others who can deny emotional ties to the patient. Thoroughly exposed, the patient is expected patiently to submit to all manner of indignities (Cooper, 1978, p. 43).

If this is the way you approach a medical examination or treatment, you may be in danger of becoming what has been referred to by health psychologists as a "good patient" (Taylor, 1982).

What's wrong with being a "good patient"? In the present context, quite a bit, for although good patients are often popular with medical staff, they are of little help to themselves. Good patients appear to be compliant with medical treatment; they do not complain much and they do not ask for much. Overall they are rather passive, making the jobs of medical staff easier.

But there is another side to such patient behavior. Beneath the facade of compliance and cooperation, many patients conceal a strong desire for attention and information, as well as concern about their medical condition. However, because of their perception of what being a good patient requires, they rarely attempt to affect the course of treatment that they are receiving and may be misinformed about their condition. As a result, they may experience helplessness, anxiety, and depression. Obviously, then, what may be seen as good adjustment from the point of view of a health caretaker may not be so healthy from the perspective of the patient.

What *is* a patient to do? One alternative is to adopt the "bad patient" role. In the view of medical staff, bad patients make constant efforts to obtain information and attention from the staff through complaints, questions, and anger vented at the health-care providers. Ultimately, the anger may grow so intense that patients sabotage their own chances for recovery, behaving in a way that is counterproductive to their treatment. Moreover, the staff may react with condescension—simply ignoring or placating such a patient—or may decide that the patient's agitation requires medication. In extreme cases, health-care providers may decide that patients require psychological counseling, or they may discharge such patients from the hospital prematurely, just to relieve the burden they impose on the staff.

Obviously, there is a middle road: Patients should be neither "good" nor "bad" (DiMatteo & DiNicola, 1982; Pellegrino, 1973). Among the char-

Patients who seek information about their condition have a better chance of successful recovery. (*Joel Gordon.*)

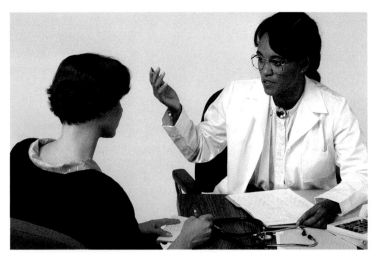

acteristics of reasonable patient behavior and expectations identified by health psychologists are the following:

▶ Individuals should seek out health-care providers who consider effective communication of information a central part of their role. Technical expertise therefore should not be the sole criterion when choosing a physician, since a physician's ability to convey warmth and understanding has been shown to influence a patient's recovery in a positive direction.

▶ Patients should seek as much information as they can about their medical condition in a way that recognizes the greater knowledge and experience of health-care providers.

▶ Informed consumers should view medical care as a partnership between physician and patient. Rather than delegating sole responsibility for their health to a physician, they must be aware that they, as well as their physicians, must accept responsibility for their treatment.

To summarize, people should try—and, in fact, expect—to experience a sense of control over the course of their medical treatment.

RECAP AND REVIEW III

Recap

◀ Problems in communication affect the success with which a physician can diagnose and treat medical problems.

◀ Patients often construct their own—sometimes inaccurate—theories or explanations of their illness.

◀ Patient compliance can be increased when patients are persuaded that they are in a partnership with their physician and have some control over their medical condition, as well as when physicians are warmer and friendlier and keep patients well informed.

◀ "Good" patients are compliant and cooperative on the surface, but they may be overly dependent and reluctant to divulge their concern about their medical condition.

Review

1. Many health psychologists believe that the biggest problem in health care is
   a. lack of communication between doctor and patient.
   b. incompetent health-care providers.
   c. rising health-care costs.
   d. scarcity of medical research funding.
2. A good physician is one who can
   a. make an accurate diagnosis on the basis of physical examination alone.
   b. provide information and advice in technical terms.
   c. explain to the patient every decision that is made in his or her care, without considering patient input.
   d. provide good medical skills and sufficient information to the patient.
3. Following a physician's instructions for self-care is called _____ .
4. James Pennebaker found that writing essays about emotions relating to deeply personal traumatic events
   a. made subjects feel better immediately afterward.
   b. resulted in reports of better health months after writing the essays.
   c. caused some subjects to seek psychological help.
   d. was beneficial only if the subjects reviewed their essays from time to time.

(Answers to review questions are on page 544.)

◀ LOOKING BACK

1. The field of health psychology considers how psychology can be applied to the prevention, diagnosis, and treatment of medical problems.
2. Stress is a response to threatening or challenging environmental conditions. People's lives are filled with stressors—the circumstances that produce stress—of both a positive and negative nature.
3. Stress produces immediate physiological reactions, including a rise in hormonal secretions, heart-rate and blood-pressure elevations, and changes in the electrical conductance of the skin. In the short term, these reactions may be adaptive, but in the long term they may have negative consequences, including the development of psychosomatic disorders. The consequences of stress

can be explained in part by Selye's general adaptation syndrome (GAS), which suggests there are three stages to stress responses: alarm and mobilization, resistance, and exhaustion.

4. Stress factors are not universal—the way an environmental circumstance is interpreted affects whether it will be considered stressful. Still, there are general classes of events that tend to provoke stress: cataclysmic events, personal stressors, and background stressors or daily hassles. Stress is reduced by the presence of uplifts, minor positive events that make people feel good—even if only temporarily.

5. Stress can be reduced by developing a sense of control over one's circumstances. In some cases, however, people develop a state of learned helplessness—a response to uncontrollable situations that produces the feeling that no behavior will be effective in changing the situation; therefore no response is even attempted. Coping with stress can take a number of forms, including the unconscious use of defense mechanisms and the use of emotion-focused or problem-focused coping strategies.

6. Coronary heart disease, cancer, and smoking are major health problems studied by health psychologists. Research has shown that coronary heart disease is linked to a specific type of behavior pattern known as Type A. In contrast to Type B people, Type A individuals tend to be competitive, show a sense of time urgency and hurriedness, are hostile and aggressive, and seem to be driven.

7. There is increasing evidence that people's attitudes and emotional responses affect the course of a disease. Although the exact mechanism underlying this link is not well understood, it appears that people's emotional responses affect their immune system, the body's natural defenses that attack disease.

8. Smoking, the leading preventable health problem, has proved to be difficult to control, even though most smokers are aware of the dangerous consequences of the behavior. People go through four stages in becoming habitual smokers: preparation, initiation, becoming a smoker, and maintaining the habit.

9. Although patients often expect physicians to be able to make a diagnosis from only a physical examination, in fact communicating one's problem to the physician is equally critical. Among the reasons that patients may find it difficult to communicate openly with their doctors are the high social prestige of physicians and the technical nature of medical information.

10. Problems in communication can be attributed to the behavior of physicians and other health-care workers as well: These professionals may fail to communicate treatment requirements adequately to their patients, thereby lowering patient compliance. Compliance is also related to satisfaction with medical care and to the kinds of theories patients may develop to explain their medical conditions.

11. "Good" patients are compliant and cooperative on the surface, but may be overly dependent and reluctant to divulge their concern about their medical condition. "Bad" patients, in contrast, are uncooperative and vent their anger at health-care providers. A more reasonable course is to view medical care as a partnership between physician and patient.

KEY TERMS AND CONCEPTS ▶

health psychology (p. 516)
immune system (516)
stress (517)
stressors (517)
psychosomatic disorders (518)
general adaptation syndrome (518)
alarm and mobilization stage (519)
resistance stage (519)

exhaustion stage (520)
cataclysmic events (521)
posttraumatic stress syndrome (522)
personal stressors (522)
background stressors (522)
uplifts (523)
learned helplessness (524)
coping (525)

defense mechanisms (525)
emotion-focused coping (526)
problem-focused coping (526)
hardiness (526)
social support (527)
inoculation (528)
Type A behavior (529)
Type B behavior (529)

FOR FURTHER STUDY AND APPLICATION ▶

Borysenko, J. (1987). *Minding the body, mending the mind.* Reading, MA: Addison-Wesley.

This work offers a new introduction to the old question of the relationship between mind and body.

Taylor, S. E. (1986). *Health psychology.* New York: Random House.

Gatchel, R. J., & Baum, A. (1983). *An introduction to health psychology.* Reading, MA: Addison-Wesley.

Two readable overviews of the field of health psychology, both books are useful for understanding theory and applications of psychological research on major health problems.

Nieves, L. R. (1984). *Coping in college: Successful strategies.*

ANSWERS (REVIEW III):
1. a **2.** d **3.** Compliance **4.** b

Princeton, NJ: Educational Testing Service.

This book provides a practical, comprehensive guide to the stresses of college, including challenges of both an academic and a personal nature.

American Cancer Society (1989). *FreshStart: 21 days to stop smoking*. New York: Simon & Schuster.

This audio- and videocassette, available at many bookstores, presents the American Cancer Society's program to help smokers quit. It includes techniques for overcoming two of the largest obstacles to quitting: stress and weight gain.

Brown, B. (1984). *Between health and illness*. Boston: Houghton Mifflin.

This is a layperson's guide to stress. Written in a breezy style, the book contains a good deal of scientifically sound, practical information relating to ways of coping with the stress of daily living.

DiMatteo, M. R., & Friedman, H. S. (1982). *Social psychology and medicine*. Cambridge, MA: Oelgeschlager, Gunn & Hain.

This is a fine overview of the social factors that affect patient care, especially in terms of physician-patient interaction.

CHAPTER

16

ABNORMAL BEHAVIOR

After being released from the hospital through the intervention of a civil-rights organization, Joyce Brown worked for a short time as an office volunteer. (Chester Higgins, Jr./The New York Times.)

PROLOGUE:
JOYCE BROWN

There was nothing out of place in the scene of the secretary expertly fielding calls to the office. Well-dressed, intelligent, and attractive, Joyce Brown, 40 years old, looked as if she had spent years polishing her secretarial skills. Yet just a few months earlier, Brown had spent her days and nights on a New York City sidewalk over a hot-air vent in front of a restaurant. She hurled insults and obscenities at passers-by and used the street as her bathroom.

Her background gave no clue to the unusual transformation that she had undergone during the course of her life. Brown grew up in Elizabeth, New Jersey, where, after graduating from high school, she held a series of jobs at Bell Laboratories and at the local Human Rights Commission. At some point, though, she became dependent on heroin and later cocaine. Her mental health deteriorated, and she was eventually hospitalized. After her release, she fought with her family and moved to New York, where she eventually found her way to the heating grate that was her "home" for about a year.

She gained notoriety when she became the first person chosen by New York City mental health professionals to be hospitalized under a program in which severely mentally ill street people were forcibly removed from the streets and treated. Yet once she was hospitalized, Brown, with the help of lawyers from the American Civil Liberties Union, eloquently argued that she had a constitutional right to be free—and a judge accepted her arguments. After twelve weeks of hospitalization and refusal to accept treatment, she was allowed to leave the hospital, and she quickly gained celebrity status.

Brown dined in the best restaurants and shopped at Bloomingdale's and Lord & Taylor; people stopped her and asked for her autograph. She was interviewed on national television and received a number of movie and book offers.

However, there remained suggestions that all was not well with her. Her former roommate at a residence for homeless women reported that, although basically considerate and nonargumentative, Brown talked to herself. Others overheard her mumbling racial slurs. And a few weeks after lecturing at Harvard Law School on the plight of the homeless, she was back on the street, begging for money and shouting obscenities.

Brown had explanations for these apparent setbacks. When asked why she panhandled, she said she did so only because she had run out of money—not because she was mentally disordered. She admitted using obscenities, but only as a reaction to being harassed by people who passed by her on the street (Barbanel, 1988).

To Brown, her behavior was no more abnormal than anyone else's.

LOOKING AHEAD ▶

Many of us would disagree with Joyce Brown's own assessment of her behavior as "quite normal." Yet her case presents a series of perplexing questions. Why did she live in the streets, hurling obscenities? Why did she spurn housing in shelters provided for the homeless and instead choose to live over a hot-air vent? Was she correct in claiming her behavior was normal? What factors in her background led to her behavior? Could she have been spared a life in the streets through early treatment? How do we distinguish normal from abnormal behavior, and how can Brown's behavior be categorized and classified and the specific nature of her problem pinpointed?

Although these questions cannot be answered definitively, especially with a case as complex as Brown's, we can start to address some of the issues raised by her atypical behavior in this and the following chapter. We begin by discussing the distinction between normal and abnormal behavior, considering the subtle distinctions that must be made. We examine the various approaches that have been used to explain abnormal behavior, ranging from explanations based on superstition to those based on contemporary, scientific approaches, and apply these approaches to the case of Joyce Brown, showing how the various explanations complement one another.

The heart of the chapter consists of a description of the various types of abnormal behaviors. Using a classification system employed by mental health practitioners, we examine the most significant kinds of disorders. The chapter also includes a discussion of the problems and dangers of self-diagnosis, and the signals people might see in themselves that could lead them to consider seeking help from a mental health professional.

In sum, after reading this chapter, you will have the answers to several fundamental questions about mental health:

▶ How can we distinguish normal from abnormal behavior?

▶ What are the major models of abnormal behavior used by mental health professionals?

▶ How can we apply these approaches to specific cases, such as that of Joyce Brown?

▶ What is the classification system used to categorize abnormal behavior, and what are the major mental health disorders?

▶ What are the major indicators that signal a need for the help of a mental health practitioner?

NORMAL VERSUS ABNORMAL: MAKING THE DISTINCTION

Universally that person's acumen is esteemed very little perceptive concerning whatsoever matters are being held as most profitable by mortals with sapience endowed to be studied who is ignorant of that which the most in doctrine erudite and certainly by reason of that in them high mind's ornament deserving of veneration constantly maintain when by general consent they affirm that other circumstances being equal by no exterior splendour is the prosperity of a nation more efficaciously asserted than by the measure of how far forward may have progressed the tribute of its solicitude for that proliferent continuance which of evils the original if it be absent when fortunately present constitutes the certain sign of omnipollent nature's incorrupted benefaction.

It would be easy to conclude that these words were the musings of a madman; the passage does not seem, at least at first consideration, to make any sense at all. But literary scholars would disagree; in actuality this passage is from James Joyce's classic *Ulysses,* which has been hailed as one of the major works of twentieth-century literature (Joyce, 1934, p. 377).

As this example illustrates, making a cursory examination of a person's writing is insufficient to determine the degree to which he or she is "normal." But even when we consider more extensive samples of a person's behavior, we find that there may be only a fine line between behavior that is considered normal and that which is considered abnormal.

APPROACHES TO ABNORMALITY

The difficulty in distinguishing normal from abnormal behavior has led to a diversity of approaches for devising a precise, scientific definition of "abnormal behavior." Over the years, in fact, the definitions of what constitutes normal and abnormal behavior have taken a number of twists. We examine next the four major approaches employed at one time or another.

Different Equals Abnormal: Deviation from the Average

Perhaps the most obvious approach defines abnormality as deviation from the average—a statistical definition. In order to determine abnormality, we simply observe what behaviors are rare or infrequent in a given society or culture and label these deviations from the norm as abnormal (Ullman & Krasner, 1975).

Although such a definition may be appropriate in some instances, its drawback is that some behaviors that are statistically rare clearly do not lend themselves to classification as abnormal. If most people prefer to have orange juice with breakfast, but you prefer apple juice, this hardly makes your behavior abnormal. Similarly, such a conception of abnormality would unreasonably necessitate labeling a person who has an unusually high IQ as abnormal, because it is statistically rare to have a high IQ. A definition of abnormality that rests on deviation from the average, then, is insufficient by itself.

Although membership in a cult such as the Hare Krishna is statistically rare, it would be inaccurate to classify all Hare Krishnas as abnormal. (Bonnie Freer/Photo Researchers.)

Aiming for Perfection: Deviation from the Ideal

An alternative approach to defining abnormality is one that takes into account not what most people do (the average), but the standard toward which most people are striving—the ideal. Under this sort of definition, behavior is considered abnormal if it deviates a sufficient degree from some kind of ideal or standard (Jahoda, 1958). Unfortunately, the definition suffers from even more difficulties than the deviation-from-the-average definition, since society has so few standards about which people agree. Moreover, the standards that do arise tend to change over time, leaving the deviation-from-the-ideal approach inadequate.

Normal Feels Right: Abnormality as a Sense of Subjective Discomfort

Given the drawbacks of both the deviation-from-the-average and deviation-from-the-ideal definitions of normality, we must turn to more subjective approaches. In fact, one of the most useful definitions of abnormal behavior is one that concentrates on the psychological consequences of the behavior for the individual. In this approach, behavior is considered abnormal if it produces a sense of distress, anxiety, or guilt in an individual—or if it is harmful to others in some way.

Of course, even a definition that rests on subjective discomfort has its drawbacks, for in some particularly severe forms of mental disturbance people report feeling euphoric and on top of the world—yet to others, their behavior is bizarre. In this case, then, there is a subjective state of well-being, yet the behavior is clearly within the realm of what most people would consider abnormal—suggesting that a definition of abnormality that does not consider people's ability to function effectively is inadequate. Thus psychologists have developed one final approach to distinguishing normal and abnormal behavior.

Getting Along in the World: Abnormality as the Inability to Function Effectively

Most people are able to feed themselves, hold a job, get along with others, and in general live as productive members of society. Yet there are those who are unable to adjust to the demands of society or function effectively.

According to this last view of abnormality, people who are unable to function effectively and adapt to the demands of society are considered abnormal. For example, an unemployed, homeless woman living on the street—such as Joyce Brown—might be considered unable to function effectively; therefore her behavior would be considered abnormal, even if she had made the choice to live in this particular fashion. It is her inability to adapt to the requirements of society that makes her "abnormal," according to this approach.

DRAWING THE LINE ON ABNORMALITY:
The Continuum of Abnormal and Normal Behavior

None of the four definitions alone is sufficiently broad to cover all instances of abnormal behavior, and the division between normal and abnormal behavior often remains indistinct, sometimes even to trained professionals (see the Research Classics box). Probably the best way to deal with this imprecision is to consider abnormal and normal behavior not as absolute states but rather as marking the two ends of a *continuum* (or scale) of behavior, with completely normal functioning at one end and totally abnormal behavior at the other. Obviously, behavior will often fall somewhere between these two extremes.

Because the difference between normal and abnormal behavior is indistinct, the issue of when society should intervene and require treatment of people displaying abnormal behavior is also ambiguous. For example, did Joyce Brown, whose behavior was clearly out of the ordinary but who presented little danger to others, warrant the intervention of New York City officials who demanded that she receive treatment?

There is no clear-cut answer to the question, both in Brown's case and in those of many others. However, lawyers and forensic psychologists—psychologists who specialize in the law—have attempted to define the circumstances under which legal intervention in cases of abnormal behavior is appropriate. In most states, a person must meet four criteria prior to intervention (Schwitzgebel & Schwitzgebel, 1980): The person must be (1) dangerous to himself or herself; (2) incapable of providing for basic physical needs; (3) unable to make reasonable decisions about whether treatment is required; and (4) require treatment or care. Of course, these four criteria still do not clearly answer the question of when treatment should be provided to an individual since the criteria are fraught with ambiguity. The

WHO IS ABNORMAL?

Even trained professionals may have difficulty distinguishing between abnormal and normal behavior, as an intriguing study by psychologist David Rosenhan (1973) reveals. In the study, Rosenhan and seven of his colleagues presented themselves at the doors of separate mental hospitals across the United States and sought admission. The reason, they each stated, was that they were hearing voices—"unclear voices" which said "empty," "hollow," and "thud." Aside from changing their names and occupations, *everything* else they did and said was representative of their true behavior, including the responses they gave during extensive admission interviews and answers to the battery of tests they were asked to complete. In fact, as soon as they were admitted, they said they no longer heard any voices. In sum, each of the pseudo-patients acted in a "normal" way.

One would assume that Rosenhan and his colleagues would have been quickly discovered as the impostors they were, but this was not the case. In fact, each of them was diagnosed as severely abnormal on the basis of observed behavior. Most

were labeled as schizophrenic, and they were kept in the hospital from three to fifty-two days, with the average stay being nineteen days. In most cases, they were not allowed to leave without the assistance of people outside the hospital. Even when they were discharged, most of the patients left with the label "schizophrenia—in remission," meaning that the abnormal behavior had only temporarily subsided and could recur at any time.

Most disturbing of all is the fact that none of the pseudo-patients were identified by the staff of the hospitals as impostors. On the other hand, a number of actual patients realized that the investigators were not actually suffering from a mental problem. One patient said, "You're not crazy. You're a journalist or a professor. You're checking up on the hospital" (Rosenhan, 1973, p. 252). This insight came from the fact that the pseudo-patients were openly making notes—a behavior that, when noticed by the hospital staff, was viewed as a sign of mental disorder.

Although the results of the study are instructive, critics have pointed out several cogent drawbacks (Millon, 1975; Spitzer, 1975; Farber, 1975). First, it is a one-time demonstration and not a true experiment; no control or comparison groups were included. Furthermore, there were justifiable explanations of the hospital staff's behavior. They were forced to use all the information they were provided, which included the "patients'" own reports of hearing voices. To simply discount such information and label the patients normal would hardly seem reasonable. Moreover, the diagnosis of "schizophrenia—in remission" is a relatively rare one and indicated a response to the singular nature of the pseudo-patients' behavior. Finally, the study raises ethical concerns in terms of duping the staff of a mental hospital.

Despite these drawbacks, the surprising results of Rosenhan's study suggest that the differences between normal and abnormal behavior can be sufficiently subtle to elude detection even in situations where behavior is—or at least should be—the focus of attention.

determination, then, of when society should intervene in the presence of abnormal behavior is clearly a difficult one to make.

THE MENTAL STATE OF THE UNION: The Prevalence of Mental Disorders

Given the difficulties in satisfactorily defining abnormality, it should come as no surprise that determining the number of people showing signs of abnormal behavior is no simple task. But a survey conducted by the U.S. government in the mid-1980s does provide a sense of how many Americans show signs of mental disorder (Reiger et al., 1984; 1988).

The survey, conducted in five communities and including about 18,000 Americans, found that close to 20 percent of the adults queried had a mental disorder, and that the rates were about equal for men and women. In individual interviews that lasted two hours, each subject answered 200 questions about particular kinds of problems, such as feeling panicky when leaving the house and losing interest in normally pleasant activities. By using standard categories of mental disturbance that we will explore later in the chapter, the researchers were able to produce a statistical profile of the "mental state of the union."

Projecting the results to the nation as a whole indicates that over 29 million Americans have one or more mental disorders or have suffered from one within the past six months. For example, 13 million have difficulties related to anxiety, 10 million abuse alcohol or some other drug, and some 11 million have irrational fears. (Because subjects could report more than one problem, there is overlap in these statistics.) Surprisingly, just one in five of those with a problem seek help.

These results suggest that abnormal behavior is far from rare. Moreover, in further surveys now under way, researchers are obtaining information about which mental disorders benefit most from treatment and which ones simply go away on their own, as well as information on how major life events (such as marriage and death in the family) influence mental disorders. This work offers the promise of identifying specific events that trigger abnormal behavior and of finding ways to prevent their occurrence.

RECAP AND REVIEW I

Recap

◄ Distinctions between normal and abnormal behavior are not always readily apparent.

◄ Definitions of abnormality include those based on deviation from the average, deviation from the ideal, the psychological consequences of the behavior for the individual, and the individual's ability to function effectively and adapt as a member of society.

◄ Abnormal and normal behavior may best be viewed as marking the two ends of a continuum or scale.

Review

1. According to the approach that abnormality is defined by a sense of subjective discomfort or by causing harm to others, which of the following people is most likely to need treatment?
   a. An executive is afraid to accept a promotion because it would require moving from his ground-floor office to the top floor of a tall office building.
   b. A woman quits her job and chooses to live on the street.
   c. A man believes that UFOs visit his house every Thursday.

   d. A photographer lives with nineteen cats in a small apartment.
2. Karl's family is worried about his decision to live in a tree house—unheard-of behavior in their wealthy neighborhood. What approach to defining abnormality is Karl's family using?
3. A scale of behavior ranging from "most abnormal" to "most normal" is an example of a(n) _____.
4. Virginia's mother thinks that Virginia's behavior is clearly abnormal because, despite being offered admission to medical school, she decides to become a waitress. What approach is Virginia's mother using to define abnormal behavior?
5. David Rosenhan's 1973 study that placed "normal" people in mental institutions most convincingly proved which of the following?
   a. Patients in mental institutions do not receive adequate care or attention.
   b. In any institution it is very difficult to act normally.
   c. The differences between normal and abnormal behaviors are sometimes too subtle to be detected, even by specialists.
   d. Normal and abnormal behaviors are so similar it can take several days of observation to determine a patient's classification.

(Answers to review questions are on page 554.)

MODELS OF ABNORMALITY:
FROM SUPERSTITION TO SCIENCE

The disease occurred at the height of the summer heat. People, asleep or awake, would suddenly jump up, feeling an acute pain like the sting of a bee. Some saw the spider, others did not, but they knew that it must be the tarantula. They ran out of the house into the street, to the marketplace, dancing in great excitement. Soon they were joined by others who like them had been bitten, or by people who had been stung in previous years. . . .

Thus groups of patients would gather, dancing wildly in the queerest attire. . . . Others would tear their clothes and show their nakedness, losing all sense of modesty. . . . Some called for swords and acted like fencers, others for whips and beat each other. . . . Some of them had still stranger fancies, liked to be tossed in the air, dug holes in the ground, and rolled themselves into the dirt like swine. They all drank wine plentifully and sang and talked like drunken people . . . (Sigerist, 1943, pp. 103, 106–107).

This description of a peculiar form of abnormal behavior that occurred during the thirteenth century—behavior attributed, at the time, to the bite of a real or imagined tarantula spider—indicates that mental disturbance and theories about its causes are nothing new. Yet our understanding of the causes of such behavior has become considerably more sophisticated.

For much of the past, abnormal behavior was linked to superstition and witchcraft; people displaying abnormal behavior were accused of being possessed by the devil or some sort of demonic god (Howells & Osborn, 1984). Authorities felt justified in "treating" abnormal behavior by attempting to drive out the source of the problem. This typically involved whipping, immersion in hot water, starvation, or other forms of torture in which the cure was often worse than the affliction.

Contemporary approaches to abnormal behavior take a more enlightened view, and five major models of abnormal behavior predominate: the medical model, the psychoanalytic model, the behavioral model, the humanistic model, and the sociocultural model. These models suggest not only different causes of abnormal behavior but—as we shall see in the next chapter—different treatment approaches as well.

ABNORMAL BEHAVIOR AS A BIOLOGICAL DISEASE: The Medical Model

Medical model of abnormality: The model that suggests that when an individual displays symptoms of abnormal behavior, the cause is physiological

When a person displays the symptoms of tuberculosis, we generally find the tuberculin germ in his or her body tissue. In the same way, the **medical model of abnormality** suggests that when an individual displays the symptoms of abnormal behavior, the root cause will be found in an examination of some physical aspect of the individual, such as a hormonal imbalance, a chemical deficiency, or an injury to part of the body. Indeed, when we speak of mental "illness," the "symptoms" of abnormal behavior, and mental "hospitals," we are using terminology related to the medical model.

As we will discuss later, because many sorts of abnormal behaviors have been linked to physiological causes, the medical model would seem to be a reasonable approach. In fact, the medical model does represent a major advance over explanations of abnormal behavior based on superstitions. Yet serious criticisms have been leveled against it. For one thing, there are many instances in which no physiological cause has been identified for abnormal behavior, thus negating the basic assumption of the medical model. Other

ANSWERS (REVIEW I):
1. a **2.** Deviation from the average **3.** Continuum **4.** Deviation from the ideal **5.** c

criticisms have equally important, though less obvious, implications. For instance, some critics have argued that the use of the term "illness" implies that there is something "wrong" with a person, something that is in need of a cure (Szasz, 1982; 1987). Using such terms suggests that people displaying abnormal behavior hold little control over their actions and have no responsibility for them—and that any "cure" is entirely in the hands of someone else (who, given the assumptions of the medical model, would presumably be a physician).

CONFLICTING CAUSES OF ABNORMAL BEHAVIOR: The Psychoanalytic Model

On the surface, Joyce Brown's background shows little difference from that of anyone else. Yet could certain aspects of her past, of which she was unaware, have brought about her unusual behavior? Such a possibility is suggested by the psychoanalytic model of abnormal behavior.

Whereas the medical model suggests that physiological causes are at the root of abnormal behavior, the **psychoanalytic model of abnormality** holds that abnormal behavior stems from childhood conflicts over opposing wishes regarding sex and aggression. As we discussed in Chapter 14, Freud believed that children pass through a series of stages in which sexual and aggressive impulses take different forms that require resolution. If the conflicts of childhood are not successfully dealt with, they remain unresolved in the unconscious and eventually bring about abnormal behavior during adulthood.

In order to understand the roots of a person's disordered behavior, the psychoanalytic model scrutinizes his or her early life history. For example, if we knew more details of Joyce Brown's childhood, we might discover experiences that produced unresolved insecurities and conflicts in adulthood. Of course, it would be difficult to prove a direct link between her childhood experiences and later abnormal behavior—pointing to one of the major objections that critics have raised regarding psychoanalytic theorizing. Because there is no conclusive way of linking people's childhood experi-

Psychoanalytic model of abnormality: The model that suggests that abnormality stems from childhood conflicts over opposing desires

Abnormal behavior is not just a modern phenomenon, as this seventeenth-century French woodcut of moonstruck ("lunatic") women illustrates. (Bettmann Archive.)

Until the twentieth century, abnormal be-havior was blamed on "evil spirits." As a result, its treatment involved (a) religious ceremonies or (b) bizarre paraphernalia designed to drive out the demons. (Bettmann Archive.)

ences with the abnormal behaviors they display as adults, we can never be sure that the mechanisms suggested by psychoanalytic theory are accurate. Moreover, psychoanalytic theory, like the medical model, paints a picture of people as having little control over their behavior and of behavior as being guided by unconscious impulses, implying that the treatment of abnormal behavior is dependent on people other than those exhibiting the behavior.

On the other hand, the contributions of psychoanalytic theory have been great. More than any other approach to abnormal behavior, it highlights the fact that people can have a rich, involved inner life and that prior experiences can have a profound effect on current psychological functioning.

WHEN BEHAVIOR ITSELF IS THE PROBLEM: The Behavioral Model

Behavioral model of abnormality: The model that suggests that abnormal be-havior itself is the problem to be treated, rather than viewing behavior as a symptom of some underlying medical or psychological problem

The medical model and the psychoanalytic model display a common approach to behavior disorders: They both look at abnormal behaviors as *symptoms* of some underlying problem. In contrast, the **behavioral model of abnormality** looks at the behavior itself as the problem. According to theorists using this approach, one need not look beyond a person's display of abnormal behavior or past the environment to be able to understand and ultimately change that behavior.

Using the principles of learning we discussed in Chapter 5, behavioral theorists can thus explain why people behave abnormally—or normally. Both normal and abnormal behaviors are seen as responses to a set of stimuli, responses that have been learned through past experience and are guided in the present by the stimuli that one finds in one's environment. Indeed, in its most extreme form, the behavioral model rejects the notion that it is important to understand what a person is thinking. What is critical is analyzing how an abnormal behavior has been learned and observing the circumstances in which it is displayed in order to explain why such behavior is occurring. For example, a behavioral approach would explain an individual's inability to get work done on time as being due to a lack of skill in time management. This could be remedied by teaching the individual techniques for working more efficiently. Other approaches, in contrast, would try to determine the underlying causes of the person's inability to manage time.

The emphasis on overt observable behavior represents both the greatest strength and the greatest weakness of the behavioral approach to abnormal behavior. Because of its emphasis on the present, the behavioral approach is the most precise and objective in examining manifestations of abnormal behavior. Rather than hypothesizing elaborate, underlying, unobservable mechanisms to explain abnormal behavior, behavioral theorists concentrate on immediate behavior. They have developed many techniques (presented in the next chapter) to modify such behavior successfully.

On the other hand, the behavioral approach has received its share of criticism. For example, behavioral theories, like medical and psychoanalytic explanations, tend to view people's behavior as being caused by factors largely outside of their own control, although for different reasons. Moreover, according to critics, one cannot overlook the very real fact that people have complex unobservable thoughts that influence their behavior. This latter criticism has led some behavioral theorists to modify their position and consider approaches in which a change in cognitions—people's thoughts and beliefs—is the goal of treatment, rather than a direct change in overt behavior. For example, they may teach a student who, on taking every exam, thinks, "This exam is crucial to my future," to modify her thoughts to make them more realistic (and less threatening and less potentially debilitating): "My entire future is not dependent on this one exam." The basic principles of learning theory are still used; what is different is the target of behavior change. Although not all behavioral theorists subscribe to these views, the behavioral model has been broadened by the addition of such cognitive approaches.

PUTTING THE PERSON IN CONTROL: The Humanistic Model

You might wonder if there is any model of abnormal behavior that considers a person to be in complete control of her or his behavior, and in fact this is a reasonable question in light of the three models we have discussed. In each of these models the individual is seen, to a greater or lesser degree, as something of a pawn, beset by physiological difficulties, unconscious conflicts, or environmental stimuli that direct and motivate behavior.

Psychologists who subscribe to the humanistic approach, in contrast, emphasize the control and responsibility that people have for their own behavior—even when such behavior is abnormal. The **humanistic model of abnormality** concentrates on what is uniquely human, viewing people as basically rational, oriented toward a social world, and motivated to get along with others (Rogers, 1980).

Humanistic model of abnormality: The model that suggests that people are basically rational, and that abnormal behavior results from an inability to fulfill human needs and capabilities

Although diverse in many ways, humanistic approaches to abnormal behavior focus on the relationship of the individual to the world, on the ways people view themselves in relation to others and see their place in the world in a philosophical sense. People have an awareness of life and of themselves that leads them to search for meaning and self-worth. So-called abnormal behavior is basically a sign of a person's inability to fulfill his or her human needs and capabilities. Moreover, humanistic approaches take a much less judgmental view of atypical behavior than other models. Rather than assuming that a "cure" is required, the humanistic model suggests that individuals can, by and large, set their own limits of what is acceptable behavior. As long as they are not hurting others and do not feel personal distress, people should be free to choose the behaviors they engage in. It is only if *they* feel that their behavior needs some correction that they ought to consider taking responsibility for modifying it, and the way to bring about such modification is by exploring ways to reach higher levels of self-fulfillment.

Humanistic models consider abnormal behavior, then, in a less negative light than the models we discussed earlier. Rather than assuming there is something wrong with an individual, humanistic theorists view abnormal behavior as an understandable reaction to circumstances arising in the person's daily life. Moreover, the humanistic model suggests that people have a relatively high degree of control over their lives and can make informed and rational choices to overcome their difficulties.

The humanistic model is not without its detractors. For instance, it has been criticized for its reliance on unscientific, unverifiable information, as well as for its vague, almost philosophical formulation related to such concepts as "human striving" and "fulfillment of human needs." Despite these criticisms, the humanistic model offers a view of abnormal behavior that stresses the unique aspects of being human and provides a number of important suggestions for helping those with psychological problems.

SOCIETY AS THE CAUSE OF ABNORMAL BEHAVIOR:
The Sociocultural Model

Sociocultural model of abnormality: The model that suggests that people's behavior, both normal and abnormal, is shaped by family, society, and cultural influences

Sociocultural approaches to abnormal behavior make the assumption that people's behavior—both normal and abnormal—is shaped by the kind of family group, society, and culture in which they live. We all are part of a social network of family, friends, acquaintances, and even strangers, and the kinds of relationships that evolve with others may support abnormal behaviors and even cause them to occur. According to the **sociocultural model of abnormality**, then, the kinds of stresses and conflicts people experience—not in terms of unconscious processes, but as part of their daily interactions with those around them—can promote and maintain abnormal behavior.

In fact, some proponents of this view take the extreme position that there really is no such thing as abnormal behavior. Although people who violate social rules may be labeled by society as showing abnormal behavior, in reality there is nothing wrong with such individuals. Rather, there is something wrong with a society that is unwilling to tolerate deviant behavior.

To support the position that sociocultural factors shape abnormal behavior, theorists say statistics show that certain kinds of abnormal behavior are far more prevalent among certain social classes than others, and poor economic times tend to be linked to general declines in psychological functioning (Pines, 1982). For instance, diagnoses of schizophrenia tend to be higher among members of lower socioeconomic classes than among members of more affluent groups (Hollingshead & Redlich, 1958). The reason may relate to the way in which abnormal behavior is interpreted by diagnosticians, who tend to be psychiatrists and psychologists from upper socioeconomic classes. Alternatively, it may be that stresses on members of lower socioeconomic classes are greater than those on people in higher classes. Whatever the reason, there is frequently a link between sociocultural factors and abnormal behavior, suggesting the possibility of a cause-and-effect sequence.

As with the other theories, the sociocultural model does not have unequivocal support. Alternative explanations abound for the association between abnormal behavior and social factors. For example, people of lower classes may be less likely than those of higher classes to seek help until their symptoms become relatively severe and warrant a more serious diagnosis (Gove, 1982). Moreover, sociocultural explanations provide relatively little in the way of direct guidance for the treatment of individuals showing mental disturbance, since the focus is on broader societal factors.

APPLYING THE MODELS: The Case of Joyce Brown

We began this chapter by discussing Joyce Brown's case. Perhaps you are wondering which of these models brings us closer to understanding the reasons for her behavior. Indeed, you may be looking for the answer to a more encompassing question: Which of these approaches provides the best model for explaining abnormal behavior in general?

The most appropriate answer to both questions is, in fact, that *all* of them can be reasonably and profitably used. As in other branches of their field, psychologists have found that there is more than one workable approach to the problems of abnormal behavior; as we shall see, effective and worthwhile approaches to resolving psychological problems have been made using each of the different models. Indeed, it is possible to address various parts of a given problem simultaneously using each model.

Consider the case of Joyce Brown. We might first use the medical model to examine whether Brown had any physical problems—such as continued dependence on heroin or cocaine, a brain tumor, a chemical imbalance in the brain, or some type of disease—that could possibly account for her unusual behavior.

A psychoanalytic theorist would take a very different approach, seeking out information about Brown's past, concentrating on her childhood and probing her memories to determine the nature of conflicts residing in her unconscious. A behavioral theorist would take still another approach, concentrating on the nature of the rewards and punishments that Brown received for behaving in the way she did, as well as the stimuli in the environment that maintained or reinforced her behavior. For instance, Brown's street life certainly made her a center of attention in the neighborhood in which she lived. Finally, humanistic and sociocultural approaches would concentrate on Brown's view of herself, in relation to other people and to the world in general.

Humanistic theories might suggest that, by living on the streets and refusing to stay in the mental hospital, Brown had made a series of choices—although unconventional ones—about the way she wanted to lead her life. Sociocultural approaches, in contrast, would focus on the ways society contributed to Brown's problems, looking at how her relationships with others, possible economic difficulties, family structure, and cultural background influenced her behavior. Taking an extreme view, a sociocultural theorist might suggest that living over a hot-air grate was a legitimate alternative lifestyle and that society should not intervene in Brown's preferences. In fact, this argument was raised by her public defense lawyers, who argued that she had a constitutional right to choose whether she wanted treatment and that legally she could not be held against her will in a mental hospital. (For consideration of another legal issue associated with abnormal behavior, see the Psychology at Work box.)

As you can see, finding support for one or another of these approaches does not automatically make the others wrong; each focuses on somewhat different aspects of Brown's behavior and life. Of course, if her background were analyzed in depth, one approach ultimately might provide a better explanation than any other. But because the theories consider abnormal behavior at different levels, and because people's lives are made up of so many facets, a single approach may be insufficient to provide a full explanation for a person's abnormal behavior.

WHEN LAW AND PSYCHOLOGY MIX: THE INSANITY DEFENSE

When 26-year-old John Hinckley pulled the trigger and shot Ronald Reagan early in Reagan's first term, he did more than almost kill the former president. Ultimately, he set into motion a series of events that came close to dealing a lethal blow to the legal plea of insanity. For when Hinckley was found not guilty by reason of insanity, the public outrage at the verdict was so intense that Congress soon considered legislation to change the way in which that defense could be used.

Whether or not he had shot Reagan was never an issue, of course, during Hinckley's trial. Millions of people had witnessed the shooting on videotapes that were played repeatedly on television following the incident. What was at issue was Hinckley's state of mind: Was he legally insane at the time of the shooting?

According to law in twenty-two states, insanity—which is a legal, not a psychological term—means that defendants at the time they commit a criminal act cannot understand the difference between right and wrong. In twenty-six other states, however, a somewhat different definition is used; defendants are considered insane if they are substantially confused or unable to control themselves. And two other states—Idaho and Montana—do not accept insanity pleas at all.

As a defendant in a federal crime, Hinckley had to prove that he was incapable of knowing that his actions were wrong when he shot President Reagan. To prove this, the defense called expert witness after expert witness to the stand to portray Hinckley as a man overcome by schizophrenia, as well as an assortment of other severe mental problems. On the other hand, expert witnesses for the prosecution contended that Hinckley had made a conscious and rational decision to shoot Reagan, and that although he was self-centered and manipulative, he suffered from only minor mental health problems. To the jury, the task of determining which side was right seemed impossible; one juror, Maryland Copelin, said afterward, "If the expert psychiatrists could not decide whether the man was sane, then how are we supposed to decide?" (*Time*, July 5, 1982, p. 25).

In the end, the jury decided that Hinckley had been legally insane. The verdict produced rage and indignation, with a clear majority of people polled in an ABC news survey maintaining that the verdict was unjust. Some individuals called for drastic modification of the plea. For example, the *Denver Post* editorialized, "It's the system which found him innocent that's insane." Others called for complete abolition of the insanity plea. Their outrage increased a few years later, when Hinckley received several weekend passes from the mental hospital in which he had been confined after the jury decision.

Nonetheless, most people, while acknowledging the drawbacks to a plea about which even experts could not agree, believed that it was unreasonable to abolish the plea completely. Surely there was *something* wrong with Hinckley, whether or not he met the legal criteria for insanity, and abolishing the plea might prove to be like throwing out the baby with the bath water. Hopefully, as our understanding of abnormal behavior advances, it will be possible to provide more conclusive answers about the nature of a person's state of mind. Until that happens, however, we are going to have to grapple with the issues raised by Hinckley's trial (Rogers, 1987).

THE INFORMED CONSUMER OF PSYCHOLOGY: Do You Feel Abnormal?

Medical student's disease: The feeling that symptoms and illnesses about which one studies are characteristic of oneself

As we conclude this introduction to abnormal behavior and begin to consider its specific classifications and treatment, it is important to note a phenomenon that has long been known to medical students, and one that you, too, may find yourself susceptible to—a phenomenon called **medical student's disease**. Although in the present case it might be more aptly labeled "psychology student's disease," the basic symptoms are the same: deciding that you suffer from the same sorts of problems you are studying.

Most often, of course, your concerns will be unwarranted. As we have discussed, the differences between normal and abnormal behavior are often so fuzzy that it is easy to jump to the conclusion that one has the same symptoms that are involved in serious forms of mental disturbance.

Before coming to such a conclusion, though, it is important to keep in mind that from time to time we all experience a wide range of emotions and subjective experiences, and it is not unusual to feel deeply unhappy, to fantasize about bizarre situations, or to feel anxiety about life's circumstances. It is the persistence, depth, and consistency of such behavior that sets normal reactions apart from abnormal ones. If you have not previously had serious doubts about the normality of your behavior, it is unlikely that reading about others' abnormality should prompt you to reevaluate your earlier conclusion.

RECAP AND REVIEW II

Recap

◀ Historically, abnormal behavior was first linked to superstition and witchcraft.

◀ Current theories view abnormality in terms of five major models: the medical, psychoanalytic, behavioral, humanistic, and sociocultural models.

◀ The question of which model provides the best explanation of abnormal behavior can be answered most reasonably by noting that each model can be profitably used.

Review

1. Which of the following is a strong argument against the medical model?
   a. Physiological abnormalities are almost impossible to identify.
   b. There is no conclusive way to link past experience and behavior.
   c. The medical model rests too heavily on the effects of nutrition.
   d. Assigning behavior to a physical problem takes responsibility away from the individual.

2. The _____ model suggests that behavior is shaped by a person's interactions with others.

3. If we say that Tom's lingering depression is due to his inability to find meaning in his life, we are using a _____ model.

4. Cheryl is painfully shy. According to the behavioral approach to psychology, the best way to help her "abnormal" behavior is to
   a. treat the underlying physical problem.
   b. use the principles of learning theory to modify her shy behavior.
   c. express a great deal of caring.
   d. uncover her negative past experiences through hypnosis.

5. Sigmund Freud is most closely associated with the
   a. medical model.
   b. psychoanalytic model.
   c. behavioral model.
   d. humanistic model.

6. Imagine that a wealthy acquaintance of yours was recently arrested for shoplifting an $8.95 necktie. Briefly explain this behavior in terms of *each* of the following:
   a. The medical model
   b. The psychoanalytic model
   c. The behavioral model
   d. The humanistic model
   e. The sociocultural model

7. Experiencing another person's problems as a result of reading about them is called _____ .

(Answers to review questions are on page 562.)

THE ABCs OF DSM-III-R:
CLASSIFYING TYPES OF ABNORMAL BEHAVIOR

Crazy. Nutty as a fruitcake. Loony. Insane. Neurotic. Strange. Demented. Odd. Possessed.

Society has long placed labels on people displaying abnormal behavior. Unfortunately, most of the time these labels have been pejorative, and they have been used without giving much thought to what the label signifies.

Providing appropriate and specific names and classifications for abnormal behavior has presented a major challenge to psychologists. It is not too hard to understand why, given the difficulties we discussed earlier in simply distinguishing normal from abnormal behavior. Yet classification systems are

Diagnostic and Statistical Manual of Mental Disorders, Third Edition— Revised (DSM-III-R): A manual that presents comprehensive definitions of more than 230 separate diagnostic categories for identifying problems and behaviors

necessary in order to be able to describe and ultimately understand abnormal behavior.

Over the years many different classification systems have been used, varying in terms of their utility and how universally they have been accepted by mental health workers. Today, however, one standard system—devised by the American Psychiatric Association—has emerged and is employed by most professionals to classify abnormal behavior. The classification system is known as *DSM-III-R*—the **Diagnostic and Statistical Manual of Mental Disorders, Third Edition—Revised**.

Published in 1987, *DSM-III-R* presents comprehensive and relatively precise definitions for more than 230 separate diagnostic categories. By following the criteria presented in the system, diagnosticians can provide a clear description of the specific problem an individual is experiencing. (Table 16-1 provides a brief outline of the major diagnostic categories.)

DSM-III-R evaluates a person's behavior according to five dimensions, or axes. The first three axes assess the person's present condition according to the particular maladaptive behaviors being exhibited; the nature of any long-standing personality problems in adults or any specific developmental problems in children and adolescents that may be relevant to treatment; and any physical disorders or illnesses that may also be present. The fourth and fifth axes take into account a broader consideration of the person, focusing on the severity of stressors present and the general level of functioning over the past year in social relationships, work, and the use of leisure time.

One particularly noteworthy feature of *DSM-III-R* is that it is meant to be primarily descriptive and devoid of suggestions as to the underlying causes of an individual's behavior and problems (Klerman, 1984). Hence, the term "neurotic"—a label that is commonly used by people in their everyday descriptions of abnormal behavior—is not listed as a *DSM-III-R* category. The reason is that "neurotic" derives directly from Freud's theory of personality (discussed in Chapter 14). Because the term refers to problems with a specific cause and theoretical approach, neurosis is no longer listed as a category.

DSM-III-R has the advantage, then, of providing a descriptive system that does not specify the cause or reason behind the problem. Instead, it paints a picture of the behavior that is being manifested. Why should this be important? For one thing, it allows communication between mental health professionals of diverse backgrounds and approaches and does not immediately suggest that there is only one appropriate treatment. Another important point is that precise classification enables researchers to go forward and to explore the causes of a problem. If the manifestations of an abnormal behavior cannot be reliably described, researchers will be hard-pressed to find ways of investigating the difficulties. Finally, *DSM-III-R* provides a kind of conceptual shorthand through which professionals can describe the behaviors that tend to occur simultaneously in an individual.

It is also important to note that the *DSM* is designed to be revised

---

TABLE 16-1

Major *DSM-III-R* Diagnostic Categories

The following list of disorders represents the major categories from DSM-III-R, presented in the order in which they are discussed in the text. This is only a partial list of the 230 disorders found in DSM-III-R.

Anxiety disorders   (problems in which anxiety impedes daily functioning)
   Subcategories: generalized anxiety disorder, panic disorder, phobic disorder, obsessive-compulsive disorder, posttraumatic stress disorder

Somatoform disorders   (psychological difficulties displayed through physical problems)
   Subcategories: hypochondriasis, conversion disorder

Dissociative disorders   (the splitting apart of crucial parts of personality that are usually integrated)
   Subcategories: multiple personality, psychogenic amnesia, psychogenic fugue

Mood disorders   (emotions of depression or euphoria that are so strong they intrude on everyday living)
   Subcategories: major depression, bipolar disorder

Schizophrenia   (declines in functioning, thought, and language disturbances, perception disorders, emotional disturbance, and withdrawal from others)
   Subcategories: disorganized, paranoid, catatonic, undifferentiated, residual

Personality disorders   (problems that create little personal distress but that lead to an inability to function as a normal member of society)
   Subcategories: antisocial (sociopathic) personality disorder, narcissistic personality disorder

Sexual disorders   (problems related to sexual arousal from unusual objects or problems related to sexual functioning)
   Subcategories: paraphilias, sexual dysfunction

Psychoactive substance-use disorders   (problems related to drug dependence and abuse)
   Subcategories: alcohol, cocaine, hallucinogens, marijuana

Organic mental disorders   (problems produced by physical deterioration of the brain)
   Subcategories: Alzheimer's disease, delirium, dementia

---

periodically. Reflecting the fact that changes in society affect what behaviors are viewed as abnormal, *DSM-IV* is scheduled to be completed in the early 1990s. (For a sense of the role that societal factors play in the classification of abnormal behavior, see the Cutting Edge box.)

Of course, *DSM-III-R* has its drawbacks, as does any classification system (Vaillant, 1984). Perhaps the strongest criticism is its possible overreliance on a medical model. Because it was drawn up by psychiatrists—who are physicians—it was criticized as viewing abnormal behaviors primarily in terms of symptoms of some underlying physiological disorder. Moreover, some critics suggest that *DSM-III-R* pigeonholes people into inflexible categories, and that it would be more reasonable to use systems that classify people along some sort of continuum or scale.

Other concerns with *DSM-III-R* are more subtle but equally important. For instance, Szasz (1961) argues that labeling an individual as a deviant provides a lifetime stigma that is dehumanizing. Moreover, there is a

DSM-III-R DELETIONS

You might feel that the 230 disorders covered in *DSM-III-R* are more than sufficient to cover the spectrum of abnormal behaviors. In fact, this number excludes three categories that, just before publication, were part of the latest version of the document. The reasons for their absence provide a telling commentary on the importance of social factors in defining abnormal behavior.

The three deleted categories, which were the source of much controversy during the revision process, are "late luteal phase dysphoric disorder," "self-defeating personality disorder," and "sadistic personality disorder." The late luteal phase disorder is sometimes termed "premenstrual syndrome" and refers to symptoms associated with women's menstrual periods. It drew criticism because of concerns that menstruation is a normal part of life for women, and that mood swings associated with menstrual periods should not be considered disordered behavior.

The self-defeating personality disorder is thought by some to occur when an individual is drawn to situations or relationships in which he or she will suffer or to situations that undermine pleasurable experiences or prevent others from helping him or her (Baumeister & Scher, 1988). Because in clinical settings it applies primarily to women, critics saw the category as sexist. Moreover, critics suggested that it was a societal problem and not a characteristic of disordered behavior.

Finally, the sadistic personality disorder is characterized as a pervasive pattern of cruel, demeaning, and aggressive behavior. Because this category applies primarily to men, particularly to those who abuse their wives, it too was seen as sexist. In addition, some critics felt that such abusive behavior represented a criminal act and should not be made to seem legitimate by being labeled a psychological disorder.

The controversy surrounding these three categories illustrates once again that the definition of what constitutes abnormal behavior is not always obvious. Social, political, cultural, and historical factors all have an impact on how we categorize abnormal behavior.

tendency for a diagnosis itself to be mistaken for an explanation of a problem. Saying, for instance, that a woman with schizophrenia hears voices may make it seem as though schizophrenia is an *explanation* for her behavior—when in fact schizophrenia is simply a label that gives no clue as to *why* the woman hears voices (Rosenhan, 1975). Furthermore, after an initial diagnosis is made, other diagnostic possibilities may be overlooked by mental health professionals, who concentrate on the initial diagnostic category.

Despite these drawbacks, *DSM-III-R* remains the major categorization system in use today. It has increased both the reliability and validity of diagnostic categorization; it also provides a logical way to organize our examination of the major types of mental disturbance, to which we turn next.

In our discussion of the major disorders, we will consider the disorders that are most common, serious, or debilitating. We begin with disorders in which anxiety plays a predominate role, those in which psychological difficulties take on a physical form, and disorders in which the parts of personality are no longer integrated. Although these disorders are discussed in a dispassionate manner, it is important to keep in mind that each represents a very human set of difficulties that influence and in some cases play havoc with people's lives.

THE MAJOR DISORDERS

I remember walking up the street, the moon was shining and suddenly everything around me seemed unfamiliar, as it would be in a dream. I felt panic rising inside me, but managed to push it away and carry on. I walked a quarter of a mile or so, with the panic getting worse every minute. ... By now, I was sweating, yet trembling; my heart was pounding and my legs felt like jelly. . . . Terrified, I stood not knowing what to do. The only bit of sanity left in me told me to get home. Somehow this I did very slowly, holding onto the fence in the road. I cannot remember the actual journey back, until I was going into the house, then I broke down and cried helplessly (Melville, 1977, pp. 1, 14).

ANXIETY WITHOUT REASON: Anxiety Disorders

All of us, at one time or another, experience **anxiety**, a feeling of apprehension or tension, in reaction to stressful situations. There is nothing "wrong" with such anxiety; everyone feels it to some degree, and usually it is a reaction to stress that helps, rather than hinders, our daily functioning. Without anxiety, for instance, most of us would not be terribly motivated to study hard, to undergo physical exams, or to spend long hours at our jobs.

But some people—such as the person who wrote the passage above—experience anxiety in situations in which there is no external reason or cause. When anxiety occurs without external justification and begins to impede people's daily functioning, it is considered a psychological problem known as an **anxiety disorder**. There are four main types of anxiety disorders: generalized anxiety disorder, panic disorder, phobic disorder, and obsessive-compulsive disorder.

Generalized Anxiety Disorder

As the name implies, **generalized anxiety disorder** refers to a disorder in which an individual experiences long-term, consistent anxiety without knowing why. Such people feel afraid of *something*, but are unable to articulate what it is. Because of their anxiety they are unable to function normally. They cannot concentrate and cannot set their fears aside, and their lives become centered around their anxiety. Such anxiety may eventually result in the development of physiological problems. Because of heightened muscle tension and arousal, individuals with generalized anxiety disorder may begin to experience headaches, dizziness, heart palpitations, or insomnia. The most frequent symptoms are given in Table 16-2.

Panic Disorder

In another type of anxiety disorder, **panic disorder**, there are instances of **panic attacks** that last from a few seconds to as much as several hours. During

Anxiety: A feeling of apprehension or tension

Anxiety disorder: The occurrence of anxiety without obvious external cause, intruding on daily functioning

Generalized anxiety disorder: The experience of long-term anxiety with no explanation

Panic disorder: Anxiety that manifests itself in the form of panic attacks

Panic attack: Sudden anxiety characterized by heart palpitations, shortness of breath, sweating, faintness, and great fear

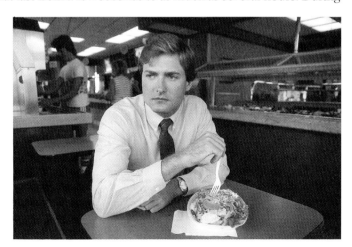

A person with a generalized anxiety disorder experiences long-term, consistent anxiety, without knowing the reason why. (Cary Wolinski/Stock Boston.)

TABLE 16-2

Frequency of Symptoms in Cases of Generalized Anxiety Disorder

Symptom	Percentage of Cases in Which Symptom Occurs
Unable to relax	97
Difficulty concentrating	86
Tense	86
Frightened	79
Fear of losing control	76
Jumpy	72
Fear of being rejected	72
Unable to control thoughts	72
Confusion	69
Mind blurred	66
Unsteady	62
Weakness all over	59
Inability to recall	55
Terrified	52
Hands sweating	52
Heart racing	48
Face flushed	48
Wobbly	45
Sentences disconnected	45
Speech blocked	45
Sweating all over	38
Fear of being attacked	35
Fear of dying	35
Difficulty breathing	35
Urgent need to urinate	35
Hands trembling	31
Body swaying	31
Nausea	31
Diarrhea	31
Faint/dizzy feeling	28
Facial paleness	24
Stuttering	24
Feeling of choking	14
Actual fainting	3

Source: Adapted from Beck & Emery, 1985, pp. 87–88.

an attack, such as the one described at the start of this section of the chapter, the anxiety that a person has been chronically experiencing suddenly rises to a peak, and the individual feels a sense of impending, unavoidable doom. Although symptoms differ from person to person, they may include heart palpitations, shortness of breath, unusual amounts of sweating, faintness and dizziness, an urge to urinate, gastric sensations and—in extreme cases—a sense of imminent death (Lader & Matthews, 1970). After an attack such as this, it is no wonder that people tend to feel exhausted.

Phobic Disorder

Claustrophobia. Acrophobia. Xenophobia. Although these sound like characters in a Greek tragedy, they are actually members of a class of psychological disorders known as **phobias**. Phobias are intense, irrational fears of spe-

Phobic disorder: A disorder characterized by unrealistic fears (phobias) that may keep people from carrying out routine daily behaviors

Phobias: Intense, irrational fears of specific objects or situations cific objects or situations. For example, claustrophobia is a fear of enclosed places, acrophobia a fear of high places, and xenophobia a fear of strangers. Although the objective danger posed by an anxiety-producing stimulus (which can be just about anything, as you can see from the list in Table 16-3) is typically small or nonexistent, to the individual suffering from the phobia it represents great danger, and a full-blown panic attack may follow exposure to the stimulus. Phobic disorders differ from generalized anxiety disorders and panic disorders in that there is a specific, identifiable stimulus that sets off the anxiety reaction.

Phobias may have only a minor impact on people's lives if the people who suffer from them can avoid the things they fear. Unless one is a professional fire fighter or tightrope walker, for example, a fear of heights may have little impact on one's daily life. On the other hand, a fear of strangers presents a more debilitating problem. In one extreme case, a Washington housewife left her home just three times in thirty years—once to visit her family, once for an operation, and once to purchase ice cream for a dying companion (Adler, 1984).

To Virginia Artus or anyone else suffering from acrophobia (the fear of heights), climbing or descending even a short flight of stairs may present major difficulties. (James Wilson/Woodfin Camp & Assoc.)

Obsessive-compulsive disorder: A disorder characterized by obsessions or compulsions

Obsession: A thought or idea that keeps recurring

Obsessive-Compulsive Disorder

In **obsessive-compulsive disorder**, people are plagued by unwanted thoughts, called obsessions, or feel that they must carry out some actions, termed compulsions, against their will.

An **obsession** is a thought or idea that keeps recurring in one's mind. For example, a student may not be able to stop feeling that he has neglected to put his name on a test and may think about it constantly for the two weeks it takes to get the paper back; a man may go on vacation and wonder the whole time whether he locked his house; a woman may hear the same tune running through her head over and over again. In each case, the thought or idea is unwanted and difficult to put out of mind. Of course, many of us

TABLE 16-3

Giving Fear a Proper Name

Phobia	Stimulus	Phobia	Stimulus
Acrophobia	Heights	Herpetophobia	Reptiles
Aerophobia	Flying	Hydrophobia	Water
Agoraphobia	Open spaces	Mikrophobia	Germs
Ailurophobia	Cats	Murophobia	Mice
Amaxophobia	Vehicles, driving	Mysophobia	Dirt or germs
Anthophobia	Flowers	Numerophobia	Numbers
Anthrophobia	People	Nyctophobia	Darkness
Aquaphobia	Water	Ochlophobia	Crowds
Arachrophobia	Spiders	Ophidiophobia	Snakes
Astraphobia	Lightning	Ornithophobia	Birds
Brontophobia	Thunder	Phonophobia	Speaking out loud
Claustrophobia	Closed spaces	Pyrophobia	Fire
Cynophobia	Dogs	Thanatophobia	Death
Dementophobia	Insanity	Trichophobia	Hair
Gephyrophobia	Bridges	Xenophobia	Strangers

suffer from mild obsessions from time to time, but usually such thoughts persist for a short period only. For people with serious obsessions, however, the thoughts persist for days or months and may consist of bizarre, troubling images. In one classic case of an obsession, the patient

> complained of having "terrible thoughts." When she thought of her boyfriend she wished he were dead; when her mother went down the stairs, she "wished she'd fall and break her neck"; when her sister spoke of going to the beach with her infant daughter, the patient "hoped that they would both drown." These thoughts "make me hysterical. I love them; why should I wish such terrible things to happen? It drives me wild, makes me feel I'm crazy and don't belong to society" (Kraines, 1948, p. 199).

Compulsion: An urge to repeatedly carry out an act that even the sufferer realizes is unreasonable

As part of an obsessive-compulsive disorder, people may also experience **compulsions**, urges to repeatedly carry out some act that seems strange and unreasonable, even to them. Whatever the compulsive behavior, people experience extreme anxiety if they cannot carry it out, even if it is something they want to stop. The acts involved may be relatively trivial, such as repeatedly checking the stove to make sure all the burners are turned off, or more unusual, such as a continuous need to wash oneself (Rachman & Hodgson, 1980). For example, consider this case report of a 27-year-old woman with a cleaning ritual:

> Bess would first remove all of her clothing in a preestablished sequence. She would lay out each article of clothing at specific spots on her bed, and examine each one for any indications of "contamination." She would then thoroughly scrub her body, starting at her feet and working meticulously up to the top of her head, using certain washcloths for certain areas of her body. Any articles of clothing that appeared to have been "contaminated" were thrown into the laundry. Clean clothing was put in the spots that were vacant. She would then dress herself in the opposite order from which she took the clothes off. If there were any deviations from this order, or if Bess began to wonder if she had missed some contamination, she would go through the entire sequence again. It was not rare for her to do this four or five times in a row on certain evenings (Meyer & Osborne, 1982, p. 156).

Unfortunately for people experiencing an obsessive-compulsive disorder, there is no reduction of anxiety from carrying out a compulsive ritual. They tend to lead lives filled with unrelenting tension.

WHEN THE PSYCHOLOGICAL LEADS TO THE PHYSICAL: Somatoform Disorders

Most of us know people who cannot wait to regale us with their latest physical problems; even an innocent "How are you?" brings a long list of complaints in response. People who consistently report physical problems, have a preoccupation with their health, and have unrealistic fears of disease may be experiencing a problem known as **hypochondriasis**. In hypochondriasis there is a constant fear of illness, and physical sensations are misinterpreted as

Hypochondriasis (HY po kon DRY a sis): A constant fear of illness and misinterpretation of normal aches and pains signs of disease. It is not that the "symptoms" are faked; hypochondriacs actually experience the aches and pains that most of us feel as we go through an active existence (Costa & McCrae, 1985). It is the misinterpretation of these sensations as symptoms of some dread disease—often in the face of unarguable medical evidence to the contrary—that characterizes hypochondriasis.

Hypochondriasis is just one example of a class of disorders known as **somatoform disorders**—psychological difficulties that take on a physical (somatic) form of one sort or another. Even though an individual reports physical symptoms, there is no underlying physical problem, or, if a physical problem does exist, the person's reaction greatly exaggerates what would be expected from the medical problem alone. Only when a physical examination rules out actual physiological difficulties can a diagnosis of somatoform disorder be made.

Somatoform disorder: Psychological difficulties that take on physical (somatic) form

In addition to hypochondriasis, the other major somatoform disorder is **conversion disorder**. In contrast to hypochondriasis, in which there is no actual physical problem, conversion disorders involve an actual physical disturbance such as the inability to use a sensory organ or the complete or partial inability to move an arm or leg. The *cause* of such a physical disturbance is purely psychological; there is no biological reason for the problem. Some of Freud's classic cases involved conversion disorders. For instance, one patient of Freud's was suddenly unable to use her arm, without any apparent physiological cause; later, just as abruptly, she regained its use.

Conversion disorder: Psychological disturbances characterized by actual physical disturbances, such as the inability to speak or move one's arms

Conversion disorders are often characterized by their rapid onset. People wake up one morning blind or deaf, or they experience numbness that is restricted to a certain part of the body. A person's hand, for example, might become entirely numb, while an area above the wrist—controlled by the same nerves—remains inexplicably sensitive to touch. Such a condition is referred to as "glove anesthesia," because the area that is numb is the part of the hand covered by a glove, and not a region related to pathways of the nervous system (see Figure 16-1).

Interestingly, one of the characteristics of conversion disorders is a surprising lack of concern over the symptoms that one would expect to be highly anxiety-producing. For instance, a person in good health who wakes up blind might react in a bland, matter-of-fact way. Considering how most people would feel if it happened to them, this reaction hardly seems appropriate.

Most conversion disorders occur when an individual is under emotional stress that can be reduced by a physical symptom. The physical condition allows the person to escape or reduce the source of stress. An emotional problem is turned, then, into a physical ailment that acts to relieve the source of the original emotional problem.

In large-scale example of conversion disorder, Mucha and Reinhardt (1970) found that some 16 percent of the student aviators at the U.S. Naval Aerospace Medical Institute suffered symptoms for which there was no underlying physical problem. The difficulties most frequently included blurred vision, double vision, and the development of blind spots and focusing trouble. Investigation revealed that the students found outright quitting an unacceptable response to the stress they were experiencing and instead developed physical responses that allowed them to avoid the demands of the program. Their stress was thus relieved through a face-saving physical problem.

FIGURE 16-1

A person who suffered from actual nerve damage in the arm would show numbness in the entire area shown in (*a*). However, a person with "glove anesthesia" would experience numbness in just the area that would be covered by a glove (*b*), which is a region of the body that is unrelated to the pathways of the nervous system. Therefore, the phenomenon can only be attributed to psychological causes.

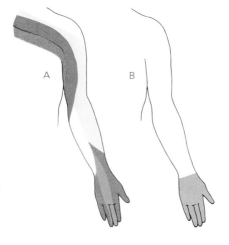

ONE BECOMES TWO (OR MORE): Dissociative Disorders

Dissociative disorders: The splitting apart of critical personality facets, allowing stress avoidance by escape

Multiple personality: A disorder in which a person displays characteristics of two or more distinct personalities

Psychogenic amnesia: A failure to remember past experience

Although in reality quite rare, the disorder of multiple personality has been featured in many novels and films. For instance, movie buffs will recall *Sybil*, the story of a girl who, as her psychiatrist eventually discovered, had no fewer than sixteen separate personalities. (Photo Fest.)

The most dramatic and celebrated cases of psychological dysfunctioning—although they are actually quite rare—have been **dissociative disorders**. The movie *The Three Faces of Eve,* the book *Sybil* (about a girl with sixteen personalities), and cases of people found wandering the streets with no notion of who they are or where they came from exemplify dissociative disorders. The key factor in such problems is the splitting apart (or dissociation) of critical parts of personality that are normally integrated and work together. This lack of integration acts to allow certain parts of a personality to avoid stress—since another part can be made to face it. By dissociating themselves from key parts of their personality, individuals with the disorder can eliminate anxiety.

There are three major types of dissociative disorders: multiple personality, psychogenic amnesia, and psychogenic fugue. A person with a **multiple personality** displays characteristics of two or more distinct personalities. Each personality has a unique set of likes and dislikes and its own reactions to situations. In fact, some people with multiple personalities carry several pairs of glasses because their vision changes with each personality (Braun, 1985). Moreover, each individual personality can be well adjusted, when considered on its own.

The problem, of course, is that there is only one body available to the various personalities, forcing the personalities to take turns. Because there can be strong variations in personalities, the person's behavior—considered as a whole—can appear very inconsistent. For instance, in the famous case portrayed in *The Three Faces of Eve,* the meek, bland Eve White provided a stunning contrast to the dominant and carefree Eve Black (Nunes, 1975).

Psychogenic amnesia, another dissociative disorder, is a failure or inability to remember past experiences. Psychogenic amnesia is unlike simple amnesia, which, as we discussed in Chapter 6, involves an actual loss of information from memory, typically due to a physiological cause. In contrast, in cases of psychogenic amnesia, the "forgotten" material is still present in memory—it simply cannot be recalled.

In the most severe forms, individuals cannot recall their names, are unable to recognize parents and other relatives, and do not know their addresses. In other respects, though, they may appear quite normal: Apart from an inability to remember certain facts about themselves, they may be able to recall skills and abilities that they developed earlier. For instance, even though a chef may not remember where he grew up and received training, he may still be able to prepare gourmet meals.

In some cases of psychogenic amnesia, the memory loss is quite profound. For example, a woman—dubbed Jane Doe by her rescuers—was found by a Florida park ranger in the early 1980s. Incoherent, thin, and only partially clothed, Doe was unable to recall her name, her past, and even how to read and write. On the basis of her accent, authorities thought the woman was from Illinois, and interviews conducted under drugs revealed that she had had a Catholic education. However, the childhood memories she revealed were so universal that her background could not be further pinpointed. In a desperate attempt to rediscover her identity, she appeared on the television show *Good Morning America,* and ultimately a couple from Roselle, Illinois, whose daughter had moved to Florida, stepped forward, saying that they were her parents. However, Jane Doe never regained her memory (Carson, Butcher & Coleman, 1988).

This woman, identified only as "Jane Doe" by the hospital where she was treated, was a victim of psychogenic amnesia. (Susan Greenwood/Liaison Agency.)

A more unusual form of amnesia is a condition known as **psychogenic fugue**. In this state, people take an impulsive, sudden trip, often assuming a new identity. After a period of time—days, months, or sometimes even years—they suddenly realize that they are in a strange place and completely forget the time that they have spent wandering. Their last memories are those just before they entered the fugue state.

Psychogenic fugue: An amnesiac condition in which people take sudden, impulsive trips, sometimes assuming a new identity

What the dissociative disorders have in common is that they allow people to escape from some anxiety-producing situation. Either the person produces a new personality to deal with stress, or the situation that caused the stress is forgotten or left behind as the individual journeys to some new—and perhaps less anxiety-ridden—situation.

RECAP AND REVIEW III

Recap

◄ Although they have their drawbacks, classification systems are necessary to describe and ultimately understand abnormal behavior.

◄ The *Diagnostic and Statistical Manual of Mental Disorders, Third Edition—Revised (DSM-III-R)* provides a description of some 230 separate diagnostic categories of abnormal behavior.

◄ Anxiety disorders occur when anxiety is so great that it impedes people's everyday functioning.

◄ Somatoform disorders are psychological problems that take on a physical form.

◄ Dissociative disorders occur when there is a splitting apart of normally integrated parts of personality.

Review

1. *DSM-III-R* is intended to both describe abnormal behaviors and suggest their underlying causes. True or false?

_____

2. The experience of long-term, consistent anxiety without a clear cause is known as _____

_____ _____ .

3. Kathy is terrified by elevators. She is likely to be suffering from a(n)

a. obsessive-compulsive disorder.
b. phobic disorder.
c. panic disorder.
d. generalized anxiety disorder.

4. John described an incident in which his anxiety rose suddenly to a peak and he felt a sense of impending doom. He had experienced a(n) _____

_____ .

5. Troubling thoughts which persist for days or months are known as

a. obsessions.   c. rituals.
b. compulsions.   d. panic attacks.

6. An overpowering urge to carry out a strange ritual is called a(n) _____ .

7. In what major way does conversion disorder differ from hypochondriasis?

8. The splitting apart of the personality, providing escape from stressful situations, is the key factor in _____ disorders.

9. Sue Ann has no memory of the time since she moved to another town and changed her identity. She probably suffers from

a. psychogenic fugue.   c. variable personality.
b. psychogenic amnesia.   d. multiple personality.

I do not care for anything. I do not care to ride, for the exercise is too violent. I do not care to walk, for walking is too strenuous. I do not care to lie down, for I should either have to remain lying, and I do not care to do that, or I should have to get up again, and I do not care to do that either. . . . I do not care at all.

Have you ever taken a test for which you had studied for days and days, felt afterward that you had done well, but later found that you had received a very low grade? Although the reactions you experienced were probably not as strong as those felt by the Danish philosopher Søren Kierkegaard, who wrote the passage above, it is likely that you experienced a feeling of depression, an emotional reaction of sadness and melancholy. More than likely, however, you soon returned to a more pleasant frame of mind.

We all experience mood swings. Sometimes we are happy, perhaps even euphoric; at other times we feel upset, saddened, or depressed. Such changes in mood are a normal part of everyday life. In some people, however, moods are so pronounced and so long-lasting that they interfere with the ability to function effectively. In extreme cases a mood may become life-threatening, and in others it may cause the person to lose touch with reality. Situations such as these represent **mood disorders**, disturbances in emotional feelings strong enough to intrude on everyday living.

Mood disorders: Affective disturbances severe enough to interfere with normal living

Feeling Down: Major Depression

Moses. Rousseau. Dostoevsky. Queen Victoria. Lincoln. Tchaikovsky. Freud.

The common link among these people? Each suffered from periodic attacks of **major depression**, one of the most common forms of mood disorders. In fact, the percentage of people who are likely to experience major depression during their lifetime is 8 to 12 percent for men and 20 to 26 percent for women (Boyd & Weissman, 1981). Depression is the most frequent problem diagnosed in outpatient clinics, affecting about one-third of the patients (Woodruff, Clayton & Guze, 1975; Winokur, 1983). Furthermore, the rate of depression is increasing, with people experiencing much more depression than they did two generations ago. Even children can display depression; for instance, a sample of 3000 third-, fourth-, and fifth-graders found that around 5 percent were depressed (Lefkowitz & Tesiny, 1985; Seligman, 1988).

Major depression: A severe form of depression that interferes with concentration, decision making, and sociability

When psychologists speak of major depression they do not mean the sadness that comes from experiencing one of life's disappointments. Some depression is normal following the break-up of a long-term relationship, the death of a loved one, or the loss of a job. It is even normal for less serious problems: doing badly in school or not getting into the college of one's choice. In fact, many college students experience some form of "normal" depression during their years in school. Blatt, D'Afflitti, and Quinlan (1976) studied cases of "normal" depression in college students and found that depression tended to be characterized by three sets of factors: dependence

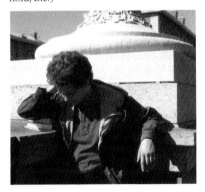

While temporary depression is a normal response to one of life's disappointments, in some cases depression is so severe and lingering that it represents a major psychological disorder. (Richard Choy/Peter Arnold, Inc.)

on others' help and support, exaggeration of one's faults, and the sense that one is not in control of one's life. (For more information on the kinds of psychological difficulties college students experience, see the Psychology at Work box.)

Individuals who suffer from major depression experience similar sorts of feelings, but the severity tends to be considerably greater. They may feel useless, worthless, and lonely and may despair over the future—feelings that may continue for months and years. They may have uncontrollable crying jags and disrupted sleep. The depth of such behavior and the length of time it lasts are the hallmarks of major depression.

Ups and Downs: Mania and Bipolar Disorders

While some people are sinking into the depths of depression, others are emotionally soaring high, experiencing what is called mania. **Mania** refers to

Mania: An extended state of intense euphoria and elation

PSYCHOLOGY AT WORK

THE SPECIAL PROBLEMS OF COLLEGE STUDENTS

I remember my first week at college. My parents drove me to the campus. It was rainy and dark. I felt sort of scared 'cause I'd come from a small town. All my high school teachers said I'd do great at college. I wasn't so sure. What if they were wrong? What if I was really just a "big fish in a little pond"? Well, the day was rainy, the other students walked around aimlessly as did I. I remember the sick feeling I had when my parents drove off and left me. I was left to grow up. Even with all the fighting and hate that went on in our house over the previous two years, and even though I couldn't wait to get away, I was scared, sad, unbelievably lonely (Duke & Nowicki, 1979, p. 517).

Have you ever experienced similar feelings during your college career? In fact, such emotions are relatively common and represent one of the special psychological difficulties of college students—the freshman adjustment reaction. Students with this problem are depressed and severely homesick and may be anxious and withdrawn from others. The reaction often is most severe in students who had perceived themselves as particularly successful high school seniors—either socially or academically—and suddenly find

themselves without status or authority and looked down upon by upperclassmen. The cure? Often just the passage of time is enough, especially since time passing by inevitably brings the next class of freshmen to campus. In severe cases, however, counseling may be appropriate.

Psychologists have identified other problems that are particularly prevalent among college students (Duke & Nowicki, 1979, 1986; Wechsler, Rohman, & Solomon, 1981). They include:

● For male students:
Grades
Social life
Vocational decisions
The future
Sexual relationships
Peer pressures
Adjusting to a new environment
Leaving family for the first time
Competition
Depression

● For female students:
What to do with their lives

Developing sexual and emotional relationships
Strain from too much work
Grades
Adjustment
Gaining independence
Identity
Pressure from parents
Peer pressures
Morals

How prevalent are these problems? One survey found that 47 percent of the students queried said that they had at least one psychological issue of concern to them (Wechsler, Rohman & Solomon, 1981). Furthermore, certain subgroups of students showed particular problems. For example, students who were overweight reported a greater frequency of psychological apprehensions, and minority women displayed a higher frequency of motivational problems than white women.

As you can see from the list, many of the problems students experience are unique to the specific demands of college and the particular stage of a student's life. However, knowing that others are going through the same sorts of problems may be a step in alleviating the stress brought on by such difficulties, which are fairly universal among college students.

an extended state of intense euphoria and elation. People experiencing mania feel intense happiness, power, invulnerability, and energy. They may become involved in wild schemes, believing that they will succeed at anything they attempt. There are many cases on record of people squandering all their money while in a state of mania; consider, for example, the following description of an individual who experienced a manic episode:

> Mr. O'Reilly took a leave of absence from his civil service job. He purchased a large number of cuckoo clocks and then an expensive car, which he planned to use as a mobile showroom for his wares, anticipating that he would make a great deal of money. He proceeded to "tear around town" buying and selling clocks and other merchandise, and when he was not out, he was continuously on the phone making "deals." He rarely slept and, uncharacteristically, spent every evening in neighborhood bars drinking heavily and, according to him, "wheeling and dealing." . . . He was $3000 in debt and had driven his family to exhaustion with his excessive activity and talkativeness. He said, however, that he felt "on top of the world" (Spitzer, Skodol, Gibbon & Williams, 1983, p. 115).

Bipolar disorder: A disorder in which a person alternates between euphoric feelings of mania and bouts of depression

Mania is often found paired with bouts of depression. This alternation of mania and depression is called **bipolar disorder** (or, as it used to be known, manic-depressive disorder). The swings between highs and lows may occur as frequently as a few days apart or they may alternate over a period of years. In addition, the periods of depression tend to be longer in most individuals than the periods of mania, although this pattern is reversed in some.

Interestingly, it has been suggested that some of society's most creative individuals may suffer from a mild form of bipolar disorder (Fieve, 1975). The imagination, drive, excitement, and energy that they display during manic stages allows them to make unusually creative contributions. On the other hand, most people who display mania go beyond the bounds of what would generally be considered normal, and their behavior clearly causes self-harm.

Causes of Mood Disorders

Because they represent a major mental health problem, mood disorders—in particular, depression—have received a good deal of study, and a number of approaches have been used to explain their occurrence (Clayton & Barrett,

Historical and biographical information has enabled experts to diagnose these three Romantic composers as sufferers of bipolar disorder: Robert Schumann, Hector Berlioz, and Gustav Mahler. (Bettmann Archive.)

1983). Psychoanalytic approaches, for example, see depression as the result of anger at oneself. In this view, people feel responsible for the bad things that happen to them and direct their anger inward. On the other hand, there is convincing evidence that heredity plays a role in depression, since major depression seems to run in certain families (Rosenthal, 1970; Wender et al., 1986; Egeland et al., 1987).

Furthermore, some researchers have found a chemical imbalance in the brains of some depressed patients: Certain abnormalities have been identified in the chemical substances involved in the transmission of electrical charges across the gaps between nerve cells (Wender & Klein, 1981). Other research has identified a genetic defect that provides evidence that bipolar disorder is linked to inherited factors (Egeland et al., 1987). This chemical and genetic evidence suggests that people's moods may be determined in part by biological factors rather than the psychological factors suggested by psychoanalytic approaches (McNeal & Cimbolic, 1986).

There are still other explanations for mood disorders. For instance, Seligman (1975) suggests that depression is a response to learned helplessness, a state in which a person perceives and eventually learns that there is no way to escape from or cope with stress and simply gives up fighting it—a proposition that has received a good deal of research support (Robins, 1988).

One of the most puzzling questions about depression is why there has been an increase in its incidence over past generations. Martin Seligman (1988) suggests that the increase is due to a change in societal values, in which individuals now feel an increased commitment to themselves and a lowered commitment to the traditional institutions of religion, family, the nation, and the community. In the past, such institutions helped people from feeling despair at times of personal failure. Without these institutions to lean on in time of stress, people sink into depression more readily than in earlier years.

Societal factors also may provide the elusive answer to another difficult question facing researchers: Why is the incidence of depression almost two times higher for women than for men? One possibility is that the stress experienced by women may be greater than men at certain points in women's lives—such as cases in which a woman must simultaneously earn a living and be primary caretaker for her children (McGrath, 1988). But biological factors may also explain some women's depression. For example, 25 to 50 percent of women who take oral contraceptives report symptoms of depression, and depression that occurs following the birth of a child is linked to hormonal changes (Strickland, 1988).

It is clear, though, that researchers have discovered no definitive solutions to the puzzle of depression, and there are many alternative explanations (e.g., Hyland, 1987; Pyszczynski, Holt & Greenberg, 1987). Most likely, mood disorders are caused by a complex interaction of several factors.

WHEN REALITY IS LOST: Schizophrenia

For many years she has heard voices, which insult her and cast suspicion on her chastity. They mention a number of names she knows, and tell her she will be stripped and abused. The voices are very distinct, and, in her opinion, they must be carried by a telescope or a machine from her home. Her thoughts are dictated to her; she is obliged to think them, and hears them repeated after her. She is interrupted in her work, and has all kinds of uncomfortable sensations in her body, to which some-

Schizophrenia: A class of disorders characterized by a severe distortion of reality, resulting in antisocial behavior, silly or obscene behavior, hallucinations, and disturbances in movement

thing is "done." In particular, her "mother parts" are turned inside out, and people send a pain through her back, lay ice water on her heart, squeeze her neck, injure her spine, and violate her (Kraepelin, 1904).

The label given to the most severe forms of mental disturbance, such as that described in the famous case study above, is **schizophrenia**. Schizophrenics make up by far the largest percentage of those hospitalized for mental disorders and in most respects are the least likely to recover from their difficulties.

Schizophrenia refers to a class of disorders in which severe distortion of reality occurs. Thinking, perception, and emotion may deteriorate; there may be a withdrawal from social interaction; and there may be displays of bizarre behavior. Although several types of schizophrenia (see Table 16-4) have been observed, the distinctions between them are not always clear-cut (e.g., Zigler & Glick, 1988). Moreover, the symptoms displayed by a schizophrenic person may vary considerably over time, and people with schizophrenia show significant differences in the pattern of symptoms even when they are labeled with the same diagnostic category. Nonetheless, a number of characteristics reliably distinguish schizophrenia. They include:

▶ Decline from a previous level of functioning. An individual can no longer carry out activities he or she was once able to do.

▶ Disturbances of thought and language. Schizophrenics use logic and language in a peculiar way; their thinking does not make sense and they do not follow conventional linguistic rules. Consider, for example, the following response to the question "Why do you think people believe in God?"

TABLE 16-4

The Major Types of Schizophrenia

Type	Symptoms
Disorganized (hebephrenic) schizophrenia	Inappropriate laughter and giggling, silliness, incoherent speech, infantile behavior, strange and sometimes obscene behavior
Paranoid schizophrenia	Delusions and hallucinations of persecution or of greatness, loss of judgment, erratic and unpredictable behavior
Catatonic schizophrenia	Major disturbances in movement; in some phases, loss of all motion, with patient frozen into a single position, remaining that way for hours and sometimes even days; in other phases, hyperactivity and wild, sometimes violent, movement
Undifferentiated schizophrenia	Variable mixture of major symptoms of schizophrenia; classification used for patients who cannot be typed into any of the more specific categories
Residual schizophrenia	Minor signs of schizophrenia following a more serious episode

FIGURE 16-2

This excerpt from the diary of Sirhan Sirhan, the killer of Robert F. Kennedy, shows the disturbances of thought and language characteristic of schizophrenia. (Wide World Photos.)

Uh, let's, I don't know why, let's see, balloon travel. He holds it up for you, the balloon. He don't let you fall out, your little legs sticking down through the clouds. He's down to the smokestack, looking through the smoke trying to get the balloon gassed up you know. Way they're flying on top that way, legs sticking out. I don't know, looking down on the ground, heck, that'd make you so dizzy you just stay and sleep you know, hold down and sleep there. I used to be sleep outdoors, you know, sleep outdoors instead of going home (Chapman & Chapman, 1973, p. 3).

As this selection illustrates, although the basic grammatical structure may be intact, the substance of schizophrenics' thinking is often illogical, garbled, and lacking in meaningful content (see Figure 16-2).

▶ Delusions. People with schizophrenia often have **delusions**, firmly held, unshakable beliefs with no basis in reality. Among the most frequent ones are the beliefs that they are being controlled by someone else, that they are being persecuted by others, and that their thoughts are being broadcast so that others are able to know what they are thinking.

Delusions: Firmly held beliefs with no basis in reality

▶ Perceptual disorders. Schizophrenics do not perceive the world as most other people do. They may see, hear, or smell things differently from others (see Figure 16-3) and do not even have a sense of their bodies in the way that others do. Some reports suggest that schizophrenics have difficulty determining where their own bodies stop and the rest of the world begins (Ritzler & Rosenbaum, 1974). They may also have **hallucinations**, the experience of perceiving things that do not actually exist.

Hallucinations: Perceptions of things that do not actually exist

Process schizophrenia: One course of schizophrenia in which symptoms begin early in life and develop slowly and subtly

Reactive schizophrenia: One course of schizophrenia in which the onset of symptoms is sudden and conspicuous

▶ Emotional disturbances. People with schizophrenia sometimes show a bland lack of emotion in which even the most dramatic events produce little or no emotional response. Conversely, they may display emotion that is inappropriate to a situation. For example, a schizophrenic might laugh uproariously at a funeral or may react with anger when being helped by someone.

▶ Withdrawal. Schizophrenics tend to have little interest in others. They tend not to socialize or hold real conversations with others, although they may talk *at* another person. In the most extreme cases they do not even acknowledge the presence of other people, appearing to be in their own isolated world.

The symptoms of schizophrenia follow two primary courses. In **process schizophrenia**, the symptoms develop relatively early in life, slowly and subtly. There may be a gradual withdrawal from the world, excessive daydreaming, a blunting of emotion, until eventually the disorder reaches the point where others cannot overlook it. In other cases—known as **reactive schizophrenia**—the onset of symptoms is sudden and conspicuous. The treatment outlook for reactive schizophrenia is relatively favorable; process schizophrenia has proved to be much more difficult to treat.

A relatively recent addition to the classifications used in schizophrenia distinguishes positive-symptom from negative-symptom schizophrenia (Opler et al., 1984; Andreasen, 1985). Negative-symptom schizophrenia means an absence or loss of normal functioning, such as social withdrawal or blunted emotions. In contrast, positive-symptom schizophrenia is indicated by the presence of disordered behavior such as hallucinations, delusions, and extremes of emotionality. The distinction, although controversial, is becoming increasingly important because it suggests that two different underlying processes may explain the roots of schizophrenia—which remains one of the greatest mysteries facing psychologists who deal with abnormal behavior.

Solving the Puzzle: The Causes of Schizophrenia

Although it is clear that schizophrenic behavior departs radically from normal behavior, its causes are less apparent. It does appear, however, that schizophrenia has genetic, biochemical, and environmental components at its roots (Mirsky & Duncan, 1986; Watt, 1985).

GENETIC COMPONENTS   Because schizophrenia is more common in some families than in others, genetic factors seem to be involved in producing at least a susceptibility to or readiness for developing schizophrenia (Faraone & Tsuang, 1985). For example, researchers have found evidence of a link between schizophrenia and an abnormally functioning gene (Gurling et al., 1988). In addition, some studies show that people who have been classified as suffering from schizophrenia have about a 25 percent chance of having children with severe psychological problems. Furthermore, if one of a pair of identical twins has schizophrenia, the other has as much as a 42 percent chance of developing it (Gottesman & Schields, 1972; Kringlen, 1978). However, if genetics alone were entirely accountable, the chance of the other identical twin having schizophrenia would be 100 percent, since identical twins share the same genetic makeup. The development of schizophrenia, then, is due to more than just genetic factors.

BIOCHEMICAL COMPONENTS   One of the most intriguing hypotheses to explain schizophrenia is that there is some sort of biochemical imbalance in the brains of people with the disorder (Asnis & Ryan, 1983; Noll & Davis, 1983). One form of this theory suggests that schizophrenia occurs when a person's body in a condition of stress produces chemicals that cause hallucinations or disorganized thought—similar to the effects of a drug such as LSD—in a sort of self-induced chemical overdose (Carson, 1983).

On the other hand, alternative theories resting on the notion of a biochemical imbalance are also plausible. For instance, the **dopamine hypothesis** suggests that schizophrenia occurs when there is excess activity in those areas of the brain that use the chemical dopamine to transmit impulses across nerve cells (Wong et al., 1988; Snyder, 1978). This hypothesis came to light after the discovery that drugs that block dopamine action in brain pathways can be highly effective in reducing the symptoms of schizophrenia.

Unfortunately, the dopamine hypothesis does not provide the whole story. Drugs that block dopamine action produce a biological reaction in just a few hours after they're taken—yet the symptoms of schizophrenia don't subside for weeks. If the hypothesis were entirely correct, we would expect an immediate improvement in schizophrenic symptoms. Moreover, these drugs are effective in reducing symptoms not only in schizophrenics but also in those suffering from very different sorts of psychological problems such as mania and depression (Carson, 1983). Nevertheless, the dopamine hypothesis provides a starting point in understanding biochemical factors in schizophrenia. (Additional biological factors are discussed in the Cutting Edge box.)

ENVIRONMENTAL COMPONENTS   Given that genetic and biochemical factors do not provide a full explanation for schizophrenia, we need to consider past and current experiences found in the environments of people who develop the disturbance (Keith & Matthews, 1983). Psychoanalytic approaches suggest that schizophrenia is a form of regression to earlier ex-

Dopamine hypothesis: A theory that suggests that schizophrenia occurs when there is excess activity in those areas of the brain using dopamine to transmit nerve impulses

Although diagnoses of schizophrenia are typically made on the basis of an individual's behavior, an exciting new approach to diagnosis—as well as an important advance in understanding the causes of schizophrenia—suggests that the brains of schizophrenics have structural abnormalities that someday could be used to predict when a person will show behaviors typical of schizophrenia.

The notion that there are abnormalities in the brains of people with schizophrenia is based on research being done in the laboratories of Arnold Scheibel and Joyce Kovelman of the University of California's Brain Research Institute in Los Angeles. Scheibel and Kovelman have found that they are able to distinguish between the brains of schizophrenics and normal individuals by examining microscopic photographs of brain samples taken from the hippocampus, an area of the brain related to the expression of emotions.

In their initial work, they took specimens from ten long-term schizophrenics and eight normal people who had died when they were between the ages of 25 and 67. They later studied the samples—without knowing from which population they came—and were able to distinguish between the two groups. The major

SCHIZOPHRENIA: A BEHAVIORAL OR BIOLOGICAL PROBLEM?

difference was in the organization of cells: In normal people, the nerve cells were arranged in orderly rows, whereas the cells of those with schizophrenia were in disarray. Not only were some of the cells of those with schizophrenia rotated about 90 degrees from their normal orientation, but some of the dendrites of the nerve cells were disorganized. Moreover, further research has revealed that there is a rough correlation between the severity of cell disorganization and schizophrenia symptoms: The greater the disorganization, the more severe are the symptoms (Scheibel, 1984; Altshuler et al., 1987).

Although we cannot rule out that the structural problems in the brain were a consequence of schizophrenia—rather than its cause, as Scheibel and Kovelman suggest—the findings do represent the first clear demonstration that problems exist in the configuration of portions of the brains of some people with schizophrenia. Scheibel suggests that the symptoms of schizophrenia may

have their origin as early as the first three months of pregnancy, when the nerve cells of the developing embryo are supposed to align themselves appropriately (Scheibel, 1986).

Other evidence suggests that certain kinds of schizophrenic symptoms may be related to specific kinds of brain abnormalities. For example, schizophrenics classified as having negative symptomology—such as social withdrawal—are apt to have brains with structural abnormalities, whereas people with positive-symptom schizophrenia—those who experience hallucinations or exaggerated emotionality—are more likely to have brains without structural abnormalities (Crow, 1980).

When this research is added to other current work that uses CAT and PET scans (discussed in Chapter 2) to assess the brains of schizophrenics, it becomes increasingly clear that someday biological techniques may be developed to accurately and reliably diagnose schizophrenia—and perhaps, in addition, other forms of mental disturbance. Ultimately, it may be possible to do prenatal genetic screening to test for schizophrenia. Just as today blood tests are taken for granted, in the not-so-distant future use of brain-cell tests may become routine.

periences and stages of life. Freud said, for instance, that people with schizophrenia lack strong enough egos to cope with their unacceptable impulses. They regress to the oral stage—a time in which the id and ego are not yet separated. Therefore, individuals suffering from schizophrenia essentially lack an ego and act out impulses without concern for reality.

Although this is theoretically reasonable, there is little evidence to support psychoanalytic explanations. More compelling are theories that look toward the family and other major figures in the lives of people with schizophrenia. One influential theory, known as the **double-bind hypothesis**, states that individuals with schizophrenia may have received simultaneous messages from their mothers that contradicted one another (Bateson, 1960). Consider, for example, how you would react if someone told you to "come here," and then, as you approached, waved you away. According to the hypothesis, this is essentially what happens in some families: The mother is warm and loving on a verbal level but anxious and rejecting on an emotional

Double-bind hypothesis: A theory that suggests that people suffering from schizophrenia may have received simultaneous contradictory messages from their mothers and never learned what behavior was appropriate and nonverbal level. The results are so devastating to the child that eventually he or she develops schizophrenia.

Although the details of the double-bind hypothesis have not received considerable support, there is firm evidence that families with members who have schizophrenia often have abnormal communication patterns (Wynne, Singer, Bartko & Toohey, 1975). These families may differ on a number of other dimensions as well, including socioeconomic status, anxiety level, and general degree of stress present (Lidz, 1973; Lidz & Fleck, 1985).

Theorists taking a behavioral perspective believe these differences support a **learned-inattention theory** of schizophrenia (Ullmann & Krasner, 1975). According to the learned-inattention view, schizophrenia is a learned behavior consisting of a set of inappropriate responses to social stimuli. Instead of responding to others, people with schizophrenia have learned to ignore appropriate stimuli and pay attention instead to stimuli that are not related to normal social interaction. Because this results in bizarre behavior, others respond to them in a negative way, leading to social rejection and unpleasant interactions and ultimately to an even less appropriate response by the individual in the future. Eventually, the individual begins to "tune out" appropriate stimuli and develops schizophrenic characteristics.

Learned-inattention theory (of schizophrenia): A theory that suggests that schizophrenia is a learned behavior consisting of a set of inappropriate responses to social stimuli

THE CAUSES OF SCHIZOPHRENIA—NOT ONE, BUT MANY?   As we have seen, there is research supporting genetic, biochemical, and environmental causes of schizophrenia. It is likely, then, that not just one but several causes jointly explain the onset of the problem. The predominant approach used today, the **predisposition model**, considers a number of factors simultaneously (Zubin & Spring, 1977). This model suggests that individuals may inherit a predisposition or an inborn sensitivity to schizophrenia which makes them particularly vulnerable to stressful factors in the environment. The stressors may vary—a poor family environment, social rejection, or dysfunctional communication patterns—but if they are sufficiently strong and are coupled with a genetic predisposition, the result will be the onset of schizophrenia (see Figure 16-4). Similarly, if the genetic predisposition is strong enough, schizophrenia may occur even when the environmental stressors are relatively weak.

In sum, schizophrenia may be produced by several different combinations of biological predisposition and environmental stress. It is increasingly clear, then, that schizophrenia is not produced by any single factor but is an amalgamation of interrelated problems.

Predisposition model (of schizophrenia): A model that suggests that individuals may inherit a predisposition toward schizophrenia that makes them particularly vulnerable to stressful factors in the environment

FIGURE 16-4

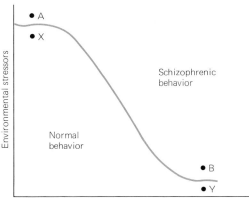

Predisposition to schizophrenia

According to the predisposition model of schizophrenia, schizophrenic behavior occurs when environmental stressors are particularly high, even if the predisposition is relatively low (person A). Similarly, schizophrenic behavior can occur if the predisposition is relatively high, even if stressors are relatively low (person B). On the other hand, even though the stress level is high, person X will not display schizophrenic behavior, because the predisposition is sufficiently low. Similarly, person Y will behave normally, despite the strong predisposition, because the stress is low. (Adapted from Zubin & Spring, 1977.)

I had always wanted lots of things; as a child I can remember wanting a bullet that a friend of mine had brought in to show the class. I took it and put it into my school bag and when my friend noticed it was missing, I was the one who stayed after school with him and searched the room, and I was the one who sat with him and bitched about the other kids and how one of them took his bullet. I even went home with him to help him break the news to his uncle, who had brought it home from the war for him.

But that was petty compared with the stuff I did later. I wanted a Ph.D. very badly, but I didn't want to work very hard—just enough to get by. I never did the experiments I reported; hell, I was smart enough to make up the results. I knew enough about statistics to make anything look plausible. I got my master's degree without even spending one hour in a laboratory. I mean, the professors believed anything. I'd stay out all night drinking and being with my friends, and the next day I'd get in just before them and tell 'em I'd been in the lab all night. They'd actually feel sorry for me. I did my doctoral research the same way, except it got published and there was some excitement about my findings. The research helped me get my first college teaching job. There my goal was tenure.

The rules at my university were about the same as at any other. You had to publish and you had to be an effective teacher. "Gathering" data and publishing it was never any problem for me, so that was fine. But teaching was evaluated on the basis of forms completed by students at the end of each semester. I'm a fair-to-good teacher, but I had to be sure that my record showed me as excellent. The task was simple. Each semester, I collected the evaluation forms, took out all the fair-to-bad ones and replaced them with doctored ones. It would take me a whole evening, but I'd sit down with a bunch of different colored pens and pencils and would fill in as many as 300 of the forms. Needless to say, I was awarded tenure (Duke & Nowicki, 1979, pp. 309–310).

Before you think that all college professors are like the one describing himself above, it should be stated that this person represents a clear example of someone with a **personality disorder**. Personality disorders are different from the other problems that we have discussed in this chapter, because there is often little sense of personal distress associated with the psychological maladjustment of those affected. In fact, people with personality disorders frequently lead seemingly normal lives—until one looks just below the surface. There one finds a set of inflexible, maladaptive personality traits that do not permit the individual to function appropriately as a member of society.

The best-known type of personality disorder is the **antisocial** or **sociopathic personality disorder**. Individuals with this disorder tend to display no regard for the moral and ethical rules of society or for the rights of others. Although they appear intelligent and are usually likeable at first, they can be seen as manipulative and deceptive upon closer examination. Moreover, they tend to share certain other characteristics (Coleman, Butcher & Carson, 1988):

▶ A lack of conscience, guilt, or anxiety over transgressions. When those with an antisocial personality behave in a way that injures someone else,

Personality disorder: A mental disorder characterized by a set of inflexible, maladaptive personality traits that keep a person from functioning properly in society

Antisocial (sociopathic) personality disorder: A disorder in which individuals display no regard for moral and ethical rules or for the rights of others they understand intellectually that they have caused the harm but feel no remorse.

▶ Impulsive behavior and an inability to withstand frustration. Antisocial personalities are unable to withstand frustration without reacting in some way—which may include violating the rights of others, if doing so allows them to remove the frustration.

▶ Manipulation of others. Antisocial personalities frequently have very good interpersonal skills: They are charming, engaging, and able to convince others to do what they want. In fact, some of the best con men have antisocial personalities and are able to get people to hand over their life savings without a second thought. The misery that follows in the wake of such activities is not cause for concern to the antisocial personality.

What causes such an unusual constellation of problems? A variety of factors have been suggested, ranging from a biological inability to experience emotions to problems in family relationships (e.g., Newman & Kosson, 1986). For example, in many cases of antisocial behavior the individual has come from a home in which a parent has died or left, or one in which there is a lack of affection, a lack of consistency in discipline, or outright rejection. Other explanations concentrate on sociocultural factors, since an unusually high proportion of antisocial personalities come from lower socioeconomic groups. Some researchers have suggested that the breakdown of societal rules, norms, and regulations that may be found in severely deprived economic environments may encourage the development of antisocial personalities (Melges & Bowlby, 1969). Still, no one has been able to pinpoint the specific causes of antisocial personalities, and it is likely that some combination of factors is responsible.

Another example of a personality disturbance is the **narcissistic personality disorder**, which is characterized by an exaggerated sense of self-importance. Those with the disorder expect special treatment from others, while at the same time they disregard others' feelings. In some ways, in fact, the main attribute of the narcissistic personality is an inability to experience empathy for other people.

Narcissistic personality disorder: A personality disorder characterized by an exaggerated sense of self and an inability to experience empathy for others

There are several other categories of personality disorder, ranging in severity from individuals who may simply be regarded by others as eccentric, obnoxious, or difficult, to people who act in a manner that is criminal and dangerous to others. Although they are not out of touch with reality in the way that schizophrenics are, people with personality disorders lead lives that are on the fringes of society.

Beyond the Major Disorders

The various forms of abnormal behavior described in DSM-III-R cover much wider ground than we have been able to discuss in this chapter. Some we have covered in earlier parts of the book, such as **sexual disorders**, in which one's sexual activity is unsatisfactory (discussed in Chapter 10), and **psychoactive substance-use disorder**, in which problems arise from the abuse of drugs (covered in Chapter 11). Another important class of disorders that we have previously touched on is **organic mental disorders**, problems that have a purely biological basis. Other disorders we have not mentioned at all, and each of the classes we have discussed can be divided into several subcategories.

Sexual disorders: A form of abnormal behavior in which one's sexual activity is unsatisfactory

Psychoactive substance-use disorder: Disordered behavior involving drug abuse

Organic mental disorders: Problems having a purely biological basis

In some ways, then, our discussion of psychological disturbances has only touched the surface. The challenge facing psychologists interested in abnormal behavior is to improve their understanding of the nature and causes of these psychological disorders in order to improve the lives of those who suffer from them, as well as to prevent their occurrence in the first place—issues we discuss in the next chapter.

THE INFORMED CONSUMER OF PSYCHOLOGY:
Deciding When You Need Help

 After you consider the range and variety of psychological disturbances that can afflict people, it would not be surprising if you felt that you were suffering from one (or more) of the problems we have discussed. This is a perfectly natural reaction, for, as we mentioned earlier, people often conclude that they have the same problems they are studying—the classic medical student's disease. Because this is such a common phenomenon, it is important that you be well aware of the pitfalls of self-diagnosis.

One of the truisms of the legal profession is that a lawyer who defends himself has a fool for a client. Similarly we might say that people who try to categorize their own mental disorders are making a foolish mistake. With categories that are subjective under the best of circumstances, and with problems that can be elusive and fleeting even to well-trained, experienced mental health professionals, it is unreasonable to expect that after reading a chapter in an introductory psychology book anyone could make a valid diagnosis.

On the other hand, there are guidelines you can use to determine when some kind of professional help is warranted. The following signals suggest the possible necessity of outside intervention:

▶ Long-term feelings of psychological distress that interfere with your sense of well-being, competence, and ability to function effectively in daily activities

▶ Occasions in which you experience overwhelmingly high stress, accompanied by feelings of inability to cope with the situation

▶ Prolonged depression or feelings of hopelessness, particularly when they do not have any clear cause (such as the death of someone close)

▶ Withdrawal from other people

▶ A chronic physical problem for which no physical cause can be determined

▶ A fear or phobia that prevents you from engaging in normal everyday activities

▶ Feelings that other people are out to get you or are talking about and plotting against you

▶ The inability to interact effectively with others, preventing the development of friendships and loving relationships

The above criteria can serve as a rough set of guidelines for determining when the normal problems of everyday living are beyond the point that you are capable of dealing with them yourself. In such situations, the least reasonable approach would be to pore over the psychological disorders we have discussed in an attempt to pigeonhole yourself into a specific category. A more reasonable strategy is to consider seeking professional help—a possibility that we discuss in the next chapter.

RECAP AND REVIEW IV

Recap

◄ Affective disorders are characterized by mood disturbances that are so great they impede daily living.

◄ Schizophrenia represents the most common diagnosis for those hospitalized for mental disturbance.

◄ People with personality disorders do not feel the personal distress associated with other disorders, but they do have maladaptive traits that prevent them from functioning as normal members of society.

◄ Other forms of abnormal behavior include sexual disorders, psychoactive substance-use disorders, and organic mental disorders.

Review

1. Henry's feelings of deep despair, worthlessness, and loneliness have persisted for months. His symptoms are indicative of
   a. an adjustment reaction.
   b. normal depression.
   c. major depression.
   d. affective depression.

2. States of extreme euphoria and energy paired with severe depression characterize _____ disorder.

3. Arthur's belief that his thoughts are being controlled by beings from outer space is an example of a _____ .

4. List five characteristics that reliably distinguish schizophrenia from other mental disturbances.

5. Because of support for the notion that several factors cause schizophrenia, the predominant approach used today is
   a. the double-bind hypothesis.
   b. regression theory.
   c. the predisposition model.
   d. learned inattention theory.

6. Celeste believes that she deserves special attention from other people, and that she owes them nothing in return. She shows signs of having a _____ personality disorder.

7. A disregard for the moral and ethical rules governing society and the rights of others characterizes the _____ or _____ personality disorder.

8. Having read and studied this chapter, you should now feel confident about making valid diagnoses. True or false? _____

(Answers to review questions are on page 587.)

◄ LOOKING BACK

1. The most satisfactory definition of abnormal behavior is one based on the psychological consequences of the behavior, which is thought of as abnormal if it produces a sense of distress, anxiety, or guilt, or if it is harmful to others. Another useful definition considers people who cannot adapt to society and who are unable to function effectively to be abnormal.

2. No single definition is totally adequate; therefore it is reasonable to consider abnormal and normal behavior as marking two ends of a continuum, or scale, with completely normal functioning at one end and completely abnormal behavior at the other.

3. The medical model of abnormal behavior views abnormality as a symptom of an underlying disease that requires a cure. Psychoanalytic models suggest that abnormal behavior is caused by conflicts in the unconscious stemming from past experience. In order to resolve psychological problems, people need to resolve the unconscious conflicts.

4. In contrast to the medical and psychoanalytic models, behavioral approaches view abnormal behavior not as a symptom of some underlying problem, but as the problem itself. To resolve the problem, one must change the behavior. Although traditional behavioral models ignore a person's "inner life" and focus instead on overt behavior, some behavioral theorists suggest it is appropriate to take a cognitive approach in which the modification of cognitions (thoughts and beliefs) is carried out.

5. Humanistic approaches view people as rational and motivated to get along with others; abnormal behavior is seen as a difficulty in fulfilling one's needs. People are considered to be in control of their lives and able to resolve their own problems.

6. Sociocultural approaches view abnormal behavior in terms of difficulties arising from family and other social relationships. The sociocultural model concentrates on such factors as socioeconomic status and the social rules society creates to define normal and abnormal behavior.

586

7. Students of psychology are susceptible to the same sort of "disease" that afflicts medical students: the perception that they suffer from the problems about which they are studying. Unless their psychological difficulties are persistent, have depth, and are consistent, however, it is unlikely that their concerns are valid.

8. The system for classifying abnormal behaviors that is used most widely today is *DSM-III-R—Diagnostic and Statistical Manual of Mental Disorders, Third Edition—Revised.*

9. Anxiety disorders are present when a person experiences so much anxiety that it impedes daily functioning. Specific types of anxiety disorders include generalized anxiety disorder, panic disorder, phobic disorder, and obsessive-compulsive disorder. Generalized anxiety disorder occurs when a person experiences long-term anxiety with no apparent cause. Panic disorders are marked by panic attacks, which are sudden, intense feelings of anxiety. Phobic disorders are characterized by intense, irrational fears of specific objects or situations. People with obsessive-compulsive disorders display obsessions (recurring thoughts or ideas) or compulsions (repetitious, unwanted behaviors).

10. Somatoform disorders refer to psychological difficulties that are displayed through physical problems. An example is hypochondriasis, in which there is a constant fear of illness and a preoccupation with disease. Another somatoform disorder is conversion disorder, in which there is an actual physical difficulty that occurs without a physiological cause.

11. Dissociative disorders are marked by the splitting apart, or dissociation, of crucial parts of personality that are usually integrated. The three major kinds of dissociative disorders are multiple personality, psychogenic amnesia, and psychogenic fugue.

12. Mood disorders are characterized by emotions of depression or euphoria so strong that they intrude on everyday living. In major depression, people experience sorrow so deep that they may become suicidal. In bipolar disorder, stages of mania, in which there is an extended sense of elation and powerfulness, alternate with depression.

13. Schizophrenia is one of the most severe forms of mental illness. The manifestations of schizophrenia include declines in functioning, thought and language disturbances, perceptual disorders, emotional disturbance, and withdrawal from others. There is strong evidence linking schizophrenia to genetic, biochemical, and environmental factors. According to the predisposition model, there is likely to be an interaction among various factors.

14. People with personality disorders experience little or no personal distress, but they do suffer from an inability to function as normal members of society. The best-known type of personality disorder is the antisocial or sociopathic personality disorder, in which the moral and ethical rules of society are ignored. The narcissistic personality is characterized by an exaggerated sense of importance.

15. There are many other categories of disorders, including sexual disorders, psychoactive substance-use disorders, and organic mental disorders.

16. A number of signals indicate a need for professional help. These include long-term feelings of psychological distress, feelings of inability to cope with stress, withdrawal from others, prolonged feelings of hopelessness, chronic physical problems with no apparent causes, phobias and compulsions, paranoia, and an inability to interact with others.

KEY TERMS AND CONCEPTS ▶

medical model of abnormality (p. 554)
psychoanalytic model of abnormality (555)
behavioral model of abnormality (556)
humanistic model of abnormality (557)
sociocultural model of abnormality (558)
medical student's disease (560)
DSM-III-R (562)
anxiety (565)
anxiety disorder (565)
generalized anxiety disorder (565)
panic disorder (565)
panic attack (565)
phobic disorder (566)

phobia (566)
obsessive-compulsive disorder (567)
obsession (567)
compulsion (568)
hypochondriasis (568)
somatoform disorder (569)
conversion disorder (569)
dissociative disorder (570)
multiple personality (570)
psychogenic amnesia (570)
psychogenic fugue (571)
mood disorder (572)
major depression (572)
mania (573)
bipolar disorder (574)
schizophrenia (576)
delusions (577)

hallucinations (577)
process schizophrenia (578)
reactive schizophrenia (578)
dopamine hypothesis (579)
double-bind hypothesis (580)
learned-inattention theory of schizophrenia (581)
predisposition model of schizophrenia (581)
personality disorder (582)
antisocial (sociopathic) personality disorder (582)
narcissistic personality disorder (583)
sexual disorders (583)
psychoactive substance-use disorder (583)
organic mental disorders (583)

FOR FURTHER STUDY AND APPLICATION ▶

Carson, R. C., Butcher, J. N., & Coleman, J. C. (1988). *Abnormal psychology and modern life* (8th ed.). Glenview, IL: Scott, Foresman.

A classic overview of abnormal behavior, now in its eighth edition, this volume covers the full sweep and depth of abnormal psychology.

Sutherland, N. S. (1976). *Breakdown*. New York: Stein & Day.

If you have ever wondered what it is like to experience a mental breakdown, read this book. Written by a psychologist, it is an autobiographical narration of the author's breakdown and subsequent recovery.

American Psychiatric Association. (1987). *Diagnostic and statistical manual of mental disorders, third edition—revised (DSM-III-R)*. Washington, D.C.: American Psychiatric Association.

This is the major diagnostic categorization system used by mental health workers. Although the manual is technical, it provides a feeling for the range and comprehensiveness of the system.

Meyer, R. & Osborne, Y. (1987). *Case studies in abnormal behavior* (2nd ed.). Boston: Allyn & Bacon.

This book presents fascinating case studies of individuals who suffer from many of the problems discussed in the chapter, along with explanations for the disorders.

Schreiber, F. R. (1974). *Sybil*. New York: Warner.

Thigpen, C. H., & Cleckley, H. M. (1954). *The three faces of Eve*. Kingsport, TN: Kingsport Press.

These two works describe women with very rare multiple personality disorders.

ANSWERS (REVIEW IV):
1. c **2.** Bipolar **3.** Delusion **4.** Decline from previous level of functioning; disturbances of thought and language; perception disorders; emotional disturbances; withdrawal **5.** c **6.** Narcissistic **7.** Antisocial, sociopathic **8.** False; diagnosis of mental illness is a serious matter that should be left to professionals

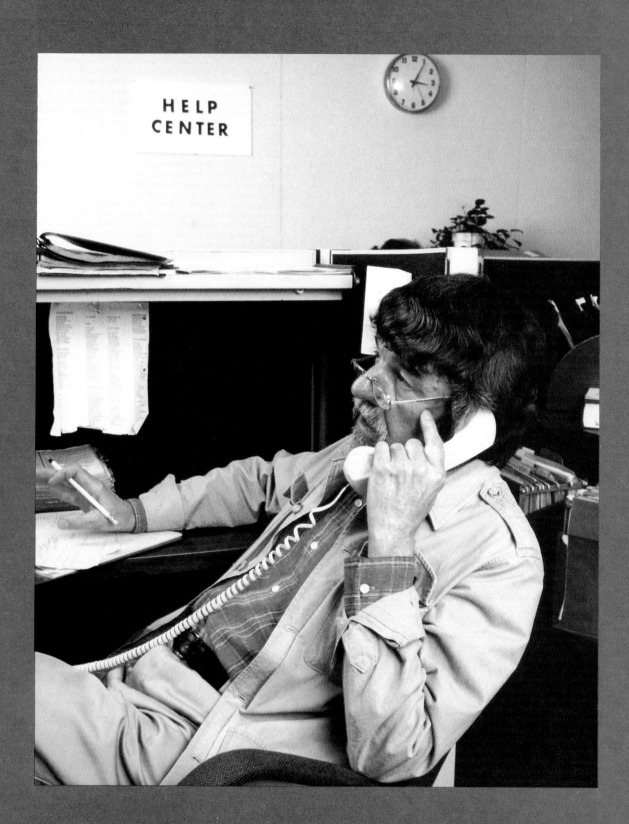

CHAPTER

TREATMENT OF ABNORMAL BEHAVIOR

Though many psychotherapy sessions may look alike, the content of what is said is likely to vary greatly according to the training of the therapist and the needs of the client.

PROLOGUE:
JOANNA

Joanna: I just feel nervous a lot of the time.

Therapist: What is the feeling like?

Joanna: I don't know. It's hard to describe. . . . I just feel nervous.

Therapist: [*I think I'm going to have some difficulty in getting her to elaborate on her problems. Maybe I'll hold off on trying to push for specifics for a little bit, and instead try to get her to feel more comfortable about describing and elaborating on her feelings, and just talking in general.*] So you know what the feeling is like, but it's kind of difficult to describe it in words.

Joanna: Yes, it is. You know, it's just a feeling of uneasiness and apprehension. Like when you know something bad may happen, or at least you're afraid that it might.

Therapist: So emotionally, and perhaps physically, there's a fear that something might happen, although you may not be certain exactly what.

Joanna: Yes.

Therapist: When you're feeling that way, what do you experience physically?

Joanna: Well, my heart starts pounding and I feel myself tense up all over. It's not always that bad; sometimes it's only mild.

Therapist: [*I can make a smooth transition at this point and try to find out the situations in which the intensity of her anxiety varies.*] In other words, depending upon the circumstances, you may feel more or less anxious.

Joanna: Yes.

Therapist: Tell me something about the situations that make you *most* anxious.

Joanna: Well, it's usually when I deal with other people.

Therapist: I would find it particularly helpful to hear about some typical situations that may upset you.

Joanna: It's hard to come up with something specific.

Therapist: [*I'm having doubts as to how hard to press her for details. If she has too much difficulty in coming up with specifics, the whole process of questioning might just make our relationship too aversive. I sense by the expression on her face that she may be somewhat uneasy about her inability to give me the information I want. I should probably attend to that before moving on.*] I can understand how it may be hard to come up with specific examples right on the spot. That's not at all uncommon. Let me see if I can help to make it a little easier for you. Let's take the past week or so. Think of what went on either at work or at home, or when you were out socially, that might have upset you.

Joanna: OK. Something just occurred to me. We went out to a party last weekend, and as we were driving to the place where the party was being held, I felt myself starting to panic.

Therapist: Can you tell me more about that situation?

Joanna: Well, the party was at . . . (Goldfried & Davison, 1976, pp. 40–42).

LOOKING AHEAD ▶

This actual transcript of an initial therapy session represents the view that most people have of what treatment for psychological disorders is all about. Popularized by the media, the notion that treatment always involves a therapist asking a series of probing questions and a client searching for answers to a difficult problem has come to represent society's general view of the nature of therapy.

In fact—although many kinds of therapy do encompass the situation described in the transcript—treatment approaches are much broader than this example of an initial interview with a person experiencing anxiety might suggest. Therapists today use over 250 different kinds of treatment, ranging from informal one-session discussions to long-term treatments involving powerful drugs. However, no matter what type of therapy is employed, all have a common goal: the relief of psychological disorder, ultimately enabling individuals to achieve richer, more meaningful, and more fulfilling lives.

This chapter explores a number of important issues related to abnormal behavior: How do we treat individuals with psychological disorders? Who is the most appropriate person to provide treatment? What is the future like for people with severe disturbances? What is the most reasonable therapeutic approach to use? Is one form of therapy better than others? Does any therapy *really* work? How does a person choose the "right" kind of therapy and therapist?

Most of the chapter focuses on the various approaches used by providers of treatment for psychological disturbances—approaches which, despite their diversity, boil down to two main categories: psychologically based and biologically based therapy. Psychologically based therapy, or **psychotherapy**, is the process in which a patient (often referred to as the client) and a professional attempt to remedy psychological difficulties. In psychotherapy, the emphasis is on change as a result of discussions and interactions between therapist and client. In contrast, biologically based therapy uses drugs and other medical procedures to improve psychological functioning.

As we discuss the various approaches to therapy, it is important to keep in mind that, although the distinctions may seem clear-cut, there is a good deal of overlap in the classifications and procedures employed, and even in the training and titles of various kinds of therapists (see Table 17-1). In fact, many therapists today use a variety of methods with a given person, in what is referred to as an **eclectic approach to therapy** (Karasu, 1982). Assuming that abnormal behavior is often the product of both psychological and biological processes, eclectic therapists may draw from several perspectives simultaneously, merging them into a "package" of treatment procedures that address both psychological and biological aspects of a person's problems.

After reading this chapter, then, you will be able to answer the following questions:

▶ What are the differences between psychologically and biologically based treatment approaches?

Psychotherapy: The process in which a patient (client) and a professional attempt to remedy the client's psychological difficulties

Eclectic approach to therapy: An approach to therapy that uses a variety of treatment methods rather than just one

TABLE 17-1

Getting Help from the Right Person

Clinical psychologist	Ph.D. who specializes in assessment and treatment of psychological difficulties
Counseling psychologist	Psychologist with Ph.D. or master's who usually treats day-to-day adjustment problems in a counseling setting, such as a university mental health clinic
Psychiatrist	M.D. with postgraduate training in abnormal behavior who can prescribe medication as part of treatment
Psychoanalyst	Either an M.D. or a psychologist who specializes in psychoanalysis, a treatment technique first developed by Freud
Psychiatric social worker	Professional with a master's degree and specialized training in treating people in home and community settings

Each of these trained professionals could be expected to give helpful advice and direction, although the nature of the problem a person is experiencing may make one or the other more appropriate. For example, a person who is suffering from severe disturbance and has lost touch with reality will typically require some sort of biologically based drug therapy. In that case, a psychiatrist—who is a physician—would clearly be the professional of choice. On the other hand, those suffering from milder disorders, such as difficulty in adjusting to the death of a family member, have a broader choice that might include any of the professionals listed above. The decision can be made easier because mental health facilities in communities, colleges, and health organizations often provide guidance, during an initial consultation, in selecting an appropriate therapist.

▶ What are the basic kinds of psychotherapies, and how do we evaluate them?

▶ How are drug, electroconvulsive, and psychosurgical techniques used today in the treatment of mental disorders?

▶ What is the best kind of therapy and therapist for a given situation?

PSYCHOTHERAPY: PSYCHOLOGICAL APPROACHES TO TREATMENT

Although diverse in many respects, all psychological approaches see treatment as a way of solving psychological problems by modifying people's behavior and helping them gain a better understanding of themselves and their past, present, and future. We will consider three major kinds of psychotherapies: psychodynamic, behavioral, and humanistic, all of which are based on the different models of abnormal behavior we discussed in Chapter 16.

PIERCING THE UNCONSCIOUS: Psychodynamic Treatment

Psychodynamic therapy is based on the premise, first suggested by Freud, that the primary source of abnormal behavior is unresolved past conflicts and anxiety over the possibility that unacceptable unconscious impulses will enter the conscious part of a person's mind. To guard against this undesirable possibility, individuals employ **defense mechanisms**—psychological strategies that protect them from these unconscious impulses (see Chapter 14). Even though repression, the most common defense mechanism (in which threatening conflicts and impulses are pushed back into the unconscious), typically occurs, our unacceptable conflicts and impulses can never be completely buried. Therefore, some of the anxiety associated with them can produce abnormal behavior in the form of what Freud called **neurotic symptoms**.

How does one rid oneself of the anxiety caused by the repression of unconscious, unwanted impulses and drives? To Freud, the answer was to confront the conflicts and impulses by bringing them out of the unconscious part of the mind and into the conscious part. Freud assumed that, by this technique, anxiety over the past would be reduced and the patient could participate in his or her daily life more effectively.

The challenge facing a psychodynamic therapist, then, is how to facilitate patients' attempts to explore and understand their unconscious. The technique that has evolved has a number of components, but basically it consists of leading patients to consider and discuss their past experiences from the time of their first memories, in explicit detail. Through this process, it is assumed that patients will eventually stumble upon long-hidden crises, traumas, and conflicts that are producing anxiety in their adult lives. They will then be able to "work through"—understand and rectify—these difficulties.

Freud's Therapy: Psychoanalysis

Classic Freudian psychodynamic therapy—called **psychoanalysis**—tends to be a lengthy and expensive affair. Patients typically meet with their therapists

Psychodynamic therapy: Therapy based on the notion that the basic sources of abnormal behavior are unresolved past conflicts and anxiety

Defense mechanisms: Psychological strategies that protect people from unconscious impulses

Neurotic symptoms: According to Freud, abnormal behavior brought about by anxiety associated with unwanted conflicts and impulses

Psychoanalysis: Psychodynamic therapy that involves frequent sessions and often lasts for many years

(Drawing by Modell, © 1981 The New Yorker Magazine, Inc.)

"And then I say to myself, 'If I really wanted to talk to her, why do I keep forgetting to dial 1 first?'"

Psychodynamic therapy attempts to uncover long-suppressed conflicts through an exploration of past experiences and relationships. Some therapists encourage their clients to use physical symbols and exercises to represent persons, places, or situations. (Innervisions.)

Free association: A Freudian therapeutic technique in which a patient says everything that comes to mind to give the therapist a clue to the workings of the patient's unconscious

Dream interpretation: An examination of a patient's dreams to find clues to the unconscious conflicts and problems being experienced

Manifest content: The surface description and interpretation of a dream

Latent content: The "true" message hidden within a dream

Resistance: An inability or unwillingness to discuss or reveal particular memories, thoughts, or motivations

Transference: A patient's transfer of certain strong feelings for others to the analyst

an hour a day, four to six days a week, for several years. In their sessions, they often use a technique developed by Freud called **free association**. Patients are told to say whatever comes to mind, regardless of its apparent irrelevance or senselessness. In fact, they are urged *not* to try to make sense of things or impose logic upon what they are saying, since it is assumed that the ramblings evoked during free association actually represent important clues to the unconscious, which has its own logic. It is the analyst's job to recognize and label the connections between what is being said and the patient's unconscious.

Another important tool of the therapist is **dream interpretation**. As we discussed in Chapter 11, this is an examination of the patients' dreams to find clues to the unconscious conflicts and problems being experienced. According to Freud, dreams provide a closer look at the unconscious because people's defenses tend to be lowered when they are asleep. But even in dreaming there is a censoring of thoughts; events and people in dreams are usually represented by symbols. Because of this, one must move beyond the surface description of the dream—the **manifest content**—and consider its underlying meaning—the **latent content**—which reveals the true message of the dream.

The processes of free association and dream interpretation do not always move easily forward. The same unconscious forces that initially produced repression may work to keep past difficulties out of the conscious, producing resistance. **Resistance** is an inability or unwillingness to discuss or reveal particular memories, thoughts, or motivations. Resistance can be expressed in a number of ways. For instance, patients may be discussing a childhood memory and suddenly forget what they were saying, or they may completely change the subject. It is the therapist's job to pick up instances of resistance and to interpret their meaning, as well as to ensure that patients return to the subject—which is likely to hold difficult or painful memories for them.

Because of the close, almost intimate interaction between patient and psychoanalyst, the relationship between the two often becomes emotionally charged and takes on a complexity unlike most others. In fact, patients may come to see the analyst as symbolic of significant others in their past, perhaps a parent or a lover, and apply some of their feelings for that person to the analyst—a phenomenon known as **transference**.

Transference can be used by a therapist to help the patient recreate past relationships that were psychologically difficult. For instance, if a patient undergoing transference views his therapist as symbolic of his father—with whom he had a difficult relationship—the patient and therapist may "redo" an earlier interaction, this time including more positive aspects. Through this process, conflicts regarding the real father may be resolved.

Contemporary Alternatives to Psychoanalysis: Is Freud Dead?
If time is money, patients in psychoanalysis need a lot of both. As you can imagine, few people have the time, money, or patience that participating in years of traditional psychoanalysis requires. Moreover, there is no conclusive evidence that psychoanalysis, as originally conceived by Freud, works better than other, more contemporary versions of psychodynamic therapy. Today, for instance, psychodynamic therapy tends to be shorter, usually lasting no longer than three months or twenty sessions. The therapist takes a more active role than Freud would have liked, controlling the course of therapy and prodding and advising the patient with considerable directness. Finally, there is less emphasis on a patient's past history and childhood. Instead, a more here-and-now approach is used, in which the therapist concentrates on an individual's current relationships and level of functioning (Parloff, 1976; Reppen, 1981; Strupp, 1981).

Even with its current modifications, psychodynamic therapy has its critics. It is still relatively time-consuming and expensive, especially in comparison with other forms of psychotherapy that we will discuss later. Moreover, only certain kinds of patients tend to be well suited for this method: those who suffer from anxiety disorders and those who are highly articulate—characteristics enshrined in a (facetious) acronym, YAVIS, for the perfect patient: young, attractive, verbal, intelligent, and successful (Schofield, 1964).

Ultimately, the most important concern about psychodynamic treatment is whether it actually works, and here we find no pat answer. Psychodynamic treatment techniques have been controversial since Freud introduced them. Part of the problem is the difficulty in establishing whether or not patients have improved following psychodynamic therapy. One must depend on reports from the therapist or the patients themselves, reports that are obviously open to bias and subjective interpretation (Luborsky & Spence, 1978; Peterfreund, 1984).

Critics have questioned the entire theoretical basis of psychodynamic theory, maintaining that there is no proof that such constructs as the unconscious exist. Despite the considerable criticism, though, the psychodynamic treatment approach has remained a viable technique, not only providing effective treatment in many cases of psychological disturbances but permitting the potential development of an unusual degree of insight into and understanding of people's lives.

LEARNING THE GOOD AND UNLEARNING THE BAD:
Behavioral Approaches to Treatment

Perhaps, as a child, you would be rewarded by your parents with an ice cream cone if you were especially good ... or sent to your room if you misbehaved. As we saw in Chapter 5, the principles behind such a child-rearing strategy is quite valid: Good behavior is maintained by rewards, and unwanted behavior can be eliminated by punishment.

These principles represent the basic underpinnings of behavioral treatment approaches. Building upon the fundamental processes of learning—

Behavioral treatment approaches: Approaches to abnormal behavior that assume that both normal and abnormal behaviors are learned and that treatment consists of learning new behavior or unlearning maladaptive behavior

classical and operant conditioning—**behavioral treatment approaches** make a fundamental assumption: both abnormal and normal behavior is *learned* (Craighead, Kazdin & Mahoney, 1981; Karoly & Kanfer, 1982). People who display abnormal behavior have either failed to learn the skills needed to cope with the problems of everyday living or they have acquired faulty skills and patterns that are being maintained through some form of reinforcement. To modify abnormal behavior, then, people must learn new behavior to replace the faulty skills they have developed and unlearn their maladaptive behavior patterns.

To behavioral psychologists, it is not necessary to delve into people's pasts or dig into their psyches; rather than viewing abnormal behavior as a symptom of some underlying problem, they consider the abnormal behavior itself as the problem in need of modification. Changing people's behavior to allow them to function more effectively solves the problem—with no need for concern about the underlying cause. In this view, then, if you can change abnormal behavior, you've cured it.

Learning to Hate What You Love and Love What You Hate: Classical Conditioning Approaches

Suppose you bite into your favorite candy bar and find that it is infested with ants and that you've swallowed a bunch of them. You immediately become sick to your stomach and throw up. Your long-term reaction? You never eat that kind of candy bar again; in fact, it may be months before you eat any type of candy.

This simple example hints at how classical conditioning might be used to modify behavior. You might remember from our discussion in Chapter 5 that, when a stimulus that naturally evokes a negative response (such as an unpleasant taste or a puff of air in the face) is paired with a previously neutral stimulus (such as the sound of a bell), a state of affairs is produced in which the neutral stimulus can bring about a similar negative reaction by itself. Using this procedure, first developed by Ivan Pavlov, we may create unpleasant reactions to stimuli that previously were enjoyed—possibly to excess—by an individual. The technique, known as **aversive conditioning**, has been used in cases of alcoholism, drug abuse, and smoking.

Aversive conditioning: A technique used to help people break unwanted habits by associating the habits with very unpleasant stimuli

One treatment for people who want to stop smoking involves aversive conditioning, in which smoking and cues relating to smoking are repeatedly paired with unpleasant stimuli. (Lester Sloan/Woodfin Camp & Assoc.)

The basic procedure in aversive conditioning is relatively straightforward. For example, a person with a drinking problem might be given an alcoholic drink along with a drug that causes severe nausea and vomiting. After these two are paired a few times, the alcohol alone becomes associated with the vomiting and loses its appeal. In fact, what typically happens is that just the sight or smell of alcohol triggers the aversive reaction.

Although aversion therapy works reasonably well to inhibit substance-abuse problems such as alcoholism and certain kinds of sexual deviation, its long-term effectiveness is questionable. Moreover, there are important ethical drawbacks to aversion techniques employing such potent stimuli as electric shock—used only in the most extreme cases (for example, self-mutilation)—instead of drugs that merely induce gastric discomfort (Russo, Carr & Lovaas, 1980; Sulzer-Azaroff & Mayer, 1985). It is clear, though, that aversion therapy is an important procedure for eliminating maladaptive responses for some period of time—which provides, even if only temporarily, the opportunity to encourage more adaptive behavior patterns.

The most successful treatment based on classical conditioning is known as systematic desensitization. In **systematic desensitization**, a stimulus that evokes pleasant feelings is repeatedly paired with a stimulus that evokes anxiety in the hope that the positive feelings will eventually become associated with the anxiety-producing stimulus, thereby alleviating the anxiety (Rachman & Hodgson, 1980; Wolpe, 1969).

Suppose, for instance, you were afraid of flying. In fact, the very thought of being in an airplane made you begin to sweat and shake, and you'd never even been able to get yourself near enough to an airport to know how you'd react if you actually had to fly somewhere. Using systematic desensitization to treat your problem, you would first be trained in muscle-relaxation techniques by a behavior therapist (see Table 17-2), learning to relax your body fully—a highly pleasant state, as you might imagine. The next step would involve the construction of a **hierarchy of fears**—a list, in order of increasing severity, of the things that are associated with your fears. For instance, your hierarchy might resemble the one at the top of the next page.

Systematic desensitization: A procedure in which a stimulus that evokes pleasant feelings is repeatedly paired with a stimulus that evokes anxiety in the hope that the anxiety will be alleviated

Hierarchy of fears: A list, in order of increasing severity, of the things that are associated with one's fears

Learning to Relax

To get a sense of how behavior therapists train people to relax, try this procedure developed by Herbert Benson (1975).
1. Sit quietly in a comfortable position.
2. Close your eyes.
3. Deeply relax all your muscles, beginning at your feet and progressing to your face—keep them relaxed.
4. Breathe through your nose. Become aware of your breathing. As you breathe out, say the word "one" silently to yourself. For example, breathe in . . . out, "one"; in . . . out, "one"; and so on. Breathe easily and naturally.
5. Continue for ten to twenty minutes. You may open your eyes to check the time, but do not use an alarm. When you finish, sit quietly for several minutes, at first with your eyes closed and later with your eyes open. Do not stand up for a few minutes.
6. Do not worry about whether you are successful in achieving a deep level of relaxation. Maintain a passive attitude and permit relaxation to occur at its own pace. When distracting thoughts occur, try to ignore them by not dwelling upon them, and return to repeating "one."

With practice, the response should come with little effort. Practice the techniques once or twice daily, but not within two hours after any meal, since the digestive processes seem to interfere with the elicitation of the relaxation response (Benson, 1975, pp. 114–115).

PHYSICAL AND MENTAL HEALTH

▶ Watching a plane fly overhead

▶ Going to an airport

▶ Buying a ticket

▶ Stepping into the plane

▶ Seeing the plane door close

▶ Having the plane taxi down the runway

▶ Taking off

▶ Being in the air

Once this hierarchy had been developed and you had learned relaxation techniques, the two sets of responses would be associated with each other. To do this, your therapist might ask you to put yourself into a relaxed state and then to imagine yourself in the first situation identified in your hierarchy. After you were able to consider that first step while remaining relaxed, you would move on to the next situation, eventually moving up the hierarchy in gradual stages until you could imagine yourself being in the air without experiencing anxiety. In some cases, all this would take place in a psychologist's office, while in others people are actually placed in the fear-evoking situation. Thus, it would not be surprising if you were brought, finally, to an airplane to use your relaxation techniques.

Systematic desensitization has proved to be an effective treatment for a number of problems, including phobias, anxiety disorders, and even impotence and fear of sexual contact (Karoly & Kanfer, 1982; Kennedy & Kimura, 1974). As you see, we *can* learn to enjoy the things we once feared.

Following the "Fearless Peer": Observational Learning and Modeling

If we had to be hit by a car in order to learn the importance of looking both ways before we crossed the street, the world would likely be suffering from a serious underpopulation problem. Fortunately, this is not necessary, for we learn a significant amount through **observational learning**, by **modeling** the behavior of other people.

Observational learning: Learning by watching others' behavior and the consequences of that behavior

Modeling: Imitating the behavior of others (models)

Behavior therapists have used modeling to systematically teach people new skills and ways of handling their fears and anxieties. For example, some people have never learned fundamental social skills such as maintaining eye contact with those they are speaking to. A therapist can model the appropriate behavior and thereby teach it to someone deficient in such skills (Sarason, 1976). Children with dog phobias have also been able to lose their fears by watching another child—called the "Fearless Peer"—repeatedly walk up to a dog, touch it, pet it, and finally play with it (Bandura, Grusec & Menlove, 1967). Modeling, then, can play an effective role in resolving some kinds of behavior difficulties, especially if the model is rewarded for his or her behavior.

Reward the Good, Extinguish the Bad: Operant Conditioning Approaches

Consider the A we get for a good paper . . . the raise for fine on-the-job performance . . . the gratitude for helping an elderly person cross the street. Such rewards for our behavior produce a greater likelihood that we will repeat that behavior in the future. Similarly, behavioral approaches using operant conditioning techniques (which demonstrate the effects of rewards and punishments on future behavior) are based on the notion that we should reward people for carrying out desirable behavior, and extinguish behavior—either through ignoring or punishing it—that we wish to eliminate.

Probably the best example of the systematic application of operant conditioning principles is the **token system**, whereby a person is rewarded with a token such as a poker chip or some kind of play money for desired behavior. The behavior may range from such simple things as keeping one's room neat to personal grooming to interacting with other people. The tokens that are earned for such behavior can then be exchanged for some desired object or activity, such as snacks, new clothes, or in extreme cases, being able to sleep in one's own bed (as opposed to on the floor).

Token system: A procedure whereby a person is rewarded for performing certain desired behaviors

Although it is most frequently employed in institutional settings for individuals with relatively serious problems, the system is not unlike what parents do when they give children money for being well behaved—money that they can later exchange for something they want. In fact, **contingency contracting**, a variant of the more extensive token system, has proved quite effective in producing behavior modification. In contingency contracting, a written agreement is drawn up between a therapist and patient (or teacher and student or parent and child). The contract states a series of behavioral goals that the patient hopes to attain. It also specifies the consequences for the patient if the goals are reached—usually some explicit reward such as money or additional privileges. Contracts frequently state negative consequences if the goals are not met.

Contingency contracting: Acting upon a written contract between a therapist and a patient (or parent and child, etc.) that sets behavioral goals, with rewards for achievement

For instance, suppose a person is having difficulty quitting smoking. He and his therapist might devise a contract in which he would pledge that for every day he went without a cigarette he would receive a reward. On the other hand, the contract could include punishments for failure. If the patient smoked on a given day, the therapist might send a check—written out in advance by the patient and given to the therapist to hold—to a cause the patient had no interest in supporting (for instance, the National Rifle Association if the patient is a staunch advocate of gun control).

Albert Ellis is the founder and Executive Director of the Institute for Rational-Emotive Therapy. (Courtesy of Albert Ellis.)

Where Thinking Better Leads to Feeling Better:
Cognitive-Behavioral Approaches and Rational-Emotive Therapy
Consider the following assumptions:

▶ It is necessary to be loved or approved by virtually every significant other person for everything we do.

▶ We should be thoroughly competent, adequate, and successful in all possible respects if we are to consider ourselves worthwhile.

▶ It is horrible when things don't turn out the way we want them to.

Although each of these statements verges on the absurd, psychologist Albert Ellis suggests that many people lead unhappy and sometimes even psychologically disordered lives because they harbor these very kinds of irrational, unrealistic ideas about themselves and the world (Ellis, 1962, 1975). In developing a treatment approach based on this premise—called **rational-emotive therapy**—he has suggested that the goal of therapy should be to restructure a person's belief system into a more realistic, rational, and logical set of views of the world.

Rational-emotive therapy: Psychotherapy based on Ellis's suggestion that the goal of therapy should be to restructure one's belief into a more realistic, rational, and logical system

In order to make their clients adopt more effective thinking, rational-emotive therapists take an active, directive role during therapy, openly challenging patterns of thought that appear to be dysfunctional. For example, a therapist might bluntly dispute the logic employed by a person in treatment by saying, "Why does the fact that your girlfriend left you mean that *you* are a bad person?" or "How does failing an exam indicate that you have *no* good qualities?" By pointing out the problems in clients' logic, therapists employing this form of treatment believe that people can come to adopt a more realistic view of themselves and their circumstances (Ellis & Dryden, 1987; Bernard & Joyce, 1984).

Cognitive-behavioral therapy: A process by which people's faulty cognitions about themselves and the world are changed to more accurate ones

Rational-emotive techniques exemplify an approach known as **cognitive-behavioral therapy** (McMullin, 1986; Beck, 1983). Rather than relying exclusively on overt behaviors as indicators of psychological disorder, cognitive-behavioral therapists attempt to change faulty cognitions that people hold about the world and themselves. Cognitive-behavioral therapists, then, bring an eclectic point of view to behavioral therapy, combining ideas derived from cognitive psychology with a behavioral approach.

The Crucial Question: How Does Behavior Therapy Stack Up?

Behavior therapy is quite good for certain kinds of problems. Depending on the specific problem being addressed, the success rate can range from 50 percent to as high as 90 percent (Kazdin & Wilson, 1978). For instance, behavior therapy works well for phobias and compulsions, for establishing control over impulses, and for learning complex social skills to replace maladaptive behavior. More than any of the other therapeutic techniques, it has produced methods that can be employed by nonprofessionals to change their own behavior (see the Psychology at Work box). Moreover, it tends to be economical in terms of time, since it is directed toward the solution of carefully defined problems (Marks, 1982; Wilson et al., 1987).

PSYCHOLOGY AT WORK

A fellow student, whom you don't know all that well, asks to borrow your class notes. This is the fourth time this semester he has asked you, and you feel that it is grossly unfair. But, feeling that he might become angry at you if you refuse his request, you quietly hand over your notebook.

This is not the first time you've felt that others take advantage of you, and you begin to wonder if you have a serious problem with lack of assertiveness. In fact, you begin to feel so bad about your inability to be assertive that you think about entering therapy. One day, though, a friend mentions that she was able to become more assertive entirely on her own, without professional assistance, through a technique known as behavioral self-management—and she assures you that you can do the same thing yourself.

WHEN BEING YOUR OWN THERAPIST WORKS: SELF-MANAGEMENT THROUGH BEHAVIOR MODIFICATION

Although the dangers of self-diagnosis and treatment have been emphasized a number of times—and caution should indeed always be used—there is one treatment approach that specifically allows people suffering from minor problems to "cure" themselves: behavioral self-management. In **behavioral self-management** people are taught to identify their problems and design their own ways of resolving them by using behavioral techniques.

Using techniques derived from behavioral treatment approaches, self-management has been shown to be effective in many cases for a variety of problems, including alcoholism, drug dependence, high blood pressure, stress control, poor study habits, and insomnia. Although many different strategies have been employed, they basically consist of altering the cues that promote an undesirable behavior, directly modifying a response that should be changed, and/or providing reinforcement or punishment for desirable or undesirable behavior.

The problems associated with self-assertion provide an excellent illustration of a problem that is responsive to self-management techniques. In a typical procedure, people are first asked to identify the cues and circumstances associated with a lack of assertiveness. For a student named Jim, such cues included being unable to refuse when asked for a favor and being unable to talk to strangers at a party.

To remedy his lack of assertiveness, the general strategy employed was to find some way to modify his reaction to cues that had become associated with unassertiveness. To do this, a number of goals and "rules" were set up about when, where, and how Jim should be assertive. For example, he set a goal of initiating conversations with at least two strangers at any party he went to. To accomplish this, he made a list of ways to initiate conversations, such as asking a question or making a comment on the situation, complimenting a person, and asking for help, advice, information, or an opinion.

Jim also used role playing to learn strategies for dealing with situations in which he was asked a favor. For example, he practiced scenarios in his mind—and sometimes out loud with a close friend—in which, when asked a favor, he requested time to think it over, asked for more information before agreeing or disagreeing, or simply said no to the person asking the favor.

Jim also developed a system of self-reinforcement, in which he would reward himself after acting assertively by treating himself to a movie. Moreover, he used self-punishment; when he hadn't acted assertively, he forced himself to send a check for $5 to a political party whose views he completely opposed.

By using such self-management procedures, Jim was able to become more assertive. Behavioral self-management techniques provide a means by which people can, in a sense, be their own therapists.

Behavioral self-management: A procedure in which people learn to identify and resolve their problems using techniques based on learning theory

---

Recap

◀ Psychotherapy is psychologically based therapy in which the emphasis is on producing change through discussion and interaction between client and therapist. Biologically based therapy uses drugs and other medical procedures.

◀ Psychodynamic therapy is based on Freud's notion that abnormal behavior is caused by unconscious conflicts and anxiety. To treat psychological problems, it is necessary to probe the unconscious and bring old difficulties to the surface through free association and dream interpretation.

◀ Behavioral approaches to therapy are built on the premise that people who display abnormal behavior either have failed to acquire appropriate skills or have learned faulty or maladaptive skills. To remedy the problem, it is necessary to learn new, more adaptive behaviors or unlearn old, faulty patterns of behavior.

◀ Among the approaches used by behavioral therapists are classical conditioning, including aversive conditioning and systematic desensitization; modeling; operant conditioning; and rational-emotive therapy, a cognitive-behavioral approach.

Review

1. The main purpose of psychoanalysis is to uncover repressed experiences that are causing abnormal behavior or anxiety. True or false? _____

2. Systematic desensitization, pairing a stimulus that evokes pleasant feelings with a stimulus that evokes anxiety, is used to
   a. combat the anxiety through a positive association.
   b. teach control by alternating pleasure with anxiety.
   c. break down the components of past experiences.
   d. replace pain with pleasure.

3. Six-year-old Robin watches her mother make a peanut butter sandwich. The next day, when she gets hungry, she makes one for herself. Robin has demonstrated _____ learning.

4. The practice of obtaining desired behavior by offering rewards is called a _____ system.

5. Rational-emotive therapy is a type of
   a. psychoanalysis.   c. eclectic therapy.
   b. free association.   d. cognitive-behavioral therapy.

6. To overcome your habit of biting your nails, you develop a program to monitor and control the habit. This is an example of
   a. free association.   c. aversive conditioning.
   b. resistance.   d. self-management.

(Answers to review questions are on page 602.)

As you know from your own experience, it is impossible to master the material covered in a course without some hard work, no matter how good the teacher and the textbook are. It is *you* who must take the time to study, to memorize the vocabulary, to learn the concepts. Nobody else can do it for you. If you choose to put in the effort, you'll succeed; if you don't, you'll fail. The responsibility is primarily yours.

Humanistic therapy draws upon this philosophical point of view of self-responsibility in developing treatment techniques. Although many different types of therapy fit into this category, the ideas that underlie them are the same: We have control of our own behavior; we can make choices about the kinds of lives we want to live, and it is up to us to solve the difficulties that we encounter in our daily lives. Instead of being the directive figures they are in some psychodynamic and behavioral approaches, humanistic therapists view themselves as guides or facilitators, leading people to realizations about themselves and to ways of changing in order to come closer to the ideal they hold for themselves. In this view, abnormal behavior is one result of people's inability to find meaning in life, of feeling lonely and unconnected with others, and of believing that they are pawns in a world that acts upon them without their being able to respond adequately.

Client, Heal Thyself: Client-centered Therapy

Consider the following dialogue between a therapist and a client named Alice who is seeking treatment:

Alice: I was thinking about this business of standards. I somehow devel-

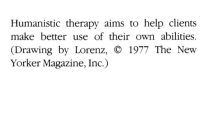

Humanistic therapy: Therapy in which the underlying assumption is that people have control of their behavior, can make choices about their lives, and are essentially responsible for solving their own problems

Humanistic therapy aims to help clients make better use of their own abilities. (Drawing by Lorenz, © 1977 The New Yorker Magazine, Inc.)

"Of course you have strengths, dear. It's just that you don't communicate them."

ANSWERS (REVIEW I):
1. True **2.** a **3.** Observational **4.** Token **5.** d **6.** d

oped a sort of a knack, I guess, of—well—habit—of trying to make people feel at ease around me, or to make things go along smoothly. . . .

Counselor: In other words, what you did was always in the direction of trying to keep things smooth and to make other people feel better and to smooth the situation.

Alice: Yes. I think that's what it was. Now the reason why I did it probably was—I mean, not that I was a good little Samaritan going around making other people happy, but that was probably the role that felt easiest for me to play. I'd been doing it around home so much. I just didn't stand up for my own convictions, until I don't know whether I have any convictions to stand up for.

Counselor: You feel that for a long time you've been playing the role of kind of smoothing out the frictions or differences or what not. . . .

Alice: M-hm.

Counselor: Rather than having any opinion or reaction of your own in the situation. Is that it?

Alice: That's it. Or that I haven't been really honest being myself, or actually knowing what my real self is, and that I've been just playing a sort of false role . . . (Rogers, 1951, pp. 151–153).

If you carefully consider the responses of the counselor, you will see that they are not interpretations or answers to questions that the client has raised. Instead, they tend to clarify or reflect back in some way what the client has said. This therapeutic technique is known as **nondirective counseling**, and it is at the heart of client-centered therapy. First practiced by Carl Rogers (1951, 1980), **client-centered therapy** is the best-known and most frequently used type of humanistic therapy.

The goal of client-centered therapy is to enable people to better reach the potential for self-actualization that is assumed to be characteristic of everyone. By providing a warm and accepting environment, therapists hope to motivate clients to air their problems and feelings, which, in turn, will enable people to make realistic and constructive choices and decisions about the things that bother them in their current lives. Instead of directing the choices clients make, then, the therapist provides what Rogers calls **unconditional positive regard**—expressing acceptance and understanding, regardless of the feelings and attitudes the client expresses—thereby creating an atmosphere in which clients are able to come to decisions that can improve their lives. It does not mean that the therapist must approve of everything the client says or does; rather, it means that the therapist must convey that the client's thoughts and behaviors are seen as genuine reflections of what the client is experiencing (Lietaer, 1984).

It is relatively rare for client-centered therapy to be used today in its purest form. Contemporary approaches are apt to be somewhat more directive, nudging clients toward insights rather than merely reflecting back their statements. However, clients' insights are still seen as central to the therapeutic process.

Freeing the Fear of Freedom: Existential Therapy

What is the meaning of life? We have all probably pondered this thought at

Nondirective counseling: A therapeutic technique in which the therapist creates a warm, supportive environment to allow the client to better understand and work out his or her problems

Client-centered therapy: Therapy in which the therapist reflects back the patient's statements in a way that causes the patient to find his or her own solutions

Unconditional positive regard: Supportive behavior from another individual, regardless of one's words or actions

Existential therapy: A humanistic approach that addresses the meaning of life, allowing a client to devise a system of values that gives purpose to his or her life

one time or another, but for some people it is a central issue in their daily existence. For those individuals who experience psychological problems as a result of difficulty in finding a satisfactory answer, existential therapy is one particularly appropriate place to turn, because this question is central to existential therapeutic techniques.

In contrast to other humanistic approaches that view humans' unique freedom and potential as a positive force, **existential therapy** is based on the premise that the inability to deal with such freedom can produce anguish, fear, and concern (May, 1969). In existential therapy, the goal is to allow individuals to come to grips with the freedom they have, to begin to understand how they fit in with the rest of the world, and to devise a system of values that permits them to give meaning to their lives. Existential therapists try to make their patients aware of the importance of free choice and the fact that they have the ultimate responsibility for making their own choices about their lives.

The specific processes used in existential therapy are more varied than in client-centered approaches. The therapist is considerably more directive in existential therapy, probing and challenging the client's views of the world. In addition, therapists will try to establish a deep and binding relationship with their clients, attempting to be as open with them about their own feelings and points of view as possible. Their objective is to allow clients to see that they share in the difficulties and experiences that arise in trying to deal with the freedom that is part of being human.

Making People Whole in a Fragmented World: Gestalt Therapy

Have you ever thought back to some childhood incident in which you were treated unfairly and again felt the rage that you had experienced at that time? To therapists working in a gestalt perspective, the healthiest thing for you to do psychologically might be to act out that rage—by hitting a pillow, kicking a chair, or yelling in frustration. In fact, this sort of activity represents an important part of what goes on in gestalt therapy sessions, in which the client is encouraged to act out past conflicts and difficulties.

The rationale for this approach to treatment is that it is necessary for people to integrate their thoughts, feelings, and behaviors into a gestalt, the German term for "whole" (as we discussed in reference to perception in Chapter 4). According to Fritz Perls (1967, 1970), who developed **gestalt therapy**, the way to do this is for people to examine their earlier experience and complete any "unfinished business" from their past that still affects and colors present-day relationships. Specifically, Perls assumed that people should reenact the specific conflicts that they experienced earlier. For instance, a client might first play the part of his angry father, and then play himself when his father yelled at him, in order to experience the different parts of a conflict. By increasing their perspectives on a situation, clients are better able to understand their problems and to experience life in a more unified, honest, and complete way.

Gestalt therapy: An approach that attempts to integrate thoughts, feelings, and behavior into a whole

Can You Become More Human in the Consulting Room?: Humanistic Approaches in Perspective

You may be bothered by the lack of specificity of the humanistic treatments, and this is a problem that has also troubled its critics. Humanistic approaches are, in fact, not very precise and are probably the least scientifically and theoretically developed type of treatment. Moreover, this form of treatment

In gestalt therapy, people closely examine, and sometimes try to recreate, experiences from their childhood. (Alex Webb/Magnum.)

is best suited for the same type of highly verbal client who profits most from psychoanalytic treatment.

On the other hand, the emphasis of humanistic approaches on what is uniquely human and their acknowledgment that the freedom we possess can lead to psychological difficulties work to provide an unusually supportive environment for therapy. In turn, this atmosphere can aid in finding solutions to difficult psychological problems.

GROUP THERAPY

Although most treatment takes place with a single individual and therapist, some forms of therapy involve groups of people seeking treatment. In **group therapy**, several unrelated people meet with a therapist to discuss some aspect of their psychological functioning.

Group therapy: Therapy in which people discuss problems with a group

People typically discuss their problems with the group, which is often centered around a particular difficulty, such as alcoholism or a lack of social skills. The other members of the group provide emotional support, as well as dispensing advice on ways in which they have coped effectively with similar problems (Lewis, 1987).

Groups vary a great deal not only in the particular model that is employed (there are psychoanalytic groups, humanistic groups, and groups corresponding to the other therapeutic aproaches) but also in the degree of guidance the therapist provides. In some groups, the therapist is quite directive; in others, the members of the group set their own agenda and determine how the group will proceed.

Because several people are treated simultaneously in group therapy, it is a much more economical means of treatment than individual psychotherapy. On the other hand, critics argue that group settings do not afford the individual attention inherent in one-to-one therapy, and especially shy and withdrawn individuals may not receive the necessary attention in a group.

Family Therapy

One specialized form of group therapy is family therapy. As the name implies, **family therapy** involves two or more members of the same family, one (or

Family therapy: An approach that focuses on the family as a whole unit to which each member contributes more) of whose problems led to treatment. But rather than focusing simply on members of the family who present the initial problem, family therapists consider the family as a whole unit, to which each member contributes. By meeting with the entire family simultaneously, family therapists attempt to obtain a sense of how the family members interact with one another.

Family therapists view the family as a "system," and they assume that the separate individuals in the family cannot improve without understanding the conflicts that are to be found in the interactions of the family members. Thus each member is expected to contribute to the resolution of individual problems.

Many family therapists assume that family members fall into rigid roles or set patterns of behavior, with one person acting as the scapegoat, another as a bully, and so forth. In their view, family disturbances are perpetuated by the system of roles. One goal of this type of therapy, then, is to get the family to adopt new, more constructive patterns of roles (Minuchin, 1974).

COMPARING PSYCHOTHERAPEUTIC APPROACHES

We have seen that there are a variety of forms of psychotherapy. In order to compare them, we can classify them along several dimensions. Among the most important are (Carson, Butcher & Coleman, 1988):

▶ Directive versus nondirective. In some forms of therapy, the therapist takes considerably more responsibility for the person being treated than in others. In directive therapy, the therapist takes an active role, whereas in nondirective therapy, the therapist acts more as a facilitator, helping clients clarify their own feelings. Among the most directive are the behavioral approaches. In contrast, psychodynamic and humanistic approaches are considerably less directive.

▶ Inner control of behavior versus outer control of behavior. In the psychodynamic and humanistic approaches, behavior is seen as largely under the control of the individual. In contrast, behavioral approaches to therapy view behavior primarily as the result of environmental factors. Cognitive-behavioral approaches take an intermediate view, seeing behavior determined not only by environmental factors but by internal cognitions as well.

▶ Long-term versus short-term therapy. Therapeutic approaches vary widely in terms of the typical length of treatment. Traditional psychoanalysis is the longest lasting, potentially stretching on for years. Today, however, most therapy is considerably shorter and may take as few as two or three sessions, depending on the nature of the problem being addressed.

▶ Historical focus versus here-and-now focus. Some kinds of therapy pay primary attention to events from the past that are assumed to be affecting current behavior. Psychodynamic approaches fall into such a category. In contrast, behavioral approaches stress the present, minimizing the consequences of early experiences. Other approaches fall in between.

▶ Cognitive change versus behavior change. Some kinds of therapy, particularly psychodynamic and cognitive-behavioral approaches, emphasize changes in attitudes, perceptions, feelings, and cognitions about the world and assume that a change in those characteristics will produce more adaptive behavior. In contrast, behavioral approaches emphasize the change of behavior itself.

It is important to remember, although they are presented in an either/ or fashion, that each of these dimensions of therapy marks the end point of a continuum. Most therapeutic approaches will not fall squarely on one or the other end of the continuum but rather will lie somewhere in between.

EVALUATING PSYCHOTHERAPY

Your best friend at school, Colette, comes to you because she just hasn't been feeling right about things lately. She's upset because she and her boy-friend aren't getting along, but her difficulties go beyond that. She can't concentrate on her studies, has a lot of trouble getting to sleep, and—this is what really bothers her—she's begun to think that people are ganging up on her, talking about her behind her back. It just seems that no one really cares about or understands her or makes any effort to see why she's become so miserable.

Colette is aware that she ought to get *some* kind of help, but she is not sure where to turn. She is fairly skeptical of psychologists and psychiatrists, thinking that a lot of what they say is just mumbo-jumbo, but she's willing to put her doubts aside and try anything to feel better. She also knows there are many different types of therapy, and she doesn't have a clue as to which would be best for her. She turns to you for advice, since she knows you are taking a psychology course. She asks, "Which kind of therapy works best?"

Such a question requires a complex response, for there is no easy answer. In fact, identifying which form of treatment is most appropriate is a controversial, and still unresolved, task for psychologists specializing in abnormal behavior. For example, even before considering whether any one form of therapy works better than another, we need to determine whether therapy in *any* form is effective in alleviating psychological disturbances.

Fortunately, most psychologists agree: Therapy does work. Several recent comprehensive reviews indicate that therapy brings about greater improvement than does no treatment at all—although it represents a surprisingly controversial issue, as the Research Classics box suggests (Luborsky, Singer & Luborsky, 1975; Smith, Glass & Miller, 1980; Garfeld, 1983; Landman & Dawes, 1984; Bowers & Clum, 1988). Furthermore, the rate of **spontaneous remission**—recovery without treatment—is fairly low; in most cases the symptoms of abnormal behavior do not go away by themselves if left untreated (Bergin & Lambert, 1978).

Spontaneous remission: Recovery without treatment

Which Kind of Therapy Works Best?

Although most psychologists feel confident that psychotherapeutic treatment *in general* is more effective than no treatment at all, the question of whether any specific form of treatment is superior to any others has yet to be answered definitively (Bowers & Clum, 1988; Orwin & Condray, 1984). In part, this is due to methodological issues. For instance, it is difficult to equate the "cures" that various forms of treatment produce, because qualitatively they may be very different. Is the reduction of depression-related anxiety obtained from psychodynamic treatment equivalent to the reduction of phobia-related anxiety brought about by behavior therapy? In both cases the problems are alleviated—but, if we were keeping a tally of cures versus noncures for the two forms of treatment, would they each receive one point? You can see the difficulties involved in comparing types of treatment.

The problems, however, are not insurmountable. One solution has been

DOES PSYCHOTHERAPY WORK?

Until the 1950s most people simply assumed that therapy, on the face of it, was an effective strategy for resolving psychological difficulties. But in 1952 psychologist Hans Eysenck published an influential article, reviewing the published literature on the subject, which challenged this widely held assumption. He claimed that people who received psychodynamic treatment and related therapies were no better off at the end of treatment than those people who were placed on a waiting list for treatment—but never received it. According to his analysis, about two-thirds of the people who reported suffering from "neurotic" symptoms believed that those symptoms had disappeared after two years, regardless of whether or not they had been in therapy. Eysenck concluded that people suffering from neurotic symptoms would go into spontaneous remission, recovery without treatment, if they were simply left alone—certainly a cheaper and simpler process.

As you can imagine, Eysenck's review was controversial from the start, and its conclusions were quickly challenged. Critics pointed to the inadequacy of the data he reviewed, suggesting that he was basing his conclusions on studies that contained a number of flaws.

Many potential sources of error exist in studies of the effectiveness of psychotherapy. Most often, the data are based on therapist and patient self-reports, which may be biased and unreliable. All the parties involved are motivated to see themselves as successful, so all may report an improvement in psychological functioning when none really exists. Only when independent judges are used to determine how much progress a person has made can we be assured that the self-report is accurate. Even the use of judges has its drawbacks, however, since no well-agreed-upon set of criteria exists to determine what constitutes good and bad mental health. For all these reasons, then, critics of Eysenck's review rejected his findings.

Nonetheless, Eysenck's early review did serve to stimulate a continuing stream of better-controlled, carefully crafted studies on the effectiveness of psychotherapy, and today we can say, with confidence, that psychotherapy *is* effective.

to compare the "cure" rate for a particular form of treatment with the "cure" rate for a group of untreated controls. Next, we could do the same thing with another type of treatment and compare this cure rate with its own untreated control. Finally, we could see which of the two forms of therapy produced a higher cure rate. For instance, we could take a sample of people who, because of the nature of their problems, would be "eligible" for psychodynamic treatment, treat half of them, and compare their results to the untreated half. By following the same procedure with a group of people "eligible" for another form of treatment, we could infer which kind of treatment was most successful.

Using this kind of procedure, Smith, Glass & Miller (1980) came to the conclusions displayed in Figure 17-1. As you can see, although there is some variation among the success rates of the various treatment forms, most are fairly close to one another, ranging from about 70 to 85 percent greater success for treated than for untreated individuals. There is a slight tendency for behavioral approaches and cognitive-behavioral approaches to be a bit more successful, although this may be due to differences in the severity of cases treated (Orwin & Condray, 1984). In sum, research generally finds only minor differences among the success rates for various types of therapy (Berman, Miller & Massman, 1985).

This finding does not mean that every problem will be resolved equally well by different sorts of therapy. Recall the way that therapy-comparison studies are typically carried out: They initially consider only problems appropriate for a given treatment approach, and then compare treated versus untreated people within that specific approach to see which group of people

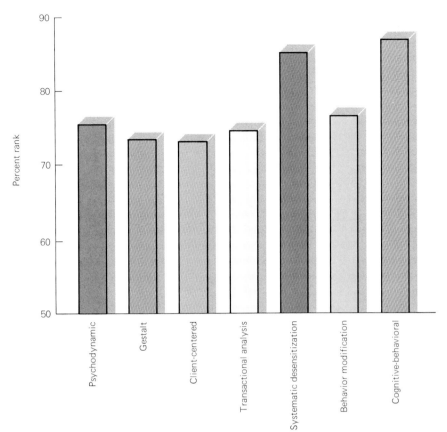

FIGURE 17-1

Estimates of the effectiveness of different types of treatment, in comparison to control groups of untreated people. The percentile score shows how much more effective a particular type of treatment is for the average patient than is no treatment. For example, people given psychodynamic treatment score, on average, more positively on outcome measures than about 75 percent of untreated people. (Adapted from Smith, Glass, & Miller, 1980.)

does better. Such studies say little about whether specific sorts of problems are better treated by one approach or another (Garfield, 1983). Furthermore, in some cases—perhaps as many as 10 percent—psychotherapy actually *hurts* participants: They would have been better off if they had not undertaken it (Lambert, Shapiro & Bergin, 1986; Luborsky, 1988).

It is clear, then, that particular kinds of therapies are more appropriate for some problems than for others—a point made when we considered each of the specific treatment approaches earlier (Klerman, 1983). For example, if someone is suffering from the kind of general unhappiness and anxiety described by Colette in the earlier scenario, psychodynamic or humanistic approaches, which emphasize gaining insight into one's problems, would probably be most appropriate. On the other hand, if Colette's problems had been focused more on a particular set of circumstances that brought about her anxiety—such as a phobia or a lack of good study skills that was preventing her from doing well in school—then a behavioral approach might be more reasonable.

Similarly, it might be more appropriate for therapists with certain personal characteristics to work with particular people, and certain kinds of people may be more appropriately treated by one approach than another. For example, a behavioral approach may be more suitable for people who have difficulty expressing themselves verbally or who lack the patience or ability to engage in sustained introspection, qualities that are necessary for a psychodynamic approach.

Finally, there are an increasing number of eclectic approaches to therapy, in which a therapist uses techniques taken from a variety of approaches to treat a person's problems. By using eclectic procedures, the therapist is able to choose the appropriate mix in accordance with the specific needs of the individual (Nelson, 1983).

The question of which therapy works best, then, cannot be answered without reference to the specific type of psychological problem that is being treated. The accuracy of the match between individual problems and therapeutic methods best determines the likelihood of success. Overall, though, it is clear that psychotherapy, in general, provides an effective means for solving psychological difficulties.

Given the general agreement that psychotherapy is effective, some recent research efforts have been devoted to answering the question of whether the judgments of clinical psychologists relating to the diagnosis and treatment of abnormal behavior are best made on the basis of "clinical" versus "actuarial" methods (Dawes, Faust, & Meehl, 1989). In "clinical" methods—the traditional judgment technique—decisions are made on the basis of knowledge, prior experience, and information available in the psychologist's head.

In contrast, "actuarial" judgments are based on a formal statistical rule or formula in which specific information is combined in a predetermined way. The particular rule or formula that is employed is developed on the basis of the prior collection of data relevant to the decision. For example, a psychologist using an actuarial judgment process might administer a series of standardized tests and, using a rule based on earlier research, combine the test results and define anyone who scored above a certain level on each of the tests as being severely depressed. Such a procedure would contrast with the more traditional "clinical" approach, in which the psychologist would make more intuitive judgments, based on his or her previous experience and understanding of how test scores fit together (Garb, 1989).

Because the actuarial method challenges more traditional clinical practices, its use has been controversial. While some clinical psychologists argue that it provides a more objective, scientific means of making diagnoses and treatment judgments, critics respond that subjective appraisal is a critical component of treatment for psychological disorders and that applying statistics about groups to individuals ignores the individuality of particular cases. Furthermore, critics suggest that the use of actuarial methods dehumanizes patients.

It is far too early to tell if actuarial methods will come to replace clinical techniques, and clinical judgment approaches remain the choice of most psychologists. Still, if actuarial approaches become more sophisticated and are developed to cover a wide domain of psychological disorders, their use is likely to increase (Dawes, Faust, & Meehl, 1989).

Recap

◄ Humanistic approaches view therapy as a way to help people solve their own problems; the therapist merely acts as a guide or facilitator.

◄ Among the types of humanistic therapies are client-centered therapy, existential therapy, and gestalt therapy.

◄ The major dimensions along which therapies can be evaluated are directive versus nondirective, inner control of behavior versus outer control of behavior, long-term versus short-term, historical focus versus here-and-now focus, and cognitive change versus behavior change.

◄ A long-standing issue is whether psychotherapy is effective, and, if it is, whether one kind is superior to others.

Review

1. Match the names of the following treatment strategies with the statements you might expect to hear from a therapist.
   a. Gestalt therapy
   b. Group therapy
   c. Unconditional positive regard
   d. Behavioral therapy
   e. Nondirective counseling
   ____ "In other words, you don't get along with your mother because she hates your dog, is that right?"

____ "I want you all to take turns talking about why you decided to come, and what you hope to gain in therapy."
____ "I can understand why you wanted to wreck your friend's car after she hurt your feelings. Now, can you tell me more about the accident?"
____ "That's not appropriate behavior. Let's work on replacing it with something else."
____ "Remember the anger you felt and scream until you feel better."

2. Reconciling a client with his or her concerns about free will and the meaning of life is an aim of _____ therapy.

3. _____ therapy emphasizes the integration of thoughts, feelings, and behaviors.

4. Hans Eysenck's conclusions about the effectiveness of psychotherapy suggest that
   a. no one method is superior to the others.
   b. people receiving no treatment fare as well as those receiving treatment.
   c. the humanistic approach is the most client-sensitive kind of therapy.
   d. the humanistic approach results in longer-lasting results.

5. Treatments that combine methodology from all theoretical approaches are called _____ procedures.

(Answers to review questions are on page 612.)

THE MEDICAL MODEL AT WORK: BIOLOGICAL TREATMENT APPROACHES

If you get a kidney infection, you're given some penicillin and, with luck, about a week later your kidney is as good as new. If your appendix becomes inflamed, a surgeon removes it and your body functions normally once more. Could an analogous approach, focusing on the body's physiology, be taken with psychological disturbances?

According to biological approaches to treatment, the answer is affirmative. In fact, biologically based treatments are used routinely for certain kinds of problems. The basic model suggests that, rather than focusing on a patient's psychological conflicts, past traumas, or environmental factors that may support abnormal behavior, it is more appropriate in certain cases to treat brain chemistry and other neurological factors directly. This can be done through the use of drugs, electric shock, or surgery.

MEDICINE FOR MENTAL DISTURBANCES: Drug Therapy

Are we close to the day when we will take a pill each morning to maintain good psychological health, in the same way that we now take a vitamin pill to help us stay physically healthy? Although that day has not yet arrived, there are quite a few forms of **drug therapy** that successfully alleviate symptoms of a number of psychological disturbances.

Drug therapy: Control of psychological problems through drugs

PART 6

Antipsychotic drugs: Drugs that temporarily alleviate psychotic symptoms such as agitation and overactivity

Chlorpromazine (klor PRO mah zeen): An antipsychotic drug that is used in the treatment of schizophrenia

Antipsychotic Drugs

Probably no greater change has occurred in mental hospitals than the successful introduction in the mid-1950s of **antipsychotic drugs**—drugs used to alleviate psychotic symptoms such as agitation and overactivity. Previously, mental hospitals typically fulfilled all the stereotypes of the insane asylum—with screaming, moaning, clawing patients displaying the most bizarre behaviors. Suddenly, in just a matter of months, the hospital wards became considerably calmer environments in which professionals could do more than just try to get the patients through the day without serious harm to themselves or others.

This dramatic change was brought about by the introduction of a drug from the phenothiazine family called **chlorpromazine**. This drug, and others of similar type, rapidly became the most popular—and successful—treatment for schizophrenia. Today drug therapy is the preferred treatment for most cases of severely abnormal behavior, used for almost 90 percent of all hospitalized patients (Carson, 1983; MacDonald & Tobias, 1976).

How do antipsychotic drugs work? They seem to function by blocking the production of dopamine at the sites where electric impulses travel across nerve receptors, a process we discussed in Chapter 16 (Kane, 1983). Unfortunately, they do not produce a "cure" in the same way that, say, penicillin cures an infection—because as soon as the drug is withdrawn, the original symptoms tend to reappear. Moreover, such drugs can have long-term side effects, such as dryness of the mouth and throat, dizziness, and even the development of tremors and loss of muscle control that may continue even after drug treatments are stopped (Kane & Siris, 1983).

Perhaps even more devastating than these physical side effects are the numbing effects of antipsychotic drugs on the emotional responses of patients. For example, Mark Vonnegut (son of author Kurt Vonnegut) describes his reactions to the use of the antipsychotic drug Thorazine while he was institutionalized for schizophrenia:

> What the drug is supposed to do is keep away hallucinations. What I think it does is just fog up your mind so badly you don't notice the hallucinations or much else.... On Thorazine everything's a bore. Not

Antipsychotic drugs have alleviated the symptoms of several different types of serious mental disturbances. (Kenneth Karp.)

a bore, exactly. Boredom implies impatience. You can read comic books
… you can tolerate talking to jerks forever…. The weather is dull, the
flowers are dull, nothing's very impressive (Vonnegut, 1975, pp.
196–197).

Antidepressant Drugs

As you might guess from the name, **antidepressant drugs** are a class of medications used in cases of severe depression to improve the moods of patients.
They were discovered quite by accident: It was found that patients suffering
from tuberculosis who were given the drug iproniazid suddenly became
happier and more optimistic. When the same drug was tested on people
suffering from depression, a similar result occurred, and drugs became an
accepted form of treatment for depression (McNeal & Cimbolic, 1986).

Most antidepressant drugs work by allowing an increase in the concentration of certain neurotransmitters in the brain (see Chapter 2). For example,
tricyclic drugs modify the amount of norepinephrine and serotonin within
the brain; others, such as bupropion, operate by affecting the neurotransmitter dopamine (Schmeck, 1988). Although antidepressant drugs may produce side effects such as drowsiness and faintness, the overall success rate
is quite good (Prien, 1983; Siris & Rifkin, 1983). In fact, unlike antipsychotic
drugs, antidepressants can produce lasting, long-term recoveries from
depression; in many cases, even after the drugs are no longer being taken,
the depression does not return.

Lithium, a form of simple mineral salts, is another drug that has been
used very successfully in cases of bipolar disorders. Although no one knows
definitely why it works (it has no known physiological function), it is very
effective in reducing manic episodes, ending manic behavior some 70 percent of the time. On the other hand, its effectiveness in resolving depression
is not as impressive. It works only in certain cases, and, like other antidepressants, it can produce a number of side effects (Coopen, Metcalfe & Wood,
1982).

Lithium has a quality that sets it apart from other drug treatments: It
represents, more than any other drug, a *preventive* treatment. People who
have been subject to manic-depressive episodes in the past often can, after
returning to a normal state, take a daily dose of lithium that prevents a
recurrence of their symptoms. Lithium, then, presents one thought-provoking vision of the future, suggested by medical-model aproaches to abnormal
behavior: a future in which people take drugs regularly to make them psychologically healthier. The reality, though, is that for better or for worse,
such a future is far away.

The Minor Tranquilizers: Antianxiety Drugs

Valium, Miltown, Librium—perhaps you are familiar with these drug names,
which are among the most common of all the drugs physicians prescribe. A
cure for infection? Relief of the common cold? On the contrary, these drugs
have nothing to do with physical symptoms. Instead, they are members of a
class of drugs known as **antianxiety drugs** (sometimes known as minor tranquilizers) which are prescribed—often by family physicians—to alleviate the
stress and anxiety experienced by patients during particularly difficult periods of their lives. In fact, more than half of all Americans have a family
member who has taken such a drug at one time or another.

As the name implies, antianxiety drugs reduce the level of anxiety experienced, essentially by reducing excitability and in part by increasing drow-

Antidepressant drugs: Medication that improves a depressed patient's mood and feeling of well-being

Lithium (LITH ee um): A drug used in the treatment of bipolar disorders

Antianxiety drugs: Drugs that alleviate stress and anxiety siness. They are used not only to reduce general tension in people who are experiencing temporary difficulties but also to aid in the treatment of more serious anxiety disorders.

Although the popularity of antianxiety drugs suggests that they are relatively risk-free, in fact they can produce a number of potentially serious side effects. For instance, they can cause fatigue, and long-term use can lead to dependence. Moreover, taken in combination with alcohol, some antianxiety drugs can become lethal. But a more important question concerns their use to suppress anxiety. Since almost every theoretical approach to psychological disturbance views continuing anxiety as a symptom of some sort of problem, drugs that mask anxiety may be hiding difficulties that might be more appropriately faced and solved—rather than simply being glossed over.

ELECTROCONVULSIVE THERAPY (ECT)

If you thought that people who have epilepsy—a disorder characterized by seizures and convulsions—were immune to schizophrenia, what might you conclude? A number of psychiatrists in the 1930s, who mistakenly believed that a relationship did exist, concluded that if some way could be found to actually induce convulsions in patients with schizophrenia, they might be cured. To this end, two Italian physicians, Cerletti and Bini (Bini, 1938) tried to induce convulsions by administering shocks to the heads of patients suffering from schizophrenia—and reported some success in alleviating its symptoms.

Electroconvulsive therapy (ECT): Treatment involving the administration of an electric current to a patient's head to treat depression

The use of **electroconvulsive therapy (ECT)** has continued to the present, although the way in which it is administered has been improved. An electric current of 70 to 150 volts is passed through the head of a patient for about a second and a half, causing the patient to lose consciousness and often experience a seizure. Usually the patient is sedated and receives muscle relaxants prior to administration of the current, helping to prevent violent contractions. The typical patient receives about ten such treatments in the course of a month (Breggin, 1979; Weiner, 1982).

Dr. Richard B. Weiner of Duke University Medical Center reads a patient's EEG as technicians administer electroconvulsive therapy. ECT is used in the treatment of severe depression. (Will McIntyre/Photo Researchers.)

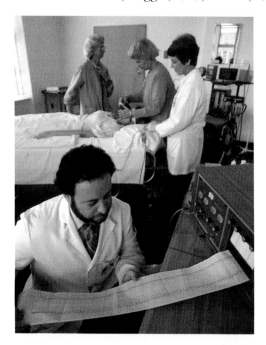

As you might expect, ECT is a controversial technique. Apart from the obvious distastefulness of a treatment that evokes images of capital punishment, there are frequent side effects. For instance, following treatment, patients often experience disorientation, confusion, and sometimes memory loss that may remain for months. Moreover, many patients fear ECT, even though they are anesthetized during the actual treatment and thus experience no pain. Finally, we still do not know how or why ECT works, and although it has never been proved, there is the reasonable fear that the treatment may produce permanent neurological damage to the brain (Fisher, 1985).

Given the drawbacks to ECT, why is it used at all? The basic reason is that in many cases it still seems to be an effective treatment for severe cases of depression (Sackheim, 1985). Indeed, although it is less popular today than it once was, some surveys suggest that the use of ECT rose in the 1980s (Harvard Medical School, 1987). Still, ECT tends to be used only in cases when other treatments have proved ineffective.

PSYCHOSURGERY

If ECT strikes you as a questionable procedure, the use of **psychosurgery**—brain surgery in which the object is to alleviate symptoms of mental disorder—will likely appear even more so. A technique that has largely disappeared, psychosurgery was first introduced as a treatment of "last resort" in the 1930s. The procedure—specifically, a **prefrontal lobotomy**—consists of surgically destroying or removing certain parts of a patient's frontal lobes, which control emotionality. The rationale for this procedure was that destroying the connections between various parts of the brain would make patients less subject to emotional impulses, and their general behavior would improve.

In fact, psychosurgery often did improve a patient's behavior—but not without drastic side effects. For along with remission of symptoms of mental disorder, patients sometimes suffered personality changes, becoming bland, colorless, and unemotional. In other cases, patients became aggressive and unable to control their impulses; in the worst cases, the patients died from treatment.

Despite these problems—and the obvious ethical questions regarding the appropriateness of forever altering someone's personality—psychosurgery was used in thousands of cases in the 1930s and 1940s. In fact, the treatment became so routine that in some places fifty patients a day received psychosurgery (Freeman, 1959).

With the advent of effective drug treatments, psychosurgery became practically obsolete. It is still used, in modified form, in very rare cases when all other procedures have failed and the patient's behavior presents a high risk to self and others or when there is severe, uncontrollable pain in terminal cases. When psychosurgery is used today, more precise techniques are employed, and only extremely small areas of brain tissue are destroyed. Still, even in these cases, important ethical issues are raised, and psychosurgery remains a highly controversial treatment (Valenstein, 1980).

Psychosurgery: Brain surgery, once used to alleviate symptoms of mental disorder but rarely used today

Prefrontal lobotomy: The surgical destruction of certain areas of a patient's frontal lobes to improve the control of emotionality

CAN ABNORMAL BEHAVIOR BE CURED?:
Biological Treatment in Perspective

In some respects, there has been no greater revolution in the field of mental health than that represented by the biological approaches to treatment. Mental hospitals have been able to concentrate more on actually helping patients and less on custodial functions as previously violent, uncontrollable patients have been calmed by the use of drugs. Similarly, patients whose lives have been disrupted by depression or manic-depressive episodes have been able to function normally, and other forms of drug therapy in particular have shown remarkable results. Furthermore, innovative forms of biological treatment are continually being developed (as discussed in the Cutting Edge box).

On the other hand, biological therapies can be criticized. For one thing, in many cases they merely provide relief of the *symptoms* of mental disorder; as soon as the drugs are withdrawn, the symptoms return. Although it is

THE CUTTING EDGE

LET THE LIGHT SHINE IN: NEW TREATMENTS FOR DEPRESSION

In treatment for severe depression, the patient lay down in a small room in the early morning hours. As she comfortably reclined on the bed, a series of bright lights were lit. For two hours, the patient stayed in the room, bathed in the artificial light. Then, her therapy over for the day, she left, knowing that the next morning she would return for another treatment.

Experimental evidence has begun to accumulate suggesting a new treatment for certain kinds of depression: exposure to light. In a study reported by a team of researchers at the Oregon Health Sciences University, a group of patients who regularly suffered from depression in the winter—when the length of the days shortens—were exposed to bright lights at various parts of the day. The results showed that when the patients were exposed to two hours of bright light in the early morning, their depression lifted. In contrast, bright-light exposure in the evening had no effect (Lewy, Sack, Miller & Hoban, 1987).

The antidepressive effects of morning exposure to bright light were accompanied by a shift in the timing of the patients' production of the chemical melatonin, which typically follows a predictable pattern during the day. It appears, then, that the exposure to light produced a change in the patients' natural biological rhythms, and this suggests

that their depression may have stemmed from disorders in their natural biological rhythms, which exposure to light—at the appropriate time—corrected.

If the potential of light exposure as a treatment for certain kinds of depression becomes realized—and it should be stressed that the technique is experimental at this point— it will join several other new forms of therapy that are being devised for the treatment of psychological disorders. Of course, the implementation of new therapies raises the issue, once more, of which type of therapy is the most effective in treating abnormal behavior—an issue that is being addressed continually by researchers.

For example, one study examined the question of which type of therapy is optimal for the treatment of depression, and the results were immediately controversial. In a major study presented at a meeting of the American Psychiatric Association, a team of researchers found that two forms of psychotherapy were as effective as a standard drug regimen in treating depression (Boffey, 1986; Elkin et al., 1986). The study found that both cognitive behavior therapy

and a type of treatment labeled "interpersonal" psychotherapy—which focuses on patients' interpersonal problems and social functioning— were at least as effective as drug therapy in reducing the symptoms of depression and improving the functioning of patients.

In the study, 250 patients who were either moderately or severely depressed were divided randomly into three experimental groups and an untreated control group. The patients assigned to the two psychotherapy groups were given sixteen weeks of treatment; the third experimental group was given an antidepressant drug. The control group received a biologically inactive placebo, plus informal weekly support consultations with a therapist.

Approximately 50 to 60 percent of the patients in the treatment groups became fully recovered, in contrast to less than 30 percent in the untreated control group. No significant differences in recovery rates were found among the three treatment groups.

The study is continuing, with eighteen-month follow-ups planned. It is clear from even these preliminary results, however, that the question of which therapy approach is most effective is far from being answered with certainty, and that new techniques will continue to be developed.

considered a major step in the right direction, biological treatment does not solve the underlying problem that may continue to haunt a patient even while he or she is undergoing treatment. Moreover, biological therapies can have numerous side effects, ranging from physical reactions to the development of *new* symptoms of abnormal behavior (Elkin, 1986). For these reasons, then, biologically based treatment approaches do not represent a cure-all for psychological disorders.

FOCUS ON PREVENTION: Community Psychology

All the treatments that we have reviewed in this chapter have a common element: They are "restorative" treatments, aimed at alleviating psychological difficulties that already exist. However, a new movement, dubbed **community psychology**, is geared toward a different aim: to prevent or minimize psychological disorders.

Community psychology: A movement aimed toward preventing or minimizing psychological disorders in the community

Community psychology came of age in the 1960s, when plans were developed for a nationwide network of community mental-health centers. These centers were meant to provide low-cost mental-health services, including short-term therapy and community educational programs. Moreover, over the last thirty years, the population of mental hospitals plunged, as drug treatments made physical restraint of patients unnecessary. The influx of former mental patients into the community, known as **deinstitutionalization**, further spurred the community psychology movement, which was concerned with ensuring not only that the deinstitutionalized received proper treatment but that their civil rights were maintained (Melton & Garrison, 1987).

Deinstitutionalization: The transfer of former mental patients from institutions into the community

Although the original goals of the field of community psychology have not yet been met—the incidence of mental disorders has shown no decline, for instance, and many people who need treatment do not get it (Shapiro et al., 1984)—the movement has yielded several encouraging by-products. One of these is the installation of telephone "hot lines" in cities throughout the United States. People undergoing acute stress can call a telephone number at any time of day or night and talk to a trained, sympathetic listener who can give immediate—although quite limited—treatment.

The college crisis center is another innovation to grow out of the community psychology movement. Modeled after suicide prevention hotline centers (places for potential suicide victims to call and speak to someone about their difficulties), campus crisis centers provide callers with the opportunity to discuss life crises with a sympathetic listener, who is most often a student volunteer.

Although not professionals, the volunteers receive careful training in telephone counseling. They role-play particular problems and are told how to respond to the difficulties they may confront with callers. The volunteers also hold group meetings to discuss the kinds of problems they are encountering and to share experiences about the kinds of strategies that are most effective.

Because they are not professionals, the staff members of college crisis centers do not, of course, offer long-term therapy to those who contact them. But they are able to provide callers with a supportive, constructive response—often when it is most needed. They are also able to refer callers to appropriate agencies on and off campus to get the long-term help they need.

Suppose your friend Colette, who sought your advice on the most effective kind of therapy, decides on the general nature of the treatment that she wants and begins therapy. How does she know that she has chosen the right therapist?

Once again, there is no simple answer. There are, however, a number of factors that informed consumers of psychological services can and should take into consideration to determine whether they have made the right choice.

▶ The relationship between client and therapist should be a comfortable one; the client should not be afraid or in awe of the therapist but should trust the therapist and feel free to discuss the most personal issues without fearing a negative reaction.

▶ The therapist should have appropriate training and credentials for the type of therapy that he or she is conducting and should be licensed by appropriate state and local agencies. Far from being a breach of etiquette to ask a therapist on an initial visit about the kind of training that he or she received, it behooves a wise consumer of psychological services to make such an inquiry.

▶ Clients should feel that they are making progress toward resolving their psychological difficulties after therapy has begun, despite occasional setbacks (Goleman, 1988). Although there is no set timetable, the most obvious changes resulting from therapy tend to occur relatively early in the course of treatment (Howard & Zola, 1988). (Later, however, change may take longer, as more deep-seated problems are attacked.) If a client has no sense of improvement after repeated visits, this issue should be frankly discussed, with an eye toward the possibility of making a change. Most therapy today is of fairly brief duration, especially that involving college students—who average just five therapy sessions (Nowicki & Duke, 1978).

▶ Clients should be aware that they will have to put in a great deal of effort in therapy. Although ours is a culture that promises quick cures for any problem—as anyone who has perused the self-help shelves of bookstores knows—in reality solving difficult problems is far from easy (Rosen, 1987). People must be committed to making therapy work and should know that it is they, and not the therapist, who must do most of the work to resolve their problems. The potential is there for the effort to pay off handsomely—as people experience more positive, fulfilling, and meaningful lives.

Recap

◀ Biological treatment approaches encompass drug therapy, electric-shock therapy, and surgical therapy.

◀ Drug therapy has produced dramatic reductions in psychotic behavior. Among the medications used are antipsychotic drugs, antidepressant drugs, and antianxiety drugs.

◀ Electroconvulsive therapy (ECT) consists of passing an electric current through the brain of patients suffering from severe psychological disturbances, particularly schizophrenia and depression.

◀ The most extreme form of biological therapy is psychosurgery, in which patients undergo brain surgery. Although rarely used today, prefrontal lobotomies were once a common form of treatment.

◀ Community psychology aims to prevent or minimize psychological disorders.

Review

1. Like penicillin, antipsychotic drugs have provided effective, long-term, and complete cures for schizophrenia. True or false? _____

2. One of the most effective biological treatments for psychological disorders, used mainly to arrest and prevent manic-depressive episodes, is
   a. chlorpromazine.
   b. lithium.
   c. Librium.
   d. Valium.

3. Originally a treatment for schizophrenia, _____ _____ involves administering electric current to a patient's head.

4. Psychosurgery has grown in popularity as a method of treatment as surgical techniques have become more precise. True or false? _____

5. The trend toward releasing more patients from mental hospitals into the community is known as _____.

(Answers to review questions are on page 620.)

1. Although the specific treatment types are diverse, psychologically based therapy, known as psychotherapy, and biologically based therapy share the goal of resolving psychological problems by modifying people's thoughts, feelings, expectations, evaluations, and ultimately their behavior.

2. Psychoanalytic treatment is based on Freud's psychodynamic theory. It seeks to bring unresolved past conflicts and unacceptable impulses from the unconscious into the conscious, where the problems may be dealt with more effectively. To do this, patients meet frequently with their therapists and use techniques such as free association and dream interpretation. The process can be a difficult one, because of patient resistance and transference, and there is no unquestioned evidence that the process works.

3. Behavioral approaches to treatment view abnormal behavior itself as the problem, rather than viewing the behavior as a symptom of some underlying cause. In order to bring about a "cure," this view suggests that the outward behavior must be changed. In aversive conditioning, unpleasant stimuli are linked to a behavior that the patient enjoys but wants to stop. Systematic desensitization uses the opposite procedure: A stimulus that evokes pleasant feelings is repeatedly paired with a stimulus that evokes anxiety in order to reduce that anxiety.

4. Observational learning is another behavioral treatment used to teach new, more appropriate behavior, as are

◀ **LOOKING BACK**

techniques such as token systems. Rational-emotive therapy is an example of a class of behavioral treatments known as cognitive-behavioral therapy. It suggests that the goal of therapy should be a restructuring of a person's belief system into a more realistic, rational, and logical view of the world. Behavioral therapy in general has been shown to be relatively successful, although critics argue that behavioral approaches may produce symptom substitution.

5. Humanistic therapy is based on the premise that people have control of their behavior, that they can make choices about their lives, and that it is up to them to solve their own problems. Humanistic therapists take a nondirective approach, acting more as guides who facilitate a client's search for answers. One example of humanistic therapy is Carl Rogers's client-centered therapy, in which the goal is to allow people to reach the potential good assumed to be characteristic of every human being. Existential therapy helps people cope with the unique freedom and potential that human existence offers, whereas gestalt therapy is directed toward aiding people in the integration of their thoughts, feelings, and behavior.

6. Most research suggests that, in general, therapy is more effective than no therapy, although how much more effective is not known. The answer to the more difficult question of which therapy works best is even less clear, in part because the therapies are so qualitatively different and in part because the definition of "cure" is so

vague. It is indisputable, though, that particular kinds of therapy are more appropriate for some problems than for others.

7. Biological treatment approaches suggest that therapy ought to focus on the physiological causes of abnormal behavior, rather than considering psychological factors. Drug therapy, the best example of biological treatments, has been effective in bringing about dramatic reductions in the appearance of severe signs of mental disturbance.

8. Antipsychotic drugs such as chlorpromazine are very effective in reducing psychotic symptoms, although they can produce serious side effects. Antidepressant drugs reduce depression. The antianxiety drugs, or minor tranquilizers, are among the most frequently prescribed medications of any sort; they act to reduce the experience of anxiety.

9. Electroconvulsive therapy (ECT) consists of passing an electric current of 70 to 150 volts through the head of a patient, who loses consciousness and has a strong seizure. This procedure is an effective treatment for severe cases of schizophrenia and depression. Another biological treatment is psychosurgery. The typical procedure consists of surgically destroying certain parts of a patient's brain in an operation known as a prefrontal lobotomy. Given the grave ethical problems and possible adverse side effects, the procedure is rarely used today.

10. Community psychology aims to prevent or minimize psychological disorders. The movement was spurred in part by deinstitutionalization, in which previously hospitalized mental patients were released into the community. A notable by-product of the movement has been the installation of telephone hot lines and campus crisis centers throughout the country.

KEY TERMS AND CONCEPTS ▶

psychotherapy (p. 591)
eclectic approach to therapy (591)
psychodynamic therapy (593)
defense mechanisms (593)
neurotic symptoms (593)
psychoanalysis (593)
free association (594)
dream interpretation (594)
manifest content (594)
latent content (594)
resistance (594)
transference (594)
behavioral treatment approaches (596)
aversive conditioning (596)
systematic desensitization (597)

hierarchy of fears (597)
observational learning (598)
modeling (598)
token system (599)
contingency contracting (599)
rational-emotive therapy (599)
cognitive-behavioral therapy (600)
behavioral self-management (601)
humanistic therapy (602)
nondirective counseling (603)
client-centered therapy (603)
unconditional positive regard (603)
existential therapy (604)
gestalt therapy (604)
group therapy (605)

family therapy (605)
spontaneous remission (607)
drug therapy (611)
antipsychotic drugs (612)
chlorpromazine (612)
antidepressant drugs (613)
lithium (613)
antianxiety drugs (613)
electroconvulsive therapy (ECT) (614)
psychosurgery (615)
prefrontal lobotomy (615)
community psychology (617)
deinstitutionalization (617)

FOR FURTHER STUDY AND APPLICATION ▶

Meyer, R. G., & Osborne, Y. H. (1987). *Case studies in abnormal behavior* (2nd ed.). Boston: Allyn & Bacon.

This series of fascinating case histories of individuals suffering from a variety of mental disorders includes discussions of how they were treated.

Hunt, M. (1987, August 30). Navigating the therapy maze. *The New York Times Magazine*, pp. 28–30, 37–49.

This concise yet thorough introduction to the varieties of therapy provides advice on how to make the best choices.

Karoly P., & Kanfer, F. H. (1982). *Self-management and behavior change*. New York: Pergamon Press.

This is an excellent guide to behavior-modification techniques that you can apply to yourself, with step-by-step instructions.

Moos, R. H. (Ed.). (1986). *Coping with life crises*. New York: Plenum.

In a series of articles, various sorts of life crises are discussed, and ways of coping with the stress and anxiety they bring about are presented.

ANSWERS (REVIEW III):
1. False; schizophrenia can be controlled, but not cured, by medication **2.** b
3. Electroconvulsive therapy (ECT) **4.** False; psychosurgery is now used only as a treatment of last resort **5.** Deinstitutionalization

Williams, J. B. W., & Spitzer, R. L. (1983). *Psychotherapy research: Where are we and where should we go?* New York: Guilford Press.

In a series of technical but readable chapters written by experts, this book provides an excellent overview of the kinds of psychotherapy and the research findings that support them. Of particular interest are chapters discussing the issue of how well psychotherapy works.

Kanfer, F. H., & Goldstein, A. P. (Eds.). (1986). *Helping people change* (3rd ed.). New York: Pergamon Press.

This book provides a clear overview of the various techniques that are currently used to treat people with psychological difficulties.

Higginboth, H. N., West, S. G., & Forsyth, D. R. (1988). *Psychotherapy and behavior change: Social, cultural, and methodological perspectives.* New York: Pergamon Press.

This volume describes the links between basic theory and research and the treatment of psychological disorders.

PART SEVEN
THE SOCIAL FOUNDATIONS OF BEHAVIOR

We now turn to the social world, of which we are all a part. We meet an admitted murderer, whose defense rests on blaming his victim. We view a jungle scene, in which hundreds of people line up to drink from a cauldron filled with poison that they know will bring them, and their children, an agonizing death. And we meet a scientist who asks people to give electric shocks to others—and finds ready acceptance of his request.

In this part of the book, we consider the social world and how it affects people's behavior. We focus on how we decide what other people are like and the reasons why they behave in the way they do. We examine what psychologists have learned about social influence and how our everyday activities are affected by the behavior of others. Finally, we consider the reasons why we like and fall in love with particular people, and we look at two contradictory forms of human behavior: aggression and helping behavior.

In Chapter 18, we examine attitudes and persuasion, how people understand what others are like, and how people understand the causes behind others'—and their own—behavior.

In Chapter 19, the focus is on the ways in which we interact with others in a social world, as we explore conformity, liking and loving, aggression, and helping behavior.

CHAPTER

18

SOCIAL PSYCHOLOGY: THE INDIVIDUAL IN A SOCIAL WORLD

PROLOGUE:
ROBERT CHAMBERS

No one disputed the basic facts. At 4:30 on an August morning, 19-year-old Robert Chambers left a bar on New York City's Upper East Side with Jennifer Levin, 18, and walked into Central Park. A few hours later, Chambers strangled Levin with his bare hands.

At issue is exactly why Levin was killed by Chambers, a handsome six-footer who had dropped out of college. According to his version, Chambers unintentionally killed her during a wild, rough sexual encounter. In this scenario, Levin grabbed Chambers so hard during sex that he was momentarily blinded with pain and flipped Levin over, crushing her throat. In support of this explanation, medical personnel testified at Chambers's trial that it could take only five seconds for someone to die if choked in the particular way that Chambers described the incident.

To friends and family of Levin, however, Chambers's explanation was grotesquely hollow. They pointed out that the grisly injuries she sustained during her last moments suggested a prolonged struggle.

More important, the suggestion that Levin provoked Chambers represented a classic "blame the victim" argument. Lawyers using this explanation for a defendant's actions attempt to make it appear that it was the victim's behavior that was at fault, not the defendant's. By employing a blame-the-victim strategy, lawyers portray victims as responsible for and even deserving of whatever harm has come their way (Linden, 1988).

Robert Chambers was sentenced to five to fifteen years in prison for murdering Jennifer Levin. (Top, James Hamilton/Sygma; bottom, Sygma.)

Social psychology: The branch of psychology concerned with how people's thoughts, feelings, and actions are affected by others

LOOKING AHEAD ▶

We'll probably never know what really happened that night in Central Park. We can be sure about what happened to Chambers, though: While the jury in his trial was deliberating, he struck a deal with the prosecution and agreed to plead guilty to a first-degree manslaughter charge without waiting for the jury's decision. He is currently serving a five- to fifteen-year sentence in prison.

The pivotal question faced by the jurors in Chambers's trial was this: How does one identify the reasons behind his behavior? In fact, all of us face the problem of understanding other people and the causes of their behavior on a daily basis, and to one branch of psychology—social psychology—these issues are central. **Social psychology** is the study of how people's thoughts, feelings, and actions are affected by others. Social psychologists consider the nature and causes of individual behavior in social situations.

The broad scope of social psychology is conveyed by the kinds of questions social psychologists ask, such as: How can we convince people to change their attitudes or to adopt new ideas and values? In what ways do we come to understand what others are like? How are we influenced by what others do and think? Why do people display such violence, aggression, and cruelty toward others that people throughout the world live in fear of annihilation? And why, at other times, do people place their own lives at risk to help others?

In this chapter and the next, we explore social psychological approaches to these and other issues. Not only do we examine those processes that underlie social behavior; we also discuss solutions and approaches to a variety of problems and issues that all of us face—ranging from achieving a better understanding of persuasive tactics to forming more accurate impressions of others.

We begin with a look at attitudes, our evaluations of people and other stimuli. Next, we discuss the ways people form judgments about others and the causes of their behavior. Finally, we examine the way we glean the meaning of others' behavior and the kinds of biases that affect our understanding of others. We will see how our interpretation of the causes of other people's behavior affects the way we treat them.

In sum, after reading this chapter you'll have the answers to these questions:

▶ What are attitudes and how are they formed, maintained and changed?

▶ How do we form impressions of what others are like and the causes of their behavior?

▶ What are the biases that color the way in which we view others' behavior?

▶ How can our judgments about others be made more accurately?

ATTITUDES, BEHAVIOR, AND PERSUASION

"You can't beat the feeling." "It's a good time for the great taste of . . ." "You've come a long way baby." "Who can ask for anything more?"

You've heard it all before, and you know you'll hear it over and over again. We are constantly bombarded with advertisements designed to persuade us to purchase specific products. In fact, these attempts illustrate basic principles that have been articulated by social psychologists who study **attitudes**, learned predispositions to respond in a favorable or unfavorable manner to a particular person or object (Fishbein & Ajzen, 1975; Ajzen, 1988).

Attitudes, of course, are not restricted to consumer products; they also relate to specific individuals, as well as to more abstract issues. For example, when you think of the various people in your life, you no doubt hold vastly differing attitudes toward them, depending on the nature of your interactions with them. These attitudes may range from highly positive, as in the case of a lover, to extremely negative, as with a despised rival. Attitudes are also likely to vary in importance. Whereas our attitudes toward friends, family, and peers are generally central to our interactions in the social world, our attitudes toward, say, television newscasters may be relatively insignificant.

Social psychologists generally consider attitudes to follow the **ABC model**, suggesting that an attitude has three components: affect, behavior, and cognition. The **affect component** encompasses our positive or negative emotions about something—how we feel about it. The **behavior component** consists of a predisposition or intention to act in a particular manner that is relevant to our attitude. Finally, the **cognition component** refers to the beliefs and thoughts we hold about the object of our attitude. For example, someone's attitude toward Bruce Springsteen may consist of a positive emotion (the affect component), an intention to buy his latest recording (the behavior component), and the belief that he is a good singer (the cognition component).

Attitudes: Learned predispositions to respond in a favorable or unfavorable manner to a particular object

ABC model: The model suggesting that an attitude has three components: affect, behavior, and cognition

Affect component: That part of an attitude encompassing how one feels about the object of one's attitude.

Behavior component: A predisposition to act in a way that is relevant to one's attitude

Cognition component: The beliefs and thoughts held about the object of one's attitude

Advertising is often designed to appeal to the emotions of the buying public. This engaging photo has been used to sell dozens of products and services including picture frames, wine, real estate, employment counseling, and garden hoses. (Comstock, Inc.)

Every attitude has these three interrelated components, although they vary in terms of which element predominates and in the nature of their relationship. All attitudes, however, develop according to the general principles that social psychologists have discovered about their formation, maintenance, and change—principles that we discuss next.

FORMING AND MAINTAINING ATTITUDES

Although people do not enter the world holding well-defined attitudes toward any particular person or object, anyone who has seen an infant smile at her parents knows that at least certain attitudes develop quickly. Interestingly, some of the same principles governing how attitudes in the youngest of children are acquired and develop continue to operate throughout life.

Classical Conditioning and Attitudes

One of the basic processes that underlie attitude formation and development relates to learning principles (McGuire, 1985). Research has shown that the same classical conditioning processes that made Pavlov's dogs salivate at the sound of a bell (see Chapter 5) can explain how attitudes are acquired. In one experiment, for example, subjects were exposed to paired auditory and visual stimuli in which the names of particular countries were paired with words that had positive connotations (such as "gift" and "happy"), neutral connotations, or negative connotations. When the name of a country toward which the experimenter wanted the subjects to form a positive attitude was flashed on a screen, the experimenter said a word with a positive connotation.

After repeated trials in which each country's name appeared eighteen times, subjects' attitudes toward each of the nationalities were assessed. In general, the results showed that subjects held more positive attitudes toward the nationalities associated with positive words and more negative attitudes toward nationalities that had been associated with negative words. In technical terms, the nationalities became conditioned stimuli, evoking conditioned responses in the form of new attitudes (Staats, 1967; Staats & Staats, 1958).

Advertisers are well aware of results such as these, and often try to link a product they want consumers to buy with a positive feeling or event (Alsop, 1988). For instance, many advertisements feature young, attractive, healthy men and women using a product—even if it is one as uninteresting as toothpaste. The idea behind such advertisements is to create a classically conditioned response to the product, so that just seeing a tube of Crest toothpaste evokes a positive feeling.

Praise for the "Right" Attitude: Reinforcement Approaches to Attitude Acquisition

Another basic learning process, operant conditioning, underlies attitude acquisition. Attitudes that are reinforced, either verbally or nonverbally, tend to be maintained, whereas a person who states an attitude that elicits ridicule from others may modify or abandon the attitude. But it is not only direct reinforcement or punishment that can influence attitudes. **Vicarious learning**, in which a person learns something through the observation of others, also accounts for attitude development—particularly when the individual has no direct experience with the object about which the attitude is held. It is through vicarious learning processes that children pick up the prejudices of

Vicarious learning: Learning by observing others

their parents. For example, even if they have never met a blind person, children whose parents say that "blind people are incompetent" may adopt such attitudes themselves.

We also learn attitudes vicariously through television, films, and other media. For instance, movies that glorify violence reinforce positive attitudes regarding aggression (as we discuss more in Chapter 19), and portrayals of women as subservient to men shape and bolster sexist attitudes (Tuchman, 1978).

PERSUASION: Changing Attitudes

What is it about Bill Cosby that leads people to buy more Jell-O? How does Michael Jackson get people to drink more Pepsi?

According to professionals working in the field of advertising, each of these is a carefully selected match between the product and the individual chosen to represent it. It is not just a matter of finding a well-known celebrity; the person must also be believable, trustworthy, and representative of the qualities that advertisers want their particular product to project (Alwitt, Barnet & Mitchell, 1985; Kanner, 1989).

The work of advertisers draws heavily upon findings from social psychology regarding persuasion. This research has identified a number of factors (see Figure 18-1) that promote effective persuasion—many of which you will recognize if you consider for a moment some of the advertisements with which you are most familiar.

▶ Message source. The individual who delivers a persuasive message has a major impact on the effectiveness of that message (Wu & Shaffer, 1987). Communicators who are both physically and socially attractive seem to produce greater attitude change (Chaiken, 1979). Moreover, the expertise and trustworthiness of a communicator are related to the impact of a message—except in situations in which the communicator is believed to have an ulterior motive. If a prestigious communicator seems to be benefiting from persuading others, the message may be discounted (Hovland, Janis & Kelly, 1953; Eagly, Wood, & Chaiken, 1978). For example, a prestigious scientist who argues in favor of opening a nuclear power plant would generally be a

FIGURE 18-1

In this model of the critical factors affecting persuasion, the message source and message characteristics are shown to influence the recipient or target of a persuasive message.

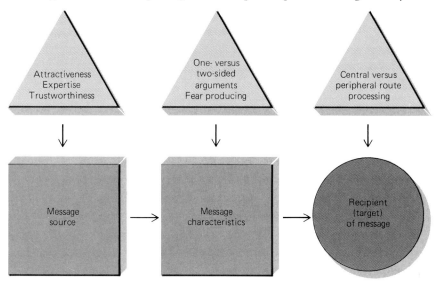

particularly influential source, unless it is revealed that the scientist owns stock in the power plant and stands to benefit financially from its opening.

▶ Characteristics of the message. As you might expect, it is not just *who* delivers a message but *what* the message is like that affects attitude and behavior change. One-sided arguments—in which only the communicator's side is presented—are probably best if the communicator is initially viewed favorably by the audience. But if the audience receives a message presenting an unpopular viewpoint, two-sided messages—which include both the communicator's position and the one he or she is arguing against—are more effective, probably because they are seen as more precise and thoughtful (Karlins & Abelson, 1979). In addition, fear-producing messages ("If you don't use our dental floss, your teeth are sure to fall out") are effective only if they include precise recommendations for actions to avoid danger. Otherwise, messages that arouse fear tend to evoke people's defense mechanisms and may be ignored (Leventhal, 1970).

▶ Characteristics of the recipient or target. Once a message has been communicated, the characteristics of the audience of the message determine whether it will be accepted. For example, we might expect that recipients' intelligence would be related to their persuasibility—and it is, although the relationship is complex. High intelligence both aids and hinders persuasion. Because higher intelligence enables people to understand a message better and later recall it more easily, persuasion is more likely. On the other hand, greater intelligence is associated with more confidence in one's own opinions, and therefore messages of opposing viewpoints are more likely to be rejected. Therefore, in many cases, these two factors cancel each other out, and intelligence is unrelated to persuasibility (McGuire, 1968).

Some gender differences in persuasibility also seem to exist. For instance, social psychologist Alice Eagly (1989) has found that women are somewhat more easily persuaded than men, particularly when they have less knowledge of the message topic. However, the magnitude of the differences between men and women are not large.

One factor that is important in determining whether a message is accepted is the nature of information processing carried out by the recipient. There are two routes to persuasion: central and peripheral (Petty & Cacioppo, 1981; Cialdini, 1984; Eagly, 1983). **Central route processing** occurs when the recipient thoughtfully considers the issues and arguments involved in persuasion. **Peripheral route processing**, in contrast, occurs when the recipient uses more easily understood information that requires less thought, such as the nature of the source or other information less central to the issues involved in the message itself (Mackie, 1987; Petty & Cacioppo, 1986).

In general, central route processing results in the most lasting attitude change. However, if central route processing cannot be employed (for instance, if the target is inattentive, bored, or distracted), then the nature of the message becomes less important, and peripheral factors more critical (Petty & Cacioppo, 1984). Advertising that uses celebrities to sell a product, then, tends to produce change through the peripheral route. In fact, it is possible that well-reasoned, carefully crafted messages will be *less* effective when delivered by a celebrity than by an anonymous source—if the target pays greater attention to the celebrity (leading to peripheral route processing) than to the message (which would have led to central route processing).

Central route processing: Message interpretation characterized by thoughtful consideration of the issues and arguments used to persuade

Peripheral route processing: Message interpretation characterized by consideration of the source and related general information rather than of the message itself

On the other hand, since recipients of advertising messages are often in a fairly inattentive state, the use of celebrities is probably an excellent strategy. Advertisers are correct, then, in their assumption that well-known individuals can have a significant persuasive impact.

THE LINK BETWEEN ATTITUDES AND BEHAVIOR:
Striving for Consistency

Not surprisingly, attitudes influence behavior. If you like hamburgers (the affect component), are predisposed to eat at McDonald's or Burger King (the behavior component), and believe hamburgers are healthy for you (the cognitive component), it is hardly surprising that you will eat hamburgers frequently. The strength of the link between particular attitudes and behavior varies, of course (see the Research Classics box), but generally people strive for consistency between their attitudes and their behavior. Furthermore, people tend to be fairly consistent in the different attitudes they hold: You would probably not hold the attitude that eating meat is immoral and still have a positive attitude toward hamburgers.

Interestingly, the consistency that leads attitudes to influence behavior sometimes works the other way around, for in some cases it is our behavior that shapes our attitudes. Consider, for instance, the following incident:

RESEARCH CLASSICS

DISCREPANCIES BETWEEN ATTITUDES AND BEHAVIOR

If you had polled residents of the West Coast of the United States in the 1930s, you would have found a deep-seated prejudice against the Chinese. For instance, it was not uncommon for people of Chinese extraction to be denied lodging and service at hotels and restaurants merely on the basis of their ethnic background.

To Richard LaPiere, this state of affairs represented a useful opportunity to investigate the relationship between people's attitudes and their behavior. LaPiere (1934) arranged a three-month, 10,000-mile trip with a Chinese couple that took him up and down the West Coast and across the country. In all, the three stopped at some 250 hotels and restaurants. To his surprise, they received service at all but one establishment.

To see how well the proprietors' attitudes matched their behavior, LaPiere sent a questionnaire to all the hotels and restaurants at which they had stopped, asking whether each establishment would serve

Chinese patrons. About 50 percent of the establishments responded, and contrary to the Chinese couple's experience, almost 92 percent of those responding flatly said "no"—with the rest saying "perhaps." LaPiere took these results as a clear indication of the discrepancy between attitudes and behavior.

However, before accepting the results of this study—which is considered an early research classic—as confirmation that attitudes are unrelated to behavior, we must consider several alternative explanations. For one thing, we do not know whether the people who answered the letters were the same ones who actually allowed the couple to spend the night in their establishment.

An even more telling criticism can be made. Because it is much more difficult to turn away a nicely

dressed couple who are standing at your doorstep than to turn them down in a letter, LaPiere's measures of attitude and behavior are not equivalent to each other. Thus the two measures lack direct correspondence, making the comparison ambiguous. It also may be that the couple was subtly rejected in person through unpleasant verbal or nonverbal behavior or through assignment to poorer tables or rooms. Had this been the case, the study might actually have demonstrated congruence between attitude and behavior.

The LaPiere study is clearly not definitive, and it is remembered most for its early importance in raising the issue of how well attitudes correspond to behavior. In fact, most researchers on attitudes now reject the question of *whether* attitudes and behavior are congruent and instead concentrate on the issue of *under what circumstances* the two are related (Aizen, 1988).

THE SOCIAL FOUNDATIONS
OF BEHAVIOR

Cognitive dissonance: The conflict that arises when a person holds contrasting cognitions

Cognitions: Attitudes, thoughts, or beliefs

You've just spent what you feel is the most boring hour of your life, turning pegs for a psychology experiment. Just as you're finally finished and about to leave, the experimenter asks you to do him a favor. He tells you that he needs a confederate to tell subsequent subjects about the task. All you have to do is tell them how interesting it was. For this, you'll be paid $1.

If you agree to such a request, you may be setting yourself up for a state of psychological tension that is known as **cognitive dissonance.** According to a major social psychologist, Leon Festinger (1957), cognitive dissonance occurs when a person holds two attitudes or thoughts (referred to as **cognitions**) that contradict each other. For example, a smoker who knows that smoking leads to lung cancer holds contradictory cognitions: (1) I smoke; and (2) smoking leads to lung cancer. The theory predicts that these two thoughts will lead to a state of cognitive dissonance. More important, it predicts that the individual will be motivated to reduce such dissonance by one of the following methods: (1) modifying one or both of the cognitions; (2) changing the perceived importance of one cognition; (3) adding cognitions; or (4) denying that the two cognitions are related to each other. Hence the smoker might decide that he really doesn't smoke all that much (modifying the cognition), that the evidence linking smoking to cancer is weak (changing the importance of a cognition), that the amount of exercise he gets compensates for the smoking (adding cognitions), or that there is no evidence linking smoking and cancer (denial). Whatever technique is used, the result is a reduction in dissonance (see Figure 18-2).

If we consider the situation in which a subject in an experiment is paid just $1 to tell someone else that a boring task was interesting, as in the situation described above, we have set up classic dissonance-producing circumstances. A subject in such a situation is left with two contradictory

As this cartoon aptly illustrates, cognitive dissonance arising from the two contradictory cognitions of "I want a drink" and "I can't afford a drink" may be reduced by deciding that one really doesn't want a drink after all. (Drawing by B. Tobey, © 1978 The New Yorker Magazine, Inc.)

"Nothing there appeals to me."

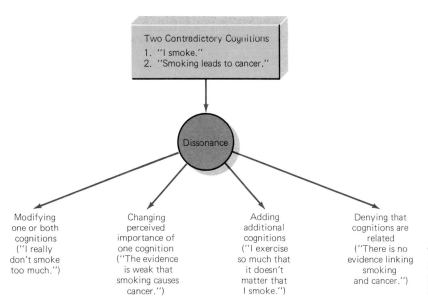

FIGURE 18-2

The presence of two contradictory cognitions ("I smoke" and "Smoking leads to cancer") produces dissonance, which may be reduced through several methods.

thoughts: (1) I believe the task is boring; but (2) I said it was interesting with only little justification (one dollar's worth).

According to the theory, dissonance should be aroused. But how can such dissonance be reduced? One can't very well deny having said that the task was interesting without making a fairly strong break with reality. But, relatively speaking, it is easy to change one's attitude toward the task—and thus the theory predicts that dissonance will be reduced as the subjects change their attitudes to be more positive.

This prediction was confirmed in a classic experiment (Festinger & Carlsmith, 1959). The experiment followed essentially the same procedure outlined earlier, in which a subject was offered $1 to describe a boring task as interesting. In addition, as a control, a condition was included in which subjects were offered $20 to say that the task was interesting. The reasoning behind this condition was that $20 was so much money that subjects in this condition had a good reason to be telling something that was incorrect; dissonance would *not* be aroused, and *less* attitude change would be expected. The results supported this notion: Subjects changed their attitudes more (becoming more positive toward the peg-turning task) when they were paid $1 than subjects who were paid $20.

We now know that dissonance explains a number of everyday occurrences involving attitudes and behavior. For example, consider what happens when you decide to make a major purchase, such as a new car. First you will probably get as much information as possible about a range of models by talking to people and reading about different cars. But after you make your decision, what happens? Most people experience some degree of dissonance because the car they've chosen has some undesirable characteristics, whereas those models that were rejected have some positive features. What typically happens to reduce such dissonance, after a decision has been reached, is that people's attitudes toward the rejected models become *more* negative, while their attitudes toward the chosen model become *more* positive (Converse & Cooper, 1979). Moreover, a **selective exposure** phenomenon occurs: In order to minimize dissonance, people selectively expose themselves to

Selective exposure: An attempt to minimize dissonance by exposing oneself only to information that supports one's choice

THE SOCIAL FOUNDATIONS
OF BEHAVIOR

Self-perception theory: Bem's theory that people form attitudes by observing their own behavior and applying the same principles to themselves as they do to others

information that supports their own choice and attempt to avoid information that is contrary to their choice (Sears, 1968; Sweeney & Gruber, 1984).

Since its development in the late 1950s, dissonance theory has generated a tremendous amount of research, most of which has supported the theory. Research continues today, with investigators examining the specific physiological reactions induced by the state of dissonance (Croyle & Cooper, 1983). However, the theory has not been without its critics. Some psychologists have criticized the methodology used in dissonance experiments, while others have suggested alternative theoretical explanations.

One of the most plausible alternatives was suggested by Darryl Bem (1967, 1972) in his **self-perception theory**. Bem put forth the idea that people form attitudes by observing their own behavior, using the same principles that they use when they observe others' behavior to draw conclusions about others' attitudes. In other words, people are sometimes unclear about the reasons for which they have just demonstrated a certain behavior. In those instances, they will look at their behavior and try to figure out just why they did what they did.

For example, if I were the subject who received $1 for saying that a task I hated was actually very interesting, I might look at what I said and try to figure out why I said it. The most likely explanation is "Well, if I agreed to say I liked the task for a paltry $1, then I probably didn't dislike it all that much. In fact, I probably liked it." Therefore, when asked by the experimenter to indicate my attitude, I might respond with a relatively positive attitude toward the task. Of course, this is the same result that dissonance theory would predict—more positive attitude change in the lower-incentive condition ($1) than in the higher-incentive condition ($20)—but the underlying reason is different. Whereas the dissonance explanation suggests that attitude change is due to the presence (in the $1 condition) of the unpleasant state of dissonance that a subject tries to overcome, the self-perception theory suggests it is due to an active search for understanding one's behavior.

Although we cannot be sure whether dissonance or self-perception theory provides the more accurate description of how people react to inconsistencies between their attitudes and their behavior, it is clear most of us try to make sense of our own attitudes and behavior and maintain consistency between them. When we behave in a way that is inconsistent with our attitudes, we tend to change our attitudes to make them fit better with our behavior.

RECAP AND REVIEW I

Recap

◄ Attitudes are learned predispositions to respond in a favorable or unfavorable manner to a particular object. They have three components: affect, behavior, and cognition.

◄ Both classical conditioning and operant conditioning underlie attitude acquisition.

◄ The major factors promoting persuasion relate to the message source, characteristics of the message, and characteristics of the recipient or target.

◄ People strive to fit their attitudes and behavior together in a logical framework, and they attempt to overcome any inconsistencies that they perceive.

◄ Cognitive dissonance, a state of psychological tension, occurs when a person holds two attitudes or thoughts (known as cognitions) that contradict each other. Self-perception theory provides an alternative explanation to dissonance theory.

Review

1. A learned predisposition to respond in a favorable or an unfavorable manner to a particular object is called a(n) _____ .

2. Name the three components of attitudes making up the ABC model.

3. Someone who believes that Jell-O is better than other brands because Bill Cosby promotes it has been persuaded by _____ route processing.
4. Jim firmly believes what his doctor said about his need to lose weight and reduce his cholesterol intake. The tension he feels as he finishes his second bowl of ice cream is known as
   a. selective exposure.
   b. cognitive dissonance.

c. negative reinforcement.
d. vicarious learning
5. The theory which suggests that people form attitudes by observing and trying to understand their own behavior is called
   a. operant conditioning.
   b. cognitive dissonance.
   c. vicarious learning.
   d. self-perception.

(Answers to review questions are on page 636.)

UNDERSTANDING OTHERS: SOCIAL COGNITION

Regardless of whether they agreed with his policies and ideology, in spite of how they felt he garbled the facts at news conferences, and irrespective of the trouble his subordinates found themselves in, most Americans genuinely *liked* President Ronald Reagan. Reagan's unfavorable experiences never seemed to adhere to him, and he was dubbed the "Teflon president" by the press. Perceived as a "nice guy," he remained one of the most popular presidents of the century through the end of his second term.

Phenomena such as these illustrate the power of our impressions and suggest the importance of determining how people develop an understanding of others. In fact, one of the dominant areas of study in social psychology during the last few years has focused on learning how people come to understand what others are like and to explain the reasons underlying others' behavior (Ross & Fletcher, 1985).

UNDERSTANDING WHAT OTHERS ARE LIKE

Consider for a moment the enormous amount of information about other people to which we are exposed. How are we able to decide what is im-

Regardless of whether they agreed or disagreed with President Reagan's specific policies, most people had a positive impression of him as a person. (UPI/Bettmann Newsphotos.)

Social cognition: The processes that underlie our understanding of the social world

Schemas: Sets of cognitions about people and social experiences

portant and what is not and to make judgments about the characteristics of others? Social psychologists interested in this question study **social cognition**—the processes that underlie our understanding of the social world. They have learned that individuals have highly developed **schemas**, sets of cognitions about people and social experiences. These schemas organize information stored in memory, represent in our minds the way the social world operates, and give us a framework to categorize and interpret information relating to social stimuli (Fiske & Taylor, 1983).

We typically hold schemas for particular types of people in our environments. Our schema for "teacher," for instance, generally consists of a number of characteristics: knowledge of the subject matter he or she is teaching, a desire to impart that knowledge, and an awareness of the student's need to understand what is being said. Or we may hold a schema for "mother" that includes the characteristics of warmth, nurturance, and caring. Regardless of their accuracy—and, as we shall see, very often their inaccuracies—schemas are important because they organize the way in which we recall, recognize, and categorize information about others. Moreover, they allow us to make predictions of what others are like on the basis of relatively little information, since we tend to fit people into schemas even when there is not much concrete evidence to go on (Smith, 1984; Snyder & Cantor, 1979).

Impression Formation

Impression formation: The process by which an individual organizes information about another individual to form an overall impression of that person

How do we decide that Gail is a flirt, or Andy is a jerk, or Jon is a really nice guy? The earliest work on social cognition was designed to examine **impression formation**, the process by which an individual organizes information about another individual to form an overall impression of that person. In one classic study, for instance, students were told that they were about to hear a guest lecturer (Kelley, 1950). One group of students was told that the lecturer was "a rather warm person, industrious, critical, practical, and determined," while a second group was told that he was "a rather cold person, industrious, critical, practical, and determined."

The simple substitution of "cold" for "warm" was responsible for drastic differences in the way the students in each group perceived the lecturer, even though he gave the same talk in the same style in each condition. Students who had been told he was "warm" rated him considerably more positively than students who had been told he was "cold."

Central traits: The major traits considered in forming impressions of others

The findings from this experiment led to a good deal of research on impression formation that focused on the way people pay particular attention to certain unusually important traits—known as **central traits**—to help them form an overall impression of others. According to this work, the presence of a central trait alters the meaning of other traits (Asch, 1946; Widmey & Loy, 1988). Hence the description of the lecturer as "industrious" presumably meant something different according to whether it was associated with the central trait "warm" or "cold."

Other work on impression formation has used information-processing approaches (see Chapter 7) to develop mathematically oriented models of how individual personality traits are combined to create an overall impression (Anderson, 1974). Generally, the results of this research suggest that, in forming an overall judgment of a person, we use a psychological "average"

ANSWERS (REVIEW I):
1. Attitude **2.** Affect, behavior, cognition **3.** Peripheral **4.** b **5.** d

of the individual traits we see, in a manner that is analogous to finding a mathematical average of several numbers (Kaplan, 1975).

Of course, as we gain more experience with people and see them exhibiting behavior in a variety of situations, our impressions of them become more complex (Anderson & Klatzky, 1987; Gilbert, Pelham & Krull, 1987). But, because there usually are gaps in our knowledge of others, we still tend to fit them into personality schemas that represent particular "types" of people. For instance, we might hold a "gregarious person" schema, made up of the traits of friendliness, aggressiveness, and openness. The presence of just one or two of these traits might be sufficient to make us assign a person to a particular schema.

Unfortunately, as illustrated in the Cutting Edge box, the schemas that we employ are susceptible to a variety of factors that affect the accuracy of our judgments (Kenny & Albright, 1987; Gordon & Wyer, 1987; DePaulo et al., 1987). For example, our mood affects how we perceive others. People who are happy form more favorable impressions and make more positive judgments than people who are sad (Forgas & Bower, 1987).

Even when schemas are not entirely accurate, they serve an important function. They allow us to develop expectations about how others will behave, permitting us to plan our interactions with others more easily, and serving to simplify a complex social world.

THE CUTTING EDGE

MAKING A GOOD IMPRESSION: JUDGING TRIAL DEFENDANTS

In the typical trial seen on television or in the movies, the defendant is good-looking and modest, facing a prosecuting attorney who is cold and callous. In real life, however, the defendant's attractiveness may vary quite a bit—a fact that has triggered a good deal of research. For it turns out that, quite apart from the merits of a particular case and absolutely contrary to law, defendants may be judged by juries on the basis of their attractiveness.

One of the first experiments demonstrating the importance of the general appearance of a defendant was carried out by psychologist Eliott Aronson and colleagues (Landy & Aronson, 1969), who examined how a defendant's general social attractiveness related to the length of sentence awarded by mock jurors for the crime of vehicular homicide in which the defendant was negligent. In one condition, the defendant was described as a stable 64-year-old insurance adjuster who had been employed with the same firm for twenty-four years,

whose wife had died of cancer, and who had been spending Christmas with his son and daughter-in-law. In the other condition, the defendant was described as an unstable 33-year-old janitor, twice divorced, who had been spending Christmas Eve with his girlfriend. The results were clear: the more attractive the general description of the defendant, the lighter the sentence.

Subsequent laboratory experiments have examined the components of social attractiveness more precisely and found that such factors as attractiveness, personality, and attire are related to sentence length, with greater attractiveness generally leading to more lenient treatment—all other factors being equal (Monahan & Loftus, 1982).

One the other hand, in some situations attractiveness on the part of the defendant can have a detrimen-

tal effect. For instance, one study found that if the defendant's physical attractiveness appears to have been used profitably during a criminal activity—as in a swindle that was successful in part because of the defendant's good looks—jurors will give harsher sentences to more attractive defendants than to less attractive ones (Sigall & Ostrove, 1975). Attorneys for Robert Chambers, whose case we discussed at the beginning of the chapter, were worried about this effect: Chambers's good looks and affluent background could have been held against him in a trial in which sexual activity played such a central role.

Attractiveness is just one characteristic that influences juror decisions about the guilt or innocence of defendants; such factors as the defendant's nonverbal behavior, race, and socioeconomic status also affect the judgments that are made. In sum, the same factors and processes that influence a person's perception in everyday life also operate within the courtroom.

THE NEGATIVE SIDE OF SOCIAL COGNITION: Stereotypes

Stereotype: A kind of schema in which beliefs and expectations about members of a group are held simply on the basis of their membership in that group

What do we think of when someone says, "He's black," or "She's Chinese," or "woman driver"? If we're honest, most of us would have to admit we tend to form some sort of immediate impression of what that individual is like. This fact illustrates an important point: Although schemas can be helpful in organizing the social world, they also have a negative side—particularly when they promote an oversimplified understanding of other people. **Stereotypes**, beliefs and expectations about members of groups held simply on the basis of their membership in those groups, represent one particularly damaging instance of this approach to impression formation.

Some of the most prevalent stereotypes have to do with racial and ethnic categorizations. Over the years, various groups have been called, for example, "lazy" or "shrewd" or "cruel" with varying degrees of regularity by nongroup members (Katz & Brayly, 1933; Weber & Crocker, 1983). But stereotypes are by no means confined to racial and ethnic groups. Sex and age stereotyping—which we discussed in Chapters 10 and 12, respectively— are all too common as well. There is even a general stereotype relating to *any* group, known as the **ingroup–outgroup bias** (Brewer, 1979; Evans & Dovido, 1983; Ng & Cram, 1988). We tend to hold less favorable opinions about members of groups of which we are not a part (**outgroups**) and more favorable opinions about members of groups to which we belong (**ingroups**).

Ingroup-outgroup bias: The tendency to hold less favorable opinions about groups to which we do not belong (outgroups), while holding more favorable opinions about groups to which we do belong (ingroups)

Outgroups: Groups to which an individual does not belong

Ingroups: Groups to which an individual belongs

Discrimination: Negative behavior toward members of a particular group

Although there is little evidence to support the accuracy of most stereotypes, they can have harmful consequences. When negative stereotypes are acted on, they result in **discrimination**—negative behavior toward members of a particular group. Discrimination can produce exclusion from jobs, neighborhoods, or educational opportunities, and may result in members of particular groups receiving lower salaries and benefits.

Self-fulfilling prophecy: An expectation about the occurrence of an event or behavior that increases the likelihood that the event or behavior will happen

Stereotypes not only produce overt discrimination; they can actually *cause* members of stereotyped groups to behave in ways that reflect the stereotype through a phenomenon known as a **self-fulfilling prophecy** (Archibald, 1974). Self-fulfilling prophecies are expectations about the occurrence of a future event or behavior that act to increase the likelihood that

Ingroup-outgroup bias is the tendency to hold less favorable opinions of those who belong to groups we are not part of. (Drawing by Ziegler, © 1983 The New Yorker Magazine, Inc.)

"I'm surprised, Marty. I thought you were one of us."

the event or behavior *will* occur. For example, if people think that members of a particular group are lazy, they may treat them in a way that actually brings about their laziness (Skrypnek & Snyder, 1982). Similarly, people holding a stereotype may be "primed" to interpret the behavior of the stereotyped group as representative of the stereotype, even when the behavior depicts something entirely different (Slusher & Anderson, 1987).

The knowledge that others hold a stereotype about you can cause you to behave in a way that is representative of that stereotype in order to make a positive impression on those holding the stereotype—even if the behavior is not typical for you. For instance, researchers found that women interacting with an attractive, desirable male whom they thought stereotyped women as passive and dependent tended to espouse views that were more passive and dependent than women who thought the attractive male held an untraditional view of women. In contrast, when the male was unattractive, the women's behavior was not affected by the nature of the stereotype they thought he held. In sum, only when they felt motivated to make a good impression did they behave according to the stereotype (Zanna & Pack, 1974).

Reverse Discrimination.

Stereotyping can sometimes lead to **reverse discrimination**, in which people holding some degree of prejudice compensate for their prejudice by treating members of a particular group *more* favorably than if they did not belong to the group. In a sense, they bend over backwards to avoid seeming to be prejudiced.

Reverse discrimination: Behavior in which people prejudiced toward a group compensate for their prejudice by treating the group's members more favorably than others

Psychologist Daniel Fajardo found an example of the phenomenon of reverse discrimination in a study he carried out in a public school setting (Fajardo, 1985). He asked teachers to rate a series of essays that were constructed to be of poor, low-average, high-average, or excellent quality. The teachers were also provided with information indicating in one condition that the student authors were white, and in another condition that they were black. As you can see in Figure 18–3, at every quality level, the same essay

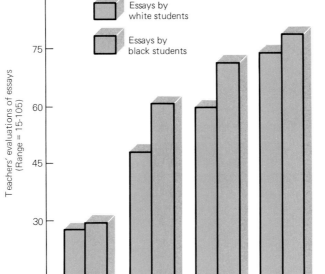

FIGURE 18-3

In an example of reverse discrimination, teachers in an experiment rated essays more positively when they thought they were written by black students than when they thought they were written by white students, regardless of the level of quality of the essay. (Fajardo, 1985.)

was rated more positively when it was supposedly written by a black student than by a white student. In addition, the teachers' tendency to favor the black students was strongest with moderate-level essays. In sum, it was average students who were most susceptible to reverse discrimination.

Why was there a discrepancy between the ratings given to "black" versus "white" students' essays? When asked, the teachers reported using different grading strategies for black students, reading their essays more carefully and grading them more leniently.

As you might imagine, reverse discrimination may often be as damaging as outward, negative discrimination. People who are the recipients of reverse discrimination may feel as if they are "tokens," treated specially not because of their own talents but because of their membership in a special group. Furthermore, in academic situations, their special treatment may result in their being passed from grade to grade, without any real effort being made to teach them skills that they might be lacking. Ultimately, such "positive" treatment becomes detrimental.

It is clear from research on stereotyping, then, that the processes of social cognition leading to the creation of schemas both help and hinder social interaction. Although schemas allow us to simplify an otherwise complex social world, they can also lead to oversimplification; we may assume that individuals possess certain traits associated with a group—just because of their membership in that group (Jussim, Coleman & Lerch, 1987).

RECAP AND REVIEW II

Recap

◄ Social cognition is concerned with the processes that underlie our understanding of the social world. This understanding can be held in the form of schemas—sets of cognitions about people and our social experience.

◄ We often form impressions of others by relying on basic, central traits to combine individual traits into an overall impression or by mathematically averaging individual traits into a general impression.

◄ Stereotypes are beliefs and expectations about members of a group formed simply on the basis of their membership in that group.

◄ Stereotypes are frequently held about members of racial, ethnic, sex, and age groups. Although they have little validity, they can produce difficulties in social interaction because of discrimination and self-fulfilling prophecies.

Review

1. The sets of cognitions we have about particular types of people—lawyers, secretaries, and football players, for example—are called _____ .

2. One approach to explaining impression formation states that people pay particular attention to certain unusually important characteristics, called _____ _____ . Another approach holds that people take a mathematical average of the many traits they observe in a person. This is called the _____ _____ approach.

3. During the bank robbery, Estelle's job was to flirt with the security guard, distracting him until the robbers were finished. At her trial, Estelle's beauty will probably hurt her case. True or false? _____

4. Negative behavior toward or negative treatment of members of a particular group is known as
   a. ingroup-outgroup bias.
   b. stereotyping.
   c. self-fulfilling prophecy.
   d. discrimination.

5. Floyd is afraid of appearing prejudiced, so he acts especially friendly toward members of minority groups, although he is normally quiet and shy. Floyd's behavior is an example of _____ _____ .

(Answers to review questions are on page 642.)

UNDERSTANDING THE CAUSES OF BEHAVIOR:
ATTRIBUTION PROCESSES

When Barbara Washington, a new employee at the Staditron Computer Company, completed a major staffing project two weeks early, her boss, Marian, was delighted. At the next staff meeting, she announced how pleased she was with Barbara and explained that *this* was an example of the kind of performance she was looking for in her staff. The other staff members looked on resentfully, trying to figure out why Barbara had worked night and day to finish the project not just on time, but two weeks early. She must be an awfully compulsive person, they decided.

Most of us have, at one time or another, puzzled over the reasons behind someone's behavior. Perhaps it was in a situation similar to the one above, or it may have been under more formal circumstances, such as the task faced by the jurors in the Robert Chambers trial described at the beginning of the chapter. In contrast to work on social cognition, which describes how people develop an overall impression about others' personality traits, **attribution theory** seeks to explain how we decide, on the basis of samples of an individual's behavior, what the specific causes of the person's behavior are (Harvey & Weary, 1985; Weiner, 1985).

When trying to understand the causes underlying a given behavior, individuals typically try first to determine whether the cause is situational or dispositional (Heider, 1958). **Situational causes** are those brought about by something in the environment. For instance, someone who knocks over a quart of milk and then cleans it up is probably doing so not because he or she is a terribly neat person, but because the *situation* is one that requires it. In contrast, a person who spends hours shining the kitchen floor is probably doing so because he or she *is* a neat person—hence, the behavior has a **dispositional cause**, prompted by the person's disposition (his or her internal traits or personality characteristics).

In our example involving Barbara, her fellow employees, in trying to attribute her behavior to either the situation or her disposition, assumed that her disposition was the cause. But from a logical standpoint, it is equally plausible that there was something about the situation that caused the behavior. If asked, Barbara might attribute her accomplishment to situational factors, explaining that she had so much other work to do that she just had to get the project out of the way, or that the project was not all that difficult and that it was easy to complete ahead of schedule. To her, then, the reason for her behavior might not be dispositional at all; it could be situational.

How do we determine whether Barbara's behavior is motivated by situational or dispositional factors? Harold Kelley (1967) suggested that people use three types of information to answer this question. First, there is **consensus** information—the degree to which other people behave similarly in the same situation. For instance, if most people would have completed the project two weeks early, Barbara's behavior would be high in consensus, but if most people would have procrastinated, her behavior would be low in consensus. Second, there is **consistency** information—the degree to which an individual would behave similarly in a similar situation. If Barbara always gets her work in early on the job, no matter what the project, she is high in consistency. Finally, there is **distinctiveness** information, the extent to which

Attribution theory: The theory that seeks to explain how we decide, on the basis of samples of an individual's behavior, what the specific causes of that behavior are

Situational causes of behavior: Causes of behavior that are based on environmental factors

Dispositional causes of behavior: Causes of behavior that are based on internal traits or personality factors

Consensus information: The degree to which people behave similarly in the same situation

Consistency information: The degree to which an individual behaves similarly in similar situations

Distinctiveness information: The extent to which a given behavior occurs across different situations

Behavior   Type of Information   Attribution

Barbara is the only one who gets her work in on time. → Low consensus

Barbara always gets her work in on time. → High consistency

Barbara does everything early. → Low distinctiveness

Dispositional attribution: Barbara's behavior is characteristic of her personality.

All employees finish their work early. → High consensus

Barbara always gets her work in on time. → High consistency

Barbara gets her work in on time, but is late in other situations. → High distinctiveness

Situational attribution: Barbara's behavior is due to the situation.

FIGURE 18-4

An illustration of Kelley's model of attribution. Learning that Barbara's behavior represents low consensus, high consistency, and low distinctiveness leads to a dispositional attribution. In contrast, determining that Barbara's behavior represents high consensus, high consistency, and high distinctiveness leads to a situational attribution.

the behavior occurs across other situations. If Barbara gets her work done early only on her job but procrastinates everywhere else, her behavior is high in distinctiveness.

By simultaneously considering all three kinds of information, people are able to make an attribution that is based primarily on dispositional factors or on situational factors. As shown in Figure 18-4, information that is high in consensus, high in consistency, and high in distinctiveness leads to attributions that are situational: In our example, Barbara's behavior would be attributed to the demands of the job. But with situations in which consensus and distinctiveness are low and consistency is high, people tend to make dispositional attributions, assuming the behavior is related to one's personality.

TO ERR IS HUMAN: Biases in Attribution

If we always processed information in the rational manner that Kelley's model suggests, the world might run a lot more smoothly. Unfortunately, although Kelley's attribution formulation generally makes accurate predictions—at least for cases in which people have concrete, firsthand knowledge of consensus, consistency, and distinctiveness (Wells & Harvey, 1978; Orvis, 1982)—people do not always process information about others in as logical a fashion as the theory seems to suggest (Funder, 1987; Gilbert, Jones, & Pelham, 1987). In fact, research shows that there tend to be consistent biases in the way attributions are made. Among the most typical:

ANSWERS (REVIEW II):
1. Schemas   **2.** Central traits, information-processing   **3.** True   **4.** d   **5.** Reverse discrimination

▶ *The fundamental attribution bias.* One of the most common biases in people's attributions is the tendency to attribute others' behavior to dispositional causes—but one's own behavior to situational causes. Known as the **fundamental attribution bias**, this tendency is quite prevalent (Watson, 1982). For example, an analysis of letters and advice in newspaper columns such as "Dear Abby" and "Ann Landers" showed that writers tended to attribute their own problems to situational factors, while they described the problems of others as due to dispositional causes (Schoeneman & Rubanowitz, 1985). In our own example, we saw how Barbara attributed her behavior to constraints of the environment (situational factors), while Barbara's colleagues thought her behavior was due to her personality characteristics (dispositional factors).

> **Fundamental attribution bias:** A tendency to attribute others' behavior to dispositional causes but to attribute one's own behavior to situational causes

Why should the fundamental attribution bias be so common? One reason has to do with the nature of information that is available to the people making an attribution. When we view the behavior of another person in a particular setting, the information that is most conspicuous is the person's behavior itself. Because the individual's environment is relatively stable and invariant, the person is the center of our attention. But when we consider our own behavior, changes in the environment are going to be more obvious, and we are more likely to make attributions based on situational factors.

One consequence of the fundamental attribution bias is that we may excuse our own failures by attributing them to extenuating circumstances ("I couldn't finish my paper because the library didn't have the book I needed"), but when others have a problem we blame their personality flaws ("He's just too lazy to finish his paper on time"; Snyder & Higgins, 1988).

▶ *The halo effect.* Harry is intelligent, kind, and loving. Is he also conscientious?

If you were to hazard a guess, your most likely response would be "yes." Your guess reflects the **halo effect**, a phenomenon in which an initial understanding that a person has positive traits is used to infer other uniformly positive characteristics (Cooper, 1981). The opposite would also hold true: Learning that Harry was unsociable and argumentative would probably lead you to assume he was lazy as well.

> **Halo effect:** A phenomenon in which an initial understanding that a person has positive traits is used to infer other uniformly positive characteristics

The reason for the halo effect is that we hold **implicit personality theories**, theories reflecting our notions of what traits are found together in individuals. These theories are based on a combination of experience and logic. Our perception of the world may be flawed, however, because application of our theory can be singularly inappropriate for a given individual, or it may simply be wrong. Most people have neither uniformly positive nor uniformly negative traits but instead possess a combination of the two.

> **Implicit personality theories:** Theories reflecting our notions of what traits are found together in individuals

▶ *The Pollyanna effect.* In some respects, people have a blind optimism that is not too different from that of Pollyanna, the heroine of Eleanor Porter's 1913 novel who could see no evil in the world. Because we are typically motivated to view the world as a pleasant, enjoyable place, our perceptions of others are colored in a positive direction (Sears, 1982). This **Pollyanna effect** produces a tendency to rate others in a generally positive manner.

> **Pollyanna effect:** The tendency to rate others in a generally positive manner

There are several examples of the Pollyanna effect. For instance, the public's evaluation of the U.S. president and other public figures historically is generally positive. Similarly, ratings of other people made by subjects in experiments normally fall in the positive range—even when the people have just met. Humorist Will Rogers may have been reflecting a widespread feeling when he claimed, "I never met a man I didn't like."

Assumed-similarity bias: The tendency to think of people as being similar to oneself

▶ *Assumed-similarity bias.* How similar to you—in terms of attitudes, opinions, and likes and dislikes—are your friends and acquaintances? Most people feel that their friends and acquaintances are fairly similar to themselves. But this feeling goes beyond just people we know; there is a general tendency—known as the **assumed-similarity bias**—to think of people as being similar to oneself, even when meeting them for the first time (Ross, Greene & House, 1977; Hoch, 1987; Marks & Miller, 1987).

If other people are, in fact, different from oneself, the assumed-similarity bias reduces the accuracy of the judgments being made. Moreover, it suggests an interesting possibility: It may be that a judgment about another individual better defines the judge's characteristics than those of the person being rated. In some cases, then, the portrait we draw of another person—particularly one about whom we have little information—may in reality be a sketch of the way we view ourselves.

UNDERSTANDING OUR OWN BEHAVIOR: Self-Perception Theory

The fundamental attribution bias illustrates an important point about attributional processes: People not only make attributions about others; they can sometimes act as observers of their *own* behavior and make attributions on the basis of what they see themselves doing. As we discussed earlier in the chapter in reference to attitudes, Bem's theory of self-perception suggests that people monitor their own behavior and make judgments about themselves on the basis of what they see themselves doing (Bem, 1967). The theory suggests, then, that when situational cues are weak or past experience does not provide relevant information, people will look to their own behavior to make attributions about themselves.

How does the theory work? Suppose you are asked to handle advertising for a play being produced by the campus drama club during the next term. You are pleased to be asked but not too sure you can spare the time, so you tell the person making the request you will get back to her with your decision in a few days. As the days drag on, though, you never seem to have the time to call her back, and you just can't make up your mind. After a few weeks have gone by, you begin to wonder why you can't reach a decision. As you ponder the question, you conclude that your reluctance indicates that you are unenthusiastic and really don't want the job.

Your decision to decline the request is based on self-perception. Using your own behavior as an indication of your underlying motivation, you determine that the hesitancy you observe in yourself is based on a lack of desire to take on the job. Here you are acting much like an outside observer, making an inference on the basis of your behavior. In sum, self-perception theory suggests that we derive knowledge about ourselves by examining our own actions.

Another facet of self-perception is illustrated by research showing that people habitually use a particular style in explaining events in their lives. For example, some of us tend to be more optimistic in explaining bad events in our lives, whereas others tend to be more pessimistic. Pessimists typically see unfavorable events, such as failing a test, as being due to a personal deficit that will plague them for the rest of their lives. Optimists, in contrast, may view the failure as a temporary setback, one that can be remedied by making changes in their lives.

The kinds of explanations we employ have important consequences on many areas of our lives. For example, people who employ more optimistic explanations enjoy better health, have greater job success, and actually seem to live longer than those who are more pessimistic (Scheier, 1987; Peterson, Seligman & Vaillant, 1988). The explanation for these consequences may be that people who characteristically use pessimistic explanations may act more passively in the face of adversity. When they are ill, for example, they may not seek medical advice or may not follow it once they receive it. In contrast, optimists may feel more strongly that their own actions can in fact have an impact upon their future health and consequently may be more receptive to and compliant with medical advice. (For another application of self-perception theory, see the Psychology at Work box.)

THE VALUE OF ILLUSIONS

The fact that there are psychological benefits to making certain kinds of inaccurate attributions—such as having a consistently optimistic attributional style—tends to fly in the face of much traditional theorizing about the nature of good mental health. A central dictum is that accurate perceptions of the world are a sign of good mental health and that inaccurate or distorted perceptions of reality signify psychological difficulties.

However, there is increasing evidence to the contrary: Accurate perceptions of reality, at least in terms of oneself, are not always as beneficial as

---

PSYCHOLOGY AT WORK

IMPROVING YOUR GRADES BY IMPROVING YOUR ATTRIBUTIONS

If you are like most people, when you first began college, you were concerned about whether you'd be able to make the grade. Could you do well enough to meet the competition of your classmates? Would you be able to meet the standards set by your professors? Would you, in short, be smart enough to do well?

For some first-year students, these concerns become so great that they produce anxiety that interferes with work. Any difficulties that such students experience early in their college careers are viewed as confirmations that they are ill-equipped to do college-level work. This attribution leads to further disruption of their studying and ultimately to even poorer performance (Peterson & Barrett, 1987).

In actuality, statistics show that *most* students' performance improves over the course of their college careers, so it is not unusual to expect that first-year performance will be less than optimal. This finding

led social psychologists Timothy Wilson and Patricia Linville (1982, 1985) to devise a program to change the way first-year college students who were concerned about their grades attributed the causes of their academic performance.

Wilson and Linville hypothesized that academic performance would improve by exposing students to information that showed that poor first-year performance was likely caused by temporary factors that were susceptible to change, rather than by permanent, unchangeable conditions. To test this reasoning, Wilson and Linville carried out a series of simple experiments. In them, university freshmen who had expressed concern about their first-year grades viewed videotapes of interviews with

juniors and seniors who stated that their grades had improved since they had started college. In addition, the freshmen were given statistical information indicating that grades typically improve among college students in general.

The program showed clear success. In contrast to a control group for students who received no treatment, students who viewed the videotapes and were exposed to the information showed an improvement in their grades in the semester following the study, and also had a lower dropout rate.

In sum, exposure to a one-time program designed to change attributions was sufficient to produce better performance. These results are promising, as are those for similar programs (Försterling, 1985), for other everyday problems may be solved simply by changing people's attributions regarding the causes of their behavior (Baumgardner, Heppner & Arkin, 1986).

we might first think. Specifically, social psychologist Shelley Taylor concludes that three basic illusions are profitable: holding an unrealistically positive self-evaluation, having an exaggerated perception of control, and being unrealistically optimistic (Taylor & Brown, 1988). Such illusions tend to be associated with better psychological functioning on an everyday basis.

In sum, certain inaccuracies in our perceptions of ourselves may turn out to be beneficial. On the other hand, it is typically better to be precise in our understanding of others. We turn now to ways in which our impressions of others can be made more accurate.

THE INFORMED CONSUMER OF PSYCHOLOGY:
Forming more Accurate Impressions

At one time or another, we've all been guilty of forming an impression of someone and later finding out we were completely off base. For although people try to use the information available to them to construct a meaningful, orderly social world for themselves, there is ample opportunity in both the development of schemas and in attributional processes to make errors, to oversimplify, and thereby to misperceive other people. This would not be of much concern were it not for the fact that once individuals make decisions about others, they act upon these decisions—sometimes with very undesirable consequences. As a result, social psychologists have designed a number of techniques to increase the accuracy with which people can make judgments about others. They have paid particular attention to strategies for reducing the negative effects of stereotyping. Among the most useful of those strategies are the following:

▶ Increasing contact between the target of stereotyping and the holder of the stereotype. A good deal of research has shown that increasing the amount of interaction between people can reduce negative stereotyping (Amir, 1976; Miller & Brewer, 1984). But certain kinds of contact are more likely than others to lead to the development of more accurate schemas: Situations where there is relatively intimate contact, where the individuals are of equal status, or where participants are dependent on one another are most likely to bring about a reduction of stereotyping. The explanation for the effectiveness of contact seems to be that schemas regarding stereotyped groups become more detailed, individualized, and accurate as the amount of interaction increases. This finding provides part of the basis for such social practices as school integration and fair housing laws.

▶ Making positive values more conspicuous, rather than relying on contact to change the nature of schemas and stereotypes, this approach suggests that people be shown the inconsistencies between values they hold regarding equality and fair treatment of others on one hand, and negative stereotyping on the other. Rokeach (1971) found that if people were simply made to see that the values they held regarding equality and freedom were inconsistent with some of their perceptions of minority group members, the people were more likely to later join a group organized to further minorities and to register for a class in ethnic relations.

▶ Providing information about the objects of stereotyping. Probably the most direct means of changing schemas about the objects of stereotyping is through education, by teaching people to be more aware of the positive characteristics of objects of stereotyping (Langer, Bashner & Chanowitz, 1985). For instance, if the meaning behind puzzling behavior that is quite common to members of a stereotyped group is pointed out to people who hold the stereotypes, they may come to understand the significance of the behavior—although it may still appear foreign and perhaps even threatening (Fiedler, Mitchell & Triandis, 1971; Landis, Day, McGrew, Thomas & Miller, 1976).

Figure 18–5 shows an example of a teaching aid—called a **cultural assimilator**—devised to decrease racial prejudice among military personnel through better understanding the meaning of others' behavior. In the procedure, trainees read about an incident and are then presented with explanations for the behavior that occurred, only one of which is accurate. The assimilator provides a rationale for both right and wrong choices, and by going through a large number of such incidents, the trainee develops a more accurate understanding of the causes behind behavior of minority group members. Ultimately, this results in a more precise schema pertaining to members of different groups.

Each of these strategies for forming more accurate impressions—although not invariably effective—serves to illustrate a major approach taken

Cultural assimilator: A teaching aid designed to minimize racial prejudice through understanding of others' behavior

FIGURE 18-5

An example of a cultural assimilator used to decrease racial prejudice. (Landis, Day, McGrew, Thomas, & Miller, 1976.)

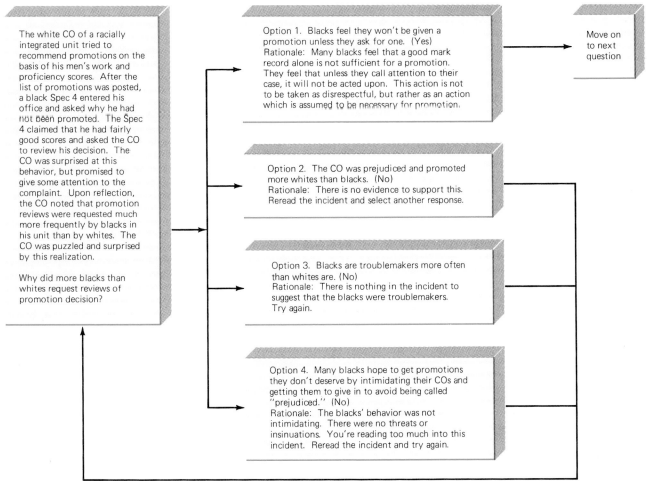

by social psychologists. The ultimate goal of this work, of course, is to increase the quality of social interaction—something which should follow after people develop a more accurate understanding of one another—and which we discuss further in the next chapter.

RECAP AND REVIEW III

Recap

◀ Attribution theory explains the processes that underlie how we attribute the causes of others' behavior, particularly in terms of situational versus dispositional causes. This is typically done using consensus, consistency, and distinctiveness information.

◀ Attribution processes are affected by a number of biases, including the fundamental attribution bias, the halo effect, the Pollyanna effect, and the assumed-similarity bias.

◀ Self-perception theory suggests that we monitor our own behavior to identify its causes, just as we make attibutions about others' behavior, and that people have characteristic attributional styles.

◀ Among the ways of increasing the accuracy of impressions and reducing stereotyping are increasing contact, making positive values conspicuous, and providing information about the targets of stereotyping.

Review

1. Chris is always late for his study group meeting, which is scheduled right after chemistry class. The other members of the group probably think he is somewhat irresponsi-

ble, attributing his lateness to _____ factors. Chris himself probably blames _____ factors.

2. If the members of the study group discover that Chris is usually on time for other meetings and classes, what type of information have they received?
   a. Consensus
   c. Situational
   b. Dispositional
   d. Distinctiveness

3. Fran hears from a friend that Irene is friendly and outgoing. Fran decides to ask her if she will participate in a community service project requiring a great deal of responsibility. Fran's judgment of Irene's character is based on the _____ _____ .

4. Attributing our own failures to situational circumstances while attributing the shortcomings of others to personality flaws is known as the _____ _____ _____ .

5. Social psychologists have proposed several techniques to increase the accuracy with which people make judgments about others and thereby reduce stereotyping. Name three such techniques.

(Answers to review questions are on page 649.)

◀ LOOKING BACK

1. In this chapter, we discussed social psychology, the study of the way people's thoughts, feelings, and actions are affected by others, and the nature and causes of individual behavior in social situations.

2. Attitudes, a central area of study in social psychology, are learned predispositions to respond in a favorable or unfavorable manner to a particular object. The ABC model of attitudes suggests that they have three components: the affect component, the behavior component, and the cognition component. We acquire attitudes through classical conditioning processes, in which a previously neutral object begins to evoke the attitudes associated with another object due to repeated pairings, and through operant conditioning.

3. A number of theories suggest that people try to maintain consistency between attitudes. Cognitive dissonance occurs when two cognitions—attitudes or thoughts—contradict each other and are held simultaneously by an individual. To resolve the contradiction, the person may modify the cognition, change its importance, or deny it, thereby bringing about a reduction in dissonance. How-

ever, alternative explanations based on self-perception theory have been proposed to explain dissonance phenomena.

4. Impressions of others are formed through social cognition—the study of the processes that underlie our understanding of the social world. People develop schemas, which organize information about people and social experiences in memory. Such schemas represent our social life and allow us to interpret and categorize information about others.

5. One of the ways in which people form impressions of others is through the use of central traits, personality characteristics that are given unusually heavy weight when an impression is formed. Information-processing approaches have found that we tend to average sets of traits to form an overall impression.

6. Stereotypes are beliefs and expectations about members of groups held on the basis of membership in those groups. Although they most frequently are used for racial and ethnic groups, stereotypes are also found in categorizations of sex- and age-group membership.

Stereotyping can lead not only to discrimination but to self-fulfilling prophecies, expectations about the occurrence of future events or behaviors that act to increase the likelihood that the event or behavior will actually occur.

7. Attribution theory tries to explain how we understand the causes of behavior, particularly with respect to situational or dispositional factors. To determine causes, people use consensus, consistency, and distinctiveness information.

8. Even though logical processes are involved, attribution is still prone to error, as the fundamental attribution bias and the prevalence of stereotyping demonstrate. Other biases include the halo effect, in which the initial understanding that a person has positive traits is used to infer other positive characteristics; the Pollyanna effect, the tendency to rate others in a generally positive manner; and the assumed-similarity bias, the tendency to think of people as being similar to oneself.

9. Self-perception theory suggests that attribution processes similar to those we use with others may be used to understand the causes of our own behavior. Furthermore, people have characteristic attributional styles, such as the tendency to be optimistic or pessimistic about bad events in their lives. This tendency has consequences for jobs and health.

10. Accurate perception of reality, at least in terms of oneself, is not always beneficial. For example, there is increasing evidence that three sorts of illusions—unrealistic positive self-evaluation, exaggerated perceptions of control, and unrealistic optimism—may be adaptive.

11. Among the ways of increasing the accuracy of attributions and impressions are increasing contact, making values apparent, and providing information about the target of the attribution or stereotype.

KEY TERMS AND CONCEPTS ▶

social psychology (p. 626)
attitudes (627)
ABC model of attitudes (627)
affect component (of attitudes) (627)
behavior component (of attitudes) (627)
cognition component (of attitudes) (627)
vicarious learning (628)
central route processing (630)
peripheral route processing (630)
cognitive dissonance (632)
cognitions (632)

selective exposure (633)
self-perception theory (634)
social cognition (636)
schemas (636)
impression formation (636)
central traits (636)
stereotypes (638)
ingroup-outgroup bias (638)
outgroup (638)
ingroup (638)
discrimination (638)
self-fulfilling prophecy (638)
reverse discrimination (639)

attribution theory (641)
situational causes of behavior (641)
dispositional causes of behavior (641)
consensus information (641)
consistency information (641)
distinctiveness information (641)
fundamental attribution bias (643)
halo effect (643)
implicit personality theory (643)
Pollyanna effect (643)
assumed-similarity bias (644)
cultural assimilator (647)

FOR FURTHER STUDY AND APPLICATION ▶

Ajzen, I. (1988). *Attitudes, personality, and behavior.* Pacific Grove, CA: Brooks/Cole.

This volume provides an interesting overview of the field of attitudes. It does a fine job of integrating various theories.

Kleinke, C. (1987). *Meeting and understanding people.* New York: Freeman.

Drawing on current research and theory, this book provides a summary of how we form perceptions regarding those we encounter and practical ways of making our impressions more accurate.

Shaver, P. (1984). *An introduction to attribution processes.* Hillsdale, NJ: Erlbaum.

This is an excellent guide to attribution theory, written in a way that makes a complex theory clear and lucid.

Fiske, S. T., & Taylor, S. E. (1991). *Social cognition* (2nd ed.). New York: McGraw-Hill.

This book provides a good overview of the latest work on social cognition, particularly in terms of implications for future research.

Katz, P. A., & Taylor, D. A. (1988). *Eliminating racism: Profiles in controversy.* New York: Plenum.

This book presents several approaches to understanding and eliminating prejudice based on race.

Feldman, R. S. (1985). *Social psychology: Theory, research, and applications.* New York: McGraw-Hill.

This is a comprehensive overview of the field, emphasizing the applications drawn from social psychological theories.

ANSWERS (REVIEW III):
1. Dispositional, situational **2.** d **3.** Halo effect **4.** Fundamental attribution error
5. Increasing contact between the target of stereotyping and the holder of the stereotype; making relevant values noticeable; providing information about the targets of stereotyping.

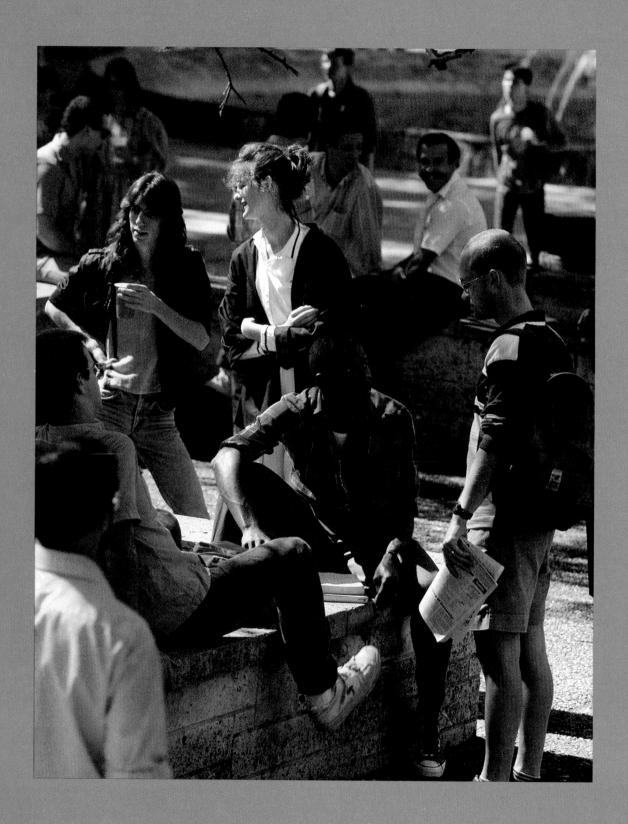

CHAPTER
19

SOCIAL PSYCHOLOGY: INTERACTING WITH OTHERS

PROLOGUE:
JIM JONES

The scene was from another world. Amid the vast beauty of the dense South American jungle, a group of people stood in line to reach a cauldron of soda laced with cyanide. As they neared, they could see the people who had preceded them writhing in agony on the ground as the poison began its deadly work.

Reverend Jim Jones, the leader of the religious cult that made its home in the settlement, urged people forward, assuring them that mass suicide was the only reasonable action to take, and that they should step forward and meet their deaths with eagerness. Whole families moved through the line together, with mothers feeding the poison to their children. Jones's exhortations were effective: When it was all over, some 900 people—the entire population of the settlement—were dead.

LOOKING AHEAD ▷

The mass suicide was no less bizarre than the lives the members of the cult had already been leading. Most had given up all their worldly possessions— and even their children—to Jones and his so-called People's Temple. They had subjected themselves obediently to his dictatorial rule, which had included public humiliation and horrific beatings for infractions of the most minor and arbitrary rules.

When we consider a situation as strange as this, it is tempting to conclude that it is a unique occurrence unrelated to everyday life. Yet it provides a disturbing example of the power of one individual to influence the behavior of others—different in magnitude but similar in kind to many everyday situations.

For instance, how often do we follow the directions of a parent, teacher, or employer, doing things that we feel are inappropriate or incorrect because the order came from someone with authority? How often do we purchase

The grim aftermath of the People's Temple mass suicide illustrates the power of one individual to influence the behavior of others. (Tim Chapman/Black Star.)

clothing because "everybody else" is wearing the same sort of clothes? And how often do we come away from a store having spent more than we intended because of the influence of a persuasive salesperson?

This chapter examines people's interactions and social relationships with one another. We begin with a discussion of **social influence**, the area of social psychology that considers situations in which the actions of an individual (or a group) affect the behavior of others. We explore how what others do and say affects our everyday activities, including circumstances in which we are submissive—or resistant—to authority. Next we consider more special and exclusive forms of social relationships: liking and loving. We examine what social psychologists have learned about the ways people become attracted to one another, form relationships, and fall in love. The chapter concludes with a look at the factors that underlie some of the most negative and positive social behaviors: aggression and helping.

When you finish reading this chapter, you will be able to answer the following questions about our interactions with others:

▶ What are the major sources of social influence and the tactics that are used to bring them about?

▶ What are the best strategies for resisting social pressure?

▶ Why are we attracted to certain people?

▶ What factors underlie aggression and prosocial behavior?

Social influence: The area of social psychology concerned with situations in which the actions of an individual or group affect the behavior of others

SOCIAL INFLUENCE

You have just transferred to a new college and are attending your first class. When the professor enters, you find that your fellow classmates all rise, bow down, and then face the back of the room. You have no understanding of this behavior. Is it more likely that you will (1) jump up to join the rest of the class or (2) remain seated?

Based on what research has told us about social influence, the answer to such a question would almost always be (1). As you undoubtedly know from your own experience, pressures to conform can be painfully strong, and they can bring about changes in behavior that, when considered in perspective, would never have otherwise occurred.

DOING WHAT OTHERS DO: Conformity

Conformity is a change in behavior or attitudes brought about by a desire to follow the beliefs or standards of other people. The classic demonstration of pressure to conform comes from a series of studies carried out in the 1950s by Solomon Asch (Asch, 1951). In the experiments, subjects thought they were participating in a test of perceptual skills with a group of six other subjects. The subjects were shown one card with three lines of varying length and a second card which had a fourth line that matched one of the first three (see Figure 19-1). The task was seemingly straightforward: The subjects had

Conformity: A change in behavior or attitudes brought about by a desire to follow the beliefs or standards of other people

FIGURE 19-1

FIGURE 19-1

Subjects in Asch's conformity experiment were first shown a "standard" line and then asked to identify which of the three comparison lines was identical in length. As this example illustrates, there was always an obvious answer.

to announce aloud which of the first three lines was identical in length to a "standard" line. Because there was always an obvious answer, the task seemed easy to the participants.

Indeed, since the subjects all agreed on the first few trials, the procedure was quite a simple one. But then something odd began to happen. From the perspective of the subject in the group who got to answer last, all of the first six subjects' answers seemed to be wrong—in fact, unanimously wrong. And this continued: Over and over again, the first six subjects provided answers that contradicted what the last subject felt was the correct one. The dilemma that this situation posed for the last subject was whether to follow his or her own perceptions or to follow the group and repeat the answer that everyone else was giving.

As you might have guessed, the situation in the experiment was more contrived that it first appeared. The first six subjects were actually confederates of the experimenter and had been instructed to give unanimously erroneous answers in many of the trials. And the study had nothing to do with perceptual skills. Instead, the issue under investigation was that of conformity.

What Asch found was that in about one-third of the trials, subjects conformed to the unanimous but erroneous group answer, with about 75 percent of all subjects conforming at least once. However, there were strong individual differences: Some subjects conformed nearly all the time, whereas others never did so.

Since Asch's pioneering work, literally hundreds of studies have examined the factors affecting conformity, and we now know a great deal about the phenomenon (Moscovici, 1985; Tanford & Penrod, 1984). Among the most important variables producing conformity are the following:

▶ The nature of the group. The more attractive the group, the greater its ability to produce conformity. The lower the **status**—the social rank held within a group—of a person and the greater the similarity of the individual to the group, the greater is the power of the group over the individual's behavior.

Status: The social rank held within a group

▶ The nature of the individual's response. Conformity is considerably higher when people must make a response publicly than when they can respond privately, as our founding fathers noted when they authorized secret ballots in voting.

▶ The kind of task. People working on tasks and questions that are ambiguous (having no clear answer) are more susceptible to social pressure. Giving an opinion, such as on what type of clothing is fashionable, is more likely to produce conformity than answering a question of fact. Moreover, tasks at which an individual is less competent relative to the group create conditions in which conformity is more likely.

▶ Unanimity of the group. Conformity pressures are most pronounced in groups that are unanimous in their support of a position. But what of the case in which people with dissenting views have an ally in the group—known as a **social supporter**—who agrees with them? Having just one person present who shares the unpopular point of view is sufficient to reduce conformity pressures (Allen, 1975).

Social supporter: A person who shares an unpopular opinion or attitude of another group member, thereby encouraging nonconformity

Gender Differences in Conformity

One of the most inconsistent findings to emerge from the work on conformity relates to gender differences. For many years, the prevailing wisdom was that women were more easily influenced than men—a view that held until the late 1970s (Allen, 1965). At that time, however, research conducted by social psychologist Alice Eagly (1978) suggested that the difference was more apparent than real. For example, it seemed that the tasks employed in conformity experiments often were more familiar to men than to women, leading females to conform because of differences in their perceived lack of expertise (Eagly, 1983; Eagly & Carli, 1981).

More recent reviews of the literature, however, seem to support the earlier point of view: women do seem to conform more to others than do men, relatively independent of the topic at hand (Eagly, 1989). Thus, the best summation of the research on conformity to date is an old one: women are more susceptible to social influence than men. Still, the topsy-turvy nature of the interpretation of the conformity research suggests that we have not heard the last word on this issue.

DOING WHAT OTHERS TELL US TO DO: Compliance

When we discuss conformity, we are usually talking about a phenomenon in which the social pressure is not in the form of a direct order. But in some situations social pressure is much more obvious, and there is direct, explicit pressure to endorse a certain point of view or to behave in a particular way. Social psychologists call the type of behavior that occurs in response to direct social pressure **compliance**.

Compliance: Behavior that occurs in response to direct social pressure

When a Small Request Leads to a Larger One: The Foot in the Door

A salesperson comes to your door and asks you to accept a small sample. You agree, thinking you have nothing to lose. A little while later comes a larger request, which, because you have already agreed to the first one, you have a harder time turning down.

The salesperson in this case is employing a tried-and-true strategy that social psychologists call the foot-in-the-door technique. According to the **foot-in-the-door technique**, you first ask that a person agree to a small request and later ask the person to comply with a more important one. It turns out that compliance with the ultimate request increases significantly when the person first agrees to the smaller favor.

Foot-in-the-door technique: A technique in which compliance with an important request is more likely following compliance with a smaller, previous request

The foot-in-the-door phenomenon was first demonstrated in a study in which a number of experimenters went door to door asking residents to sign a petition in favor of safe driving (Freedman & Fraser, 1966). Almost everyone complied with this small, benign request. However, a few weeks later, different experimenters contacted the residents again and asked for a much larger request: that they erect a huge sign reading "Drive Carefully" on their front lawns. The results were clear: 55 percent of those who had signed the petition agreed to the request, whereas only 17 percent of people in a control group who had not been asked to sign the petition agreed.

Subsequent research has confirmed the effectiveness of the foot-in-the-door technique (Beaman et al., 1983). Why does it work? One reason is that involvement with the small request leads to an interest in an issue, and taking an action—any action—makes the individual more committed to the issue, thereby increasing the likelihood of future compliance. Another explanation revolves around people's self-perceptions. By complying with the initial request, individuals may come to see themselves as the kind of person who provides help when asked. Then, when confronted with the larger request, they agree in order to maintain the kind of consistency in attitudes and behavior that we discussed in Chapter 18. Although we don't know which of these two explanations is more accurate, it is clear that the foot-in-the-door strategy is an effective one.

Where a Large Request Leads to a Smaller One: The Door-in-the-Face

A fund raiser comes to your door and asks for a $500 contribution. You laughingly refuse, telling her that the amount is way out of your league. She then asks for a $10 contribution. What do you do? If you are like most people, you'll probably be a lot more compliant than if she hadn't asked for the huge contribution first. The reason lies in the **door-in-the-face technique**, in which a large request, refusal of which is expected, is followed by a smaller one. Clearly a totally opposite strategy to the foot-in-the-door approach, the door-in-the-face technique has also proved to be effective.

One example of its success was shown in a field experiment in which college students were stopped on the street and asked to agree to a substantial favor—acting as unpaid counselors for juvenile delinquents two hours a week for two years (Cialdini et al., 1975). Not surprisingly, no one agreed to such an outrageous request. But when they were later asked the considerably smaller favor of taking a group of delinquents on a two-hour trip to the zoo, half the people complied. In comparison, only 17 percent of a control group of subjects who had not first received the larger request agreed.

The use of this technique is widespread in everyday life. For instance, children who ask their parents for an increase in their allowance would be well advised to ask for a very large increase and later settle for less. Similarly, television writers sometimes sprinkle their scripts with obscenities that they know will be cut out by network censors, hoping to keep other key phrases intact (Cialdini, 1988).

Why is the door-in-the-face procedure effective? Two explanations have been suggested (Baron & Byrne, 1987). One possibility rests on reciprocal concessions between the person making the request and the individual being asked. In **reciprocal concessions**, requesters are seen to make a compromise (reducing their initial request), thereby inviting a compromise on the part of those who initially refused the request. The result is that people are more willing to comply with the smaller request.

Another explanation rests in our desire to present ourselves well to others. When we first refuse, we feel we have acted reasonably, but a second refusal can make us feel that we are coming across as unreasonable. We comply, then, to enhance the way we present ourselves to others.

Door-in-the-face technique: A strategy in which a large request, refusal of which is expected, is followed by a smaller request

Reciprocal concessions: A phenomenon in which requesters are perceived as compromising their initial request, thereby inviting a compromise from the individual being asked to comply

Obedience to Authority: Testing the Limits of Compliance

Both the foot-in-the-door and the door-in-the-face techniques provide a means by which people are gently led toward agreement with another person's request. In some cases, however, requests are couched in terms of **obedience**, a change in behavior that is due to the commands of others. Although obedience is considerably less common than conformity and compliance, it does occur in several specific kinds of relationships. For example, we may show obedience to our boss, teacher, or parent, merely because of the power they hold to reward or punish us.

In some cases, obedience reaches unusual extremes, such as the People's Temple disaster described at the beginning of the chapter. Although obedience is difficult to study under controlled conditions, at least one series of experiments, described in the Research Classics box on p. 658, has examined the phenomenon.

Obedience: A change in behavior due to the commands of others

THE INFORMED CONSUMER OF PSYCHOLOGY:
Strategies for Maintaining Your Own Point of View

We have seen how susceptible people are to the influence of others, whether it be relatively indirect, as with subtle conformity pressure, or direct, as with a straightforward order. How can one remain independent in the face of these sorts of pressures? Social psychological theory and research have suggested a number of techniques for helping one to remain faithful to one's own point of view:

▶ Inoculation. To avoid smallpox, people receive a shot containing a small dose of smallpox germs. This injection produces antibodies in the body that can repel a major invasion of smallpox germs, should the individual be exposed to the disease in the future. Similarly, one procedure for helping people remain independent of future attempts at persuasion is for them to expose themselves to a sample of counterarguments to which they might be subjected in the future. In an example of this technique, William McGuire (1964) showed that subjects could be made more resistant to persuasion if they were first exposed to a sample of opposing arguments along with information that refuted those arguments. Exposure to the opposing arguments—**inoculation**, as he called it—led to less subsequent change in beliefs than exposing subjects to information that bolstered their own initial views.

Inoculation: Exposure to arguments opposing one's beliefs, making the subject more resistant to later attempts to change those beliefs

▶ Forewarning. Telling people that a persuasive message is coming and what that message involves, a strategy called **forewarning**, is sometimes sufficient to reduce social influence, even if counterarguments are not provided. This is particularly true if the issues are important and the target of influence has a large amount of information available (Cacioppo & Petty, 1979; Petty & Cacioppo, 1977). Simply knowing that a persuasive message is likely to be received without knowing the specific content of the upcoming message can reduce subsequent attitude change. The reason? When people are aware that they are going to receive information counter to their attitudes, they tend to develop their own arguments in support of their original attitudes. Forewarned is thus forearmed.

Forewarning: A procedure in which a subject is told in advance that a persuasive message is forthcoming, sometimes reducing the effects of social influence

▶ Consistency. One technique that is not only effective in reducing persuasibility but that can actually change the attitude of the persuader is **consistency**. Under certain conditions, particularly in group settings where a

Consistency: The persistence of those holding an unpopular view, eventually bringing about a change in the attitude of the majority

WOULD YOU SHOCK A STRANGER?: OBEDIENCE TO AUTHORITY

Think, for a moment, about how you might respond if a stranger said to you:

I've devised a new way of improving memory. All I need is for you to teach people a list of words and then give them a test. The test procedure requires only that you give learners a shock each time they make a mistake on the test. To administer the shocks you will use a "shock generator" that gives shocks ranging from 30 to 450 volts. You can see that the switches are labeled from "slight shock" through "danger: severe shock" at the top level, where there are three red X's. But don't worry; although the shocks may be painful, they will cause no permanent damage.

Presented with this situation, you would likely think that neither you, nor anyone else, would go along with the stranger's unusual request. Clearly, it lies outside the bounds of what we consider good sense.

Or does it? Suppose the stranger asking for your help were a psychologist conducting an experiment. Or suppose it were your teacher, your employer, or your military commander—all people in authority with some seemingly legitimate reason for their request.

If you still think it unlikely that you would comply, you might reconsider. For the situation represented

above describes a now-classic experiment conducted by social psychologist Stanley Milgram in the 1960s (Milgram, 1974). In the study, subjects were placed in a situation in which they were told by an experimenter to give increasingly strong shocks to another person as part of a study on learning (see Figure 19-2). In reality, the experiment had nothing to do with learning; the real issue under consideration was the degree to which subjects would comply with the experimenter's requests. In fact, the person supposedly receiving the shocks was actually a confederate who never really received any punishment.

Most people who hear a description of the experiment feel that it is unlikely that *any* subject would give the maximum level of shock—or, for that matter, any shock at all. Even a group of psychiatrists who had the situation described to them predicted that fewer than 2 percent of the subjects would comply completely and administer the strongest shocks. However, the actual results contradicted both experts' and nonexperts' predictions: Almost two-thirds of the subjects eventually used the highest setting on the

shock generator to "electrocute" the learner.

Why did so many individuals comply fully with the experimenter's demands? Extensive interviews carried out with subjects following the experiment showed that they were obedient primarily because they believed that the experimenter would be responsible for any potential ill effects that befell the learner. The experiment's orders were accepted, then, because the subjects thought that they personally could not be held accountable for their actions—they could always blame the experimenter.

Although the Milgram experiment has been criticized for creating an extremely trying set of circumstances for the subjects—thereby raising serious ethical questions—and on methodological grounds (Miller, 1986; Orne & Holland, 1968), it remains one of the strongest laboratory demonstrations of compliance. We need only consider actual instances of compliance to authority to witness some frightening real-life parallels. A major defense of Nazi officers after World War II, for instance, was that they were "only following orders." Jim Jones's cult members uniformly complied with his orders—though it meant their own deaths. Milgram's results force each of us to consider how able we would be to withstand the intense power of authority.

majority is attempting to influence a minority, the unyielding persistence of the minority in its point of view can actually bring about a change in the majority's attitudes (Moscovici & Mugny, 1983; Tanford & Penrod, 1984). Apparently, the unyielding repetition of one's own point of view can cause others to rethink their position and, ultimately, to be persuaded by the minority's opinion.

On the other hand, some evidence suggests that a somewhat different approach is more appropriate. Social psychologist Edwin Hollander (1980) has addressed situations in which a minority is attempting to remain independent of a majority position. He suggests a strategy in which individuals

FIGURE 19-2

This impressive-looking "shock generator" was used to lead participants to believe they were administering electric shocks to another person, who was connected to the generator by electrodes that were attached to the skin. (Copyright © 1965 by Stanley Milgram. From the film *Obedience*, distributed by the New York University Film Library and Pennsylvania State University, PCR.)

conform initially to the views of the source of influence. After doing so, which establishes them as competent and reasonable group members, they can behave more independently and espouse views that are contrary to the majority's views. According to Hollander's theory, instead of remaining consistently firm in a deviant position, as Moscovici's consistency approach suggests, people should first conform—but after establishing their "credentials," they should then press their minority views.

Experimental evidence supports both approaches (Maass & Clark, 1984; Wold, 1985). Such research makes it clear that social influence is not a one-way street; when we are the targets of social influence, we have a fighting chance to remain independent.

RECAP AND REVIEW I

Recap

◄ Social influence encompasses situations in which the actions of one individual or group affect the behavior of another.

◄ Conformity is a change in attitude or behavior brought about by a desire to follow the beliefs or standards of others.

◄ Compliance is a change in behavior made in response to more explicit social pressure. Obedience, in contrast, is a change in behavior resulting from a direct command.

◄ Among the primary techniques for remaining independent from group pressure are inoculation, forewarning, and consistency.

Review

1. When social psychologists discuss _____, they are referring to a change in behavior resulting from a desire to follow the beliefs or standards of others. However, when a change in behavior occurs in response to social pressure in the form of a direct order, the change is called _____ .

2. List four of the most important variables producing conformity.

3. What was the primary reason that subjects in Milgram's compliance experiment gave increasingly painful shocks to another person?
   a. They believed that they were not responsible for what happened to the other person.
   b. They were predisposed to cruel behavior.
   c. They were afraid they wouldn't get paid if they didn't complete the experiment.
   d. They knew the experiment was faked.

4. Preliminary exposure to opposing arguments is a method of resisting persuasion called
   a. forewarning.   c. consistency.
   b. inoculation.   d. injection.

5. Describe an alternative to the consistency technique for persuading a majority of a minority's views.

(Answers to review questions are on page 660.)

Interpersonal attraction: Positive feelings for others

Proximity: Nearness to another, one cause for liking

The proximity of neighbors is one factor that leads us to like them. We tend to be attracted to those who are geographically close to us. (Innervisions.)

LIKING AND LOVING: INTERPERSONAL ATTRACTION AND THE DEVELOPMENT OF RELATIONSHIPS

When nineteenth-century poet Elizabeth Barrett Browning wrote "How do I love thee? Let me count the ways," she was expressing feelings about a topic that is central to most people's lives—and one that has developed into a major subject of investigation by social psychologists: loving and liking. Known more formally as the study of **interpersonal attraction** or **close relationships**, this topic encompasses the factors that lead to positive feelings for others.

HOW DO I LIKE THEE? Let Me Count the Ways

By far the greatest amount of research has focused on liking, probably because it has always proved easier for investigators conducting short-term experiments to produce states of liking in strangers who have just met than to promote and observe loving relationships over long periods of time. Hence traditional studies have given us a good deal of knowledge about the factors that initially attract two people to each other (Berscheid, 1985). Among the most important factors considered by social psychologists are the following:

▶ Proximity. If you live in a dormitory or an apartment, consider the friends you made when you first moved in. Chances are you became friendliest with those who lived geographically closest to you. In fact, this is one of the best-established findings in the interpersonal attraction literature; **proximity** leads to liking (Festinger, Schachter & Back, 1950; Nahome & Lawton, 1976).

ANSWERS (REVIEW I):
1. Conformity, obedience   **2.** Nature of the group; nature of the individual's response; kind of task; unanimity of group   **3.** a   **4.** b   **5.** Initially conform with majority to establish credibility, then present minority views

► Mere exposure. Repeated exposure to a person is often sufficient to produce attraction. Interestingly, repeated exposure to *any* stimulus—be it a person, picture, record, or what have you—most frequently makes us like the stimulus more (Birnbaum & Mellers, 1979; Zajonc, 1968). Becoming familiar with a stimulus can evoke positive feelings; these positive feelings stemming from familiarity are then transferred to the stimulus itself. There are exceptions, though: In cases in which the initial interactions are strongly negative, repeated exposure is unlikely to cause us to like another person more; instead, we may end up disliking such an individual more the more we are exposed to him or her.

► Similarity. We tend to like those who are similar to us; discovering that others are similar in terms of attitudes, values, or traits promotes liking for them (Byrne, 1969; Hill & Stull, 1981; Meyer & Pepper, 1971). Moreover, the more similar others are, the more we like them. One reason behind the relationship between similarity and interpersonal attraction is that we assume that people with similar attitudes will evaluate us positively (Condon & Crano, 1988). Because there is a strong **reciprocity-of-liking effect** (a tendency to like those who like us), knowing that someone evaluates us positively will promote attraction to that person. In addition, we assume that when we like someone else, that person likes us in return (Metee & Aronson, 1974; Tagiuri, 1958).

Reciprocity-of-liking effect: The tendency to like those who like us

► Need complementarity. There are exceptions to the general case that similarity and attraction are found together. People don't always seek out others like themselves: Some people seem to be attracted to others who are unlike them. One reason for this may be that we are attracted to those people who fulfill the greatest number of needs for us. Thus a dominant person may seek out someone who is submissive; at the same time, the submissive individual may be seeking someone who is dominant. Although their dissimilarity often makes others expect them to be incompatible, by forming a relationship they are able to fulfill each other's complementary needs.

The hypothesis that people are attracted to others who fulfill their needs—dubbed the **need-complementarity hypothesis**—was first proposed in the late 1950s in a classic study which found that a sample of married couples appeared to have complementary needs (Winch, 1958). However, there has been little evidence since that time to support the hypothesis, with most studies finding that attraction is related more to similarity in needs than to complementarity (e.g., Meyer & Pepper, 1977). In general, then, similarity—be it in attitudes, values, or personality traits—remains one of the best predictors of whether two people will be attracted to each other.

Need-complementarity hypothesis: The hypothesis that people are attracted to others who fulfill their needs

► Physical attractiveness. For most people, the equation *beautiful = good* is a very real one. As a result, people who are physically attractive are more popular than those who are physically unattractive, if all other factors are equal. This finding, which contradicts the values that most people would profess, is apparent even in childhood—with nursery-school-age children rating popularity on the basis of attractiveness (Dion & Berscheid, 1974)—and continues into adulthood. Indeed, physical attractiveness may be the single most important element promoting initial liking in college dating situations, although its influence decreases when people get to know each other better (Berscheid & Walster, 1974; Hatfield & Sprecher, 1986).

Physical attractiveness is a drawback in some cases, however. Although good looks lead to more positive impressions of men in job-related situa-

THE PROPORTIONS OF BEAUTY

The importance of physical attractiveness in both friendships and romantic relationships has raised the question of just what people mean when they say that someone is beautiful, and recent research is beginning to find an answer to the question.

According to the results of a series of experiments by psychologist Michael Cunningham, there is remarkable agreement on the specific dimensions of facial configuration that lead people to find a face attractive (Cunningham, 1986). In the research, a group of 150 white male college students rated that attractiveness and social attributes of 50 women from pictures of their faces. About half the women—most of them white, some black or Asian—were finalists in a Miss Universe contest.

From the ratings of the faces, Cunningham was able to quantify the perceived ideal female face. For example, the ideal face had an eye width that was three-tenths the width of the face at the level of the eyes. Chin length was one-fifth the height of the face. The distance from the center of the eye to the bottom of the eyebrow was one-tenth the height of the face, and the height of the eyeball was one-fourteenth the height of the face (see Figure 19-3).

It is important to understand, of course, that such proportions represent composite ideals, not those dimensions found in any particular individual. Furthermore, the emphasis on facial configuration discounts the influence of personality traits on the way in which individuals are perceived.

Still, the influence of beauty clearly is an important one in everyday interactions, and there is even evidence suggesting that we may be born with preferences for attractive faces. In one experiment, a group of infants between the ages of 6 and 8 months was shown pairs of photos—one of a woman judged attractive and the other of a woman judged unattractive (Langlois et al., 1987). The infants spent significantly more time looking at the attractive faces than the unattractive faces, suggesting that the attractive faces were more interesting to them. The results clearly support the notion that there are universal standards of attractiveness, and that the way we judge attractiveness may be at least partially innate. Beauty, then, is also in the eye of the baby.

tions, beauty can work against women in managerial positions. The reason is a common (although totally unfounded) stereotype that successful, attractive women attain their position as a result of looks rather than ability (Heilman & Stopek, 1985).

In general, though, physical attractiveness is an asset in social situations. It is a powerful factor in determining to whom people are attracted and the kind of social life they will have (Reis, 1982; Hatfield & Sprecher, 1986). Furthermore, as discussed in the Cutting Edge box, high agreement exists in society's definition of attractiveness.

The factors that we have discussed are not, of course, the only constituents of liking. For example, survey research has sought to identify the factors critical in friendships. In one questionnaire answered by some 40,000 respondents, the qualities that were most valued in a friend were identified as the ability to keep confidences, loyalty, and warmth and affection, followed closely by supportiveness, frankness, and a sense of humor (Parlee, 1979). The results are summarized in Figure 19-4.

HOW DO I LOVE THEE? Let Me Count the Ways

Whereas our knowledge of what makes people like one another is extensive, our understanding of love is a more limited and relatively recent phenomenon. For some time, many social psychologists believed that love represents a phenomenon too difficult to observe and study in a controlled, scientific way. However, love is such a central issue in most people's lives that, in time, social psychologists could not resist its allure and became infatuated with the topic (Sternberg & Grajek, 1984).

FIGURE 19-3

In order to determine the facial configuration that was seen as most attractive, researchers measured each of the numbered distances on a series of photos that had been previously rated by a group of judges according to how physically and socially attractive they appeared. The results showed that there was surprising uniformity across judges and that several common proportions existed. For example, the "ideal" female face had a chin length that was one-fifth the height of the face. Of course, emphasis on facial configuration discounts the influence of personality traits on the way in which individuals are perceived. (Cunningham, 1986.)

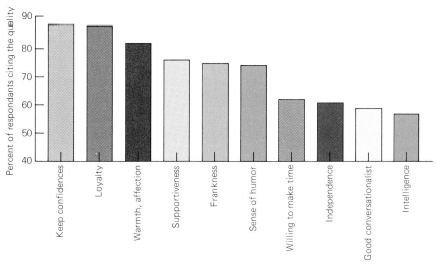

FIGURE 19-4

These are the key qualities looked for in a friend, according to some 40,000 respondents to a questionnaire.

As a first step, researchers tried to identify the distinguishing characteristics between mere liking and full-blown love (Sternberg, 1987). Using this approach, they discovered that love is not simply liking of a greater quantity, but a qualitatively different psychological state (Walster & Walster, 1978). For instance, at least in its early stages, love includes relatively intense physiological arousal, an all-encompassing interest in another individual, fantasizing about the other, and relatively rapid swings of emotion. Similarly, Davis

TABLE 19-1

Loving and Liking

Sample love items:
I feel that I can confide in _____ about virtually everything.
I would do almost anything for _____ .
I feel responsible for _____ 's well-being.

Sample liking items:
I think that _____ is unusually well adjusted.
I think that _____ is one of those people who quickly wins
respect.
_____ is one of the most likable people I know.

Source: Rubin, 1973

(1985) suggests that love has elements of fascination, exclusiveness, sexual desire, and intense caring that liking lacks.

Social psychologist Zick Rubin (1970, 1973) has tried to differentiate between love and liking using a paper-and-pencil scale. As can be seen from the sample items in Table 19-1, each question refers to the person to whom the individual is attracted.

Researchers have found that couples scoring high on the love scale differ considerably from those with low scores. They gaze at each other more, and their relationships are more likely to be intact six months later than are the relationships of those who score low on the scale.

Other experiments have found evidence suggesting that the heightened physiological arousal hypothesized to be characteristic of loving is indeed present when a person reports being in love. Interestingly, though, it may not be just arousal of a sexual nature. Berscheid & Walster (1974) have theorized that when we are exposed to *any* stimulus that increases physiological arousal—such as danger, fear, or anger—our feelings for another person present at the time of the arousal may be labeled as love, if there are situational cues that suggest that "love" is an appropriate label for the feelings being experienced. In sum, we perceive we are in love when instances of general physiological arousal are coupled with the thought that the cause of the arousal is most likely love.

This theory explains why a person who keeps being rejected or hurt by another can still feel "in love" with that person. If the rejection leads to physiological arousal, but the arousal still happens to be attributed to love—and not to rejection—then a person will still feel "in love."

Other researchers have theorized that there are actually several kinds of love (Hendrick, Hendrick & Adler, 1988; Hendrick & Hendrick, 1988). Some distinguish between two main types of love: passionate love and companionate love. **Passionate (or romantic) love** represents a state of intense absorption in someone. It includes intense physiological arousal, psychological interest, and caring for the needs of another. In contrast, **companionate love** is the strong affection that we have for those with whom our lives are deeply involved. The love we feel for our parents, other family members, and even some close friends falls into the category of companionate love.

According to psychologist Robert Sternberg (1986), an even finer differentiation between types of love is in order. He proposes that love is made up of three components: an intimacy component, encompassing feelings of

Passionate (or romantic) love: A state of intense absorption in someone that is characterized by physiological arousal, psychological interest, and caring for another's needs

Companionate love: The strong affection we have for those with whom our lives are deeply involved

TABLE 19-2

The Kinds of Love

	Component*		
	Intimacy	**Passion**	**Decision/Commitment**
Nonlove	−	−	−
Liking	+	−	−
Infatuated love	−	+	−
Empty love	−	−	+
Romantic love	+	+	−
Companionate love	+	−	+
Fatuous love	−	+	+
Consummate love	+	+	+

*+ = component present; − = component absent.
Source: Sternberg, 1986, Table 2.

closeness and connectedness; a passion component, made up of the motivational drives relating to sex, physical closeness, and romance; and a decision/commitment component, encompassing the cognition that one loves someone (in the short term) and longer-term feelings of commitment to maintain love. As can be seen in Table 19-2, particular combinations of the three components produce eight kinds of love.

THE RISE AND FALL OF LIKING AND LOVING:
Understanding the Course of Relationships

With one out of two marriages ending in divorce and broken love affairs a common phenomenon, it is not surprising that social psychologists have begun to turn their attention increasingly toward understanding how relationships develop, are maintained—and, in some cases, dissolve (Ickes, 1984; Hays, 1985; Snyder, Berscheid & Glick, 1985; Clark & Reis, 1988).

The behavior of couples in developing relationships changes in fairly predictable patterns (Berscheid, 1985; Burgess & Huston, 1979). The most frequent pattern follows this course:

▶ People interact more often, for longer periods of time, and in a widening array of settings.

▶ They seek each other's company.

▶ They increasingly "open up" to each other, disclosing secrets and sharing physical intimacies. They are more willing to share both positive and negative feelings and are increasingly willing to provide praise and criticism.

▶ They begin to understand each other's point of view and way of looking at the world.

▶ Their goals and behavior form greater synchrony, and they begin to share greater similarity in attitudes and values.

▶ Their investment in the relationship—in terms of time, energy, and commitment—increases.

▶ They begin to feel that their psychological well-being is tied to the well-being of the relationship. The relationship comes to be seen as unique and irreplaceable.

▶ They start behaving as a couple, rather than as two separate individuals.

Although these transitions in relationships are typical, it is difficult to predict the exact point at which each will occur. One important reason is that at the same time the relationship is evolving, the two individuals may be going through personal growth and change themselves.

Once a relationship has evolved, how can we distinguish successful ones from those that will ultimately fail? Some answers come from a study by Jeanette and Robert Lauer (1985), who surveyed couples who reported being happily married for 15 years or more. When asked to indicate what it was that had made their marriages last, both the husbands and the wives gave remarkably similar responses. As you can see in Table 19-3, the most frequently named reason was perceiving one's spouse as one's best friend and

TABLE 19-3

Most-often-cited Reasons* for Success in Marriage

Cited by Husbands	Cited by Wives
My spouse is my best friend.	My spouse is my best friend.
I like my spouse as a person.	I like my spouse as a person.
Marriage is a long-term commitment.	Marriage is a long-term commitment.
Marriage is sacred.	Marriage is sacred.
We agree on aims and goals.	We agree on aims and goals.
My spouse has grown more interesting.	My spouse has grown more interesting.
I want the relationship to succeed.	I want the relationship to succeed.
An enduring marriage is important to social stability.	We laugh together.
We laugh together.	We agree on a philosophy of life.
I am proud of my spouse's achievements.	We agree on how and how often to show affection.
We agree on a philosophy of life.	An enduring marriage is important to social stability.
We agree about our sex life.	We have a stimulating exchange of ideas.
We agree on how and how often to show affection.	We discuss things calmly.
I confide in my spouse.	We agree about our sex life.
We share outside hobbies and interests.	I am proud of my spouse's achievements.

*In order of frequency.
Source: Lauer & Lauer, 1985.

liking him or her "as a person." There was also a strong belief in marriage as a commitment and a desire to make the relationship work, as well as agreement about aims and goals. On the other hand, there was not blind commitment to the other person: People acknowledged their partner's flaws, but they tended to overlook them. As one husband said, "She isn't perfect. But I don't worry about her weak points, which are very few. Her strong points overcome them too much" (Lauer & Lauer, 1985).

Another factor affecting the long-term success of loving relationships concerns the rate at which the various components of love develop. According to Sternberg's theory of love, the three individual components of love—intimacy, passion, and decision/commitment—vary in their influence over time and follow distinct courses, as illustrated in Figure 19-5. In strong loving relationships, the level of commitment peaks and then remains stable, while intimacy continues to grow over the course of a relationship. Passion, on the other hand, shows a marked decline over time, reaching a plateau fairly early in a relationship. Still, it remains an important component of loving relationships.

The Decline of a Relationship

What is it that causes some relationships to flounder? Social psychologist George Levinger (1983) has speculated on the reasons behind the deterioration of relationships. One important factor appears to be a change in judgments about the meaning of a partner's behavior. Behavior that was once viewed as "charming forgetfulness" becomes seen as "boorish indifference," and the partner becomes less valued. In addition, communications may be disrupted; rather than listening to what the other person is saying, each partner becomes bent on justifying himself or herself, and communication deteriorates. Eventually, a partner may begin to invite and agree with criticism of the other partner from people outside the relationship and look to others for the fulfillment of basic needs that were previously met by the partner.

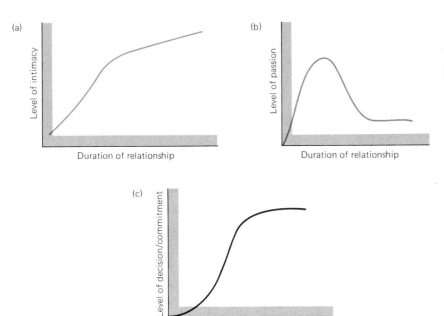

FIGURE 19-5

The changing ingredients of love. The three components of love vary in strength over the course of a relationship. (Sternberg, 1986.)

"*When I fell in love with you, suddenly your eyes didn't seem close together. Now they seem close together again.*"

When relationships begin to deteriorate, flaws that were previously viewed as charming come to be perceived in a more negative light. (Drawing by Wm. Hamilton, © 1976 The New Yorker Magazine, Inc.)

Interpsychic phase: The first phase in the decline of a relationship, characterized by a focus on the other person's behavior and an evaluation of the extent to which this behavior provides reason for terminating the relationship

Dyadic phase: The second phase in the decline of a relationship, in which a person confronts a partner and determines whether to attempt to repair, redefine, or terminate the relationship

Social phase: The third phase in the decline of a relationship, in which there is public acknowledgment that the relationship is being dissolved, and others are given an account of events that led to the relationship's termination

Grave-dressing phase: The fourth and final stage in the decline of a relationship, in which the relationship is physically and psychologically ended

Just as developing relationships tend to follow a common pattern, relationships that are on the decline conform to a pattern of stages (Duck, 1982). The first phase occurs when a person decides that he or she can no longer tolerate being in a relationship. During this stage, called the **interpsychic phase**, there is a focus on the other person's behavior and an evaluation of the extent to which this behavior provides a basis for terminating the relationship.

In the **dyadic phase**, a person decides to confront the partner and determines whether to attempt to repair, redefine, or terminate the relationship. For example, a redefinition might encompass a qualitative change in the level of the relationship. ("We can still be friends" might replace "I'll love you forever.")

If the decision is made to terminate the relationship, the person then enters the **social phase**, in which there is public acknowledgment that the relationship is being dissolved and an accounting is made to others regarding the events that led to the termination of the relationship. The last stage is the **grave-dressing phase**, in which the major activity is to physically and psychologically end the relationship. One of the major concerns of this period is to rethink the entire relationship, making what happened seem reasonable and in keeping with one's self-perceptions.

RECAP AND REVIEW II

Recap

◄ Studies of interpersonal attraction and close relationships consider liking and loving.

◄ Among the most important elements that affect liking are proximity, mere exposure, similarity, and physical attractiveness.

◄ Love is assumed to be differentiated from liking in qualitative, as well as quantitative, respects. In addition, several different kinds of love can be distinguished.

◄ Social psychologists have begun to pay increasing attention to the factors relating to the maintenance and decline of relationships.

Review

1. What five factors are among the most important in determining how much we like another person?

2. Research has shown that "beauty is in the eye of the beholder"—that each person has a different opinion about what constitutes physical attractiveness. True or false?

_____

3. Name the three components of love proposed by Sternberg.

4. The stages through which relationships decline include the _____ phase, the _____ phase, the _____ phase, and the _____ - _____ phase.

(Answers to review questions are on page 670.)

HURTING AND HELPING OTHERS: AGGRESSION AND PROSOCIAL BEHAVIOR

A 22-year-old woman who stopped in a bar for a drink late one evening was sexually assaulted and repeatedly raped on a pool table by a group of four men. Despite her desperate pleas to at least nine bystanders, no one came to her aid. In fact, instead of helping her, the other people in the bar simply stood by, and some even cheered.

▲ ▲ ▲

When he saw a man slumped in the seat of a burning car, Darrell Van Etten rushed to save him, "just as any other . . . human being would have done." Aware that the car could blow up at any second, Van Etten struggled to remove the unconscious man from the flaming vehicle. His efforts came just in time: When he was eight feet away from the car, it exploded.

In these two incidents, we see the best and the worst of humanity. In the first—a true sequence of events dramatized in the film *The Accused*—we see violence unrestrained by bystanders. In the second, we get a considerably more positive view of the world, in a deed that won a Carnegie award for heroism.

Psychologists have long pondered the issues of what motivates helping behavior and its counterpart, aggression. Much of the work was inspired by an incident—described in Chapter 1—that occurred some twenty years ago when a young woman named Kitty Genovese was heard screaming, "Oh, my God, he stabbed me," and "Please help me," by no fewer than thirty-eight of her neighbors. Not one witness came forward to help, and it was not until thirty minutes had gone by that even one person bothered to call the police. Genovese subsequently died in an alleyway before the police arrived—the victim of a vicious attack by a mugger.

If events such as these foster only a negative, pessimistic interpretation of human capacities, other, equally dramatic incidents promote a more optimistic view of humankind. In addition to dramatic incidents of heroism such as those performed by Darrell Van Etten, ponder the cases of people like Raoul Wallenberg, who risked death to help Jews escape from the Nazis in German-occupied countries during World War II. Or consider the simple kindnesses of life: lending a valued recording, stopping to help a child who has fallen off her bicycle, or merely sharing a candy bar with a friend. Such instances of helping are no less characteristic of human behavior than the more distasteful examples. In this part of the chapter we explore the work that social psychologists have done in an effort to explain instances of both aggressive and helping behavior.

We need look no further than our daily paper or the nightly news to be bombarded with examples of aggression, both on a societal level (war, invasion, assassination) and on an individual level (crime, child abuse, and the many petty cruelties that humans are capable of inflicting on one another). Is such aggression an inevitable part of the human condition, or is aggression primarily a function of particular circumstances that might be alleviated by changing the conditions that cause it?

Social psychologists investigating this issue have begun by attempting to define the term "aggression" (Krebs & Miller, 1985). This is not as simple as it may at first appear, since many examples of inflicted pain or injury may or may not qualify as aggression, depending upon one's definition (see Table 19-4). Although it is clear, for instance, that a rapist is acting aggressively toward his victim, it is less certain that a physician carrying out an emergency medical procedure without an anesthetic, thereby causing incredible pain to the patient, should be considered aggressive.

Aggression: Intentional injury or harm to another person

Most social psychologists define aggression in terms of the intent and purpose behind the behavior: **Aggression** is intentional injury of or harm to another person (Berkowitz, 1974). Under this definition, it is clear that the rapist in our example is acting aggressively, whereas the physician causing pain during a medical procedure is not.

Aggression as a Release: Instinct Approaches

If you have ever punched an adversary in the nose, you may have experienced a certain satisfaction, despite your better judgment. Instinct theories, noting the prevalence of aggression not only in humans but in animals as well, propose that aggression is primarily the outcome of innate—or inborn—urges.

The major proponent of the instinct approach is Konrad Lorenz, an ethologist (a scientist who studies animal behavior) who suggested that humans, along with members of other species, have a fighting instinct, which in earlier times ensured protection of food supplies and weeded out the weaker of the species (Lorenz, 1966, 1974). The controversial notion arising from Lorenz's instinct approach is the idea that aggressive energy is constantly being built up within an individual until it is finally discharged in a process called **catharsis**. The longer the energy is built up, says Lorenz, the greater will be the magnitude of the aggression displayed when it is discharged.

Catharsis: The notion that aggression is built up and must be discharged through violent acts

Probably the most controversial idea to come out of instinct theories of aggression is Lorenz's proposal that society ought to provide acceptable means of catharsis through, for instance, participation in sports and games, in order to prevent its discharge in less socially desirable ways. However, although the notion makes logical sense, there is no possible way to devise an adequate experiment to test it. In fact, relatively little support exists for instinct theories in general because of the difficulty in finding evidence for

---

ANSWERS (REVIEW II):
1. Proximity, exposure, similarity, need complementarity, physical attractiveness **2.** False; research has provided evidence that there may be universal components of physical attractiveness **3.** Intimacy, passion, decision/commitment **4.** Interpsychic, dyadic, social, grave-dressing

TABLE 19-1

Is This Aggression?

To see for yourself the difficulties involved in defining aggression, consider each of the following acts and determine whether it represents aggressive behavior—according to your own definition of aggression.

1. A spider eats a fly.
2. Two wolves fight for the leadership of the pack.
3. A soldier shoots an enemy at the front line.
4. The warden of a prison executes a convicted criminal.
5. A juvenile gang attacks members of another gang.
6. Two men fight for a piece of bread.
7. A man viciously kicks a cat.
8. A man, while cleaning a window, knocks over a flower pot, which, in falling, injures a pedestrian.
9. A girl kicks a wastebasket.
10. Mr. X, a notorious gossip, speaks disparagingly of many people of his acquaintance.
11. A man mentally rehearses a murder he is about to commit.
12. An angry son purposely fails to write to his mother, who is expecting a letter and will be hurt if none arrives.
13. An enraged boy tries with all his might to inflict injury on his antagonist, a bigger boy, but is not successful in doing so. His efforts simply amuse the bigger boy.
14. A woman daydreams of harming her antagonist but has no hope of doing so.
15. A senator does not protest the escalation of bombing to which she is morally opposed.
16. A farmer beheads a chicken and prepares it for supper.
17. A hunter kills an animal and mounts it as a trophy.
18. A dog snarls at a mail carrier but does not bite.
19. A physician gives a flu shot to a screaming child.
20. A boxer gives his opponent a bloody nose.
21. A girl scout tries to assist an elderly woman but trips her by accident.
22. A bank robber is shot in the back while trying to escape.
23. A tennis player smashes her racket after missing a volley.
24. A person commits suicide.
25. A cat kills a mouse, parades around with it, and then discards it.

Source: Benjamin, 1985, p. 41.

any kind of pent-up reservoir of aggression (Berkowitz, 1974; Geen & Donnerstein, 1983). Most social psychologists suggest that we should look to other approaches to explain aggression.

Aggression as a Reaction to Frustration: Frustration-Aggression Approaches

Have you ever worked painstakingly on a model or puzzle, only to have someone clumsily knock it over and ruin it just as you were about to complete it? The feelings you experienced toward the person who destroyed your work probably placed you on the verge of real aggression, and you no doubt seethed inside.

Frustration-aggression theory tries to explain aggression in terms of events such as the one described above. When first put forward, the theory said flatly that frustration *always* led to aggression of some sort, and that aggression was *always* the result of some frustration, where **frustration** is

Frustration: A state produced by the thwarting or blocking of some ongoing, goal-directed behavior

PART 7

THE SOCIAL FOUNDATIONS
OF BEHAVIOR

Aggressive cues: Stimuli that have been associated with aggression in the past

After observing an adult model behaving aggressively, angered children carried out behaviors remarkably similar to those they had seen earlier. (Courtesy of Albert Bandura, Stanford University.)

defined as the thwarting or blocking of some ongoing, goal-directed behavior (Dollard, Doob, Miller, Mowrer & Sears, 1939). More recent formulations, however, have modified the original one, suggesting instead that frustration produces anger, leading to a *readiness* to act aggressively. Whether or not actual aggression occurs depends on the presence of **aggressive cues**, stimuli that have been associated in the past with actual aggression or violence and that will trigger aggression again (Berkowitz, 1984; Josephson, 1987). In addition, frustration is assumed to produce aggression only to the extent that the frustration produces negative feelings (Berkowitz, 1989).

What kinds of stimuli act as aggressive cues? They can range from the most overt, such as the presence of weapons, to the most subtle, such as the mere mention of the name of an individual who has behaved violently in the past. For example, in one experiment angered subjects behaved significantly more aggressively when in the presence of a rifle and revolver than in a comparable situation in which the guns were not present (Berkowitz & LePage, 1967). Similarly, frustrated subjects in an experiment who had viewed a violent movie were more aggressive to a confederate with the same name as the star of the movie than to a confederate with a different name (Berkowitz & Geen, 1966). It appears, then, that frustration does lead to aggression, at least when aggressive cues are present.

Learning to Hurt Others: Observational Learning Approaches
Do we learn to be aggressive? The observational learning (sometimes called "social learning") approach to aggression says we do. Taking an almost opposite view from the instinct theories, which focus on the innate aspects of aggression, observational learning theory (which we discussed first in Chapter 5) emphasizes how social and environmental conditions can teach individuals to be aggressive. Aggression is seen not as inevitable, but rather as a learned response that can be understood in terms of rewards and punishments (Bandura, 1973; Zillman, 1978).

Suppose, for instance, that a girl hits her younger brother when he damages one of her new toys. Whereas instinct theory would suggest that the aggression had been pent up and was now being discharged, and frustration-aggression theory would examine the girl's frustration at no longer being able to use her new toy, observational learning theory would look for a previous reinforcement that the girl had received for being aggressive. Perhaps she had learned that aggression resulted in her getting attention from her parents, or perhaps in the past her brother had apologized after being hit. In either case, observational learning theory views the aggression as a result of past rewards the girl had obtained for such behavior.

Observational learning theory pays particular attention not only to direct rewards and punishments that individuals themselves receive, but to the rewards and punishments that models—individuals who provide a guide to appropriate behavior—receive for their aggressive behavior. According to observational learning theory, people observe the behavior of models and the subsequent consequences of the behavior. If the consequences are positive, the behavior is likely to be imitated when the observer finds himself or herself in a similar situation.

This basic formulation of observational learning theory has received wide support. For example, nursery-school-age children who have watched an adult behave aggressively display the same behavior themselves if they have been previously angered (Bandura, Ross & Ross, 1963). It turns out, though, that exposure to models typically leads to spontaneous aggression only if the observer has been angered, insulted, or frustrated after exposure (Bandura, 1973). This finding has important implications for understanding the effects of aggression observed in the media.

Does It Hurt to Watch TV?: Media Aggression

The average American child between the ages of 5 and 15 is exposed to no fewer than 13,000 violent deaths on television; the number of fights and aggressive sequences that children view is still higher. Even Saturday mornings, once filled with relatively peaceful fare, now include cartoons sporting titles such as "Teenage Mutant Ninja Turtles" and "The Transformers," which include long sequences of aggressive action (Gerbner et al., 1978; Berkowitz, 1984; Freedman, 1984).

Does observation of this kind of violent television fare, as well as observation of aggression in other forms of media, suggest that our world is destined to become even more violent than it already is? Because observational learning research on modeling shows that people frequently learn and imitate the aggression that they observe, this question is one of the most important being addressed by social psychologists.

Most research suggests that there is a significant association between watching violent television programs and displaying aggressive behavior (Eron, 1982; Huesmann & Eron, 1986). For example, one experiment showed that subjects who watched a lot of television as third-graders became more aggressive adults than those who didn't watch so much TV (Eron, Huesmann, Lefkowitz & Walden, 1972). Of course, these results cannot prove that viewing television was the *cause* of the adult aggression; some additional factor, such as socioeconomic status, may have led both to higher levels of television viewing and to increased aggression.

Still, most experts agree that watching media violence can lead to a greater readiness to act aggressively, if not invariably to acting overtly with direct aggression, and to desensitization to the suffering of victims of violence (Linz, Donnerstein, & Penrod, 1989). Several reasons, beyond mere modeling, help explain why the observation of media violence may produce aggression. For one thing, watching violence seems to lower inhibitions against the performance of aggression—watching television portrayals of violence makes aggression seem a legitimate response to particular situations. Furthermore, viewing violence may make our understanding of the meaning of others' behavior shift: We may be predisposed to view even nonaggressive acts of others as aggressive after watching media aggression, and subsequently may act upon these new interpretations by responding aggressively. Finally, a continual diet of aggression may leave us desensitized to violence, and what previously would have repelled us now produces little emotional response. The pain and suffering brought about by aggression may be lost, and we may find it easier to act aggressively ourselves (Geen & Donnerstein, 1983). For more on the connection between media violence and aggression, see the Psychology at Work box on the next page.

Reducing and Preventing Aggression

Billy, a seventh-grader, gets into fights almost weekly on the school playground. His teacher thinks he ought to get involved in football in order to, as she says, "get rid of his aggression." His father thinks Billy is frustrated over his inability to read very well. His mother thinks they ought to withhold

674

Does viewing pornography that includes violence against women lead to subsequent actual violence toward women? This question is a complex one, but recent evidence suggests that there may, in fact, be a link between certain kinds of erotic material and aggression.

In an experiment examining this issue, angered male subjects who viewed an erotic movie that contained violence toward a woman showed significantly more subsequent aggression toward a female than those who viewed an erotic movie that contained no violence (Donnerstein & Berkowitz, 1981). Other experiments have found that long-term exposure to violent and sexually degrading depictions of women lead to emotional and physiological desensitization. In one study, for example, subjects who saw a series of R-rated violent "slasher" movies later showed less anxiety and depression when exposed to violence against women, and they were less sympathetic toward rape victims than subjects who

THE LINK BETWEEN AGGRESSIVE PORNOGRAPHY AND VIOLENCE TOWARD WOMEN

saw nonviolent films (Linz, Donnerstein, & Penrod, 1987; Linz, Donnerstein, & Adams, 1989).

Overall, research in this area suggests that viewing pornography that contains violence toward women leads to emotional and physiological desensitization regarding aggression directed at women and an increased likelihood of actual aggression toward women (Donnerstein, Linz & Penrod, 1987). What appears to be particularly critical is whether the pornography contains violence toward women; aggressive content in erotic materials clearly raises the level of aggression subsequently displayed by those exposed to it.

On the other hand, in some cases even nonviolent X-rated movies showing sex between consenting adults may be sufficient to produce

unwanted effects. In one study, a group of subjects was shown a series of six 8-minute films during six weekly sessions (Zillman & Bryant, 1984). Some subjects saw films that were entirely sexual in content; others saw half sexual and half nonsexual films; a third group saw only nonsexual films. At the end of the six weeks, subjects completed a questionnaire that described a rapist who had been convicted, and were asked to recommend a sentence. As you can see in Figure 19-6, the greater the exposure to the films with sexual content, the lower the recommended sentence. Exposure to even nonviolent pornography, then, can result in a decrease in the perceived repugnance of the crime of rape.

Whether these findings mean that pornography should be banned is a debatable question—such a move would certainly infringe on first-amendment rights to free speech—but they do alert us to the danger of exposure to pornography depicting aggression against women.

FIGURE 19-6

The greater the exposure of subjects to films with a sexual content, the lower was the sentence they recommended for a convicted rapist. (Based on Zillman & Bryant, 1984.)

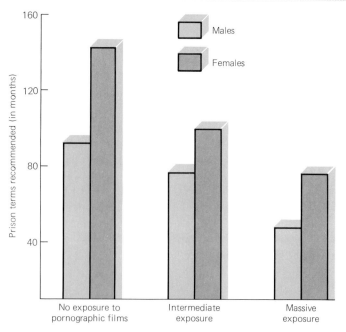

Billy's allowance until he has gone without a fight for two weeks. The school counselor suggests still another approach: Every week that Billy displays no aggression, he should receive a $5 reward.

Who is right? Looking back at the different explanations of aggression, we find that each of these approaches may have some merit. Instinct theories of aggression suggest that aggression builds up until it is discharged; this hypothesis—known as the catharsis hypothesis, and expressed by the teacher's point of view that Billy should play football—suggests that by behaving aggressively in socially acceptable ways people can relieve aggressiveness that would otherwise be expressed in less desirable ways. Unfortunately, the scientific evidence in support of the theory is quite inconsistent (Ebbesen, Duncan & Konĕcni, 1975), and the only circumstance in which catharsis is seemingly effective is when a person's aggression is directed toward an individual who caused that person to be angry (Doob & Wood, 1972). Moreover, as we discussed earlier, exposure to aggression in media forms can actually lead to an increase in aggression. In sum, instinct approaches have not garnered much scientific support.

More promising approaches to reducing aggression are provided by frustration-aggression and observational learning theories. As suggested by the father's point that Billy's inability to read leads to frustration, removing frustration is effective in reducing aggression. However, the difficulty with such a technique is that life is full of all sorts of frustrations, and removing them all is an impossibility. One cannot create an environment completely free of frustration, and techniques for reducing aggression that are based on frustration-aggression theory may not be practical.

To date, the most promising approach to reducing aggression comes from learning theory, which deals with the modification of the rewards and punishments that follow aggression. The mother's suggestion to withhold Billy's allowance is an example of the most frequently used technique to control aggression and is built on observational-learning-theory approaches: the use of punishment following aggressive behavior. Interestingly, though, the use of punishment turns out to be a relatively ineffective technique for reducing aggression. One reason is that the people who do the punishing, especially when they use physical punishment, can actually serve as aggressive models themselves and thereby increase the likelihood of future aggression. Moreover, research shows that in most cases the effects of punishment tend to be relatively transitory (Sulzer-Azaroff & Mayer, 1986).

There is clear evidence, however, in support of the school counselor's strategy of reinforcing Billy's nonaggressive behavior, for research demonstrates that providing rewards for nonaggressive behavior can lead to a reduction in aggression. In fact, even exposure to nonaggressive models leads to reduced aggression, at least in laboratory studies (Baron & Kepner, 1970). Moreover, work on changing people's interpretations of models' behavior has shown that aggression can be minimized (Huesmann, Eron, Klein, Brice & Fischer, 1983).

In one study, a group of first- and third-graders was taught that the behavior of television characters was not representative of the way that most people behaved and that people generally resolved their problems without resorting to aggression. Furthermore, they were told how special effects and camera techniques were used to create the illusion that aggression was occurring. Finally, the children were explicitly taught that watching television violence was undesirable and that they should refrain from imitating the behavior they saw on television (Huesmann, et al. 1983; Eron & Huesmann, 1985).

In comparison to a control group of children who did not receive the special training, the children participating in the study were rated by their classmates as showing significantly less aggression. In addition, the children's attitudes toward media aggression became less favorable.

In sum, it seems that the procedure was effective, demonstrating that the effects of exposure to media aggression can be reduced by changing people's understanding of the meaning of the aggression they view. Although we don't know how lasting the effects of such programs are, they are encouraging in suggesting that aggression, in general, is not inevitable and can be reduced.

HELPING OTHERS: The Brighter Side of Human Nature

Prosocial behavior: Helping behavior

Turning away from aggression, we move now to the opposite—and brighter—side of the coin of human nature: helping behavior. Helping behavior, or **prosocial behavior** as it is more formally known, has been investigated under many different approaches, but the question that has been looked at most closely relates to bystander intervention in emergency situations. What are the factors that lead someone to give help to a person who is in need?

Diffusion of responsibility: The tendency for people to feel that responsibility for helping is shared among those present

As we noted in Chapter 1, one critical factor relates to the number of others present. When more than one person bears witness to an emergency situation, there can be a sense of diffusion of responsibility among bystanders. **Diffusion of responsibility** is the tendency for people to feel that responsibility for acting is shared, or diffused, among those present. The more people present in an emergency, then, the less personally responsible each individual feels—and therefore the less help is provided (Latané & Nida, 1981).

FIGURE 19-7

The basic steps of helping. (Based on Latané & Darley, 1970.)

Although the majority of research on helping behavior supports the diffusion-of-responsibility formulation, other factors clearly are involved in helping behavior. According to a model developed by Latané and Darley (1970), the process of helping involves four basic steps (see Figure 19-7).

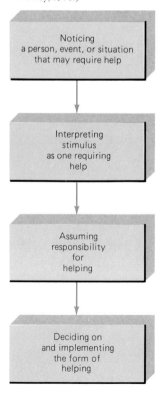

▶ Noticing a person, event, or situation that may require help.

▶ Interpreting the event as one that requires help. Even if an event is noticed, it may be sufficiently ambiguous to be interpreted as a non-emergency situation (Shotland, 1985). It is here that the presence of others first affects helping behavior: The presence of inactive others may indicate to the observer that a situation does not require help—a judgment not necessarily made if the observer is alone.

▶ Assuming responsibility for taking action. It is at this point that diffusion of responsibility is likely to occur if others are present. Moreover, a bystander's particular expertise is apt to play a role in whether helping occurs. For instance, if people with training in medical aid or lifesaving techniques are present, untrained bystanders are less apt to intervene because they feel they have less expertise. This point was well illustrated in a study by Jane and Irving Piliavin (1972), who conducted a field experiment in which an individual seemed to collapse in a subway car with blood trickling out of the corner of his mouth. The results of the experiment showed that bystanders were less likely to help when a person (actually a confederate) appearing to be an intern was present than when the "intern" was not present.

▶ Deciding on and implementing the form of assistance. After an individual assumes responsibility for helping, the decision must be made as to how assistance will be provided. Helping can range from very indirect forms of intervention, such as calling the police, to more direct forms, such as giving first aid or taking the victim to a hospital. Most social psychologists use a **rewards-costs approach** for helping to predict the nature of assistance that a bystander will choose to provide. The general notion is that the rewards of helping, as perceived by the bystander, must outweigh the costs if helping is to occur (Lynch & Cohen, 1978), and most research tends to support this notion.

Rewards-costs approach: The notion that, in a situation requiring help, a bystander's perceived rewards must outweigh the costs if helping is to occur

After the nature of assistance is determined, there is still one step remaining: the actual implementation of the assistance. A rewards-costs analysis suggests that the least costly form of implementation is the most likely to be used. However, this is not the whole story: In some cases, people behave altruistically. **Altruism** is helping behavior that is beneficial to others but clearly requires self-sacrifice. For example, an instance in which a person runs into a burning house to rescue a stranger's child might be considered altruistic, particularly when compared with the alternative of simply calling the fire department.

Altruism: Helping behavior that is beneficial to others while requiring sacrifice on the part of the helper

Some research suggests that individuals who intervene in emergency situations tend to have certain personality characteristics that differentiate them from nonhelpers. For example, Shotland (1984) suggests that helpers tend to be more self-assured. Other research has found that individuals who are characteristically high in **empathy**—a personality trait in which an individual observing another person experiences the emotions of that person—are more likely to respond to others' needs (Eisenberg-Berg, 1978; Cialdini et al., 1987; Eisenberg & Miller, 1987). Still, most social psychologists agree that there is no single set of attributes that differentiate helpers from nonhelpers; situational factors play the predominant role in determining whether an individual intervenes in a situation requiring aid (e.g., Carlson, Charlin & Miller, 1988).

Empathy: One person's experiencing of another's emotions, leading to an increased likelihood of responding to the other's needs

The model provided by this person helping an elderly woman is likely to encourage passers-by to act more compassionately. (Erika Stone/Peter Arnold, Inc.)

THE INFORMED CONSUMER OF PSYCHOLOGY: Learning to Be Helpful

Our earlier description of the attack on Kitty Genovese and the reluctance of bystanders to help raises a crucial question. Are there ways in which our society can promote prosocial behavior to prevent the recurrence of such episodes?

Social psychologists specializing in helping behavior have suggested a number of approaches to teaching the virtues of helping. Among the most important of those approaches are the following:

▶ Providing helpful models. Growing out of work on observational learning theory, one approach suggests that the presence of models who are rewarded for their prosocial behavior can lead to increased prosocial behavior on the part of observers. For example, research shows that viewing another person behaving generously will lead to increased generosity on the part of the observer. Similarly, viewing a selfish model results in more selfish behavior (Rushton, 1975; Staub, 1971).

A now-classic experiment demonstrated quite directly the effects of modeling on helping. In the study, subjects in one condition passed by a man helping a woman change a flat tire on a busy highway. A quarter of a mile later, subjects came across another woman with a flat tire, but this time she was alone and appeared to be in need of assistance. The experimental question was how many people would stop to help, in comparison with a condition in which the passersby had not first seen a helpful model. The results showed that the model was effective in producing helping behavior. In the no-model condition, only 35 of 4,000 passersby stopped, whereas more than double that figure stopped to offer aid to the second woman in the model condition (Bryan & Test, 1967).

▶ Using moral admonitions. Another approach to promoting prosocial behavior relies on the use of moral admonitions. When parents teach their children the golden rule, or politicians say, "Do what is best for your country, not for yourselves," they are providing a form of moral education. How effective are such moral admonitions? Unfortunately, most research suggests that they do not work particularly well. In fact, most work shows that compared with individuals who actually behave helpfully, models who just *preach* prosocial behavior are considerably less effective in eliciting helping behavior in observers (Grusec & Skubiski, 1970).

▶ Teaching moral reasoning. One further approach to promoting prosocial behavior is to try to actually teach moral reasoning. Based on Kohlberg's model of moral reasoning (see Chapter 13), the technique presents moral dilemmas, creating conflicts between various solutions to the dilemmas and helping people take the perspective of those involved in the dilemmas in order to illustrate that many points of view must be considered simultaneously (Hersh, Paolitto & Reimer, 1979).

Each of these techniques is promising, although there are as yet no definitive data indicating their long-term effectiveness in actually raising the incidence of prosocial behavior (Kaplan, 1983). Still, considered together, they do appear to be reasonable approaches to bringing about a society in which helping behavior is the rule instead of the exception.

RECAP AND REVIEW III

Recap

◀ Aggression refers to intentional injury of or harm to another person. Some theories view aggression as instinctual, whereas others view it as a reaction to frustration. Another approach, based on observational learning theory, concentrates on the way in which aggression is learned and modeled from others.

◀ Strong evidence links aggression viewed in the media—both in television programs and in pornographic materials—to subsequent aggression, although a cause-and-effect relationship has yet to be established.

◀ Helping involves four steps: (1) noticing a person, event, or situation that may require help; (2) interpreting the event as one that requires help; (3) assuming responsibility for taking action; and (4) deciding on and implementing the form of assistance.

◀ Helping behavior can be increased by providing helpful models, using moral admonitions, and teaching moral reasoning.

Review

1. According to recent formulations of the frustration-aggression approach, aggression is viewed as a reaction to frustration, but its actual occurrence depends on the presence of
   a. a model.
   b. aggressive cues.
   c. pent-up aggressive urges.
   d. innate urges.

2. Observational learning theories state that a person is most likely to imitate the aggressive behavior of a model if the

consequences of the model's behavior are

a. positive.
b. negative.
c. expected.
d. neutral.

3. Research shows that exposure to violent, pornographic material is associated with the likelihood of increased violence or tolerance of violence toward women. True or false? _____

4. The phenomenon that helping behavior is less likely when more people are present at an emergency is called _____ .

5. Rodney jumped into the river to rescue a child who had fallen in and was approaching a waterfall. This type of helping behavior is called _____ .

6. List three approaches suggested by social psychologists for teaching the virtues of prosocial behavior.

(Answers to review questions are on page 680.)

1. Social influence is the area of social psychology concerned with situations in which the actions of an individual or group affect the behavior of others.

2. Conformity refers to changes in behavior or attitudes that occur as the result of a desire to follow the beliefs or standards of others. Among the factors affecting conformity are the nature of the group, the nature of the response required, the kind of task, and the unanimity of the group.

3. Compliance is behavior that occurs as a result of direct social pressure. Two means of eliciting compliance are the foot-in-the-door technique, in which people are initially asked to agree to a small request but later asked to respond to a larger one, and the door-in-the-face procedure, in which a large request, designed to be refused, is followed by a smaller one. In contrast to compliance, obedience is a change in behavior that results from the commands of others. Among the ways to remain independent of group pressure are inoculation, forewarning, and consistency.

4. The study of interpersonal attraction, or close relationships, considers liking and loving. Among the primary determinants of liking are proximity, mere exposure, similarity, and physical attractiveness.

5. Love is distinguished from liking by the presence of intense physiological arousal, an all-encompassing interest in another, fantasies about the other, rapid swings of emotion, fascination, sexual desire, exclusiveness, and strong feelings of caring. According to one approach, love can be distinguished into two types: passionate and romantic.

◀ LOOKING BACK

Sternberg's theory further subdivides love into eight kinds.

6. Recent work has examined the development, maintenance, and deterioration of relationships. Partners in lasting marriages tend to be remarkably similar in their perceptions of what makes their marriage endure.

7. Aggression is intentional injury of or harm to another person. Instinct approaches suggest that humans have an innate drive to behave aggressively and that if aggression is not released in socially desirable ways, it will be discharged in some other form—a point for which there is relatively little research support. Frustration-aggression theory suggests that frustration produces a readiness to be aggressive—if aggressive cues are present. Finally, observational learning theory hypothesizes that aggression is learned through reinforcement—particularly reinforcement that is given to models. Each of these approaches suggests means of reducing aggressive behavior.

8. Helping behavior in emergencies is determined in part by the phenomenon of diffusion of responsibility, which results in a lower likelihood of helping when more people are present. Deciding to help is the outcome of a four-stage process consisting of noticing a possible need for help, interpreting the situation as requiring aid, assuming responsibility for taking action, and deciding on and implementing a form of assistance. Techniques for promoting prosocial behavior include providing helpful models, using moral admonitions, and teaching moral reasoning.

KEY TERMS AND CONCEPTS ▶

social influence (p. 653)
conformity (653)
status (654)
social supporter (655)
compliance (655)
foot-in-the-door technique (655)
door-in-the-face technique (656)
reciprocal concessions (656)
inoculation (657)

forewarning (657)
consistency (657)
obedience (658)
interpersonal attraction (660)
proximity (660)
reciprocity-of-liking effect (661)
need-complementarity hypothesis (661)
passionate (or romantic) love (664)

companionate love (664)
interpsychic phase (of relationship dissolution) (668)
dyadic phase (of relationship dissolution) (668)
social phase (of relationship dissolution) (668)
grave-dressing phase (of relationship dissolution) (668)

aggression (670) aggressive cues (672) rewards-costs approach (677)
catharsis (670) prosocial behavior (676) altruism (677)
frustration (671) diffusion of responsibility (676) empathy (677)

FOR FURTHER STUDY AND APPLICATION ▶

Aronson, E. (1988). *The social animal* (5th ed.). New York: Freeman.

This book offers a beautifully written overview of the major threads of social psychology.

Cialdini, R. (1988). *Social influence* (2nd ed.). Glenview, IL: Scott, Foresman.

A very readable, informative, and enjoyable book, this text is filled with practical insights regarding persuasion and other forms of social influence.

Hendrick, C., & Hendrick, S. (1983). *Liking, loving, and relating.* Monterey, CA: Brooks/Cole.

This is an excellent overview of the topics of liking and loving, written in an open and accessible fashion. The rise and fall of relationships are clearly described.

Nadler, A., Fisher, J. D., & DePaulo, B. M. (1983). *Applied research in help-seeking and reactions to aid.* New York: Academic Press.

This volume contains a number of applications relating to helping behavior, especially in field settings. Although there are many technical details, the layperson can get a good sense of the work.

Donnerstein, E., Linz, D., & Penrod, S. (1987). *The question of pornography.* New York: Free Press.

Readers interested in the current state of knowledge regarding the relationship between pornography and aggression should refer to this book.

ANSWERS (REVIEW III):
1. b **2.** a **3.** True **4.** Diffusion of responsibility **5.** Altruism **6.** Providing helpful models; using moral admonitions; teaching moral reasoning

PART EIGHT

THE PSYCHOLOGICAL CONTEXT OF THE WORLD AROUND US

PART
EIGHT

THE PSYCHOLOGICAL CONTEXT OF THE WORLD AROUND US

As we reach the end of our journey through an exploration of the science of psychology, we meet an employee whose job produces severe health and emotional problems. We watch as the President of the United States, despite advice from the best minds of the country, blunders into a wrong decision. And we consider the consequences of a computer prank gone wrong.

In the final chapters of the book, we focus on several of the most important psychological influences in the world around us. We see how our membership in groups and organizations affects the way in which we view the world. We explore how groups make decisions. We consider satisfaction with careers and work. And we examine how twentieth-century technology and the physical environment in which we live, as well as the threat of nuclear war, affects the day-to-day quality of our lives.

In Chapter 20, we look at organizations and the workplace, concentrating on the findings of industrial-organizational psychologists.

In Chapter 21, we turn to technology and environmental psychology, considering how the technological and physical world in which we live influences our behavior.

CHAPTER
20
ORGANIZATIONS AND THE WORKPLACE

PROLOGUE:
ROBERT HEARSCH

Robert Hearsch, whose job took on night-marish qualities. (Lester Sloan/Woodfin Camp & Assoc.)

For Robert Hearsch, it was a nightmare that wouldn't end. For four years Hearsch had been a successful supervisor for Hughes Aircraft. Then General Motors took over the company—and his career took a nose dive. As part of the restructuring, he was put in charge of buying pens and pencils. He found orders backlogged and records in disarray. He spent most of his days appeasing angry secretaries. He stayed on gamely, arriving early, leaving late, working through his breaks. But, as Hearsch tells the story, things only got worse. His supervisors hinted that his position might be phased out. They ignored his diligence and recorded small mistakes into his file. They even left him off the guest list for the department office party.

The pressure took its toll. Hearsch lost 20 pounds. His marriage hit the skids. . . . The strain got to his colleagues as well. One day, Hearsch says, a co-worker showed up at the office brandishing a handgun. Hearsch finally filed a workers' compensation claim, blaming his health and emotional problems on Hughes, . . . [finally accepting] a $20,000 settlement from the company, which refuses to comment on the case. The money, he says, is small consolation. "I lost my wife, my house, and my career" (Miller, 1988, p. 40).

LOOKING AHEAD ▶

Although at its most basic level work provides us with a way of earning a living, it is much more, as we see in Robert Hearsch's horrific description of his job. For other, luckier people, work offers some of life's most important satisfactions, providing us not only with financial gain but also with a sense of purpose and self-fulfillment. Consider, for instance, this worker's description of his job:

Why do I work? Well, there are the obvious reasons: money for shelter, food, and the other necessities of life. I like to feel that I'm doing something for society, too, contributing in even a small way. But when it comes down to it, I *like* to work. I enjoy the things I do at the office; I like to talk to people on the job. I enjoy working with other folks, and, although I hate to admit it, I'm happy that I achieve things that other people don't. I'm awfully competitive, and I'm always trying to outdo my fellow employees. Oh, there are days when I'd rather not get out of bed in the morning; my job certainly isn't perfect. But when it comes down to it, I have more fun doing my job than a lot of other things I do in life.

As this description shows, work has an importance that extends far beyond simply earning a living. Because of this, the study of work and organizations has grown into a major area of psychology. **Industrial-organizational psychologists**—psychologists who study the workplace—have investigated such issues as the interaction of workers on the job, how jobs can be designed to prevent stress and fatigue, how worker morale is best maintained, and how organizations can motivate employees to do their best.

This chapter explores these questions and others relating to organiza-

Industrial-organizational psychologists: Psychologists who study the workplace and organizations

Job satisfaction does not always depend on receiving a fat paycheck, as this forest ranger at Muir Woods National Monument would probably attest. (Lawrence Migdale/ Photo Researchers.)

tions and the workplace. We first examine the nature of groups in organizations and the influence they exert over the way individuals respond to their jobs. The discussion then turns to how people react to the demands of the workplace, identifying the major sources of problems and stress on the job. Finally, we consider ways of modifying organizations—and changing people's behavior—to produce a better fit between people and their jobs.

As we discuss these topics, it will become evident that psychological factors have a major effect on people's reactions to organizations and their work, and that psychologists have devised a number of useful techniques for improving the quality of people's work lives. Given that most of us spend a major portion of our adult lives working, these findings hold major importance.

After reading this chapter, you'll have the answers to such questions as these:

▶ What are the defining characteristics of groups and organizations?

▶ How can we improve the quality of decisions made in organizations?

▶ What are the characteristics of jobs that produce difficulties for workers?

▶ How can we reduce job-related problems and stress?

GROUPS AT WORK

Jack was delighted to get a job as a graphic designer in a large publishing company. Although his ultimate career goal went well beyond drawing graphs for high school textbooks—he was aiming for a management position—he thought that this job would be a good steppingstone to a better job. He'd show his supervisors how motivated he was to succeed, and they would soon realize that he was an employee to be reckoned with.

In fact, Jack found that after his first week on the job he was easily exceeding the production of his co-workers by almost 50 percent. Yet it was clear that something else was happening. His fellow workers, who

THE PSYCHOLOGICAL CONTEXT
OF THE WORLD AROUND US

had initially greeted him warmly, had begun to act coldly and angrily toward him. Even his supervisor didn't seem all that pleased that he was outproducing his co-workers by such a large margin.

Rethinking his behavior, Jack decided that perhaps he had been taking the wrong approach. He slowed down his rate of production to the level of everyone else and noticed that the climate changed immediately. Co-workers became friendlier and his boss seemed relieved— telling him that he seemed to have learned the ropes pretty quickly.

Although Jack's behavior and the reactions of his co-workers may at first seem unusual, they are quite predictable if we consider research findings of organizational and industrial psychologists on the effects of group membership in the workplace. These investigators have established a large body of research on **group dynamics**, the scientific study of groups and group processes relevant to successful organizational functioning.

Group dynamics: The scientific study of groups and group processes

GROUPS: The Building Blocks of Organizations

To understand the role of group dynamics in workplace organizations, we need first to formally define what we mean by group. To psychologists, a **group** is not just a collection of people: rather, groups in a formal sense have certain psychological characteristics that include:

Group: A collection of individuals in which there is (1) interaction among members, (2) perception of group membership, (3) shared norms and goals, and (4) fate interdependence

▶ Interaction among group members. People involved in a group must interact, although this interaction need not take place with the members physically present. For instance, some groups are made up of people whose only interaction is through written correspondence.

▶ Perception of group membership. Group members perceive themselves, and are perceived by others, as being part of a group

▶ Shared norms and goals. One of the most critical components of group membership—especially in relationship to organizations and the workplace—is the sharing of important norms and goals. **Norms** are informal rules that are followed by group members regarding what is—and is not— appropriate behavior. Norms describe the "shoulds" and "ought to's" of group members' behavior.

Norms: Informal rules regarding the appropriateness of behavior followed by group members

The norms held by group members can be as overt and trivial as dress standards or they can be more subtle—and crucial—as when they determine what the performance levels of group members ought to be. For example, one study showed that good students began to show declines in academic performance when they joined class groups in which there were subtle norms *against* good academic performance (Hargreave, 1963).

The goals of group members do not always relate to the reasons for starting the group initially; they may develop informally over time and have little to do with the formal purpose of the group. For example, a group whose original goal is to help the needy may evolve into a social group whose major purpose is to provide a meeting place where friends can socialize. Similarly, people working together in organizational settings may begin to view themselves as part of a closely knit, social group—rather than as part of a work group sharing the norms of the business that employs them.

▶ Fate interdependence. This feature of a group signifies that what happens to one group member affects other group members, and what happens to the group as a whole affects the individual members. If a group is successful, the individual group members share in the feeling of success; if an individual group member fails in an activity related to the goal of the group, the other group members share in the failure. For instance, the fortunes of the individual members of an engineering team whose goal is to produce a new form of computer chip will ride on whether each member upholds his or her part of the task.

GROUPS IN ORGANIZATIONS

Organizations—groups of people working together to attain common goals—contain both formal and informal groups. **Formal groups** are work units set up by the management of the organization, designed to carry out some specific task; **informal groups** evolve as a result of the interests and needs of the individuals making up the organization (Frost et al., 1985).

Informal groups can exert as much, or more, influence on the activities and success of an organization as formal groups, as we saw in the earlier example of the graphics designer who cut his production and became better accepted by his co-workers. This phenomenon first was demonstrated in a series of pioneering studies carried out in a telephone manufacturing plant, known as the Hawthorne studies (described in the Research Classics box).

The Hawthorne studies revealed for the first time how sensitive workers were to the behavior of others in their work groups and confirmed that informal norms regarding appropriate behavior can readily supplant the formal rules and regulations provided by the company. In fact, the studies found cases in which employees' loyalty to their co-workers and to the informal norms of their work groups was more powerful than even their own personal financial interests and those of the company.

Why would employees behave in a way that works against their best financial interests? The answer is related to the concept of group cohesiveness. **Cohesiveness** is the degree to which group members are attracted to the group as a whole, and to other members individually (Forsyth, 1983). High levels of group cohesiveness result in a number of important consequences, including greater influence of the group over its members, higher self-esteem for group members, higher likelihood of maintaining membership in the group, and greater adherence to the group's norms. Furthermore, if the norms of the group are supportive of high performance, highly cohesive groups will be more productive (Druckman & Swets, 1988).

On the other hand, cohesiveness does not invariably produce positive results. Because cohesiveness is associated with greater influence by a group over its members, people who express views or behave in a way that deviates from the group norms may be ignored or even rejected. Thus innovative or creatives ideas may be lost.

Similarly, if group norms run counter to those of the organization, the performance of the group may suffer—as in the switchboard wiring room described in the Research Classics box, in which a relatively low rate of production was maintained. In such situations—with relatively high cohesiveness within people's own work groups but low cohesiveness in terms of the organization as a whole—workers may be likely to follow the lower production norms of the informal group than to follow formal organizational goals that call for higher output (Berkowitz, 1954; Schachter, Ellertson, McBride & Gregory, 1951).

Organizations: Groups of people working together to attain common goals

Formal groups: Work units set up by the management of an organization, designed to carry out some specific task

Informal groups: Groups that develop as a result of the interests and needs of the individuals making up an organization

Cohesiveness: The degree to which group members are attracted to the group as a whole and to other members individually

THE HAWTHORNE STUDIES

In its heyday during the early part of the twentieth century, the Hawthorne plant of the Western Electric Company near Chicago was a major producer of telephone components. It was also the site of one of the first research programs that identified the importance of psychological factors in determining how productive workers could be (Mayo, 1933; Whitehead, 1938; Roethlisberger & Dickson, 1939).

Although the research started with only modest goals, it soon blossomed into a series of multiyear experiments on the psychological factors related to worker behavior in organizational settings. The initial studies conducted at the Hawthorne plant were designed simply to examine the effects of changes in illumination intensity on the productivity of workers assembling telephone components. Gradual increases in lighting were made, and each change brought increased productivity. Surprisingly, however, productivity increased even when the researchers went beyond a reasonable point and brought illumination to a level that was abnormally bright. Even more intriguing was the fact that when they began to decrease the lighting, productivity still rose slightly! It seemed clear that something other than illumination per se was playing a role in the workers' productivity.

A subsequent experiment at the Hawthorne plant shed some light on the reasons for the productivity increases. Using a group of six women, the researchers made a number of changes in working con-

ditions, such as varying the rest pauses and rates of compensation. Once again, productivity increases occurred independent of the nature of the specific change. It almost seemed as if change itself could produce increases in productivity.

In fact, the explanation that the subjects themselves came up with was that the special attention they had received from the investigators, their own interest in the experimental results, and the uniqueness of their situation as participants in the study all contributed to their increased productivity. Change and special attention, then, rather than the specific nature of the situational modifications, led to increases in productivity. This concept has become known as the **Hawthorne effect**, and it signifies that any time subjects know they are in an experiment their behavior may change simply as a function of the special attention they are receiving and not necessarily because of any of the experimental manipulations.

The Hawthorne research illuminated several other important issues relating to group performance in organizations. For instance, in one part of the telephone plant in which the research was carried out—the switchboard wiring room—the formal management goal was for each worker to wire $2\frac{1}{2}$ switchboards per day. Invariably, however, most workers completed only 2 per day. Those workers who were above or below

this informal norm received verbal and sometimes even physical punishment by co-workers. Workers who produced fewer than 2 switchboards per day were called chislers, whereas overproducers were called speed kings or rate busters. Moreover, overproducers were sometimes punched in the arms by co-workers in a not-so-subtle attempt to punish their overenthusiastic rate of production. Such techniques easily maintained the informal norm of 2 switchboards per day, even though workers were fully capable of producing more—and by so doing making more money for themselves, since their pay was dependent on their productivity. Thus, even though it worked against their own financial interests, workers encouraged a lower rate of production than they were capable of achieving.

Although the Hawthorne studies can be criticized for their unsophisticated methodology—for example, they lacked appropriate control groups—they made an important contribution to our understanding of how people behave in business settings (Parsons, 1974; Sonnenfeld, 1982). It may not seem so revolutionary to us today, but the idea that psychological factors must be taken into account in the workplace was a new one in the 1930s.

Hawthorne effect: The concept that when subjects know they are in an experiment, their behavior may change as a function of the special attention they receive

Solving the Problem: Change Cohesiveness or Change Norms?

At first glance, the most direct way to solve the problem of worker underproduction in cohesive work groups seems to be to modify the cohesiveness of the group by weakening the social bonds of co-workers and increasing their loyalty to the organization and its goals. However, a more logical solution might be to encourage continued high cohesiveness toward the informal group, but to change the content of the norms relevant to productivity

(Zander, 1977). Making workers feel it is important to maintain high productivity so that they will profit not only financially but from the social support of their peers ought to lead to higher worker productivity.

Of course, modifying worker norms is easier said than done (Druckman & Swets, 1988), but at least one technique has proved to be useful: worker participation in goal setting. Because involving workers in the setting of specific, formal production goals motivates them to accept and attain more ambitious goals, it is likely that involved workers will eventually produce informal production norms more consistent with the formal goals of the organization (Vroom & Yetton, 1973; Tuttle, 1983).

MORE THAN JUST A LIVING: The Functions of Work

The importance of informal norms in job settings demonstrates a critical point about work that was illustrated in the case of Robert Hearsch at the beginning of the chapter: Jobs hold a significance that extends well beyond merely providing financial support.

For example, many people subscribe to the **Protestant work ethic**, the notion that work is important in and of itself. According to this view, the act of earning a living is of value and can provide satisfaction to workers. The Protestant work ethic is a norm that is widely held in American society and has sometimes been cited as a reason for the economic success of cultures that live by it.

But work also provides individuals with personal satisfactions that are related to their own particular needs (Repetti, 1987). For instance, one's job provides a source of personal identity. Consider, for example, the kinds of questions we ask people when we first meet them. After we find out their names and where they live, the question that we ask most frequently usually has to do with their occupational roles. To a large extent, people define themselves according to the jobs that they hold.

Work also affects people's social lives. Because we spend so much of our time in work settings, important relationships often develop there. Friendships at work often spill over into nonwork-related areas of people's lives, and the quality of the social environment at work is related to people's general psychological well-being (Repetti, 1987).

The kinds of work people do is reflected in their personal values and interests. Individuals in a given profession tend to show similarities in their attitudes, and their values tend to mirror those of their co-workers (Huntley & Davis, 1983). For example, one survey found that business executives tended to place particular emphasis on economic and political values, whereas college professors and high school teachers were particularly concerned with social and religious values.

Of course, we cannot tell for sure whether holding similar values is a consequence of working in a certain profession, or whether holding particular values initially leads people to choose their professions. Nonetheless, it is clear that people's sense of what is and is not important tends to be shared by their co-workers.

The nature of our jobs also has an important effect on our **status**—the evaluation by others of the roles we play in society. As you can see in Table 20-1, there are significant differences in the status of various professional roles, with physicians and college teachers at the top of the list and ushers and shoe shiners falling at the bottom. In addition, there is a clear relation-

Protestant work ethic: The notion that work is important in and of itself

Status: The evaluation by others of the roles we play in society

TABLE 20-1

Occupational Status for Different Occupations

In a series of national surveys conducted between 1972 and 1982, a variety of occupations were ranked in terms of prestige. The highest possible score was 90, the lowest 10. Some of the results are presented below.

Occupation	Score	Occupation	Score
Physician	82	Bank teller	50
College teacher	78	Electrician	49
Lawyer	76	Police officer	48
Dentist	74	Insurance agent	47
Bank officer	72	Secretary	46
Airline pilot	70	Air-traffic controller	43
Clergy	69	Mail carrier	42
Sociologist	66	Farm owner	41
Secondary school teacher	63	Restaurant manager	39
Registered nurse	62	Automobile mechanic	37
Pharmacist	61	Baker	34
Elementary school teacher	60	Sales clerk	29
Accountant	56	Gas station attendant	22
Painter	56	Waiter and waitress	20
Librarian	55	Laundry operator	17
Actor	55	Garbage collector	17
Funeral director	52	Janitor	16
Athlete	51	Usher	15
Reporter	51	Shoe shiner	12

(Source: NORC, 1982, pp. 299–314.)

ship between a job's status and people's attitudes toward their work: The higher the status of people's jobs, the more likely they are to say that they would choose those jobs again (Yankelovich, 1974). Moreover, the status of the entire family can be influenced by the job held by the head of the household.

RECAP AND REVIEW I

Recap

◀ Groups, as psychologists use the term, have four characteristics: interaction among group members, perception of group membership among the members, shared goals and norms, and fate interdependence.

◀ Groups in organizations may be formal or informal in nature. Both exert an influence on worker morale and productivity, as the Hawthorne studies demonstrate.

◀ Group cohesiveness is the degree to which group members are attracted to the group and its members. Cohesiveness may either raise or lower productivity, depending on the nature of the group norms.

◀ People work not only to earn money but for reasons related to the Protestant work ethic, personal identity, and their social lives, values, and status.

Review

1. What four characteristics do psychologists use to define groups?
2. The Hawthorne studies showed that productivity increased as a result of
   a. good management.
   b. bright lighting.
   c. involvement in an experiment.
   d. cohesiveness.
3. Informal rules regarding appropriate behavior within a group are called _____ .
4. The president of a company chose twelve individuals from several departments to work together and design a new product. Three of the members began to meet together to discuss a part of the project that especially in-

terested them. The group of twelve is an example of a(n) _____ group, and the group of three is an example of a(n) _____ group.

5. Judging from what we know about group norms, the most logical approach to increasing organization productivity is to
   a. weaken the cohesiveness among co-workers and attempt to strengthen their loyalty to organizational goals.
   b. selectively reward workers who exceed current production norms.
   c. change the norms of the informal group by having workers participate in goal setting.
   d. reprimand workers who seem to be keeping productivity low.

(Answers to review questions are on page 694.)

MAKING THE RIGHT CHOICES: STRATEGIES FOR DECISION MAKING IN ORGANIZATIONS

It seemed like a good idea at the time. When Coca-Cola decided, with much fanfare and millions of dollars in costs, to reformulate the ingredients in its popular soft drink, it was banking on the assumption that the public's tastes had changed and that people would prefer the sweeter, less tangy taste of "New Coke." Instead, the public outcry at the change was far greater than the company ever thought possible, and within a few months the original formulation was reintroduced as "Classic Coke." In a news conference, the company chair admitted that Coke had completely miscalculated the public's loyalty to its original formula.

As the above example illustrates, organizations, like individuals, are not immune from making bad decisions. In fact, even though decisions in organizations tend to be carefully scrutinized and are often made only after months of deliberation, they still are sometimes based on erroneous assumptions and faulty logic—and the results, as we see above, can be disastrous.

Organizational and industrial psychologists have sought to answer a number of questions regarding decision making, including who is best equipped to make a decision, whether decisions ought to be made by individuals or groups, and whether those people who have to implement the decisions should be involved in the decision-making process (Lorsch, 1987). We explore some of their findings next.

WHO MAKES THE DECISIONS: One or Many?

Consider how you might feel if you were told by the president of your company that you must reduce your staff by 20 percent in order to reduce expenses. "Sure," you say to yourself, "it's easy for her to make a decision like this. *She* doesn't have to carry it out. Anyway, why wasn't I included when the decision was made? How can one person decide on the best way to cut

Group decision making has both advantages and drawbacks, depending on the kind of decision to be made. (Ray Ellis/ Photo Researchers.)

Participative decision making: A decision-making technique in which the people involved in implementing a decision are involved in making it

costs? Everybody knows that group decisions are better: Groups have more facts and information at their disposal, they have a broader perspective, and they can suggest more solutions."

Would you be right in your criticisms of the company president?

Answering this question is not a simple task. Consider, for example, the question of whether **participative decision making**, in which the people involved in implementing a decision are involved in making it, is superior to nonparticipative decision making. Most research suggests that the specifics of each situation must be taken into account. For example, one review of literature on the question found that participative decision making had a positive effect on productivity about as often as it had a negative effect—and more than half of the studies reviewed showed no effect at all (Locke & Schweiger, 1979). On the other hand, most research does support the notion that the satisfaction and morale of individuals involved in implementing the decisions are higher when they participate in making the decisions than when they are not involved. If one is concerned with worker morale, then, participative decision making seems superior.

Clearly, it is not possible to say that participative decision making is invariably effective. Before one can determine whether participative decision making does work, it is necessary to specify the nature of the problem to be decided (Vroom, 1976; Vroom & Yetton, 1973). Highly structured problems—those having clear issues and questions, and solutions that will be readily accepted by the people carrying them out—may call for very different decision-making procedures than unstructured problems having solutions that subordinates will have difficulty accepting.

Moreover, participation can take many forms: It can involve a group coming to a joint decision, an advisory group making a recommendation to a manager who then makes the ultimate decision, or someone providing information and potential solutions to a manager, without making a specific recommendation. In sum, the question of whether decisions should be made with the input of those who must implement them is not easily resolved.

Equally complex is the question of whether decisions are, in general,

---

ANSWERS (REVIEW I):
1. interaction among group members; perception of group membership; shared norms and goals; fate interdependence **2.** c **3.** Norms **4.** Formal, informal **5.** c

better made in groups or by individuals. As we suggested in the hypothetical situation in which the company president decides to reduce staff size by 20 percent, group decisions *can* have certain, clear advantages. Groups generally have greater knowledge and information as well as a broader perspective, and they generally produce a greater quantity of solutions (Maier, 1967).

At the same time, group decision making has several disadvantages: Groups are less efficient at making decisions, they have a tendency to adopt compromises that may ultimately lead to poor decisions, and they may be unduly influenced by one or a few powerful individuals. Moreover, they may act too slowly to be able to respond effectively in situations that require immediate action.

We see, then, that group decision making has both advantages and drawbacks. There are, however, several summary statements that may be helpful in determining whether group or individual decision making is more likely to be superior (Harrison, 1975):

▶ For establishing objectives, groups are generally better than individuals because of their collective knowledge.

▶ For identifying the greatest number of alternative solutions to a problem, a set of individuals working alone is superior to a group working together — to ensure that nothing is overlooked.

▶ For evaluating alternatives, group judgments are superior, since a wider range of information is brought into play.

▶ For choosing an alternative, involvement of group members helps ensure a greater stake in the outcome — and greater acceptance of it.

▶ For implementing the choice, individuals tend to be superior to groups; decisions are usually carried out more effectively when a single person has responsibility than when a group does.

THE INFORMED CONSUMER OF PSYCHOLOGY:
Improving Decision-making Performance

Obviously the question "Are groups better than individuals at reaching decisions?" cannot be answered with a simple "yes" or "no." The answer depends on the kind of decision being made, the nature of the situation, and several other important factors (e.g., Kaplan & Miller, 1987). However, in conjunction with organizational experts, psychologists have developed a number of techniques to improve the quality of decision making, particularly in group settings. These procedures include brainstorming, nominal group techniques, and acting to promote controversy.

Brainstorming

The principle behind brainstorming is to manipulate the norms that prevent people in groups from putting forth new, unconventional, and unusual ideas for fear of ridicule or embarrassment. Such norms frequently restrain and inhibit the presentation of new ideas in group settings.

To overcome these inhibitions, **brainstorming** is a technique in which group members are strongly encouraged to express any and all new ideas that they can think of without being afraid that their ideas will be criticized or considered impractical. Other group participants are not allowed to make

Brainstorming: A technique of decision making in which group members express any new ideas they can think of, no matter how outlandish, with evaluation occurring only after all ideas have been voiced

PART 8

critical or negative comments of any sort until all ideas have been suggested. Only after no new ideas are forthcoming is evaluation allowed, and then the group can decide upon the most reasonable solution. Group norms are changed to ensure that the creation of new ideas is the most highly valued activity of the group members and that criticism of even the most outlandish notion is discouraged. It is assumed that the freedom this process promotes will produce creative, high-quality decisions and solutions (Osborne, 1957; Rubeck, Dabbs & Hopper, 1985; Diehl & Stroebe, 1987).

Nominal Group Techniques

Nominal group technique: A technique of decision making in which group members write down ideas in private and then present arguments for the ideas to the group, with evaluation made by secret ballot only after all ideas have been presented and discussed one at a time

Whereas brainstorming conjures up the vision of almost uncontrolled, vigorous conversation as participants throw out their suggestions (which may not have been thoroughly thought out), the **nominal group technique** is considerably more sedate and controlled. The major difference between brainstorming and this method is that with the nominal group technique group members first write down their ideas in private. They then act as advocates of each idea, presenting the virtues of the course of action they have proposed in a systematic manner. Not until all the ideas have been put forward are they discussed by the group for clarification and individual evaluation. Finally, after all the solutions have been presented and discussed, a secret ballot is held in which group members rank-order the solutions. The ultimate decision is based on a mathematical evaluation of the results of the balloting (Delbecq, Van de Ven, & Gustafson, 1975).

Delphi method: A variation of the nominal group technique in which experts on a given problem are asked to complete a series of detailed questionnaires

Several variants of the nominal group technique have been suggested. Probably the most important is the **Delphi method**, in which group members never meet in a face-to-face setting. Instead, all contact is limited to written communication in the form of detailed questionnaires. With this method, experts on a given problem are identified and asked to complete a questionnaire on the topic. On the basis of their responses, a new survey form is developed, one that presents the results of the first questionnaire and assesses the experts' reactions. Finally, the results are summarized and returned to the experts for a rank-ordering of the possible solutions, and a final decision is made through a mathematical analysis of the solutions.

Nominal group techniques offer several advantages. They overcome the problems sometimes associated with public discussions, such as the restraints imposed by the presence of a powerful leader or the undue influence of a high-status individual in the organizational hierarchy (further described in the accompanying Psychology at Work box). Moreover, in more typical group situations, the participants may reach decisions prematurely, without due regard for the evidence that is being presented, or they may pay more attention to matters unrelated to the decision that needs to be made, such as maintenance of interpersonal social relationships. Because they evaluate information in a relatively objective manner, nominal group techniques surmount such difficulties.

Promoting Controversy

Although one rationale behind the use of groups in decision making is to reach a consensus agreeable to group members, research suggests that decisions based on controversy may prove to be more effective. In one study, for example, business executives who were encouraged to reach a cooperative decision by engaging in controversial, provocative discussions—in which a "frank discussion of differences" was to take place—made more

697

(Washington, D.C.) President John F. Kennedy today admitted that a group of 1400 men, who invaded the Bay of Pigs area of Cuba in an attempt to overthrow the Castro Communist government, were supported by funds and arms from the United States. In fact, it was learned that plans for the invasion were debated extensively by the President and his advisers, and had his personal go-ahead. The invasion, which turned out to be a military and public relations fiasco, was expected to draw support from the Cuban people and easily defeat the Cuban military forces. Instead, within three days most of the invaders were captured. President Kennedy was reported to say in private, "How could we have been so stupid?" (*Washington Post,* April 18, 1961).

With the hindsight that some thirty years affords us, it is clear that Kennedy's decision to allow an ill-equipped group of Cuban refugees to invade a neighboring country that had been well armed by the Soviet Union was the height of folly. How could such a poor decision have been made?

A phenomenon known as **groupthink** provides an explanation. Groupthink is a type of thinking that members of highly cohesive groups sometimes engage in. In such instances, members share such strong motivation to achieve consensus that they lose the ability to critically evaluate alternative points of view (Janis, 1972). Such thinking is apt to occur in situations in which there is a popular or powerful leader

WHEN GROUPS MAKE THE WRONG DECISIONS: GROUPTHINK AT WORK

who is surrounded by individuals who are of lower status—obviously the case with any U.S. President and his advisers, but also true in a myriad of other organizations.

The phenomenon of groupthink is apt to occur in several types of situations:

● There is an illusion that the group is invulnerable and cannot make major errors in judgment.

● Information that is contradictory to the dominant group view tends to be ignored, discounted, or minimized.

● Pressures are placed on group members to conform to the majority view—although the pressures may be relatively subtle (such as those discussed in Chapter 19 in reference to conformity)

● The pressure to conform discourages minority viewpoints from being brought before the group; consequently, there *appears* to be unanimity in the group, even if this is not really the case.

● There is an illusion of morality. Because the group views itself as representing something just and moral (in the case of the Bay of Pigs invasion, it was the American cause), members assume that any judgment that is reached by the group will be just and moral as well.

The consequences of groupthink are numerous, and nearly always negative. Groups tend to limit their list of possible solutions to just a few, and they spend relatively little time considering any alternatives once the leader seems to be leaning toward a particular solution. In fact, they may completely ignore information that challenges a developing consensus.

Groupthink, which appears to have resulted in numerous errors in judgment throughout history, can be overcome, however. One way is to increase the quantity and quality of information available to the group. Another is to put together decision-making groups that contain a wide diversity of views.

In addition, groups containing a strong leader should encourage open criticism and give-and-take when decisions are made, and the leader should refrain from voicing a preference. Finally, subgroups could be formed to examine and encourage one particular solution each, then the various subgroups could be brought together, with each subgroup advocating its position to the group as a whole. These strategies would ensure that divergent opinion was thoroughly aired in the group before a final decision was reached, thereby avoiding the pitfalls of groupthink (Flowers, 1977; Janis, 1972).

Groupthink: A phenomenon that occurs when members of a highly cohesive group share such strong motivation to achieve consensus that they lose the ability to critically evaluate alternative points of view

effective decisions than did groups that were encouraged to avoid controversy and to smooth over their differences (Tjosvold, 1982).

The reason that controversy ultimately seems to produce better decisions is that group members begin to understand opposing views more fully as they learn more about the nature of arguments in their support. In addition, controversy provokes greater initial uncertainty about the problem—and this makes group participants think more actively about the problem and develop solutions of higher quality (Johnson & Johnson, 1979; Tjosvold & Deewar, 1980). Promoting controversy in the initial phases of group discussion, then, can lead to better decisions than when a problem is approached in a routine, consensus-seeking way.

RECAP AND REVIEW II

Recap

◀ In order to determine whether participative or nonparticipative decision making is superior, the nature of the specific situation must be considered, as well as the type of participation.

◀ In general, group decision making is better for establishing objectives, evaluating alternatives, and choosing alternatives. Individuals are generally better at identifying alternatives and implementing decisions—all other factors being equal.

◀ Decision making can be improved through brainstorming, adopting nominal group techniques, and promoting controversy.

Review

1. A doctor realizes that a more efficient system of record-keeping is necessary and calls a meeting of the office staff to decide on a new system. The doctor is using a technique called _____ _____ _____ .

2. A problem-solving technique in which group members never meet but communicate through detailed questionnaires is called
   a. the Delphi method.
   b. the nominal group technique.
   c. participative decision making.
   d. brainstorming.

3. Groups are generally better than individuals at establishing objectives. True or false? _____

4. Name five factors that may promote groupthink.

(Answers to review questions are on page 700.)

THE JOYS OF THE JOB: SATISFACTION AT WORK

When Patricia Alford reports to work each day as a health claims processor for the Equitable Life Assurance Company of New York, she knows exactly what she will do for the next nine hours: sit in front of a computer terminal. Except for two fifteen-minute breaks and an hour off for lunch, Ms. Alford is tied to her terminal—making for a workday filled with tedium, loneliness, and stress. In fact, she doesn't even know how much she will be paid in a given week because her salary depends on how many claims she processes. The pay standards are so complicated that her pay can vary from between $217 to $400 per week, giving her a surprise each week when she opens her pay envelope. Moreover, she is closely scrutinized by supervisors. If she stops working, one immediately comes over and asks why (*New York Times*, March 28, 1984).

Were it not for the mention of a computer terminal, Patricia Alford's job description would be reminiscent of an impression of work that Charles Dickens often conveyed in his novels. In this view, the sole goal of work is to be as productive as possible, in order that the employer can earn the maximum amount of money. Job satisfaction, if it is considered at all, is important only insofar as it is related to higher productivity—a relationship that, as we will discuss later, has yet to be demonstrated.

Most organizational and industrial psychologists, on the other hand, have

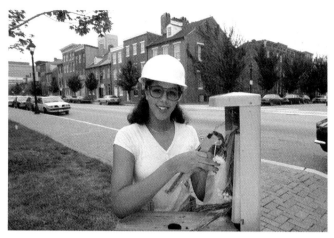

Wendy Thorpe's satisfaction in installing telephone equipment may result in higher productivity—although not necessarily. (Stacy Pick/Stock Boston.)

suggested that work plays such a fundamental role in most people's lives that it should be satisfying in its own right—regardless of whether it is associated with higher productivity. Taking this perspective, they have investigated the factors that have an impact on job satisfaction.

THE ORGANIZATION'S INFLUENCE ON JOB SATISFACTION

One of the major influences on how satisfied people are with their jobs is the nature of the organization for which they work. When company policies and procedures are perceived as fair and administered without bias, workers tend to feel greater satisfaction with their jobs.

In addition, the nature of decision making permitted within an organization is an important factor. Employees who feel that decision making is **decentralized**, meaning that authority extends throughout the organization, have greater job satisfaction than those in organizations that are **centralized**, meaning that power and authority rest in the hands of just a few people at the top of the organization (Cummings & Berger, 1976). In one example of decentralization, for instance, some manufacturing plants permit all employees to shut down the assembly line rolling past them if they have a problem that they cannot otherwise resolve. Such authority is particularly significant because it provides workers with the power to stop the entire plant's production, and having such responsibility results in workers who feel particularly satisfied with their jobs (Holden, 1986). (For more on worker satisfaction, see the Cutting Edge box.)

Decentralized decision making: Decision making in which the distribution of authority extends throughout the organization

Centralized decision making: Decision making in which authority is controlled by a few people at the top of the organization

THE CUTTING EDGE

IMITATING THE JAPANESE: INVOLVING WORKERS IN THE ORGANIZATION

It would have been an unusual spectacle in any part of the United States, but it looked particularly incongruous in the rural Arkansas town of Forrest City: Some 500 employees of a television manufacturing plant, all wearing company T-shirts, shouted "Good morning" in unison to the company president, and then began an afternoon of relay races, tugs-of-war, and other games. With executives and workers participating side by side, the afternoon was devoted to celebrating the success of their plant, which only seven years earlier had been near bankruptcy (Serrin, 1983, p. B-14).

How had the company managed to turn its fortunes around? The major reason was the implementation of a management system similar to that found in the typical Japanese organization—a system based largely on findings of psychologists interested in organizations and the workplace. Seven years earlier, the plant, which made television sets for Sears, Roebuck & Company, was losing money and on the verge of closing. At that time, however, the factory was bought by the Sanyo Manufacturing Corporation, and it adopted a Japanese management system in which concern for the company employees became a dominant focus.

Heralded by some as the wave of the future and by others as dictatorial and paternalistic, the Japanese management style has become the topic of much debate in this country. The major reason for this interest is that the Japanese economy has witnessed an enormous growth in the last two decades—a rate of growth that has outpaced that in the United States. According to advocates, the success of Japanese technology is due in no small measure to the organizational principles the Japanese use.

Several strategies characterize Japanese management systems (Hatvany & Pucik, 1981; Holden, 1986; Imai, 1986).

● Doing things according to the principle of *kaizen*. The Japanese term *kaizen* refers to the constant search for improvement, a norm that is at the heart of Japanese management models. One goal is to produce as much as possible in as little time as possible, but an equally important objective is to produce a high-quality product that is constantly improving. And it is not just products that are expected to progress; employees, too, are constantly striving to improve themselves.

● Developing employees. Employees are hired right after graduation from high school or college, and it is assumed that they will stay with the same company until retirement. Consequently, companies develop their own labor pool, which remains stable and becomes well trained in the particular operations of the company. Moreover, Japanese companies tend to have relatively rapid job rotation, whereby an employee is placed in numerous different jobs within the company. Coupled with a slow promotion policy—most job changes do not result in a change in status—this means that the majority of employees gain wide experience in a number of positions. In contrast, employees in the United States feel little loyalty to their employer and frequently move from one company to another.

● Providing a unique philosophy for the company. A conscious effort is made to create a cohesive, family-like atmosphere among employees. Workers are encouraged to live together in company housing, to take vacations together, and to socialize during their spare time. Such group activity fosters a strong sense of group cohesiveness and motivates workers to adopt the formal norms of the organization. Rather than giving allegiance to informal groups within the organization, a worker will adopt the norms of the company as a whole. The high cohesiveness serves in this case to increase the influence of the organization over the individual.

● Encouraging strong socialization into the organization. **Socialization** is the process by which an individual learns the rules and norms of appropriate behavior during development. Similarly, **organizational socialization** occurs when a worker learns to behave and adopt attitudes similar to others in the organization.

Japanese organizations tend to promote socialization through intensive training programs that may last as long as six months. In these programs, employees are exposed to all aspects of the company, not just to the jobs for which they were hired. The result, again, is to build loyalty to the company as a whole rather than to a small subunit of the organization. Socialization on one level begins even before the official training program: Potential employees are probed during job interviews to determine whether they hold initial attitudes that are compatible with those the organization wants to see in its employees.

These strategies foster employee attitudes that are very different from those of employees in typical American companies. Instead of developing an individualistic orientation (following personal goals and being concerned with their own career advancement), employees of companies using Japanese management strategies tend to be committed to the workplace and *its* goals. Of course, this does not mean that the Japanese management style will work in every organizational setting in the United States, as there are vast differences between the two cultures (Latham, 1988; Suzuki, 1986). It does suggest, however, that the Japanese management style is worth considering as a potential way to improve the functioning of organizations in this country.

Socialization: The developmental process by which an individual learns the rules and norms of appropriate behavior

Organizational socialization: The process by which a worker learns to behave like others in the organization and to adopt similar attitudes

---

ANSWERS (REVIEW II):
1. Participative decision making   **2.** a   **3.** True   **4.** Illusion of invulnerability; ignoring information contrary to majority opinion; pressure to conform to majority view; apparent unanimity resulting from discouragement of minority views; illusion of morality

The supervisory style of a worker's boss represents another important factor affecting job satisfaction. Employees who perceive their boss as considerate of their own needs tend to have greater satisfaction with their work than do those who view their supervisor as insensitive (Stogdill, 1974).

Conversely, the job satisfaction of supervisors is affected by the behavior and attitudes of the people they are supervising. As a supervisor, one must constantly balance the demands of the organization for both high productivity and high quality in output against the task of motivating and meeting the needs of employees. Under some conditions, the balancing act can prove to be difficult. Because employees may not even be well qualified for their jobs, they may need to receive on-the-job training that the supervisor is poorly equipped to provide. Furthermore, employees may hold the supervisor personally responsible for the problems they face—even when those problems are not under the supervisor's control. In some situations, then, supervisory responsibilities can lead to lower job satisfaction.

In most cases, however, holding a supervisory position results in a higher level of job satisfaction than being supervised by others. For one thing, bosses tend to have greater responsibility and control over their day-to-day activities than do the people under them, and—as we have seen several times before— a sense of control provides important psychological benefits. Furthermore, supervisors have higher status than their subordinates, providing them with higher prestige than the people that they supervise. Finally, bosses have greater power than subordinates to make decisions and to reward and punish others. For all these reasons, it is better to give supervision than to receive it—at least in terms of job satisfaction.

Back to the Future?: Electronic Supervision

For some workers, the issue is not *who* their supervisor is but *what* it is, for their every keystroke is monitored by the computer terminal at which they work.

Today's technology has brought an unheard-of degree of sophistication to the tools that managers have to oversee worker productivity, and some experts estimate that between 4 and 6 million clerical workers are currently being monitored electronically at least part of the day (Booth, 1987). In addition to being able to monitor the rate of computer keyboard use—and

Because they have more power to make decisions, supervisors generally have a higher level of job satisfaction than those they supervise. (Curtis Compton/Stock South.)

Classical (or bureaucratic) model. A management theory in which explicit rules, regulations, and procedures govern every task

the specific nature of what is being entered into the computer at a given moment—managers can use the telephone to check on workers. For instance, most telephone operators in the United States are subject to "service observation," which means that a supervisor can listen in on them at any time.

Ironically, electronic monitoring marks a return to a **classical (or bureaucratic) model** of managing employees, a largely discredited management theory in which explicit rules, regulations, and procedures govern every task. In such a system, a rigid division of labor exists, in which people have well-specified and defined jobs that can be carried out with a maximum degree of competence and efficiency. Careful monitoring of employees' every move is seen as the key to increased productivity (Weber, 1952).

The drawback to such a view of supervision is that it ignores the social nature of the workplace. In settings that follow the classical model, workers easily experience alienation, a loss of a sense of control, and develop informal norms that are contrary to the formal management goals. The ultimate result is a decline of efficiency and organizational dysfunction (Katz & Kahn, 1978).

Human relations model: A view of management which emphasizes the social context of work and people's interactions with one another

Because of these difficulties with the classical model, then, most organizations today follow a **human relations model**, a view of management that places greater emphasis on the social context of work and people's interactions with one another. For example, rather than seeking to control employees, supervisors in many organizations are taught to act as facilitators, helping workers to carry out their jobs with a sense of independence and control. The human relations model recognizes the importance of work in people's lives.

It is difficult to see how the capability to electronically monitor employees can be integrated into the human relations view of management. Although it is too early to determine the consequences of such monitoring of employees, the potential of being observed at any moment would hardly be expected to be positive.

BEING HAPPY WITH WHAT YOU DO:
Satisfaction and the Nature of the Job

Consider what it would be like to walk into a large corporation your first day on the job and be told that your boss is out of town for the next three

Workers under the classical model of management may feel alienated and experience a loss of a sense of control. (Larry Mulvehill/ Photo Researchers.)

weeks, and that you should use the time for deciding what you will do and how you are going to get it done. Although some might relish the challenge, most of us would find such a situation difficult, at best.

The degree of explicitness of the rules that determine what is expected of a worker is called **job clarity**. Jobs that have very well-defined expectations have a high degree of clarity, while those that lack clear-cut definitions tend to be low in clarity. The greater the clarity, the more satisfied employees tend to be.

A lack of job clarity is most frequently found in managerial jobs in which there are many different ways to meet a goal—and often no clear-cut goals for which to strive (Kahn et al., 1964). But even relatively low-status positions can produce low clarity, such as the example of an administrative assistant who is not told by his boss what it is he is supposed to do.

Job clarity: The degree of explicitness of the rules which determine what is expected of a worker

"Nobody Can Do All I'm Asked to Do": Role Conflict

Another factor that has an important impact on job satisfaction is **role conflict**, which arises when job expectations are defined in a way that makes it impossible to carry out the job properly. An individual faced with role conflict must respond to two or more sets of pressures or demands that contradict one another—so that if one set of requirements is followed, the other cannot be complied with (Kahn et al., 1964). For example, consider the job of foreman in a manufacturing plant. Suppose one of the foreman's responsibilities is to increase the productivity of his workers. At the same time, he may be told that he must keep the employees happy in order to prevent them from wanting to unionize. This can clearly be a no-win situation. If he forces an increase in productivity he is likely to upset the workers, leading them closer to unionization, but if he tolerates lower productivity, which might prevent the initiation of a unionization drive, he will not be meeting his production goals.

Role conflict: A conflict which arises when an individual is faced with two or more sets of demands that contradict one another

There are other kinds of role conflicts as well. In some cases, the role a person holds outside an organization can produce conflict. A classic example is that of a woman who is simultaneously a mother, a homemaker, and a professional. The job conflicts can create powerful dilemmas. For example, a woman whose child is ill and must be left at home while she makes a business trip experiences conflict no matter what she chooses to do. If she cancels the trip her career and salary may suffer, but if she chooses to go, her child may be hurt (Hammond & Fong, 1988).

As you might expect, role conflict produces a number of serious consequences for individuals and the organizations that employ them (VanSell, Brief & Schuler, 1981). Not only is job satisfaction generally lower for people in such situations, but they report feeling tense and anxious and have lower confidence in supervisors and managers above them in the organizational hierarchy. There are also concrete behavioral consequences: Job turnover is higher and productivity lower when people experience job conflict.

SHOULD THE JOB FIT THE PERSON OR THE PERSON FIT THE JOB?: Increasing Employee Job Satisfaction

Because job satisfaction has been viewed as so important to employees as well as the organizations for which they work, organizational and industrial psychologists have looked for ways in which it can be promoted. They have

THE PSYCHOLOGICAL CONTEXT
OF THE WORLD AROUND US

Job enrichment: Techniques for improving the quality of the activities involved in a job

identified three main approaches: changing the nature of the job, changing people so they are better matched to the requirements of a particular job, and changing both the jobs and the people that fill them in order to produce a more appropriate match between person and job.

Changing the Job

Obviously, if one wants to increase job satisfaction, a logical starting point is the job itself. Role ambiguity and conflict can be reduced by providing carefully delineated job descriptions that describe the specific duties and responsibilities of a given position.

Another strategy relates to the concept of **job enrichment**, techniques for improving the quality of the activities involved in a job (Hackman & Oldham, 1976; Katzell & Guzzo, 1983). These include:

▶ Increasing the variety of skills that must be used in a given position

▶ Modifying what a job entails in order to allow each person to complete a specific, whole, identifiable product

▶ Increasing the degree to which a person has influence over others

▶ Increasing the precision with which an individual receives feedback about his or her performance.

When jobs are redesigned to take these dimensions into account, it is possible to increase the meaningfulness of work and the degree to which workers feel responsibility for what they have produced. Ultimately, this results not only in higher satisfaction but in increased worker motivation, higher-quality work, lower absenteeism and turnover, and a decrease in job-related stress. These effects can be dramatic; for example, one division of Monsanto found that productivity increased by 75 percent after it started a job-enrichment program (Mares & Simmons, 1985; Umstot, Bell & Mitchell, 1976).

Changing the Person

In some cases it is impossible to change the nature of a job. Assembly lines, for instance, tend to require people to carry out repetitive activities under unrelenting time constraints, and the job by its very nature cannot be changed very much without revamping the whole assembly-line concept. In situations such as these, an alternative solution is to change people's reactions to the job characteristics that cause low satisfaction (Latham, 1988).

One approach has been the introduction of sensitivity training in organizations to teach members to be more aware of their own feelings and values, as well as those of others. During such training, participants engage in face-to-face interactions in which they discuss their feelings and emotions about themselves and the other members of a group in a "safe" setting.

The goals of sensitivity training are to promote greater sensitivity to others' perspectives and to explore different varieties of social interaction. Advocates assume that the greater understanding brought about by this process will enable people to be more at ease with the restraints of their jobs—although the evidence supporting such an assumption is decidedly mixed. It is unclear whether the insights gained from participation in sensitivity training generalize to work settings, and, even if they do, whether they ultimately enhance workers' lives (Goldstein, 1986).

Some organizations also use role-playing exercises for employees, in which an incident is described and an individual is assigned to play the role of one of the participants in the incident. Through this activity, role players come to a better understanding of how *they* might react to being in a similar situation. For example, the role player might have to act out the firing of an employee and would get a chance to see what the reactions of the person receiving the news might be. In this way, he or she might be better able to cope with a similar—and real—incident in the future, ultimately relieving some of the stress that the job entails.

Matching the Person to the Job

Rather than expecting to change either the job or the individual who fills it, the most reasonable approach to enhancing job satisfaction is to produce as close a fit as possible between the person in a given position and the position itself. People differ in the degree to which they can tolerate ambiguity and conflict in their jobs: Some people thrive in supervisory roles; others work best under the close supervision of others, without having supervisory responsibilities themselves. As we mentioned in Chapter 14 when discussing the use of personality measures in employee selection, it is at least theoretically possible to keep stress at manageable levels by examining worker personality characteristics and attitudes and precisely defining the nature of a given job.

SATISFACTION MAY NOT EQUAL PRODUCTIVITY: A Final Note

Implicit in much of the research that psychologists have carried out in studying job satisfaction is the assumption that there is a link between job satisfaction and worker performance (Petty, McGee & Cavender, 1984; Druckman & Swets, 1988). Shouldn't a happy worker be a more productive worker?

In fact, the answer seems to be "not necessarily." There is only a slight relationship between workers' satisfaction and their productivity (Iaffaldano & Muchinsky, 1985). What this suggests is that organizations seeking to increase both worker productivity and worker satisfaction—two worthy goals—must use different means to achieve the two ends.

Despite the lack of association between productivity and satisfaction, the solutions that have been suggested to increase job satisfaction—changing the job, changing the person, and optimizing the job-person match—still make sense. Indeed, it is reasonable to say that any technique that produces an increase in employee satisfaction is likely to produce a better workplace and organization—one in which the goal of having a satisfied, psychologically well-adjusted workforce can be met.

RECAP AND REVIEW III

Recap

◀ Because work plays such an important role in most people's lives, organizational and industrial psychologists have focused on work satisfaction.

◀ The policies and procedures that are part of an organization affect employee satisfaction. For instance, organizations with more decentralized decision making generally have higher worker satisfaction.

◀ Job satisfaction is related to the kind of supervisor one has, the nature of the work situation, job clarity, and role conflict.

◀ Approaches to increasing satisfaction in the workplace include changing the nature of the job, changing the person who fills the job, and/or changing both.

◀ Productivity is only minimally related to job satisfaction.

706

Review

1. Japanese organizations encourage a process, called _____ _____ , in which a worker learns to behave and adopt attitudes similar to other members in the organization.
2. Name four job enrichment techniques.
3. Mike generally enjoys good rapport with the employees he supervises, an important requirement of his job. A problem arises when every so often he is asked to issue written warnings regarding the employees' past performance. "How can I do this and maintain my rapport?" he wonders. His dissatisfaction centers around the issue of
   a. participation.
   b. job clarity.
   c. role conflict.
   d. job enrichment.
4. We can be confident that a happy, satisfied worker will also be a productive worker. True or false?

_____

(Answers to review questions are on page 707.)

◀ **LOOKING BACK**

1. In this chapter, we have discussed some of the major issues relating to organizations and the workplace. We started with an exploration of groups, the building blocks of organizations. According to psychologists, groups have four characteristics that distinguish them from mere aggregates of people: interaction among the group members, perception of membership, shared goals and norms, and interdependence of fate. Organizations have two kinds of groups: formal (work units set up by management) and informal (groups that evolve as a result of the interests and needs of the individuals within the organization).

2. The Hawthorne studies showed that informal group membership, and the informal group's norms and goals, can have a greater effect on productivity and worker morale than the formal groups within the organization to which a worker belongs. This is especially true if group cohesiveness—the degree of attraction members feel to the group or to other members—is higher for the informal group than for the organization as a whole.

3. Some research has sought to determine whether participative or nonparticipative decision making is superior. Although the results in terms of productivity are mixed, it is clear that participative decision making is better for worker morale. The issue of whether individuals or groups make better decisions is also unresolved; in part, it depends on the nature of the decision being made.

4. The factors that increase job satisfaction have been a major focus for organizational and industrial psychologists. One factor that is related to satisfaction is the nature of the organization: Organizations with policies and procedures that are equitably administered foster satisfaction. Moreover, organizations in which decision making is decentralized are apt to have employees with greater job satisfaction.

5. Supervision that is considerate of workers' needs produces higher job satisfaction. Although some circumstances produce dissatisfaction among supervisors, they generally report a relatively high level of satisfaction, since supervisory positions tend to have greater responsibility and higher status within the organization—factors that are related to satisfaction.

6. Electronic monitoring of employees marks a return to the classical (or bureaucratic) model of management, in which explicit rules, regulations, and procedures govern every task. This view of supervision contrasts with human relations models, which place greater emphasis on the social context of work and people's interactions in the workplace.

7. Several approaches have been used to increase job satisfaction. Among them are changing the nature of the job (for example, through job enrichment programs), changing the people who fill the jobs (through sensitivity training or role playing), and matching specific people to specific jobs more effectively.

8. Despite the fact that there is only a modest relationship between job satisfaction and productivity, increasing worker satisfaction is likely to have a beneficial impact on work organizations.

KEY TERMS AND CONCEPTS ▶

industrial-organizational psychologists (p. 686)

group dynamics (688)

group (688)

norms (688)

organizations (689)

formal group (689)

informal group (689)

Hawthorne effect (689)

cohesiveness (689)

Protestant work ethic (691)

status (691)

participative decision making (694)

brainstorming (695)

nominal group technique (696)

Delphi method (698)

groupthink (697)

decentralized decision making (699)

centralized decision making (699)

socialization (700)

organizational socialization (700)

classical (or bureaucratic) model (of management) (702)

human relations model (of management) (702)

job clarity (703)

role conflict (703)

job enrichment (704)

FOR FURTHER STUDY AND APPLICATION ▶

Forsyth, D. (1983). *An introduction to group dynamics.* Monterey, CA: Brooks/Cole.

In a readable, scholarly volume, the author presents an overview of group dynamics, including many applications of groups in such areas as education and the workplace.

Zander, A. (1977). *Groups at work.* San Francisco: Jossey-Bass.

A clear guide to the use of groups in applied settings, this text is written by one of the experts in group process research and theory.

Landy, F. J. (1985). *Psychology of work behavior.* Homewood, IL: Dorsey.

This clear, detailed, and well-written introduction describes the relationship between psychological issues and work settings.

Kossen, S. (1987). *The human side of organizations* (4th ed.). New York: Harper & Row.

Steers, R. M. (1988). *Introduction to organizational behavior* (3rd ed.). Glenview, IL: Scott, Foresman.

These two volumes present a clear picture of how the structure, makeup, and policies of industrial organizations affect the productivity and satisfaction of their employees.

Frost, P. J., Mitchell, V. F., & Nord, W. R. (1986). *Organizational reality reports from the firing line* (3rd ed.). Chicago: Scott, Foresman.

To get a sense of what it is really like to work in an organization, read this volume, which provides firsthand accounts from workers in a wide variety of settings.

ANSWERS (REVIEW III):

1. Organizational socialization **2.** Increasing the variety of skills necessary for a given position; modifying a job so that each employee completes an identifiable project; increasing an employee's influence; increasing the precision with which an employee receives feedback **3.** c **4.** False; there is only a slight relationship between satisfaction and performance

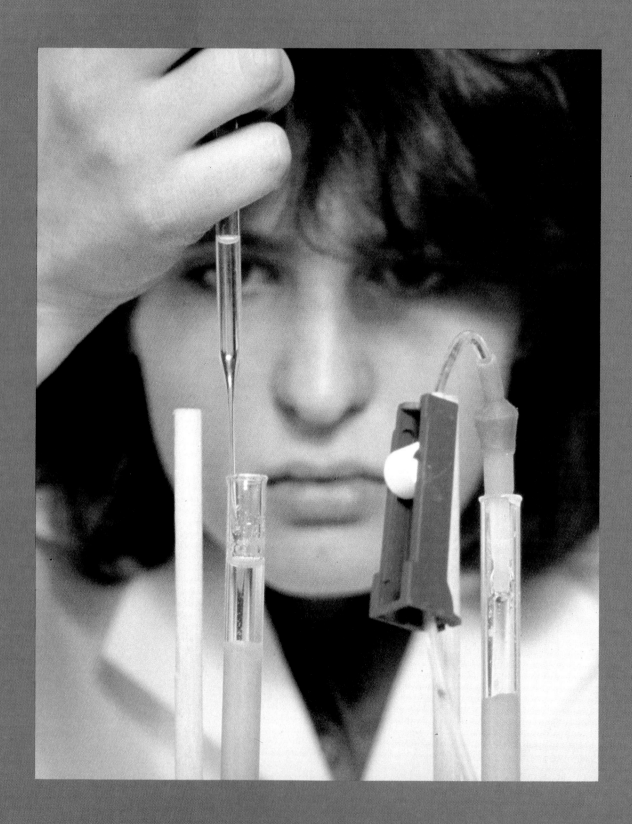

CHAPTER

TECHNOLOGY AND CONTEMPORARY SOCIETY

Robert T. Morris, Jr., who devised a computer virus that got out of control. (J. L. Atlan/Sygma.)

PROLOGUE:
ROBERT T. MORRIS, JR.

It began as just a prank. But by the time the computer virus devised by 23-year-old Robert T. Morris, Jr., made its way across the United States, the infection brought work to a virtual standstill in thousands of computer centers and produced enormous costs.

Morris, a computer science graduate student, faced possible criminal indictment for his injection of a highly infectious computer virus that was designed to replicate itself, moving over an electronic network that connected computers throughout the country. Analogous to viruses in humans, computer viruses are programs that are designed to reproduce themselves, taking control over the computers in which they reside. Less damaging viruses merely make copies of certain programs, slowly clogging a computer's memory until there is no room left in the machine for legitimate users. More malignant viruses, in contrast, actually erase programs and files of host computers, rendering permanent damage.

Morris claimed his program was intended to cause no harm and that his purpose was merely to demonstrate that the highly sophisticated security measures meant to prevent such viral attacks were inadequate. However, a tiny programming error made his virus replicate at such a rapid rate that it quickly clogged the computers of tens of thousands of researchers.

If Morris's attack had a virtue, it was to bring about a careful reexamination of the art of computer defense and a tightening of computer security. After all, for many computer "hackers," the world's computers remain fair game (Elmer-Dewitt, 1988).

LOOKING AHEAD ▶

Whether you consider it as merely a prank or as a malicious act, the virus unleashed by Robert Morris raises some intriguing issues for psychologists to grapple with. What is the motivation behind viral attacks? What is it about computers that makes them such a source of interest and even obsession to some people? Why do other people view computers with fear, apprehension, and real anxiety?

In fact, the use of computers is just one example—although one of the most obvious—of the impact of technological advances on our lives. The technology of the twentieth century has brought advances that have made life considerably easier. At the same time, it has brought dangers that were unimaginable just fifty years ago, including the threat that looms over all our lives: the destruction of the human race through nuclear warfare.

These technological changes have had a profound psychological impact. As the world becomes more complex, we are increasingly less able to understand its workings, making uncertainty more common and decreasing our feelings of mastery and control. Technological advances also force us to perpetually modify our definitions of what is and is not possible, leading to a further inability to understand the world in which we live. Furthermore, we are continually affected by an earth that is growing more crowded every day, an earth over which the threat of nuclear war hangs like a sword on a thin string.

This chapter considers the effects of technology and the environment around us. We begin by examining the psychological effects of technology, focusing on the interaction between machines and their users and on human reactions to computers. Next, we discuss work in a relatively new branch of the field known as environmental psychology. **Environmental psychology** considers the relationship between the environment and people's behavior and their sense of well-being. We consider the influence of the social and physical environments on our everyday existence, exploring the impact on our lives of some of the most important characteristics of the physical environment, including crowding, air temperature, air quality, and noise. Finally, we discuss disasters and catastrophes—artificial and natural—as well as considering some of the ways that psychologists contribute to issues of war and peace.

After reading this chapter, then, you'll have the answers to such questions as these:

▶ How does the design of everyday objects affect how we use them?

▶ Why do some people fear computers, and what effects has the increased use of computers had on people's lives?

▶ Why does crowding produce negative consequences?

▶ What major aspects of the physical environment affect behavior?

▶ What are the psychological consequences of surviving a disaster?

▶ What contributions can psychologists make to the prevention of war and the promotion of peace?

Environmental psychology: The branch of psychology that studies the relationship between people and their physical environment

PSYCHOLOGY MEETS THE FUTURE: TECHNOLOGY IN THE 1990s

The lights dimmed in the university auditorium, the students' chatter subsided, and the professor from California, psychologist Donald A. Norman, began his lecture. The topic: how people interact with things. The student in charge of showing Norman's slides pushed the control button, and *crash!* The tray shot out of the projector, fell onto the floor, and disgorged all the slides. For fifteen minutes Norman struggled to put them back in order. When he resumed his talk and the student began pressing the control button again, the slides refused to move the right way. The harder the student pressed to ensure that the switch was making contact, the worse the mix-up became. Later a technician explained that a brief push of the button prompted a slide to the front, while a long one caused it to reverse. Norman's rueful comment: "What an elegant design. Why, it managed to do two functions with only one button. But how was a first-time user of the projector to know this?" (Blake, 1988, p. 48.)

To any of us who have struggled to master the controls of a VCR or pushed on a door that slides open automatically, it is easy to understand Norman's frustration. As humans continue to display amazing ingenuity in producing new contrivances to make life easier, the world paradoxically may become a progressively more complex place in which to live. Here we will consider two major psychological aspects of technology: the interaction of people and machines and the omnipresence of computers in our society.

HUMANS VERSUS MACHINES: The Psychology of Everyday Technologies

One of the reasons that the technological world presents an increasing number of challenges is that insufficient attention is paid to the interaction between machines and their users. Psychologists examining **ergonomics**, the study of how people's behavior and abilities affect the design of tools, machines, and environments for effective use, have found that even everyday objects which we all employ could be designed in a way that makes them considerably easier to utilize.

For example, psychologist Donald Norman (1988) points to several common objects whose design makes them difficult to operate (see Figure 21-1). Car stereos often include rows of buttons so tiny that a driver must lean toward the radio to read them, a maneuver that makes driving at highway speeds a particularly challenging endeavor. Similarly, the single-control shower faucet found in newer houses, hotels, and dormitories presents users with the opportunity to savor the unknown, for it is typically unclear whether scalding or icy water will come from the spigot, and whether it will come out in a trickle or a torrent.

Ergonomics: The study of how people's behavior and abilities affect the design of tools, machines, and environments for effective use

Well-designed objects, in contrast, possess **visibility**, visual cues to their operation that are inherent in the design. Visibility enhances accurate perception and cognitive understanding of mechanisms, permitting them to be used effectively with a minimum of thought.

Visibility: Visual cues to the operation of an object that are inherent in the object's design

A central feature of visibility is **natural mapping**, a design that relies on an analogy between the physical appearance of a device and the physical actions that are required to operate it. For example, the controls for the separate burners on a stove are often laid out in a straight line, whereas the burners themselves are laid out in a square. A stove that conformed to the principle of natural mapping would situate the controls in a square design, corresponding to the layout of the burners.

Natural mapping: A design relying on an analogy between a device's physical appearance and the actions required to operate it

In some cases, the design of objects can produce deadly consequences. For example, in the late 1980s, Audi 5000 cars were plagued with a problem of sudden, uncontrolled acceleration. According to one U.S. government report, part of the blame for the problem was the location, shape, and feel

FIGURE 21-1

The "visibility" of everyday objects affects the ease of their use. For example, it is considerably more difficult to know which knobs control particular burners on the stove-top at left than the one at right, on which the knobs mirror the configuration of the burners. Similarly, it is easier to understand the use of traditional two-faucet controls than the single faucet pictured at left.

of the gas pedal. The government suggested that the pedal design led drivers to "misapply" their feet to the pedal, producing the surge in acceleration (Levin, 1989).

Given the difficulty in designing everyday objects that are simple, safe, and easy to use, it is hardly surprising that technologically sophisticated machinery presents even more of a challenge to designers—and users. We turn now to the technological advance that has had perhaps the biggest impact in the last decade: the computer.

LIVING WITH COMPUTERS

We all encounter computers in our daily lives, whether we're playing a game at a video arcade, using a word processor, registering for university classes, withdrawing money from an automatic teller, or making a long distance phone call. However, some of us interact with computers with far greater ease than others. Certain people do their best to avoid them; others—like Robert Morris, Jr., whose virus attack paralyzed computers around the United States—view them as a humanity-over-machine challenge to be tested. These individual differences, as well as the increasing prevalence of computers, have led psychologists to turn their attention to the ways in which people adapt to computers.

Computers in the Workplace

The workplace is one of the areas that has attracted the most interest, because businesses have been eager to embrace the efficiency and other benefits that computers can offer (see the Psychology at Work box). At the same time, computers have produced several unanticipated (and unfavorable) side effects in the workplace. For instance, workers who have portions of their jobs replaced by computers may feel that their skills are not necessary or not valuable, leading to declines in morale. Workers may also lose a sense of control over their environment, as activities over which they once had governance are no longer under their personal direction. As we have noted in several chapters, a sense of control is an important component of psychological well-being (Rodin, 1987), and its loss in the workplace can be devastating.

Some people have an actual fear of computers, sometimes labeled **cyberphobia**. Faced with learning a new terminology, dealing with an unfamiliar piece of machinery, and handling new ways of thinking about problems, employees may be overwhelmed and may experience anxiety. Negative reactions to computers can take several forms. For example, one organization that specializes in training workers has found several distinguishable types of reactions (Carroll, 1988). The "puppydogs" slap away at the keys without apparent purpose. "Hoverers" keep their fingers just above the keyboard, almost as if the keys were hot, while "delegators" wait for someone else to hit the keys for them. Worst are the "cellists"—a name that comes from a scene in a Woody Allen movie in which a cello teacher says that some students have no concept of the instrument, as a person holds a cello up to his mouth and blows on it.

Although we have been focusing on the potential disadvantages of computerization in the workplace, it does offer the promise of improvement in people's work-related lives. For instance, once computers are introduced, they can facilitate the upgrading of jobs. Removal of the boring, tedious, and

Cyberphobia: Fear of computers

714

COMPUTER THERAPY

My first reaction was "A machine? You want me to sit down with a machine? I thought it would take a lot of the personalness out of it." (Ravo, 1988, p. B-1).

The "it" about which Lyn Conlan is speaking is an encounter with Dr. Bob—the nickname given to a computer at the corporate headquarters of UST, a manufacturer of wine and smokeless tobacco. Dr. Bob's function is to serve as an adjunct therapist for employees such as Conlan who are suffering from minor, but draining, stress-related problems.

The computer asks a series of questions to which employees respond using the computer keyboard. For example, it opens with the statement "I feel stress in my . . . ," to which a user must respond with up to four of the following choices:

"work life, social life, emotional life, family life, school life, day-to-day life, and physical health."

The questions are aimed at discovering the source of stress and developing a strategy for dealing with the stress. Input is recorded on a floppy disk, which, to preserve privacy, users keep following a session. The entire program lasts for ten one-hour sessions. Human therapists make evaluations of the sessions following the second, sixth, and final hours. They may intervene at any time, suggesting further treatment or the use of a human therapist if the problems warrant it.

The computer program, called the Therapeutic Learning Program, is clearly not for everyone. People with serious problems are screened out initially. Furthermore, the long-term effects of the program have yet to be formally evaluated, so it is still unclear how effective the program is in resolving even minor problems. Still, employee response to the program has been favorable, and the head of the company that produced it, psychiatrist Roger Gould, claimed that 80 percent of the program's users needed no further counseling (Ravo, 1988).

Whether computer-therapists become a standard feature of the workplace remains to be seen. In the meantime, the prevalence of computers in people's lives shows no signs of abating.

repetitive aspects of job activities can leave workers with the more interesting and rewarding components of their jobs. Workers may even find that the quality of their work improves as they incorporate computers into their jobs. We still don't know, however, what the long-term psychological consequences of computerization in the workplace will be and whether the negative or the positive consequences will predominate (Atwell & Rule, 1984).

Computers in Educational Settings

In Chapter 5, we discussed the use of programmed instruction in educational settings. But in many respects this is only a small part of the impact of computers on students (Lepper & Gurtner, 1989). For instance, it is now almost as routine for college students to use their own computers to produce papers as it once was for them to sit down at a typewriter.

On most college campuses where the use of computers is commonplace, a "computer culture" exists to which some (but not all) students belong. To the "hackers" who are part of the culture, a set of norms specifies what is and isn't appropriate behavior. For example, the computer culture typically encompasses several characteristics that led to the efforts of Robert Morris, Jr., to produce his virus (Dubrovsky, Kiesler, Sproull & Zubrow, 1986; Soukanhov, 1989).

▶ Tricks, pranks, and games that appear in computers are tolerated and, in some cases, encouraged.

▶ Hackers are often unconventional, impolite, adventurous, and irreverent.

▶ Individuals engage in mild forms of larceny, such as stealing computer time, copying software, and breaking into systems without being authorized.

▶ Special language is used—words such as "quux," "bagbiter," "glork," and "hungus."

▶ Social cooperation is deemphasized, and individual performance is the norm. People compete to see who can write the biggest, the most powerful, and the fastest programs.

▶ Idiosyncrasy—in both people and computer systems—is valued. Committed members of the culture may be found at a terminal or in the computer center day and night. Status is confirmed through titles given to people—such as hackers, wizards, and losers.

One of the reasons for the development of such a specialized culture is that computer science courses differ in several fundamental ways from other, more traditional courses (Dubrovsky et al., 1986). In most courses, students are free to pick out the time and place they wish to work; in computer courses, students must schedule their time according to the availability of the computer center. When a pencil point breaks, a student can sharpen it, but when a monitor screen goes blank, there is little the user can do except wait for someone else to fix the system. Feedback differs in its immediacy. A mistake in a mathematics assignment does not provoke the flood of error messages that a mistake in a program does. Furthermore, with an English essay, for example, students can stop when *they* are satisfied that they have reached an appropriate level of quality. In completing a software programming assignment, in contrast, students can't stop until the program actually runs.

All these characteristics leave newcomers to the computer culture overwhelmed by the experience, feeling shock and disorientation. For example, in a survey of first-time computer users, one person wrote, "I sat down at this computer and started hitting the buttons and it started making all this noise and people kept looking at me. I didn't know what I was doing. I didn't know it was on" (Sproull, Kiesler & Zubrow, 1984, p. 31). Another commented, "I feel like I'm in *1984*—cells right next to each other. It's like Russia. You've got to just get as many people as you can, crammed in there. [The walls] are all white. And all they have are computer information on them. Maybe they could have a Picasso picture. Anything just to break the monotony. All you see are computer geeks and computers and the Xerox machines and white on the walls" (Dubrovsky et al., 1986, p. 319).

Perceptions of expert computer users are often negative. In an exaggerated view, newcomers see computer experts as "strange" and unable to function outside the computer culture. As one survey respondent said, "They can't relate to anything but the computer. They can't talk to a guy. Even when they talk, they talk computer language. It's like they've turned into a computer" (Dubrovsky et al., 1986, p. 321).

Computers and Privacy

One of the most important issues raised by the use of computers throughout society is that of privacy. One study conducted in the late 1970s by the Senate Subcommittee on Constitutional Rights found that in the federal government alone there were close to 1,000 data banks containing more than 1.25 billion records on individuals. Furthermore, hundreds of nongovernment agencies, ranging from banks to magazine publishers, maintain records on every one of us.

Given the magnitude and scope of the data currently retained by various organizations, the possibility for mishandling information is a real one. For example, people who apply for reimbursement for medical or psychological treatment must complete a form that allows insurance companies to disseminate the information about their treatment to other insurance companies. Once this information becomes part of someone's file, it is permanent, and such material may be shared routinely with other insurance companies in the future, seriously compromising an individual's privacy.

Even seemingly harmless information about the use of a check, bank cash card, or credit card allows someone to trace your whereabouts and behavior in a comprehensive manner. Paying in cash provides no traceable information, but writing a check creates a record of payer, payee, and the amount of the transaction. When you use a bank card to withdraw or deposit money, a record of time, location, and the nature of the transaction is prepared. Furthermore, the use of a credit card can be tracked. Credit card companies can then sell information about patterns of credit card use to mail-order retailers, who send catalogs to potential customers on the basis of their prior purchases of certain kinds of merchandise. In sum, personal privacy can be compromised by the availability of information in computer data banks.

RECAP AND REVIEW I

Recap

◀ Ergonomics is the study of how people's behavior and abilities affect the design of tools, machines, and environments for effective use. Everyday objects that have visual cues to their operation allow for natural mapping, in which there is an analogy between the appearance of an object and the actions required to operate it.

◀ New users of computers may exhibit cyberphobia, or fear of computers. For members of the computer culture, a set of well-established norms regulates appropriate behavior.

◀ The ability of computers to store large amounts of data presents the opportunity for violations of privacy.

Review

1. An object designed with inherent cues to its operation has a quality that environmental psychologists call _____ .

2. Which of the following are possible consequences of using computers in the workplace?
   a. Workers may feel a loss of control as computers take over some tasks.
   b. Tedious jobs can be done by computer, leaving the more interesting and challenging jobs for workers.
   c. Declines in morale can occur as workers feel that their skills are no longer valuable.
   d. Computers may reduce error and lead to higher-quality work.
   e. All of the above

3. A debilitating fear of computers is known as _____ .

4. Which of the following is *not* a typical characteristic of the computer culture?
   a. Tricks, pranks and games are common.
   b. Hackers work together for common goals.
   c. Eccentricity is valued.
   d. Hackers engage in unauthorized and irreverent behavior.

(Answers to review questions are on page 718.)

PEOPLE AND THE WORLD AROUND US:
THE SOCIAL AND PHYSICAL ENVIRONMENT

My first image of Chicago was of the train station—enormous and cavernous, filled with rushing people. As I left the station, the sensation of anxiety that had been gnawing at me from the time I left my home in rural Kansas, for the first time really, grew into what could only be called fear. There were so many people—all striding purposefully toward some destination unknown to me. As I walked down Michigan Avenue, buffeted by a freezing wind, it seemed that people kept bumping into me, or I into them. The buildings looked so tall, the people so numerous; there just seemed to be no space at all. I was overcome by a feeling of suffocation, which only got worse when I boarded a crowded bus. I felt light-headed; I couldn't make sense of anything; and thoughts of returning home to Kansas—escaping—ran incessantly through my head. I yearned for the solitude of the country.

▲ ▲ ▲

Here I was at last—back in a city, after four years stuck in the farmland of Kansas. Although I had never been to Chicago before, having been raised in New York and then going to school in Kansas, I felt I was back where I belonged as soon as I stepped off the train onto a crowded station filled with rushing travelers. And then to experience the thrill of walking up bustling Michigan Avenue, where I pushed my way through crowds of people—I was so excited I felt like a little kid. What a wonderful feeling to see all those tall buildings, to be an anonymous individual among so many, to feel the hustle of big-city life. As I crowded onto the bus, shoving my way into the only empty seat, I felt exhilarated and more alive than I had in years. Clearly, I had missed the stimulation of life in the city, and I had no regrets about leaving the solitude of Kansas.

What would you feel upon arriving in a large city like Chicago? Would you, like the person from the country, feel overwhelmed by the stimuli of

A newcomer to Chicago, coming from a rural or suburban environment, will likely be overwhelmed by the bustle on the streets. On the other hand, a visitor raised in a big city might welcome the stimulation. (Roger A. Clarke, Jr./Photo Researchers.)

the city and yearn for the quiet of rural Kansas, or would your reaction be more like that of the second traveler, who is excited and stimulated by the crowds and is glad to have left the solitude of the country?

It is likely that your own response to encountering a city environment will depend on the psychological meaning you give to the various elements of urban life, which in turn is related to your past history and the kinds of experiences you have had. Nowhere is this better illustrated than by one of the primary features of life in cities: the experience of crowding.

BEING ONE OF MANY: The Social Environment and Crowding

Crowding is one of the major social issues of our time. Consider this fact: The population of the world increases by some 100 million people every year, and by a billion people every ten years. Add to this the fact that 50 percent of the United States population lives on just 1 percent of the land, and you can see why crowding has become a problem of increasing seriousness.

Defining the Issue: Crowding versus Density

Although most of us know all too well what it is like to feel crowded, environmental psychologists have had considerable difficulty in devising a precise scientific definition. One reason is that the experience of crowding is not just a function of figuring the number of people in a given area. For instance, even though we might not feel crowded at a party in a small living room or at a rock concert in which every seat is taken, we might report feeling crowded on a beach where there were only a few people—if we were used to swimming on a deserted beach.

To overcome this definitional difficulty, most environmental psychologists make a distinction between density and crowding (Fisher, Bell & Baum, 1984). **Density** refers to the purely physical and spatial characteristics of an environment: the number of people per unit of space. In contrast, **crowding** is an unpleasant psychological and subjective state relating to how a person *reacts* to the physical density of the environment.

High density alone, then, does not inevitably lead to the experience of crowding. Instead, other factors—including a person's prior experience, the nature of the situation (such as the degree of control that can be exercised), and social conditions (such as the kinds of relationships people have with those around them)—interact with density to determine whether crowding will be experienced.

What are the specific factors that cause a certain density to be considered crowding, and why is crowding such an unpleasant experience? A number of explanations have been suggested, all of which may contribute to our understanding of the phenomenon.

▶ The **stimulus-overload explanation**. Just as our Kansan was overwhelmed by the stimulation of the "big city," people may find that situations characterized by high density produce so much stimulation that they are unable to process the information effectively. This inability to sort out and consider competing stimuli leads to psychological stress. Until a person is able to

Density: Number of people per unit of space

Crowding: An unpleasant psychological and subjective state involving people's reaction to the density of their environment

Stimulus-overload explanation of crowding: An explanation based on the fact that stress can lead to withdrawal from the "crowded" situation cope, such stress may lead to physical withdrawal from the situation or to attempts to ignore the presence of others.

▶ The **loss-of-control explanation**. When there are many individuals in a small area, people may feel they have less control over the situation and that their behavioral freedom has been reduced. Loss-of-control models of crowding, then, suggest that the unpleasant experience of crowding is due to the feeling that one is unable to control and change one's environment (Burger, Oakman & Bullard, 1983).

▶ The **focus-of-attention explanation**. One thing that happens when we are with many people in a small area is that others may approach us closely, producing a sense of invasion. When this happens, a typical reaction is to become psychologically and physiologically aroused. According to the focus-of-attention model, people will then become motivated to determine why they are aroused. If they attribute their arousal to the presence of others—"That guy sure is standing close to me"—they will experience crowding. But if their attention is focused on some other aspect of the situation—"I drank a lot of wine," "I ate too much cake," "That ugly wallpaper is driving me crazy"—then crowding will not be experienced. Crowding is dependent, then, on where a person's attention is focused (Worchel & Brown, 1984; Webb et al., 1986).

▶ The **density-intensity explanation**. Consider the last good party you went to. Chances are the room was filled with people—and yet you still had a good time and probably never felt crowded during the course of the evening. It is even possible that the presence of many others added to your enjoyment.

According to the density-intensity explanation, high density does not automatically lead to unpleasant consequences; in fact, it is just as likely to result in positive effects. In essence, if something about the situation is unpleasant, high density increases the feelings of unpleasantness; if something about the situation is pleasant, high density magnifies the pleasantness (Freedman, 1979). If we like the people we are with, high density will increase our liking for them, but if we dislike them, high density will lead us to feel even more negative toward them.

The Consequences of Crowding

Crowding, by definition, results in an unpleasant state. But does it have consequences beyond just a negative emotional response?

In fact, crowding has wide-ranging effects upon our behavior in several

Although the physical density is so high in this Tokyo subway train that conductors are employed to shove people in, the experience of crowding may be low depending on the psychological reactions and expectations of the riders. Conversely, a farm family may feel crowded by the encroachment of a suburban mall or housing tract located miles from their home. (H. W. Silvester/Photo Researchers.)

Loss-of-control explanation of crowding: An explanation that suggests that the unpleasantness of crowding is due to the feeling that people cannot control their surroundings

Focus-of-attention explanation of crowding. An explanation based on the fact that an attempt to determine what aspect of a stimulating situation is causing one's arousal can lead to a feeling of being crowded or of being comfortable

Density-intensity explanation of crowding: An explanation based on the fact that "crowded" situations that seem negative become more negative, whereas those that seem positive become more positive

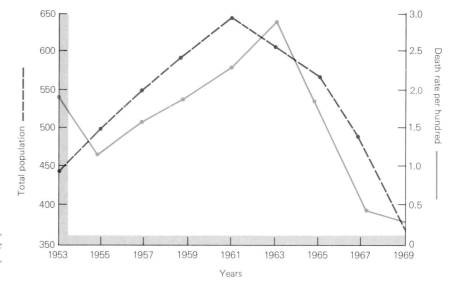

FIGURE 21-2

As the population of this prison increased, so did the death rate, indicating one of the more startling outcomes of crowding. (Cox, Paulus, & McCain, 1984.)

ways—some of which are surprisingly powerful. For example, higher rates of stress and illness are related to crowding in a variety of settings (Fleming, Baum & Weiss, 1987). One study showed that college students who live in dormitories of higher density pay more visits to the student health center than those living in low-density housing (Baron, Mandel, Adams & Griffen, 1976). Even more striking are findings showing that the death rates for inmates in a state psychiatric prison were related to the population density. As the prison population grew, so did the per-capita death rate; as it fell, the death rate followed suit, as shown in Figure 21-2 (Paulus & McCain, 1983; Paulus, McCain & Cox, 1978). Although these relationships are based on correlations and thus do not demonstrate cause-and-effect relationships (Ruback & Innes, 1988), the associations they report are provocative.

Crowding has a similar—although not as deadly—relationship with interpersonal attraction: People are less likely to like one another under conditions of high density than under lower-density conditions. For instance, college students housed in rooms built for two who were forced to cram in a third person liked their roommates less and viewed one another as less cooperative than those in less crowded conditions (Baron et al., 1976). Even when density is lower, people prefer double rooms over triple rooms; in triples, there is a tendency for two of the roommates to form a close relationship, isolating the third one and leaving all three less satisfied with the situation (Aiello, Baum & Gormley, 1980). (For more on dormitory living, see the Research Classics box.)

RESEARCH CLASSICS

Complaints about dormitory living are often a standard part of college life. However, a classic study on the effects of the configuration of dormitories shows that several things can be done to improve the quality of life of their occupants.

DESIGNING A DORMITORY

In a series of experiments, Andrew Baum and Stuart Valins (1977, 1979) investigated various dormitory

floor plans at the State University of New York at Stony Brook. The major comparison was between residents assigned to dormitories arranged in a typical pattern—a series of bedrooms located along a long corridor, with a central bathroom and shared lounge—and residents assigned to dormitories in which three to four bedrooms were arranged in a suite, with a bath and living room shared only by the occupants of the few bedrooms (see Figure 21-3).

Although the floor plans varied greatly, each resident had virtually identical square footage. But, as you might suspect, the effects on the occupants were dramatic. Residents of the corridor-style dormitory reported feeling significantly greater crowding, felt they had less privacy, and reported the desire to avoid others considerably more frequently than residents of the suite-style dormitories. In addition, although suite dwellers reported no differences in perceptions of crowding according to which room they had in the suite, there were strong differences in re-

ported crowding according to the location of corridor-style dorm dwellers. Students who lived near the bathroom or the lounge reported feeling considerably more crowded than those farther away from the two areas. Finally, corridor residents felt that they were forced into interactions with others much more frequently. They were less sure of what their neighbors thought about them, and they were less apt to perceive similarity in attitudes between themselves and their neighbors.

One of the most intriguing findings to emerge from the study was that the effect of the configuration of the living quarters lingered even after the residents left the setting (Baum & Gatchel, 1981). When students participated in a laboratory study outside the dorm, residents of

the corridor-style dormitory tended to sit farther away from a confederate and looked at the confederate less. They also performed worse than suite residents on a task that required cooperation, and better when the task required a lower level of interpersonal involvement.

Why should suite residents come out so far ahead of corridor residents? The major reason seems to be that corridor residents have far less control over their social interactions with others. In order to cope with the situation, corridor residents tend to withdraw from social interaction with their peers.

If you ever have your choice of dormitory rooms, you might consider these results. Clearly, where you live has an important effect on how you live.

FIGURE 21-3

Floor plans of traditional corridor-style and suite-style dormitories. Although similar in square footage, the configurations of the two floor plans had dramatic effects upon their occupants. (Baum & Valins, 1977.)

Finally, crowding leads to decreases in helping behavior, increases in aggression, and declines in the level of performance on various tasks (Holahan, 1982). Despite the seemingly unrelenting negative view of crowding, however, the picture is not universally gloomy. For instance, field studies of residential areas in which social density is extremely high—such as in Hong Kong, one of the most densely populated areas of the world—show little or no negative effects that can be attributed to housing density (Mitchell, 1982). It may be that people eventually adapt to crowded conditions, particularly when their neighbors are living under the same circumstances.

EARTH, WIND, AND FIRE: The Physical Environment

Tempers are not the only things that flare when the weather is hot; so does the incidence of aggressive crime. At least that is the conclusion of a comprehensive, two-year analysis of rapes and murders in the Houston, Texas, metropolitan area (Anderson & Anderson, 1984). As you can see in Figure 21-4, the mean number of murders and rapes tended to rise sharply as the temperature increased.

These findings are consistent with other research findings suggesting that air temperature is related to the incidence of riots—a common explanation for the large-scale urban rioting that occurred during the 1960s. Indeed, laboratory research supports the view that aggression is related to air temperature, although the relationship is complex (Baron & Ransberger, 1978). Specifically, aggression seems to rise as air temperature increases, but only up to a certain level. When it gets *too* hot, people may prefer flight over fight, simply leaving the situation (Anderson, 1989).

Air temperature is just one example of how physical factors of the environment are related to behavior; for example, the quality of air also affects our behavior in several ways. Consider the effects of high concentrations of carbon monoxide, which is emitted by automobiles. People exposed to large amounts of this invisible gas have problems with vision and hearing, may experience headaches and memory loss, and even—when the concentrations are sufficiently large—show symptoms of psychosis (Garland & Pearce, 1967).

FIGURE 21-4

By examining crime and weather records in Houston, Texas, researchers found that as temperatures rose, so did the level of aggressive crime. (Anderson & Anderson, 1984.)

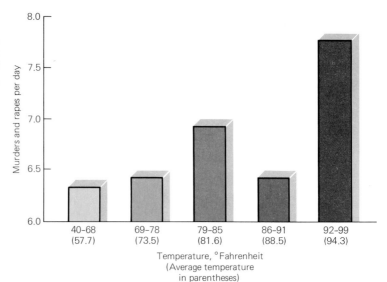

Even the electromagnetic charge of the air affects our behavior: The presence of a higher-than-average number of negatively charged ions in the air increases aggression. Moreover, the quality of the air has an impact on how much we are attracted to others and affects our performance in a variety of tasks (Baron, 1987; Baron, Russell & Arms, 1985; Rotton & Frey, 1985). For example, moderate levels of polluted, smelly air increase aggression—although at very high levels of pollution, aggression actually decreases as people become incapacitated (Rotton et al., 1977).

THE INFORMED CONSUMER OF PSYCHOLOGY:
Living Well with Your Environment

Is there anything you can do to make your own personal environment more livable?

In fact, there probably is. There are a number of ways in which the physical world might be made more livable and our interactions with others more positive. Several explicit suggestions can be made:

▶ Stake out your territory. Everyone needs places and spaces that he or she can call their own. Even if it is only a corner of a room or a desktop, it is important to have some area that is used by no one else but you.

▶ Personalize your environment. You will probably feel more comfortable and at home in spaces in which you have placed pictures, posters, and other objects that are yours and yours alone than in spaces where you cannot "personalize" the walls.

▶ Lower the density of high-density settings. Because, by and large, the effects of high density lead to the experience of crowding, and are thereby unpleasant, you might attempt to modify situations in which there is high density. While there are likely to be constraints involved—you can't just tell a roommate to find another place to live because you're trying to lower the density of your living quarters—you can make architectural and decorating changes that modify the perception of crowding.

For instance, you could keep the amount of furniture in a small room to a minimum, giving the feeling of less crowding. Moreover, it would be important to choose furniture that is movable, so that you can control and change its placement—leading to feelings of greater control over the situation. You might also decorate crowded areas with bright colors and pictures on the walls, focusing attention away from the crowded conditions and toward other features of the environment.

While none of these suggestions can guarantee that your environment will be perfect—because of architectural decisions made long ago, there are still many factors in most people's lives over which they have no control—the suggestions do give you some idea of how to approach the environment in which you live, and make it a more pleasant place.

Recap

◄ Density and crowding refer to two distinct concepts.

◄ The major explanation for the effects of crowding are based on stimulus-overload, loss-of-control, focus-of-attention, and density-intensity theories.

◄ Crowding can result in higher rates of illness and death, lower interpersonal attraction, decreases in helping, increases in aggression, and declines in performance levels—although crowding does not inevitably lead to negative consequences.

◄ Temperature, noise level, and quality of air all influence behavior.

Review

1. A situation of high density may cause a person to have difficulty sorting out and processing so much information, and to try to escape from the situation. This is the _____ explanation of crowding.

2. Bill and Sara, arriving at a party, find people standing elbow to elbow in a small room. Bill is pleasantly stimulated as he squeezes his way through the group, stopping to converse with several people. Sara, on the other hand, soon feels dizzy and nauseated and makes a beeline for the door. Sara, in comparison to Bill, could be said to be suffering from
   a. density-intensity.
   b. density.
   c. crowding.
   d. antisocial behavior.

3. After the party, Bill states happily that he met several good friends. Sara replies that she knew very few people at the party, and the few she did know she disliked. Which explanation best describes the discrepancy in Bill's and Sara's experience?
   a. Stimulus overload
   b. Loss of control
   c. Bill drank more liquor than Sara
   d. Density-intensity

4. Increases in heat or air pollution [increase/decrease] aggressive behavior. (circle one)

(Answers to review questions are on page 726.)

CATASTROPHES AND CRISES: DISASTERS, WAR, AND PEACE

The 1988 earthquake in Soviet Armenia brought devastation in psychological, as well as physical, terms. (Sygma.)

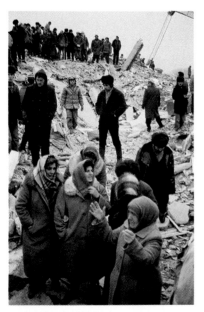

The first tremor shook at 11:41 A.M. on a December day in 1988. When the earth finally stopped shaking a few minutes later, the devastation was on a scale difficult to comprehend. With tens of thousands dead, survivors of the Armenian earthquake walked in a daze, crying out for lost loved ones and clawing through the ruins of what once were their homes. For those who were spared, their ordeal had only begun.

Disasters, such as the Armenian earthquake that killed nearly 100,000 people, are an unfortunate part of our daily existence. Furthermore, the looming threat of war or nuclear holocaust hangs like a dark cloud above the world, affecting the way we perceive one another and our futures. We consider now the ways in which people react to disaster and some of the ways psychological findings might help prevent them and promote a more peaceful existence.

DISASTER: Psychological Reactions and Outcomes

In the aftermath of a major disaster, victims' psychological worlds collapse in much the same way as their physical worlds did. The exact impact depends on the nature and magnitude of the disaster, as well as on the psychological characteristics of the victims.

The most critical result of disaster is a loss of one's sense of control. As we have discussed several times previously, a sense of control is an important component of psychological well-being, and finding oneself a victim of a major catastrophe threatens many of the things that organize one's life—home, family, neighborhood, friends. Moreover, some of our most basic assumptions about the world—that it is basically benevolent and that we are invulnerable to major disasters—are shattered by catastrophic events (Janoff-Bulman, 1988).

Some research suggests that reactions to disasters tend to follow a reasonably predictable course (see Figure 21-5), although individuals may follow somewhat different patterns (Horowitz, 1985). The first response is an outcry of fear, sadness, or rage, when victims rail against their fates. It is followed closely by a state of daze and shock. This is the beginning of the defense mechanism of denial, in which people block the facts and details

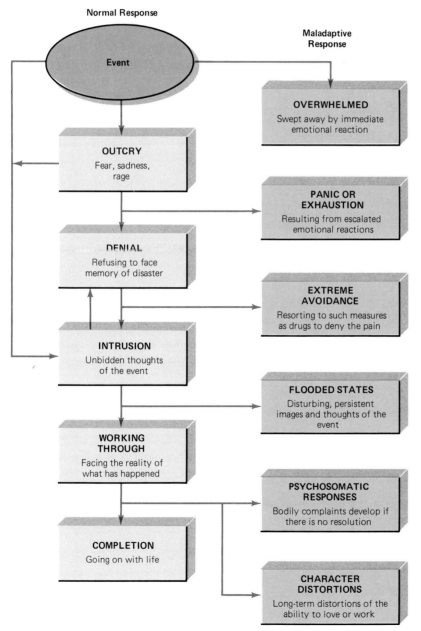

FIGURE 21-5

The normal response to disaster follows the course indicated in the first column. When the recovery is unsatisfactory, the maladaptive responses illustrated in the second column may occur. [Source: Horowitz, M. (1986). *Stress response syndrome*. 2nd ed. p. 41.]

about the catastrophe. Normally, reality begins to intrude, and people come face-to-face with the actual, unpleasant facts of the situation. In these cases, they are then able to work through the circumstances of the disaster and eventually get on with their lives.

In other cases, however, the process of dealing with the situation goes awry, and severe problems can occur. For instance, the event may be so overwhelming that people are unable to deal with it effectively. They may be overcome with emotions that lead them to exhaustion and inaction. Conversely, their denial may be so strong that they are unable to experience emotions at all. Eventually, if the psychological process of coming to grips with the disaster is never completed, the individual may experience reactions such as a deterioration of physical or mental health—as the accompanying Cutting Edge box explains.

Natural Disasters Versus Technological Disasters

If you had your choice of being the victim of a natural disaster, such as a flood, or a technological one, such as the failure of a nuclear power plant, which would you prefer? Though you might reasonably say you'd skip both, if you had to choose one, your preference should probably be the flood. There is increasing evidence that victims of natural disasters fare better physically and emotionally than victims of human-induced, technological disasters.

In one experiment, psychologist Andrew Baum and colleagues studied a group of people who were inadvertently exposed to chemicals leaking from a waste dump as a result of technological failure. This group was compared with one involved in a flood that caused widespread community damage and disruption (Baum, 1988). Close to a year later, the people living near the toxic waste dump expressed significantly greater distress and showed physiological reactions as well. In contrast, the flood victims reported relatively little continuing distress and showed only a few physiological changes related to stress.

Why should reactions to natural disasters be more fleeting? One reason is that technological accidents provide victims with someone to blame, opening up the possibility of continuing lawsuits that keep memories of the disasters fresh. Natural disasters, on the other hand, give people no one to blame (and no one, hence, to sue), permitting the recollections of the misfortune to fade.

Similarly, feelings of loss of control differ between natural and technological disasters. In a natural disaster, none of us has any control, so we have little sense of it to lose. In contrast, technological disasters produce a considerably stronger sense of a loss of control, since we tend to assume that technology is under human control, and not the other way around.

Finally, natural disasters usually have a clear beginning and a clear end. When a storm starts, it gradually intensifies, does its worst damage, and then subsides. A technological disaster, on the other hand, may have no clear starting date, and its effects may linger indefinitely. For example, people exposed to chemical wastes may wonder for the rest of their lives whether they were personally contaminated and whether any ill health or other symptoms they experience later are due to the exposure.

ANSWERS (REVIEW III)
1. Stimulus-overload **2.** c **3.** d **4.** Increase

LIVING WITH AN OUT-OF-ORDER NUCLEAR POWER PLANT

When the nuclear power plant at Three Mile Island in Pennsylvania malfunctioned in the late 1970s, it presented a unique set of circumstances to residents living nearby. The accident, which attracted worldwide attention, brought the plant to the brink of a dreaded meltdown in which huge quantities of nuclear material would have been released into the atmosphere. It also provoked a series of ongoing questions: Were the people nearby being exposed to constant radiation? Was it too late to do anything about the situation? Should residents move away from the area? Just *what* was happening at the plant, which was shut down immediately after the accident?

Clear answers to these and other questions were difficult, if not impossible, to obtain, and the plant remained a constant threat to nearby residents. The situation thus presented an opportunity to study the long-term effects of a technological accident. Researcher Andrew Baum and his colleagues embarked on an ongoing research program, studying the effects of stress that result from technological advances.

In one study, they assessed the emotional, behavioral, and physiological effects of long-term stress at Three Mile Island (Baum, Gatchel & Schaeffer, 1983). In the experiment, conducted about a year and a half after the accident, they compared residents living close to the damaged nuclear plant with a control group living close to an undamaged plant, a group living relatively far away from any plant, and a group living near a traditional coal-fired power plant.

The results showed a number of stress-related behaviors unique to the group living close to the Three Mile Island plant. Nearby residents reported suffering from a significantly greater number of symptoms of emotional distress, including a higher rate of anxiety. They also performed more poorly on a number of behavioral tasks devised by the experimenters, such as proofreading a sample passage. Finally, there were physiological differences as well. People living close to the plant showed higher levels of catecholamines, chemicals that are released as a result of stress, in their urine.

In sum, more than a year after the nuclear accident, residents living near the plant showed signs of ongoing stress related to the damaged reactor. Furthermore, although the absolute levels of stress were not exceedingly high, Baum and his colleagues argue that the stress continues to this day, and is unlikely to dissipate as long as the plant presents a threat. For instance, radioactive water remains in the reactor, and the core of the reactor has not been removed. There is also talk of reopening the plant.

Not everyone was equally affected by the reactor breakdown. Three main factors distinguished those who showed the most symptoms from those who showed the fewest: their coping style, the social support they received from others, and the degree of responsibility they assumed (Baum, 1988). Specifically, those who actively sought to control their negative emotions showed the fewest symptoms, whereas those who actively attempted to bring about changes in the situation—for example, by demonstrating against the reopening of the plant—showed significantly more symptoms. Also, the greater the social support in the form of friends and family, the lower the degree of reported symptoms. Finally, those people who accepted the greatest responsibility for what happened to them after the accident showed fewer symptoms than those who blamed outside factors.

Psychologists continue to monitor the symptoms displayed by the people living near the Three Mile Island plant. In doing so, they hope to better understand the pressures experienced by those of us who live under threats unique to our technological age. In addition, psychologists are developing treatments that may help alleviate the symptoms.

In sum, there are several reasons that technological accidents provoke stronger reactions than natural ones. Of course, the challenge for psychologists is to develop techniques for diminishing the harmful effects of both.

UNNATURAL DISASTERS: Terrorism and Hostages

One of the most morally difficult human-induced disasters is one with which governments and law enforcement agencies have become increasingly familiar during the last two decades: political terrorism and the taking of innocent hostages. Terrorists with political aims have found that taking hostages

How to deal with hostage-taking terrorists is a question upon which psychologists, as well as other experts, disagree. Pictured here are spokesmen for the hijackers of a TWA plane in 1985. (Vieljeux/Sygma.)

provides tremendous (free) publicity for whatever cause they represent, a sense of personal martyrdom and heroism for themselves, adulation from their followers, and a powerful negotiating chip.

Understanding how best to deal with hostage-taking terrorists has proved to be a difficult task that raises several important psychological—as well as moral—issues. Psychologists themselves are divided on the best course of action (Jenkins, 1983; Merari, 1985; Pruitt & Rubin, 1986; Baron & Byrne, 1988).

The most obvious and direct approach to a hostage taking is to use force to free those being held. The drawback, of course, is the danger to the lives of the hostages, either from the deliberate actions of their captors or from the unintended actions of their would-be rescuers. Although force has occasionally been used—as with the Israeli commando rescue of airplane passengers being held in Entebbe airport in Uganda in the 1970s—in most cases the hostages are so heavily guarded that the possibility of loss of life is unacceptably high.

A second approach is to assume that the hostages' lives must be saved at any cost. If this proposition is followed, the demands of the terrorists are met, within some limits, and they may be provided with publicity, freedom for jailed compatriots, money, or the opportunity to escape without punishment. Although this strategy often leads to the release of hostages, it has a major drawback: It provides a model to other would-be terrorists, illustrating the success of terrorism. As we know from Chapter 5, observers learn from the observation of rewarded models. Over the long-run, then, rewarding terrorists by meeting their demands leads to more terrorism by those and other terrorists.

A third approach is to refuse to deal with terrorists under any circumstances, no matter how many hostages have been taken—a stance adopted as official United States policy in the late 1980s (although not carried out all that effectively in practice). According to this strategy, terrorists who are ignored by government authorities present models who are not rewarded, thereby decreasing the probability of modeling effects and ultimately reducing terrorism over the long term. The disadvantage of such a policy, of course, is that it provides little in the way of hope or consolation for hostages and their families at the time of the crisis, and it may in fact increase the likelihood of injury or death at the hands of the terrorists.

There is, however, an intermediate approach in which negotiations between terrorists and authorities would occur under a total news blackout (Rubin & Friedland, 1986). Terrorists are thus denied the reinforcement of press coverage and are unable to act as models for others. Moreover, negotiatiors insist on the release of hostages, and terrorists are made responsible and are ultimately tried for any criminal acts such as murder and kidnapping. Authorities must then follow through by pursuing terrorists, trying them in court, and sending them to prison.

The difficulty with such an approach is that it ignores many of the political realities of terrorism. For example, political leaders may face almost irresistable pressures to do everything in their power to release hostages, especially when hostages make well-publicized, pitiful pleas to be saved. Furthermore, what is best in the long run may not be optimal in the short term. Clearly, dealing with terrorists is a difficult exercise for negotiators—not to mention the torturous ordeal faced by the hostages themselves.

WAR AND PEACE

Although no looming disaster is more dangerous to the human race than nuclear war, it is only recently that psychologists have begun to consider the ways in which their field can have an impact on this issue. Important psychological issues underlying the nuclear arms race include the way we perceive our enemies, reactions to the possibility of nuclear war, and psychological approaches to promoting peace and preventing war.

Misperceiving the Enemy

In the next minute, the world will spend around one million dollars arming itself. In a year it will spend more than half its population, combined, will earn. The purpose, we are told, is to protect us from our enemies.

Yet our views of who our enemies are, what they are like, and the reasons behind their behavior are often ill formed. Psychologist Ralph White has argued that in many situations our understanding of our enemies is so distorted that it causes serious strategic miscalculation. As a specific case, White cites the following distortions that affected the United States' decision to enter the war in Vietnam:

▶ *An image of the enemy as diabolical.* Americans viewed the communist Vietnamese as inscrutable and deceptive, people who were capable of horrible atrocities and fiendish aggression.

▶ *A virile self-image.* Americans saw themselves and their military policy as determined, correct, and strong.

▶ *An overconfident military.* Having never "lost" a war, Americans believed they could win any confrontation in which they participated. It always seemed that just one more battle would bring a final victory.

▶ *Lack of empathy for the enemy.* There was no clear understanding of what the enemy felt, how it perceived the situation, or even why it was fighting.

▶ *Selective inattention.* The United States consistently ignored facts and events that might have changed its position on or understanding of the war. For example, widespread corruption in the South Vietnamese army, the

United States' ally, was ignored, as were South Vietnam's undemocratic policies.

▶ *A moral self-image.* The United States viewed itself not only as militarily superior but as morally superior as well.

Such misperceptions of our enemies are not restricted to the war in Vietnam; citizens and leaders of the world powers still tend to mischaracterize one another's pronouncements, and deciphering the meaning of another's words is a formidable task (Tetlock, 1988; White, 1984).

Reactions to Nuclear War

My friend has cancer. She has reason to believe that she has a 1-in-3 chance of dying from it. Although she understands this diagnosis, her possible death remains somewhat hypothetical to her. She imagines her death mostly in the abstract, and she talks about missing the city and her occasional trips into the country. Strangely, she does not talk so much about missing the people in her life. She also believes she cannot do anything to change her odds. She does not worry about the cancer very often.... She goes on about her normal life. Some people say she is marvelous, remarkable, life-affirming, brave, and adaptable. Other people say she is suppressing her fear, denying reality, and becoming desensitized to her own death (Fiske, 1987, p. 207).

The "friend" discussed above is the average American citizen; her "cancer" is the possibility of a nuclear war.

When psychologist Susan Fiske drew the analogy presented above, she sought to dramatize the way most American citizens react to the threat of nuclear war. Drawing on a composite of some fifty surveys, she found that beliefs about nuclear war have remained remarkably stable over the past four decades, since the bombing of Hiroshima and Nagasaki in 1945. Most people view the chances of nuclear war within the next ten years as not unlikely, with estimates ranging from one chance in three to one chance in two (Fiske, Pratto & Pavelchak, 1983; Tyler & McGraw, 1983). When asked to assume that a war will occur, people's perceptions are bleak: They expect the world's population to be wiped out, although they tend to focus more on physical damage to buildings than on the death of specific individuals. Most people do not expect to survive.

People do not think about nuclear war very often. This fact seems surprising: If you thought you had a 1-in-3 chance of contracting and dying of cancer in the next ten years, you might be expected to think about it often and to take preventive measures. Yet this does not occur with the possibility of a nuclear holocaust; most people take no concrete steps to stop the threat.

Several possibilities explain the discrepancy between people's beliefs and negative emotional responses to nuclear war, and their lack of action to stop it. One is that the threat of a nuclear holocaust is so devastating that people are psychologically unable to deal with it, repressing their fears out of their conscious awareness. Another explanation is, as research has indicated, that a single citizen, acting alone, rarely makes a difference in government policy; even large numbers of citizens working collectively have only a minor influence on the decisions made by government leaders (Rosenau, 1967).

Finally, there is the question of what strategy is best for reducing the threat of a nuclear war. Several differing (and contradictory) strategies have been proposed—ranging from a ban on all nuclear weapons to an increase in their numbers so large that their use would ensure total destruction, thereby theoretically (and paradoxically) reducing their chances of being used. Thus it is not surprising that people find it difficult to identify the most appropriate course of action—a problem which psychologists have recently begun to address.

Psychological Approaches to Reducing
The Threat of Nuclear War

One of the major political issues of the 1980s was nuclear arms control. Many people suggested the implementation of a nuclear arms "freeze," in which the world's political superpowers would pledge to build no new nuclear weapons—which already existed in sufficient quantities to destroy the world many times over. After the freeze took hold, advocates reasoned, the superpowers would be able to hold arms reduction talks to decrease the size of their nuclear arsenals (Plous, 1988).

The notion of a weapons freeze runs counter to the strategy of deterrence that the superpowers have traditionally employed. **Deterrence** is the notion that threats of large-scale retaliation against an enemy attack are the most effective means of preventing the attack in the first place. According to this view, the most suitable means of defense is an arms buildup. This ensures that retaliation would completely wipe out the attacking country—a concept known as MAD: mutually assured destruction (Morgan, 1977; Jervis, Lebow & Stein, 1985).

Deterrence: The notion that threats of large-scale retaliation against an enemy attack are the most effective means of preventing the attack in the first place

Does deterrence work? The question is difficult to answer, given the impossibility of doing controlled, experimental research in a highly complex world. Furthermore, the focus of such research is the behavior of abstract entities—countries—which are, in reality, made up of the behaviors of many individuals. Finally, it is often impossible to know, after the fact, the information that leaders had available to them when decisions were made about issues of war and peace.

Despite these difficulties, careful analyses of historical instances of deterrence suggest that it has not been terribly effective in preventing military conflict (Lebow & Stein, 1987). For example, an analysis of military policies over 2000 years of history found that countries that used a military buildup as a means of preventing war were subsequently more likely to become involved in wars than countries that had not armed themselves (Naroll, Bullough & Naroll, 1974). Furthermore, it seems that the ready availability of weapons brought about by an arms race can lead policymakers to include military action among their options much more readily than if so many arms were not accessible.

In sum, an arms buildup can act as a self-fulfilling prophecy: A country may expect to need arms to defend itself and, to meet this expected need, may produce and stockpile huge quantities of arms. Later the presence of the arms results in the perception that the use of weapons is an appropriate option to resolve crises and foreign policy disputes. Ultimately, this perception increases the probability that the arms will be used, until at some point they are. The initial expectation that arms may be necessary, then, results in their being used—which is just the opposite of the intended outcome.

Psychology and The Promotion of Peace

> ... Since wars begin in the minds of men, it is in the minds of men that the defenses of peace must be constructed.

In spite of such a statement (adopted by UNESCO just after World War II), the study of peace has remained largely outside the realm of psychology, being left primarily to political scientists and historians (Blight, 1987). Yet there are several areas in which a growing number of psychologists are making contributions to the prevention of war and the promotion of peace. The most important areas of research include (Intriligator & Brito, 1988):

▶ *Attitudes toward other nations.* Social psychologists have studied how our attitudes toward other nations arise and affect how we perceive them. For example, why have Americans' attitudes toward the Soviet Union, which just a few years ago were quite negative, become considerably more positive?

▶ *Defense-related decisions.* Cognitive psychologists have examined the ways in which decisions are made. As we discussed in Chapter 7, biases in cognitive processes may lead to miscalculation and inappropriate decisions, such as the invasion of the Bay of Pigs in Cuba in the 1960s.

▶ *Behavior in times of crisis.* The way national leaders behave during crises has been the focus of many studies. By better understanding leaders' reactions to unusual events, psychologists potentially can provide guidance for future crises.

▶ *Accidental war.* Psychologists in the military have devised the Personnel Reliability Program to ensure that people working with nuclear weapons are appropriately trained and will not be inclined to use such weapons without authorization (Maszak, 1988). Furthermore, they have studied such issues as the likelihood that a given set of circumstances may bring about accidents in weapons systems.

▶ *Negotiation and prevention.* There has been a focus on negotiation skills and, in some ways even more important, on the prevention of international incidents. For instance, psychologists have developed simulations in which participants play the roles of national leaders facing a crisis in order to identify workable strategies that might be employed to end actual conflicts.

Although psychological approaches to avoiding war and promoting peace are being developed, few have been implemented (Blight, 1988). But the promise is there, and many psychologists are continuing their quest to devise alternatives to traditional approaches to war and peace.

RECAP AND REVIEW III

Recap

◀ One of the most critical results of a disaster is the loss of a sense of control. In addition, victims of a disaster have reactions that move through a predictable course. However, the nature of their reactions varies according to whether the disaster is natural or caused by the failure of human technology.

◀ Dealing with hostage-taking terrorists may involve using force, negotiating to save the hostages' lives at any cost, refusing to deal with the hostages, or adopting an intermediate approach.

◀ Although people believe that a nuclear war is not unlikely, they rarely take any concrete actions to prevent one.

Review

1. Rage, shock, and blocking facts and details in the wake of a catastrophe are signs of a defense mechanism called _____ .

2. Which of the following has *not* been shown to reduce distress after a catastrophe?
   a. Seeking to control negative emotions
   b. Accepting responsibility for one's situation after the event
   c. Taking out lawsuits against those responsible for the catastrophe
   d. Having strong ties to friends and family

3. One of the most important considerations for terrorists is
   a. receiving money in return for releasing hostages.
   b. free plane trips.
   c. convincing more people to join the terrorist group.
   d. media attention.

4. Ralph White has argued that misperceptions of the enemy may affect decisions made in times of conflict. Name three possible misperceptions.

5. The notion that an enemy attack can be prevented by threats of retaliation is called _____ .

(Answers to review questions are on page 734.)

◀ LOOKING BACK

1. In this chapter, we considered the psychological consequences of the technological growth of our world. We began by examining the interaction of people and machines. Ergonomics is the study of how people's behavior and abilities affect the design of tools, machines, and environments for effective use.

2. Well-designed objects possess visibility—visual cues to their operation that are inherent in their design. One of the central features of visibility is natural mapping—a design that relies on an analogy between the physical appearance of a device and the physical actions that are required to operate it.

3. Computers, a rapidly growing feature of modern society, have brought about many changes in the workplace. For example, workers may perceive that their skills are unnecessary or not valued, leading to declines in morale. Furthermore, workers may experience a lack of control over their environment. Some workers, in fact, have an overriding fear of computers (cyberphobia). On the other hand, computers may permit an upgrading of jobs and an increase in job quality, but it is still too early to gauge the full psychological impact of computerization in the workplace.

4. Computer cultures have arisen on many college campuses. These cultures have specific characteristics, including a set of norms regarding what is appropriate behavior. Computer cultures arise, in part, because of the differences between computer courses and more traditional academic courses.

5. With the growing magnitude and scope of computer records, privacy has become an important issue. Once information about an individual is placed in a data bank, it may be permanently stored and shared with outsiders. People and organizations with access to others' computerized records can trace a person's whereabouts and certain aspects of his or her behavior.

6. Most environmental psychologists distinguish between density and crowding. Density refers to the purely physical and spatial characteristics of an environment: the number of people per unit of space. Crowding is an unpleasant psychological and subjective state relating to how a person reacts to the physical density of an environment.

7. High density alone does not always lead to the experience of crowding. When crowding is experienced, it may be explained by one of a number of theories: stimulus overload (the inability to sort out the many stimuli present in a setting); loss of control (difficulties due to the inability to control the environment); focus of attention (psychological and physiological arousal due to the presence of others); and density-intensity (situations that seem negative become more negative and those that seem positive become more positive, owing to the presence of others). Whatever the specific causes of crowding, among its outcomes are higher rates of illness and death, declines in liking others, and decreases in helping behavior.

8. The physical environment plays an important role in influencing behavior. For instance, air temperature, noise, and air quality are related to aggression and other indicators of the quality of life.

9. There are a number of things people can do to improve their environments and interactions. Among them are staking out their territory, personalizing their environment, and lowering the density of high-density settings.

10. Disasters, both technological and natural, produce a loss of a sense of control. Other reactions follow a predictable course. Initially there is fear, sadness, or rage, followed by denial. The reality of the occurrence later intrudes, and people ultimately face the reality of what has happened. In normal cases, people then go on with their lives, but in extreme cases the disaster continues to affect its victims. Furthermore, victims of technological disasters tend to show more severe reactions than do survivors of natural disasters.

11. Psychologists have suggested several approaches to

dealing with the taking of hostages. Among them are employing force to free hostages, attempting to save the hostages' lives at any cost (which includes meeting the demands of terrorists), refusing to deal with terrorists under any circumstances, and choosing a middle ground in which negotiations occur in the context of a total news blackout.

12. One theory holds that people's misperceptions about their enemies act as hindrances to peace. Possible distortions include an image of the enemy as diabolical, a virile self-image, an overconfident military, lack of empathy for the enemy, selective inattention to facts, and a moral self-image.

13. Beliefs about nuclear war have remained stable over the past forty years. Most people feel that the likelihood of nuclear war ranges from one chance in three to one chance in two. Although they do not expect to survive a nuclear war, most people take no steps to stop the threat.

14. Several psychological issues relate to reducing the threat of nuclear war. The notion of a nuclear freeze, in which countries build no new nuclear weapons, runs counter to the notion of deterrence, which suggests that threats of retaliation against an enemy are the most effective means of preventing an attack in the first place. Research suggests, however, that deterrence has been relatively ineffective.

15. Psychologists have made contributions to the prevention of war and the promotion of peace by studying such topics as attitudes toward other nations, defense-related decisions, behavior in times of crisis, avoidance of accidental war, and negotiation skills.

KEY TERMS AND CONCEPTS ▶

environmental psychology (p. 711)
ergonomics (712)
visibility (712)
natural mapping (712)
cyberphobia (713)
density (718)

crowding (718)
stimulus-overload explanation of crowding (718)
loss-of-control explanation of crowding (719)

focus-of-attention explanation of crowding (719)
density-intensity explanation of crowding (719)
deterrence (731)

FOR FURTHER RESEARCH AND STUDY ▶

Norman, D. A. (1988). *The psychology of everyday things.* New York: Basic Books.

A psychologist looks at the way in which the design of common objects, ranging from hot water faucets to radios, affects the way in which we use them.

Fisher, J. D., Bell, P. A., & Baum, A. S. (1984). *Environmental psychology* (2nd ed.). New York: Holt, Rinehart and Winston.

This clear, easy-to-understand introduction to the field of environmental psychology was written by some of the best-known researchers in the field.

Altman, I., & Werner, C. J. (Eds.) (1985). *Home environments.* New York: Plenum.

This book illustrates how research and theory drawn from environmental psychology can be used to provide recommendations to architects and designers.

Stokols, D., & Altman, I. (Eds.) (1986). *Handbook of environmental psychology.* New York: Wiley.

This volume presents a series of chapters, written by experts, on an array of topics central to the field of environmental psychology.

White, R. K. (Ed.). (1986). *Psychology and the prevention of nuclear war.* New York: New York University Press.

This guidebook presents a series of chapters on the ways in which psychology can advance the search for peace and prevent nuclear war.

ANSWERS (REVIEW III):
1. Denial **2.** c **3.** d **4.** The misperceptions referred to in the text are image of the enemy as diabolical; virile self-image; overconfident military; lack of empathy for the enemy; selective inattention; moral self-image **5.** Deterrence

APPENDIX

GOING BY THE NUMBERS: STATISTICS IN PSYCHOLOGY

Selma Vorwerk, shortly after her immigration to the United States. (Photo courtesy of K. E. Vorwerk.)

Statistics: The branch of mathematics concerned with collecting, organizing, analyzing, and drawing conclusions from numerical data

PROLOGUE: SELMA VORWERK

As the boat moved closer to shore, the outline of the Statue of Liberty was plainly visible in the distance. Closer and closer it came, sending a chill down the spine of Selma Vorwerk. A symbol of America, the statue represented the hopes she carried from her native Europe in the early 1900s—hopes of liberty, of success, of a life free of economic and social strain.

Yet as the boat moved closer to Ellis Island, the first point of arrival in the United States, Vorwerk did not realize that her very presence—and that of the other thousands of immigrants seeking their fortune in a land of opportunity—was threatened. A strong political movement was growing in the country on which she was pinning her hopes. This movement sought, by using information collected by psychologists, to stem the flow of immigrants through "scientific" analysis of data.

The major assertion of this group was that a flood of mentally deficient immigrants was poisoning the intellectual capacity of the United States. To proponents of this view, unless drastic measures were taken, it would not be too many years before western civilization collapsed from a lack of collective intelligence.

To support this assertion, Lathrop Stoddard, a member of the anti-immigration movement, reported the results of a study of intelligence in which tests were administered to a group of 82 children and 400 adults. On the basis of these test results, he concluded that the average mental age of Americans was only 14 years—proof to him that unlimited immigration had already seriously eroded American mental capacity.

LOOKING AHEAD ▶

Fortunately for immigrants such as Selma Vorwerk, observers in favor of immigration pointed out the fallacy of using data from a relatively small sample—when a considerably larger set of intelligence test data was available. Specifically, the Army had been collecting intelligence data for years and had the test scores of 1.7 million men available. When these scores were analyzed, it was immediately apparent that the claim that the average mental age of American adults was 14 years was completely without merit.

A debate reminiscent of this earlier one rages today, as some observers suggest that an unrestrained flow of immigrants—this time from Latin America and Asia—would seriously damage the United States. This time, though, the debate is based more on analyses of social and economic statistics, with opponents of immigration suggesting that the social fabric of the country will be changed and that jobs are being taken away from longer-term residents because of the influx of immigrants. Equally vehement proponents of immigration suggest that the relevant statistics are being misinterpreted, and that *their* analyses of the situation result in a quite different conclusion.

Statistics, the branch of mathematics concerned with collecting, organizing, analyzing, and drawing conclusions from numerical data, is a part of all our lives. For instance, all of us are familiar with the claims and counterclaims regarding the effects of smoking. The U.S. government requires that cigarette manufacturers include a warning that smoking is dangerous to people's health on every package of cigarettes and in their advertisements; the government's data show clear statistical links between smoking and disease.

At the same time, the American Tobacco Institute questions in its advertisements that there is any scientific validity to the claim that smoking is dangerous, for, according to its statistics, the data are inconclusive.

Statistics also lie at the heart of a considerable number of debates within the field of psychology. How do we determine the nature and strength of the effects of heredity on behavior? What is the relationship between learning and schedules of reinforcement? How do we know if the "double standard" of male and female sexual practices has shifted over time? These questions, and most others of interest to psychologists, cannot be answered without a reliance on statistics.

In this appendix, we consider the basic approaches to statistical measurement. We first discuss approaches to summarizing data that allow us to describe sets of observations. Next, we consider techniques for deciding how different one set of scores is from another. Finally, we examine approaches to measuring the relationship between two sets of scores.

After reading this material, then, you will be able to answer these questions:

▶ What measures can we use to summarize sets of data?

▶ What are the strengths and weaknesses of basic statistical procedures?

▶ How can we determine the nature of a relationship and the significance of differences between two sets of scores?

DESCRIPTIVE STATISTICS

Suppose, as a teacher of college psychology, you wanted to evaluate your class's performance on its initial exam. Where might you begin?

You would probably start by using **descriptive statistics**, the branch of statistics that provides a means of summarizing data. For instance, you might first simply list the scores the pupils had received on the test:

72 78 78 92 69 73

85 49 86 86 72 59

58 85 89 80 83 69

78 90 90 96 83

Descriptive statistics: The branch of statistics that provides a means of summarizing data

Viewed in this way, the scores are a jumble of numbers that are difficult to make any sense of. However, there are several methods by which you could begin to organize the scores in a more meaningful way. For example, you might sort them in order of highest to lowest score, as is done in Table A-1. By indicating the number of people who obtained each score, you would have produced what is called a **frequency distribution**, an arrangement of scores from a sample that indicates how often a particular score is present.

Another way of summarizing the scores is to consider them visually. For example, you could construct a **histogram** or bar graph, shown in Figure A-1. In the histogram, the number of people obtaining a given score is represented pictorially. The scores are ordered along one dimension of the graph, and the number of people obtaining each score along the other dimension.

Frequency distribution: An arrangement of scores from a sample that indicates how often a particular score is present

Histogram: A bar graph used to represent data graphically

TABLE A-1

A Sample Frequency Distribution

Score	Number of People Attaining that Score
96	1
92	1
90	2
89	1
86	2
85	2
83	2
80	1
78	3
73	1
72	2
69	2
59	1
58	1
49	1

FIGURE A-1

In this histogram, the number of people obtaining each score is represented by a bar.

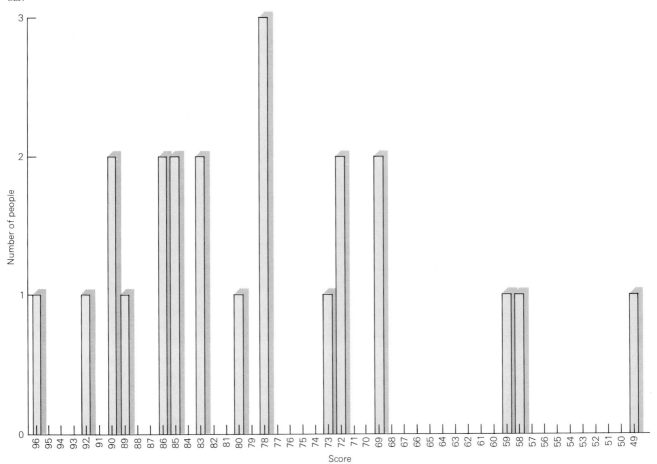

Arranging the scores from the highest to lowest allows us to visually interpret the data. Most often, however, visual inspection is insufficient. For one thing, there may be so many scores in a sample that it is impossible to construct a meaningful visual representation. For another, as the research that we discussed in Chapter 4 suggests, our perceptions of the meaning of stimuli are often biased and inaccurate; more precise, mathematically based measures would seem to be preferable. In cases in which a precise means of summarizing the data is desirable, then, psychologists turn to measures of **central tendency**, the most representative score in a distribution of scores. There are three major measures of central tendency: the mean, the median, and the mode.

Central tendency: The most representative score in a distribution of scores (the mean, median, and mode are measures of central tendency)

FINDING THE AVERAGE: The Mean

The most familiar measure of central tendency is the mean. A **mean** is the technical term for an average, which is simply the sum of all the scores in a set, divided by the number of scores making up the set. For example, to calculate the mean of the sample we have been using, begin by adding each of the numbers (96 + 92 + 90 + 90 + 89 + · · · and so forth). When you have the total, divide this sum by the number of cases, which is 23. This calculation, 1800 ÷ 23 = 78.26, produces a mean score, or average, for our sample, then, of 78.26.

Mean: The average of all scores, arrived at by adding scores together and dividing by the number of scores

In general, the mean is an accurate reflection of the central score in a set of scores; as you can see from the histogram in Figure A-1, our mean of 78.26 falls roughly in the center of the distribution of scores. Yet the mean does not always provide the best measure of central tendency. For one thing, the mean is very sensitive to extreme scores. As an example, imagine that we added two additional scores of 20 and 22 to our sample scores. The mean would now become 1842 ÷ 25, or 73.68, a drop of almost 5 points. Because of its sensitivity to extreme scores, then, the mean can sometimes present a deceptive picture of a set of scores, especially where the mean is based on a relatively small number of scores.

FINDING THE MIDDLE: The Median

A measure of central tendency that is less sensitive to extreme scores than the mean is the median. The **median** is the point in a distribution of scores that divides the distribution exactly in half. For example, consider a distribution of five scores 10, 8, 7, 4, and 3. The point that divides the distribution exactly in half is the score 7: Two scores in the distribution lie above the 7 score, while two scores lie below it. If there are an even number of scores in a distribution—in which case there would be no score lying in the middle—the two middle scores would be averaged. If our distribution consisted of scores of 10, 8, 7, 6, 4, and 3, then, we would average the two middle scores of 7 and 6 to form a median of 7 + 6 divided by 2, or 13 ÷ 2 = 6.5.

Median: The point in a distribution of scores that divides the distribution exactly in half when the scores are listed in numerical order

In our original sample test scores, there are twenty-three scores. The score that divides the distribution exactly in half will be the twelfth score in the frequency distribution of scores, since the twelfth score has eleven scores above it and eleven below it. If you count down to the twelfth score in the distribution depicted in Table A-1 you will see the score is 80. Therefore, the median of the distribution is 80.

One advantage of the median as a measure of central tendency is that it is insensitive to extreme scores. For example, adding the scores of 20 and

22 to our distribution would change the median no more than adding scores of 48 and 47 to the distribution. The reason is clear: The median divides a set of scores in half, and the magnitude of the scores is of no consequence in this process.

The median is often used instead of the mean when extreme scores might be misleading. For example, government statistics on income are typically presented using the median as the measure of central tendency, since the median corrects for the small number of extreme cases of very wealthy individuals, whose high incomes might otherwise inflate the mean income.

FINDING WHAT IS MOST FREQUENT: The Mode

Mode: The most frequently occurring score in a set of scores

The final measure of central tendency is the mode. The **mode** is the most frequently occurring score in a set of scores. If you return to the distribution in Table A-1, you can see that three people scored 78, and the frequency of all of the other scores is either 2 or 1. The mode for the distribution, then, is 78.

Some distributions, of course, might have more than one score occurring most frequently. For instance, we could imagine that if the distribution had an additional score of 86 added to the two that are already there, there would be two most frequently occurring categories: 78 and now 86. In this instance, we would say there are two modes—a case known as a **bimodal distribution**.

Bimodal distribution: Cases in which a frequency distribution includes two modes

The mode is often used as a measure of preference or popularity. For instance, if teachers wanted to know who was the most popular child in their elementary school classrooms, they might develop a questionnaire which asked the students to choose someone with whom they would like to participate in some activity. After the choices were tallied, the mode would probably provide the best indication of which child was most popular.

COMPARING THE THREE M's: Mean versus Median versus Mode

Normal distribution: A distribution of scores that produces a bell-shaped, symmetrical curve

If a sample is sufficiently large, there is generally little difference between the mean, median, and mode. The reason is that with large samples, scores typically form what is called a normal distribution. A **normal distribution** is a distribution of scores that produces the bell-shaped curve displayed in Figure A-2, in which the right half mirrors the left half.

Most large distributions, those containing many scores, produce a normal curve. For instance, if you asked a large number of students how many hours a week they studied, you might expect to find that most studied within a similar range of hours, while there would be a few who studied many, many hours, and some very few who studied not at all. There would be many

FIGURE A-2

In a normal distribution, the mean, median, and mode are identical, falling at the center of the distribution.

Mean
Median
Mode

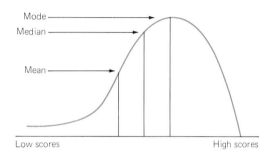

FIGURE A-3

In this skewed distribution, most scores are low.

FIGURE A-4

In this example of a skewed distribution, there tend to be more high scores than low ones.

scores in the center of the distribution of scores, then, and only a few at the extremes—producing a normal distribution. Many phenomena of interest to psychologists produce a normal curve when graphed. For example, if you turn to Figure 8-1 in Chapter 8, where the distribution of intelligence scores is given, you can see the pattern of scores falls into a normal distribution.

The mean, median, and the mode fall at exactly the same point in a normal distribution. This means that in a normal distribution of scores, the mean score will divide the distribution exactly in half (the median), and it will be the most frequently occurring score in the distribution (the mode).

The mean, median, and mode differ, however, when distributions are not normal. In cases in which the distributions are **skewed**, or not symmetrical, there is a "hump" at one end or the other (see Figures A-3 and A-4). For instance, if we gave a calculus exam to a group of students enrolled in an elementary algebra class, we would expect that most students would fail the test, leading to low scores being overrepresented in the distribution, as in Figure A-3. On the other hand, if we gave the same students a test of elementary addition problems, the scores would probably form a distribution in which high scores predominated, such as in Figure A-4. Both distributions are skewed, although in opposite directions, and the mean, median, and mode are different from one another.

Skewed distribution: A distribution that is not normal and therefore creates a curve that is not symmetrical

RECAP AND REVIEW I

Recap

◀ Statistics is the branch of mathematics concerned with collecting, organizing, analyzing, and drawing conclusions from numerical data.

◀ Descriptive statistics is the branch of statistics that provides a means of summarizing data.

◀ Measures of central tendency provide an index of where the centermost point in a distribution of scores lies. The most common measures of central tendency are the mean, median, and mode.

Review

1. A frequency distribution of numbers could be displayed pictorially by constructing a bar graph, or _____ .

2. Match each item in the left-hand column with the corresponding item in the right-hand column.

a. ____ Mean = 10.0   1. 2, 8, 10, 12, 13, 18
b. ____ Median = 11   2. 4, 5, 10, 10, 15, 16
c. ____ Mode = 12   3. 4, 5, 12, 12, 12, 16

3. The mean, median, and mode are measures of _____
    _____ .

4. Professor Peters explains to the class that most of the forty

exam scores fell within a B range, but there were two
extremely high scores. Should she report the median or
the mean as a measure of central tendency?

5. The mean, median, and mode will differ in a normal
    distribution. True or false? _____

(Answers to review questions are at the bottom of page 744.)

MEASURES OF VARIABILITY

Although measures of central tendency provide us with information about
where the center of a distribution lies, often this information is insufficient.
For example, suppose a psychologist was interested in determining the nature of people's eye movements while they were reading in order to perfect
a new method of teaching reading. It would not be enough to know how
most people moved their eyes (information that a measure of central
tendency would provide); it would also be important to know how much
individual people's eye movements differed or varied from one another.

Variability: The spread, or dispersion, of scores in a distribution

A second important characteristic of a set of scores provides this information: variability. **Variability** is a term that refers to the spread of scores in
a distribution. Figure A-5 contains two distributions of scores that have identical means, but which differ in variability. Measures of variability provide a
means of describing the spread of scores in a distribution.

HIGHEST TO LOWEST: The Range

Range: The highest score in a distribution minus the lowest score

The simplest measure of variability is the range. A **range** is the highest score
in a distribution minus the lowest score. In the set of scores presented in
Table A-1 the distribution has a range of 47 ($96 - 49 = 47$).

The fact that a range is simple to calculate is about the only virtue it has.
The problem with this particular measure of variability is that it is based
entirely on extreme scores, and a single score that is very different from the
others in a distribution can distort the picture of the distribution as a whole.
For example, the addition of a score of 20 to the test score distribution in
Table A-1 would almost double the range measure, even though the variability of the remaining scores in the distribution has not changed at all.

DIFFERENCES FROM THE MEAN: The Standard Deviation

Standard deviation: An index of how far
an average score in a distribution of
scores deviates from the distribution's
center

The most frequently used method of characterizing the variability of a distribution of scores is the **standard deviation**. The standard deviation bears a

FIGURE A-5

Although the mean is identical in these two
distributions, the variability, or spread of
scores, is very different.

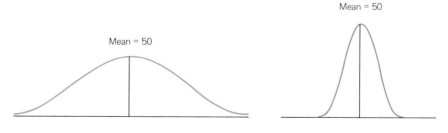

conceptual relationship to a mean. You will recall that the mean is the average score in a distribution of scores. A standard deviation is related to the mean in that it provides an index of how far an average score in a distribution of scores deviates from the center of the distribution.

Consider, for instance, the distributions in Figure A-5. The distribution on the left is widely dispersed and on the average an individual score in the distribution can be thought of as deviating quite a bit from the center of the distribution. Certainly the scores in the distribution on the left are going to deviate more from the center of the distribution than those in the distribution on the right.

On the other hand, in the distribution on the right, the scores are closely packed together and there is little deviation of a typical score from the center of the distribution. Based on this analysis, then, it would be expected that a good measure of variability would yield a larger value for the distribution on the left than it would for the one on the right—and, in fact, a standard deviation would do exactly this by indicating how far away a typical score lies from the center of the distribution.

The calculation of the standard deviation follows the logic of calculating the difference of individual scores from the mean of the distribution, and the exact technique is presented in Table A-2. It provides an excellent indicator of the variability of a set of scores because it is based on all of the

TABLE A-2

Calculating a Standard Deviation

1. The calculation of a standard deviation begins with the calculation of the mean of distribution. In the following distribution of scores on a psychology student's weekly quizzes, the mean is 84.5: 82, 88, 71, 86, 96, 84. (As you recall, the mean is the sum of the scores divided by the number of scores in the distribution, or 507 ÷ 6 = 84.5.)
2. The next step is to produce a deviation score for each score in the distribution. A deviation score is simply an original score minus the mean of all the scores in a distribution. This has been done in the second column below:

Original Score	Deviation Score*	Deviation Score Squared
82	− 2.5	6.25
88	3.5	12.25
71	− 13.5	182.25
86	1.5	2.25
96	11.5	132.25
84	− .5	.25

*Original score minus the mean of 84.5.

3. In the third step, the deviation scores are squared (multiplied by themselves) to eliminate negative numbers. This has been carried out in the third column above.
4. The squared deviation scores are then added together, and this sum is divided by the number of scores. In the example above, the sum of the deviation score is 6.25 + 12.25 + 182.25 + 2.25 + 132.25 + .25 = 335.50, and 335.50 ÷ 6 = 55.916.
5. The final step is to take the square root of the resulting number. The square root of 55.916 is 7.4777—which is the standard deviation of the distribution of scores.

scores within a set and because it is not highly sensitive to extreme scores. Moreover, the standard deviation provides a means for converting initial scores on standardized tests such as the Scholastic Aptitude Test (SAT) into the scales used to report results. In this way, it is possible to make a score of 585 on the verbal section of the SAT exam, for example, equivalent from one year to the next, even though the specific test items differ from year to year.

RECAP AND REVIEW II

Recap

◀ Measures of variability provide an index of the dispersion, or spread, of a distribution of scores.

◀ The range and standard deviation are the most commonly used measures of variability.

Review

1. A measure of variability based solely on the distance between the most extreme scores is the
   a. Spread
   b. Standard deviation
   c. Deviation score
   d. Range

2. By simply eyeing the following sets of numbers, predict which will have a higher standard deviation:
   a. 6, 8, 10, 10, 11, 12, 13
   b. 2, 5, 8, 11, 16, 17, 18

3. Calculate the mean and standard deviation for set **a** and **b** in the previous question.

4. The standard deviation is highly sensitive to extreme scores. True or false? _____

(Answers to review questions are at the bottom of page 746.)

USING STATISTICS TO ANSWER QUESTIONS: INFERENTIAL STATISTICS AND CORRELATION

Suppose you were a psychologist who was interested in whether there was a relationship between smoking and anxiety. Would it be reasonable to simply look at a group of smokers and measure their anxiety using some rating scale? Probably not, since—as we discussed in Chapter 1—it would clearly be more informative if you compared their anxiety to the anxiety exhibited by a group of nonsmokers.

Once you had decided to observe anxiety in two groups of people, you would have to determine just who would be your subjects. In an ideal world with unlimited resources, you might contact *every* smoker and nonsmoker, since these are the two populations with which you are concerned. A **population** consists of all the members of a group of interest. Obviously, however, this would be impossible, given the all-encompassing size of the two groups; instead, you would limit your subjects to a sample of smokers and nonsmokers. A **sample**, in formal statistical terms, is a subgroup of a population of interest that is representative of the larger population. Once you had identified samples representative of the population of interest to you, it would be possible to carry out your study, yielding two distributions of scores—one from the smokers and one from the nonsmokers.

The obvious question is whether the two samples differ in the degree of anxiety displayed by their members. The statistical procedures that we

Population: All the members of the group being studied

Sample: A subgroup of a population of interest

ANSWERS (REVIEW I):
1. Histogram   **2.** a.2; b.1; c.3   **3.** Central tendency   **4.** The median; the mean is too sensitive to extreme scores.   **5.** False; they will be equal.

have been discussing earlier are helpful in answering this question, since each of the two samples can be examined in terms of central tendency and variability. The more important question, though, is whether the magnitude of difference between the two distributions is sufficient to conclude that the distributions truly differ from one another, or if, instead, the differences are attributable merely to chance.

To answer the question of whether samples are truly different from one another, psychologists use **inferential statistics**, the branch of statistics that uses data from samples to make predictions about a larger population. To take a simple example, suppose you had two coins that were each flipped 100 times. Suppose further that one coin came up heads forty-one times and the other came up heads sixty-five times. Are both coins fair? We know that a fair coin should come up heads about fifty times in 100 flips. But a little thought would also suggest that it is unlikely that even a fair coin would come up heads exactly fifty times in 100 flips. The question is, then, how far could a coin deviate from fifty heads before the coin would be considered unfair?

Questions such as this—as well as whether the results found are due to chance or represent unexpected, nonchance findings—revolve around how "probable" certain events are. Using coin flipping as an example, fifty-three heads in a hundred flips would be a highly probable outcome since it departs only slightly from the expected outcome of fifty heads. In contrast, if a coin was flipped 100 times and 90 of those times it came up heads, it would be a highly improbable outcome. In fact, 90 heads out of 100 flips should occur by chance only one time in 2 million trials of 100 flips of a fair coin. Ninety heads in a hundred flips, then, is an extremely improbable outcome; if ninety heads did appear, the odds would be that the coin or the flipping process was rigged.

Inferential statistics are used to mathematically determine the probability of observed events. Using inferential statistics to evaluate the result of an experiment, psychologists are able to calculate the likelihood of whether the difference is a reflection of a true difference between populations. For example, suppose we find that the mean on an anxiety scale is 68 for smokers, and 48 for nonsmokers. Inferential statistical procedures allow us to determine whether this difference is really meaningful, or whether we might expect the same difference to occur merely because of chance factors.

Results of inferential statistical procedures are described in terms of measures of significance. To a psychologist, a **significant outcome** is one in which the observed outcome would be expected to occur by chance less than five times out of a hundred. Put another way, a significant difference between two means says that there is a 95 percent or better probability that the difference an experimenter has found is due to real differences between two groups rather than to chance.

MEASURING RELATIONSHIPS: The Correlation Coefficient

How do we know if television viewing is related to aggression, if reading romance novels is related to sexual behavior, or if mothers' IQs are related to their daughters' IQs?

Each of these questions revolves around the issue of the degree of relationship between two variables. One way of answering them is to draw a **scatterplot**, a means of graphically illustrating the relationship between two

Inferential statistics: The branch of statistics that uses data from samples to make predictions about the larger population from which the sample is drawn

Significant outcome: An outcome expected to occur by chance less than 5 percent of the time

Scatterplot: A means of graphically illustrating the relationship between two variables

(a) Positive relationship: As values of one variable rise, values of the social variable increase.

Attraction to another (Y)

Number of shared attitudes with another (X)

(b) Negative relationship: As values of one variable rise, the second declines.

Amount of helping behavior (Y)

Number of bystanders witnessing an emergency (X)

(c) No relationship: There is no relationship between the two variables.

Aggression toward victim (Y)

Intelligence of victim (X)

FIGURE A-6

Scatterplots representing (a) a positive relationship between two variables, (b) a negative relationship, and (c) no clear relationship between two variables.

Positive relationship: A relationship established by data that shows high values of one variable corresponding with high values of another, and low values of the first variable corresponding with low values of the other

Negative relationship: A relationship established by data that shows high values of one variable corresponding with low values of the other

TABLE A-3

IQ Scores of Mothers and Daughters

Mother's IQ	Daughter's IQ
135	122
128	130
125	110
120	132
114	100
110	116
102	108
96	89
90	84
86	92

variables. We would first collect two sets of paired measures and assign one score to the horizontal axis (variable X) and the other score to the vertical axis (variable Y). Then we would draw a dot at the place where the two scores meet on the graph. The three scatterplots illustrated in Figure A-6 present typical situations. In the first, there is a **positive relationship**, in which high values of variable X are associated with high values of variable Y and low values of X are associated with low values of Y. In the second, there is a **negative relationship**: As values of variable X increase, the values of variable Y decrease. The third panel of the figure illustrates a situation in which no clear relationship between variable X and variable Y exists.

It is also possible to consider scores in terms of their mathematical relationship to one another, rather than simply the way they appear on a scatterplot. Suppose, for example, a psychologist was interested in the degree to which a daughter's IQ was related to the mother's IQ—specifically, if a mother with a high IQ tended to have a daughter who also had a high IQ, and whether a mother with a low IQ tended to have a daughter with a low IQ. To examine the issue, suppose the psychologist measured the IQs of ten mothers and daughters and arranged their IQs as presented in Table A-3.

An inspection of the data present in the table indicates that the mothers and daughters obviously do not have the same IQs. Moreover, they do not even have IQs that are rank-ordered the same in the two columns. For example, the mother with the highest IQ does not have the daughter with the highest IQ, and the mother with the lowest IQ does not have the daughter with the lowest IQ. It is apparent, then, that there is not a *perfect* relationship between the IQ of the mother and the IQ of the daughter. However, it would be a mistake to conclude that there is a *zero*, or no, relationship between the IQs of the mothers and daughters, since it is clear that there is a tendency for mothers who have high IQs to have daughters with high IQs, and that mothers with low IQs tend to have daughters with low IQs.

The statistic that provides a precise mathematical index of the degree to which two variables are related is the correlation coefficient. A **correlation**

coefficient is a number that indicates the extent of the relationship between two variables. It ranges in value from + 1.00 to − 1.00. A value of + 1.00 would indicate that two variables had a perfect positive relationship with one another, meaning that the highest score on one variable would be associated with the highest score on the other variable, the second highest score on the first variable would be associated with the second highest score on the second variable, and so on. A value of − 1.00 would indicate that there was a perfect negative relationship between the two variables; the highest score on the first variable would be associated with the lowest score on the second variable, the second highest score would be associated with the second lowest score, and so forth.

Correlation coefficients around zero indicate that there is no relationship between the two variables. In such cases, there is no tendency for high values on one variable to be associated with either high or low values on the second variable.

Correlation coefficients that range between zero and ± 1.00 reflect varying degrees of relationship between the two variables. For instance, a value of + .20 or − .20 would indicate that there was a slight relationship between the two variables, a value of around + .50 or − .50 would indicate a moderate relationship, and a value of + .80 or − .80 would indicate a relatively strong relationship between the variables. As an example, if we were to calculate the correlation of the two sets of variables in Table A-3, we would find a correlation which is quite strong: The coefficient is + .86.

It is important to note that finding a strong correlation between two variables does *not* in any way indicate that one variable *causes* changes in another—only that they are associated with one another. While it might seem plausible to us, for example, that it is the mother's intelligence that causes higher intelligence in a daughter, it is just as possible that a daughter's intelligence affects how the mother performs on an IQ test. (Perhaps the daughter's behavior affects the general home environment, affecting the mother's performance on IQ tests.) It is even plausible that some other unmeasured— and previously unconsidered—third variable is causing both mother's and daughter's IQs to increase or decrease simultaneously. In a clear example of this possibility, even if we found that ice cream sales and violent crimes are correlated with one another (as they happen to be), we would not presume that they were causally related. In this case, it is likely they are both influenced by a third factor—the weather.

The crucial point is that even if we find a perfect correlation between two sets of variables, we would not be able to say that the two variables were linked causally—only that they were strongly related to one another.

Correlation coefficient: A number that indicates the relationship between two variables

THE INFORMED CONSUMER OF PSYCHOLOGY: Evaluating Statistics

It has been said that statisticians are the kind of people who could sit with their heads in a refrigerator and their feet in an oven and report that, on the average, they feel fine. Yet despite many people's personal feelings regarding statistics, the science of psychology is built on a statistical foundation. A glance at any report of research in the psychology literature will confirm that analysis of data represents an indispensable element in the advance of the science.

Just because someone publishes a statistical result, however, does not mean that either the statistic or the conclusions based on it are necessarily appropriate. Although it is difficult for a person who is not well versed in statistics to argue effectively with the kind of sophisticated mathematics that you are likely to see in published research articles, there are certain basic questions that you can ask yourself when considering the results of research that are based on statistical tests. Among the most important are the following:

▶ Is the sample appropriate? The sample should be representative of the population for which conclusions are being made. The results of an experiment that uses only college sophomores as subjects might well be considered inapplicable to poor, unemployed, unskilled workers. Moreover, it is important to consider the size of the sample; very small samples may produce results that are not representative of the population at large.

▶ Are the measures used in the study appropriate? Statistics are only as good as the measures on which they are based, and no statistical machinations can produce something useful if the measures are not initially valid and reliable.

▶ Are the conclusions made from the statistical analyses drawn directly from the statistical tests? Research reports vary in terms of how closely the conclusions are built upon the results of tests. Investigators who are eager to distance their conclusions from their analyses should be treated with suspicion.

▶ Do results have practical, as well as statistical, meaning? It is possible to find a statistically significant difference between two means that are mathematically very close if a sufficiently large sample is used. At the same time, the practical significance of such differences may be relatively minor. It is crucial to attempt to determine the practical, as well as statistical, meaning of experimental results.

Statistical procedures represent important weapons in the arsenal of psychologists. As such, they should be treated with respect. At the same time, it is important to remember that statistics are no more infallible than the people who use them. The better informed you are about statistics and the way that they are employed, the better able you will be to make use of the findings of the science of psychology.

RECAP AND REVIEW III

Recap

◀ Inferential statistical analysis is a technique that uses data from samples to make predictions about a larger population.

◀ Statistical significance occurs when the probability that a difference between means is due to chance is less than 5 in 100.

◀ Measures of relationship provide an index of the degree to which two variables are related. The most frequently used measure is the correlation coefficient.

Review

1. Researchers would like to estimate the level of stress for college freshmen for a given year at a large university. A stress index is given to a randomly assigned group of 500 freshmen. The class size is 6000 for that year. In this example the group of 500 is known as a _____, and the entire class of freshmen is known as the _____ .

2. Dr. Sanders states that the results of his experiment show a difference between the two groups, and that there is a

90 percent probability that the results are due to a true difference between the groups and not by chance. Are his results statistically significant?

3. A hypothetical set of data for college freshmen at a university might indicate that as rate of caffeine consumption increases, amount of sleep decreases. The scatterplot for this data is apt to show a _____ relationship.

4. What would the value of the correlation coefficient be for
   a. A perfect negative relationship?
   b. A perfect positive relationship?
   c. No relationship?

5. If we observed a correlation coefficient of $-.90$ in item 3, we would probably be safe in saying that caffeine consumption *causes* lack of sleep in college students. True or false? _____

6. The researchers in item 3 want to extend their findings to include all college students. As an informed consumer, would you accept their generalization? Why or why not?

(Answers to review questions are at the bottom of page 750.)

◀ **LOOKING BACK**

1. Statistics is concerned with collecting, organizing, analyzing, and drawing conclusions from numerical data. One branch of statistics, descriptive statistics, provides a means of summarizing data.

2. A frequency distribution arranges scores from a sample by indicating how often a particular score is presented. A histogram, or bar graph, presents the same data pictorially.

3. There are three major measures of central tendency, which is the most representative score in a distribution of scores. The mean (or average) is generally the best measure of central tendency. It is calculated by summing the scores in a distribution and dividing by the number of scores. The median is the point or score in a distribution that divides the distribution in half, so that half the scores are higher and half are lower. The third measure of central tendency is the mode. The mode is the most frequently occurring score in a distribution of scores. Distributions sometimes have more than one mode.

4. The range and standard deviation are two measures of variability, which is the spread of scores in a distribution. The range is the highest score in a distribution minus the lowest score. The standard deviation is an index of the extent to which the average score in a distribution deviates from the center of the distribution. The range is a very limited measure of variability because of its sensitivity to extreme scores. The standard deviation, however, is an excellent measure of variability.

5. Inferential statistics, techniques that use data from samples to make predictions about a larger population, are useful in deciding whether differences between distributions of data are attributable to real differences or to chance variation. Usually, if a difference would occur by chance more than 5 times in 100, the difference is attributed to chance. On the other hand, if the difference would occur by chance fewer than 5 times in 100, it is attributed to a true difference brought about by an experimental manipulation.

6. Measures of relationship provide a numerical index of the extent to which two variables are related. The correlation coefficient ranges in value from $+1.00$ to -1.00, with a $+1.00$ indicating a perfect positive relationship and -1.00 a perfect negative relationship. Correlations close to or at zero indicate there is little or no relationship between two variables. It is critical to realize that even when correlations are close to perfect one cannot assume that two variables are related in a causal sense.

KEY TERMS AND CONCEPTS ▶

statistics (p. 736)
descriptive statistics (737)
frequency distribution (737)
histogram (737)
central tendency (739)
mean (739)
median (739)
mode (740)

bimodal distribution (740)
normal distribution (740)
skewed distribution (741)
variability (742)
range (742)
standard deviation (742)
population (744)

sample (744)
inferential statistics (745)
significant outcome (745)
scatterplot (745)
positive relationship (746)
negative relationship (746)
correlation coefficient (747)

FOR FURTHER STUDY AND APPLICATION ▶

Ferguson, G. A., & Takane, Y. (1989). *Statistical analysis in psychology and education*. (6th ed.) New York: McGraw-Hill.

If your statistical appetite has been whetted by the material discussed in this appendix, you might want to look at this volume, which provides a more in-depth overview of statistics.

Kimble, G. (1978). *How to use (and misuse) statistics*. Englewood Cliffs, NJ: Prentice-Hall.

This book is filled with practical advice on how to make use of statistics. It is particularly useful in terms of how to evaluate the statistics presented to you by others.

Pagano, R. R. (1982). *Understanding statistics in the behavioral sciences*. St. Paul: West.

A clear overview of how scientists in psychology and related fields use statistics to interpret research findngs.

ANSWERS (REVIEW III)

1. Sample; population **2.** No, at least not at the .05 level. **3.** Negative **4.** a. −1.00; b. +1.00; c. 0 **5.** False; we cannot assume a causal relation, only an association. **6.** No, the sample (freshmen) does not represent the population (all college students).

GLOSSARY

(Numbers in parentheses indicate the chapters where the terms are discussed. *A* indicates the Appendix.)

ABC model The model suggesting that an attitude has three components: affect, behavior, and cognition (18)

absolute refractory period The period following the triggering of a neuron in which the neuron recovers and prepares for another impulse (2)

absolute threshold The smallest amount of physical intensity by which a stimulus can be detected (3)

accommodation The ability of the lens to vary its shape in order to focus incoming images on the retina (3)

acetylcholine A common neurotransmitter that produces contractions of skeletal muscles (2)

achievement test A test intended to determine a person's level of knowledge in a given subject (8)

acquired immune deficiency syndrome (AIDS) A fatal, sexually transmitted disease that is caused by a virus that destroys the body's immune system and has no known cure (10)

action potential An electric nerve impulse that travels through a neuron when it is set off by a "trigger," changing the cell's charge from negative to positive (2)

activity theory of aging A theory that suggests that the elderly who age most successfully are those who maintain the interests and activities they had during middle age (13)

acupuncture A Chinese technique of relieving pain through the placement of needles in specific areas of the body (3)

adaptation An adjustment in sensory capacity following prolonged exposure to stimuli (3)

addictive drugs Drugs that produce a physical or physiological dependence in the user (11)

adolescence The developmental stage between childhood and adulthood during which many physical, cognitive, and social changes take place (13)

affect component That part of an attitude encompassing how one feels about the object of one's attitude (18)

affective disorders Mood disturbances severe enough to interfere with normal living (16)

afterimage The image appearing when one moves one's eyes from a particular image to a blank area (3)

age of viability The point at which a fetus can survive if born prematurely (12)

aggression Intentional injury of or harm to another person (19)

aggressive cues Stimuli that have been associated with aggression in the past (19)

Ainsworth strange situation A sequence of events involving a child and his or her mother that provide a measurement of attachment (12)

alarm and mobilization stage In Selye's general adaptation syndrome, a person's initial awareness of the presence of a stressor (15)

algorithm A set of rules that, if followed, guarantee a problem's solution, though the reason they work may not be understood (7)

all-or-none law The principle governing the state of neurons, which are either on (firing) or off (resting) (2)

altered states of consciousness Experiences of sensation or thought that differ from one's normal experience (11)

altruism Helping behavior that is beneficial to others while requiring sacrifice on the part of the helper (19)

Alzheimer's disease An illness associ-

ated with aging that includes severe memory loss, physical deterioration, and loss of language abilities (6, 13)

amnesia Memory loss unaccompanied by other mental difficulties (6)

amphetamines Strong stimulants that cause a temporary feeling of confidence and alertness but may increase anxiety and appetite loss and, taken over a period of time, suspiciousness and feelings of persecution (11)

anal stage According to Freud, a stage, from 12–18 months to 3 years of age, in which a child's pleasure is centered on the anus (14)

androgens Male sex hormones (10)

androgynous A state in which gender roles encompass characteristics thought typical of both sexes (18)

anorexia nervosa An eating disorder usually striking young women in which symptoms include self-starvation or near self-starvation in an attempt to avoid obesity (9)

anorgasmia A female's lack of orgasm (10)

anterograde amnesia Memory loss of events following an injury (6)

antianxiety drugs Drugs that alleviate stress and anxiety (17)

antidepressant drugs Medication that improves a patient's mood and feeling of well-being (17)

antipsychotic drugs Drugs that temporarily alleviate psychotic symptoms such as agitation and overactivity (17)

antisocial (sociopathic) personality disorder A disorder in which individuals display no regard for moral and ethical rules or for the rights of others (16)

anvil A tiny bone in the middle ear that transfers vibrations to the stirrup (3)

anxiety A feeling of apprehension or tension (14, 16)

anxiety disorder The occurrence of anxiety without obvious external cause, intruding on daily functioning (16)

aphasia A disorder resulting in problems with verbal expression due to brain injury (2)

apraxia The inability to perform activities in a logical way (2)

aptitude test A test designed to predict ability in a particular line of work (8)

archetypes According to Jung, universal, symbolic representations of a particular person, object, or experience (14)

archival research The examination of written records for the purpose of understanding behavior (1)

arousal theory The belief that we try to maintain certain levels of stimulation and activity, increasing or reducing them as necessary (9)

arrangement problems Problems whose solution requires the rearrangement of a group of elements in order to satisfy a certain criterion (7)

artificial intelligence Intelligence demonstrated by computers and other sophisticated machines (8)

association area One of the major areas of the brain, the site of the higher mental processes such as thought, language, memory, and speech (2)

assumed-similarity bias The tendency to think of people as being similar to oneself (18)

attachment The positive emotional bond that develops between parents and their children (12)

attitudes Learned predispositions to respond in a favorable or unfavorable manner to a particular object (18)

attribution theory The theory that seeks to explain how we decide, on the basis of samples of an individual's behavior, what the specific causes of that behavior are (18)

auditory canal A tubelike passage in the ear through which sound moves to the eardrum (3)

authoritarian parents Parents who are firm and punitive and who value unquestioning obedience from their children (12)

authoritative parents Parents who are firm, set clear limits, reason with and explain things to their children (12)

autonomic division The part of the nervous system that controls involuntary movement (the actions of the heart, glands, lungs, and other organs) (2)

autonomy - versus - shame - and - doubt stage The period during which, according to Erikson, toddlers (ages 18 months to 3 years) develop independence and autonomy if exploration and freedom are encouraged, or shame and self-doubt if they are restricted and overprotected (12)

aversive conditioning A technique used to help people break unwanted habits by associating the habits with very unpleasant stimuli (17)

aversive stimuli unpleasant or painful stimuli (5)

axon A long, slim, tubelike extension from the end of a neuron that carries messages (2)

babble speechlike but meaningless sounds (7)

Babinski reflex The reflex action in which an infant fans out its toes in response to a stroke on the outside of its foot (12)

background stressors Daily hassles, such as being stuck in traffic, that cause minor irritations but no long-term ill effects, unless they continue or are compounded by other stressful events (15)

barbiturates Depressants used to induce sleep and reduce stress, the abuse of which, especially when combined with alcohol, can be deadly (11)

basilar membrane A structure dividing the cochlea into an upper and a lower chamber (3)

behavior component (of attitude) A predisposition to act in a way that is relevant to one's attitude (18)

behavior modification A formalized technique for promoting the frequency of desirable behaviors and decreasing the incidence of unwanted ones (5)

behavioral assessment Direct measures of an individual's behavior used to describe characteristics indicative of personality (5)

behavioral model The psychological model that suggests that observable behavior should be the focus of study (17)

behavioral model of abnormality The model that suggests that abnormal behavior itself is the problem to be treated, rather than viewing behavior as a symptom of some underlying medical or psychological problem (16)

behavioral self-management A procedure in which people learn to identify and resolve their problems using techniques based on learning theory (17)

behavioral treatment approaches Approaches to abnormal behavior that assume that both normal and abnormal behaviors are learned and that treatment consists of learning new behavior or unlearning maladaptive behavior (17)

bimodal distribution Cases in which a frequency distribution includes two modes (A)

binocular disparity The difference between the images that reach the retina of each eye; this disparity allows the brain to estimate distance (4)

biofeedback A technique for learning to control internal physiological processes through conscious thought (2)

biological constraints Built-in limitations in an organism's ability to learn particular behaviors (12)

biological model The psychological model that views behavior in terms of biological functioning (1)

biopsychologists Psychologists who study the ways biological structures and body functions affect behavior (1)

biopsychology The branch of psychology that studies the biological basis of behavior (2)

bipolar cells Nerve cells leading to the brain that are triggered by nerve cells in the eye (3)

bipolar disorder A disorder in which a person alternates between euphoric feeling of mania and bouts of depression (16)

bisexuality A sexual attraction to members of both sexes (10)

bottom-up processing Recognition and processing of individual components of a stimulus (4)

brain electrical activity mapping

(BEAM) A computerized scan technique that indicates electrical activity within the brain (2)

brain scan A method of "photographing" the brain without opening the skull (2)

brainstorming A technique of decision making in which group members express any new ideas they can think of, no matter how outlandish, with evaluation occurring only after all ideas have been voiced (20)

Broca's aphasia A syndrome in which speech production is disturbed (2)

bulimia An eating disorder characterized by a vast intake of food that may be followed by self-induced vomiting (9)

caffeine A stimulant found most abundantly in coffee, soda, and chocolate (11)

Cannon-Bard theory of emotion The belief that both physiological and emotional arousal are produced simultaneously by the same nerve impulse (9)

cardinal trait A single personality trait that directs most of a person's activities (e.g., greed, lust, kindness) (14)

case study An in-depth interview of an individual in order to better understand that individual and to make inferences about people in general (1)

cataclysmic events Strong stressors that occur suddenly, affecting many people at once (e.g., natural disasters) (15)

catharsis The notion that aggression is built up and must be discharged through violent acts (16)

central core The "old brain," which controls such basic functions as eating and sleeping and is common to all vertebrates (2)

centralized decision making Decision making in which authority is controlled by a few people at the top of the organization (20)

central nervous system (CNS) The system that includes the brain and the spinal cord (2)

central route processing Message interpretation characterized by thoughtful consideration of the issues and arguments used to persuade (18)

central tendency The most representative score in a distribution of scores (the mean, median, and mode are measures of central tendency) (A)

central traits A set of major characteristics that make up the core of a person's personality forming impressions of others (14, 18)

cerebellum The part of the brain that controls bodily balance (2)

cerebral cortex The "new brain," responsible for the most sophisticated information processing in the brain; contains the lobes (2)

channels Paths along which verbal and nonverbal behavioral messages are communicated (e.g., facial expressions, eye contact, body movements) (9)

chlamydia An STD which initially produces no symptoms in women but which can lead to pelvic inflammation and sterility, and produces in men painful urination and discharge from the penis (10)

chlorpromazine An antipsychotic drug that is used in the treatment of schizophrenia (17)

chromosomes Rod-shaped structures that contain basic hereditary information (12)

chronological A person's physical age (8)

chunk A meaningful grouping of stimuli that can be stored as a unit in short-term memory (6)

classical conditioning A kind of learning in which a previously neutral stimulus comes to elicit a response through its association with a stimulus that naturally brings about the response (5)

classical (or bureaucratic) model A management theory in which explicit rules, regulations, and procedures govern every task (20)

client-centered therapy therapy in which the therapist reflects back the patient's statements in a way that causes the patient to find his or her own solutions (17)

clinical psychology The branch of psychology that studies diagnosis and treatment of abnormal behavior (1, 17)

clitoris The small and very sensitive organ in the female's external genitals (10)

close relationships See interpersonal attraction (19)

closure The tendency to group according to enclosed or complete figures rather than open or incomplete ones (4)

cocaine A stimulant that initially creates feelings of confidence, alertness, and well-being, but eventually causes mental and physical deterioration (11)

cochlea A coiled tube filled with fluid that receives sound via the oval window or through bone conduction (3)

cognition The higher mental processes through which we understand the world, process information, make judgments and decisions, and communicate knowledge to others (7, 18)

cognition component (of attitude) The belief and thoughts held about the object of one's attitude (18)

cognitive-behavioral therapy A process by which people's faulty cognitions about themselves and the world are changed to more accurate ones (17)

cognitive complexity The use of and preference for elaborate, intricate, and complex stimuli and thinking patterns (7)

cognitive development The process by which a child's understanding of the world changes as a function of age and experience (12)

cognitive dissonance The conflict that arises when a person holds contrasting cognitions (18)

cognitive learning theory The study of the thought processes that underlie learning (5)

cognitive map A mental "picture" of locations and directions (5, 21)

cognitive model The psychological model that focuses on how people know, understand, and think about the world (1)

cognitive psychology The branch of psychology that considers higher mental processes including thinking, language, memory, problem solving, knowing, reasoning, judging, and decision making (1, 5)

cohesiveness The degree to which group members are attracted to the group as a whole and to other members individually (20)

collective unconscious A concept developed by Jung proposing that we inherit certain personality characteristics from our ancestors and the human race as a whole (14)

community psychology A branch of psychology aimed at preventing and treating psychological disorders in the community (17)

companionate love The strong affection felt for those with whom our lives are deeply involved (18)

compliance Behavior that occurs in response to direct social pressure (19)

compulsion An urge to repeatedly carry out an act that even the sufferer realizes is unreasonable (16)

computerized axial tomography (CAT) scan A scanning procedure that shows the structures within the brain (2)

concept A categorization of objects, events, or people that share common properties (7)

conception Process by which an egg cell is fertilized by a sperm cell (12)

concrete operational stage According to Piaget, the period from 7 to 12 years of age that is characterized by logical thought and a loss of egocentrism (12)

conditioned response (CR) A response that, after conditioning, follows a previously neutral stimulus (e.g., salivation at the sound of a tuning fork) (5)

conditioned stimulus (CS) A once-neutral stimulus that has been paired with an unconditioned stimulus to bring about a response formerly caused only by the unconditioned stimulus (5)

cones Cone-shaped, light-sensitive receptor cells in the retina that are responsible for sharp focus and color perception, particularly in bright light (3)

confederate A participant in an experiment who has been instructed to behave in ways that will affect the responses of other subjects (1)

confirmation bias A bias in problem solving favoring an initial hypothesis and disregarding contradictory information suggesting alternative solution (7)

conformity A change in behavior or attitudes brought about by a desire to follow the beliefs or standards of other people (19)

conscience The part of the superego that prevents us from doing what is morally wrong (14)

consciousness A person's awareness of the sensations, thoughts, and feelings that he or she is experiencing at a given moment (11)

consensus information The degree to which people behave similarly in the same situation (18)

conservation, principle of The knowledge that quantity is unrelated to the arrangement and physical appearance of objects (12)

consistency information The degree to which an individual behaves similarly in similar situations (18)

constructive processes Processes in which memories are influenced by the interpretation and meaning we give to events (6)

consumer psychology The branch of psychology that considers our buying habits and the effects of advertising on buyer behavior (1)

context-dependent memory The phenomenon by which memory of information is enhanced when recalled under the same conditions as when it was learned (6)

contingency contracting Acting upon a written contract between a therapist and a patient (or parent and child, etc.) that sets behavioral goals, with rewards for achievement (17)

continuous reinforcement The reinforcing of a behavior every time it occurs (5)

control group The experimental group receiving no treatment (1)

convergent thinking A type of thinking which produces responses based on knowledge and logic (7)

conversion disorder Psychological disturbances characterized by actual physical disturbances, such as the inability to speak or move one's arms (16)

coping The efforts to control, reduce, or learn to tolerate the threats that lead to stress (15)

cornea A transparent, protective window into the eyeball (3)

correlation coefficient A number that indicates the relationship between two variables (A)

correlational research Research to de-

termine whether there is a relationship between certain behaviors and responses (1)

counseling psychology The branch of psychology that focuses on educational, social, and career adjustment issues (17)

creativity The combining of responses or ideas in novel ways (7)

critical period The first of several stages of development in which specific kinds of growth must occur to enable further crucial development (12)

cross-sectional research A research method in which people of different ages are compared at the same point in time (12)

cross-sequential research A research method which combines cross-sectional and longitudinal research (12)

crowding An unpleasant psychological and subjective state involving people's reaction to the density of their environment (21)

crystallized intelligence Intelligence based on the store of specific information, skills, and strategies that people have acquired through experience (8,13)

cultural assimilator A teaching aid designed to minimize racial prejudice through understanding of others' behavior (18)

culture-fair IQ test A test that does not discriminate against members of any minority culture group (8)

cumulative recorder A device that automatically records and graphs the pattern of responses made in reaction to a particular reinforcement schedule (5)

cyberphobia Fear of computers (21)

dark adaptation A heightened sensitivity to light resulting from being in low-level light (3)

date rape Rape in which rapist is either a date or an acquaintance (10)

daydreams Fantasies people construct while awake (11)

decay The loss of information through nonuse (6)

decentralized decision making Decision making in which the distribution of authority extends throughout the organization (20)

decibel A measure of sound loudness or intensity (3)

declarative knowledge The body of knowledge that concerns facts—faces, dates, names, etc. (16)

defense mechanisms Psychological strategies that protect people from unconscious impulses (14, 15, 17)

deinstitutionalization The transfer of former mental patients from institutions into the community (17)

delphi method A variation of the nominal group technique in which experts on a given problem are asked to complete a series of detailed questionnaires (20)

delusion Firmly held beliefs with no basis in reality (16)

dendrites Fibers at one end of a neuron that receive messages from other neurons (2)

denial A refusal to accept or acknowledge anxiety-producing information (14)

density number of people per unit of space (21)

density-intensity explanation of crowding An explanation based on the fact that "crowded" situations that seem negative become more negative, while those that seem positive become more positive (21)

dependent variable The variable that is measured and is expected to change as a result of experimenter manipulation of the independent variable (1)

depressants Drugs that slow down the nervous system (11)

depth perception The ability to view the world in three dimensions and to perceive distance (4)

descriptive statistics The branch of statistics that provides a means of summarizing data (A)

determinism The view suggesting that people's behavior is shaped primarily by factors outside their control (14)

deterrence The view that threats of large-scale retaliation against an enemy attack are an effective means of preventing the attack in the first place (21)

developmental psychology The branch of psychology that studies people's growth and change over the life span (1, 12)

deviation IQ score A calculation of an IQ score that allows one person's performance to be measured in relation to others' (8)

Diagnostic and Statistical Manual of Mental Disorders, *Third Edition—Revised* A manual that presents comprehensive definitions of more than 230 separate diagnostic categories for identifying problems and behaviors (16)

dichotic listening A procedure in which an individual wears earphones through which different messages are sent to each ear at the same time (4)

difference threshold The smallest detectable difference between two stimuli (3)

diffusion of responsibility The tendency for people to feel that responsibility for helping is shared among those present (19)

discriminative stimulus A stimulus to which an organism learns to respond as part of stimulus control training (5)

disengagement theory of aging A theory that suggests that aging is a gradual withdrawal from the world on physical, psychological, and social levels (13)

displacement The expression of an unwanted feeling or thought, directed toward a weaker person instead of a more powerful one (14)

display rules Learned rules that inform us about the appropriateness of showing emotions nonverbally (9)

dispositional causes of behavior Causes of behavior that are based on internal traits or personality factors (18)

dissociative disorders The splitting apart of critical personality facets, allowing stress avoidance by escape (16)

distinctiveness information The extent to which a given behavior occurs across different situations (18)

divergent thinking The ability to generate unusual, but appropriate, responses to problems or questions (7)

door-in-the-face technique A strategy in which a large request, refusal of which is expected, is followed by a smaller request (18)

dopamine (DA) A common neurotransmitter that inhibits certain neurons and excites others (2)

dopamine hypothesis A theory that suggests that schizophrenia occurs when there is excess activity in those areas of the brain using dopamine to transmit nerve impulses (16)

double-bind hypothesis A theory that suggests that people suffering from schizophrenia may have received simultaneous contradictory messages from their mothers and never learned what behavior was appropriate (16)

double-blind procedure The technique by which both the experimenter and the subject are kept from knowing which subjects received a drug, making any observed behavior variations more reliable (1)

double standard The view that premarital sex is permissible for males but not for females (10)

Down's syndrome A disorder caused by the presence of an extra chromosome, resulting in mental retardation (8, 12)

dream interpretation An examination of a patient's dreams to find clues to the unconscious conflicts and problems being experienced (17)

drive A motivational tension or arousal that energizes behavior in order to fulfill a need (9)

drive-reduction theory The theory which claims that drives are produced to obtain our basic biological requirements (9)

drug therapy Control of psychological problems through drugs (17)

dyadic phase The second phase in the decline of a relationship, in which a person confronts a partner and determines whether to attempt to repair, redefine, or terminate the relationship (18)

dyslexia A disability with a perceptual basis that can result in the reversal of letters during reading and writing, confusion between left and right, and difficulties in spelling (4)

eardrum The part of the ear that vibrates when sound waves hit it (3)

echoic memory The storage of information obtained from the sense of hearing (16)

eclectic approach to therapy An approach to therapy that uses a variety of treatment methods rather than just one (17)

ecological theory A theory suggesting that the relationship between objects in a scene gives clues about the objects' sizes (4)

educational psychology The branch of psychology that considers how the educational process affects students (5)

ego The part of personality that provides a buffer between the id and the outside world according to Freud (14)

egocentric thought Viewing the world entirely from one's own perspective (12)

ego-ideal The part of the superego that motivates us to do what is morally proper (14)

ego-integrity-versus-despair stage According to Erikson, a period from late adulthood until death during which we review life's accomplishments and failures (13)

ejaculation The expulsion of semen through the penis (10)

elaborative rehearsal Organizing information into a logical framework to assist in recalling it (6)

electroconvulsive therapy Treatment involving the administration of an electric current to a patient's head to treat depression (17)

electroencephalogram A measure of the brain's electrical activity (2, 11)

embryo A developed zygote that has a heart, a brain, and other organs (12)

emotion-focused coping The conscious regulation of emotion as a means of dealing with stress (15)

emotions Feelings (such as happiness and sorrow) that generally have both physiological and cognitive elements and that influence behavior (9)

empathy One person's experiencing of another's emotions, leading to an increased likelihood of responding to the other's needs (19)

encoding The process by which information is initially recorded in a form usable to memory (6)

endocrine system A chemical communication network that sends messages throughout the nervous system and secretes hormones that affect body growth and functioning (2)

endorphins Chemicals produced by the body that interact with an opiate receptor to reduce pain (2)

engram (See memory trace) (6)

environmental influence Influences on behavior that occur in the world around us—family, friends, school, nutrition, and many other factors (12)

environmental psychology The branch of psychology that considers the relationship between people and their physical environment (1, 21)

episodic memories Stored information relating to personal experiences (6)

erectile failure A male's inability to achieve or maintain an erection (10)

ergonomics The study of how people's behavior and abilities affect the design of tools, machines, and environments for effective use (21)

erogenous zones Areas of the body that are particularly sensitive because of an unusually rich array of nerve receptors (10)

erotic Sexually stimulating (10)

estrogen The female sex hormone (10)

excitatory message A chemical secretion that "tells" a receiving neuron to fire (2)

excitement phase A period during which the body prepares for sexual intercourse (10)

exhaustion stage The third stage of Selye's general adaptation syndrome: failure to adapt to a stressor, leading to physical, psychological, and emotional problems (15)

existential therapy A humanistic approach that addresses the meaning of life, allowing a client to devise a system of values that gives purpose to his or her life (17)

experiment A study carried out to investigate the relationship between two or more factors in order to establish causality (1)

experimental bias Factors that could lead an experimenter to an erroneous conclusion about the effect of the independent variable on the dependent variable (1)

experimental manipulation The intentional alteration of factors in an experiment to affect responses or behaviors (1)

experimental psychology The branch of psychology that studies the processes of sensing, perceiving, learning, and thinking about the world (1)

experimenter expectations An experi-

menter's unintentional message to a subject about results expected from the experiment (1)

extinction The weakening and eventual disappearance of a learned response (5)

extramarital sex Sexual activity between a married person and someone who is not his or her spouse (10)

extrinsic motivation Motivation by which people participate in an activity for a tangible reward (9)

facial-affect program The activation of a set of nerve impulses that make the face display the appropriate expression (9)

facial-feedback hypothesis The notion that facial expressions are involved in determining the experience of emotions and in labeling them (9)

factor analysis A statistical technique for combining traits into broader, more general patterns of consistency (14)

familial retardation Mental retardation in which there is a history of retardation in a family but no evidence of biological causes (8)

family therapy An approach that focuses on the family as a whole unit to which each member contributes (17)

fear of success A fear that being successful will have a negative influence on the way one is perceived (9)

feature detection The activation of neurons in the cortex by visual stimuli of specific shapes or patterns (4)

fetal alcohol syndrome An ailment producing mental and physical retardation in a baby as a result of the mother's high alcohol intake while pregnant (12)

fetus A developing child, from nine weeks after conception until birth (12)

figure/ground Figure refers to the object being perceived, whereas ground refers to the background of or spaces within the object (4)

fixation Behavior reflecting an earlier stage of development (14)

fixed-interval schedule A schedule whereby a reinforcer is given at established time intervals (5)

fixed-ratio schedule A schedule whereby reinforcement is given only after a certain number of responses are made (5)

flashbulb memories Memories of a specific event that are so clear that they seem like "snapshots" of the event (6)

fluid intelligence The ability to deal with new problems and situations (8, 13)

focus-of-attention explanation of crowding An explanation based on the fact that an attempt to determine what aspect of a stimulating situation is causing one's arousal can lead to a feeling of being crowded or of being comfortable (21)

foot-in-the-door technique A technique in which compliance with an important request is more likely following compliance with a smaller, previous request (19)

forensic psychology The branch of psychology that studies insanity and other legal issues (1)

forewarning A procedure in which a subject is told in advance that a persuasive message is forthcoming, sometimes reducing the effects of social influence (19)

formal groups Work units set up by the management of an organization, designed to carry out some specific task (20)

formal operational stage According to Piaget, the period from age 12 to adulthood that is characterized by abstract thought (12)

fovea A very sensitive region of the retina that aids in focusing (3)

free association A Freudian therapeutic technique in which a patient says everything that comes to mind to give the therapist a clue to the workings of the patient's unconscious (17)

free will The human ability to make decisions about one's own life (1)

frequency The number of wave crests occurring each second in any particular sound (3)

frequency distribution An arrangement of scores from a sample that indicates how often a particular score is present (A)

frequency theory of hearing The theory that suggests that the entire basilar membrane acts like a microphone, vibrating in response to sound (3)

frontal lobes The brain structure located at the front center of the cortex containing major motor and speech and reasoning centers (2)

frustration A state produced by the thwarting or blocking of some ongoing, goal-directed behavior (19)

functional fixedness The tendency to think of an object in terms of its most typical use (7)

functionalism An early approach to psychology that considered the role of mental activity in adapting to one's environment (1)

fundamental attribution bias A tendency to attribute others' behavior to dispositional causes but to attribute one's own behavior to situational causes (18)

gag reflex An infant's reflex to clear its throat (12)

ganglion cells Nerve cells that collect and summarize information from rods and carry it to the brain (3)

gate-control theory of pain The theory that suggests that particular nerve receptors lead to specific areas of the brain related to pain; when these receptors are activated by an injury or bodily malfunction, a "gate" to the brain is opened and pain is sensed (3)

gender The sense of being male or female (10)

gender roles Societal expectations about appropriate behavior for women and men (10)

gender schema A cognitive framework that organizes and guides a child's understanding of gender (10)

general adaptation syndrome (GAS) A theory developed by Selye that suggests that a person's response to stress consists of three stages: alarm and mobilization, resistance, and exhaustion (15)

generalized anxiety disorder The experience of long-term anxiety with no explanation (16)

generativity-versus-stagnation stage According to Erikson, a period in middle adulthood during which we take stock of our contributions to family and society (13)

genes The parts of a chromosome through which genetic information is transmitted (12)

genetic Pertaining to the biological factors that transmit hereditary information (12)

genetic preprogramming theories of aging Theories that suggest a built-in time limit to the reproduction of human cells (13)

genital herpes A noncurable virus producing small blisters or sores around the genitals (10)

genital stage According to Freud, a period from puberty until death, marked by mature sexual behavior (i.e., sexual intercourse) (14)

genitals The male and female sex organs (10)

gerontologists Specialists who study aging (13)

gestalt laws of organization A series of principles that describe how we organize pieces of information into meaningful wholes; they include closure, proximity, similarity, and simplicity (14)

gestalt psychology An approach to psychology that focuses on the organization of perception and thinking in a "whole" sense, rather than on the individual elements of perception (1)

gestalts Patterns studied by the gestalt psychologists (1)

gestalt therapy An approach that attempts to integrate thoughts, feelings, and behavior into a whole (17)

glaucoma A dysfunction of the eye in which fluid pressure builds up and causes a decline in visual acuity (3)

gonorrhea An STD which leads to infertility and infection (10)

g or g-factor A single general factor accounting for mental ability (8)

grammar The framework of rules that determine how our thoughts can be expressed (7)

grave-dressing phase The fourth and final stage in the decline of a relationship in which the relationship is physically and psychologically ended (18)

group A collection of individuals in which there is (1) interaction among members, (2) perception of group membership, (3) shared norms and goals, and (4) fate interdependence (20)

group dynamics The scientific study of groups and group processes (20)

group therapy Therapy in which people discuss problems with a group (17)

groupthink A phenomenon that occurs when members of a highly cohesive group share such strong motivation to achieve consensus that they lose the ability to critically evaluate alternative points of view (20)

habituation A decrease in responding to repeated presentations of the same stimulus (12)

hair cells Tiny cells covering the basilar membrane that, when bent by vibrations entering the cochlea, transmit neural messages to the brain (3)

hallucinations Perceptions of things that do not actually exist (16)

hallucinogen A drug that is capable of producing changes in perception, or hallucinations (11)

halo effect A phenomenon in which an initial understanding that a person has positive traits is used to infer other uniformly positive characteristics (18)

hammer A tiny bone in the middle ear that transfers vibrations to the anvil (3)

hardiness A personality characteristic associated with a lower rate of stress-related illness, consisting of three components: commitment, challenge, and control (15)

Hawthorne effect The concept that when subjects know they are in an experiment, their behavior may change as a function of the special attention they receive (20)

health psychology The branch of psychology that explores the relationship of physical and psychological factors (1, 15)

hemispheres Symmetrical left and right halves of the brain (2)

heredity Influences on behavior that are transmitted biologically from patients to a child (12)

heritability A measure of the degree to which a characteristic is related to genetic, inherited factors, as opposed to environmental factors (8)

heroin A powerful depressant, usually injected, that gives an initial rush of good feeling but leads eventually to anxiety and depression; extremely addictive (11)

heuristic A rule of thumb that may bring about a solution to a problem but is not guaranteed to do so (7)

heterosexuality Sexual behavior between a man and a woman (10)

hierarchy of fears A list, in order of increasing severity, of the things that are associated with one's fears (17)

higher-order conditioning A form of conditioning that occurs when an already-conditioned stimulus is paired with a neutral stimulus until the neutral stimulus evokes the same response as the conditioned stimulus (5)

histogram A bar graph used to represent data graphically (A)

homeostasis The process by which an organism tries to maintain an internal biological balance or steady state (9)

homosexuality A sexual attraction to a member of one's own sex (10)

hormones Chemicals that circulate throughout the blood and affect the functioning and growth of parts of the body (2)

human relations model A view of management which emphasizes the social context of work and people's interactions with one another (20)

humanistic model The psychological model that suggests that people are in control of their lives (1)

humanistic model of abnormality The model that suggests that people are basically rational, and that abnormal behavior results from an inability to fulfill human needs and capabilities (16)

humanistic theory (of personality) The theory emphasizing people's basic goodness and their natural tendency to rise to higher levels of functioning (14)

humanistic therapy Therapy in which the underlying assumption is that people have control of their behavior, can make choices about their lives, and are essentially responsible for solving their own problems (17)

hypnosis A state of heightened susceptibility to the suggestions of others (11)

hypochondriasis A constant fear of illness and misinterpretation of normal aches and pains (16)

hypothalamus Located below the thalamus of the brain, its major function is to maintain homeostasis (2, 9)

hypothesis A prediction that can be tested experimentally (1)

iconic memory The storage of visual information (6)

id The raw, unorganized, inherited part of personality whose purpose is to reduce tension created by biological drives and irrational impulses (14)

identical twins Twins with identical genetic makeup (12)

identification A child's attempt to be similar to his or her same-sex parent (14)

identity The distinguishing character of the individual: who each of us is, what our roles are, and what we are capable of (13)

identity-versus-role-confusion stage According to Erikson, a time in adolescence of testing to determine one's own unique qualities (13)

idiographic approaches to personality A study of personality emphasizing what makes one person different from others and unique (14)

imaginal code Memory storage based on visual images (6)

immune system The body's natural defenses that fight disease (15)

implicit personality theories Theories reflecting our notions of what traits are found together in individuals (18)

impression formation The process by which an individual organizes information about another individual to form an overall impression of that person (18)

incentive An external stimulus anticipated as a reward which directs and energizes behavior (9)

incentive theory The theory explaining motivation in terms of external stimuli (9)

independent variable The variable that is manipulated in an experiment (1)

inducing structure problems Problems whose solution requires the identification of existing relationships among elements presented so as to construct a new relationship among them (7)

industrial-organizational psychology The branch of psychology that studies the psychology of the workplace, considering productivity, job satisfaction, and related issues (1, 20)

industry-versus-inferiority stage According to Erikson, the period during which children aged 6 to 12 years may develop positive social interactions with others or may feel inadequate and become less sociable (12)

inferential statistics The branch of statistics that uses data from samples to make predictions about the larger population from which the sample is drawn (A)

inferiority complex A phenomenon whereby adults have continuing feelings of weakness and insecurity (14)

inferred process A process, not directly observable, whose occurrence is revealed in changed behaviors (5)

informal groups Groups that develop as a result of the interests and needs of the individuals making up an organization (20)

information processing The way in which people take in, use, and store information (7)

information overload The phenomenon that occurs in situations in which we receive so much physical and visual stimulation that we are unable to process and comprehend important information around us (21)

informed consent A document signed by subjects prior to an experiment in which the study and conditions and risks of participation are explained (1)

ingroup-outgroup bias The tendency to hold less favorable opinions about groups to which we do not belong (outgroups), while holding more favorable opinions about groups to which we do belong (ingroups) (18)

ingroups Groups to which an individual belongs (18)

inhibited ejaculation A male's inability to ejaculate when he wants to, if at all (10)

inhibitory message A chemical secretion that prevents a receiving neuron from firing (2)

initiative-versus-guilt stage According to Erikson, the period during which children aged 3 to 6 years experience conflict between independence of action and the sometimes negative results of that action (12)

innate Inborn, biologically determined (12)

inner ear The interior structure that changes sound vibrations into a form that can be transmitted to the brain (13)

inoculation Exposure to arguments opposing one's beliefs, making the subject more resistant to later attempts to change those beliefs (19)

inoculation (for stress) Preparation for stress before it is encountered (15)

insight Sudden awareness of the relationships among various elements that had previously appeared to be independent of one another (7)

insomnia An inability to get to sleep or stay asleep (11)

instinct An inborn pattern of behavior that is biologically determined (9)

instinctual drives Infantile wishes, desires, demands, and needs hidden from conscious awareness (14)

intellectually gifted Individuals characterized by higher-than-average intelligence, with IQ scores above 130 (8)

intelligence The capacity to understand the world, think rationally, and use resources effectively when faced with challenges (8)

intelligence quotient (IQ) score A measure of intelligence that takes into account an individual's mental and chronological ages (8)

intelligence tests A battery of measures to determine a person's level of intelligence (8)

intensity A feature of wave patterns that allows us to distinguish between loud and soft sounds (3)

interactionist One believing that a combination of genetic predisposition and environmental influences determine the course of development (12)

interference The phenomenon by which recall is hindered because of other information in memory (6)

interneurons Neurons that transmit information between sensory and motor neurons (2)

interpersonal attraction Positive feelings for others (19)

interpsychic phase The first phase in the decline of a relationship, characterized by a focus on the other person's behavior and an evaluation of the extent to which this behavior provides reason for terminating the relationship (18)

intimacy-versus-isolation stage According to Erikson, a period during early adulthood on developing close relationships (13)

intoxication A state of drunkenness (11)

intrinsic motivation Motivation by which people participate in an activity for their own enjoyment, not for the reward it will get them (9)

introspection A method in which subjects are asked to describe in detail their thoughts and feelings (1)

introversion-extroversion According to Eysenck, a dimension of personality traits encompassing the shyest to the most sociable people (14)

iris The colored part of the eye (3)

James-Lange theory of emotion The belief that emotional experience is a reaction to bodily events occurring as a result of an external situation ("I feel sad because I am crying") (9)

job clarity The degree of explicitness of the rules which determine what is expected of a worker (20)

job enrichment Techniques for improving the quality of the activities involved in a job (20)

just noticeable difference (See difference threshold) (3)

keyword technique The pairing of a foreign word with a common, similar-sounding English word to aid in remembering the new word (6)

Korsakoff's syndrome A disease among long-term alcoholics involving memory impairment (6)

language The systematic arrangement of symbols to convey meaning (7)

language-acquisition device A neural system of the brain hypothesized to permit understanding of language (7)

lanugo A soft fuzz covering the body of a newborn (12)

latency period According to Freud, the period, between the phallic stage and puberty, during which children's sexual concerns are temporarily put aside (14)

latent content The "true" message hidden within a dream (11, 17)

latent learning Learning in which a new behavior is acquired but not readily demonstrated until reinforcement is provided (5)

lateral hypothalamus The part of the brain which, when damaged, results in an organism's starving to death (9)

lateralization The dominance of one hemisphere of the brain in specific functions (2)

law of effect Thorndike's theory that responses that satisfy are more likely to be repeated, and those that don't satisfy will be discontinued (5)

learned helplessness An organism's learned belief that it has no control of the environment (5, 15)

learned-inattention theory (of schizophrenia) A theory that suggests that schizophrenia is a learned behavior consisting of a set of inappropriate responses to social stimuli (16)

learning A relatively permanent change in behavior brought about by experience (5)

least-restrictive environment The official phrase from PL94-142 that guarantees the right of full education for retarded people in an environment that is most similar to the educational environment of typical children (8)

lens The part of the eye located behind the pupil that bends rays of light to focus them on the retina (3)

levels-of-processing theory The theory which suggests that the way information is initially perceived and learned determines recall (6)

light The stimulus that produces vision (3)

light adaptation The eye's temporary insensitivity to light dimmer than that to which it has become accustomed (3)

limbic system The part of the brain located outside the "new brain" that controls eating and reproduction (2)

linear perspective The phenomenon by which distant objects appear to be closer together than nearer objects (9)

linguistic code Memory storage relying on language (7)

linguistic-relativity hypothesis The theory claiming that language shapes and may even determine the way people perceive and understand the world (7)

lithium A drug used in the treatment of bipolar disorders (17)

lobes Areas of the brain (2)

longitudinal research A research method which investigates behavior as subjects age (12)

long-term memory The storage of information on a relatively permanent basis, although retrieval may be difficult (6)

loss-of-control explanation of crowding An explanation that suggests that the unpleasantness of crowding is due to the feeling that people cannot control their surroundings (21)

lysergic acid diethylamide (LSD) One of the most powerful hallucinogens, affecting the operation of neurotransmitters in the brain and causing brain cell activity to be altered (11)

magnitude The strength of a stimulus (3)

mainstreaming The integration of retarded people into regular classroom situations (8)

major depression A severe form of depression that interferes with concentration, decision making, and sociability (16)

mania An extended state of intense euphoria and elation (16)

manifest content of dreams According to Freud, the surface description of dreams (11, 17)

mantra A sound, word, or syllable repeated over and over to take one into a meditative state (11)

marijuana A common hallucinogen, usually smoked (11)

masturbation Sexual self-stimulation (10)

maturation The unfolding of biologically predetermined patterns of behavior due to aging (5, 12)

mean The average of all scores, arrived at by adding scores together and dividing by the number of scores (A)

means-ends analysis Repeated testing to determine and reduce the distance between real and desired outcomes in problem solving (7)

median The point in a distribution of scores that divides the distribution exactly in half when the scores are listed in numerical order (A)

medical model of abnormality The model that suggests that when an individual displays symptoms of abnormal behavior, the cause is physiological (16)

medical student's disease The feeling that symptoms and illnesses about which one studies are characteristic of oneself (16)

meditation A learned technique for refocusing attention that brings about an altered state of consciousness (11)

medulla The part of the central core of the brain that controls functions such as breathing and heartbeat (2)

memory The capacity to record, retain, and retrieve information (6)

memory trace A physical change in the brain corresponding to the memory of material (6)

menopause The point at which women stop menstruating, generally at around age 45 (13)

mental age The typical intelligence level found for people at a given chronological age (8)

mental retardation A significantly subaverage level of intellectual functioning accompanying deficits in adaptive behavior (9)

mental set The tendency for old patterns of problem solving to persist (5)

metabolism Rate at which energy is produced and expended by the body (9)

metacognition An awareness and understanding of one's own cognitive processes (12)

methadone A chemical used to detoxify heroin addicts (11)

method of loci Assigning words or ideas to places, thereby improving recall of the words by envisioning those places (6)

middle ear A tiny chamber containing three bones—the hammer, the anvil, and the stirrup—which transmit vibrations to the oval window (3)

midlife crisis The negative feelings that accompany the realization that we have not accomplished in life what we had hoped to (13)

midlife transition Beginning around the age of 40, a period during which we come to the realization that life is finite (13)

mild retardation Mental retardation characterized by an IQ between 55 and 69 and the ability to function independently (8)

Minnesota Multiphasic Personality Inventory (MMPI) A test used to identify people with psychological difficulties (14)

mnemonics Formal techniques for organizing material to increase the likelihood of its being remembered (6)

mode The most frequently occurring score in a set of scores (A)

model A person serving as an example to an observer; if a model's behavior is rewarded, the observer may imitate that behavior (5, 12)

modeling Imitating the behavior of others (models) (5, 12)

moderate retardation Mental retardation characterized by an IQ between 40 and 54 (8)

monocular cues Signals that allow us to perceive distance and depth with just one eye (4)

mood disorders Disturbances severe enough to interfere with normal living (16)

Moro (startle) reflex The reflex action in which an infant, in response to a sudden noise, flings it arms, arches its back, and spreads its fingers (12)

morphine Derived from the poppy flower, a powerful depressant that reduces pain and induces sleep (11)

motion parallax The movement of the image of objects on the retina as the head moves, providing a monocular cue to distance (11)

motivation The factors that direct and energize behavior (9)

motives Desired goals that prompt behavior (9)

motor code Memory storage based on physical activities (6)

Müller-Lyer illusion An illusion in which two lines of the same length appear to be of different lengths because of the direction of the arrows at the ends of each line; the line with arrows pointing out appears shorter than the line with arrows pointing in (4)

multiple personality A disorder in which a person displays characteristics of two or more distinct personalities (16)

myelin sheath An axon's protective coating, made of fat and protein (2)

narcissistic personality disorder A personality disorder characterized by an exaggerated sense of self and an inability to experience empathy for others (17)

narcolepsy An uncontrollable need to sleep for short periods during the day (11)

natural concepts Simple concepts that represent familiar objects and share a set of characteristic features (7)

natural mapping A design relying on an analogy between a device's physical appearance and the actions required to operate it (21)

naturalistic observation Observation without interference, in which the researcher records information about a naturally occurring situation in a way that does not influence the situation (1)

nature-nurture question The issue of the degree to which environment and heredity influence behavior (12)

need-complementarity hypothesis The hypothesis that people are attracted to others who fulfill their needs (19)

need for achievement A stable, learned characteristic in which satisfaction comes from striving for and achieving a level of excellence (9)

need for affiliation A need to establish and maintain relationships with other people (9)

need for power A tendency to want to make an impression or have an impact on others in order to be seen as a powerful individual (9)

negative reinforcer A stimulus whose removal is reinforcing, leading to a greater probability that the response bringing about this removal will occur again (5)

negative relationship A relationship established by data that shows high values of one variable corresponding with low values of the other (A)

neo-Freudian psychoanalysts (neo-Freudians) Theorists who place greater emphasis than did Freud on the functions of the ego and its influence on our daily activities (14)

neonate A newborn child (12)

nervous system The brain and its pathways extending throughout the body (2)

neurometrics The study of brain electrical activity, allowing for the comparison of brain functioning in normal and disordered individuals (2)

neurons The basic elements of the nervous system that carry messages (2)

neuroscientists Individuals from diverse fields who study the nervous system (1)

neurotic anxiety Anxiety caused when irrational impulses from the id threaten to become uncontrollable (14)

neuroticism-stability Eysenck's personality spectrum encompassing people from the moodiest to the most even-tempered (14)

neurotic symptoms According to Freud, abnormal behavior brought about by anxiety associated with unwanted conflicts and impulses (16)

neurotransmitter A chemical, secreted when a nerve impulse comes to the end of an axon, that carries messages between neurons (2)

neutral stimulus A stimulus that, before conditioning, has no effect on the desired response (5)

nicotine A stimulant present in cigarettes (11)

nightmares Unusually frightening dreams (11)

night terrors Profoundly frightening nightmares which wake the dreamer (11)

noise Background stimulation that interferes with the perception of other stimuli (3)

nominal group technique A technique of decision making in which group members write down ideas in private and then present arguments for the ideas to the group, with evaluation made by secret ballot only after all ideas have been presented and discussed one at a time (20)

nomothetic approaches to personality A study of personality accentuating the broad uniformities across behavior (14)

nondirective counseling A therapeutic technique in which the therapist creates a warm, supportive environment to allow the client to better understand and work out his or her problems (17)

normal distribution A distribution of

scores that produces a bell-shaped, symmetrical curve (A)

norms Informal rules regarding the appropriateness of behavior followed by group members (20)

norms (for tests) Standards of test performance (14)

nuclear magnetic resonance (NMR) scan A scan produced by a magnetic field which shows brain structure in great detail (2)

obesity The state of being more than 20 percent above the average weight for a person of a particular height (9)

obedience A change in behavior due to the commands of others (19)

object permanence The awareness that objects do not cease to exist if they are out of sight (12)

observational learning Learning through observation of others (models) (5, 14, 17)

obsession A thought or idea that keeps recurring (16)

obsessive-compulsive disorder A disorder characterized by obsessions or compulsions (16)

occipital lobes The structures of the brain lying behind the temporal lobes (2)

Oedipal conflict A child's sexual interests in his or her opposite-sex parent, typically resolved through identification with the same-sex parent (14)

olfactory cells The receptor cells of the nose (3)

operant The learning process involving one's operation of the environment (see operant conditioning) (5)

operant conditioning Learning that occurs as a result of certain positive or negative consequences; the organism operates on its environment in order to produce a result (5)

operationalization The process of translating a hypothesis into experimental procedures (1)

opiate receptor A neuron that acts to reduce the experience of pain (2)

opponent-process theory The theory that suggests that increases in arousal produce a calming reaction in the nervous system, and vice versa (9)

opponent-process theory of color vision The theory that suggests that members of pairs of different receptor cells are linked together to work in opposition to each other (3)

optic chiasma A point between and behind the eyes at which nerve impulses from the optic nerves are reversed and "righted" in the brain (3)

optic nerve A bundle of ganglion axons in the back of the eyeball that carry visual information to the brain (3)

oral stage According to Freud, a stage from birth to 12–18 months, in which an infant's center of pleasure is the mouth (14)

organic mental disorders Problems having a purely biological basis (16)

organizational socialization The process by which a worker learns to behave like others in the organization and to adopt similar attitudes (20)

organizations Groups of people working together to attain common goals (20)

orgasm The peak of sexual excitement during which time rhythmic muscular contractions occur in the genitals (10)

otoliths Crystals in the semicircular canals that sense body acceleration (3)

outer ear The visible part of the ear that acts as a sound collector (3)

outgroups Groups to which an individual does not belong (18)

oval window A thin membrane between the middle ear and the inner ear that transmits vibrations while increasing their strength (3)

ovaries The female reproductive organs (10)

overlearning Rehearsing material beyond the point of mastery to improve long-term recall (6)

overregularization Applying rules of speech in instances in which they are inappropriate (7)

ovulation The monthly release of an egg from an ovary (10)

panic attack Sudden anxiety characterized by heart palpitations, shortness of breath, sweating, faintness, and great fear (16)

panic disorder Anxiety that manifests itself in the form of panic attacks (16)

parallel search Searching the memory for stored information all at once (6)

paranoid schizophrenia Mental disorder characterized by delusions of persecution or of greatness; loss of judgment and unpredictable behavior (16)

paraplegia The inability, as a result of injury to the spinal cord, to move any muscles in the lower half of the body (2)

parasympathetic division The part of the autonomic division of the peripheral nervous system that calms the body, bringing functions back to normal after an emergency has passed (2)

parietal lobes The brain structure to the rear of the frontal lobes; the center for bodily sensations (2)

partial reinforcement The reinforcing of a behavior some, but not all of the time (5)

participative decision making A decision-making technique in which the people involved in implementing a decision are involved in making it (20)

passionate (or romantic) love A state of intense absorption in someone that is characterized by physiological arousal, psychological interest, and caring for another's needs (19)

penis The primary male sex organ (10)

penis envy According to Freud, a girl's wish, developing around age 3, that she had a penis (14)

perception The sorting out, interpretation, analysis, and integration of stimuli from our sensory organs (4)

perceptual constancy The phenomenon by which physical objects are perceived as unvarying despite changes in their appearance or the surrounding environment (4)

peripheral nervous system All parts of the nervous system except the brain and the spinal cord (includes somatic and autonomic divisions) (2)

peripheral route processing Message interpretation characterized by consideration of the source and related general information rather than of the message itself (18)

peripheral vision The ability to see objects behind the eye's main center of focus (3)

permissive parents Parents who are lax, inconsistent, and undemanding, yet warm toward their children (12)

personality The sum total of characteristics that differentiate people, or the stability in a person's behavior across different situations (14)

personality disorder A mental disorder characterized by a set of inflexible, maladaptive personality traits that keep a person from functioning properly in society (16)

personality psychology The branch of psychology that studies consistency and change in people's behavior and the characteristics that differentiate people (1)

personal stressors Major life events, such as the death of a family member, that have immediate negative consequences which generally fade with time (15)

phallic stage According to Freud, a period beginning around age 3 during which a child's interest focuses on the genitals (14)

phencyclidine (PCP) A powerful hallucinogen that alters brain-cell activity (11)

phenylketonuria (PKU) The inability to produce an enzyme that resists certain poisons, causing profound mental retardation (12)

pheromones Chemicals that produce a reaction in other members of a species (3)

phobias Intense, irrational fears of specific objects or situations (16)

phobic disorder Disorders characterized by unrealistic fears (phobias) that may keep people from carrying out routine daily behaviors (16)

phonemes The smallest units of sound used to form words (7)

phonology The study of the sounds we make when we speak and of how we use those sounds to produce meaning by forming them into words (7)

pitch The "highs" and "lows" in sound (3)

pituitary gland The "master gland," the major component of the endocrine system, which secretes hormones that control growth (2)

placebo A biologically ineffective pill used in an experiment to keep subjects, and sometimes experimenters, from knowing whether or not the subjects have received a behavior-altering drug (1)

place theory of hearing The theory that states that different frequencies are responded to by different areas of the basilar membrane (3)

plateau phase A period in which the maximum level of arousal is attained, the penis and clitoris swell with blood, and the body prepares for orgasm (10)

pleasure principle The principle by which the id operates, in which the person seeks the immediate reduction of tension and the maximization of satisfaction (14)

Poggendorf illusion An illusion involving a line that passes diagonally through two parallel lines (4)

Pollyanna effect The tendency to rate others in a generally positive manner (18)

polygraph An electronic device that measures bodily changes which may signal that a person is lying; often called a lie detector (9)

pons The part of the brain that joins the halves of the cerebellum, transmitting motor information to coordinate muscles and integrate movement between the right and left sides of the body (2)

population All the members of the group being studied (A)

positive reinforcer A stimulus added to the environment that brings about an increase in the response that preceded it (5)

positive relationship A relationship established by data that shows high values of one variable corresponding with high values of another, and low values of the first variable corresponding with low values of the other (A)

positron emission tomography (PET) scan A scan technique which indicates how the brain is functioning at a given moment (2)

posttraumatic stress syndrome A phenomenon in which victims of major catastrophes reexperience the original stress event and associated feelings in flashbacks or dreams (15)

practical intelligence A person's style of thought and approach to problem solving, which may differ from traditional measures of intelligence (8)

predisposition model (of schizophre-

nia) A model that suggests that individuals may inherit a predisposition toward schizophrenia that makes them particularly vulnerable to stressful factors in the environment (16)

prefrontal lobotomy The surgical destruction of certain areas of a patient's frontal lobes to improve the control of emotionality (17)

premature ejaculation A male's inability to delay ejaculation (10)

preoperational stage According to Piaget, the period from 2 to 7 years of age that is characterized by language development (12)

primary drives Biological needs such as hunger, thirst, fatigue, and sex (9)

primary erectile failure A long-term inability to achieve or maintain an erection (10)

primary orgasmic dysfunction A female's long-term inability to achieve orgasm (10)

primary reinforcer A reward that satisfies a biological need (e.g., hunger or thirst) and works naturally (5)

proactive interference The phenomenon by which information stored in memory interferes with recall material learned later (6)

problem-focused coping The management of a stressful stimulus as a way of dealing with stress (15)

process schizophrenia One course of schizophrenia in which symptoms begin early in life and develop slowly and subtly (16)

profound retardation mental retardation characterized by an IQ below 25 and an inability to function independently (8)

program evaluation The assessment of large-scale programs to determine their effectiveness in meeting their goals (1)

programmed instruction Development of learning by building gradually on basic knowledge, with review and reinforcement when appropriate (5)

projection A defense mechanism in which people attribute their own inadequacies or faults to someone else (14)

projective personality test An ambiguous stimulus presented to a person for the purpose of determining personality characteristics (14)

prosocial behavior Helping behavior (19)

Protestant work ethic The notion that work is important in and of itself (20)

prototypes Typical, highly representative examples of a concept (7)

proximity The tendency to group together those elements that are close together (4)

psychoactive drugs Drugs that influence a person's emotions, perceptions, and behavior (11)

psychoactive substance-use disorder Disordered behavior involving drug abuse (16)

psychoanalysis Psychodynamic therapy that involves frequent sessions and often lasts for many years (17)

psychoanalysis Physicians or psychologists who specialize in psychoanalysis (17)

psychoanalytic model of abnormality The model that suggests that abnormality stems from childhood conflicts over opposing wishes (16)

psychoanalytic theory Freud's theory that unconscious forces act as determinants of personality (14)

psychodynamic model The psychological model based on the belief that behavior is brought about by unconscious inner forces over which an individual has little control (1)

psychodynamic therapy Therapy based on the notion that the basic sources of abnormal behavior are unresolved past conflicts and anxiety (17)

psychogenic amnesia A failure to remember past experience (16)

psychogenic fugue An amnesiac condition in which people take sudden, impulsive trips, sometimes assuming a new identity (16)

psychological tests Standard measures devised to objectively assess behavior (14)

psychology The scientific study of behavior and mental processes (1)

psychophysics The study of the relationship between the physical nature of stimuli and a person's sensory responses to them (3)

psychosocial development Development of individuals' interactions and understanding of each other and of their knowledge and understanding of themselves as members of society (12)

psychosomatic disorders Medical problems caused by an interaction of psychological, emotional, and physical difficulties (15)

psychosurgery Brain surgery, once used to alleviate symptoms of mental disorder but rarely used today (17)

psychotherapy The process in which a patient (client) and a professional attempt to remedy the client's psychological difficulties (17)

puberty The period during which maturation of the sexual organs occurs (13)

punishment An unpleasant or painful stimulus that is added to the environment after a certain behavior occurs, decreasing the likelihood that the behavior will occur again (5)

pupil A dark hole in the center of the eye's iris which changes size as the amount of incoming light changes (3)

random assignment to condition The assignment of subjects to given conditions on a chance basis alone (1)

range The highest score in a distribution minus the lowest score (A)

rape The act whereby one person forces another to submit to sexual activity (10)

rapid eye movement (REM) sleep Sleep occupying around 20 percent of an adult's sleeping time, characterized by increased heart rate, blood pressure, and breathing rate; erections; eye movements; and the experience of dreaming (11)

rational-emotive therapy Psychotherapy based on Ellis's suggestion that the goal of therapy should be to restructure one's beliefs into a more realistic, rational, and logical system (17)

rationalization A defense mechanism whereby people justify a negative situation in a way that protects their self-esteem (14)

reactive schizophrenia One course of schizophrenia in which the onset of symptoms is sudden and conspicuous (16)

reality principle The principle by which the ego operates, in which instinctual energy is restrained in order to maintain an individual's safety and integration into society (14)

rebound effect An increase in REM sleep after one has been deprived of it (11)

recall drawing from memory a specific piece of information for a specific purpose (6)

reciprocal concessions A phenomenon in which requesters are perceived as compromising their initial request, thereby inviting a compromise from the individual being asked to comply (19)

reciprocity-of-liking effect The tendency to like those who like us (19)

recognition Acknowledging prior exposure to a given stimulus, rather than recalling the information from memory (6)

reflexes Unlearned, involuntary responses to certain stimuli (12)

refractory period Entered by a male after the resolution stage, a temporary period during which he cannot be sexually aroused again (10)

regression Behavior reminiscent of an earlier stage of development, carried out in order to have fewer demands put upon oneself (14)

rehearsal The transfer of material from short- to long-term memory via repetition (6)

reinforcer Any stimulus that increases the probability that a preceding behavior will be repeated (5)

relative refractory period The period during which a neuron, not yet having returned to its resting state, requires more than the normal stimulus to be set off (2)

relative size The phenomenon by which, if two objects are the same size, the one that makes a smaller image on the retina is perceived to be farther away (4)

reliability Consistency in the measurements made by a test (14)

replication The repetition of an experiment in order to verify the results of the original experiment (1)

representativeness heuristic A rule in which people and things are judged by the degree to which they represent a certain category (7)

repression The primary defense mechanism, in which unacceptable or unpleasant id impulses are pushed back into the unconscious (14)

research Systematic inquiry aimed at discovering knowledge (1)

resistance An inability or unwillingness to discuss or reveal particular memories, thoughts, or motivations (17)

resistance stage The second stage of Selye's general adaptation syndrome: coping with the stressor (10)

resolution stage The final stage of sexual arousal during which the body returns to its normal state (2)

resting state The nonfiring state of a neuron when the charge equals about −70 millivolts (2)

reticular formation A group of nerve cells in the brain that arouses the body to prepare it for appropriate action and screens out background stimuli (2)

retina The part of the eye that converts the electromagnetic energy of light into useful information for the brain (3)

retrieval The process by which material in memory storage is located, brought into awareness, and used (6)

retrieval cue A stimulus such as a word, smell, or sound that allows one to more easily recall information located in long-term memory (6)

retroactive interference The phenomenon by which new information interferes with the recall of information learned earlier (6)

retrograde amnesia Memory loss of occurrences prior to some event (6)

reuptake The reabsorption of neurotransmitters by a terminal button (2)

reverse discrimination Behavior in which people prejudiced toward a group compensate for their prejudice by treating the group's members more favorably than others (18)

rewards-costs approach The notion that, in a situation requiring help, a bystander's perceived rewards must outweigh the costs if helping is to occur (19)

rhodopsin A complex reddish-purple substance that changes when energized by light, causing a chemical reaction (3)

rods Long, cylindrical, light-sensitive receptors in the retina that perform well in poor light but are largely insensitive to color and small details (3)

role conflict A conflict which arises when an individual is faced with two or more sets of demands that contradict one another (20)

rooting reflex A neonate's tendency to turn its head toward things that touch its cheek (12)

Rorschach test A test consisting of inkblots of indefinite shapes, the interpretation of which is used to assess personality characteristics (14)

rubella German measles; when contracted by pregnant women, it can cause severe birth defects (12)

sample A subgroup of a population of interest (A)

scatterplot A means of graphically illustrating the relationship between two variables (A)

Schachter-Singer theory of emotion The belief that emotions are determined jointly by a nonspecific kind of physiological arousal and its interpretation, based on environmental cues (9)

schedules of reinforcement The frequency and timing of reinforcement following desired behavior (5)

schemas Sets of cognitions about people and social experiences (18)

schizophrenia A class of disorders characterized by a severe distortion of reality, resulting in antisocial behavior, silly or obscene behavior, hallucinations, and disturbances in movement (16)

school psychology Branch of psychology that considers the academic and emotional problems of elementary and secondary school students (1)

secondary drives Drives in which no biological need is fulfilled (e.g., need for achievement) (9)

secondary erectile failure A male's temporary inability to achieve or maintain an erection (10)

secondary orgasmic dysfunction A female's temporary inability to achieve orgasm or her ability to achieve orgasm only under certain conditions (such as masturbation) (10)

secondary reinforcer A stimulus that becomes reinforcing by its association with a primary reinforcer (e.g., money, which allows us to obtain food, a primary reinforcer) (5)

secondary traits Less important personality traits (e.g., preferences for certain clothes or movies) that do not affect behavior as much as central and cardinal traits do (14)

selective attention The perceptual process of choosing a stimulus to attend to (4)

selective exposure An attempt to minimize dissonance by exposing oneself only to information that supports one's choice (18)

self-actualization In Maslow's theory, a state of self-fulfillment in which people realize their highest potential (9, 14)

self-concept The impression one holds of oneself (14)

self-fulfilling prophecy An expectation about the occurrence of an event or behavior that increases the likelihood that the event or behavior will happen (18)

self-perception theory Bem's theory that people form attitudes by observing their own behavior and applying the same principles to themselves as they do to others (18)

self-report measures A method of gathering data about people by asking them questions about a sample of their behavior (14)

semantic memories Stored, organized facts about the world (e.g., mathematical and historical data) (6)

semantics The rules governing the meaning of words and sentences (7)

semen A fluid containing sperm that is ejaculated through the penis during orgasm (10)

semicircular canals part of the inner ear containing fluid that moves when the body moves to control balance (3)

senility A broad, imprecise term used in reference to elderly people who experience progressive deterioration of mental abilities, including memory loss, confusion of time and place, and general disorientation (13)

sensate focus A method of sexual therapy in which attention is directed away from intercourse and toward other pleasurable behaviors (10)

sensation The process by which an organism responds to a stimulus (3)

sensorimotor stage According to Piaget, the stage from birth to 2 years during which a child has little competence in representing the environment using images, language, or other symbols (12)

sensory area The site in the brain of the tissue that corresponds to each of the senses, the degree of sensitivity relating to amount of tissue (2)

sensory memory The initial, short-lived storage of information recorded as a meaningless stimulus (6)

sensory (afferent) neurons Neurons that transmit information from the body to the nervous system (2)

serial reproduction The passage of interpretive information from person to person, often resulting in inaccuracy through personal bias and misinterpretation (6)

serial search A method of retrieving information from memory one piece at a time (6)

severe retardation Mental retardation characterized by an IQ between 25 and 39 and difficulty in functioning independently (8)

sexism Negative attitudes toward a person based on that person's sex (10)

sexual disorders A form of abnormal behavior in which one's sexual activity is unsatisfactory (10)

sexually transmitted disease (STD) A disease spread primarily through sexual contact (10)

shadowing A technique used during dichotic listening in which a subject is asked to repeat one of the messages aloud as it comes into one ear (4)

shaping The process of teaching a complex behavior by rewarding closer and closer approximations of the desired behavior (5)

short-term memory The storage of information for fifteen to twenty-five seconds (6)

sickle-cell anemia A disease of the blood that affects about 10 percent of America's black population (12)

signal detection theory The theory that addresses the questions of whether a person can detect a stimulus and whether a stimulus is actually present at all (3)

significant outcome An outcome expected to occur by chance less than 5 percent of the time (A)

similarity The tendency to group to-gether those elements that are similar in appearance (4)

simplicity The tendency to perceive a pattern in the most basic, straightforward, organized manner possible—the overriding gestalt principle (4)

situational causes of behavior Causes of behavior that are based on environmental factors (18)

skewed distribution A distribution that is not normal and therefore creates a curve that is not symmetrical (A)

skin senses The senses that include touch, pressure, temperature, and pain (3)

sleep apnea A sleep disorder characterized by difficulty in breathing and sleeping simultaneously (11)

soap opera effect The phenomenon by which memory of a prior event involving a person is more reliable when we understand that person's motivations (6)

social clock The psychic timepiece that indicates major milestones in adult life (12)

social cognition The processes that underlie our understanding of the social world (18)

social influence The area of social psychology concerned with situations in which the actions of an individual or group affect the behavior of others (19)

socialization The developmental process by which an individual learns the rules and norms of appropriate behavior (10, 20)

social learning theory (of personality) The theory that suggests that personality develops through observational learning (17)

social phase The third phase in the decline of a relationship in which there is public acknowledgment that the relationship is being dissolved, and others are given an account of events that led to the relationship's termination (18)

social psychology The branch of psychology that studies how people's thoughts, feelings, and actions are affected by others (1, 18)

social support Knowledge of being part of a mutual network of caring, interested others (19)

sociocultural model of abnormality The model that suggests that people's behavior, both normal and abnormal, is shaped by family, society, and cultural influences (16)

social supporter A person who shares an unpopular opinion or attitude of another group member, thereby encouraging nonconformity (19)

somatic division The part of the nervous system that controls voluntary movements of the skeletal muscles (2)

somatoform disorder Psychological difficulties that take on a physical (somatic) form (16)

somatosensory area The area within the cortex corresponding to the sense of touch (2)

sound The movement of air molecules brought about by the vibration of an object (3)

source traits The sixteen basic dimensions of personality that Cattell identified as the root of all behavior (14)

spinal cord A bundle of nerves running along the spine, carrying messages between the brain and the body (2)

split-brain patient A person who suffers from independent functioning of the two halves of the brain, as a result of which the sides of the body work in disharmony (2)

spontaneous recovery The reappearance of a previously extinguished response after a period of time during which the conditioned stimulus has been absent (5)

spontaneous remission Recovery without treatment (17)

stage 1 sleep The state of transition between wakefulness and sleep (11)

stage 2 sleep A sleep deeper than that of stage 1, characterized by sleep spindles (11)

stage 3 sleep Sleep characterized by slow brain waves, with greater peaks and valleys in the wave pattern (11)

stage 4 sleep The deepest stage of sleep, during which we are least responsive to outside stimulation (11)

standard deviation An index of how far an average score in a distribution of scores deviates from the distribution's center (A)

Stanford-Binet test A test of intelligence that includes a series of items varying in nature according to the age of the person being tested (8)

statistics The branch of mathematics concerned with collecting, organizing, analyzing, and drawing conclusions from numerical data (A)

status The evaluation by others of the roles we play in society (19)

stereotype A kind of schema in which beliefs and expectations about members of a group are held simply on the basis of their membership in that group (18)

stimulants Drugs that affect the central nervous system, causing increased heart rate, blood pressure, and muscle tension (11)

stimulus A source of physical energy that activates a sense organ (3)

stimulus control training Training in which an organism is reinforced in the presence of a certain specific stimulus, but not in its absence (5)

stimulus discrimination The process by which an organism learns to differentiate among stimuli, restricting its response to one in particular (5)

stimulus generalization Response to a stimulus similar to but different from a conditioned stimulus; the more similar the two stimuli, the more likely generalization is to occur (5)

stimulus-overload explanation of crowding An explanation based on the fact that stress can lead to withdrawal from the situation (21)

stirrup A tiny bone in the middle of the ear that transfers vibrations to the oval window (3)

storage The location in the memory system in which material is saved (6)

stress The response to events that are threatening or challenging (15)

stressors Circumstances that produce threats to our well-being (15)

Stroop task An exercise requiring the division of our attention between two competing stimuli—the meaning of words and the colors in which they are written (7)

structuralism An early approach to psychology which focused on the fundamental elements underlying thoughts and ideas (1)

structure-of-intellect model A model of intelligence based on performance along three different dimensions: task content, task requirements, and product (8)

subject A participant in research (1)

subject expectations A subject's interpretation of what behaviors or responses are expected in an experiment (1)

sublimation A defense mechanism, considered healthy by Freud, in which a person diverts unwanted impulses into socially acceptable thoughts, feelings, or behaviors (14)

sucking reflex A reflex that prompts an infant to suck at things that touch its lips (12)

sudden infant death syndrome A disorder in which seemingly healthy infants die in their sleep (11)

superego The part of personality that represents the morality of society as presented by parents, teachers, and others (14)

superstitious behavior The mistaken belief that particular ideas, objects, or behavior will cause certain events to occur, learning based on the coincidental association between the idea, object, or behavior and subsequent reinforcement (5)

surface traits According to Cattell, clusters of a person's related behavior that can be observed in a given situation (14)

survey research Sampling a group of people by assessing their behavior, thoughts, or attitudes, then generalizing the findings to a larger population (1)

sympathetic division The part of the autonomic division of the peripheral nervous system that prepares the body to respond in stressful emergency situations (2)

synapse The gap between neurons through which chemical messages are communicated (2)

syntax The rules that indicate how words are joined to form sentences (7)

syphilis An STD which, if untreated, may affect brain, heart, and developing fetus and can be fatal (10)

systematic desensitization A procedure in which a stimulus that evokes pleasant feelings is repeatedly paired with a stimulus that evokes anxiety in the hope that the anxiety will be alleviated (5, 17)

taste buds The location of the receptor cells of the tongue (3)

Tay-Sachs disease A genetic defect preventing the body from breaking down fat and typically causing death by the age of 3 or 4 (12)

telegraphic speech Sentences containing only the most essential words (7)

temperament Basic, innate dispositions (12)

temporal lobes The portion of the brain located beneath the frontal and parietal lobes (2)

terminal buttons Small branches at the end of an axon that relay messages to other cells (2)

testes The male reproductive organs responsible for secreting androgens (10)

thalamus The part of the brain's central core that transmits messages from the sense organs to the cerebral cortex and from the cerebral cortex to the cerebellum and medulla (2)

Thematic Apperception Test (TAT) A test consisting of a series of ambiguous pictures about which a person is asked to write a story, which is then taken to be a reflection of the writer's personality (9, 14)

theories Broad explanations and predictions concerning phenomena of interest (1)

time management A method of planning our time to make the most efficient use of it (5)

tip-of-the-tongue phenomenon The inability to recall information that one realizes one knows (6)

token system A procedure whereby a person is rewarded for performing certain desired behaviors (17)

top-down processing Perception guided by knowledge, experience, expectations, and motivations (4)

traits Enduring dimensions of personality characteristics differentiating people from one another (14)

trait theory A model that seeks to identify the basic traits necessary to describe personality (14)

transcendental meditation (TM) A popular type of meditation practiced by followers of Maharishi Mahesh Yogi (11)

transcutaneous electrical nerve stimulation A method of providing relief from pain by passing a low-voltage electric current through parts of the body (3)

transference A patient's transferal of certain strong feelings for others to the analyst (17)

transformation problems Problems to be solved using a series of methods to change an initial state into a goal state (7)

treatment The manipulation implemented by the experimenter to influence results in a segment of the experimental population (1)

treatment group The experimental group receiving the treatment, or manipulation (1)

triarchic theory of intelligence A theory suggesting three major aspects of intelligence: componential, experiential, and contextual (8)

trichromatic theory of color vision The theory that suggests that the retina has three kinds of cones, each responding to a specific range of wavelengths, perception of color being influenced by the relative strength with which each is activated (3)

trust-versus-mistrust stage According to Erikson, the first stage of psychosocial development, occurring from birth to 18 months of age, during which time infants develop feelings of trust or lack of trust (12)

tunnel vision An advanced stage of glaucoma in which vision is reduced to the narrow circle directly in front of the eye (3)

Type A behavior A pattern of behavior characterized by competitiveness, impatience, tendency toward frustration, and hostility (15)

Type B behavior A pattern of behavior characterized by noncompetitiveness, nonaggression, and patience in times of potential stress (15)

unconditional positive regard Supportive behavior from another individual, regardless of one's words or actions (14, 17)

unconditioned response (UCR) A response that is natural and needs no training (e.g., salivation at the smell of food) (5)

unconditioned stimulus (UCS) A stimulus that brings about a response without having been learned (5)

unconscious A part of the personality of which a person is unaware and which is a potential determinant of behavior (14)

unconscious inference theory A theory stating that unconscious inferences about an object's location are made on the basis of prior experience with the object's size (4)

universal grammar An underlying structure shared by all languages, the basis of Chomsky's theory that certain language characteristics are based in the brain's structure and are, therefore, common to all people (7)

uplifts Minor positive events that make one feel good (15)

vagina The female canal into which the penis enters during sexual intercourse (10)

validity The ability of a test to measure what it is supposed to measure (14)

variability The spread or dispersion of scores in a distribution (A)

variable A behavior or event that can be changed (1)

variable-interval schedule A schedule whereby reinforcement is given at various times, usually causing a behavior to be maintained more consistently (5)

variable-ratio schedule A schedule whereby reinforcement occurs after a varying number of responses rather than after a fixed number (5)

ventromedial hypothalamus The part of the brain which, when injured, results in extreme overeating (9)

vernix A white lubricant that covers a fetus, protecting it during birth (12)

vicarious learning Learning by observing others (18)

visability Visual cues to the operation of an object that are inherent in the object's design (21)

visceral experience The "gut" reaction experienced internally, triggering an emotion (see James-Lange theory) (9)

visual illusion A physical stimulus that consistently produces errors in perception (often called an optical illusion) (4)

visual spectrum The range of wavelengths to which humans are sensitive (3)

von Restorff effect The phenomenon by which distinctive stimuli are recalled more readily than less distinctive ones (6)

wear-and-tear theories of aging Theories that suggest that the body's mechanical functions cease efficient activity and, in effect, wear out (13)

Weber's law The principle that states that the just noticeable difference is a constant proportion of the magnitude of an initial stimulus (3)

Wechsler Adult Intelligence Scale—Revised (WAIS-R) A test of intelligence consisting of verbal and nonverbal performance sections, providing a relatively precise picture of a person's specific abilities (8)

Wechsler Intelligence Scale for Children—Revised (WISC-R) An intelligence test for children; see Wechsler Adult Intelligence Scale—Revised (8)

weight set point The particular level of weight the body strives to maintain (9)

Wernicke's aphasia A syndrome involving problems with understanding language, resulting in fluent but nonsensical speech (7)

Yerkes-Dodson law The theory that a particular level of motivational arousal produces optimal performance of a task (9)

Yerkish A language system, taught to chimpanzees, that consists of about 225 geometric symbols representing English words (7)

zygote The one-celled product of fertilization (12)

REFERENCES

Abrahamson, L. Y., Garber, J., & Seligman, M. E. P. (1980). Learned helplessness in humans: An attributional analysis. In J. Garber and M. E. P. Seligman (Eds.), *Human helplessness: Theory and applications.* New York: Academic Press.

Ackley, D. H., Hinton, G. E., & Sejnowski, T. J. (1985). A learning algorithm for Boltzmann Machines. *Cognitive Science, 9,* 147–169.

Adam, K., & Oswald, I. (1977). Sleep is for tissue restoration. *Journal of the Royal College of Physicians, 11,* 376–388.

Adams, M. J. (1989). Thinking skills curricula: Their promise and progress. *Educational Psychologist, 24,* 25–77.

Adams, P. R., & Adams, G. R. (1984). Mount Saint Helen's ashfall: Evidence for a disaster stress reaction. *American Psychologist, 39,* 252–260.

Adelmann, P. K., & Zajonc, R. B. (1989). Facial efference and the experience of emotion. *Annual Review of Psychology, 40,* 249–280.

Adler, J. (1984, April 23). The fight to conquer fear. *Newsweek,* pp. 66–72.

Adler, J. (1985, March 25). A teen-pregnancy epidemic. *Newsweek,* p. 90.

Adler, J. (1985, September 23). The AIDS conflict. *Newsweek,* pp. 18–24.

Aiello, J. R., Baum, A., & Gormley, F. P. (1980). *Social determinants of residential crowding.* Unpublished manuscript, Rutgers University, New Brunswick, NJ.

Ainsworth, M. D. (1989). Attachments beyond infancy. *American Psychologist, 44,* 709–716.

Ainsworth, M. D. S., Blehar, M. C., Waters, E., & Wall, S. (1978). *Patterns of attachment: A psychological study of the strange situation.* Hillsdale, New Jersey: Erlbaum.

Ajzen, I. (1988). *Attitudes, personality, and behavior.* Stratford, England: Open University Press.

Akmajian, A., Demers, R. A., & Harnish, R. M. (1984). *Linguistics.* Cambridge, MA: MIT Press.

Albee, G. W. (1978, February 12). I.Q. tests on trial. *New York Times,* p. E-13.

Aldwin, C. M., & Revenson, T. A. (1987). Does coping help? A reexamination of the relation between coping and mental health. *Journal of Personality and Social Psychology, 53,* 337–348.

Alkon, D. L. (1987). *Memory traces in the brain.* New York: Cambridge University Press.

Allen, M. (1988, January 25). When jurors are ordered to ignore testimony, they ignore the order. *Wall Street Journal,* p. 33.

Allen, V. L. (1965). Situational factors in conformity. In L. Berkowitz (Ed.), *Advances in experimental social psychology,* Vol. 1. New York: Academic Press.

Allen, V. L. (1975). Social support for nonconformity. In L. Berkowitz (Ed.), *Advances in experimental and social psychology* (Vol. 8). New York: Academic Press.

Allen Gutmacher Institute (1988). *Report on family planning practices.* New York: Allen Gutmacher Institute.

Allore, R., O'Hanlon, D., Price, R., Neilson, K., Willard, H. F., Cox, D. R., Marks, A., & Dunn, R. J. (1988, March 11). Gene encoding of the B-subunit of S100 protein is on chromosome 21: Implications for Down's syndrome. *Science, 239,* 1311–1313.

Allport, G. W., & Postman, L. J. (1958). The basic psychology of rumor. In E. D. Maccoby, T. M. Newcomb, & E. L. Hartley (Eds.), *Readings in social psychology* (3rd ed.). New York: Holt, Rinehart and Winston.

Allport, G. W. (1961). *Pattern and growth in personality.* New York: Holt, Rinehart and Winston.

Allport, G. W. (1966). Traits revisited. *American Psychologist, 21,* 1–10.

Allred, K. D., & Smith T. W. (1989). The hardy personality: Cognitive and physiological responses to evaluative threat. *Journal of Personality and Social Psychology, 56,* 257–266.

Alsop, R. (1988, May 13). Advertisers put consumers on the couch. *Wall Street Journal,* p. 21.

Altman, I. (1975). *The environment and social behavior.* Monterey, CA: Brooks/Cole.

Altman, I. (1987). Community psychology twenty years later: Still another crisis in psychology? *American Journal of Community Psychology, 15,* 613–627.

Altshuler, L. L., Conrad, A., Kovelman, J. A., & Scheibel, A. (1987). Hippocampal pyramidal cell orientation in schizophrenia. *Archives of General Psychiatry, 44,* 1094–1096.

Alwitt, L., & Mitchell, A. A. (1985). *Psychological processes and advertising effects: Theory, research, and applications.* Hillsdale, NJ: Erlbaum.

Amabile, T. M. (1985). Motivation and creativity: Effects of motivational orientation on creative writers. *Journal of Personality and Social Psychology, 48,* 393–399.

Amabile, T. M., Hennessey, B. A., & Grossman, B. S. (1986). Social influences on creativity: The effects of contracted for reward. *Journal of Personality and Social Psychology, 50,* 14–23.

American Psychological Association. (1980). *Careers in psychology.* Washington, DC: American Psychological Association.

American Psychological Association. (1981). *Ethical principles of psychologists.* Washington, DC: American Psychological Association.

American Psychological Association. (1986, March). Council resolution on polygraph tests. *APA Monitor.*

American Psychological Association (1987). *PsychINFO training manual.* Washington, DC: American Psychological Association.

American Psychological Association (1988). *Behavioral research with animals.* Washington, DC: American Psychological Association.

Amir, Y. (1976). The role of intergroup contact in change of prejudice and ethnic relations. In P. Katz (Ed.), *Towards the elimination of racism.* New York: Pergamon.

Anastasi, A. (1982). *Psychological testing* (5th ed.). New York: Macmillan.

Anderson, B. F. (1980). *The complete thinker: A handbook of techniques for creative and critical problem solving.* Englewood Cliffs, NJ: Prentice-Hall.

Anderson, C. A. (1989). Temperature and aggression: Ubiquitous effects of heat on occurrence of human violence. *Psychological Bulletin, 106,* 74–96.

Anderson, C. A., & Anderson, D. C. (1984). Ambient temperature and violent crime: Tests of the linear and curvilinear hypotheses. *Journal of Personality and Social Psychology, 46,* 91–97.

Anderson, E. (1987). Preoperative preparation for cardiac surgery facilitates recovery, reduces psychological distress, and reduces the incidence of acute postoperative hypertension. *Journal of Consulting and Clinical Psychology, 55,* 513–520.

Anderson, J. R., & Bower, G. H. (1972). Recognition and retrieval processes in free recall. *Psychological Review, 79,* 97–123.

Anderson, J. R., & Bower, G. H. (1973). *Human associative memory.* Washington, DC: Winston.

Anderson, N. H. (1974). Cognitive algebra integration theory applied to social attribution. In L. Berkowitz (Ed.), *Advances in experimental social psychology* (Vol. 7, pp. 1–101). New York: Academic Press.

Anderson, S. M., & Klatzky, R. L. (1987). Traits and social stereotypes: Levels of categorization in person perception. *Journal of Personality and Social Psychology, 53*, 235–246.

Andreasen, N. C. (1985). Positive vs. negative schizophrenia: A critical evaluation. *Schizophrenia, 11*, 380–389.

Andreasen, N. C. (1987). Creativity and mental illness: Prevalence rates in writers and their first-degree relatives. *American Journal of Psychiatry, 144*, 1288–1292.

Angell, M. (1985). Disease as a reflection of the psyche [editorial]. *New England Journal of Medicine, 312*, 1570–1572.

Angleitner, A., & Wiggins, J. S. (Eds.) (1986). *Personality assessment via questionnaires: Current issues in theory and measurement.* Berlin: Springer-Verlag.

Angoff, W. H. (1988). The nature-nurture debate, aptitudes, and group differences. *American Psychologist, 43*, 713–720.

Annett, M. (1985). *Left, right, hand, and brain: The right shift theory.* Hillsdale, NJ: Erlbaum.

Appleyard, D. (1976). *Planning a pluralistic city.* Cambridge, MA: MIT Press.

Apter, A., Galatzer, A., Beth-Halachmi, N., & Laron, Z. (1981). Self-image in adolescents with delayed puberty and growth retardation. *Journal of Youth and Adolescence, 10*, 501–505.

Arafat, I., & Cotton, W. L. (1974). Masturbation practices of males and females. *Journal of Sex Research, 10*, 293–307.

Archibald, W. P. (1974). Alternative explanations for the self-fulfilling prophecy. *Psychological Bulletin, 81*, 74–84.

Arena, J. M. (1984, April). A look at the opposite sex. *Newsweek on Campus*, p. 21.

Aronoff, J., Barclay, A. M., & Stevenson, L. A. (1988). The recognition of threatening facial stimuli. *Journal of Personality and Social Psychology, 54*, 647–655.

Aronson, E. (1988). *The social animal* (3rd ed.). San Francisco: W. H. Freeman.

Asch, S. E. (1946). Forming impressions of personality. *Journal of Abnormal and Social Psychology, 41*, 258–290.

Asch, S. E. (1951). Effects of group pressure upon the modification and distortion of judgments. In H. Guetzkow (Ed.), *Groups, leadership, and men.* Pittsburgh: Carnegie Press.

Asch, S. E., & Zukier, H. (1984). Thinking about persons. *Journal of Personality and Social Psychology, 46*, 1230–1240.

Aslin, R. N. (1987). Visual and auditory development in infancy. In J. Osofsky (Ed.), *Handbook of infant development* (2nd ed.). New York: Wiley.

Aslin, R. N., & Smith, L. B. (1988). Perceptual development. *Annual Review of Psychology, 39*, 435–473.

Asnis, G., & Ryan, N. D. (1983). The psychoneuroendocrinology of schizophrenia. In A. Rifkin (Ed.), *Schizophrenia and effective disorders: Biology and drug treatment* (pp. 205–236). Boston: John Wright.

Astington, J. W., Harris, P. L., & Olson, D. R. (1988). Developing theories of mind. Cambridge, England: Cambridge University Press.

Atkinson, J. W., & Feather, N. T. (1966). *Theory of achievement motivation.* New York: Krieger.

Atkinson, J. W., & Litwin, G. H. (1960). Achievement motive and test anxiety conceived as motive to approach success and motive to avoid failure. *Journal of Abnormal and Social Psychology, 60*, 52–63.

Atkinson, J. W., & Raynor, J. O. (Eds.) (1974). *Motivation and achievement.* Washington, DC: Winston.

Atkinson, R. C., & Shiffrin, R. M. (1968). Human memory: A proposed system and its control processes. In K. W. Spence and J. T. Spence (Eds.), *The psychology of learning and motivation: Advances in research and theory* (Vol. 2, pp. 80–195). New York: Academic Press.

Atwater, E. (1983). *Adolescence.* Englewood Cliffs, NJ: Prentice-Hall.

Atwell, P., & Rule, J. (1984). Computing and organizations: What we know and what we don't know. *Communications of the ACM, 27*, 1184–1192.

Averill, J. R. (1975). A semantic atlas of emotional concepts. *Catalog of Selected Documents in Psychology, 5*, 330.

Azrin, N. H., & Holt, N. C. (1966). Punishment. In W. A. Honig (Ed.), *Operant behavior: Areas of research and application* (pp. 380–447). New York: Appleton.

Azrin, N. H., & Foxx, R. M. (1974). *Toilet training in less than a day.* New York: Simon & Schuster.

Bach-Y-Rita, P. (1982). Sensory substitution in rehabilitation. In L. Illis, M. Sedwick, & H. Granville (Eds.), *Rehabilitation of the neurological patient* (pp. 361–382). Oxford, England: Blackwell Press.

Baddeley, A. (1982). *Your memory: A user's guide.* New York: Macmillan.

Baddeley, A., & Wilson, B. (1985). Phonological coding and short-term memory in patients without speech. *Journal of Memory and Language, 24*, 490–502.

Baer, J. S., Donovan, D. M., & Kivlahan, D. R. (1988). Addictive behaviors: Etiology and treatment. *Annual Review of Psychology, 39*, 223–252.

Backer, T. E., Batchelor, W. F., Jones, J. M., & Mays, V. M. (1988). Introduction to the special issue: Psychology and AIDS. *American Psychologist, 43*, 835–836.

Bahill, T. A., & Laritz, T. (1984). Why can't batters keep their eyes on the ball? *American Scientist, 72*, 249–253.

Baker, J. N. (1987, July 27). Battling the IQ-test ban. *Newsweek*, p. 53.

Bales, J. (1988, April). Polygraph screening banned in Senate bill. *A.P.A. Monitor*, 10.

Ballard, D. H., Hinton, G. E., & Sejnowski, T. J. (1983). Parallel vision computation. *Nature, 306*, 21–26.

Ballinger, C. B. (1981). The menopause and its syndromes. In J. G. Howells (Ed.), *Modern perspectives in the psychiatry of middle age* (pp. 279–303). New York: Brunner/Mazel.

Baltes, P. B., & Schaie, K. W. (1974, March). The myth of the twilight years. *Psychology Today*, pp. 35–38ff.

Bandura, A. (1973). *Aggression: A social learning analysis.* Englewood Cliffs, NJ: Prentice-Hall.

Bandura, A. (1977). *Social learning theory.* Englewood Cliffs, NJ: Prentice-Hall.

Bandura, A. (1981). In search of pure unidirectional determinants. *Behavior Therapy, 12*, 30–40.

Bandura, A. (1986). *Social foundations of thought and action: A social cognitive theory.* Englewood Cliffs, NJ: Prentice-Hall.

Bandura, A., Grusec, J. E., & Menlove, F. L. (1967). Vicarious extinction of avoidance behavior. *Journal of Personality and Social Psychology, 5*, 16–23.

Bandura, A., Ross, D., & Ross, S. (1963). Imitation of film-mediated aggressive models. *Journal of Abnormal and Social Psychology, 66*, 3–11.

Bandura, A., Ross, D., & Ross, S. (1963). Vicarious reinforcement and imitative learning. *Journal of Abnormal and Social Psychology, 67*, 601–607.

Bannatyne, A. (1971). *Language, reading, and learning disabilities.* Springfield, IL: Thomas.

Barbanel, J. (1988, February 15). Joyce Brown's ascent from anonymity. *New York Times*, pp. B-1, B-4.

Barber, T. X. (1970). Who believes in hypnosis? *Psychology Today, 4*, 20, 24–27, 84.

Barber, T. X. (1975). Responding to "hypnotic" suggestions: An introspective report. *American Journal of Clinical Hypnosis, 18*, 6–22.

Barber, T. X. (1981). *Hypnosis: A scientific approach.* South Orange, NJ: Power.

Barker, L. M., Best, M. E., & Domjan, M. (Eds.) (1977). *Learning mechanisms in food selection.* Waco, TX: Baylor University Press.

Barland, G. H., & Raskin, D. C. (1975). An evaluation of field techniques in detection of deception. *Psychophysiology, 12*, 321–330.

Barmash, I. (1983, January 9). Getting more for less. *New York Times.*

Barnes, D. M. (1988). The biological tangle of drug addiction. *Science, 24*, 415–417.

Baron, J. B., & Sternberg, R. J. (1986). *Teaching thinking skills.* New York: Freeman.

Baron, R. A. (1987). Effects of negative air ions on interpersonal attraction: Evidence for intensification. *Journal of Personality and Social Psychology, 52*, 547–553.

Baron, R. A., & Byrne, D. (1987). *Social psychology: Understanding human interaction* (5th ed.). Boston: Allyn & Bacon.

Baron, R. A., & Kepner, C. R. (1970). Model's behavior and attraction toward the model as determinants of adult aggressive behavior. *Journal of Personality and Social Psychology, 14*, 335–344.

Baron, R. A., & Ransberger, V. M. (1978). Ambient temperature and the occurrence of collective violence: The long, hot summer revisited. *Journal of Personality and Social Psychology, 36,* 351–360.

Baron, R. A., Russell, G. W., & Arms, R. L. (1985). Negative ions and behavior: Impact on mood, memory, and aggression among Type A and Type B persons. *Journal of Personality and Social Psychology, 48,* 746–754.

Baron, R. M., Mandel, D.R., Adams, C. A., & Greiffen, L. M. (1976). Effects of social density in university residential environments. *Journal of Personality and Social Psychology, 34,* 434–446.

Barron, F. (1969). *Creative person and creative process.* New York: Holt.

Barron, F., & Harrington, D. M. (1981). Creativity, intelligence, and personality. *Annual Review of Psychology, 32,* 439–476.

Bartlett, F. (1932). *Remembering: A study in experimental and social psychology.* Cambridge, England: Cambridge University Press.

Bartoshuk, L. M. (1971). The chemical senses: I. Taste. In J. N. Kling & L. A. Riggs (Eds.), *Experimental psychology* (3rd ed.). New York: Holt, Rinehart and Winston.

Baruch, G. K., & Barnett, R. C. (1980). On the well-being of adult women. In L. A. Bond & J. C. Rosen (Eds.), *Competence and coping during adulthood.* Hanover, NH: University Press of New England.

Bateson, G. (1960). Minimal requirements for a theory of schizophrenia. *Archives of General Psychiatry, 2,* 477–491.

Baum, A. (1988, April). Disasters, natural and otherwise. *Psychology Today,* pp. 57–60.

Baum, A., Fleming, R., & Singer, J.E. (1983). Coping with technological disaster. *Journal of Social Issues, 39,* 117–138.

Baum, A., & Gatchel, R. J. (1981). Cognitive determinants of reaction to uncontrollable events: Development of reactance and learned helplessness. *Journal of Personality and Social Psychology, 40,* 1078–1089.

Baum, A., Gatchel, R. J., & Schaeffer, M. A. (1983). Emotional, behavioral, and physiological effects of chronic stress at Three Mile Island. *Journal of Consulting and Clinical Psychology, 51,* 565–572.

Baum, A., & Valins, S. (1977). *Architecture and social behavior: Psychological studies of social density.* Hillsdale, NJ: Erlbaum.

Baum, A., & Valins, S. (1979). Architectural mediation of residential density and control: Crowding and the regulation of social contact. In L. Berkowitz (Ed.), *Advances in experimental social psychology* (Vol. 12). New York: Academic Press.

Bauman, L. J., & Siegel, K. (1987). Misperception among gay men of the risk for AIDS associated with their sexual behavior. *Journal of Applied Social Psychology, 17,* 329–350.

Baumeister, R. F., & Scher, S. J. (1988). Self-defeating behavior patterns among normal individuals: Review and analysis of common self-destructive tendencies. *Psychological Bulletin, 104,* 3–22.

Baumgardner, A. H., Heppner, P. P., & Arkin, R. M. (1986). Role of causal attribution in personal problem solving. *Journal of Personality and Social Psychology, 50,* 636–643.

Baumrind, D. (1971). Current patterns of parental authority. *Developmental Psychology Monographs, 4* (1, Pt. 2).

Beaman, A. L., Cole, C. M., Preston, M., Klentz, B., & Steblay, N. M. (1983). Fifteen years of foot-in-the-door research: A meta-analysis. *Personality and Social Psychology Bulletin, 9,* 181–196.

Beaton, A. (1986). *Left side, right side: A review of laterality research.* New Haven: Yale University Press.

Bear, M. F., Cooper, L. N., & Ebner, F. F. (1987). A physiological basis for a theory of synapse modification. *Science, 237,* 42–48.

Beck, A. (1984). Cognitive approaches to stress. In R. L. Woolfolk & P. M. Lehrer (Eds.), *Principles and practice of stress management.* New York: Guilford Press.

Beck, A. T. (1985). Cognitive therapy of depression: New perspectives. In P. J. Clayton & J. E. Barrett (Eds.), *Treatment of depression: Old controversies and new approaches* (pp. 265–290). New York: Raven Press.

Beck, A. T., & Emery, G., with Greenberg, R. L. (1985). *Anxiety disorders and phobias: A cognitive perspective.* New York: Basic Books.

Beck, A. T., Rush, A. J., Shaw, B., & Emery, G. (1979). *Cognitive therapy of depression: A treatment manual.* New York: Guilford Press.

Beck, J., Hope, B., & Rosenfeld, A. (Eds.) (1983). *Human and machine vision.* New York: Academic Press.

Bednar, R. L., & Kaul, T. J. (1978). Experimental group research: Current perspectives. *Handbook of Psychotherapy and Behavior Change: An empirical analysis* (2nd ed.). New York: Wiley.

Bee, H. L. (1985). *The developing child* (4th ed.). New York: Harper & Row.

Bell, A., & Weinberg, M. S. (1978). *Homosexuality: A study of diversities among men and women.* New York: Simon & Schuster.

Bell, S. M., & Ainsworth, M. D. S. (1972). Infant crying and maternal responsiveness. *Child Development, 43,* pp. 1171–1190.

Belsky, J. (1985). Two waves of day-care research: Developmental effects and conditions of quality. In R. Ainslie (Ed.), *The child and the day-care setting.* New York: Praeger.

Belsky, J. (1988). The 'effects' of infant day care reconsidered. *Early Childhood Research Quarterly, 3,* 235–272.

Belsky, J., & Rovine, M. (1988). Nonmaternal care in the first year of life and infant-parent attachment security. *Child Development, 59,* 157–167.

Bem, D. J. (1967). Self-perception: An alternative interpretation of cognitive dissonance phenomena. *Psychological Review, 74,* 183–200.

Bem, D. (1972). Self-perception theory. In L. Berkowitz (Ed.), *Advances in experimental social psychology* (Vol. 6, pp. 1–62). New York: Academic Press.

Bem, S. (1987). Gender schema theory and its implications for child development: Raising gender-aschematic children in a gender-schematic society. In M. R. Walsh (Ed.), *The Psychology of Women: Ongoing Debates.* New Haven: Yale University Press.

Benbow, C. P. (1988). Physiological correlates of extreme intellectual precocity. *Neuropsychologia, 24,* 719–725.

Benjamin, L. T., Jr. (1985, February). Defining aggression: An exercise for classroom discussion. *Teaching of Psychology, 12* (1), 40–42.

Benjamin, L. T., Jr. (1988). A history of teaching machines. *American Psychologist, 43,* 703–712.

Bennett, W., & Gurin, J. (1982). *The dieter's dilemma: Eating less and weighing more.* New York: Basic Books.

Ben-Sira, Z. (1976). The function of the professional's affective behavior in client satisfaction: A revised approach to social interaction theory. *Journal of Health and Social Behavior, 17,* 3–11.

Benson, H. (1975). *The relaxation response.* New York: Morrow.

Benson, H., & Friedman, R. (1985). A rebuttal to the conclusions of Davis S. Holme's article, "Meditation and somatic arousal reduction." *American Psychologist,* 725–726.

Benson, H., Kotch, J. B., Crassweller, K. D., & Greenwood, M. (1977). Historical and clinical considerations of the relaxation response. *American Scientist, 65,* 441–445.

Berg, J. H. (1984). Development of friendship between roommates. *Journal of Personality and Social Psychology, 46,* 346–356.

Bergener, M., Ermini, M., & Stahelin, H. B. (Eds.). (1985, February). *Thresholds in aging.* The 1984 Sandoz Lectures in Gerontology (Basel, Switzerland).

Berger, J. (1984, December 12). Two Bronx brothers, two different lives. *New York Times.*

Berger, J. (1988, March 16). Teachers of the gifted fight accusations of elitism. *New York Times,* p. 36.

Bergin, A. E., & Lambert, M. J. (1978). The evaluation of therapeutic outcomes. *Handbook of psychotherapy and behavior change: An empirical analysis* (2nd ed.). New York: Wiley.

Berkowitz, L. (1954). Group standards, cohesiveness and productivity. *Human Relations, 7,* 509–519.

Berkowitz, L. (1974). Some determinants of impulsive aggression: The role of mediated associations with reinforcements for aggression. *Psychological Review, 81,* 165–176.

Berkowitz, L. (1979). *A survey of social psychology* (2nd ed.). New York: Holt, Rinehart and Winston.

Berkowitz, L. (1983). Some parallels and differences in research with animals and humans. *American Psychologist, 38,* 1135–1144.

Berkowitz, L. (1984). Aversive conditioning as stimuli to aggression. In R. J. Blanchard & C. Blanchard (Eds.), *Advances in the study of aggression* (Vol. 1). New York: Academic Press.

Berkowitz, L. (1989). Frustration-aggression hypothesis. *Psychological Bulletin, 106,* 59–73.

Berkowitz, L., & Geen, R. G. (1966). Film violence and the cue properties of available targets. *Journal of Personality and Social Psychology, 3,* 525–530.

Berkowitz, L., & LePage, A. (1967). Weapons as aggression-eliciting stimuli. *Journal of Personality and Social Psychology, 7,* 202–207.

Berlyne, D. (1967). Arousal and reinforcement. In D. Levine (Ed.), *Nebraska symposium on motivation.* Lincoln: University of Nebraska Press.

Berman, J. S., Miller, R. C., & Massman, P. J. (1985). Cognitive therapy versus systematic desensitization: Is one treatment superior? *Psychological Bulletin, 97,* 451–461.

Bernard, M. E., & Joyce, M. R. (1984). *Rational-emotive therapy with children and adolescents.* Somerset, NJ: Wiley.

Berscheid, E. (1985). Interpersonal attraction. In G. Lindzey & E. Aronson (Eds.), *Handbook of social psychology* (3rd ed.). New York: Random House.

Berscheid, E., & Walster, E. (1974). Physical attractiveness. In L. Berkowitz (Ed.), *Advances in experimental social psychology* (Vol. 7, pp. 157–215). New York: Academic Press.

Best, C. T. (Ed.). (1985). *Hemispheric function and collaboration in the child.* New York: Academic Press.

Bieber, I., et al. (1962). *Homosexuality: A psychoanalytic study.* New York: Basic Books.

Biederman, I., & Shiffrar, M. M. (1987). Sexing day-old chicks: A case study and expert systems analysis of a difficult perceptual-learning task. *Journal of Experimental Psychology: Learning, Memory, and Cognition, 13,* 640–645.

Binet, A., & Simon, T. (1916). *The development of intelligence in children* (The Binet-Simon Scale). Baltimore, MD: Williams & Wilkins.

Bini, L. (1938). Experimental research on epileptic attacks induced by the electric current. *American Journal of Psychiatry,* Supplement 94, 172–183.

Birch, H. G. (1945). The role of motivation factors in insightful problem solving. *Journal of Comparative Psychology, 38,* 295–317.

Birnbaum, M. H., & Mellers, B. A. (1979). Stimulus recognition may mediate exposure effects. *Journal of Personality and Social Psychology, 37,* 391–394.

Bishop, J. E. (1988, March 2). Memory on trial: Witnesses of crimes are being challenged as frequently fallible. *Wall Street Journal,* pp. 1, 18.

Bjorklund, D. F. (1985). The role of conceptual knowledge in the development of organization in children's memory. In C. J. Brainerd & M. Pressley (Eds.), *Basic process in memory development.* New York: Springer-Verlag.

Blake, P. (1988, July 4). How machines can defeat people. *Time,* pp. 48–49.

Blakeslee, S. (1984, August 14). Scientists find key biological causes of alcoholism. *New York Times,* p. C-1.

Blanchard, R. J., & Blanchard, L. (1984). *Advances in the study of aggression* (Vol. 1). New York: Academic Press.

Blank, J. P. (1983, October). "I can see feeling good." *Readers Digest, 123,* 98–104.

Blank, T. O. (1981). The incomplete social psychology of aging: A psychologist's perspective. *International Journal of Aging and Human Development, 14,* 307–318.

Blatt, S. J., D'Afflitti, J. P., & Quinlan, D. M. (1976). Experiences of depression in normal young adults. *Journal of Abnormal Psychology, 85,* 383–389.

Blau, Z. S. (1973). *Old age in a changing society.* New York: New Viewpoints.

Blight, J. G. (1987). Toward a policy-relevant psychology of avoiding nuclear war: Lessons for psychologists from the Cuban missile crisis. *American Psychologist, 42,* 12–29.

Blight, J. G. (1988). Must the psychology of avoiding nuclear war remain free and insignificant? *American Psychologist, 43,* 326–329.

Block, J. H. (1983). Differential premises arising from differential socialization of the sexes: Some conjectures. *Child Development, 54,* 1335–1354.

Block, V., Hennevin, E., & LeConte, P. (1977). Interaction between post-trial reticular stimulation and subsequent paradoxical sleep in memory consolidation processes. In R. R. Drucker-Colin & J. L. McGlaugh (Eds.), *Neurobiology of sleep and memory.* New York: Academic Press.

Bloom, B. (1985). *Developing talent in young people.* New York: Ballantine

Blumenfeld, M., Levy, N. B., & Kaplan, D. (1979). The wish to be informed of a fatal illness. *Omega, 9,* 323–326.

Blumstein, P. W., & Schwartz, P. (1983). *American couples.* New York: Morrow.

Bluth, B. J. (1984, January–February). The human uses of outer space. *Society,* pp. 31–36.

Blusztajn, J. K., & Wurtman, R. J. (1983). Choline and cholinergic neurons. *Science, 221,* 614–620.

Boakes, R. A., Popplewell, D. A., & Burton, M. J. (Eds.) (1987). *Eating habits: Food, physiology, and learned behaviour.* New York: Wiley.

Boffey, P. M. (1986, May 14). Psychotherapy is as good as drugs in curing depression, study finds. *New York Times,* pp. A-1, A-17.

Blyle, C. M. (1970). Differences between patient's and doctor's interpretations of some common medical terms. *British Medical Journal, 2,* 286–289.

Bolles, R. N. (1987). *What color is your parachute?* Berkeley, CA: Ten Speed Press.

Bolles, R. C., & Fanselow, M. S. (1982). Endorphins and behavior. *Annual Review of Psychology, 33,* 87–101.

Booth, W. (1988, January 15). CDC paints a picture of HIV infection in U.S., *Science, 239,* 253.

Booth, W. (1987, October 2). Big brother is counting your keystrokes. *Science, 238,* 17.

Booth, W. (1988, March 4). The long, lost survey on sex. *Science, 239,* 1084–1085.

Booth, W. (1989). Asking America about its sex life. *Science, 243,* 304.

Bootzin, R. R. (1975). *Behavior modification and therapy: An introduction.* Cambridge, MA: Winthrop Press.

Boring, E. G., Langfeld, H. S., & Weld, H. P. (1948). *Foundations of psychology.* New York: Wiley.

Borland, J. H. (1989). *Planning and implementing programs for the gifted.* New York: Teachers College Press.

Bornstein, M. H. (1984). Habituation of attention as a measure of visual information processing in human infants: Summary, systematization, and synthesis. In G. Gottleib & N. A. Krasnegor (Eds.), *Measurement of audition and vision in the first year of postnatal life: A methodological overview.* Norwood, NJ: Ablex.

Bornstein, M. H. (1984). Perceptual development. In M. H. Bornstein & M. E. Lamb (Eds.), *Developmental psychology: An advanced textbook.* Hillsdale, NJ: Erlbaum.

Bornstein, M. H. (1989). Sensitive periods in development: Structural characteristics and causal interpretations. Psychological Bulletin, 105, 179–197.

Bornstein, M. H., & Sigman, M. D. (1986). Continuity in mental development from infancy. *Child Development, 57,* 251–274.

Bornstein, M. H. (1987). *Sensitive periods in development: Interdisciplinary perspectives.* Hillsdale, NJ: Erlbaum.

Botstein, D. (1986, April 11). The molecular biology of color vision. *Science, 232,* 142–143.

Botwinick, J. (1978). *Aging and behavior: A comprehensive integration of research findings* (2nd ed.). New York: Springer-Verlag.

Bourne, L. E., Dominowski, R. L., Loftus, E. F., & Healy, A. F. (1986). *Cognitive processes* (2nd ed.). Englewood Cliffs, NJ: Prentice Hall.

Bower, G., & Cohen, P. R. (1982). Emotional influences in memory and thinking: Data and theory. In M. S. Clark & S. T. Fiske (Eds.), *Affect and cognition.* Hillsdale, NJ: Erlbaum.

Bowers, T. G., & Clum, G. A. (1988). Relative contribution of specific and nonspecific treatment effects: Meta-analysis of placebo-controlled behavior therapy research. *Psychological Bulletin, 103,* 315–323.

Boyd, J. H., & Weissman, M. M. (1981). Epidemiology of affective disorders: A re-examination and future directions. *Archives of General Psychiatry, 38,* pp. 1039–1045.

Boynton, R. M. (1988). Color vision. *Annual Review of Psychology, 39,* 69–100.

Bradburn, N. M., Rips, L. J., & Shevell, S. K. (1987). Answering autobiographical questions: The impact of memory and inference on surveys. *Science, 236,* 157–161.

Brady, J. V. (1958, October). Ulcers in "executive monkeys." *Scientific American.*

Bransford, J. D., & Johnson, M. K. (1972). Contextual prerequisites for understanding: Some investigations of comprehension and recall. *Journal of Verbal Learning and Verbal Behavior, 11,* 717–721.

Braun, B. (1985, May 21). Interview by D. Goleman: New focus on multiple personality. *New York Times,* p. C-1.

Brazelton, T. B. (1969). *Infants and mothers: Differences in development.* New York: Dell.

Breckler, S. J. (1984). Empirical validation of affect, behavior, and cognition as distinct components of attitude. *Journal of Personality and Social Psychology, 47,* 1191–1205.

Breggin, P. R. (1979). *Electroshock: Its brain-disabling effects.* New York: Springer-Verlag.

Breisacher, P. (1971). Neuropsychological effects of air pollution. *American Behavioral Scientist, 14,* 837–864.

Breland, K., & Breland, M. (1961). Misbehavior of organisms. *American Psychologist, 16,* 681–684.

Brehm, J. W., & Self, E. A. (1989). The intensity of motivation. *Annual Review of Psychology, 40,* 109–131.

Breskin, A. (1984, November 8). *Rolling Stone Magazine,* p. 26.

Brewer, M. B. (1979). Ingroup bias in the minimal intergroup situation: A cognitive motivational analysis. *Psychological Bulletin, 86,* 307–324.

Brewer, W. F., & Dupree, D. A. (1983). Use of plan schemata in the recall and recognition of goal-directed actions. *Journal of Experimental Psychology: Learning, Memory, and Cognition, 9,* 117–129.

Bridges, J. S. (1988). Sex differences in occupational performance expectations. *Psychology of Women Quarterly, 12,* 75–90.

Broad, N. J. (1984, January 10). Pentagon is said to focus on ESP for wartime use. *New York Times,* pp. C-1, C-7.

Broad, N. J. (1984, September 25). *New York Times,* p. C-1.

Brody, G. H., Neubaum, E., & Forehand, R. (1988). Serial marriage: A heuristic analysis of an emerging family form. *Journal of Personality and Social Psychology, 103,* 211–222.

Brody, J. (1982). *New York Times guide to personal health.* New York: Times Books.

Brody, J. E. (1986, August 19). Widely used mental test undergoing treatment *New York Times,* pp. C-1, C-3.

Brody, J. E. (1987, May 5). Talking to the baby: Some expert advice. *New York Times,* p. C-11.

Brody, J. E. (1987, March 24). Research lifts blame from many of the obese. *New York Times,* pp. C-1, C-6.

Brody, J. E. (1987, November 19). Encouraging news for the absent-minded: Memory can be improved, with practice. *New York Times,* p. C-1.

Brody, N. (1983). *Human motivation.* New York: Academic Press.

Broverman, I. K., Vogel, S. R., Broverman, D. M., Clarkson, F. E., & Rosenkrantz, P. S. (1972). Sex-role stereotypes: A current appraisal. *Journal of Social Issues, 28,* 59–78.

Brown, B. (1984). *Between health and illness.* Boston: Houghton Mifflin.

Brown, B. B. (1977). *Stress and the art of biofeedback.* New York: Harper & Row.

Brown, M. S., & Tanner, C. (1988, May–June). Type A behavior and cardiovascular responsivity in preschoolers. *Nursing Research, 37,* 152.

Brown, P. K., & Wald, G. (1964). Visual pigments in single rod and cones of the human retina. *Science, 144,* pp. 45–52.

Brown, R. (1958). How shall a thing be called? *Psychological Review, 65,* 14–21.

Brown, R., & Fraser, C. (1963). The acquisition of syntax. In C. N. Cofer & B. Musgrave (Eds.), *Verbal behavior and learning: Problems and processes* (pp. 158–201). New York: McGraw-Hill.

Brown, R., & Kulik, J. (1977). Flashbulb memories. *Cognition, 5,* 73–99.

Browne, A., & Finkelhor, D. (1986). Impact of child sexual abuse: A review of the research. *Psychological Bulletin, 99,* 66–77.

Bruce, C., Desimone, R., & Gross, C. (1986). Both striate cortex and superior colliculus contribute to visual properties of neurons in superior temporal polysensory area of macaque monkey. *Journal of Neurophysiology, 55,* 1057–1075.

Bruce, V., & Green, P. (1984). *Visual perception: Physiology, psychology, and ecology.* Hillsdale, NJ: Erlbaum.

Bruch, H. (1973). *Eating disorders.* New York: Basic Books.

Brumberg, J. J. (1988). *Fasting girls: The emergence of anorexia nervosa as a modern disease.* Cambridge, MA: Harvard University Press.

Bruner, J. S. (1969). Foreword. In T. B. Brazelton, *Infants and mothers: Differences in development.* New York: Dell.

Bronson, B. I., & McKee, K. D. (1982). Crisis intervention and stress management: Giving resident advisors what they need. *Journal of College Student Personnel, 23,* 547–548.

Bryan, J. H., & Test, M. A. (1967). Models and helping: Naturalistic studies in aiding behavior. *Journal of Personality and Social Psychology, 6,* 400–407.

Buckhout, R. (1975). Eyewitness testimony. *Scientific American,* pp. 23–31.

Budiansky, S. (1987, June 29). Taking the pain out of pain. *U.S. News and World Report,* pp. 50–57.

Burbules, N. C., & Linn, M. C. (1988). Response to contradiction: Scientific reasoning during adolescence. *Journal of Educational Psychology, 80,* 67–75.

Burger, J. M., Oakman, J. A., & Ballard, N. G. (1983). Desire of control and the perception of crowding. *Personality and Social Psychology Bulletin, 9,* 475–479.

Burgess, A. W., & Holmstrom, L. L. (1979). *Rape: Crisis and recovery.* Bowie, MD: Robert J. Brady.

Burgoon, J. K. (1985). Nonverbal signals. In M. L. Knapp & W. K. Stevens, *Handbook of interpersonal communication.* Beverly Hills, CA: Sage.

Burnham, D. K. (1983). Apparent relative size in the judgment of apparent distance. *Perception, 12,* 683–700.

Butcher, J. N., & Owen, P. L. (1978). Objective personality inventories: Recent research and some contemporary issues. In B. B. Wolman (Ed.), *Clinical diagnosis of mental disorders: A handbook.* New York: Plenum Press.

Butler, R. A. (1954). Incentive conditions which influence visual exploration. *Journal of Experimental Psychology, 48,* 19–23.

Byers, P., and Byers, H. (1972). Nonverbal communication and the education of children. In C. B. Cazden, V. P. John, & D. Hynes (Eds.), *Functions of language in the classroom.* New York: Teachers College Press.

Byrne, D. (1969). Attitudes and attraction. In L. Berkowitz (Ed.), *Advances in experimental social psychology* (Vol. 4, pp. 35–89). New York: Academic Press.

Byrne, D., & Kelley, L. (1981). *An introduction to personality* (3rd ed.). Englewood Cliffs, NJ: Prentice-Hall.

Cacioppo, J. T., Martzke, J. S., Petty, R. E., and Tassinary, L. G. (1988). Specific forms of facial EMG response index emotions during an interview: From Darwin to the continuous-flow hypothesis of affect-laden information processing. *Journal of Personality and Social Psychology, 54,* 592–604.

Cacioppo, J. T., & Petty, R. E. (1979). Attitudes and cognitive response: An electrophysiological approach. *Journal of Personality and Social Psychology, 37,* 2181–2199.

Cairns, H. S., & Cairns, C. E. (1976). *Psycholinguistics: A cognitive view of language.* New York: Holt, Rinehart and Winston.

Candee, D., & Kohlberg, L. (1987). Moral judgment and moral action: A reanalysis of Haan, Smith, and Block's (1968) free-speech data. *Journal of Personality and Social Psychology, 52,* 554–564.

Cannon, W. B. (1929). Organization for physiological homeostatics. *Physiological Review, 9,* 280–289.

Carlson, M., Charlin, V., & Miller, N. (1988). Positive mood and helping behavior: A test of six hypotheses. *Journal of Personality and Social Psychology, 55,* 211–229.

Caroll, J. B. (1982). The measurement of intelligence. In R. J. Sternberg (Ed.), *The handbook of human intelligence* (pp. 29–120). Cambridge, MA: Cambridge University Press.

Carroll, P. B. (1988, June 18). The tough job of training computerphobic managers. *Wall Street Journal,* p. 17.

Carson, R. C. (1983). The schizophrenias. In H. E. Adams & P. B. Sutker (Eds.), *Handbook of clinical behavior therapy.* New York: Plenum Press.

Carson, R. C., Butcher, J. N., & Coleman, J. C. (1988). *Abnormal psychology and modern life* (8th ed.). Glenview, IL: Scott, Foresman.

Cartwright, D. (1968). The nature of group cohesiveness. In D. Cartwright & A. Zandu (Eds.), *Group dynamics: Research and theory* (3rd ed.). New York: Harper & Row.

Cartwright, R. D. (1978). *A primer on sleep and dreaming.* Reading, MA: Addison-Wesley.

Cartwright, R. D., Lloyd, S., Knight, S., & Trenholme, I. (1984). Broken dreams: A study of the effects of divorce and depression on dream content. *Psychiatry, 47,* 251–259.

Case, R. (1985). *Intellectual development: Birth to adulthood.* New York: Academic Press.

Casey, K. L., & Morrow, T. J. (1983). Ventral posterior thalamic neurons differentially responsive to noxious stimulation of the awake monkey. *Science, 223,* 675–677.

Casey, R. J., & Berman, J. S. (1985). The outcome of psychotherapy with children. *Psychological Bulletin, 98,* 388–400.

Cataldo, C. Z. (1987). Parent education for early childhood. New York: Columbia University Press.

Catania, A. C. (1984). *Learning* (2nd ed.). Englewood Cliffs, NJ: Prentice-Hall.

Cattell, R. B. (1963). Theory of fluid and crystallized intelligence: A critical experiment. *Journal of Educational Psychology, 54,* 1–22.

Cattell, R. B. (1967). *The scientific analysis of personality.* Baltimore: Penguin.

Cattell, R. B. (1987). *Intelligence: Its structure, growth, and action.* Amsterdam: North-Holland.

Ceci, S. J., Peters, D., & Plotkin, J. (1985). Human subjects review: Personal values and the regulation of social science research. *American Psychologist, 40,* 994–1002.

Cerella, J. (1985). Information-processing rates in the elderly. *Psychological Bulletin, 98,* 67–83.

Chafetz, M. (1976). *Why drinking can be good for you.* New York: Stein & Day.

Chaiken, S. (1979). Communicator physical attractiveness and persuasion. *Journal of Personality and Social Psychology, 37,* 1387–1397.

Chambers, M. (1985, June 29). Torres is guilty in the slaying of actress. *New York Times,* p. 29.

Chandler, M. J. (1976). Social cognition and life-span approaches to the study of child development. In H. W. Reese & L. P. Lipsitt (Eds.), *Advances in child development and behavior* (Vol. 11), New York: Academic Press.

Chapman, L. J., & Chapman, J. P. (1973). *Disordered thought in schizophrenia.* New York: Appleton-Century Crofts.

Charlier, M. (1988, February 24). Fasting plans are fast becoming a popular way to combat obesity. *Wall Street Journal,* p. 28.

Chavez, C. J., Ostrea, E. M., Stryker, J. C., & Smialek, Z. (1979). Sudden infant death syndrome among infants of drug-dependent mothers. *Journal of Pediatrics, 95,* 407–409.

Check, J. V. P., & Malamuth, N. M. (1986). Pornography and sexual aggression: A social learning theory analysis. In M. L. McLaughlin (Ed.), *Communication yearbook 9.* Beverly Hills, CA: Sage.

Check, J. V. P., Malamuth, N. M., Elias, B., & Barton, S. A. (1985, April). On hostile ground. *Psychology Today,* pp. 56–61.

Cherry, E. C. (1953). Some experiments on the recognition of speech with one and two ears. *Journal of the Acoustical Society of America, 25,* 975–979.

Chomsky, N. (1968). *Language and mind.* New York: Harcourt Brace Jovanovich.

Chomsky, N. (1969). *The acquisition of syntax in children from five to ten.* Cambridge, MA: MIT Press.

Chomsky, N. (1978). On the biological basis of language capacities. In G. A. Miller & E. Lennenberg (Eds.), *Psychology and biology of language and thought* (pp. 199–220). New York: Academic Press.

Chwalisz, K., Diener, E., & Gallagher, D. (1988). Autonomic arousal feedback and emotional experience: Evidence from the spinal-cord injured. *Journal of Personality and Social Psychology, 54,* 820–828.

Christensen, L. (1988). Deception in psychological research: When is its use justified? *Personality and Social Psychology Bulletin, 14,* 664–675.

Cialdini, R. B. (1984). *Social influence.* New York: William Morrow.

Cialdini, R. B. (1988). *Influence: Science and practice* (2nd ed.). Glenview, IL: Scott, Foresman.

Cialdini, R. B., Schaller, M., Houlihan, D., Arps, K., Fultz, J., & Beaman, A. L. (1987). Empathy-based helping: Is it selflessly or selfishly motivated? *Journal of Personality and Social Psychology, 52,* 749–758.

Clark, K. B., & Clark, M. P. (1947). Racial identification and preference in Negro children. In T. M. Newcomb & E. L. Hartley (Eds.), *Readings in social psychology.* New York: Holt, Rinehart and Winston.

Clark, L. A., & Watson, D. (1988). Mood and the mundane: Relations between daily life events and self-reported mood. *Journal of Personality and Social Psychology, 54,* 296–308.

Clark, M. (1987, November 9). Sweet music for the deaf. *Newsweek,* 73.

Clark, M. S., & Reis, H. T. (1988). Interpersonal processes in close relationships. *Annual Review of Psychology, 39,* 609–672.

Clarke-Stewart, A., & Friedman, S. (1987). *Child development: Infancy through adolescence.* New York: Wiley.

Clarke-Stewart, K. A. (1989). Infant day care: Maligned or malignant? *American Psychologist, 44,* 266–273.

Cleary, M. (1988, September 2). On the job: Behind the scenes. *Hampshire Life,* pp. 6–9, 46.

Clement, J. (in press). Nonformal reasoning in physics: The use of analogies and extreme cases. In J. Voss, D. N. Perkins, & J. Segal (Eds.), *Informal reasoning.* Hillsdale, NJ: Erlbaum.

Cohen, D. B. (1979). *Sleep and dreaming: Origins, nature, and functioning.* New York: Pergamon.

Cohen, L. B., DeLoache, J. S., & Strauss, M. S. (1979). Infant visual perception. In J. D. Osopsky (Ed.), *Handbook of infant development* (pp. 393–438). New York: Wiley-Interscience.

Cohen, T. E., & Lasley, D. J. (1986). Visual sensitivity. In Rosenzweig & Porter (Eds.), *Annual Review of Psychology, 37.* Palo Alto, CA: Annual Reviews.

Colby, A., & Damon, W. (1987). Listening to a different voice: A review of Gilligan's *In a different voice.* In M. R. Walsh (Ed.), *The Psychology of Women.* New Haven, CT: Yale University Press.

Colby, A., & Kohlberg, L. (1987). *The measurement of moral judgment.* Cambridge, England: Cambridge University Press.

Colby, A., Kohlberg, L., Gibbs, J., & Lieberman, M. (1983). A longitudinal study of moral judgment. *Monographs of the Society for Research in Child Development, 48,* 77.

Coleman, J. C., Butcher, J.N., & Carson, R. C. (1984). *Abnormal psychology and modern life.* Glenview, IL: Scott, Foresman.

Coleman, J., George, R., & Holt, G. (1977). Adolescents and their parents: A study of attitudes. *Journal of Genetic Psychology, 130,* 239–245.

Coleman, J., et al. (1977). Adolescents and their parents: A study of attitudes. *Journal of Genetic Psychology, 130,* 239–245.

Coles, R., & Stokes, G. (1985). *Sex and the American teenager.* New York: Harper & Row.

Colligan, R. C., & Offord, K. P. (1987, April). *Normal teenagers and the MMPI: Response patterns from the 1980s.* Paper presented at the annual meeting of the Eastern Psychological Association.

Compas, B. E. (1987). Coping with stress during childhood and adolescence. *Psychological Bulletin, 101,* 393–403.

Condon, J. W., & Crano, W. D. (1988). Inferred evaluation and the relation between attitude similarity and interpersonal attraction. *Journal of Personality and Social Psychology, 54,* 789–797.

Connors, M. M., Harrison, A. A., & Akins, F. R. (1986). Psychology and the resurgent space program. *American Psychologist, 41,* 906–913.

Converse, J., Jr., & Cooper, J. (1979). The importance of decisions and free-choice attitude change: A curvilinear finding. *Journal of Experimental Social Psychology, 15,* 48–61.

Coombs, W. N., & Schroeder, H. E. (1985). *Psychological preparation for stressful medical procedures: A meta-analysis.* Paper presented at the meeting of the American Psychological Association.

Cooper, A. M. (1984). Psychoanalysis at one hundred: Beginnings of maturity. *Journal of American Psychoanalytical Association, 32,* 245–268.

Cooper, C., & Payne, R. (1978). *Stress at work.* London: John Wiley.

Cooper, H. M. (1986). On the social psychology of using research reviews: The case of desegregation and black achievement. In R. S. Feldman (Ed.), *The social psychology of education: Current research and theory* (pp. 341–363). Cambridge, England: Cambridge University Press.

Cooper, I. S. (1981). *Living with chronic neurological disease.* New York: Norton.

Cooper, J., & Fazio, R. H. (1984). A new look at dissonance theory. In L. Berkowitz (Ed.), *Advances in experimental social psychology* (Vol. 17). New York: Academic Press.

Cooper, J. D., Heron, T. E., & Heward, W. L. (1987). *Applied behavior analysis.* Columbus, OH: Merrill.

Cooper, W. H. (1981). Ubiquitous halo. *Psychological Bulletin, 90,* 218–244.

Coppen, A., Metcalfe, M., & Wood, K. (1982). Lithium. In E. S. Paykel (Ed.), *Handbook of affective disorders.* New York: Guilford Press.

Corballis, M. C., & Beale, I. L. (1976). *The psychology of left and right.* Hillsdale, NJ: Erlbaum.

Corballis, M. C., & Beale, I. L. (1983). *The ambivalent mind: The neuro-psychology of left and right.* Chicago: Nelson-Hall.

Coren, S., Porac, C., & Ward, L. M. (1979). *Sensation and perception.* (1st ed.) New York: Academic Press.

Coren, S., & Porac, C. (1983). The creation and reversal of the Müller-Lyer illusion through attentional manipulation. *Perception, 12,* 49–54.

Coren, S., Porac, C., & Ward, L. M. (1984). *Sensation and perception* (2nd ed.). New York: Academic Press.

Cornelius, S. W., & Caspi, A. (1987). Everyday problem solving in adulthood and old age. *Psychology and Aging, 2,* 144–153.

Cornsweet, T. N. (1970). *Visual perception.* New York: Academic Press.

Coryell, W., & Winokur, G. (1982). Course and outcome. In E. S. Paykel (Ed.), *Handbook of affective disorders.* New York: Guilford Press.

Costa, P. T., Jr., & McCrae, R. R. (1985). Hypochondriasis, neuroticism, and aging. *American Psychologist, 40,* 19–28.

Council of Scientific Affairs (1985, April 5). Scientific status of refreshing recollection by the use of hypnosis. *Journal of the American Medical Association, 253*(13).

Covington, M. V., & Omelich, C. L. (1987). "I knew it cold before the exam": A test of the anxiety-blockage hypothesis. *Journal of Educational Psychology, 79,* 393–400.

Cowan, N. (1988). Evolving conceptions of memory storage, selective attention, and their mutual constraints within the human information-processing system. *Psychological Bulletin, 104,* 163–191.

Cox, V. C., Paulus, P. B., & McCain, G. (1984). Prison crowding research. *American Psychologist, 39,* 1148–1160.

Craighead, W. E., Kazdin, A. E., & Mahoney, M. J. (1981). *Behavior modification: Principles, issues, and applications.* Boston: Houghton Mifflin.

Craik, F. I. M. (1977). Age differences in human memory. In J. E. Birren & K. W. Schaie (Eds.). *Handbook of the psychology of aging.* New York: Van Nostrand Reinhold.

Craik, F. I., & Lockhart, R. S. (1972). Levels of processing: A framework for memory research. *Journal of Verbal Behavior, 11,* 671–684.

Cramer, P. (1987). The development of defense mechanisms. *Journal of Personality, 55,* 597–614.

Crandall, C. S. (1988). Social contagion of binge eating. *Journal of Personality and Social Psychology, 55,* 588–598.

Crapo, L. (1985). *Hormones: Messengers of life.*

Crocetti, G. (1983). *GRE: Graduate record examination general aptitude test.* New York: Arco.

Crook, T. H., & Miller, N. E. (1985). The challenge of Alzheimer's disease. *American Psychologist, 40*(11), 1245–1250.

Crow, T. J. (1980). Molecular pathology of schizophrenia: More than one disease process? *British Medical Journal, 280,* 66–68.

Croyle, R. T., & Cooper, J. (1983). Dissonance arousal: Physiological evidence. *Journal of Personality and Social Psychology, 45,* 782–791.

Cummings, E. E. (1972). *Complete poems.* New York: Harcourt Brace Jovanovich.

Cummings, E., & Henry, W. E. (1961). *Growing old.* New York: Basic Books.

Cummings, J. (1987, October 6). An earthquake aftershock: Calls to mental health triple. *New York Times,* p. A-1.

Cummings, L. L., & Berger, C. J. (1976). Organization structure: How does it influence

attitudes and performance? *Organizational Dynamics, 5,* 34 49.

Cunningham, M. R. (1986). Measuring the physical in physical attractiveness: Quasi-experiments on the sociobiology of female facial beauty. *Journal of Personality and Social Psychology, 50,* 925–935.

Curtis, R. C., & Miller, K. (1986). Believing another likes or dislikes you: Behaviors making the beliefs come true. *Journal of Personality and Social Psychology, 51,* 284–290.

Cusack, O. (1984, April). Pigeon posses. *Omni,* p. 34.

Cutler, B. L., & Penrod, S. D. (1988). Improving the reliability of eyewitness identification: Lineup construction and presentation. *Journal of Applied Psychology, 73,* 281–290.

Cutler, B. L., Penrod, S. D., & Martens, T. K. (1987). The reliability of eyewitness identification: The role of system and estimator variables. *Law and Human Behavior, 11,* 233–258.

Cyert, R., & March, J. G. (1963). *A behavioral theory of the firm.* Englewood Cliffs, NJ: Prentice-Hall.

Daehler, M., & Bukato, D. (1985). *Cognitive development.* New York: Random House.

Damon, W. (1989). *The moral child: Nurturing children's natural moral growth.* New York: The Free Press.

Darley, J. M., & Latané, B. (1968). Bystander intervention in emergencies: Diffusion of responsibility. *Journal of Personality and Social Psychology, 8,* 377–383.

Darwin, C. J., Turvey, M. T., & Crowder, R. G. (1972). An auditory analogue of the Sperling partial-report procedure: Evidence for brief auditory storage. *Cognitive Psychology, 3,* 255–267.

Davidson, R. J. (1984). Hemispheric asymmetry and emotion. In K. R. Scherer & P. Ekman (Eds.), *Approaches to emotion* (pp. 39–57). Hillsdale, NJ: Erlbaum.

Davis, H. P., & Squire, L. R. (1984). Protein synthesis and memory: A review. *Psychological Bulletin, 96,* pp. 518–559.

Davis, R. (1986). Assessing the eating disorders. *The Clinical Psychologist, 39,* 33–36.

Dawes, R. M., Faust, D., & Meehl, P. E. (1989, March 31). Clinical versus actuarial judgment. *Science, 243,* 1668–1674).

Deane, V. K., & Waters, E. (1985). *Monograph for the society for research in child development, 50,* 110–135.

Deaux, K., & Lewis, L. L. (1984). The structure of gender stereotypes: Interrelationships among components and gender label. *Journal of Personality and Social Psychology, 46,* 991–1004.

DeCarlo, N. A. (1983). *Psychological games.* New York: Facts on File.

DeCasper, A. J., & Fifer, W. D. (1980). Of human bonding: Newborns prefer their mothers' voices. *Science, 208,* 1174–1176.

DeCharms, R., & Moeller, G. H. (1962). Values expressed in American children's readers, 1800–1950. *Journal of Abnormal and Social Psychology, 64,* 136–142.

Deci, E. L., & Ryan, R. M. (1985). *Intrinsic motivation and self-determination in human behavior.* New York: Plenum Press.

deGroot, A. D. (1966). Perception and memory versus thought: Some old ideas and recent findings. In B. Kleinmuntz (Ed.), *Problem solving: Research, method, and theory.* New York: Wiley.

Dehn, N., & Shank, R. (1982). Artificial and human intelligence. In R. J. Sternberg (Ed.), *Handbook of human intelligence* (pp. 352–391). Cambridge, MA: Cambridge University Press.

Delbeckq, A., Van DeVen, A., & Gustafson, D. (1975). *Group techniques for program planning.* Glenview, IL: Scott, Foresman.

DeLeon, P. H. (1988). Public policy and public service: Our professional duty. *American Psychologist, 43,* 309–315.

DeLongis, A., Folkman, S., & Lazarus, R. S. (1988). The impact of daily stress on health and mood: Psychological social resources as mediators. *Journal of Personality and Social Psychology, 54,* 486–495.

Dement, W. C. (1976). *Some must watch while some must sleep.* New York: Norton.

Dement, W. C. (1979). Two kinds of sleep. In D. Goleman & R. J. Davidson (Eds.), *Consciousness: Brain, states of awareness, and mysticism* (pp. 72–75). New York: Harper & Row.

Dement, W. C., & Wolpert, E. A. (1958). The relation of eye movements, body mobility, and external stimuli to dream content. *Journal of Experimental Psychology, 55,* 543–553.

Denmark, F. L. (1989). Back to the future in the education and training of psychologists. *American Psychologist, 44,* 725–730.

Dent, J. (1984, March). *Readers Digest, 124,* 38.

Dentzer, S. (1986, May 5). Can you pass the job test? *Newsweek,* pp. 46–53.

DePaulo, B. M., & Fisher, J. (1980). The costs of asking for help. *Basic and Applied Social Psychology, 1,* 23–35.

DePaulo, B. M., Kenny, D. A., Hoover, C. W., Webb, W., & Oliver, P. V. (1987). Accuracy of person perception: Do people know what kinds of impressions they convey? *Journal of Personality and Social Psychology, 52,* 303–315.

Deregowski, J. B. (1973). Illusion and culture. In R. L. Gregory & G. H. Combrich (Eds.), *Illusion in nature and art* (pp. 161–192). New York: Scribner.

Desimone, R., Albright, T. D., Gross, C. G., & Bruce, C. (1984). Stimulus-selective properties of inferior temporal neurons in the Macaque. *The Journal of Neuroscience, 4,* 2051–2062.

Deutsch, M. (1985). *The historical context and the challenge of Head Start.* Keynote presentation for the twentieth-anniversary celebration of Head Start. New York: Loeb Student Center.

Deutsch, M., Jordan, T. J., & Deutsch, C. (1985). *Long-term effects of early intervention: Summary of selected findings.* Unpublished manuscript. New York: NYU Institute for Developmental Studies.

deVilliers, J. G., & deVilliers, P. A. (1978). *Language acquisition.* Cambridge, MA: MIT Press.

Deyo, R. A., Straube, K. T., & Disterhoft, J. F. (1989, February 10). Nimodipine facilitates associative learning in aging rabbits. *Science, 243,* 809–811.

Diaconis, P. (1978). Statistical problems in ESP research. *Science, 201,* 131–136.

Diehl, M., & Stroebe, W. (1987). Productivity loss in brainstorming groups: Toward the solution of a riddle. *Journal of Personality and Social Psychology, 53,* 497–509.

DiMatteo, M. R., & DiNicola, D. D. (1982). *Achieving patient compliance: The psychology of the medical practitioner's role.* New York: Pergamon.

Dion, K. L., & Dion, K. K. (1987). Belief in a just world and physical attractiveness stereotyping. *Journal of Personality and Social Psychology, 52,* 775–780.

Dion, K. K., & Berscheid, E. (1974). Physical attractiveness and peer perception among children. *Sociometry, 37,* 1–12.

Dohrenwend, B. S., Dohrenwend, B. P., Dodson, M., & Shrout, P. E. (1984). Symptoms, hassles, social supports, and life events: The problem of confounded measures. *Journal of Abnormal Psychology, 93,* 222–230.

Dolce, J. J., & Raczynski, J. M. (1985). Neuromuscular activity and electromyography in painful backs: Psychological and biomechanical models in assessment and treatment. *Psychological Bulletin, 97,* 502–520.

Dollard, J., Doob, L., Miller, N., Mower, O. H., & Sears, R. R. (1939). *Frustration and aggression.* New Haven, CT: Yale University Press.

Dollard, J., & Miller, N. E. (1950). *Personality and psychotherapy: An analysis in terms of learning, thinking and culture.* New York: McGraw-Hill.

Donnerstein, E., & Berkowitz, L. (1981). Victim reactions in aggressive erotic films as a factor in violence against women. *Journal of Personality and Social Psychology, 41,* 710–724.

Donnerstein, E., Linz., D., & Penrod, S. (1987). *The question of pornography: Research findings and policy implications.* New York: Free Press.

Doob, A. N., & Wood, L. (1972). Catharsis and aggression: The effects of annoyance and retaliation on aggressive behavior. *Journal of Personality and Social Psychology, 22,* 156–162.

Dore, F. Y., & Dumas, C. (1987). Psychology of animal cognition: Piagetian studies. *Psychological Bulletin, 102,* 219–233.

Doty, R. L. (1986). Development and age-related changes in human olfactory func-

tion. In W. Breipohl & R. Apfelbach (Eds.), *Ontogeny of olfaction in vertebrates.* Berlin: Springer-Verlag.

Douglas, W. K. (1984). *Human performance issues arising from manned space station missions.* Huntington Beach, CA: McDonnell Douglas Astronautics Company.

Dove, A. (1968, July 15). Taking the chitling test. *Newsweek.*

Dovidio, J. F., & Ellyson, S. L. (Eds.) (1985). *Power, dominance, and nonverbal behavior.* New York: Springer-Verlag.

Dovidio, J. F., Ellyson, S. L., Keating, C. F., Heltman, K., & Brown, C. E. (1988). The relationship of social power to visual displays of dominance between men and women. *Journal of Personality and Social Psychology, 54,* 233–242.

Dreyer, P. H. (1982). Sexuality during adolescence. In B. B. Wolman (Ed.), *Handbook of developmental psychology.* Englewood Cliffs, NJ: Prentice-Hall.

Druckman, D., & Swets, J. A. (Eds.) (1988). *Enhancing human performance: Issues, theories, and techniques.* Washington, DC: National Academy Press.

Dubrovsky, V., Kiesler, S., Sproull, L., & Zubrow, D. (1986). Socialization to computing in college: A look beyond the classroom. In R. S. Feldman (Ed.), *The social psychology of education: Current research and theory.* Cambridge, England: Cambridge University Press.

Duck, S. W. (Ed.). (1982). *Personal relationships: Vol. 4. Dissolving personal relationships.* New York: Academic Press.

Duke, M., & Nowicki, S., Jr. (1979). *Abnormal psychology: Perspectives on being different.* Monterey, Ca: Brooks/Cole.

Duke, M. P., & Nowicki, S., Jr. (1986). *Abnormal psychology: A new look.* New York: Holt, Rinehart and Winston.

Duncker, K. (1945). On problem solving. *Psychological Monographs, 58,* (5, whole no. 270).

Dunkel-Schetter, C., Folkman, S., & Lazarus, R. S. (1987). Correlates of social support receipt. *Journal of Personality and Social Psychology, 53,* 71–80.

Dunne, E. J., McIntosh, J. L., & Dunne-Maxim, K. (Eds.) (1987). *Suicide and its aftermath: Understanding and counseling the survivors.* New York: Norton.

Dutton, D. G., & Aron, A. P. (1974). Some evidence for heightened sexual attraction under conditions of high anxiety. *Journal of Personality and Social Psychology, 30,* 510–517.

Dweck, C. (1986). Motivational processes affecting learning. *American Psychologist, 41,* 1040–1048.

Dworkin, R. H., & Widom, C. S. (1977). Undergraduate MMPI profiles and the longitudinal prediction of adult social outcome. *Journal of Consulting and Clinical Psychology, 45,* 620–625.

Dywan, J., & Bowers, K. (1983). The use of hypnosis to enhance recall. *Science, 222,* 184–185.

Eagly, A. (1989, May). Meta-analysis of sex differences. Annual conference on adversity. University of Massachusetts, Amherst, Massachusetts.

Eagly, A. H. (1978). Sex differences in influenceability. *Psychological Bulletin, 85,* 86–116.

Eagly, A. H. (1983). Gender and social influence: A social psychological analysis. *American Psychologist, 38,* 971–981.

Eagly, A. H., & Carlie, L. L. (1981). Sex of researchers and sex-typed communications as determinants of sex differences in influenceability: A meta-analysis of social influence studies. *Psychological Bulletin, 90,* 1–20.

Eagly, A., & Steffen, V. J. (1986). Gender and aggressive behavior: A meta-analytic review of the social psychological literature. *Psychological Bulletin, 100,* 309–330.

Eagly, A. H., Wood, W., & Chaiken, S. (1978). Causal inferences about communicators and their effect on opinion change. *Journal of Personality and Social Psychology, 36,* 424–435.

Ebbinghaus, H. (1885/1913). *Memory: A contribution to experimental psychology.* (H. A. Roger & C. E. Bussenius, Trans.) New York: Columbia University Press.

Eberts, R., & MacMillan, A. C. (1985). Misperception of small cars. In R. Eberts & C. Eberts (Eds.), *Trends in ergonomics/human factors, III.* Amsterdam: Elsevier.

Ebbesen, E. B., Duncan, B., & Konečni, V. J. (1975). Effects of content of verbal aggression on future verbal aggression: A field experiment. *Journal of Experimental Social Psychology, 11,* 192–204.

Eccles, J. S. (1987). Gender roles and women's achievement-related decisions. *Psychology of Women Quarterly, 11,* 135–171.

Eckenrode, J. (1984). Impact of chronic and acute stressors on daily reports of mood. *Journal of Personality and Social Psychology, 46,* 907–918.

Eckholm, E. (1988, April 17). Exploring the forces of sleep. *New York Times Magazine,* pp. 26–34.

Edmonston, W. E., Jr. (1986). *The induction of hypnosis.* New York: Wiley.

Egan, D. E., & Schwartz, B. J. (1979). Chunking in recall of symbolic drawings. *Memory and Cognition, 7,* 149–158.

Egan, J. P. (1975). *Signal detection theory and ROC analysis.* New York: Academic Press.

Egeland, J. A., Gerhard, D. S., Pauls, D. L., Sussex, J. N., Kidd, K. K., Allen, C. R., Hostetter, A. M., & Housman, D. E. (1987). Bipolar effective disorders linked to DNA markers on chromosome 11. *Nature, 325,* 783–787.

Eisenberg, N. (Ed.) (1987). *Contemporary topics in developmental psychology.* New York: Wiley.

Eisenberg, N., & Miller, P. A. (1987). The relation of empathy to prosocial and related behaviors. *Psychological Bulletin, 101,* 91–119.

Eisenberg-Berg, N., & Mussen, P. (1978). Empathy and moral development in adolescence. *Developmental Psychology, 14,* 185–186.

Ekman, P. (1972). Universals and cultural differences in facial expressions of emotion. In J. Cole (Ed.), *Darwin and facial expression: A century of research in review* (pp. 169–222). New York: Academic Press.

Ekman, P. (1984). Expression and the nature of emotion. In K. Scherer & P. Ekman, P. (Eds.). *Approaches to emotion.* Hillsdale, N.J.: Lawrence Erlbaum Associates.

Ekman, P. (1985). *Telling lies.* New York: Norton.

Ekman, P., Friesen, W. V., & Ellsworth, P. (1972). *Emotion in the human face.* Elmsford, NY: Pergamon Press.

Ekman, P., Herman, C. P., & Polivy, J. (1975). Anxiety, restraint, and eating behavior. *Journal of Abnormal Psychology, 84,* 666–672.

Ekman, P., Friesen, W. V., O'Sullivan, M., Chan, A., Diacoyanni-Tarlatzis, I., Heider, K., Krause, R., LeCompte, W. A., Pitcairn, T., Ricci-Bitti, P. E., Scherer, K., Tomita, M., & Tzavaras, A. (1987). Universals and cultural differences in the judgments of facial expressions of emotion. *Journal of Personality and Social Psychology, 53,* 712–717.

Ekman, P., Levenson, R. W., & Friesen, W. V. (1983, September 16). Autonomic nervous system activity distinguishes among emotions. *Science, 223,* 1208–1210.

Elkin, I. (1986, May). *NIMH treatment of depression: Collaborative research program.* Paper presented at the annual meeting of the American Psychiatric Association (Washington, DC).

Elkind, D. (1981). *The hurried child.* Reading, MA: Addison-Wesley.

Ellis, A. (1962). *Reason and emotion in psychotherapy.* New York: Lyle Stuart.

Ellis, A. (1975). Creative job and happiness: The humanistic way. *The Humanist, 35* (1), 11–13.

Ellis, A., & Dryden, W. (1987). *The practice of rational-emotive therapy (RET).* New York: Springer.

Elmer-DeWitt, P. (1988, November 14). "The kid put us out of action." *Time,* p. 76.

Engen, T. (1982). *Perception of odors.* New York: Academic Press.

Engen, T. (1987, September–October). Remembering odors and their names. *American Scientist, 75,* 497–503.

Epp, H., Kalin, M., & Miller, D. (1988, May 6). PC software for artificial intelligence applications. *Science, 240,* 824–830.

Epperson, S. E. (1988, September 16). Studies link subtle sex bias in schools with women's behavior in the workplace. *Wall Street Journal,* p. 19.

Epstein, A. N., Fitzsimons, J. T., & Roys, B. J. (1970). Drinking induced by injection of angiotensin into the brain of the rat. *Journal of Physiology, 210,* 457–474.

Epstein, L. (1986). Childhood obesity. *Science, 232,* 20–21.

Epstein, R. (1987). The spontaneous interconnection of four repertoires of behavior in a pigeon. *Journal of Comparative Psychology, 101,* 197–201.

Epstein, S., & Meier, P. (1989). Constructive thinking: A broad coping variable with specific components. *Journal of Personality and Social Psychology, 57,* 332–350.

Epstein, S., & O'Brien, E. J. (1985). The person-situation debate in historical and current perspective. *Psychological Bulletin, 98,* 513–537.

Erickson, E. H. (1963). *Childhood and society* (2nd ed.). New York: Norton.

Eron, L. D. (1982). Parent-child interaction, television violence, and aggression of children. *American Psychologist, 37,* 197–211.

Eron, L. D. (1986). Interventions to mitigate the psychological effects of media violence on aggressive behavior. *Journal of Social Issues, 3,* 155–169.

Eron, L. D., & Huesmann, L. R. (1985). The control of aggressive behavior by changes in attitude, values, and the conditions of learning. In R. J. Blanchard and C. Blanchard (Eds.), *Advances in the study of aggression.* New York: Academic Press.

Eron, L. D., Huesmann, L. R., Lefkowitz, M. M., & Walden, L. O. (1972). Does television cause aggression? *American Psychologist, 27,* 253–263.

Evans, C. (1984). *Landscapes of the night: How and why we dream.* New York: Viking Press.

Evans, G. W. (1974). An examination of the information overload mechanism of personal space. *Man-Environment Systems, 4,* 61.

Evans, N. J., & Dovido, J. F. (1983, April). *Evaluation processing of racial stereotypes.* Paper presented at the 54th Annual Meeting of the Eastern Psychological Association (Philadelphia).

Ewen, R. B. (1980). *An introduction to theories of personality.* New York: Academic Press.

Eysenck, H. J. (1952). The effects of psychotherapy: An evaluation. *Journal of Consulting Psychology, 16,* 319–324.

Eysenck, H. J. (1973). *Eysenck on extraversion.* New York: Wiley.

Eysenck, H. J. (1985). Race, social class, and individual differences in IQ. *Personality and Individual Differences, 6,* 287.

Eysenck, H. J., & Eysenck, S. B. G. (1975). *Manual of the Eysenck personality questionnaire.* San Diego, CA: Educational and Industrial Testing Service.

Eysenck, H. J., & Eysenck, M. W. (1985). *Personality and individual differences: A natural science approach.* New York: Plenum.

Fajardo, D. M. (1985). Author race, essay quality, and reverse discrimination. *Journal of Applied Social Psychology, 15,* 255–268.

Fanelli, R. J., Burright, R. G., & Donovick,

P. J. (1983). A multivariate approach to the analysis of genetic and septal lesion effects on maze performance in mice. *Behavioral Neuroscience, 97,* 354–369.

Faraone, S. V., & Tsuang, M. T. (1985). Quantitative models of the genetic transmission of schizophrenia. *Psychological Bulletin, 98,* 41–66.

Farber, I. E. (1975). Sane and insane: Constructions and misconstructions. *Journal of Abnormal Psychology, 84,* 589–620.

Farley, F. (1986, May). The big T in personality. *Psychology Today,* pp. 44–52.

Fay, R. E., Turner, C. F., Klassen, A. D., & Gagnon, J. H. (1989). Prevalence and patterns of same-gender sexual contact among men. *Science, 243,* 338–348.

Fayol, H. (1949). *General and industrial management.* London: Pitman.

Fazio, R. H., Zanna, M. P., & Cooper, J. (1977). Dissonance and self-perception: An integrative view of each theory's proper domain of application. *Journal of Experimental Social Psychology, 13,* 464–479.

Feifel, H. (1963). In N. L. Farberow (Ed.), *Taboo topics* (pp. 8–12). New York: Atherton.

Feingold, A. (1988). Cognitive gender differences are disappearing. *American Psychologist, 43,* 95–103.

Feldman, R. S. (1982). *Development of nonverbal behavior in children.* New York: Springer-Verlag.

Festinger, L. (1957). *A theory of cognitive dissonance.* Stanford, CA: Stanford University Press.

Festinger, L., & Carlsmith, J. M. (1959). Cognitive consequences of forced compliance. *Journal of Abnormal and Social Psychology, 58,* 203–210.

Festinger, L., Schachter, S., & Back, K. W. (1950). *Social pressure in informal groups.* New York: Harper.

Feynman, R. P. (1988, February). An outsider's view of the *Challenger* inquiry. *Physics Today,* pp. 26–37.

Fiedler, F. E., Mitchell, R., & Triandis, H. C. (1971). The culture assimilator: An approach to cross-cultural training. *Journal of Applied Psychology, 55,* 95–102.

Field, T. (1982). Individual differences in the expressivity of neonates and young infants. In R. S. Feldman (Ed.), *Development of nonverbal behavior in children.* New York: Springer-Verlag.

Field, T. M. (1978). Interaction of primary versus secondary caretaker fathers. *Developmental Psychology, 14,* 183–184.

Fieve, R. R. (1975). *Moodswing.* New York: Morrow.

Fineberg, H. V. (1988, October). The social dimensions of AIDS. *Scientific American, 259,* 128–134.

Fink, A., & Kosecoff, J. (1985). *How to conduct surveys: A step-by-step guide.* Beverly Hills, CA: Sage.

Finkelhor, D. (1979). *Sexually victimized children.* New York: Free Press.

Fischman, M. (1985, August). *Cocaine use: Laboratory perspective on a growing*

health problem. Paper presented at the annual meeting of the American Psychological Association, Los Angeles.

Fischoff, B. (1977). Perceived informativeness of facts. *Journal of Experimental Psychology: Human Perception and Performance, 3,* 349–358.

Fishbein, M., & Ajzen, I. (1975). *Belief, attitude, intention, and behavior: An introduction to theory and research.* Reading, MA: Addison-Wesley.

Fisher, J. D., Bell, P. A., & Baum, A. S. (1984). *Environmental psychology* (2nd ed.). New York: Holt, Rinehart and Winston.

Fisher, K. (1985, March). ECT: New studies on how, why, who. *APA Monitor,* pp. 18–19.

Fisher, S., Raskin, A., & Uhlenhuth, E. H. (Eds.) (1987). *Cocaine: Classical and biobehavioral aspects.* New York: Oxford University Press.

Fiske, E. B. (1984, November 11). Learning Disabled: A New Awareness. *New York Times.* Section 12, pp. 1, 44, 58.

Fiske, S. T. (1988). People's reactions to nuclear war: Implications for psychologists. *American Psychologist, 42,* 207–217.

Fiske, S. T., Pratto, F., & Pavelchak, M. A. (1983). Social science and the politics of the arms race. *Journal of Social Issues, 39,* 161–180.

Fiske, S. T., & Taylor, S. E. (1983). *Social cognition.* Reading, MA: Addison-Wesley.

Fitzsimons, J. T. (1961). Drinking by rats depleted of body fluid without increase in osmotic pressure. *Journal of Physiology, 159,* 297–309.

Fleming, I., Baum, A., & Weiss, L. (1987). Social density and perceived control as mediators of crowding stress in high-density residential neighborhoods. *Journal of Personality and Social Psychology, 52,* 899–906.

Fleming, R., Baum, A., & Singer, J. E. (1984). Toward an integrative approach to the study of stress. *Journal of Personality and Social Psychology, 46,* 939–949.

Flood, J. F., Smith, G. E., & Morley, J. E. (1987). Modulation of memory processing by cholecystokinin: Dependence on the vagus nerve. *Science, 236,* 832–834.

Flor, H., & Turk, D. C. (1989). Psychophysiology of chronic pain: Do chronic pain patients exhibit symptom-specific psychophysiological responses? *Psychological Bulletin, 105,* 215–259.

Flowers, M. A. (1977). A laboratory test of some implications of Janis's groupthink hypotheses. *Journal of Personality and Social Psychology, 35,* 888–896.

Flynn, J. R. (1987). Massive IQ gains in 14 nations: What IQ tests really measure. *Psychological Bulletin, 101,* 171–191.

Foa, E. B., & Kozak, M. S. (1986). Emotional processing of fear: Exposure to corrective information. *Psychological Bulletin, 99,* 20–35.

Fodor, E. M. (1985). The power motive, group conflict, and physiological arousal.

Journal of Personality and Social Psychology, 49, 1408–1415.

Foley, J. E., & Cohen, A. J. (1984). Working mental representations of the environment: Spatial perception, cognitive maps, estimation, school environment. *Environment and Behavior, 16,* 713–729.

Folkman, S. (1984). Personal control and stress and coping processes: A theoretical analysis. *Journal of Personality and Social Psychology, 46,* 839–852.

Folkman, S., & Lazarus, R. S. (1980). An analysis of coping in a middle-aged community sample. *Journal of Health and Social Behavior, 21,* 219–239.

Folkman, S., & Lazarus, R. S. (1988). Coping as a mediator of emotion. *Journal of Personality and Social Psychology, 54,* 466–475.

Folkman, S., Lazarus, R. S., Dunkel-Schetter, C., DeLongis, A., & Green, R. J. (1986). Dynamics of a stressful encounter: Cognitive appraisal, coping, and encounter outcome. *Journal of Personality and Social Psychology, 50,* 992–1003.

Fordyce, W. E. (1988). Pain and suffering: A reappraisal. *American Psychologist, 43,* 276–283.

Forer, B. (1949). The fallacy of personal validation: A classroom demonstration of gullibility. *Journal of Abnormal and Social Psychology, 44,* 118–123.

Forgas, J. P., & Bower, G. H. (1987). Mood effects on person-perception judgments. *Journal of Personality and Social Psychology, 53,* 53–60.

Forsyth, D. R. (1983). *An introduction to group dynamics.* Monterey, CA: Brooks/Cole.

Försterling, F. (1985). Attributional retraining: A review. *Psychological Bulletin, 98,* 495–512.

Frable, D. E. S., & Bem, S. L. (1985). If you are gender schematic, all members of the opposite sex look alike. *Journal of Personality and Social Psychology, 49,* 459–468.

Frankenburg, W. K., & Dodds, J. B. (1967). The Denver developmental screening test. *Journal of Pediatrics, 71,* 181–191.

Franks, L. (1985, October 20). A new attack on alcoholism. *New York Times Magazine,* pp. 47–50, 61–65, 69.

Frauk, B. M., & Noble, J. P. (1984). Field independence-dependence and cognitive restructuring. *Journal of Personality and Social Psychology, 47,* 1129–1135.

Frederikson, N. (1986). Toward a broader conception of human intelligence. *American Psychologist, 41,* 445–452.

Freedman, J. L. (1979). Reconciling apparent differences between responses to humans and other animals to crowding. *Psychological Review, 86,* 80–85.

Freedman, J. L. (1984). Effects of television violence on aggressiveness. *Psychological Bulletin, 96,* 227–246.

Freedman, J. L., & Fraser, S. C. (1966). Compliance without pressure: The foot-in-the-door technique. *Journal of Personality and Social Psychology, 4,* 195–202.

Freeman, W. (1959). Psychosurgery. In *American handbook of psychiatry* (Vol. 2, pp. 1521–1540). New York: Basic Books.

Freeman, F. R. (1981). *Organic mental disease.* New York: Spectrum.

French, J. R. P. (1976, September). *Job demands and worker health.* Paper presented at the 84th Annual Convention of the American Psychological Association.

French, J. R. P., & Caplan, R. D. (1972). Organizational stress and individual strain. In *The failure of success.* New York: Amacom.

Freud, S. (1900). *The interpretation of dreams.* New York: Basic Books.

Freud, S. (1922/1959). *Group psychology and the analysis of the ego.* London: Hogarth.

Frey, D., & Wicklund, R. A. (1978). A clarification of selective exposure: The impact of choice. *Journal of Experimental Social Psychology, 14,* 132–139.

Friedman, H. S., & DiMatteo, M. R. (1982). *Interpersonal issues in health care.* New York: Academic Press.

Friedman, H. S., Hall, J. A., & Harris, M. J. (1985). Type A behavior, nonverbal expressive style, and health. *Journal of Personality and Social Psychology, 48,* 1299–1315.

Friedman, M., Thoresen, C. E., Gill, J. J., Powell, L. H., Ulmer, D., Thompson, L., Price, V. A., Rabin, D. D., Breall, W. S., Dixon, T., Levy, R., & Bourg, E. (1984). Alteration of type: A behavior and reduction in cardiac recurrences in postmyocardial infarction patients. *American Heart Journal, 108* (2), 237–248.

Friedman, M., Thoresen, C. E., Gill, J. J., Ulmer, D., Leonti, T., Powell, L., Price, V., Elek, S. R., Robin, D. D., Breall, W. S., Piaget, G., Dixon, T., Bourg, E., Levy, R. A., & Tasto, D. L. (1982). Feasibility of altering type A behavior pattern after myocardial infarction. *Circulation, 66,* 83–92.

Friedman, M., & Ulmer, D. (1985). *Type A behavior and your heart.* New York: Fawcett.

Frijda, N. H. (1988). The laws of emotion. *American Psychologist, 43,* 349–358.

Friedman, H. S., & Booth-Kewley, S. (1988). Validity of the Type A construct: A reprise. *Psychological Bulletin, 104,* 381–384.

Frost, P. J., Moore, L. F., Louis, M. R., Lundberg, C. C., & Martin, J. (Eds.) (1985). *Organizational culture.* Beverly Hills, CA: Sage.

Funder, D. C. F. (1987). Errors and mistakes: Evaluating the accuracy of social judgment. *Psychological Bulletin, 101,* 75–90.

Gagnon, G. H. (1977). *Human sexualities.* Glenview, IL: Scott, Foresman.

Galaburda, A. M. (1988, February). Dyslexia. Paper presented at the annual meeting of the American Association for the Advancement of Science (Boston).

Galanter, E. (1962). Contemporary psychophysics. In R. Brown, E. Galanter, E. Hess,

& G. Maroler (Eds.), *New directions in psychology.* New York: Holt, 87–157

Gallant, D. M. (1987). *Alcoholism: A guide to diagnosis, intervention, and treatment.* New York: Norton.

Gallup, G. G., Jr., & Suarez, S. D. (1985). Alternatives to the use of animals in psychological research. *American Psychologist, 40,* 1104–1111.

Gama, E. M. P. (1985). Achievement motivation of women: Effects of achievement and affiliation arousal. *Psychology of Women, 9,* 89–103.

Garb, H. N. (1989). Clinical judgment, clinical training, and professional experience. *Psychological Bulletin, 105,* 387–396.

Garber, H. L. (1988). *The Milwaukee Project: Preventing mental retardation in children at risk.* Washington, DC: American Association on Mental Retardation.

Garcia, J., Hankins, W. G., & Rusniak, K. W. (1974). Behavioral regulation of the milieu intern in man and rat. *Science, 185,* 824–831.

Gardell, G. (1976). *Arbetsinnehall och livskvalitet.* Stockholm: Prisma.

Gardner, H. (1975). *The shattered mind: The person after brain damage.* New York: Knopf.

Gardner, H. (1983). *Frames of mind: The theory of multiple intelligences.* New York: Basic Books.

Garfield, S. L. (1983). Psychotherapy: Efficacy, generality, and specificity. In J. B. N. Williams & R. L. Spitzer (Eds.), *Psychotherapy research: Where are we and where should we go?* (pp. 295–305). New York: Guilford Press.

Garland, H., & Pearce, J. (1967). Neurological complications of carbon monoxide poisoning. *Quarterly Journal of Medicine, 36,* 445–455.

Gartell, N. N. (1982). Hormones and homosexuality. In W. Paul et al. (Eds.), *Homosexuality: Social, psychological, and biological issues.* Beverly Hills, CA: Sage.

Gatchel, R. J., & Baum, A. (1983). *An introduction to health psychology.* Reading, MA: Addison-Wesley.

Gawin, F. H., & Ellinwood, E. H. (1988). Cocaine and other stimulants: Actions, abuse, and treatment. *New England Journal of Medicine, 18,* 1173.

Gazzaniga, M. S. (1967). The split brain in man. *Scientific American, 217,* 24–29.

Gazzaniga, M. S. (1970). *The bisected brain.* New York: Plenum Press.

Gazzaniga, M. S. (1983). Right-hemisphere language following brain bisection: A twenty-year perspective. *American Psychologist, 38,* 525–537.

Gazzaniga, M. S. (1985, November). The social brain. *Psychology Today,* pp. 29–38.

Gazzaniga, M. S. (1988). Mind matters: How mind and brain interact to create our conscious lives. Boston: Houghton Mifflin.

Geen, R. G. (1984). Human motivation: New perspectives on old problems. In A. M. Rogers & C. J. Scheirer (Eds.), *The G.*

Stanley Hall Lecture Series (Vol. 4). Washington, DC: American Psychological Association.

Geen, R. G., & Donnerstein, E. (1983). *Aggression: Theoretical and empirical reviews.* New York: Academic Press.

Geller, E. S., Winnett, R. A., & Everett, P. B. (1982). *Preserving the environment: New strategies for behavior change.* New York: Pergamon.

Gelman, D. (1989, February 20). Roots of addiction. *Newsweek, 113,* 52–57.

Gelman, R., & Baillargeon, R. (1983). A review of some Piagetian concepts. In J. H. Flavell & E. M. Markman (Eds.), *Handbook of child psychology: Vol. 3, Cognitive development* (4th ed.). New York: Wiley.

Gerbner, G., Gross, L., Jackson-Beeck, M., Jeffries-Fox, S., & Signorielli, N. (1978). Cultural indicators: Violence profile No. 9. *Journal of Communication, 28,* 176–207.

Gerrard, M. (1988). Sex, sex guilt, and contraceptive use revisited: The 1980s. *Journal of Personality and Social Psychology, 57,* 973–980.

Gerschwind, N. (1985). Cerebral lateralization: Biological mechanisms, associations, and pathology: III. A hypothesis and a program for research. *Archives of Neurology, 42,* 634–654.

Gerschwind, N., & Galuburda, A. M. (1985). Cerebral lateralization. Biological mechanisms, associations, and pathology: I. A hypothesis and a program for research. *Archives of Neurology, 17,* 128–457.

Gescheider, G. A. (1985). *Psychophysics: Method, theory, and application.* Hillsdale, NJ: Erlbaum.

Gfeller, J. D., Lynn, S. J., & Pribble, W. E. (1987). Enhancing hypnotic susceptibility: Interpersonal and rapport factors. *Journal of Personality and Social Psychology, 52,* 586–595.

Gholson, J. B., & Rosenthal, T. L. (Eds.). (1984). *Application of cognitive development theory.* New York: Academic Press.

Gibbs, M. E., & Ng, K. T. (1977). Psychobiology of memory: Towards a model of memory formation. *Behavioral Reviews, 1,* 113–136.

Gibson, E. J. (1988). Explanatory behavior in the development of perceiving, acting, and the acquiring of knowledge. *Annual Review of Psychology, 39,* 1–41.

Gibson, J. J. (1979). *The ecological approach to visual perception.* Boston: Houghton Mifflin.

Gilbert, D. T., Jones, E. E., & Pelham, B. W. (1987). Influence and inference: What the active perceiver overlooks. *Journal of Personality and Social Psychology, 52,* 861–870.

Gilbert, D. T., Pelham, B. W., & Krull, D. S. (1987). On cognitive busyness: When person perceivers meet persons perceived. *Journal of Personality and Social Psychology, 54,* 733–740.

Gilbert, A. N., & Wysocki, C. J. (1987, October). The smell survey results. *National Geographic, 172,* 514–525.

Gilligan, C. (1987). In a different voice: Women's conception of self and of morality. In M. R. Walsh (Ed.), *The psychology of women.* New Haven, CT: Yale University Press.

Ginsberg, A. (1977). *Mind breaths.* San Francisco: City Lights.

Ginsburg, H. P., & Opper, S. (1988). *Piaget's theory of intellectual development* (3rd ed.). Englewood Cliffs, NJ: Prentice-Hall.

Gladue, B. (1984). Hormone markers for homosexuality. *Science, 225,* 198.

Gladwin, T. (1964). Culture and logical process. In N. Goodenough (Ed.), *Explorations in cultural anthropology: Essays in honor of George Peter Murdoch.* New York: McGraw-Hill.

Glass, A., & Holyoak, K. J. (1985). *Cognition* (2nd ed.). Reading, MA: Addison-Wesley.

Glass, D. C. (1976). *Behavior patterns, stress, and coronary disease.* Hillsdale, NJ: Erlbaum.

Glass, D. C., & Singer, J. E. (1972). *Urban stress.* New York: Academic Press.

Glenn, N. D. (1987, October). Marriage on the rocks. *Psychology Today,* pp. 20–21.

Glick, P., Zion, C., & Nelson, C. (1988). What mediates sex discrimination in hiring decisions? *Journal of Personality and Social Psychology, 55,* 178–186.

Golberg, S. (1983). Parent-infant bonding: Another look. *Child Development, 54,* 1355–1382.

Gold, P. W., Gwirtsman, H., Avgerinos, P. C., Nieman, L. K., Gallucci, W. T., Kaye, W., Jimerson, D., Ebert, M., Rittmaster, R., Loriaux, L., & Chrousos, G. P. (1986). Abnormal hypothalmic-pituitary-adrenal function in anorexia nervosa. *New England Journal of Medicine, 314,* 1335–1342.

Goldfried, M., & Davison, G. (1976). *Clinical behavior therapy.* New York: Holt, Rinehart and Winston.

Goldstein, I. L. (1986). *Training in organizations: Needs assessment, development, and evaluation* (2nd ed.). Pacific Grove, CA: Brooks/Cole.

Goleman, D. (1984, February 21). The aging mind proves capable of lifelong growth. *New York Times,* pp. C-1–C-3.

Goleman, D. (1985, February 5). Mourning: New studies affirm its benefits. *New York Times,* pp. C-1–C-2.

Goleman, D. (1987, August 2). Girls and math: Is biology really destiny? *New York Times,* Education section, pp. 42–46. (a)

Goleman, D. (1987, October 13). Thriving despite hardship: Key childhood traits identified. *New York Times,* pp. C-1, C-11. (b)

Goleman, D. (1988, January 21). Physicians may bungle key part of treatment: The medical interview. *New York Times,* p. B-16. (a)

Goleman, D. (1988, February 2). The experience of touch: Research points to a critical role. *New York Times,* pp. C-1, C-4. (b)

Goleman, D. (1988, March 29). Study of normal mourning process illuminates grief gone awry. *New York Times,* pp. C-1, C-6. (c)

Goleman, D. (1988, October 9). When to challenge the therapist—and why. *New York Times Good Health Magazine,* pp. 37–40. (d)

Goodall, J. (1987, November–December). A plea for chimpanzees. *American Scientist, 75,* 574–577.

Googans, B., & Burden, D. (1987). Vulnerability of working parents: Balancing work and home roles. *Social Work, 32,* 295–300.

Gordon, S. E., & Wyer, R. S., Jr. (1987). Person memory: Category-set-size effects on the recall of a person's behaviors. *Journal of Personality and Social Psychology, 53,* 648–662.

Gorenstein, E. E. (1984). Debating mental illness. *American Psychologist, 39,* 50–56.

Gormezano, I., Prokasy, W. F., & Thompson, R. F. (Eds.). (1987). *Classical conditioning* (3rd ed.). Hillsdale, N.J.: Erlbaum.

Gottesman, I. I., & Shields, J. (1972). *Schizophrenia and genetics.* New York: Academic Press.

Gottfried, A. W. (Ed.). (1984). *Home environment and early cognitive development.* New York: Academic Press.

Gottfried, A. E., & Gottfried, A. W. (Eds.). (1988). *Maternal employment and children's development.* New York: Plenum.

Gough, H. G., Fioravanti, M., & Lazzari, R. (1979). A cross-cultural unisex ideal self scale for the adjective checklist. *Journal of Clinical Psychology, 35,* 314–319.

Gould, P., & White, R. (1974). *Mental maps.* New York: Penguin.

Gould, R. L. (1978). *Transformations.* New York: Simon and Schuster.

Gove, W. R. (1982). Labeling theory's explanation of mental illness: An update of recent evidence. *Deviant Behavior, 3,* 307–327.

Green, R. (1978). Sexual identity of 37 children raised by homosexual or transsexual parents. *American Journal of Psychiatry, 135,* 687–692.

Green, R. (1982). Gender identity disorders and transvestism. In J. Greist, J. Jefferson, & R. Spitzer (Eds.), *Treatment of mental disorders.* New York: Oxford University Press.

Green, R. (1987). The "sissy boy syndrome" and the development of homosexuality. New Haven, CT: Yale University Press.

Greenberg, P. T. (1977, April). The thrill seekers. *Human Behavior, 6,* 17–21.

Greenblatt, M. (1978). The grieving spouse. *American Journal of Psychiatry, 135,* 43–47.

Greeno, J. G. (1978). Natures of problem-solving abilities. In W. K. Estes (Ed.), *Handbook of learning and cognitive processes.* Hillsdale, NJ: Erlbaum.

Greenspan, B. (1988, September 11). The highs, the lows of Greg Louganis. *Parade Magazine,* pp. 4–7.

Gregory, R. L. (1978). *The psychology of seeing* (3rd ed.). New York: McGraw-Hill.

Greist-Bousquet, S., & Schiffman, H. R. (1986). The basis of the Poggendorff effect: An additional clue for Day and Kasperczyk. *Perception and Psychophysics, 39,* 447–448.

Griffit, N., & Veitch, R. (1971). Hot and crowded: Influences of population density on interpersonal affective behavior. *Journal of Personality and Social Psychology, 17,* 92–98.

Griffith, R. M., Miyago, O., & Tago, A. (1958). The universality of typical dreams: Japanese vs. Americans. *American Anthropologist, 60,* 1173–1179.

Groner, R., Groner, M., & Bischof, W. F. (Eds.) (1983). *Methods of heuristics.* Hillsdale, NJ: Erlbaum.

Gross, C. G., Rocha-Miranda, C. E., & Bender, D. B. (1972). Visual properties of neurons in inferotemporal cortex of the macaque. *Journal of Neurophysiology, 35,* 96–111.

Gross, C. G., Deimone, R., Albright, T. D., & Schwartz, E. L. (1985). Inferior temporal cortex and pattern recognition. In C. Chagas, R. Gattass, & C. Gross (Eds.), *Pattern and recognition mechanisms.* New York: Springer-Verlag.

Grossman, H. J. (Ed.) (1983). *Classification in mental retardation.* Washington, DC: American Associations on Mental Deficiency.

Groth, A. N. (1979). *Men who rape: The psychology of the offender.* New York: Plenum Press.

Gruenberg, B. (1980). The happy workers: An analysis of educational and occupational differences in determinants of job satisfaction. *American Journal of Sociology, 86,* 247–271.

Grusec, J. E., Kuczynski, L., Rushton, J. P., & Simutis, Z. M. (1979). Learning resistance to temptation through observation. *Developmental Psychology, 15,* 223–240.

Grusec, J. E., & Skubiski, S. L. (1970). Model nurturance, demand characteristics of the modeling experiment, and altruism. *Journal of Personality and Social Psychology, 14,* 352–359.

Gubrium, J. G. (1973). *The myth of the golden years: A socio-environmental theory of aging.* Springfield, IL: Thomas.

Guilford, J. P. (1968). The structure of intelligence. In D. K. White (Ed.), *Handbook of measurement and assessment in behavioral sciences.* Reading, MA: Addison-Wesley.

Guilford, J. P. (1982). Cognitive psychology's ambiguities: Some remedies. *Psychological Review, 89,* 48–59.

Gur, R. C., Gur, R. E., Obrist, W. D., Hungerbuhler, J. P., Younkin, D., Rosen, A. D., Skilnick, B. E., & Reivich, M. (1982). Sex and handedness differences in cerebral blood flow during rest and cognitive activity. *Science, 217,* 659–661.

Gustavson, C. R., Garcia, J., Hankins, W. G., & Rusniak, K. W. (1974). Coyote predation control by aversive conditioning. *Science, 184,* 581–583.

Haber, R. N. (1983). Stimulus information processing mechanisms in visual space perception. In J. Beck, B. Hope, & A. Rosenfeld (Eds.), *Human and machine vision.* New York: Academic Press.

Hackman, J. R., & Oldham, G. R. (1976). Motivation through the design of work: Test of a theory. *Organizational Behavior and Human Performance, 16,* 250–279.

Hagen, E., Sattler, J. M., & Thorndike, R. L. (1985). *Stanford-Binet test.* Chicago: Riverside.

Hahn, W. K. (1987). Cerebral lateralization of function: From infancy through childhood. *Psychological Bulletin, 10,* 376–392.

Hainline, L., & Lemerise, E. (1982). Infants' scanning of geometric forms varying in size. *Journal of Experimental Child Psychology, 33,* 235–256.

Hall, E. T. (1966). *The hidden dimension.* Garden City, NY: Doubleday.

Hall, E. T. (1976). *Beyond culture.* New York: Anchor/Doubleday.

Hall, J. A. (1978). Gender effects in decoding nonverbal cues. *Psychological Bulletin, 85,* 845–857.

Hall, J. A., Roter, D. L., & Katz, N. R. (1988). Task versus socioemotional behaviors in physicians. *Medical Care, 25,* 399–412.

Hall, J. A., Roter, D. L., & Katz, N. R. (1988). Meta-analysis of correlates of provider behavior in medical encounters. *Medical Care, 26,* 657–675.

Hamburg, D. A., Elliott, G. R., & Parion, D. L. (1980). *Health and behavior: Frontiers of research in the biobehavioral sciences.* Washington, DC: National Academy Press.

Hammond, L., & Fong, M. L. (1988, August). Mediators of stress and satisfaction in multiple-role persons. Paper presented at the annual meeting of the American Psychological Association (Atlanta).

Hanna, G. (1988, February). Mathematics and gender differences. Paper presented at the annual meeting of the American Association for the Advancement of Science (Boston).

Hannon, R., Butler, C. P., Day, C. L., Khan, S. A., Quitoriano, L. A., Butler, A. M., & Meredith, L. A. (1985). Alcohol use and cognitive functioning in men and women college students. In M. Galanter (Ed.), *Recent developments in alcoholism* (Vol. 3, pp. 241–252). New York: Plenum Press.

Hansen, W. B., & Altman, I. (1976). Decorating personal places: A descriptive analysis. *Environment and Behavior, 8,* 491–504.

Hargreaves, D. H. (1967). Social relations in a secondary school. New York: Humanities Press.

Harlow, H. F., Harlow, M. K., & Meyer, D. R. (1950). Learning motivated by a manipulation drive. *Journal of Experimental Psychology, 40,* 228–234.

Harlow, H. F., & Zimmerman, R. R. (1959). Affectional responses in the infant monkey. *Science, 130,* 421–432.

Harlow, J. M. (1869). Recovery from the passage of an iron bar through the head. *Massachusetts Medical Society Publication, 2,* 329–347.

Harris, G. M., & Johnson, S. B. (1983). Coping imagery and relaxation instructions in a covert modeling treatment for test anxiety. *Behavior Therapy, 14,* 144–159.

Harris, L. (1987). *Inside America.* New York: Vintage.

Harris Poll: National Council on the Aging (1975). *The myth and reality of aging in America.* Washington, DC: National Council on the Aging.

Hart, N. A., & Keidel, G. C. (1979). The suicidal adolescent. *American Journal of Nursing,* 80–84.

Harte, R. A., Travers, J. A., & Savich, P. (1948). Voluntary caloric intake of the growing rat. *Journal of Nutrition, 36,* 667–679.

Hartmann, E. (1967). *The biology of dreaming.* Springfield, IL: Thomas.

Hartmann, E. (1982). From the biology of dreaming to the biology of the mind. Psychoanalytic Study of the Child, 37, 303–335.

Hartup, W. W. (1989). Social relationships and their developmental significance. *American Psychologist, 44,* 120–126.

Hartmen, W., & Fithian, M. (1984). *Any man can.* New York: St. Martin's Press.

Harvard Medical School (1987, December). *Mental health letter,* p. 4.

Harvey, J. G., & Weary, G. (Eds.). (1985). *Attribution: Basic issues and applications.* Orlando, FL: Academic Press.

Hassett, J., & Dukes, S. (1986, September). The new employee trainer: A floppy disk. *Psychology Today, 20,* 30–34.

Hastie, R., Penrod, S., & Pennington, N. (1983). *Inside the jury.* Cambridge, MA: Harvard University Press.

Hatfield, E., & Sprecher, S. (1986). *Mirror, mirror: The importance of looks in everyday life.* Albany: State University of New York Press.

Hathaway, B. (1984, July). Running to ruin. *Psychology Today,* pp. 14–15.

Hathaway, S. R., Monachesi, E., & Salasin, S. (1970). A follow-up study of MMPI high 8, schizoid children. In M. Roff & D. F. Ricks (Eds.), *Life history research in psychopathology.* Minneapolis: University of Minnesota Press.

Hatvany, N., & Pucik, V. (1981). An integrated management system: Lessons from the Japanese experience. *Academy of Management Review, 6,* 469–480.

Havighurst, R. J. (1973). Social roles, work, leisure, and education. In C. Eisdorfer & M. P. Lawton (Eds.), *The psychology of adult development and aging.* Washington, DC: American Psychological Association.

Hay, D. F. (1986). Infancy. *Annual Review of Psychology, 37.*

Hay, J. (1989). *Psychworld* (2nd ed. software). New York: McGraw-Hill.

Hayes, J. R. (1966). Memory, goals, and problem solving. In B. Kleinmuntz (Ed.), *Problem solving: Research, method, and theory.* New York: Wiley.

Hayes, S. C., Johnson, V. S., & Cone, J. D. (1975). The marked-item technique: A practical procedure for litter control. *Journal of Applied Behavior Analysis, 8,* 381–386.

Hayflick, L. (1974). The strategy of senescence. *Journal of Gerontology, 14,* 37–45.

Haymes, M., Green, L., & Quinto, R. (1984). Maslow's hierarchy, moral development, and prosocial behavioral skills within a child psychiatric population. *Motivation and Emotion, 8,* 23–31.

Hays, R. B. (1985). A longitudinal study of friendship development. *Journal of Personality and Social Psychology, 48,* 909–924.

Hearst, N., & Hulley, S. B. (1988, April 22–29). Preventing the heterosexual spread of AIDS: Are we giving our patients the best advice? *Journal of the American Medical Association, 259,* 2428–2432.

Hebb, D. O. (1955). Drive and the CNS. *Psychological Review, 62,* 243–254.

Hechinger, F. M. (1985, February 12). How talent can be nurtured. *New York Times,* p. C5.

Heckhausen, H., Schmalt, H. D., & Schneider, K. (1985). *Achievement motivation in perspective.* (M. Woodruff & R. Wicklund, Trans.) Orlando, FL: Academic Press.

Heider, F. (1958). *The psychology of interpersonal relations.* New York: Wiley.

Heilman, M. E., & Stopeck, M. H. (1985). Attractiveness and corporate success: Different causal attributions for men and women. *Journal of Applied Psychology, 70,* 379–388.

Hellerstein, D. (1988, May 22). Plotting a theory of the brain. *New York Times Magazine,* pp. 17–19, 27–28, 55–64.

Helmreich, R. L. (1983). Applying psychology in outer space: Unfulfilled promise revisited. *American Psychologist, 38,* 445–450.

Helson, R., & Moane, G. (1987). Personality change in women from college to midlife. *Journal of Personality and Social Psychology, 53,* 176–186.

Hendrick, C., & Hendrick, S. (1986). A theory and method of love. *Journal of personality and social psychology, 50,* 392–402.

Hendrick, C., & Hendrick, S. S. (1989). Research on love: Does it measure up? *Journal of Personality and Social Psychology, 56,* 784–794.

Hendrick, S. S., Hendrick, C., & Adler, N. L. (1988). Romantic relationships: Love, satisfaction, and staying together. *Journal of Personality and Social Psychology, 54,* 980–988.

Herink, R. (Ed.). *The psychotherapy handbook.* New York: New American Library.

Herman, L. M., & Forestell, P. H. (1985). Reporting presence or absence of named objects by a language-trained dolphin. *Neuroscience & Biobehavioral Reviews, 9,* 667–681.

Hermans, H. J. M. (1987). The dream in the process of valuation: A method of interpretation. *Journal of Personality and Social Psychology, 53,* 163–175.

Hersh, R. H., Paolitto, D. P., & Reimer, J. (1979). *Promoting moral growth.* New York: Longmans.

Hetherington, E. M. (1986, April). Introduction. In E. M. Hetherington (Chair), *Coping with divorce and remarriage.* Symposium conducted at the meeting of the Southern Conference on Human Development (Nashville).

Hetherington, E. M., Cox, M., & Cox, R. (1978). The aftermath of divorce. In J. H. Stevens, Jr., & M. Matthews (Eds.), *Mother-child, father-child relations.* Washington, DC: National Association for the Education of Young Children.

Hetherington, E. M., & Parke, R. D. (1986). *Child psychology: A contemporary viewpoint* (3rd ed.). New York: McGraw-Hill.

Heyward, W. L., & Curran, J. W. (1988, October). The epidemiology of AIDS in the U.S. *Scientific American,* 72–81.

Higbee, K. L., & Kunihira, S. (1985). Cross-cultural applications of Yodni mnemonics in education. *Educational Psychologist, 20,* 57–64.

Hilgard, E. R. (1974). Imaginative involvement: Some characteristics of the highly hypnotizable and the nonhypnotizable. *International Journal of Clinical and Experimental Hypnosis, 22,* 138–156.

Hilgard, E. R. (1975). Hypnosis. *Annual Review of Psychology, 26,* 19–44.

Hilgard, E. R. (1980). Consciousness in contemporary psychology. *Annual Review of Psychology, 31,* 1–26.

Hill, C. T., & Stull, D. E. (1981). Sex differences in effects of social and value similarity in same-sex friendship. *Journal of Personality and Social Psychology, 41,* 488–502.

Hinton, G. E., & Sejnowski, T. J. (1985). A learning algorithm for Boltzmann machines. *Cognitive Science, 9,* 147–169.

Hinz, L. D., & Williamson, D. A. (1987). Bulimia and depression: A review of the affective-variant hypothesis. *Psychological Bulletin, 102,* 150–158.

Hiroto, D. S., & Seligman, M. E. P. (1975). Generality of learned helplessness in man. *Journal of Personality and Social Psychology, 31,* 311–327.

Hirsch, J., & Leibel, R. (1988, February 25). New light on obesity. *New England Journal of Medicine, 318,* 467–472.

Hirschman, R. S., Leventhal, H., & Glynn, K. (1984). The development of smoking behavior: Conceptualization and supportive cross-sectional survey data. *Journal of Applied Social Psychology, 14,* 184–206.

Hite, S. (1976). *The Hite report.* New York: Macmillan.

Hobson, J. A. (1988). *The dreaming brain.* New York: Basic Books.

Hobson, J. A., & McCarley, R. W. (1977). The brain as a dream state generator: An activation-synthesis hypothesis of the dream process. *American Journal of Psychiatry, 134,* 1335–1348.

Hoch, S. J. (1987). Perceived consensus and predictive accuracy: The pros and cons of projection. *Journal of Personality and Social Psychology, 53,* 221–234.

Hochberg, J. E. (1978). *Perception.* Englewood Cliffs, NJ: Prentice-Hall.

Hoffman, C., Lau, I., & Johnson, D. R. (1986). The linguistic relativity of person cognition: An English–Chinese comparison. *Journal of Personality and Social Psychology, 51,* 1097–1105.

Hoffman, L. W. (1989). Effects of maternal employment in the two-parent family. *American Psychologist, 44,* 283–292.

Holahan, C. J. (1982). *Environmental psychology.* New York: Random House.

Holahan, C. J., & Dobrowolny, M. B. (1978). Cognitive and behavioral correlates of the spatial environment: An interactional analysis. *Environment and Behavior, 10,* 317–334.

Holahan, C. J., & Moos, R. H. (1987). Personal and contextual determinants of coping strategies. *Journal of Personality and Social Psychology, 52,* 946–955.

Holden, C. (1985, January). Genes, personality, and alcoholism. *Psychology Today,* pp. 38–44.

Holden, C. (1986, July 18). New Toyota–GM plant is U.S. model for Japanese management. *Science, 233,* 273–277. (a)

Holden, C. (1986, August 22). Youth suicide: New research focuses on a growing social problem. *Science, 233,* 839–840. (b)

Holden, C. (1986, September 19). Researchers grapple with problems of updating classic psychological test. *Science, 233,* 1249–1251. (c)

Holden, C. (1987, August 7). The genetics of personality. *Science, 237,* 598–601. (a)

Holden, C. (1987, October 9). Why do women live longer than men? *Science, 238,* 158–160. (b)

Holden, C. (1988, January 29). Animal stealer convicted. *Science, 239,* 458.

Hollander, E. P. (1980). Leadership and social exchange processes. In K. J. Gargon, M. Greenberg & R. S. Willis (Eds.), *Social exchange: Advances in theory and research.* New York: Plenum Press.

Hollingshead, A. B., & Redich, F. C. (1958). *Social class and mental illness.* New York: Wiley.

Hollis, K. L. (1984). The biological function of Pavlovian conditioning: The best defense is a good offense. *Journal of Experimental Psychology: Animal Behavior Processes, 10,* 413–425.

Holmes, D. S. (1985). To meditate or rest?: The answer is rest. *American Psychologist, 40,* 728–731.

Holmes, T. H., & Rahe, R. H. (1967). The social readjustment rating scale. *Journal of Psychosomatic Research, 11,* 213–218.

Holmes, T. S., & Holmes, T. H. (1970). Short-term intrusions into the life style routine. *Journal of Psychosomatic Research, 14,* 121–132.

Holzman, A. D., & Turk, D. C. (1985). *Pain management: A handbook of psychological treatment approaches.* New York: Pergamon.

Honts, C. R., Hodes, R. L., & Raskin, D. C. (1985). Effects of physical countermeasures on the physiological detection of deception. *Journal of Applied Psychology, 70,* 177–187.

Honts, C. R., Raskin, D. C., & Kircher, J. C. (1987). Effects of physical countermeasure and their electromyographic detection during polygraphy tests for deception. *Journal of Psychophysiology, 1,* 241–247.

Hoon, P. W., Bruce, K., & Kinchloe, B. (1982). Does the menstrual cycle play a role in sexual arousal? *Psychophysiology, 19,* 21–26.

Horn, J. L. (1980). Concepts of intellect in relation to learning and adult development. *Intelligence, 4,* 285–317.

Horn, M. C., & Bachrach, C. A. (1985). *1982 National Survey of Family Growth.* Washington, DC: National Center for Health Statistics.

Horner, M. (1972). Toward an understanding of achievement-related conflicts in women. *Journal of Social Issues, 28,* 157–175.

Horney, K. (1937). *Neurotic personality of our times.* New York: Norton.

Horowitz, F. D., & O'Brien, M. (Eds.) (1987). *The gifted and talented: Developmental perspectives.* Washington, DC: American Psychological Association.

Horowitz, M. J. (1976). *Stress response syndrome.* New York: Jason Aronson.

Hostetler, A. J. (1988, April). Exploring the "gatekeeper" of memory. *APA Monitor, 19,* 3.

Houston, L. N. (1981). Romanticism and eroticism among black and white college students. *Adolescence, 16,* 263–272.

Hovland, C., Janis, I., & Kelly, H. H. (1953). *Communication and persuasion.* New Haven, CT: Yale University Press.

Howard, A., Pion, G. M., Gottfredson, G. D., Flattau, P. E., Oskamp, S., Pfafflin, S. M., Bray, D. W., & Burstein, A. D. (1986). The changing face of American psychology: A report from the committee on employment and human resources. *American Psychologist, 41,* 1311–1327.

Howard, K. I., & Zola, M. A. (1988). Paper presented at the annual meeting of the Society for Psychotherapy Research.

Howells, J. G., & Osborn, M. L. (1984). *A reference companion to the history of abnormal psychology.* Westport, CT: Greenwood Press.

Hoyenga, K., & Hoyenga, K. (1984). *Motivation.* Monterey, CA: Brooks-Cole.

Hubel, D. H., & Wiesel, T. N. (1979). Brain mechanisms of vision. *Scientific American, 241,* 150–162.

Hudson, W. (1960). Pictorial depth perception in subcultural groups in Africa. *Journal of Social Psychology, 52,* 183–208.

Huesmann, L. R., & Eron, L. D. (Eds.) (1986). *Television and the aggressive child: A cross-national comparison.* Hillsdale, NJ: Erlbaum.

Huesmann, L. R., Eron, L. D., Klein, R., Brice, P., & Fischer, P. (1983). Mitigating the imitation of aggressive behaviors by changing children's attitudes about media violence. *Journal of Personality and Social Psychology, 5,* 899–910.

Hughes, J. (1987). *Cancer and emotion: Psychological preludes and reactions to cancer.* Chichester, England: John Wiley.

Hull, C. L. (1943). *Principles of behavior.* New York: Appleton-Century-Crofts.

Hull, J. G., VanTreuren, R. R., & Virnelli, S. (1987). Hardiness and health: A critique and alternative approach. *Journal of Personality and Social Psychology, 53,* 518–530.

Humphries, C., Carver, C. S., Neumann, P. G. (1983). Cognitive characteristics of the type A coronary-prone behavior pattern. *Journal of Personality and Social Psychology, 44,* 177–187.

Hunt, M. (1974). *Sexual behaviors in the 1970s.* New York: Dell.

Hunt, W. A., & Matarazzo, J. A. (1982). Changing smoking behavior. In R. J. Gatchel, A. Baum, & J. E. Singer (Eds.), *Behavioral medicine and clinical psychology: Overlapping areas.* Hillsdale, NJ: Erlbaum.

Huntley, C. W., Davis, F. (1983). Undergraduate study of value scores as predictors of occupation 25 years later. *Journal of Personality and Social Psychology, 45,* 1148–1155.

Hurvich, L., & Jameson, D. (1974). Opponent processes as a model of neural organization. *American Psychologist, 29,* 88–102.

Hurlburt, A. C., & Poggio, T. A. (1988, January 29). Synthesizing a color algorithm from examples. *Science, 239,* 482–485.

Hurst, R. (1984). *Pilot error.* London: Granada.

Huston, A. C. (1983). Sex-typing. In P. H. Mussen (Ed.), *Handbook of child psychology* (4th ed.). New York: Wiley.

Hutchison, J. B. (Ed.) (1978). *Biological determinants of sexual behavior.* New York: Wiley.

Hyde, J. A., & Linn, M. C. (1988). Gender differences in verbal ability: A meta-analysis. *Psychological Bulletin, 104,* 53–69.

Hyde, J. S. (1984). How large are gender differences in aggression? A developmental meta-analysis. *Developmental Psychology, 20,* 722–736.

Hyland, M. E. (1987). Control theory interpretation of psychological mechanisms of depression: Comparison and integration of several theories. *Psychological Bulletin, 102,* 109–121.

Iaffaldano, M. T., & Muchinsky, P. M. (1985). Job satisfaction and job performance: A meta-analysis. *Psychological Bulletin, 97,* 151–173.

Ickes, W. (Ed.) (1984). *Compatible and incompatible relationships.* New York: Springer-Verlag.

Imai, M. (1986). *Kaizen: The key to Japan's competitive success.* New York: Random House.

Ingelfinger, F. J. (1944). The late effects of total and subtotal gastrectomy. *New England Journal of Medicine, 231,* 321–377.

Institute of Medicine. (1982). *Marijuana and health.* Washington, DC: National Academy Press.

Intriligator, M. D., & Brito, D. L. (1988). The potential contribution of psychology to nuclear war issues. *American Psychologist, 43,* 318–321.

Isen, A. M., Daubman, K. A., & Nowicki, G. P. (1987). Positive affect facilitates creative problem solving. *Journal of Personality and Social Psychology, 52,* 1122–1131.

Izard, C. (1988, August). The structure and function of human emotions. Paper presented at the annual meeting of the American Psychological Association.

Izard, C. E. (1977). *Human emotions.* New York: Plenum.

Jacklin, C. N. (1989). Female and male: Issues of gender. *American Psychologist, 44,* 127–133.

Jackson, J. M., Buglione, S. A., & Glenwick, D. S. (1988). Major league baseball performance as a function of being traded: A drive theory analysis. *Personality and Social Psychology Bulletin, 14,* 46–56.

Jacobs, B. L. (1987, July–August). How hallucinogenic drugs work. *American Scientist, 75,* 386–392.

Jacobs, J. (1971). *Adolescent suicide.* New York: Wiley.

James, W. (1890). *The principles of psychology,* New York: Holt.

Janis, I. (1972). *Victims of groupthink: A psychological study of foreign policy decisions and fiascoes.* Boston: Houghton Mifflin.

Janis, I. (1984). Improving adherence to medical recommendations: Descriptive hypothesis derived from recent research in social psychology. In A. Baum, J. E. Singer, & S. E. Taylor (Eds.), *Handbook of medical psychology* (Vol. 4). Hillsdale, NJ: Erlbaum.

Janis, I. L., & Mann, L. (1976). *Decision making.* New York: Holt, Rinehart and Winston.

Janis, I. L., & Rodin, J. (1979). Attribution, control, and decision making: Social psychology and health care. In *Health psychology: A handbook.* San Francisco: Jossey-Bass.

Janoff-Bulman, R. (1988, August). Adaptiveness of illusions: A structural analysis of people's conceptual systems. Paper presented at the annual meeting of the American Psychological Association (Atlanta).

Jaroff, L. (1987, July 13). Steps toward a brave new world. *Time,* pp. 56–57.

Jarvik, M. E. (1973). Further observations on nicotine as a reinforcing agent in smoking. In W. L. Dunn, Jr. (Ed.), *Smoking behavior: Motives and incentives.* Washington, DC: Winston.

Jemmott, J. B., III, & Locke, S. E. (1984). Psychosocial factors, immunologic mediation, and human susceptibility to infectious disease: How much do we know? *Psychological Bulletin, 95,* 78–108.

Jencks, C., et al. (1972). *Inequality.* New York: Basic Books.

Jenkins, B. M. (1983). Some reflections on recent trends in terrorism. Santa Monica, CA: Rand Corporation.

Jenkins, S. R. (1987). Need for achievement and women's careers over 14 years: Evidence for occupational structure effects. *Journal of Personality and Social Psychology, 53,* 922–932.

Jennings, J., Geis, F. L., & Brown, V. (1980). Influence of television commercials on women's self-confidence and independent judgment. *Journal of Personality and Social Psychology, 38,* 203–210.

Jensen, A. How much can we boost IQ and scholastic achievement? *Harvard Educational Review, 39,* 785–795.

Jensen, M. R. (1987). Psychobiological factors predicting the course of breast cancer. *Journal of Personality, 55,* 317–342.

Jervis, R., Lebow, R. N., & Stein, J. G., with Moragan, P. M., & Snyder, J. L. (1985). *Psychology and deterrence.* Baltimore: Johns Hopkins University Press.

John, E. R., Prichep, L. S., Fridman, J., & Easton, P. (1988, January 8). Neurometrics: Computer-assisted differential diagnosis of brain dysfunction. *Science, 239,* 162–169.

Johnson, D. M., Parrott, G. R., & Stratton, R. P. (1968). Production and judgment of solutions to five problems. *Journal of Educational Psychology Monograph Supplement, 59* (6, pt. 2).

Johnson, D. W., & Johnson, R. T. (1979). Conflict in the classroom: Controversy and learning. *Review of Educational Research, 49,* 51–70.

Johnson, J. T., Cain, L. M., Falke, T. L., Hayman, J., & Perillo, E. (1985). The "Barnum Effect" revisited: Cognitive and motivational factors in the acceptance of personality descriptions. *Journal of Personality and Social Psychology, 49,* 1378–1391.

Johnson, T. E. (1986, March 17). Kids and cocaine. *Newsweek,* pp. 58–65.

Jones, G. N., Brantley, P. J., & Gilchrist, J. C. (1988, August). The relation between daily stress and health. Paper presented at the annual meeting of the American Psychological Association (Atlanta).

Jones, L. V. (1984). White-black achievement differences: The narrowing gap. *American Psychologist, 39,* 1207–1213.

Josephson, W. L. (1987). Television violence and children's aggression: Testing the priming, social script, and disinhibition predictions. *Journal of Personality and Social Psychology, 53,* 882–890.

Joyce, C. (1984, May). Space travel is no joyride. *Psychology Today, 18,* 30–37.

Joyce, J. (1934). *Ulysses.* New York: Random House.

Jusczyk, P. W. (1986). Toward a model of the

development of speech perception. In J. S. Perkell & D. H. Klatt (Eds.), *Invariance and Variability in speech processes*. Hillsdale, NJ: Erlbaum.

Jusczyk, P. W., & Derrah, C. (1987). Representation of speech sounds by young infants. *Developmental Psychology, 23,* 648–654.

Jussim, L., Coleman, L. M., & Lerch, L. (1987). The nature of stereotypes: A comparison and integration of three theories. *Journal of Personality and Social Psychology, 52,* 536–546.

Kagan, J. (1989). Temperamental contributions to social behavior. *American Psychologist, 44,* 668–674.

Kagan, J., Kearsley, R. B., & Zelazo, P. R. (1978). *Infancy: Its place in human development.* Cambridge, MA: Harvard University Press.

Kagan, J., & Moss, H. (1962). *Birth to maturity.* New York: Wiley.

Kagan, J., Reznick, J. S., & Snidman, N. (1988, April 8). Biological bases of childhood shyness. *Science, 240,* 167–171.

Kahn, R. L., Wolfe, D. M., Quinn, R. P., Snoek, J. D., & Rosenthal, R. A. (1964). *Organizational stress: Studies in role conflict and ambiguity.* New York: Wiley.

Kahn, S., Zimmerman, G., Csikszentmihalyi, M., & Getzels, J. W. (1985). Relations between identity in young adulthood and intimacy at midlife. *Journal of Personality and Social Psychology, 49,* 1316–1322.

Kahneman, D., & Tversky, A. (1973). On the psychology of prediction. *Psychology Review, 80,* 237–251.

Kahneman, D., & Tversky, A. (1972). Subjective probability: A judgment of representativeness. *Cognitive Psychology, 3,* 430–454.

Kamin, L. J. (1974). *The science and politics of IQ.* New York: Wiley.

Kamin, L., with Eysenck, H. J. (1981). *The intelligence controversy.* New York: Wiley.

Kandel, E. R., & Schwartz, J. H. (1982). Molecular biology of learning: Modulation or transmitter release. *Science, 218,* 433–442.

Kane, J. M. (1983). Hypotheses regarding the mechanism of action of antidepressant drugs: Neurotransmitters in affective disorders. In A. Rifkin (Ed.), *Schizophrenia and affective disorders: Biology and drug treatment* (pp. 19–34). Boston: John Wright.

Kanfer, F. H., & Goldstein, A. P. (Eds.). (1985). *Helping people change: A textbook of methods* (3rd ed.). New York: Pergamon.

Kanner, A. D., Coyne, J. C., Schaefer, C., & Lazarus, R. (1981). Comparison of two modes of stress measurement: Daily hassles and uplifts versus major life events. *Journal of Behavioral Medicine, 4,* 14.

Kaplan, H. S. (1974). *The new sex therapy.* New York: Brunner-Mazel.

Kaplan, H. S. (1979). *Disorders of sexual desire.* New York: Simon & Schuster.

Kaplan, M. F. (1975). Information integration in social judgment: Interaction of judge and informational components. In M. Kaplan & S. Schwartz (Eds.), *Human development and decision processes.* New York: Academic Press.

Kaplan, M. F. (1983, May). *Effect of training on reasoning in moral choice.* Paper presented at the meeting of the Midwestern Psychological Association.

Kaplan, M. F., & Miller, C. E. (1987). Group decision making and normative versus informational influence: Effects of type of issue and assigned decision rule. *Journal of Personality and Social Psychology, 53,* 306–313.

Karasu, T. B. (1982). Psychotherapy and psychopharmacology: Toward an integrative model. *American Journal of Psychiatry, 139,* 1102–1113.

Karlins, M., & Abelson, H. I. (1979). *How opinions and attitudes are changed.* New York: Springer-Verlag.

Karoly, P., & Kanfer, F. H. (1982). *Self-management and behavior change.* New York: Pergamon.

Karp, D. A. (1988). A decade of remembrances: Changing age consciousness between fifty and sixty years old. *The Gerontologist, 28,* 727–738.

Kasa, P. (1986). The cholinergic systems in brain and spinal cord. *Progress in Neurobiology, 26,* 211–272.

Kassin, S. M. (1985). Eyewitness identification: Retrospective self-awareness and the accuracy-confidence correlation. *Journal of Personality and Social Psychology, 41,* 878–893.

Kastenbaum, R. (1975). Is death a life crisis? On the confrontation with death in theory and practice. In N. Datan & L. H. Ginsberg (Eds.), *Life-span developmental psychology: Normative life crisis.* New York: Academic Press.

Katz, D., & Braly, K. W. (1933). Racial stereotypes of 100 college students. *Journal of Abnormal and Social Psychology, 4,* 280–290.

Katz, D., & Kahn, R. (1978). *The social psychology of organizations* (2nd ed.). New York: Wiley.

Katzell, R. A., & Guzzo, R. A. (1983). Psychological approaches to productivity improvement. *American Psychologist,* 468–472.

Kaufman, J., Schaffer, H., & Burglass, M. E. (1983). The clinical assessment and diagnosis of addiction. In T. Bratter & G. Forrest (Eds.), *Current treatment of substance abuse and alcoholism.* New York: Macmillan.

Kazdin, A. E. (1983). Treatment of conduct disorders. In J. B. W. Williams & R. L. Spitzer (Eds.), *Psychotherapy research: Where are we and where should we go?* (pp. 3–28). New York: Guilford Press.

Kazdin, A. E., & Wilson, G. T. (1978). *Evaluation of behavior therapy: Issues, evidence, and research strategies.* Cambridge, MA: Ballinger.

Keating, D. P., & Clark, L. V. (1980). Development of physical and social reasoning in adolescence. *Developmental Psychology, 16,* 23–30.

Keerdoja, E. (1985, July 8). Scaling the walls of silence. *Newsweek,* p. 66.

Keesey, R. E., & Powley, T. L. (1986). The regulation of body weight. *Annual Review of Psychology,* p. 37.

Keith, S. J., & Matthews, S. M. (1983). Schizophrenia: A review of psychosocial treatment strategies. In J. W. W. Williams & R. L. Spitzer (Eds.), *Psychotherapy research: Where are we and where should we go?* (pp. 70–88). New York: Guilford Press.

Keith-Spiegel, P., & Koocher, G. P. (1985). *Ethics in psychology.* San Francisco: Random House-Knopf.

Kelley, H. (1950). The warm-cold variable in first impressions of persons. *Journal of Personality and Social Psychology, 18,* 431–439.

Kelley, H. H. (1967). Attribution theory in social psychology. In D. Levine (Ed.), *Nebraska Symposium on Motivation.* Lincoln: University of Nebraska Press.

Kelley, H. H. (1979). *Close relationships: Their structures and processes.* Hillsdale, NJ: Erlbaum.

Kemeny, M. (1985, August). *Stress and psychosocial factors predicting immunity and genital herpes recurrence.* Paper presented at the annual convention of the American Psychological Association (Los Angeles).

Kendig, F. (1983, April). A conversation with Roger Schank. *Psychology Today,* pp. 28–36.

Kendrick, D. T., & Funder, D. C. (1988). Profiting from controversy: Lessons from the person-situation debate. *American Psychologist, 43,* 23–34.

Kennedy, T. D., & Kumura, H. K. (1974). Transfer, behavioral improvement, and anxiety reduction in systematic desensitization. *Journal of Consulting and Clinical Psychology, 42,* 720–728.

Kenny, D. A., & Albright, L. (1987). Accuracy in interpersonal perception: A social relations analysis. *Psychological Bulletin, 102,* 390–402.

Kerouac, J. (1959). *Mexico City blues.* New York: Grove Press.

Kertesz, A. E. (1983). Cyclofusion and stereopsis. *Perception and Psychophysics, 33,* 99–101.

Kiecolt-Glaser, J. K., & Glaser, R. (1986). Behavioral influences on immune function: Evidence for the interplay between stress and health. In T. Field, P. McCabe, & N. Schneiderman (Eds.), *Stress and coping* (Vol. 2). Hillsdale, NJ: Erlbaum.

Kienker, P. K., Sejnowski, T. J., Hinton, G. E., & Schumacher, L. E. (1986). Separating figure from ground with a parallel network. *Perception, 15,* 197–216.

Kiester, E., Jr. (1986, March). Spare parts for damaged brains. *Science 86, 7,* 33–38.

Kihlstrom, J. F. (1987, September 18). The cognitive unconscious. *Science, 237,* 1445–1452.

Kilpatrick, D. G., Resick, P. A., & Veronen, L. J. (1981). Effects of rape experience: A longitudinal study. *Journal of Social Issues, 3*, 105–122.

Kimble, G. A. (1989). Psychology from the standpoint of a generalist. *American Psychologist, 44*, 491–499.

Kimura, D. (1983). Sex differences in cerebral organization for speech and praxic functions. *Canadian Journal of Psychology, 37*, 19–35.

Kinsey, A. C., Pomeroy, W. B., & Martin, C. E. (1948). *Sexual behavior in the human male.* Philadelphia: Saunders.

Kinsey, A. C., Pomeroy, W. B., Martin, C. E., & Gebhard, P. H. (1953). *Sexual behavior in the human female.* Philadelphia: Saunders.

Kirby, D. (1977). The methods and methodological problems of sex research. In J. S. DeLora & C. A. B. Warren (Eds.), *Understanding sexual interaction.* Boston: Houghton Mifflin.

Klaus, H. M., & Kennell, J. H. (1976). *Maternal-infant bonding.* St. Louis, MO: Mosby.

Klein, G. S. (1970). *Perception, motives, and personality.* New York: Knopf.

Kleinmuntz, B. (1967). *Personality measurement: An introduction.* Homewood, IL: Dorsey Press.

Klerman, G. L. (1983). Evaluating the efficacy of psychotherapy. In P. J. Clayton & J. E. Barret (Eds.), *Treatment of depression: Old controversies and new approaches* (pp. 291–298). New York: Raven Press.

Klerman, G. L. (1984). The advantages of DSM-III. *American Journal of Psychiatry, 141*, 539–542.

Klima, E. S., & Bellugi, U. (1973). Teaching apes to communicate. In G. A. Miller (Ed.), *Communication, language and meaning: Psychological perspectives* (pp. 76–106). New York: Basic Books.

Kline, P. (1987). The experimental study of the psychoanalytic unconscious. *Personality and Social Psychology Bulletin, 13*, 363–378.

Klinger, E. (1987, October). The power of daydreams. *Psychology Today*, pp. 37–44.

Kloos, P. (1971). *The Maroni River caribs of Surinam.* Assen. The Netherlands: Van Gorcum.

Knittle, J. L. (1975). Early influences on development of adipose tissue. In G. A. Bray (Ed.), *Obesity in perspective.* Washington, DC: U.S. Government Printing Office.

Kobasa, S. C. (1979). Stressful life events, personality, and health: An inquiry into hardiness. *Journal of Personality and Social Psychology, 37*, 1–11.

Kobasa, S. C. (1982). The hardy personality: Toward a social psychology of stress and health. In G. S. Sanders & J. Suls (Eds.), *Social psychology of health and illness.* Hillsdale, NJ: Erlbaum.

Kohlberg, L. (1969). Stage and sequence: The cognitive-developmental approach to socialization. In D. Goslin (Ed.), *Handbook of socialization theory and research.* Chicago: Rand McNally.

Kohlberg, L. (1976). Stages and moralization: the cognitive-developmental approach. In T. Liskona (Ed.), *Moral development and behavior: Theory, research and social issues.* New York: Holt, Rinehart and Winston.

Kohlberg, L. (1984). *The psychology of moral development: Essays on moral development* (Vol. 2). San Francisco: Harper & Row.

Kohn, A. (1988, April). What they say. *Psychology Today*, pp. 36–41.

Köhler, W. (1927). *The mentality of apes.* London: Routledge & Kegan Paul.

Kolata, G. (1986, December 5). New drug counters alcohol intoxication. *Science, 234*, 1198–1199.

Kolata, G. (1987, May 15). Early signs of school-age IQ. *Science, 236*, 774–775. (a)

Kolata, G. (1987, August 14). What babies know, and noises parents make. *Science, 237*, 726. (b)

Kolata, G. (1987, November 10). Alcoholism: Genetic links grow clearer. *New York Times*, p. C-1. (c)

Kolata, G. (1988, February 25). New obesity studies indicate metabolism is often to blame. *New York Times*, pp. A-1, B-5.

Konner, M. (1988, January 17). Caffeine high. *New York Times Magazine*, pp. 47–48.

Konnold, C. (1985). Personal communication.

Koop, C. E. (1988). *The health consequences of smoking.* Washington, DC: Government Printing Office.

Korsch, B. M., & Negrete, V. F. (1972). Doctor-patient communication. *Scientific American*, 66–74.

Koss, M. P. (in press). Hidden rape: Incidence, prevalence, and descriptive characteristics of sexual aggression in a national sample of college students. In A. W. Burgess (Ed.), *Sexual assault* (Vol. 2). New York: Garland.

Koss, M. P., & Burkhart, B. R. (1989). A conceptual analysis of rape victimization. *Psychology of Women Quarterly, 13*, 27–40.

Koss, M. P., Dinero, T. E., Seibel, C. A., & Cox, S. L. (1988). Stranger and acquaintance rape: Are there differences in the victim's experience? *Psychology of Women's Quarterly, 12*, 1–24.

Kosslyn, S. M. (1988). Aspects of a cognitive neuroscience of mental imagery. *Science, 240*, 1621–1626.

Koveceses, Z. (1987). *The container metaphor of emotion.* Paper presented at the University of Massachusetts, Amherst.

Kraepelin, E. (1904–1968). *Lectures on clinical psychiatry.* New York: Hafner.

Kraft, C. L., & Elworth, C. L. (1969). Measurement of aircrew performance: The flight deck workload and its relation to pilot performance (NTIS70-19779/A; 699934-DTIC).

Kraines, S. H. (1948). *The therapy of the neuroses and psychoses* (3rd ed.). Philadelphia: Lea and Febiger.

Krantz, D., Baum, A., & Wideman, M. V. (1980). Assessment of preferences for self-treatment and information in health care. *Journal of Personality and Social Psychology, 39*, 977–990.

Krantz, D. S., Glass, D. C., Schaeffer, M. A., & Davia, J.E. (1982). Behavior patterns and coronary disease: A critical evaluation. In J. T. Cacioppo & R. E. Petty (Eds.), *Focus on cardiovascular psychophysiology* (pp. 315–346). New York: Guilford Press.

Kravitz, E. A. (1988). Hormonal control of behavior: Amines and the biasing of behavioral output in lobsters. *Science, 241*, 1775–1782.

Krebs, D. L., & Miller, D. T. (1985). Altruism and aggression. In G. Lindzey & E. Aronson (Eds.), *Handbook of social psychology,* (3rd ed.). New York: Random House.

Kringlen, E. (1978). Adult offspring of two psychotic parents, with special reference to schizophrenia. In L. C. Wynne, R. L. Cromwell, & S. Matthysee (Eds.), *The nature of schizophrenia: New epidemiological-clinical twin study.* Oslo: Univesitsforlaget.

Krippner, S. (Ed.). (1982). *Advances in parapsychological research* (Vol. 3). New York: Plenum Press.

Kroger, W. S., & Fexler, W. D. (1976). *Hypnosis and behavior modification: Imagery conditioning.* Philadelphia: Lippincott.

Kübler-Ross, E. (1969). *On death and dying.* New York: Macmillan.

Kucharski, D., & Hall, W. G. (1987). New routes to early memories. *Science, 238*, 786–788.

Kulik, J. A., Bangert-Drowns, R. L., & Kulik, C. C. (1984). Effectiveness of coaching for aptitude tests. *Psychological Bulletin, 95*, 179–188.

Kurtines, W. M., & Gewirtz, J. L. (Eds.). (1987). *Moral development through social interaction.* New York: Wiley.

Lader, M., & Matthews, A. (1970). Physiological changes during spontaneous panic attacks. *Journal of Psychosomatic Research, 14*, 377–382.

LaFrance, M., & Mayo, C. (1978). *Moving bodies: Nonverbal communication in social relationships.* Monterey, CA: Brooks/Cole.

Lakey, B., & Heller, K. (1985). Response biases and the relation between negative life events and psychological symptoms. *Journal of Personality and Social Psychology, 49*, 1662–1668.

Lamal, P. A. (1979). College students' common beliefs about psychology. *Teaching of Psychology, 6*, 155–158.

Lamb, M. (1982). The bonding phenomenon: Misinterpretations and their implications. *Journal of Pediatrics, 101*, 555–557.

Lamb, M., & Bornstein, M. H. (1987). *The father's role.* Hillsdale, N.J.: Erlbaum.

Lamb, M. E. (1982). Paternal influences on early socio-emotional development. *Journal of Child Psychology and Psychiatry and Allied Disciplines, 23*, 185–190.

Lamb, M. E. (Ed.) (1987). *The father's role.* Hillsdale, NJ: Erlbaum.

Lambert, M. J., Shapiro, D. A., & Bergin, A. E. (1986). The effectiveness of psychotherapy. In S. L. Garfield & A. E. Bergin (Eds.), *Handbook of psychotherapy and behavior change* (3rd ed.). New York: Wiley.

Landesman, S., & Ramey, C. (1989). Developmental psychology and mental retardation: Integrating scientific principles with treatment practices. *American Psychologist, 44,* 409–415.

Landis, D., Day, H. R., McGrew, P. L., Thomas, J. A., & Miller, A. B. (1976). Can a black "culture assimilator" increase racial understanding? *Journal of Social Issues, 32,* 169–183.

Landman, J., & Dawes, R. M. (1984). Reply to Orwin and Cordray. *American Psychologist, 39,* 72–73.

Landy, D., & Aronson, E. (1969). The influence of the character of the criminal and his victim on the decisions of simulated jurors. *Journal of Experimental Social Psychology, 5,* 141–152.

Lang, J. S. (1987, April 13). Happiness is a reunited set of twins. *U.S. News and World Report,* pp. 63–66.

Langer, E. J. (1983). *The psychology of control.* Beverly Hills, CA: Sage.

Langer, E., Bashner, R. S., & Chanowitz, B. (1985). Decreasing prejudice by increasing discrimination. *Journal of Personality and Social Psychology, 49,* 113–120.

Langer, E., & Janis, I. (1979). *The psychology of control.* Beverley Hills, CA: Sage.

Langer, E., Janis, I. L., & Wolfer, J. A. (1975). Reduction of psychological stress in surgical patients. *Journal of Experimental Social Psychology, 11,* 155–165.

Langlois, J. H., Roggman, L. A., Casey, R. J., Ritter, J. M., et al. (1987). Infant preferences for attractive faces: Rudiments of a stereotype? *Developmental Psychology, 23,* 363–369.

LaPiere, R. T. (1934). Attitudes and actions. *Social Forces, 13,* 230–237.

Lashley, K. S. (1950). In search of the engram. *Symposia of the Society for Experimental Biology, 4,* 454–482.

Latané, B., & Darley, J. M. (1970). *The unresponsive bystander: Why doesn't he help?* New York: Appleton-Century-Crofts.

Latané, B., & Nida, S. (1981). Ten years of research on group size and helping. *Psychological Bulletin, 89,* 308–324.

Latham, G. P. (1988). Human resource training and development. *Annual Review of Psychology, 39,* 545–582.

Lauer, J., & Lauer, R. (1985, June). Marriages made to last. *Psychology Today,* pp. 22–26.

Layton, B. D., & Turnbull, B. (1975). Belief, evaluation, and performance in an ESP task. *Journal of Experimental Social Psychology, 11,* 166–179.

Lazarus, A. A. (1961). Group therapy of phobic disorders by systematic desensitization. *Journal of Abnormal and Social Psychology, 63,* 504–510.

Lazarus, R. S. (1984). On the primacy of cognition. *American Psychologist, 39,* 124–129.

Lazarus, R. S., & Cohen, J. B. (1977). Environmental stress. In I. Altman & J. F. Wohlwill (Eds.), *Human behavior and the environment: Current theory and research* (Vol. 2). New York: Plenum Press.

Lazarus, R. S., DeLongis, A., Folkman, S., & Gruen, R. (1985). Stress and adaptational outcomes: The problem of confounded measures. *American Psychologist, 40,* 770–779.

Lebow, R. N., & Stein, J. G. (1987). Beyond deterrence. *Journal of Social Issues, 43,* 5–71.

Lechtenberg, R. (1982). *The psychiatrist's guide to diseases of the nervous system.* New York: Wiley.

Lefkowitz, M. M., & Tesiny, E. P. (1985). Depression in children: Prevalence and correlates. *Journal of Consulting and Clinical Psychology, 53,* 647–656.

Lehman, D. R., & Taylor, S. E. (1988). Date with an earthquake: Coping with a probable, unpredictable disaster. *Personality and Social Psychology Bulletin, 13,* 546–555.

Leigh, H., & Reiser, M. F. (1980). *The patient.* New York: Plenum Press.

Lenfant, C., & Schweizer, M. (1985). Contributions of health-related biobehavioral research to the prevention of cardiovascular diseases. *American Psychologist, 40,* 217–220.

Lepper, M. R. (1985). Microcomputers in education: Motivational and social issues. *American Psychologist, 40,* 1–18.

Lepper, M. R., Greene, D., & Nisbett, R. E. (1973). Undermining children's intrinsic interest with extrinsic reward: A test of the overjustification hypothesis. *Journal of Personality and Social Psychology, 23,* 129–137.

Lepper, M. R., & Gurner, J. (1989). Children and computers: Approaching the twenty-first century. *American Psychologist, 44,* 170–178.

Lertola, J. (1988, August 8). Learning through mistakes (Figure). *Time Magazine.*

Levant, R. F., & Shlien, L. M. (1984). *Client-centered therapy and the person-centered approach.* New York: Praeger.

Leventhal, H. (1970). Findings and theory in the study of fear communications. In L. Berkowitz (Ed.), *Advances in experimental social psychology* (Vol. 5). New York: Academic Press.

Leventhal, H., & Cleary, P. D. (1980). The smoking problem: A review of the research and theory in behavioral risk modification. *Psychological Bulletin, 88,* 370–405.

Leventhal, H., Nerenz, D., & Leventhal, E. (1985). Feelings of threat and private views of illness: Factors in dehumanization in the medical care system. In A. Baum and J. E. Singer (Eds.), *Advances in environmental psychology* (Vol. 4). Hillsdale, NJ: Erlbaum.

Leventhal, H., & Tomarken, A. J. (1986). Emo-

tion: Today's problems. *Annual Review of Psychology, 37,* 565–610.

Levin, D. P. (1989, March 11). Audi gets a lift from safety study. *New York Times,* D-1.

Liebert, R. M., & Sprafkin, J. (1988). *The early window: effects of television on children and youth* (3rd ed.). New York: Pergamon.

Levin, R. J. (1975, October). The *Redbook* report on premarital and extramarital sex: The end of the double standard? *Redbook,* pp. 38–44, 190–192.

Levinger, G. (1983). Development and change. In H. H. Kelley et al., *Close relationships.* San Francisco: Freeman.

Levinson, D. J. (1986). A conception of adult development. *American Psychologist, 41,* 3–13.

Levinson, D. J., Darrow, C. N., Klein, E. B., Levinson, M. H., & McKee, B. (1978). *The seasons of a man's life.* New York: Knopf.

Levy, J. (1980). Cerebral asymmetry and the psychology of man. In M. C. Wittrock (Ed.), *The brain and psychology.* New York: Academic Press.

Levy, J. (1985). Language, cognition, and the right hemisphere: A response to Gazzaniga. *American Psychologist, 38,* 538–541.

Levy, S. M., Lee, J., Bagley, C., & Lippman, M. (1988). Survival hazards analysis in first recurrent breast cancer patients: Seven-year follow-up. *Psychosomatic Medicine, 50,* 520–528.

Levy, W. B., Anderson, J. A., & Lehmkuhle, S. (1984). *Synaptic modification, neuron selectivity, and nervous system organization.* Hillsdale, NJ: Erlbaum.

Lewin, R. (1987, July 17). Dramatic results with brain grafts. *Science, 237,* 245–247.

Lewin, R. (1988, April 22). Cloud over Parkinson's therapy. *Science, 240,* 390–392.

Lewis, P. (1987). Therapeutic change in groups: An interactional perspective. *Small Group Behavior, 18,* 548–556.

Lewis, M., Feiring, C., McGuffog, C., & Jaskir, J. (1984). Predicting psychopathology in six-year-olds from early social relations. *Child Development, 55,* 123–136.

Lewy, A. J., Sack, R. L., Miller, L. S., & Hoban, T. M. (1987, January 16). Antidepressant and circadian phase-shifting effects of light. *Science, 235,* 352–353.

Ley, D., & Cybriwsky, R. (1974). Urban graffiti as territorial markers. *Annals of the Association of American Geographers, 64,* 491–505.

Ley, P., & Spelman, M. S. (1967). *Communicating with the patient.* London: Staples Press.

Lichtenstein, E. (1982). The smoking problem: A behavioral perspective. *Journal of Consulting and Clinical Psychology, 50,* 804–819.

Lichtenstein, E., & Penner, M. D. (1977). Long-term effects of rapid smoking treatment for dependent cigarette smokers. *Addictive Behaviors, 2,* 109–112.

Lidz, T. (1973). *The origin and treatment of schizophrenic disorders.* New York: Basic Books.

Lidz, T., & Fleck, S. (1985). *Schizophrenia and the family* (2nd ed.). New York: International Universities Press.

Lieberman, M. A. (1982). The effects of social supports on responses to stress. In L. Goldberger & L. Breznitz (Eds.), *Handbook of stress.* New York: Free Press.

Lieberman, M. A., & Bond, G. R. (1978). Self-help groups: Problems of measuring outcome. *Small Group Behavior, 9,* 222–241.

Lietaer, G. (1984). Unconditional positive regard: A controversial basic attitude in client-centered therapy. In R. F. Levant & L. M. Shlien (Eds.), *Client-centered therapy and the person-centered approach.* New York: Praeger.

Linden, E. (1988, April 4). The preppie killer cops a plea. *Time,* p. 22.

Lindsay, P. H., & Norman, D. A. (1977). *Human information processing* (2nd ed.). New York: Academic Press.

Linz, D., Donnerstein, E., & Adams, S. M. (1989). Physiological desensitization and judgments about female victims of violence. *Human Communication Research,* 15.

Linz, D. G., Donnerstein, E., & Penrod, S. (1988). Effects of long-term exposure to violent and sexually degrading depictions of women. *Journal of Personality and Social Psychology, 55,* 758–768.

Lisak, D., & Roth, S. (1988). Motivational factors in nonincarcerated sexually aggressive men. *Journal of Personality and Social Psychology, 55,* 795–802.

Livingston, M., & Hubel, D. (1988, May 6). Segregation of form, color, movement, and depth: Anatomy, physiology, and perception. *Science, 240,* 740–749.

Livingstone, M. S. (1988, January–February). Art, illusion, and the visual system. *Scientific American,* pp. 78–85.

Lobsenz, M. M. (1975). *Sex after sixty-five.* Public Affairs Pamphlet #519, New York Public Affairs Committee.

Lochhead, J. (1985). Teaching analytic reasoning skills through pair problem solving. In J. W. Segal, S. F. Chipman, & R. Glaser (Eds.), *Thinking and learning skills* (Vol. 1). Hillsdale, NJ: Erlbaum.

Locke, E. A., & Schweiger, D. M. (1979). Participation in decision making: One more look. In B. Staw (Ed.), *Research in organizational behavior* (Vol. 1). Greenwich, CT: JAI Press.

Loeb, G. E. (1985, February). The functional replacement of the ear. *Scientific American,* pp. 104–111.

Loehlin, J. C., Willerman, L., & Horn, J. M. (1987). Personality resemblance in adoptive families: A 10-year follow-up. *Journal of Personality and Social Psychology, 53,* 961–969.

Loftus, E. F., & Palmer, J. C. (1974). Reconstruction of automobile destruction: An example of the interface between language and memory. *Journal of Verbal Learning and Verbal Behavior, 13,* 585–589.

Long, A. (1987, December). What is this thing called sleep? *National Geographic, 172,* 786–821.

Long, G. M., & Beaton, R. J. (1982). The case for peripheral persistence: Effects of target and background luminance on a partial-report task. *Journal of Experimental Psychology: Human Perception and Performance, 8,* 383–391.

Long, P. (1986, January). Medical mesmerism. *Psychology Today.*

Lorenz, K. (1966). *On aggression.* New York: Harcourt Brace Jovanovich.

Lorenz, K. (1974). *Civilized man's eight deadly sins.* New York: Harcourt Brace Jovanovich.

Lorsch, J. W. (Ed.) (1987). *Handbook of organization behavior.* Englewood Cliffs, NJ: Prentice-Hall.

Lovaas, O. I., & Koegel, R. (1973). Behavior therapy with autistic children. In C. Thoreson (Ed.), *Behavior Modification and Education.* Chicago: University of Chicago Press.

Luborsky, L. (1988). *Who will benefit from psychotherapy?* N.Y.: Basic Books

Luborsky, L., Singer, B., & Luborsky, L. (1975). Comparative studies of psychotherapies: Is it true that everyone has won and all must have prizes? *Archives of General Psychiatry, 32,* 995–1008.

Luborsky, L., & Spence, D. P. (1978). Quantitative research on psychoanalytic therapy. In S. L. Garfield & A. E. Bergin (Eds.), *Handbook of psychotherapy and behavior change: An empirical analysis* (2nd ed.). New York: Wiley.

Luchins, A. S. (1946). Classroom experiments on mental set. *American Journal of Psychology, 59,* 295–298.

Ludwick-Rosenthal, R., & Neufeld, R. W. J. (1988). Stress management during noxious medical procedures: An evaluative review of outcome studies. *Psychological Bulletin, 104,* 326–342.

Ludwig, A. M. (1969). Altered states of consciousness. In C. T. Tart (Ed.), *Altered states of consciousness.* New York: Wiley.

Lunn, J. H. (1948). Chick sexing. *American Scientist, 36,* 280–287.

Luria, A. R. (1968). *The mind of a mnemonist.* New York: Basic Books.

Lynch, J. G., Jr., & Cohen, J. L. (1978). The use of subjective expected utility theory as an aid to understanding variables that influence helping behavior. *Journal of Personality and Social Psychology, 36,* 1138–1151.

Lynn, S. J., & Rhue, J. (1985, September). Daydream believers. *Psychology Today,* 14–15.

Lynn, S. J., & Rhue, J. W. (1988). Fantasy-proneness: Hypnosis, developmental antecedents, and psychopathology. *American Psychologist, 43,* 35–44.

Lynn, S. J., & Snodgrass, M. (1987). Goal-directed fantasy, hypnotic susceptibility, and expectancies. *Journal of Personality and Social Psychology, 53,* 933–938.

Lyons, R. D. (1984, June 12). Take your eye off the ball, scientist coaches sluggers. *New York Times,* p. C-3.

Maass, A., & Clark, R. D., III (1984). Hidden impact of minorities: Fifteen years of minority influence research. *Psychological Bulletin, 95,* 428–450.

Maccoby, E. E., & Jacklin, C. N. (1974). *The psychology of sex differences.* Stanford, CA: Stanford University Press.

MacDonald, M. L., & Tobias, L. L. (1976). Withdrawal causes relapse? Our response. *Psychological Bulletin, 83,* 448–451.

MacDonald, M. R., & Kuiper, N. A. (1983). Cognitive-behavioral preparations for surgery: Some theoretical and methodological concerns. *Clinical Psychology Review, 3,* 27–39.

MacEvoy, B., Lambert, W. W., Karlberg, P., Karlberg, J., Klackenberg-Larsson, I., & Klackenberg, G. (1988). Early affective antecedents of adult Type A behavior. *Journal of Personality and Social Psychology, 54,* 108–116.

MacFadyen, J. T. (1987, November). Educated monkeys help the disabled help themselves. *Smithsonian,* pp. 125–133.

Mackenzie, B. (1984). Explaining race differences in IQ: The logic, the methodology, and the evidence. *American Psychologist, 39,* 1214–1233.

Mackie, D. M. (1987). Systematic and nonsystematic processing of majority and minority persuasive communications. *Journal of Personality and Social Psychology, 53,* 41–52.

MacQueen, G., Marshall, J., Perdue, M., Siegel, S., & Bienenstock, J. (1989). Pavlovian conditioning of rat mucosal mast cells to secrete rat mast cell protease II. *Science, 243,* 83–85.

Maddi, S. R., Barone, P. T., & Puccetti, M. C. (1987). Stressful events are indeed a factor in physical illness: Reply to Schroeder and Costa (1984). *Journal of Personality and Social Psychology, 52,* 833–843.

Maeroff, G. I. (1977, August 21). The unfavored gifted few. *New York Times Magazine.*

Magnusson, D., & Endler, N. S. (1977). Interactional psychology: Present status and future prospects. In D. Magnusson & N. S. Endler (Eds.), *Personality at the crossroads: Current issues in interactional psychology.* Hillsdale, NJ: Erlbaum.

Mahoney, E. R. (1983). *Human Sexuality.* New York: McGraw-Hill.

Maier, N. R. F. (1967). Assets and liabilities in group problem solving: The need for an integrative function. *Psychological Review, 47,* 239–249.

Major, B., & Konar, E. (1984). An investigation of sex differences in pay expectations and their possible causes. *Academy of Management Journal, 27,* 777–792.

Malamuth, N. M. (1981). Rape proclivity among males. *Journal of Social Issues, 37,* 138–157.

Malamuth, N., & Donnerstein, E. (1982). The effects of aggressive-pornographic mass media stimuli. In L. Berkowitz (Ed.), *Advances in experimental social psychology* (Vol. 15). New York: Academic Press.

Malamuth, N. M., & Donnerstein, E. (1984). *Pornography and sexual aggression.* New York: Academic Press.

Malanka, P. A. (1986, February). Quit smoking for someone you love. *Health, 18,* 27–36.

Malin, J. T. (1979). Information-processing load in problem solving by network search. *Journal of Experimental Psychology: Human Perception and Performance, 5,* 379–390.

Malinak, D. P., Hoyt, M. F., & Patterson, V. (1979). Adults' reactions to the death of a parent: A preliminary study. *American Journal of Psychiatry, 136,* 1152–1156.

Malinowski, C. I., & Smith, C. P. (1985). Moral reasoning and moral conduct: An investigation prompted by Kohlberg's theory. *Journal of Personality and Social Issues, 49,* 1016–1027.

Mandl, H., & Lesgold, A. (1988). *Learning issues for intelligent tutoring systems.* New York: Springer-Verlag.

Manis, F., Keating, D. P., & Morrison, F. J. (1980). Developmental differences in the allocation of processing capacity. *Journal of Experimental Child Psychology, 29,* 156–159.

Markman, E. M., & Callanan, M. S. (1984). An analysis of hierarchical classification. In R. Sternberg (Ed.), *Advances in the psychology of human intelligence* (Vol. 2, pp. 345–365). Hillsdale, NJ: Erlbaum.

Marks, G., & Miller, N. (1987). Ten years of research on the false-consensus effect: An empirical and theoretical review. *Psychological Bulletin, 102,* 72–90.

Marks, I. M. (1982). Toward an empirical clinical science: Behavioral psychotherapy in the 1980s. *Behavioral Therapies, 13,* 63–81.

Marlatt, G. A., Baer, J. S., Donovan, D. M., & Kivlahan, D. R. (1988). Addictive behaviors: Etiology and treatment. *Annual Review of Psychology, 39,* 223–252.

Marr, D. C. (1982). *Vision.* New York: Freeman.

Marshall, G., & Zimbardo, P. (1979). The affective consequences of "inadequately explained" physiological arousal. *Journal of Personality and Social Psychology, 37,* 970–988.

Martin, C. L. (1987). A ratio measure of sex stereotyping. *Journal of Personality and Social Psychology, 52,* 489–499.

Martin, J. B. (1987, November 6). Molecular genetics: Applications to the clinical neurosciences. *Science, 238,* 765–772.

Martindale, C. (1981). *Cognition and consciousness.* Homewood, IL: Dorsey Press.

Martinez del Rio, C., & Stevens, B. R. (1989). Physiological constraint of feeding behavior: Intestinal membrane disaccaridases of the starling. *Science, 243,* 794.

Marting, B. A., (1989). Gender differences in salary expectations when current salary information is provided. *Psychology of Women Quarterly, 13,* 87–96.

Marvel Comics Group (1981). *See no evil.* New York: Marvel.

Marx, M. B., Garrity, T. F., & Bowers, F. R. (1975). The influence of recent life experience on the health of college freshmen. *Journal of Psychosomatic Research, 19,* 87–98.

Marx, M. H., & Hillix, W. A. (1987). *Systems and theories in psychology* (4th ed.). New York: McGraw-Hill.

Masland, R. L., Sorason, S. B., & Gladwyn, T. (1958). *Mental subnormality.* New York: Basic Books.

Maslow, A. H. (1987). *Motivation and personality* (3rd ed.). New York: Harper & Row.

Mason, J. W. (1974). Specificity in the organization of neuroendocrine response profiles. In P. Seeman and G. M. Brown (Eds.), *Frontiers in neurology and neuroscience research.* First International Symposium of the Neuroscience Institute. Toronto: University of Toronto Press.

Mason, J. W. (1975). A historical view of the stress field. *Journal of Human Stress, 1,* 6–12, 22–37.

Masters, W. H., & Johnson, V. E. (1966). *Human sexual response.* Boston: Little, Brown.

Masters, W. H., & Johnson, V. E. (1970). *Human sexual inadequacy.* Boston: Little, Brown.

Masters, W. H., & Johnson, V. E. (1979). *Homosexuality in perspective.* Boston: Little, Brown.

Masters, W. H., Johnson, V. E., & Kolodny, R. C. (1985). *Human sexuality.* Boston: Little, Brown.

Masters, W. H., Johnson, V. E., & Kolodny, R. C. (1988). *CRISIS: Heterosexual behavior in the age of AIDS.* New York: Grove Press.

Mastropierei, M. A., & Scruggs, T. (1987). *Effective instruction for special education.* Boston: College-Hill Press/Little, Brown.

Maszak, M. (1988, June). Minding the missiles. *Psychology Today,* pp. 52–56.

Mathes, E. W. (1975). The effects of physical attractiveness and anxiety on heterosexual attraction over a series of five encounters. *Journal of Marriage and the Family,* 769–773.

Matlin, M. M. (1987). *The psychology of women.* New York: Holt.

Matrazzo, J. D. (1987). There is only one psychology, no specialties, but many applications. *American Psychologist, 42,* 893–903.

Matsumoto, D. (1987). The role of facial response in the experience of emotion: More methodological problems and a meta-analysis. *Journal of Personality and Social Psychology, 52,* 769–774.

Matthews, K. A. (1982). Psychological perspectives on the Type A behavior pattern. *Psychological Bulletin, 91,* 293–323.

Matthews, K. A. (1988). Coronary heart disease and Type A behaviors: Update on and alternative to the Booth-Kewley and Friedman (1987) quantitative review. *Psychological Bulletin, 104,* 373–380.

Matthews, K. A., & Siegel, J. (1987). Type A behavior pattern in children and adolescents. In A. Baum & J. Singer (Eds.), *Handbook of psychology and health.* Hillsdale, NJ: Erlbaum.

Mawhinney, V. T., Boston, D. E., Loaws, O. R., Blumenfeld, G. T., & Hopkins, B. L. (1971). A comparison of students' studying behavior produced by daily, weekly, and three-week testing schedules. *Journal of Applied Behavior Analysis, 4,* 257–264.

May, R. (1969). *Love and will.* New York: Norton.

Mayer, R. E. (1982). Different problem-solving strategies for algebra word and equation problems. *Journal of Experimental Psychology: Learning, Memory, and Cognition, 8,* 448–462.

Mayo, E. (1933). *The human problems of an industrial civilization.* New York: Macmillan.

McAlister, A., Puska, P., Koskela, K., Pallonen, U., & Maccoby, N. (1980). Mass communication and community organization for public health education. *American Psychologist, 35,* 375–379.

McCanne, T. R., & Anderson, J. A. (1987). Emotional responding following experimental manipulation of facial electromyographic activity. *Journal of Personality and Social Psychology, 52,* 759–768.

McClelland, D. C. (1978). Managing motivation to expand human freedom. *American Psychologist, 33,* 201–210.

McClelland, D. C. (1985). How motives, skills, and values determine what people do. *American Psychologist, 40,* 812–825.

McClelland, D. C. (1985). *Human motivation.* Glenview, IL: Scott, Foresman.

McClelland, D. C., Atkinson, J. W., Clark, R. A., & Lowell, E. L. (1953). *The achievement motive.* New York: Appleton-Century-Crofts.

McClelland, D. C., & Winter, D. G. (1971). *Motivating economic achievement.* New York: Free Press.

McCloskey, M., Wible, C. G., & Cohen, N. J. (1988). Is there a special flashbulb-memory mechanism? *Journal of Experimental Psychology: General, 117,* 171–181.

McConnell, J. V. (1985). On Gazzaniga and right hemisphere language. *American Psychologist, 40,* 1273.

McDonald, K. (1988, March). Sex under glass. *Psychology Today,* pp. 58–59.

McDougall, W. (1908). *Introduction to social psychology.* London: Methuen.

McGlone, J. (1980). Sex differences in human brain asymmetry: A critical survey. *The Behavioral and Brain Sciences, 3,* 215–263.

McGrath, E. (1988, August). A different kind of treatment: Medicine, education and research. Paper presented at the annual meeting of the American Psychological Association (Atlanta).

McGraw, K. M., & Bloomfield, J. (1987). Social influence on group moral decisions: The interactive effects of moral reasoning and sex-role orientation. *Journal of Personality and Social Psychology, 53,* 1080–1087.

McGuire, W. J. (1964). Inducing resistance to persuasion. In L. Berkowitz (Ed.), *Advances in experimental social psychology* (Vol. 1). New York: Academic Press.

McGuire, W. J. (1968). Personality and susceptibility to social influence. In E. F. Borgatta & W. W. Lambert (Eds.), *Handbook of personality theory and research.* Chicago: Rand McNally.

McGuire, W. J. (1985). Attitudes and attitude change. In G. Lindzey & E. Aronson (Eds.), *Handbook of social psychology* (Vol. 2, 3rd ed.). New York: Random House.

McKean, K. (1982, April). Anatomy of an air crash. *Discover,* pp. 19–21.

McKinley, J. B. (1975). Who is really ignorant—physician or patient? *Journal of Health and Social Behavior, 16,* 3–11.

McKusick, L., Coates, T., & Horstman, W. (1985). *HTLV-III transmitting behavior and desire for HTLV-III: Antibody testing in San Francisco on men at risk from AIDS, 1982–1985.* Report from the AIDS Behavioral Research Project. The Public Health Department of the City and County of San Francisco.

McKusick, L., Horstman, W., & Coates, T. J. (1985). AIDS and sexual behavior reported by gay men in San Francisco. *American Journal of Public Health, 75,* 493–496.

McMillan, J. R., et al. (1977). Women's language: Uncertainty or interpersonal sensitivity and emotionality? *Sex Roles, 3,* 545–560.

McNeal, E. T., & Cimbolic, P. (1986). Antidepressants and biochemical theories of depression. *Psychological Bulletin, 99,* 361–374.

McNeil, J. C. (1975). Feminism, femininity, and the television series: A content analysis. *Journal of Broadcasting, 19,* 259–271.

Meaney, M. J., Aitken, D. H., Van-Berkel, C., Bhatnager, S., et al. (1988). Effect of neonatal handling on age-related impairments associated with the hippocampus. *Science, 239,* 766–768.

Mednick, S. A., Higgins, J., & Kirschbaum, J. (1974). *Psychology: Explorations in behavior and experiences.* New York: Wiley.

Melges, F. T., & Bowlby, J. (1969). Types of hopelessness in psychopathological process. *Archives of General Psychiatry, 70,* 690–699.

Melville, J. (1977). *Phobias and obsessions.* New York: Coward, McCann.

Melzack, R., & Wall, P. D. (1965). Pain mechanisms: A new theory. *Science, 150,* pp. 971–979.

Melton, G. B., & Garrison, E. G. (1987). Fear, prejudice, and neglect: Discrimination against mentally disabled persons. *American Psychologist, 42,* 1007–1026.

Mentzer, S. J., & Snyder, M. L. (1982). The doctor and the patient: A psychological

perspective. In G. S. Sanders and J. Suls (Eds.), *Social psychology of health and illness* (pp. 161–181). Hillsdale, NJ: Erlbaum.

Merai, A. (Ed.) (1985). *On terrorism and combating terrorism.* College Park, MD: University Publications of America.

Merzenich, M. M., & Kass, J. H. (1980). Principles of organization of sensory-perceptual systems in mammals. In J. M. Sprague & A. N. Epstein (Eds.), *Progress in psychology and physiological psychology* (Vol. 9). New York: Academic Press.

Messick, S., & Jungeblut, A. (1981). Time and method in coaching for the SAT. *Psychological Bulletin, 89,* 191–216.

Metcalfe, J. (1986). Premonitions of insight predict impending error. *Journal of Experimental Psychology: Learning, Memory, and Cognition, 12,* 623–634.

Metee, D. R., & Aronson, E. (1974). Affective reactions to appraisal from others. In T. L. Huston (Ed.), *Foundations of interpersonal attraction* (pp. 235–283). New York: Academic Press.

Meyer, J. P., & Pepper, S. (1977). Need compatibility and marital adjustment in young married couples. *Journal of Personality and Social Psychology, 35,* 331–342.

Meyer, R. G., & Osborne, Y. V. H. (1987). *Case studies in abnormal behavior.* (2nd ed.) Boston: Allyn & Bacon.

Meyerhoff, M. K., & Whilte, B. L. (1986, September). Making the grade as parents. *Psychology Today,* pp. 38–45.

Michelmore, P. (1984, March). You're too young to die. *Readers Digest,* pp. 117–121.

Middlebrook, P. (1974). *Social psychology and modern life.* New York: Knopf.

Mihal, W. L., & Barrett, G. V. (1976). Individual differences in perceptual information processing and their relation to automobile accident involvement. *Journal of Applied Psychology, 61,* 229–233.

Mikhail, A. (1981). Stress: A psychophysiological conception. *Journal of Human Stress, 7,* 9–15.

Miles, R. H., & Perreault, W. D. (1976). Organizational role conflict: Its antecedents and consequences. *Organizational Behavior and Human Performance, 17,* 19–44.

Milewski, A. E. (1976). Infants' discrimination of internal and external pattern elements. *Journal of Experimental Child Psychology, 22,* 229–246.

Milgram, S. (1974). *Obedience to authority.* New York: Harper & Row.

Miller, D., & Starr, M. (1967). *The structure of human decisions.* Englewood Cliffs, NJ: Prentice-Hall.

Miller, A. (1988, April 25). Stress on the job. *Newsweek,* pp. 40–45.

Miller, A. G. (1986). *The obedience experiments: A case study of controversy in social science.* New York: Praeger.

Miller, G. A. (1956). The magical number seven, plus or minus two: Some limits on our capacity for processing information. *Psychology Review, 63,* 81–97.

Miller, G. R., & Knapp, M. L. (Eds.). (1985). *Handbook of interpersonal communication.* Beverly Hills, CA: Sage.

Miller, J. D. (1984, June). *Psychology Today,* p. 18.

Miller, L. L. (Ed.). (1975). *Marijuana: Current research.* New York: Academic Press.

Miller, M. W. (1986, September 19). Effects of alcohol on the generation and migration of cerebral cortical neurons. *Science, 2133,* 1308–1310.

Miller, N., & Brewer, M. B. (1984). *Groups in contact: The psychology of desegregation.* New York: Academic Press.

Miller, N. E. (1980). Applications of learning and biofeedback to psychiatry and medicine. In H. I. Kaplan, A. M. Freedman, & B. J. Sadock (Eds.), *Comprehensive textbook of psychiatry III.* Baltimore: Williams & Wilkins.

Miller, N. E. (1985a, February). Rx: Biofeedback. *Psychology Today, 19,* pp. 54–59.

Miller, N. E. (1985b). The value of behavioral research on animals. *American Psychologist, 40,* 423–440.

Miller, S. M., Brody, D. S., & Summerton, J. (1988). Styles of coping with threat: Implications for health. *Journal of Personality and Social Psychology, 54,* 142–148.

Miller, S. M., & Mangan, C. E. (1983). Interacting effects of information and coping style in adapting to gynecologic stress: Should the doctor tell all? *Journal of Personality and Social Psychology, 45,* 223–236.

Miller-Jones, D. (1989). Culture and testing. *American Psychologist, 44,* 360–366.

Millon, T. (1975). Reflections on Rosenhan's "On being sane in insane places." *Journal of Abnormal Psychology, 84,* 589–620.

Milloy, C. (1986, June 22). Crack user's highs, lows. *Washington Post,* p. A-1.

Milner, B. (1966). Amnesia following operation on temporal lobes. In C. W. M. Whitty & P. Zangwill (Eds.), *Amnesia.* London: Butterworth.

Mineka, S., & Henderson, R. W. (1985). Controllability and predictability in acquired motivation. *Annual Review of Psychology, 36,* 495–529.

Minuchin, S. (1974). *Families and family therapy.* Cambridge, MA: Harvard University Press.

Mirsky, A. F., & Duncan, C. C. (1986). Etiology and expression of schizophrenia: Neurological and psychosocial factors. *Annual Review of Psychology, 37.*

Mischel, W. (1968). *Personality and assessment.* New York: Wiley.

Mischel, W. (1984). Convergences and challenges in the search for consistency. *American Psychologist, 39,* 351–364.

Mischel, W., & Peake, P. K. (1982). Analyzing the construction of consistency in personality. *Nebraska Symposium on Motivation,* 233–262.

Mischel, W., & Peake, P. K. (1982). Beyond deja vu in the search for cross-situational consistency. *Psychological Review, 89,* 730–755.

Mischel, W., & Peake, P. K. (1983). Some facets of consistency: Replies to Epstein, Funder, and Bem. *Psychological Review, 90*. 394–402.

Mitchell, R. E. (1971). Some social implications of high-density housing. *American Sociological Review, 36*, 18–29.

Mitchel, T. R. (1982). *People in organizations: An introduction to organizational behavior* (2nd ed.). New York: McGraw-Hill.

Mobley, W. H. (1982). *Employee turnover: Causes, consequences, and control.* Reading, MA: Addison-Wesley.

Mollon, J. D., & Sharpe, L. T. (Eds.). (1983). *Colour vision: Physiology and psychophysics.* New York: Academic Press.

Molotsky, I. (1984, November 30). Implant to aid the totally deaf is approved. *New York Times,* pp. 1, B-10.

Monahan, J., & Loftus, E. F. (1982). The psychology of law. *Annual Reviews, 33,* 441–475.

Monahan, J., & Walker, L. (1988). Social science research in law: A new paradigm. *American Psychologist, 43,* 465–472.

Money, J. (1986). *Lovemaps: Clinical concepts of sexual/erotic health and pathology, paraphilia, and gender transposition in childhood, adolescence, and maturity.* New York: Irvington.

Money, J. (1987). Sin, sickness, or status? Homosexuality, gender identity, and psychoneuroendocrinology. *American Psychologist, 42,* 384–399.

Monmaney, T. (1987, December 7). Keeping it in the family. *Newsweek,* p. 81.

Montemayor, P. (1983). Parents and adolescents in conflict: All families some of the time and some families most of the time. *Journal of Early Adolescence, 3,* 83–103.

Morgan, P. M. (1977). *Deterrence: A conceptual analysis.* Beverly Hills, CA: Sage.

Morgan, M. (1982). Television and adolescents' sex-role stereotypes: A longitudinal study. *Journal of Personality and Social Psychology, 43,* 947–955.

Morin, S. F., Charles, K. A., & Malyon, A. K. (1984). The psychological impact of AIDS on gay men. *American Psychologist, 39,* 1288–1293.

Morse, N., & Skinner, B. F. (1957). A second type of "superstition" in the pigeon. *American Journal of Psychology, 70,* 308–311.

Moscovici, S. (1985). Social influence and conformity. In G. Lindzey & E. Aronson (Eds.), *Handbook of social psychology* (3rd ed.). New York: Random House.

Moscovici, S., & Mugny, G. (1983). Minority influence. In P. B. Paulus (Ed.), *Basic group processes.* New York: Springer-Verlag.

Mosher, D. L., & Anderson, R. D. (1986). Macho personality, sexual aggression, and reactions to guided imagery of realistic rape. *Journal of Research in Personality, 20,* 77–94.

Motley, M. T. (1987, February). What I meant to say. *Psychology Today,* pp. 25–28.

Mucha, T. F., & Reinhardt, R. F. (1970). Conversion reactions in student aviators. *American Journal of Psychiatry, 127,* 493–497.

Muehlenhard, C. L., & Hollabaugh, L. C. (1988). Do women sometimes say no when they mean yes? The prevalence and correlates of women's token resistance to sex. *Journal of Personality and Social Psychology, 54,* 872–879.

Mueller, E., & Lucas, T. (1975). A developmental analysis of peer interaction among toddlers. In M. Lewis & L. A. Rosenblum (Eds.), *Friendship and peer relations.* New York: Wiley-Interscience.

Mumford, M. D., & Gustafson, S. B. (1988). Creativity syndrome: Integration, application, and innovation. *Psychological Bulletin, 103,* 27–43.

Munnichs, U., Mussen, P., Olbrich, E., & Coleman, P. (Eds.). (1985). *Life-span and change in a gerontological perspective.* New York: Academic Press.

Murstein, B. I. (1974). *Love, sex, and marriage.* New York: Springer-Verlag.

Mussen, P. H., & Jones, M. C. (1957). Self-conceptions, motivations, and interpersonal attitudes of late- and early-maturing boys. *Child Development, 28,* 243–256.

Nahome, L., & Lawton, M. P. (1975). Similarity and propinquity in friendship formation. *Journal of Personality and Social Psychology, 32,* 205–213.

Namir, S., Wolcott, D. L., Fawzy, F. I., & Alumbaugh, M. J. (1987). Coping with AIDS: Psychological and health implications. *Journal of Applied Social Psychology, 17,* 309–328.

Naroll, R., Bullough, V. L., & Naroll, F. (1974). *Military deterrence in history: A pilot cross-historical survey.* Albany: State University of New York Press.

Nash, M. (1987). What, if anything, is regressed about hypnotic age regression? A review of the empirical literature. *Psychological Bulletin, 102,* 42–52.

Nathans, J., Piantanidu, T. P., Eddy, R. L., Shows, T. B., & Hogness, D. S. (1986, April 11). Molecular genetics of inherited variation in human color vision. *Science, 232,* pp. 203–210.

National Center for Health Statistics. (1986). *Annual report.* Washington, D.C.: Government Printing Office.

National Institute of Drug Abuse. (1986). *Annual survey of drug use.* Washington, D.C.: Government Printing Office.

National Opinion Research Center (NORC). (1982). *General social surveys, 1972–1982.* Chicago: National Opinion Research Center.

Nauta, W. J. H., & Feirtag, M. (1979, September). The organization of the brain. *Scientific American,* p. 102.

Navon, R., & Proia, R. L. (1989, March 17). The mutations in Ashkenazi Jews with adult G(M2) Gangliosidosis, the adult form of Tay-Sachs Disease. *Science, 243,* 1471–1474.

Nelson, B. (1983, April 2). Despair among jobless is on rise, studies find. *New York Times,* p. 22.

Neugarten, B. L. (1979). Time, age, and the life cycle. *American Journal of Psychiatry, 136,* 887–894.

New York Times. (1984, May 20). The new addicts. *New York Times,* p. 50.

New York Times. (1989, February 2). Musician's death at 75 reveals he was a woman. A-18.

Newman, J. P., & Kosson, D. S. (1986). Passive avoidance learning in psychopathic and nonpsychopathic offenders. *Journal of Abnormal Psychology, 95,* 252–256.

Ng, S. H., & Cram, F. (1988). Intergroup bias by defensive and offensive groups in majority and minority conditions. *Journal of Personality and Social Psychology, 55,* 749–757.

Nickerson, R. S., Perkins, D. N., & Smith, E. E. (1985). *Teaching thinking.* Hillsdale, NJ: Erlbaum.

Ninokur, G. (1983). Controversies in depression, or do clinicians know something after all? In P. J. Clayton & J. E. Barret (Eds.), *Treatment of depression: Old controversies and new approaches* (pp. 153–168). New York: Raven Press.

Nisbett, R. E. (1968). Taste, deprivation, and weight determinants of eating behavior. *Journal of Personality and Social Psychology, 10,* 107–116.

Nisbett, R. E. (1972). Hunger, obesity and the ventromedial hypothalamus. *Psychological Review, 79,* 433–453.

Nisbett, R. E., Fong, G. T., Lehman, D. R., & Cheng, P. W. (1987, October 30). Teaching reasoning. *Science, 238,* 625–631.

Nogrady, H., McConkey, K. M., & Perry, C. (1985). Enhancing visual memory: Trying hypnosis, trying imagination, and trying again. *Journal of Abnormal Psychology, 94,* 105–204.

Noll, K. M., & Davis, J. M. (1983). Biological theories in schizophrenia. In A. Rifkin (Ed.), *Schizophrenia and affective disorders: Biology and drug treatment* (pp. 139–204). Boston: John Wright.

Norcia, A. M., & Tyler, C. W. (1985). Spatial frequency sweep VEP: Visual acuity during the first year of life. *Vision Research, 25,* 1399–1408.

Norman, D. A. (1988). *The psychology of everyday things.* New York: Basic Books.

Norvell, N., & Worchel, S. (1981). A reexamination of the relation between equal status contact and intergroup attraction. *Journal of Personality and Social Psychology, 41,* 902–908.

Novak, M. A., & Suomi, S. J. (1988). Psychological well-being of primates in captivity. *American Psychologist, 43,* 765–773.

Nowicki, S., & Duke, M. (1978). An examination of counseling variables within a social learning framework. *Journal of Counseling Psychology, 25,* 1–7.

O'Brien, C. P., et al. (1988). Pharmacological and behavioral treatments of cocaine dependence: Controlled studies. *Journal of Clinical Psychiatry, 49,* 17.

Olds, J., & Milner, P. (1954). Positive reinforcement produced by electrical stimulation of septal area and other regions of rat brain. *Journal of Comparative and Physiological Psychology, 47,* 411–427.

O'Leary, V., & Smith, D. (1988, August). Sex makes a difference: Attributions for emotional cause. Paper presented at the annual meeting of the American Psychological Association (Atlanta).

Opler, L. A., Kay, S. R., Rosado, V., & Lindenmayer, J. P. (1984). Positive and negative syndromes in chronic schizophrenic inpatients. *Journal of Nervous and Mental Disease, 172,* 317–325.

Orlafsky, J., Marcia, J., & Lasser, I. (1973). Ego identity status and intimacy vs. isolation crisis of young adulthood. *Journal of Personality and Social Psychology, 27,* 211–219.

Orne, M. T., & Holland, C. C. (1968). On the ecological validity of laboratory deceptions. *International Journal of Psychiatry, 6,* 282–293.

Ornstein, P. A., & Naus, M. J. (1988). Effects of the knowledge base on children's memory strategies. In H. W. Reese (Ed.), *Advances in Child Development and Behavior* (Vol. 19). New York: Academic Press.

Ornstein, R. E. (1977). *The psychology of consciousness* (2nd ed.). New York: Harcourt Brace Jovanovich.

Orwin, R. G., & Condray, D. S. (1984). Smith and Glass' psychotherapy conclusions need further probing: On Landman and Dawes' re-analysis. *American Psychologist, 39,* 71–72.

Orzek, A. M. (1983). Use of rape crisis center services by a university community. *Journal of College Student Personnel, 24,* 465–466.

Osborne, A. F. (1957). *Applied imagination.* New York: Scribner.

Oskamp, S. (1984). *Applied social psychology.* Englewood Cliffs, NJ: Prentice-Hall.

Oskamp, S. (1988). Nontraditional employment opportunities for applied psychologists. *American Psychologist, 43,* 484–485.

Ouchi, W. (1981). *Theory Z.* Reading, MA: Addison-Wesley.

Owens, J., Bower, G. H., & Black, J. (1979). The "soap opera" effect in story recall. *Memory and Cognition, 7,* 185–191.

Packer, J., & Bain, J. D. (1978). Cognitive style and teacher student compatibility. *Journal of Educational Psychology, 70,* 864–871.

Painter, C. (1985). *Gifts of age.* San Francisco: Chronicle Books.

Paivio, A. (1971). *Imagery and verbal processes.* New York: Holt, Rinehart and Winston.

Palladino, J. J., & Carducci, B. J. (1984). Students' knowledge of sleep and dreams. *Teaching of Psychology, 11,* 189–191.

Panek, P. E. (1982). Do beginning psychology of aging students believe 10 common

myths about aging? *Teaching of Psychology, 9,* 104–105.

Papalia, D., & Olds, S. (1986). *Human development* (3rd ed.). New York: McGraw-Hill.

Papalia, D., & Tennent, S. S. (1975). Vocational aspirations in preschoolers: A manifestation of early sex-role stereotyping. *Sex Rules, 1,* 197–199.

Parke, R. D. (1981). *Fathers.* Cambridge, MA: Harvard University Press.

Parlee, M. B. (1979, October). The friendship bond. *Psychology Today, 13,* pp. 43–45.

Parloff, M. B. (1976, February 21). Shopping for the right therapy. *Saturday Review, 14–20.*

Parsons, H. M. (1974). What happened at Hawthorne? *Science, 183,* 922–932.

Parsons, T. (1975). The sick role and the role of the physician reconsidered. *Milbank Memorial Fund Quarterly/Health and Society, 53,* 257–278.

Paterson, R. J., & Neufeld, R. W. J. (1987). Clear danger: Situational determinants of the appraisal of threat. *Psychological Bulletin, 101,* 404–416.

Patterson, F. G. (1978). The gestures of a gorilla: Language acquisition in another pongid. *Brain and Language, 5,* 72–97.

Patterson, M. (1987). Presentational and affect-management functions of nonverbal involvement. *Journal of Nonverbal Behavior, 11,* 110–122.

Paul, S. (1986, December 5). A selective imidazobenzodiazepine antagonist of ethanol in the rat. *Science, 234,* 1245.

Paulus, P. B. (1983). *Basic group processes.* New York: Springer-Verlag.

Paulus, P. B. (1983). Crowding in jails. *Basic and Applied Psychology, 4,* 89–107.

Paulus, P. B., & McCain, G. (1983). Crowding in jails. *Basic and Applied Social Psychology, 4,* 89–107.

Paulus, P. B., McCain, G., & Cox, V. C. (1978). Death rates, psychiatric commitments, blood pressure, perceived crowding as a function of institutional crowding. *Environmental Psychology and Nonverbal Behavior, 3,* 107–116.

Pavlidis, G. T., & Fisher, D. F. (1986). *Dyslexia: Its neuropsychology and treatment.* New York: Wiley.

Pavlov, I. P. (1927). *Conditioned reflexes.* London: Oxford University Press.

Payne, D. G. (1986). Hyperamnesia for pictures and words: Testing the recall level hypothesis. *Journal of Experimental Psychology: Learning, Memory, and Cognition, 12,* 16–29.

Pechacek, T. F. (1979). Modification of smoking behavior. In *Smoking and health: A report of the surgeon general.* Washington, DC: U.S. Department of Health, Education, and Welfare, Public Health Service.

Pearl, J. (1987). Embracing causality in formal reasoning. *Proceedings of AAAI-87, The Sixth National Conference on Artificial Intelligence* (p. 369).

Peck, J. W. (1978). Rats defend different body weights depending on palatability

and accessibility of their food. *Journal of Comparative and Physiological Psychology, 91,* 555–570.

Pelligrino, E. D. (1973). Toward an expanded medical ethics: The Hippocratic ethic revisited. In J. Bulger (Ed.), *Hippocrates revisited* (pp. 133–147). New York: Med Com.

Penfield, W., & Rasmussen, T. (1950). *The cerebral cortex of man.* New York: Macmillan.

Pennebaker, J. W., & Beall, S. (1986). Confronting a traumatic event: Toward an understanding of inhibition and disease. *Journal of Abnormal Psychology, 95,* 274–281.

Pennebaker, J. W., Hughes, C. F., & O'Heeron, R. C. (1987). The psychophysiology of confession: Linking inhibitory and psychosomatic processes. *Journal of Personality and Social Psychology 52,* 781–793.

Pennebaker, N. N., Burnam, M. A., Schaeffer, N. A., & Harper, D. C. (1977). Lack of control as a determinant of perceived physical symptoms. *Journal of Personality and Social Psychology, 35,* 167–174.

Peper, R. J., & Mayer, R. E. (1978). Note taking as a generative activity. *Journal of Educational Psychology, 70,* 514–522.

Peplau, L. A., Rubin, Z., & Hill, C. T. (1977). Sexual intimacy in dating relationships. *Journal of Social Issues, 2,* 86–109.

Pereira, P. (1987, November 18). Effects of date rape linger while she tries to forget. *Massachusetts Daily Collegian, 119,* 1.

Pereira-Smith, O., Smith, J., et al. (1988, August). Paper presented at the annual meeting of the International Genetics Congress (Toronto)

Perkins, D. N. (1983). Why the human perceiver is a bad machine. In J. Beck, B. Hope & A. Rosenfeld (Eds.), *Human and machine vision.* New York: Academic Press.

Perkins, D. N., Lochhead, J., & Bishop, J. (Eds.) (1987). *Thinking: The Second International Conference.* Hillsdale, NJ: Erlbaum.

Perlmutter, M. (1979). Age differences in adults' free recall, cued recall, and recognition. *Journal of Gerontology, 34,* 533–539.

Perlmutter, M., & Mitchell, D. B. (1986). The appearance and disappearance of age differences in adult memory. In I. M. Craik & S. Trehub (Eds.), *Aging and cognitive processes.* New York: Plenum Press.

Perls, F. S. (1967). Group vs. individual therapy. *ETC: A review of general semantics, 34,* 306–312.

Perls, F. S. (1970). *Gestalt therapy now: Therapy, techniques, applications.* Palo Alto, CA: Science and Behavior Books.

Pervin, L. A. (1985). Personality: Current controversies, issues and directions. *Annual Review of Psychology, 36.*

Peterson, A. C. (1988, September). Those gangly years. *Psychology Today,* pp. 28–34.

Peterson, C., & Barrett, L. C. (1987). Explanatory style and academic performance among university freshmen. *Journal of*

Personality and Social Psychology, 53, 603–607.

Peterson, C., & Raps, C. S. (1984). Helplessness and hospitalization: More remarks. *Journal of Personality and Social Psychology, 46,* 82–83.

Peterson, C., Seligman, M. E. P., & Vaillant, G. E. (1988). Pessimistic explanatory style is a risk factor for physical illness: A thirty-five-year longitudinal study. *Journal of Personality and Social Psychology, 55,* 23–27.

Peterson, L. R., & Peterson, M. J. (1959). Short-term retention of individual items. *Journal of Experimental Psychology, 58,* 193–198.

Pettingale, K. W., Morris, T., Greer, S., & Haybittle, J. L. (1985). Mental attitudes to cancer: An additional prognostic factor. *Lancet,* 750.

Petty, M. M., McGee, G. W., & Cavender, J. W. (1984). A meta-analysis of the relationships between individual job satisfaction and individual performance. *Academy of Management, 9,* 712–721.

Petty, R. E., & Cacioppo, J. T. (1977). Cognitive responding and resistance to persuasion. *Journal of Personality and Social Psychology, 35,* 645–655.

Petty, R. E., & Cacioppo, J. T. (1981). *Attitudes and persuasion: Classic and contemporary approaches.* Dubuque, IA: Brown.

Petty, R. E., & Cacioppo, J. T. (1984). The effects of involvement on responses to argument quantity and quality: Central and peripheral routes to persuasion. *Journal of Personality and Social Psychology, 46,* 69–81.

Petty, R. E., & Cacioppo, J. T. (1986). The elaboration likelihood model of persuasion. In L. Berkowitz (Ed.), *Advances in experimental social psychology* (Vol. 10). New York: Academic Press.

Piaget, J. (1970). Piaget's theory. In P. H. Mussen (Ed.), *Carmichael's manual of child psychology* (Vol. I, 3rd ed.). New York: John Wiley.

Piaget, J., & Inhelder, B. (1958). *The growth of logical thinking from childhood to adolescence.* Translated by A. Parsons & S. Seagrin. New York: Basic Books.

Piccione, C., Hilgard, E. R., & Zimbardo, P. G. (1989). On the degree of stability of measured hypnotizability over a 25-year period. *Journal of Personality and Social Psychology, 56,* 289–295.

Piliavin, J. A., & Piliavin, I. M. (1972). Effect of blood on reactions to a victim. *Journal of Personality and Social Psychology, 23,* 353–362.

Pion, G. M., & Lipsey, M. W. (1984). Psychology and society: The challenge of change. *American Psychologist, 39,* 739–754.

Pi-Sunyer, F. X. (1987). Exercise effects on caloric intake. In R. Wurtman (Ed.), *Obesity.* New York: New York Academy of Science.

Plomin, R. (1989). Environment and genes: Determinants of behavior. *American Psychologist, 44,* 105–111.

Plous, S. (1988). Disarmament, arms control, and peace in the nuclear age: Political objectives and relevant research. *Journal of Social Issues, 44,* 133–154.

Plutchik, R. (1984). Emotion. In K. Scherer & P. Ekman, (Eds.), *Approaches to emotion.* Hillsdale, NJ: Erlbaum.

Polivy, J., & Herman, L. P. (1985). Dieting and binging: A causal analysis. *American Psychologist, 40,* 193–201.

Pollack, A. (1987, September 15). More human than ever, computer is learning to learn. *New York Times,* pp. C-1, C-6.

Pomerleau, O. F. (1979). Behavioral factors in the establishment, maintenance and cessation of smoking. In *Smoking and health: A report of the Surgeon General.* Washington, DC: U.S. Department of Health, Education and Welfare. Public Health Service.

Pomerleau, O., Adkins, D., & Pertschuk, M. (1978). Predictors of outcome and recidivism in smoking cessation treatment. *Addictive Behaviors, 3,* 65–70.

Pomerleau, O. F., Pertschuk, M., Adkins, D., & Brady, J. A. (1978). A comparison of behavioral traditional treatment of middle income problem drinkers. *Journal of Behavioral Medicine, 1,* 187–200.

Pomerleau, O. F., & Pomerleau, C. S. (1977). *Breaking the smoking habit: A behavioral program for giving up cigarettes.* Champaign, IL: Research Press.

Porter, R. H., Cernich, J. M., & McLaughlin, F. J. (1983). Maternal recognition of neonates through olfactory cues. *Physiology and Behavior, 30,* 151–154.

Posner, M. I., & Presti, D. E. (1987). Selective attention and cognitive control. *Trends in Neurosciences, 10,* 13–17.

Power, T. G., & Parke, R. D. (1982). Play as a context for early learning: Lab and home analyses. In L. M. Laosa & I. E. Sigal (Eds.), *The family as a learning environment.* New York: Plenum.

Premack, D. (1965). Reinforcement theory. In D. Levine (Ed.), *Nebraska Symposium on Motivation.* Lincoln: University of Nebraska Press.

Premack, D. (1985). "Gavagai!" or the future history of the animal language controversy. *Cognition, 19,* 207–296.

Pressley, M., Levin, J., & Ghatala, E. S. (1984). Memory strategy monitoring in adults and children. *Journal of Verbal Learning and Verbal Behavior, 23,* 270–288.

Pressley, M. (1987). Are keyword method effects limited to slow presentation rates? An empirically based reply to Hall and Fuson (1986). *Journal of Educational Psychology, 79,* 333–335.

Pribram, K. H. (1984). Emotion: A neurobehavioral analysis. In K. R. Scherer & P. Ekman (Eds.), *Approaches to emotion,* Hillsdale, NJ: Erlbaum.

Pribram, K. H. (1986). The cognitive revolution and mind/brain issues. *American Psychologist, 41,* 507–520.

Prien, R. F. (1983). Lithium and the long-term maintenance treatment of tricyclic antidepressant drugs and therapeutic response. In P. J. Clayton & J. E. Barret (Eds.), *Treatment of depression: Old controversies and new approaches* (pp. 105–114). New York: Raven Press.

Proxmire, W. (1975). Press release, U.S. Senate.

Pruitt, D. G., & Rubin, J. Z. (1986). *Social conflict: Escalation, stalemate, and settlement.* New York. Random House.

Pyszczynski, T., Holt, K., & Greenberg, J. (1987). Depression, self-focused attention, and expectancies for positive and negative future life events for self and others. *Journal of Personality and Social Psychology, 52,* 994–1001.

Rachman, S., & Hodgson, R. (1980). *Obsessions and compulsions.* Englewood Cliffs, NJ: Prentice-Hall.

Ragland, D. R. (1988, January 14). Type A behavior and mortality from coronary heart disease. *New England Journal of Medicine, 318,* 65.

Ragozin, A. S. (1980). Attachment behavior of day care children: Naturalistic and laboratory observations. *Child Development, 51,* 409–415.

Rahe, R. H., & Arthur, R. J. (1978). Life change and illness studies: Past history and future directions. *Human Stress, 4,* 3–15.

Ramey, C. T. (1981). Consequences of infant day care. In B. Weissbound & J. Musick (Eds.), *Infants: Their social environments.* Washington, DC: National Association for the Education of Young Children.

Rand, J. (1978, January). The psychology of conjuring. *Technology Review, 80,* 56–63.

Raphael, B. (1976). *The thinking computer.* San Francisco: Freeman.

Rasmussen, J. (1981). Models of mental strategies in process control. In J. Rasmussen & W. Rouse (Eds.), *Human detection and diagnosis of system failures.* New York: Plenum Press.

Ratner, H. H., Schell, D. A., Crimmins, A., Mittelman, D., et al. (1987). Changes in adults' prose recall: Aging or cognitive demands? *Developmental Psychology, 23,* 521–525.

Ravo, N. (1988, December 14). For those who need something to talk to. *New York Times,* pp. B-1, B-12.

Ravussin, E., Lillioja, S., Knowler, W. C., Christin, L., Freymond, D., Abbott, W. G. H., Boyce, V., Howard, B. V., & Bogardus, C. (1988, February 25). Reduced rate of energy expenditure as a risk factor for body-weight gain. *New England Journal of Medicine, 318,* 467–472.

Reed, C. F. (1984). Terrestrial passage theory of the moon illusion. *Journal of Experimental Psychology: General, 113,* 489–500.

Reed, S. K. (1988). *Cognition: Theories and applications* (2nd ed.). Monterey, CA: Brooks/Cole.

Reese, H.W., Parnes, S. J., Treffinger, D. J., & Kaltsounis, G. (1976). Effects of a creative studies program on structure-of-intellect factors. *Journal of Educational Psychology, 68,* 401–410.

Reich, P. A. (1986). *Language development.* Englewood Cliffs, NJ: Prentice-Hall.

Regier, D. A., Boyd, J. H., Burke, J. D., Jr., Rae, D. S., Myers, J. K., Kramer, M., Robins, L. N., George, L. K., Karno, M., & Locke, B. Z. (1988). One-month prevalence of mental disorders in the United States. *Archives of General Psychiatry, 45,* 977–986.

Reiger, D. A., Myers, J. K., Kramer, M., Robins, L. N., Blazer, D. G., Hough, R. L., Eaton, W. W., & Lock, B. Z. (1984). The NIMH epidemiological catchment area program. *Archives of General Psychiatry, 41,* 934–941.

Reiman, E. M., Fusselman, M. J., Fox, P. T., & Raichle, M. E. (1989, February 24). Neuroanatomical correlates of anticipatory anxiety. *Science, 243,* 1071–1074.

Reinhardt-Rutland, A. H. (1988). Induced movement in the visual modality: An overview. *Psychological Bulletin, 103,* 57–71.

Reinke, B. J., Holmes, D. S., & Harris, R. L. (1985). The timing of psychosocial changes in women's lives: The years 25 to 45. *Journal of Personality and Social Psychology, 48,* 1353–1364.

Reis, H. T., Wheeler, L., Spiegel, N., Kerris, M. H., Nezlek, J., & Perri, M. (1982). Physical attractiveness in social interaction: II. Why does appearance affect social experience? *Journal of Personality and Social Psychology, 43,* 979–996.

Reis, S. M. (1989). Reflections on policy affecting the education of gifted and talented students. *American Psychologist, 44,* 399–408.

Reisenzein, R. (1983). The Schachter theory of emotion. Two decades later. *Psychological Bulletin, 94,* 239–264.

Reiss, B. F. (1980). Psychological tests in homosexuality. In J. Marmor, (Ed.), *Homosexual behavior* (pp. 296–311). New York: Basic Books.

Reitman, J. S. (1965). *Cognition and thought.* New York: Wiley.

Repetti, R. L. (1987). Individual and common components of the social environment at work and psychological well-being. *Journal of Personality and Social Psychology, 52,* 710–720.

Rescorla, R. A. (1988). Pavlovian conditioning: It's not what you think it is. *American Psychologist, 43,* 151–160.

Reuman, D. A., Alwin, D. F., & Veroff, J. (1984). Assessing the validity of the achievement motive in the presence of random measurement error. *Journal of Personality and Social Psychology, 47,* 1347–1362.

Reyner, A. (1984, April). The nose knows. *Science,* p. 26.

Reynolds, C., & Mann, L. (Eds.) (1987). *Encyclopedia of special education.* New York: Wiley.

Reynolds, R. I., & Takooshian, H. (1988, January). Where were you August 8, 1985? *Bulletin of the Psychonomic Society, 26,* 23–25.

Rhue, J. W., & Lynn, S. J. (1987). Fantasy-proneness and psychopathology. *Journal of Personality and Social Psychology, 53,* 327–336.

Rice, A. (1984, May). Imagination to go. *Psychology Today,* pp. 48–52.

Rice, B. (1981, December). Call-in therapy: Reach out and shrink someone. *Psychology Today,* pp. 39–47, 87.

Rice, M. L. (1989). Children's language acquisition. *American Psychologist, 44,* 149–156.

Richards, R., Kinney, D. K., Benet, M., & Merzel, A. P. C. (1988). Assessing everyday creativity: Characteristics of the lifetime creativity scales and validation with three large samples. *Journal of Personality and Social Psychology, 54,* 476–485.

Riegel, K. F., & Riegel, R. M. (1972). Development, drop, and death. *Developmental Psychology, 6,* 306–319.

Rifkin, A., & Siris, S. G. (1983). Long-term drug treatment of schizophrenia. In A. Rifkin (Ed.), *Schizophrenia and affective disorders: Biology and drug treatment* (pp. 299–322). Boston: John Wright.

Rinn, W. E. (1984). The neuropsychology of facial expression: A review of neurological and psychological mechanisms for producing facial expressions. *Psychological Bulletin, 95,* 52–77.

Ristau, C. A., & Robbins, D. (1982). Language in the great apes. In J. S. Rosenblatt, R. A. Hinde, C. Beer, & M. Busnel (Eds.), *Advances in the study of behavior.* New York: Academic Press.

Ritzler, B., & Rosenbaum, G. (1974). Proprioception in schizophrenics and normals: Effects of stimulus intensity and interstimulus interval. *Journal of Abnormal Psychology, 83,* 106–111.

Rivers, P. C. (Ed.) (1986). Alcohol and addictive behavior. *Nebraska Symposium on Motivation, 34,* 1–346.

Robbins, M., & Jensen, G. D. (1978). Multiple orgasm in males. *Journal of Sex Research, 14,* 21–26.

Robbins, W. J. (1929). *Growth.* New Haven, CT: Yale University Press.

Roberto, L. G. (1983). Issues in diagnosis and treatment of transsexualism. *Archives of Sexual Behavior, 12,* 445–473.

Roberts, A. H. (1985). Biofeedback: Research, training, and clinical roles. *American Psychologist, 40,* 938–941.

Roberts, L. (1988, January 1). Zeroing in on the sex switch. *Science, 239,* 21–23. (a)

Roberts, L. (1988, July 8). Vietnam's psychological toll. *Science, 241,* 159–161. (b)

Roberts, R. (1989). Are neural nets like the human brain? *Science, 243,* 481–482.

Roberts, S. B., Savage, J., Coward, W. A., Chew, B., & Lucas, A. (1988, February 25). Energy expenditure and intake in infants born to lean and overweight mothers. *New England Journal of Medicine, 318,* 461–466.

Robins, C. J. (1988). Attributions and depression: Why is the literature so inconsistent?

Journal of Personality and Social Psychology, 54, 880–889.

Rock, I. (1983). *The logic of perception.* Cambridge, MA: MIT Press.

Rodin, J. (1981). Current status of the internal-external hypothesis of obesity: What went wrong? *American Psychologist, 34,* 361–372.

Rodin, J. (1985). Insulin levels, hunger, and food intake: An example of feedback loops in body-weight regulation. *Health Psychology, 4,* 1–18.

Rodin, J. (1986, September 19). Aging and health: Effects of the sense of control. *Science, 233,* 1271–1276.

Rodin, J., & Janis, I. L. (1979). The social power of health care practitioners as agents of change. *The Journal of Social Issues, 35,* 60–81.

Rodin, J., & Langer, E. (1980). Aging labels: The decline of control and the fall of self-esteem. *Journal of Social Issues, 36,* 12–29.

Rodin, J., & Langer, E. (1977). Long-term effects of a control-relevant intervention with the institutionalized aged. *Journal of Personality and Social Psychology, 35,* 897–902.

Rodin, J., & Salovey, P. (1989). Health psychology. *Annual Review of Psychology, 40,* 533–579.

Roethlisberger, F. J., & Dickson, W. V. (1939). *Management and the worker.* Cambridge, MA: Harvard University Press.

Roffwarg, H. F., Muzio, J. N., & Dement, W. C. (1966). Ontogenetic development of the human sleep-dream cycle. *Science, 152,* 604–619.

Rogers, C. R. (1951). *Client-centered therapy.* Boston: Houghton-Mifflin.

Rogers, C. R. (1971). A theory of personality. In S. Maddi (Ed.), *Perspectives on personality.* Boston: Little, Brown.

Rogers, C. R. (1980). *A way of being.* Boston: Houghton Mifflin.

Rogers, E. M., & Rogers, R. A. (1976). *Communication in organizations.* New York: The Free Press.

Rogers, M. (1988, February 15). The return of 3-D movies—on TV. *Newsweek,* pp. 60–62. (a)

Rogers, M. (1988, October 3). Here comes hypermedia. *Newsweek,* pp. 44–45. (b)

Rogers, R. (1987). APA's position on the insanity defense. *American Psychologist, 42,* 840–848.

Rohter, L. (1987, July 21). Inside the operating room: A day of bold brain surgery. *New York Times,* pp. C-17, C-20.

Rokeach, M. (1971). Long-range experimental modification of values, attitudes, and behavior. *American Psychologist, 26,* 453–459.

Rorschach, H. (1921). *Psychodiagnosis.* Berne: Hans Huber.

Rorschach, H. (1924). *Psychodiagnosis: A diagnostic test based on perception.* New York: Grune and Stratton.

Rosch, E. (1974). Linguistic relativity. In A. Silverstein (Ed.), *Human communication:*

Theoretical explorations (pp. 95–121). New York: Halstead Press.

Rosch, E. (1975). Cognitive representations of semantic categories. *Journal of Experimental Psychology—General, 104,* 192–233.

Rose, R. J., Koskenvuo, M., Kaprio, J., Sarna, S., & Langinvainio, H. (1988). Shared genes, shared experiences, and similarity of personality: Data from 14,288 adult Finnish co-twins. *Journal of Personality and Social Psychology, 54,* 161–171.

Rosen, A. (1958). Differentiation of diagnostic groups by individual MMPI scales. *Journal of Consulting Psychology, 22,* 453–457.

Rosen, G. M. (1987). Self-help treatment books and the commercialization of psychotherapy. *American Psychologist, 42,* 46–51.

Rosenberg, M. B., Friedmann, T., Robertson, R. C., Tuszynski, M., Wolff, J. A., Breakefield, X. O., & Gage, F. H. (1988). Grafting genetically modified cells to the damaged brain: Restorative effects of NGF expression. *Science, 242,* 1575–1578.

Rosenau, J. N. (1967). Introduction. In J. N. Rosenau (Ed.), *Domestic sources of foreign policy.* New York: Free Press.

Rosenhan, D. L. (1973). On being sane in insane places. *Science, 179,* 250–258.

Rosenhan, D. L. (1975). The contextual nature of psychiatric diagnosis. *Journal of Abnormal Psychology, 84,* 462–474.

Rosenmon, R. H., Brond, R. J., Sholtz, R. I., & Friedman, M. (1976). Multivariate prediction of coronary heart disease during 8.5 year follow-up in the Western collaborative group study. *American Journal of Cardiology, 37,* 903–910.

Rosenthal, D. (1970). *Genetic theory and abnormal behavior.* New York: McGraw-Hill.

Rosenthal, R., & Rosnow, R. L. (1984). Applying Hamlet's question to the ethical conduct of research: A conceptual addendum. *American Psychologist, 39,* 561–563.

Rosenweig, M. R. (1984). Experience, memory, and the brain. *American Psychologist, 39,* 365–376.

Rosenweig, M. R., & Leiman, A. L. (1989). *Physiological psychology.* (2nd ed.). New York: Random House.

Ross, M., & Fletcher, G. J. O. (1985). Attribution and social perception. In G. Lindzy & E. Aronson (Eds.), *Handbook of social psychology* (3rd ed.). New York: Random House.

Ross, L., Greene, D., & House, P. (1977). The false consensus effect: An egocentric bias in social perception and attribution processes. *Journal of Experimental Social Psychology, 13,* 279–301.

Rotter, J. B. (1966). Generalized expectancies for internal versus external control of reinforcement. *Psychological Monographs, 80* (Whole No. 609).

Rotton, J., Barry, T., Frey, J., & Soler, E. (1978). Air pollution and interpersonal attraction. *Journal of Applied Social Psychology, 8,* 57–71.

Rotton, J., & Frey, J. (1985). Air pollution, weather, and violent crimes: Concomitant time-series analysis of archival data. *Journal of Personality and Social Psychology, 49,* 1207–1220.

Rotton, J., Frey, J., Barry, T., Milligan, M., & Fitzpatrick, M. (1977). *Modeling, malodorous air pollution, and interpersonal aggression.* Paper presented at the meeting of the Midwestern Psychological Association (Chicago).

Rouse, W. B., & Morris, N. M. (1986). On looking into the black box: Prospects and limits in the search for mental models. *Psychological Bulletin, 100,* 349–363.

Routtenberg, A., & Lindy, J. (1965). Effects of the availability of rewarding septal and hypothalmic stimulation on bar pressing for food under conditions of deprivation. *Journal of Comparative and Physiological Psychology, 60,* 158–161.

Rovner, S. (1984, June 22). Healthtalk: Overcoming disaster. *Washington Post,* p. B-5.

Rowe, J. W., & Kahn, R. L. (1987, July 10). Human aging: Usual and successful. *Science, 237,* 143–149.

Rowlison, R. T., & Felner, R. D. (1988). Major life events, hassles, and adaptation in adolescence: Confounding in the conceptualization and measurement of life stress and adjustment revisited. *Journal of Personality and Social Psychology, 55,* 432–444.

Royer, J. M., & Feldman, R. S. (1984). *Educational psychology: Applications and theory.* New York: Knopf.

Rozin, P. (1977). The significance of learning mechanisms in food selection: Some biology, psychology and sociology of science. In L. M. Barker, M. R. Best, & M. Donijan (Eds.), *Learning mechanisms in food selection.* Waco, TX: Baylor University Press.

Rubeck, R. B., Dabbs, J. M., Jr., & Hopper, C. H. (1984). The process of brainstorming: An analysis with individual and group vocal parameters. *Journal of Personality and Social Psychology, 47,* 558–567.

Rubeck, R. B., & Innes, C. A. (1988). The relevance and irrelevance of psychological research: The example of prison crowding. *American Psychologist, 43,* 683–693.

Rubenstein, C. (1982, July). Psychology's fruit flies. *Psychology Today,* pp. 83–84.

Rubin, D. C. (1985, September). The subtle deceiver: Recalling our past. *Psychology Today, 19,* pp. 39–46.

Rubin, D. C. 1986). *Autobiographical memory.* Cambridge: Cambridge University Press.

Rubin, J. Z., & Friedland, N. (1986). Theater of terror. *Psychology Today, 20,* 18–19, 22, 24, 26–28.

Rubin, Z. (1970). Measurement of romantic love. *Journal of Personality and Social Psychology, 16,* 265–273.

Rubin, Z. (1973). *Liking and loving.* New York: Holt, Rinehart and Winston.

Ruble, D. N., Fleming, A. S., Hackel, L. S., & Stangor, C. (1988). Changes in the marital relationship during the transition to first-time motherhood: Effects of violated expectations concerning division of household labor. *Journal of Personality and Social Psychology, 55,* 78–87.

Ruble, T. L. (1983). Sex stereotypes: Issues of change in the 1970s. *Sex Roles, 9,* 397–402.

Rushton, J. P. (1975). Generosity in children: Immediate and long-term effects of modeling, preaching, and moral judgment. *Journal of Personality and Social Psychology, 31,* 459–466.

Rushton, J. P., Fulker, D. W., Neale, M. C., Nias, D. K. B., & Eysenck, H. J. (1986). Altruism and aggression: The heritability of individual differences. *Journal of Personality and Social Psychology, 50,* 1192–1198.

Russ, N. W., Harwood, M. K., & Geller, E. S. (1986). Estimating alcohol impairment in the field: Implications for drunk driving. *Journal of Studies on Alcohol, 47,* 237–240.

Russ, N. W., & Geller, E. S. (1987). Training bar personnel to prevent drunken driving: A field evaluation. *American Journal of Public Health, 77,* 952–954.

Russell, D. E. H., & Howell, N. (1983). The prevalence of rape in the United States revisited. *Signs, 8,* 688–695.

Russell, M. A. H. (1979). Tobacco dependence: Is nicotine rewarding or aversive? In N. A. Krasnegor (Ed.), *Cigarette smoking as a dependence process* (NIDA Research Monograph No. 23, U.S. Department of Health, Education, and Welfare, Publication No. [ADM] 79-800). Rockville, MD: National Institute on Drug Abuse.

Russo, D. C., Carr, E. G., & Lovaas, O. I. (1980). Self-injury in pediatric populations. *Comprehensive handbook of behavioral medicine* (Vol. 3: Extended applications and issues). Holliswood, NY: Spectrum.

Russo, N. (1981). In L. T. Benjamin, Jr., & K. D. Lowman (Eds.), *Activities handbook for the teaching of psychology.* Washington, DC: American Psychological Association.

Rutter, M. (1982). Social-emotional consequences of day-care for preschool children. In E. F. Zigler & E. W. Gordon (Eds.), *Day-care: Scientific and social policy issues.* Boston: Auburn House.

Sackheim, H. A. (1985, June). The case for E.C.T. *Psychology Today,* pp. 36–40.

Salber, E. J., Freeman, H. E., & Abelin, T. (1968). Needed research on smoking: Lessons from the Newton study. In E. F. Borgatta & R. R. Evans (Eds.), *Smoking, health, and behavior.* Chicago: Aldine.

Sanders, M. S., & McCormick, E. J. (1987). *Human factors in engineering and design* (6th ed.). New York: McGraw-Hill.

Sanders, C. M. (1988). Risk factors in bereavement outcome. *Journal of Social Issues, 44,* 97–111.

Sank, L. T. (1979). Community disasters: Primary prevention and treatment in a health maintenance organization. *American Psychologist, 34,* 334–338.

Sarafino, E. P. (1979). An estimate of nationwide incidence of sexual offenses against children. *Child Welfare, 58,* 127–134.

Sarason, I. G. (1976). A modeling and informational approach to delinquency. In E. Ribes-Inesta & A. Bandura (Eds.), *Analysis of Delinquency and Aggression.* Hillsdale, NJ: Erlbaum.

Saufley, W. H., Otaka, S. R., & Bavaresco, J. L. (1985). Context effects: Classroom tests and context independence. *Memory and Cognition, 13,* 522–528.

Saul, E. V., & Kass, T. S. (1969). Study of anticipated anxiety in a medical school setting. *Journal of Medical Education, 44,* 526.

Savage-Rumbaugh, E. S., Rumbaugh, D. M., & Boysen, S. (1980). Do apes use language? *American Scientist, 68,* 49–61.

Saxe, L., Dougherty, D., & Cross, T. (1985). The validity of polygraph testing. *American Psychologist, 40,* 355–366.

Scarr, S. (1984). *Mother care/other care.* New York: Basic Books.

Scarr, S. (1986, August). Child-care decisions and working mothers' dilemmas. Address given at the annual meeting of the American Psychological Association (Washington, DC).

Scarr, S., & Carter-Saltzman, L. (1982). Genetics and intelligence. In R. J. Sternberg (Ed.), *Handbook of human intelligence* (pp. 792–896). Cambridge: Cambridge University Press.

Scarr, S., & Weinberg, R. A. (1976). I.Q. test performance of black children adopted by white families. *American Psychologist, 3,* 726–739.

Schachter, S. (1959). *The psychology of affiliation.* Stanford, CA: Stanford University Press.

Schachter, S. (1971). Some extraordinary facts about obese humans and rats. *American Psychologist, 26,* 129–144.

Schachter, S., Ellertson, N., McBride, D., & Gregory, D. (1951). An experimental study of cohesiveness and productivity. *Human Relations, 4,* 229–238.

Schachter, S., Goldman, R., & Gordon, A. (1968). Effects of fear, food deprivation, and obesity on eating. *Journal of Personality and Social Psychology, 10,* 91–97.

Schachter, S., & Singer, J. E. (1962). Cognitive, social, and physiological determinants of emotional state. *Psychological Review, 69,* 379–399.

Schaefer, C., Coyne, J. C., & Lazarus, R. S. (1981). The health-related functions of social support. *Journal of Behavioral Medicine, 4,* 381–406.

Schaie, K. W. (1985). *Longitudinal studies of psychological development.* New York: Guilford Press.

Schaie, K. W. (1988). Ageism in psychological research. *American Psychologist, 43,* 179–183.

Schaie, K. W., & Willis, S. L. (1985, August). *Differential ability decline and its remedia-*tion in late adulthood. Paper presented at annual meeting of the American Psychological Association (Los Angeles).

Schaie, K. W., & Willis, S. L. (1986). Can decline in adult intellectual functioning be reversed? *Developmental Psychology, 22,* 223–232.

Schanberg, S. M., & Field, T. M. (1987). Sensory deprivation stress and supplemental stimulation in the rat pup and preterm human neonate. *Child Development, 58,* 1431–1447.

Schank, R. (1985). *The cognitive computer.* New York: McGraw-Hill.

Scharf, B., & Buus, S. (1986). Audition. In K. R. Boff, L. Kaufman, & J. P. Thomas (Eds.), *Handbook of perception and human performance* (Vol. 1). New York: Wiley.

Scheff, T. J. (1985). The primacy of affect. *American Psychologist, 40,* 849–850.

Scheibel, A. (1984). Personal communication.

Scheibel, A. (1986). Personal communication.

Scheier, M. F. (1986). Coping with stress: Divergent strategies of optimists and pessimists. *Journal of Personality and Social Psychology, 51,* 1257–1264.

Scherer, K. R. (1984). Les émotions: Fonctions et composantes. [Emotions: Functions and components.] *Cahiers de psychologie cognitive, 4,* 9–39.

Scherer, K. R. (Ed.) (1988). *Facets of emotion.* Hillsdale, N.J.: Erlbaum.

Scherer, K. R., & Ekman, P. (Eds.). (1984). *Approaches to emotion.* Hillsdale, NJ: Erlbaum.

Schickedanz, J. A., Schickedanz, D. I., & Forsyth, P. D. (1982). *Toward understanding children.* Boston: Little, Brown.

Schiffman, H. R. (1982). *Sensation and perception: An integrated approach* (2nd ed.). New York: Wiley.

Schmeck, H. M., Jr. (1984, March 6). Explosion of data on brain cell reveals its great complexity. *New York Times,* pp. C-1–C-2.

Schmeck, H. M., Jr. (1987, December 29). New light on the chemistry of dreams. *New York Times,* pp. C-1, C-2.

Schmeck, H. M., Jr. (1988, February 16). Depression: Studies bring new drugs and insights. *New York Times,* pp. C-1, C-10.

Schneiderman, N. (1983). Animal behavior models of coronary heart disease. In D. S. Krantz, A. Baum, & J. E. Singer (Eds.), *Handbook of psychology and health* (Vol. 3). Hillsdale, NJ: Erlbaum.

Schneidman, E. S. (1987). A psychological approach to suicide. In G. R. VandenBos & B. K. Bryant (Eds.), *Cataclysms, crises, and catastrophes: Psychology in action.* Washington, DC: American Psychological Association.

Schnelle, J. F., Gendrich, J. G., Beegle, G. P., Thomas, M. M., & McNess, M. (1980). Mass media techniques for prompting behavior change in the community. *Environment and Behavior, 12,* 157–166.

Schoeneman, T. J., & Rubanowitz, D. E. (1985). Attributions in the advice columns: Actors and observers, causes and reasons. *Journal of Personality and Social Psychology, 11,* 315–325.

Schofield, W. (1964). *Psychotherapy: The purchase of friendship.* Englewood Cliffs, NJ: Prentice-Hall.

Schofield, W., & Vaughan-Jackson, P. (1913). *What a boy should know.* New York: Cassell.

Schonche, D. A. (1974, August). The emotional aftermath of "the largest tornado ever." *Today's Health,* pp. 16–19, 61–63.

Schwartz, G. E., Davidson, R., & Maer, F. (1975). Right hemisphere lateralization for emotion in the human brain: Interactions with cognition. *Science,* 286–288.

Schwartz, S. H., & Inbar-Saban, N. (1988). Value self-confrontation as a method to aid in weight loss. *Journal of Personality and Social Psychology, 54,* 396–404.

Schwitzgabel, R. L., & Schwitzgabel, R. K. (1980). *Law and psychological practice.* New York: Wiley.

Seagraves, R. T., & Schoenberg, H. W. (1985). *Diagnosis and treatment of erectile disturbances.* New York: Plenum Press.

Sears, D. D. (1968). The paradox of de facto selective exposure without preferences for supportive information. In R. P. Abelson (Ed.), *Theories of cognitive consistency.* Chicago: Rand McNally.

Sears, D. O. (1982). The person-positivity bias. *Journal of Personality and Social Psychology, 44,* 233–250.

Sears, D. O. (1986). College sophomores in the laboratory: Influences of a narrow data base on social psychology's view of human nature. *Journal of Personality and Social Psychology, 51,* 515–530.

Sears, R. R. (1977). Sources of life satisfaction of the Terman gifted men. *American Psychologist, 32,* 119–128.

Segall, M. H., Campbell, D. T., & Herskovits, M. J. (1966). *The influence of culture on visual perception.* New York: Bobbs-Merrill.

Seligman, M. E. P. (1975). *Helplessness: On depression, development, and death.* San Francisco: Freeman.

Seligman, M. E. P. (1988, October). Baby boomer blues. *Psychology Today,* p. 54.

Selman, R. L., Schorin, M. Z., Stone, C. R., & Phelps, E. (1983). A naturalistic study of children's social understanding. *Developmental Psychology, 19,* 82–102.

Selye, H. (1976). *The stress of life.* New York: McGraw-Hill.

Serrin, W. (1983, November 3). Japanese turn Arkansas plant into a success. *New York Times,* pp. A-1, B-14.

Shapiro, S., Skinner, E. A., Kessler, L. G., VonKorff, M., German, P. S., Shapiro, D. H., & Walsh, R. N. (Eds.) (1984). *Meditation: Classical and contemporary perspectives.* New York: Aldine.

Sharpe, L. T., Fach, C., Nordby, K., & Stockman, A. (1989, April 21). *Science, 244,* 354–356.

Shaver, P., Schwartz, J., Kirson, D., & O'Connor, C. (1987). Emotion knowledge: Further exploration of a prototype approach. *Journal of Personality and Social Psychology, 52*, 1061–1086.

Shaw, M. E. (1954). Some effects of problem complexity upon problem solution efficiency in different communication nets. *Journal of Experimental Psychology, 48*, 211–217.

Shaw, M. E. (1964). Communication networks. In L. Berkowitz (Ed.), *Advances in experimental social psychology* (Vol. 1, pp. 111–147). New York: Academic Press.

Shaw, M. E. (1981). *Group dynamics: The psychology of small group behavior* (3rd ed.). New York: McGraw-Hill.

Shock, N. W. (1962, January). The physiology of aging. *Scientific American*, 100–110.

Shotland, R. L. (1984, March). Paper presented at the Catherine Genovese Memorial Conference on Bad Samaritanism, Fordham University.

Shotland, R. L. (1985, June). When bystanders just stand by. *Psychology Today, 19*, pp. 50–55.

Sifakis, C. (1987). *The mafia encyclopedia.* New York: Facts on File.

Sigall, H., & Ostrove, N. (1975). Beautiful but dangerous: Effects of offender attractiveness and nature of the crime on juridic judgment. *Journal of Personality and Social Psychology, 29*, 497–508.

Sigerist, H. E. (1943). *Civilization and disease.* Ithaca, NY: Cornell University Press.

Simmons, J. V., Jr. (1981). U.S. patent document #4, 261, 284.

Simmons, J. V., Jr. (1984). U.S. Patent Office Document #4,261,284 (1981). Washington, D.C.: U.S. Government Printing Office.

Simmons, J., & Mares, W. (1985). *Working together: Employee participation in action.* New York: University Press.

Simon, H. A. (1957). *Administrative behavior* (2nd ed.). New York: Free Press.

Singer, J. L. (1975). *The inner world of daydreaming.* New York: Harper & Row.

Sinoway, C. G., Raupp, C. D., & Newman, J. (1985). *Binge eating and bulimia: Comparing incidence and characteristics across universities.* Paper presented at annual meeting of the American Psychological Association, Los Angeles.

Siris, S. G., & Rifkin, A. (1983). Side effects of drugs used in the treatment of affective disorders. In A. Rifkin (Ed.), *Schizophrenia and affective disorders: Biology and drug treatment* (pp. 117–138). Boston: John Wright.

Skeels, H. M. (1966). Adult status of children with contrasting early life experiences: A follow-up study. *Monographs of the Society for Research in Child Development, 31* (3, whole no. 105).

Skinner, B. F. (1948). *Walden Two.* New York: Macmillan.

Skinner, B. F. (1957). *Verbal behavior.* New York: Appleton-Century-Crofts.

Skinner, B. F. (1975). The steep and thorny road to a science of behavior. *American Psychologist, 30*, 42–49.

Skinner, B. F. (1986). Programmed instruction revisited. *Phi Delta Kappan, 68*, 103–110.

Skinner, B. F., & Krakower, S. A. (1968). *Handwriting with write and see.* Chicago: Lyons & Carnahan.

Skrypnek, B. J., & Snyder, M. (1982). On the self-perpetuating nature of stereotypes about women and men. *Journal of Experimental Social Psychology, 18*, 277–291.

Sloane, R. B., Staples, F. R., Criostal, A. H., Yorkston, W. J., & Whipple, K. (1975). *Psychotherapy vs. behavior therapy.* Cambridge, MA: Harvard University Press.

Slusher, M. P., & Anderson, C. A. (1987). When reality monitoring fails: The role of imagination in stereotype maintenance. *Journal of Personality and Social Psychology, 52*, 653–662.

Smith, C. A., & Ellsworth, P. C. (1987). Patterns of appraisal and emotion related to taking an exam. *Journal of Personality and Social Psychology, 52*, 475–488.

Smith, E. (1988, May). Fighting cancerous feelings. *Psychology Today*, pp. 22–23.

Smith, E. R. (1984). Attributions and other inferences: Processing information about the self versus others. *Journal of Experimental Social Psychology, 20*, 97–115.

Smith, L. (1987). From global similarities to kinds of similarities: The construction of dimensions in development. In S. Voniadou & A. Ortony (Eds.), *Similarity and analogy.* Cambridge, England: Cambridge University Press.

Smith, M. L., Glass, G. V., & Miller, T. J. (1980). *The benefits of psychotherapy.* Baltimore: John Hopkins.

Snarey, J. R. (1985). Cross-cultural universality of social-moral development: A critical review of Kohlbergian research. *Psychological Bulletin, 97*, 202–232.

Snyder, C. R., & Higgins, R. L. (1988). Excuses: Their effective role in the negotiation of reality. *Psychological Bulletin, 104*, 23–35.

Snyder, C. R., & Shenk, R. J. (1975). The P. T. Barnum effect. *Psychology Today, 8*, 52–54.

Snyder, M., Berscheid, E., & Glick, P. (1985). Focusing on the exterior and the interior: The investigations of the initiation of personal relations. *Journal of Personality and Social Psychology, 48*, 1427–1439.

Snyder, M., & Cantor, N. (1979). Testing hypotheses about other people: The use of historical knowledge. *Journal of Experimental Social Psychology, 15*, 330–343.

Snyder, S. H. (1978). Dopamine and schizophrenia. In L. C. Wynne, R. L. Cromwell, & S. Matthysse (Eds.), *The nature of schizophrenia: New approaches to research and treatment* (pp. 87–94). New York: Wiley.

Snyder, S. H. (1980). *Biological aspects of mental disorder.* New York: Oxford University Press.

Snyder, S. H. (1984). Drug and neurotransmitter receptors in the brain. *Science, 224*, pp. 22–31.

Snyder, S. H. (1987, April 30). Parkinson's disease: A cure using brain transplants? *Nature, 326*, 824–825.

Soelberg, P. O. (1967). Unprogrammed decision making. *Industrial Management Review*, 19–29.

Solomon, R. L., & Corbit, J. D. (1974). An opponent-process theory of motivation: I. Temporal dynamics of affect. *Psychological Review, 81*, 119–145.

Sommer, R. (1969). *Personal space: The behavioral basis of design.* Englewood Cliffs, NJ: Prentice-Hall.

Sommer, R., & Becker, F. D. (1969). Territorial defense and the good neighbor. *Journal of Personality and Social Psychology, 11*, 85–92.

Sonnenfeld, J. (1982). Clarifying critical confusion in the Hawthorne hysteria. *American Psychologist, 37*, 1397–1399.

Soukhanov, A. A. (1989, January). Word watch. *Atlantic*, 124.

Spanos, N. P. (1986). Hypnotic behavior: A social psychological interpretation of amnesia, analgesia, and "trance logic." *Behavioral and Brain Science, 9*, 449–467.

Spanos, N. P., Cross, W. P., Menary, E. P., Brett, P. J., & deGroic, M. (1987). Attitudinal and imaginal ability predictors of social cognitive skill-training enhancements in hypnotic susceptibility. *Personality and Social Psychology Bulletin, 13*, 379–398.

Spearman, C. (1927). *The abilities of man.* London: Macmillan.

Spence, J. T. (1985, August). *Achievement American style: The rewards and costs of individualism.* Presidential address. 93rd Annual Convention of the American Psychological Association (Los Angeles).

Spence, J. T. (1987). Centrifugal versus centripetal tendencies in psychology: Will the center hold? *American Psychologist, 42*, 1052–1054.

Spence, J. T., Deaux, K., & Helmreich, R. L. (1985). Sex roles in contemporary American society. In G. Lindzey & E. Aronson (Eds.), *Handbook of social psychology: Vol. II* (3rd ed.). New York: Random House.

Spence, M. J., & DeCasper, A. J. (1982, March). Human fetuses perceive maternal speech. Paper presented at the meeting of the International Conference on Infant Studies (Austin, Texas).

Sperling, G. (1960). The information available in brief visual presentation. *Psych Monographs, 74* (whole no. 498).

Sperry, R. (1982). Some effects of disconnecting the cerebral hemispheres. *Science, 217*, pp. 1223–1226.

Spiegel, D., Cutcomb, S., Ren, C., & Pribram, K. (1985). Hypnotic hallucination alters evoked potentials. *Journal of Abnormal Psychology, 94*, 249–255.

Spiegel, H. (1987). The answer is: Psychotherapy plus. Special Issue: Is hypnotherapy a placebo? *British Journal of Experimental and Clinical Hypnosis, 4,* 163–164.

Spitzer, R. L. (1975). On pseudoscience in science, logic in remission, and psychiatric diagnosis: A critique of Rosenhan's "On being sane in insane places." *Journal of Abnormal Psychology, 84,* 442–452.

Spitzer, R. L., Skodol, A. E., Gibbon, M., & Williams, J. B. W. (1983). *Psychopathology: A case book.* New York: McGraw-Hill.

Springer, S. P., & Deutsch, G. (1985). *Left brain, right brain.* San Francisco: Freeman.

Sproull, L. S., & Kiesler, S. B. (1983). *Encounters with the alien culture.* Paper presented at the American Psychological Association annual meeting. Berkeley, CA.

Sproull, L., Kiesler, S., & Zubrow, D. (1984). Encountering an alien culture. *Journal of Social Issues, 40,* 31–48.

Squire, L. (1986, June 27). Mechanisms of memory. *Science, 232,* 1612–1619.

Squire, L. (1987). *Memory and brain.* New York: Oxford University Press.

Squire, L. (1988, February). *Memory.* Paper presented at the annual meeting of the American Association for the Advancement of Science (Boston).

Squire, L., & Butters, N. (Eds.). (1985). *Neuropsychology of memory.* New York: Guilford Press.

Sroufe, L. A., Fox, N. E., & Pancake, V. R. (1983). Attachment and dependency in a developmental perspective. *Child Development, 54,* 1615–1627.

Staats, A. W. (1967). Outline of an integrated learning theory of attitude formation and function. In M. Fishbein (Ed.), *Attitude theory and measurement.* New York: Wiley.

Staats, A. W., & Staats, C. K. (1958). Attitudes established by classical conditioning. *Journal of Abnormal and Social Psychology, 57,* 37–40.

Stanley, J. C. (1980). On educating the gifted. *Educational Researcher, 9,* 8–12.

Stanley, J. C., & Benbow, C. P. SMPY's first decade: Ten years of posing problems and solving them. *Journal of Special Education, 17,* 11–25.

Stapp, J., Fulcher, R., & Wicherski, M. (1984). The employment of 1981 and 1982 doctorate recipients in psychology. *American Psychologist, 39,* 1408–1423.

Stapp, J., Tucker, A. M., & VandenBos, G. R. (1985). Census of psychology personnel. *American Psychologist, 40,* 1317–1351.

Stark, E. (1985, May). Breaking the pain habit. *Psychology Today,* pp. 31–36.

Staub, E. (1971). A child in distress: The influence of nurturance and modeling on children's attempts to help. *Developmental Psychology, 5,* 124–133.

Stava, L. J., & Jaffa, M. (1987). Some operationalizations of the neodissociation concept and their relationship to hypnotic susceptibility. *Journal of Personality and Social Psychology, 54,* 989–996.

Steele, C. M., & Southwick, L. (1985). Alcohol and social behavior I: The psychology of

drunken excess. *Journal of Personality and Social Psychology, 48,* 18–34.

Steers, R. M. (1984). *Introduction to organizational behavior.* Glenview, IL: Scott, Foresman.

Stein, A. H., & Bailey, M. M. (1973). The socialization of achievement orientation in females. *Psychological Bulletin, 80,* 345–366.

Stein, J. A., Newcomb, M. D., & Bentler, P. M. (1987). An 8-year study of multiple influences on drug use and drug-use consequences. *Journal of Personality and Social Psychology, 53,* 1094–1105.

Steinberg, L. (1989). *Adolescence* (2nd ed.). New York: Knopf.

Steinberg, L. (1987, September). Bound to bicker. *Psychology Today,* pp. 36–39.

Steiner, J. E. (1979). Human facial expressions in response to taste and smell stimulation. In H. Reese & L. P. Lipsitt (Eds.), *Advances in child development and behavior* (Vol. 13). New York: Academic Press.

Sternbach, R. A. (Ed.) (1987). *The psychology of pain.* New York: Raven Press.

Sternberg, R. J. (1981). Testing and cognitive psychology. *American Psychologist, 36,* 1181–1189.

Sternberg, R. J. (1982). Reasoning, problem solving, and intelligence. In R. J. Sternberg (Ed.), *Handbook of human intelligence* (pp. 225–307). Cambridge, MA: Cambridge University Press.

Sternberg, R. J. (1985). Implicit theories of intelligence, creativity, and wisdom. *Journal of Personality and Social Psychology, 49,* 607–627.

Sternberg, R. (1985). *Beyond IQ: A triarchic theory of human intelligence.* New York: Cambridge University Press.

Sternberg, R. J. (1986). Triangular theory of love. *Psychological Review, 93,* 119–135.

Sternberg, R. J. (1987). Liking versus loving: A comparative evaluation of theories. *Psychological Bulletin, 102,* 331–345.

Sternberg, R. J., Conway, B. E., Ketron, J. L., & Bernstein, M. (1981). Peoples' conceptions of intelligence. *Journal of Personality and Social Psychology, 41,* 37–55.

Sternberg, R. J., & Davidson, J. E. (Eds.) (1986). *Conceptions of giftedness.* New York: Cambridge University Press.

Sternberg, R. J., & Detterman, D. (1986). *What is intelligence?* Norwood, NJ: Ablex.

Sternberg, R. J., & Grajek, S. (1984). The nature of love. *Journal of Personality and Social Psychology, 47,* 312–329.

Sternberg, R. J., & Wagner, R. K. (Eds.) (1986). *Practical intelligence: Nature and origins of competence in the everyday world.* New York: Cambridge University Press.

Sternberg, S. (1966, August 5). High-speed scanning in human memory. *Science, 153,* 652–654.

Sternberg, S. (1969). Mental processes revealed by reaction time experiments. *American Scientist, 57,* 421–457.

Stevens, C. F. (1979, September). The neuron. *Scientific American,* p. 36.

Stiles, W. B., Shapiro, D. A., & Elliot, R. (1986). Are all psychotherapies equivalent? *American Psychologist, 41,* 165–180.

Stogdill, R. (1974). *Handbook of leadership.* New York: The Free Press.

Stoller, S., & Field, T. (1982). Alteration of mother and infant behavior and heart rate during a still-face perturbation of face-to-face interaction. In T. Field & A. Fogel (Eds.), *Emotion and interactions.* New York: Erlbaum.

Storandt, M., et al. (1984). Psychometric differentiation of mild senile dementia of the Alzheimer type. *Archives of Neurology, 41,* 497–499.

Storm, C., & Storm, T. (1987). A taxonomic study of the vocabulary of emotion. *Journal of Personality and Social Psychology, 53,* 805–816.

Streufert, S. (1984, October). The stress of excellence. *Across the Board,* 9–16.

Stricker, E. M., & Zigmond, M. J. (1976). Recovery of function after damage to catecholamine-containing neurons: A neurochemical model for hypothalmic syndrome. In J. M. Sprague & A. N. Epstein (Eds.), *Progress in psychobiology and physiological psychology* (Vol. 6). New York: Academic Press.

Strickland, B. (1988, August). Winning the battle against depression: Strategies for women. Paper presented at the annual meeting of the American Psychological Association (Atlanta).

Strong, L. D. (1978). Alternative marital and family forms: Their relative attractiveness to college students and correlates of willingness to participate in nontraditional forms. *Journal of Marriage and the Family, 40,* 493–503.

Stroop, J. R. (1935). Studies of interference in serial verbal reactions. *Journal of Experimental Psychology, 18,* 643–662.

Strupp, H. H. (1981). Clinical research, practice, and the crisis of confidence. *Journal of Consulting and Clinical Psychology, 49,* 216–219.

Strupp, H. H. (1981). Toward a refinement of time-limited dynamic psychotherapy. *Forms of brief therapy.* New York: Guilford Press.

Stunkard, A. J. (1980). *Obesity.* Philadelphia: Saunders.

Stunkard, A. J., Foch, T. T., & Hrubec, Z. (1986). A twin study of human obesity. *Journal of the American Medical Association, 256,* 51–54.

Stunkard, A. J., Sorensen, T., Hanis, C., Teasdale, T. W., Chakraborty, R., Schull, W. J., & Schulsinger, F. (1986). An adoption study of human obesity. *New England Journal of Medicine, 314,* 193–198.

Sue, D. (1979). Erotic fantasies of college students during coitus. *Journal of Sex Research, 15,* 299–305.

Sugarman, S. (1988). *Piaget's construction of*

the child's reality. Cambridge, England: Cambridge University Press.

Sullivan, B. (1985). *Double standard.* Paper presented at the annual meeting of the Society for the Scientific Study of Sex (San Diego).

Sullivan, W. (1984, September). Transplanting cells into brain offers promise of therapy. *New York Times,* pp. C-1–C-2.

Sulzer-Azaroff, B., & Mayer, G. R. (1986). *Achieving educational excellence with behavioral strategies.* New York: Holt, Rinehart and Winston.

Super, C. M. (1980). Cognitive development: Looking across at growing up. In C. M. Super & S. Harakness (Eds.), *New directions for child development: Anthropological perspectives on child development* (pp. 59–69). San Francisco: Jossey-Bass.

Suzuki, N. (1986). Problems and prospect of Japanese companies' training programmes. *Asia Pacific Journal of Management, 3,* 110–120.

Svanum, S., Bringle, R. G., & McLaughlin, J. E. (1982). Father absence and cognitive performance in a large sample of six- to eleven-year-old children. *Child Development, 53,* 136–143.

Svarstad, B. (1976). Physician-patient communication and patient conformity with medical advice. In D. Mechanic (Ed.), *The growth of bureaucratic medicine.* New York: Wiley.

Swan, G. E., & Denk, C. E. (1988). Risk factors for late relapse in male and female ex-smokers. *Addictive Behaviors, 13,* 253–266.

Sweeney, P. D., & Gruber, L. L. (1984). Selective exposure: Voter information preferences and the Watergate affair. *Journal of Personality and Social Psychology, 46,* 1208–1221.

Sweet, E. (1985, October). Date rape: The story of an epidemic and those who deny it. *Ms/Campus Times,* pp. 56–59.

Sweetland, R. C., & Keyser, D. J. (1988). *Tests: A comprehensive reference for assessments in psychology, education, and business.* Kansas City: Test Corporation of America.

Swets, J. A. (1982). Indexes of discrimination or diagnostic accuracy. *Psychological Bulletin, 99,* 100–117.

Szasz, T. (1977). *Psychiatric slavery.* New York: Free Press.

Szasz, T. (1982). The psychiatric will: A new mechanism for protecting persons against "psychosis" and psychiatry. *American Psychologist, 37,* 762–770.

Szasz, T. (1987). *Insanity and its consequences.* New York: Wiley.

Szasz, T. S. (1961). *The myth of mental illness.* New York: Harper & Row.

Szasz, T. S. (1970). *The manufacture of madness.* New York: Harper & Row.

Szilagyi, A. D. (1981). *Management and performance.* Glenview, IL: Scott, Foresman.

Tagiuri, R. (1958). Social preference and its perception. In R. Tagiuri & L. Petrullo (Eds.), *Person, perception, and interpersonal behavior* (pp. 316–336). Stanford, CA: Stanford University Press.

Tanford, S., & Penrod, S. (1984). Social influence model: A formal integration of research on majority and minority influence processes. *Psychological Bulletin, 95,* 189–225.

Tanner, J. M. (1978). *Education and physical growth* (2nd ed.). New York: International Universities Press.

Tavris, C. (1983). *Anger: The misunderstood emotion.* New York: Simon & Schuster.

Tavris, C., & Sadd, S. (1977). *The Redbook report on female sexuality.* New York: Delacorte.

Taylor, S. E. (1982). Hospital patient behavior: Reactance, helplessness, or control. In H. S. Friedman & M. R. DiMatteo (Eds.), *Interpersonal issues in health care.* New York: Academic Press.

Taylor, S. E. (1986). *Health psychology.* New York: Random House.

Taylor, S. E., & Brown, J. D. (1988). Illusion and well-being: A social psychological perspective on mental health. *Psychological Bulletin, 103,* 193–210.

Tellegen, A., Lykken, D. T., Bouchard, T. J., Jr., Wilcox, K. J., Segal, N. L., & Rich, S. (1988). Personality similarity in twins reared apart and together. *Journal of Personality and Social Psychology, 54,* 1031–1039.

Terkel, S. (1974). *Working.* New York: Avon.

Terman, L. M., & Oden, M. H. (1947). *Genetic studies of genius, IV: The gifted child grows up.* Stanford, CA: Stanford University Press.

Terrace, H. S. (1985). In the beginning was the "name." *American Psychologist, 40,* 1011–1028.

Terrace, H. S., Petitto, L. A., Sanders, R. J., & Bever, T. G. (1981). Commentary on ape language. *Science, 221,* pp. 87–88.

Tetlock, P. E. (1988). Monitoring the integrative complexity of American and Soviet policy rhetoric: What can be learned? *Journal of Social Issues, 44,* 101–131.

Thatcher, R. W., Walker, R. A., & Giudice, S. (1987, May 29). Human cerebral hemispheres develop at different rates and ages. *Science, 236,* 1110–1114.

Thigpen, C., & Cleckley, H. M. (1985). *Three faces of eve.* Augusta, GA: Cleckley-Thigpen.

Thomas, A., Chess, S., Birch, H. G., Hartzig, M. E., & Korn, J. (1963). *Behavioral individuality in early childhood.* New York: New York University Press.

Thomas, C. B., Duszynski, K. R., & Schaffer, J. W. (1979). Family attitudes reported in youth as potential predictors of cancer. *Psychosomatic Medicine, 4,* 287–302.

Thompson, S. C. (1988, August). *An intervention to increase physician-patient communication.* Paper presented at the annual meeting of the American Psychological Association, Atlanta.

Thorndike, E. L. (1932). *The fundamentals of learning.* New York: Teachers College.

Thorndike, R. L., Hagan, E., & Sattler, J. (1986). *Stanford-Binet* (4th ed.). Chicago: Riverside.

Thurstone, L. L. (1928). Attitudes can be measured. *American Journal of Sociology, 33,* 529–554.

Tierney, J. (1988, May 15). Wired for stress. *New York Times Magazine,* pp. 49–85.

Time. (1976, September). Svengali squad: L.A. police. *Time,* p. 76.

Time. (1987, July 13). One in two? Not true. *Time,* p. 21.

Timnick, L. (1985, August 25). The *Times* poll: 22% in survey were child abuse victims. *Los Angeles Times,* pp. 1, 34.

Tischler, G. L., Leaf, P. J., Beham, L., Cottler, L., & Legler, D. A. (1984). Utilization of health and mental-health services. *Archives of General Psychiatry, 41,* 971–978.

Tjosvold, D. (1982). Effects of approach to controversy on superiors' incorporation of subordinates' information in decision making. *Journal of Applied Psychology, 67,* 189–193.

Tjosvold, D., & Deemer, D. K. (1980). Effects of controversy within a cooperative or competitive context on organizational decision making. *Journal of Applied Psychology, 65,* 590–595.

Tolman, E. C., & Honzik, C. H. (1930). Introduction and removal of reward and maze performance in rats. *University of California Publications in Psychology, 4,* 257–275.

Tomlinson-Keasey, C. (1985). *Child development: Psychological, sociological, and biological factors.* Homewood, IL: Dorsey.

Tomlinson-Keasey, C., Eisert, D. C., Kahle, L. R., Hardy-Brown, K., & Keasey, B. (1979). The structure of concrete operations. *Child Development,* 1153–1163.

Toynbee, P. (1977). *Patients.* New York: Harcourt Brace Jovanovich.

Treisman, A., & Gormican, S. (1988). Feature analysis in early vision: Evidence from search asymmetries. *Psychological Review, 95,* 15–48.

Treisman, M. (1960). Motion sickness: An evolutionary hypothesis. *Science,* pp. 493–495.

Trinder, J. (1988). Subjective insomnia without objective findings: A pseudo-diagnostic classification. *Psychological Bulletin, 107,* 87–94.

Tross, S., & Hirsch, D. A. (1988). Psychological distress and neuropsychological complications of HIV infection and AIDS. *American Psychologist, 43,* 924–934.

Trost, C. (1988). Men, too, wrestle with career-family stress. *Wall Street Journal,* p. B-1.

Tuchman, G. (1978). The symbolic annihilation of women by the mass media. In G. Tuchman, A. K. Daniels, & J. Benet (Eds.), *Hearth and home: Images of women in the mass media.* New York: Oxford University Press.

Tuller, D. (1985, February 24). What's new in employment testing? *New York Times,* p. 17.

Tucker, B. J., Megenity, D., & Virgil, L. (1970). Anatomy of a campus crisis center. *Personnel and Guidance Journal, 48,* 343–348.

Tulving, E. (1972). Episodic and semantic memory. In E. Tulving and W. Donaldson (Eds.), *Organization of memory.* New York: Academic Press.

Tulving, E. (1983). *Elements of episodic memory.* New York: Oxford University Press.

Tulving, E., & Psotka, J. (1971). Retroactive inhibition in free recall: Inaccessibility of information available in the memory store. *Journal of Experimental Psychology, 87,* 1–8.

Tulving, E., & Thompson, D. M. (1973). Encoding specificity and retrieval processes in episodic memory. *Psychological Review, 80,* 352–373.

Turkington, C. (1985, September). Computer unlocks secrets in folds, functions of brain. *APA Monitor.*

Turkington, C. (1986, August). Pot and the immune system. *APA Monitor,* p. 22.

Turkington, C. (1987, September). Special talents. *Psychology Today,* pp. 42–46.

Turner, C. R., Miller, H. B., & Moses, L. E. (Eds.). (1989). *AIDS: Sexual behavior and intravenous drug use.* Washington, DC: National Academy Press.

Tuttle, T. C. (1983). Organizational productivity: A challenge for psychologists. *American Psychologist, 38,* 479–486.

Tversky, B. (1981). Distortions in memory for maps. *Cognitive Psychology, 13,* 407–433.

Tversky, A., & Kahneman, D. (1974). Judgment under uncertainty: Heuristics and biases. *Science, 185,* 1124–1131.

Tyler, T. R., & McGraw, K. M. (1983). The threat of nuclear war: Risk interpretation and behavioral response. *Journal of Social Issues, 39,* 25–40.

Udolf, R. (1981). *Handbook of hypnosis for professionals.* New York: Van Nostrand.

Udolf, R. (1983). *Drugs, society, and human behavior* (3rd ed.). St. Louis: Mosby.

Ullman, L. P., & Krasner, L. (1975). *A psychological approach to abnormal behavior* (2nd ed.). Englewood Cliffs, NJ: Prentice-Hall.

Umstot, D. D., Bell, C. H., & Mitchell, T. R. (1976). Effects of job enrichment and task goals on satisfaction and productivity: Implications for job design. *Journal of Applied Psychology, 61,* 379–394.

Ungson, G., & Braunstein, D. (1982). *Design making.* Boston: Kent.

U.S. Census Bureau. (1985). *Marital status and living arrangement.* Washington, DC: Government Printing Office.

U.S. Census Bureau. (1988). *Current population reports.* Washington, D.C.: U.S. Government Printing Office.

U.S. Department of Health, Education, and Welfare. (1979). *Smoking and health: A report of the Surgeon General* (DHEW Publication No. (PHS) 79-50066). Washington, DC: Public Health Service.

U.S. Department of Health and Human Services. (1981). *The health consequences of smoking for women: A report of the Surgeon General.* Washington, DC: Public Health Service.

U.S. Department of Labor. (1985, February). *Employment and earnings.* Washington, DC: Government Printing Office.

U.S. Bureau of Labor Statistics (1987, August). Press release (No. 87-345). Washington, DC: U.S. Department of Labor.

U.S. Surgeon General (1988, May). *Report on Smoking.* Washington, DC: Government Printing Office.

Uttal, W. R. (1983). *Visual form detection in three-dimensional space.* Hillsdale, NJ: Erlbaum.

Vaillant, G. E. (1984). The disadvantages of DSM-III outweigh its advantages. *American Journal of Psychiatry, 141,* 542–545.

Valenstein, E. S. (Ed.). (1980). *The psychosurgery debate: Scientific, legal, and ethical perspectives.* San Francisco: Freeman.

Vance, E. B., & Wagner, N. W. (1976). Written descriptions of orgasm: A study of sex differences. *Archives of Sexual Behavior, 5,* 87–98.

VanHoesen, G. W. (1988, February). Memory. Paper presented at the annual meeting of the American Association for the Advancement of Science (Boston).

VanSell, M., Brief, A. P., & Schuler, R. S. (1981). Role conflict and role ambiguity: Integration of the literature and directions for future research. *Human Relations, 34,* 43–71.

Veroff, J. (1982). Assertive motivations: Achievement versus power. In A. J. Steward (Ed.), *Motivation and Society.* San Francisco: Jossey-Bass.

Verplanck, W. S. (1955). The control of the content of conversation: Reinforcement of statements of opinion. *Journal of Abnormal and Social Psychology, 51,* 668–676.

Vonnegut, M. (1975). *The Eden express.* New York: Bantam.

VonRestorff, H. (1933). Uber die wirking von bereichsbildumgen im Spurenfeld. In W. Kohler & H. VonRestorff, *Analyse von vorgangen in Spurenfeld. I. Psychologische forschung, 18,* 299–342.

Vroom, V. H. (1976). Leadership. In M. D. Dunnette (Ed.), *Handbook of industrial and organizational psychology.* Chicago: Rand McNally.

Vroom, V. H., & Yetton, P. W. (1973). *Leadership and decision making.* Pittsburgh: University of Pittsburgh Press.

Wagner, H. L., MacDonald, C. J., & Manstead, A. S. R. (1986). Communication of individual emotions by spontaneous facial expressions. *Journal of Personality and Social Psychology, 50,* 737–743.

Wagner, R., & Sternberg, R. (1985). Alternate conceptions of intelligence and their implications for education. *Review of Educational Research, 54,* 179–223.

Waid, W. M., & Orne, M. T. (1982). The phys-

iological detection of deception. *American Scientist, 70,* pp. 402–409.

Waldrop, M. M. (1987, September 11). Causality, structure, and common sense. *Science, 237,* 1297–1299.

Waldrop, M. M. (1988). Toward a unified theory of cognition. *Science, 241,* 27–29.

Walker, E., & Emory, E. (1985). Commentary: Interpretive bias and behavioral genetic research. *Child Development, 56,* 775–778.

Wall, P. D., & Melzack, R. (Eds.) (1984). *Textbook of pain.* Edinburgh, Scotland: Churchill Livingstone.

Wallace, R. K., & Benson, H. (1972, February). The physiology of meditation. *Scientific American,* pp. 84–90.

Wallis, C. (1984, June 11). Unlocking pain's secrets. *Time,* pp. 58–60.

Walster, E., & Walster, G. W. (1978). *Love.* Reading, MA: Addison-Wesley.

Wanous, J. P., Reichers, A. E., & Malik, S. D. (1984). Organization socialization and group development: Toward an integrative perspective. *Academy of Management Review, 9,* 670–683.

Ward, W. C., Kogan, N., & Pankove, E. (1972). Incentive effects in children's creativity. *Child Development, 43,* 669–67

Warga, C. (1987, August). Pain's gatekeeper. *Psychology Today,* pp. 51–56.

Warner, K. E. (1977). The effects of the anti-smoking campaign on cigarette consumption. *American Journal of Public Health, 67,* 645–650.

Washton, A. M., & Gold, M. S. (Eds.) (1987). *Cocaine: A clinician's handbook.* New York: Guilford.

Waters, H. F., & Huck, J. (1989, March 13). Networking women. *Newsweek, 113,* 48–55.

Watkins, L. R., & Mayer, D. J. (1982). Organization of endogenous opiate and non-opiate pain control systems. *Science, 216,* pp. 1185–1192.

Watson, D. (1982). The actor and the observer: How are their perceptions of causality divergent? *Psychological Bulletin, 92,* 682–700.

Watson, J. B. (1924). *Behaviorism.* New York: Norton.

Watson, J. B., & Rayner, R. (1920). Conditioned emotional reactions. *Journal of Experimental Psychology, 3,* 1–14.

Watt, N. (Ed.). (1985). *Children at risk for schizophrenia.* Cambridge, England: Cambridge University Press.

Waynbaum, I. (1907). *La physionomie humaine: Son mecanisme et son rôle social.* Paris: Alcan.

Webb, B., Worchel, S., Riechers, L., & Wayne, W. (1986). The influence of categorization on perceptions of crowding. *Personality and Social Psychology Bulletin, 12,* 539–546.

Webb, W. B. (1979). Sleep and dreams. In B. B. Wolman (Ed.), *Handbook of general psychology* (pp. 734–748). Englewood Cliffs, NJ: Prentice-Hall.

Weber, M. (1952). The essentials of bureaucratic organization: An ideal-type construction. In R. K. Merton et al. (Eds.), *A reader in bureaucracy*. Glencoe, IL: Free Press.

Weber, R., & Crocker, J. (1983). Cognitive processes in the revision of stereotypic beliefs. *Journal of Personality and Social Psychology, 45,* 961–977.

Wechsler, D. (1975). Intelligence defined and undefined. *American Psychologist, 30,* 135–139.

Wechsler, H., Rohman, M., & Solomon, R. (1981). Emotional problems and concerns of New England college students. *American Journal of Orthopsychiatry, 51,* 719.

Weinberg, C. (1979). *Self-creation*. New York: Avon.

Weinberg, R. A. (1989). Intelligence and IQ: Landmark issues and great debates. *American Psychologist, 44,* 98–104.

Weinberg, S. (1984). *Cyberphobia*. Unpublished manuscript, St. John's College.

Weinberger, N. M., McGaugh, J. L., & Lynch, G. (Eds.) (1985). *Memory systems of the brain*. New York: Guilford.

Weiner, B. (1985). *Human motivation*. New York: Springer-Verlag.

Weiner, B. (1985). "Spontaneous" causal thinking. *Psychological Bulletin, 97,* 74–84.

Weiner, I. B., & Hess, A. K. (Eds.) (1987). *Handbook of forensic psychology*. New York: Wiley.

Wiener, E. L., & Nagel, D. C. (Eds.). (1988). *Human factors in aviation*. New York: Academic Press.

Weiner, R. (1982). Another look at an old controversy. *Contemporary Psychiatry, 1,* 61–62.

Weinstein, C. E. (1986). Assessment and training of student learning strategies. In R. R. Schmeck (Ed.), *Learning styles and learning strategies*. New York: Plenum Press.

Weisman, S. R. (1984, April 29). Will the magic prevail? *New York Times Magazine,* pp. 39–56.

Weiss, L. (1985). *Dream analysis in psychotherapy*. New York: Pergamon.

Weiss, R. S. (1988). Loss and recovery. *Journal of Social Issues, 44,* 37–52.

Weizenbaum, J. (1966). ELIZA—a computer program for the study of natural language communication between man and machine. *Communications of the ACM, 9,* 36–45.

Wells, G. L., & Harvey, J. H. (1978). Naive attributors' attributions and predictions: What is informative and when is an effect an effect? *Journal of Personality and Social Psychology, 36,* 483–490.

Wells, G. L., & Loftus, E. A. (Eds.). (1984). *Eyewitness testimony: Psychological perspectives*. New York: Cambridge University Press.

Wender, P. H., & Klein, D. F. (1981, February). The promise of biological psychiatry. *Psychology Today,* pp. 25–41.

Wender, P. H., Kety, S. S., Rosenthal, D., Schulsinger, F., & Ortmann, J. (1986). Psy-

chiatric disorders in the biological and adoptive families of adopted individuals with affective disorders. *Archives of General Psychiatry, 43,* 923–929.

Wertheimer, M. (1923). Untersuchuugen zur lehre von der Gestalt. II. *Psychol. Forsch., 5,* pp. 301–350. In Beardsley and M. Wertheimer (Eds.) (1958), *Readings in perception*. New York: Van Nostrand.

West, S. G., Higginbotham, H. N., & Forsyth, D. R. (1985). *Psychotherapy and behavior change: Social and cultural perspectives*. New York: Pergamon.

Westoff, C. F. (1974). Coital frequency and contraception. *Family Planning Perspectives, 8,* 54–57.

Whalen, D. H., & Liberman, A. M. (1987, July 10). Speech perception takes precedence over nonspeech perception. *Science, 237,* 169–171.

Wheeler, D., & Janis, J. L. (1980). *A practical guide for making decisions*. New York: Free Press.

Whitaker, M. (1984, December 17). It was like breathing fire. *Newsweek,* pp. 26–32.

White, L. A., Fisher, W. A., Byrne, D., & Kingma, R. (1977, May). *Development and validation of a measure of affective orientation to erotic stimuli: The sexual opinion survey*. Paper presented at the meeting of the Midwestern Psychological Association (Chicago).

Whitam, F. L. (1977). The homosexual role: A reconsideration. *Journal of Sex Research, 13,* 1–11.

Whitbourne, S. K. (1986). *Adult development* (2nd ed.). New York: Praeger.

White, R. (1984). *Fearful warriors: A psychological profile of U.S.–Soviet relations*. New York: Free Press.

Whitehead, T. N. (1938). *The industrial worker*. Cambridge, MA: Harvard University Press.

Whorf, B. L. (1956). *Language, thought, and reality*. New York: Wiley.

Wickens, C. D. (1984). *Engineering psychology and human performance*. Columbus, OH: Merrill.

Widmeyer, W. N., & Loy, J. W. (1988). When you're hot, you're hot! Warm-cold effects in first impressions of persons and teaching effectiveness. *Journal of Educational Psychology, 80,* 118–121.

Wiederhold, W. C. (Ed.). (1982). *Neurology for non-neurologists*. New York: Academic Press.

Wielkiewicz, R. M. (1985). *Behavior management in the schools: Principles and procedures*. New York: Pergamon.

Wiener, E. L., & Nagel, D. C. (1988). Human factors in aviation. Orlando, FL: Academic Press.

Wildman, R. W., Wildman, R. W., II, Brown, A., & Trice, C. (1976). Note on males' and females' preference for opposite-sex body parts, bust sizes, and bust-revealing clothing. *Psychological Reports, 38,* 485–486.

Wilkinson, A. C. (Ed.) (1983). *Classroom*

computers and cognitive science. New York: Academic Press.

Williams, S. W., & McCullers, J. C. (1983). Personal factors related to typicalness of career and success in active professional women. *Psychology of Women Quarterly, 7,* 343–357.

Wilson, G. T., Franks, C. M., Kendall, P. C., & Foreyt, J. P. (1987). *Review of behavior therapy: Theory and practice* (Vol. 11). New York: Guilford Press.

Wilson, T. D., & Linville, P. N. (1982). Improving academic performance of college freshmen: Attribution therapy revisited. *Journal of Personality and Social Psychology, 42,* 367–376.

Wilson, T. D., & Linville, P. W. (1985). Improving the performance of college freshmen with attributional techniques. *Journal of Personality and Social Psychology, 49,* 287–293.

Winch, R. F. (1958). *Mate selection: A study of complementary needs*. New York: Harper & Row.

Winokur, G. (1983). Alcoholism and depression. *Substance and Alcohol Actions/Misuse, 4,* 111–119.

Winter, D. G. (1973). *The power motive*. New York: Free Press.

Winter, D. G. (1976, July). What makes the candidate run? *Psychology Today,* pp. 45–92.

Winter, D. G. (1988). The power motive in women—and men. *Journal of Personality and Social Psychology, 54,* 510–519.

Witelson, S. (1989, March). *Sex differences*. Paper presented at the annual meeting of the New York Academy of Sciences, New York.

Witkin, H. A., Moore, C. A., Goodenough, D. R., & Cox, P. N. (1977). Field-dependent and field-independent cognitive styles and their educational implications. *Review of Educational Research, 47,* 1–64.

Wolf, S. (1985). Manifest and latent influence of majorities and minorities. *Journal of Personality and Social Psychology, 48,* 899–908.

Wolman, B. (1968). *The unconscious mind: The meaning of Freudian psychology*. Englewood Cliffs, NJ: Prentice-Hall.

Wolozin, B. L., Pruchnicki, A., Dickson, D. W., & Davies, P. (1986). A neuronal antigen in the brains of Alzheimer patients. *Science, 232,* 648–650.

Wolpe, J. (1969). *The practice of behavior therapy*. New York: Pergamon.

Wong, D. F., Gjedde, A., Wagner, H. M., Jr., Dannals, R. F., Links, J. M., Tune, L. E., & Pearlson, G. D. (1988, February 12). Response to Zeeberg, Gibson, and Reba. *Science 239,* 790–791.

Wong, D. F., Wagner, H. N., Jr., Tune, L. E., Dannals, R. F., Pearlson, G. D., Links, J. M., Tamminga, C. A., Broussolle, E. P., Ravert, H. T., Wilson, A. A., Toung, T., Malat, J., Williams, J. A., O'Tuama, L. A., Snyder, S. H., Kuhar, M. J., & Gjedde, A. (1986, December 19). Positron emission tomography reveals elevated D2 Dopamine receptors in drug-naive schizophrenics. *Science, 234*, 1558–1563.

Woodhead, M. (1988). When psychology informs public policy: The case of early childhood intervention. *American Psychologist, 43*, 443–454.

Woodruff, R. A., Clayton, P. J., & Guze, S. B. (1975). Is everyone depressed? *American Journal of Psychiatry, 132*, 627–628.

Woolfolk, R. L. (1975, October). Psychophysiological correlates of meditation. *Archives of General Psychiatry, 32*, 1326–1333.

Woolfolk, R. L., & McNulty, T. F. (1983). Relaxation treatment for insomnia: A component analysis. *Journal of Consulting and Clinical Psychology, 4*, 495–503.

Worchel, S., & Brown, E. H. (1984). The role of plausibility in influencing environmental attributions. *Journal of Experimental Social Psychology, 20*, 86–96.

Worley, P. F., Heller, W. A., Snyder, S. H., & Baraban, J. M. (1988, March 18). Lithium blocks of phosphoinositide-mediated cholinergic response in hippocampal slices. *Science, 239*, 1428–1429.

Wright, J. D. (1978). Are working women really more satisfied?: Evidence from several national surveys. *Journal of Marriage and the Family, 40*, 301–313.

Wright, L. (1988). The Type A behavior pattern and coronary artery disease. *American Psychologist, 43*, 2–14.

Wu, C., & Shaffer, D. R. (1987). Susceptibility to persuasive appeals as a function of source credibility and prior experience with the attitude object. *Journal of Personality and Social Psychology, 52*, 677–688.

Wundt, W. (1874). *Grundzüge der physiologischen Psychologie.*

Wyden, B. (1971, December). Growth: 45 crucial months. *Life*, pp. 93–95.

Wynne, L. C., Singer, M. T., Bartko, J. J., & Toohey, M. L. (1975). Schizophrenics and their families: Recent research on parental communication. *Psychiatric Research: The Widening Perspective.* New York: International Universities Press.

Yalom, I. D. (1975). *The theory and practice of group psychotherapy* (2nd ed.). New York: Basic Books.

Yamamato, T., Yuyama, N., & Kawamura, Y. (1981). Cortical neurons responding to tactile, thermal and taste stimulations of the rat's tongue. *Brain Research, 22*, 202–206.

Yancey, W. L. (1972). Architecture, interaction and social control: The case of a large-scale housing project. In J. G. Wohlwill & D. H. Carson (Eds.), *Environment and the social sciences: Perspectives and applications.* Washington, DC: American Psychological Association.

Yankelovich, D. (1974). *The new morality.* New York: McGraw-Hill.

Yarnold, P. R., Grimm, L. G., & Mueser, K. T. (1986). Social conformity and the Type A behavior pattern. *Perceptual and Motor Skills, 62*, 99–104.

Yates, A. J. (1980). *Biofeedback and the modification of behavior.* New York: Plenum Press.

Yerkes, R. M., & Margulis, S. (1909). The method of Pavlov in animal psychology. *Psychological Bulletin, 6*, 257–273.

Youkilis, H., & Bootzin, R. R. (1981). A psychophysiological perspective on the etiology and treatment of insomnia. In S. M. Haynes & L. A. Gannon (Eds.), *Psychosomatic disorders: A psychophysiological approach to etiology and treatment.* New York: Praeger.

Yukl, G. (1974). Effects of the opponent's initial offer, concession magnitude, and concession frequency on bargaining behavior. *Journal of Personality and Social Psychology, 30*, 323–335.

Yussen, S. R. (1984). *Intellectual development: Birth to adulthood.* New York: Academic Press.

Zajonc, R. B. (1968). The attitudinal effects of mere exposure. *Journal of Personality and Social Psychology, 9*, 1–27.

Zajonc, R. B. (1984). On the primacy of affect. *American Psychologist, 39*, 117–123.

Zajonc, R. B. (1985). Emotion and facial efference: A theory reclaimed. *Science, 228*, 15–21.

Zander, A. (1977). *Groups at work.* San Francisco: Jossey-Bass.

Zanna, M. P., & Pack, S. J. (1974). On the self-fulfilling nature of apparent sex differences in behavior. *Journal of Experimental Social Psychology, 11*, 583–591.

Zigler, E., & Glick, M. (1988). Is paranoid schizophrenia really camouflaged depression? *American Psychologist, 43*, 284–290.

Zika, S., & Chamberlain, K. (1987). Relation of hassles and personality to subjective well-being. *Journal of Personality and Social Psychology, 53*, 155–162.

Zilbergeld, B., & Ellison, C. R. (1980). Desire discrepancies and arousal problems in sex therapy. In S. R. Leiblum & L. A. Pervin (Eds.), *Principles and practices of sex therapy.* New York: Guilford Press.

Zillman, D. (1978). *Hostility and aggression.* Hillsdale, NJ: Erlbaum.

Zillman, D., & Bryant, J. (1984). Effects of massive exposure to pornography. In N. Malamuth & E. Donnerstein (Eds.), *Pornography and sexual aggression.* Orlando, FL: Academic Press.

Zimmer, J. (1984). Courting the Gods of sport: Athletes use superstition to ward off the devils of injury and bad luck. *Psychology Today, 18*, 36–39.

Zivin, G. (Ed.) (1985). *The development of expressive behavior: Biology-environmental interactions.* New York: Academic Press.

Zubin, J., & Spring, B. (1977). Vulnerability: New view of schizophrenia. *Journal of Abnormal Psychology, 86*, 103–126.

Zuckerman, M., & Wheeler, L. (1975). To dispel fantasy about the fantasy-based measure of fear of success. *Psychological Bulletin, 82*, 932–946.

Zuckerman, M. (1978). The search for high sensation. *Psychology Today*, 30–46.

Zuckerman, M. et al. (1978). On the importance of self-determination for intrinsically-motivated behavior. *Personality and Social Psychology Bulletin, 4*, 443–446.

Acknowledgments

Today, 11, 38-46. Reprinted with permission from *Psychology Today Magazine.* Copyright © 1978 (PT Partners, L.P.).

Figure 9-3 from Motivation and Personality by Abraham H. Maslow. Copyright 1954, © 1987 by Harper & Row, Publishers, Inc. Copyright © 1970 by Abraham H. Maslow. Reprinted by permission of Harper & Row, Publishers, Inc.

Figure 9-7 from Plutchick, R., Emotion, in *Approaches to Emotion,* K. Scherer and D. Ekman, Editors. Copyright © 1984 by Erlbaum, Lawrence, Associates, Inc. Reprinted with permission of the publisher.

Table 10-2 adapted from Broverman, I. K., Wogel, S. R., Broverman, D. M., Clarkson, F. E., & Rosenkrantz, P. S., Sex-role stereotypes: A current appraisal. *Journal of Social Issues, 28.* Copyright 1972 by the Society for the Psychological Study of Social Issues. Reprinted with permission of the publisher and author.

Figure 10-7 adapted with permission of The Alan Guttmacker Institute, 1985.

Figure 10-8 adapted from Kinsey, A. C., Pomeroy, W. B., & Martin, C. E., *Sexual Behavior in the Human Male.* Copyright © 1948 by The Institute of Sex Research. Adapted with permission of the publisher.

Quote, Chapter 10, from Pereira, P., Effects of date rape linger while she tries to forget. *Massachusetts Daily Collegian, 119,* November 18, 1987.

Figure 10-10 adapted from Mahoney, E. R., *Human Sexuality,* 1983. New York: McGraw-Hill Book Co.

Figure 11-4 from Roffwarg, H. R., Muzio, J. N., & Dement, W. C., Development of human sleep dream cycle. *Science, 152,* Copyright © 1966 by the American Association for the Advancement of Science. Reprinted by permission of the publisher and author.

Figure 11-5 reproduced by permission of the *American Anthropologist, 60: 6,* 1958. Not for further reproduction.

Quotation, Chapter 11, from *Washington Post,* June 22, 1986, p. A1. "Crack users, highs, lows. C. Milloy. Reprinted by permission.

Figure 11-9 © 1984 by The New York Times Company. Reprinted by permission.

Figure 12-7 from Weissbound, B., & J. Musick (Eds.), Consequences of infant daycare, *Infants: Their Social Environment.* Washington, D.C.: National Association for the Education of the Young Children (1981).

Figure 12-8 adapted from Piaget, J., & Inhelder, B. (1948), *The Child's Conception of Space,* with the permission of Humanities Press, Inc.

Figure 13-1 from Tanner, J. M., *Education and Physical Growth,* 2nd ed., Madison, CT: International University Press, 1978.

Table 13-1 from Kohlberg, L., Stage and sequence: The cognitive developmental approach to specialization, in *Handbook of Socialization Theory and Research,* David A. Goslin, Editor. Copyright © 1969 by Houghton Mifflin Company. Reprinted with permission.

Figure 13-3 from Levinson, D. J., A conception of adult development. *American Psychologist, 41,* 3. Copyright © 1986 by the American Psychological Association. Reprinted with permission of the author.

Figure 13-5 from Googins, B., & Burden, D., Vulnerability of working parents: Balancing work and home roles. *Social Work, 32,* 295. Copyright © 1987 by the National Association of Social Workers, Inc. Reprinted by permission of the publisher and author.

Figure 13-6 from Schaie, W., *Longitudinal Studies of Psychological Development* (1985). New York: Guilford Press.

Figure 14-2 adapted from Catell, Eber, & Tatsuoka. Copyright © 1970 by the Institute for Personality and Ability Testing. Reproduced by permission.

Figure 14-3 from Eysenck, H. J., *Eysenck on Extraversion.* Collins Professional and Technical Books, Ltd., 1973.

Figure 14-4 copyright © 1986 by the New York Times Company. Reprinted by permission.

Figure 14-5 from Graser, J. E., Kuczynski, L., Rushton, J. P., & Simutis, Z. M., Learning resistance to temptation through observation. *Developmental Psychology, 15,* 223. Copyright © 1979 by the American Psychological Association. Reprinted with permission of the publisher.

Table 15-2 from Kanner, A. D., Coyne, J. C., Schaefer, C., & Lazarus, R. S., Comparison of two modes of stress measurements: Daily hassles and uplifts versus major life events. *Journal of Behavioral Medicine, 4,* 14. Copyright © 1981 by Plenum Publishing Corp. Reprinted with permission.

Figure 15-2 from Pettingale, K. W., Morris, T., Greer, S., & Haybittle, J. L., Mental attitudes to cancer: An additional prognostic factor. *Lancet,* p. 750. Copyright © 1985 by *The Lancet.* Reprinted with permission.

Table 16-2 from Beck, A. T. & Emery, G., *Anxiety Disorders and Phobias: A Cognitive Perspective.* New York: Basic Books, Inc. 1985.

Quote, Chapter 16, from Kraines, S. H., *The Therapy of the Neuroses and Psychoses* (3rd ed.). Philadelphia, PA: Lea and Febinger, 1948.

Quotation, Chapter 16, from Spitzer, R. L., Skodol, A. E., Gibbon, M., & Williams, J. B. W. *Psychopathology: A Case Book.* New York: McGraw-Hill Book Co. (1983).

Figure 16-4 from Zubin, J., & Spring B., A new view of schizophrenia. *Journal of Abnormal Psychology, 86,* 103. Copyright © 1977 by the American Psychological Association. Reprinted with permission.

Quote, Chapter 17, from *Clinical Behavior Therapy* by Goldfried, M. R., & Davison, G. C. Copyright © 1976 by Holt, Rinehart and Winston.

Table 17-2 from *The Relaxation Response* by Herbert Benson, M.D. Copyright © 1975 by William Morrow and Company, Inc.

Figure 18-3 adapted from Fajardo, D. M., Author race, essay quality, and reverse discrimination. *Journal of Applied Social Psychology, 15,* 255. Copyright © 1985 by V. H. Winston and Sons, Inc.

Figure 18-5 adapted from Landis, D., Day, H. R., McGraw, P. L., Thomas, J. A., & Miller, A. B., "Can a Black 'Culture Assimilator' Increase Racial Understanding?" *Journal of Social Issues, 32* (2), 169-183.

Figure 19-3 from Cunningham, M. R., Measuring the physical in physical attractiveness: Quasi-experiments on the sociobiology of female facial beauty, *Journal of Personality and Social Psychology, 50,* 928. Copyright © 1986 by the American Psychological Association. Reprinted by permission.

Figure 19-4 from Parlee, M. B. The friendship bond. *Psychology Today,* October 3, 1979. Reprinted with permission from *Psychology Today Magazine.* Copyright © 1979 (PT Partners, L.P.).

Table 19-1 excerpted from *Liking and Loving: An Invitation to Social Psychology* by Zick Rubin. Copyright © 1973 by Holt, Rinehart, and Winston, Inc. Reprinted by permission by the publisher.

Tables 19-2 & 19-5 from Sternberg, R. J., Triangular theory of love. *Psychological Review, 93,* 119. Copyright © 1986 by the American Psychological Association. Reprinted by permission of the publisher and the author.

Table 19-3 from Laver, J., & Laver, R., Marriages made to last. *Psychology Today, 19,* (16), 22-26. Reprinted with permission from *Psychology Today Magazine.* Copyright © 1985 (PT Partners, L.P.).

Table 19-4 from Benjamin, L. T., Jr., Defining aggression: An exercise for the classroom. *Teaching of Psychology, 12,* (1), 41. Copyright © 1985 by Erlbaum, Lawrence, Associates, Inc. Reprinted with permission of the publisher and author.

Table 20-1 copyright © 1982 by the National Opinion Research Center. Reprinted by permission.

Quotation in Chapter 20 copyright © 1988 by *Time,* Inc. Reprinted by permission.

Figure 21-3 from Baum, A., & Valine, S., *Architecture and Social Behavior: Psychological Studies of Social Density.* Hillsdale, NJ: Erlbaum, Lawrence, Associates, Inc. (1977).

Figure 21-5 adapted from Horowitz, M. (1986). *Stress response syndromes.* (Aronson Press) with permission of the author.

PART-OPENING PHOTOGRAPHS

One   © Richard Wood/The Picture Cube
Two   © Jeffry W. Myers/Stock, Boston

Three   © Frank Siteman/Stock, Boston
Four   © 1985 Joel Gordon
Five   © 1986 Susan Lapides

Six   © Phaneuf/Gurdziel, The Picture Cube
Seven   Jack Spratt/The Image Works
Eight   © 1983 Jack Spratt/The Image Works

CHAPTER-OPENING PHOTOGRAPHS

1 © 1989 David Perdew/Stock, South
2 © 1987 Bill Gallery/Stock, Boston
3 Innervisions, © 1989
4 © 1981 Joel Gordon
5 Innervisions, © 1989
6 Innervisions, © 1989

7 © Dan Walsh/The Picture Cube
8 © 1983 Joel Gordon
9 © Bob Daemmrich/The Image Works
10 R. Michael Stuckey/Comstock
11 Innervisions, © 1989
12 © Sally Cassidy/The Picture Cube
13 © Jonathan Rawle/Stock, Boston
14 © Gary Haynes/The Image Works
15 © Frank Siteman/The Picture Cube

16 © David Hughes/Stock, Boston
17 Innervisions, © 1989
18 © The Image Works
19 © Bob Daemmrich/The Image Works
20 © Bob Daemmrich/The Image Works
21 © Richard Wood/The Picture Cube
Appendix Katherine E. Vorwerk

NAME INDEX

I-4 NAME INDEX

Horney, K., 489
Horowitz, F. D., 279
Horowitz, M. J., 725
Horstman, W., 366
Hostetler, A. S., 221
Houston, L. N., 354
Hovland, C., 629
Howard, A., 24
Howard, K. I., 618
Howell, N., 363
Howells, J. G., 554
Hoyenga, K., 298
Hoyt, M. F., 474
Hrubec, Z., 308
Hubel, D. H., 102, 137
Hudson, W., 147
Huesmann, L. R., 673, 675, 676
Hughes, C. F., 539
Hughes, J., 534
Hull, C. L., 295
Hull, J. G., 527
Hulley, S. B., 365
Hunt, M., 354, 359
Huntley, C. W., 691
Hurlbert, A. C., 102
Hurst, R., 144
Huston, A. C., 342
Hutchinson, J. B., 360
Hyde, J., 339, 341
Hyland, M. E., 575

Iaffaldano, M. T., 705
Ickes, W., 665
Imai, M., 700
Inbar-Saban, N., 310
Ingelfinger, F. J., 304
Inhelder, B., 440
Innes, C. A., 720
Institute of Medicine, 402
Intriligator, M. D., 732
Isen, A. M., 243
Izard, C. E., 323, 327

Jacklin, C. N., 339, 340, 341, 342
Jackson, J. M., 297
Jacobs, B. L., 403
Jacobs, J., 457
Jaffa, M., 390
James, W., 320
Janis, I. L., 15, 528, 541, 629, 697
Janoff-Bulman, R., 725
Jaroff, L., 77
Jarvik, M. E., 535
Jemmott, J. B., III, 534
Jencks, C., 284
Jenkins, B. M., 728
Jenkins, S. R., 312
Jennings, J., 342
Jensen, A., 284
Jensen, G. D., 350
Jervis, R., 731
John, E. R., 66, 67
Johnson, D. M., 237
Johnson, D. R., 254
Johnson, D. W., 698
Johnson, J. T., 503
Johnson, M. K., 214

Johnson, R. T., 698
Johnson, T. E., 23
Johnson, V. E., 348, 350, 351, 360, 365, 369
Jones, B. W., 642
Jones, G. N., 523
Jones, L. V., 285
Jones, M. C., 451
Jordan, T. J., 433
Josephson, W. L., 672
Joyce, J., 550
Joyce, M. R., 600
Jung, C., 488
Jungeblut, A., 274
Jusczyk, P. W., 427
Jussim, L., 640

Kagan, J., 417, 421, 494
Kahn, R. L., 468, 471, 702, 703
Kahn, S., 454
Kahneman, D., 235, 240, 241
Kalin, M., 246
Kamin, L. J., 284
Kanfer, F. H., 596, 598
Kanner, A. D., 523, 524
Kaplan, D., 541
Kaplan, H. S., 348, 368
Kaplan, M. F., 637, 678, 695
Karasu, T. B., 591
Karlins, M., 630
Karoly, P., 596, 598
Karp, D. A., 462
Kasa, P., 57
Kass, J. H., 104
Kass, T. S., 541
Kassin, S. M., 215
Kastenbaum, R., 474
Katz, D., 638, 702
Katzell, R. A., 704
Kazdin, A. E., 596, 600
Kearsley, R. B., 421
Keating, D. P., 440, 442
Keerdoja, E., 252, 253
Keesey, R. E., 304
Keidel, G. C., 457
Keith, S. J., 579
Keith-Spiegel, P., 38
Kelley, H., 629, 636, 641, 642
Kellogg, J. W., 352
Kemeny, M., 534
Kendig, F., 246
Kendrick, D. T., 496
Kennedy, T. D., 598
Kennell, J. H., 428
Kenny, D. A., 637
Kepner, C. R., 675
Kertesz, A. E., 74
Ketron, J. L. 265
Keyser, D. J., 507
Kiecolt-Glaser, J. K., 518
Kienker, P. K., 129
Kierkegaard, S., 572
Kiesler, S., 714, 715
Kihlstrom, J. F., 488
Kilpatrick, D. G., 364
Kinchloe, B., 346
Kinney, D. K., 243, 244
Kinsey, A. C., 353, 359, 360

Kirby, D., 353
Kirschbaum, J., 128
Klatzky, R. L., 637
Klaus, H. M., 428
Klein, D. F., 575
Klein, R., 675
Kleinmuntz, B., 505
Klerman, G. L., 562, 609
Klima, E. S., 253
Kline, P., 488
Klinger, E., 386
Knittle, J. L., 307
Kobasa, S. C., 526
Koegel, R., 170
Kohlberg, L., 451, 452, 453, 678
Köhler, W., 236
Kohn, A., 8, 292
Kolata, G., 280, 309, 399, 401, 426
Kolodny, R. C., 351, 365
Konar, E., 338
Konečni, V. J., 675
Konner, M., 395
Konnold, C., 245
Koocher, G. P., 38
Koop, C. E., 395
Korsch, B. M., 540
Kosecoff, J., 28
Koss, M. P., 363, 364
Kosslyn, S. M., 79
Kosson, D. S., 583
Kotch, J. B., 392
Koveces, Z., 318
Kovelman, J., 580
Kozak, M. S., 323
Kraepelin, E., 576
Kraft, C. L., 144
Krantz, D. S., 531
Krasner, L., 550, 581
Kravitz, E. A., 69
Krebs, D. L., 670
Kringlen, E., 579
Krull, D. S., 637
Kübler-Ross, E., 473, 474
Kucharski, D., 80
Kuiper, N. A., 528
Kulik, C. C., 274
Kulik, J., 211, 274
Kumura, H. K., 598
Kunihira, S., 204

Lader, M., 566
Lakey, B., 519
Lamal, P. A., 8
Lamb, M., 414, 429, 431
Lambert, M. J., 607, 609
Landesman, S., 278
Landis, D., 647
Landman, J., 607
Landy, D., 637
Lang, J. S., 412
Lange, C., 320
Langer, E., 525, 541, 647
Langfeld, H. S., 129
Langlois, J. H., 662
LaPiere, R. T., 631
Lashley, K. S., 220
Lasley, D. J., 99

Latané, B., 27, 31–32, 33, 34, 35, 36, 37, 676
Latham, G. P., 700, 704
Lau, I., 254
Lauer, J., 666, 667
Lauer, R., 666, 667
Lawton, M. P., 660
Lazarus, R. S., 317, 519, 521, 522, 523, 524, 526, 527
Lebow, R. N., 731
Lechtenberg, R. R., 77
Lefkowitz, M. M., 572, 673
Lehman, D. R., 526
Lehmkuhle, S., 51
Leibel, R., 308
Leigh, H., 537
Lemerise, E., 426
LePage, A., 672
Lepper, M. R., 299, 714
Lerch, L., 640
Lesgold, A., 179
Levenson, R. W., 327, 328
Leventhal, E., 540
Leventhal, H., 323, 534, 535, 540, 630
Levin, D. P., 713
Levinson, D. J., 460
Levy, J., 78
Levy, N. B., 541
Levy, S. M., 533
Levy, W. B., 51
Lewin, R., 48, 76
Lewis, L. L., 337–338
Lewis, M., 431
Lewis, P., 605
Lewy, A. J., 616
Ley, P., 539
Liberman, A. M., 138
Lichtenstein, E., 535
Lidz, T., 581
Liebert, R. M., 342
Lietaer, G., 603
Linden, E., 626
Lindsay, P. H., 102, 131, 206
Lindy, J., 71
Linn, M. C., 341, 440
Linville, P., 645
Linz, D., 674
Linz, D. G., 673, 674
Lisak, D., 363
Livingstone, M. S., 137
Lobsenz, M. M., 468
Lochhead, J., 244, 245
Locke, E. A., 694
Locke, S. E., 534
Lockhart, R. S., 204, 206
Loehlin, J. C., 494
Loftus, E., 215, 637
Long, A., 376
Long, G. M., 200
Long, P., 391
Lorenz, K., 670
Lorsch, J. W., 693
Lovaas, O. I., 170, 597
Lowell, E. L., 311
Loy, J. W., 636
Luborsky, L., 595, 607, 609
Lucas, T., 432
Luchins, A. S., 239
Ludwig, A. M., 377

SUBJECT INDEX